An easy way to help students learn, collaborate, and grow.

Designed to engage today's student, WileyPLUS Learning Space will transform any course into a vibrant, collaborative learning community.

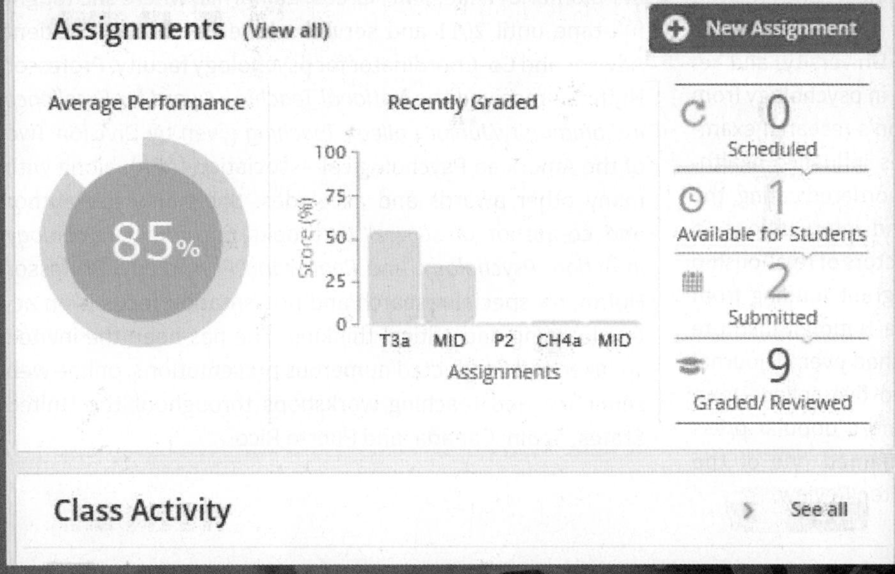

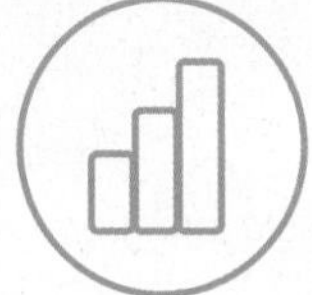

Identify which students are struggling early in the semester.

Educators assess the real-time engagement and performance of each student to inform teaching decisions. Students always know what they need to work on.

Facilitate student engagement both in and outside of class.

Educators can quickly organize learning activities, manage student collaboration, and customize their course.

Measure outcomes to promote continuous improvement.

With visual reports, it's easy for both students and educators to gauge problem areas and act on what's most important.

www.wileypluslearningspace.com

About the Authors

Courtesy of Catherine Sanderson

Courtesy of Karen Huffman

CATHERINE A. SANDERSON is the Manwell Family Professor of Life Sciences (Psychology) at Amherst College. She received a bachelor's degree in psychology, with a specialization in Health and Development, from Stanford University, and received both masters and doctoral degrees in psychology from Princeton University. Professor Sanderson's research examines how personality and social variables influence health-related behaviors such as safer sex and disordered eating, the development of persuasive messages and interventions to prevent unhealthy behavior, and the predictors of relationship satisfaction. This research has received grant funding from the National Science Foundation and the National Institute of Health. Professor Sanderson has published over 25 journal articles and book chapters in addition to five college textbooks, a high school health textbook, and a popular press book on parenting. In 2012, she was named one of the country's top 300 professors by the Princeton Review.

KAREN HUFFMAN is an emeritus professor of psychology at Palomar College, San Marcos, California, where she taught full-time until 2011 and served as the Psychology Student Advisor and Co-Coordinator for psychology faculty. Professor Huffman received the *National Teaching Award for Excellence in Community/Junior College Teaching* given by Division Two of the American Psychological Association (APA), along with many other awards and accolades. She's also the author and co-author of several textbooks, including *Psychology in Action*, *Psychology*, and *Real World Psychology*. Professor Huffman's special research and presentation focus is on active learning and critical thinking. She has been the invited speaker and conducted numerous presentations, online web seminars, and teaching workshops throughout the United States, Spain, Canada, and Puerto Rico.

Real World Psychology

Second Edition

CATHERINE A. SANDERSON
Amherst College

KAREN HUFFMAN
Palomar College

WILEY

VICE PRESIDENT AND DIRECTOR	George Hoffman
DIRECTOR	Verona Visentin
PRODUCT DESIGNER	Wendy Ashenberg
ASSISTANT DEVELOPMENT EDITOR	Emma Townsend-Merino
SENIOR CONTENT MANAGER	Dorothy Sinclair
SENIOR PRODUCTION EDITOR	Sandra Rigby
SENIOR PHOTO EDITOR	Mary Ann Price
PHOTO RESEARCHER	Margaret Sidlosky
SENIOR DESIGNER	Wendy Lai
SENIOR MARKETING MANAGER	Glenn Wilson
PRODUCTION SERVICES	Furino Production

Cover photos: Chameleon © GlobalP/iStockphoto, Footprints © TPopova/iStockphoto
This book was set in Garamond 10/12 pts by MPS Limited, and printed and bound by Quad Graphics/Versailles.

This book is printed on acid-free paper. ∞

Founded in 1807, John Wiley & Sons, Inc. has been a valued source of knowledge and understanding for more than 200 years, helping people around the world meet their needs and fulfill their aspirations. Our company is built on a foundation of principles that include responsibility to the communities we serve and where we live and work. In 2008, we launched a Corporate Citizenship Initiative, a global effort to address the environmental, social, economic, and ethical challenges we face in our business. Among the issues we are addressing are carbon impact, paper specifications and procurement, ethical conduct within our business and among our vendors, and community and charitable support. For more information, please visit our website: www.wiley.com/go/citizenship.

ePub ISBN: 978-1-119-29501-3

The inside back cover will contain printing identification and country of origin if omitted from this page. In addition, if the ISBN on the back cover differs from the ISBN on this page, the one on the back cover is correct.

Printed in the United States of America

10 9 8 7 6 5 4 3 2 1

Brief Contents

Contents

Preface

TPopova/iStockphoto

© GlobalP/iStockphoto

People who believe they have the power to exercise some measure of control over their lives are healthier, more effective and more successful than those who lack faith in their ability to effect changes in their lives.

—Albert Bandura

Why did we, the authors of this text, choose to start our Preface with this particular quote from psychologist Albert Bandura? It's because we strongly agree that having faith in our ability to effect change is all important. We also firmly believe that the field of psychology is the single-best route for gaining some measure of control over our lives, and why we're so happy to "give psychology away" in this Second Edition of *Real World Psychology (RWP)*!

© GlobalP/iStockphoto

In keeping with this focus on change, did you notice the colorful chameleon on the cover of this book? Have you ever wondered why authors or publishers choose certain images for their books? In our case, we chose the chameleon as RWP's brand image because of its famous ability to change. Our second reason for choosing the chameleon is due to its 360-degree range of vision—making it remarkably adaptive to the environment! We believe that recognizing and adapting to the world around us is essential to survival and success, as reflected by our text's focus on real world examples and in the title, *Real World Psychology (2e)*.

In addition to discussing our foundational belief in the power of change and adapting to the real-world environment, we want to explain our text's central theme and essence—*Student Engagement*. How can a textbook engage and inspire today's students? Most would agree that good teaching largely depends on the commitment and excitement of the teacher, and we believe the same can be said about a textbook and its authors. As you'll see in the next section, we've done everything we can in this Second Edition to engage and inspire the reader. Psychology has always been a deep passion and love for both of us. After a combined total of more than 50 years of teaching introductory psychology, we truly believe that understanding ourselves and others can enrich and improve virtually every aspect of our lives—work, play, home, college, national and international affairs.

Unfortunately, studies find that this first class in general psychology is the only formal course in psychology that most students will ever encounter, and the field is so large and complex that it's a constant juggling act to try to cover all the major concepts and theories. How can one text, *Real World Psychology (RWP 2e)*, capture all the essential content, while still engaging and inspiring you—our readers and professors?

Designed for introductory psychology teachers and their students, this text is *concise, comprehensive,* and *comprehensible* (see the following details):

- **Concise** When textbook chapters (or classroom lectures) are too long, attention strays and educational goals are lost. But brevity is more than just fewer words. The true goal of concise writing is clarity. Textbooks and teachers must be as brief and clear as possible because *brevity with clarity matters*!
- **Comprehensive** Knowing that the overarching goal of all instructors is to present the essentials of our field, this text is dedicated to comprehensive coverage of all the core concepts because *content matters!* For example, given that the scientific method and its various components is one of the most common learning objectives in psychology, we believe students need more practice and exposure than just the basic introductory material most texts traditionally provide.

Therefore, we include a special **PsychScience** feature that offers an expanded discussion of the latest research on various "Hot Topics," such as the impact of distracted driving and whether or not animals have distinct personalities. The detailed example is then followed by a special, interactive *Research Challenge*, which asks the reader to identify the research method, independent variable (IV), dependent variable (DV), and so on. This exercise helps reinforce the core learning objective on research methods, while also building student appreciation and engagement with the latest research. Answers are provided in Appendix B. (See three **PsychScience** boxes below.)

PS Psych**Science**

Does Wearing Red Increase Your Sex Appeal?

To examine this question, researchers recruited women who had on-line dating profiles expressing interest in meeting a man, and had posted color photographs (Guéguen & Jacob, 2014). Through the magic of photoshop, the researchers changed the color of the woman's shirt in the photograph every 12 weeks: the color rotated at random through red, black, white, yellow, blue, and green. The women were asked to notify the researchers of how many emails they received from men during the eight to nine-month period of the study. As hypothesized, women received more contacts from men when they wore red (see photo) as opposed to any of the other five colors. In fact, they received about a five percent increase in emails.

Does the color red also impact a man's sex appeal? In a related study, researchers showed female college students photographs of a man who was wearing a red, white, blue, or green shirt (Elliot et al., 2010). They then asked the women to rate his attractiveness, as well as their interest in dating, kissing, and engaging in other types of sexual activity with him. As predicted, men who were wearing a red shirt seemed more powerful, attractive, and sexually desirable. This effect was also seen across a variety of cultures, including the United States, England, Germany, and China, suggesting that these links between the color red and perceptions of attractiveness are partially rooted in our biology, not merely social learning.

Reggie Casagrande/Getty Images

Research Challenge

1. Based on the information provided, did this research (Guéguen & Jacob, 2014; Elliot et al., 2010) use descriptive, correlational, and/or experimental research? (Tip: Be sure to look for two separate answers for the two different studies.)
2. If you chose:
   - *descriptive research*, is this a naturalistic observation, survey/interview, case study, and/or archival research?
   - *correlational research*, is this a positive, negative, or zero correlation?
   - *experimental research*, label the IV, DV, experimental groups(s), and control group.
   - both *descriptive* and *correlational*, answer the corresponding questions for both.

Check your answers with those provided.

Note: The information provided in this study is a[…] level of detail is similar to what is presented in n[…] reports of research findings. Answering these que[…] ing your answers to those provided, will help yo[…] thinker and consumer of scientific research.

PS Psych**Science**

Can Watching Movies Prevent Divorce?

As we all know, roughly half of all U.S. marriages end in divorce. Numerous secular and religious institutions have attempted to reduce this rate with various early marriage intervention programs. To examine whether simple self-help strategies, such as watching and discussing movies about relationships, might offer some of the same benefits as these professionally led intervention programs, researchers randomly assigned 174 couples to one of four groups (Rogge et al., 2013):

- Group 1 (control) received no training or instructions.
- Group 2 (conflict management) learned active listening strategies to help discuss heated issues.
- Group 3 (compassion and acceptance training) learned strategies for finding common ground and showing empathy.
- Group 4 (minimal intervention—movie and talk) attended a 10-minute lecture on relationship awareness and how watching couples in movies could help increase awareness of their own behaviors.

Following this initial assignment to groups, Group 1 received no training at all, but members of this group were similar to those in the three other groups in terms of age, education, ethnicity, relationship satisfaction, and other dimensions. Groups 2 and 3 attended weekly lectures, completed homework assignments, and met with a trained therapist periodically. In contrast, Group 4 only attended a 10-minute lecture, watched a romantic comedy, and then discussed 12 questions about the screen couple's interactions (such as, "Did they try using humor to keep things from getting nasty?"). They were then sent home with a list of 47 relationship-oriented movies and allowed to choose their favorite one to watch and discuss once a week for the next month.

The researchers then followed up with all couples 3 years later to see which of these approaches was most effective for preventing divorce. Much to their surprise, couples in all three of the intervention groups were much less likely to get divorced compared to those in the control group. Specifically, 24% of couples in the control group were divorced, compared to only 11% of those in any of the other three groups. Even more surprising, this study shows that a simple self-help strategy of watching and discussing five relationship movies over 1 month's time can be just as effective at reducing the divorce or separation rate as more intensive early marriage counseling programs led by trained psychologists.

MAD_Production / Shutterstock

Do you see how this study has exciting wide-scale, national applications? If "movie date night" can double as therapy, many U.S. couples might be saved from the very high emotional and financial costs of divorce. What about your own current or future relationships? If simply sharing and discussing a relationship movie now and then with your romantic partner might strengthen that relationship, why not try it? You can learn more about this study (and see a list of recommended movies with guided discussion questions) at: www.couples-research.com.

Research Challenge

1. Based on the information provided, did this study (Rogge et al., 2013) use descriptive, correlational, and/or experimental research?
2. If you chose:
   - *descriptive research*, is this a naturalistic observation, survey/interview, case study, and/or archival research?
   - *correlational research*, is this a positive, negative, or zero correlation?
   - *experimental research*, label the IV, DV, experimental group(s), and control group.
   - both *descriptive* and *correlational*, answer the corresponding questions for both.

Check your answers with those provided.

Note: The information provided in this study is admittedly limited, but the level of detail is similar to what is presented in most textbooks and public reports of research findings. Answering these questions, and then comparing your answers to those provided, will help you become a better critical thinker and consumer of scientific research.

PS Psych**Science**

Can Taking Photos Impair Our Memories?

Researchers interested in this and related questions set up two studies using participants who were led on a guided tour of an art museum (Henkel, 2014). During the tour participants were asked to take note of certain objects, either by photographing them or by simply observing them. The next day their memory for the specific objects was tested. As you may have suspected, participants were less accurate in recognizing the objects they had photographed, and weren't able to answer as many questions about the objects' details, compared to those they had only observed.

However, when participants were asked to zoom in and photograph a specific part of the object, their subsequent recognition and detail memory was not impaired. Furthermore, participants' memories for features that were NOT zoomed in on were just as strong as memory for features that were zoomed in on. Can you see how this finding suggests that the selective attention and deeper levels of processing engaged by this focused activity improve overall encoding, and may eliminate the photo-taking-impairment effect?

This research has important implications. Given that it's difficult to always be paying full focused attention, we need to keep in mind that while we're mindlessly taking numerous "selfies" and other photos we may encode fewer details. This means that taking photos the whole time we're on vacation or during a child's dance recital may not only interfere with our full enjoyment of the event, but our actual memories of those special occasions as well! (Study Tip: While reading this and other college texts and/or listening to lectures, you can improve your learning and memory by consciously directing your brain to pay focused, selective attention to important details. You can also process the material at a deeper level by "zooming in" on important details.)

Owen Franken/Getty Images

Research Challenge

1. Based on the information provided, did this study (Henkel, 2014) use descriptive, correlational, and/or experimental research?
2. If you chose:
   - *descriptive research*, is this a naturalistic observation, survey/interview, case study, and/or archival research?
   - *correlational research*, is this a positive, negative, or zero correlation?
   - *experimental research*, label the IV, DV, experimental group(s), and control group.
   - both *descriptive* and *correlational*, answer the corresponding questions for both.

Check your answers with those provided.

Note: The information provided in this study is admittedly limited, but the level of detail is similar to what is presented in most text books and public reports of research findings. Answering these questions, and then comparing your answers to those provided, will help you become a better critical thinker and consumer of scientific research.

- **Comprehensible** A good textbook must be more than concise and comprehensive. It must organize and present complex topics in a manner that is easily read and understood by the reader. However, comprehension and retention of abstract concepts is difficult for many students unless they are clearly linked to their daily lives. Therefore, *RWP* uses numerous real world examples and real world applications to scaffold the content of psychology onto the reader's existing schemas (see the two samples on the next page). This real world focus increases comprehension, while at the same time showing our readers why *studying psychology matters*!

Real World **Psychology**—Understanding the World

Subliminal Music and Food Choices

© Matthew Ennis/iStockphot

In a recent study, researchers placed 10 volunteers in different rooms with music playing in the background from one of three regions—the United States, China, or India (North et al., 2016). While listening to different types of music, each participant looked at a menu for 5 minutes with 30 dinner options (10 from each country). The scientists then asked them to recall as many dishes from the menu as they could, and then to choose one dish to order as a meal. Perhaps thanks to subliminal stimuli from the music, participants better remembered and chose dishes that reflected the music they had listened to before looking at the menu. For example, those who listened to American music ("California Girls," "Surfin' U.S.A.," and "Good Vibrations" by the Beach Boys) chose foods like hamburgers and hot dogs (see photo).

Psychology and **You**—Understanding Yourself

Sexual Response Reflexes

Reflexes even influence our sexual responses. Certain stimuli, such as the stroking of the genitals, can lead to arousal and the reflexive muscle contractions of orgasm in both men and women. However, in order for us to have the passion, thoughts, and emotion we normally associate with sex, the sensory information from the stroking and orgasm must be carried on to the appropriate areas of the brain that receive and interpret these specific sensory messages.

Kovalchynskyy Mykola/Shutterstock

For even more real world applications that are tied in with core psychology topics, we've added a **NEW** feature, **PositivePsych**–see the sample below. Psychology has a long history of focusing primarily on dysfunction versus function and negative versus positive outcomes. To offset this imbalance, and further engage our readers, we offer numerous examples and applications from the field of positive psychology, which emphasizes optimal human functioning.

PP **Positive**Psych

Would You Donate a Kidney to a Stranger?

In what is a particularly remarkable act of altruism, each year people donate one of their kidneys to strangers (people they aren't related to and don't know). They receive nothing in return, and generally experience serious pain and discomfort, along with a somewhat lengthy period of recovery. What prompts this type of generosity? Under what conditions would you donate a kidney to a stranger? Some research suggests that people who feel good about themselves overall are more likely to engage in other types of prosocial behavior, such as volunteering and giving money to charity, which might explain organ donation.

To examine this idea, researchers in the United States compared rates of kidney donations in different states with each state's overall level of well-being (Brethel-Haurwitz & Marsh, 2014). As predicted, states with higher rates of kidney donation tended to have higher rates of well-being. This finding held true even after the researchers took into account other factors that could explain this relationship, such as household income, age, education, religion, and mental and physical health.

PA images/Alamy Stock Photo

What do you think? Beyond giving a kidney while you're alive, are you registered as an organ donor upon your death? Given the thousands of people who die each year who are on waiting lists for donor organs, should we adopt policies like considering everyone to be a donor unless they officially "opt-out?" If you'd like more information on the facts and myths about organ donation, visit: http://www.americantransplantfoundation.org/about-transplant/facts-and-myths/

As you can see, we feel passionate about our second edition and believe that our B (Brevity) and three Cs (Concise, Comprehensive, and Comprehensible) can turn "B" and "C" students into "A"s! We're eager to share our passion for psychology with all instructors and their students. If you have suggestions or comments, please feel free to contact us directly: Catherine Sanderson (casanderson@amherst.edu) and Karen Huffman (khuffman@palomar.edu).

What's New in the Second Edition?

Real World Psychology, Second Edition, includes over 1500 new research citations, a fresh new design and layout, new photos, figures, and tables, and some chapter reorganizations. As in the previous edition, numerous integrated cross cultural examples are found throughout the text, along with **Think Critically** discussion sections generally placed in the "Self-Tests" and sprinkled throughout each chapter.

General Changes—The following list includes the most significant, general changes we incorporated throughout the Second Edition:

- Expanded the *Chapter Overview* to include a summary of the entire chapter.
- Updated and expanded learning objectives for each chapter.
- Reconfigured some figures and/or created NEW **Process Diagrams** for each chapter to better illustrate the step-by-step processes of certain key concepts.
- Replaced "minority" and "minorities" with "person of color" and "people of color."
- Changed references to "African-Americans" and "Caucasians" to "Black" and "White."
- Due to recent findings, which better reflect the actual response of the autonomic nervous system (ANS), we changed "fight or flight" to "fight-flight-freeze."
- In response to reviewer suggestions, we deleted the previous *Voices from the Classroom*, which also allowed us space to include our NEW **PositivePsych** feature in each chapter.
- Each *Self-Test* following the major headings has been updated and expanded to include additional and new questions, as well as changes in the **Think Critically** sections.
- Updated and refined all key term definitions using full sentences.
- Expanded details within each end-of-chapter, narrative **Summary**.

Specific Changes—Below, you will find a listing of the **specific content changes** in each chapter of RWP(2e). Note that the top section highlights the changes to the "Things you'll learn," as well as providing the titles of the NEW and continuing **PositivePsych** and **PsychScience** sections.

Chapter 1 Introduction and Research Methods

Real World **Psychology**
Things you'll learn in Chapter 1
[Q1] How does your culture influence what you look for in a romantic partner?
[Q2] Can a change in posture make you more attractive?
[Q3] Do breast-fed babies have higher IQs?
[Q4] Can a diet high in fats and sugars impair learning and memory?
[Q5] Are older people happier than younger people?
[Q6] What are the two best study techniques for improving your exam performance?

Throughout the chapter, margin icons for Q1–Q6 indicate where the text addresses these questions.

PositivePsych What Makes Us Happy?
PsychScience Why Do Men and Women Lie About Sex?

- Expanded discussion of *pseudopsychology* (p. 2).
- Updated and added new activity to Table 1.1 (p. 5).
- Expanded discussion of evolutionary psychology and added new key term for **natural selection** (pp. 5-6).
- Expanded coverage of *Gender and People of Color* section (p. 6).
- Updated and moved *Psychology's Research Ethics* (pp. 13-15) from previous *Research Methods* to the *Science of Psychology* section.
- Revised Table 1.5 (p. 16) "Psychology's Three Major Research Methods."
- Revised two sections, *Limits of Correlations* and *The Value of Correlations* (pp. 19–20), including two new key terms—the **third-variable problem** and **illusory correlation**. Removed *confounding variable* as a key term.
- NEW Table 1.6 (p. 20) "Superstitions as Illusory Correlations."
- NEW example of "texting while driving" in **Process Diagram 1.2** (p. 21).
- NEW Figure 1.12 (p. 23) "Can a horse, add, multiply, and divide?"
- Revised drawing of Figure 1.13 (p. 24) to better reflect the single- and double-blind set up.
- Added new key term, **placebo effect** (p. 24).
- Significantly revised and expanded *Strategies for Student Success section* (pp. 26–30) to include:
    - NEW **Psychology and You** (p. 26) "Skills for Student Success Checklist."
    - NEW Test Yourself (Stroop effect) "The Importance of Focus and Active Reading" (p. 27).
    - NEW section (pp. 29–30) *Grade Improvement.*
    - NEW section (p. 30) *A Final Word About College Success.*

Chapter 2 Neuroscience and Biological Foundations

Real World **Psychology**
Things you'll learn in Chapter 2
[Q1] Does spending the first few months of life in an orphanage lead to long-term problems in cognitive functioning?

[Q2] How can singing and/or dancing make you feel closer to strangers and also raise your pain threshold?
[Q3] Why does eye contact with your dog make you feel good?
[Q4] How might stem cell injections have saved "Superman"?
[Q5] Can playing video games be good for your brain?
[Q6] Why are former NFL athletes at increased risk of depression, dementia, and suicide?

Throughout the chapter, margin icons for Q1–Q6 indicate where the text addresses these questions.

PositivePsych The Power of Positive Coaching
PsychScience Phineas Gage—Myths Versus Facts

- Due to reviewer suggestions and chapter length, moved section on *Our Genetic Inheritance* to Chapters 9 and 11, along with these key terms: *behavioral genetics, evolutionary psychology, gene, heritability*, and *natural selection*.
- Added NEW and expanded section, *Understanding the Neuron* (pp. 34–35).
- Added NEW narrative discussion of the three steps of communication within the neuron, and the three steps of communication between neurons (pp. 35, 37).
- Added NEW key term, **all-or-nothing principle** (p. 37).
- Added glutamate to Table 2.1 (p. 39).
- Added NEW Figure 2.5, "Lou Gehrig's disease or repeated head trauma?" (p. 43).
- Expanded and moved the previous section on the *Cerebral Cortex* to the end of the chapter for better chapter coverage and balance.
- Expanded discussion of frontal lobes (pp. 54–56).
- Added NEW **Psychology and You**—"Testing Your Motor Cortex and Somatosensory Cortex" (p. 58).
- Significantly revised part E of Figure 2.19 (p. 59).
- Created new **Applying Real World Psychology** feature and photo (p. 61).

Chapter 3 Stress and Health Psychology

Real World **Psychology**
Things you'll learn in Chapter 3

[Q1] Does frequent checking of your email and social media increase your stress?
[Q2] Can the stress of growing up in poverty cause changes in your brain?
[Q3] Does watching televised coverage of natural disasters increase symptoms of posttraumatic stress disorder?
[Q4] Could thinking about the "silver linings" of a stressful event, or sharing it with others, reduce depression?
[Q5] Are people with stressful jobs at increased risk of experiencing a heart attack?

Throughout the chapter, margin icons for Q1–Q5 indicate where the text addresses these questions.

PositivePsych Mindfulness and Your GPA
PsychScience When Losers Actually Win

- Added NEW Myth Busters feature (p. 63).
- Changed the name of the previous section on *Chronic Stress* to *Acute/Chronic Stress*, and added NEW key term, **acute stress** (p. 64).
- Updated Table 3.1, "Types of Conflict" (p. 66), with new graphics and text.
- Expanded research discussion of cataclysmic events (p. 67).
- Added NEW term of *fight-flight-freeze* to replace previous *fight or flight*, and NEW research discussion of gender differences in reaction to stress (p. 68).
- Added NEW Figure 3.3, "Our brain under chronic stress," and NEW section, *Benefits of Stress*, and two NEW key terms, **distress** and **eustress** (p. 71).
- Added NEW Figure 3.4, "Stress and task complexity," and discussion of the so-called "advantages" of mass trauma events compared to individual-level trauma (p. 72).
- Removed discussion of *Type A* and *Type B behavior patterns* and as key terms from the previous section on *Cardiovascular Disorders*.
- Expanded discussion of PTSD and added two new tables, "Key Characteristics of PTSD" and "Seven Important Tips for Coping with Crisis" (pp. 75–76).
- Added NEW **Real World Psychology** feature—"Helping Someone with PTSD" (pp.76–77).
- Added NEW section, *Cognitive Appraisal* (pp. 78–79).
- Revised previous Figure 3.11 to make it **Process Diagram 3.3** (p. 78).
- Added NEW section, *Personality and Individual Differences*, to include *locus of control, positive affect*, and *optimism* (pp. 79-80).
- Added NEW key term, **optimism** (p. 80).
- Added NEW **Real World Psychology** feature—"Why Are Optimists Healthier?" (p. 80).
- Added NEW **Psychology and You**—"Practicing Progressive Relaxation" (p. 82).
- Moved and revised previous section, *Health Psychology and Stress Management*, to the end of chapter, with NEW sections on *Health Psychology at Work* and *Coping with Job and Technostress* (pp. 85-86).
- Added NEW key term for **technostress** (p. 85).
- Added NEW **Psychology and You**—"Workplace Stress" (p. 86).

Chapter 4 Sensation and Perception

Real World **Psychology**
Things you'll learn in Chapter 4
[Q1] Do athletes have a higher pain tolerance than non-athletes?
[Q2] Can looking at a photograph of a loved one lead you to feel less pain?
[Q3] Can using a lower-pitched voice affect your perceived influence and power?
[Q4] How can listening to loud music on headphones damage your hearing?
[Q5] Why do babies (and adults) need skin-to-skin contact?
[Q6] Are Black football players more likely to be penalized for touch-down celebrations than White football players?

Throughout the chapter, margin icons for Q1–Q6 indicate where the text addresses these questions.

PositivePsych Can Bouncing a Baby Increase Helping?
PsychScience Does Wearing Red Increase Your Sex Appeal?

- Added NEW Figure 4.1, "Sensation and perception" (p. 90).
- Moved discussion of *bottom-up* and *top-down processing* from end of chapter to opening as tie ins and examples of sensation vs. perception (p. 90).
- Slightly revised Table 4.1, "Sensation and Perception" (p. 91).
- Added NEW Figure 4.3, "Why is our difference threshold important?" (p. 92).
- Expanded section on Subliminal Stimuli, and added NEW key term, **priming** (pp. 93–94).
- Added NEW **Real World Psychology** feature—"Subliminal Music and Food Choices" (p. 94).
- Added NEW Figure 4.6, "Treating phantom limb pain" (p. 95).
- In response to reviewers, we move moved *Color Vision* from the perception section at the end of the chapter to the vision section (pp. 98-100).
- Added NEW Figure 4.9, "Primary colors" (p. 99).
- Removed previous Table 4.3, and added research and discussion on the NEW key term, **volley principle for hearing** (p. 102).
- Expanded discussion of taste and smell receptors (p. 104).
- Added NEW Figure 4.15, "Infant benefits from kangaroo care" (p. 107).
- Added new discussion of the distinction between *sensory adaptation* and *habituation* (p. 110).
- Replaced Figure a. from Figure 4.19, "Form perception and "impossible figures" and expanded discussion (p. 110).
- Expanded discussion with NEW research on *depth perception,* and added NEW Figure 4.23, "Visual cues for depth perception" (p. 112).
- Updated and expanded discussion of *Ames room illusion,* Figure 4.28 (p. 114).
- Removed discussion of *fallacy of positive instances* (p. 116).

Chapter 5 States of Consciousness

Real World **Psychology**
Things you'll learn in Chapter 5
[Q1] Could you fail to notice a clearly visible brutal assault (or a person in a gorilla suit) if you were otherwise distracted?
[Q2] Can using a computer or iPad late at night make it harder to fall asleep?
[Q3] Are you addicted to Facebook?
[Q4] Does binge drinking reduce condom use?
[Q5] Can using marijuana decrease your IQ?
[Q6] Can hypnosis decrease the pain of childbirth?

Throughout the chapter, margin icons for Q1–Q6 indicate where the text addresses these questions.

PositivePsych Can Meditation Increase Helping Behaviors?
PsychScience The Very Real Hazards of Distracted Driving

- Added NEW #2 heading, *Understanding Consciousness* (p. 120).
- Expanded discussion of *selective attention* (p. 120).
- Added NEW key term, **inattentional blindess** (p. 120).
- Added NEW section on *Levels of Awareness*, and two NEW key terms, **controlled processes** and **automatic processes** (p. 121).
- Added NEW #2 heading, *Understanding Sleep and Dreams* (p. 123).
- Rearranged and added NEW Part c. to Figure 5.2 (p. 124).
- In response to NEW research, changed the stages of NREM sleep from 4 stages to 3 stages, and adjusted Figure 5.3 (p. 126).
- Added NEW **Think Critically** questions to Table 5.1 (p. 129).
- Changed category of "Opiates" to "Opiates/Opiods" in text, key term, and Table 5.3 to reflect current usage (pp. 134, 137).
- Added NEW Figure 5.8, "Alcohol and rape" discussing the controversy over Brock Turner's light sentence, and added **Think Critically** questions (p. 136).
- Changed and updated photo of Cory Monteith and "High cost of drug abuse" to photo of Prince (p. 138).
- Expanded discussion on the controversial research on marijuana (p. 138).
- Updated section on *Club Drugs* (pp. 138–139).
- Updated section on *Meditation and Hypnosis* (pp. 139–142).

Chapter 6 Learning

Real World **Psychology**
Things you'll learn in Chapter 6
[Q1] Why can simply hearing the sound of a drill in a dentist's office—even if that drill is nowhere near you—make you feel anxious?
[Q2] Can off ering cash incentives and gift cards to smokers actually help them to quit?
[Q3] Why do gamblers have such trouble quitting, even when they continue to lose money?
[Q4] Can children learn anti-fat prejudice and math anxiety from their parents?
[Q5] Why can even young children recognize a picture of a snake much faster than a picture of a frog or caterpillar?
Throughout the chapter, margin icons for Q1–Q5 Indicate where the text addresses these questions.
PositivePsych The Impressive Powers of Prosocial Media
PsychScience Can Television Exposure Change Body Size Preference?

- Expanded discussion of the *six principles of classical conditioning* (pp. 150–152).
- In response to reviewers, removed the word "stimulus" from key terms of **generalization** and **discrimination** and added the words "in classical conditioning" to the term (pp. 150–151).
- Expanded discussion of Skinner's response to Thorndike and his definition of reinforcement and punishment as observable behaviors. Updated Table 6.2, "How Reinforcement Increases (or Strengthens) Behavior" (pp. 154–155).
- Expanded discussion of *primary* and *secondary reinforcers* and *positive* and *negative punishment*, deleted *Premack principle* as a key term, and updated Table 6.3, "How Punishment Decreases (or Weakens) Behavior" (pp. 155–157).
- Added NEW **Real World Psychology** feature (p. 159) discussing the "Effective Use of Reinforcement and Punishment."
- NEW Table 6.4 (p. 158) "Potential Side Effects of Punishment" with NEW **Think Critically** questions.
- Reorganized and added six NEW *Principles of Operant Conditioning* section with NEW key term—**acquisition** (pp. 158–161).
- Added NEW Figure 6.8, "Shaping in action" (p. 159).
- Added NEW Figure 6.9, "Gambling-a partial schedule of reinforcement" and updated Table 6.5, "Four Schedules of Partial (Intermittent) Reinforcement" (p. 160).
- Added NEW Figure 6.10, "Which schedule is best?" (p. 161).
- Updated Part a. of Figure 6.11, "Operant conditioning in everyday life" (p. 161).
- Updated Table 6.6, "Comparing Classical and Operant Conditioning" (p. 162).
- Added and expanded NEW section, *Cognitive-Social Learning and Everyday Life* (pp. 164–167).
- Added NEW **Psychology and You** (p. 167) "Using Learning Principles to Succeed in College."
- Added NEW Figure 6.16 (p. 168) "How our brains respond to reinforcement versus punishment."
- Added NEW **Think Critically** questions to **Psychology and You** (p. 170).

Chapter 7 Memory

Real World **Psychology**
Things you'll learn in Chapter 7
[Q1] Do video game players have better working-memory skills?
[Q2] How can taking a nap improve your memory?
[Q3] Why do we remember President Lincoln better than President Truman?
[Q4] How might exposure to pornography interfere with memory?
[Q5] Could someone falsely convince you as an adult that you committed a serious crime as a teenager?
Throughout the chapter, margin icons for Q1–Q5 indicate where the text addresses these questions.
PositivePsych Memory and Age-Related Happiness
PsychScience Can Taking Photos Impair Our Memories?

- Moved previous **Psychology and You** personal memory test from end of chapter to first pages to demonstrate constructive nature of memory (p. 175).
- Added NEW key term—**levels of processing** (p. 176).
- Added NEW discussion regarding infant memories and NEW key term—**age-related positivity effect** (pp. 180-181).
- Added NEW **Psychology and You** on "Improving Elaborative Rehearsal" (p. 183).
- Updated previous **Psychology and You**, which used the "Penny Test" to demonstrate encoding failure, and replaced it with a test of the "Apple Logo" (p. 187).
- Removed *sleeper effect* as a key term.
- Added NEW **Real World Psychology** feature—"High Price of Forgetting" (p. 188).
- Added NEW **Psychology and You**—"Common FBMs" (p. 191).
- Added NEW **Real World Psychology** feature—"How Emotional Arousal May Threaten Our Survival!" (p. 192).
- Added NEW section on *Traumatic Brain Injury* (TBI) with a NEW **Real World Psychology** feature—"Professional Sports and Brain Damage" (p. 193).

- Added expanded section on *Eyewitness Testimony* and a NEW Figure 7.19 (pp. 196-197).
- Expanded section on *False Versus Repressed Memories*, and a NEW Figure 7.20 on brain scans that detect true versus false memories (p. 198).
- Added NEW section *Memory Improvement—Strategies for Student Success*, which summarizes specific tips found throughout the chapter (pp. 199–201).

Chapter 8 Thinking, Language, and Intelligence

Real World **Psychology**
Things you'll learn in Chapter 8
[Q1] Why might some medical treatments be judged as more effective than they really are?
[Q2] Can outdoor activities or simply taking a walk improve your creativity?
[Q3] Do babies begin to learn language even before they are born?
[Q4] Does speaking multiple languages make you smarter?
[Q5] Can personal traits and character strengths be better predictors of achievement than IQ?
[Q6] Will watching TV dramas increase your emotional intelligence?
Throughout the chapter, margin icons for Q1–Q6 indicate where the text addresses these questions.
PositivePsych Why Talk or Read to Babies?
PsychScience The Power of Words

- In response to reviewers, removed *concept, artificial concept*, and *mental image* as key terms.
- Added NEW **Psychology and You**—"Problem Solving and Your Career" (p. 206).
- Added NEW Table 8.1, "Three Problem-Solving Heuristics and Your Career" (p. 208).
- Added NEW section, *Strategies for Better Problem Solving* (p. 210).
- In response to reviewers, changed Table 8.2 to use Nikola Tesla versus Thomas Edison as an exemplar for creative thinking (p. 211).
- Added NEW key term—**convergent thinking** (p. 211).
- Updated Table 8.3, "Resources of Creative People" with new resource and applied to Lady Gaga (p. 212).
- Added NEW **Real World Psychology** feature—"Language Distortions" (p. 215).
- Updated Table 8.4, "Language Acquisition," and in response to reviewers removed *cooing, babbling, overextension, overgeneralization*, and *telegraphic speech* as key terms (p. 216).
- To balance content in the previous *Intelligence* section, we divided it into two sections, *Intelligence* and *Intelligence Controversies*. We then moved *Measuring Intelligence* up in the first section and Sternberg, Gardner, and Goleman's EI into the second section.
- Added two NEW key terms—**mental age (MA)** and **normal distribution** (p. 220).
- Removed *savant syndrome* as a key term.
- Added NEW discussion of gender differences in IQ, NEW Figure 8.13, "Brain sex differences," and NEW Table 8.6, "Problem-Solving Tasks Favoring Women and Men" (pp. 225–226).
- Updated discussion of research on controversial issues in IQ differences (pp. 226–228).
- Added NEW key term—**triarchic theory of intelligence** (p. 229).
- Added NEW **Psychology and You** feature—"Key Traits for Emotional Intelligence (EI)" (p. 230).
- Added NEW **Psychology and You** feature—"Optimizing Your Well-Being" (p. 231).

Chapter 9 Life Span Development

Real World **Psychology**
Things you'll learn in Chapter 9
[Q1] Why are young people more supportive of gay marriage than older adults?
[Q2] Does prenatal exposure to smoke increase the risk of obesity later in life?
[Q3] Why do teenagers sleep so much?
[Q4] Do babies learn faster when they're sitting up than when they're lying down?
[Q5] Does the taking and posting of self-portraits ("selfies") increase narcissism?
[Q6] Do today's college students want women to propose marriage?
Throughout the chapter, margin icons for Q1–Q6 indicate where the text addresses these questions.
PositivePsych Adults Need Hugs Too!
PsychScience Deprivation and Development

- Removed *maturation* as a key term (p. 236).
- Updated Figure 9.1 from Lorenz and geese to cranes (p. 236).
- Updated Figure 9.3, "Cross-sectional versus longitudinal research" (p. 238).
- Added NEW **Psychology and You**—"Want to be Happier? Grow Older!" (pp. 239–240).
- Added NEW section on genetics with NEW key terms, **chromosomes, DNA, gene, behavioral genetics,** and **epigenetics** (pp. 241–242).

- Updated Table 9.2, "Sample Prenatal Environmental Conditions that Endanger a Child." Added new discussion of *fetal alcohol spectrum disorder (FASD)*, and removed *fetal alcohol syndrome (FAS)* as a key term (pp. 243–244).
- Added NEW **Real World Psychology** feature—"Puberty and Oversleeping" (p. 246).
- Moved previous discussion of teenage brain from *Cognitive Development* section up to *Physical Development* (p. 246).
- Added NEW section and NEW key term **emerging adulthood** (p. 247).
- Added NEW discussion of theories of aging and why we die, along with a new section, *Late Adulthood brain* (p. 248).
- Added the late Justice Scalia to **Real World Psychology** feature (p. 249).
- Updated previous Table 9.3 and made it **Process Diagram 9.2** (p. 251).
- Expanded discussion and examples of *Preoperational Stage* (p. 252).
- Expanded discussion and examples of *Formal Operational Stage* (p. 254).
- Expanded discussion and examples of *Attachment* (p. 257).
- Updated and added NEW drawings to Figure 9.20, "Research on infant attachment" (p. 259)
- Added NEW discussion of father's role in parenting styles (p. 260).
- In response to reviewers, removed *conventional level, preconventional level*, and *postconventional level* as key terms (pp. 261–262).
- Added NEW section, *Thomas and Chess's Temperament Theory* and NEW key term—**temperament** (pp. 263–264).

Chapter 10 Motivation and Emotion

Real World **Psychology**
Things you'll learn in Chapter 10
[Q1] Is paying students to get good grades a good idea?
[Q2] How can just looking at pictures of high-fat foods make you feel hungry?
[Q3] Is motivation a better predictor of success than IQ?
[Q4] Does sexual frequency predict greater well-being?
[Q5] Can airport security agents increase their effectiveness by simply talking to passengers?
[Q6] Are our emotions contagious?

Throughout the chapter, margin icons for Q1–Q6 indicate where the text addresses these questions.

PositivePsych Can Long-Distance Relationships Survive?
PsychScience Does Your Smile Tell Others Where You're From?

- Expanded discussion of optimal-arousal theory, added NEW Figure 10.3, "The Yerkes-Dodson law," and NEW key term—**Yerkes-Dodson law** (pp. 272–273).
- Added NEW **Psychology and You**—"Test Yourself/Need for Achievement" (p. 281).
- Added discussion of personal control and achievement, and two NEW key terms—**growth mindset** and **grit** (p. 281).
- Moved section on *Extrinsic Versus Intrinsic Motivation* up before sexuality (pp. 281–283).
- Added NEW **Psychology and You**—"Tips for Increasing Motivation" (p. 283).
- Updated Table 10.3, "Sexual Orientation Myths," to include 2015 Obergefell v. Hodges decision legalizing gay marriage (p. 285).
- Added new discussion of Orlando, Florida 2016 attacks on gays as latest example of sexual prejudice (p. 285).
- For better balance in length of #2 heads, we broke the previous *Components and Theories of Emotion* into two *Components and Theories of Emotion* (pp. 286–291) and *Experiencing Emotions* (pp. 292–298).
- Added NEW Figure 10.12, "The three components of emotion—in action!" (p. 286).
- Moved previous Figure 10.18 (p. 296) to this section (p. 287).
- Added NEW section, *Evaluating Theories of Emotion* (pp. 290–291).
- Added NEW information on the 6-12 emotions, and later research that limits it to four—happy, sad, afraid/surprised, and angry/disgusted (pp. 292–293).
- Added NEW Table 10.4, "Sample Basic Emotions," comparing four different groups of theorists with a Test Yourself to identify six photos of infant emotions (p. 293).
- Added NEW section, *The Psychology of Happiness*, which discusses the latest research (pp. 296–298).
- Added NEW **Psychology and You**—"Five Tips for Increased Happiness" (pp. 296-297).
- Added NEW key term—**adaptation-level phenomenon** (p. 297)

Chapter 11 Personality

Real World **Psychology**
Things you'll learn in Chapter 11
[Q1] Are some people with highly negative attitudes toward gay people repressing their own sexual desires?
[Q2] Which personality traits are most important for your career and academic success?
[Q3] What parenting skills are also associated with increased marital satisfaction?
[Q4] Can spending time in a foreign country change your personality?
[Q5] Do our genes predict how much we will give to charity?
[Q6] Can social media postings be used to measure your personality?

Throughout the chapter, margin icons for Q1–Q6 indicate where the text addresses these questions.

PositivePsych Can (and Should) We Improve Our Personality Traits?
PsychScience Do Nonhuman Animals Have Unique Personalities?

- Deleted *pleasure principle, reality principle*, and *morality principle* as key terms (pp. 302–303).
- Expanded narrative discussion of psychosexual stages of development (pp. 303–306).
- Updated previous Figure 11.5 and made it **Process Diagram 11.1** (p. 305).
- Added NEW **Real World Psychology** feature—"Freud and Modern Western Culture" (p. 306).
- Added NEW **Psychology and You**—"Constructing Your Own Personality Profile" (p. 309).
- Added NEW **Real World Psychology** feature—"The Stanford Marshmallow Test" (p. 319).
- Added NEW section, *Personality and Behavioral Genetics*, added NEW Figure 11.12, "Identical versus fraternal twins," and NEW Figure 11.14, "Adoption studies" (pp. 321–322).
- Added NEW discussion of social media outlets as a measure of personality, and added NEW Figure 11.18, "Facebook test of your personality" (p. 324).
- Deleted previous Table 11.3, "Subscales of the MMPI-2."
- Replaced previous term of *fallacy of positive instances* with more accurate term of *confirmation bias* in the **Psychology and You** section (p. 328).

Chapter 12 Psychological Disorders

Real World **Psychology**
Things you'll learn in Chapter 12
[Q1] How can media coverage of mass shootings create negative misperceptions about people with mental illness?
[Q2] What is the most "contagious" psychological disorder?
[Q3] Can internet and cell phone use increase mental health problems?
[Q4] Are children who experience trauma at increased risk of developing schizophrenia later in life?
[Q5] How do changes in the brain help explain severe antisocial personality disorder?
[Q6] Are symptoms of depression in women more distressing, deserving of sympathy, and difficult to treat than the same signs in men?

Throughout the chapter, margin icons for Q1–Q6 indicate where the text addresses these questions.

PositivePsych Resilience in Children and Adults
PsychScience Creativity and Bipolar Disorder

- Updated Table 12.1, "Common Myths About Mental Illness" (p. 333).
- Added NEW Figure 12.2, "Witchcraft or mental illness" (p. 333).
- Updated Figure 12.4, "The insanity plea—guilty of a crime or mentally ill," with Eddie Ray Routh's shooting of "American Sniper" Chris Kyle and Chad Littlefield (p. 335).
- Added NEW section, *The Dangers and Stigma of Mental Illness* (pp. 335, 337).
- Added NEW **Real World Psychology** feature—"The Media, Myths, and Mental Illness" (p. 337).
- Updated psychological factors of anxiety disorders with discussion of anxiety as the "most contagious" of all disorders (pp. 339–341).
- Rearranged previous two Psychology and You features, "Danger Signs for Suicide," and "What to Do if You Think Someone is Suicidal." And created NEW Table 12.3, "Common Myths About Suicide," a Test Yourself, "Danger Signs for Suicide," and a NEW **Real World Psychology** feature—"What to do if You Think Someone is Suicidal," with a new photo and description of Robin William's suicide (pp. 346–347).
- Added NEW section, *Prenatal and Other Environmental Factors*, to cover new research on schizophrenia (pp. 350–351).
- Removed previous discussion of James Holmes as an example of antisocial personality disorder.

Chapter 13 Therapy

Real World **Psychology**
Things you'll learn in Chapter 13
[Q1] Can changing your irrational thoughts and self-talk make you feel better about your body?
[Q2] How might accepting fears and worries rather than trying to eliminate them decrease PTSD?
[Q3] Could therapy help you hold a tarantula?
[Q4] Does simply watching other children play with dogs reduce dog phobias in young children?
[Q5] Do psychedelic drugs cause psychosis?
[Q6] Can therapy that is delivered over the telephone lead to lower levels of depression?

Throughout the chapter, margin icons for Q1–Q6 indicate where the text addresses these questions.

PositivePsych Protecting Your Mental Health
PsychScience Can Watching Movies Prevent Divorce?

- Expanded discussion of *psychotherapy* (p. 362).
- Added NEW Figure13.3, "The five key techniques for psychoanalysis" (p. 364).
- Added NEW Figure 13.3, "Freud's free association" (p. 364).
- Added NEW **Psychology and You**—"Overcoming Irrational Misconceptions" (p. 368).
- Updated **Psychology and You**, "A Cognitive Approach to Lifting Depression," and changed "magnification" to "magnification and minimization," and added "personalization" (p. 370).
- Updated Table 13.2, "Psychotherapeutic Drug Treatments for Psychological Disorders" (p. 376).

- Added NEW **Real World Psychology** feature—“Do Psychedelic Drugs Cause Psychosis” (p. 378).
- Updated and rearranged section on *Evaluating Biomedical Therapies*, and placed deep brain stimulation (DBS) in the psychosurgery section 379–380).
- Updated the *Gender and Therapy* section, and added gender-role conflict as part of the unique gender concerns (pp. 385–386).
- Added NEW key term—**well-being therapy (WBT)** (p. 387).

Chapter 14 Social Psychology

Real World **Psychology**

Things you'll learn in Chapter 14

[Q1] Why do athletes often blame their losses on bad officiating?
[Q2] How can taking a pain pill reduce attitude change?
[Q3] Can reading books about Harry Potter increase positive feelings toward gay people?
[Q4] If popular high-school students are anti-bullying and anti-drinking, does that reduce these behaviors among their peers?
[Q5] Why are we so surprised when our preferred presidential candidate loses?
[Q6] How does simple nearness (proximity) influence attraction?

Throughout the chapter, margin icons for Q1–Q6 indicate where the text addresses these questions.

PositivePsych Would You Donate a Kidney to a Stranger?
PsychScience Can a 10-Minute Conversation Reduce Prejudice?

- Updated and added three NEW myths to **Psychology and You**—“How Much Do You Know About the Social World?” (p. 392).
- Added NEW Figure 114.1 “Attribution in action” (p. 393).
- Updated, rearranged, and added NEW *Attributional Errors and Biases* section (p. 393).
- Added NEW **Psychology and You**—“Reducing Attributional Biases” (p. 394).
- Expanded discussion of cognitive dissonance (pp. 395–396).
- Change the previous Figure 14.3 to **Process Diagram 14.1** and added new “Overall Summary” at the bottom of the figure (p. 397).
- To balance the length of the three major headings and improve the flow of the chapter, we moved the topic of prejudice from the end of the chapter to the first, right after attitudes (pp. 396–402).
- In response to reviewers, removed “discrimination” from the title of “Prejudice and Discrimination” section, but kept the distinction.
- Added NEW Figure 14.8, “The high price of prejudice” with a recent photo of the Orlando, FL massacre in 2016 (p. 399).
- Added NEW section on *Empathy Induction* as one of the five methods for reducing prejudice (p. 401).
- Added two NEW Figures—14.10, “Breaking the Gay barrier” and 14.11, “Harry Potter reduces prejudice?” (p. 401).
- Added NEW “norm violation” exercise to the **Real World Psychology** feature on cultural norms for personal space (p. 404).
- Added NEW “Adherence to ideologies” section to the factors that influence obedience (p. 407).
- Added NEW section on how to prevent or minimize groupthink (p. 410).
- Updated **Real World Psychology** feature—“Aggression in Sports” to include Italian soccer player biting another player (p. 411).
- Deleted previous (and outdated) **frustration-aggression hypothesis**, and expanded section on *Reducing Aggression* (p. 412).
- Added NEW sections on *When and Why Do We Help?* and *Why Don't We Help?* with discussion of Kitty Genovese case (pp. 412–413).
- Added NEW key term—**diffusion of responsibility** (p. 414).
- Added expanded discussion on flirting with references to helpful websites (p. 416).
- Added NEW research on oxytocin as a link between proximity and attraction (p. 416).
- Added a NEW “sign off” note to students to close this chapter, this text, and their first course in psychology (p. 419).
- Deleted five previous key terms throughout the chapter—**interpersonal attraction, mere-exposure effect, social cognition, social influence, and social relations.**

A list of the “What's NEW?” changes for Chapters 15 and 16 is available upon request.

Teaching and Learning Program

Real World Psychology is accompanied by a full menu of ancillary materials designed to enrich instructor teaching effectiveness and increase student mastery of psychology.

WileyPLUS Learning Space with ORION

WileyPLUS Learning Space is a research-based online environment for the most effective and efficient teaching and learning. From multiple study paths, to self-assessment, to a wealth of interactive resources—including the complete online textbook—*WileyPLUS Learning Space* gives you (the instructor) everything you need to personalize the teaching and learning experience while giving your students more value for their money. Students achieve concept mastery in a rich environment that is available 24/7. Instructors personalize and manage their course more effectively with assessment, assignments, grade tracking, and more. Powered by a proven technology, *WileyPLUS Learning Space* has enriched the education of millions of students in over 20 countries around the world.

WileyPLUS Learning Space is equipped with an interactive teaching and learning module called ORION. Based on the latest findings in cognitive science, *WileyPLUS Learning Space* with ORION, provides students with a personal, adaptive learning experience, which personalizes (adapts) the educational material according to their specific learning needs. With this individualized, immediate feedback, students can build on their strengths, overcome their weaknesses, and maximize their study time.

WileyPLUS Learning Space with ORION is great as:

- an adaptive pre-lecture tool that assesses your students' conceptual knowledge so they to come to class better prepared;
- a personalized study guide that helps students understand their strengths, as well as areas where they need to invest more time, especially in preparation for quizzes and exams.

Unique to ORION, students begin their study of each chapter with a quick diagnostic test. This test provides invaluable feedback to each student regarding his or her current level of mastery for the chapter's key terms and contents, while also identifying specific areas where they need to do additional study.

Additional Instructor Resources Available with WileyPLUS Learning Space *WileyPLUS Learning Space with Orion* provides reliable, customizable resources that reinforce course goals inside and outside of the classroom as well as instructor visibility into individual student progress.

Powerful multimedia resources for classroom presentations:

- More than 50 **Wiley Psychology Videos** are available, which connect key psychology concepts and themes to current issues in the news.
- **NEW** series of **Wiley Psychology Animations**, embedded within the e-text of *WileyPlus Learning Space*, which illustrate difficult-to-learn concepts from a real world perspective.
- More than 30 **Tutorial Videos**, featuring author Karen Huffman and Katherine Dowdell of Des Moines Area Community College, provide students with explanations and examples of some of the most challenging concepts in psychology. These 3 to 5 minute videos reflect the richness and diversity of psychology, from the steps of the experimental method to the interaction of genes and our environment, to the sources of stress.
- 20 **Virtual Field Trips** allow students to view psychology concepts in the real world as they've never seen them before. These 5 to 10 minute virtual field trips include visits to places such as a neuroimaging center, a film studio where 3-D movies are created, and a sleep laboratory, to name only a few.
- More than 20 **Visual Drag-and-Drop Exercises** that allow students a different, and more interactive, way to visualize and label key structures and important concepts.

Ready-to-go teaching materials and assessments help instructors optimize their time:

- The **Instructor's Manual,** revised by Vicki Ritts, St. Louis Community College is carefully crafted to help instructors maximize student learning. It provides teaching suggestions for each chapter of the text, including lecture starters, lecture extensions, classroom discussions and activities, out of the classroom assignments, Internet and print resources, and more!
- **NEW Visual Instructor's Guide** for classroom demonstrations and presentations. Prepared by Melissa Patton, Eastern Florida State College, these videos provide a step-by-step, visual illustration of ways to incorporate engaging and relevant classroom demonstrations in each chapter of the text.
- Every chapter contains a **Lecture PowerPoint™ Presentation,** prepared by Joseph Miller, Pennsylvania College of Technology, with a combination of key concepts, figures and tables, and examples from the textbook.
- **Media Enriched PowerPoint™ Presentations,** also prepared by Joseph Miller, are only available in *WileyPLUS Learning Space*. They contain up-to-date, exciting embedded links to multimedia sources, both video and animation, and can be easily modified according to your needs.
- **Instructor's Test Bank,** updated by Jason Spiegelman, The Community College of Baltimore County, is available in Word document format or Respondus. Instructors can easily alter or add new questions or answer options. They also can create multiple versions of the same test by quickly scrambling the order of all questions found in the Word version of the test bank. The test bank has over 2000 multiple choice questions, including approximately 10 essay questions for each chapter. Each multiple-choice question has been linked to a specific, student learning outcome, and the correct answer is provided with section references to its source in the text.
- **Gradebook:** *WileyPLUS Learning Space* provides instant access to reports on trends in class performance, student use of course materials, and progress toward learning objectives, helping inform decisions and drive classroom discussions.

For more information, visit www.wileypluslearningspace.com

Additional Student Resources Available with WileyPLUS Learning Space A wide variety of personalized resources are readily available 24/7, including:

- **Digital Version of the Complete Textbook** with integrated videos, animations, and quizzes.
- **Chapter Exams,** prepared by Paulina Multhaupt, Macomb Community College, give students a way to easily test themselves on course material before exams. Each chapter exam contains page referenced fill-in-the-blank, application, and multiple-choice questions. The correct answer for each question is provided, which allows immediate feedback and increased understanding. All questions and answers are linked to a specific learning objective within the book to further aid a student's concept mastery.
- **Interactive Flashcards** allow students to easily test their knowledge of key vocabulary terms.
- **Handbook for Non-Native Speakers** clarifies idioms, special phrases, and difficult vocabulary, which has a documented history of significantly improving student performance—particularly for those who do not use English as their first language.

Create a Custom Text Wiley Custom offers you an array of tools and services *designed to put content creation back in your hands.* Our suite of custom products empowers you to create high-quality, economical education solutions tailored to meet your individual classroom needs. Adapt or augment an existing text, combining individual chapters from across our extensive Wiley library to ensure content matches your syllabus. *Real World Psychology, Second Edition* is ready for immediate customization with two supplementary chapters not part of the standard text: "Gender and Human Sexuality" and "Industrial/Organizational Psychology." Visit wiley.com/college/custom to review these chapters today.

Enhance Your Book Add your personal, departmental, or institutional content. We can even deliver part of the proceeds of the custom title back to help fund content development, scholarship funds, student activities, or purchase supplies. Ask your Wiley sales representative about customizing *Real World Psychology* to fit your course!

Acknowledgments

Reviewers: To the professors who reviewed material and who gave their time and constructive criticism, we offer our sincere appreciation. We are deeply indebted to the following individuals and trust that they will recognize their contributions throughout the text.

Kojo Allen, *Metropolitan Community College of Omaha*
Patrick Allen, *College of Southern Maryland*
Dennis Anderson, *Butler Community College, Andover Campus*
Roxanna Anderson, *Palm Beach State College*
Sheryl Attig, *Tri-County Technical College*
Pamela Auburn, *University of Houston-Downtown*
Christine Bachman, *University of Houston-Downtown*
Linda Bajdo, *Macomb Community College*
Michelle Bannoura, *Hudson Valley Community College*
Elizabeth Becker, *Saint Joseph's University*
Karen Bekker, *Bergen Community College*
Jamie Borchardt, *Tarleton State University*
Debi Brannan, *Western Oregon University*
Alison Buchanan, *Henry Ford College*
Donald Busch, *Bergen Community College*
Elizabeth Casey, *SUNY Onondaga Community College*
April Cobb, *Macomb Community College*
Jennifer Cohen, *Metropolitan Community College of Omaha*
Frank Conner, *Grand Rapids Community College*
Lisa Connolly, *Ivy Tech Community College - Bloomington*
Katrina Cooper, *Bethany College*
Kristi Cordell-McNulty, *Angelo State University*
Kristen Couture, *Manchester Community College*
Stephanie Ding, *Del Mar College*
Denise Dunovant, *Hudson County Community College*
Judith Easton, *Austin Community College*
Gary Freudenthal, *Florida Southwestern State College*
Betty Jane Fratzke, *Indiana Wesleyan University*
Lenore Frigo, *Shasta College*
Adia Garrett, *University of Maryland, Baltimore County*
Michael K. Garza, *Brookhaven College*
Nichelle Gause, *Clayton State University*
Bryan Gibson, *Central Michigan University*
Jeffrey Gibbons, *Christopher Newport University*
Cameron Gordon, *University Of North Carolina, Wilmington*
Peter Gram, *Pensacola State College*
Keith Happaney, *CUNY Lehman College*
Sidney Hardyway, *Volunteer State Community College*
Jaime Henning, *Eastern Kentucky University*
Sandra Holloway, *Saint Joseph's University*
Amy Houlihan, *Texas A&M University Corpus Christi*
Cory Howard, *Tyler Junior College*
Sayeedul Islam, *Farmingdale State College*
Nita Jackson, *Butler Community College, Andover Campus*
Michael James, *Ivy Tech Community College - Bloomington*
Judy Jankowski, *Grand Rapids Community College*
Margaret Jenkins, *Seminole State College of Florida*
Deana Julka, *University of Portland*
Kiesa Kelly, *Tennessee State University*
Dana Kuehn, *Florida State College at Jacksonville*
Robert Lawyer, *Delgado Community College*
Juliet Lee, *Cape Fear Community College*
Marvin Lee, *Tennessee State University*

Robin Lewis, *California Polytechnic State University*
Shayn Lloyd, *Tallahassee Community College*
Wade Lueck, *Mesa Community College*
Lisa Lynk-Smith, *College of Southern Maryland*
Mike Majors, *Delgado Community College*
Jason McCoy, *Cape Fear Community College*
Bradley McDowell, *Madison Area Technical College of Florida*
Valerie Melburg, *SUNY Onondaga Community College*
Jan Mendoza, *Golden West College*
Steven Mewaldt, *Marshall University*
Yesimi Milledge, *Pensacola State College*
Joseph Miller, *Pennsylvania College of Technology*
Tal Millet, *Bergen Community College*
Kristie Morris, *Rockland Community College*
Brendan Morse, *Bridgewater State University*
Elizabeth Moseley, *Pensacola State College*
Ronald Mulson, *Hudson Valley Community College*
Bill Overman, *University Of North Carolina, Wilmington*
Justin Peer, *University of Michigan-Dearborn*
Andrea Phronebarger, *York Technical College*
Susan Pierce, *Hillsborough Community College*
Harvey Pines, *Canisius College*
Lydia Powell, *Vance Granville Community College*
Sandra Prince-Madison, *Delgado Community College*
Sadhana Ray, *Delgado Community College*
Vicki Ritts, *St. Louis Community College*
Angela Sadowski, *Chaffey College*
Monica Schneider, *SUNY Geneseo*
John Schulte, *Cape Fear Community College*
Mary Shelton, *Tennessee State University*
Barry Silber, *Hillsborough Community College*
Deirdre Slavik, *Northwest Arkansas Community College*
Theodore Smith, *University of Louisiana, Lafayette*
Jonathan Sparks, *Vance Granville Community College*
Jessica Streit, *Northern Kentucky University*
William Suits, *Seminole State College of Florida*
Griffin Sutton, *University of North Carolina, Wilmington*
Regina Traficante, *Community College of Rhode Island*
Rebekah Wanic, *Grossmont College*
Mark Watman, *South Suburban College*
Keith Williams, *Oakland University*
Michelle Williams, *Holyoke Community College*
Stacy Wyllie, *Delgado Community College*

Class Testers: A number of professors class tested chapters with their students and provided us with invaluable feedback and constructive recommendations. We benefitted greatly from this class testing and offer our sincere appreciation to these individuals for their helpful feedback.

Roxanna Anderson	Palm Beach State College
Christine Bachman	University of Houston-Downtown
Amy Beeman	San Diego Mesa College
Shannon Bentz	Northern Kentucky University
Vivian Bergamotto	Manhattan College
Jamie Borchardt	Tarleton State University
Amber Chenoweth	Hiram College
Jennifer Cohen	Metropolitan Community College of Omaha, Nebraska
Lisa Connolly	Ivy Tech Community College-Bloomington
Katrina Cooper	Bethany College
Kristi Cordell-McNulty	Angelo State University
Maureen Donegan	Delta College
Lauren Doninger	GateWay Community College
Denise Dunovant	Hudson County Community College
Daniella Errett	Pennsylvania Highlands Community College
Lenore Frigo	Shasta College
Kim Glackin	Metropolitan Community College-Blue River
Jonathan Golding	University of Kentucky
Justin Hackett	University of Houston-Downtown
Brett Heintz	Delgado Community College
Amy Houlihan	Texas A&M University–Corpus Christi
Mildred Huffman	Virginia Western Community College
Andrew Johnson	Park University
James Johnson	Illinois State University
Deana Julka	University of Portland
Marvin Lee	Tennessee State University
Wade Lueck	Mesa Community College
Claire Mann	Coastline Community College
Monica Marsee	University of New Orleans
Robert Martinez	University of the Incarnate Word
T. Darin Matthews	The Citadel, The Military College of South Carolina
Jason McCoy	Cape Fear Community College
Valerie Melburg	SUNY Onondaga Community College
Jan Mendoza	Golden West College
Dan Muhwezi	Butler Community College, Andover Campus
Paulina Multhaupt	Macomb Community College
Jennifer Ortiz-Garza	University of Houston–Victoria
Alexandr Petrou	CUNY Medgar Evers College
Sandra Prince-Madison	Delgado Community College
Sadhana Ray	Delgado Community College
Vicki Ritts	St. Louis Community College, Meramec
Brendan Rowlands	College of Southern Idaho
Spring Schafer	Delta College
Kelly Schuller	Bethany College
Randi Shedlosky-Shoemaker	York College of Pennsylvania
Barry Silber	Hillsborough Community College–Dale Mabry
Jonathan Sparks	Vance-Granville Community College
Laura Thornton	University of New Orleans
Virginia Tompkins	The Ohio State University at Lima
Rebekah Wanic	University of California, San Diego
Mark Watman	South Suburban College
Molly Wernli	College of Saint Mary
Khara Williams	University of Southern Indiana
Carl Wilson	Ranken Technical College
Stacy Wyllie	Delgado Community College
Gary Yarbrough	Arkansas Northeastern College

Acknowledgments from the Authors

We'd like to offer our very special thank you to the superb editorial and production teams at John Wiley and Sons. Like any cooperative effort, writing a book requires an immense support team, and we are deeply grateful to this remarkable group of people: Sandra Rigby, Senior Production Editor; Dorothy Sinclair, Senior Content Manager; Mary Ann Price, Senior Photo Editor; Wendy Lai, Senior Designer; Wendy Ashenberg, Product Designer; Karen Ehrmann who carefully guided us through the tricky world of permissions, and a host of others. Each of these individuals helped enormously throughout the production of this second edition.

This second edition text particularly benefited from the incredible patience, wisdom, and insight of Emma Townsend-Merino. Her title, "Assistant Development Editor," does not reflect the scope of her responsibilities and contributions. Her patience, wisdom, and prompt professionalism literally made all of this possible. As Jason Spiegelman (our Test Bank author) noted, "she's awesome"!

- Our deepest gratitude also goes out to Veronica Visentin, our Executive Editor, who recently joined the team at Wiley and added her energy and personal touch to this Second Edition. We're also deeply indebted to Glenn Wilson, who also recently joined us as the Senior Marketing Manager. He handles all the ins and outs of marketing and was instrumental in the creative ideas for the cover design, and capturing the "chameleon's voice" for our book.
- *Real World Psychology* would simply not exist without a great ancillary author team. We gratefully acknowledge the expertise and immense talents of our Video Tutorials director, Katherine Dowdell, and her teammates; Test Bank author, Jason Spiegelman, The Community College of Baltimore County; Instructor's Manual author, Vicki Ritts of St. Louis Community College; PowerPoint author, Joseph Miller of Pennsylvania College of Technology; Practice Test author, Paulina Multhaupt of Macomb Community College, and our dear friend and collaborator, Katie Townsend-Merino, who carefully crafted the scripts for the NEW psychology animations.
- The staff at Furino Production deserves a special note of thanks. Their careful and professional approach was critical to the successful production of this book. Jeanine Furino, the Project Manager, should be particularly commended for her infinite patience, gracious handholding, and personal support. Even during unusual challenges and crises in her family life, Jeanine maintained her professionalism and incredible work ethic—never missing a single date in the schedule!
- We'd also like to express our heartfelt appreciation to the hundreds of faculty across the country who contributed their constructive ideas to this second edition and to our many students over all the years. They've taught us what students want to know and inspired us to write this book.
- Finally, we'd like to acknowledge that all the writing, producing, and marketing of this book would be wasted without an energetic and dedicated sales staff! We wish to sincerely thank all the publishing representatives for their tireless efforts and good humor. It's a true pleasure to work with such a remarkable group of people.

Authors' Personal Notes!

- The writing of this text has been a group effort involving the input and support of all our wonderful families, friends, and colleagues. To each person we offer our sincere thanks: Sky Chafin, Haydn Davis, Tom Frangicetto, Mike Garza, Teresa Jacob, Jim Matiya, Lou Milstein, Kandis Mutter, Tyler Mutter, Roger Morrissette, Katie Townsend-Merino, Maria Pok, Fred Rose, and Kathy Young. They provided careful feedback and a unique sense of what should and should not go into an introduction to psychology text.
- A special note of appreciation goes to Beverly Peavler, who graciously and professionally tracked the changes from previous editions and checked all the references, along with Chris Roll, who patiently and carefully formatted all the references for each chapter of the text.
- *From Catherine Sanderson:* Thank you to my husband, Bart Hollander, who supported me in taking on this immense challenge, even though he understood it would require considerable late night writing, a (very) messy study, and even more take-out dinners. I also want to express my appreciation to my children—Andrew, Robert, and Caroline—who sometimes allowed me peace and quiet with which to write.
- *From Karen Huffman:* A big hug and continuing appreciation to my family, friends, and students who supported and inspired me. I also want to offer my deepest gratitude to Richard Hosey. His careful editing, constructive feedback, professional research skills, and shared authorship were essential to this revision. Having saved the truly best for last, I want to thank my dear friend and beloved husband, Bill Barnard—may the magic continue.

© Olga Danylenko/iStockphoto

CHAPTER **1**

Introduction and Research Methods

Uniquely India/Getty Images

Real World **Psychology**

Things you'll learn in Chapter 1

[Q1] How does your culture influence what you look for in a romantic partner?

[Q2] Can a change in posture make you more attractive?

[Q3] Do breast-fed babies have higher IQs?

[Q4] Can a diet high in fats and sugars impair learning and memory?

[Q5] Are older people happier than younger people?

[Q6] What are the two best study techniques for improving your exam performance?

Throughout the chapter, margin icons for Q1–Q6 indicate where the text addresses these questions.

Chapter Overview

Welcome to **Real World Psychology!** As our title suggests, we believe psychology's unique contributions to the scientific world are best shown through every day, real-life examples. Our innermost thoughts, our relationships, our politics, our "gut" feelings, and our deliberate decisions are all shaped by a complex psychological system that affects us at every level, from the cellular to the cultural. Psychology encompasses not only humankind but our nonhuman compatriots as well—from rats and pigeons to cats and chimps.

Given that this first chapter is an overview of the entire field of psychology, we begin with a formal definition of psychology, followed by its brief history as a scientific discipline. Next, we discuss the seven major perspectives of modern psychology, as well as its many different specialties and career options. Then, we explore the science of psychology, the scientific method and how psychologists apply it when conducting research. Following this, we examine the four major goals of psychology. We close with a section called, *Strategies for Student Success,* that provides proven, research-based techniques for improving your study habits, time management, and grades. These techniques will help you enjoy and master the material in this and all your other college textbooks and courses.

We invite you to let us know how your study of psychology (and this text) affects you and your life. You can reach us at casanderson@amherst.edu and khuffman@palomar.edu. We look forward to hearing from you.

CHAPTER OUTLINE

Warmest regards,

courtesy of Catherine Sanderson

Courtesy of Karen Huffman

Cathy A. Sanderson Karen R. Huffman

1.1 Introducing Psychology

LEARNING OBJECTIVES

Retrieval Practice While reading the upcoming sections, respond to each Learning Objective in your own words.

Summarize psychology, its past and present.

- **Define** psychology, critical thinking, and pseudopsychologies.
- **Review** structuralism, functionalism, and the psychoanalytic perspectives.
- **Discuss** modern psychology's seven major perspectives, and the contributions of women and people of color.
- **Describe** the biopsychosocial model, along with individualistic and collectivistic cultures.
- **Summarize** psychology's major career options and specialties.

Psychology The scientific study of behavior and mental processes.

The term **psychology** derives from the roots *psyche*, meaning "mind," and *logos*, meaning "word." Modern psychology is most commonly defined as the *scientific study of behavior and mental processes. Scientific* is a key feature of the definition because psychologists follow strict scientific procedures to collect and analyze their data. *Behavior* (such as crying, hitting, and sleeping) can be directly observed. *Mental processes* are private, internal experiences that cannot be directly observed (like feelings, thoughts, and memories).

Critical thinking The process of objectively evaluating, comparing, analyzing, and synthesizing information.

Psychology also places high value on *empirical evidence* that can be objectively tested and evaluated. In addition, psychologists emphasize **critical thinking**, *the process of objectively evaluating, comparing, analyzing, and synthesizing information* (Caine et al., 2016; Halpern, 2014).

Be careful not to confuse psychology with *pseudopsychologies*, which are based on common beliefs, folk wisdom, or superstitions. (*Pseudo* means "false.") These sometimes give the appearance of science, but they do not follow the basics of the scientific method. Examples include purported psychic powers, horoscopes, mediums, and self-help and "pop psych" statements such as "I'm mostly right brained" or "We use only 10% of our brains." For some, horoscopes or palmists are simple entertainment. Unfortunately, some true believers seek guidance and waste large sums of money on charlatans purporting to know the future or to speak with the deceased (e.g., Wilson, 2015b). Broken-hearted families also have lost valuable time and emotional energy on psychics claiming they could locate their missing children. As you can see, distinguishing scientific psychology from pseudopsychology is vitally important (Lilienfeld et al., 2010, 2015; Loftus, 2010). Given the popularity of these misleading beliefs, be sure to test your own possible myths in the *Test Yourself* section.

Psychology and **You**—Understanding Yourself

Test Yourself | Psychology Versus Pseudopsychology

True or False?

________ **1.** The best way to learn and remember information is to "cram," or study it intensively during one concentrated period.

________ **2.** Advertisers and politicians often use subliminal persuasion to influence our behavior.

________ **3.** Most brain activity stops when we're asleep.

________ **4.** Punishment is the most effective way to permanently change behavior.

________ **5.** Eyewitness testimony is often unreliable.

________ **6.** Polygraph ("lie detector") tests can accurately and reliably reveal whether a person is lying.

________ **7.** Behaviors that are unusual or violate social norms may indicate a psychological disorder.

________ **8.** People with schizophrenia have multiple personalities.

________ **9.** Similarity is one of the best predictors of satisfaction in long-term relationships.

________ **10.** In an emergency, as the number of bystanders increases, your chance of getting help decreases.

Henry Groskinsky/Time Life Pictures/Getty Images

The magician James Randi has dedicated his life to educating the public about fraudulent pseudopsychologists. Along with the prestigious MacArthur Foundation, Randi has offered $1 million to "anyone who proves a genuine psychic power under proper observing conditions" (Randi, 2014; The Amazing Meeting, 2011). Even after many years, the money has never been collected, and the challenge has since been terminated. For details, please see—http://web.randi.org/home/jref-status

Answers: 1. False (Chapter 1), 2. False (Chapter 4), 3. False (Chapter 5), 4. False (Chapter 6), 5. True (Chapter 7), 6. False (Chapter 10), 7. True (Chapter 12), 8. False (Chapter 12), 9. True (Chapter 14), 10. True (Chapter 14)

Psychology's Past

Although people have long been interested in human nature, it was not until the first psychological laboratory was founded in 1879 that psychology as a science officially began. As interest in the new field grew, psychologists adopted various perspectives on the "appropriate" topics for psychological research and the "proper" research methods. These diverse viewpoints and subsequent debates molded and shaped modern psychological science.

Psychology's history as a science began in 1879, when Wilhelm Wundt [VILL-helm Voont], generally acknowledged as the "father of psychology," established the first psychological laboratory in Leipzig, Germany. Wundt and his followers were primarily interested in how we form sensations, images, and feelings. Their chief methodology was termed "introspection," and it relied on participants' self-monitoring and reporting on conscious experiences (Freedheim & Weiner, 2013; Goodwin, 2012).

A student of Wundt's, Edward Titchener, brought his ideas to the United States. Titchener's approach, now known as *structuralism*, sought to identify the basic building blocks, or "structures," of mental life through introspection and then to determine how these elements combine to form the whole of experience. Because introspection could not be used to study animals, children, or more complex mental disorders, however, structuralism failed as a working psychological approach. Although short-lived, it did establish a model for studying mental processes scientifically.

Structuralism's intellectual successor, *functionalism*, studied the way the mind functions to enable humans and other animals to adapt to their environment. William James was the leading force in the functionalist school (**Figure 1.1**). Although functionalism also eventually declined, it expanded the scope of psychology to include research on emotions and observable behaviors, initiated the psychological testing movement, and influenced modern education and industry. Today, James is widely considered the "father" of American psychology.

During the late 1800s and early 1900s, while functionalism was prominent in the United States, the **psychoanalytic perspective** was forming in Europe. Its founder, Austrian physician Sigmund Freud, believed that a part of the human mind, the unconscious, contains thoughts, memories,

Psychoanalytic perspective An earlier approach to psychology developed by Sigmund Freud, which focuses on unconscious processes, unresolved conflicts, and past experiences.

Bettmann/Getty Images

FIGURE 1.1 William James (1842–1910) William James founded the perspective, known as functionalism, and established the first psychology laboratory in the United States, at Harvard University. In modern times, he is commonly referred to as the "father" of American psychology, whereas Wundt is considered the "father" of all psychology.

and desires that lie outside personal awareness yet still exert great influence. For example, according to Freud, a man who is cheating on his wife might slip up and say, "I wish you were her," when he consciously planned to say, "I wish you were here." Such seemingly meaningless, so-called "Freudian slips" supposedly reveal a person's true unconscious desires and motives.

Freud also believed many psychological problems are caused by unconscious sexual or aggressive motives and conflicts between "acceptable" and "unacceptable" behaviors (Chapter 11). His theory led to a system of therapy known as *psychoanalysis* (Chapter 13).

Modern Psychology

As summarized in **Table 1.1**, contemporary psychology reflects seven major perspectives: *psychodynamic*, *behavioral*, *humanistic*, *cognitive*, *biological*, *evolutionary*, and *sociocultural*. Although there are numerous differences among these seven perspectives, most psychologists recognize the value of each orientation and agree that no one view has all the answers.

Freud's nonscientific approach and emphasis on sexual and aggressive impulses have long been controversial, and today there are few strictly Freudian psychoanalysts left. However, the broad features of his theory remain in the modern **psychodynamic perspective**. The general goal of psychodynamic psychologists is to explore unconscious *dynamics*—internal motives, conflicts, and past experiences.

In the early 1900s, another major perspective appeared that dramatically shaped the course of modern psychology. Unlike earlier approaches, the **behavioral perspective** emphasizes objective, observable environmental influences on overt behavior. Behaviorism's founder, John B. Watson (1913), rejected the practice of introspection and the influence of unconscious forces. Instead, Watson adopted Russian physiologist Ivan Pavlov's concept of *conditioning* (Chapter 6) to explain behavior as a result of observable stimuli (in the environment) and observable responses (behavioral actions).

Most early behaviorist research was focused on learning; nonhuman animals were ideal participants for this research. One of the best-known behaviorists, B. F. Skinner, was convinced that behaviorist approaches could be used to "shape" human behavior (**Figure 1.2**). As you'll discover in Chapters 6 and 13, therapeutic techniques rooted in the behavioristic perspective have been most successful in treating observable behavioral problems, such as those related to phobias and alcoholism (Anker et al., 2016; Botella et al., 2014; Tyner et al., 2016).

Although the psychoanalytic and behavioral perspectives dominated U.S. psychology for some time, in the 1950s a new approach emerged—the **humanistic perspective**, which stresses *free will* (voluntarily chosen behavior) and *self—actualization* (an inborn drive to develop all one's talents and capabilities). According to Carl Rogers and Abraham Maslow, two central figures with this perspective, all individuals naturally strive to develop and move toward self-actualization. Like psychoanalysis, humanistic psychology developed an influential theory of personality, and its own form of psychotherapy (Chapters 11 and 13). The humanistic approach also led the way to a contemporary research specialty known as **positive psychology**—the study of optimal human functioning, as shown in the following **PositivePsych** special feature (Diener et al., 2015; Lopez et al., 2015; Seligman, 2003, 2015).

One of the most influential modern approaches, the **cognitive perspective**, emphasizes the mental processes we use in thinking, knowing, remembering, and communicating (Goldstein, 2015; Greene, 2016). These mental processes include perception, memory, imagery, concept formation, problem solving, reasoning, decision making, and language. Many cognitive psychologists also use an *information-processing approach*, likening the mind to a computer that sequentially takes in information, processes it, and then produces a response.

During the past few decades, scientists have explored the role of biological factors in almost every area of psychology. Using sophisticated tools and technologies, scientists who adopt this **biological perspective** examine behavior through the lens of genetics and biological processes in the brain and other parts of the

Psychodynamic perspective A modern approach to psychology that emphasizes unconscious dynamics, motives, conflicts, and past experiences; based on the psychoanalytic approach, but focuses more on social and cultural factors, and less on sexual drives.

Behavioral perspective A modern approach to psychology that emphasizes objective, observable, environmental influences on overt behavior.

Humanistic perspective A modern approach to psychology that perceives human nature as naturally positive and growth seeking; it emphasizes free will and self-actualization.

Positive psychology The study of optimal human functioning; emphasizes positive emotions, traits, and institutions.

Cognitive perspective A modern approach to psychology that focuses on the mental processes used in thinking, knowing, remembering, and communicating.

Nina Leen/Time & Life Pictures/GettyImages

FIGURE 1.2 B. F. Skinner (1904–1990) B. F. Skinner was one of the most influential psychologists of the twentieth century. Here he uses the so-called "Skinner box" to train a rat to press a lever for a reward.

TABLE 1.1 Modern Psychology's Seven Major Perspectives

Perspectives	Major Emphases	Sample Research Questions
Psychodynamic	Unconscious dynamics, motives, conflicts, and past experiences	How do adult personality traits or psychological problems reflect unconscious processes and early childhood experiences?
Behavioral	Objective, observable, environmental influences on overt behavior; stimulus–response (S-R) relationships and consequences for behavior	How do reinforcement and punishment affect behavior? How can we increase desirable behaviors and decrease undesirable ones?
Humanistic	Free will, self-actualization, and human nature as naturally positive and growth seeking	How can we promote a client's capacity for self-actualization and understanding of his or her own development? How can we promote international peace and reduce violence?
Cognitive	Mental processes used in thinking, knowing, remembering, and communicating	How do our thoughts and interpretations affect how we respond in certain situations? How can we improve how we process, store, and retrieve information?
Biological	Genetic and biological processes in the brain and other parts of the nervous system	How might changes in neurotransmitters or damage to parts of the brain lead to psychological problems and changes in behavior and mental processes?
Evolutionary	Natural selection, adaptation, and reproduction	How does natural selection help explain why we love and help certain people, but hurt others? Do we have specific genes for aggression and altruism?
Sociocultural	Social interaction and the cultural determinants of behavior and mental processes	How do the values and beliefs transmitted from our social and cultural environments affect our everyday psychological processes?
		Why do we need multiple perspectives? What do you see in this figure? Is it two profiles facing each other, a white vase, or both? Your ability to see both figures is similar to a psychologist's ability to study behavior and mental processes from a number of different perspectives.

nervous system. For example, research shows that genes influence many aspects of our behavior, including how kind we are to other people, whom we vote for in elections, and even whether or not we decide to purchase a handgun (Barnes et al., 2014; Ksiazkiewicz et al., 2016; Wilson, 2015a).

Biological perspective A modern approach to psychology that focuses on genetics and biological processes.

The **evolutionary perspective** stresses natural selection, adaptation, and reproduction (Buss, 2011, 2015; Dawkins, 2016; Goldfinch, 2015). This perspective stems from the writings of Charles Darwin (1859), who suggested that natural forces select traits that aid an organism's survival. This process of **natural selection** occurs when a particular genetic trait gives an organism a reproductive advantage over others. Because of natural selection, the fastest, strongest, smartest, or otherwise most fit organisms are most likely to live long enough to reproduce and thereby pass on their

Evolutionary perspective A modern approach to psychology that stresses natural selection, adaptation, and reproduction.

PP PositivePsych

What Makes Us Happy?

One of the most consistent findings in positive psychology is that other people make us happy! "Simply" building and maintaining relationships tends to significantly improve our overall happiness and well-being (Diener & Tay, 2015; Galinha et al., 2016; Gander et al., 2016). As shown in the photo, even just talking with strangers leads to higher levels of happiness. Researchers who asked riders on trains and buses to either quietly sit alone or to talk to a stranger found that those who talked to a stranger reported more positive feelings than those who sat alone (Epley & Schroeder, 2014). In addition, contrary to the popular belief that "money buys happiness," research shows that once we have enough income to meet our basic needs, additional funds do not significantly increase our levels of happiness and well-being (Kushlev et al., 2015; Whillans et al., 2016). Furthermore, when adults are given money and told to spend it on others, they experience higher levels of happiness than do those who are told to spend it on themselves (Dunn et al., 2008). In short, powerful evidence suggests that forming and maintaining human connections and giving to others are very important predictors of happiness. (Recognizing the increasing research focus on positive psychology, as well as its direct applicability to the real world and your everyday life, we have included a special **PositivePsych** feature in each chapter of this text. We hope you enjoy them.)

Hill Street Studios/Getty Images

Natural selection Darwin's principle of an evolutionary process in which heritable traits that increase an organism's chances of survival or reproduction are more likely to be passed on to succeeding generations.

Sociocultural perspective A modern approach to psychology that emphasizes social interaction and the cultural determinants of behavior and mental processes.

genes to the next generation. According to the evolutionary perspective, there's even an evolutionary explanation for the longevity of humans over other primates–it's grandmothers! Without them, a mother who has a two-year-old and then gives birth would have to devote her time and resources to the newborn at the expense of the older child. Grandmothers act as supplementary caregivers.

Finally, the **sociocultural perspective** emphasizes social interactions and cultural determinants of behavior and mental processes. Although we are often unaware of their influence, factors such as ethnicity, religion, occupation, and socioeconomic class, all have an enormous psychological impact on our mental processes and behavior. For example, in countries with low levels of gender equality, women are more likely to be attracted by their partner's resources and men by physical attractiveness (Zentner & Mitura, 2012). [Q1]

Surprisingly, recent studies conducted within the U.S. found that both men and women with bigger postures—outstretched arms and spread apart legs—were judged as more romantically appealing than those with limbs held tight (Vacharkulksemsuk et al., 2016). Why? The researchers suggested that this type of expansive posture signals dominance, which is socially and culturally desirable in the U.S., and thereby increases an individual's chance of being selected as a potential mate. Note that this research was conducted via speed dating and smartphone-based dating applications. The results may not hold up past a second date! [Q2]

Gender and People of Color During the late 1800s and early 1900s, most colleges and universities provided little opportunity for women and people of color, either as students or as faculty members. One of the first women to be recognized in the field of psychology was Mary Calkins. Her achievements are particularly noteworthy, considering the significant discrimination that she overcame. For example, married women could not be teachers or professors in co-educational settings during this time in history. In Mary Calkins' case, even after she completed all the requirements for a Ph.D. at Harvard University in 1895, and was described by William James as his brightest student, the university refused to grant the degree to a woman. Nevertheless, Calkins went on to perform valuable research on memory, and in 1905 served as the first female president of the American Psychological Association (APA). The first woman to receive her Ph.D. in psychology was Margaret Floy Washburn from Cornell University in 1894. She also wrote several influential books and served as the second female president of the APA.

Library of Congress Prints and Photographs Division

FIGURE 1.3 Kenneth Clark (1914–2005) and Mamie Phipps Clark (1917–1985) Kenneth Clark and Mamie Phipps Clark conducted experiments with Black and White dolls to study children's attitudes about race. This research and their expert testimony contributed to the U.S. Supreme Court's ruling that racial segregation in public schools was unconstitutional.

Francis Cecil Sumner became the first Black person to earn a Ph.D. in psychology (Clark University, 1920). Dr. Sumner later chaired one of the country's leading psychology departments, at Howard University. In 1971, one of Sumner's students, Kenneth B. Clark, became the first person of color to be elected APA president. Clark's research with his wife, Mamie Clark, documented the harmful effects of prejudice and directly influenced the Supreme Court's landmark 1954 ruling against racial segregation in schools, Brown v. Board of Education (**Figure 1.3**).

Calkins, Washburn, Sumner, and Clark, along with other important people of color and women, made significant and lasting contributions to psychology's development. Today, women earning doctoral degrees in psychology greatly outnumber men, but, unfortunately, people of color are still underrepresented (American Psychological Association, 2014; Willyard, 2011).

Biopsychosocial Model The seven major perspectives, as well as women and people of color, have all made significant contributions to modern psychology. This explains why most contemporary psychologists do not adhere to one single intellectual perspective. Instead, a more integrative, unifying theme—the **biopsychosocial model**—has gained wide acceptance. This model views biological processes (genetics, neurotransmitters, evolution), psychological factors (learning, personality, motivation), and social forces (family, culture, gender, and ethnicity) as interrelated. It also sees all three factors as influences inseparable from the seven major perspectives (**Figure 1.4**).

Biopsychosocial model An integrative, unifying theme of modern psychology that sees biological, psychological, and social processes as interrelated and interacting influences.

Why is the biopsychosocial model so important? As the old saying goes, "A fish doesn't know it's in water." Similarly, as individuals living alone inside our own heads, we're often unaware of the numerous, interacting factors that affect us—particularly cultural forces. For example, most North Americans and Western Europeans are raised to be very individualistic and are surprised to learn that over 70% of the world's population lives in collectivistic cultures. As you can see in **Table 1.2**, in *individualistic cultures*, the needs and goals of the individual are emphasized over the needs and goals of the group. When asked to complete the statement "I am . . . ," people from individualistic cultures tend to respond with personality traits ("I am shy"; "I am outgoing") or their occupation ("I am a teacher"; "I am a student").

In *collectivistic cultures*, however, the person is defined and understood primarily by looking at his or her place in the social unit (Conway et al., 2014; Fang et al., 2016; Saucier et al., 2015). Relatedness, connectedness, and interdependence are valued, as opposed to separateness, independence, and individualism. When asked to complete the statement "I am . . . ," people from collectivistic cultures tend to mention their families or nationality ("I am a daughter"; "I am Chinese"). Keep in mind, however, that these sample countries and their sample values exist on a continuum, and that within each country there is a wide range of individual differences.

Looking again at the photos from the cultures in Figure 1.4, can you see how learning more about the biopsychosocial model offers increased understanding of ourselves, our friends, and our families, and how it may improve our understanding and sensitivity to other

FIGURE 1.4 The biopsychosocial model **Real** World **Psychology**

When we consider people as individuals (**Figure a**), we don't always get a complete picture of their emotions and motivations. Stepping back to see the same individuals in a broader context (**Figure b**) can provide new insights. With this "bigger picture" (the child's immediate surroundings and his or her group's behavior) in mind, can you better understand why each child might be feeling and acting as he or she is? The biopsychosocial model recognizes that there is usually no single cause for our behavior or our mental states (**Figure c**). For example, our moods and feelings are often influenced by genetics and neurotransmitters (biological), our learned responses and patterns of thinking (psychological), and our socioeconomic status and cultural views of emotion (sociocultural).

A

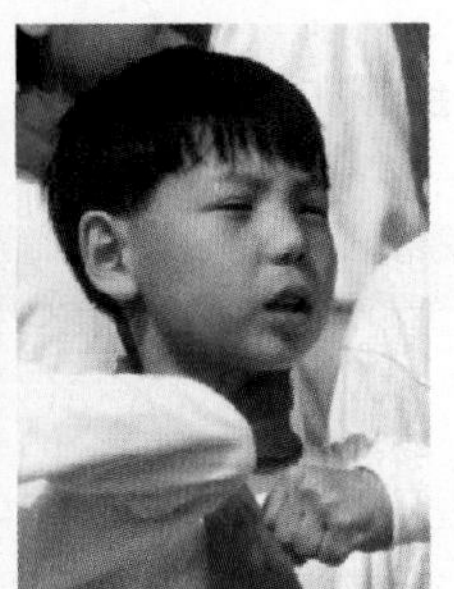

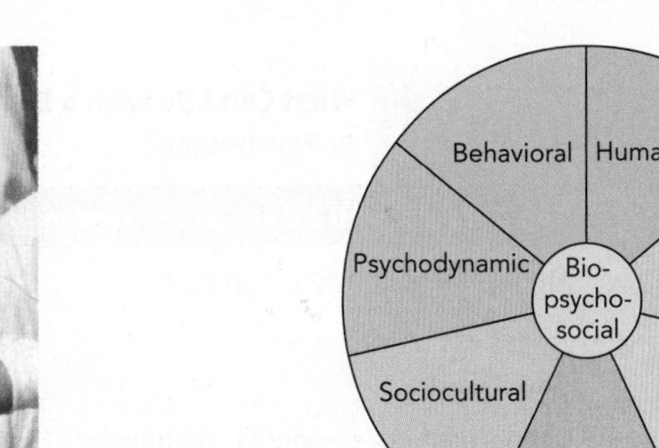

C

B

© Bonnie Jacobs/iStockphoto

© Jurgen Schulzki/Imagebroker/Age Fotostock America, Inc.

TABLE 1.2 A Comparison Between Individualistic and Collectivistic Cultures **Real** World **Psychology**

Sample Individualistic Countries	Sample Collectivistic Cultures
United States	Korea
Australia	China
Great Britain	India
Canada	Japan
The Netherlands	West Africa region
Germany	Thailand
New Zealand	Taiwan
Sample Individualistic Values	**Sample Collectivistic Values**
Independence	Interdependence
Individual rights	Obligations to others
Self-sufficiency	Reliance on group
Individual achievement	Group achievement
Independent living	Living with kin
Personal failure leads to shame and guilt	Failing the group leads to shame and guilt

cultures? For example, Americans generally define *sincerity* as behaving in accordance with our inner feelings, whereas people from collectivist cultures tend to see their equivalent word for sincerity as behavior that conforms to a person's role expectations and duties (Yamada, 1997). This explains why collectivistic behaviors might appear insincere to Americans.

Careers and Specialties in Psychology

Many people think of psychologists only as therapists, and it's true that the fields of clinical and counseling psychology do make up the largest specialty areas. However, many psychologists have no connection with therapy. Instead, we work as researchers, teachers, or consultants in academic, business, industry, and government settings, or in a combination of settings. As you can see in **Table 1.3**, there are several career paths and valuable life skills associated with

TABLE 1.3 What Can I Do with a Bachelor's Degree in Psychology? **Real** World **Psychology**

Top Careers with a Bachelor's Degree in Psychology
Management and administration
Sales
Social work
Labor-relations, personnel and training
Sample Skills Gained from a Psychology Major
Real estate, business services, insurance
Improved ability to predict and understand behavior
Better understanding of how to use and interpret data
Increased communication and interpersonal skills
Increased ability to manage difficult situations and high-stress environments
Enhanced insight into problem behavior
Note that the U.S. Department of Labor predicts only an average rate of growth for psychologists in the next decade. However, the good news is that a degree in our field, and this course in general psychology, will provide you with invaluable lifetime skills.

a bachelor's degree in psychology. Of course, your options are even greater if you go beyond the bachelor's degree and earn your master's degree, Ph.D., or Psy.D.—see **Table 1.4**. For more information about what psychologists do—and how to pursue a career in psychology—check out the websites of the American Psychological Association (APA) and the Association for Psychological Science (APS).

TABLE 1.4 Sample Careers and Specialties in Psychology **Real World Psychology**

CAREER/SPECIALTY	DESCRIPTION
Biopsychologist/neuroscientist	Investigates the relationship between biology, behavior, and mental processes, including how physical and chemical processes affect the structure and function of the brain and nervous system
Clinical psychologist	Specializes in the evaluation, diagnosis, and treatment of psychological disorders
Cognitive psychologist	Examines "higher" mental processes, including thought, memory, intelligence, creativity, and language
Comparative psychologist	Studies the behavior and mental processes of nonhuman animals; emphasizes evolution and cross-species comparisons
Counseling psychologist	Overlaps with clinical psychology, but generally works with less seriously disordered individuals and focuses more on social, educational, and career adjustment
Cross-cultural psychologist/psychological anthropologist	Studies similarities and differences in and across various cultures and ethnic groups
Developmental psychologist	Studies the course of human growth and development from conception to death
Educational psychologist	Studies the processes of education and works to promote the academic, intellectual, social, and emotional development of children in the school environment
Environmental psychologist	Investigates how people affect and are affected by the physical environment
Experimental psychologist	Examines processes such as learning, conditioning, motivation, emotion, sensation, and perception in humans and other animals (Note that psychologists working in almost all other areas of specialization also conduct research.)
Forensic psychologist	Applies principles of psychology to the legal system, including jury selection, psychological profiling, assessment, and treatment of offenders
Gender and/or cultural psychologist	Investigates how men and women and different cultures vary from one another and how they are similar
Health psychologist	Studies how biological, psychological, and social factors affect health, illness, and health-related behaviors
Industrial/organizational psychologist	Applies principles of psychology to the workplace, including personnel selection and evaluation, leadership, job satisfaction, employee motivation, and group processes within the organization
Personality psychologist	Studies the unique and relatively stable patterns in a person's thoughts, feelings, and actions
Positive psychologist	Examines factors related to optimal human functioning
School psychologist	Collaborates with teachers, parents, and students within the educational system to help children with special needs related to a disability and/or their academic and social progress; also provides evaluation and assessment of a student's functioning and eligibility for special services
Social psychologist	Investigates the role of social forces in interpersonal behavior, including aggression, prejudice, love, helping, conformity, and attitudes
Sport psychologist	Applies principles of psychology to enhance physical performance

Zigy Kaluzny/Stone/Getty Images

Jeffrey L. Rotman/Getty Images

Retrieval Practice 1.1 | Introducing Psychology

SELF-TEST Completing this self-test, and then checking your answers by clicking on the answer button or by looking in Appendix B, will provide immediate feedback and helpful practice for exams.

1. Psychology is defined as the ____.
   a. science of conscious and unconscious forces
   b. empirical study of the mind and behavior
   c. scientific study of the mind
   d. scientific study of behavior and mental processes
2. ____ relies on common beliefs, folk wisdom, or even superstitions and do not follow the basics of the scientific method.
   a. Pseudopsychology b. Astrophysics
   c. Astronomy d. None of these options
3. ____ is generally acknowledged to be the father of psychology.
   a. Sigmund Freud b. B. F. Skinner
   c. Wilhelm Wundt d. William Tell
4. Which of the following terms do not belong together?
   a. structuralism, unconscious behavior
   b. behaviorism, observable behavior
   c. psychoanalytic, unconscious conflict
   d. humanism, free will
5. The ____ views biological processes, psychological factors, and social forces as interrelated influences, and it is one of the most widely accepted themes of modern psychology.
   a. eclectic perspective b. nature-nurture model
   c. interactionist position d. biopsychosocial model

Think Critically

1. Psychologists are among the least likely to believe in psychics, palmistry, astrology, and other paranormal phenomena. Why might that be?
2. Which of the seven modern perspectives of psychology do you most agree with? Why?
3. How might the biopsychosocial model explain difficulties or achievements in your own life?

Real World **Psychology**

How does your culture influence what you look for in a romantic partner?

Can a change in posture make you more attractive?

HINT: LOOK IN THE MARGIN FOR **[Q1]** AND **[Q2]**

1.2 The Science of Psychology

LEARNING OBJECTIVES

Retrieval Practice While reading the upcoming sections, respond to each Learning Objective in your own words.

Discuss the key principles underlying the science of psychology.

- **Compare and contrast** the fundamental goals of basic and applied research.
- **Describe** the scientific method, its key terms, and its six steps.
- **Review** psychology's four main goals.
- **Discuss** the ethical concerns and guidelines for psychological research.

Basic and Applied Research

Basic research A type of research primarily conducted to advance core scientific knowledge; most often conducted in universities and research laboratories.

Applied research A type of research primarily conducted to solve practical, real world problems; generally conducted outside the laboratory.

In science, research strategies are generally categorized as either *basic* or *applied*. **Basic research** is most often conducted to advance core scientific knowledge, whereas **applied research** is generally designed to solve practical ("real world") problems (**Figure 1.5**). As you'll see in Chapter 6, classical and operant conditioning principles evolved from numerous *basic research* studies designed to advance the general understanding of how human and nonhuman animals learn. In Chapters 12 and 13, you'll also discover how *applied research* based on these principles has been used to successfully treat psychological disorders, such as phobias. Similarly, in Chapter 7, you'll see how basic research on how we create, store, and retrieve our memories has led to practical applications in the legal field, such as a greater appreciation for the fallibility of eyewitness testimony.

Keep in mind that basic and applied research approaches are not polar opposites. Instead, they frequently share similar goals, and their outcomes interact, with one building on the other.

FIGURE 1.5 Applied research in psychology Note how psychological research has helped design safe and more reliable appliances, machinery, and instrument controls (*Psychology Matters*, 2006).

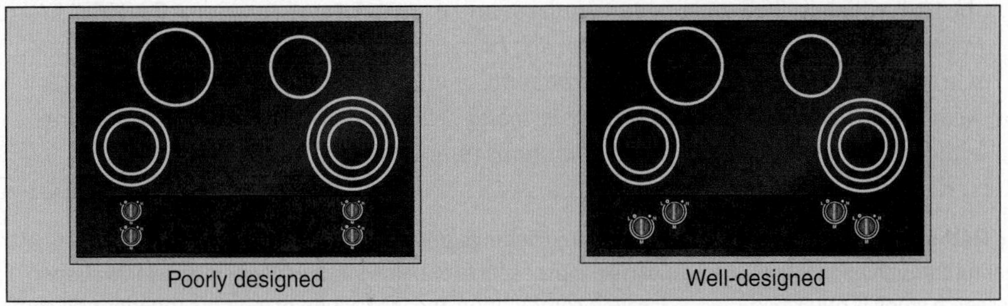

a. Spatial correspondence Controls for stovetops should be arranged in a pattern that corresponds to the placement of the burners.

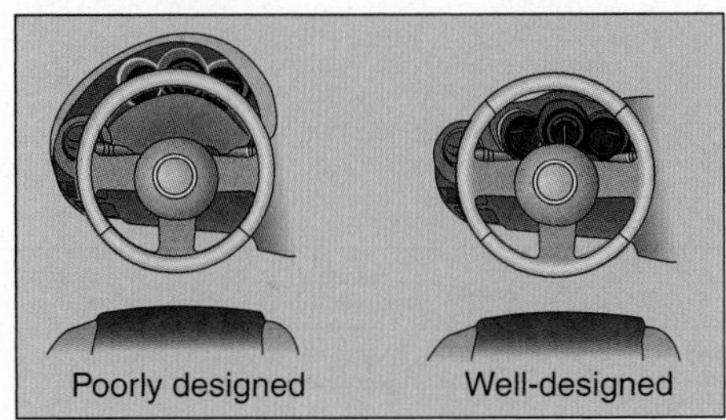

b. Visibility Automobile gauges for fuel, temperature, and speed should be easily visible to the driver.

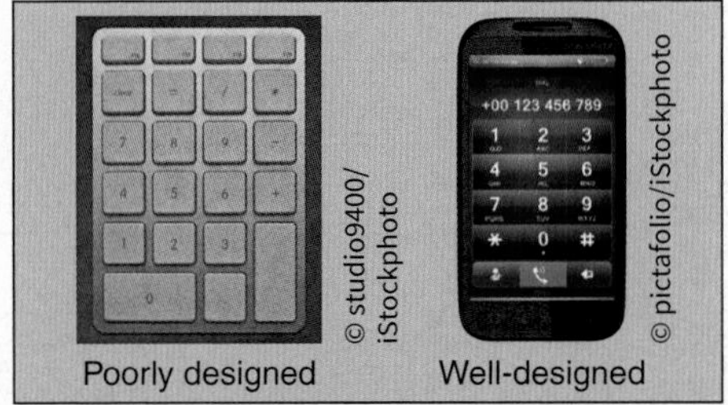

c. Arrangement of numbers A top-down arrangement of numbers on a cell phone is more efficient than the bottom-up arrangement on a computer's key board.

The Scientific Method

While conducting either basic or applied research, psychologists follow strict, standardized procedures so that others can understand, interpret, and repeat or test their findings. Most scientific investigations consist of six basic steps, collectively based on the **scientific method** (**Process Diagram 1.1**).

Scientific method The cyclical and cumulative research process used for gathering and interpreting objective information in a way that minimizes error and yields dependable results.

For example, are you wondering whether completing the *Retrieval Practice* exercises that follow the Learning Objectives, Self-Test, and Key Terms in each chapter of this text is worth your time? Have you thought, "Will I get a better grade on my exams if I do these exercises?" How would you use the scientific method to answer these general questions? Starting with Step 1, you could go to professional journals and read up on the research about retrieval practice that already exists. To complete Step 2, you would first form an educated guess based on your literature review in Step 1. You would then turn this guess into a statement, called a **hypothesis**, which provides predictions that can be tested in some way. You would then need to explicitly state how each of your variables in your hypothesis will be **operationally defined** (observed, manipulated, and measured). For example, a better grade on my exams might be operationally defined as earning one letter grade higher than the letter grade on my previous exam.

Hypothesis A tentative and testable explanation (or "educated guess") about the relationship between two or more variables; a testable prediction or question.

Operational definition A precise description of how the variables in a study will be observed, manipulated, and measured.

Using your initial question about the value of the Retrieval Practice exercises, your hypothesis and operational definitions might be: "Students who spend two hours studying Chapter 1 in this text and one hour completing the three Retrieval Practice exercises will earn higher scores on a standard academic exam than students who spend three hours studying Chapter 1 without completing the Retrieval Practice exercises."

For Step 3, you would then most likely choose an experimental research design and solicit 100 volunteers from various classes, 50 of whom should be randomly assigned to Group 1 (Retrieval Practice) and the other 50 to Group 2 (no Retrieval Practice). After both groups study for three hours, you would present and score a 20-point quiz, followed by a statistical analysis (Step 4) to determine whether the difference in test scores between the two groups is **statistically significant**. To be statistically significant, the difference between the groups must be large enough that the result is probably not due to chance.

Statistical significance A statistical statement of how likely it is that a study's result occurred merely by chance.

STOP! This Process Diagram contains essential information NOT found elsewhere in the text, which is likely to appear on quizzes and exams. Be sure to study it CAREFULLY! *Research has shown that diagrams showing how a process works result in higher performance on tests than having no diagrams at all, or just a text outline of the process (Bui & McDaniel, 2015). This research and others, along with our own experiences as educators, explains why we've included process diagrams throughout out text.*

PROCESS DIAGRAM 1.1 **The Scientific Method** Scientific knowledge is constantly evolving and self-correcting through application of the scientific method. As soon as one research study is published, the cycle almost always begins again. The ongoing, circular nature of theory building often frustrates students. In most chapters, you will encounter numerous, and sometimes conflicting, scientific theories and research findings. You'll be tempted to ask: "Which one is right?" But, like most aspects of behavior, the "correct" answer is almost always a combination and interaction of multiple theories and competing findings. The good news is that such complex answers lead to a fuller and more productive understanding of behavior and mental processes.

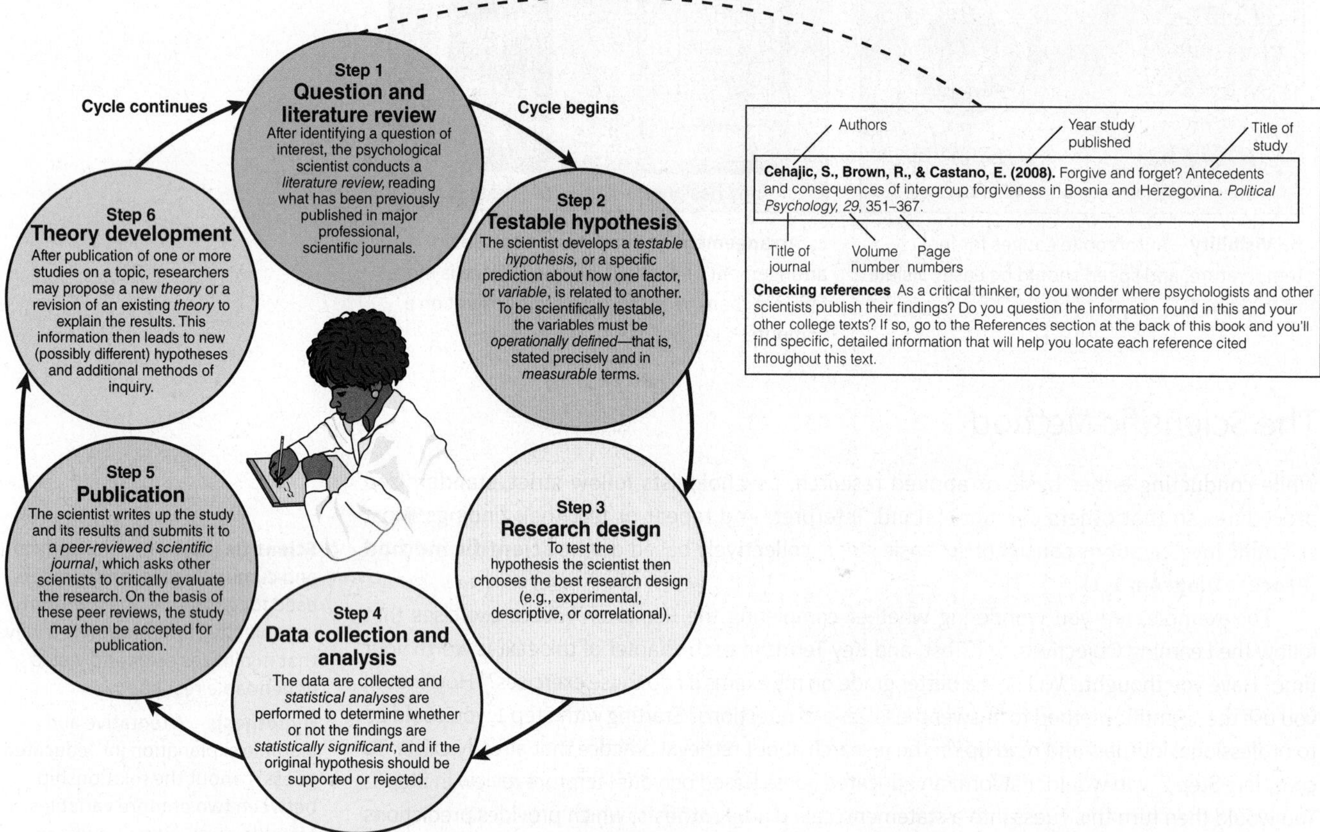

In Step 5, you could publish your research, and then you go on to further investigate additional study techniques that might contribute to theory development on the most effective study methods, Step 6. [You'll be interested to know that research does exist on the superiority of retrieval practice on retention of material and improved exam scores (Dunlosky & Rawson, 2015; Trumbo et al., 2016; Weinstein et al., 2016), which is why they're emphasized in this text.]

Note also in Figure 1.6 that the scientific method is cyclical and cumulative. Scientific progress comes from repeatedly challenging and revising existing theories and building new ones. If numerous scientists, using different procedures or participants in varied settings, can repeat, or *replicate*, a study's findings, there is increased scientific confidence in the findings. If the findings cannot be replicated, researchers look for other explanations and conduct further studies. When different studies report contradictory findings, researchers may average or combine the results of all such studies and reach conclusions about the overall weight of the evidence, a popular statistical technique called **meta-analysis**. For example, one recent meta-analysis found that babies who are breast-fed have higher IQs (on average 3.44 points) than babies who are not breast-fed (Horta et al., 2015). [Q3]

After many related findings have been collected and confirmed, scientists may generate a **theory** to explain the data through a systematic, interrelated set of concepts. In common usage,

Meta-analysis A statistical technique for combining and analyzing data from many studies in order to determine overall trends.

Theory A well-substantiated explanation for a phenomenon or a group of facts that have been repeatedly confirmed by previous research.

the term *theory* is often assumed to mean something is only a hunch or someone's personal opinion. In reality, scientific theories are based on empirical evidence, rigorously tested, and self-correcting (**Figure 1.6**).

Psychology's Four Main Goals

In contrast to *pseudopsychologies*, which we discussed earlier and which rely on unsubstantiated beliefs and opinions, psychology is based on rigorous scientific methods. When conducting their research, psychologists have four major goals—to *describe*, *explain*, *predict*, and *change* behavior and mental processes:

1. **Description** Description tells what occurred. In some studies, psychologists attempt to *describe*, or name and classify, particular behaviors by making careful scientific observations. Description is usually the first step in understanding behavior. For example, if someone says, "Boys are more aggressive than girls," what does that mean? The speaker's definition of aggression may differ from yours. Science requires specificity.
2. **Explanation** An explanation tells why a behavior or mental process occurred. *Explaining* a behavior or mental process requires us to discover and understand its causes. One of the most enduring debates in science is the **nature–nurture controversy**. Are we controlled by biological and genetic factors (the nature side) or by the environment and learning (the nurture side)? As you will see throughout the text, psychology (like all other sciences) generally avoids "either or" positions and focuses instead on *interactions*. Today, almost all scientists agree that most psychological, and even physical, traits reflect an interaction between nature and nurture. For example, research suggests numerous interacting causes or explanations for aggression, including culture, learning, genes, brain damage, and testosterone (Bushman, 2016; Gerring & Vasa, 2016; Lippa, 2016).
3. **Prediction** Psychologists generally begin with description and explanation (answering the "whats" and "whys"). Then they move on to the higher-level goal of *prediction*, identifying "when" and under what conditions a future behavior or mental process is likely to occur. For instance, knowing that alcohol leads to increased aggression (de Bruijn & de Graaf, 2016; Woodin et al., 2016; Zinzow & Thompson, 2015), we can predict that more fights will erupt in places where alcohol is consumed than in places where it isn't.
4. **Change** For some people, change as a goal of psychology brings to mind evil politicians or cult leaders brainwashing unknowing victims. However, to psychologists, *change* means applying psychological knowledge to prevent unwanted outcomes or bring about desired goals. In almost all cases, change as a goal of psychology is positive. Psychologists help people improve their work environments, stop addictive behaviors, become less depressed, improve their family relationships, and so on. Furthermore, as you may know from personal experience, it is very difficult (if not impossible) to change someone's attitude or behavior against her or his will. (*Here is an old joke*: Do you know how many psychologists it takes to change a light bulb? *Answer*: None. The light bulb has to want to change.)

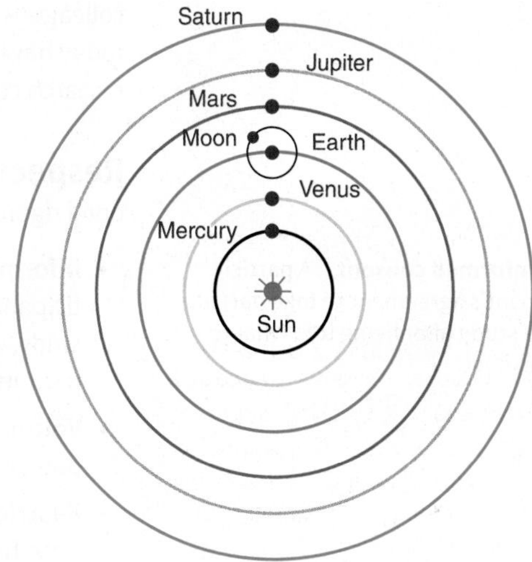

a.

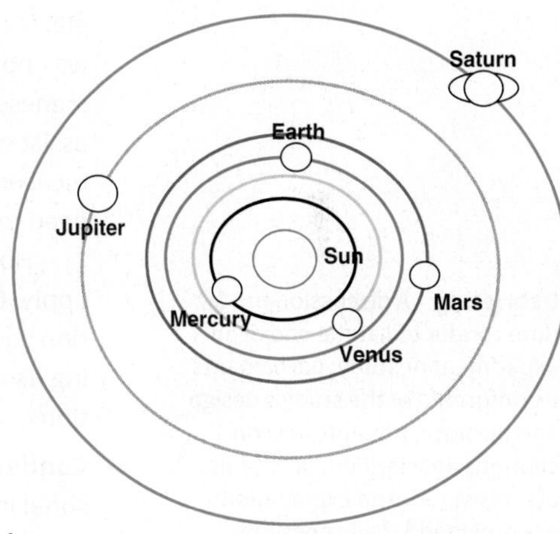

b.

FIGURE 1.6 Opinions versus facts—science to the rescue! Early experiments, conducted primarily by Nicolaus Copernicus (1473–1543), led to a collection of facts and the ultimate theory that the Earth was not the center of the universe (as generally assumed at the time) **(Figure a)**. Instead, it rotated around the sun with the other planets in concentric circles. Later scientists (astronomers Johannes Kepler and Tycho Brahe) built on this Copernican (heliocentric) theory with additional experiments that led to a revised theory, in which the orbits were not circular, but rather elliptical. **(Figure b)**. Today, researchers have expanded the theory even further by demonstrating that our sun is not the center of the universe, but only a part of a galaxy that in turn is only one of many billions. Can you see how these incremental changes illustrate the value of scientific theories and their ever changing, and self-correcting nature?

Psychology's Research Ethics

So far, we've discussed applied versus basic research, the scientific method, and the four basic goals of psychology. Now we need to examine the general ethics that guide psychological research. The two largest professional organizations of psychologists, the American Psychological Association (APA) and the Association for Psychological Science (APS), both recognize the importance of maintaining high ethical standards in research, therapy, and all other areas of professional psychology. The preamble to the APA's publication *Ethical Principles of Psychologists and Code of Conduct* (2016) requires psychologists to maintain their competence, to retain objectivity in applying their skills, and to preserve the dignity and best interests of their clients,

Nature–nurture controversy An ongoing dispute about the relative contributions of nature (heredity) and nurture (environment) in determining the development of behavior and mental processes.

colleagues, students, research participants, and society. In addition, colleges and universities today have institutional review boards (IRBs) that carefully evaluate the ethics and methods of research conducted at their institutions.

Respecting the Rights of Human Participants

The APA and APS have developed rigorous guidelines regulating research with human participants, including:

Informed consent A participant's agreement to take part in a study after being told what to expect.

- **Informed consent** Researchers must obtain an **informed consent** agreement from all participants *before* initiating an experiment. Participants are made aware of the nature of the study, what to expect, and significant factors that might influence their willingness to participate, including all physical risks, discomfort, and possibly unpleasant emotional experiences.
- **Voluntary participation** Participants must be told that they're free to decline to participate, or to withdraw from the research at any time.
- **Restricted use of deception, followed by debriefing.** If participants knew the true purpose behind certain studies, they might not respond naturally. In one of psychology's most famous, and controversial, studies (Milgram, 1963), researchers ordered participants to give electric shocks to another participant (who was really a confederate of the researcher, and was not actually receiving any shocks). Although this study was testing participants' willingness to follow orders, they were told that the study was examining the use of shocks to assist with learning. Obviously in this case, participants' behavior could not be accurately measured if they were told the real focus of the study. Therefore, researchers occasionally need to temporarily deceive participants about the actual reason for the experiment.

  However, when deception is necessary, important guidelines and restrictions still apply. One of the most important is **debriefing**, which is conducted once the data collection has been completed. The researchers provide a full explanation of the research, including its design and purpose, any deception used, and then clarify participants' misconceptions, questions, or concerns.

Debriefing A discussion procedure conducted at the end of an experiment or study; participants are informed of the study's design and purpose, possible misconceptions are clarified, questions are answered, and explanations are provided for any possible deception.

- **Confidentiality** Whenever possible, participants are provided anonymity and all personal information acquired during a study must be kept private, and not published in such a way that an individual's right to privacy is compromised.

Respecting the Rights of Nonhuman Animals

Although they are used in only 7 to 8% of psychological research (APA, 2009; ILAR, 2009; MORI, 2005), nonhuman animals—mostly rats and mice—have made significant contributions to almost every area of psychology. Without nonhuman animals in *medical research*, how would we test new drugs, surgical procedures, and methods for relieving pain? *Psychological research* with nonhuman animals has led to significant advances in virtually every area of psychology—the brain and nervous system, health and stress, sensation and perception, sleep, learning, memory, motivation, and emotion. For example, one recent study found that rats who are fed a diet high in fats and sugars show impairment in their learning and memory (Tran & Westbrook, 2015). This study could have very important real-world implications for people, but do you see why this type of research would be unethical and impossible to conduct using human subjects? [Q4]

Nonhuman animal research has also produced significant gains for some animal populations, such as the development of more natural environments for zoo animals, and more successful breeding techniques for endangered species.

Despite the advantages, using nonhuman animals in psychological research remains controversial. While debate continues about ethical issues in such research, psychologists take great care in handling research animals. Researchers also actively search for new and better ways to minimize any harm to the animals (APA Congressional Briefing, 2015; Morling, 2015; Pope & Vasquez, 2011).

Respecting the Rights of Psychotherapy Clients

Professional organizations, such as the APA and APS, as well as academic institutions, and state and local agencies, all may require that therapists, like researchers, maintain the highest ethical standards. Therapists must also uphold their clients' trust. All personal information and therapy records must be kept confidential. Furthermore, client records are only made available to authorized persons, and with the client's permission. However, therapists are legally required to break confidentiality if a client threatens violence to him or herself or to others, if a client is suspected of abusing a child or an elderly person, and in other limited situations (Fisher, 2013; Kress et al., 2013; Tyson et al., 2011).

A Final Note on Ethical Issues What about ethics and beginning psychology students? Once friends and acquaintances know you're taking a course in psychology, they may ask you to interpret their dreams, help them discipline their children, or even ask your opinion on whether they should start or end their relationships. Although you will learn a great deal about psychological functioning in this text, and in your psychology class, take care that you do not overestimate your expertise. Also remember that the theories and findings of psychological science are circular and cumulative—and continually being revised.

David L. Cole, a recipient of the APA Distinguished Teaching in Psychology Award, reminds us that, "Undergraduate psychology can, and I believe should, seek to liberate the student from ignorance, but also the arrogance of believing we know more about ourselves and others than we really do" (Cole, 1982, p. 24).

Retrieval Practice 1.2 | The Science of Psychology

SELF-TEST Completing this self-test, and then checking your answers by clicking on the answer button or by looking in Appendix B, will provide immediate feedback and helpful practice for exams.

1. If you conducted a study on areas of the brain most affected by drinking alcohol, it would be _____ research.
   a. unethical b. basic
   c. pseudopsychology d. applied
2. Label the six steps in the scientific method.

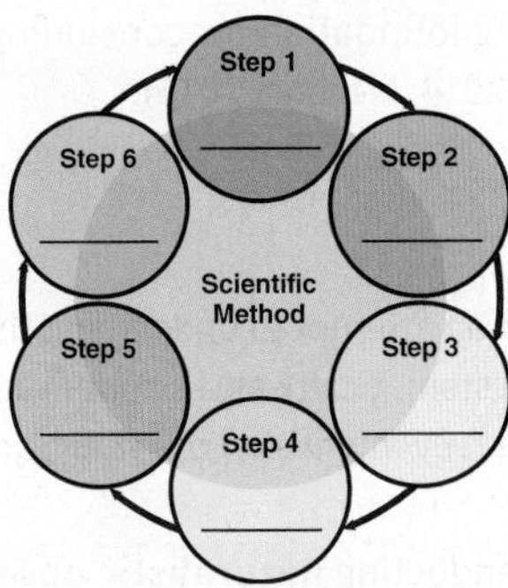

3. A(n) _____ provides a precise definition of how the variables in a study will be observed and measured.
   a. meta-analysis b. theory
   c. independent observation d. operational definition
4. The goal of _____ is to tell what occurred, whereas the goal of _____ is to tell when.
   a. health psychologists; biological psychologists
   b. description; prediction
   c. psychologists; psychiatrists
   d. pseudopsychologists; clinical psychologists
5. A participant's agreement to take part in a study after being told what to expect is known as _____.
   a. psychological standards b. an experimental contract
   c. debriefing d. informed consent

Think Critically

1. What is the difference between a scientific theory, an opinion, and a hunch?
2. If you had a million dollars to contribute to either basic or applied research, which one would you choose? Why?
3. Which group's rights—human participants, nonhuman animals, or psychotherapy clients—are the most important to protect? Why?

Real World Psychology

Do breast-fed babies have higher IQs?

Can a diet high in fats and sugars impair learning and memory?

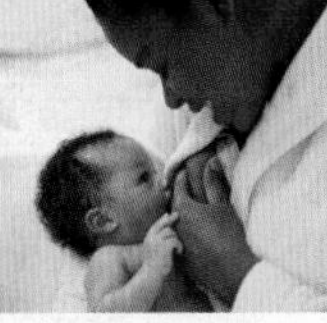
Camille Tokerud/ Getty Images

matthewennisphotography/ Getty Images

HINT: LOOK IN THE MARGIN FOR **[Q3]** AND **[Q4]**

1.3 Research Methods

LEARNING OBJECTIVES

Retrieval Practice While reading the upcoming sections, respond to each Learning Objective in your own words.

Summarize psychology's three major research methods.

- **Review** descriptive research and its four key methods.
- **Discuss** correlational research and the correlation coefficient.
- **Identify** the key terms and components of experimental research.

TABLE 1.5 Psychology's Three Major Research Methods

Method	Purpose	Advantages	Disadvantages
Descriptive (naturalistic observation, survey/interview, case study, archival research)	Observe, collect, and record data (meets psychology's goal of *description*)	Minimizes artificiality, makes data collection easier, allows description of behavior and mental processes as they occur	Little or no control over variables, potential biases, cannot identify cause and effect
Correlational (statistical analyses of relationships between variables)	Identify strength and direction of relationships and assess how well one variable predicts another (meets psychology's goal of *prediction*)	Helps clarify relationships between variables that cannot be examined by other methods and allows prediction	Little or no control over variables, cannot identify cause and effect, possible illusory correlation or third-variable problem, and potential biases
Experimental (manipulation and control of variables)	Identify cause and effect (meets psychology's goal of *explanation*)	Allows researchers to have precise control over variables, and provides explanation of the causes of behavior and mental processes	Ethical concerns, practical limitations, artificiality of lab conditions, uncontrolled variables may confound results, potential biases

Note that the three methods are not mutually exclusive. Researchers may use one, two, or all three methods to explore the same topic.

Having studied the scientific method and psychology's four main goals, we can now examine how psychologists conduct their research. Psychologists generally draw on three major research methods—*descriptive*, *correlational*, and *experimental* (**Table 1.5**). Each of these approaches has advantages and disadvantages, and psychologists often use variations of all three methods to study a single problem. In fact, when multiple approaches lead to similar conclusions, scientists have an especially strong foundation for concluding that one variable does affect another in a particular way (Cohen, 2014; Morling, 2015).

Descriptive Research

Descriptive research A type of research that systematically observes and records behavior and mental processes without manipulating variables; designed to meet the goal of *description*.

Naturalistic observation A descriptive research technique that observes and records behavior and mental processes in a natural, real-world setting.

Almost everyone observes and describes others in an attempt to understand them, but in conducting **descriptive research**, psychologists do so systematically and scientifically. The key types of descriptive research are *naturalistic observation*, *survey/interview*, *case study*, and *archival research*.

Naturalistic Observation When conducting **naturalistic observation**, researchers systematically observe and record participants' behavior in their natural setting, without interfering. Many settings lend themselves to naturalistic observation, from supermarkets to airports to outdoor settings. For example, Jane Goodall's classic naturalistic observations of wild chimpanzees provided invaluable insights into their everyday lives, such as their use of tools, acts of aggression, demonstrations of affection, and, sadly, even the killing of other chimps' babies (infanticide). In Chapter 14, you'll read about an observational study that examined if bus drivers would allow passengers whose fare card didn't have enough money to ride for free (Mujcic & Frijters, 2013)? If so, would they allow more free passes to Whites than Blacks? Can you guess what they found?

The chief advantage of naturalistic observation is that researchers can obtain data about natural behavior rather than about behavior that is a reaction to an artificial experimental situation. But naturalistic observation can be difficult and time-consuming, and the lack of control by the researcher makes it difficult to conduct observations for behavior that occurs infrequently.

For a researcher who wants to observe behavior in a more controlled setting, *laboratory observation* has many of the advantages of naturalistic observation, but with greater control over the variables (**Figure 1.7**).

Survey/interview A descriptive research technique that questions a large sample of people to assess their behaviors and mental processes.

Survey/Interview Psychologists use **surveys/interviews** to ask people to report their behaviors, opinions, and attitudes. In Chapter 3, you'll read about survey research showing that even a single close childhood friendship can protect vulnerable children in lower socioeconomic circumstances from several psychological risk factors (Graber et al., 2015). One key advantage of this approach is that researchers can gather data from many more people than is generally possible with other research designs.

Unfortunately, most surveys/interviews rely on self-reported data, and not all participants are honest. As you might imagine, people are especially motivated to give less-than-truthful answers when asked about highly sensitive topics, such as infidelity, drug use, and pornography.

Jeffrey Greenberg/Photo Researchers

FIGURE 1.7 **Laboratory observation** In this type of observation, the researcher brings participants into a specially prepared room in the laboratory, with one-way mirrors, or inconspicuous, hidden cameras and microphones. Using such methods, the researcher can observe school children at work, families interacting, or other individuals and groups in various settings.

Case Study

What if a researcher wants to investigate photophobia (fear of light)? In such a case, it would be difficult to find enough participants to conduct an experiment or to use surveys/interviews or naturalistic observation. For rare disorders or phenomena, researchers try to find someone who has the problem and study him or her intensively. This type of in-depth study of a single research participant, or a small group of individuals, is called a **case study**. In Chapter 9, we'll share a fascinating case study that examined the impact of severe neglect during childhood on language acquisition. This study obviously could not be conducted using another method, for ethical reasons, and because of the rarity of such severe deprivation.

Case study A descriptive research technique involving an in-depth study of a single research participant or a small group of individuals.

Archival Research

The fourth type of descriptive research is **archival research**, in which researchers study previously recorded data. For example, archival data from 30,625 Himalayan mountain climbers from 56 countries found that expeditions from countries with hierarchical cultures, which believe that power should be concentrated at the top and followers should obey leaders without question, had more climbers reach the summit than did climbers from more egalitarian cultures (Anicich et al., 2015). Sadly, they also had more climbers die along the way. The researchers concluded that hierarchical values impaired performance by preventing low-ranking team members from sharing their valuable insights and perspectives. (If you're wondering about how America ranked, we're a little below midpoint in hierarchical values.)

Interestingly, the new "digital democracy," based on spontaneous comments on Twitter or Facebook, may turn out to be an even better method of research than the traditional random sampling of adults. Researchers who used a massive archive of billions of stored data from Twitter found "tweet share" predicted the winner in 404 out of 435 competitive races in the U.S. House elections in 2010 (DiGrazia et al., 2013). Apparently, just the total amount of discussion—good or bad—is a very good predictor of votes.

"What I drink and what I tell the pollsters I drink are two different things."

Archival research A descriptive research technique that studies existing data to find answers to research questions.

Correlational Research

As mentioned before, data collected from descriptive research provides invaluable information on behavior and mental processes because they describe the dimensions of a phenomenon or behavior, in terms of who, what, when, and where it occurred. However, if we want to know *whether* and *how* two or more variables change together, we need **correlational research**. As the name implies, the purpose of this approach is to determine whether any two variables are

Correlational research A type of research that examines possible relations between variables; designed to meet the goal of *prediction*.

co-related, meaning a change in one is accompanied by a change in the other. If one variable increases, how does the other variable change? Does it increase or decrease?

[Q5] For example, a careful analysis of over 30 years of descriptive data, using archival research, discovered a link between happiness and age in a sample of more than 5,000 people across the United States (Sutin et al., 2013). This study revealed that, contrary to common stereotypes, increases in age are accompanied by increases in happiness!

Correlational research is also very popular because it allows us to make predictions about one variable based on the knowledge of another. For instance, suppose scientists noted a relationship between the hours of television viewing and performance on exams. The researchers could then predict exam grades based on the amount of TV viewing. The researchers also could determine the direction and strength of the relationship using a statistical formula that gives a **correlation coefficient**, which is a number from −1.00 to +1.00 that indicates the direction and strength of a relationship between two variables (**Figure 1.8**).

Correlation coefficient A number from −1.00 to +1.00 that indicates the direction and strength of the relationship between two variables.

Chris Carroll/Corbis Images

Direction of the correlation	Strength of the correlation	
High	+1.00	Perfect positive relationship (100% of the variance)
Maternal smoking	+.80 to +.99	Very strong positive relationship (64–98% of the variance)
	+.60 to +.79	Strong positive relationship (36–62% of the variance)
Low Fetal defects	+.40 to +.59	Moderate positive relationship (16–35% of the variance)
Positive correlation	+.20 to +.39	Weak positive relationship (4–15% of the variance)
High	0.00	No relationship (0% of the variance)
Intelligence	−.20 to −.39	Weak negative relationship (4–15% of the variance)
Low Shoe size	−.40 to −.59	Moderate negative relationship (16–35% of the variance)
Zero correlation	−.60 to −.79	Strong negative relationship (36–62% of the variance)
	−.80 to −.99	Very strong negative relationship (64–98% of the variance)
High	−1.00	Perfect negative relationship (100% of the variance)
Exam scores; Low Class absences; Negative correlation		

Think Critically

Can you identify whether each of the following pairs most likely has a positive, negative, or zero correlation?

1. Health and exercise
2. Hours of TV viewing and student grades
3. Happiness and helpfulness
4. Hours of sleep and number of friends
5. Extraversion and loneliness

Answers: 1. positive, 2. negative, 3. positive, 4. zero, 5. negative

FIGURE 1.8 Interpreting a correlation coefficient A correlation coefficient is a number from −1.00 to +1.00 that represents the direction and strength of a relationship between two variables. Understanding that this number corresponds to the direction and strength of a relationship between two variables is crucial to becoming an educated consumer of research.

- **Direction of the correlation** (left-hand column) The + or − sign in the correlation coefficient indicates the *direction* of the correlation, either positive or negative. When two factors vary in the same direction, meaning they increase or decrease together, it is called a *positive correlation*. In contrast, when two factors vary in opposite directions, one increasing as the other decreases, it's known as a *negative correlation*. When there is NO relation between the two variables, it is called a *zero correlation*. These three forms of correlation are often depicted in graphs called *scatterplots* (shown in the left column of the table below). Each dot on these graphs represents one participant's score on both variables.
- **Strength of the correlation** (right-hand column) A correlation of +1.00 and a −1.00 magnitude both indicate the strongest possible relationship. As the number decreases and gets closer to 0.00, the relationship weakens. We interpret correlations close to zero as representing NO relationship between the variables—like the "relationship" between broken mirrors and supposed years of bad luck.

Limits of Correlations As you've just seen, correlations are sometimes confusing, or not particularly useful. In addition, sometimes a mathematical correlation can be found between two events or variables that have no direct connection—yet people may wrongly infer that they do. Therefore, it's very important to note two major cautions concerning correlations.

1. **Correlation does NOT prove causation!** Cities with a higher number of churches have a higher crime rate. Does this mean that an increase in churches leads to more crime? Of course not! Instead, a *third variable* (increased population) is the real source of the link between more churches and more crime. A similar problem exists with the correlational finding that sales of ice cream are higher when the rate of drownings is highest (**Figure 1.9**). This mistake of confusing correlation with causation is referred to as the **third-variable problem**, which refers a situation in which a variable that has not been measured accounts for a relationship between two or more other variables. Would you like a less obvious and more commonly confused example? See **Figure 1.10**.
2. **Correlations are sometimes illusory—meaning they don't exist!** In this second problem, there is NO factual connection between two variables—the relationship is the result of random coincidence and/or misperception. Popular beliefs, such as infertile couples often conceiving after an adoption, or that certain slot machines are more likely to pay off than others, are called **illusory** (false) **correlations** (Bleske-Rechek et al., 2015; Lilienfeld et al., 2015).

FIGURE 1.9 Revisiting correlation versus causation Ice cream consumption and drowning are highly correlated. Obviously, eating ice cream doesn't cause people to drown. A third factor, such as high temperatures, increases both ice cream consumption and participation in water-based activities.

Third-variable problem A situation in which a variable that has not been measured accounts for a relationship between two or more other variables; also known as a problem of confounding.

Illusory correlation A mistaken perception that a relationship exists between variables when no such relationship actually exists.

If you're confused about these two problems with correlations, note that with the *third-variable problem*, an actual correlation does exist between two or more variables, but a third factor might be responsible for their connection. In contrast, with an *illusory correlation* there is NO factual connection between two variables—the apparent connection is totally FALSE.

Interestingly, superstitions, such as breaking a mirror supposedly leading to 7 years of bad luck, or sports fans who always wears their lucky team sports jackets because they believe it will bring the team good luck, are additional examples of illusory correlations. We mistakenly perceive an association that factually does not exist. Unfortunately, these and other well-known superstitions (**Table 1.6**) persist despite logical reasoning and scientific evidence to the contrary.

Why are beliefs in illusory correlations so common? As you'll discover in upcoming chapters, we tend to focus on the most noticeable (salient) factors when explaining the causes of behavior. Paying undue attention to the dramatic (but very rare) instances when infertile couples conceive after adoption, or when a gambler wins a large payout on one specific slot machine, are both examples of the *saliency bias* (see Chapter 14). In addition to this saliency bias, we also more often note and remember events that confirm our expectations and ignore the "misses." This is known as the *confirmation bias*.

The important thing to remember while reading research reports in this or any textbook, or reports in the popular media, is that observed correlations may be illusory and that correlational research can NEVER provide a clear cause and effect relationship between variables. Always consider that a third factor might be a better explanation for a perceived correlation. To find causation, we need the experimental method.

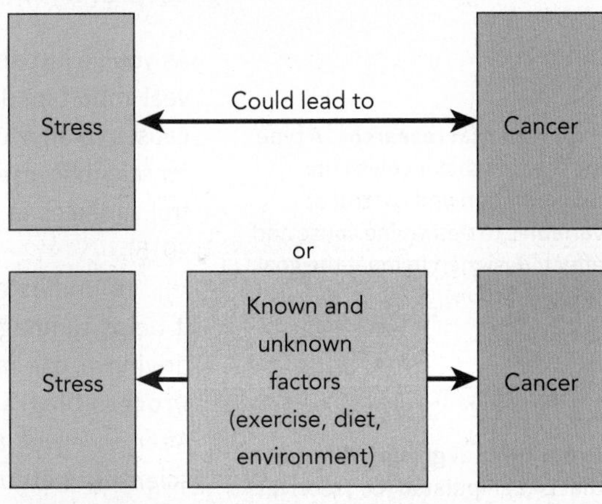

FIGURE 1.10 Correlation versus causation—The third-variable problem Research has found a strong correlation between stress and cancer (Chapter 3). However, this correlation does not tell us whether stress causes cancer, whether cancer causes stress, or whether other known and unknown factors, such as smoking, drinking, or pesticides, could contribute to both stress and cancer. Can you think of a way to study the effects of stress on cancer that is not correlational—and still ethical?

TABLE 1.6 Superstitions as Illusory Correlations

Behavior	Superstition
Wedding plans: *Why do brides wear something old, and something borrowed?*	The something old is usually clothing that belongs to an older woman who is happily married. Thus, the bride will supposedly transfer that good fortune to herself. Something borrowed is often a relative's jewelry. This item should be golden, because gold represents the sun, which was once thought to be the source of life.
Spilling salt: *Why do some people throw a pinch of salt over their left shoulder?*	Years ago, people believed good spirits lived on the right side of the body, and bad spirits on the left. If someone spilled salt, it supposedly meant that a guardian spirit had caused the accident to warn him or her of evil nearby. At the time, salt was scarce and precious. Therefore, the person was advised to bribe the bad spirits with a pinch of salt thrown over his or her left shoulder.
Knocking on wood: *Why do some people knock on wood when they're speaking of good fortune or making predictions?*	Down through the ages, people have believed that trees were homes of gods, who were kind and generous if approached in the right way. A person who wanted to ask a favor of the tree god would touch the bark. After the favor was granted, the person would return to knock on the tree as a sign of thanks.

The Value of Correlations After discussing the limits of correlational research, it's important to point out that it's still an incredibly valuable research method. A correlation can tell us if a relationship exists between variables, as well as its strength and direction. If we know the value of one variable, we can predict the value of the other.

In addition to providing more accurate predictions, correlational studies often point to *possible* causation, which can then be followed up with later experiments. For example, smoking cigarettes and drinking alcohol while pregnant are highly correlated with birth defects (Doulatram et al., 2015; Mason & Zhou, 2015; Roozen et al., 2016). Conducting experiments on pregnant women would be obviously impossible and illegal. However, evidence from this strong correlation, and other research, has helped convince women to avoid these drugs while pregnant—likely preventing many birth defects.

Experimental Research

As you've just seen, both descriptive and correlational studies are important because they reveal important data, insights, and practical applications. However, to determine *causation* (what causes what), we need **experimental research**. Experiments are considered the "gold standard" for scientific research because only through an experiment can researchers manipulate and control variables to determine cause and effect (Cohen, 2014; Goodwin & Goodwin, 2013; Morling, 2015).

Experimental research A type of research that involves the manipulation and control of variables to determine cause and effect; designed to meet the goal of *explanation*.

To understand all the important key terms, and the general set up for an experiment, it helps to imagine yourself as a psychologist interested in determining how texting while driving a car might affect the number of traffic accidents. You begin by reviewing the **Process Diagram 1.1** for the scientific method, which we discussed earlier in this chapter. After *reviewing the literature* and developing your *testable hypothesis* (Steps 1 and 2 of the scientific method), you then decide to use an experiment for your *research design* (Step 3 of the scientific method).

Experimental group The group that is manipulated (i.e., receives treatment) in an experiment; participants who are exposed to the independent variable (IV).

Control group The group that is not manipulated (i.e., receives no treatment) during an experiment; participants who are NOT exposed to the independent variable (IV).

Now carefully study the very simple experimental set up in the **Process Diagram 1.2**. You start by developing your *hypothesis*, which we defined earlier as a tentative and testable explanation (or "educated guess") about the relationship between two or more variables. Then you assign your research participants to either the **experimental group**, who receive the drug or treatment under study, or the **control group**, participants who do NOT receive the drug or treatment under study. Note that having at least two groups allows the performance of one group to be compared with that of another.

STOP! This Process Diagram contains essential information NOT found elsewhere in the text, which is likely to appear on quizzes and exams. Be sure to study it CAREFULLY!

PROCESS DIAGRAM 1.2 **Experimental Research Design** When designing an experiment, researchers must follow certain steps to ensure that their results are scientifically meaningful. In this example, researchers want to test whether people texting on cell phones while driving had more traffic accidents than those who didn't text while driving.

Step 1 The experimenter begins by identifying the hypothesis.

Step 2 In order to avoid sample bias, the experimenter first selects research participants who constitute a representative sample of the entire population of interest. Next, the experimenter randomly assigns these participants to two different groups.

Step 3 Having an experimental group, who receives the treatment, and a control group, who does not receive the treatment, allows a baseline comparison of responses between the two groups.

Step 4 Both the experimental and control groups are assigned to a driving simulator. The experimental group then texts while driving, whereas the control group does not text. Texting or not texting is the independent variable (IV). And the number of simulated traffic accidents is the dependent variable (DV). It's called "dependent" because the behavior (or outcome) exhibited by the participants is assumed to depend on manipulations of the IV.

Step 5 The experimenter then counts the number of simulated traffic accidents for each group, and then analyzes the data.

Step 6 The experimenter writes up his or her report, and submits it to scientific journals for possible publication.

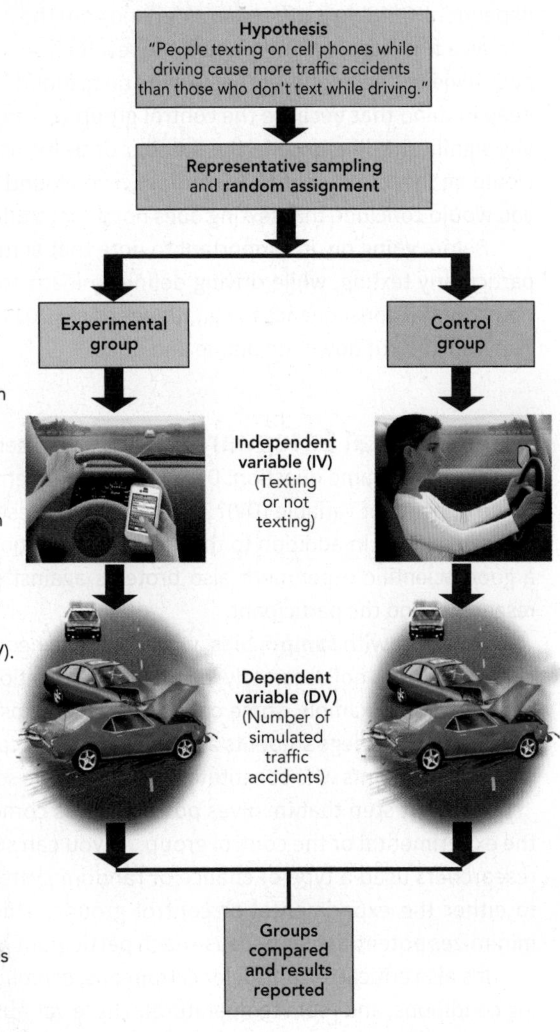

Study tip: To help you understand and differentiate between the independent and dependent variables (IV and DV), carefully study these drawings, and create a visual picture in your own mind of how:

The experimenter "manipulates" the IV to determine its causal effect on the DV.

The experimenter "measures" the DV, which "depends" on the IV.

Independent variable (IV) The variable that is manipulated and controlled by the experimenter to determine its causal effect on the dependent variable; also called the treatment variable.

Dependent variable (DV) The variable that is observed and measured for change; the factor that is affected by (or dependent on) the independent variable.

Next, you arrange the factors, or *variables*, you manipulate, which are called **independent variables (IV)**. You also decide which variables you plan to measure and examine for possible change, known as **dependent variables (DV)**. Participants who are assigned to the *experimental group* receive the IV, which is the treatment under study, and the variable being manipulated by you—the experimenter. Those assigned to the *control group* will be treated in every way just like the experimental group. The only difference is that they would NOT text while driving.

You, the experimenter, would then ask all participants to drive for a given amount of time (e.g., 30 minutes in the driving simulator). While they're driving, you would record the number of simulated traffic accidents (the DV). [Note: The goal of any experiment is to learn how the dependent variable is *affected by* (depends on) the independent variable.]

As a final step, you'll compare the results from both groups, and report your findings to a peer-reviewed scientific journal like the ones found in the reference list at the end of this book. Keep in mind that because the control group was treated exactly like the experimental group, any significant difference in the number of traffic accidents (the DV) between the two groups would be the result of the IV. In contrast, if you found little or no difference between the groups, you would conclude that texting does not affect traffic accidents.

Before going on, it's important to note that actual research does find that cell phone use, particularly texting, while driving definitely leads to increased accidents, and potentially serious or fatal consequences (e.g., Klauer et al., 2014; Rumschlag et al., 2015). In other words: "Let's all just put down the phone and drive."

Experimental Safeguards

As you've seen, every experiment is designed to answer essentially the same question: Does the independent variable (IV) *cause* the predicted change in the dependent variable (DV)? To answer this question, the experimenter must establish several safeguards. In addition to the previously mentioned controls within the experiment itself, a good scientific experiment also protects against potential sources of error from both the researcher and the participant.

Sample bias A bias that may occur when research participants are unrepresentative of the larger population.

Let's start with **sample bias**, which occurs when the researcher recruits and/or selects participants who do not accurately reflect the composition of the larger population from which they are drawn. For example, some critics suggest that psychological literature is biased because it too often uses college students as participants. We can counteract potential sample bias by selecting participants who constitute a *representative sample* of the entire population of interest.

Random assignment A research technique for assigning participants to experimental or control conditions so that each participant has an equal chance of being in either group; minimizes the possibility of biases or preexisting differences within or between the groups.

The next step that involves potential bias comes when assigning participants to either the experimental or the control group. As you can see in Step 2 of **Process Diagram 1.2**, the researchers used a type of chance or random system, such as a coin toss, to assign people to either the experimental or control groups. This is called **random assignment** and it minimizes potential bias because each participant has an equal chance to be in either group.

It's also critical to control for extraneous, *confounding variables* (such as time of day, lighting conditions, and room temperature). These variables must be held constant across both the experimental and control groups. Otherwise, if not controlled, these variables might contaminate your research results (**Figure 1.11**).

Experimenter bias A bias that occurs when a researcher influences research results in the expected direction.

In addition, if experimenters' beliefs and expectations are not controlled for, they can affect participants' responses, producing flawed results. Imagine what might happen if an experimenter breathed a sigh of relief when a participant gave a response that supported the researcher's hypothesis. A good example of this comes from the case of *Clever Hans*, the famous mathematical "wonder horse" (**Figure 1.12**). One way to prevent such **experimenter bias** from destroying the validity of participants' responses is to establish objective methods for collecting and recording data, such as using computers to present stimuli and record responses.

Ethnocentrism The belief that one's culture is typical of all cultures; also, viewing one's own ethnic group (or culture) as central and "correct" and judging others according to this standard.

Experimenters also can skew their results if they assume that behaviors typical in their own culture are typical in all cultures—a bias known as **ethnocentrism**. One way to avoid this problem is to have researchers from two cultures each conduct the same study twice, once with their own culture and once with at least one other culture. This kind of *cross-cultural sampling* isolates group differences in behavior that might stem from any researchers' ethnocentrism.

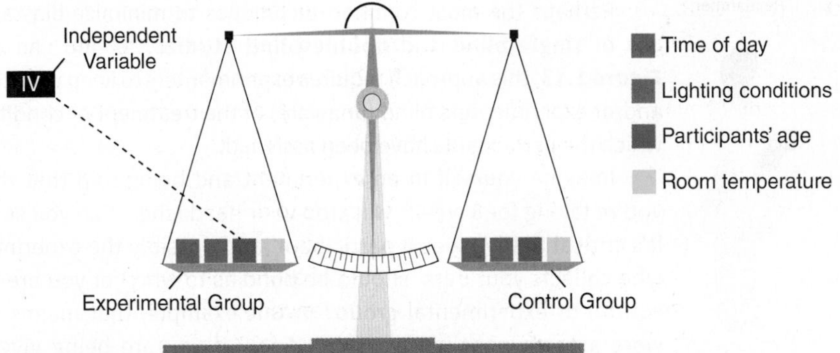

FIGURE 1.11 **Controlling for confounding variables** Recognizing that certain outside variables may affect their experimental findings, researchers strive for balance between the experimental and control groups, making sure the variables are the same for both. Once balance is achieved, and the independent variable (IV) is added to the experimental group, the experimenters check to see if the scale's balance is significantly disrupted. If so, they can then say that the IV *caused* the change. However, if the IV is not "heavy" enough to make a significant difference, then the experiment "failed," and experimenters go back to further refine their approach, start over, or go on to a new project.

Participant bias A bias that occurs when a research participant contaminates research results.

We've seen that researchers can inadvertently introduce error (the experimenter bias). Unfortunately, participants also can produce a similar error, called **participant bias**. For example, research measuring accuracy of reports of alcohol consumption demonstrates that heavy drinkers tend to under-report how much alcohol they are consuming (Northcote & Livingston, 2011; Wetterling et al., 2014). In this case, participants obviously tried to present themselves in a good light—called the *social desirability* response (as described in the **Real World Psychology** feature below).

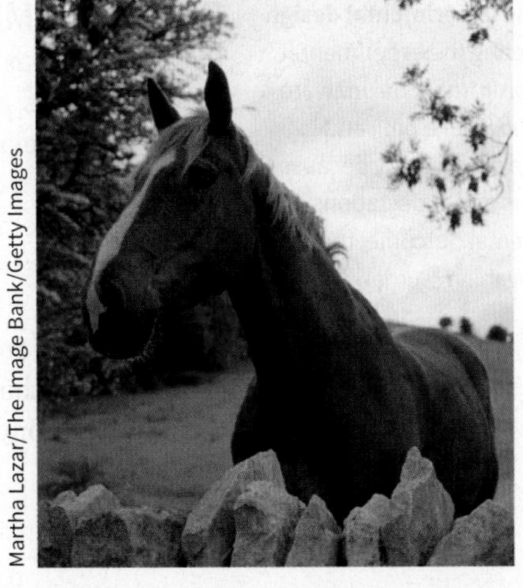
Martha Lazar/The Image Bank/Getty Images

FIGURE 1.12 **Can a horse add, multiply, and divide?** Clever Hans and his owner, Mr. Von Osten, convinced many people that this was indeed the case (Rosenthal, 1965). When asked to multiply 6 times 8, minus 42, Hans would tap his hoof 6 times. Or if asked to divide 48 by 12, add 6, and take away 6, he would tap 4 times. Even when Hans's owner was out of the room and others asked the question, he was still able to answer correctly. How did he do it? Researchers eventually discovered that all questioners naturally lowered their heads to look at Hans's hoof at the end of their question. And Hans had learned that this was a signal to start tapping. When the correct answer was approaching, the questioners also naturally looked up, which signaled Hans to stop. Can you see how this provided an early example of experimenter bias?

As you discovered in the previous section on ethical guidelines, researchers attempt to control for participant bias by offering anonymous participation, along with guarantees of privacy and confidentiality. In addition, one of the most effective (and controversial) ways of preventing participant bias is to temporarily deceive participants about the true nature of the research project. For example, in studies examining when and how people help others, participants may not be told the true goal of the study because they might try to present themselves as more helpful than they actually would be in real life.

Real World **Psychology**—Understanding the World

Clarifying Social Desirability

Imagine you're participating in a study that asks you about sensitive and highly personal behaviors, such as whether you've ever abused drugs, cheated on a test, or shoplifted. Can you see why participants might give dishonest answers to such questions, either due to fear of the consequences or personal embarrassment?

Runzelkorn/Shutterstock

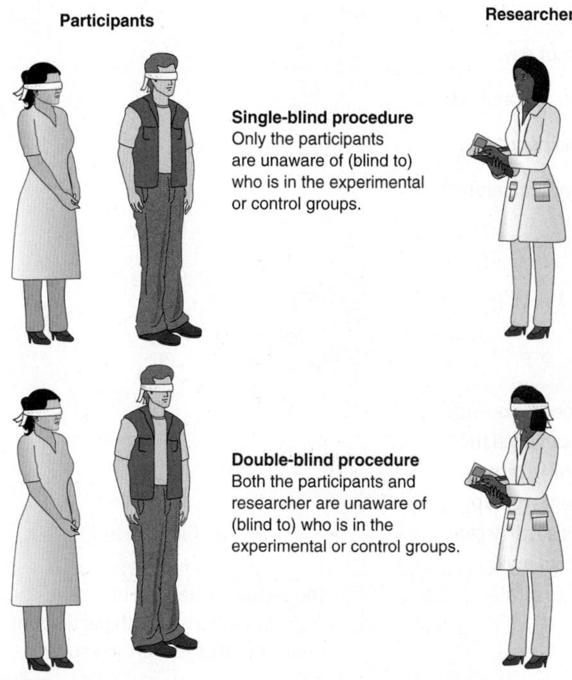

FIGURE 1.13 A single- or double-blind experimental design To test a new drug, researchers administering the experimental drug, and/or the participants taking the drug, must be unaware of (or "blind" to) who is receiving a *placebo* (a fake pill), and who is receiving the drug itself. Placebos are necessary because researchers know that participants' beliefs and expectations can change their responses, and the experimental outcome, the so-called "placebo effect" (Brown, 2013; Draganich & Erdal, 2014).

Perhaps the most common techniques to minimize bias are the use of **single-blind** and **double-blind studies**. As you can see in **Figure 1.13**, this approach requires experimenters to keep participants and/or experimenters blind (unaware) of the treatment or condition to which the participants have been assigned.

Imagine yourself in an experiment and being told that the pill you're taking for 8 weeks will stop your headaches. Can you see how it's critical that you, as a participant, and possibly the experimenter who collects your data, should be blind as to whether you are in the control or experimental group? In this example, that means if you were a participant you wouldn't know if you are being given the actual, experimental drug, or a harmless, **placebo** pill that has no physiological effect. Researchers do this because your expectations or beliefs, rather than the experimental treatment, can produce a particular outcome, called a **placebo effect**. Giving members of the control group a placebo, while giving the experimental group a pill with the active ingredients, allows researchers to determine whether changes are due to the pill that's being tested, or simply to the participants' expectations.

Research Methods—Final Take Home Message

Recognizing that we've offered a large number of research problems and safeguards associated with the various research methods (descriptive, correlational, and experimental), we've gathered them all into **Figure 1.14**. Be sure to study it carefully. In addition, note that the problems and safeguards connected with descriptive and correlational research described earlier also apply to experimental research.

If you'd like additional information about research methods and statistical analyses, see Appendix A. Note also that each chapter of this text offers an in-depth analysis of a hot topic in research (**PsychScience**), along with it's own, built-in, self-grading quiz (*Research Challenge*).

Single-blind study An experimental technique in which only the participants are unaware of (blind to) who is in the experimental or control groups.

Double-blind study An experimental technique in which both the researcher and the participants are unaware of (blind to) who is in the experimental or control groups.

Placebo An inactive substance or fake treatment used as a control technique in experiments; often used in drug research.

Placebo effect A change that occurs when a participant's expectations or beliefs, rather than the actual drug or treatment, cause a particular experimental outcome.

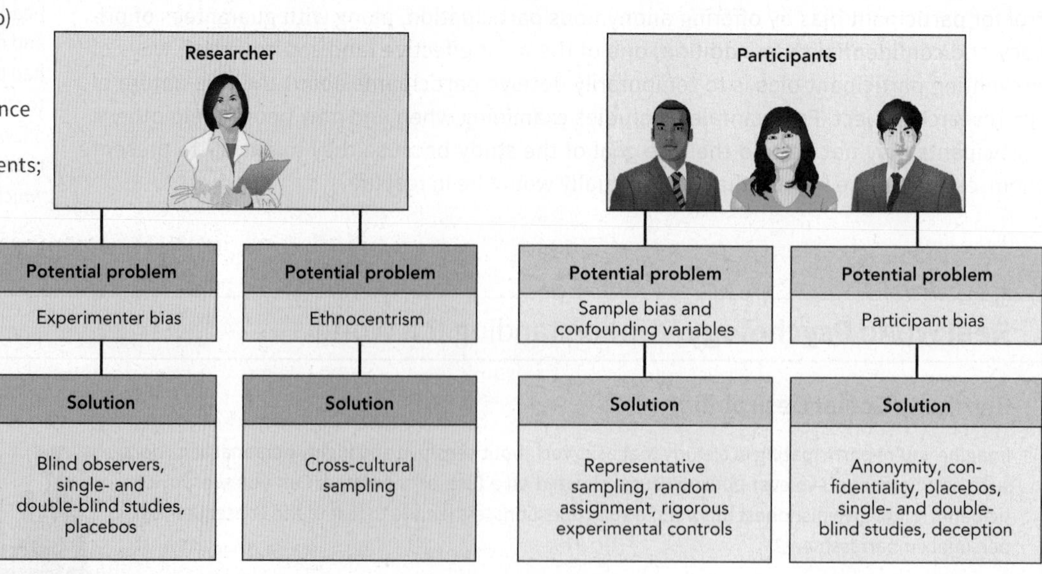

FIGURE 1.14 Potential research problems and solutions

PS PsychScience

Why Do Men and Women Lie About Sex?

As discussed earlier in this chapter, one of the biggest research challenges is seen when participants distort their responses in an attempt to present themselves in a positive light—the *social desirability response*. This is particularly true when we study sexual behaviors. An interesting example comes from a study that asked college students to complete a questionnaire regarding how often they engaged in 124 different gender-typical behaviors (Fisher, 2013). Some of these behaviors were considered more typical of men (such as wearing dirty clothes and telling obscene jokes), whereas other behaviors were more common among women (such as writing poetry and lying about their weight). Half of the participants completed these questionnaires, while attached to what they were told was a polygraph machine (or lie detector), although in reality this machine was not working. The other half completed the questionnaires without being attached to such a machine.

Can you predict how students' answers differed as a function of their gender, and whether they were (or were NOT) attached to the supposed lie detector? Among those who were attached to a supposed lie detector, and believed that it could reliably detect their lies, men were more likely to admit that they sometimes engaged in behaviors seen as more appropriate for women, such as writing poetry. In contrast, women were more likely to admit that they sometimes engaged in behaviors judged more appropriate for men, such as telling obscene jokes. Even more interesting, men reported having had more sexual partners when they weren't hooked up to the lie detector than when they were. The reverse is true for women! They reported fewer partners when they were not hooked up to the lie detector than when they were.

How does the *social desirability response* help explain these differences? We're all socialized from birth to conform to norms (unwritten rules) for our culturally approved male and female behaviors. Therefore, participants who were NOT attached to the supposed lie detector provided more "gender appropriate" responses. Men admitted telling obscene jokes and reported having more sexual partners, whereas women admitted lying about their weight and reported having fewer sexual partners.

Inti St Clair/Getty Images

The fact that these findings were virtually reversed, when participants believed they were connected to a machine that could detect their lies, provides a strong example of the dangers of the social desirability response. It also reminds us, as either researchers or consumers, to be very careful when interpreting findings regarding sexual attitudes and behaviors. Gender roles may lead to inaccurate reporting, and exaggerated gender differences.

Research Challenge

1. Based on the information provided, did this study (Fisher, 2013) use descriptive, correlational, and/or experimental research?
2. If you chose:
   - *descriptive research*, is this a naturalistic observation, survey/interview, case study, and/or archival research?
   - *correlational research*, is this a positive, negative, or zero correlation?
   - *experimental research*, label the IV, DV, experimental group(s), and control group.
   - both *descriptive* and *correlational*, answer the corresponding questions for both.

Check your answers by clicking on the answer button or by looking in Appendix B.

Note: The information provided in this study is admittedly limited, but the level of detail is similar to what is presented in most text books and public reports of research findings. Answering these questions, and then comparing your answers to those provided, will help you become a better critical thinker and consumer of scientific research.

Retrieval Practice 1.3 | Research Methods

SELF-TEST Completing this self-test, and then checking your answers by clicking on the answer button or by looking in Appendix B, will provide immediate feedback and helpful practice for exams.

1. In a case study, a researcher is most likely to ____.
   a. interview many research participants who have a single problem or disorder
   b. conduct an in-depth study of a single research participant
   c. choose and investigate a single topic
   d. use any of these options, which describe different types of case studies
2. When a researcher observes or measures two or more variables to find relationships between them, without directly manipulating them or implying a causal relationship, he or she is conducting ____.
   a. experimental research **b.** a correlational study
   c. non-causal metrics **d.** a meta-analysis
3. When participants are not exposed to any amount or level of the independent variable, they are members of the ____ group.
   a. control **b.** experimental
   c. observation **d.** out-of-control
4. If researchers gave participants varying amounts of a new memory drug and then gave them a story to read and measured their scores on a quiz, the ____ would be the IV, and the ____ would be the DV.
   a. response to the drug; amount of the drug
   b. experimental group; control group
   c. amount of the drug; quiz scores
   d. researcher variables; extraneous variables

5. When both the researcher and the participants are unaware of who is in the experimental or control group, the research design can be called _____.

a. reliable b. double-blind
c. valid d. deceptive

Think Critically

1. Which form of research would you most trust, descriptive, correlational, experimental, or a meta-analysis? Why?
2. Cigarette companies have suggested that there is no scientific evidence that smoking causes lung cancer. How would you refute this claim?

Real World Psychology

Are older people happier than younger people?

Kurhan/Shutterstock

HINT: LOOK IN THE MARGIN FOR **[Q5]**

1.4 Strategies for Student Success

LEARNING OBJECTIVES

Retrieval Practice While reading the upcoming sections, respond to each Learning Objective in your own words.

Review the key strategies for student success.

- **Describe** the steps you can take to improve your study habits.
- **Discuss** ways to improve your time management.
- **Discuss** the key factors in grade improvement.

In this section, you will find several important, well-documented study tips and techniques guaranteed to make you a more efficient and successful college student. Before we begin, be sure to complete the following *skills checklist*.

Psychology and You—Understanding Yourself

Skills for Student Success Checklist

(Answer true or false to each item. Then for each answer that you answered "True," pay particular attention to the corresponding headings in this *Strategies for Student Success* section.)

© Zastavkin/iStockphoto

Study Habits

_____ **1.** While reading, I often get lost in all the details, and can't pick out the most important points.

_____ **2.** When I finish studying a chapter, I frequently can't remember what I've just read.

_____ **3.** I generally study with either the TV or music playing in the background.

_____ **4.** I tend to read each section of a chapter at the same speed, instead of slowing down on the difficult sections.

Time Management

_____ **5.** I can't keep up with my reading assignments given all the other demands on my time.

_____ **6.** I typically wait to study, and then "cram" right before a test.

_____ **7.** I go to almost all my classes, but I generally don't take notes, and often find myself texting, playing games on my computer, or daydreaming.

Grade Improvement

_____ **8.** I study and read ahead of time, but during a test I frequently find that my mind goes blank.

_____ **9.** Although I study and read before tests, and think I'll do well, I often find that the exam questions are much harder than I expected.

_____ **10.** I wish I could perform better on tests, and read faster or more efficiently.

Study Habits

If you sometimes read a paragraph many times, yet remember nothing from it, try these four ways to successfully read (and remember) information in this and most other texts:

1. **Familiarization** The first step to good study habits is to familiarize yourself with the general text so that you can take full advantage of its contents. Scanning through the Table of Contents will help give you a bird's-eye view of the overall text. In addition, as you're familiarizing yourself with these features, be sure to also note the various tables, figures, photographs, and special feature boxes, all of which will enhance your understanding of the subject.
2. **Active Reading** The next step is to make a conscious decision to *actively* read and learn the material. Reading a text is *not* like reading a novel, or fun articles on the Internet! You must tell your brain to slow down, focus on details, and save the material for future recall (see the following *Test Yourself*).

   Another way to read actively is to use the **SQ4R method**, which was developed by Francis Robinson (1970). The initials stand for six steps in effective reading: Survey, Question, Read, Recite, Review, and wRite. As you might have guessed, this text was designed to incorporate each of these steps (**Process Diagram 1.3**).

SQ4R method A study technique based on six steps: Survey, Question, Read, Recite, Review, and wRite.

3. **Avoid highlighting and rereading** Marking with a yellow highlighter, or underlining potentially important portions of material, as well as rereading text material after initial reading, are common techniques students use while studying. Unfortunately, they are almost always a waste of time! Research clearly shows that highlighting and rereading are among the LEAST effective of all the major study techniques, whereas *distributed practice* and *practice testing* (explained later in the grade improvement section) are the MOST effective (Dunlosky et al., 2013). As previously discussed, you need to actively focus on your reading. Highlighting and rereading generally encourage passive reading.
4. **Take notes** While reading and listening to classroom lectures, ask yourself, "What is the main idea?" Write down key ideas and supporting details and examples. Effective note taking depends on active reading and active listening. Also, pay attention to the amount of pages and lecture time your text or instructors spend on various topics—It's generally a good indication of what they consider important for you to know.

Psychology and You—Understanding Yourself

Test Yourself | The Importance of Focus and Active Reading

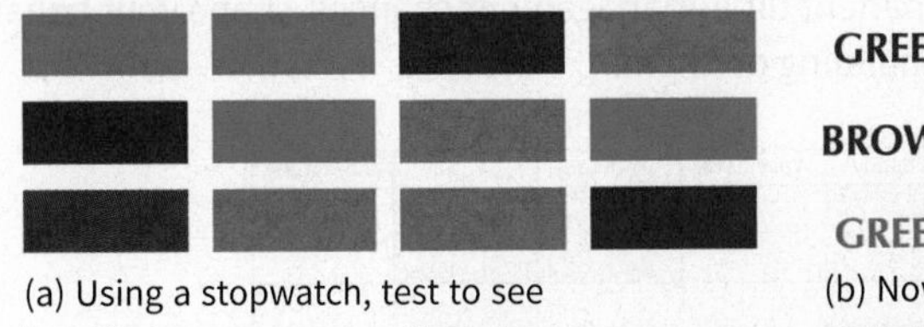

(a) Using a stopwatch, test to see how fast you can name the color of each rectangular box.

GREEN RED BROWN RED

BROWN GREEN GREEN BLUE

GREEN BROWN RED BLUE

(b) Now, time yourself to see how fast you can state the color of ink used to print each word, ignoring what each word says.

How did you do? Interestingly, young children who have learned their colors, but have not yet learned to read, easily name the colors in both sections in about the same amount of time. However, virtually every adult takes more time, and makes more errors on (b) than on (a). This is because, over time, our well-learned ability to read words overrides the less common task of naming the colors. We include this demonstration, known as the *Stroop effect*, here because it helps illustrate the importance of active reading. If you passively read a chapter in a text once, or even several times, you'll still do poorly on an exam. Just as it takes more time to state the color in part (b), it will take you more time to override your well-learned passive reading, and focus on the details to truly learn and master the material.

Time Management

If you find that you can't always strike a good balance between work, study, and social activities, or that you aren't always good at budgeting your time, here are four basic time-management strategies:

STOP! This Process Diagram contains essential information NOT found elsewhere in the text, which is likely to appear on quizzes and exams. Be sure to study it CAREFULLY!

PROCESS DIAGRAM 1.3 **Using the SQ4R Method** Follow these steps to improve your reading efficiency.

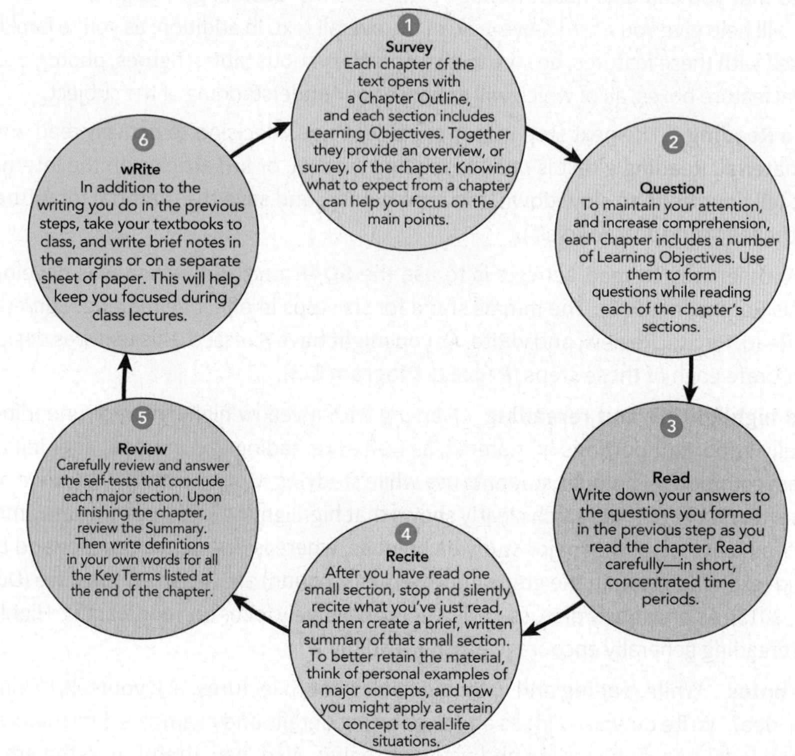

1
Survey
Each chapter of the text opens with a Chapter Outline, and each section includes Learning Objectives. Together they provide an overview, or survey, of the chapter. Knowing what to expect from a chapter can help you focus on the main points.
2
Question
To maintain your attention, and increase comprehension, each chapter includes a number of Learning Objectives. Use them to form questions while reading each of the chapter's sections.
3
Read
Write down your answers to the questions you formed in the previous step as you read the chapter. Read carefully—in short, concentrated time periods.
4
Recite
After you have read one small section, stop and silently recite what you've just read, and then create a brief, written summary of that small section. To better retain the material, think of personal examples of major concepts, and how you might apply a certain concept to real-life situations.
5
Review
Carefully review and answer the self-tests that conclude each major section. Upon finishing the chapter, review the Summary. Then write definitions in your own words for all the Key Terms listed at the end of the chapter.
6
wRite
In addition to the writing you do in the previous steps, take your textbooks to class, and write brief notes in the margins or on a separate sheet of paper. This will help keep you focused during class lectures.

- **Establish a baseline.** Before attempting any changes, simply record your day-to-day activities for one to two weeks (see the sample in **Figure 1.15**). You may be surprised at how you spend your time.
- **Set up a realistic schedule.** Make a daily and weekly "to do" list, including all required activities, basic maintenance tasks (like laundry, cooking, child care, and eating), and a reasonable amount of down time. Then create a daily schedule of activities that includes time for each of these. To make permanent time-management changes, shape your behavior, starting with small changes and building on them.

	Sunday	Monday	Tuesday	Wednesday	Thursday	Friday	Saturday
7:00		Breakfast		Breakfast		Breakfast	
8:00		History	Breakfast	History	Breakfast	History	
9:00		Psychology	Statistics	Psychology	Statistics	Psychology	
10:00		Review History & Psychology	Campus Job	Review History & Psychology	Statistics Lab	Review History & Psychology	
11:00		Biology		Biology		Biology	
12:00		Lunch / Study		Exercise	Lunch	Exercise	
1:00		Bio Lab	Lunch	Lunch	Study	Lunch	
2:00			Study	Study			

FIGURE 1.15 **Sample record of daily activities** To help manage your time, draw a grid similar to this, and record your daily activities in appropriate boxes. Then fill in other necessities, such as daily maintenance tasks and "downtime."

- **Reward yourself.** Give yourself immediate, tangible rewards for sticking with your daily schedule, such as calling a friend, getting a snack, or checking your social media.
- **Maximize your time.** To increase your efficiency, begin by paying close attention to the amount of time you spend on true, focused studying versus the time you waste worrying, complaining, and/or fiddling around getting ready to study ("fretting and prepping").

Time experts also point out that people often overlook important *time opportunities*—spare moments that normally go to waste that you might use productively. When you use public transportation, review notes, or read your textbook. While waiting for doctor or dental appointments, or to pick up your kids after school, take out your text and study for 10 to 20 minutes. Hidden moments count! (Can you see how this also is a form of distributed practice?)

In addition, time management is equally important during class lectures. Students often mistakenly believe that they can absorb information, and do well on exams, by simply going to class. They fail to realize that casually listening to the professor, while also texting, playing computer games, or talking to other classmates, is largely a waste of their valuable time. As you just discovered in the Study Habits section, it's very important to stay focused while studying AND during class lectures. Given that the professor generally lectures on what he or she considers most important (and will include on exams), paying full attention, and taking detailed notes during each class session, is the most efficient and profitable use of your time—and far better than what you can accomplish while studying on your own.

Grade Improvement

Here are five very important strategies for grade improvement and overall test taking skills. Each of these strategies will have a direct impact on your overall grade point average (GPA) in all your college classes, and your mastery of the material. However, research has clearly shown that the last two techniques—*distributed practice* and *practice testing*—are the MOST important keys to grade improvement.

1. **Improve your general test-taking skills.** Expect a bit of stress but don't panic. Pace yourself but don't rush. Focus on what you know. Skip over questions when you don't know the answers, and then go back if time allows. On multiple-choice exams, carefully read each question, and all the alternative answers, before responding. Answer all questions and make sure you have recorded your answers correctly.

   Also, bear in mind that information relevant to one question is often found in another test question. Do not hesitate to change an answer if you get more information—or even if you simply have a better guess about an answer. Contrary to the popular myth widely held by many students (and faculty) that "your first hunch is your best guess," research suggests this is NOT the case (Benjamin et al., 1984; Lilienfeld et al., 2010, 2015). Changing answers is far more likely to result in a higher score (**Figure 1.16**).

2. **Overlearn.** Many people tend to study new material just to the point where they can recite the information, but they do not attempt to understand it more deeply. For best results, however, you should *overlearn*. In other words, be sure to fully understand how key terms and concepts are related to one another, and also be able to generate examples other than the ones in the text. In addition, you should repeatedly review the material (by visualizing the phenomena that are described, and explained in the text, and by rehearsing what you have learned) until the information is firmly locked in place. Overlearning is particularly important if you suffer from test anxiety.

   Would you like a quick demonstration of why it's so important to overlearn? See **Figure 1.17**. You'll undoubtedly have trouble picking out the true penny, even though you've handled and undoubtedly bought many things involving pennies your entire life. The point is that if you're going to take a test on pennies, or any material in this text, you need to carefully study to the point of overlearning in order to do well.

3. **Take study skills courses.** Improve your reading speed and comprehension, and your word-processing/typing skills, by taking additional courses designed to develop these specific abilities. Also, don't overlook important human resources. Your instructors, roommates, classmates, friends, and family members often provide useful tips and encouragement.

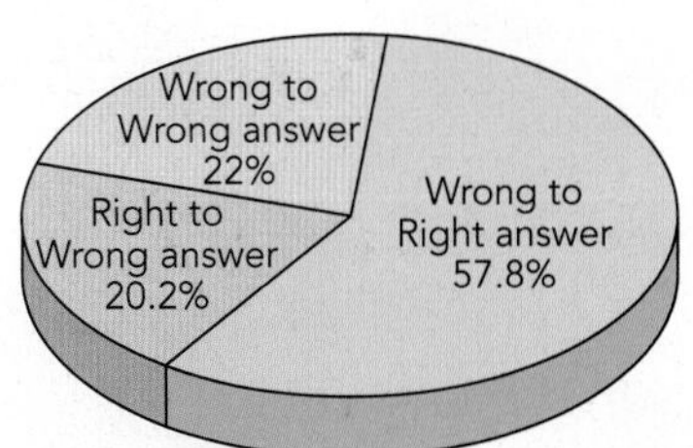

FIGURE 1.16 Should you change your answers? Yes! Research clearly shows that answer changes that go from a wrong to a right answer (57.8 percent) greatly outnumber those that go from a right to a wrong answer (20.2 percent). *Source:* Benjamin et al., 1984.

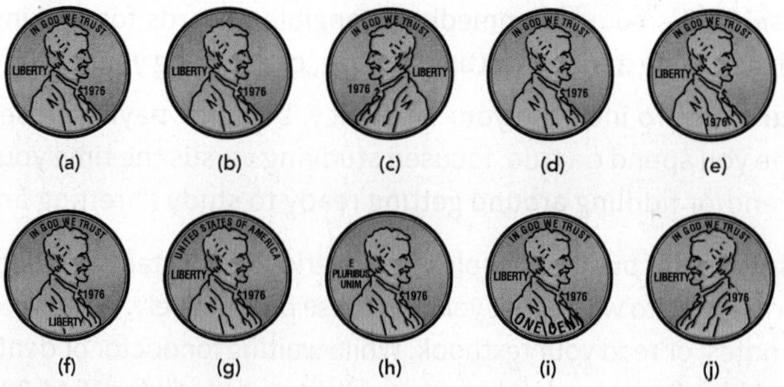

(a) (b) (c) (d) (e)

(f) (g) (h) (i) (j)

Nickerson, R. S., & Adams, M. J. (1979)

Answers: Coin a is the duplicate of a real

FIGURE 1.17 Which one of these 10 pennies is an exact duplicate of a real U.S. penny? Unless you're a coin collector, you probably can't easily choose the correct one without comparing it to a real coin—despite having seen it thousands of times. Why? As you will discover later in the text (Chapter 7), you must encode (or process) the information in some way before it will be successfully stored in your long-term memory.

4. **Distributed practice.** Spreading your study sessions out over time (distributed practice) is far more efficient than waiting until right before an exam, and cramming in all the information at once (massed practice) (Chapter 7). If you were a basketball player, you wouldn't wait until the night before a big play-off game to practice. The same is true for exam preparation. Keep in mind that distributed practice is NOT simply rereading the chapter several times over a few days. As mentioned earlier, you need to actively focus and study what you're reading.
5. **Practice test taking.** For most of us, taking tests is NOT one of our favorite activities. However, it's important to note that, as we mentioned several times, research has clearly shown that *practice test taking* and *distributed practice* are two of the most efficient ways to study and learn—and thereby improve your exam performance (Bourne & Healy, 2014; Dunlosky et al., 2013; Trumbo et al., 2016). Just as you need to repeatedly practice your free throw shot to become a good basketball player, you need to repeatedly practice your test-taking skills. [Q6]

If you think practice testing only applies to sports, consider this study conducted in actual introduction to psychology courses! Researchers (who were psych professors doing this study in their own classes) compared students who took brief, multiple-choice quizzes at the start of each class, which made up the bulk of their final grade, to those in a typical class with final grades being based entirely on four big exams (Pennebaker et al., 2013). As predicted by the previously mentioned value of practice test taking, the researchers found that this type of frequent testing led to higher grades (on average a half a letter grade increase) not only in this psychology class, but also in the students' subsequent college classes. Beyond the value of practice testing itself, how would you explain this grade increase? Students in the daily quiz condition showed higher class attendance, which included lectures over the material included on quizzes and exams. In addition, the researchers discovered that frequent testing required students to diligently keep up with the material, which led to better study skills and time management.

Based on this growing body of research, and our own teaching success with frequent testing, we've designed this text to include numerous opportunities for practice testing sprinkled throughout each chapter. As you're actively reading and studying each chapter, be sure to complete all these self-tests. When you miss a question, it's very helpful, and important, to immediately go back and reread the sections of the text that correspond to your incorrect response. You also can easily access the free flashcards, and other forms of self-testing in your Learning Space course.

A final word about college success. Some students may believe they can pass college courses by simply attending class and doing the assignments. This may have worked for *some* students in *some* classes in high school. But many college professors don't assign homework, and may not notice if you skip class. They assume students are independent, self-motivated adult learners, and that grades for their course should generally reflect knowledge and performance—not effort. Although hard work and perseverance are the true keys to overall life success (Chapter 10), your college grades are primarily based on your scores on quizzes and exams. This is why we included this section at the end of this first chapter. We want you to be successful in this and all your college courses.

Retrieval Practice 1.4 | Strategies for Student Success

SELF-TEST Completing this self-test, and then checking your answers by clicking on the answer button or by looking in Appendix B, will provide immediate feedback and helpful practice for exams.

1. Which of the following is NOT one of the recommended study habits?

a. active reading **b.** familiarization
c. highlighting **d.** note taking

2. List the six steps in the SQ4R method.

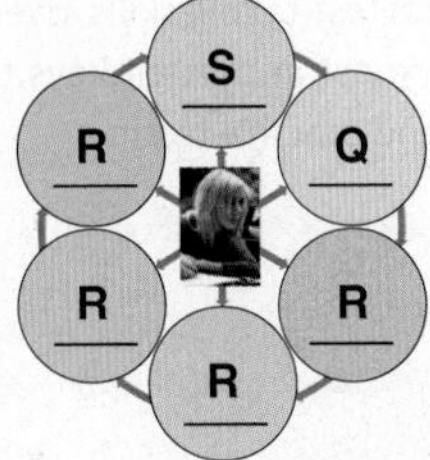

3. One of the clearest findings in psychology is that _____ practice is a much more efficient way to study and learn than _____ practice.

a. spaced (distributed); massed
b. active; passive
c. applied; basic
d. none of these options

4. _____ is particularly important if you suffer from test anxiety.

a. Overlearning **b.** Hyper-soma control
c. Active studying **d.** Passive listening

5. Research suggests that _____ might be two of the most important keys to improving your grades.

a. highlighting and rereading
b. personal control and better time management
c. active studying and the SQ4R method
d. distributed practice and practice testing

Think Critically

1. What topic or tip for student success do you consider most valuable? Why?

2. What prevents you, or other students you know, from fully employing the strategies for student success presented in this chapter?

Real World Psychology

What are the two best study techniques for improving your exam performance?

HINT: LOOK IN THE MARGIN FOR **[Q6]**

Summary

1.1 Introducing Psychology 2

- **Psychology** is the scientific study of *behavior* and *mental processes*. The discipline places high value on *empirical evidence* and **critical thinking**. *Pseudopsychologies*, such as belief in psychic powers, are not based on scientific evidence.
- Wilhelm Wundt, considered the father of psychology, and his followers were interested in studying conscious experience. Their approach, *structuralism*, sought to identify the basic structures of mental life through introspection.
- The *functionalism* perspective, led by William James, considered the father of American psychology, studied the way the mind functions to enable humans and nonhuman animals to adapt to their environment.
- The **psychoanalytic perspective**, founded by Sigmund Freud, emphasized the influence of the unconscious mind, which lies outside personal awareness.
- Contemporary psychology reflects the ideas of seven major perspectives: **psychodynamic, behavioral, humanistic, cognitive, biological, evolutionary,** and **sociocultural**.
- Despite early societal limitations, women and people of color have made important contributions to psychology. Pioneers include Mary Calkins, Margaret Floy Washburn, Francis Cecil Sumner, and Kenneth and Mamie Clark. Most contemporary psychologists embrace a unifying perspective known as the **biopsychosocial model**.
- Psychologists work as therapists, researchers, teachers, and consultants, in a wide range of settings.

1.2 The Science of Psychology 10

- **Basic research** is conducted to advance core scientific knowledge, whereas **applied research** works to address practical, real-world problems.
- Most scientific investigations consist of six basic steps, collectively known as the **scientific method**. Scientific progress comes from repeatedly challenging and revising existing **theories** and building new ones.
- Psychology's four basic goals are to *describe, explain, predict*, and *change* behavior and mental processes through the use of the scientific method. One of psychology's most enduring debates is the **nature-nurture controversy**.
- Psychologists must maintain high ethical standards, including respecting the rights of therapy clients and research participants (both human and nonhuman). **Informed consent**, voluntary participation, restricted deception (followed by **debriefing**), and confidentiality are critical elements of research using human participants. Psychologists also take care to protect research animals. U.S. researchers and clinicians are held professionally responsible by the APA and APS, their research institutions, and local and state agencies.

1.3 Research Methods 15

- **Descriptive research** systematically observes and records behavior and mental processes to meet the goal of *description*, without manipulating variables. The four major types of descriptive research are **naturalistic observation, survey, case study,** and **archival research**.

• **Correlational research** measures the relationship between two variables, and it provides important information about those relationships and valuable predictions. Researchers analyze their results using a **correlation coefficient**. Correlations can be *positive*, when they vary in the same direction, or *negative*, meaning they vary in opposite directions. A *zero* correlation occurs when there is no relationship between the variables. A correlation between two variables does not necessarily mean that one causes the other. It could be a **third-variable problem** or an **illusory correlation**. It's important to remember that *correlation does not prove causation.*

• **Experimental research** manipulates and controls variables to determine cause and effect. An experiment has several critical components: **hypothesis, independent** and **dependent variables** and **experimental** and **control groups**. A good scientific experiment protects against potential sources of *bias* (or error) from both the researcher and the participants through rigorous experimental controls, including **sample bias, random assignment, experimenter bias, ethnocentrism, participant bias, single-** and **double-blind studies,** and **placebos**.

1.4 Strategies for Student Success 26

• To improve your study habits, try familiarization, active reading (including the SQ4R method), and avoiding highlighting and rereading. While studying or listening to lectures, also be sure to take careful notes.

• For better time management, you can establish a baseline, set up a realistic schedule, reward yourself, and maximize your time.

• To improve your grades, work on your general test-taking skills, overlearn, and take study skills courses. The two most important keys to grade improvement are distributed practice and practice testing.

Applying **Real** World **Psychology**

We began this chapter with six intriguing Real World Psychology questions, and you were asked to revisit these questions at the end of each section. Questions like these have an important and lasting impact on all of our lives. See if you can answer these additional critical thinking questions related to real world examples.

Jonathan Selig/Getty Images

1. Nonhuman animals, like the mice in this photo, are sometimes used in psychological research when it would be impractical or unethical to use human participants. Do you believe nonhuman animal research is ethical? Why or why not?
2. What research questions might require the use of nonhuman animals? How would you ensure the proper treatment of these animals?
3. Imagine you designed an experiment to test whether watching violent TV might increase aggression in children. Assuming that you did find a significant increase, can you think of reasons the findings might not generalize to real world situations?
4. You may have heard that dog owners are healthier than cat owners, which leads some to believe that getting a dog would improve their health. Given this chapter's repeated warning that "correlation does not prove causation," can you think of an alternative explanation for why dog owners might be healthier?
5. People often confuse critical thinking with simply being critical and argumentative. How would you explain the true meaning and value of critical thinking?
6. How does psychology's emphasis on the scientific method contribute to critical thinking?

Key Terms

Retrieval Practice Write your own definition for each term before turning back to the referenced page to check your answer.

Fred Goldstein/
Shutterstock

CHAPTER **2**

Neuroscience and Biological Foundations

© George Peters/iStockphoto

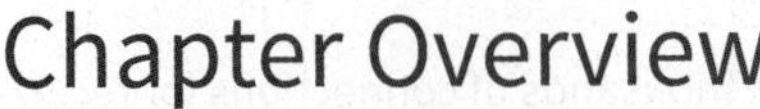

Real World **Psychology**

Things you'll learn in Chapter 2

[Q1] Does spending the first few months of life in an orphanage lead to long-term problems in cognitive functioning?

[Q2] How can singing and/or dancing make you feel closer to strangers and also raise your pain threshold?

[Q3] Why does eye contact with your dog make you feel good?

[Q4] How might stem cell injections have saved "Superman"?

[Q5] Can playing video games be good for your brain?

[Q6] Why are former NFL athletes at increased risk of depression, dementia, and suicide?

Throughout the chapter, margin icons for Q1–Q6 indicate where the text addresses these questions.

Chapter Overview

The brain is the last and grandest biological frontier, the most complex thing we have yet discovered in our universe. It contains hundreds of billions of cells interlinked through trillions of connections. The brain boggles the mind.

—James Watson
(Nobel Prize Winner)

Ancient cultures, including the Egyptian, Indian, and Chinese, believed the heart was the center of all thoughts and emotions. Today we know that the brain and the rest of the nervous system are the center of virtually all parts of our life. This chapter introduces you to the important and exciting field of *neuroscience* and *biopsychology*, which involve the scientific study of the *biology* of behavior and mental processes.

We begin this chapter with a look at the neuron, which is the foundation of the brain and nervous system. Next, we explore how neurons communicate, and how their chemicals (called neurotransmitters) affect us. Then, we examine the importance of hormones and our endocrine system. Following this, we discuss the overall organization of our entire nervous system—the central and peripheral systems. We conclude with a brief tour of the tools used in biological research, and the major structures

CHAPTER OUTLINE

and functions of our mysterious and magical human brain. Be aware that this chapter does contain a high number of new biological terms, which some students find a bit overwhelming. However, it's very important to master this material because it provides an essential foundation for topics we'll cover throughout this text. More importantly, knowing the proper terms and functions of your own brain and nervous system will help you understand and make better choices about the care of these vital structures.

2.1 Neural and Hormonal Processes

LEARNING OBJECTIVES

Retrieval Practice While reading the upcoming sections, respond to each Learning Objective in your own words.

Describe the key features and functions of the nervous and endocrine systems.

- **Describe** the neuron's key components and their respective functions.
- **Explain** how neurons communicate throughout the body.
- **Describe** the roles of hormones and the endocrine system.

Stop for a moment and consider your full human body. Did you know that your brain and nervous system are responsible for receiving, transmitting, and interpreting all the sensory information from your internal and the external environment? Are you surprised to learn that your body is composed of about 10 trillion cells divided into about 200 different types—muscle cells, heart cells, etc.? For psychologists, the microscopic nerve cells, called **neurons**, are the most important because they are essential to understanding who we are as individuals and how we behave. In other words, our every thought, mood, or action is a biological experience. To fully appreciate these neural bases of behavior, we must start with the *neuron*.

Neuron The basic building block (nerve cell) of the nervous system; responsible for receiving, processing, and transmitting electrochemical information.

Understanding the Neuron

Each neuron is a tiny information-processing system with thousands of connections for receiving and sending electrochemical signals to other neurons. Each human body may have as many as 1 *trillion* neurons.

Neurons are held in place and supported by **glial cells**, which make up about 90% of the brain's total cells. They also supply nutrients and oxygen, perform cleanup tasks, and insulate one neuron from another so that their neural messages are not scrambled. In addition, they play a direct role in nervous system communication and our immune system (Garrett, 2015; McCarthy et al., 2015; Sénécal et al., 2016). In short, our neurons simply could not function without glial cells. However, the "star" of the communication show is still the neuron.

It's important to recognize that there are different types of neurons, but they generally share three basic features: **dendrites**, the **cell body**, and an **axon** (**Figure 2.1**). *Dendrites* look like leafless branches of a tree. In fact, the word *dendrite* means "little tree" in Greek. Each neuron may have hundreds or thousands of dendrites, which act like antennas to receive electrochemical information from other nearby neurons. The information then flows into the *cell body*, or *soma* (Greek for "body"). If the cell body receives enough information/stimulation from its dendrites, it will pass the message on to a long, tube-like structure, called the *axon* (from the greek word for "axle"). The axon then carries information away from the cell body to the *terminal buttons*.

The **myelin sheath**, a white, fatty coating around the axons of some neurons, is not considered one of the three key features of a neuron, but it plays the essential roles of insulating and speeding neural impulses. As you'll discover in the next section, our human body is essentially an information-processing system dependent upon electrical impulses

Glial cells The cells that provide structural, nutritional, and other functions for neurons; also called glia or neuroglia.

Dendrites The branching fibers of neurons that receive neural impulses from other neurons and convey impulses toward the cell body.

Cell body The part of a neuron that contains the cell nucleus and other structures that help the neuron carry out its functions; also known as the soma.

Axon A long, tube-like structure that conveys impulses away from a neuron's cell body toward other neurons or to muscles or glands.

Myelin sheath The layer of fatty insulation wrapped around the axon of some neurons that increases the rate at which neural impulses travel along the axon.

FIGURE 2.1 Key parts and functions of a neuron Red arrows in the figure on the left indicate direction of information flow: dendrites → cell body → axon → terminal buttons of axon.

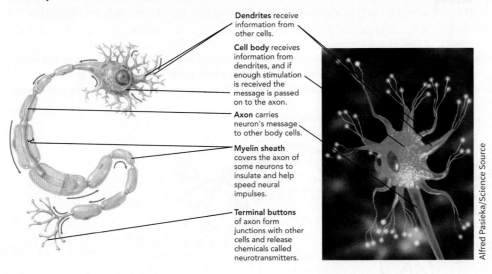

Dendrites receive information from other cells.

Cell body receives information from dendrites, and if enough stimulation is received the message is passed on to the axon.

Axon carries neuron's message to other body cells.

Myelin sheath covers the axon of some neurons to insulate and help speed neural impulses.

Terminal buttons of axon form junctions with other cells and release chemicals called neurotransmitters.

Alfred Pasieka/Science Source

Note: To remember the three key parts of a neuron, picture your hand and arm:

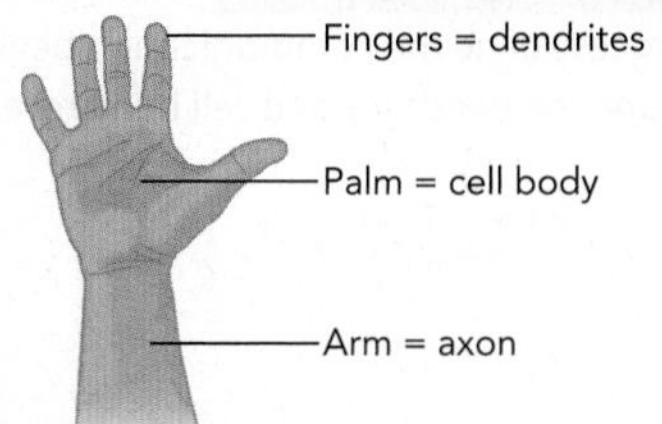

To understand how information travels through the neuron, think of the three key parts in reverse alphabetical order: Dendrite → Cell Body → Axon (D, C, B, A).

and chemical messengers. Just as the wires in data cables are insulated from one another by plastic, the myelin sheath provides insulation and separation for the numerous axons that travel throughout our bodies. And just as the data cable wires are bundled together into larger cables, our myelin-coated axons are bundled together into "cables" called *nerves*. The importance of myelin sheaths becomes readily apparent in certain diseases, such as *multiple sclerosis,* in which myelin progressively deteriorates and the person gradually loses muscular coordination. Thankfully, the disease often goes into remission, but it can be fatal if it strikes the neurons that control basic life-support processes, such as breathing or heartbeat. Myelin is also very important in the first few weeks and months of life. Research shows that social isolation during these critical periods (as occurs for babies
[Q1] who are neglected in some orphanages, see photo) prevents cells from producing the right amount of myelin. Sadly, this loss of normal levels of myelin leads to long-term problems in cognitive functioning (Makinodan et al., 2012).

Fred Goldstein/Shutterstock

Having described the structure, function, and importance of the neuron itself, we also need to explain that we have two general types of neurons—sensory and motor. Our *sensory neurons* respond to physical stimuli by sending neural messages to our brains and nervous systems. In contrast, our *motor neurons* respond to sensory neurons by transmitting signals that activate our muscles and glands. For example, light and sound waves from the text messages that we receive on our cell phones are picked up by our sensory neurons, whereas our motor neurons allow our fingers to almost instantaneously type reply messages.

Communication Within the Neuron

As we've just seen, the basic function of our neurons is to transmit information throughout the nervous system. But exactly how do they do it? Neurons "speak" in a type of electrical and chemical language. The communication begins within the neuron itself, when the dendrites and cell body receive electrical signals from our senses (sight, sound, touch) or from chemical messages from other nearby neurons. If the message is sufficiently strong, it will instruct the neuron to "fire"—to transmit information to other neurons. As you can see in **Process Diagram 2.1**, this type of electrical communication is admittedly somewhat confusing. Therefore, we'll also briefly explain it here in narrative form:

Step 1 Neurons are normally at rest and ready to be activated, which explains why this resting stage is called the "resting potential."

Step 2 If a resting neuron receives a combined signal (from the senses or other neurons) that exceeds the minimum threshold, it will be activated and "fire," thus transmitting an

STOP! This Process Diagram contains essential information NOT found elsewhere in the text, which is likely to appear on quizzes and exams. Be sure to study it CAREFULLY!

PROCESS DIAGRAM 2.1 Communication *Within* the Neuron The process of neural communication begins within the neuron itself, when the dendrites and cell body receive information, and conduct it toward the axon. From there, the information moves down the entire length of the axon via a brief, traveling electrical charge called an action potential, which can be described in the following three steps:

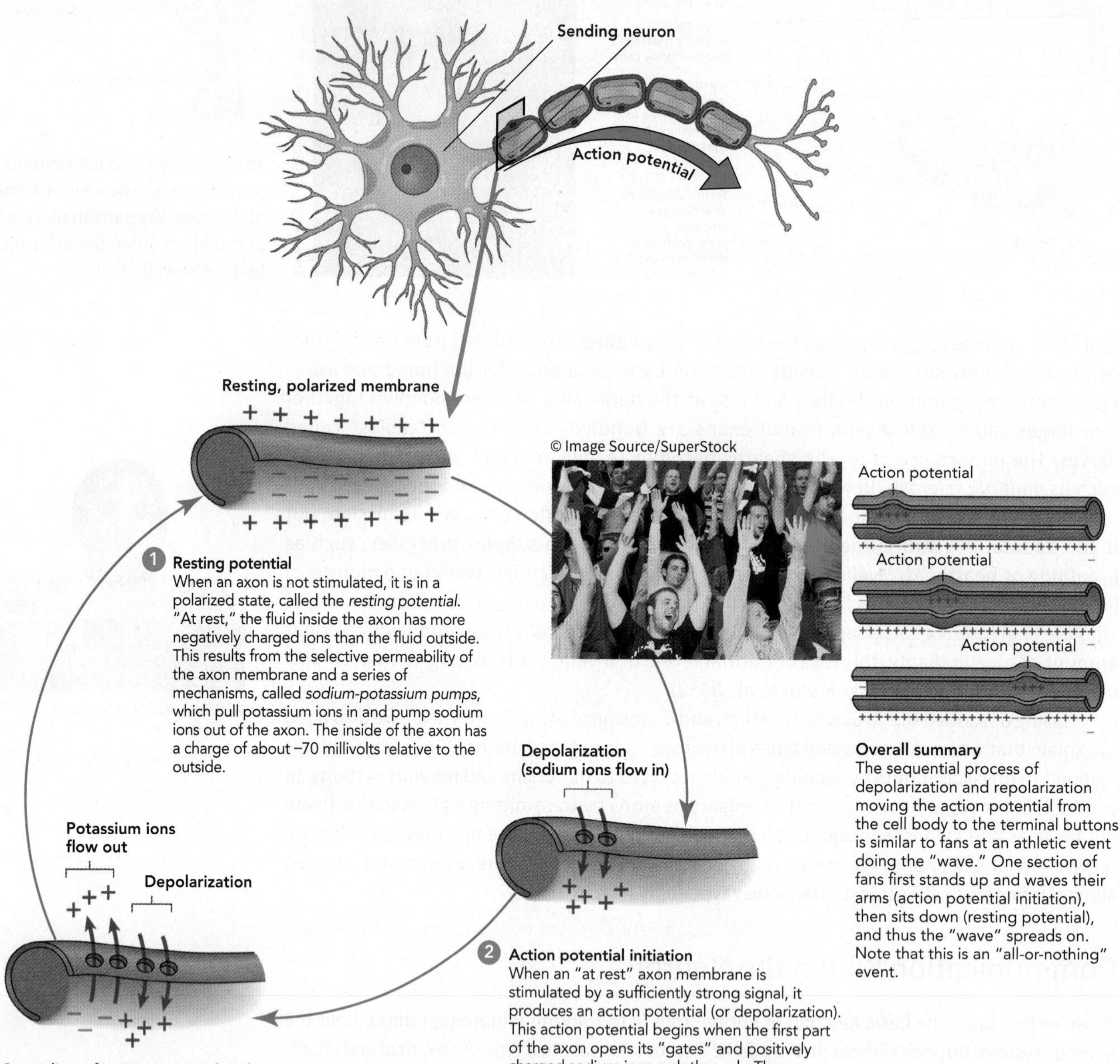

1 Resting potential
When an axon is not stimulated, it is in a polarized state, called the *resting potential.* "At rest," the fluid inside the axon has more negatively charged ions than the fluid outside. This results from the selective permeability of the axon membrane and a series of mechanisms, called *sodium-potassium pumps,* which pull potassium ions in and pump sodium ions out of the axon. The inside of the axon has a charge of about −70 millivolts relative to the outside.

2 Action potential initiation
When an "at rest" axon membrane is stimulated by a sufficiently strong signal, it produces an action potential (or depolarization). This action potential begins when the first part of the axon opens its "gates" and positively charged sodium ions rush through. The additional sodium ions change the previously negative charge inside the axon to a positive charge—thus depolarizing the axon.

3 Spreading of action potential and repolarization
The initial depolarization (or action potential) of Step 2 produces a subsequent imbalance of ions in the adjacent axon membrane. This imbalance thus causes the action potential to spread to the next section. Meanwhile, "gates" in the axon membrane of the initially depolarized section open and potassium ions flow out, thus allowing the first section to repolarize and return to its resting potential.

Overall summary
The sequential process of depolarization and repolarization moving the action potential from the cell body to the terminal buttons is similar to fans at an athletic event doing the "wave." One section of fans first stands up and waves their arms (action potential initiation), then sits down (resting potential), and thus the "wave" spreads on. Note that this is an "all-or-nothing" event.

electrical impulse (called an **action potential**). (Note that in Process Diagram 2.1, we're only demonstrating how an action potential "fires"—also known as "excitation." However, this resting neuron also receives simultaneous messages telling it NOT to fire—a process called "inhibition." Given these contradictory messages, the neuron does something simple—it goes with the majority! If it receives more excitatory messages than inhibitory, it fires—and vice versa.)

Action potential A neural impulse, or brief electrical charge, that carries information along the axon of a neuron; movement is generated when positively charged ions move in and out through channels in the axon's membrane.

Step 3 The beginning action potential then spreads and travels down the axon. As the action potential moves toward the terminal buttons, the areas on the axon left behind return to their resting state. Note that this firing of an action potential is similar to a light switch, where once you apply the minimum amount of pressure needed to flip the switch, the light comes on. There is no "partial firing" of a neuron. It's either on or off. This neural reaction of either firing with a full-strength response or not at all is known as the **all-or-nothing principle**. But if this is true, how do we detect the intensity of a stimulus, such as the difference between a rock and a butterfly landing on our hand? A strong stimulus (like the rock) causes more neurons to fire and to fire more often than does a butterfly.

All-or-nothing principle The principle that a neuron's response to a stimulus is either to fire with a full-strength response or not at all; also known as the all-or-none law.

Now that we understand how communication occurs within the neuron, we need to explain how it works between neurons.

Communication Between Neurons

As you discovered in the overall summary and photo in Process Diagram 2.1, neural transmission (via *action potentials*) within the neuron can be compared to a crowd's behavior doing the "wave" in a stadium. The analogy helps explain how the action potential travels down the axon in a "wave-like" motion. However, the comparison breaks down when we want to know how the message moves from one neuron to another—or how the "wave" in a stadium gets across the aisles. The answer is that within the neuron, messages travel electrically, whereas between neurons the messages are carried across the **synapse** via chemicals called **neurotransmitters**—see **Process Diagram 2.2**.

Synapse The gap between the axon tip of the sending neuron and the dendrite and/or cell body of the receiving neuron; during an action potential, neurotransmitters are released and flow across the synapse.

Neurotransmitter A chemical messenger released by neurons that travels across the synapse and allows neurons to communicate with one another.

Like Process 2.1, this procedure is complicated, so we'll also briefly summarize it in narrative form here:

Beginning with Step 1, note how the *action potential* travels down the axon and on to the knob-like terminal buttons. These buttons contain small tiny vesicles (sacs) that store the neurotransmitters. These neurotransmitters then travel across the *synapse*, or gap between neurons, to bind to receptor sites on the nearby receiving neurons. (The neuron that delivers the neurotransmitter to the synapse is called a *pre-synaptic neuron*.)

Now in Step 2, like a key fitting into a lock, the neurotransmitters then unlock tiny channels in the receiving neuron, and send either excitatory ("fire") or inhibitory ("don't fire") messages. (The receiving neuron is called a *post-synaptic neuron*.)

Finally in Step 3, after delivering its message, the neurotransmitters must be removed from the receptor sites before the next neural transmission can occur. Note how some of the neurotransmitters are used up in the transmission of the message. However, most of the "leftovers" are reabsorbed by the axon and stored until the next neural impulse—a process known as *reuptake*. In other cases, the "leftovers" are dealt with through enzymes that break apart the neurotransmitters to clean up the synapse.

Appreciating Neurotransmitters While researching how neurons communicate, scientists have discovered numerous neurotransmitters with differing effects on us that will be discussed here and in later chapters. For instance, we now know that some **agonist drugs** enhance or "mimic" the action of particular neurotransmitters, whereas **antagonist drugs** block or inhibit the effects (**Figure 2.2**)

Agonist drug A substance that binds to a receptor and triggers a response that mimics or enhances a neurotransmitter's effect.

Antagonist drug A substance that binds to a receptor and triggers a response that blocks a neurotransmitter's effect.

In addition to knowing how drugs and other chemicals can alter neurotransmission, we also know that neurotransmitters play important roles in certain medical problems. For example, decreased levels of the neurotransmitter dopamine are associated with Parkinson's disease (PD), whereas excessively high levels of dopamine appear to contribute to some forms

STOP! This Process Diagram contains essential information NOT found elsewhere in the text, which is likely to appear on quizzes and exams. Be sure to study it CAREFULLY!

PROCESS DIAGRAM 2.2 Communication *Between* Neurons

Within the neuron, messages travel electrically (see Process Diagram 2.1). Between neurons, messages are transmitted chemically. The three steps shown here summarize this chemical transmission.

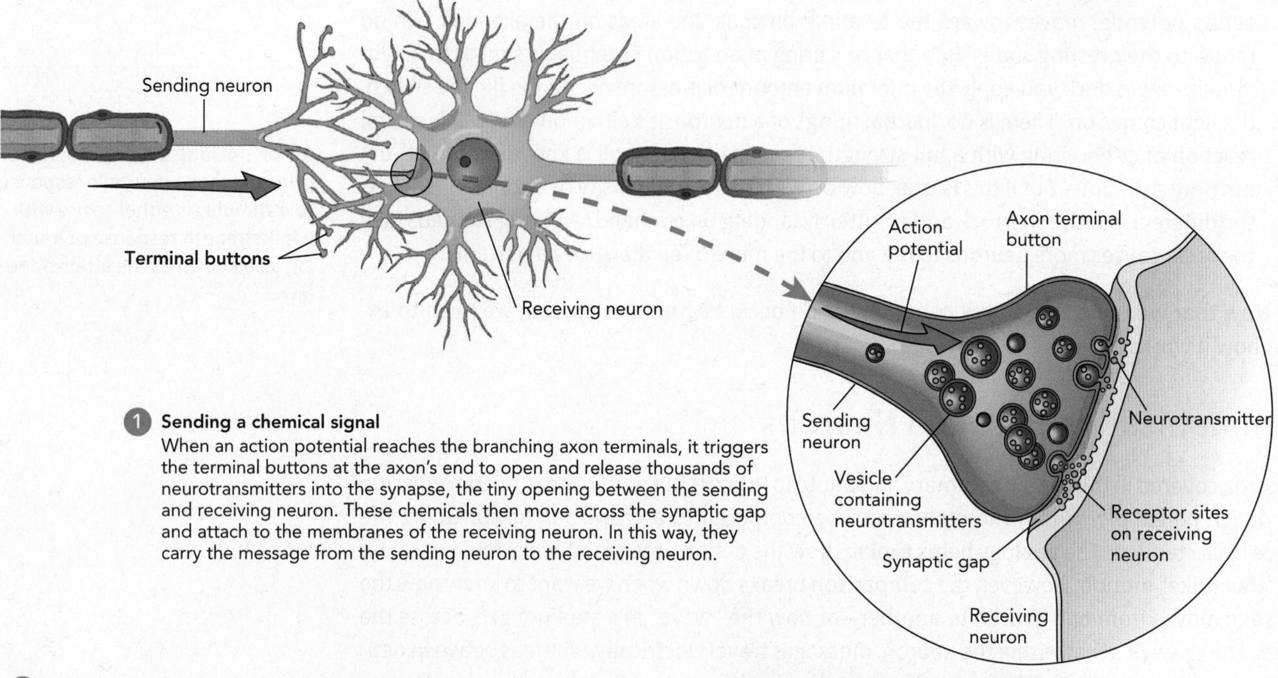

1 Sending a chemical signal
When an action potential reaches the branching axon terminals, it triggers the terminal buttons at the axon's end to open and release thousands of neurotransmitters into the synapse, the tiny opening between the sending and receiving neuron. These chemicals then move across the synaptic gap and attach to the membranes of the receiving neuron. In this way, they carry the message from the sending neuron to the receiving neuron.

2 Receiving a chemical signal
After a chemical message flows across the synaptic gap, it attaches to the receiving neuron. It's important to know that each receiving neuron gets multiple neurotransmitter messages. As you can see in this close-up photo, the axon terminals from thousands of other nearby neurons almost completely cover the cell body of the receiving neuron. It's also important to understand that neurotransmitters deliver either excitatory ("fire") or inhibitory ("don't fire") messages. The receiving neurons will only produce an action potential and pass along the message if the number of excitatory messages outweigh the inhibitory messages.

Receiving neuron (cell body)

Sending neurons (axon terminal buttons)

Science Source

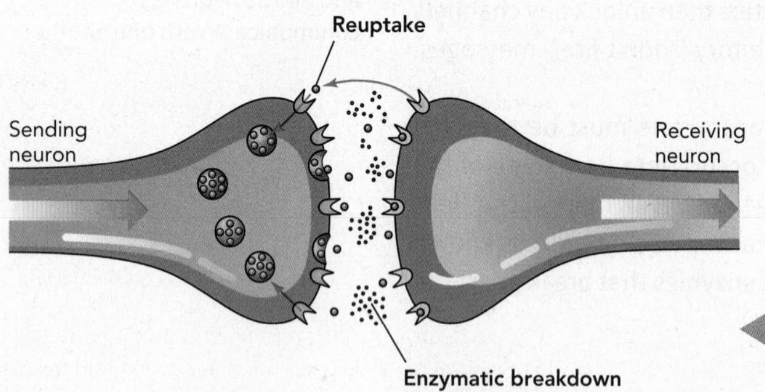

3 Dealing with leftovers
Given that some neurons have thousands of receptors, which are only responsive to specific neurotransmitters, what happens to excess neurotransmitters or to those that do not "fit" into the adjacent receptor sites? The sending neuron normally reabsorbs the excess (called "reuptake"), or they are broken down by special enzymes.

Endorphin A chemical substance in the nervous system similar in structure and action to opiates; involved in pain control, pleasure, and memory.

of schizophrenia. **Table 2.1** presents additional examples of how some of the most common neurotransmitters affect us.

Perhaps the best-known neurotransmitters are the endogenous opioid peptides, commonly known as **endorphins** (a contraction of *endogenous* [self-produced] and *morphine*). These chemicals mimic the effects of opium-based drugs such as morphine: They elevate mood and reduce pain (Antunes et al., 2016; Fan et al., 2016). In fact, drinking alcohol causes

FIGURE 2.2 How poisons and drugs affect neural transmission

Foreign chemicals, like poisons and drugs, can mimic or block ongoing actions of neurotransmitters, thus interfering with normal functions.

Altrendo Images/Stockbyte/Getty Images

Most snake venom and some poisons, like *botulinum* toxin (Botox®), seriously affect normal muscle contraction. Ironically, these same poisons are sometimes used to treat certain medical conditions involving abnormal muscle contraction—as well as for some cosmetic purposes.

Normal neurotransmission

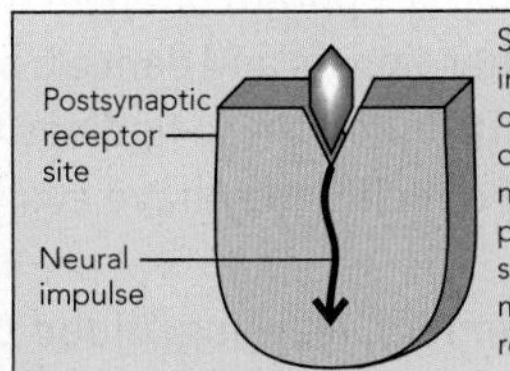

Somewhat like a key fitting into a lock, receptor sites on receiving neurons' dendrites recognize neurotransmitters by their particular shape. When the shape of the neurotransmitter matches the shape of the receptor site a message is sent.

A Normal neurotransmitter activation

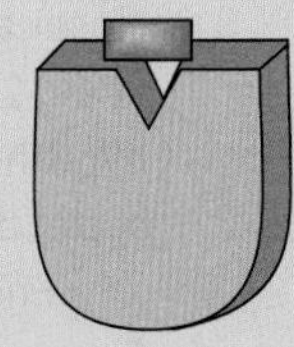

Neurotransmitters without the correct shape won't fit the receptors, so they cannot stimulate the dendrite, and that neurotransmitter's message is blocked.

B Blocked neurotransmitter activation

How poisons and drugs affect neurotransmission

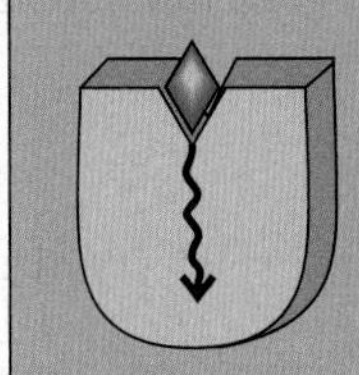

Some *agonist drugs*, like the nicotine in cigarettes (and the poison from a black widow spider bite), are similar enough in structure to a specific neurotransmitter (in this case, acetylcholine) that they mimic its effects on the receiving neuron, and a message is sent.

C Agonist drug "mimics" neurotransmitter

Some *antagonist drugs or poisons (like curare)* block neurotransmitters like acetylcholine, which is vital in muscle action. Blocking it paralyzes muscles, including those involved in breathing, which can be fatal.

D Antagonist drug fills receptor space and blocks neurotransmitter

TABLE 2.1 How Neurotransmitters Affect Us

Cameron Spencer/Getty Images

Which neurotransmitters best explain the skills of a professional tennis player, like Maria Sharapova (pictured here), or those involved in your own athletic abilities?

NEUROTRANSMITTER	SAMPLE AGONIST/ ANTAGONIST ACTING DRUGS	KNOWN OR SUSPECTED EFFECTS
Acetylcholine (ACh)	Nicotine, amphetamines, LSD, PCP, marijuana	Muscle action, learning, attention, memory, REM (rapid-eye-movement) sleep, emotion; decreased ACh plays a suspected role in Alzheimer's disease
Dopamine (DA)	Cocaine, methamphetamine, LSD, GHB, PCP, marijuana, Ecstasy (MDMA), L-Dopa (treatment for Parkinson's disease), chlorpromazine (treatment for schizophrenia)	Movement, attention, memory, learning, emotion; excess DA associated with schizophrenia; too little DA linked with Parkinson's disease; key role in addiction and the reward system
Endorphins	Heroin, morphine and oxycodone (treatments for pain)	Mood, pain, memory, learning, blood pressure, appetite, sexual activity
Epinephrine (or adrenaline)	Amphetamines, ecstasy (MDMA), cocaine	Emotional arousal, memory storage, metabolism of glucose necessary for energy release
GABA (gamma-aminobutyric acid)	Alcohol, GHB, rohypnol, valium (treatment for anxiety)	Learning, anxiety regulaton; key role in neural inhibition in the central nervous system; tranquilizing drugs, like Valium, increase GABA's inhibitory effects and thereby decrease anxiety
Glutamate	Alcohol, phencyclidine, PCP, ketamine (an anesthetic)	Learning, movement, memory; key role in neural excitation in the central nervous system; factor in migraines, anxiety, depression
Norepinephrine (NE) [or noradrenaline (NA)]	Cocaine, methamphetamine, amphetamine, ecstasy (MDMA), Adderall (treatment for ADHD)	Attention, arousal learning, memory, dreaming, emotion, stress; low levels of NE associated with depression; high levels of NE linked with agitated, manic states
Serotonin	Ecstasy (MDMA), LSD, cocaine, SSRIs, like Prozac (treatment for depression)	Mood, sleep, appetite, sensory perception, arousal, temperature regulation, pain suppression, impulsivity; low levels of serotonin associated with depression

endorphins to be released in parts of the brain that are responsible for feelings of reward and pleasure (Mitchell et al., 2012).

jonya/Getty Images

Surprisingly, researchers have even found that when we sing in choirs and/or move in synchrony with others (e.g., dancing, see photo) our pain thresholds are higher and we tend to feel closer to others—even if the other singers and dancers are strangers (Tarr et al., 2016; Weinstein et al., 2016). The researchers attributed these findings to the release of endorphins. They also hypothesized that singing and dancing may have evolved over time because they encourage social bonding with strangers! [Q2]

Endorphins also affect memory, learning, blood pressure, appetite, and sexual activity. For example, rats injected with an endorphin-like-chemical eat considerably more M&Ms than they would under normal conditions, even consuming as much as 17 grams (more than 5% of their body weight; DiFeliceantonio et al., 2012). Although this may not seem like a lot of chocolate to you, it is the equivalent of a normal-sized adult eating 7.5 pounds of M&Ms in a single session!

Hormones and the Endocrine System

Hormone Chemical messengers manufactured and secreted by the endocrine glands, which circulate in the bloodstream to produce bodily changes or maintain normal bodily functions.

Endocrine system A network of glands located throughout the body that manufacture and secrete hormones into the bloodstream.

We've just seen how the nervous system uses neurotransmitters to transmit messages. We also have a second type of communication system that uses **hormones** as its messengers. This second system is made up of a network of glands, called the **endocrine system** (**Figure 2.3**).

Why do we need two communication systems? Neurotransmitters are like emails that we only send to certain people—they only deliver messages to certain receptors. Hormones, in contrast, are like a global e-mail message that we send to everyone in our address book.

Another difference between the two communication systems is that neurotransmitters are released from a neuron's terminal buttons into the synapse, whereas hormones are released from endocrine glands directly into our bloodstream. These slower hormonal messages are then carried by the blood throughout our bodies to any cell that will listen. Like our global e-mail recipients who may forward our message on to other people, messages from hormones

FIGURE 2.3 The endocrine system This figure shows the major endocrine glands, along with some internal organs to help you locate the glands.

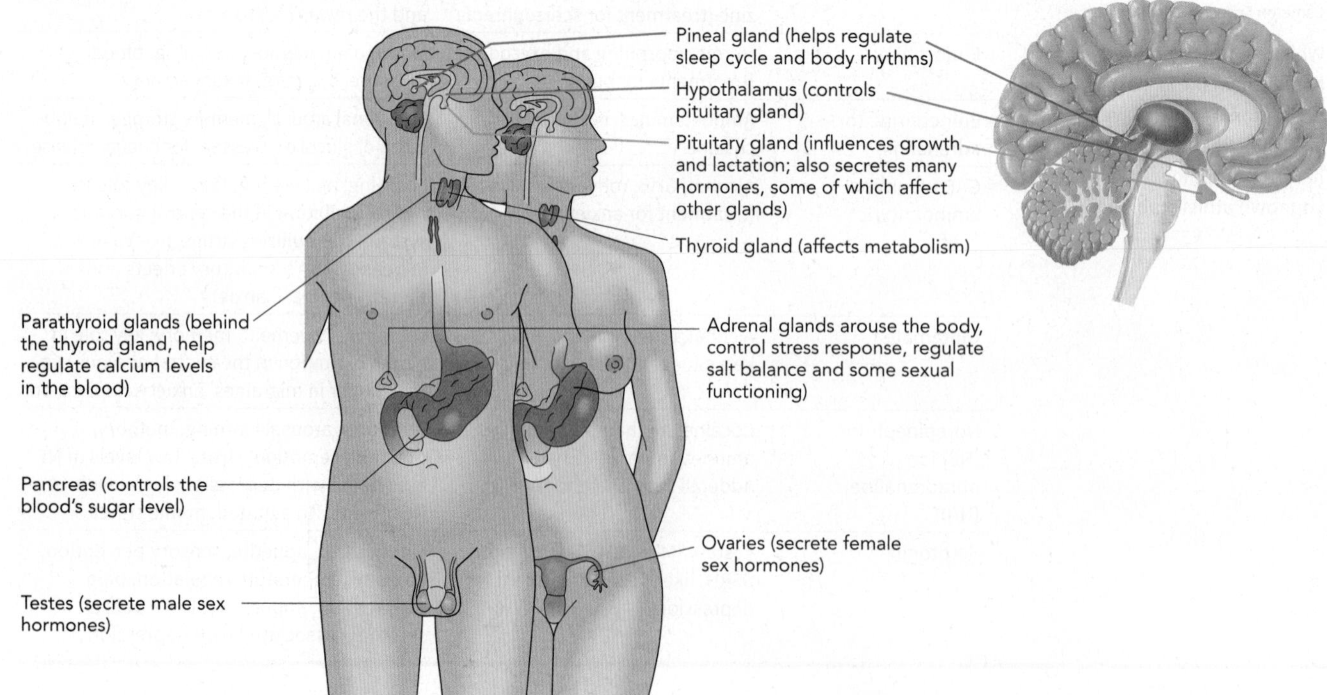

are often forwarded on to other parts of the body. For example, a small part of the brain called the hypothalamus releases hormones that signal the pituitary gland, which in turn stimulates or inhibits the release of other hormones.

Our hormone-releasing endocrine system has several important functions. It helps regulate long-term bodily processes, such as growth and sexual characteristics, while also changing or maintaining short-term processes, such as digestion and elimination.

Before going on, it's important to know that in spite of the previously mentioned differences between the nervous system and the endocrine system, they're actually close relatives that are intricately interconnected. In times of crisis, the hypothalamus sends messages through two pathways—the neural system and the endocrine system (primarily the pituitary gland). The pituitary sends hormonal messages to the adrenal glands (located right above the kidneys). As you'll discover in Chapter 3, the adrenal glands then release *cortisol*, a stress hormone that boosts energy and blood sugar levels, *epinephrine* (commonly called adrenaline), and *norepinephrine* (or nonadrenaline). (Remember that these same chemicals also can serve as neurotransmitters.)

The pituitary gland also releases another important hormone, *oxytocin*, which plays a very interesting role in love, attachment, and social bonding. Oxytocin enables contractions during birth, nursing, and sexual orgasm, and high oxytocin levels are also found during hugging, cuddling, and emotional bonding with romantic partners. One study even discovered that men who receive a spray of the hormone oxytocin rate their female partners as more attractive than unfamiliar women—thus suggesting oxytocin may increase faithfulness (Scheele et al., 2013). Perhaps even more interesting is the research showing that dogs who stare at their owners show elevated levels of oxytocin (see photo), and after receiving these dog gazes, the human's level of oxytocin also increases (Nagasawa et al., 2015)! Can you see why this might explain why we feel so good after sharing eye contact with our dogs? [Q3]

Arthur Baensch/Getty Images

Retrieval Practice 2.1 | Neural and Hormonal Processes

SELF-TEST Completing this self-test, and then checking your answers by clicking on the answer button or by looking in Appendix B, will provide immediate feedback and helpful practice for exams.

1. The three major parts of a neuron are the ____.

a. glia, dendrites, and myelin
b. myelin, dendrites, and axon
c. dendrites, cell body, and axon
d. axon, glia, and myelin

2. An action potential is ____.

a. the likelihood that a neuron will take action when stimulated
b. the tendency for a neuron to be potentiated by neurotransmitters
c. the firing of a nerve, either toward or away from the brain
d. a neural impulse that carries information along the axon of a neuron

3. According to the all-or-nothing principle, the ____.

a. neuron cannot fire again during the refractory period
b. neurotransmitter either attaches to a receptor site or is destroyed in the synapse
c. neuron either fires completely or not at all
d. none of these options

4. Chemical messengers that are released by neurons and travel across the synapse are called ____.

a. chemical agonists **b.** neurotransmitters
c. synaptic transmitters **d.** neuroactivists

5. Chemicals manufactured and secreted by endocrine glands and circulated in the bloodstream to change or maintain bodily functions are called ____.

a. vasopressors **b.** neurotransmitters
c. hormones **d.** chemical antagonists

Think Critically

1. Why is it valuable for scientists to understand how neurotransmitters work at a molecular level?

2. What are some examples of how hormones affect your daily life?

Real World Psychology

Does spending the first few months of life in an orphanage lead to long-term problems in cognitive functioning?

How can singing and/or dancing make you feel closer to strangers and also raise your pain threshold?

jonya/Getty Images

Why does eye contact with your dog make you feel good?

Arthur Baensch/Getty Images

HINT: LOOK IN THE MARGIN FOR **[Q1]**, **[Q2]**, AND **[Q3]**

2.2 Nervous System Organization

LEARNING OBJECTIVES

Retrieval Practice While reading the upcoming sections, respond to each Learning Objective in your own words.

Summarize the major divisions and functions of our nervous system.

- **Explain** the key features and role of our central nervous system (CNS).
- **Define** neuroplasticity and neurogenesis.
- **Describe** the key components and role of our peripheral nervous system (PNS).

Have you heard the expression "Information is power"? Nowhere is this truer than in the human body. Without information, we could not survive. Neurons within the nervous system must take in sensory information from the outside world and then pass it along to the entire human body. Just as the circulatory system handles blood, which conveys chemicals and oxygen, the nervous system uses chemicals and electrical processes to convey information.

The nervous system is divided and subdivided into several branches (**Figure 2.4**). The main branch includes the brain and a bundle of nerves that form the *spinal cord*. Because this system is located in the center of the body (within the skull and spine), it is called the

FIGURE 2.4 **Our nervous system**

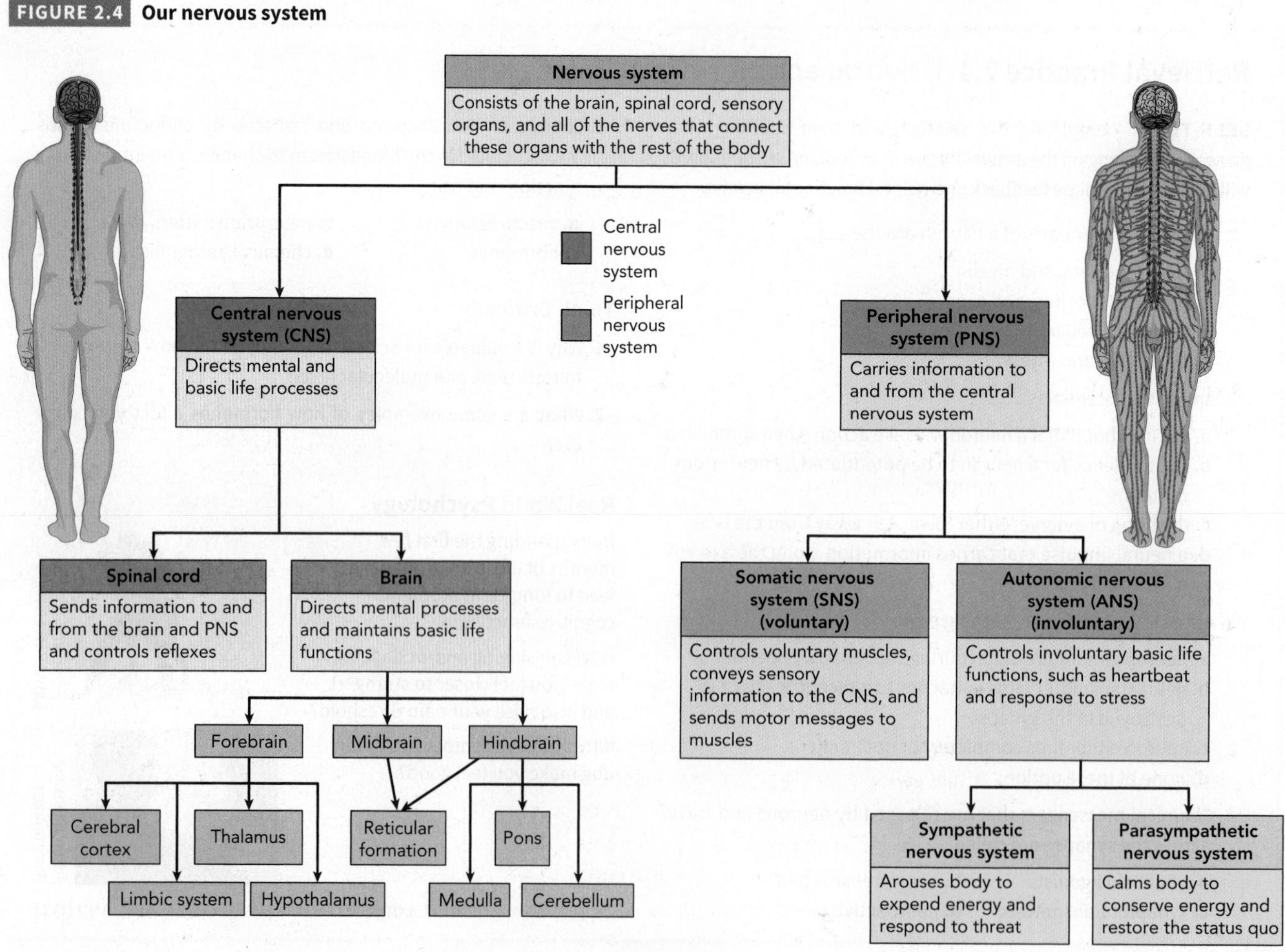

FIGURE 2.5 Lou Gehrig's disease or repeated head trauma?

Lou Gehrig was a legendary player for the New York Yankees from 1925 to 1939. Tragically, he had to retire while still in his prime when he developed symptoms of *amyotrophic lateral sclerosis (ALS)*, a neurological disease caused by degeneration of motor neurons (later commonly called "Lou Gehrig's disease"). However, scientists now think that Lou Gehrig may not have had ALS. Instead, he may have developed symptoms that were similar to those of ALS because he was so often hit in the head with baseballs. (Gehrig played before batting helmets were required.) Like Lou Gehrig, many athletes, including football players, soccer players, and boxers, may have been similarly diagnosed with ALS, Parkinson's disease, early onset dementia, or Alzheimer's disease (AD). Many researchers now believe that certain sports-related symptoms are most likely caused by repeated concussions, which may in turn lead to the development of these and other serious brain diseases (Branch, 2014; Eade & Heatton, 2016; McKee et al., 2013, 2014).

MLB Photos/Getty Images, Inc.

central nervous system (CNS). The CNS is primarily responsible for processing and organizing information.

The second major branch of the nervous system includes all the nerves outside the brain and spinal cord. This **peripheral nervous system (PNS)** carries messages (action potentials) to and from the CNS to the periphery of the body. Now, let's take a closer look at the CNS and the PNS.

Central nervous system (CNS) The part of the nervous system consisting of the brain and spinal cord.

Peripheral nervous system (PNS) The part of the nervous system composed of the nerves and neurons connecting the central nervous system (CNS) to the rest of the body.

Neuroplasticity The brain's lifelong ability to reorganize and change its structure and function by forming new neural connections.

Neurogenesis The formation (generation) of new neurons.

Stem cells Immature (uncommitted) cells that have the potential to develop into almost any type of cell, depending on the chemical signals they receive.

Central Nervous System (CNS)

The central nervous system (CNS) is the branch of the nervous system that makes us unique. Most other animals can smell, run, see, and hear far better than we can. But thanks to our CNS, we can process information and adapt to our environment in ways that no other animal can. Unfortunately, our CNS is also incredibly fragile. Unlike neurons in the PNS that can regenerate and require less protection, neurons in the CNS can suffer serious and permanent damage. As we'll see later in this chapter, repeated head trauma, particularly when associated with loss of consciousness, can lead to debilitating and potentially fatal illnesses (**Figure 2.5**).

However, the brain may not be as "hardwired" and fragile as we once thought. In the past, scientists believed that after the first two or three years of life damaged neurons within the brain or spinal cord of most animals, including humans, were impossible to repair or replace. However, we now know that the brain is capable of lifelong *neuroplasticity* and *neurogenesis*.

Neuroplasticity

Rather than being a fixed, solid organ, the brain is capable of changing its structure and function as a result of usage and experience (Ben-Soussan et al., 2015; Kim et al., 2016b; Presti, 2016). This "rewiring," officially known as **neuroplasticity**, is what makes our brains so wonderfully adaptive. In later chapters, we'll discuss how neuroplasticity remodels our brains after learning and experience. But here we'll look at how it helps the brain modify itself after damage. For example, when infants suffer damage to the speech area of their left hemisphere, the right hemisphere can reorganize and pick up some language abilities. Remarkably, this rewiring has even helped "remodel" the adult brain following strokes. Psychologist Edward Taub and his colleagues (2004, 2014) have had notable success working with stroke patients (**Figure 2.6**).

Courtesy Taub Therapy Clinc/UAB Media Relations

FIGURE 2.6 A breakthrough in neuroscience

By immobilizing the unaffected arm or leg and requiring rigorous and repetitive exercise of the affected limb, psychologist Edward Taub and colleagues "*recruit*" stroke patients' intact brain cells to take over for damaged cells (Taub et al., 2004, 2014). The therapy has restored function in some patients as long as 21 years after their strokes.

Neurogenesis

Whereas *neuroplasticity* refers to the brain's ability to restructure itself, **neurogenesis** is achieved through the formation (generation) of new neurons in the brain. The source of these newly created cells is **stem cells**—rare, immature cells that can grow and develop into any type of cell. Their fate depends on the chemical signals they receive. Experiments and clinical trials on both human and nonhuman animals have used stem cells for bone marrow transplants, and to repopulate or replace cells devastated by injury or disease (see the **Real World Psychology** feature). This research offers hope to patients suffering from strokes, Alzheimer's, Parkinson's, epilepsy, stress, and depression (Alenina & Klempin, 2015; Belkind-Gerson et al., 2016; Kim et al., 2016a). In addition, stem cell injections into the eyes of patients with untreatable eye diseases and severe visual problems have led to dramatic improvements in vision (Chucair-Elliott et al., 2015; Fahnehjelm et al., 2016; Song & Bharti, 2016).

Real World **Psychology**—Understanding the World

Stem Cell Therapy

Will stem cell transplants allow people paralyzed from spinal cord injuries to walk again? Scientists have had some success transplanting stem cells into spinal cord–injured nonhuman animals (Gao et al., 2016; Raynald et al., 2016; Sandner et al., 2015). When the damaged spinal cord was viewed several weeks later, the implanted cells had survived and spread throughout the injured area. More important, the transplant animals also showed some improvement in previously paralyzed parts of their bodies. Medical researchers are also testing the safety of embryonic stem cell therapy for human paralysis patients, and future trials may determine whether these cells will repair damaged spinal cords and/or improve sensation and movement in paralyzed areas (Granger et al., 2014; Presti, 2016; Robbins, 2013).

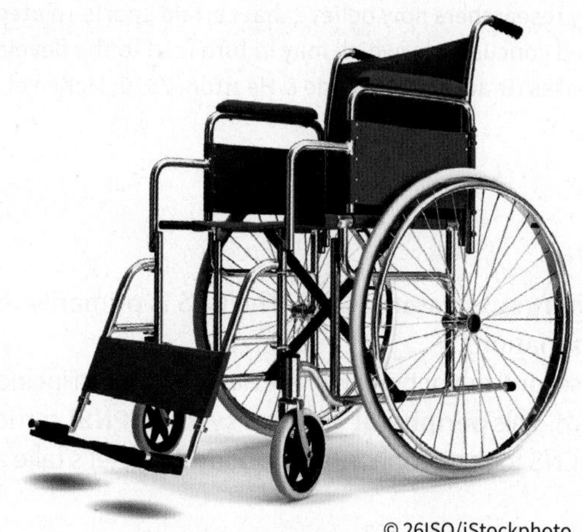

© 26ISO/iStockphoto

Before going on, it's important to note that neuroplasticity and neurogenesis are NOT the same as *neuroregeneration*, which refers to the regrowth or repair of neurons, glia, or synapses. This process is fairly common within the peripheral nervous system (PNS). You've undoubtedly watched a cut heal on your skin and/or known of someone who slowly regained his or her feeling and function after a serious motor vehicle accident or severe fall. In contrast, regeneration after damage within the central nervous system (CNS) is far less common. However, scientists have made significant advances in promoting axon growth, preventing scar formation, and enhancing compensatory growth on uninjured neurons. Actor Christopher Reeve's well-publicized partial recovery after serious damage to his spinal cord following a horse riding accident in 1995 is a welcome example of this type of regeneration (Maddox, 2015). Sadly, "Superman" Christopher Reeve (see photo) never regained full mobility and died in 2004 reportedly due to sepsis ("blood poisoning") and/or a fatal reaction to an antibiotic (Clifford, 2015; Hutchinson, 2015). [Q4]

© AF archive/Warner Bros/Alamy Stock Photo

Now that we've discussed neuroplasticity and neurogenesis within the central nervous system (CNS), let's take a closer look at the spinal cord. Because of its central importance for psychology and behavior, we'll discuss the brain in more detail in the next major section.

Reflex An innate, automatic response to a stimulus that has a biological relevance for an organism (for example, knee-jerk reflex).

Spinal Cord

Beginning at the base of our brains and continuing down our backs, the spinal cord carries vital information from the rest of the body into and out of the brain. But the spinal cord doesn't simply relay messages. It can also initiate certain automatic behaviors on its own. We call these involuntary, automatic behaviors **reflexes**, or *reflex arcs*, because the response to the incoming stimuli is automatically sent to the spinal cord, and then "reflected" back to the appropriate muscles. This allows an immediate action response without the delay of routing signals first to the brain.

As you can see in the simple reflex arc depicted in **Process Diagram 2.3**, a sensory receptor first responds to stimulation and initiates a neural impulse that travels to the spinal cord. This signal then travels back to the appropriate muscle, which reflexively contracts. The response is automatic and immediate in a reflex because the signal travels only as far as the spinal cord before action is initiated, not all the way to the brain. The brain is later "notified" of the action when the spinal cord sends along the message.

STOP! This Process Diagram contains essential information NOT found elsewhere in the text, which is likely to appear on quizzes and exams. Be sure to study it CAREFULLY!

PROCESS DIAGRAM 2.3 How the Spinal Reflex Operates In a simple reflex arc, a sensory receptor responds to stimulation and initiates a neural impulse that travels to the spinal cord. This signal then travels back to the appropriate muscle, which then reflexively contracts. Note that the reflex response is automatic and immediate because the signal only travels as far as the spinal cord before action is initiated, not all the way to the brain. The brain is later "notified" when the spinal cord sends along the message, which, in this case of the hot pan, leads to a perception of pain. What might be the evolutionary advantages of the reflex arc?

1. In a simple reflex circuit, like this hand/heat withdrawal reflex, skin receptors in the fingertips detect heat from the hot handle of the sauce pan. These receptors then send neural messages to sensory neurons.

2. Sensory neurons then send messages to interneurons, in the spinal cord, which in turn connect with motor neurons.

3. Next, motor neurons send messages to hand muscles, causing a withdrawal reflex away from the hot handle of the pan–and possibly the dropping of the sauce pan! (This occurs before the brain perceives the actual sensation of pain.)

4. While the simple reflex is occurring within the spinal cord, messages are also being sent up the spinal cord to the brain.

5. A small structure in the brain, the thalamus, then relays incoming sensory information to the higher, cortical areas of the brain.

6. Finally, an area of the brain, known as the somatosensory cortex, receives the message from the thalamus and interprets it as PAIN!

Red = sensory neuron
Blue = motor neuron

Spinal cord (cross section)

We're all born with numerous reflexes, many of which fade over time (**Figure 2.7**). But even as adults, we still blink in response to a puff of air in our eyes, gag when something touches the back of the throat, and urinate and defecate in response to pressure in the bladder and rectum.

Think Critically

1. What might happen if infants lacked these reflexes?
2. Can you explain why most infant reflexes disappear within the first year?

FIGURE 2.7 Testing for reflexes

If you have a newborn or young infant in your home, you can easily (and safely) test for these simple reflexes. (Most infant reflexes disappear within the first year of life. If they reappear in later life, it generally indicates damage to the central nervous system.)

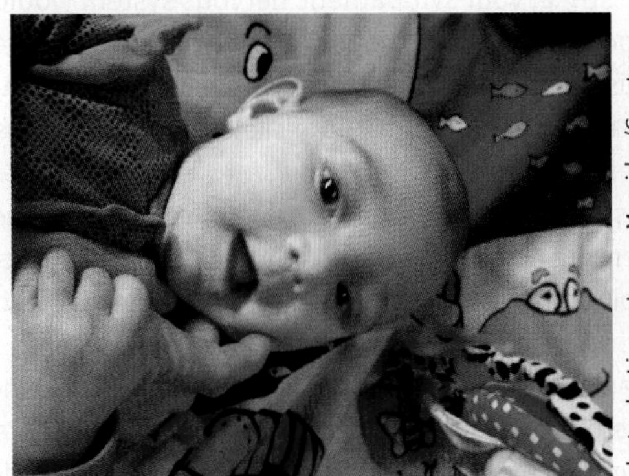

photos by Linnea Leaver Mavrides/Courtesy Catherine Sanderson

A Rooting reflex
Lightly stroke the cheek or side of the mouth, and watch how the infant automatically (reflexively) turns toward the stimulation and attempts to suck.

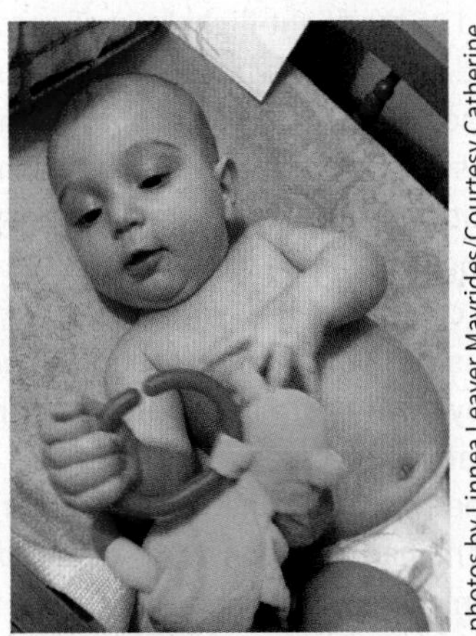

photos by Linnea Leaver Mavrides/Courtesy Catherine Sanderson

B Grasping reflex
Place your finger or an object in the infant's palm and note his or her automatic grasping reflex.

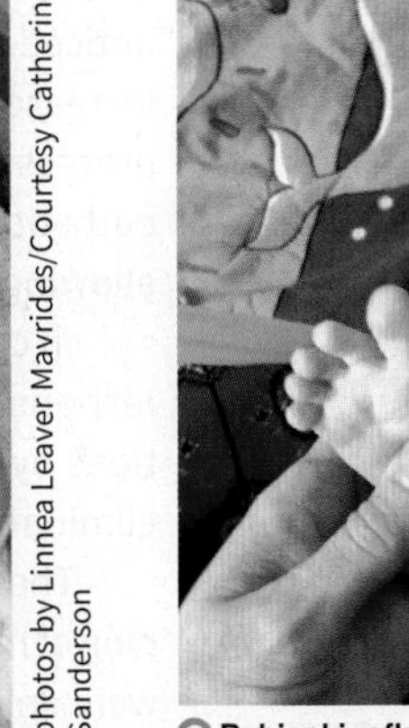

photos by Linnea Leaver Mavrides/Courtesy Catherine Sanderson

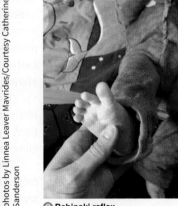

C Babinski reflex
Lightly stroke the sole of the infant's foot, and the big toe will move toward the top of the foot, while the other toes fan out.

Psychology and **You**—Understanding Yourself

Sexual Response Reflexes

Reflexes even influence our sexual responses. Certain stimuli, such as the stroking of the genitals, can lead to arousal and the reflexive muscle contractions of orgasm in both men and women. However, in order for us to have the passion, thoughts, and emotion we normally associate with sex, the sensory information from the stroking and orgasm must be carried on to the appropriate areas of the brain that receive and interpret these specific sensory messages.

Kovalchynskyy Mykola/Shutterstock

Peripheral Nervous System (PNS)

The peripheral nervous system (PNS) is just what it sounds like—the part that involves nerves *peripheral* to (or outside) the brain and spinal cord. The chief function of the peripheral nervous system (PNS) is to carry information to and from the central nervous system (CNS). It links the brain and spinal cord to the body's sense receptors, muscles, and glands.

Somatic nervous system (SNS) A subdivision of the peripheral nervous system (PNS) that connects the central nervous system (CNS) to sensory receptors and controls skeletal muscles.

Looking back at Figure 2.4, note that the PNS is subdivided into the somatic nervous system and the autonomic nervous system. The **somatic nervous system (SNS)** consists of all the nerves that connect to sensory receptors and skeletal muscles. The name comes from the term *soma*, which means "body," and the somatic nervous system plays a key role in communication throughout the entire body. In a kind of two-way street, the somatic nervous system (also called the skeletal nervous system) first carries sensory information to the brain and spinal cord (CNS) and then carries messages from the CNS to skeletal muscles.

Autonomic nervous system (ANS) The subdivision of the peripheral nervous system (PNS) that controls the body's involuntary motor responses; it connects the sensory receptors to the central nervous system (CNS) and the CNS to the smooth muscle, cardiac muscle, and glands.

The other subdivision of the PNS is the **autonomic nervous system (ANS)**. The ANS is responsible for involuntary tasks, such as heart rate, digestion, pupil dilation, and breathing. Like an automatic pilot, the ANS can sometimes be consciously overridden. But as its name implies, the autonomic system normally operates on its own (autonomously).

The ANS is further divided into two branches, the sympathetic and parasympathetic, which tend to work in opposition to each other to regulate the functioning of such target organs as the heart, the intestines, and the lungs. Like two children on a teeter-totter, one will be up while the other is down, but they essentially balance each other out. **Figure 2.8** illustrates a familiar example of the interaction between the sympathetic and parasympathetic nervous systems.

Sympathetic nervous system The subdivision of the autonomic nervous system (ANS) that is responsible for arousing the body and mobilizing its energy during times of stress; also called the "fight-flight-freeze" system.

During stressful times, either mental or physical, the **sympathetic nervous system** arouses and mobilizes bodily resources to respond to the stressor. This emergency response is often called the "fight or flight" response. (Note this response has recently been expanded and relabeled as the "fight-flight-freeze" response, which will be fully discussed in Chapter 3.) If you noticed a dangerous snake coiled and ready to strike, your sympathetic nervous system would increase your heart rate, respiration, and blood pressure; stop your digestive and eliminative processes; and release hormones, such as cortisol, into the bloodstream. The net result of sympathetic activation is to get more oxygenated blood and energy to the skeletal muscles, thus allowing you to cope with the stress—to either fight or flee.

Parasympathetic nervous system The subdivision of the autonomic nervous system (ANS) that is responsible for calming the body and conserving energy.

In contrast to the sympathetic nervous system, the **parasympathetic nervous system** is responsible for calming our bodies and conserving energy. It returns our normal bodily functions by slowing our heart rate, lowering our blood pressure, and increasing our digestive and eliminative processes.

The sympathetic nervous system provides an adaptive, evolutionary advantage. At the beginning of human evolution, when we faced a dangerous bear or an aggressive human attacker, there were only three reasonable responses—fight, flight, or freeze. The automatic mobilization of bodily resources can still be critical, even in modern times. However, less life-threatening events, such as traffic jams, also activate our sympathetic nervous system. As the next chapter discusses, ongoing sympathetic system response to such chronic, daily stress can become detrimental to our health. For a look at how the autonomic nervous system affects our sexual lives, see **Figure 2.9**.

FIGURE 2.8 Actions of the autonomic nervous system (ANS) The ANS is responsible for a variety of independent (autonomous) activities, such as salivation and digestion. It exercises this control through its two divisions—the sympathetic and parasympathetic branches.

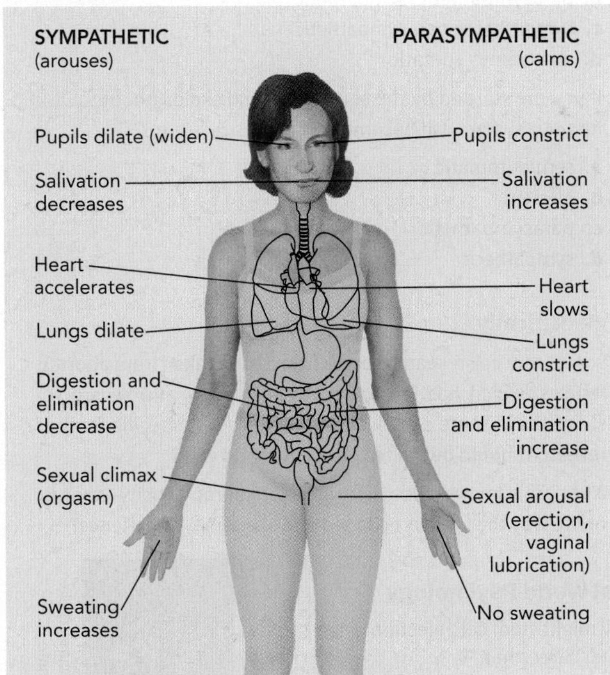

Sympathetic dominance

Beto Hacker/Getty Images, Inc.

Parasympathetic dominance

Geri Lavrov/Photographer's Choice/ Getty Images, In

FIGURE 2.9 Autonomic nervous system and sexual arousal

The complexities of sexual interaction—and, in particular, the difficulties couples sometimes have in achieving sexual arousal or orgasm—illustrate the balancing act between the sympathetic and parasympathetic nervous systems.

Piotr Marcinski/Shutterstock

a. Parasympathetic dominance Sexual arousal and excitement require that the body be relaxed enough to allow increased blood flow to the genitals—in other words, the nervous system must be in *parasympathetic dominance*. Parasympathetic nerves carry messages from the central nervous system directly to the sexual organs, allowing for a localized response (increased blood flow and genital arousal).

© 4774344sean/iStockphoto

b. Sympathetic dominance During strong emotions, such as anger, anxiety, or fear, the body shifts to *sympathetic dominance*, which causes blood flow to the genitals and other organs to decrease because the body is preparing for "fight, flight, or freeze." As a result, the person is unable (or less likely) to become sexually aroused. Any number of circumstances—performance anxiety, fear of unwanted pregnancy or disease, or tensions between partners—can trigger sympathetic dominance.

Retrieval Practice 2.2 | Nervous System Organization

SELF-TEST Completing this self-test, and then checking your answers by clicking on the answer button or by looking in Appendix B, will provide immediate feedback and helpful practice for exams.

1. The major divisions of the nervous system are the _____.
   - **a.** sympathetic and parasympathetic
   - **b.** somatic and autonomic
   - **c.** gray matter and white matter
   - **d.** central and peripheral
2. The central nervous system _____.
   - **a.** consists of the brain and spinal cord
   - **b.** is responsible for the "fight, flight, or freeze" response
   - **c.** includes the automatic and somatic nervous systems
   - **d.** all these options
3. The peripheral nervous system is _____.
   - **a.** composed of the spinal cord and peripheral nerves
   - **b.** less important than the central nervous system
   - **c.** contained within the skull and spinal column
   - **d.** a combination of all the nerves and neurons outside the brain and spinal cord
4. The _____ nervous system is responsible for the fight, flight, or freeze response, whereas the _____ nervous system is responsible for maintaining or restoring calm.
   - **a.** central; peripheral
   - **b.** parasympathetic; sympathetic
   - **c.** sympathetic; parasympathetic
   - **d.** autonomic; somatic
5. If you are startled by the sound of a loud explosion, the _____ nervous system will become dominant.
   - **a.** semiautomatic
   - **b.** afferent
   - **c.** parasympathetic
   - **d.** sympathetic

Think Critically

1. Some stem cell research comes from tissue taken from aborted fetuses, which has led to great controversy and severe restrictions in some states. Do you believe this specific form of research should be limited? If so, how and why?
2. What are some everyday examples of neuroplasticity—that is, of the way the brain is changed and shaped by experience?

Real World Psychology

How might stem cell injections have saved "Superman"?

© AF archive/Warner Bros/Alamy Stock Photo

HINT: LOOK IN THE MARGIN FOR **[Q4]**

2.3 A Tour Through the Brain

LEARNING OBJECTIVES

Retrieval Practice While reading the upcoming sections, respond to each Learning Objective in your own words.

Review the tools used in biological research, along with the brain's key structures and functions.

- **Identify** the tools neuroscientists use to study the brain and nervous system.
- **Describe** the major structures of the hindbrain, midbrain, and forebrain, as well as their respective functions.

We begin our exploration of the brain with a discussion of the tools that neuroscientists use to study it. Then we offer a quick tour of the brain, beginning at its lower end, where the spinal cord joins the base of the brain, and then moving upward, all the way to the top of the skull. As we move from bottom to top, "lower," basic processes, such as breathing, generally give way to more complex mental processes.

Biological Tools for Research

How do we know how the brain and nervous system work? Beginning in early times, scientists have *dissected* the brains and other body parts of human and nonhuman animals. They've also used *lesioning* techniques (systematically destroying bodlily tissue to study the effects on behavior and mental processes). By the mid-1800s, this research had produced a basic map of the nervous system, including some areas of the brain. Early researchers also relied on clinical observations and case studies of living people who had experienced injuries, diseases, and disorders that affected brain functioning.

Modern researchers still use such methods, but they also employ other techniques to examine biological processes that underlie our behavior (**Table 2.2**). For example, recent advances in brain science have led to various types of brain-imaging scans, which can be used in both clinical and laboratory settings. Most of these methods are relatively *noninvasive*—that is, their use does not involve breaking the skin or entering the body (see the following **PositivePsych**).

PP PositivePsych

The Power of Positive Coaching

Have you ever watched some coaches harshly yelling at their young athletes, and wondered how those children felt? If so, you'll be happy to know that the tools we regularly use to study the brain can provide interesting information and insights. For example, in one study, researchers used fMRI brain imaging scans to study which parts of the brain are most active during interviews emphasizing either positive or negative visions (Jack et al., 2013). All participants underwent two distinct types of interviews. One interview focused on positive messages, such as: "If everything worked out ideally in your life, what would you be doing in 10 years?" The other interview focused on negative messages, such as: "What challenges have you encountered or do you expect to encounter in your experience here? How are you doing with your courses? Are you doing all of the homework and readings?"

As you might expect, during the positive interview, students showed more brain activity in the parts of the brain associated with positive emotions, including empathy, positive affect, and emotional security. In contrast, during the negative interview, students showed more activity in brain areas linked with the sympathetic nervous system and negative feelings. Can you see how this research has powerful implications for coaches, instructors, and parents, as well as in management and organizational practices? As the authors of this research suggest, "effective coaching and mentoring is crucial to the success of individuals and organizations."

KidStock/Getty Images

What's the take home message? For the best emotional responses in all our interactions, we need to emphasize positive messages. The value and effectiveness of reinforcement compared to the limits and serious problems with punishment is further detailed in Chapter 6.

Brain Organization

Having studied the tools scientists use for exploring the brain, we can now begin our tour (see photo). Let's talk first about brain size and complexity, which vary significantly from species to species. For example, fish and reptiles have smaller, less complex brains than do cats and dogs. The most complex brains belong to whales, dolphins, and higher primates, such as chimps, gorillas, and humans. The billions of neurons that make up the human brain control much of what we think, feel, and do. Certain brain structures are specialized to perform certain tasks, a process known as *localization of function*. However, most parts of the brain perform integrating, overlapping functions.

As you can see in **Figure 2.10**, scientists typically divide and label the human brain into three major sections: *the hindbrain, midbrain, and forebrain.*

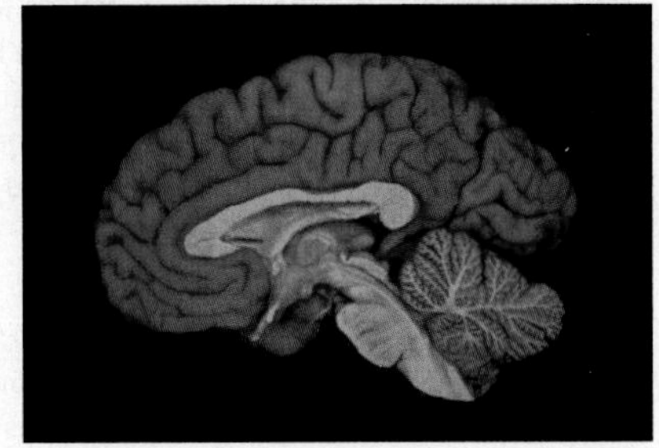

Science Pictures Limited/Photo Researchers

A photo of the human brain
This brain has been sliced down the center to reveal the inner sections. Like the diagram below, only the right half of the brain is shown in this photo.

Hindbrain

Picture this: You're asleep and in the middle of a frightening nightmare. Your heart is racing, your breathing is rapid, and you're attempting to run away but find you can't move! Suddenly, your nightmare is shattered by a buzzing alarm clock. All your automatic behaviors and survival responses in this scenario are controlled or influenced by parts of the hindbrain. The **hindbrain** includes the medulla, pons, and cerebellum.

The **medulla** is essentially an extension of the spinal cord, with many neural fibers passing through it carrying information to and from the brain. Because the medulla controls many essential automatic bodily functions, such as respiration and heart rate, serious damage to this area is most often fatal.

Hindbrain The lower or hind region of the brain; collection of structures including the medulla, pons, and cerebellum.

Medulla The hindbrain structure responsible for vital, automatic functions, such as respiration and heartbeat.

TABLE 2.2 Sample Tools for Biological Research

TOOL	DESCRIPTION	PURPOSE
Electrical recordings Electrical activity throughout the brain sweeps in regular waves across its surface, and the electroencephalogram (EEG) is a read out of this activity.	Using electrodes attached to the skin or scalp, brain activity is detected and recorded on an EEG.	Reveals areas of the brain most active during particular tasks or mental states such as reading or sleeping; also traces abnormal brain waves caused by brain malfunctions, such as epilepsy or tumors. Larry Mulvehill/Science Source
CT (computed tomography) scan This CT scan used X-rays to locate a brain tumor, which is the deep purple mass at the top left.	Computer-created cross-sectional X-rays of the brain or other parts of the body produce 3-D images. Least expensive type of imaging and widely used in research.	Reveals the effects of strokes, injuries, tumors, and other brain disorders. Mehau Kulyk/Science Source
PET (positron emission tomography) scan	A radioactive form of glucose is injected into the bloodstream; a scanner records the amount of glucose used in particularly active areas of the brain and produces a computer-constructed picture of the brain.	Originally designed to detect abnormalities, now used to identify brain areas active during ordinary activities (such as reading or singing). N.I. H/Science Source
MRI (magnetic resonance imaging) Note the fissures and internal structures of the brain. The throat, nasal airways, and fluid surrounding the brain are dark.	Using a powerful magnet and radio waves linked to a computer, a scanner creates detailed, cross-sectional images.	Produces high-resolution 3-D pictures of the brain useful for identifying abnormalities and mapping brain structures and function. Scott Camazine/Science Source
fMRI (functional magnetic resonance imaging) The yellow highlighted areas in this fMRI are "lit up," which tells us that oxygen from the blood is being heavily used in this region.	Newer, faster version of MRI that detects blood flow by picking up magnetic signals from blood, which has given up its oxygen to activate brain cells.	Measures blood flow, which indicates areas of the brain that are active and inactive during ordinary behaviors or responses (like reading or talking); also shows changes associated with various disorders. Science Photo Library/Science Source
Other methods: (a) Cell body or tract (myelin) staining, (b) Microinjections, and (c) Intrabrain electrical recordings	(a) Colors/stains selected neurons or nerve fibers. (b) Injects chemicals into specific areas of the brain. (c) Records activity of one or a group of neurons inside the brain.	Increases overall information of structure and function through direct observation and measurement. Intrabrain wire probes allow scientists to "see" individual neuron activity.

Pons The hindbrain structure involved in respiration, movement, waking, sleep, and dreaming.

Cerebellum The hindbrain structure responsible for coordinating fine muscle movement, balance, and some perception and cognition.

The **pons** is involved in respiration, movement, sleeping, waking, and dreaming (among other things). It also contains axons that cross from one side of the brain to the other (*pons* is Latin for "bridge").

The cauliflower-shaped **cerebellum** (Latin for "little brain") is, evolutionarily, a very old structure. It coordinates fine muscle movement and balance (**Figure 2.11**). Researchers using functional magnetic resonance imaging (fMRI) have shown that parts of the cerebellum [Q5]

FIGURE 2.10 The human brain Note on the left side of this figure how the forebrain, midbrain, and hindbrain radically change in their size and placement during prenatal development. The profile drawing in the middle highlights key structures and functions of the right half of the adult brain. As you read about each of these structures, keep this drawing in mind and refer to it as necessary. (The diagram shows the brain structures as if the brain were split vertically down the center and the left hemisphere were removed.)

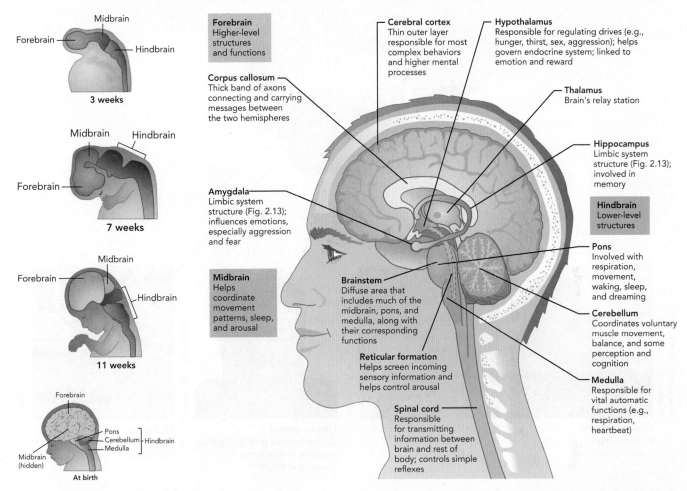

Midbrain
Forebrain
Hindbrain
3 weeks

Midbrain
Hindbrain
Forebrain
7 weeks

Midbrain
Forebrain
Hindbrain
11 weeks

Forebrain
Pons
Cerebellum
Medulla
Hindbrain
Midbrain (hidden)
At birth

Forebrain Higher-level structures and functions

Corpus callosum Thick band of axons connecting and carrying messages between the two hemispheres

Cerebral cortex Thin outer layer responsible for most complex behaviors and higher mental processes

Hypothalamus Responsible for regulating drives (e.g., hunger, thirst, sex, aggression); helps govern endocrine system; linked to emotion and reward

Thalamus Brain's relay station

Hippocampus Limbic system structure (Fig. 2.13); involved in memory

Amygdala Limbic system structure (Fig. 2.13); influences emotions, especially aggression and fear

Hindbrain Lower-level structures

Pons Involved with respiration, movement, waking, sleep, and dreaming

Midbrain Helps coordinate movement patterns, sleep, and arousal

Brainstem Diffuse area that includes much of the midbrain, pons, and medulla, along with their corresponding functions

Cerebellum Coordinates voluntary muscle movement, balance, and some perception and cognition

Reticular formation Helps screen incoming sensory information and helps control arousal

Medulla Responsible for vital automatic functions (e.g., respiration, heartbeat)

Spinal cord Responsible for transmitting information between brain and rest of body; controls simple reflexes

[Q5] also are important for memory, sensation, perception, cognition, language, learning, and even "multitasking" (Garrett, 2015; Ng et al., 2016; Presti, 2016). Interestingly, researchers have found that people who play videogames for 30 minutes a day for 2 months show increases in gray matter in the cerebellum, right hippocampus, and the right prefrontal cortex (see photo) (Kühn et al., 2014). Gray matter is critical for higher cognitive functioning, and we'll study more about these three brain areas in the next section. For now it's enough to know that these brain sections are largely responsible for spatial navigation, strategic planning, and fine motor skills in the hands. In short, research suggests that playing video games may actually be good for your brain!

Blend Images - KidStock/ Getty Images

Midbrain The collection of structures in the middle of the brain responsible for coordinating movement patterns, sleep, and arousal.

Midbrain

The **midbrain** helps us orient our eye and body movements to visual and auditory stimuli, and it works with the pons to help control sleep and level of arousal. It also contains a small structure, the *substantia nigra*, that secretes the neurotransmitter dopamine. Parkinson's disease, an age-related degenerative condition, is related to the deterioration of neurons in the substantia nigra and the subsequent loss of dopamine.

Running through the core of the hindbrain and midbrain is the **reticular formation (RF)**. This diffuse, finger-shaped network of neurons helps screen incoming sensory

Getty Images, Inc.

FIGURE 2.11 Walk the line Asking drivers to perform tasks like walking the white line is a somewhat common part of a field sobriety test for possible intoxication. Why? The cerebellum, responsible for smooth and precise movements, is one of the first areas of the brain to be affected by alcohol.

FIGURE 2.12 Structures of the forebrain

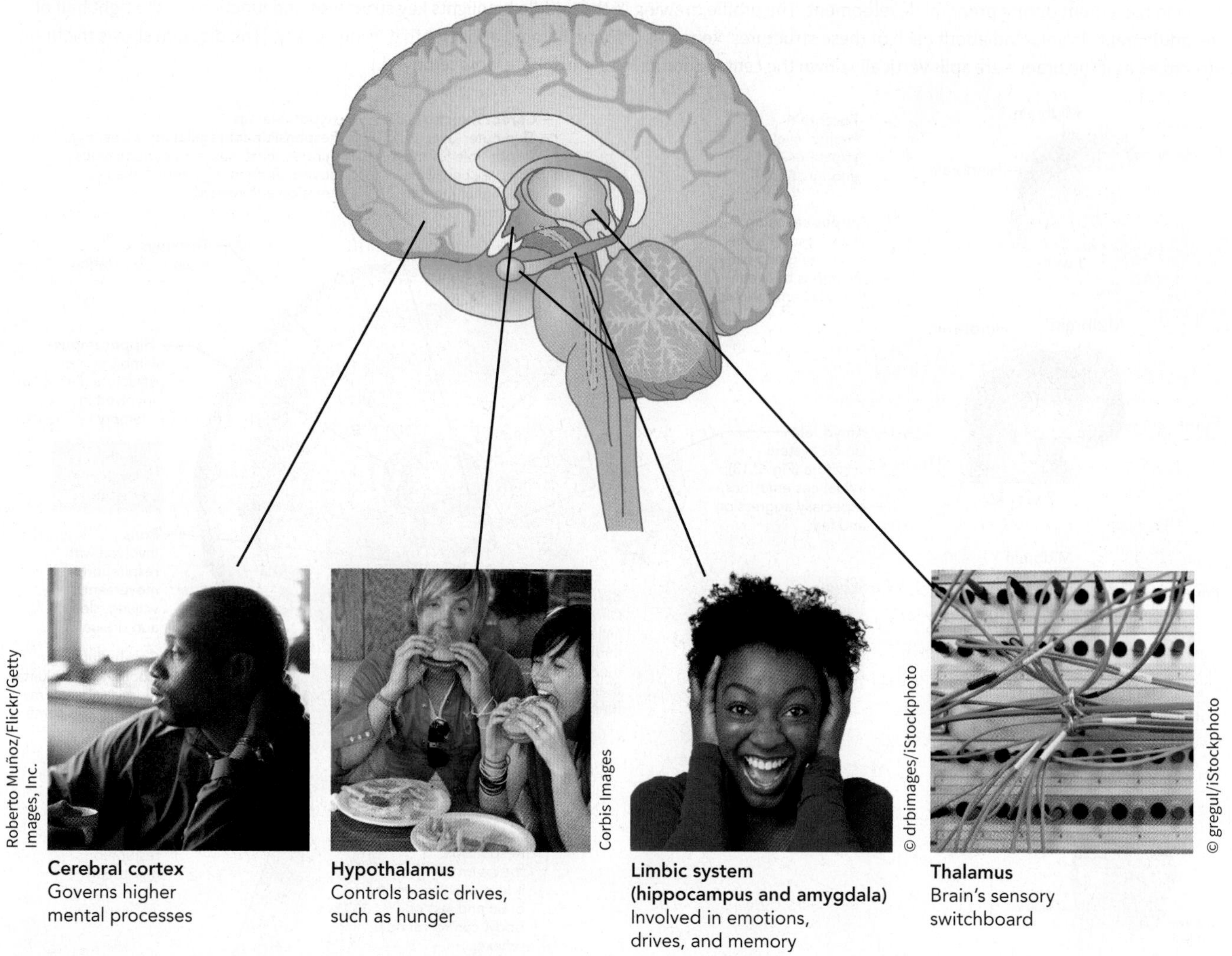

Roberto Muñoz/Flickr/Getty Images, Inc.

Cerebral cortex
Governs higher mental processes

Corbis Images

Hypothalamus
Controls basic drives, such as hunger

© drbimages/iStockphoto

Limbic system (hippocampus and amygdala)
Involved in emotions, drives, and memory

© gregul/iStockphoto

Thalamus
Brain's sensory switchboard

Reticular formation The diffuse set of neurons that helps screen incoming information and helps control arousal.

Brainstem A diffuse, stem-shaped area of the brain, including much of the midbrain, pons, and medulla; responsible for automatic survival functions, such as respiration and heartbeat.

information and alert the higher brain centers to important events. Without our reticular formation, we would not be alert or perhaps even conscious.

Before going on, it's important to note that the reticular formation passes through the diffuse, stem-shaped area of the midbrain, known as the **brainstem**, which also includes the pons and medulla in the hindbrain (see again Figure 2.10). At its lower end, the brainstem connects with the spinal cord, and at its upper end it attaches to the thalamus.

Forebrain

The **forebrain** is the largest and most prominent part of the human brain. It includes the cerebral cortex, limbic system, thalamus and hypothalamus (**Figure 2.12**). The last three are located near the top of the brainstem. The cerebral cortex (discussed separately, in the next section) is wrapped above and around them. (*Cerebrum* is Latin for "brain," and *cortex* is Latin for "covering" or "bark.")

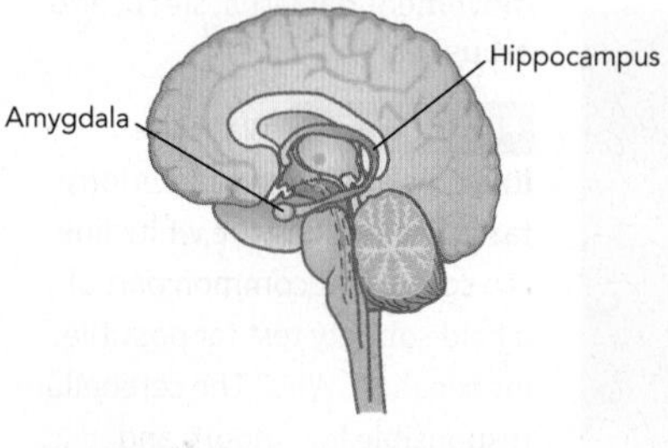

An interconnected group of forebrain structures, known as the **limbic system**, is located roughly along the border between the cerebral cortex and the lower-level brain structures (**Figure 2.13**). Although opinion is divided upon whether other structures, such as the hypothalamus and thalamus, should be included as part of the limbic sytem, its two most important structures are the hippocampus and amygdala. The limbic system is generally responsible for emotions, drives, and memory. In Chapter 7, you'll discover how the **hippocampus**, a key part of the limbic system, is involved in forming and retrieving our memories. However, the limbic system's major focus of interest is the **amygdala**, which is linked to the production and regulation of emotions–especially aggression and fear (Cohen et al., 2016; LeDoux, 1998, 2007; Meletti, 2016).

Hippocampus
Amygdala

FIGURE 2.13 Most important major brain structures commonly associated with the limbic system

The **thalamus** is located at the top of the brainstem. It integrates input from the senses, and it may also function in learning and memory (McCormick et al., 2015; Schroll et al., 2015; Zhou et al., 2016). The thalamus receives input from nearly all sensory systems, except smell, and then directs the information to the appropriate cortical areas. The thalamus also transmits some higher brain information to the cerebellum and medulla. Think of the thalamus as the switchboard in an air traffic control center that receives information from all aircraft and directs them to appropriate landing or takeoff areas.

Because the thalamus is the brain's major sensory relay center to the cerebral cortex, damage or abnormalities in the thalamus might cause the cortex to misinterpret or not receive vital sensory information. As you'll discover in Chapter 12, brain-imaging research links thalamus abnormalities to schizophrenia, a serious psychological disorder characterized by problems with sensory filtering and perception (Buchy et al., 2015; Kim et al., 2015; Ramsay & MacDonald, 2015).

Beneath the thalamus lies the kidney bean–sized **hypothalamus**. (*Hypo-* means "under.") This organ has been called the "master control center" for emotions and for many basic motives such as hunger, thirst, sex, and aggression (Falkner & Lin, 2014; Maggi et al., 2015; Presti, 2016). See the **Psychology and You** feature. The hypothalamus also controls the body's internal environment, including temperature, which it accomplishes by regulating the endocrine system.

Another well-known function of the hypothalamus is its role as part of the so-called "pleasure center," a set of brain structures whose stimulation leads to highly enjoyable feelings (Naneix et al., 2016; Olds & Milner, 1954; Stopper & Floresco, 2015). Even though the hypothalamus and other structures and neurotransmitters are instrumental in emotions, the frontal lobes of the cerebral cortex also play an important role.

Hanging down from the hypothalamus, the *pituitary gland* is usually considered the master endocrine gland because it releases hormones that activate the other endocrine glands. The hypothalamus influences the pituitary through direct neural connections and through release of its own hormones into the blood supply of the pituitary. The hypothalamus also directly influences some important aspects of behavior, such as eating and drinking patterns.

Forebrain The collection of upper-level brain structures including the cerebral cortex, limbic system, thalamus, and hypothalamus.

Limbic system The interconnected group of forebrain structures involved with emotions, drives, and memory; its two most important structures are the hippocampus and amygdala.

Hippocampus The seahorse-shaped part of the limbic system involved in forming and retrieving memories.

Amygdala A part of the limbic system linked to the production and regulation of emotions—especially aggression and fear.

Thalamus The forebrain structure at the top of the brainstem that relays sensory messages to and from the cerebral cortex.

Hypothalamus The small brain structure beneath the thalamus that helps govern drives (hunger, thirst, sex, and aggression) and hormones.

Psychology and You—Understanding Yourself

Diet and the Hypothalamus

Have you ever gone on a diet to try to lose weight or lost weight but then struggled to maintain your new weight? One of the reasons long-term weight loss is so hard for many people is that eating a high-fat diet can lead to long-term changes in the hypothalamus (Cordeira et al., 2014; Stamatakis et al., 2016; Zhang et al., 2015). These changes make it harder for the body to regulate its weight, meaning that you will continue to feel hungry even when you have just eaten plenty of food. Sadly, this process makes it hard to stick to a diet and thereby increases the risk of obesity, which in turn can lead to cognitive impairment (Miller & Spencer, 2014).

© donmedia/iStockphoto

Retrieval Practice 2.3 | A Tour Through the Brain

SELF-TEST Completing this self-test, and then checking your answers by clicking on the answer button or by looking in Appendix B, will provide immediate feedback and helpful practice for exams.

1. Label the following structures/areas of the brain:

a. corpus callosum **b.** amygdala
c. cerebellum **d.** thalamus
e. hippocampus **f.** cerebral cortex

2. Damage to the medulla can lead to loss of ______.

a. vision **b.** respiration
c. hearing **d.** smell

3. The pons, cerebellum, and the medulla are all ______.

a. higher-level brain structures
b. cortical areas
c. association areas
d. a part of the hindbrain

4. The brainstem is primarily involved with your ____.

   a. sense of smell and taste **b.** sense of touch and pain
   c. automatic survival functions **d.** emotional behavior

5. An interconnected group of forebrain structures particularly responsible for emotions is known as the ____.

   a. subcortical center **b.** homeostatic controller
   c. limbic system **d.** master endocrine gland

Think Critically

1. Which tool for biological research do you consider the least invasive and damaging? Which would be the most dangerous?
2. Given that the limbic system is largely responsible for our emotional arousal and expression, do you think people with significant damage to this section should be held less responsible for violent crimes? Why or why not?

Real World Psychology

Can playing videogames be good for your brain?

Blend Images - KidStock/ Getty Images

HINT: LOOK IN THE MARGIN FOR **[Q5]**

2.4 The Cerebral Cortex

LEARNING OBJECTIVES

Retrieval Practice While reading the upcoming sections, respond to each Learning Objective in your own words.

Summarize the key features and major divisions of the cerebral cortex.

- **Discuss** the location and functions of the eight lobes of the cerebral cortex.
- **Describe** the brain's two specialized hemispheres and split-brain research.

Cerebral cortex The thin surface layer on the cerebral hemispheres that regulates most complex behavior, including sensations, motor control, and higher mental processes.

The gray, wrinkled **cerebral cortex**, the surface layer of the cerebral hemispheres, is responsible for most complex behaviors and higher mental processes. It plays such a vital role that many consider it the essence of life itself.

© George Peters/iStockphoto

Although the cerebral cortex is only about one-eighth of an inch thick, it's made up of approximately 30 billion neurons and nine times as many glial cells. Its numerous wrinkles, called *convolutions*, significantly increase its surface area. Damage to the cerebral cortex is linked to numerous problems, including suicide, substance abuse, and dementia (Flores et al., 2016; Presti, 2016; Sharma et al., 2015). Evidence suggests that such trauma is particularly common in athletes who experience head injuries in sports like football (see photo), ice hockey, boxing, and soccer (**Figure 2.14**). [Q6]

NICHOLAS KAMM/AFP/Getty Images

FIGURE 2.14 Damage to the brain In 2014, many professional soccer organizations enacted a new rule requiring doctors (instead of coaches) to determine whether a player can safely return to the game after experiencing a head injury. This rule was enacted following several high profile cases, in which players appeared to suffer a concussion during World Cup games, yet quickly returned to the match. In this photo, you see Morgan Brian of the U.S. Women's National Team colliding in the semi-finals of the 2015 Women's World Cup.

The full cerebral cortex and the two cerebral hemispheres beneath it closely resemble an oversized walnut. The division, or *fissure*, down the center marks the separation between the left and right *hemispheres* of the brain, which make up about 80% of the brain's weight. The hemispheres are mostly filled with axon connections between the cortex and the other brain structures. Each hemisphere controls the opposite side of the body (**Figure 2.15**).

Lobes of the Brain

The cerebral hemispheres are each divided into four distinct areas, or lobes (**Figure 2.16**). Like the lower-level brain structures, each lobe specializes in somewhat different tasks, another example of localization of function. However, some functions overlap two or more lobes.

Frontal Lobes By far the largest of the cortical lobes, the two **frontal lobes** are located at the top front portion of the two brain hemispheres—right behind the forehead. The frontal lobes receive and coordinate messages from all other lobes of the cortex, while also being responsible for at least three additional functions:

1. *Speech production* Broca's area, located in the *left* frontal lobe near the bottom of the motor control area, plays a crucial role in speech production. In 1865, French physician Paul Broca discovered that damage to this area causes difficulty in speech, but not language comprehension. This type of impaired language ability is known as *Broca's aphasia*.
2. *Motor control* At the very back of the frontal lobes lies the *motor cortex*, which sends messages to the various muscles that instigate voluntary movement. When you want to call your friend on your cell phone, the motor control area of your frontal lobes guides your fingers to press the desired sequence of numbers.
3. *Higher functions* Most complex, higher functions, such as thinking, personality, and memory, are controlled primarily by the frontal lobes. Damage to the frontal lobe also affects motivation, drives, creativity, self-awareness, initiative, and reasoning. Abnormalities in the frontal lobes are often observed in patients with schizophrenia (Chapter 12). For example, patients with schizophrenia often show overall loss of gray matter, as well as increases in cerebrospinal fluid in the frontal lobes (DeRosse et al., 2015; Kubera et al., 2014; Schnack et al., 2014).

At this point in the chapter, you may be feeling inundated with the large number of terms and functions of the various parts of your brain and nervous system. If so, please understand

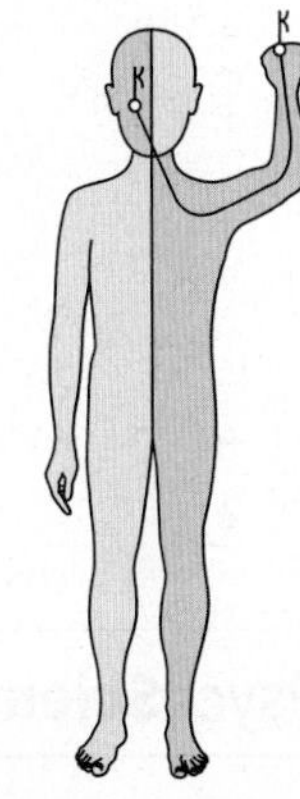

FIGURE 2.15 Information crossover Our brains' right hemisphere controls the left side of our bodies, whereas the left hemisphere controls the right side.

Frontal lobes The two lobes at the front of the brain that govern motor control, speech production, and higher functions, such as thinking, personality, emotion, and memory.

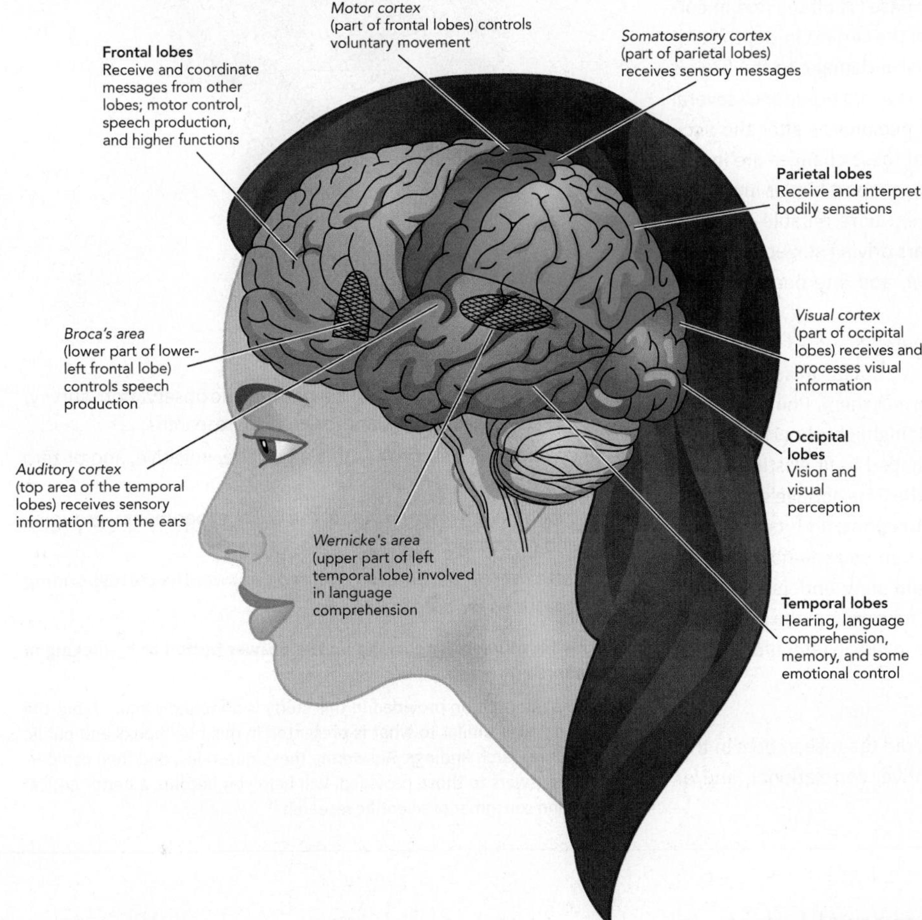

FIGURE 2.16 Lobes of the brain This is a view of the brain's left hemisphere showing its four lobes—*frontal, parietal, temporal*, and *occipital*. The right hemisphere has the same four lobes. Divisions between the lobes are marked by visibly prominent folds. Keep in mind that Broca's and Wernicke's areas occur only in the left hemisphere.

that mastering this information is essential to every chapter of this text and to the entire field of psychology. More importantly, recognizing that your brain is YOU—all your personality, thoughts, and your very life—will undoubtedly increase your motivation to study and protect it. Just as we routinely wear shoes to protect our feet, we need seat belts and helmets to protect our far more fragile brains! On a more encouraging note, updated information on the famous case of Phineas Gage, which is discussed in the following **PsychScience**, indicates that damage to the brain may not be as permanent as we once thought, thanks to the two processes we discussed earlier—*neuroplasticity* and *neurogenesis*.

PS PsychScience

Phineas Gage—Myths Versus Facts

In 1848, a 25-year-old railroad foreman named Phineas Gage had a metal rod (13½ pounds, 3 feet 7 inches long, and 1¼ inches in diameter) accidentally blown through the front of his face, destroying much of his brain's left frontal lobe. Amazingly, Gage was immediately able to sit up, speak, and move around, and he did not receive medical treatment until about 1½ hours later. After his wound healed, he tried to return to work, but was soon fired. The previously friendly, efficient, and capable foreman was now "fitful, impatient, and lacking in deference to his fellows" (Macmillan, 2000). In the words of his friends: "Gage was no longer Gage" (Harlow, 1868).

This so-called "American Crowbar Case" is often cited in current texts and academic papers as one of the earliest in-depth studies of an individual's survival after massive damage to the brain's frontal lobes. The evidence is clear that Gage did experience several dramatic changes in his behavior and personality after the accident, but the extent and permanence of these changes are in dispute. Most accounts of post-accident Gage report him as impulsive and unreliable until his death. However, more reliable evidence later showed that Gage spent many years driving stagecoaches—a job that required high motor, cognitive, and interpersonal skills (Griggs, 2015; Macmillan, 2010).

So why bother reporting this controversy? As you'll note throughout this text, we discuss several popular misconceptions in psychology in order to clarify and correct them. Phineas Gage's story is particularly important because it highlights how a small set of reliable facts can be distorted and shaped to fit existing beliefs and scientific theories. For example, at the time of Gage's accident, little was known about how the brain functions, and damage to it was believed to be largely irreversible. Can you see how our current research techniques along with our new understanding of *neurogenesis* and *neuroplasticity*, might now explain the previously ignored evidence of Gage's significant recovery in later life?

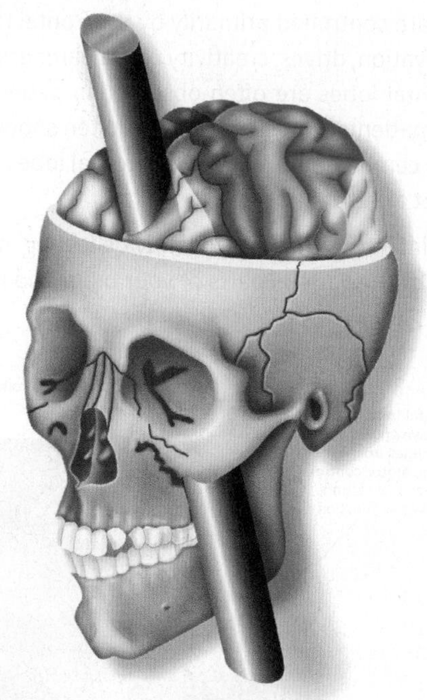

Research Challenge

1. Based on the information provided, did the researchers in this study of Phineas Gage use descriptive, correlational, and/or experimental research?
2. If you chose:
   - *descriptive research*, is this a naturalistic observation, survey/interview, case study, and/or archival research?
   - *correlational research*, is this a positive, negative, and or zero correlation?
   - *experimental research*, label the IV, DV, experimental group(s), and control group.
   - both *descriptive* and *correlational*, answer the corresponding questions for both.

Check your answers by clicking on the answer button or by looking in Appendix B.

Note: The information provided in this study is admittedly limited, but the level of detail is similar to what is presented in most textbooks and public reports of research findings. Answering these questions, and then comparing your answers to those provided, will help you become a better critical thinker and consumer of scientific research.

Temporal lobes The two lobes on each side of the brain above the ears that are involved in audition (hearing), language comprehension, memory, and some emotional control.

Temporal Lobes

The **temporal lobes** are responsible for hearing, language comprehension, memory, and some emotional control. The *auditory cortex*, which processes sound, is located at the top front of each temporal lobe. This area is responsible for receiving incoming sensory information and sending it on to the parietal lobes, where it is combined with other sensory information.

A part of the left temporal lobe called *Wernicke's area* aids in language comprehension. About a decade after Broca's discovery, German neurologist Carl Wernicke noted that patients with damage in this area could not understand what they read or heard, but they could speak quickly and easily. However, their speech was often unintelligible because it contained made-up words, sound substitutions, and word substitutions. This syndrome is now referred to as *Wernicke's aphasia*.

Occipital Lobes The **occipital lobes** are responsible for, among other things, vision and visual perception. Damage to the occipital lobes can produce blindness, even if the eyes and their neural connection to the brain are perfectly healthy.

Occipital lobes The two lobes at the back of the brain that are primarily responsible for vision and visual perception.

Parietal Lobes The **parietal lobes** receive and interpret bodily sensations including pressure, pain, touch, temperature, and location of body parts. A band of tissue on the front of the parietal lobes, called the *somatosensory cortex*, receives information about touch in different body areas. Areas of the body with more somatosensory and motor cortex devoted to them (such as the hands and face) are most sensitive to touch and have the most precise motor control (**Figure 2.17**). See the **Psychology and You** feature.

Parietal lobes The two lobes located at the top of the brain in which bodily sensations are received and interpreted.

Association Areas One of the most popular myths in psychology is that we use only 10% of our brains. This myth might have begun with early research which showed that approximately three-fourths of the cortex is "quiet" (with no precise, specific function responsive to electrical brain stimulation). These areas are not dormant, however. They are clearly engaged in interpreting, integrating, and acting on information processed by other parts of the brain. They are called **association areas** because they associate, or connect, various areas and functions of the brain. The association areas in the frontal lobes, for example, help in decision making and planning. Similarly, the association area right in front of the motor cortex aids in the planning of voluntary movement.

Association areas The "quiet" areas in the cerebral cortex involved in interpreting, integrating, and acting on information processed by other parts of the brain.

FIGURE 2.17 Body representation of the motor cortex and somatosensory cortex This drawing shows a vertical cross section taken from the left hemisphere's motor cortex and right hemisphere's somatosensory cortex. If body areas were truly proportional to the amount of tissue on the motor and somatosensory cortices that affect them, our bodies would look like the oddly shaped human figures draped around the outside edge of the cortex.

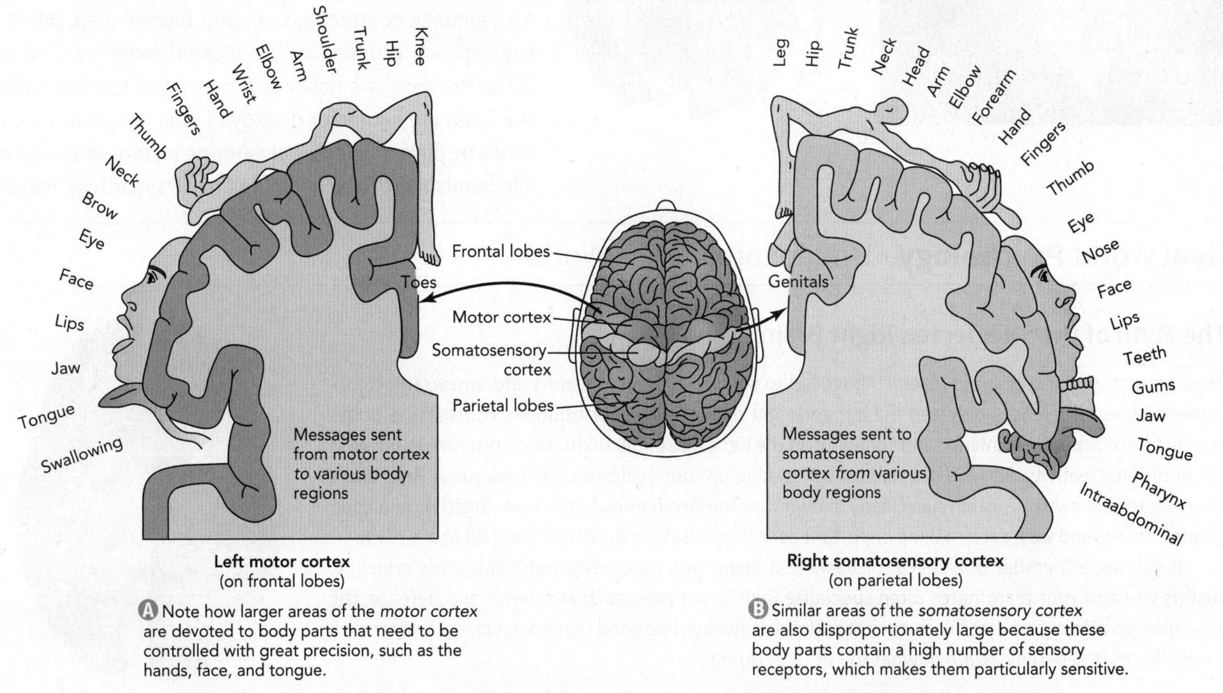

A Note how larger areas of the *motor cortex* are devoted to body parts that need to be controlled with great precision, such as the hands, face, and tongue.

B Similar areas of the *somatosensory cortex* are also disproportionately large because these body parts contain a high number of sensory receptors, which makes them particularly sensitive.

Psychology and You—Understanding Yourself

Testing Your Motor Cortex and Somatosensory Cortex

1. ***Motor cortex*** Try wiggling each of your fingers one at a time. Now try wiggling each of your toes. Note on Figure 2.17 how the area of your motor cortex is much larger for your fingers than for your toes, thus explaining the greater control in your fingers.
2. ***Somatosensory cortex*** Ask a friend to close his or her eyes. Using a random number of fingers (one to four), press down on the skin of your friend's back for 1 to 2 seconds. Then ask, "How many fingers am I using?" Repeat the same procedure on the palm or back of the hand. Note the increased accuracy of reporting after pressing on the hand, which explains why the area of the somatosensory cortex is much larger for the hands than for the back, as well as the greater sensitivity in our hands versus our backs.

Split-brain surgery The cutting of the corpus callosum to separate the brain's two hemispheres; used medically to treat severe epilepsy; also provides information on the functions of the two hemispheres.

Corpus callosum A bundle of neural fibers that connects the brain's two hemispheres.

Two Brains in One?

We mentioned earlier that the brain's left and right cerebral hemispheres control opposite sides of the body. Each hemisphere also has separate areas of specialization. This is another example of localization of function, technically referred to as *lateralization*.

Early researchers believed the right hemisphere was subordinate or nondominant to the left, with few special functions or abilities. In the 1960s, landmark **split-brain surgeries** began to change this view.

The primary connection between the two cerebral hemispheres is a thick, ribbon-like band of neural fibers under the cortex called the **corpus callosum** (**Figure 2.18**). In some rare cases of severe epilepsy, when other forms of treatment have failed, surgeons cut the corpus callosum to stop the spread of epileptic seizures from one hemisphere to the other. Because this operation cuts the only direct communication link between the two hemispheres, it reveals what each half of the brain can do in isolation from the other. The resulting research has profoundly improved our understanding of how the two halves of the brain function.

FIGURE 2.18 Views of the corpus callosum In the side-view photo on the left, a human brain was sliced vertically from the top to the bottom to expose the corpus callosum, which conveys information between the two hemispheres of the cerebral cortex. The top-down illustration on the right shows how fibers, or *axons*, of the corpus callosum link to both the right and left hemispheres. Note: The deep, extensive cuts shown in these images are to reveal the corpus callosum. In split-brain surgeries on live patients, only fibers within the corpus callosum itself are cut.

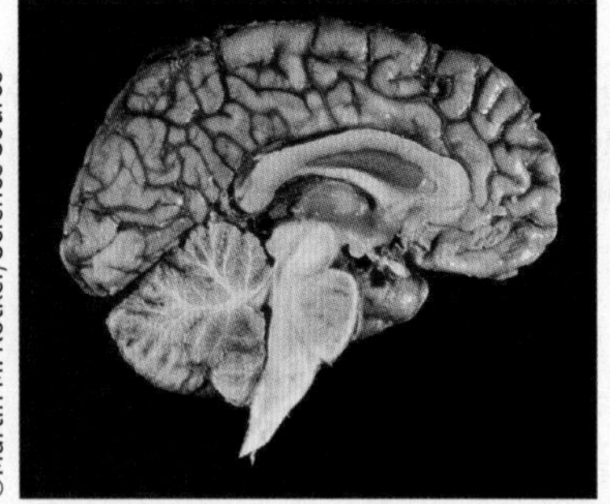
©Martin M. Rotker/Science Source

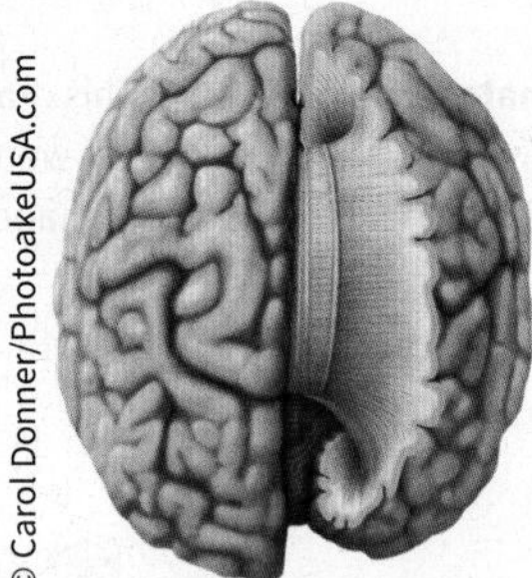
© Carol Donner/PhotoakeUSA.com

For example, when someone has a brain stroke and loses his or her language comprehension or ability to speak, we know this generally points to damage on the left hemisphere, because this is where *Wernicke's area*, which is responsible for language comprehension, and *Broca's area*, which controls speech production, are located (refer back to Figure 2.16). However, we now know that when specific regions of the brain are injured or destroyed their functions can sometimes be picked up by a neighboring region—even the opposite hemisphere (see the **Real World Psychology** feature).

Real World Psychology—Understanding the World

The Myth of the "Neglected Right Brain"

Popular accounts of split-brain research have led to some exaggerated claims and unwarranted conclusions about differences between the left and right hemispheres. For example, courses and books directed at "right-brain thinking" and "drawing on the right side of the brain" often promise to increase our intuition, creativity, and artistic abilities by "waking up" our neglected and underused right brain. Contrary to this myth, research has clearly shown that the two hemispheres work together in a coordinated, integrated way, each making important contributions (Garrett, 2015; Lilienfeld et al., 2015).

If you are a member of a soccer or basketball team, you can easily understand this principle. Just as you and your teammates often specialize in different jobs, such as offense and defense, the hemispheres also somewhat divide their workload. However, like good team players, each of the two hemispheres is generally aware of what the other is doing.

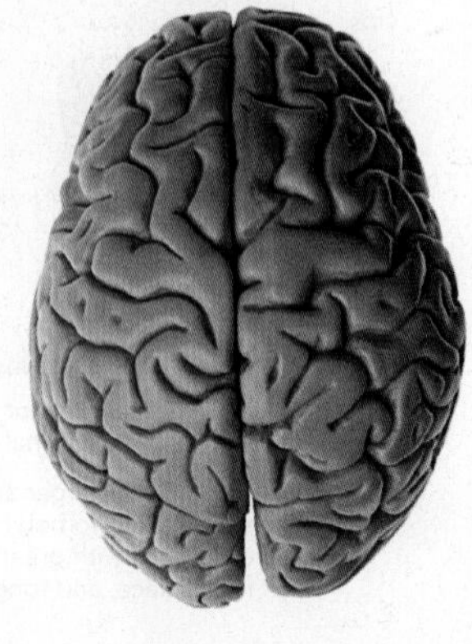
© Debbi Smirnoff/iStockphoto

Although most split-brain surgery patients generally show very few outward changes in their behavior, other than fewer epileptic seizures, the surgery does create a few unusual responses. For example, one split-brain patient reported that when he dressed himself, he sometimes pulled his pants down with his left hand and up with his right (Gazzaniga, 2009). The subtle changes in split-brain patients normally appear only with specialized testing. See **Figure 2.19** for an

FIGURE 2.19 Split-brain research Experiments on split-brain patients often present visual information to only the patient's left or right hemisphere, which leads to some intriguing results.

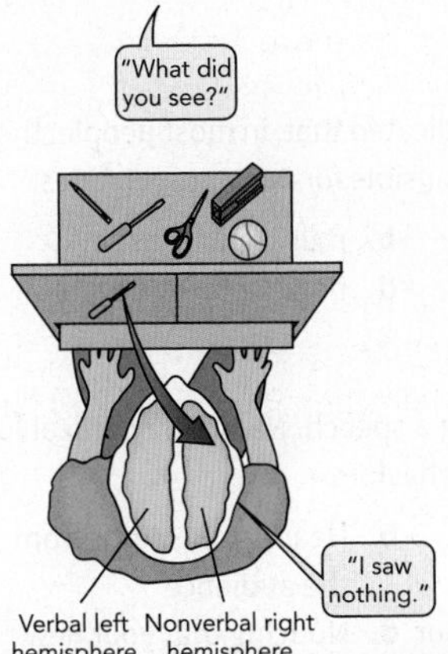

Ⓐ When a split-brain patient is asked to stare straight ahead while a photo of a screwdriver is flashed only to the right hemisphere, he will report that he "saw nothing."

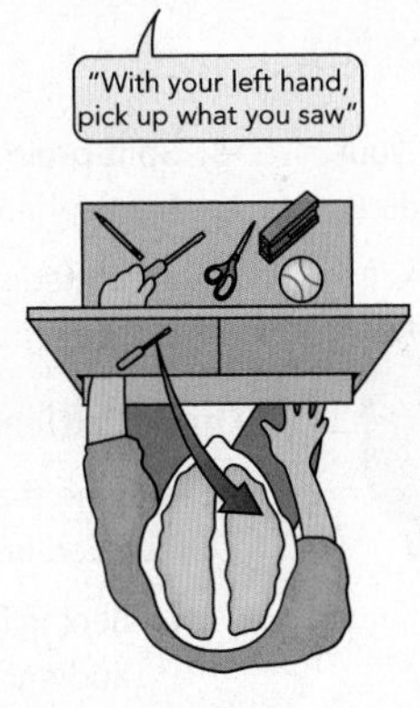

Ⓑ However, when asked to pick up with his left hand what he saw, he can reach through and touch the items hidden behind the screen and easily pick up the screwdriver.

Ⓒ When the left hemisphere receives an image of a baseball, the split-brain patient can easily name it.

Assuming you have an intact, nonsevered corpus callosum, if the same photos were presented to you in the same way, you could easily name both the screwdriver and the baseball. Can you explain why? The answers lie in our somewhat confusing visual wiring system (as shown in drawings d and e below).

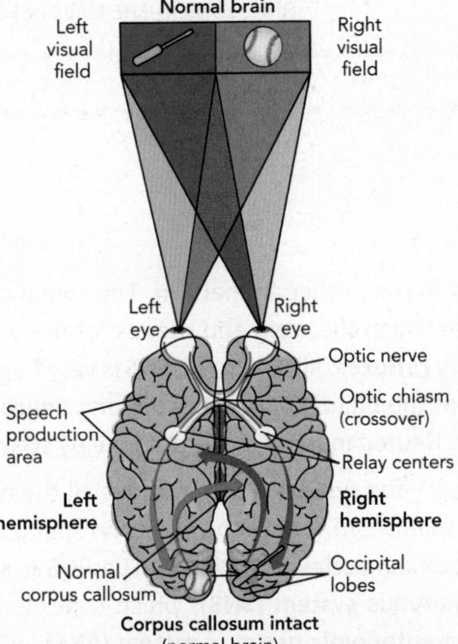

Corpus callosum intact (normal brain)

Ⓓ As you can see, our eyes normally connect to our brains in such a way that, when we look straight ahead, information from the left visual field travels to our right hemisphere (the blue line). In contrast, information from the right visual field travels to our left hemisphere (the red line). The messages received by either hemisphere are then quickly sent to the other across the corpus callosum (the red and blue arrows).

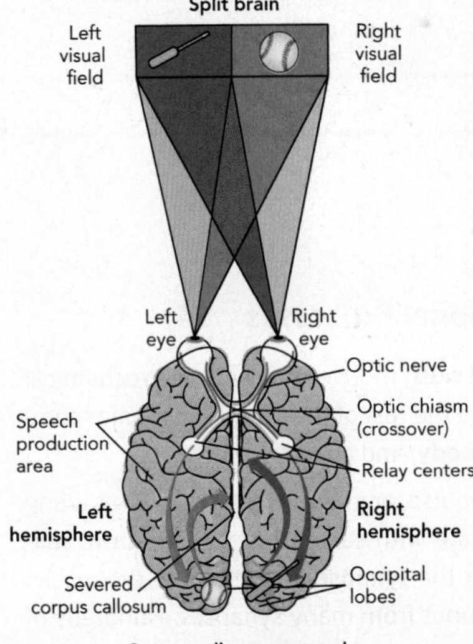

Corpus callosum severed (split brain)

Ⓔ When the corpus callosum is severed (note the white line down the middle of the two hemispheres), a split-brain patient cannot state out loud the name of what he sees in the left visual field (in this case "screwdriver"). Why? It's because the image from the left visual field is sent to both eyes, but only to the right side of the brain. For most people, the speech-control center is in the left hemisphere, and information from either hemisphere is normally passed quickly to the other hemisphere across the corpus callosum. However, in the split-brain patient, the corpus callosum is severed and communication between the two hemispheres is blocked. (Compare how the red and blue arrows cross over to the opposite hemisphere in Figure D versus how the same arrows are limited to only one hemisphere here in Figure E.)

illustration and description of this type of specialized test. Keep in mind that in actual split-brain surgery on live patients, only some fibers within the corpus callosum are cut (*not* the lower brain structures), and this surgery is performed only in rare cases of uncontrollable epilepsy.

In our tour of the nervous system, the principles of localization of function, lateralization, and specialization recur: Dendrites receive information, the occipital lobes specialize in vision, and so on. Keep in mind, however, that all parts of the brain and nervous system also play overlapping and synchronized roles.

Retrieval Practice 2.4 | The Cerebral Cortex

SELF-TEST Completing this self-test, and then checking your answers by clicking on the answer button or by looking in Appendix B, will provide immediate feedback and helpful practice for exams.

1. Label the four lobes of the brain:
   a. frontal **b.** parietal
   c. temporal **d.** occipital
2. The _____ lobes are largely responsible for motor control, speech production, and higher functions, such as thinking, personality, and memory.
   a. cortical **b.** frontal
   c. parietal **d.** occipital
3. Specialization of the left and right hemispheres of the brain for particular operations is known as _____.
   a. centralization **b.** asymmetrical processing
   c. normalization of function **d.** lateralization
4. Although the left and right hemispheres sometimes perform different, specialized functions, they are normally in close communication and share functions, thanks to the _____.
   a. thalamus system **b.** sympathetic nervous
   c. corpus callosum **d.** cerebellum
5. Split-brain research has indicated that, in most people, the left hemisphere is largely responsible for our _____ abilities.
   a. athletic and spatial **b.** music and artistic
   c. speech and language **d.** none of these options

Think Critically

1. Imagine that you are giving a speech. Name the cortical lobes involved in the following behaviors:
   a. Seeing faces in the audience **b.** Hearing questions from the audience
   c. Remembering where your car is parked when you are ready to go home **d.** Noticing that your new shoes are too tight and hurting your feet
2. What are some everyday examples of the different functions of the two hemispheres?

Real World Psychology

Why are former NFL athletes at increased risk of depression, dementia, and suicide?

HINT: LOOK IN THE MARGIN FOR **[Q6]**

Summary

2.1 Neural and Hormonal Processes 34

- **Neurons**, supported by **glial cells**, receive and send electrochemical signals to other neurons and to the rest of the body. Their major components are **dendrites**, a **cell body**, and an **axon**.
- Within a neuron, a neural impulse, or **action potential**, moves along the axon. Neurons communicate with each other using **neurotransmitters**, which are released at the **synapse** and attach to the receiving neuron. Neurons receive input from many synapses. Hundreds of different neurotransmitters regulate a wide variety of physiological processes. Many **agonist** and **antagonist drugs** and poisons act by mimicking or interfering with neurotransmitters.
- The **endocrine system** uses **hormones** to broadcast messages throughout the body. The system regulates long-term bodily processes, maintains ongoing bodily processes, and controls the body's response to emergencies.

2.2 Nervous System Organization 42

- The **central nervous system (CNS)** includes the brain and spinal cord. The CNS allows us to process information and adapt to our environment in ways that no other animal can. The spinal cord transmits information between the brain and the rest of the body, and it initiates involuntary **reflexes**. Although the CNS is very fragile, recent research shows that the brain is capable of lifelong **neuroplasticity** and **neurogenesis**. Neurogenesis is made possible by **stem cells**.
- The **peripheral nervous system (PNS)** includes all the nerves outside the brain and spinal cord. It links the brain and spinal cord to the body's sense receptors, muscles, and glands. The PNS is subdivided into the **somatic nervous system (SNS)**, which controls voluntary movement, and the **autonomic nervous system (ANS)**, which is responsible for automatic behavior.
- The ANS includes the **sympathetic nervous system** and the **parasympathetic nervous system**. The sympathetic nervous system mobilizes the body's fight-flight-freeze response. The parasympathetic nervous system returns the body to its normal functioning.

2.3 A Tour Through the Brain 48

- Neuroscientists have developed several tools to explore the human brain and nervous system. Early researchers used dissection and other methods like clinical observation and case studies of living people. Recent scientific advances include newer brain imaging scans, which have improved scientists' ability to examine these processes and to do so noninvasively.

- The brain is divided into the **hindbrain**, **midbrain**, and **forebrain**. Certain brain structures are specialized to perform certain tasks thanks to *localization of function*.
- The hindbrain, including the **medulla, pons,** and **cerebellum**, controls automatic behaviors and survival responses.
- The midbrain helps us orient our eye and body movements, helps control sleep and arousal, and is involved with the neurotransmitter dopamine. The **reticular formation (RF)** runs through the core of the hindbrain, midbrain, and brainstem, and is responsible for screening information and managing our levels of alertness.
- Forebrain structures, including the **cerebral cortex, limbic system, thalamus**, and **hypothalamus**, integrate input from the senses, control basic motives, regulate the body's internal environment, and regulate emotions, learning, and memory.

2.4 The Cerebral Cortex 54

- The **cerebral cortex**, part of the forebrain, governs most higher processing and complex behaviors. It is divided into two hemispheres, each controlling the opposite side of the body. The **corpus callosum** links the hemispheres.
- Each hemisphere is divided into **frontal, parietal, temporal**, and **occipital lobes**. Each lobe specializes in somewhat different tasks, but a large part of the cortex is devoted to integrating actions performed by different brain regions.
- **Split-brain** research shows that each hemisphere performs somewhat different functions, although they work in close communication.

Applying **Real** World **Psychology**—Understanding the World

We began this chapter with five intriguing Real World Psychology questions, and you were asked to revisit these questions at the end of each section. Questions like these have an important and lasting impact on all of our lives. See if you can answer these additional critical thinking questions related to real world examples.

1. Given that neglect in the first few months of life leads to lasting problems, what can we do as a society to increase parental bonding and infant security?
2. If you were one of the parents in this photo, what might you do to protect and maximize your infant's brain development?
3. If neuroscientists were able to use brain scans to determine what a person is thinking, what might be the ethical considerations of this type of research?
4. Imagine that your friend "John" has suffered a major automobile accident, and now has right-sided paralysis. Given that he has lost his ability to speak, can you identify the specific section of the brain and which hemisphere was most likely damaged in the accident?

Kei Uesugi/Getty Images

5. Some research suggests that women are better than men at multitasking. What part(s) of the brain would explain this possible difference?

Key Terms

Retrieval Practice Write your own definition for each term before turning back to the referenced page to check your answer.

- action potential 37
- agonist drug 37
- all-or-nothing principle 37
- amygdala 53
- antagonist drug 37
- association areas 57
- autonomic nervous system (ANS) 46
- axon 34
- brainstem 52
- cell body 34
- central nervous system (CNS) 43
- cerebellum 50
- cerebral cortex 54
- corpus callosum 58
- dendrites 34
- endocrine system 40
- endorphin 38
- forebrain 53
- frontal lobes 55
- glial cells 34
- hindbrain 49
- hippocampus 53
- hormone 40
- hypothalamus 53
- limbic system 53
- medulla 49
- midbrain 51
- myelin sheath 34
- neurogenesis 43
- neuron 34
- neuroplasticity 43
- neurotransmitter 37
- occipital lobes 57
- parasympathetic nervous system 46
- parietal lobes 57
- peripheral nervous system (PNS) 43
- pons 50
- reflex 44
- reticular formation (RF) 52
- somatic nervous system (SNS) 46
- split-brain surgery 58
- stem cells 43
- sympathetic nervous system 46
- synapse 37
- temporal lobes 56
- thalamus 53

CHAPTER 3

© JuSun/iStockphoto

Stress and Health Psychology

erikreis/Getty Images

Real World Psychology

Things you'll learn in Chapter 3

[Q1] Does frequent checking of your email and social media increase your stress?

[Q2] Can the stress of growing up in poverty cause changes in your brain?

[Q3] Does watching televised coverage of natural disasters increase symptoms of posttraumatic stress disorder?

[Q4] Could thinking about the "silver linings" of a stressful event, or sharing it with others, reduce depression?

[Q5] Are people with stressful jobs at increased risk of experiencing a heart attack?

Throughout the chapter, margin icons for Q1–Q5 indicate where the text addresses these questions.

CHAPTER OUTLINE

Chapter Overview

Do you recall the 2013 dramatic rescue of the three women held hostage in a suburban house in Cleveland, Ohio? Despite having been raped, beaten, and caged under horrific conditions for over a decade, these women apparently survived with their physical and emotional health relatively intact. As you might expect, stress exists on a continuum, and it's often in the eye of the beholder. We would all agree that what these women endured was extreme, unimaginable stress. In comparison, if you've done poorly on previous exams and are only just now reading this chapter at the last minute before an exam, you may be experiencing personally high levels of stress. But, if you're a student who's generally well prepared and performs well on exams, you're probably experiencing little or no stress. In short, stress is largely dependent on our interpretations of events and our perceived resources for coping with them.

In this chapter, we begin with a general description of stress, along with its sources, effects, and surprising benefits. Then we explore the numerous ways we typically cope with stress, personality effects on coping, and resources for healthy living. We close with a discussion of the field of health psychology, its contribution to our understanding of stress, and health psychology in the workplace.

3.1 Understanding Stress

LEARNING OBJECTIVES

Retrieval Practice While reading the upcoming sections, respond to each Learning Objective in your own words.

Summarize the major issues and discoveries concerning stress.

- **Define** stress and stressors.
- **Identify** the major sources of stress.
- **Describe** our physical and cognitive reactions to stress.
- **Review** the benefits of stress.

Everyone experiences **stress**, and we generally know what a person means when he or she speaks of being "stressed." But scientists typically define stress as *the interpretation of specific events,* called **stressors**, *as threatening or challenging*. The resulting physical and psychological reactions to stressors are known as the *stress response* (Anisman, 2016; Sanderson, 2013; Selye, 1936, 1983). Using these definitions, can you see how an upcoming exam on this material could be called a stressor, whereas your physical and psychological reactions are your stress response? In this section, we'll discuss the key sources of stress and how it affects us. Before going on, test your general knowledge of stress and health in the following **Myth Busters**.

Stress The interpretation of specific events, called *stressors*, as threatening or challenging; the physical and psychological reactions to stress, known as the *stress response*.

Stressor A trigger or stimulus that induces stress.

MYTH BUSTERS

True or False?

_____ **1.** Even positive events, like graduating from college and getting married, are major sources of stress.

_____ **2.** Small, everyday hassles can impair your immune system functioning.

_____ **3.** Police officers, nurses, doctors, social workers, and teachers are particularly prone to "burnout."

_____ **4.** Stress causes cancer.

_____ **5.** Having a positive attitude can prevent cancer.

_____ **6.** Optimistic personality types may cope better with stress.

_____ **7.** Ulcers are caused primarily or entirely by stress.

_____ **8.** Friendship is one of your best health resources.

_____ **9.** Prolonged stress can lead to death.

_____ **10.** You can control, or minimize, most of the negative effects of stress.

Shannon Fagan/The Image Bank/Getty Images

Answers: Three out of the 10 questions are false. Looking for the false answers, while reading the chapter, will improve your mastery of the material.

Sources of Stress

Although literally hundreds of things can cause stress in all our lives, psychological science has focused on seven major sources (**Figure 3.1**).

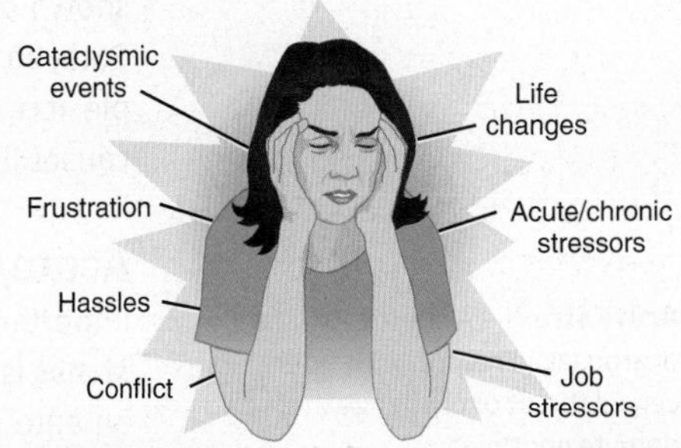

FIGURE 3.1 Seven major sources of stress

Life Changes Early stress researchers Thomas Holmes and Richard Rahe (1967) believed that any *life change* that required some adjustment in behavior or lifestyle could cause some degree of stress. They also believed that exposure to numerous stressful events in a short period could have a direct, detrimental effect on health.

Psychology and You—Understanding Yourself

Test Yourself | Measuring Life Changes

To score yourself on the Social Readjustment Rating Scale (SRRS), add up the "life change units" for all life events you have experienced during the last year and compare your score with the following standards: 0–150 = No significant problems; 150–199 = Mild life crisis (33% chance of illness); 200–299 = Moderate life crisis (50% chance of illness); 300 and above = Major life crisis (80% chance of illness).

LIFE EVENTS	LIFE CHANGE UNITS
Death of spouse	100
Divorce	73
Marital separation	65
Jail term	63
Death of a close family member	63
Personal injury or illness	53
Marriage	50
Fired at work	47
Marital reconciliation	45
Retirement	45
Change in health of family member	44
Pregnancy	40
Sex difficulties	39
Gain of a new family member	39
Business readjustment	39
Change in financial state	38
Death of a close friend	37
Change to different line of work	36
Change in number of arguments with spouse	35
Mortgage or loan for major purchase	31
Foreclosure on mortgage or loan	30
Change in responsibilities at work	29
Son or daughter leaving home	29

LIFE EVENTS	LIFE CHANGE UNITS
Trouble with in-laws	29
Outstanding personal achievement	28
Spouse begins or stops work	26
Begin or end school	26
Change in living conditions	25
Revision of personal habits	24
Trouble with boss	23
Change in work hours or conditions	20
Change in residence	20
Change in schools	20
Change in recreation	19
Change in church activities	19
Change in social activities	18
Mortgage or loan for lesser purchase (car, major appliance)	17
Change in sleeping habits	16
Change in number of family get-togethers	15
Change in eating habits	15
Vacation	13
Christmas	12
Minor violations of the law	11

Source: Reprinted from the *Journal of Psychosomatic Research*, Vol. III; Holmes and Rahe: "The Social Readjustment Rating Scale," 213–218, 1967, with permission from Elsevier.

To investigate the relationship between change and stress, Holmes and Rahe created the Social Readjustment Rating Scale (SRRS), which asks people to check off all the life events they have experienced in the previous year (see **Psychology and You**). The SRRS is an easy and popular tool for measuring stress (e.g., Fabre et al., 2013), and cross-cultural studies have shown that most people rank the magnitude of their stressful events similarly (Consedine & Soto, 2014; Loving & Sbarra, 2015; Smith et al., 2014). But the SRRS is not foolproof. For example, it only shows a correlation between stress and illness; it does not prove that stress actually causes illnesses.

Acute stress A short-term state of arousal, in response to a perceived threat or challenge that has a definite endpoint.

Acute/Chronic Stress In addition to the stress caused by life-changing events, it's also important to note that the stressors can be either acute or chronic—and sometimes both. **Acute stress** is generally severe, but short term, with a definite endpoint, such as narrowly avoiding an auto accident or missing an important deadline. In modern times, this type of immediate, short-term arousal is almost a daily occurrence for most of us. Common symptoms include emotional responses (e.g., anxiety, tension, irritability), as well physical reactions (e.g., transient increases in blood pressure, heart rate, dizziness, chest pains). Thankfully, because acute stress is short term, it generally doesn't lead to the type of extensive damage associated with long-term stress.

In contrast to short-term stress, ongoing wars, a bad marriage, poor working conditions, poverty, and/or prejudice and discrimination (discussed in **Figure 3.2**), can all be significant sources of **chronic stress** (Arbona & Jimenez, 2014; Chaby et al., 2015; Vliegenthart et al., 2016). In our private lives, chronic stressors like child and spousal abuse, alcoholism, and money problems can all place severe stress on a family (Fan et al., 2015; Liang, 2015; Simons et al., 2016). Surprisingly, chronic stress can even suppress sexual desire and damage testicular cells in male rats (Hou et al., 2014). In addition, stress from persistent environmental noise is associated with negative changes in the brain and hormone levels (Fouladi et al., 2012).

© Valentin Casarsa/iStockphoto

FIGURE 3.2 Prejudice and discrimination as chronic stressors Research has found that the chronic stress resulting from prejudice and discrimination is linked to serious physical and mental problems, including being at a higher risk of heart disease, inflammation, substance abuse, and suicide (Kershaw et al., 2016; Lea et al., 2014; Tebbe & Moradi, 2016).

Chronic stress A continuous state of arousal in which demands are perceived as greater than the inner and outer resources available for dealing with them.

Our social lives also can be chronically stressful because making and maintaining friendships require considerable thought and energy (Ehrlich et al., 2016; Fox & Moreland, 2015; Vishwanath, 2015). For example, although people often use social media to maintain friendships, research suggests that your stress level increases with the more social media "friends" you have and the more time you spend on social networking sites (Bevan et al., 2014; Morin-Major et al., 2016). In addition, an online survey of college students' attitudes about Facebook revealed the following (Charles, 2011):

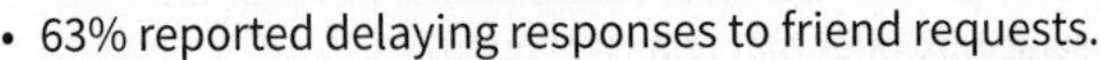

- 63% reported delaying responses to friend requests.
- 32% reported that rejecting friend requests made them feel guilty and uncomfortable.
- 12% reported that Facebook made them feel anxious.
- [Q1] 10% reported disliking receiving friend requests.

Research also shows that people who spend more time on social media (see photo) experience lower levels of day-to-day happiness, lower overall feelings of life satisfaction, and higher levels of depression due to social comparison (Brooks, 2015; Kross et al., 2013; Steers et al., 2014). Why is social comparison stressful? People may feel excluded from social events that are often described and photographed on social media, experience pressure to be entertaining when they post, and fear that they are missing important information if they don't check in repeatedly. (As you may know, this fear of missing out is so common that it has its own acronym—FOMO.) The good news is that limiting your time on social media and email checking has been shown to decrease stress and increase overall well-being (Kushlev & Dunn, 2015; Shaw et al., 2015).

Quka/Shutterstock.com

Job Stressors For many people, one of their most pressing concerns is *job stress*, which can result from unemployment, job change, and/or worries about job performance. At its worst, it can even contribute to suicide (Adams, 2015; Cartwright & Cooper, 2014; Rees et al., 2015). Studies of first responders and other high-risk professions, such as police officers, firefighters, paramedics, military and medical personnel, have found an elevated risk of suicide, suicidal thoughts and behaviors, and posttraumatic stress disorder (PTSD) (Carpenter et al., 2015; Stanley et al., 2016; Tei et al., 2015). In addition, studies have found that job stress is higher in occupations that have little job security, and make great demands on performance and concentration, with little or no allowances for creativity or opportunity for advancement (Bauer & Hämmig, 2014; Dawson et al., 2016; Sanderson, 2013).

Other common sources of job stress come from *role conflict*, being forced to take on separate and incompatible roles, or *role ambiguity*, being uncertain about the expectations and demands of your role (Lu et al., 2016; Memili et al., 2015). Being a mid-level manager who reports

Conflict A forced choice between two or more incompatible goals or impulses.

Approach–approach conflict A forced choice between two options, both of which have equally desirable characteristics.

Approach–avoidance conflict A forced choice involving one option with equally desirable and undesirable characteristics.

Avoidance–avoidance conflict A forced choice between two options, both of which have equally undesirable characteristics.

to many supervisors, while also working among the people he or she is expected to supervise, is a prime example of both role conflict and role ambiguity.

Conflict Stress can also arise when we experience **conflict**—that is, when we are forced to make a choice between at least two incompatible alternatives. There are three basic types of conflict: **approach-approach**, **approach-avoidance**, and **avoidance-avoidance** (**Table 3.1**).

Generally, approach–approach conflicts are the easiest to resolve and produce the least stress. Avoidance–avoidance conflicts, on the other hand, are usually the most difficult and take the longest to resolve because either choice leads to unpleasant results. Furthermore, the longer any conflict exists, or the more important the decision, the more stress a person will experience.

TABLE 3.1 Types of Conflict

CONFLICT	DESCRIPTION/RESOLUTION	EXAMPLE/RESOLUTION
Approach–approach + +	Forced choice between two options, both of which have equally desirable characteristics Generally easiest and least stressful conflict to resolve	Two equally desirable job offers, but you must choose one of them You make a pro/con list and/or "flip a coin"
Approach–avoidance + −	Forced choice involving one option with equally desirable and undesirable characteristics Moderately difficult choice, often resolved with a partial approach	One high-salary job offer that requires you to relocate to an undesirable location away from all your friends and family You make a pro/con list and/or "flip a coin;" if you take the job you decide to only live in the new location for a limited time (a partial approach)
Avoidance–avoidance − −	Forced choice between two options, both of which have equally undesirable characteristics Difficult, stressful conflict, generally resolved with a long delay and considerable denial	Two equally undesirable options—bad job or no job—and you must choose one of them because you're broke You make a pro/con list and/or "flip a coin" and then delay the decision as long as possible, hoping for additional job offers

Q Think Critically

The expression on this man's face indicates that he's experiencing some form of conflict.

1. Can you explain how this could be both an avoidance–avoidance and/or an approach–avoidance conflict?
2. What might be the best way resolve this conflict?

Lisa Peardon/Taxi/Getty

Hassles The minor **hassles** of daily living also can pile up and become a major source of stress. We all share many hassles, such as time pressures and financial concerns. But our reactions to them vary. Persistent hassles, among other factors, can lead to a form of physical, mental, and emotional exhaustion known as **burnout** (Cranley et al., 2016; Guveli et al., 2015; Zysberg et al., 2016). This is particularly true for some people in chronically stressful professions, such as firefighters, police officers, doctors, and nurses. Their exhaustion and "burnout" then lead to more work absences, reduced productivity, and increased risk of illness.

Some authorities believe hassles can be more significant than major life events in creating stress (Kubiak et al., 2008; Stefanek et al., 2012). Divorce is extremely stressful, but it may be so because of the increased number of hassles it brings—changes in finances, child-care arrangements, longer working hours, and so on.

Hassles The small problems of daily living that may accumulate and become a major source of stress.

Burnout A state of physical, mental, and emotional exhaustion resulting from chronic exposure to high levels of stress, with little personal control.

Frustration The unpleasant tension, anxiety, and heightened sympathetic activity resulting from a blocked goal.

Cataclysmic event A stressful occurrence that happens suddenly and generally affects many people simultaneously.

General adaptation syndrome (GAS) Selye's three-stage (alarm, resistance, exhaustion) reaction to chronic stress; a pattern of nonspecific, adaptational responses to a continuing stressor.

Frustration Like hassles, **frustration**, a negative emotional state resulting from a blocked goal, can cause stress. And the more motivated we are, the more frustrated we become when our goals are blocked. After getting stuck in traffic and being 5 minutes late to an important job interview, we may become very frustrated. However, if the same traffic jam causes us to be 5 minutes late showing up to a casual party, we may experience little or no frustration.

Cataclysmic Events Terrorist attacks and natural disasters that cause major damage and loss of life are what stress researchers call **cataclysmic events**. They occur suddenly and generally affect many people simultaneously. Politicians and the public often imagine that such catastrophes inevitably create huge numbers of seriously depressed and permanently scarred survivors (see photo).

Interestingly, relief agencies typically send large numbers of counselors to help with the psychological aftermath. However, researchers have found that because the catastrophe is shared by so many others, there is already a great deal of mutual social support from those with firsthand experience with the same disaster, which may help people cope (Aldrich & Meyer, 2015; Ginzburg & Bateman, 2008). On the other hand, these cataclysmic events are clearly devastating to all parts of the victims' lives (Alvarez, 2011; Gulliver et al., 2014; Joseph et al., 2014). In fact, people who experience extreme stress, such as a natural disaster like the 9.0 magnitude earthquake that hit Japan and caused devastating tsunami waves, show changes in the brain as long as 1 year later (Sekiguchi et al., 2014). Specifically, the hippocampus and orbitofrontal cortex are smaller following stress. Some survivors may even develop a prolonged and severe stress reaction, known as *posttraumatic stress disorder (PTSD)*, which we discuss later in this chapter (Blanc et al., 2015; Carmassi et al., 2016; Ronan et al., 2015).

Stress in Ancient Times

As shown in these ancient cave drawings, the automatic "fight-or-flight" response was adaptive and necessary for early human survival. However, in modern society, it occurs as a response to ongoing situations where we often cannot fight or flee, and this repeated arousal can be detrimental to our health. (Note that this classic term of "fight or flight" has been expanded and is now called the fight-flight-freeze response.)

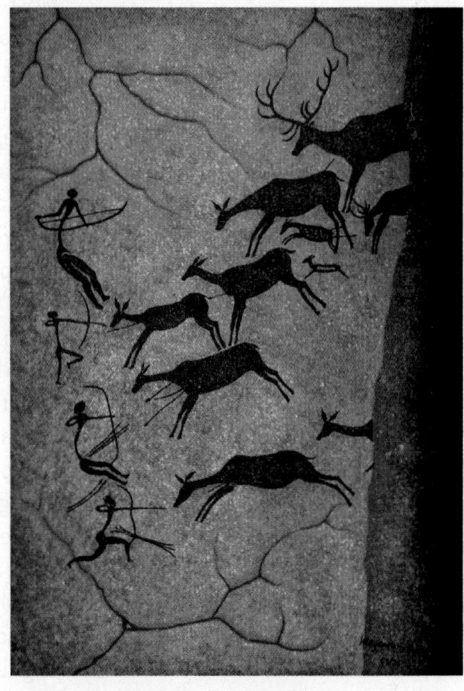

Art Resource

Reactions to Stress

As we've just seen, there are numerous factors that contribute to stress, and while it may strike without warning, it also can be a a chronic, lifelong situation. In this section, we'll take a close look at three ways our human body typically responds to both short- and long-term stress—the GAS, SAM, and HPA systems, changes in the immune system, and alterations in our cognitive functioning.

Stress and the GAS, SAM, and HPA When mentally or physically stressed, our bodies undergo several biological changes that can be detrimental to health. In 1936, Canadian physician Hans Selye (SELL-yay) described a generalized physiological reaction to stress that he called the **general adaptation syndrome (GAS)**. The GAS occurs in three phases—*alarm*, *resistance*, and *exhaustion*—activated by efforts to adapt to any stressor, whether physical or psychological (**Process Diagram 3.1**).

STOP! This Process Diagram contains essential information NOT found elsewhere in the text, which is likely to appear on quizzes and exams. Be sure to study it CAREFULLY!

PROCESS DIAGRAM 3.1 General Adaptation Syndrome (GAS)
The three phases of Selye's syndrome (*alarm, resistance,* and *exhaustion*) focus on the biological response to stress—particularly the "wear and tear" on the body that results from prolonged stress.

1 Alarm phase
When surprised or threatened, your body enters an alarm phase during which your sympathetic nervous system (SNS) is activated (e.g., increased heart rate and blood pressure) and blood is diverted to your skeletal muscles to prepare you for the "fight-flight-freeze" response (Chapter 2).

2 Resistance phase
As the stress continues, your body attempts to resist or adapt to the stressor by summoning all your resources. Physiological arousal remains higher than normal, and there is an outpouring of stress hormones. During this resistance stage, people use a variety of coping methods. For example, if your job is threatened, you may work longer hours and give up your vacation days.

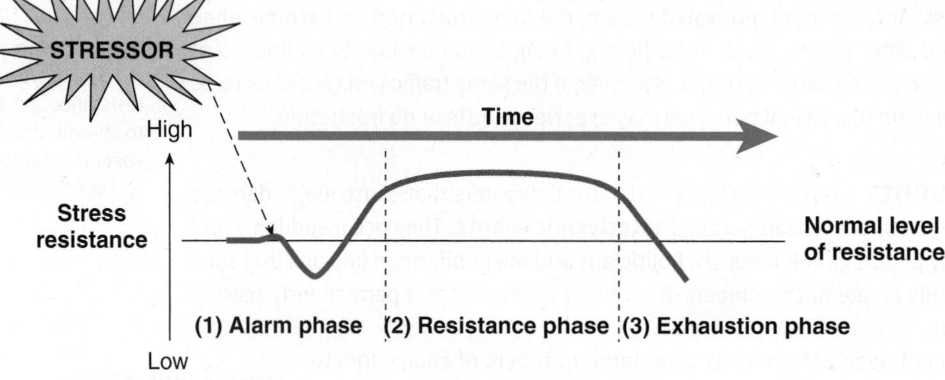

3 Exhaustion phase
Unfortunately, your body's resistance to stress can only last so long before exhaustion sets in. During this final phase, your reserves are depleted and you become more susceptible to serious illnesses, as well as potentially irreversible damage to your body. Selye maintained that one outcome of this exhaustion phase for some people is the development of *diseases of adaptation*, including asthma and high blood pressure. Unless a way of relieving stress is found, the eventual result may be complete collapse and death.

Most of Selye's ideas about the GAS pattern have proven to be correct. For example, studies have found that the primary behavioral response to stress by both men and women is to fight or flee–the classic "fight or flight" response. However, this two option response does not include situations in which we become immobile and "freeze" in the face of stress. Therefore, many researchers have now replaced the previous label of "fight or flight" with a new three option response, called *fight-flight-freeze* (Corr & Cooper, 2016; Friedman, 2015; Maack et al., 2015).

Before going on, it's important to note that different stressors evoke different responses and that people vary widely in their reactions to them. For example, women are more likely to "tend and befriend" (Cardoso et al., 2013; Taylor, 2006, 2012; von Dawans et al., 2012). This means that when under stress women more often take care of themselves and their children (tending), while also forming strong social bonds with others (befriending). Interestingly, other research has found that after being administered oxytocin, the so-called "love hormone" that increases bonding, attachment, and empathy, both men and women participants showed enhanced compassion toward women but not toward men (Palgi et al., 2015). These researchers explain their results by suggesting that the females' "tend and befriend" behaviors may have evolved from a need to help vulnerable individuals of both sexes, rather than being a result of true gender differences.

What is Selye's most important take-home message? *Our bodies are relatively well designed for temporary stress but poorly equipped for prolonged stress.* The same biological processes that are adaptive in the short run, such as the fight-flight-freeze response, can be hazardous in the long run (Papathanasiou et al., 2015; Russell et al., 2014).

To understand these dangers, we need to first describe how our bodies (ideally) respond to stress. As you can see in **Process Diagram 3.2**, once our brains identify a stressor, our **SAM** (sympatho–adreno–medullary) **system** and **HPA** (hypothalamic–pituitary–adrenocortical) **axis** then work together to increase our arousal and energy levels to deal with the stress (Anisman, 2016; Dieleman et al., 2016; Garrett, 2015). Once the stress is resolved, these systems turn off, and our bodies return to normal, baseline functioning, known as **homeostasis**.

Unfortunately, given our increasingly stressful modern lifestyle, our bodies are far too often in a state of elevated, chronic arousal, which can wreak havoc on our health. Some of the most damaging effects of stress are on our immune system and our cognitive functioning.

SAM system Our body's initial, rapid-acting stress response, involving the sympathetic nervous system and the adrenal medulla; called the sympatho–adreno–medullary (SAM) system.

HPA axis Our body's delayed stress response, involving the hypothalamus, pituitary, and adrenal cortex; also called the hypothalamic–pituitary–adrenocortical (HPA) axis.

Homeostasis Our body's tendency to maintain equilibrium, or a steady state of internal balance.

Stress and the Immune System

The discovery of the relationship between stress and our immune system has been very important. When people are under stress, the immune system is less able to regulate the normal inflammation system, which makes us more susceptible to diseases, such as bursitis, colitis, Alzheimer's disease, rheumatoid arthritis, periodontal

STOP! This Process Diagram contains essential information NOT found elsewhere in the text, which is likely to appear on quizzes and exams. Be sure to study it CAREFULLY!

PROCESS DIAGRAM 3.2 The SAM System and HPA Axis—Two Co-Actors in Our Stress Response Faced with stress, our sympathetic nervous system prepares us for immediate action—fight-flight-freeze. Our slower-acting HPA axis maintains our arousal. Here's how it happens:

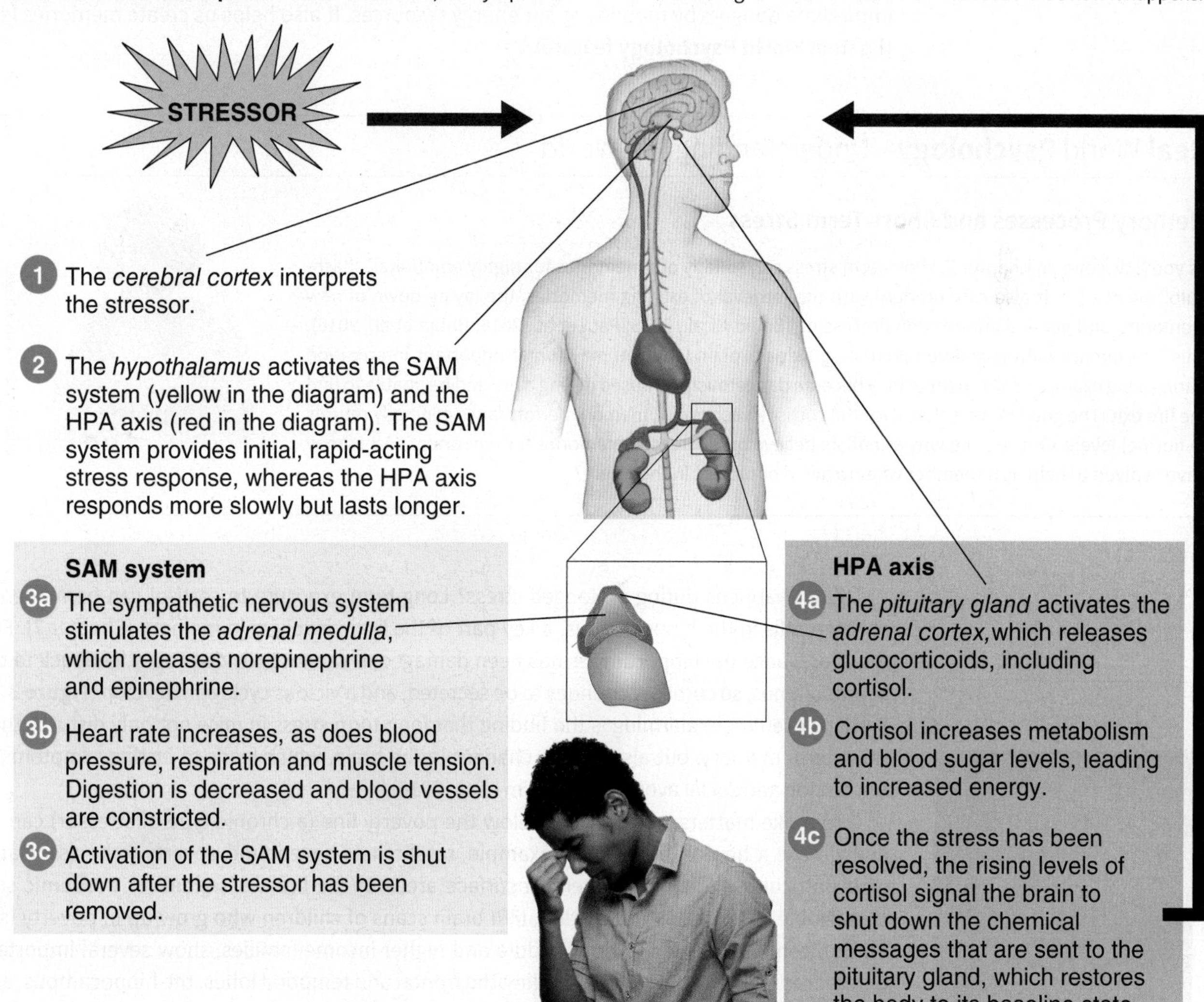

STRESSOR
1 The *cerebral cortex* interprets the stressor.
2 The *hypothalamus* activates the SAM system (yellow in the diagram) and the HPA axis (red in the diagram). The SAM system provides initial, rapid-acting stress response, whereas the HPA axis responds more slowly but lasts longer.
SAM system
3a The sympathetic nervous system stimulates the *adrenal medulla*, which releases norepinephrine and epinephrine.
3b Heart rate increases, as does blood pressure, respiration and muscle tension. Digestion is decreased and blood vessels are constricted.
3c Activation of the SAM system is shut down after the stressor has been removed.
HPA axis
4a The *pituitary gland* activates the *adrenal cortex,* which releases glucocorticoids, including cortisol.
4b Cortisol increases metabolism and blood sugar levels, leading to increased energy.
4c Once the stress has been resolved, the rising levels of cortisol signal the brain to shut down the chemical messages that are sent to the pituitary gland, which restores the body to its baseline state of *homeostasis.*

© aldomurillo/iStockphoto

disease, and even the common cold (Campbell et al., 2015; Cohen et al., 2003, 2012; Sotiropoulos et al., 2015).

Prolonged, excessive, and/or chronic stress also contributes to hypertension, depression, posttraumatic stress disorder (PTSD), drug and alcohol abuse, and even low birth weight (Guardino et al., 2016; Kim et al., 2016; Nicolaides et al., 2015). Severe or prolonged stress can even lead to premature aging and even death (Lohr et al., 2015; Prenderville et al., 2015; Simm & Klotz, 2015).

How does this happen? *Cortisol*, a key element of the HPA axis, plays a critical role in the long-term, negative effects of stress. Although increased cortisol levels initially help us fight stressors, if these levels stay high, which occurs when stress continues over time, the body's disease-fighting immune system is suppressed. For example, one study found that people who are lonely—which is another type of chronic stressor—have an impaired immune response, leaving their bodies vulnerable to infections, allergies, and many of the other illnesses cited above (Jaremka et al., 2013).

Knowledge that psychological factors have considerable control over infectious diseases has upset the long-held assumption in biology and medicine that these diseases are strictly physical. The clinical and theoretical implications are so important that a new interdisciplinary field, called **psychoneuroimmunology**, has emerged. It studies the effects of psychological and other factors on the immune system.

Psychoneuroimmunology The interdisciplinary field that studies the effects of psychological and other factors on the immune system.

Stress and Cognitive Functioning What happens to our brains and thought processes when we're under immediate stress? As we've just seen, cortisol helps us deal with immediate dangers by mobilizing our energy resources. It also helps us create memories (see the **Real World Psychology** feature).

Real World **Psychology**—Understanding the World

Memory Processes and Short-Term Stress

As you'll discover in Chapter 7, short-term stress can solidify our memories for highly emotional, "flashbulb" events. But it also can interfere with the retrieval of existing memories, the laying down of new memories, and general information processing (Banks et al., 2015; Paul et al., 2016; Rubin et al., 2016). This interference with cognitive functioning helps explain why you may forget important information during a big exam, and why people may become dangerously confused during a fire and be unable to find the fire exit. The good news is that once the cortisol washes out, memory performance generally returns to normal levels. Can you see why scientists believe our increased memories for emotional events may have evolved to help us remember what to avoid or protect in the future?

Luis Alvarez/Getty Images

What happens during prolonged stress? Long-term exposure to cortisol can permanently damage cells in the hippocampus, a key part of the brain involved in memory (Chapter 7). Furthermore, once the hippocampus has been damaged, it cannot provide proper feedback to the hypothalamus, so cortisol continues to be secreted, and a vicious cycle can develop (**Figure 3.3**). Perhaps even more alarming is the finding that long-term stress in mice not only disturbs their short-term memory, but also causes changes in the brain, which leads to lasting symptoms of depression and social avoidance (McKim et al., 2016).

John Lund/Stephanie Roeser/GettyImages

To make matters worse, living below the poverty line (a chronic type of stressor) can literally make it harder to learn. For example, researchers have found poverty to be associated with particular differences in certain surface areas of the brain essential for academic success (Noble et al., 2015). In addition, MRI brain scans of children who grow up in poverty (see photo), compared to those from middle and higher-income families, show several important differences in brain structures, including the frontal and temporal lobes, the hippocampus, and overall less gray matter (Hair et al., 2015). These areas of the brain are known to be among the most crucial for academic achievement. [Q2]

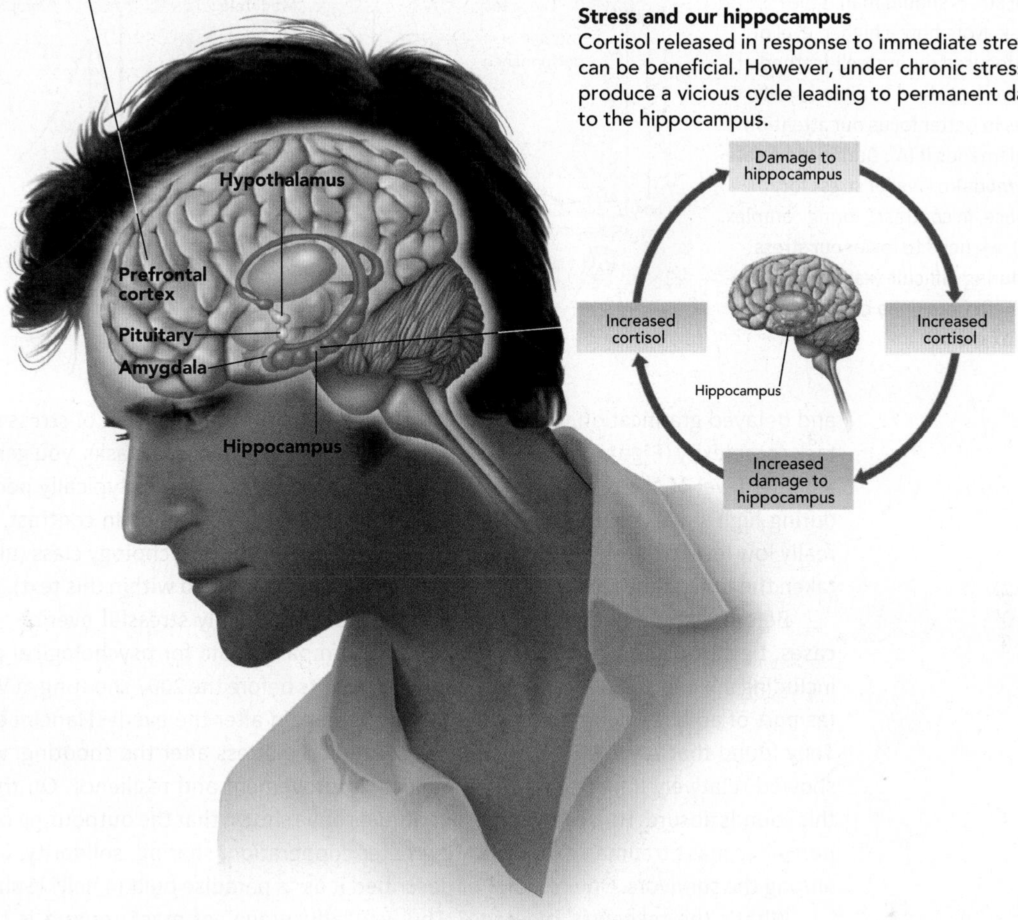
Stress and our prefrontal cortex
Chronic stress results in a reduction in the size of neurons in the prefrontal cortex and a diminished performance during cognitive tasks.
Stress and our hippocampus
Cortisol released in response to immediate stress can be beneficial. However, under chronic stress it can produce a vicious cycle leading to permanent damage to the hippocampus.
Damage to hippocampus
Increased cortisol
Increased damage to hippocampus
Increased cortisol
Hippocampus
Hypothalamus
Prefrontal cortex
Pituitary
Amygdala
Hippocampus

FIGURE 3.3 **Our brain under chronic stress**

Benefits of Stress

So far in our discussion, we've focused primarily on the harmful, negative side of stress, but there are also some positive aspects. Our bodies are nearly always in some state of stress, whether pleasant or unpleasant, mild or severe. *Anything* placing a demand on the body can cause stress. When stress is pleasant or perceived as a manageable challenge, it can be beneficial. As seen in athletes, business tycoons, entertainers, or great leaders, this type of desirable stress, called **eustress**, helps arouse and motivate us to persevere and accomplish challenging goals. Stress that is unpleasant and threatening is called **distress** (Selye, 1974).

Eustress The pleasant, desirable stress that arouses us to persevere and accomplish challenging goals.

Distress The unpleasant, undesirable stress caused by aversive conditions.

Consider large life events like graduating from college, securing a highly desirable job, and/or getting married. Each of these occasions involves enormous changes in our lives and inevitable conflicts, frustration and other sources of stress, yet for most of us they are incredibly positive events. Rather than being the source of discomfort and distress, *eustress* is pleasant and motivating. It encourages us to overcome obstacles and even enjoy the effort and work we expend toward achieving our goals. Physical exercise is an even clearer example of the benefits of eustress. When we're working out at a gym, or even just walking in a park, we're placing some level of stress on our bodies. However, this stress encourages the development and strengthening of all parts of our body, particularly our muscles, heart, lungs, and bones. Exercise also releases endorphins (Chapter 2), which helps lift depression and overall mood.

Keep in mind that all the achievements related to eustress do require considerable effort. As you well know, going through college requires long hours of study, self-discipline,

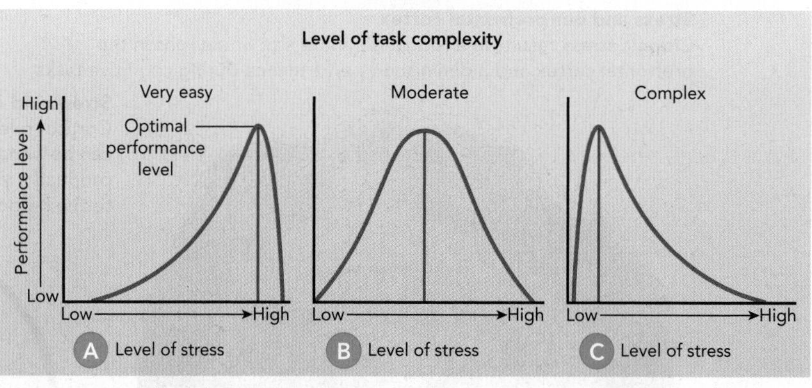

FIGURE 3.4 Stress and task complexity As you can see in this figure, stress can benefit performance. However, the level of stress should match the complexity of the task. Note how a higher level of stress helps keep us focused during well-learned, very easy tasks, but we may need to intentionally raise our stress levels to better focus our attention when the easy task demands it (A). During moderate tasks (B), we need a medium level of stress for maximum performance. In contrast, during complex, demanding tasks (C), we need to lower our stress level. For example, during difficult exams your performance will benefit from deep breathing and other methods of relaxation.

and delayed gratification. Research also shows that your optimal level of stress depends on task complexity (**Figure 3.4**). For example, during well-learned, easy tasks, you generally need a higher level of stress to perform at your best. This is why athletes typically perform better during high stakes competition—when their stress levels are higher. In contrast, you need a really low level of stress during a hard, complex exam in your psychology class (unless you've taken the time to do a lot of practice testing, like those provided within this text).

Before going on, it's important to note that even highly stressful events can, in some cases, be surprisingly beneficial. Researchers compared data for psychological adjustment, including anxiety and depression, in female students before the 2007 shooting at Virginia Tech (as part of an already on-going study), and then again after the event (Mancini et al., 2016). They found that some students suffered continued distress after the shooting, while others showed relatively long-lasting psychological improvement and resilience. On the face of it, this sounds absurd. However, numerous studies have shown that the outpouring of social support after mass traumas can promote greater cooperation, sharing, solidarity, and bonding among the survivors. One researcher described it as "a paradise built in hell" (Solnit, 2009).

What's the takeaway message? The key "advantage" of mass trauma is that it often mobilizes broad-scale public support and cooperative behaviors—as seen in the media and public outpouring of support following the horrific, Orlando, FL massacre in 2016.

Sadly, the opposite is generally true after individual-level traumas, like rape or assault. Can you see then why group therapy is often so helpful for rape and assault survivors (Chapter 13)? Or why we all need to remember to offer strong social support to survivors of both mass and individual traumas—and to actively seek it for ourselves during stressful times?

Retrieval Practice 3.1 | Understanding Stress

SELF-TEST Completing this self-test, and then checking your answers by clicking on the answer button or by looking in Appendix B, will provide immediate feedback and helpful practice for exams.

1. When John saw his girlfriend kissing another man at a party, he became very upset. In this situation, watching someone you love kiss a potential competitor is _____, and becoming upset is _____.

a. a stressor; a biological imperative
b. distressing; a life change event
c. a cataclysmic event; evidence of a burnout
d. a stressor; a stress response

2. In an approach–approach conflict, we must choose between two or more goals that will lead to _____, whereas in an avoidance–avoidance conflict, we must choose between two or more goals that will lead to _____.

a. less conflict; more ambivalence
b. frustration; hostility
c. a desirable result; an undesirable result
d. effective coping; ineffective coping

3. A state of physical, emotional, and mental exhaustion resulting from chronic exposure to high levels of stress, with little personal control is called _____.

a. primary conflict **b.** technostress
c. burnout **d.** secondary conflict

4. As Michael watches his instructor pass out papers, he suddenly realizes that this is the first major exam, and that he is unprepared. Which phase of the GAS is he most likely experiencing?

a. resistance
b. alarm
c. exhaustion
d. phase out

5. Stress that is pleasant and motivates us to accomplish challenging goals _____.

a. can be beneficial
b. is called eustress
c. both a and b
d. none of these options

Think Critically

1. What are the major sources of stress in your life?
2. How does chronic stress threaten our immune system?

Real World Psychology

Does frequent checking of your email and social media increase stress?

Quka/Shutterstock.com

Can the stress of growing up in poverty cause changes in your brain?

John Lund/Stephanie Roeser/Getty Images

HINT: LOOK IN THE MARGIN FOR **[Q1]** AND **[Q2]**

3.2 Stress and Illness

LEARNING OBJECTIVES

Retrieval Practice While reading the upcoming sections, respond to each Learning Objective in your own words.

Review how stress contributes to major illnesses.

- **Explain** how stress affects gastric ulcers.
- **Describe** the role of stress in cancer.
- **Discuss** how the development of cardiovascular disorders is affected by stress.
- **Explain** the role of stress in PTSD, and the methods used to cope with this disorder.

As we've just seen, stress has dramatic effects on our bodies. This section explores how stress is related to four serious illnesses—gastric ulcers, cancer, cardiovascular disorders, and posttraumatic stress disorder (PTSD).

Gastric Ulcers

Gastric ulcers are lesions in the lining of the stomach (and duodenum—the upper section of the small intestine) that can be quite painful. In extreme cases, they may even be life-threatening. Beginning in the 1950s, psychologists reported strong evidence that stress can lead to ulcers. Studies found that people who live in stressful situations have a higher incidence of ulcers than people who don't. And numerous experiments with laboratory animals have shown that stressors, such as shock, water-immersion, or confinement to a very small space, can produce ulcers in a few hours in some laboratory animals (e.g., Landeira-Fernandez, 2015; Shakya et al., 2015; Sun et al., 2016).

The relationship between stress and ulcers seemed well established until researchers identified a bacterium (*Helicobacter pylori*, or *H. pylori*) that appeared to be associated with ulcers. Later studies confirmed that this bacterium clearly damages the stomach wall, and that antibiotic treatment helps many patients. However, approximately 75% of normal, healthy people's stomachs also have the bacterium. This suggests that the bacterium may cause the ulcer, but only in people who are compromised by stress. Furthermore, behavior modification and other psychological treatments, used alongside antibiotics, can help ease ulcers. In other words, although stress *by itself* does not cause ulcers, it is a contributing factor, along with biological factors (Fink, 2011; Lemogne et al., 2015; Southwick & Watson, 2015).

Before going on, note that many believe ulcers are "psychosomatic," and this means they're imaginary. However, a psychosomatic illness refers to a condition in which psychological factors, particularly stress and anxiety, influence the body to aggravate or complicate an

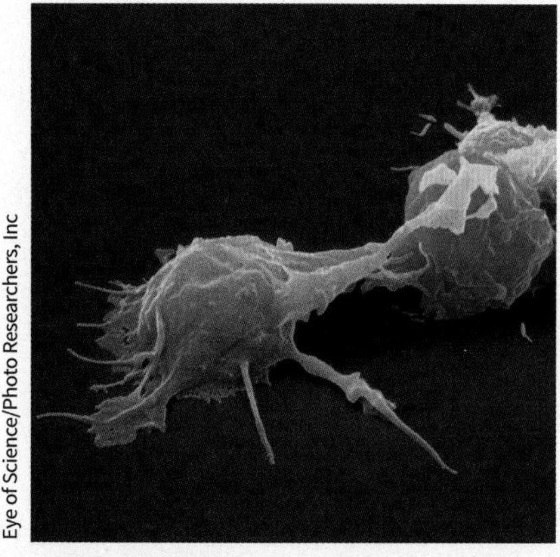

Eye of Science/Photo Researchers, Inc

FIGURE 3.5 The immune system
The actions of a healthy immune system are shown here. The round red structures are leukemia cells. Note how the yellow killer cells are attacking and destroying the cancer cells.

illness (psyche means "mind" and soma means "body"). Most researchers and health practitioners believe that almost all illnesses are partly psychosomatic in this sense.

Cancer

Cancer is among the leading causes of death for adults in the United States. It occurs when a particular type of primitive body cell begins rapidly dividing and then forms a tumor that invades healthy tissue. Unless destroyed or removed, the tumor eventually damages organs and causes death. In a healthy person, whenever cancer cells start to multiply, the immune system checks the uncontrolled growth by attacking the abnormal cells (**Figure 3.5**). More than 100 types of cancer have been identified. They appear to be caused by an interaction between environmental factors (such as diet, smoking, and pollutants) and inherited predispositions.

Note that research does *not* support the popular myths that stress directly *causes* cancer or that positive attitudes can prevent it (Chang et al., 2015; Coyne & Tennen, 2010; Lilienfeld et al., 2010, 2015). However, stress does increase the spread of cancer cells to other organs, including the bones, which decreases the likelihood of survival (Campbell et al., 2012; Klink, 2014).

But this is not to say that developing a positive attitude and reducing our stress levels aren't worthy health goals (Hays, 2014; Quick et al., 2013; Tamagawa et al., 2015). As you read earlier, prolonged stress causes the adrenal glands to release hormones that negatively affect the immune system, and a compromised immune system is less able to resist infection or to fight off cancer cells (Bick et al., 2015; Jung et al., 2015; Kokolus et al., 2014). For example, when researchers disrupted the sleep of 21 healthy people over a period of six weeks, they found increases in blood sugar and decreases in metabolism, which may lead to obesity as well as diabetes (Buxton et al., 2012).

Psychology and You—Understanding Yourself

Stress and Illness

Think about a time when you were experiencing stress, such as studying for a difficult exam, having a fight with a loved one, or struggling to pay your bills. Both minor and major stressors can decrease the effectiveness of your immune system and thereby lead to both short- and long-term health problems. Given the previous discussion of all the ill effects of stress, can you see why it's so important to not only reduce your stress levels but also to improve your personal coping skills?

© Keeweeboy/iStockphoto

Cardiovascular Disorders

Cardiovascular disorders contribute to over half of all deaths in the United States (American Heart Association, 2013). Understandably, health psychologists are concerned because stress is a major contributor to these deaths (Marchant, 2016; Orth-Gomér et al., 2015; Taylor-Clift et al., 2016).

Heart disease is a general term for all disorders that eventually affect the heart muscle and lead to heart failure. *Coronary heart disease* occurs when the walls of the coronary arteries thicken, reducing or blocking the blood supply to the heart. Symptoms of such disease include *angina* (chest pain due to insufficient blood supply to the heart) and *heart attack* (death of heart muscle tissue).

control over a stressful situation. Although you may feel like you have little or no control over exams and other common academic stressors, our students have found that by using the various study tools provided throughout this text and on our text's website, they increased their personal control and success, while also decreasing their stress levels. Do you see how this approach of studying and adopting new study skills would be a good example of *problem-focused coping*?

Many times, however, it seems that little or nothing can be done to alter the stressful situation, so we turn to **emotion-focused coping**, in which we attempt to relieve or regulate our emotional reactions. If you're dealing with the death of a loved one, the pain and stress are out of your control. To cope with your painful emotions, you might try distraction, meditation, journaling, or talking to a friend and/or therapist, which are all healthy forms of *emotion-focused coping*.

Emotion-focused coping The strategies we use to relieve or regulate our emotional reactions to a stressful situation.

Interestingly, when facing uncomfortable and/or painful stressors, Freud believed we commonly turn to another type of cognitive appraisal and response, known as **defense mechanisms**, in which we unconsciously distort reality to protect our egos and to avoid anxiety (see Chapter 11). These defense mechanisms can sometimes act as a beneficial type of emotion-focused coping. For example, when you're really angry at your boss and realize that you can't safely express that anger, you may take out your frustration by aggressively hitting a punching bag at the gym. This would be a healthy use of defense mechanisms. But if taken too far they can be destructive. If we fail to get the promotion, and then resort to elaborate excuses (rationalizations) for our failure, it may block us from seeing a situation more clearly and realistically, which in turn can prevent us from developing valuable skills. In short, occasional use of defense mechanisms can be beneficial, as long as it's not excessive and does not distort reality (Hertel et al., 2015; Levine, 2015).

Defense mechanisms Freud's term for the strategies the ego uses to reduce anxiety by unconsciously distorting reality.

Keep in mind that emotion-focused forms of coping can't change the problem, but they do make us feel better about the stressful situation (see photo). For example, teenagers who are asked to think about the "silver lining" benefits of a recent stressful event—such as hav-
[Q4] ing a traffic accident or losing a valued relationship—show increases in positive mood and decreases in negative mood (Rood et al., 2012). Interestingly, instant messaging (IM) also helps distressed teenagers share their emotions, and receive immediate social support and advice (Dolev-Cohen & Barak, 2013).

© londoneye/iStockphoto

Personality and Individual Differences

We've just seen how problem- and emotion-focused coping, as well as defense mechanisms, are used in stress management. Research has also found that various personality types and individual differences directly affect how we cope with stress. In this section, we discuss the various effects of *locus of control, positive affect,* and *optimism*.

Locus of Control Perhaps one of the most important personal resources for stress management is a sense of personal control. People who believe they are the "masters of their own destiny" have what is known as an **internal locus of control**. Believing they control their own fate, they tend to make more effective decisions and healthier lifestyle choices, are more likely to follow treatment programs, and more often find ways to positively cope with a situation.

Internal locus of control The belief that we control our own fate.

Conversely, people with an **external locus of control** believe that chance or outside forces beyond their control determine their fate. Therefore, they tend to feel powerless to change their circumstances, are less likely to make effective and positive changes, and are more likely to experience high levels of stress (e.g., Au, 2015; Rotter, 1966; Zhang et al., 2014).

External locus of control The belief that chance or outside forces beyond our control determine our fate.

Positive Affect Have you ever wondered why some people survive in the face of great stress (personal tragedies, demanding jobs, or an abusive home life) while others do not? One answer may be that these "survivors" have a unique trait called **positive affect**, meaning they experience and express positive emotions, including feelings of happiness, joy, enthusiasm,

Positive affect The experience or expression of positive feelings (affect), including happiness, joy, enthusiasm, and contentment.

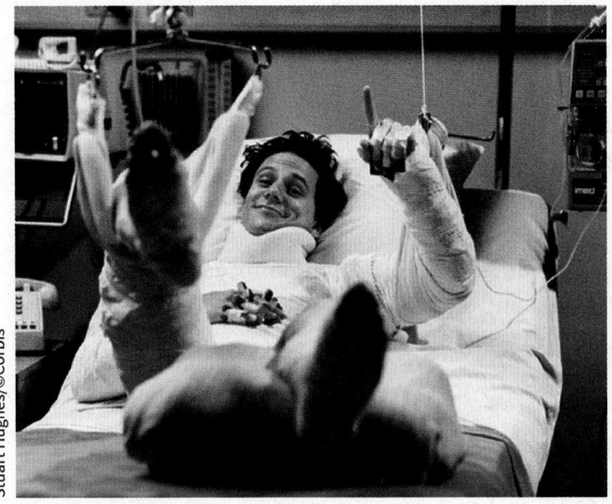

Stuart Hughes/©Corbis

FIGURE 3.7 Positive affect in action Based on his smile and cheery wave, it looks like this patient may be one of those lucky people with a naturally positive outlook on life. Can you see how this approach might help him cope and recuperate from his serious injuries?

and contentment. Interestingly, people who are high in positive affect also experience fewer colds and auto accidents, as well as better sleep, and an enhanced quality of life (Anisman, 2016; Pollock et al., 2016; Tavernier et al., 2016).

Positive states are also sometimes associated with longer life expectancy. One study of 600 patients with heart disease found that those with more positive attitudes were less likely to die during a five-year follow-up period (Hoogwegt et al., 2013). More specifically, only 9% of those with positive attitudes died five years later, compared to 16.5% of those with less positive attitudes. This study provides intriguing evidence for the mind-body link. Positive affect is also associated with a lower risk of mortality in patients with diabetes, which is a leading cause of death in the United States (Cohn et al., 2014; Moskowitz et al., 2008).

Can you see how having a positive affect is closely associated with a good sense of humor? Humor is one of the best methods you can use to reduce stress. The ability to laugh at oneself and at life's inevitable ups and downs allows us to relax and gain a broader perspective (**Figure 3.7**).

Optimism A tendency to expect the best and to see the best in all things.

Optimism Positive affect is also closely associated with **optimism**, the expectation that good things will happen in the future and bad things will not. If you agree with statements such as, "I tend to expect the best of others," or "I generally think of several ways to get out of a difficult situation," you're probably an optimist. The opposite is true if you tend to be a pessimist.

As you might expect, optimists are generally much better at stress management. Rather than seeing bad times as a constant threat and assuming personal responsibility for them, they generally assume that bad times are temporary and external to themselves. Optimists also tend to have better overall physical and psychological health, and typically have longer and overall happier lives (Denovan & Macaskill, 2016; Hernandez et al., 2015; Seligman, 2011). See the **Real World Psychology** feature.

Real World **Psychology**—Understanding the World

Why are Optimists Healthier?

To test this question, researchers in one study tracked 135 older adults (aged 60+) over six years (Jobin et al., 2014). Participants were asked about the level of stress they perceived in their day-to-day lives, and whether they would rate themselves as optimists or pessimists. Saliva samples were then collected from each individual to measure his or her current level of cortisol. Interestingly, the results revealed that compared to self-described optimists, people who described themselves as pessimists had higher cortisol levels, a higher baseline level of stress, and more difficulty coping with it.

Can you see why optimists tend to experience better overall health? Their lower cortisol levels and better coping strategies reduce the "wear-and-tear" of the biological effects of stress on their bodies.

© londoneye/iStockphoto

The good news is that according to Martin Seligman, a leader in the field of positive psychology, optimism can be learned (Seligman, 2012). In short, he believes optimism requires careful monitoring and challenging of our thoughts, feelings, and self-talk. For example, if you don't get a promotion at work or you receive a low grade on an exam, don't focus on all the negative possible outcomes and unreasonably blame yourself. Instead, force yourself to think of alternate ways to meet your goals and develop specific plans to improve your performance. Chapter 13 offers additional help and details for overcoming faulty thought processes.

Resources for Healthy Living

As we've just seen, various cognitive appraisal techniques and personality and individual differences have significant effects on our stress management. In this section, we'll provide specific, evidence-based resources for stress management. Perhaps the most researched approach comes from the recent **mindfulness-based stress reduction (MBSR)** programs, which are based on developing a state of consciousness that attends to ongoing events in a receptive, non-judgmental way. The practice of MBSR has proven to be particularly effective in managing stress and treating mood disturbances, and it's even been linked to positive, and perhaps permanent cell and brain changes (Creswell et al., 2016; Felleman et al., 2016; Mallya & Fiocco, 2016). Did you know that mindfulness training can also improve your grades? See **PositivePsych** below.

Mindfulness-based stress reduction (MBSR) A stress reduction strategy based on developing a state of consciousness that attends to ongoing events in a receptive and non-judgmental way.

PP PositivePsych

Mindfulness and Your GPA

Researchers interested in the potential usefulness of mindfulness training in academic settings assigned students either to a 7 week mental training program designed to tame the mind wandering and increase focus, or to a control group that received no training (Morrison et al., 2013). Students in the two groups did not differ at the start of the semester on levels of attention and mind wandering (two factors that lead to lower academic performance). However, by the end of the semester, people in the control group showed diminished attention and increased mind wandering. In contrast, those who participated in the mindfulness program showed significant improvements in attention and no increases in reported mind wandering.

David Malan/Getty Images

Related studies with college students who engage in mindfulness-based stress reduction (MBSR) programs show improvements in reading comprehension and working memory capacity, as well as overall better adjustment to the college environment (Mrazek et al., 2013; Ramler et al., 2016). For younger children, a school-based mindfulness program, which includes breathing and movement exercises, helps many elementary school children better manage their stress, and become more optimistic, helpful, caring, better liked by peers, and even better at math (Schonert-Reichl et al., 2015).

Another effective and frequently overlooked resource for stress management is *social support*. When we are faced with stressful circumstances, our friends and family often help us take care of our health, listen, hold our hands, make us feel important, and provide stability to offset the changes in our lives.

This support can help offset the stressful effects of chronic illness, pregnancy, physical abuse, job loss, and work overload. People who have greater social support also experience better health outcomes, including greater psychological well-being, greater physical well-being, faster recovery from illness, and a longer life expectancy (Cherry et al., 2015; Diener & Tay, 2015; Martínez-Hernáez et al., 2016). Even a single close childhood friendship seems to protect children in lower socioeconomic circumstances (which is an ongoing stressor) from several negative psychological risk factors (Graber et al., 2015).

These findings may help explain why married people live longer than unmarried people (Liu, 2009), and why a married person with cancer is 20% less likely to die from the disease than an unmarried person (Aizer et al., 2013). So what is the important take-home message from this emphasis on social support? Don't be afraid to offer help and support to others—or to ask for the same for yourself!

Six additional resources for healthy living and stress management are exercise, social skills, behavior change, stressor control, material resources, and relaxation. These resources are summarized in **Table 3.4**.

TABLE 3.4 Six Additional Stress Resources

Exercise	Exercising and keeping fit help minimize anxiety and depression, which are associated with stress. Exercise also helps relieve muscle tension; improves cardiovascular efficiency; and increases strength, flexibility, and stamina. *Those who do not find time for exercise will have to find time for illness.* —Edward Smith-Stanley	 © Rich Vintage/iStockphoto
Social skills	People who acquire social skills (such as knowing appropriate behaviors for certain situations, having conversation starters up their sleeves, and expressing themselves well) suffer less anxiety than people who do not. Social skills not only help us interact with others but also communicate our needs and desires, enlist help when we need it, and decrease hostility in tense situations.	 © Henk Badenhorst/iStockphoto/
Behavior change	When under stress, do you smoke, drink, overeat, zone out in front of the TV or computer, sleep too much, procrastinate, or take your stress out on others? If so, substitute these activities with healthier choices.	 © Hill Street Studios/BlendImages/Corbis
Stressor control	While not all stress can be eliminated, it helps to recognize and avoid unnecessary stress by: analyzing your schedule and removing nonessential tasks, and controlling your environment by avoiding people and topics that stress you. It also helps to find a less stressful job, and to give yourself permission to say "no" to extra tasks and responsibilities.	 © PK-Photos/iStockphoto
Material resources	Money increases the number of options available for eliminating sources of stress or reducing the effects of stress. When faced with the minor hassles of everyday living, acute or chronic stressors, or major catastrophes, people with more money, and the skills to effectively use it generally fare better. They experience less overall stress, and can "buy" more resources to help them cope with what stressors they do have.	 © Juanmonino/iStockphoto/
Relaxation	There are a variety of relaxation techniques. *Biofeedback* is often used in the treatment of chronic pain, but it is also useful in teaching people to relax and manage their stress. *Progressive relaxation* helps reduce or relieve the muscular tension commonly associated with stress (see the following **Psychology and You** feature).	 Dynamic GraphicsValue/SUPERSTOCK

Psychology and You—Understanding Yourself

Practicing Progressive Relaxation

You can use progressive relaxation techniques anytime and anywhere you feel stressed, such as before or during an exam. Here's how:

1. Sit in a comfortable position, with your head supported.
2. Start breathing slowly and deeply.
3. Let your entire body relax. Release all tension. Try to visualize your body getting progressively more relaxed with each breath.
4. Systematically tense and release each part of your body, beginning with your toes. Curl them tightly while counting to 10. Now, release them. Note the difference between the tense and relaxed states. Next, tense your feet to the count of 10. Then relax them and feel the difference. Continue upward with your calves, thighs, buttocks, abdomen, back muscles, shoulders, upper arms, forearms, hands and fingers, neck, jaw, facial muscles, and forehead. Try practicing progressive relaxation twice a day for about 15 minutes each time. You will be surprised at how quickly you can learn to relax—even in the most stressful situations.

Retrieval Practice 3.3 | Stress Management

SELF-TEST Completing this self-test, and then checking your answers by clicking on the answer button or by looking in Appendix B, will provide immediate feedback and helpful practice for exams.

1. Emotion-focused forms of coping are based on relieving or regulating our _____ when faced with stressful situations.
   a. feelings **b.** behavior
   c. thoughts **d.** all these options
2. Freud's term for the strategies the ego uses to reduce anxiety by unconsciously distorting reality is known as _____.
   a. "rose-colored glasses" syndrome
   b. defense mannerisms
   c. ego-denial apparatus
   d. defense mechanisms
3. Research suggests that people with a(n) _____ have less psychological stress than those with a _____.
   a. external locus of control; internal locus of control
   b. internal locus of control; external locus of control
   c. attributional coping style; person-centered coping style
   d. none of these options
4. Demonstrating positive emotions, including feelings of happiness, joy, enthusiasm, and contentment is known as _____.
   a. positive defect
   b. the positivity principle
   c. the Rogerian technique
   d. positive affect
5. Which of the following is *not* one of the ways to cope with stress outlined in the chapter?
   a. exercise **b.** sense of humor
   c. social support **d.** stimulant drugs

Think Critically

1. Do you generally prefer an emotion-focused style of coping or a problem-focused style of coping when faced with a stressful situation? Why?
2. Which of the various personality styles discussed in this section best describes you? How could you use this information to improve your stress management.

Real World **Psychology**

Could thinking about the "silver linings" of a stressful event, or sharing it with others, reduce depression?

© londoneye/iStockphoto

HINT: LOOK IN THE MARGIN FOR **[Q4]**

3.4 Health Psychology

LEARNING OBJECTIVES

Retrieval Practice While reading the upcoming sections, respond to each Learning Objective in your own words.

Summarize the field of health psychology, and the role of stress in health psychology.

- **Identify** health psychology.
- **Describe** the work of health psychologists.
- **Discuss** how health psychology can be used in the workplace.

Health psychology is the branch of psychology that studies how biological, psychological, and social factors influence health, illness, and health-related behaviors. It emphasizes wellness and the prevention of illness, as well as the interplay between our physical health and our psychological well-being. As mentioned earlier in this chapter, ulcers, cancer, cardiovascular disorders, and PTSD significantly affect our physical well-being, as well as our cognitive, emotional, and behavioral responses. In this final section, we'll discuss the work of health psychologists, followed by an exploration of stress in the workplace.

Health psychology A subfield of psychology that studies how people stay healthy, why they become ill, and how they respond when they become ill.

What Does a Health Psychologist Do?

As researchers, health psychologists are particularly interested in how changes in behavior can improve health outcomes (Anisman, 2016; Straub, 2014). They also emphasize the relationship between stress and the immune system. As we discovered earlier, a normally functioning immune system helps defend against disease. On the other hand, a suppressed immune system leaves the body susceptible to a number of illnesses.

As practitioners, health psychologists can work as independent clinicians or as consultants alongside physicians, physical and occupational therapists, and other health care workers. The goal of health psychologists is to reduce psychological distress and unhealthy behaviors. They also help patients and families make critical decisions and prepare psychologically for surgery or other treatment. Health psychologists have become so involved with health and illness that medical centers are one of their major employers (Considering a Career, 2011).

Health psychologists also educate the public about illness *prevention* and health *maintenance*. For example, they provide public information about the effects of stress, smoking, alcohol, lack of exercise, and other health issues. Tobacco use endangers both smokers and those who breathe secondhand smoke, so it's not surprising that health psychologists are concerned with preventing smoking and getting those who already smoke to stop.

Did you know that according to the U.S. Department of Health and Human Services, smoking has killed 10 times the number of Americans who died in all our nation's wars combined (Sebelius, 2014)? Thanks in large part to comprehensive mass media campaigns, smoke-free policies, restrictions on underage access to tobacco, and large price increases, adult smoking rates have fallen from about 43% in 1965 to about 18% in 2014. Unfortunately, cigarette smoking remains as the leading cause of preventable death worldwide (Centers for Disease Control, 2016).

Given that almost everyone recognizes the serious consequences of smoking, and the fact that the first puff is rarely pleasant, why do people start smoking? The answer can be found in the biopsychosocial model and the biology of addiction (**Figure 3.8**). In addition to encouraging smokers to stop, or to never start, health psychologists also help people cope with conditions such as chronic pain, diabetes, and high blood pressure, as well as unhealthful behaviors such as inappropriate anger and/or lack of assertiveness. If you're interested in a career in this field, check with your college's counseling or career center.

FIGURE 3.8 **Understanding nicotine addiction**

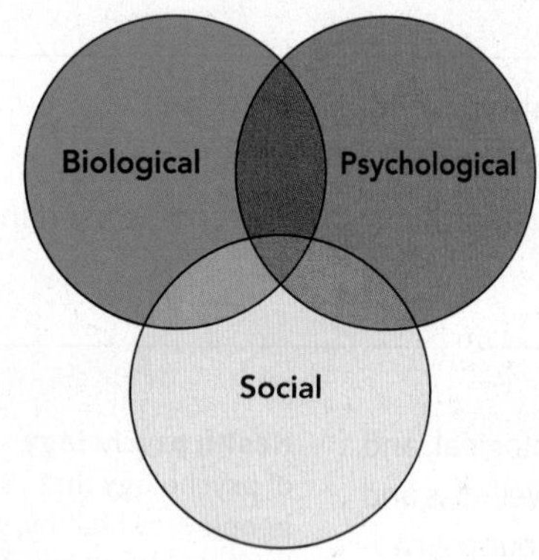

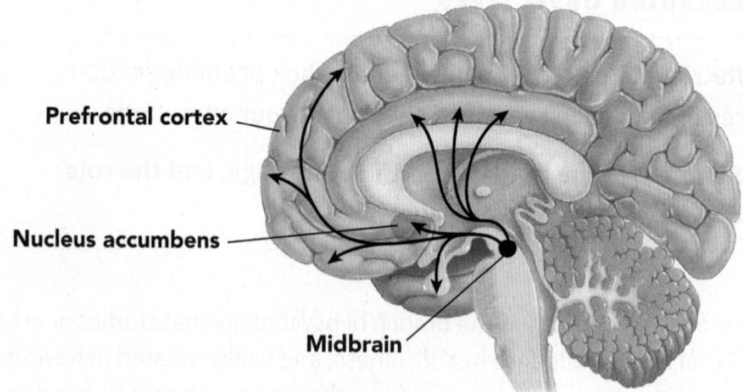

a. The biopsychosocial model of addiction

As you'll see throughout this text, the biopsychosocial model helps explain almost all human behavior, including nicotine addiction. From a psychological and social perspective, smokers learn to associate smoking with pleasant things, such as good food, friends, and sex. People also form such associations from seeing smoking in the movies, which is one reason researchers believe that requiring all movies with characters who smoke to be rated R would reduce smoking in teenagers by 20% (Sargent et al., 2012). From a biological perspective, nicotine is highly addictive. Once a person begins to smoke, there is a biological need to continue—as explained in part b of this figure.

b. The biology of addiction

Nicotine addiction appears to be very similar to heroin, cocaine, and alcohol addiction, and all four drugs are commonly associated with depression (Müller & Homberg, 2015; Torrens & Rossi, 2015; Wu et al., 2014). To make matters worse, nicotine quickly increases the release of acetylcholine and norepinephrine in our brains, increasing alertness, concentration, memory, and feelings of pleasure. Nicotine also stimulates the release of dopamine, the neurotransmitter most closely related to our brains' reward centers (shown in the figure above). This so-called "pleasure pathway" extends from an area in the midbrain, to the nucleus accumbens, and on to other subcortical structures and the prefrontal cortex.

Health Psychology at Work

Have you ever dragged yourself home from work so tired you feared you couldn't make it to your bed? Do you think your job may be killing you? You may be right! Some research suggests that job stress and overwork (see photo) can greatly increase your risk of dying from heart disease and stroke (Biering et al., 2015; Charles et al., 2014; Huang et al., 2015). In fact, a large, meta-[Q5] analysis of the correlation between job strain and coronary heart disease found that people with stressful jobs are 23% more likely to experience a heart attack than those without stressful jobs (Kivimäki et al., 2012). And the Japanese even have a specific word for this type of extreme job stress, "karoshi" [KAH-roe-she], which is translated literally as "death from overwork."

Caiaimage/Paul Bradbury/Getty Images

Intense job stressors reportedly not only increase the risk for potentially lethal physical and psychological problems, but they also leave some workers disoriented and suffering from serious stress even when they're not working (Calderwood & Ackerman, 2016; Tayama et al., 2016; Tetrick & Peiro, 2016). Stress at work can also cause serious stress at home, not only for the worker but for other family members as well. Unfortunately, in our global economy, pressures to reduce costs and to increase productivity will undoubtedly continue, and job stress may prove to be a serious and growing health risk. These risks even apply to our world's top leaders (see **PsychScience**).

PS PsychScience

When Losers Actually Win

Alex Wong/Getty Images

Can a high pressure job actually take years off your life? To test this question, researchers in one study examined life expectancy on candidates for head of country elections—meaning president or prime minister—in a number of different countries (Olenski et al., 2015). Specifically, the researchers gathered data on the number of years each candidate lived after their final campaign for office. They then compared whether candidates who won the election—and thus served as head of country—had fewer years of life than those who lost the election—and thus didn't serve in this capacity. The researchers gathered data from 17 different countries (including the United States, Australia, the United Kingdom, and Canada) over nearly 300 years (from 1722 to 2015).

As they predicted, winning an election was actually bad for your health. Candidates who lost the election lived an average of an additional 17.8 years, whereas those who won lived only an average of an additional 13.4 years. In this case, it actually hurts to win—the winning candidate lost an additional 4.4 years of life! Although this data doesn't explain exactly how winning an election led to a shorter life expectancy, researchers believe that the greater stress experienced by heads of country likely helps explain this difference.

Research Challenge

1. Based on the information provided, did this study (Olenski et al., 2015) use descriptive, correlational, and/or experimental research?
2. If you chose:
   - *descriptive research,* is this a naturalistic observation, survey/interview, case study, and/or archival research?
   - *correlational research,* is this a positive, negative, or zero correlation?
   - *experimental research,* label the IV, DV, experimental group(s), and control group.
   - both *descriptive* and *correlational,* answer the corresponding questions for both.

Check your answers by clicking on the answer button or by looking in Appendix B.

Note: The information provided in this study is admittedly limited, but the level of detail is similar to what is presented in most textbooks and public reports of research findings. Answering these questions, and then comparing your answers to those provided, will help you become a better critical thinker and consumer of scientific research.

Technostress If you're not suffering from overwork, are you hassled and stressed by the ever-changing technology at your workplace? Do the expensive machines your employers install to "aid productivity" create stress-related problems instead? Does technology in your home allow you to accomplish several things simultaneously—talking on your cell phone, checking and responding to emails, warming your dinner in the microwave, doing a load of laundry—yet you end up feeling irritable and exhausted? If so, you may be suffering from the well-documented, ill-effects of **technostress**, a feeling of anxiety or mental pressure from overexposure or involvement with technology (Joo et al., 2016; Maier et al., 2015; Tarafdar et al., 2015). Although technology is often described as a way of bringing people together, how often have

Technostress A feeling of anxiety or mental pressure from overexposure or involvement with technology; stress caused by an Inability to cope with modern technology.

you noticed busy executives frantically checking their e-mail while on vacation? It's even common to see families eating dinners at restaurants with their children playing video games or text messaging, and the parents loudly talking on separate cell phones. In fact, simply placing a cell phone on the table between two people—even if no one ever picks it up—leads to lower levels of closeness, connection, and meaning in their conversation (Przybylski & Weinstein, 2013).

Coping with Job and Technostress Experts are suggesting that we can (and must) control technology and its impact on our lives. Admittedly, we all find the new technologies convenient and useful. But how can we control technostress? First, evaluate each new technology on its usefulness for you and your lifestyle. It isn't a yes or no, "technophobe" or "technophile," choice. If something works for you, invest the energy to adopt it. Second, establish clear boundaries. Technology came into the world with an implied promise of a better and more productive life. But, for many, the servant has become the master. Like any healthy relationship, our technology interactions should be based on moderation and balance (Ashton, 2013).

In addition to evaluating technology on its personal usefulness and establishing clear boundaries, you can score your past, current, and potential future careers on several additional factors in job-related stress (see **Psychology and You**).

Psychology and You—Understanding Yourself

Workplace Stress

Start by identifying what you like and don't like about your current (and past) jobs. With this information in hand, you'll be prepared to find jobs that will better suit your interests, needs, and abilities, which will likely reduce your stress. To start your analysis, answer *Yes* or *No* to these questions:

1. Is there a sufficient amount of laughter and sociability in my workplace?
2. Does my boss notice and appreciate my work?
3. Is my boss understanding and friendly?
4. Am I embarrassed by the physical conditions of my workplace?
5. Do I feel safe and comfortable in my place of work?
6. Do I like the location of my job?
7. If I won the lottery and were guaranteed a lifetime income, would I feel truly sad if I also had to quit my job?
8. Do I watch the clock, daydream, take long lunches, and leave work as soon as possible?
9. Do I frequently feel stressed and overwhelmed by the demands of my job?
10. Compared to others with my qualifications, am I being paid what I am worth?
11. Are promotions made in a fair and just manner where I work?
12. Given the demands of my job, am I fairly compensated for my work?

Now score your answers. Give yourself one point for each answer that matches the following: 1. No; 2. No; 3. No; 4. Yes; 5. No; 6. No; 7. No; 8. Yes; 9. Yes; 10. No; 11. No; 12. No.

The questions you just answered in the *Psychology and You* are based on four factors that research shows are conducive to increased job satisfaction and reduced stress: supportive colleagues, supportive working conditions, mentally challenging work, and equitable rewards (Robbins, 1996). Your total score reveals your overall level of dissatisfaction. A look at specific questions can help identify which of these four factors is most important to your job satisfaction—and most lacking in your current job.

1. **Supportive colleagues (items 1, 2, 3):** For most people, work fills important social needs. Therefore, having friendly and supportive colleagues and superiors leads to increased satisfaction.
2. **Supportive working conditions (items 4, 5, 6):** Not surprisingly, most employees prefer working in safe, clean, and relatively modern facilities. They also prefer jobs close to home.
3. **Mentally challenging work (items 7, 8, 9):** Jobs with too little challenge create boredom and apathy, whereas too much challenge creates frustration and feelings of failure.
4. **Equitable rewards (items 10, 11, 12):** Employees want pay and promotions based on job demands, individual skill levels, and community pay standards.

Retrieval Practice 3.4 | Health Psychology

SELF-TEST Completing this self-test and comparing your answers with those in Appendix B provides immediate feedback and helpful practice for exams.

1. Which of the following is *true* of health psychology?

a. It studies the relationship between psychological well-being and physical health.
b. It studies the relationship between social factors and illness.
c. It emphasizes wellness and the prevention of illness.
d. All these statements are true.

2. According to the U.S. Department of Health and Human Services, _____ has killed 10 times the number of Americans who died in all our nation's wars combined.

a. cigarette smoking **b.** lack of exercise
c. overeating **d.** heart disease

3. An increase in acetylcholine and norepinephrine is associated with _____.

a. nicotine use **b.** any alcohol consumption
c. binge drinking **d.** stress

4. Once you begin smoking, you continue because _____.

a. nicotine is addictive
b. it increases alertness
c. it stimulates the release of dopamine
d. all of these options

5. Technostress can be defined as _____.

a. a feeling of euphoria from exposure or involvement with technology
b. anxiety or mental pressure from overexposure to loud "techno" style music.
c. stress caused by an inability to cope with modern technology.
d. none of these options

Think Critically

1. Why is it so difficult for people to quit smoking?

2. Would you like to be a health psychologist? Why or why not?

Real World Psychology

Are people with stressful jobs at increased risk of experiencing a heart attack?

Caiaimage/Paul Bradbury/ Getty Images

HINT: LOOK IN THE MARGIN FOR **[Q5]**

Summary

3.1 Understanding Stress 63

• **Stress** is the interpretation of specific events, called **stressors**, as threatening or challenging.

• The seven major sources of stress are life changes, acute/chronic stressors, job stressors, conflict, hassles, frustration, and cataclysmic events. *Life changes* require adjustment in our behaviors that cause stress. **Acute stressors** refer to a short-term state of arousal in response to a perceived threat or challenge. **Chronic stressors** produce a state of continuous physiological arousal, in which demands are perceived as greater than available coping resources. Work related **Job stressors** include role conflict and/or role ambiguity. **Conflicts** are forced choices between two or more competing goals or impulses. They are often classified as **approach-approach, avoidance-avoidance,** or **approach-avoidance. Hassles** are little everyday life problems that pile up to cause major stress, and possible **burnout. Frustration** refers to blocked goals. **Cataclysmic events** are disasters that occur suddenly and generally affect many people simultaneously.

• Hans Selye's **general adaptation syndrome (GAS)** describes our body's three-stage reaction to stress: the initial alarm reaction, the resistance phase, and the exhaustion phase (if resistance to stress is not successful). If stress is resolved, our bodies return to normal, baseline functioning, called **homeostasis.**

• The **SAM system** and the **HPA axis** control significant physiological responses to stress. The SAM system prepares us for immediate action; the HPA axis responds more slowly but lasts longer.

• Prolonged stress suppresses the immune system, which increases the risk for many diseases (e.g., colds, colitis, cancer). The new field of **psychoneuroimmunology** studies the effects of psychological and other factors on the immune system.

• During acute stress, cortisol can prevent the retrieval of existing memories, as well as the laying down of new memories and general information processing. Under prolonged stress, cortisol car permanently damage the hippocampus, a key part of the brain involved in memory.

• Our bodies are nearly always under stress, some of which has beneficial effects. **Eustress** is pleasant, desirable stress, whereas **distress** is unpleasant, undesirable stress.

3.2 Stress and Illness 73

• Scientists once believed that stress, or the H. pylori bacterium, acting alone, could cause gastric ulcers. Current psychological research shows that biopsychosocial factors, including stress, interact to increase our vulnerability to the bacterium which may then lead to gastric ulcers.

• Cancer appears to result from an interaction of heredity, environmental insults (such as smoking), and immune system deficiencies. Although stress is linked to a decreased immunity, research does *not* show that it *causes* cancer, or that a positive attitude alone will prevent it.

• Increased stress hormones can cause fat to adhere to blood vessel walls, increasing the risk of cardiovascular disorders, including heart attacks.

• Exposure to extraordinary stress can cause **posttraumatic stress disorder (PTSD)**, a type of trauma- and stressor-related disorder characterized by the persistent re-experiencing of traumatic events, which resulted from directly or indirectly experiencing actual or threatened death, serious injury, or violence.

3.3 Stress Management 77

• When facing a stressor, we generally begin with a three step cognitive appraisal: (Step 1) **primary appraisal** (deciding if a situation is harmless or potentially harmful) and (Step 2) **secondary appraisal** (assessing our resources and choosing a coping method). (Step 3) We then tend to choose either **emotion-focused coping** (managing emotional reactions to a stressor) or **problem-focused coping** (dealing directly with the stressor to decrease or eliminate it). People often combine problem-focused and emotion-focused coping strategies to resolve complex stressors or to respond to a stressful situation that is in flux.

• Freud also proposed that we commonly cope with stress with **defense mechanisms**, which are strategies the ego uses to protect itself from anxiety, but they often distort reality and may increase self-deception.

• Personality and individual differences also affect stress management. Having an **internal locus of control** (believing that we control our own fate), as opposed to having an **external locus of control** (believing that chance or outside forces beyond our control determine our fate) are all effective personal strategies for stress management. People with a **positive affect** and **optimism** tend to deal better with stress.

• **Mindfulness-based stress reduction (MBSR)** and social support are two important keys to stress management. Six additional resources include exercise, social skills, behavior change, stressor control, material resources, and relaxation.

3.4 Health Psychology 83

• **Health psychology** is a branch of psychology that studies how biological, psychological, and social factors influence health, illness, and health-related behaviors.

• Health psychologists focus on how changes in behavior can improve health outcomes. They often work as independent clinicians, or as consultants to other health practitioners, to educate the public about illness prevention and health maintenance.

• Health psychologists also study job stress and how to reduce it.

Applying **Real** World **Psychology**—Understanding the World

We began this chapter with five intriguing Real World Psychology questions, and you were asked to revisit these questions at the end of each section. Questions like these have an important and lasting impact on all of our lives. See if you can answer these additional critical thinking questions related to real world examples.

1. Are you more of an internal or external locus of control type of person? What are the advantages and disadvantages to each type?
2. How might the child in this photo be affected biologically, psychologically, and socially (the biopsychosocial model) by her mother's drinking?
3. What could a health psychologist do to improve the well-being of the mother and child in this photo?

Dennis MacDonald/PhotoEdit

4. Health psychologists often advise us to make lifestyle changes to improve our health and longevity. Do you think this is important? If so, what do you plan to change in your own life?

Key Terms

Retrieval Practice Write your own definition for each term before turning back to the referenced page to check your answer.

- acute stress 64
- approach–approach conflict 66
- approach–avoidance conflict 66
- avoidance–avoidance conflict 66
- burnout 67
- cataclysmic event 67
- chronic stress 65
- conflict 66
- defense mechanisms 79
- distress 71
- emotion-focused coping 79
- eustress 71
- external locus of control 79
- frustration 67
- general adaptation syndrome (GAS) 67
- hassle 67
- health psychology 83
- homeostasis 69
- HPA axis 69
- internal locus of control 79
- mindfulness-based stress reduction (MBSR) 81
- optimism 80
- positive affect 79
- posttraumatic stress disorder (PTSD) 75
- problem-focused coping 78
- psychoneuroimmunology 70
- SAM system 69
- stress 63
- stressor 63
- technostress 85

© maxuser/iStockphoto

Sensation and Perception

Andersen Ross/Blend Images/Getty Images

Real World **Psychology**

Things you'll learn in Chapter 4

[Q1] Do athletes have a higher pain tolerance than non-athletes?

[Q2] Can looking at a photograph of a loved one lead you to feel less pain?

[Q3] Can using a lower-pitched voice affect your perceived influence and power?

[Q4] How can listening to loud music on headphones damage your hearing?

[Q5] Why do babies (and adults) need skin-to-skin contact?

[Q6] Are Black football players more likely to be penalized for touchdown celebrations than White football players?

Throughout the chapter, margin icons for Q1–Q6 indicate where the text addresses these questions.

Chapter Overview

Imagine that your visual field has been suddenly inverted and reversed. Things you normally expect to be on your right are now on your left, and those above your head are now below. How would you ride a bike, read a book, or even walk through your home? Do you think you could ever adapt to this upside-down world?

To answer that question, psychologist George Stratton (1896) invented, and for eight days wore, special prism goggles that flipped his view of the world from up to down and right to left. For the first few days, Stratton had a great deal of difficulty navigating in this environment and coping with everyday tasks. But by the third day, he noted:

> *Walking through the narrow spaces between pieces of furniture required much less care than hitherto. I could watch my hands as they wrote, without hesitating or becoming embarrassed thereby.*

By the fifth day, Stratton had almost completely adjusted to his strange perceptual environment, but when he later removed the headgear, he quickly readapted.

What does this experiment have to do with everyday life? At this very moment, our bodies are being bombarded with stimuli from the outside world—light, sound, heat, pressure, texture, and so on—while our brains are floating in complete silence and utter darkness within our skulls. Stratton's experiment shows us that sensing the world is not enough. Our brains must receive, convert, and constantly adapt the information from our sense organs into useful mental representations of the world.

CHAPTER OUTLINE

How we get the outside world inside to our brains, and what our brains do with this information, are the key topics of this chapter. We begin with an exploration of how sensation differs from perception and three key topics involved in sensation—processing, psychophysics, and sensory adaptation. Next, we examine vision, hearing, and our other important senses—smell, taste, and body senses. We conclude with a survey of the basic processes in perception—selection, organization, and interpretation.

4.1 Understanding Sensation

LEARNING OBJECTIVES

Retrieval Practice While reading the upcoming sections, respond to each Learning Objective in your own words.

Review the key features and processes of sensation.

- **Differentiate** sensation from perception.
- **Describe** how raw sensory stimuli are processed and converted to signals sent to our brains.
- **Discuss** how and why we reduce the amount of sensory information we receive and process.
- **Explain** psychophysics and subliminal stimuli.
- **Summarize** the factors involved in sensory adaptation and pain perception.

Sensation The process of detecting, converting, and transmitting raw sensory information from the external and internal environments to the brain.

Perception The process of selecting, organizing, and interpreting sensory information into meaningful objects and events.

Bottom-up processing Information processing that starts at the "bottom" with an analysis of smaller features, and then builds on them to create complete perceptions; data-driven processing that moves from the parts to the whole.

Top-down processing Information processing that starts at the "top" with higher-level analysis (prior knowledge and expectations), and then works "down" to recognize individual features as a unified whole; conceptually driven processing that moves from the whole to the parts.

Psychologists are keenly interested in our senses because they are our mind's window to the outside world. We're equally interested in how our mind perceives and interprets the information it receives from the senses. In this chapter we separate the discussion of sensation and perception, but in our everyday life the two normally blend into one apparently seamless process. We'll start with an explanation of how they differ.

Sensation versus Perception

Sensation begins with specialized receptor cells located in our sense organs (eyes, ears, nose, tongue, skin, and internal body tissues). When sense organs detect an appropriate stimulus (light, mechanical pressure, chemical molecules), they convert it into neural impulses (action potentials) that are transmitted to our brains. Through the process of **perception**, the brain then assigns meaning to this sensory information (**Table 4.1**). Another clever way to differentiate sensation and perception is shown in **Figure 4.1**.

FIGURE 4.1 Sensation and perception When you look at this drawing, do you see a young woman looking back over her shoulder or an older woman with her chin buried in a fur collar? Younger students tend to first see a young woman, and older students first see an older woman. Although the basic sensory input (sensation) stays the same, your brain's attempt to select, organize, and interpret the sensory information (perception) turns the black and white lines and shapes into meaningful objects—either a young or old face.

How do we unknowingly and automatically combine both sensation and perception? It involves at least two processes (Johns & Jones, 2015; Sussman et al., 2016; van Ommen et al., 2016):

- In **bottom-up processing**, information processing starts at the "bottom" with an analysis of smaller features, and then builds on them to create complete perceptions. In other words, processing begins at the sensory level and works "up."
- During **top-down processing**, our brains create useable perceptions from the sensory messages based on prior knowledge and expectations. In this case, processing begins at the "top," our brain's higher-level cognitive processes, and works "down."

TABLE 4.1 Sensation and Perception

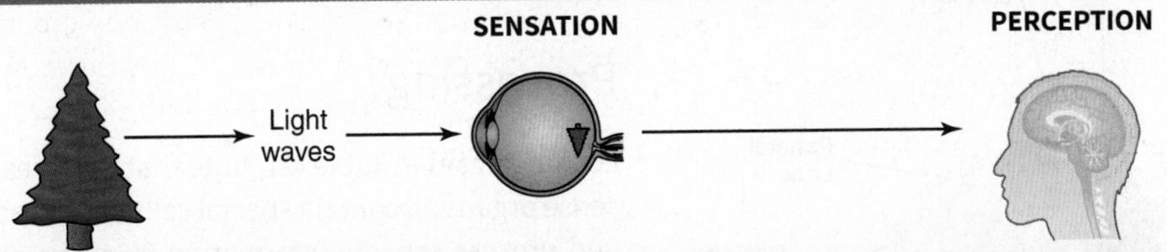

SENSE	STIMULUS	RECEPTORS	BRAIN
Vision	Light waves	Light-sensitive rods and cones in eye's retina	Visual cortex in the occipital lobe
Audition (hearing)	Sound waves	Pressure-sensitive hair cells in ear's cochlea	Auditory cortex in the temporal lobe
Olfaction (smell)	Molecules dissolved on nose's mucous membranes	Neurons in the nose's olfactory epithelium	Temporal lobe and limbic system
Gustation (taste)	Molecules dissolved on tongue	Taste buds on tongue's surface	Limbic system, somatosensory cortex, and frontal lobe
Body senses	Variety of stimuli	Variety of receptors (the drawing on the right is a model of our sensory receptor cells for touch)	Motor cortex in the frontal lobe and the somatosensory cortex in the parietal lobe

One additional way to understand the difference between bottom-up and top-down processing is to think about what happens when we "see" a helicopter flying overhead in the sky. According to the *bottom-up processing* perspective, receptors in our eyes and ears record the sight and sound of this large, loud object, and send these sensory messages on to our brains for interpretation. The other, top-down processing, approach suggests that our brains quickly make a "best guess," and interpret the large, loud object as a "helicopter," based on our previous knowledge and expectations. Given that most of our students have difficulty with this distinction, the following **Psychology and You** provides another concrete, everyday example of both bottom-up and top-down processing.

Psychology and **You**—Understanding Yourself

Bottom-Up versus Top-Down Processing

When first learning to read, you used *bottom-up processing*. You initially learned that certain arrangements of lines and "squiggles" represented specific letters. You later realized that these letters make up words that have meaning—an example of *topdown processing*.

Now, yuor aiblity to raed uisng top-dwon prcessoing mkaes it psosible to unedrstnad this sntenece desipte its mnay mssipllengis.

Jose Luis Pelaez/Iconica/Getty Images, Inc.

As you can see, the processes of sensation and perception are complex, but also very interesting. Now that you understand and appreciate the overall purpose of these

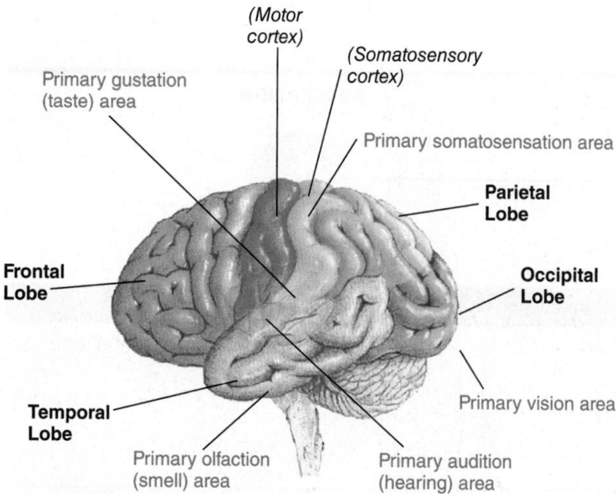

FIGURE 4.2 **Sensory processing within the brain** Neural messages from the various sense organs must travel to specific areas of the brain in order for us to see, hear, smell, and so on. Shown here in the red-colored labels are the primary locations in the cerebral cortex for vision, hearing, taste, smell, and somatosensation (which includes touch, pain, and temperature sensitivity).

two processes, let's dig deeper, starting with the first step of sensation—*processing*.

Processing

Looking again at Table 4.1, note that our eyes, ears, skin, and other sense organs all contain special cells called receptors, which receive and process sensory information from the environment. For each sense, these specialized cells respond to a distinct stimulus, such as sound waves or odor molecules. Next, during the process of **transduction**, the receptors convert the energy from the specific sensory stimulus into neural impulses, which are then sent on to the brain. For example, in hearing, tiny receptor cells in the inner ear convert mechanical vibrations from sound waves into electrochemical signals. Neurons then carry these signals to the brain, where specific sensory receptors detect and interpret the information.

How does your brain differentiate between sensations, such as sounds and smells? Through a process known as **coding**, the brain interprets different physical stimuli as distinct sensations because their neural impulses travel by different routes and arrive at different parts of the brain (**Figure 4.2**).

We also have structures that purposefully reduce the amount of sensory information we receive. In this process of *sensory reduction*, we analyze and then filter incoming sensations before sending neural impulses on for further processing in other parts of our brains. Without this natural filtering of stimuli, we would constantly hear blood rushing through our veins and feel our clothes brushing against our skin. Some level of filtering is needed to prevent our brains from being overwhelmed with unnecessary information.

All species have evolved selective receptors that suppress or amplify information for survival. Humans, for example, cannot sense ultraviolet light, electric or magnetic fields, the ultrasonic sound of a dog whistle, or infrared heat patterns from warm-blooded animals, as some other animals can.

Transduction The process of converting sensory stimuli into neural impulses that are sent along to the brain (for example, transforming light waves into neural impulses).

Coding The process in which neural impulses travel by different routes to different parts of the brain; it allows us to detect various physical stimuli as distinct sensations.

Psychophysics The study of the link between the physical characteristics of stimuli and the psychological experience of them.

Difference threshold The smallest physical difference between two stimuli that is consciously detectable 50% of the time; also called the *just noticeable difference (JND)*.

Absolute threshold The minimum amount of stimulation necessary to consciously detect a stimulus 50% of the time.

Psychophysics

How can scientists measure the exact amount of stimulus energy it takes to trigger a conscious experience? The answer comes from the field of **psychophysics**, which studies and measures the link between the physical characteristics of stimuli and the psychological experience of them.

One of the most interesting insights from psychophysics is that what is out there is not directly reproduced inside our bodies. At this moment, there are light waves, sound waves, odors, tastes, and microscopic particles touching us that we cannot see, hear, smell, taste, or feel. We are consciously aware of only a narrow range of stimuli in our environment. German scientist Ernst Weber (1795–1878) was one of the first to study the smallest difference between two weights that could be detected (Goldstein, 2014; Schwartz & Krantz, 2016).

This **difference threshold**, also known as *Weber's Law of just noticeable differences (JND)*, is the minimum difference that is consciously detectable 50% of the time (**Figure 4.3**). Another scientist, Gustav Fechner (1801–1887), expanded on Weber's law to determine what is called the **absolute threshold**, the minimum stimulation necessary to consciously detect a stimulus 50% of the time. See **Table 4.2** for a list of absolute thresholds for our various senses.

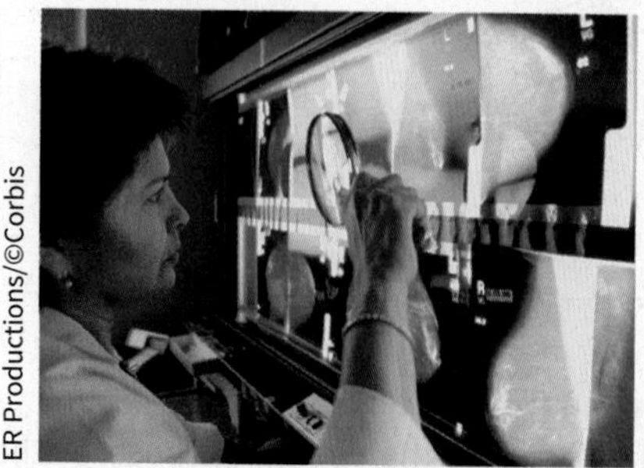
ER Productions/©Corbis

FIGURE 4.3 **Why is our difference threshold important?** This radiologist is responsible for detecting the slightest indication of a tumor in this mammogram of a female breast. The ability to detect differences between stimuli (like the visual difference between normal and abnormal breast tissue) can be improved by special training, practice, and instruments. However, it's still limited by our basic sensory difference thresholds.

To measure your senses, an examiner presents a series of signals that vary in intensity and asks you to report which signals you can detect. In a hearing test, the softest level at which you

TABLE 4.2 Examples of Human Absolute Thresholds

SENSE	ABSOLUTE THRESHOLD
Vision	A candle flame seen from 30 miles away on a clear, dark night
Audition (hearing)	The tick of an old-fashioned watch at 20 feet
Olfaction (smell)	One drop of perfume spread throughout a six-room apartment
Gustation (taste)	One teaspoon of sugar in 2 gallons of water
Body senses	A bee's wing falling on your cheek from a height of about half an inch

can consistently hear a tone is your absolute threshold. The examiner then compares your threshold with those of people with normal hearing to determine whether or not you have hearing loss (**Figure 4.4**).

Interestingly, many nonhuman animals have higher and lower thresholds than humans. For example, a dog's absolute and difference thresholds for smell are far more sensitive than those of a human. This exceptional sensitivity allows specially trained dogs to provide invaluable help in sniffing out dangerous plants, animals, drugs, and explosives; tracking criminals; and assisting in search-and-rescue operations (Porritt et al., 2015). Some researchers believe dogs can even detect hidden corrosion, fecal contamination, chemical signs of certain illnesses (such as diabetes or cancer), and possibly even predict seizures in humans (Partyka et al., 2014; Schoon, 2014; Urbanová et al., 2015). In addition, other research found that when dogs were presented with five different scents from humans and dogs, sensory receptors in the dogs' noses easily picked up all five scents (Berns et al., 2015). However, only the human scents activated a part of the dog's brain (the caudate nucleus), which has a well-known association with positive expectations. The researchers concluded that this brain activation, and the dog's positive association with human scents, point to the importance of humans in dogs' lives. A related study has shown that dogs can even discriminate among many emotional expressions on human faces (Muller et al., 2015).

Subliminal Stimuli

Have you heard some of the wild rumors about subliminal messages? During the 1970s, it was said that rock songs contained demonic messages, which could only be heard when the songs were played backwards! Similarly, in the 1990s, many suggested that some Disney films contained obscene subliminal messages. For example, in the film *Aladdin*, the lead character supposedly whispers, "all good teenagers take off your clothes," and *The Lion King* reportedly showed closeup shots of the dust with a secret spelling out of the word "sex." In addition, at one time movie theaters were reportedly flashing messages like "Eat popcorn" and "Drink Cola-Cola" on the screen. Even though the messages were so brief that viewers weren't aware of seeing them, it was believed they increased consumption of these products (Bargh, 2014; Blecha, 2004; Vokey & Read, 1985).

Subliminal perception The detection of stimuli below the absolute threshold for conscious awareness.

Priming A form of memory activation that occurs when exposure (often unconscious) to previously stored information predisposes (or *primes*) our response to related stimuli.

Can unconscious stimuli really affect our behavior? Experimental studies on **subliminal perception** have clearly shown that we *can* detect stimuli and information below our level of conscious awareness (Farooqui & Manly, 2015; Rabellino et al., 2016; Urriza et al., 2016). These studies commonly use an instrument, called a *tachistoscope*, to flash images too quickly for conscious recognition, but slowly enough to be registered by the brain. How does this happen? As we've just seen, our "absolute threshold" is the point at which we can detect a stimulus half the time. *Subliminal stimuli* are just stimuli that fall below our 50% absolute threshold, and they can be detected without our awareness. Furthermore, research on **priming** finds that certain unconscious or unnoticed stimuli can reach our brains and predispose (*prime*) us to make it easier or more difficult to recall related information already in storage (Loebnitz & Aschemann-Witzel, 2016; Xiao & Yamauchi, 2016). If a researcher shows you the words "red" and "fire engine," you'll be slightly faster to

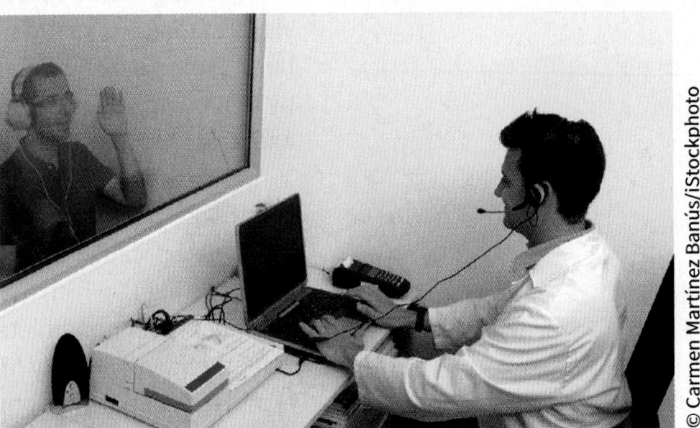

FIGURE 4.4 Measuring the absolute and difference thresholds for hearing

recognize the word "apple" because all of these words have been previously stored and closely associated in your memory.

Despite the fact that *subliminal perception* and *priming* do occur, it doesn't mean that such processes lead to significant behavioral changes. Subliminal stimuli are basically weak stimuli. However, they sometimes have an effect on indirect, more subtle reactions, such as our more casual attitudes (see the following **Real World Psychology**).

Real World **Psychology**—Understanding the World

Subliminal Music and Food Choices

© Matthew Ennis/iStockphoto

In a recent study, researchers placed 10 volunteers in different rooms with music playing in the background from one of three regions—the United States, China, or India (North et al., 2016). While listening to different types of music, each participant looked at a menu for 5 minutes with 30 dinner options (10 from each country). The scientists then asked them to recall as many dishes from the menu as they could, and then to choose one dish to order as a meal. Perhaps thanks to subliminal stimuli from the music, participants better remembered and chose dishes that reflected the music they had listened to before looking at the menu. For example, those who listened to American music ("California Girls," "Surfin' U.S.A.," and "Good Vibrations" by the Beach Boys) chose foods like hamburgers and hot dogs (see photo).

Sensory Adaptation

Imagine that friends have invited you to come visit their beautiful new baby kitten. As they greet you at the door, you are overwhelmed by the odor of the kitten's overflowing litter box. Why don't your friends do something about that smell? The answer lies in the previously mentioned sensory reduction, as well as **sensory adaptation**. When a constant stimulus is presented for a length of time, sensation often fades or disappears. Receptors in our sensory system become less sensitive. They get "tired" and actually fire less frequently.

Sensory adaptation The sensory receptors' innate tendency to fatigue and stop responding to unchanging stimuli; an example of bottom-up processing.

Sensory adaptation can be understood from an evolutionary perspective. We can't afford to waste attention and time on unchanging, normally unimportant stimuli. "Turning down the volume" on repetitive information helps the brain cope with an overwhelming amount of sensory stimuli and enables us to pay attention to change. Sometimes, however, adaptation can be dangerous, as when people stop paying attention to a small gas leak in the kitchen.

Although some senses, like smell and touch, adapt quickly, we never completely adapt to visual stimuli or to extremely intense stimuli, such as the odor of ammonia or the pain of a bad burn. From an evolutionary perspective, these limitations on sensory adaptation aid survival by reminding us, for example, to keep a watch out for dangerous predators, avoid strong odors and heat, and take care of that burn.

If we don't adapt to pain, how do athletes keep playing despite painful injuries? In certain situations, including times of physical exertion, the body releases natural, pain-killing neurotransmitters, called *endorphins* (Chapter 2), which inhibit pain perception. This is the so-called "runner's high," which may help explain why athletes have been found to have a higher pain tolerance than nonathletes (Tesarz et al., 2012). [Q1] (As a critical thinker, is it possible that individuals with a naturally high pain tolerance are just more attracted to athletics? Or might the experience of playing sports change your pain tolerance?)

Interestingly, the pain of athletes, soldiers, firefighters, and others is also greatly diminished when they're distracted by factors such as duty, competition, or fear (**Figure 4.5**).

Similarly, surgical patients who listen to music—even while under anesthesia—have less anxiety, report a 20% reduction in postsurgery pain, and need less pain medication during recovery (Hole et al., 2015). Studies have even shown that simply holding the hand of a loved one—or just looking at a photograph of him or her—can help reduce pain during a medical procedure (Master et al., 2009).

Gate-control theory of pain The theory that pain sensations are processed and altered by certain cells in the spinal cord, which act as gates to interrupt and block some pain signals while sending others on to the brain.

In addition to endorphin release and distraction, one of the most widely accepted explanations of pain perception is the **gate-control theory of pain**, first proposed by Ronald Melzack and Patrick Wall (1965). According to this theory, the experience of pain depends partly on whether the neural message gets past a "gatekeeper" in the spinal cord. Normally, the gate is kept shut, either by impulses coming down from the brain or by messages being sent from large-diameter nerve fibers that conduct most sensory signals, such as touch and pressure. However, when body tissue is damaged, impulses from smaller pain fibers open the gate (Price & Prescott, 2015; Rhudy, 2016; Zhao & Wood, 2015). Can you see how this gate-control theory helps explain why massaging an injury or scratching an itch can temporarily relieve discomfort? It's because pressure on large-diameter neurons interferes with pain signals. In addition, studies suggest that the pain gate may be chemically controlled. A neurotransmitter called *substance P* opens the pain gate, and endorphins close it (Fan et al., 2016; Krug et al., 2015; Wu et al., 2015).

In sum, endorphins, distraction, listening to music, holding a loved one's hand, pain gates, and substance P may all provide soothing comfort and pain reduction, especially for those who are very anxious (Bradshaw et al., 2012; Fan et al., 2016; Gardstrom & Sorel, 2015).

Did you know that when normal sensory input is disrupted, the brain can also generate pain and other sensations entirely on its own, as is the case with *phantom limb pain (PLP)* (Deer et al., 2015; Melzack, 1999; Raffin et al., 2016)? After an amputation, people commonly report detecting their missing limb as if it were still there with no differences at all. In fact, up to 80 percent of people who have had amputations sometimes "feel" pain (and itching, burning, or tickling sensations) in the missing limb, long after the amputation. Numerous theories attempt to explain this type of PLP, but one of the best suggests that there is a mismatch between the sensory messages sent and received in the brain.

Can you explain how this may be an example of our earlier description of how *bottom-up processes* (such as the sensory messages sent from our limbs to our brains) combine with our *top-down processes* (our brain's interpretation of these messages)? Messages are no longer being transmitted from the missing limb to the brain (bottom up), but areas of the brain responsible for receiving messages are still intact (top down). The brain's attempt to interpret the confusing messages may result in pain and other sensations.

In line with this idea of mismatched signals, when amputees wear prosthetic limbs, or when *mirror visual therapy* is used, phantom pain often disappears. In mirror therapy (**Figure 4.6**), pain relief apparently occurs because the brain is somehow tricked into believing there is no longer a missing limb (Deconinck et al., 2015; Foell et al., 2014; Hagenberg & Carter, 2014). Others believe that mirror therapy works because it helps the brain reorganize and incorporate this phantom limb into a new nervous system configuration.

Now that we've studied how we perceive pain, how we might ignore or "play through" it, and how we might misperceive it with phantom limb pain, it's important to point out that when we get anxious or dwell on our pain, we can intensify it (Lin et al., 2013; Ray et al., 2015; Wertli et al., 2014). Surprisingly, social and cultural factors, such as well-meaning friends or anxious parents who ask pain sufferers about their pain, may unintentionally reinforce and increase it (Esteve et al., 2014; Flor, 2013; Langer et al., 2014). The following **Psychology and You** offers an assessment and strategies for your personal pain management.

Ian MacNicol/Getty Images

FIGURE 4.5 Competition—a powerful pain distractor! Manteo Mitchell broke his left leg in the qualifying heats of the 4 × 400-meter relay race in the 2012 Olympics. Recalling the moment of the accident, Manteo said, "I felt it break . . . it hurt so bad . . . it felt like somebody literally just snapped my leg in half" (Moore, 2013). However, he continued running so that the American team could get into the finals.

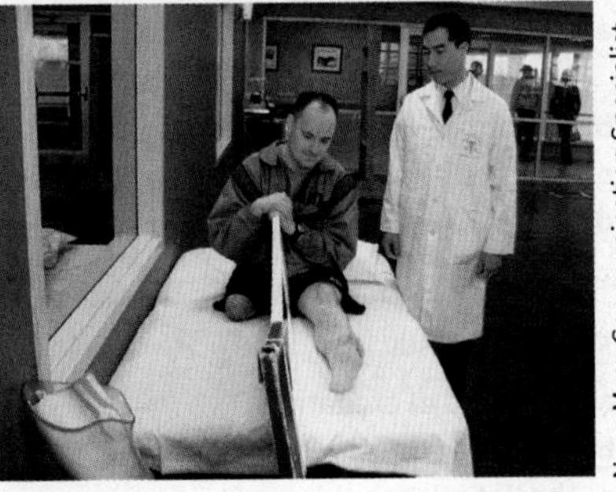

Navy Mass Communication Specialist 2nd Class Jeff Hopkins

FIGURE 4.6 Treating phantom limb pain Using mirror therapy, an amputee patient places his or her intact limb on one side of the mirror, and the amputated limb on the other. He or she then concentrates on looking into the mirror on the side that reflects the intact limb, creating the visual impression of two complete undamaged limbs. The patient then attempts to move both limbs. Thanks to the artificial feedback provided by the mirror, the patient sees the complete limb, and the reflected image of the complete limb, moving. He or she then interprets this as the phantom limb moving.

Psychology and You—Understanding Yourself

Test Yourself | How Well Do You Manage Your Pain?

Score yourself on how often you use one or more of these strategies, using the following scale:
0 = never, 1 = seldom, 2 = occasionally, 3 = often, 4 = almost always, 5 = always.

_____ **1.** I do something I enjoy, such as watching TV or listening to music.

_____ **2.** I try to be around other people.

_____ **3.** I do something active, like household chores or projects.

_____ **4.** I try to feel distant from the pain, almost as if I'm floating above my body.

_____ **5.** I try to think about something pleasant.

_____ **6.** I replay in my mind pleasant experiences from the past.

_____ **7.** I tell myself that I can overcome the pain.

_____ **8.** I don't think about the pain.

These questions are based on effective pain management techniques, such as distraction, ignoring pain, and reinterpreting it. Review those items that you checked as "never" or "seldom" and consider adding them to your pain management skills.

Retrieval Practice 4.1 | Understanding Sensation

SELF-TEST Completing this self-test, and then checking your answers by clicking on the answer button or by looking in Appendix B, will provide immediate feedback and helpful practice for exams.

1. _____ starts at the "bottom" with an analysis of smaller features.

a. Perception
b. Bottom-up processing
c. Sensation
d. Integration

2. Transduction is the process of converting _____.

a. sensory stimuli into neural impulses that are sent along to the brain
b. receptors into transmitters
c. a particular sensory stimulus into a specific perception
d. receptors into neural impulses

3. The _____ is the minimum stimulation necessary to consciously detect a stimulus.

a. threshold of excitation
b. difference threshold
c. absolute threshold
d. low point

4. Experiments on subliminal perception have _____.

a. supported its existence, but shown that it has little or no effect on behavioral change
b. shown that subliminal perception occurs only among children and some adolescents
c. shown that subliminal messages affect only people who are highly suggestible
d. failed to support the phenomenon

5. The _____ theory of pain helps explain why it sometimes helps to rub or massage an injured area.

a. sensory adaptation **b.** gate-control
c. just noticeable difference **d.** Lamaze

Think Critically

1. Sensation and perception are closely linked. What is the central distinction between the two?

2. If we sensed and attended equally to each stimulus in the world, the amount of information would be overwhelming. What sensory and perceptual processes help us lessen the din?

Real World Psychology

Do athletes have a higher pain tolerance than non-athletes?

Andersen Ross/Blend Images/ Getty Images

Can looking at a photograph of a loved one lead you to feel less pain?

© Alina Vincent Photography, LLC/iStockphoto

HINT: LOOK IN THE MARGIN FOR **[Q1]** AND **[Q2]**

4.2 How We See and Hear

LEARNING OBJECTIVES

Retrieval Practice While reading the upcoming sections, respond to each Learning Objective in your own words.

Summarize the key components and processes of vision and audition.

- **Identify** the key characteristics of light and sound waves.
- **Explain** the visual process, the key parts and functions of the human eye, and color vision.
- **Identify** vision's major problems and peculiarities.
- **Describe** audition, the key parts and functions of the human ear, and pitch perception.
- **Summarize** the two major types of hearing problems and what we can do to protect our hearing.

Many people mistakenly believe that what they see and hear is a copy of the outside world. In fact, vision and hearing are the result of what our brains create in response to light and sound waves. What we see and hear is based on wave phenomena, similar to ocean waves (**Figure 4.7**).

In addition to wavelength/frequency, waves also vary in height (technically called *amplitude*). This wave height/amplitude determines the intensity of sights and sounds. Finally, waves also vary in range, or complexity, which mixes together waves of various wavelength/frequency and height/amplitude (**Figure 4.8**).

Vision

Did you know that professional baseball batters can hit a 90-miles-per-hour fastball four-tenths of a second after it leaves the pitcher's hand? How can the human eye receive and process information that fast? To understand the marvels of vision, we need to start with the basics—that light waves are a form of electromagnetic energy and only a small part of the full *electromagnetic spectrum* (**Figure 4.9**).

To fully appreciate how our eyes turn these light waves into the experience we call *vision*, we need to first examine the various structures in our eyes that capture and focus the light waves. Then, we need to understand how these waves are transformed (transduced) into

© S. Greg Panosian/iStockphoto

FIGURE 4.7 Waves of light and sound Ocean waves have a certain distance between them (the *wavelength*), and they pass by you at intervals. If you counted the number of passing waves in a set amount of time (for example, 5 waves in 60 seconds), you could calculate the *frequency* (the number of complete wavelengths that pass a point in a given time). Longer wavelength means lower frequency and vice versa.

FIGURE 4.8 Properties of light and sound

Wavelength
The distance between successive peaks.

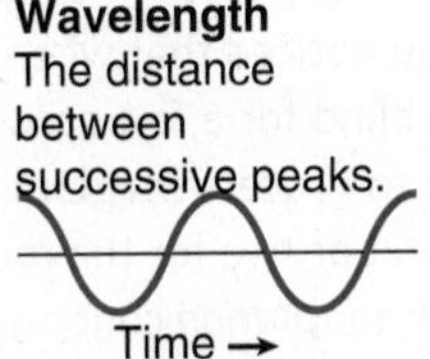

Long wavelength/ low frequency = Reddish colors/ low-pitched sounds

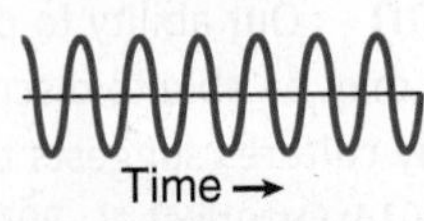

Short wavelength/ high frequency = Bluish colors/ high pitched sound

Wave amplitude
The height from peak to trough.

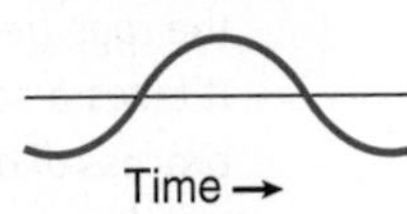

Low amplitude/ low intensity = Dull colors/ soft sounds

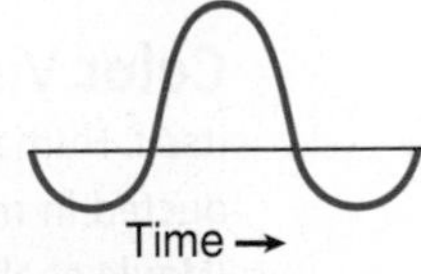

High amplitude/ high intensity = Bright colors/ loud sounds

Range of wavelengths
The mixture of waves.

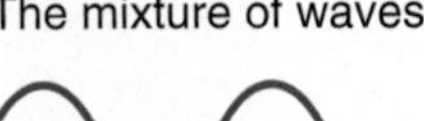

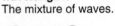

Small range/ low complexity = Less complex colors/ less complex sounds

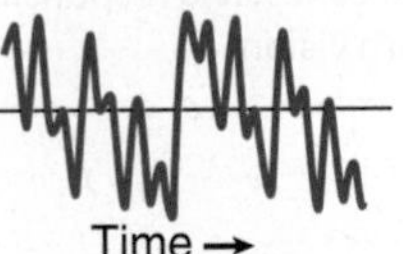

Large range/ high complexity = Complex colors/ complex sounds

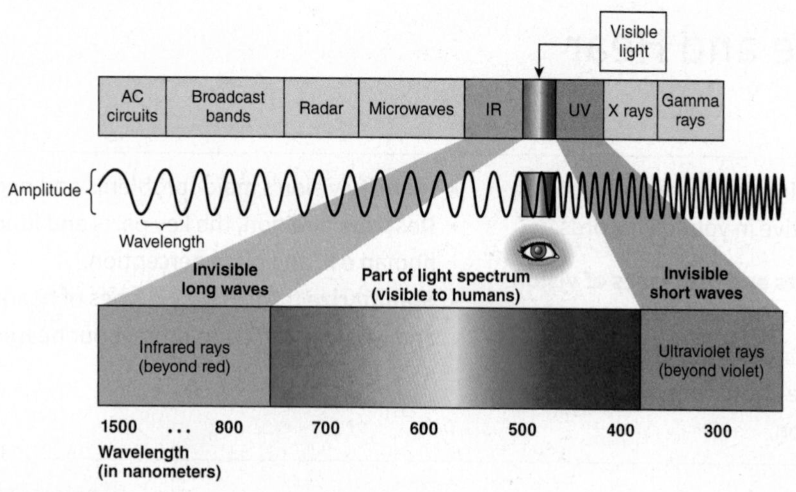

A The full spectrum of electromagnetic waves contains very long wavelength AC circuits at one end, and relatively short gamma ray waves at the other.

B Only the light waves, in the middle of the electromagnetic spectrum, can be seen by the human eye. Note that we perceive the longer visible wavelengths as red, whereas the shortest are seen as blue, with the rest of the colors in between.

FIGURE 4.9 **The electromagnetic spectrum for vision**

neural messages (action potentials) that our brains can process into images we consciously see. (Be sure to carefully study this step-by-step process in **Process Diagram 4.1.**)

Vision Problems and Peculiarities Thoroughly understanding the processes detailed in Process Diagram 4.1 offers clues that help us understand several visual peculiarities. For example, small abnormalities in the eye sometimes cause images to be focused in front of the **retina**, in the case of *nearsightedness* (myopia). In contrast, the image is focused behind the behind the retina, in the case of *farsightedness* (*hyperopia*). In addition, during middle age, most people's lenses lose elasticity and the ability to accommodate for near vision, a condition known as *presbyopia*. Corrective lenses or laser surgery can often correct all three of these visual acuity problems.

Retina The light-sensitive inner surface of the back of the eye, which contains the receptor cells for vision (rods and cones).

A visual peculiarity occurs where the optic nerve exits the eye. Because there are no receptor cells for visual stimuli in that area, we have a tiny hole, or **blind spot**, in our field of vision. (See Process Diagram 4.1 for a demonstration.)

Blind spot The point at which the optic nerve leaves the eye, which contains no receptor cells for vision—thus creating a "blind spot."

Another interesting peculiarity exists in the retina's vision receptor cells (the rods and cones). The **rods** are highly sensitive in dim light, but are less sensitive to detail and color. The reverse is true for the **cones**, which are highly sensitive to color and detail, and less sensitive in dim light. Can you see how this explains why you're cautioned to look away from bright headlights when driving or biking at night? Staring into the bright lights will activate your cones, which are less effective in dim light, whereas looking away activates the rods in your peripheral vision, which are more sensitive at night.

Rods Retinal receptor cells with high sensitivity in dim light, but low sensitivity to details and color.

Cones Retinal receptor cells with high sensitivity to color and detail, but low sensitivity in dim light.

Two additional peculiarities happen when we go from a bright to dark setting and vice versa. Have you noticed that when you walk into a dark movie theater on a sunny afternoon, you're almost blind for a few seconds? The reason is that in bright light, the pigment inside the *rods* (refer to Process Diagram 4.1) is bleached, making them temporarily nonfunctional. It takes a second or two for the rods to become functional enough again for you to see. This process of *dark adaptation* continues for 20 to 30 minutes.

In contrast, *light adaptation*, the adjustment that takes place when you go from darkness to a bright setting, takes about 7 to 10 minutes and is the work of the *cones*. Interestingly, a region in the center of the retina, called the **fovea**, has the greatest density of cones, which are most sensitive in brightly lit conditions. They're also responsible for color vision and fine detail.

Fovea A tiny pit in the center of the retina that is densely filled with cones; it is responsible for sharp vision.

Color Vision Our ability to perceive color is almost as remarkable and useful as vision itself. Humans may be able to discriminate among 7 million different hues, and research conducted in many cultures suggests that we all seem to see essentially the same colored world (Maule et al., 2014; Ozturk et al., 2013). Furthermore, studies of infants old enough to focus and move their eyes show that they are able to see color nearly as well as adults and have color preferences similar to those of adults (Bornstein et al., 2014; Yang et al., 2015).

Although we know color is produced by different wavelengths of light, the actual way in which we perceive color is a matter of scientific debate. Traditionally, there have been two

STOP! This Process Diagram contains essential information NOT found elsewhere in the text, which is likely to appear on quizzes and exams. Be sure to study it CAREFULLY!

PROCESS DIAGRAM 4.1 How Our Eyes See Various structures of your eye work together to capture and focus the light waves from the outside world. Receptor cells in your retina (rods and cones) then convert these waves into messages that are sent along the optic nerve to be interpreted by your brain.

1. Light first enters through the *cornea*, which helps protect the eye and focus incoming light rays.

2. The light then passes through the *pupil*, a small adjustable opening. Muscles in the *iris* allow the *pupil* to dilate or constrict in response to light intensity or emotional factors.

3. The muscularly controlled lens then focuses incoming light into an image on the light-sensitive *retina*, located on the back surface of the fluid-filled eyeball.

4. In the **retina**, light waves are detected and transduced into neural signals by vision receptor cells (rods and cones). Note how the image of the flower is inverted when it is projected onto the retina. Our brains later reverse the visual input into the final image that we perceive.

5. The **fovea**, a tiny pit filled with cones, is responsible for our sharpest vision.

6. **Rods** are retinal receptor cells with high sensitivity in dim light, but low sensitivity to details and color.

7. **Cones** are retinal receptor cells with sensitivity to color, but low sensitivity in dim light.

8. The optic nerve, which consists of axons of the ganglion cells, then carries the message on to the brain.

Lens
Vitreous humor
Retinal blood vessels
Retina
Lid
Iris
Sclera
Light
Light
Fovea
Pupil
Cornea
Blind spot
Optic nerve
Rod
Bipolar cells
Ganglion cells
Cone
Light
Light
Light
Visual cortex

Do you have a blind spot?
At the back of the retina lies an area that has no visual receptors at all and absolutely no vision. This **blind spot** is where blood vessels and nerves enter and exit the eyeball. To find yours, hold this book about one foot in front of you, close your right eye, and stare at the X with your left eye. Very slowly, move the book closer to you. You should see the worm disappear and the apple become whole.

theories of color vision: the trichromatic (three-color) theory and the opponent-process theory. The **trichromatic theory of color** (from the Greek word *tri*, meaning "three," and *chroma*, meaning "color") suggests that we have three "color systems," each of which is maximally sensitive to red, green, or blue (Young, 1802). The proponents of this theory demonstrated that mixing lights of these three colors could yield the full spectrum of colors we perceive (**Figure 4.10**).

However, trichromatic theory doesn't fully explain color vision, and other researchers have proposed alternative

Trichromatic theory of color The theory that color perception results from three types of cones in the retina, each most sensitive to either red, green, or blue; other colors result from a mixture of these three.

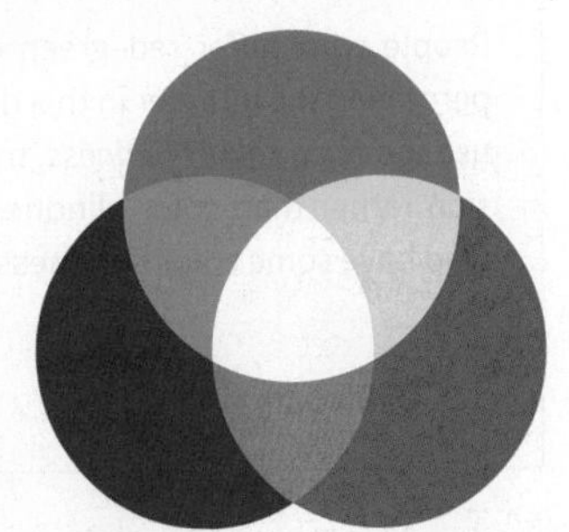

FIGURE 4.10 Primary colors Trichromatic theory found that the three primary colors (red, green, and blue) can be combined to form all colors. For example, a combination of green and red creates yellow.

Opponent-process theory of color The theory that all color perception is based on three systems, each of which contains two color opposites (red versus green, blue versus yellow, and black versus white).

theories. For example, the **opponent-process theory of color** agrees that we have three color systems, but it says that each system is sensitive to two opposing colors—blue and yellow, red and green, black and white—in an "on/off" fashion. In other words, each color receptor responds either to blue or yellow, or to red or green, with the black-or-white system responding to differences in brightness levels. This theory makes a lot of sense because when different-colored lights are combined, people are unable to see reddish greens and bluish yellow. In fact, when red and green lights or blue and yellow lights are mixed in equal amounts, we see white. This opponent-process theory also explains *color afterimages*, a fun type of optical illusion in which an image briefly remains after the original image has faded (**Psychology and You**).

Psychology and You—Understanding Yourself

Color Afterimages

Try staring at the dot in the middle of this color-distorted U.S. flag for 60 seconds. Then stare at a plain sheet of white paper. You should get interesting color aftereffects—red in place of green, blue in place of yellow, and white in place of black: a "genuine" U.S. flag. (If you don't see the afterimage, blink once or twice and try again.)

What happened? As you stared at the green, black, and yellow colors, the neural systems that process those colors became fatigued. Then when you looked at the plain white paper, which reflects all wavelengths, a reverse opponent process occurred: Each fatigued receptor responded with its opposing red, white, and blue colors! This is a good example of color afterimages—and further support for the opponent-process theory.

Think Critically

1. In what situations do you think color afterimages are more likely to occur?
2. Other than learning that our eyes can play tricks on our brain, why might illusions like this afterimage be important?

Today we know that both trichromatic and opponent-process theories are correct—they just operate at different levels in visual processing. Color vision is processed in a trichromatic fashion in the retina. In contrast, color vision during opponent processing involves the retina, optic nerve, and brain.

Color-Deficient Vision Most people perceive three different colors—red, green, and blue—and are called *trichromats*. However, a small percentage of the population has a genetic deficiency in the red–green system, the blue–yellow system, or both. Those who perceive only two colors are called *dichromats*. People who are sensitive to only the black–white system are called *monochromats*, and they are totally color blind. If you'd like to test yourself for red–green color blindness, see **Psychology and You**.

Psychology and You—Understanding Yourself

Are You Color Blind?

People who suffer red–green color deficiency have trouble perceiving the number in this design. Although we commonly use the term *color blindness*, most problems are color confusion rather than color blindness. Furthermore, most people who have some color blindness are not even aware of it.

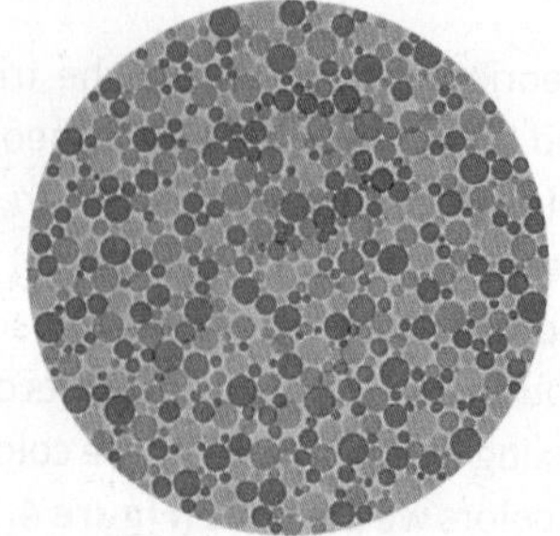

Hearing

The sense or act of hearing, known as **audition**, has a number of important functions, ranging from alerting us to dangers to helping us communicate with others. In this section we talk first about sound waves, then about the ear's anatomy and function, and finally about problems with hearing.

Like the visual process, which transforms light waves into vision, the auditory system is designed to convert sound waves into hearing. Sound waves are produced by air molecules moving in a particular wave pattern. For example, vibrating objects like vocal cords or guitar strings create waves of compressed and expanded air resembling ripples on a lake that circle out from a tossed stone. Our ears detect and respond to these waves of small air pressure changes, our brains then interpret the neural messages resulting from these waves, and we hear!

To fully understand this process, pay close attention to the step-by-step diagram in **Process Diagram 4.2**.

Audition The sense or act of hearing.

Place theory for hearing The theory that pitch perception is linked to the particular spot on the cochlea's basilar membrane that is most stimulated.

Outer ear The pinna, auditory canal, and eardrum structures, which funnel sound waves to the middle ear.

Middle ear The hammer, anvil, and stirrup structures of the ear, which concentrate eardrum vibrations onto the cochlea's oval window.

Inner ear The semicircular canals, vestibular sacs, and cochlea, which generate neural signals that are sent to the brain.

Cochlea [KOK-lee-uh] The fluid-filled, coiled tube in the inner ear that contains the receptors for hearing.

Pitch Perception

How do we determine that certain sounds are from a child's voice, and not from an adult's? We distinguish between high- and low-pitched sounds by the *frequency* of the sound waves. The higher the frequency, the higher the pitch. There are three main explanations for how we perceive *pitch*:

- According to the **place theory for hearing**, we hear different pitches because different sound waves stimulate different sections (or *places*) on our cochlea's basilar membrane

STOP! This Process Diagram contains essential information NOT found elsewhere in the text, which is likely to appear on quizzes and exams. Be sure to study it CAREFULLY!

PROCESS DIAGRAM 4.2 How Our Ears Hear The **outer ear** captures and funnels sound waves into the eardrum. Next, three tiny bones in the **middle ear** pick up the eardrum's vibrations, and transmit them to the **inner ear**. Finally, the snail-shaped **cochlea** in the inner ear transforms (transduces) the sound waves into neural messages (action potentials) that our brains process into what we consciously hear.

1. The **outer ear** captures and funnels sound waves onto the tympanic membrane (ear drum).
2. Vibrations of the tympanic membrane strike the **middle ear's** ossicles (hammer, anvil, and stirrup). Then the stirrup hits the oval window.
3. Vibrations of the oval window create waves in the **inner ear's** cochlear fluid which deflects the basilar membrane. This movement bends the hair cells.
4. The hair cells communicate with the auditory nerve, which sends neural impulses to the brain.

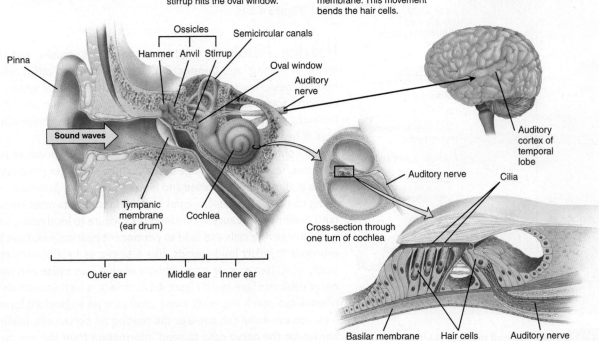

Nancy Kaszerman/ZUMAPRESS/Newscom

(see again Process Diagram 4.2). Our brains figure out the pitch of a sound by detecting the position of the hair cells that sent the neural message. High frequencies produce large vibrations near the start of the basilar membrane—next to the oval window. However, this theory does not predict well for low frequencies, which tend to excite the entire basilar membrane.

- **The frequency theory for hearing** differs from place theory because it states that we hear pitch by the *frequency* of the sound waves traveling up the auditory nerve. High-frequency sounds trigger the auditory nerve to fire more often than do low-frequency sounds. The problem with this theory is that an individual neuron cannot fire faster than 1,000 times per second, which means that we could not hear many of the notes of a soprano singer.
- The **volley principle for hearing** solves the problem of frequency theory, which can't account for the highest pitched sounds. It states that clusters of neurons take turns firing in a sequence of rhythmic *volleys*. Pitch perception depends upon the frequency of volleys, rather than the frequency carried by individual neurons.

Now that we've explored the mechanics of pitch and pitch perception, would you like a real-world example that you can apply to your everyday life? A recent experiment revealed that research participants who lowered the pitch of their voices were seen as being more influential, powerful, and intimidating (Cheng et al., 2016). This finding also held true in a second experiment in which the people only listened to audio recordings of various voices. Can you see why the famous deep-voiced actor James Earl Jones was chosen as the voice of Darth Vader in the Star Wars films (see photo)? Given that women generally tend to have higher-pitched voices, can you also see how this research might help explain why women often find it harder to gain leadership positions? [Q3]

Monkey Business Images/iStockphoto

FIGURE 4.11 Students exploiting age-related hearing loss

Interestingly, as we age, we tend to lose our ability to hear high-pitched sounds but are still able to hear low-pitched sounds. Given that young students can hear a cell phone ringtone that sounds at 17 kilohertz—too high for most adult ears to detect—they can take advantage of this age-related hearing difference and call or text one another during class (**Figure 4.11**). Ironically, the cell phone's ringtone that most adults can't hear is an offshoot of another device, called the Mosquito, which was originally designed to help shopkeepers annoy and drive away loitering teens!

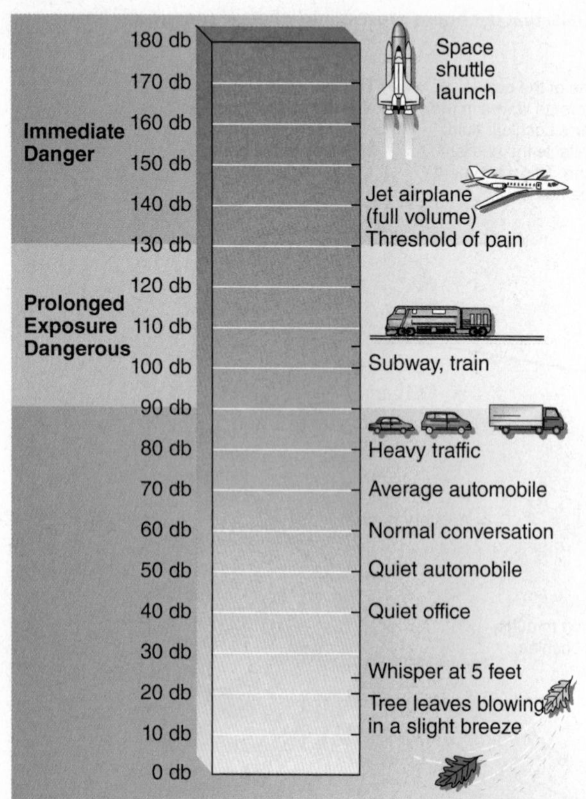

FIGURE 4.12 Beware of loud sounds The higher a sound's decibel (dB) reading, the more damaging it is to the ear.

Softness versus Loudness

How we detect a sound as being soft or loud depends on its amplitude (or wave height). Waves with high peaks and low valleys produce loud sounds; waves with relatively low peaks and shallow valleys produce soft sounds. The relative loudness or softness of sounds is measured on a scale of *decibels* (dBs) (**Figure 4.12**).

Hearing Problems

What are the types, causes, and treatments of hearing loss? **Conduction hearing loss**, also called conduction deafness, results from problems with the mechanical system that conducts sound waves to the cochlea. Hearing aids that amplify the incoming sound waves, and some forms of surgery, can help with this type of hearing loss.

In contrast, **sensorineural hearing loss**, also known as nerve deafness, results from damage to the cochlea's receptor (hair) cells or to the auditory nerve. Disease and biological changes associated with aging can result in sensorineural hearing loss. But its most common (and preventable) cause is continuous exposure to loud noise, which can damage hair cells and lead to permanent hearing loss. Even brief exposure to really loud sounds, like a stereo or headphones at full blast, a jackhammer, or a jet airplane engine, can cause permanent nerve deafness (see again Figure 4.12). In fact, a high volume on earphones can reach the same noise level as a jet engine! All forms of high volume noise can damage the coating on nerve cells, making it harder for the nerve cells to send information from the ears to the brain (Eggermont, 2015; Fagelson et al., 2016; Jiang et al., 2016). [Q4]

Although most hearing loss is temporary, damage to the auditory nerve or receptor cells is generally considered irreversible. The only treatment for auditory nerve damage is a small electronic device called a *cochlear implant*. If the auditory nerve is intact, the implant bypasses hair cells to stimulate the nerve. Currently, cochlear implants produce only a crude approximation of hearing, but the technology is improving.

Frequency theory for hearing The theory that pitch perception depends on how often the auditory nerve fires.

Volley principle for hearing An explanation for pitch perception suggesting that clusters of neurons take turns firing in a sequence of rhythmic volleys, and that pitch depends on the frequency of these volleys.

Conduction hearing loss A type of hearing loss that results from damage to the mechanical system that conducts sound waves to the cochlea; also called conduction deafness.

Sensorineural hearing loss A type of hearing loss resulting from damage to cochlea's receptor (hair) hearing cells or to the auditory nerve; also called nerve deafness.

Psychology and You—Understanding Yourself

Preventing Hearing Loss

Given the limited benefits of medicine or technology to help improve hearing following damage, it's even more important to protect our sense of hearing. We can do this by avoiding exceptionally loud noises, wearing earplugs when we cannot avoid such stimuli (see photo), and paying attention to bodily warnings of possible hearing loss, including a change in our normal hearing threshold and *tinnitus*, a whistling or ringing sensation in the ears. These relatively small changes can have lifelong benefits!

Bernd Leitner Fotodesign/ Shutterstock

Retrieval Practice 4.2 | How We See and Hear

SELF-TEST Completing this self-test, and then checking your answers by clicking on the answer button or by looking in Appendix B, will provide immediate feedback and helpful practice for exams.

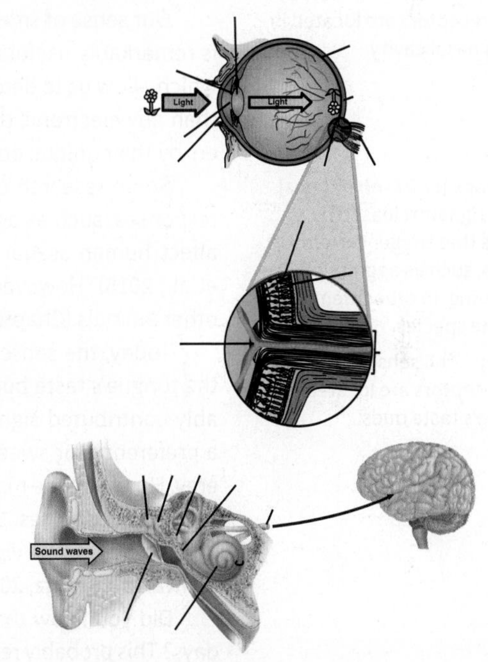

1. Identify the parts of the eye, placing the appropriate label on the figure to the right.

cornea	rod
iris	cone
pupil	fovea
lens	blind spot
retina	optic nerve

2. A visual acuity problem that occurs when the cornea and lens focus an image in front of the retina is called _____.
   a. farsightedness **b.** hyperopia
   c. myopia **d.** presbyopia
3. The _____ theory of color vision states that there are three systems of color opposites (blue-yellow, red-green, and black-white).
   a. trichromatic **b.** opponent-process
   c. tri-receptor **d.** lock-and-key
4. Identify the parts of the ear, placing the appropriate label on the figure to the right.

tympanic membrane	hammer
anvil	oval window
stirrup	cochlea

5. Chronic exposure to loud noise can cause permanent _____.
   a. auditory illusions **b.** auditory hallucinations
   c. nerve deafness **d.** conduction deafness

Think Critically

1. Which of your sensations, vision or hearing, would you most and least like to lose? Why?
2. Many people believe that blind people have supernatural hearing. How would brain plasticity explain how enhanced hearing might result from greater reliance on hearing or from just using auditory information more effectively?
3. Using what you've learned about pitch, how would you explain why an older person often has an easier time of hearing a man's voice than a woman's voice?

Real World Psychology

Can using a lower-pitched voice affect your perceived influence and power?

How can listening to loud music on headphones damage your hearing?

Nancy Kaszerman/ ZUMAPRESS/ Newscom

© maxuser/ iStockphoto

HINT: LOOK IN THE MARGIN FOR **[Q3]** AND **[Q4]**

4.3 Our Other Important Senses

LEARNING OBJECTIVES

Retrieval Practice While reading the upcoming sections, respond to each Learning Objective in your own words.

Review the processes involved in smell, taste, and the body senses.

- **Explain** the key factors in olfaction and gustation, and how the two senses interact.
- **Describe** how the body senses (skin, vestibular, and kinesthesis) work.

Vision and audition may be the most prominent of our senses, but the others—smell, taste, and the body senses—are also important for gathering information about our environment.

Smell and Taste

Smell and taste are sometimes called the *chemical senses* because they both rely on chemoreceptors that are sensitive to certain chemical molecules. Have you wondered why we have trouble separating the two sensations? Smell and taste receptors are located near each other and closely interact (**Figure 4.13**).

Olfaction The sense or act of smelling; receptors are located in the nose's nasal cavity.

Our sense of smell, **olfaction**, which results from stimulation of receptor cells in the nose, is remarkably useful and sensitive. We possess more than 1,000 types of olfactory receptors, which allow us to detect more than 10,000 distinct smells. The nose is more sensitive to smoke than any electronic detector, and—through practice—blind people can quickly recognize others by their unique odors.

Pheromones [FARE-oh-mones] Chemical signals released by organisms that trigger certain responses, such as aggression or sexual mating, in other members of the same species.

Gustation The sense or act of tasting; receptors are located in the tongue's taste buds.

Some research on **pheromones**—chemicals released by organisms that trigger certain responses, such as aggression or sexual mating, in other members of the same species—also affect human sexual responses (Baum & Cherry, 2015; Jouhanneau et al., 2014; Ottaviano et al., 2015). However, others suggest that human sexuality is far more complex than that of other animals (Chapters 10 and 14).

Today, the sense of taste, **gustation**, which results from stimulation of receptor cells in the tongue's taste buds, may be the least critical of our senses. In the past, however, it probably contributed significantly to our survival. For example, humans and other animals have a preference for sweet foods, which are generally nonpoisonous and are good sources of energy. However, the major function of taste, aided by smell, is to help us avoid eating or drinking harmful substances. Because many plants that taste bitter contain toxic chemicals, an animal is more likely to survive if it avoids bitter-tasting plants (French et al., 2015; Sagong et al., 2014; Schwartz & Krantz, 2016).

Did you know that our taste and smell receptors normally die and are replaced every few days? This probably reflects the fact that these receptors are directly exposed to the environment, whereas our vision receptors are protected by our eyeball and hearing receptors are protected by the eardrum. However, as we grow older, the number of taste cells diminishes, which helps explain why adults enjoy spicier foods than do infants. Scientists are particularly excited about the regenerative capabilities of the taste and olfactory cells because they hope to learn how to transfer this regeneration to other types of cells that are currently unable to self-replace when damaged.

Learning and Culture Many food and taste preferences are learned from an early age and from personal experiences (Fildes et al., 2014; Nicklaus, 2016; Tan et al., 2015). For example, adults who are told a bottle of wine costs $90 (rather than its real price of $10) report that it tastes better than the supposedly cheaper brand. Ironically, these false expectations actually trigger areas of the brain that respond to pleasant experiences (Plassmann et al., 2008). This means that in a neurochemical sense, the wine we believe is better does, in fact, taste better!

The culture we live in also affects our taste preferences. Many Japanese children eat raw fish, and some Chinese children eat chicken feet as part of their normal diet. Although most

FIGURE 4.13 Why we enjoy eating pizza: olfaction plus gustation When we eat pizza, the crust, cheese, sauce, and other food molecules activate taste receptor cells on our tongue, while the pizza's odors activate smell receptor cells in our nose. This combined sensory information is then sent on to our brain where it is processed in various association regions of the cortex. Interestingly, taste and smell also combine with sensory cells that respond to touch and temperature, which explains why cold, hard pizza "tastes" and "smells" different than hot, soft pizza.

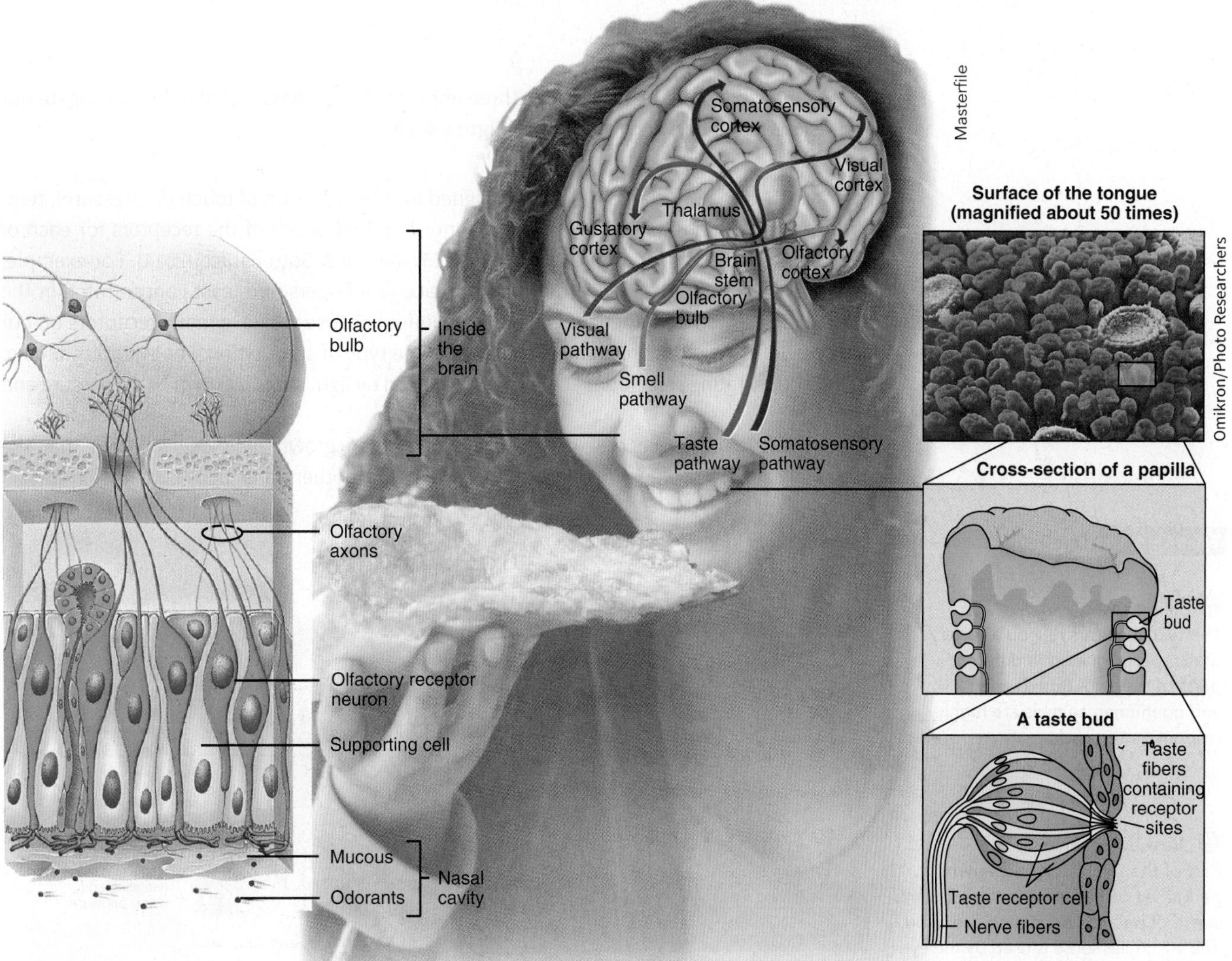

Masterfile

a. The smell pathway
Olfactory receptor neurons (shown here in blue) transduce information from odorant molecules that enter the nose. The olfactory nerve carries this information into the olfactory bulb, where most information related to smell is processed before being sent on to other parts of the brain. (Note that olfaction is the only sensory system that is NOT routed through the thalamus.)

b. The taste pathway
While eating and drinking, liquids and dissolved foods flow over the tongue's papillae (the lavender circular areas in the top photo) and into their pores. This activates the taste receptor cells, that then send messages on to the nerve fibers, which carry information on to the brain stem, thalamus, gustatory cortex, and somatosensory cortex.

U.S. children might consider these foods "yucky," they tend to love cheese, which children in many other cultures find repulsive.

Before going on, we need to update you on research findings on taste perception. It was long believed that we had only four distinct tastes: sweet, sour, salty, and bitter. However, we now know that we also have a fifth taste sense, *umami*, a word that means "delicious" or "savory" and refers to sensitivity to an amino acid called glutamate (Bredie et al., 2014; Lease et al., 2016). Glutamate is found in meats, meat broths, and monosodium glutamate (MSG).

Scientists also once believed that specific areas of the tongue were dedicated to detecting bitter, sweet, salty, and other tastes. Today we know that taste receptors, like smell receptors, respond differentially to the varying shapes of food and liquid molecules. The major taste receptors—taste buds—are distributed all over our tongues within little bumps called papillae (see again Figure 4.13).

The Body Senses

In addition to smell and taste, we have three important body senses that help us navigate our world—skin, vestibular, and kinesthesis (**Figure 4.14**).

Skin Senses Our skin is uniquely designed for the detection of touch (or pressure), temperature, and pain (**Figure 4.14a**). The concentration and depth of the receptors for each of these stimuli vary (Hsiao & Gomez-Ramirez, 2013; Ruzzoli & Soto-Faraco, 2014). For example, touch receptors are most concentrated on the face and fingers and least concentrated in the back and legs. Getting a paper cut can feel so painful because we have many receptors on our fingertips. Some receptors respond to more than one type of stimulation. For example, itching, tickling, and vibrating sensations seem to be produced by light stimulation of both pressure and pain receptors.

The benefits of touch are so significant for human growth and development that the American Academy of Pediatrics recommends that all mothers and babies have skin-to-skin

FIGURE 4.14 Our body senses—skin, vestibular, and kinesthesis

A Skin senses
The tactile senses rely on a variety of receptors located in different parts of the skin. Both human and nonhuman animals are highly responsive to touch.

© Philip Dyer/iStockphoto

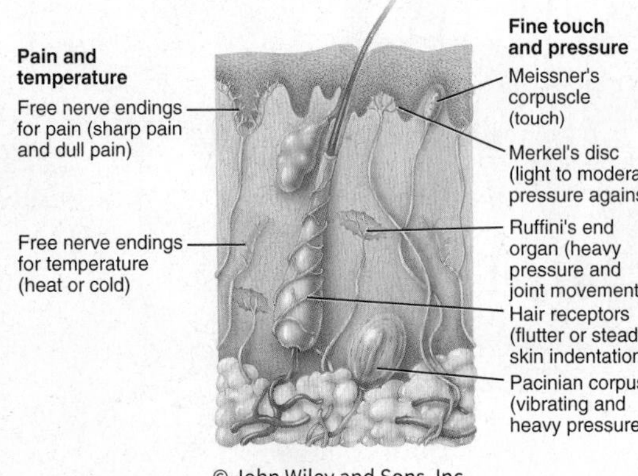

© John Wiley and Sons, Inc.

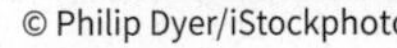

B Vestibular sense
Part of the "thrill" of amusement park rides comes from our vestibular sense of balance becoming confused. The vestibular sense is used by the eye muscles to maintain visual fixation and sometimes by the body to change body orientation. We can become dizzy or nauseated if the vestibular sense becomes "confused" by boat, airplane, or automobile motion. Children between ages 2 and 12 years have the greatest susceptibility to motion sickness.

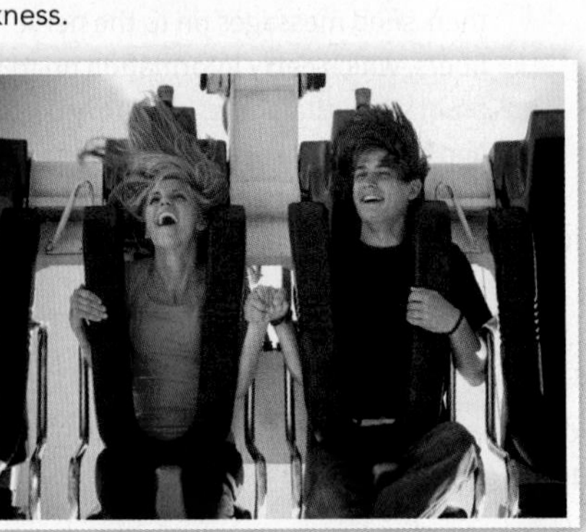

© RubberBall/Alamy Limited

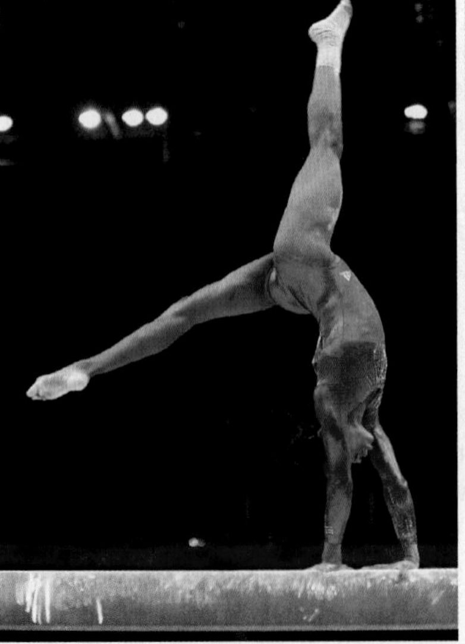

© Mike Blake/Reuters/Corbis

C Kinesthesis
This athlete's finely-tuned behaviors are the result of information provided by receptors in her muscles, joints, and tendons that detect the location, orientation, and movement of her individual body parts relative to each other.

contact in the first hours after birth. This type of contact, which is called *kangaroo care*, is especially beneficial for preterm and low-birth-weight infants, who then experience greater weight gain, fewer infections, and improved cognitive and motor development. How does kangaroo care lead to these improvements in infant health? See **Figure 4.15**.

Mike Kemp/Getty Images

FIGURE 4.15 Infant benefits from kangaroo care This type of skin-to-skin touch helps babies in several ways, including providing warmth, reducing pain (lower levels of arousal and stress increases pain tolerance and immune functioning), and better sleep quality. Other research, including a meta-analysis (which combines results from multiple studies), also found that babies who receive kangaroo care have a 36% lower likelihood [Q5] of death—as well as a lower risk of blood infection and similar positive long-term effects beyond infancy (Boundy et al., 2016; Burke-Aaronson, 2015; Castral et al., 2015; Feldman et al., 2014). As we discovered earlier in this and other chapters of this text, skin-to-skin contact, including holding hands and hugs, provides numerous physical and mental benefits for people of all ages.

Vestibular Sense

Our sense of balance, the **vestibular sense**, informs our brains of how our body (particularly our head) is oriented with respect to gravity and three-dimensional space (**Figure 4.14b**). When our head tilts, liquid in the *semicircular canals*, located in our inner ear, moves and bends hair cell receptors. In addition, at the end of the semicircular canals are *vestibular sacs*, which contain hair cells sensitive to our bodily movement relative to gravity (as shown in the amusement park ride examples in Figure 4.14b). Information from the semicircular canals and the *vestibular sacs* is converted to neural impulses that are then carried to our brains.

Vestibular sense The sense that provides information about balance and movement; receptors are located in the inner ear.

Kinesthesis

The sense that provides the brain with information about the location, orientation, and movement of individual body parts is called **kinesthesis** (**Figure 4.14c**). Kinesthetic receptors are found throughout the muscles, joints, and tendons of our body. They tell our brains which muscles are being contracted or relaxed, how our body weight is distributed, where our arms and legs are in relation to the rest of our body, and so on. For an interesting example of the unusual power of kinesthesis in young babies, see the following **PositivePsych.**

Kinesthesis The sense that provides information about the location, orientation, and movement of individual body parts relative to each other; receptors are located in muscles, joints, and tendons.

PP PositivePsych

Can Bouncing a Baby Increase Helping?

Did you know that kinesthesis may even play a role in our social behavior? Researchers in a clever study examined whether 14-month-old babies who bounced to music with another person were then more likely to assist that person (see photo) (Cirelli et al., 2014). To test this question, two researchers worked in pairs: one held a baby in a forward-facing carrier, while the second researcher stood across and facing the baby. When music started to play, both researchers gently bounced up and down (with the baby being automatically bounced as it was held in the forward-facing carrier).

Some babies were bounced at the same tempo as the researcher across from them, whereas other babies were bounced at a different tempo. When the song finished, the babies were removed from the carriers and stood on the floor. The baby then watched while the researcher, who previously stood in front of the baby in the carrier, starting drawing a picture. The researcher then "accidentally" dropped the marker she was using to draw, to see if the baby would toddle over to pick up the object and hand it back to her. (This is a standard task used to measure altruism in babies).

Can you predict what the researchers found? Surprisingly, compared to the babies who were bounced at an asynchronous, different tempo, babies who had been bounced in sync with the researcher were much more likely to toddle over, pick up the object and pass it back to the researcher. These synchronous babies also responded more quickly to the dropped pen.

Mecky/Getty Images

How would you explain these results? The researchers suggest that engaging in synchronous movement leads to feelings of shared social bonds between people, which in turn may lead to more prosocial behavior.

Think Critically

1. Could these research findings also help explain why we generally feel closer to someone after dancing with him or her?
2. Would members of a band, a dance troop, or the military feel more bonded, and thus be more likely to help? Why or why not?

Retrieval Practice 4.3 | Our Other Important Senses

SELF-TEST Completing this self-test, and then checking your answers by clicking on the answer button or by looking in Appendix B, will provide immediate feedback and helpful practice for exams.

1. _____ result(s) from stimulation of receptor cells in the nose.
   a. Audition **b.** Gustation
   c. Olfaction **d.** None of these options
2. Chemical signals released by organisms that may affect behavior, such as aggression and sexual mating, are known as _____.
   a. olfactory attractants **b.** sexual odorificants
   c. pheromones **d.** olfactory hormones
3. Most of our taste receptors are found on the _____.
   a. olfactory bulb **b.** gustatory cells
   c. frenulum **d.** taste buds
4. The skin senses include _____.
   a. pressure **b.** pain
   c. warmth and cold **d.** all of these options
5. The _____ sense is located in the inner ear and is responsible for our sense of balance.
   a. auditory **b.** vestibular
   c. kinesthetic **d.** olfactory

Think Critically

1. From an evolutionary perspective, which is more important—smell or taste?
2. From a personal perspective, which sense is most important to you—your sense of smell, taste, skin senses, vestibular, or kinesthetic?

Real World Psychology

Why do babies (and adults) need skin-to-skin contact?

Mike Kemp/Getty Images

HINT: LOOK IN THE MARGIN FOR [Q5]

4.4 Understanding Perception

LEARNING OBJECTIVES

Retrieval Practice While reading the upcoming sections, respond to each Learning Objective in your own words.

Summarize the three processes involved in perception.

- **Explain** illusions and why they're important.
- **Discuss** the process of selection and its three major factors.
- **Describe** the three ways we organize sensory data.
- **Review** the main factors in perceptual interpretation.
- **Discuss** the research findings on ESP and why so many people believe in it.

We are ready to move from *sensation* and the major senses to *perception*, the process of selecting, organizing, and interpreting incoming sensations into useful mental representations of the world.

Normally, our perceptions agree with our sensations. When they do not, the result is called an **illusion**, a false or misleading impression produced by errors in the perceptual process or by actual physical distortions, as in desert mirages. Illusions provide psychologists with a tool for studying the normal process of perception (**Figure 4.16**).

Illusion A false or misleading perception shared by others in the same perceptual environment.

Note that illusions are NOT the same as hallucinations or delusions. *Hallucinations* are false sensory experiences that occur without external stimuli, such as hearing voices during a psychotic episode or seeing particular images after using some type of hallucinogenic drug, such as LSD or hallucinogenic mushrooms. *Delusions* refer to false beliefs, often of persecution or grandeur, that may accompany drug or psychotic experiences.

Selection

In almost every situation, we confront more sensory information than we can reasonably pay attention to. Three major factors help us focus on some stimuli and ignore others: *selective attention*, *feature detectors*, and *habituation*.

Selective attention The process of focusing conscious awareness onto a specific stimulus, while filtering out a range of other stimuli occurring simultaneously.

Certain basic mechanisms for perceptual selection are built into the brain. For example, we're able to focus our conscious awareness onto a specific stimulus, while filtering out other stimuli thanks to the process of **selective attention** (**Figure 4.17**). This type of focused attention and concentration allows us to only select information that is important to us and discard the rest (Chen et al., 2016; Howell et al., 2016; Rosner et al., 2015).

FIGURE 4.16 Understanding perceptual illusions As you may have noticed, this text highlights numerous popular *myths* about psychology because it's important to understand and correct our misperceptions. For similar reasons, you need to know how illusions mislead out normal information processing and recognize that "seeing is believing, but seeing isn't always believing correctly" (Lilienfeld et al., 2010, p.7).

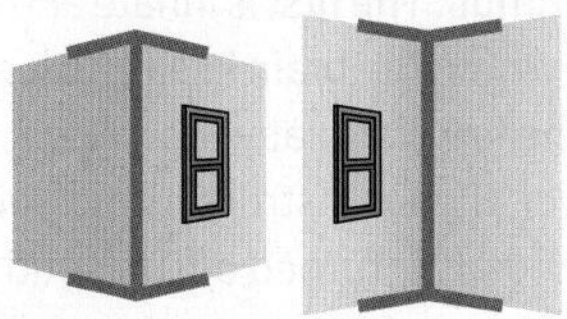

a. Müller-Lyer illusion
Which vertical line is longer? In fact, the two vertical lines are the same length, but psychologists have learned that people who live in urban environments normally see the one on the right as longer. This is because they have learned to make size and distance judgments from perspective cues created by right angles and horizontal and vertical lines of buildings and streets.

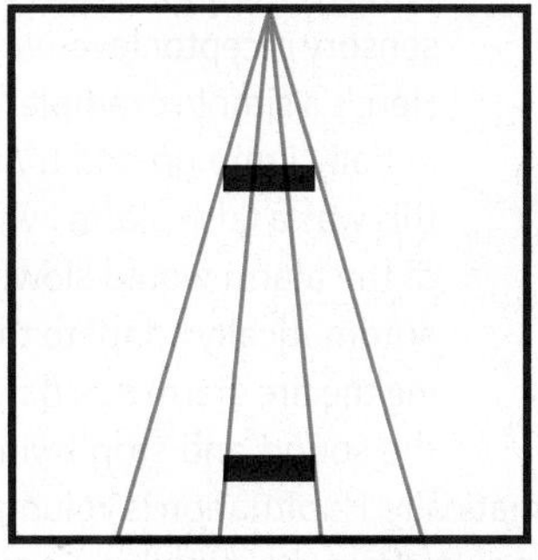

b. Ponzo illusion
Which of the two horizontal lines is longer? In fact, both lines are the exact same size, but the converging, vertical lines provide depth cues telling you that the top dark, horizontal line is farther away than the bottom line and therefore much longer.

Think Critically

1. Can you see how illusions like these might create real-world dangers for our everyday lives?
2. When you watch films of moving cars, the wheels appear to go backward. Can you explain this common visual illusion?

c. The horizontal-vertical illusion
Which is longer, the horizontal (flat) or the vertical (standing) line? People living in areas where they regularly see long straight lines, such as roads and train tracks, perceive the horizontal line as shorter because of their environmental experiences.

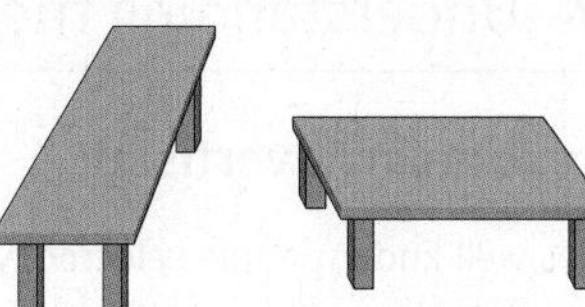

d. Shepard's tables
Do these two table tops have the same dimensions? Get a ruler and check it for yourself.

In addition to selective attention, the brains of humans and other animals contain specialized cells, called **feature detectors**, which respond only to specific characteristics of visual stimuli, such as shape, angle, or movement. For example, frogs are known to have specific "bug detector" cells that respond to small, dark, moving objects. Humans also have specific cells for detecting general motion in our peripheral vision. Interestingly, studies with humans have found feature detectors in the temporal and occipital lobes that respond maximally to faces (**Figure 4.18**). Problems in these areas can produce a condition called *prosopagnosia* (*prosopon* means "face," and *agnosia* means "failure to know"). Surprisingly, people with prosopagnosia can recognize that they are looking at a face. But they cannot say whose face is reflected in a mirror, even if it is their own or that of a friend or relative (Lohse et al., 2016; Tanzer et al., 2014; Van Belle et al., 2015).

Feature detectors Neurons in the brain's visual system that respond to specific characteristics of stimuli, such as shape, angle, or movement.

Habituation The brain's learned tendency to ignore or stop responding to unchanging information; an example of top-down processing.

Other examples of the brain's ability to filter experience occurs with **habituation**, the brain's learned tendency to ignore or stop responding to unchanging information. Apparently, the brain is "prewired" to pay more attention to changes in the environment than to stimuli that remain constant. As you'll discover in Chapter 9, developmental psychologists often use measurements of habituation to tell when a stimulus can be detected and discriminated by infants who are too young to speak. When presented with a new stimulus, infants initially pay attention, but with repetition they learn that the stimulus is unchanging and their responses weaken.

Habituation also can help explain why attention and compliments from a stranger are generally more exciting than those from a long-term romantic partner. Unfortunately, some people (who haven't taken psychology courses or read this text) may misinterpret and overvalue this new attention. They may even leave good relationships, not realizing that they will also soon habituate to the new person!

FIGURE 4.17 Selective attention Have you noticed that when you're at a noisy party, you can still select and attend to the voices of people you find interesting, or that you can suddenly pick up on another group's conversation if someone in that group mentions your name? These are prime examples of *selective attention*, also called the "cocktail party phenomenon."

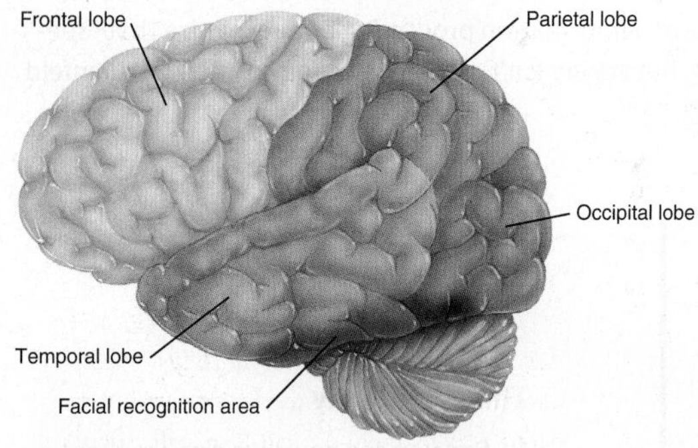

FIGURE 4.18 **Location of feature detectors**

Before going on, you may be confused about the distinction between *sensory adaptation*, which we discussed earlier, and *habituation.* If so, recall that adaptation refers to the *sensory receptors' innate* tendency to fatigue and stop responding to unchanging stimuli. In contrast, habituation is our *brain's learned* tendency to stop responding to unchanging stimuli. The first is innate and at the sensory receptor level, whereas the second is within the brain itself and learned. Here's a simple example: If someone pulled the fire alarm at your college, you'd initially jump up and try to evacuate. However, if your instructor told you that this was a false alarm, which couldn't be immediately turned off, the loud noise of the alarm would slowly start to fade because your sensory receptors would automatically adapt to the unchanging noise. In contrast, if students keep pulling the fire alarm as a dangerous prank, you and others will soon learn to ignore the sound and stop trying to evacuate. Adaptation happens to us and we respond automatically. Habituation is voluntary—we actively use our brains to deliberately redirect our attention away from the stimulus. Can you see how both sensory adaptation and habituation may have serious consequences? If you ignore the smell of leaking gas in your apartment, you'll eventually adapt—and may die from the fumes! Similarly, repeated "prank" fire alarms, lockdown drills at schools, and national "red alert" terrorist warnings may lead all of us to become complacent (and less careful). Hopefully, your increased understanding of sensory adaptation and habituation will better prepare you for a proper response when a true need arises.

Real World **Psychology**—Understanding the World

Using the Processes of Perception in Advertising

As advertisers and political operatives well know, people selectively attend to stimuli that are intense, novel, moving, contrasting, and repetitious (see photo). Why are ads so often repeated—given that sensory adaptation and habituation occur with unchanging stimuli? Advertisers know that repetition builds brand familiarity, which generally increases sales. However, they're also well aware of the *wear-in/wear-out theory* suggesting that repetition has an initial, positive effect, but too much exposure generally diminishes its effectiveness (Berlyne, 1970). Interestingly, complex and emotionally based ads tend to wear out more slowly than ads featuring simple concepts or rational appeals, and advertisers take many steps to avoid these problems (Kapexhiu, 2015). The good news is that your awareness of the psychological factors behind these persuasive techniques may help you become a more informed consumer!

©Yuri_Arcurs/iStockphoto

FIGURE 4.19 **Form perception and "impossible figures"**

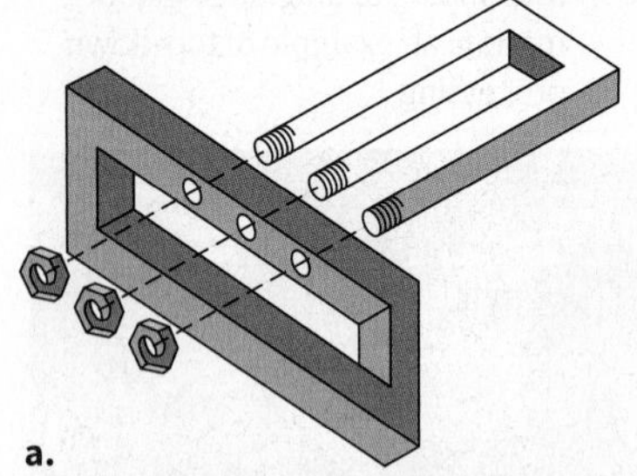
a.

b.

M.C. Escher's "Concave and Convex" © 2012 The M.C. Escher Company-Holland. All rights reserved

What do these two images teach us about form perception? When you first glance at figure (a) and the famous painting by M. C. Escher in (b), you detect specific features of the stimuli, and judge them as sensible figures. But as you try to sort and organize the different elements into a stable, well organized whole, you realize they don't add up—they're illogical or "impossible." The point of the illustration is that there is no one-to-one correspondence between your actual sensory input and your final perception. The same stimuli looked at from another perspective can lead to very different perceptions. Can you also see how this is another example of top-down versus bottom-up processing? We see both (a) and (b) as representing normal three-dimensional (3-D) figures. So we have trouble interpreting them because we're using our "higher," top-down cognitive processes or previous knowledge and expectations with normal drawings of 3-D. Our brain can only interpret (perceive) these deliberately misdrawn figures as being "impossible."

Organization

In the previous section, we discussed how we select certain stimuli in our environment to pay attention to and not others. The next step in perception is to organize this selected information into useful mental representations of the world around us. Raw sensory data are like the parts of a watch—the parts must be assembled in a meaningful way before they are useful. We organize visual sensory data in terms of *form*, *depth*, and *constancy*.

Form Perception Look at the first drawing in **Figure 4.19a**. What do you see? Can you draw a similar object on a piece of paper? This is known as an "impossible figure." Now look at **Figure 4.19b**, which shows a painting by M. C. Escher, a Dutch painter who created striking examples of perceptual distortion. Although drawn to represent three-dimensional objects or situations, the parts don't assemble into logical

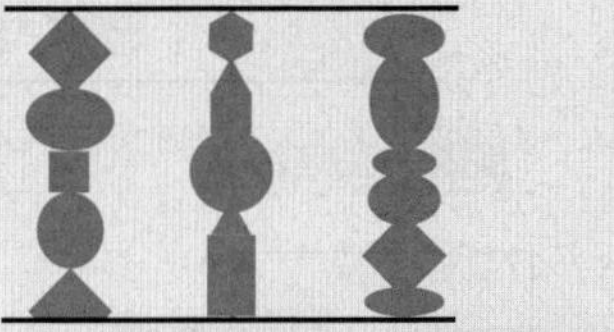

Figure–Ground:
Objects (the *figure*) are seen as distinct from the surroundings (the *gound*). (Here the red objects are the figure and the yellow backgound is the ground).

Proximity:
Objects that are physically close together are grouped together. (In this figure, we see 3 groups of 6 hearts, not 18 separate hearts.)

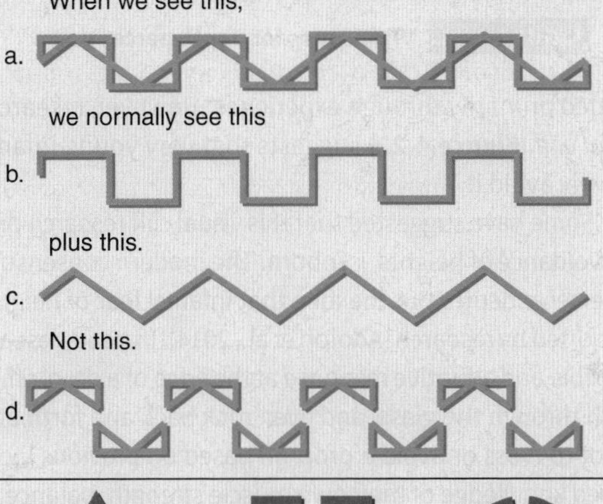

plus this.

Objects that continue a pattern are grouped together. (When we see line **a.**, we normally see a combination of lines **b.** and **c.** — not **d.**)
When we see this,

Closure:
The tendency to see a finished unit (triangle, square, or circle) from an incomplete stimulus.

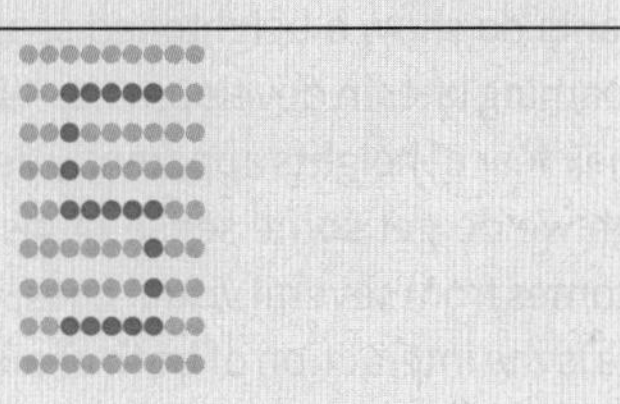

Similarity:
Similar objects are grouped together (the green colored dots are grouped together and perceived as the number 5).

FIGURE 4.20 Understanding Gestalt principles of organization Gestalt principles are based on the notion that we all share a natural tendency to force patterns onto whatever we see. Although the examples of the Gestalt principles in this figure are all visual, each principle applies to other modes of perception as well. For example, the Gestalt principle of *contiguity* cannot be shown because it involves nearness in time, not visual nearness. Similarly, the aural (hearing) effects of figure and ground aren't shown in this figure, but you've undoubtedly experienced them in a movie theater. Despite nearby conversations in the audience, you can still listen to the voices on the film because you make them your focus (the figure) versus the ground.

wholes. Like the illusions studied earlier, impossible figures and distorted paintings help us understand perceptual principles—in this case, the principle of *form perception*.

Gestalt psychologists were among the first to study form perception and how the brain organizes sensory impressions into a *gestalt*—a German word meaning "form" or "whole." They emphasized the importance of organization and patterning in enabling us to perceive the whole stimulus rather than perceive its discrete parts as separate entities. The Gestaltists proposed several laws of organization that specify how people perceive form (**Figure 4.20**).

The most fundamental Gestalt principle of organization is our tendency to distinguish between the *figure* (our main focus of attention) and *ground* (the background or surroundings).

Your sense of figure and ground is at work in what you are doing right now—reading. Your brain is receiving sensations of black lines and white paper, but your brain is organizing these sensations into black letters and words on a white background. You perceive the letters as the figure and the white as the ground. If you make a great effort, you might be able to force yourself to see the page reversed, as though a black background were showing through letter-shaped-holes in a white foreground. There are times, however, when it is very hard to distinguish the figure from the ground, as you can see in **Figure 4.21**. This is known as a *reversible figure*. Your brain alternates between seeing the light areas as the figure and seeing them as the ground.

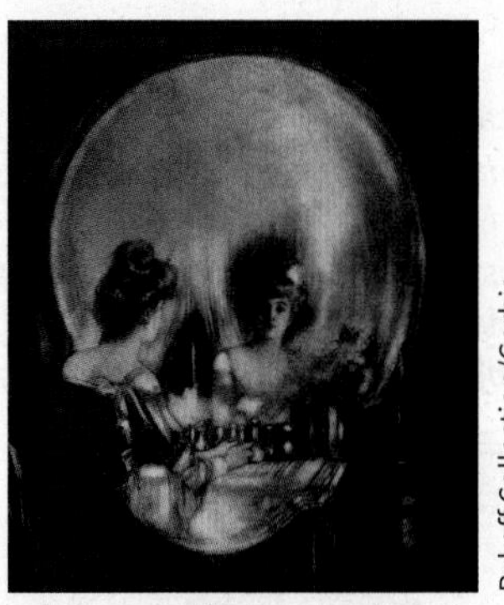
Rykoff Collection/Corbis

FIGURE 4.21 Understanding reversible figures This so-called *reversible figure* demonstrates alternating figure–ground relations. It can be seen as a woman looking in a mirror or as a skull, depending on what you see as figure or ground.

Depth Perception

In our three-dimensional world, the ability to perceive the depth and distance of objects—as well as their height and width—is essential. **Depth perception** is

Depth perception The ability to perceive three-dimensional space and to accurately judge distance.

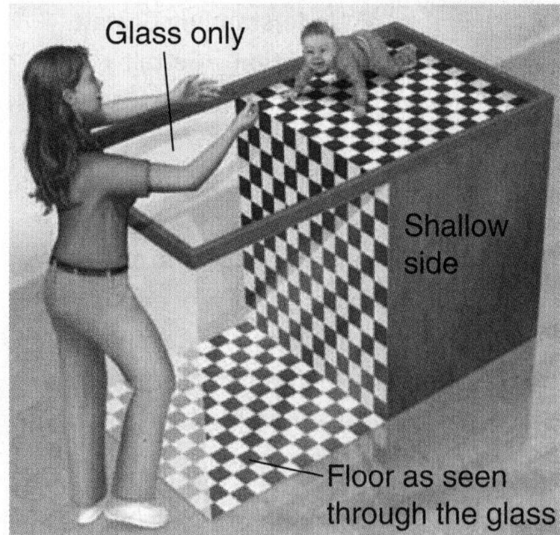

FIGURE 4.22 Visual cliff Given the desire to investigate depth perception, while also protecting infants and other experimental participants from actual falls, psychologists E. J. Gibson and R. D. Walk (1960) created a clever miniature cliff with a simulated drop off. Infants were placed on the glass surface that covered the entire table, and then encouraged (usually by their mothers) to crawl over either the shallow or the deep side. Their research showed that most crawling infants hesitate or refuse to move to the "deep end" of the visual cliff, indicating that they perceive the difference in depth.

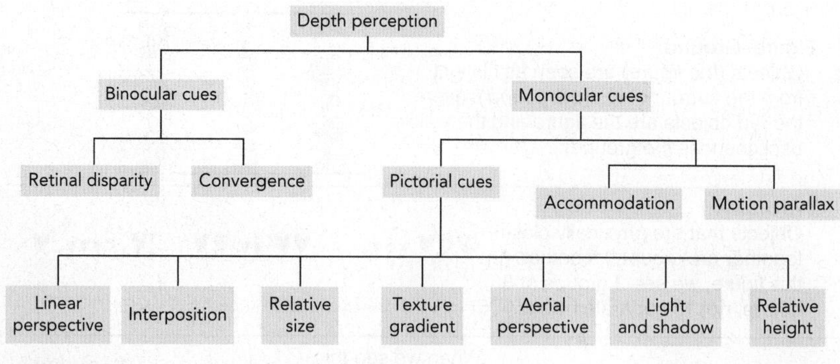

FIGURE 4.23 Visual cues for depth perception

learned primarily through experience. However, research using an apparatus called the *visual cliff* (**Figure 4.22**) suggests that very young infants can perceive depth, and will actively avoid it.

Some have suggested that this visual cliff research proves that depth perception, and an avoidance of heights, is inborn. The modern consensus is that infants are, indeed, able to perceive depth. But the idea that infants' fear of heights causes their avoidance is not supported by research (Adolph et al., 2014). Instead, researchers found that infants display a flexible and adaptive response at the edge of a drop-off. They pat the surface, attempt to reach through the glass, and even rock back and forth at the edge. They decide whether or not to cross or avoid a drop-off based on previous locomotor experiences, along with gained knowledge of their own muscle strength, balance, and other criteria.

The notion that fear of heights is NOT innate is further supported by other research showing that infants and young children willingly approach photos and videos of snakes and spiders, and even live snakes and spiders, rather than withdrawing from them (LoBue, 2013). Although infants do show a heightened sensitivity to snakes, spiders, and heights—which may facilitate fear learning later in development—they do not innately fear them. In short, infants perceive depth, but their fear of heights apparently develops over time, like walking or language acquisition.

Binocular cues Visual input from two eyes, which allows perception of depth or distance.

Although we do get some sense of distance based on hearing and even smell, most depth perception comes from several visual cues, which are summarized in **Figure 4.23**. The first mechanism we use is the interaction of both of our eyes, which produces **binocular cues** (**Figure 4.24**).

FIGURE 4.24 Binocular depth cues How do we perceive a three-dimensional world with a two-dimensional receptor system? One mechanism is the interaction of both eyes to produce binocular cues.

a. Retinal disparity

Stare at your two index fingers a few inches in front of your eyes with their tips half an inch apart. Do you see the "floating finger"? Move it farther away and the "finger" will shrink. Move it closer and it will enlarge. Because our eyes are about 2½ inches apart, objects at different distances (such as the "floating finger") project their images on different parts of the retina, an effect called *retinal disparity*. Far objects project on the retinal area near the nose, whereas near objects project farther out, closer to the ears.

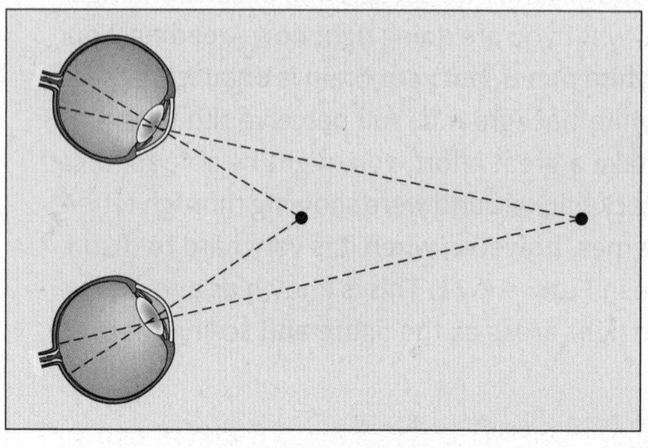

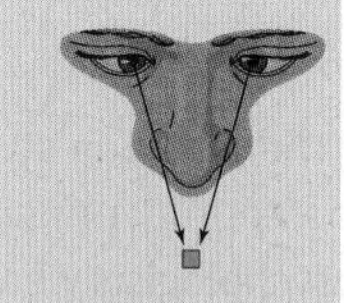

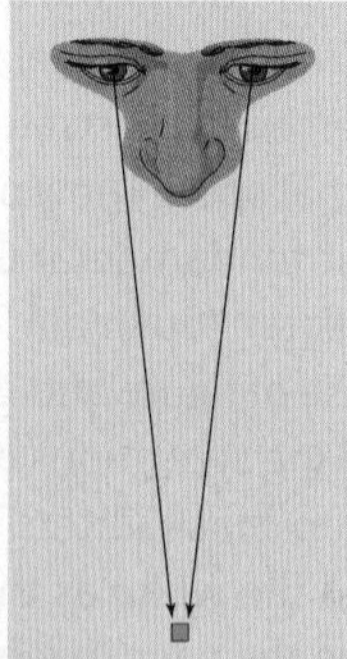

b. Convergence

Hold your index finger at arm's length in front of you and watch it as you bring it closer until it is right in front of your nose. The amount of strain in your eye muscles created by the *convergence*, or turning inward of the eyes, is used as a cue by your brain to interpret distance.

However, the binocular (two eyes) cues of **retinal disparity** and **convergence** are inadequate in judging distances longer than the length of a football field. Luckily, we have several **monocular cues**, which need only one eye to work. Imagine yourself as an artist and see whether you can identify each of the following monocular cues in this beautiful photo of the Taj Mahal, a famous mausoleum in India (**Figure 4.25**):

iStockphoto.com/adamkaz

FIGURE 4.25 **Monocular depth cues and the Taj Mahal**

- **Linear perspective** Parallel lines converge, or angle toward one another, as they recede into the distance.
- **Interposition** Objects that obscure or overlap other objects are perceived as closer.
- **Relative size** Close objects cast a larger retinal image than distant objects.
- **Texture gradient** Nearby objects have a coarser and more distinct texture than distant ones.
- **Aerial perspective** Distant objects appear hazy and blurred compared to close objects because of intervening atmospheric dust or haze.
- **Light and shadow** Brighter objects are perceived as being closer than darker objects.
- **Relative height** Objects positioned higher in our field of vision are perceived as farther away (see cartoon).

Two additional monocular cues for depth perception, **accommodation** of the lens of the eye and *motion parallax*, cannot be used by artists and are not shown in Figure 4.25. In *accommodation*, muscles that adjust the shape of the lens as it focuses on an object send neural messages to the brain, which interprets the signal to perceive distance. For near objects, the lens bulges; for far objects, it flattens. *Motion parallax* (also known as *relative motion*) refers to the fact that close objects appear to whiz by, whereas farther objects seem to move more slowly or remain stationary.

Retinal disparity The binocular cue of distance in which the separation of the eyes causes different images to fall on each retina.

Convergence A binocular depth cue in which the eyes turn inward (or converge) to fixate on an object.

Monocular cues Visual input from a single eye alone that contributes to perception of depth or distance.

Accommodation The process by which the eye's ciliary muscles change the shape (thickness) of the lens so that light is focused on the retina; adjustment of the eye's lens permitting focusing on near and distant objects.

Perceptual constancy The tendency to perceive the environment as stable, despite changes in the sensory input.

Constancies Perception

To organize our sensations into meaningful patterns, we develop **perceptual constancies**, the learned tendency to perceive the environment as stable, despite changes in an object's *size*, *color*, *brightness*, and *shape*. Without perceptual constancy, things would seem to grow as we get closer to them, change shape as our viewing angle changes, and change color as light levels change (Albright, 2015; Fleming, 2014; Stiles et al., 2015).

- **Size constancy** Regardless of the distance from us (or the size of the image it casts on our retina), *size constancy* allows us to interpret an object as always being the same size. For example, the image of the couple in the foreground of the photo (**Figure 4.26**) is much larger on our retina than the trees behind them. However, thanks to size constancy, we perceive them to be of normal size. Without this constancy, we would perceive people as "shrinking" when they move away from us, and "growing" when they move toward us. Although researchers have found evidence of size constancy in newborns, it also develops from learning and the environment. Case studies of people who have been blind since birth, and then have their sight restored, find that they initially have little or no size constancy (Sacks, 2015).
- **Color and brightness constancies** Our perception of color and brightness remain the same even when the light conditions change. Look at the two dogs' fur in this photo (**Figure 4.27**). We perceive the color and brightness as constant despite the fact that the wavelength of light reaching our retina may vary as the light changes.
- **Shape constancy** One additional perceptual constancy is the tendency to perceive an object's shape as staying constant even when the angle of our view changes (**Figure 4.28**).

BIZARRO

BIZZARO ©Dan Piraro/King Features Syndicate

Interpretation

In the previous two sections, we discussed how we select and organize all the available and incoming sensory information. Now we'll explore how our brains work to interpret this large data

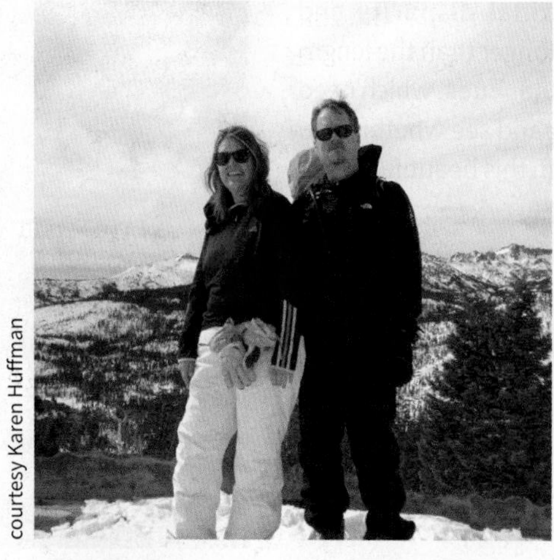

courtesy Karen Huffman

FIGURE 4.26 **Size constancy**

GK Hart/Vikki Hart/Getty Images, Inc.

FIGURE 4.27 **Color and brightness constancies**

base. This final stage of perception—*interpretation*—is influenced by several factors, including sensory adaptation, perceptual set, and frame of reference.

Stratton's experiment with the inverting goggles, discussed in the chapter overview, illustrates the critical role that *sensory adaptation* plays in the way we interpret the information that our brains gather. Without his ability to adapt his perceptions to a skewed environment, Stratton would not have been able to function. His brain's ability to retrain itself to interpret his new surroundings allowed him to create coherence from what would otherwise have been chaos.

As you can see in the following **Real World Psychology** example, our previous experiences, assumptions, and expectations also affect how we interpret and perceive the world,

FIGURE 4.28 **Shape constancy**

Note how as the coin is rotated, it changes shape, but we still perceive it as the same coin—thanks to shape constancy.

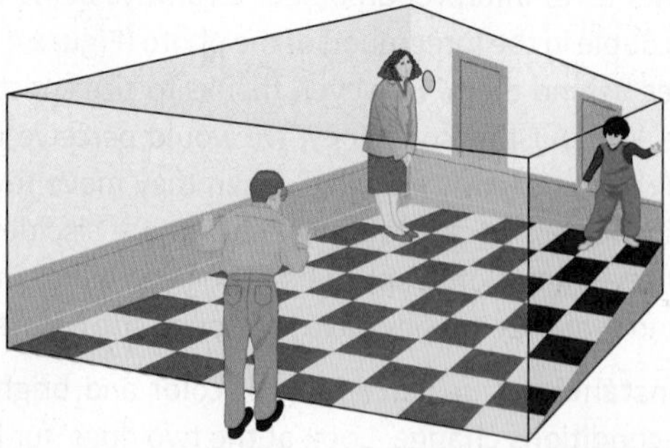

This Ames room illusion (shown in the two figures above) is found in many amusement parks. It's also been used in films, such as *The Lord of the Rings* trilogy, to make Gandalf appear much larger than the hobbits. In the first diagram, the child on the right appears to be almost the same size as his adult mother on the left. How does this illusion work? To a viewer peering through the peephole (diagram on the right), the room appears to be a normal cubic-shape. In fact, it's an artificially constructed, trapezoid-shaped room. The walls are slanted to the right, and the floor and ceiling are placed at an angle facing forward. Note also how the right corner of the room is much closer to the observer. If you're the person looking through the peephole, can you now understand why the mother and child appear to be almost the same size? If so, you'll also understand, but still be amazed, that when the two individuals walk across to exchange places, they will appear to be growing and/or shrinking! While mind-challenging and fun, this illusion illustrates what happens when our normal perceptual processes of size constancy, shape constancy, and depth perception are disrupted. We have no perceptual experience with trapezoid-shaped rooms, so we compensate by distorting the relative size of the human figures.

© OSTILL/iStockphoto

CHAPTER **5**

States of Consciousness

© Lise Gagne/iStockphoto

Real World **Psychology**

Things you'll learn in Chapter 5

[Q1] Could you fail to notice a clearly visible brutal assault (or a person in a gorilla suit) if you were otherwise distracted?

[Q2] Can using a computer or iPad late at night make it harder to fall asleep?

[Q3] Are you addicted to Facebook?

[Q4] Does binge drinking reduce condom use?

[Q5] Can using marijuana decrease your IQ?

[Q6] Can hypnosis decrease the pain of childbirth?

Throughout the chapter, margin icons for Q1–Q6 indicate where the text addresses these questions.

Chapter Overview

Control of consciousness determines the quality of life.

—Mihaly Csikszentmihaly

With the arrival of humans, it has been said, the universe has suddenly become conscious of itself. This, truly, it the greatest mystery of all.

—V. S. Ramachandran

We all commonly use the term *consciousness*, but what exactly does it mean? Is it simple awareness? What would it be like to be unaware? How can we study and understand the contents of our own consciousness when the only tool of discovery is consciousness itself?

We begin this chapter exploring our understanding of consciousness. Then we discuss the alternate states of consciousness (ASCs), including sleep, psychoactive drugs, meditation and hypnosis.

CHAPTER OUTLINE

5.1 Understanding Consciousness

LEARNING OBJECTIVES

Retrieval Practice While reading the upcoming sections, respond to each Learning Objective in your own words.

Summarize how selective attention and levels of awareness affect consciousness.

- **Define** consciousness and alternate states of consciousness (ASCs).
- **Describe** the key factors in selective attention.
- **Review** how consciousness exists on various levels of awareness.

Consciousness Our awareness of ourselves and our environment.

Alternate state of consciousness (ASC) A temporary mental state, other than ordinary waking consciousness, that occurs during sleep, dreaming, psychoactive drug use, and hypnosis.

What is **consciousness**? Most psychologists define it as a two-part awareness of both ourselves and our environment (Li, 2016; Thompson, 2015). This dual-natured awareness explains how we can be deeply engrossed in studying or a conversation with others and still hear the ping of an incoming message on our cell phones. However, if we're deeply asleep, we probably won't hear this same message ping because sleep is an **alternate state of consciousness (ASC)**, which is defined as a temporary mental state other than ordinary waking consciousness. Later in this chapter, we will discuss the ASCs of sleep, dreaming, meditation, and hypnosis. But we first need to explore the general nature of consciousness.

Selective Attention

Selective attention The process of focusing conscious awareness onto a specific stimulus, while filtering out a range of other stimuli occurring simultaneously.

William James, an important, early U.S. psychologist, likened *consciousness* to a stream that's constantly changing yet always the same. It meanders and flows, sometimes where the person wills and sometimes not. The process of **selective attention** (Chapter 4) allows us to control this *stream of consciousness* through deliberate concentration and full attention. For example, when listening to a classroom lecture, your attention may drift away to thoughts of a laptop computer you want to buy, or an attractive classmate. But you can catch and control this wandering stream of consciousness and willingly go back to selectively attending to the lecture.

Inattentional blindness The failure to notice a fully visible, but unexpected, stimulus when our attention is directed elsewhere; also known as perceptual blindness.

There's another aspect of selective attention that you may find fascinating. Sometimes when we're fully focused and selectively attending, we can fail to notice clearly visible stimuli, particularly if they're unexpected and we're otherwise distracted. For example, a Boston police officer chasing a shooting suspect on foot ran right past a brutal assault, but later claimed no memory of seeing the assault. Nevertheless, a jury convicted him of perjury and obstruction of justice (Lehr, 2009). Can you see how you might also fail to see such an assault if you were otherwise distracted? Another example of this surprising phenomenon, known as **inattentional blindness**, can be found in the popular YouTube videos in which observers fail to notice a grown man dressed in a gorilla costume as he repeatedly passes through a group of people (see the photo). These videos are based on a clever experiment that first asked participants to count the number of passes in a videotaped basketball game. Researchers then sent an assistant, dressed in a full gorilla suit, to walk through the middle of the ongoing game. Can you predict what happened? The research participants were so focused on their pass-counting task that they failed to notice the person in the gorilla suit (Simons & Chabris, 1999). [Q1]

4x6/Getty Images

Interestingly, when the participants later watched the video without having to count the basketball passes, most could not believe they had missed seeing the gorilla. Can you now see why magicians ask us to focus on a distracting element, such as a deck of cards or beautiful assistant, while they manipulate the real object of their magic, such as removing an unsuspecting volunteer's wallet or watch. On a more important note, this type of inattentional blindness can lead to serious problems for police officers focused on chasing suspects who might miss seeing an unexpected brutal assault, pilots focused on landing their plane who might fail to see a flock of birds, or a driver texting on a cell phone who fails to see the red light. In case you're wondering, this type of "blindness" also occurs in some of our other senses, such as *inattentional deafness*—failing to notice unexpected auditory stimuli when focusing on another task (Kreitz et al., 2016).

Levels of Awareness

As this example of inattentional blindness indicates, our *stream of consciousness* also varies in its level of awareness. Consciousness is not an all-or-nothing phenomenon—conscious or unconscious. Instead, it exists along a continuum, ranging from high awareness and sharp, focused alertness at one extreme, to middle levels of awareness, to low awareness or even nonconsciousness and coma at the other extreme (**Figure 5.1**).

As you can see from this figure, this continuum of levels of awareness also involves key concepts, known as *controlled* and *automatic* processes. When you're working at a demanding task or learning something new, such as how to drive a car, your consciousness is at the high end of the continuum. These **controlled processes** demand focused attention and generally interfere with other ongoing activities (Cohen & Israel, 2015; Maher & Conroy, 2016; Vidal et al., 2015).

ALTERNATE STATES OF CONSCIOUSNESS (ASCS)
Can exist on many levels of awareness, from high awareness to no awareness (e.g., drugs, sensory deprivation, sleep, dreaming, etc.)

CONTROLLED PROCESSES
Require focused, maximum attention (e.g., studying for an exam, learning to drive a car)

AUTOMATIC PROCESSES
Require minimal attention (e.g., walking to class while talking on a cell phone, listening to your boss while daydreaming)

SUBCONSCIOUS
Below conscious awareness (e.g., subliminal perception, sleeping, dreaming)

LITTLE OR NO AWARENESS
Biologically based lowest level of awareness (e.g., head injuries, anesthesia, coma; also the *unconscious mind*—a Freudian concept discussed in Chapter 11—reportedly consisting of unacceptable thoughts and feelings too painful to be admitted to consciousness)

FIGURE 5.1 **Levels of awareness**

In sharp contrast to the high awareness and focused attention required for controlled processes, **automatic processes** require minimal attention, and generally do not interfere with other ongoing activities. Think back to your teen years when you were first learning how to drive a car, and it took all of your attention (controlled processing). The fact that you can now effortlessly steer a car, and work the brakes all at one time (with little or no focused attention), is thanks to automatic processing. In short, learning a new task requires complete concentration and *controlled processing*. Once that task is well-learned, you can switch to *automatic processing*.

The following offers further insights and practical applications on the importance of selective attention and levels of awareness.

Controlled processes The mental activities that require focused attention and generally interfere with other ongoing activities.

Automatic processes The mental activities that require minimal attention and generally have little impact on other activities.

PS PsychScience

The Very Real Hazards of Distracted Driving

Thanks to repeated public service announcements and widespread media coverage, you've undoubtedly heard that cell phone use while driving, including dialing, talking, texting, reaching for the phone, etc., greatly increases your risk of accidents and near collisions. In fact, research on all such forms of "distracted driving" firmly supports the dangers of cell phone use while driving (Dingus et al., 2016; Simmons et al., 2016; Tucker et al., 2016). Given that motor vehicle crashes remain a leading cause of death and injury (LaVoie et al., 2016), and that we've all been repeatedly warned against cell phone use while driving, why is it still so common? Drivers often believe that talking on a cell phone while driving is no more dangerous than talking to another passenger. Is that true?

Using the latest in driving simulators, researchers set up four distinct driving scenarios: (1) driving alone without talking on a cell phone, (2) driving without talking on a cell phone, but talking with a passenger, (3) driving alone while speaking on a hands-free cell phone to someone in a remote location, or (4) driving under the same conditions as scenario (3), but the person in the remote condition could see the face of the driver and also observe the driving scene through a videophone (Gaspar et al., 2014).

Note that in all conditions the drivers confronted fairly challenging highway situations, such as merging and navigating around unpredictable drivers in other cars. While the drivers were confronting these challenges, researchers measured the drivers' performance, including distance from other cars, speed, and collisions.

Pamela Moore/iStock/Getty Images

What do you think happened? As you probably predicted, driving alone without talking on a cell phone (Condition 1) was the safest option. The next safest option was when drivers talked with a passenger but not on a cell phone (Condition 2). In contrast, the likelihood of a collision tripled when drivers were talking on a cell phone to a person in a remote location who had no awareness of what was going on during the drive (Condition 3). Interestingly, when the driver was talking to someone who was not in the car, but was on a specially-designed videophone, and hence could see both the driver's face and the view out the front windshield (Condition 4), the risks of collision were about the same as when the driver was just talking to a passenger (Condition 2). Can you see why? Like a passenger in the car, the remote viewer using the videophone could help the driver by stopping speaking and pointing out potentially dangerous situations while they were talking.

What's the take-home message? Most of us are unaware of the limits of our attention, and may mistakenly assume that we can safely drive while texting or talking on a cell phone. This study shows that traditional cell phone use is detrimental to driving precisely because it distracts the driver, while providing none of the assistance that a passenger in the car can typically provide.

Research Challenge

1. Based on the information provided, did this study (Gaspar et al., 2014) use descriptive, correlational, and/or experimental research?
2. If you chose:
   - *descriptive research*, is this a naturalistic observation, survey/interview, case study, and/or archival research?
   - *correlational research*, is this a positive, negative, or zero correlation?
   - *experimental research*, label the IV, DV, experimental group(s), and control group.
   - both *descriptive* and *correlational*, answer the corresponding questions for both.

Check your answers by clicking on the answer button or by looking in Appendix B.

Note: The information provided in this study is admittedly limited, but the level of detail is similar to what is presented in most text books and public reports of research findings. Answering these questions, and then comparing your answers to those provided, will help you become a better critical thinker and consumer of scientific research.

Before going on, it's important to understand how several key concepts in this section have direct, real-world applications—especially to distracted driving. First, talking with a passenger and talking or texting while driving are all risky behaviors because they require shifting your *selective attention* back and forth between what's on the road and your conversations. Second, given that people missed seeing someone dressed in a gorilla suit when they were distracted, can you see how any form of distracted driving also increases the possibility of *inattentional blindness* to serious traffic hazards? Third, inexperienced drivers should decrease all forms of distraction and use fully focused *controlled processes* while learning to drive, whereas experienced drivers are generally better equipped to handle a few distractions, such as talking to a passenger, because driving is largely an *automatic process* for them (Klauer et al., 2014). However, it's still true that distracted driving remains a serious health threat to all drivers and passengers.

What's the good news? Our ability to ignore distractions allows us to fully focus on important tasks, like listening to classroom lectures or studying. Unfortunately, this same ability can also lead to problems in situations requiring a broader focus, like driving. To minimize our risks, we should reduce unnecessary distractions, such as texting and cell phone use. Recent research also shows that mindfulness training (Chapter 3) can increase our awareness of unexpected stimuli and experiences (Schofield et al., 2015).

Retrieval Practice 5.1 | Understanding Consciousness

SELF-TEST Completing this self-test, and then checking your answers by clicking on the answer button or by looking in Appendix B, will provide immediate feedback and helpful practice for exams.

1. An organism's awareness of its own self and surroundings is known as ____.
   a. awareness **b.** consciousness
   c. alertness **d.** central processing
2. Mental states other than ordinary waking consciousness, such as sleep, dreaming, or hypnosis, are known as ____.
   a. alternate states of consciousness **b.** intentional blindness
   c. automatic processes **d.** none of these options
3. Mental activities that require minimal attention, without affecting other activities are called ____ processes.
   a. controlled **b.** peripheral
   c. conscious **d.** automatic
4. As you read this text, you should ____.
   a. be in an alternate state of consciousness (ASC)
   b. employ controlled processing
   c. let your stream of consciousness take charge
   d. employ automatic processing
5. Which of the following is TRUE?
   a. Consciousness exists on a continuum.
   b. Selective attention allows us to control our stream of consciousness.
   c. Our consciousness varies in its level of awareness.
   d. All of these options.

Think Critically

1. Can you see how selective attention and inattentional blindness might explain why some arguments with friends and love partners are impossible to resolve?
2. How would automatic processing explain how you can walk all the way from one end of your college campus to the other and not remember anything you did or saw along the way?

Real World Psychology

Could you fail to notice a clearly visible brutal assault (or a person in a gorilla suit) if you were otherwise distracted?

4x6/Getty Images

HINT: LOOK IN THE MARGIN FOR **[Q1]**

5.2 Understanding Sleep and Dreams

LEARNING OBJECTIVES

Retrieval Practice While reading the upcoming sections, respond to each Learning Objective in your own words.

Review the major processes that occur while we sleep and dream.

- **Describe** circadian rhythms and how they affect our lives.
- **Review** what happens during the various stages of sleep.
- **Compare and contrast** the key factors and theories involved in sleep and dreams.
- **Describe** the major sleep-wake disorders and their possible treatment.

Having explored the definition and description of everyday, waking consciousness and its properties of selective attention and levels of awareness, we now can explore two of our most common *alternate states of consciousness* (ASCs)—sleep and dreaming. These ASCs are fascinating to both scientists and the general public. Why are we born with a mechanism that forces us to sleep and dream for approximately a third of our lives? How can an ASC that requires reduced awareness and responsiveness to our environment be beneficial in an evolutionary sense? What are the functions and causes of sleep and dreams? To answer these questions and fully understand sleep and dreaming, we need to first discuss circadian rhythms.

Circadian Rhythms and Sleep

Most animals have adapted to our planet's cycle of days and nights by developing a pattern of bodily functions that wax and wane over each 24-hour period. For humans, our sleep cycles, alertness, core body temperature, moods, learning efficiency, blood pressure, metabolism, immune responses, and pulse rate all follow these **circadian rhythms** (Goh et al., 2016; Gumz, 2016; Hori et al., 2016). See **Figure 5.2**.

Circadian rhythm The internal, biological clock governing bodily activities, such as the sleep/wake cycle, temperature, that occur on a 24- to 25-hour cycle. (*Circa* means "about," and *dies* means "day.")

As you can see in the following **Real World Psychology**, disruptions in circadian rhythms are a particularly important problem for teenagers. However, we're all at risk of serious health issues and personal concerns, including increased risk of cancer, heart disease, autoimmune disorders, obesity, sleep disorders, and accidents, as well as decreased concentration and productivity (Situala et al., 2016; Tsimakouridze et al., 2015; Zuurbier et al., 2015). Those who suffer the most immediate and obvious ill effects from these sleep and circadian disturbances tend to be physicians, nurses, police, and others—about 20% of employees in the United States—whose occupations require rotating "shift work" schedules. Typically

Real World Psychology—Understanding the World

Circadian Challenges for Teenagers

Do you remember having trouble going to bed at a "reasonable hour" when you were a teenager and then having a really difficult time getting up each morning? This common pattern of staying up late at night and then sleeping longer in the morning appears to be a result of the natural shift in the timing of circadian rhythms that occurs during puberty (Carskadon et al., 1998; McGlinchey, 2015; Paiva et al., 2015). This shift is caused by a delay in the release of the hormone melatonin. In adults, this hormone is typically released around 10 p.m., signaling the body that it is time to go to sleep. But in teenagers, melatonin isn't released until around 1 a.m.—thus explaining why it's more difficult for teenagers to fall asleep as early as adults or younger children do.

Recognition of this unique biological shift in circadian rhythms among teenagers has led some school districts to delay the start of school in the morning. Research shows that even a 25- to 30-minute delay allows teenagers to be more alert and focused during class, and contributes to improvements in their moods and overall health (Boergers et al., 2014; Bryant & Gómez, 2015; Weintraub, 2016). Even more importantly, delaying the start of school in one large county in Kentucky was associated with a 16.5% decrease in car crashes among teenage drivers over the next two years (Danner & Philips, 2008).

FIGURE 5.2 Explaining circadian rhythms

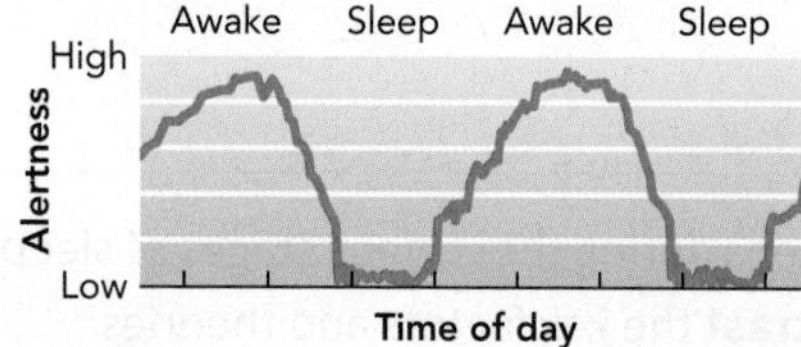

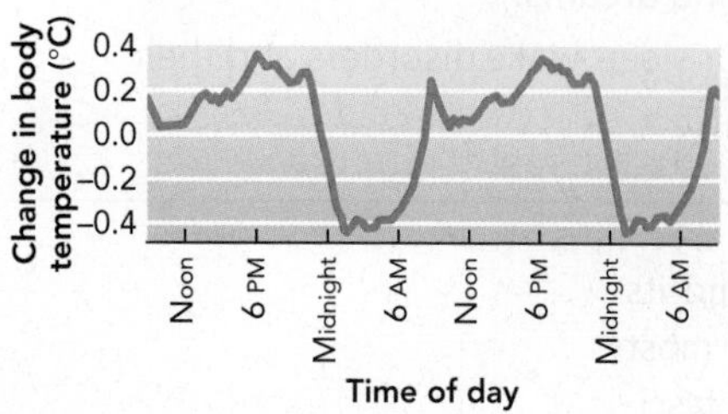

a. Note how the 24-hour daily circadian rhythm affects our degree of alertness and core body temperature, and how they rise and fall in similar ways.

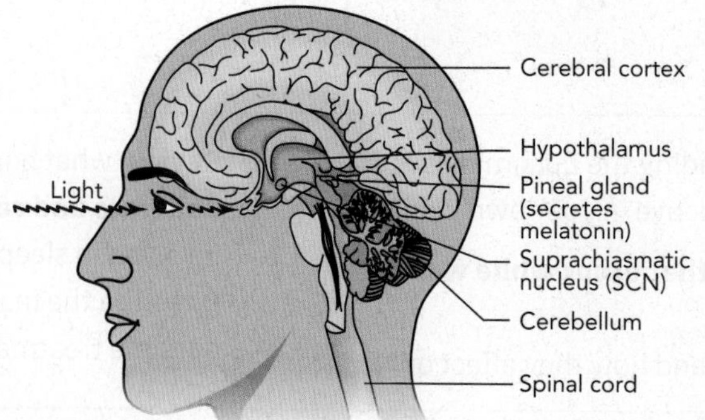

b. What controls our circadian rhythms? A part of the hypothalamus, the suprachiasmatic nucleus (SCN), receives information about light and darkness from our eyes, and then sends control messages to our *pineal gland,* which releases the hormone *melatonin.*

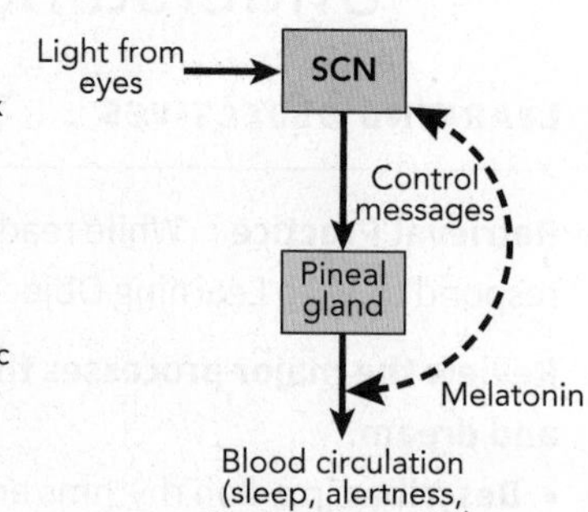

c. What regulates the melatonin? Like other feedback loops in the body, the level of melatonin in the blood is sensed by the SCN, which then adjusts the output of the pineal gland to maintain the "desired" level.

divided into a first shift (8 a.m. to 4 p.m.), second shift (4 p.m. to midnight) and a third shift (midnight to 8 a.m.), these work shifts often change from week to week, and clearly disrupt the workers' circadian rhythms. Some research suggests that productivity and safety are also believed to increase when shifts are rotated every three weeks instead of every week, and napping is allowed.

Psychology and **You**—Understanding Yourself

Jet Lag and Circadian Rhythms

Like shift work, flying across several time zones can also disrupt our circadian rhythms, and cause fatigue and irritability, decreased alertness and mental agility, as well as exacerbation of psychiatric disorders (Chiesa et al., 2015; Selvi et al., 2015; Srinivasan et al., 2014). Do you know why jet lag tends to be worse when we fly eastward rather than westward? It's because our bodies adjust more easily to going to bed later than to going to sleep earlier than normal.

© Pierivb/iStockphoto

Sleep Deprivation One of the biggest problems with disrupted circadian rhythms is the corresponding sleep deprivation that leads to reduced cognitive and motor performance, irritability and other mood alterations, and increased cortisol levels—all clear signs of stress (Arnal et al., 2016; Meldrum et al., 2015; Wright et al., 2015). Sleep deprivation also increases the risk of cancer, heart disease, and other illnesses, in addition to impairments in the immune system, which is one reason adults who get fewer than seven hours of sleep a night are four times as likely to develop a cold as those who sleep at least eight hours a night (CDC, 2016; Mezick et al., 2014; Prather et al., 2015). In addition, sleep-deprived adults are more likely to become obese. This may be because getting inadequate amounts of sleep interferes with the production of hormones that control appetite (Knutson, 2012). Interestingly, when we're sleep deprived, we're also more likely to "remember" things that did not actually happen, a phenomenon you'll learn more about in Chapter 7 (Frenda et al., 2014).

Perhaps the most frightening and immediate danger is that lapses in attention among sleep-deprived pilots, truck drivers, physicians, and other workers too often cause serious accidents and cost thousands of lives each year (see photo) (Bougard et al., 2016; Gonçalves et al., 2015; Lee et al., 2016a).

Will Vaultz Photography/AP Photo

Sleep deprivation can be fatal!

The good news is that greater enforcement of safety regulations for pilot flight times and hours of service for truck drivers and other public personnel could offset many of these public dangers. If you're concerned about your own levels of sleep deprivation, take the two-part test in the following **Psychology and You**.

Psychology and You—Understanding Yourself

Test Yourself | Sleep Deprivation

Take the following test to determine whether you are sleep deprived.

Part 1 Set up a small mirror next to this text and trace the black star pictured here, using your nondominant hand, while watching your hand in the mirror. The task is difficult, and sleep-deprived people typically make many errors. If you are not sleep deprived, it still may be difficult to trace the star, but you'll probably do it more accurately.

Part 2 Give yourself one point each time you answer yes to the following:

_____ **1.** I generally need an alarm clock or my cell phone alarm to wake up in the morning.

_____ **2.** I sometimes fall asleep unintentionally in public places.

_____ **3.** I try to only take late morning or early afternoon college classes because it's so hard to wake up early.

_____ **4.** People often tell me that I look tired and sleepy.

_____ **5.** I often struggle to stay awake during class, especially in warm rooms.

_____ **6.** I find it hard to concentrate and often nod off while I'm studying.

_____ **7.** I often feel sluggish and sleepy in the afternoon.

Pixtal/Age Fotostock America, Inc.

Effects of sleep deprivation Insufficient sleep can seriously affect your college grades, as well as your physical health, motor skills, and overall mood.

_____ **8.** I need several cups of coffee or other energy drinks to make it through the day.

_____ **9.** My friends often tell me I'm less moody and irritable when I've had enough sleep.

_____ **10.** I tend to get lots of colds and infections, especially around final exams.

_____ **11.** When I get in bed at night, I generally fall asleep within four minutes.

_____ **12.** I try to catch up on my sleep debt by sleeping as long as possible on the weekends.

The average student score is between 4 and 6. The higher your number, the greater your level of sleep deprivation.

Sources: Bianchi, 2014; Howard et al., 2014; National Sleep Foundation, 2012; Smith et al., 2012.

Stages of Sleep

The woods are lovely, dark and deep. But I have promises to keep, and miles to go before I sleep.

—Robert Frost

Having discussed our daily circadian cycle, and the problems associated with its disruption, we now turn our attention to our cyclical patterns and stages of sleep. We begin with an exploration of how scientists study sleep. Surveys and interviews can provide general information, but for more detailed and precise data researchers in sleep laboratories use a number of sophisticated instruments (**Figure 5.3**).

Imagine that you are a participant in a sleep experiment. When you arrive at the sleep lab, you are assigned one of several bedrooms. The researcher hooks you up to various physiological recording devices, which will require a night or two of adaptation before the researchers can begin to monitor your typical night's sleep (**Figure 5.3a**). After this adaptation, if you're like most sleepers, you'll begin the sleep cycle with a drowsy, presleep state followed by several distinct stages of sleep, each progressively deeper (**Figure 5.3b**). Then the sequence begins to reverse.

FIGURE 5.3 Scientific study of sleep and dreaming Data collected in sleep labs has helped scientists understand the stages of sleep.

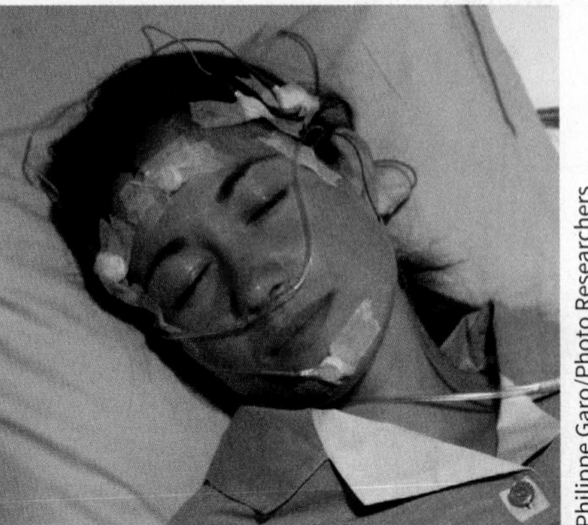

a. Participants in sleep research labs wear electrodes on their heads and bodies to measure brain and bodily responses during the sleep cycle. An electroencephalogram (EEG) detects and records brain-wave changes by means of small electrodes on the scalp. Other electrodes measure muscle activity and eye movements.

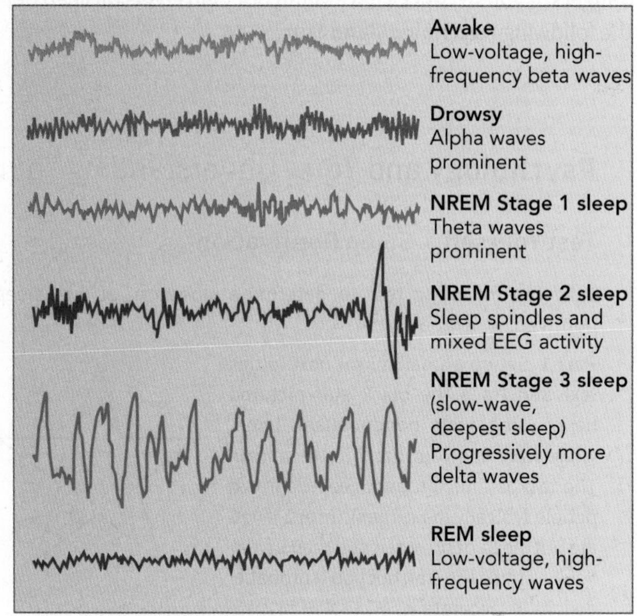

b. The stages of sleep, defined by telltale changes in brain waves, are indicated by the jagged lines. The compact brain waves of alertness gradually lengthen as you descend downward through NREM Stages 1-3. The final stage in the 90-minute sleep cycle is called REM sleep, which as you can see involves compact, faster brain waves.

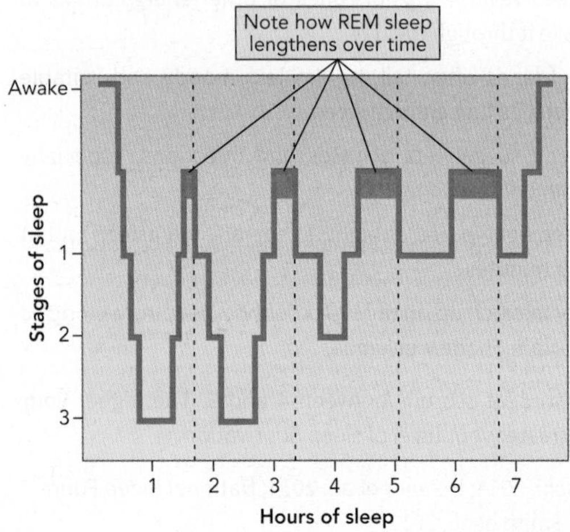

c. Your first sleep cycle generally lasts about 90 minutes from awake and alert, downward through NREM Stages 1-3, and then reverses back up through NREM Stages 3-1, followed a period of REM sleep. If you sleep 8 hours, you'll typically go through approximately four or five sleep cycles (as shown by the vertical dotted lines). Note how the overall amount of REM sleep increases as the night progresses, while the amount of deep sleep (Stage 3) decreases.

Note that we don't necessarily go through all sleep stages in this exact sequence (**Figure 5.3c**). But during the course of a night, people usually complete four to five cycles of light to deep sleep and then back up to light sleep. Each of these down and up cycles lasts about 90 minutes. Also note the two important divisions of sleep shown in Figure 5.3b and 5.3c: **non-rapid-eye-movement (NREM) sleep** (Stages 1, 2, and 3) and **rapid-eye-movement (REM) sleep.**

Non-rapid-eye-movement (NREM) sleep The sleep stages (1 through 3) during which a sleeper does not show rapid eye movements.

Rapid-eye-movement (REM) sleep The fourth stage of sleep, marked by rapid eye movements, irregular breathing, high-frequency brain waves, paralysis of large muscles, and often dreaming.

REM and NREM Sleep

During REM sleep, your brain's wave patterns are similar to those of a relaxed wakefulness stage, and your eyeballs will move up and down and from left to right. This rapid eye movement is a signal that dreaming is occurring. In addition, during REM sleep your breathing and pulse rates become fast and irregular, and your genitals may show signs of arousal. Yet your musculature is deeply relaxed and unresponsive, which many people mistakenly interpret as being in the deepest versus the actual lightest stage of sleep. Because of these contradictory qualities, REM sleep is sometimes referred to as *paradoxical sleep.*

Although dreams occur most frequently during REM sleep, they also sometimes occur during NREM sleep (Askenasy, 2016; Jones & Benca, 2013). Note how *Stage 1* of NREM sleep is characterized by theta waves and drowsy sleep. During this stage, many people experience sudden muscle movements called *myoclonic jerks* accompanied by a sensation of falling. In *Stage 2 sleep*, muscle activity further decreases and sleep spindles occur, which involve a sudden surge in brain wave frequency. Stages 1 and 2 are relatively light stages of sleep, whereas *Stage 3 sleep* involves the deepest stage of sleep, often referred to as *slow wave sleep (SWS)* or simply *deep sleep*. Sleepers during this deep sleep are very hard to awaken, and if something does wake them, they're generally confused and disoriented at first. This is also a time that sleepwalking, sleep talking, and bedwetting occur. (Note that Stage 3 sleep was previously divided into Stages 3 and 4, but the American Academy of Sleep Medicine [AASM] recently removed the Stage 4 designation.)

Why Do We Sleep and Dream?

There are many myths and misconceptions about why we sleep and dream (see **Psychology and You**). Fortunately, scientists have carefully studied what sleep and dreaming do for us and why we spend approximately 25 years of our life in these ASCs.

Psychology and You—Understanding Yourself

Test Yourself | Have You Heard These Common Myths?

Before reading the facts about each myth, place a check by any statement that you currently believe to be true.

1. ______ *Everyone needs 8 hours of sleep a night to maintain sound mental and physical health.*
2. ______ *Dreams have special or symbolic meaning.*
3. ______ *Some people never dream.*
4. ______ *Dreams last only a few seconds and occur only in REM sleep.*
5. ______ *When genital arousal occurs during sleep, it means the sleeper is having a sexual dream.*
6. ______ *Most people dream only in black and white, and blind people don't dream.*
7. ______ *Dreaming of dying can be fatal.*
8. ______ *It's easy to learn new, complicated things, like a foreign language, while asleep.*

Facts:

1. *Fact:* Although the average is 7.6 hours of sleep a night, some people get by on much less. Others may need as much as 11 hours (Blunden & Galland, 2014; Bootzin et al., 2015; Pellegrino et al., 2014).
2. *Fact:* Many people mistakenly believe that dreams can foretell the future, reflect unconscious desires, have secret meaning, reveal the truth, or contain special messages. But scientific research finds little or no support for these beliefs (Domhoff, 2010; Hobson et al., 2011; Lilienfeld et al., 2010, 2015).
3. *Fact:* In rare cases, adults with certain brain injuries or disorders do not dream (Solms, 1997). But otherwise, virtually all adults regularly dream, but many don't remember doing so. Even people who firmly believe they never dream report dreams if they are repeatedly awakened during an overnight study in a sleep laboratory. Children also dream regularly. For example, between ages 3 and 8, they dream during approximately 25% of their sleep time (Foulkes, 1993, 1999; Mindell & Owens, 2015).
4. *Fact:* Research shows that most dreams occur in real time. For example, a dream that seemed to last 20 minutes probably did last approximately 20 minutes (Dement & Wolpert, 1958). Dreams also sometimes occur in NREM sleep (Askenasy, 2016; Jones & Benca, 2013; Oudiette et al., 2012).
5. *Fact:* When sleepers are awakened during this time, they are no more likely to report sexual dreams than at other times.
6. *Fact:* People frequently report seeing color in their dreams. Those who are blind do dream, but they report visual images only if they lost their sight after approximately age 7 (Bakou et al., 2014; Meaidi et al., 2014).
7. *Fact:* This is a good opportunity to exercise your critical thinking skills. Where did this myth come from? Although many people have personally experienced and recounted a fatal dream, how would we scientifically prove or disprove this belief?
8. *Fact:* Although some learning can occur during the lighter stages (1 and 2) of sleep, processing and retention of this material is minimal (Chambers & Payne, 2015; Lilienfeld et al., 2010, 2015). Wakeful learning is much more effective and efficient.

Four Sleep Theories How do scientists explain our shared need for sleep? There are four key theories:

1. **Adaptation/protection theory** Sleep evolved because animals need to conserve energy and protect themselves from predators that are more active at night (Drew, 2013; Tsoukalas, 2012). However, as you can see in **Figure 5.4**, animals vary greatly in how much sleep they need each day. Those with the highest likelihood of being eaten by others, a higher need for food, and the lowest ability to hide tend to sleep the least.

Adaptation/protection theory of sleep The theory that sleep evolved to conserve energy and provide protection from predators.

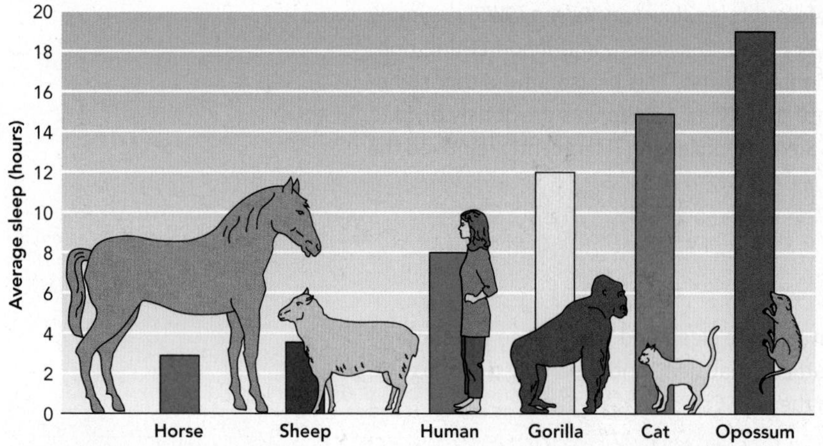

FIGURE 5.4 Average daily hours of sleep for different mammals According to the adaptation/protection theory, differences in diet and number of predators affect different species' sleep habits. For example, opossums sleep many hours each day because they are relatively safe in their environment and are able to easily find food and shelter. In comparison, sheep and horses sleep very little because their diets require almost constant foraging for food in more dangerous open grasslands.

2. **Repair/restoration theory** Sleep helps us recuperate from the depleting effects of daily waking activities. Essential chemicals and bodily tissues are repaired or replenished while we sleep, and the brain repairs and cleans itself of potentially toxic waste products that accumulate (Iliff et al., 2012; Konnikova, 2014; Underwood, 2013; Xie et al., 2013). We recover not only from physical fatigue but also from emotional and intellectual demands (Blumberg, 2015). When deprived of REM sleep, most people "catch up" later by spending more time than usual in this state (the so-called REM rebound), which further supports this theory.
3. **Growth/development theory** The percentage of deepest sleep (Stage 3) changes over the life span and coincides with changes in the structure and organization of the brain, as well as the release of growth hormones from the pituitary gland—particularly in children. As we age, our brains change less, and we release fewer of these hormones, grow less, and sleep less.
4. **Learning/memory theory** Sleep is important for learning and the consolidation, storage, and maintenance of memories (Bennion et al., 2015; Chambers & Payne, 2016; Vorster & Born, 2015). This is particularly true for REM sleep, which increases after periods of stress or intense learning. For example, infants and young children, who generally are learning more than adults, spend far more of their sleep time in REM sleep (**Figure 5.5**).

Repair/restoration theory of sleep The theory that sleep allows organisms to repair their bodies or recuperate from depleting daily waking activities.

Growth/development theory of sleep The theory that deep sleep (Stage 3) is correlated with physical development, including changes in the structure and organization of the brain; infants spend far more time in Stage 3 sleep than adults.

Learning/memory theory of sleep The theory that sleep is important for learning and for the consolidation, storage, and maintenance of memories.

Wish-fulfillment view of dreams The Freudian belief that dreams provide an outlet for unacceptable desires.

Latent content of dreams According to Freud, a dream's unconscious, hidden meaning is transformed into symbols within the dream's manifest content (story line).

Manifest content of dreams In Freudian dream analysis, the "surface," or remembered, story line, which contains symbols that mask the dream's latent content (the true meaning).

Activation–synthesis theory of dreams The theory that dreams are a by-product of random, spontaneous stimulation of brain cells during sleep, which the brain combines (synthesizes) into coherent patterns, known as dreams.

Three Dream Theories

Now let's look at three theories of why we dream—and whether dreams carry special meaning or information.

One of the oldest and most scientifically controversial explanations for why we dream is Freud's **wish-fulfillment view**. Freud proposed that unacceptable desires, which are reportedly normally repressed, rise to the surface of consciousness during dreaming. We avoid anxiety, Freud believed, by disguising our forbidden unconscious needs (what Freud called the dream's **latent content**) as symbols (**manifest content**). For example, a journey supposedly symbolizes death; horseback riding and dancing could symbolize sexual intercourse; and a gun might represent a penis.

Most modern scientific research does not support Freud's view (Domhoff, 2003, 2010; Sándor et al., 2014; Siegel, 2010). Critics also say that Freud's theory is highly subjective and that the symbols can be interpreted according to the particular analyst's view or training.

In contrast to Freud, a biological view called the **activation–synthesis theory of dreams** suggests that dreams are a by-product of random, spontaneous stimulation of brain cells during sleep, which the brain combines (synthesizes) into coherent patterns, known as dreams (Hobson, 1999, 2005; Wamsley & Stickgold, 2010). Alan Hobson and Robert McCarley (1977) proposed that specific neurons in the brain stem fire spontaneously during REM sleep and that the cortex struggles to "synthesize," or make sense of, this random stimulation by manufacturing dreams. This is *not* to say that dreams are totally meaningless. Hobson suggests that even if our dreams begin with essentially random brain activity, our individual personalities, motivations, memories, and life experiences guide how our brains construct the dream.

Have you ever dreamed that you were trying to run away from a frightening situation but found that you could not move? The activation-synthesis hypothesis might explain this dream as random stimulation of the amygdala. As you recall from Chapter 2, the amygdala is a specific brain area linked to strong emotions, especially fear. If your amygdala is randomly stimulated and you feel afraid, you may try to run. But you can't move because your major muscles are temporarily paralyzed during REM sleep. To make sense of this conflict, you might create a dream about a fearful situation in which you were trapped in heavy sand or someone was holding onto your arms and legs.

Finally, other researchers support the **cognitive view of dreams**, which suggests that dreams are simply another type of information processing that helps us organize and interpret our everyday experiences. This view of dreaming is supported by research showing strong similarities between dream content and waking thoughts, fears, and concerns (Domhoff, 2003, 2010; Malinowski & Horton, 2014; Sándor et al., 2014). Like most college students, you've probably experienced what are called "examination anxiety" dreams. You can't find your classroom, you're running out of time, your pen or pencil won't work, or you've completely forgotten a scheduled exam and show up totally unprepared. Sound familiar? Can you see how this type of dream fits best with the cognitive view of dreams?

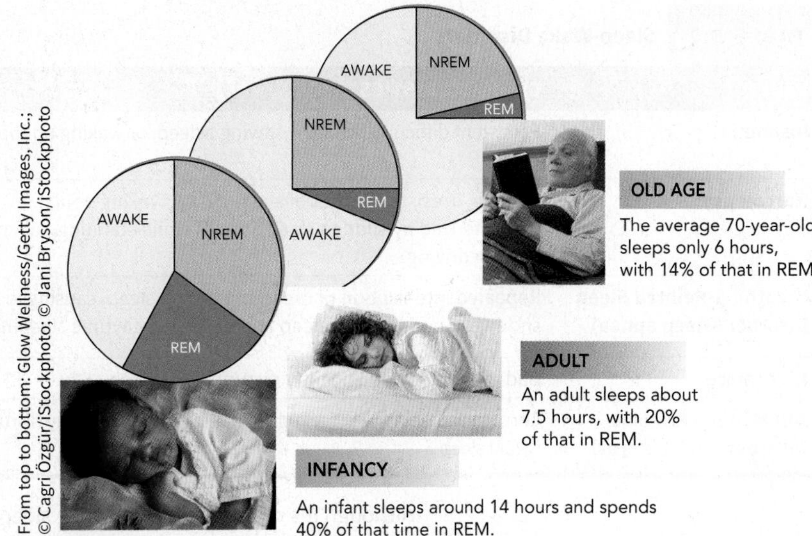
AWAKE
NREM
REM
OLD AGE
The average 70-year-old sleeps only 6 hours, with 14% of that in REM.
ADULT
An adult sleeps about 7.5 hours, with 20% of that in REM.
INFANCY
An infant sleeps around 14 hours and spends 40% of that time in REM.
From top to bottom: Glow Wellness/Getty Images, Inc.; © Cagri Özgür/iStockphoto; © Jani Bryson/iStockphoto

FIGURE 5.5 Aging and the sleep cycle Our biological need for sleep changes throughout our life span. The pie charts in this figure show the relative amounts of REM sleep, NREM sleep, and awake time the average person experiences as an infant, an adult, and an elderly person.

Gender, Culture, and Dreams

Men and women tend to share many of the common dream themes shown in **Table 5.1**. But women are more likely to report dreams of children, family members and other familiar people, household objects, and indoor events. In contrast, men tend to report dreams about strangers, violence, weapons, sexual activity, achievement, and outdoor events (Blume-Marcovici, 2010; Domhoff, 2003, 2010; Mathes et al., 2014; Mazandarani et al., 2013). (As a critical thinker, can you see how attitudes toward "proper" male and female gender roles, like caring for children, sex, weapons, and violence, might have affected what the participants were willing to report?) Interestingly, a study of WWII prisoners of war found that their dreams contained less sexuality and even less aggression than the male norms (Barrett et al., 2014).

Cognitive view of dreams The perspective that dreaming is a type of information processing that helps us organize and interpret our everyday experiences.

Dreams about basic human needs and fears (like sex, aggression, and death) seem to be found in all cultures. Children around the world often dream about large, threatening monsters or wild animals. In addition, dreams around the world typically include more misfortune than good fortune, and the dreamer is more often the victim of aggression than the cause of it (Chang, 2012; Domhoff, 2003, 2010; Yu, 2012).

TABLE 5.1 Top Ten Common Dream Themes

1. Being attacked or pursued
2. Falling
3. Sexual experiences
4. Being lost
5. Being paralyzed
6. Flying
7. Being naked in public
8. School, teachers, studying
9. Arriving too late
10. Death of a loved one or dead people as alive

Best View Stock/Getty Images, Inc.

Think Critically

1. Given that these 10 dream themes are found world wide, what might be the evolutionary advantage of such dreams?
2. Imagine that someone marketed a drug that provided complete rest and recuperation with only one hour of sleep. However, it did stop you from dreaming. Would you take the drug? Why or why not?

Sources: Mathes et al., 2014; Mazandarani et al., 2013; Yu, 2012.

Sleep–Wake Disorders

In any given year, an estimated 40 million Americans suffer from chronic sleep disorders, and another 30 million experience occasional sleep disorders serious enough to disrupt their daily activities (Larzelere & Campbell, 2016; Morin & Edinger, 2015; Ng et al., 2015).

Judging by these statistics, and your own experiences, it's not surprising to learn that almost everyone has difficulty sleeping at some point in his or her lifetime. The most common and serious of these disorders are summarized in **Table 5.2**.

TABLE 5.2 Sleep-Wake Disorders

LABEL	CHARACTERISTICS
Insomnia	Persistent difficulty falling or staying asleep, or waking up too early
Narcolepsy	Sudden, irresistible onset of sleep during waking hours, characterized by sudden sleep attacks while standing, talking, or even driving
Breathing-Related Sleep Disorder (Sleep apnea)	Repeated interruption of breathing during sleep, causing loud snoring or poor-quality sleep and excessive daytime sleepiness
Nightmare	Bad dream that significantly disrupts REM sleep
NREM Sleep Arousal Disorder (Sleep terror)	Abrupt awakening with feelings of panic that significantly disrupts NREM sleep

Although it's normal to have trouble sleeping before an exciting event, as many as 1 person in 10 may suffer from **insomnia**. Those who suffer from this disorder have persistent difficulty falling or staying asleep, or waking up too early. Nearly everybody has insomnia at some time; a telltale sign is feeling poorly rested the next day (Morin et al., 2013; Williamson & Williamson, 2015). Most people with serious insomnia have other medical or psychological disorders as well (American Psychiatric Association, 2013; Ashworth et al., 2015; Primeau & O'Hara, 2015). As a college student, you'll be particularly interested to know that students who send a high number of text messages are more likely to experience symptoms of insomnia (Murdock, 2013). Why? Researchers believe that most students feel pressured to immediately respond to texts, and may be awakened by alerts from incoming texts, which can reduce both sleep quality and quantity. On a related note, another study found that 10 to 30% of Americans experience long-term, *chronic* insomnia, compared to only 2% of hunter gatherers living in Africa and South America (Yetish et al., 2015). Could it be our American culture, filled with smart phones, television, and a hectic pace of modern life, is interfering with our need for good quality sleep?

Insomnia A sleep disorder characterized by persistent problems in falling asleep, staying asleep, or awakening too early.

Real World **Psychology**—Understanding the World

Hazards of Sleep Medication

To cope with insomnia, many people turn to nonprescription, over-the-counter sleeping pills, which generally don't work. In contrast, prescription tranquilizers and barbiturates do help people sleep, but they decrease Stage 3 and REM sleep, seriously affecting sleep quality. In the short term, limited use of drugs such as Ambien, Dalmane, Xanax, Halcion, and Lunesta may be helpful in treating sleep problems related to anxiety and acute, stressful situations. However, chronic users run the risk of psychological and physical drug dependence (Maisto et al., 2015; Mehra & Strohl, 2014; Taylor et al., 2016). The hormone *melatonin* may provide a safer alternative. Some research suggests that taking even a relatively small dose (just .3 to .4 milligrams) can help people fall asleep and stay asleep (Hajak et al., 2015; Paul et al., 2015).

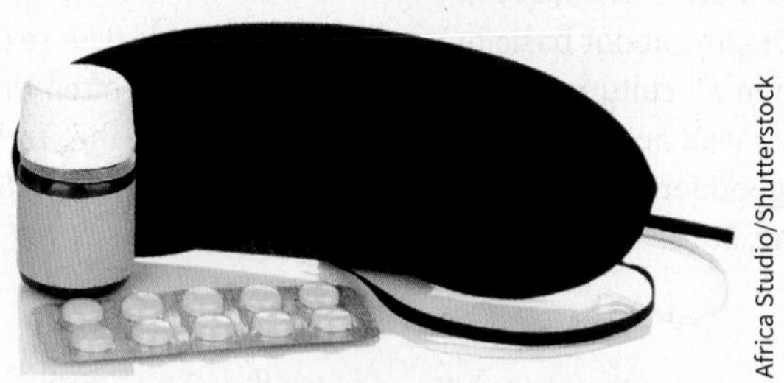
Africa Studio/Shutterstock

As you can see in the **Real World Psychology** above, many people turn to prescription or over-the-counter sleep medications to deal with their sleep disorders, but these drugs may have serious side effects. Fortunately, there are many effective strategies for alleviating sleep problems without medication. For example, research shows that watching television or using electronic devices, like your computer, iPad, eReader, or cell phone, around bedtime makes it much [Q2] harder to get to sleep (Chang et al., 2015; van der Lely et al., 2015; Wood, 2016). Why? Exposure to the light from the screens on these devices disrupts the circadian rhythm and reduces the level of melatonin in the body by about 22%, which makes it more difficult to fall asleep (especially for children and teenagers). See the following section for other recommendations about getting and staying asleep.

Psychology and You—Understanding Yourself

NATURAL SLEEP AIDS

Are you wondering what sleep experts recommend for sleep problems? Simple sleep hygiene tips and behavior therapies provide consistent benefits that you can apply in your own life (de Biase et al., 2014; Taylor et al., 2014). For example, when you're having a hard time going to sleep, don't keep checking the clock and worrying about your loss of sleep. In addition, remove all TVs, stereos, and books from your bedroom, and limit it to sleep rather than reading, watching movies, checking e-mail, and the like. If you need additional help, try some of the following suggestions.

During the Day

Exercise. Daily physical activity works away tension. But don't exercise vigorously late in the day, or you'll get fired up instead.

Keep regular hours. An erratic schedule can disrupt biological rhythms. Get up at the same time each day.

Avoid stimulants. Coffee, tea, soft drinks, chocolate, and some medications contain caffeine. Nicotine may be an even more potent sleep disrupter.

Avoid late meals and heavy drinking. Overindulgence can interfere with your normal sleep pattern.

Stop worrying. Focus on your problems at a set time earlier in the day.

Use presleep rituals. Follow the same routine every evening: listen to music, write in a diary, meditate.

Practice yoga. These gentle exercises help you relax.

In Bed

Use progressive muscle relaxation. Alternately tense and relax various muscle groups.

Use fantasies. Imagine yourself in a tranquil setting. Feel yourself relax.

Use deep breathing. Take deep breaths, telling yourself you're falling asleep.

Try a warm bath. This can induce drowsiness because it sends blood away from the brain to the skin surface.

Narcolepsy, a sleep disorder characterized by uncontrollable sleep attacks, afflicts about 1 person in 2,000 and generally runs in families (Ivanenko & Johnson, 2016; Kotagal & Kumar, 2013; Williamson & Williamson, 2015). During an attack, REM-like sleep suddenly intrudes into the waking state of consciousness. Victims may experience sudden, incapacitating attacks of muscle weakness or paralysis (known as cataplexy). They may even fall asleep while walking, talking, or driving a car. Although long naps each day and stimulant or antidepressant drugs can help reduce the frequency of attacks, both the causes and cure of narcolepsy are still unknown (**Figure 5.6**).

Perhaps the most serious sleep disorder is **sleep apnea**. People with sleep apnea may fail to breathe for a minute or longer and then wake up gasping for breath. When they do breathe during their sleep, they often snore. Sleep apnea seems to result from blocked upper airway passages and/or the brain's failure to send signals to the diaphragm, thus causing breathing to stop.

Unfortunately, people with sleep apnea are often unaware they have this disorder, and fail to understand how their repeated awakening during the night leaves them feeling tired and sleepy during the day. More importantly, they should know that sleep apnea is linked with high blood pressure, strokes, cancer, depression, and heart attacks (Kendzerska et al., 2014; Larzelere & Campbell, 2016; Lavie, 2015).

Treatment for sleep apnea depends partly on its severity. If the problem occurs only when you're sleeping on your back, sewing tennis balls to the back of your pajama top may help remind you to sleep on your side. Because obstruction of the breathing passages is related to obesity and heavy alcohol use (Tan et al., 2015; Yamaguchi et al., 2014), dieting and alcohol restriction are often recommended. For other sleepers, surgery, dental appliances that reposition the tongue, or CPAP machines that provide a stream of air to keep the airway open may provide help.

Research suggests that even "simple" snoring (without the breathing stoppage characteristic of sleep apnea) is associated with heart disease and possible death (Deeb et al., 2014; Jones & Benca, 2013). Although occasional mild snoring is fairly normal, chronic snoring is a possible warning sign that should prompt people to seek medical attention.

Two additional sleep disturbances are **nightmares** and **sleep terrors** (**Figure 5.7**). *Sleepwalking*, which sometimes accompanies sleep terrors, usually occurs during NREM sleep. (Recall that large muscles are paralyzed during REM sleep, which explains why sleepwalking normally occurs during NREM sleep.) An estimated 4% of U.S. adults—meaning over 8 million people—have at least one episode of sleepwalking each year

Narcolepsy A sleep order characterized by uncontrollable sleep attacks. (*Narco* means "numbness," and *lepsy* means "seizure.")

Sleep apnea A sleep disorder of the upper respiratory system that causes a repeated interruption of breathing during sleep; it also leads to loud snoring, poor-quality sleep, and excessive daytime sleepiness.

Nightmares The anxiety-arousing dreams that generally occur near the end of the sleep cycle, during REM sleep.

Sleep terrors The abrupt awakenings from NREM (non-rapid-eye-movement) sleep accompanied by intense physiological arousal and feelings of panic.

FIGURE 5.6 Narcolepsy Research on specially bred narcoleptic dogs has found degenerated neurons in certain areas of the brain (Siegel, 2000). Whether human narcolepsy results from similar degeneration is a question for future research. Note how this hungry puppy has lapsed suddenly from alert wakefulness to deep sleep even when offered his preferred food.

Zigy Kaluzny/Getty Images, Inc.

FIGURE 5.7 Nightmare or sleep terror? Nightmares, or bad dreams, occur toward the end of the sleep cycle, during REM sleep. Less common but more frightening are sleep terrors, which occur late in the cycle, during Stage 3 of NREM sleep. Like the child in this photo, the sleeper may sit bolt upright, screaming and sweating. They also may walk around, and talk incoherently and be almost impossible to awaken.

(Ohayon et al., 2012). *Sleep talking* can occur during any stage of sleep, but it appears to arise most commonly during NREM sleep. It can consist of single, indistinct words or long, articulate sentences. It is even possible to engage some sleep talkers in a limited conversation.

Nightmares, sleep terrors, sleepwalking, and sleep talking are all more common among young children, but they can also occur in adults, usually during times of stress or major life events (Carter et al., 2014; Ivanenko & Johnson, 2016). Patience and soothing reassurance at the time of the sleep disruption are usually the only treatment recommended for both children and adults. However, some people, such as those with *posttraumatic stress disorder (PTSD)*, suffer from such disabling and frightening nightmares that they may have suicidal thoughts or attempts, which generally requires professional intervention (Littlewood et al., 2016). See Chapters 3 and 13.

Retrieval Practice 5.2 | Understanding Sleep and Dreams

SELF-TEST Completing this self-test, and then checking your answers by clicking on the answer button or by looking in Appendix B, will provide immediate feedback and helpful practice for exams.

1. The circadian rhythm is _____.

a. patterns that repeat themselves on a twice-daily schedule
b. physical and mental changes associated with the cycle of the moon
c. circulating sleep processes in your brain
d. the biological clock governing activities that occur on a 24- to 25-hour cycle

2. The sleep stage marked by irregular breathing, eye movements, high-frequency brain waves, and dreaming is called _____ sleep.

a. beta **b.** hypnologic
c. REM **d.** transitional

3. The _____ theory says that sleep allows us to replenish what was depleted during daytime activities.

a. repair/restoration **b.** evolutionary/circadian
c. supply-demand **d.** conservation of energy

4. The _____ theory suggests dreams are by-products of random stimulation of brain cells.

a. activation-synthesis **b.** manifest-content
c. wish fulfillment **d.** information processing

5. A sleep disorder characterized by uncontrollable sleep attacks is known as _____.

a. dyssomnia **b.** parasomnia
c. narcolepsy **d.** sleep apnea

Think Critically

1. How are you affected by sleep deprivation and disruption of your circadian rhythms?

2. Which of the major theories of dreaming best explains your own dreams?

Real World Psychology

Can using a computer or an iPad late at night make it harder to fall asleep?

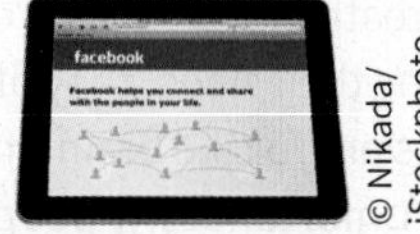

© Nikada/iStockphoto

HINT: LOOK IN THE MARGIN FOR **[Q2]**

5.3 Psychoactive Drugs

LEARNING OBJECTIVES

Retrieval Practice While reading the upcoming sections, respond to each Learning Objective in your own words.

Summarize the major issues and concepts associated with psychoactive drugs.

- **Identify** psychoactive drugs and the key terms associated with them.
- **Explain** how agonist and antagonist drugs produce their psychoactive effects.
- **Discuss** the four major categories of psychoactive drugs.

Virtually everyone routinely experiences the altered states of consciousness found in sleep and dreams. The vast majority of us also use *psychoactive drugs* (legal and/or illegal) to alter our moods, memory, concentration, and perception on a regular daily basis. As a busy college student, do you start your day with a routine cup of coffee? How about that glass of wine or a beer with your dinner that you use to help you relax after a hard day? If you're having trouble sleeping, do you reach for a couple of Tylenol PMs before going to bed? If you're like most people, you also manage to use these substances in moderation and without creating problems in your life. Therefore, you may be wondering why we're including these common drinks, pills, and behaviors as "drug use." If so, you'll be particularly interested in the next section.

Understanding Psychoactive Drugs

In our society, where the most popular **psychoactive drugs** are caffeine, tobacco, and ethyl alcohol, people often become defensive when these drugs are grouped with illicit drugs such as marijuana and cocaine. Similarly, marijuana users are disturbed that their drug of choice is grouped with "hard" drugs like heroin. Most scientists believe that there are good and bad uses of almost all drugs. The way drug use differs from drug abuse and how chemical alterations in consciousness affect a person, psychologically and physically, are important topics in psychology.

Alcohol, for example, has a diffuse effect on neural membranes throughout the nervous system. Most psychoactive drugs, however, act in a more specific way: by either enhancing a particular neurotransmitter's effect, as does an **agonist drug**, or inhibiting it, as does an **antagonist drug** (**Process Diagram 5.1**). Examples of agonist drugs are heroin and oxycodone, whereas naloxone is an example of an antagonist drug that is sometimes used to reverse a heroin overdose.

Is drug abuse the same as drug addiction? The term **drug abuse** generally refers to drug taking that causes emotional or physical harm to oneself or others. Drug consumption among abusers is also typically compulsive, frequent, and intense. **Addiction** is a broad term that refers to a condition in which a person feels compelled to use a specific drug, or engage in almost any type of compulsive activity, from working to surfing the Internet (Sdrulla et al., 2015; Smith, 2015). In fact, the latest version of the *Diagnostic and Statistical Manual (DSM-5)*, which officially classifies mental disorders, now includes *gambling disorders* as part of their substance-related and addictive disorders category. But other disorders, like "sex addiction" or "exercise addiction," were not included due to insufficient evidence at this time (American Psychiatric Association, 2013).

Psychoactive drug A chemical that changes mental processes, such as conscious awareness, mood, and perception.

Agonist drug A substance that binds to a receptor and triggers a response that mimics or enhances a neurotransmitter's effect.

Antagonist drug A substance that binds to a receptor and triggers a response that blocks a neurotransmitter's effect.

Drug abuse A type of drug taking that causes emotional or physical harm to the drug user or others.

Addiction A broad term that describes a condition in which the body requires a drug (or specific activity) in order to function without physical and psychological reactions to its absence; it is often the outcome of tolerance and dependence.

Interestingly, some evidence shows that we can even become addicted to Facebook. Researchers in one study prompted people with a series of statements, such as "You feel an urge to use Facebook more and more," and "You become restless or troubled if you are prohibited from using Facebook" (Andreassen et al., 2012). The degree to which you agree with items like these
[Q3] may indicate that you are addicted, meaning that you feel unreasonably compelled to check and use Facebook throughout the day. What explains this type of addiction? In addition to the self-reported "fear of missing out" (FOMO), researchers have found that using social media can create a high that's indistinguishable from that experienced during risky trading in the financial markets or with drug addiction (Hong & Chiu, 2016; Suissa, 2015; Zaremohzzabieh et al., 2014).

In addition to distinguishing between drug abuse and addiction, many researchers use the term **psychological dependence** to refer to the mental desire or craving to achieve a drug's effects. In contrast, **physical dependence** describes changes in bodily processes that make a drug necessary for minimum daily functioning. Physical dependence appears most clearly when the drug is withheld and the user undergoes **withdrawal** reactions, including physical pain and intense cravings.

Keep in mind that psychological dependence is no less damaging than physical dependence. The craving in psychological dependence can be strong enough to keep the user in a constant drug-induced state—and to lure an addict back to a drug habit long after he or she has overcome physical dependence. After repeated use of a drug, many of the body's physiological processes adjust to higher and higher levels of the drug, producing a decreased sensitivity called **tolerance**.

Tolerance leads many users to escalate their drug use and experiment with other drugs in an attempt to re-create the original pleasurable altered state. Sometimes using one drug increases tolerance for another, a result known as *cross-tolerance*. Developing tolerance or cross-tolerance does not prevent drugs from seriously damaging the brain, heart, liver, and other organs.

Psychological dependence The psychological desire or craving to achieve a drug's effect.

Physical dependence The changes in bodily processes that make a drug necessary for minimal functioning.

Withdrawal The discomfort and distress, including physical pain and intense cravings, experienced after stopping the use of an addictive drug.

Tolerance The bodily adjustment to continued use of a drug in which the drug user requires greater dosages to achieve the same effect.

STOP! This Process Diagram contains essential information NOT found elsewhere in the text, which is likely to appear on quizzes and exams. Be sure to study it CAREFULLY!

PROCESS DIAGRAM 5.1 **Agonist and Antagonist Drugs and Their Psychoactive Effects** Most psychoactive drugs produce their mood, energy, and perception-altering effects by changing the body's supply of neurotransmitters. Note how they can alter the synthesis, storage, or release of neurotransmitters **1.** They also can change the neurotransmitters' effects on the receiving site of the receptor neuron **2.** After neurotransmitters carry their messages across the synapse, the sending neuron normally deactivates the excess, or leftover, neurotransmitter **3.** However, when agonist drugs block this process, excess neurotransmitters remain in the synapse, which prolongs the effect of the psychoactive drug.

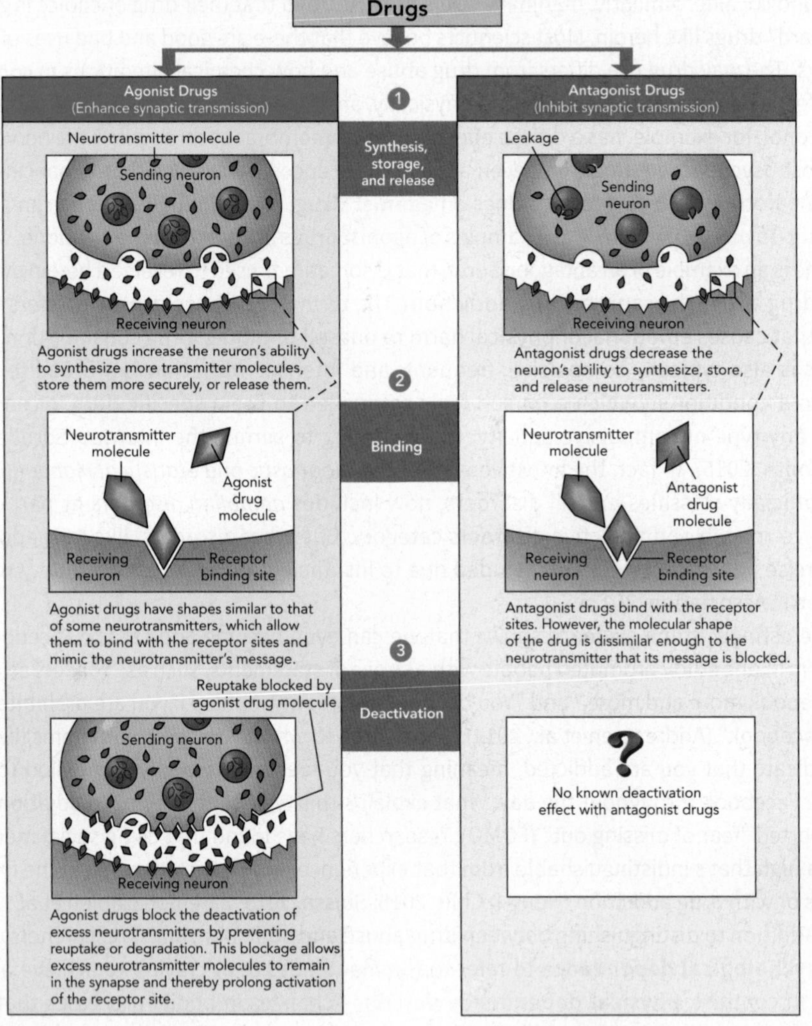

Four Drug Categories

Psychologists divide psychoactive drugs into four broad categories: *depressants, stimulants, opiates/opioids,* and *hallucinogens* (**Table 5.3**).

Depressant A drug that decreases bodily processes and overall responsiveness.

Depressants, sometimes called "downers," act on the central nervous system to suppress or slow bodily processes and reduce overall responsiveness. Because tolerance and both physical and psychological dependence are rapidly acquired with these drugs, there is strong potential for abuse.

Although alcohol is primarily a depressant, at low doses it has stimulating effects, thus explaining its reputation as a "party drug." As consumption increases, symptoms of drunkenness appear. Alcohol's effects are determined primarily by the amount that reaches the brain (**Table 5.4**). Because the liver breaks down alcohol at the rate of about 1 ounce per hour, the

TABLE 5.3 Effects of the Major Psychoactive Drugs

	CATEGORY	DESIRED EFFECTS	UNDESIRABLE EFFECTS
RICHARD NOWITZ/NG Image Collection	**Depressants (sedatives)** Alcohol, barbiturates, anxiolytics (antianxiety or tranquilizing drugs), alprazolam (xanax), flunitrazepam (rohypnol, "date-rape drug," "roofies"), ketamine (special K), gamma-hydroxybutyrate (GHB)	Tension reduction, euphoria, disinhibition, drowsiness, muscle relaxation	Anxiety, nausea, disorientation, impaired reflexes and motor functioning, amnesia, loss of consciousness, shallow respiration, convulsions, coma, death
TAYLOR S. KENNEDY/NG Image Collection	**Stimulants** Cocaine, amphetamine, ("crystal meth," "speed"), 3,4-methylene-dioxy-methamphetamine (MDMA, "ecstasy," "molly")	Exhilaration, euphoria, high physical and mental energy, reduced appetite, perceptions of power, sociability	Irritability, anxiety, sleeplessness, paranoia, hallucinations, psychosis, elevated blood pressure and body temperature, convulsions, death
	Caffeine	Increased alertness	Insomnia, restlessness, increased pulse rate, mild delirium, ringing in the ears, rapid heartbeat
SAM ABELL/NG Image Collection	Nicotine	Relaxation, increased alertness, sociability	Irritability, increased blood pressure, stomach pains, vomiting, dizziness, cancer, heart disease, emphysema
Uwe Schmid/OKAPIA/ Photo Researchers	**Opiates/opioids (narcotics)** Morphine, heroin ("H," "smack," "horse"), codeine, oxycodone	Euphoria, "rush" of pleasure, pain relief, prevention of withdrawal, sleep	Nausea, vomiting, constipation, painful withdrawal, shallow respiration, convulsions, coma, death
JOEL SARTORE//NG Image Collection	**Hallucinogens (psychedelics)** Lysergic acid diethylamide (LSD), mescaline (extract from the peyote cactus), psilocybin (extract from mushrooms)	Heightened aesthetic responses, euphoria, mild delusions, hallucinations, distorted perceptions and sensation	Panic, nausea, longer and more extreme delusions, hallucinations, perceptual distortions ("bad trips"), psychosis
	Marijuana	Relaxation, mild euphoria, nausea relief	Perceptual and sensory distortions, hallucinations, fatigue, increased appetite, lack of motivation, paranoia, possible psychosis

TABLE 5.4 Alcohol's Effect on the Body and Behavior

NUMBER OF DRINKS[a] IN TWO HOURS	BLOOD ALCOHOL CONTENT (%)[b]	EFFECT
(2)	0.05	Relaxed state; increased sociability
(3)	0.08	Everyday stress lessened
(4)	0.10	Movements and speech become clumsy
(7)	0.20	Very drunk; loud and difficult to understand; emotions unstable
(12)	0.40	Difficult to wake up; incapable of voluntary action
(15)	0.50	Coma and/or death

McPHOTO/Blickwinkel/Age Fotostock America, Inc.

[a]A drink refers to one 12-ounce beer, a 4-ounce glass of wine, or a 1.25-ounce shot of hard liquor.
[b]In the U.S., the legal blood alcohol level for "drunk driving" varies from 0.05 to 0.12.

Eric Risberg/AP Images

FIGURE 5.8 Alcohol and rape In January, 2016, 20-year-old Brock Turner was caught in the act and later convicted of sexually assaulting an unconscious woman he met earlier at a fraternity party. At the time of the rape, Turner's blood alcohol concentration was .17, twice the legal limit for driving. Turner was sentenced to six months in jail, expelled from Stanford University, and must register as a sexual offender for the rest of his life.

Think Critically

1. As you can see in the photo, numerous protests erupted following the judge's sentencing of Brock Turner to six months. Many believed that such a short jail term was inappropriate in light of his crime. What do you think?
2. Given alcohol's widely accepted social role in many college functions, what could we do to decrease its link with sexual assault?

number of drinks and the speed of consumption are both very important. People can die after drinking large amounts of alcohol in a short period of time. In addition, men's bodies are more efficient than women's at breaking down alcohol. Even after accounting for differences in size and muscle-to-fat ratio, women have a higher blood-alcohol level than men following equal doses of alcohol.

One of the most common, but seldom mentioned, risks with alcohol is that college students are more likely to have sex on days they binge drink. And they're also less likely to use condoms after binge drinking, which may lead to serious problems [Q4] such as STDs and unplanned pregnancies (Kerr et al., 2015). Sadly, overuse of alcohol and binge drinking has also been linked with major sexual crimes (**Figure 5.8**).

Before going on, it's also important to know that alcohol can be very dangerous when combined with certain other drugs. For example, combining alcohol and barbiturates—both depressants—can relax the diaphragm muscles to such a degree that the person suffocates (Marczinski, 2014). Does this information surprise you? Take the quiz in **Psychology and You** to discover if some of your other ideas about alcohol are really misconceptions.

Psychology and You—Understanding Yourself

Test Yourself | What's Your Alcohol IQ?

True or False?

_____ **1.** Alcohol increases sexual desire.

_____ **2.** Alcohol helps you sleep.

_____ **3.** Alcohol kills brain cells.

_____ **4.** It's easier to get drunk at high altitudes.

_____ **5.** Switching among different types of alcohol is more likely to lead to drunkenness.

_____ **6.** Drinking coffee and taking a cold shower are great ways to sober up after heavy drinking.

_____ **7.** Alcohol warms the body.

_____ **8.** You can't become an alcoholic if you drink only beer.

_____ **9.** Alcohol's primary effect is as a stimulant.

_____ **10.** People experience impaired judgment after drinking only if they show obvious signs of intoxication.

Answers: All these statements are false. Detailed answers are provided in this chapter and in Lilienfeld et al., 2010.

Stimulant A drug that increases overall activity and general responsiveness.

Whereas depressants suppress central nervous system activity, **stimulants**, or "uppers," increase the overall activity and responsiveness of the central nervous system. Like depressants, stimulants also involve the potential for abuse.

Cocaine is a powerful central nervous system stimulant extracted from the leaves of the coca plant. It produces feelings of alertness, euphoria, well-being, power, energy, and pleasure. But it also acts as an *agonist drug* to block the reuptake of our body's natural neurotransmitters that produce these same effects. As you can see in **Figure 5.9**, cocaine's ability to block reuptake allows neurotransmitters to stay in the synapse longer than normal—thereby artificially prolonging the effects and depleting the user's neurotransmitters.

Although cocaine was once considered a relatively harmless "recreational drug," even small initial doses can be fatal because cocaine interferes with the electrical system of the heart, causing irregular heartbeats and, in some cases, heart failure. It also can produce heart attacks, hypertension, and strokes by temporarily constricting blood vessels, as well as cognitive declines and brain atrophy (Levinthal, 2016; Siniscalchi et al., 2015; Vonmoos et al., 2014). The most dangerous form of cocaine is the smokable, concentrated version known as "crack," or "rock." Its lower price makes it affordable and attractive to a large audience. And its greater potency makes it more highly addictive.

Even legal stimulants can lead to serious problems. For example, cigarette smoking is considered to be the among the most preventable causes of death and disease in the United States, and nicotine addiction is the second leading cause of death worldwide (Herbst et al., 2014; Smith, 2015; Toll et al., 2014). Like smoking, chewing is also extremely dangerous. Sadly, in

FIGURE 5.9 Cocaine: an agonist drug in action

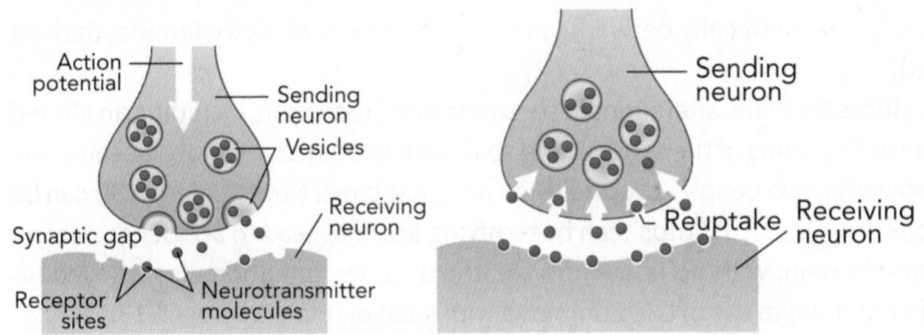

a. The two figures above depict how after releasing neurotransmitter into the synapse, the sending neuron normally reabsorbs (or reuptakes) excess neurotransmitter back into the vesicles, called terminal buttons.

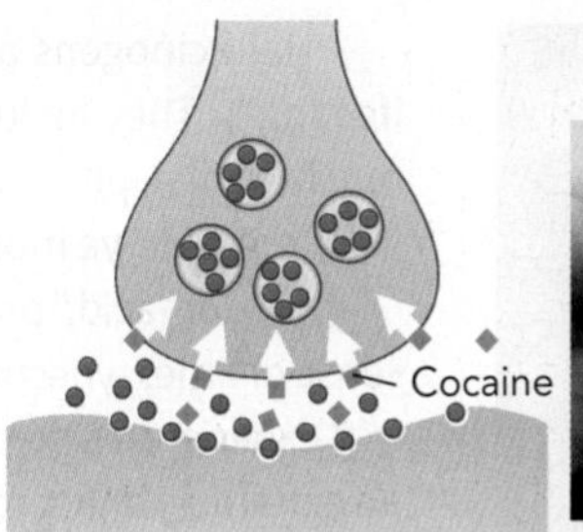

Todd Gipstein//NG Image Collection

b. This figure shows that when cocaine is present in the synapse, it will block the reuptake of dopamine, serotonin, and norepinephrine, and levels of these substances will increase. The result is overstimulation and a brief euphoric high. When the drug wears off, the depletion of the normally reabsorbed neurotransmitters may cause the drug user to "crash."

2014 fans mourned the loss of Hall of Fame baseball player Tony Gwynn, who died of mouth cancer, which he attributed to his lifelong use of chewing tobacco. Gwynn's family later filed a wrongful-death lawsuit against the tobacco industry on the grounds of negligence, fraud, and product liability (Kepner, 2016).

Given these well-known health hazards and the growing stigma against tobacco users, why do people ever start using tobacco? One of the most compelling reasons is that nicotine is highly addictive and it offers significant cognitive rewards (Castaldelli-Maia et al., 2016; Herman et al., 2014; Li et al., 2014). In fact, nicotine's effects—relaxation, increased alertness, and diminished pain and appetite—are so powerfully reinforcing that some people continue to smoke even after having a cancerous lung removed.

Opiates/opioids, or narcotics, which are derived from the opium poppy, are sometimes classified as depressants because they do depress the central nervous system (CNS). However, they also excite areas of the CNS. They're used medically to relieve pain because they mimic the brain's natural endorphins (Chapter 2), which numb pain and elevate mood (Satterly & Anitescu, 2015). This creates a dangerous pathway to drug abuse, however (see photo). After repeated flooding with opiates/opioids, the brain eventually reduces or stops the production of its own natural, pain-reducing endorphins. If the user later attempts to stop, the brain lacks both the artificial and normal level of painkilling chemicals, and withdrawal becomes excruciatingly painful (**Figure 5.10**).

Opiate/opioid A drug derived from opium that numbs the senses and relieves pain.

So far, we have discussed three of the four types of psychoactive drugs: depressants, stimulants, and opiates/opioids. Now we can explore the fourth category, known as **hallucinogens**, drugs that produce sensory or perceptual distortions, including visual, auditory, and kinesthetic hallucinations. Some cultures have used hallucinogens for religious purposes, as a way to experience "other realities" or to communicate with the supernatural. However, in Western societies, most people use hallucinogens for their reported "mind-expanding" potential.

Hallucinogen A drug that produces sensory or perceptual distortions.

FIGURE 5.10 How opiates/opioids may create physical dependence Psychoactive drugs such as opiates/opioids affect the brain and body in a variety of ways.

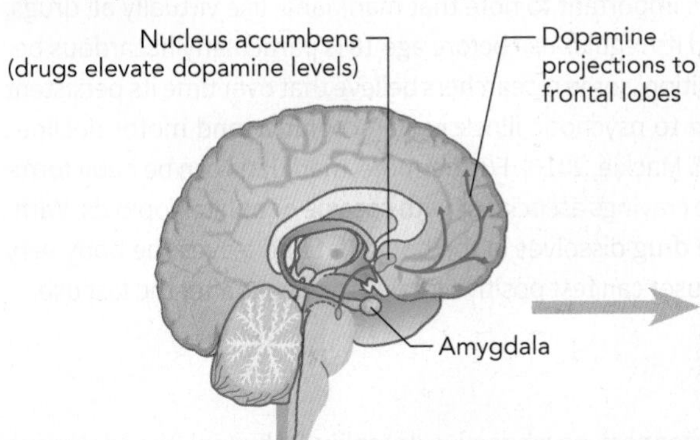

Jim Varney/Science Photo Library/Photo Researchers, Inc.

a. Most researchers believe that increased dopamine activity in this so-called *reward pathway* of the brain accounts for the reinforcing effects of most addictive drugs.

b. Absence of the drug triggers withdrawal symptoms (e.g., intense pain and cravings).

Ebet Roberts/Getty Images

The high cost of drug abuse
In May 2016, world-famous musician Prince died at the age of 57 due to an opioid overdose and possible addiction to painkillers (Eldred & Eligon, 2016; Eligon et al., 2016). Sadly, the opioid epidemic has been recently called the worst drug crisis in American history—rivaling the number of deaths from AIDS in the 1990s (Nolan & Amico, 2016).

Hallucinogens are commonly referred to as *psychedelics* (from the Greek for "mind manifesting"). They include mescaline (derived from the peyote cactus), psilocybin (derived from mushrooms), phencyclidine (chemically derived), and LSD (lysergic acid diethylamide, derived from ergot, a rye mold).

LSD, or "acid," produces dramatic alterations in sensation and perception, including an altered sense of time, synesthesia (blending of the senses), and spiritual experiences. Perhaps because the LSD experience is so powerful, few people "drop acid" on a regular basis. Nevertheless, LSD can be an extremely dangerous drug. Bad LSD "trips" can be terrifying and may lead to accidents, deaths, or suicide. One 32-year-old man, with no known psychiatric disorder, intentionally removed his own testes after the first and single use of LSD combined with alcohol (Blacha et al., 2013)!

Marijuana, also called cannabis, is generally classified as a hallucinogen even though it has some properties of a depressant—it induces drowsiness and lethargy—and some of a narcotic—it acts as a weak painkiller. In low doses, marijuana produces mild euphoria; moderate doses may lead to an intensification of sensory experiences and the illusion that time is passing slowly. High doses may produce hallucinations, delusions, and distortions of body image (Brewer & Collins, 2014; Hall & Degenhardt, 2014; Maisto et al., 2015). The active ingredient in marijuana is THC, or tetrahydrocannabinol, which attaches to receptors that are abundant throughout the brain.

Some research has found marijuana to be therapeutic in treating glaucoma (an eye disease), alleviating the nausea and vomiting associated with chemotherapy, and dealing with chronic pain and other health problems (Loflin & Earleywine, 2015; Piomelli, 2015; Wilkie et al., 2016).

In response to its potential medical benefits, and to free up police resources for fighting crime, many states have passed laws legalizing marijuana for medical and/or recreational use. However, it remains relatively controversial for a variety of reasons (Alpár et al., 2016; Pacek et al., 2015). For example, some researchers have reported several negative effects, such as increased throat and respiratory disorders, impaired lung functioning and immune response, declines in testosterone levels, reduced sperm count, and disruption of the menstrual cycle and ovulation (e.g., Harley et al., 2016; Shakoor et al., 2015; Smith et al., 2015). On the other hand, a longitudinal study that followed over a thousand cannabis versus tobacco users from the ages of 18 to 38 found no increase in physical health problems for the cannabis users, other than poorer periodontal health (Meier et al., 2016).

In addition to the conflicting research on possible health problems, some research supports the popular belief that marijuana serves as a "gateway" to other illegal drugs, whereas other studies find little or no connection (Kirisci et al., 2013; Levinthal, 2016; Mosher & Akins, 2014).

A third area with contradictory research has to do with cognitive functioning. Some studies report that marijuana use leads to decreases in IQ, educational achievement, and overall cognitive functioning (Suerken et al., 2016; Thames et al., 2014). However, these findings have been questioned by a study on over 2000 teenagers (Mokrysz et al., 2016). As discussed in Chapter 1, [Q5] correlational studies are always subject to the *third-variable problem*. The fact that other studies identified a connection between marijuana use and a lowered IQ may be because they didn't control for the influence of cigarette smoking—the third-variable. When the researchers in this last study isolated cigarette smoking, they found it to be the best predicting factor for lowered IQ.

As you can see, marijuana remains a controversial drug and more research is needed. While waiting for more conclusive research, it's important to note that marijuana, like virtually all drugs, can cause pregnancy complications, and its regular use before age 18 is particularly hazardous because the brain is still developing. In addition, some researchers believe that over time its persistent use and dependence still may be linked to psychotic illnesses and cognitive and motor declines (Alpár et al., 2016; Ganzer et al., 2016; Lu & Mackie, 2016). Furthermore, marijuana can be habit forming, but few users experience the intense cravings associated with cocaine or opiates/opioids. Withdrawal symptoms are mild because the drug dissolves in the body's fat and leaves the body very slowly, which explains why a marijuana user can test positive for days or weeks after the last use.

Club Drugs

As you may know from television or newspapers, psychoactive drugs like Rohypnol (the "date rape drug," also called "roofies"), MDMA (3,4-methylenedioxymethylamphetamine, or Ecstasy), GHB (gamma-hydroxybutyrate), ketamine ("special K"), methamphetamine ("ice" or "crystal meth"), "bath salts," and LSD, are all sometimes called "club drugs." This name reflects the fact that they're often used by teenagers and young adults at parties, bars, and nightclubs (NIDA, 2016). Unfortunately, these drugs can have very serious consequences (Dunne et al., 2015; NIDA, 2016; Weaver et al., 2015). For example, recreational use of Ecstasy is associated with potentially fatal damage to hippocampal cells in the brain, as well as a reduction in the neurotransmitter serotonin, which can lead to memory, sleep, mood, and appetite problems (Asl et al., 2015; Levinthal, 2016).

On the other hand, the club drug ketamine, *"Special K,"* shows promise as a potential treatment for major depression, suicidal behaviors, and bipolar disorders. Research has found that it appears to have an immediate and positive effect on parts of the brain responsible for executive and emotion regulation (Kishimoto et al., 2016; Lee et al., 2016b; Li et al., 2016).

Despite this one positive research finding and the positive reports of some users, it's important to note that club drugs, like all illicit drugs, are particularly dangerous because there are no truth-in-packaging laws to protect buyers from unscrupulous practices. Sellers often substitute unknown cheaper, and possibly even more dangerous, substances for the ones they claim to be selling. Also, club drugs (like most psychoactive drugs) affect the motor coordination, perceptual skills, and reaction time necessary for safe driving.

Impaired decision making is a serious problem as well. Just as "drinking and driving don't mix," club drug use may lead to risky sexual behaviors and increased risk of sexually transmitted infections. Add in the fact that some drugs, like Rohypnol, are odorless, colorless, tasteless, and can easily be added to beverages by individuals who want to intoxicate or sedate others, and you can see that the dangers of club drug use go far beyond the drug itself.

Retrieval Practice 5.3 | Psychoactive Drugs

SELF-TEST Completing this self-test, and then checking your answers by clicking on the answer button or by looking in Appendix B, will provide immediate feedback and helpful practice for exams.

1. Psychoactive drugs _____.
   a. change conscious awareness, mood, or perception
   b. are addictive, mind altering, and dangerous to your health
   c. are illegal unless prescribed by a medical doctor
   d. all these options
2. Drug taking that causes emotional or physical harm to the drug user or others is known as _____.
   a. addiction
   b. physical dependence
   c. psychological dependence
   d. drug abuse
3. _____ drugs inhibit or block a neurotransmitter's effect, whereas _____ drugs increase a neurotransmitter's effect.
   a. Antagonist; agonist
   b. Agonist; antagonist
   c. Protagonist; agonist
   d. Protagonist; co-agonist
4. _____ act on the brain and nervous system to increase overall activity and responsiveness.
   a. Stimulants
   b. Opiates/opioids
   c. Depressants
   d. Hallucinogens
5. Depressants include all the following *except* _____.
   a. antianxiety drugs
   b. alcohol
   c. tobacco
   d. Rohypnol

Think Critically

1. Which is more important in creating addiction—physical dependence or psychological dependence?
2. Do you think marijuana use should be legal in all states? Why or why not?

© Nikada/ iStockphoto

Real World Psychology

Are you addicted to Facebook?

Does binge drinking reduce condom use?

Can using marijuana decrease your IQ?

RICHARD NOWITZ/ NG Image Collection

JOEL SARTORE// NG Image Collection

HINT: LOOK IN THE MARGIN FOR **[Q3]**, **[Q4]**, AND **[Q5]**

5.4 Meditation and Hypnosis

LEARNING OBJECTIVES

Retrieval Practice While reading the upcoming sections, respond to each Learning Objective in your own words.

- **Describe** meditation and its major effects.
- **Identify** hypnosis, its key features, and its major myths.

Review the major features of meditation and hypnosis.

As we have seen, factors such as sleep, dreaming, and psychoactive drug use can create alternate states of consciousness (ASCs). Changes in consciousness also can be achieved by means of meditation and hypnosis.

Meditation

"Suddenly, with a roar like that of a waterfall, I felt a stream of liquid light entering my brain through the spinal cord . . . I experienced a rocking sensation and then felt myself slipping out of my body, entirely enveloped in a halo of light. I felt the point of consciousness that was myself growing wider, surrounded by waves of light" (Krishna, 1999, pp. 4–5).

Meditation A group of techniques generally designed to focus attention, block out distractions, and produce an alternate state of consciousness (ASC); it's believed to enhance self-knowledge and well-being through reduced self-awareness.

This is how spiritual leader Gopi Krishna described his experience with **meditation**, a group of techniques generally designed to focus attention, block out distractions, and produce an ASC (**Figure 5.11**). Most people in the beginning stages of meditation report a simpler, mellow type of relaxation, followed by a mild euphoria and a sense of timelessness. Some advanced meditators report experiences of profound rapture, joy, and/or strong hallucinations.

How can we explain these effects? Brain imaging studies suggest that meditation's requirement to focus attention, block out distractions, and concentrate on a single object, emotion, or word, reduces the number of brain cells that must be devoted to the multiple, competing tasks normally going on within the brain's frontal lobes. This narrowed focus thus explains the feelings of timelessness and mild euphoria.

PhotoAlto/Odilon Dimier/Getty Images

Research has also verified that meditation can produce dramatic changes in basic physiological processes, including heart rate, oxygen consumption, sweat gland responses, and brain activity. In addition, it's been somewhat successful in reducing pain, anxiety, and stress; lowering blood pressure; and improving overall cognitive functioning and mental health (see photo) (Crescentini et al., 2016; Heffner et al., 2016; Taylor & Abba, 2015). In fact, a meta-analysis (which combines results from multiple studies) revealed that 30 minutes of meditation may provide as much relief from anxiety and depression as antidepressants (Goyal et al., 2014).

As you can see in **Figures 5.11b** and **c**, studies have also found that meditation can change the body's sympathetic and parasympathetic responses, and increase structural support for the sensory, decision-making, emotion regulation, and attention-processing centers of the brain (Esch, 2014; Tang et al., 2014; Xue et al., 2014).

FIGURE 5.11 Benefits of meditation

Dan Dalton/Getty Images

a. Some meditation techniques, such as tai chi and hatha yoga, include body movements and postures. In other techniques, the meditator remains motionless, chanting or focusing on a single point, like a candle flame.

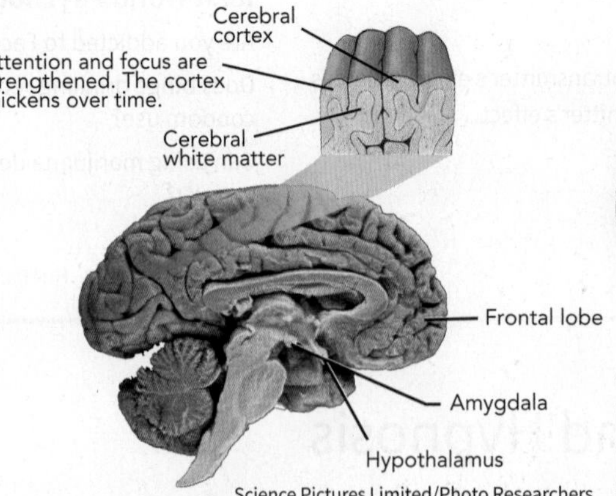

Science Pictures Limited/Photo Researchers

b. During meditation, the hypothalamus diminishes the sympathetic response and increases the parasympathetic response. Shutting down the fight-flight-freeze response in this way allows for deep rest, slower respiration, and overall relaxation.

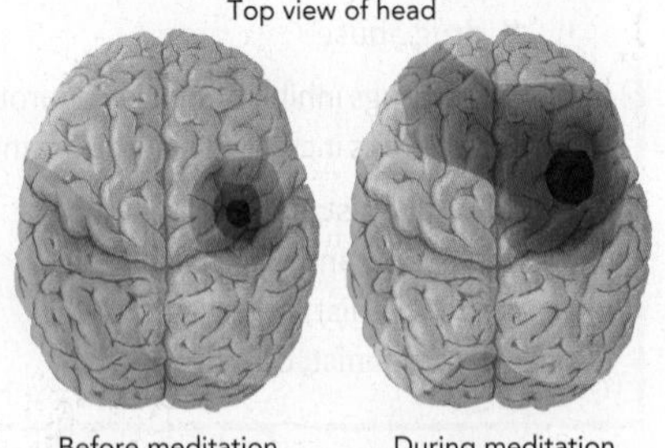

c. Researchers have found that an increased area of the brain responds to sensory stimuli during meditation, suggesting that meditation enhances the coordination between the brain hemispheres (Kilpatrick et al., 2011; Kurth et al., 2014). Note how much the blue-colored areas enlarged and spread from the right to the left hemisphere during meditation.

A number of elite athletes use meditation to help prepare for competition. To help control arousal and pregame "jitters," NBA coach Phil Jackson led his LA Lakers team in meditation before games, former MLB star Derek Jeter meditated for an hour each day on non-game days, and marathon runner Deena Kastor meditates to reduce anxiety before a big race. If you'd like more information on the positive effects of meditation, see the following **PositivePsych** feature.

PP PositivePsych

Can Meditation Increase Helping Behaviors?

To answer this question, research participants agreed to a 3-week, mobile-app training course in either mindfulness meditation or cognitive skills (Lim et al., 2015). After the training, the participants arrived at a lab to complete a supposed measure of their cognitive abilities. Upon arrival, each participant was invited to sit down in a waiting room with two other individuals, who were already seated. Another person using crutches, and appearing to be in great physical pain, then entered the room. As she did, the two previously seated individuals ignored her obvious need for a chair by fiddling with their phones, or opening a book. (The woman who entered with crutches, and the two seated individuals who ignored her, were all actually *confederates*, or secret accomplices, of the experimenter.)

As you probably suspect, the researchers were actually interested in whether the participants who took part in the meditation classes would be more likely than the non-meditators to come to the aid of the person in pain, even in the face of everyone else ignoring her. Interestingly, only about 15% of the non-meditators acted to help the woman on crutches, compared to about 50% of those who were trained in meditation. This strong helping response from both meditation groups was also particularly impressive given that they had just watched the two other people in the room ignore the woman's need for a chair.

What do you think? Given all the previously described physical and mental health benefits of meditation, along with this positive finding on increased helping behaviors, you may like to try this simple meditation/relaxation technique developed by Herbert Benson (2000):

1. Pick a focus word or short phrase that is calming and rooted in your personal value system (such as love, peace, one, shalom).
2. Sit quietly in a comfortable position, close your eyes, and relax your muscles.
3. Focusing on your breathing, breathe through your nose, and as you breathe out, say your focus word or phrase silently to yourself. Continue for 10 to 20 minutes. You may open your eyes to check the time, but do not use an alarm. When you have finished, sit quietly for several minutes, first with closed eyes and later with opened eyes.
4. Maintain a passive attitude throughout the exercise—permit relaxation to occur at its own pace. When distracting thoughts occur, ignore them and gently return to your repetition.
5. Practice the technique once or twice daily, but not within two hours after a meal—the digestive processes seem to interfere with a successful relaxation response.

Hypnosis

Relax . . . your eyelids are so very heavy . . . your muscles are becoming more and more relaxed . . . your breathing is becoming deeper and deeper . . . relax . . . your eyes are closing . . . let go . . . relax.

Hypnotists use suggestions like these to begin **hypnosis**, a trance-like state of heightened suggestibility, deep relaxation, and intense focus. Once hypnotized, some people can be convinced that they are standing at the edge of the ocean, listening to the sound of the waves and feeling the ocean mist on their faces. Invited to eat a "delicious apple" that is actually an onion, the hypnotized person may relish the flavor. Told they are watching a very funny or sad movie, hypnotized people may begin to laugh or cry at their self-created visions.

Hypnosis An alternate state of consciousness (ASC) characterized by deep relaxation and a trance-like state of heightened suggestibility and intense focus.

From the 1700s to modern times, entertainers and quacks have used (and abused) hypnosis (**Table 5.5**), but physicians, dentists, and therapists also have long employed it as a respected clinical tool. Modern scientific research has removed much of the mystery surrounding hypnosis. A number of features characterize the hypnotic state (Huber et al., 2014; Spiegel, 2015; Yapko, 2015):

- Narrowed, highly focused attention (ability to "tune out" competing sensory stimuli)
- Increased use of imagination and hallucinations

TABLE 5.5 Hypnosis Myths and Facts

MYTH	FACT
Faking Hypnosis participants are "faking it" and playing along with the hypnotist.	There are conflicting research positions about hypnosis. Although most participants are not consciously faking hypnosis, some researchers believe the effects result from a blend of conformity, relaxation, obedience, suggestion, and role playing. Other theorists believe that hypnotic effects result from a special ASC. A group of "unified" theorists suggests that hypnosis is a combination of both relaxation/role playing and a unique ASC.
Forced hypnosis People can be hypnotized against their will or hypnotically "brainwashed."	Hypnosis requires a willing, conscious choice to relinquish control of one's consciousness to someone else. The best potential subjects are those who are able to focus attention, are open to new experiences, and are capable of imaginative involvement or fantasy.
Unethical behavior Hypnosis can make people behave immorally or take dangerous risks against their will.	Hypnotized people retain awareness and control of their behavior, and they can refuse to comply with the hypnotist's suggestions.
Superhuman strength Under hypnosis, people can perform acts of special superhuman strength.	When nonhypnotized people are simply asked to try their hardest on tests of physical strength, they generally can do anything that a hypnotized person can do.
Exceptional memory Under hypnosis, people can recall things they otherwise could not.	Although the heightened relaxation and focus that hypnosis engenders improves recall for some information, it adds little (if anything) to regular memory. Hypnotized people are just more willing to guess. Because memory is normally filled with fabrication and distortion (Chapter 7), hypnosis generally increases the potential for error.

Sources: Hilgard, 1978, 1992; Huber et al., 2014; Lilienfeld et al., 2010, 2015; Polito et al., 2014.

- A passive and receptive attitude
- Decreased responsiveness to pain
- Heightened suggestibility, or a greater willingness to respond to proposed changes in perception ("This onion is an apple")

Today, even with available anesthetics, hypnosis is occasionally used in surgery and for the treatment of cancer, chronic pain, and severe burns (Adachi et al., 2014; Spiegel, 2015; Tan et al., 2015). Hypnosis has found its best use in medical areas such as dentistry and childbirth, where patients have a high degree of anxiety, fear, and misinformation (see photo). For example, some studies have found that women who use hypnosis in labor and childbirth experience lower levels of pain and a shorter duration of labor (Beebe, 2014; Madden et al., 2012). Because tension and anxiety strongly affect pain, any technique that helps the patient relax is medically useful. In psychotherapy, hypnosis can help patients relax, recall painful memories, and reduce anxiety (Alladin, 2016; Hope & Sugarman, 2015; Iglesias & Iglesias, 2014). [Q6]

One Final Note Before going on to the next chapter, we'd like to take an unusual step for authors. We'd like to offer you, our reader, a piece of caring, personal and professional advice about alternate states of consciousness (ASCs). The core problem while you're in any ASC is that you're less aware of external reality, which places you at high risk. This applies to both men and women. Interestingly, we all recognize these dangers while sleeping and dreaming, and we've developed standard ways to protect ourselves. For example, when we're driving on a long trip and start to feel sleepy, we stop for coffee, walk around, and/or rent a hotel room before allowing ourselves to fall asleep.

Our simple advice to you is to follow this same "sleepy driver" logic and standards. If you decide to use drugs, meditate, undergo hypnosis, or engage in any other form of altered consciousness, research the effects and risks of your ASC and plan ahead for the best options for dealing with it—just like you set up a designated driver before drinking. Take care and best wishes,

Catherine A. Sanderson Karen R. Huffman

Retrieval Practice 5.4 | Meditation and Hypnosis

SELF-TEST Completing this self-test, and then checking your answers by clicking on the answer button or by looking in Appendix B, will provide immediate feedback and helpful practice for exams.

1. Alternate states of consciousness (ASCs) can be achieved in which of the following ways?
   a. during sleep and dreaming
   b. via chemical channels
   c. through hypnosis and meditation
   d. all these options

2. _____ is a group of techniques designed to focus attention, block out all distractions, and produce an ASC.
   a. Hypnosis **b.** MDMA
   c. Parapsychology **d.** Meditation

3. Research on the effects of meditation has found a(n) _____.
   a. increase in blood pressure
   b. reduction in stress
   c. lack of evidence for changes in any physiological functions
   d. all of these options

4. _____ is an ASC characterized by deep relaxation and a trance-like state of heightened suggestibility and intense focus.
   a. Meditation **b.** Amphetamine psychosis
   c. Hypnosis **d.** Daydreaming

5. Which of the following is **NOT** associated with hypnosis?
   a. the use of imagination
   b. exceptional memory
   c. a passive, receptive attitude
   d. decreased pain

Think Critically

1. Why is it almost impossible to hypnotize an unwilling participant?
2. Describe the possible health benefits of hypnosis and meditation.

Real World Psychology

Can hypnosis decrease the pain of childbirth?

© Mipan/iStockphoto

HINT: LOOK IN THE MARGIN FOR **[Q6]**

Summary

5.1 Understanding Consciousness 120

- **Consciousness**, an organism's awareness of internal events and the external environment, varies in its depth and exists along a continuum. We spend most of our time in waking consciousness, but also in various **alternate states of consciousness (ASCs)**, such as sleep and dreaming.
- **Selective attention** allows us to focus our conscious awareness onto specific stimuli, whereas **inattentional blindness** blocks us from seeing unexpected stimuli.
- Consciousness varies in its depth and exists along a continuum of awareness. **Controlled processes**, which require focused attention, are at the highest level of the continuum of awareness. **Automatic processes**, which require minimal attention, are found in the middle. And, unconsciousness and coma are at the lowest level.

5.2 Understanding Sleep and Dreams 123

- Many physiological functions follow 24-hour **circadian rhythms**. Disruptions in these rhythms, as well as long-term sleep deprivation, lead to increased fatigue, cognitive and mood disruptions, and other health problems.
- During a normal night's sleep, we progress through several distinct stages of **nonrapid-eye-movement (NREM) sleep**, with periods of **rapid-eye-movement (REM) sleep** generally occurring at the end of each sleep cycle. Both REM and NREM sleep are important for our biological functioning.
- There are four major theories about why we sleep. **Adaptation/protection theory** proposes that sleep evolved to conserve energy and to provide protection from predators. The **repair/restoration theory** suggests that sleep helps us recuperate from the day's events. The **growth/development theory** argues that we use sleep for growth. The **learning/memory theory** says that we use sleep for consolidation, storage, and maintenance of memories.
- Three major theories about why we dream are Freud's **wishfulfillment view,** the **activation–synthesis hypothesis**, and the **cognitive view**. Researchers have found many similarities and differences in dream content between men and women and across cultures. How people interpret and value their dreams also varies across cultures.
- Sleep–wake disorders include **insomnia**, **narcolepsy**, **sleep apnea**, **nightmares**, and **sleep terrors**.

5.3 Psychoactive Drugs 132

- **Psychoactive drugs** influence the nervous system in a variety of ways. Alcohol affects neural membranes throughout the entire nervous system. Most psychoactive drugs act in a more specific way, by either increasing a particular neurotransmitter's effect—an **agonist drug**—or inhibiting it—an **antagonist drug**.
- The term **drug abuse** refers to drug-taking behavior that causes emotional or physical harm to oneself or others. **Addiction** refers to a condition in which a person feels compelled to use a specific drug. **Psychological dependence** refers to the mental desire or craving to achieve a drug's effects. **Physical dependence** refers to biological changes that make a drug necessary for minimum daily functioning, so as to avoid **withdrawal** symptoms (pain and intense cravings experienced after stopping the use of an addictive drug). Repeated use of a drug can produce decreased sensitivity, or **tolerance**. Sometimes, using one drug increases tolerance for another (*cross-tolerance*).

- Psychologists divide psychoactive drugs into four categories: **depressants** (such as alcohol, barbiturates, Rohypnol, and Ketamine), **stimulants** (such as caffeine, nicotine, cocaine, and amphetamines), **opiates/opioids** (such as morphine, heroin, and codeine), and **hallucinogens** (such as marijuana and LSD). Almost all psychoactive drugs may cause serious health problems and, in some cases, even death.
- Club drugs are popular due to their desirable effects, but they can also cause serious health problems and impair good decision making.

5.4 Meditation and Hypnosis 139

- **Meditation** refers to techniques designed to focus attention, block out distractions, and produce an alternate state of consciousness (ASC).
- Modern research has removed the mystery surrounding **hypnosis**, a trance-like state of heightened suggestibility, deep relaxation, and intense focus.

Applying **Real** World **Psychology**

We began this chapter with six intriguing Real World Psychology questions, and you were asked to revisit these questions at the end of each section. Questions like these have an important and lasting impact on all of our lives. See if you can answer these additional critical thinking questions related to real world examples.

Dorling Kindersley/Getty Images, Inc.

Neo Vision/Getty Images, Inc.

1. In which stage of sleep is the kitten in each photo, and how do you know?
2. Why might REM sleep serve an important adaptive function for cats?
3. Why do you think Freud's dream theory remains so popular, despite serious scientific questions and alternative modern theories?
4. Why do you think alcohol is more popular and culturally acceptable than the other drugs discussed in this chapter?
5. What are some possible ethical considerations of using hypnosis?

Key Terms

Retrieval Practice Write a definition for each term before turning back to the referenced page to check your answer.

- activation–synthesis theory of dreams 132
- adaptation/protection theory of sleep 131
- addiction 137
- agonist drug 137
- alternate state of consciousness (ASC) 124
- antagonist drug 137
- automatic processes 125
- circadian rhythm 127
- cognitive view of dreams 133
- consciousness 124
- controlled processes 125
- depressant 138
- drug abuse 137
- growth/development theory of sleep 132
- hallucinogen 141
- hypnosis 145
- inattentional blindness 124
- insomnia 134
- latent content of dreams 132
- learning/memory theory of sleep 132
- manifest content of dreams 132
- meditation 144
- narcolepsy 135
- nightmares 135
- non-rapid-eye-movement (NREM) sleep 130
- opiate/opioid 141
- physical dependence 137
- psychoactive drug 137
- psychological dependence 137
- rapid-eye-movement (REM) sleep 130
- repair/restoration theory of sleep 132
- selective attention 124
- sleep apnea 135
- sleep terrors 135
- stimulant 140
- tolerance 137
- wish-fulfillment view of dreams 132
- withdrawal 137

© Amwu/iStockphoto

CHAPTER 6

Learning

Real World Psychology

Things you'll learn in Chapter 6

[Q1] Why can simply hearing the sound of a drill in a dentist's office—even if that drill is nowhere near you—make you feel anxious?

[Q2] Can offering cash incentives and gift cards to smokers actually help them to quit?

[Q3] Why do gamblers have such trouble quitting, even when they continue to lose money?

[Q4] Can children learn anti-fat prejudice and math anxiety from their parents?

[Q5] Why can even young children recognize a picture of a snake much faster than a picture of a frog or caterpillar?

Throughout the chapter, margin icons for Q1–Q5 indicate where the text addresses these questions.

bikeriderlondon/Shutterstock

Chapter Overview

Imagine yourself in the following situations:

On your way to campus, you note a bad traffic jam up ahead and quickly decide to try a new shortcut someone mentioned several weeks ago.

Later, in your general psychology class, you watch a video on service dogs for the blind, and are amazed by these dogs opening and closing doors, helping their owners dress and undress, and even differentiating between bathrooms, escalators, and elevators.

While leaving campus and walking by the baseball field, you note that the pitcher on your college's baseball team ritualistically kicks the dirt twice with each foot, then spits in his glove, and finally taps the top of his ball cap three times before throwing each pitch.

Now ask yourself, how did you manage that new shortcut to campus? How did those guide dogs perform such amazing acts? Why did the baseball pitcher engage in such strange, superstitious rituals? All three of these sets of behavior are clearly not genetic or present at the moment of birth. Instead, they result from *learning*.

In this chapter, we begin with a focus on two of the most basic forms of learning—classical and operant conditioning. We discuss their respective beginnings and major principles. Then we look at cognitive-social learning, with an emphasis on insight, latent learning, and observational learning. We conclude with an examination of the biological factors involved in

CHAPTER OUTLINE

learning—neuroscience, mirror neurons, and evolution. Throughout the chapter, we explore how learning theories and concepts impact our everyday lives.

6.1 Classical Conditioning

LEARNING OBJECTIVES

Retrieval Practice While reading the upcoming sections, respond to each Learning Objective in your own words.

Summarize the key terms and findings in classical conditioning.

- **Define** learning and classical conditioning.
- **Describe** Pavlov's and Watson's contributions to classical conditioning.
- **Discuss** the six principles and applications of classical conditioning.
- **Identify** how classical conditioning is used in everyday life.

Learning A relatively permanent change in behavior or mental processes caused by experience.

Although most people think of learning as something formal, like what occurs in the classroom, psychologists see the term as much broader. We define **learning** as a *relatively permanent change in behavior or mental processes caused by experience*. This relative permanence applies to bad habits, like texting while driving or procrastinating about studying, as well as to useful behaviors and emotions, such as finding new shortcuts to campus, training guide dogs for the blind, or falling in love.

Learning also involves change and experience. From previous experiences, you may have learned that you "can't do well on essay exams," or that you "can't give up talking on the phone or texting while driving." The good news is that since learning is only "relatively" permanent, with new experiences, like practicing the study skills sprinkled throughout this text, and actively practicing turning off your phone in the car, mistaken beliefs and bad habits can be replaced with new, more adaptive ones (Galla & Duckworth, 2015; Gardner et al., 2016).

We begin this chapter with a study of one of the earliest forms of learning, *classical conditioning*, made famous by Pavlov's salivating dogs.

Beginnings of Classical Conditioning

Classical conditioning Learning that develops through involuntarily paired associations; a previously neutral stimulus (NS) is paired (associated) with an unconditioned stimulus (US) to elicit a conditioned response (CR).

Why does your mouth water when you stare at a large slice of delicious cake or a juicy steak? The answer to this question was accidentally discovered in the laboratory of Russian physiologist Ivan Pavlov (1849–1936). Pavlov's initial plan was to study the role of saliva in digestion by using a tube attached to dogs' salivary glands (**Figure 6.1**).

During these experiments, one of Pavlov's students noticed that even before receiving the actual food, many dogs began salivating at the mere sight of the food, the food dish, the smell of the food, or even just the sight of the person who normally delivered the food! Pavlov's genius was in recognizing the importance of this "unscheduled" salivation. He realized that the dogs were not only responding on the basis of hunger (a biological need), but also as a result of experience or learning.

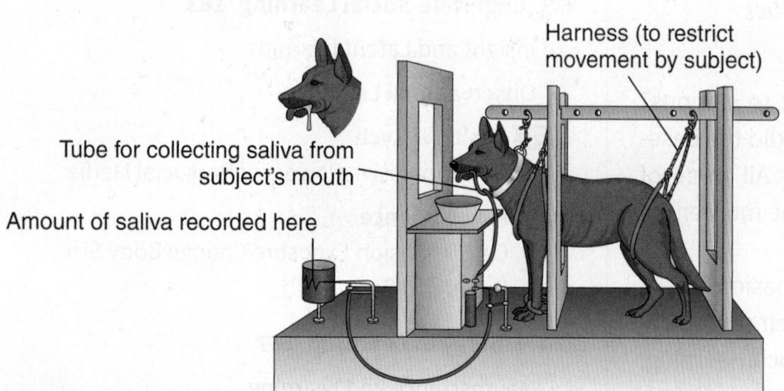

FIGURE 6.1 **Pavlov's experimental setup**

Excited by this accidental discovery, Pavlov and his students conducted several experiments, including sounding a tone on a tuning fork just before food was placed in the dogs' mouths. After several pairings of the tone and food, dogs in the laboratory began to salivate on hearing the tone alone.

Pavlov and later researchers found that many things can become conditioned stimuli for salivation if they are paired with food—a bell, a buzzer, a light, and even the sight of a circle or triangle drawn on a card. This type of learning, called **classical conditioning**, develops through involuntary, passive, paired associations. More specifically, a neutral stimulus (such as the tone on a tuning fork) comes to elicit a response after repeated pairings with a naturally occurring stimulus (like food).

To fully understand classical conditioning, and how it applies to our everyday life, the first step is to recognize that **conditioning** is simply another word for learning. Next, we need to explain that classical conditioning is a three-step process—*before*, *during*, and *after conditioning*. This process is explained in detail below, and visually summarized in **Process Diagram 6.1**.

Step 1 Before conditioning, the sound of the tone does NOT lead to salivation, which makes the tone a **neutral stimulus (NS)**. Conversely, food naturally brings about salivation, which makes food an *unlearned*, **unconditioned stimulus (US)**. The initial reflex of salivation also is *unlearned*, so it is called an **unconditioned response (UR)**.

Conditioning The process of learning associations between stimuli and behavioral responses.

Neutral stimulus (NS) A stimulus that, before conditioning, does not naturally bring about the response of interest.

Unconditioned stimulus (US) A stimulus that elicits an unconditioned response (UR) without previous conditioning.

Unconditioned response (UR) An unlearned reaction to an unconditioned stimulus (US) that occurs without previous conditioning.

STOP! This Process Diagram contains essential information NOT found elsewhere in the text, which is likely to appear on quizzes and exams. Be sure to study it CAREFULLY!

PROCESS DIAGRAM 6.1 The Beginnings and a Modern Application of Classical Conditioning Although Pavlov's initial experiment used a metronome, a ticking instrument designed to mark exact time, and later used a bell, his best-known method (depicted here) involved a tone from a tuning fork. As you can see, the basic process of classical conditioning is simple. Just as you've been classically conditioned to respond to your cell phone's tones, or possibly to just the sight of a pizza box, Pavlov's dogs learned to respond to a tuning fork's tone. Unfortunately, many students get confused by these technical terms. So here's a tip that might help: The actual stimuli (tone and meat) remain the same—only their names change from neutral to conditioned or from unconditioned to conditioned. A similar name change happens for the response (salivation)—from unconditioned to conditioned.

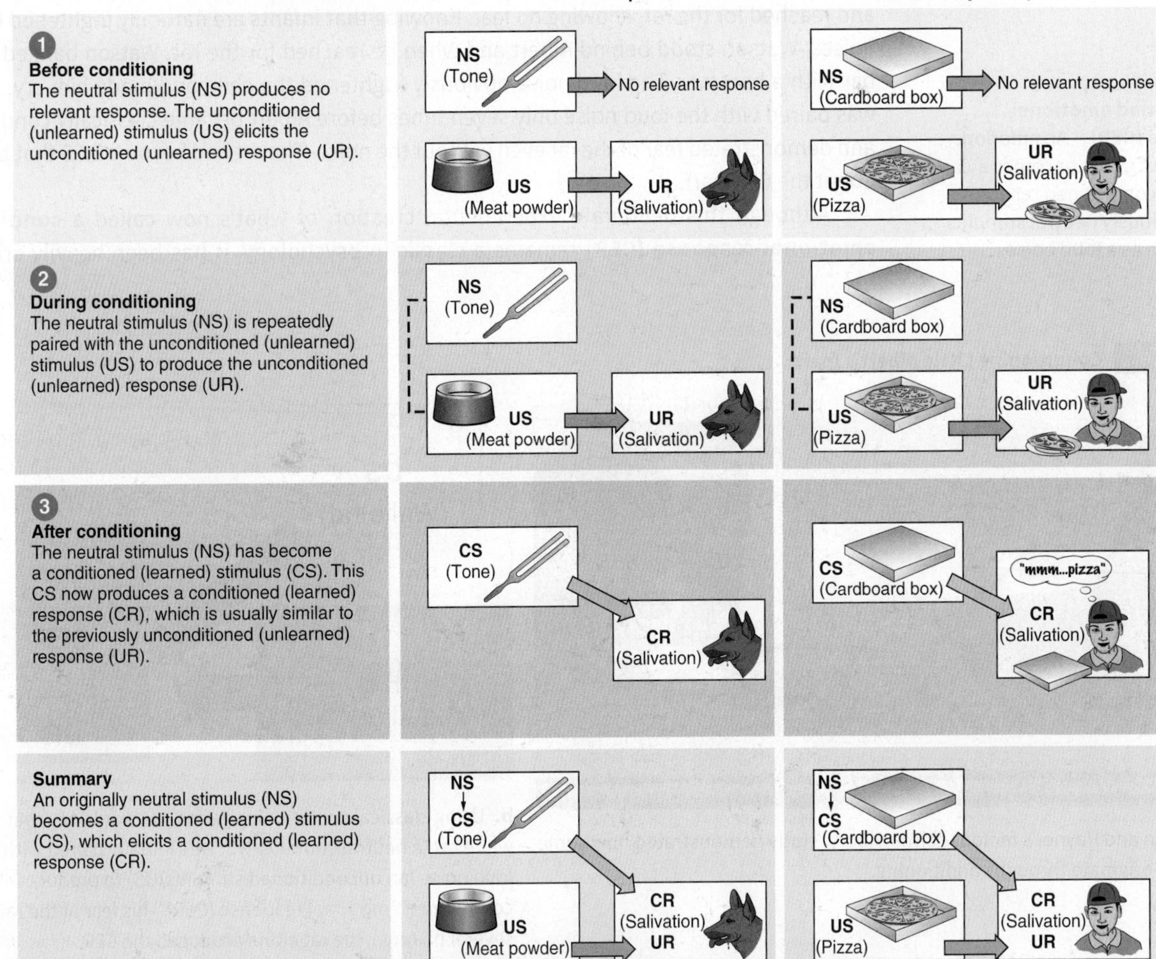
Pavlov example
Modern-day example
1
Before conditioning
The neutral stimulus (NS) produces no relevant response. The unconditioned (unlearned) stimulus (US) elicits the unconditioned (unlearned) response (UR).
NS (Tone)
No relevant response
US (Meat powder)
UR (Salivation)
NS (Cardboard box)
No relevant response
US (Pizza)
UR (Salivation)
2
During conditioning
The neutral stimulus (NS) is repeatedly paired with the unconditioned (unlearned) stimulus (US) to produce the unconditioned (unlearned) response (UR).
NS (Tone)
US (Meat powder)
UR (Salivation)
NS (Cardboard box)
US (Pizza)
UR (Salivation)
3
After conditioning
The neutral stimulus (NS) has become a conditioned (learned) stimulus (CS). This CS now produces a conditioned (learned) response (CR), which is usually similar to the previously unconditioned (unlearned) response (UR).
CS (Tone)
CR (Salivation)
CS (Cardboard box)
"mmm...pizza"
CR (Salivation)
Summary
An originally neutral stimulus (NS) becomes a conditioned (learned) stimulus (CS), which elicits a conditioned (learned) response (CR).
NS
CS (Tone)
US (Meat powder)
CR (Salivation) UR
NS
CS (Cardboard box)
US (Pizza)
CR (Salivation) UR

Conditioned stimulus (CS) A previously neutral stimulus (NS) that, after repeated pairings with an unconditioned stimulus (US), comes to elicit a conditioned response (CR).

Conditioned response (CR) A learned reaction to a conditioned stimulus (CS) that occurs after previous repeated pairings with an unconditioned stimulus (US).

Step 2 During conditioning, the tuning fork is repeatedly sounded right before the presentation of the meat (US).

Step 3 After conditioning, the tone alone will bring about salivation. At this point, we can say that the dog is *classically conditioned*. The previously neutral stimulus (NS) (the tone) has now become a *learned*, **conditioned stimulus (CS)**, that produced a *learned*, **conditioned response (CR)** (the dog's salivation). (Note that the "R" in UR in Step 1 and the CR in this Step 3 refers to both "reflex" and "response.")

In sum, the overall goal of Pavlov's classical conditioning was for the dog to learn to associate the tone with the unconditioned stimulus (meat), and then to show the same response (salivation) to the tone as to the meat.

So what does a salivating dog have to do with your everyday life? Classical conditioning is a fundamental way that all animals, including humans, learn. Just as you may have learned to salivate at the sight of a pizza box (see again Process Diagram 6.1), smokers often report cravings to smoke after watching a cigarette commercial on TV—or even after a quick glance at an ashtray. Interestingly, laboratory experiments show that smokers can be trained to develop cravings for a cigarette after seeing a simple geometric design if it was previously paired with cigarette-related cues (Deweese et al., 2016). In short, the human feelings of excitement and/or compulsion to gamble, your love for your parents (or significant other), and the almost universal fear of public speaking all largely result from classical conditioning.

How do we learn to be afraid of public speaking or of typically harmless things like mice and elevators? In a now-famous experiment, John Watson and Rosalie Rayner (1920) demonstrated how a fear of rats could be classically conditioned.

In this study, a healthy 11-month-old child, later known as "Little Albert," was first allowed to play with a white laboratory rat (**Figure 6.2**). Like most other infants, Albert was curious and reached for the rat, showing no fear. Knowing that infants are naturally frightened by loud noises, Watson stood behind Albert and when he reached for the rat, Watson banged a steel bar with a hammer. The loud noise obviously frightened the child and made him cry. The rat was paired with the loud noise only seven times before Albert became classically conditioned and demonstrated fear of the rat even without the noise. The rat had become a CS that brought about the CR (fear).

Conditioned emotional response (CER) An emotion, such as fear, that becomes a learned, conditioned response to a previously neutral stimulus (NS), such as a loud noise.

Although this deliberate experimental creation of what's now called a **conditioned emotional response (CER)** remains a classic in psychology, it has been heavily criticized

FIGURE 6.2 Conditioning Little Albert's fears

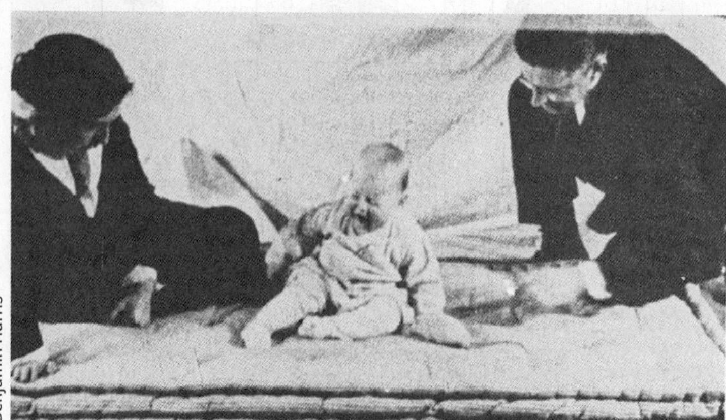

a. Watson and Rayner's famous "Little Albert" study demonstrated how some fears can originate through conditioning.

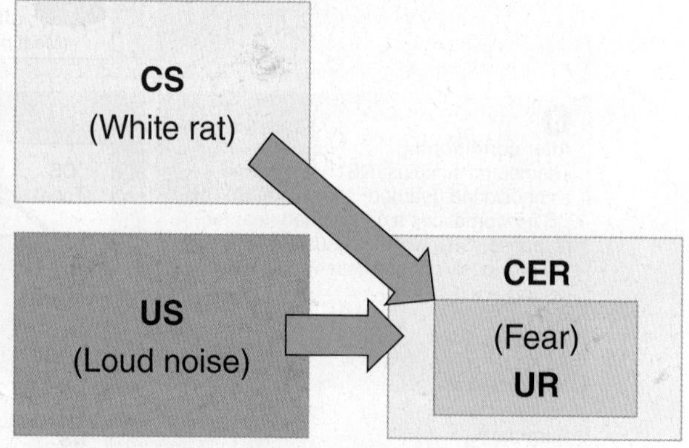

b. Using classical conditioning terms, we would say that the white rat (a neutral stimulus/NS) was initially paired with the loud noise (an unconditioned stimulus/US) to produce Albert's conditioned emotional response (CER)—his fear of the rat. After several pairings, the rat alone produced the CER.

and would never be allowed under today's experimental guidelines (Antes, 2016; Avieli et al., 2016; Ethical Principles of Psychologists, 2016). The research procedures used by Watson and Rayner violated several ethical guidelines for scientific research (Chapter 1). They not only deliberately created a serious fear in a child, but they also ended their experiment without *extinguishing* (removing) it. In addition, the researchers have been criticized because they did not measure Albert's fear objectively. Their subjective evaluation raises doubt about the degree of fear conditioned.

Despite such criticisms, this study of Little Albert and follow-up research led to our current understanding that many of our likes, dislikes, prejudices, and fears are examples of *conditioned emotional responses (CERs)*. For example, if your romantic partner always uses the same shampoo, simply the smell of that shampoo may soon elicit a positive response. In Chapter 13, you'll discover how Watson's research later led to powerful clinical tools for eliminating exaggerated and irrational fears of a specific object or situation, known as *phobias* (Ahrens et al., 2015; Donovan et al., 2015; Pear, 2016). For more examples of how classical conditioning impacts everyday life, see **Figure 6.3**.

FIGURE 6.3 Classical conditioning in everyday life

Real World **Psychology**

a. Prejudice How do children, like the one holding the KKK sign in this photo, develop prejudice at such an early age? Research shows that prejudice may be a combination of both biological and cultural factors (Hughes et al., 2016; Mallan et al., 2013). As shown in the diagram, children are naturally upset and fearful (UR) when they see that their parents are upset and afraid (US). Over time, they may learn to associate their parents' reaction with all members of a disliked group (CS), thus becoming prejudiced like their parents.

Randy Olsen/NG Image Collection

CS (Member of disliked group)
US (Parent's negative reaction)
CR (Child is upset and fearful) UR

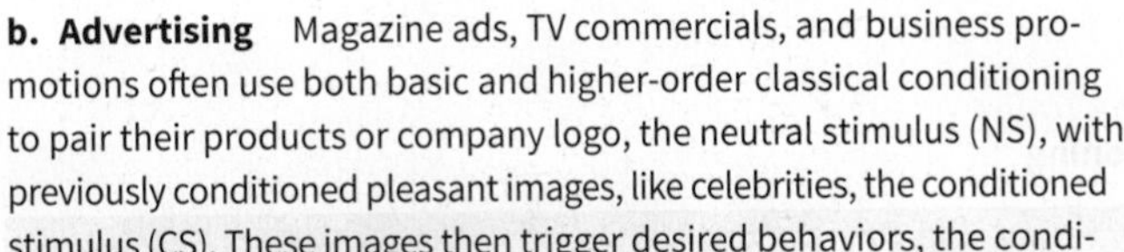

b. Advertising Magazine ads, TV commercials, and business promotions often use both basic and higher-order classical conditioning to pair their products or company logo, the neutral stimulus (NS), with previously conditioned pleasant images, like celebrities, the conditioned stimulus (CS). These images then trigger desired behaviors, the conditioned response (CR), such as purchasing their products (Chen et al., 2014; Hing et al., 2015; van der Pligt & Vliek, 2016).

© Jim Holden/Alamy Stock Photo

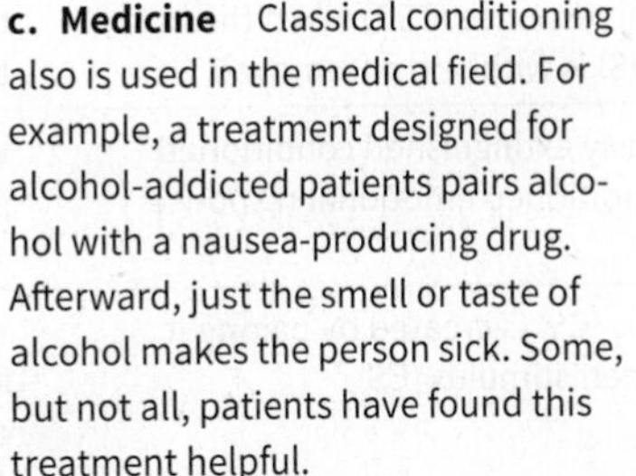

c. Medicine Classical conditioning also is used in the medical field. For example, a treatment designed for alcohol-addicted patients pairs alcohol with a nausea-producing drug. Afterward, just the smell or taste of alcohol makes the person sick. Some, but not all, patients have found this treatment helpful.

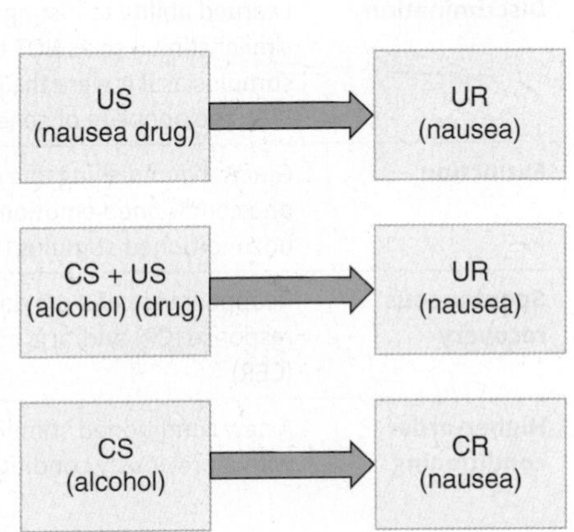

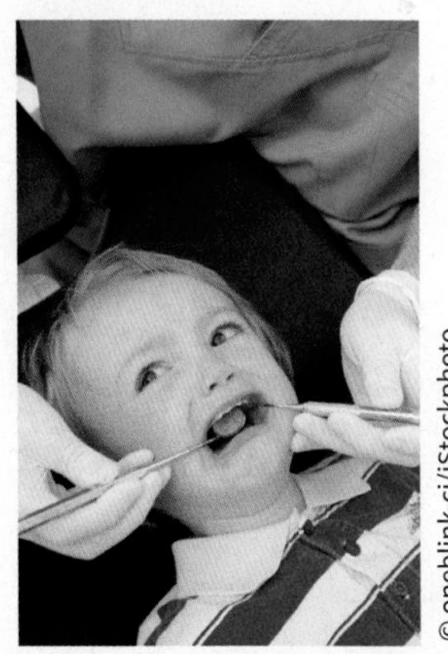
© oneblink-cj/iStockphoto

Are you afraid of dentists?

Principles of Classical Conditioning

We've just seen how a loud noise was used to condition Little Albert's fear of rats. But how would we explain common fears, such as being afraid of dentists or just the sound of a dentist's drill? How did they develop? Imagine being seated in a dental chair, and, even though the drill is nowhere near you, its sound immediately makes you feel anxious. Your anxiety is obviously not innate. Little babies don't cringe at the sound of a dental drill, unless it's very loud (see photo). Your fear of the drill, and maybe dentistry in general, involves one or more of the six principles summarized in **Table 6.1**, and discussed in detail below. (Note that dental fears and even serious dental phobias can be successfully treated—see Chapters 12 and 13.) [Q1]

Acquisition (in classical conditioning) Learning occurs (is acquired) when an organism involuntarily links a neutral stimulus (NS) with an unconditioned stimulus (US), which in turn elicits the conditioned response (CR).

Generalization (in classical conditioning) A conditioned response (CR) spreads (generalizes) and comes to be involuntarily elicited not only by the conditioned stimulus (CS), but also by stimuli similar to the CS; the opposite of discrimination.

1. **Acquisition** After Pavlov's original (accidental) discovery of classical conditioning, he conducted numerous experiments beyond the basic **acquisition** phase, which is a general term for learning that occurs (is acquired) when an organism involuntarily links a neutral stimulus (NS) with an unconditioned stimulus (US). This acquisition in turn elicits the conditioned response (CR).
2. **Generalization** One of Pavlov's most interesting findings was that stimuli similar to the original conditioned stimulus (CS) also can elicit the conditioned response (CR). For example, after first conditioning dogs to salivate to the sound of low-pitched tones, Pavlov later demonstrated that the dogs would also salivate in response to higher-pitched tones. Similarly, after Watson and Rayner's conditioning experiment, "Little Albert" learned to fear not only rats, but also a rabbit, dog, and a bearded Santa Claus mask. This process by which a conditioned response (CR) spreads (generalizes) and comes to be involuntarily elicited not only by the conditioned stimulus (CS), but also by stimuli similar to the CS is called stimulus **generalization** (Davidson et al., 2016; Okouchi et al., 2014; Pear, 2016).
3. **Discrimination** Just as Pavlov's dogs learned to generalize and respond to similar stimuli in a similar way, they also learned how to *discriminate* between similar stimuli. For example, when he gave the dogs food following a high-pitched tone, but not when he used a

TABLE 6.1 Six Principles and Applications of Classical Conditioning

PROCESS	DESCRIPTION	EXAMPLE
Acquisition	Learning occurs (is acquired) when an organism involuntarily links a neutral stimulus (NS) with an unconditioned stimulus (US), which in turn elicits the conditioned response (CR) and/or conditioned emotional response (CER)	You learn to fear (CER) a dentist's drill (CS) because you associate it with the pain of your tooth extraction (US).
Generalization	Conditioned response (CR) and/or a conditioned emotional response (CER) come to be involuntarily elicited not only by the conditioned stimulus (CS), but also by stimuli similar to the CS; the opposite of discrimination	You generalize your fear of the dentist's drill to your dentist's office and other dentists' offices.
Discrimination	Learned ability to distinguish (discriminate) between similar stimuli so as NOT to involuntarily respond to a new stimulus as if it were the previously conditioned stimulus (CS); the opposite of generalization	You are not afraid of your physician's office because you've learned to differentiate it from your dentist's office.
Extinction	Gradual diminishing of a conditioned response (CR) and/or a conditioned emotional response (CER) when the unconditioned stimulus (US) is withheld or removed	You return several times to your dentist's office for routine checkups, with no dental drill; your fear of the dentist's office (CER) gradually diminishes.
Spontaneous recovery	Reappearance of a previously extinguished conditioned response (CR) and/or a conditioned emotional response (CER)	While watching a movie depicting dental drilling, your previous fear (CER) suddenly returns.
Higher-order conditioning	A new conditioned stimulus (CS) is created by pairing it with a previously conditioned stimulus (CS)	You fear the sign outside your dentist's office, an originally neutral stimulus (NS). Why? It has become a conditioned stimulus (CS), associated with the previously conditioned stimulus (CS) of the dental drill.

low-pitched tone, he found that they learned the difference between the two tones, and only salivated to the high-pitched one. Likewise, "Little Albert" learned to recognize differences between rats and other stimuli, and presumably overcame his fear of them. This learned ability to distinguish (discriminate) between similar stimuli so as NOT to involuntarily respond to a new stimulus, as if it were the previously conditioned stimulus (CS), is known as stimulus **discrimination**.

4. **Extinction** What do you think happened when Pavlov repeatedly sounded the tone without presenting food? The answer is that the dogs' salivation gradually declined, a process Pavlov called **extinction (in classical conditioning)**. This term is defined as the gradual diminishing of a conditioned response (CR) when the unconditioned stimulus (US) is withheld or removed. Without continued association with the US, the CS loses its power to elicit the CR.

5. **Spontaneous recovery** It's important to note that extinction is not complete unlearning. It does not fully "erase" the learned connection between the stimulus and the response (González et al., 2016; John & Pineño, 2015). Pavlov found that sometimes, after a CR had apparently been extinguished, if he sounded the tone once again, the dogs would occasionally still salivate. This reappearance of a previously extinguished conditioned response (CR) is called **spontaneous recovery** (see **Psychology and You**).

6. **Higher-order conditioning** The phenomenon of **higher-order conditioning** takes basic classical conditioning one step higher. Also known as "second-order conditioning," this process refers to a situation in which a previously neutral stimulus (NS) (like a tone) was first made into a conditioned stimulus (CS) by pairing it with an unconditioned stimulus (US) (such as food). The next step of higher-order (or second order) conditioning then uses that previously CS as a basis for creating a NEW CS (like a flashing light) that produces its own conditioned response (CR). In short, a new CS is created by pairing it with a previously created CS (**Process Diagram 6.2**).

Discrimination (in classical conditioning) A learned ability to distinguish (discriminate) between similar stimuli so as NOT to involuntarily respond to a new stimulus as if it were the previously conditioned stimulus (CS); the opposite of generalization.

Extinction (in classical conditioning) The gradual diminishing of a conditioned response (CR) when the unconditioned stimulus (US) is withheld or removed.

Spontaneous recovery The reappearance of a previously extinguished conditioned response (CR).

Higher-order conditioning A new conditioned stimulus (CS) is created by pairing it with a previously conditioned stimulus (CS); also known as second-order conditioning.

Psychology and You—Understanding Yourself

Spontaneous Recovery

Have you ever felt renewed excitement at the sight of a former girlfriend or boyfriend, even though years have passed, you have a new partner, and extinction has occurred? This may be an example of *spontaneous recovery*. It also may help explain why people might misinterpret a sudden flare-up of feelings and be tempted to return to unhappy relationships. To make matters worse, when a conditioned stimulus is reintroduced after extinction, the conditioning occurs much faster the second time around—a phenomenon known as *reconditioning*.

The good news is that those who have taken general psychology (or are currently reading this book) are (hopefully) far less likely to make this mistake. Looking at **Figure 6.4**, you can see that even if you experience spontaneous recovery, your sudden peak of feelings for the old love partner will gradually return to their previously extinguished state. So don't overreact.

GoodMood Photo/Shutterstock

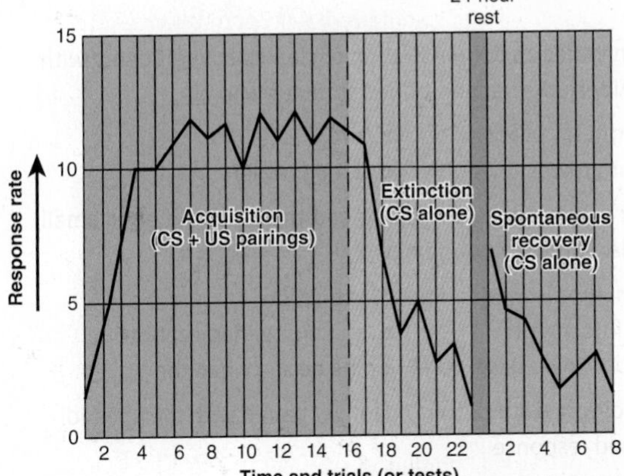

FIGURE 6.4 Three key principles of classical conditioning During acquisition, the strength of the conditioned response (CR) rapidly increases and then levels off near its maximum. During extinction, the CR declines erratically until it is extinguished. After a "rest" period in which the organism is not exposed to the conditioned stimulus (CS), spontaneous recovery may occur, and the CS will once again elicit a (weakened) CR. Note that the CR once again gradually diminishes after the spontaneous recovery because the CS is alone and not paired with the US.

STOP! This Process Diagram contains essential information NOT found elsewhere in the text, which is likely to appear on quizzes and exams. Be sure to study it CAREFULLY!

PROCESS DIAGRAM 6.2 The Power of Higher-Order Conditioning **Real World Psychology**

Children are not born salivating to the sight of McDonald's golden arches. So why do they beg adults to take them to "Mickey D's" after simply seeing an ad showing the golden arches? It's because of higher-order conditioning, which occurs when a new conditioned stimulus (CS) is created by pairing it with a previously conditioned stimulus (CS).

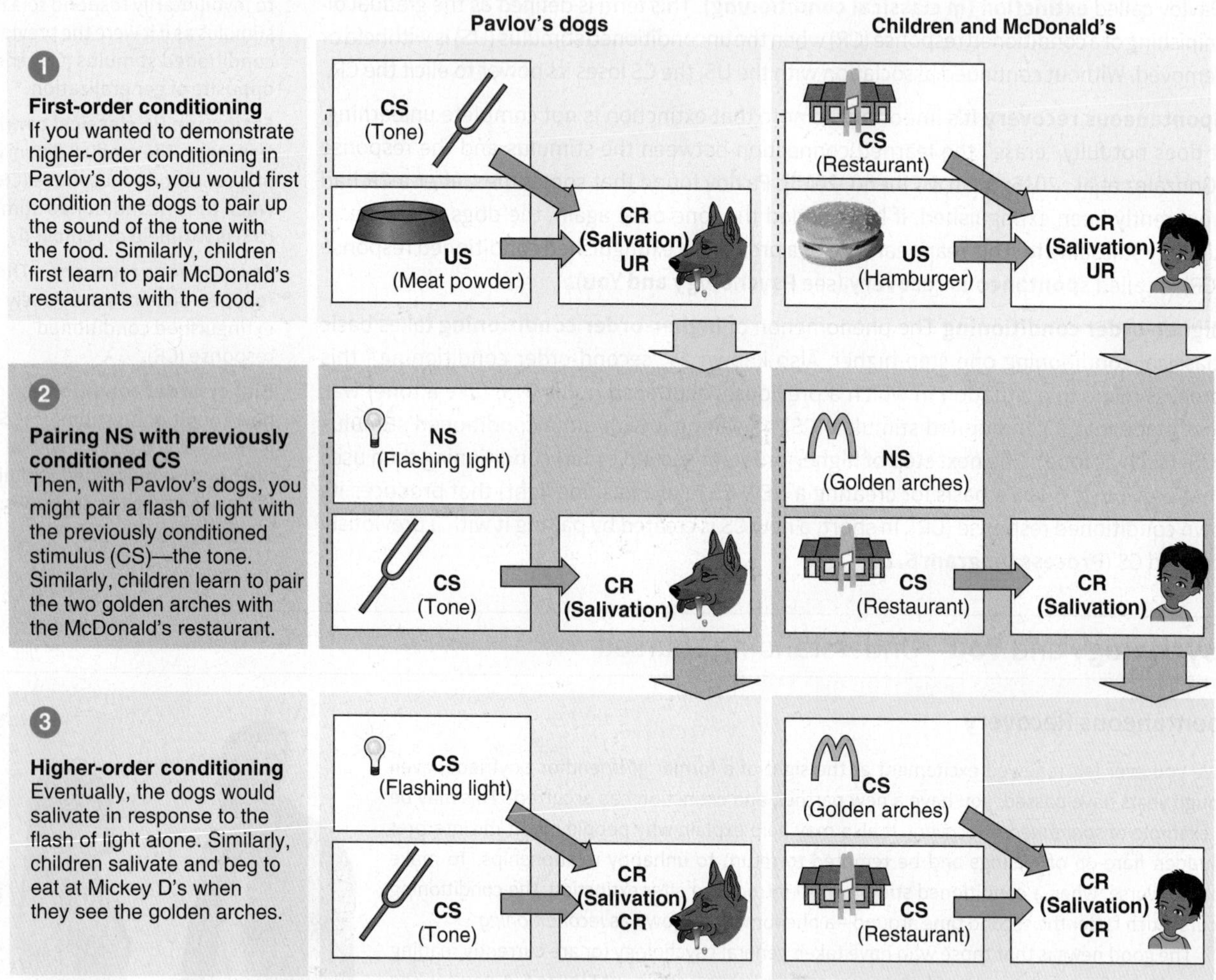

Pavlov's dogs
Children and McDonald's
1
First-order conditioning
If you wanted to demonstrate higher-order conditioning in Pavlov's dogs, you would first condition the dogs to pair up the sound of the tone with the food. Similarly, children first learn to pair McDonald's restaurants with the food.
CS (Tone)
US (Meat powder)
CR (Salivation) UR
CS (Restaurant)
US (Hamburger)
CR (Salivation) UR
2
Pairing NS with previously conditioned CS
Then, with Pavlov's dogs, you might pair a flash of light with the previously conditioned stimulus (CS)—the tone. Similarly, children learn to pair the two golden arches with the McDonald's restaurant.
NS (Flashing light)
CS (Tone)
CR (Salivation)
NS (Golden arches)
CS (Restaurant)
CR (Salivation)
3
Higher-order conditioning
Eventually, the dogs would salivate in response to the flash of light alone. Similarly, children salivate and beg to eat at Mickey D's when they see the golden arches.
CS (Flashing light)
CS (Tone)
CR (Salivation) CR
CS (Golden arches)
CS (Restaurant)
CR (Salivation) CR

Retrieval Practice 6.1 | Classical Conditioning

SELF-TEST Completing this self-test, and then checking your answers by clicking on the answer button or by looking in Appendix B, will provide immediate feedback and helpful practice for exams.

1. _____ conditioning occurs when a neutral stimulus becomes associated with an unconditioned stimulus to elicit a conditioned response.

a. Reflex **b.** Instinctive
c. Classical **d.** Basic

2. A young child learns to fear dogs after being bitten. In this situation, the unconditioned RESPONSE (UR) is the _____.

a. dog **b.** bite
c. fear **d.** none of these options

3. In John Watson's demonstration of classical conditioning with Little Albert, the unconditioned stimulus was _____.

a. symptoms of fear **b.** a rat
c. a bath towel **d.** a loud noise

4. A baby is bitten by a small dog and then is afraid of all small animals. This is an example of _____.

a. stimulus discrimination **b.** extinction
c. reinforcement **d.** stimulus generalization

5. Extinction in classical conditioning occurs when the _____.

a. conditioned stimulus is no longer paired with the unconditioned response
b. unconditioned stimulus is withheld or removed

c. conditioned response is no longer paired with the unconditioned stimulus
d. unconditioned stimulus is ambiguous

Think Critically

1. How might Watson and Rayner, who conducted the famous "Little Albert" study, have designed a more ethical study of conditioned emotional responses (CERs)?
2. Most classical conditioning is involuntary. Considering this, is it ethical for politicians and advertisers to use classical conditioning to influence our thoughts and behavior? Why or why not?

Real World Psychology

Why can simply hearing the sound of a drill in a dentist's office—even if that drill is nowhere near you—make you feel anxious?

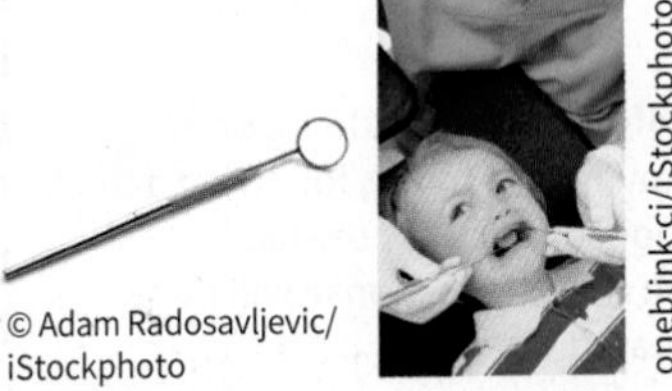

© Adam Radosavljevic/ iStockphoto

HINT: LOOK IN THE MARGIN FOR **[Q1]**

6.2 Operant Conditioning

LEARNING OBJECTIVES

Retrieval Practice While reading the upcoming sections, respond to each Learning Objective in your own words.

Discuss the key terms and findings in operant conditioning.

- **Define** operant conditioning, reinforcement, and punishment.
- **Describe** Thorndike's and Skinner's contributions to operant conditioning.
- **Explain** how reinforcement and punishment influence behavior.
- **Review** the six key principles in operant conditioning.
- **Identify** how operant conditioning is used in everyday life.
- **Summarize** the major similarities and differences between classical and operant conditioning.

Classical and operant conditioning are both known as **associative learning**. As the name implies, they occur when an organism makes a connection, or association, between two events. During classical conditioning, an association is made between two stimuli, whereas in operant conditioning the association is made between a response and its consequences.

As we've just seen, classical conditioning is based on what happens *before* we *involuntarily* respond: Something happens to us, and we learn a new response. In contrast, **operant conditioning** is based on what happens *after* we *voluntarily* perform a behavior (Chance, 2014; Pear, 2016). We do something and learn from the consequences (**Figure 6.5**).

Operant conditioning Learning through voluntary behavior and its subsequent consequences; consequences that are reinforcing increase behavioral tendencies, whereas consequences that are punishing decrease them.

Associative learning Learning that two events occur or happen together.

FIGURE 6.5 Classical versus operant conditioning Classical conditioning is based on involuntary behavior, whereas operant conditioning is based on voluntary behavior.

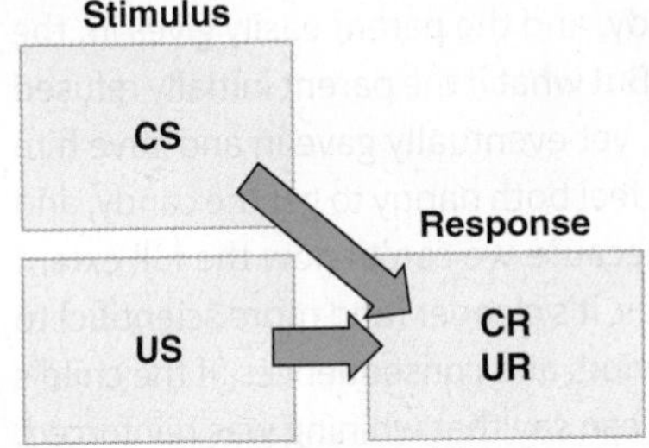

a. Classical conditioning The subject is passive, while the previously neutral stimulus (NS) is paired with an unconditioned stimulus (US). After repeated pairings, the NS becomes a conditioned stimulus (CS) that leads to a conditioned response (CR).

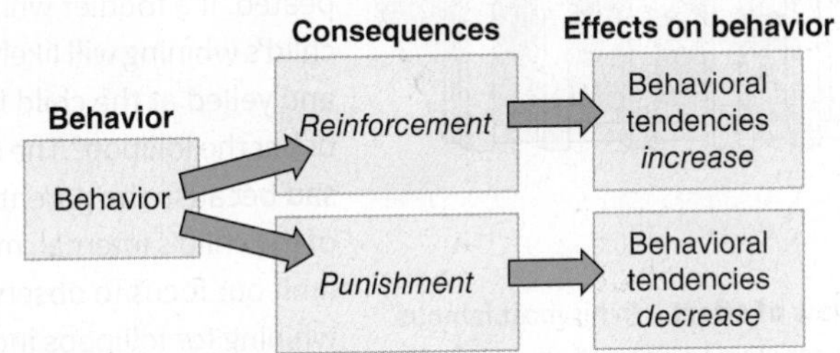

b. Operant conditioning The subject is active and voluntarily "operates" on the environment. The consequences (reinforcement or punishment) that follow the behavior determine whether the behavioral tendencies will increase or decrease.

The key point to remember is that *consequences* are the heart of operant conditioning. In classical conditioning, consequences are irrelevant—Pavlov's dogs still got to eat whether they salivated or not. But in operant conditioning, the organism voluntarily performs a behavior (an operant) that produces a consequence—either reinforcement or punishment—and the behavior either increases or decreases. It's also very important to note that **reinforcement** is the process by which adding or taking away of a stimulus following a response increases the likelihood that the response will be repeated. **Punishment**, in contrast, involves adding or taking away a stimulus following a response, which decreases the likelihood that the response will be repeated.

Reinforcement Adding or removing a stimulus following a response increases the likelihood that the response will be repeated.

Punishment Adding or removing a stimulus following a response decreases the likelihood that the response will be repeated.

We'll have much more to say about reinforcement and punishment in a later section, but for now we want to highlight how they can be used to improve your everyday life. For example, only allowing yourself to watch TV while exercising is a form of reinforcement that will improve your general physical health. Similarly, stop-smoking programs that offer reinforcement in the form of cash incentives, such as requiring a $150 deposit that is returned only to people who have successfully stopped smoking 6 months later, are nearly twice as effective at helping people stop as other approaches, such as counseling and nicotine replacement therapy (Halpern et al., 2015). Another study found that offering gift cards helps smokers quit (Kendzor et al., 2015). In contrast, using a form of punishment, such as increasing the cost of smoking—often by increasing taxes on cigarettes—reduces smoking rates (Cavazos-Rehg et al., 2012; Wilson et al., 2012). The punishing effect of increased taxes on cigarettes is particularly true for heavy smokers, who pay considerably more due to their higher consumption, and for teenagers, who tend to have less discretionary income. [Q2]

Beginnings of Operant Conditioning

In the early 1900s, Edward Thorndike, a pioneer of operant conditioning, was the first to identify that the frequency of a behavior is controlled by its consequences (Thorndike, 1911). Today this is known as Thorndike's **law of effect**, which further clarifies that any behavior followed by pleasant consequences is likely to be repeated, whereas any behavior followed by unpleasant consequences is likely to be stopped. Thorndike's findings were based on his study of cats in puzzle boxes (**Figure 6.6**).

Law of effect Thorndike's rule that any behavior followed by pleasant consequences is likely to be repeated, whereas any behavior followed by unpleasant consequences is likely to be stopped.

FIGURE 6.6 Thorndike's law of effect In his most famous experiment, Thorndike put a cat inside a specially built puzzle box. When the cat stepped on a pedal inside the box (at first by chance), the door opened, and the cat could get out and eat. Then, through trial and error, the cat learned what specific actions led to opening the door. With each additional success, the cat's actions became more purposeful, and it soon learned to open the door immediately (Thorndike, 1898).

B. F. Skinner later extended Thorndike's law of effect to more complex behaviors. However, he carefully avoided Thorndike's use of terms like *pleasant* and *unpleasant* because they are subjective, and not directly observable. Furthermore, Skinner argued that such words make unfounded assumptions about what an organism feels or wants, and imply that behavior is due to conscious choice or intention. Skinner believed that to understand behavior, we should consider only external, observable stimuli and responses. We must look outside the learner, not inside.

Skinner also talked about reinforcement and punishment in terms of *increasing* or *decreasing* the likelihood of the response being repeated. If a toddler whines for candy, and the parent easily gives in, the child's whining will likely increase. But what if the parent initially refused and yelled at the child for whining, yet eventually gave in and gave him or her the lollipop? The child might feel both happy to get the candy, and sad because the parent is upset. Because we can't know the full extent of the child's internal, mixed feelings, it's cleaner (and more scientific) to limit our focus to observable behaviors and consequences. If the child's whining for lollipops increases, we can say that whining was reinforced. If it decreases, then it was punished.

In keeping with his focus on external, observable stimuli and responses, Skinner emphasized that reinforcement and punishment should always be presented *after* the targeted behavior has occurred. This was because Skinner believed that the only way to know how we have influenced an organism's behavior is to check whether it increases or decreases. As he pointed out, we too often think we're reinforcing or punishing behavior, when we're actually doing the opposite (see **Psychology and You**).

Psychology and **You**—Understanding Yourself

The Challenge of Reinforcement

A professor may think she is encouraging shy students to talk by repeatedly praising them each time they speak up in class. But what if you are one of those shy students and are embarrassed by this extra attention? If so, you may actually decrease the number of times you talk in class. Can you see why it's important to always remember that what is reinforcing or punishing for one person may not be so for another?

Michele Cozzolino/Shutterstock

Primary reinforcer Any unlearned, innate stimulus (like food, water, or sex) that reinforces a response and thus increases the probability that it will recur.

Secondary reinforcer Any learned stimulus (like money, praise, or attention) that reinforces a response and thus increases the probability that it will recur.

Positive reinforcement A process by which adding (or presenting) a stimulus following a response increases the likelihood that the response will be repeated.

Negative reinforcement A process by which taking away (or removing) a stimulus following a response increases the likelihood that the response will be repeated.

Clarifying Reinforcement versus Punishment

Until now, we've only discussed reinforcement and punishment in general terms. But it's important to clarify exactly how they either increase or decrease behavior. To begin, you need to understand that psychologists group reinforcers into two types, primary and secondary. A **primary reinforcer** is any unlearned, innate stimulus (like food, water, or sex) that reinforces a response and thus increases the probability that it will recur. A **secondary reinforcer** is any learned stimulus (like money, praise, or attention) that reinforces a response and thus increases the probability that it will recur. The key point is that "primary" is another word for unlearned, whereas "secondary" means learned. In addition, both primary and secondary reinforcers can produce **positive reinforcement** or **negative reinforcement**, depending on whether certain stimuli are added or taken away. *Positive reinforcement* is a process by which adding (or presenting) a stimulus following a response increases the likelihood that the response will be repeated. *Negative reinforcement* is a process by which taking away (or removing) a stimulus following a response increases the likelihood that the response will be repeated (**Table 6.2**).

TABLE 6.2 How Reinforcement Increases (or Strengthens) Behavior — **Real** World **Psychology**

	POSITIVE REINFORCEMENT Stimulus added (+) and behavior increases	**NEGATIVE REINFORCEMENT** Stimulus taken away (−) and behavior increases	
PRIMARY REINFORCERS ***Unlearned, innate stimuli that reinforce and increase the probability of a response***	You put money in the vending machine, and a snack comes out. The addition of the snack makes it more likely you will put money in the vending machine in the future.	You switch from formal, dress shoes to sneakers, and your foot pain goes away. The removal of your pain makes it more likely you will wear sneakers, or more casual shoes, in the future.	 © bryanregan/iStockphoto
	You hug your baby and he smiles at you. The addition of his smile increases the likelihood that you will hug him again when he smiles.	Your baby is crying, so you hug him, and he stops crying. The removal of crying increases the likelihood that you will hug him again when he cries.	
SECONDARY REINFORCERS ***Learned stimuli that reinforce and increase the probability of a response***	Completing a quest in your video game increases your score, and unlocks desirable game items. The addition of these items increases your video game playing behavior.	You mention all the homework you have to do, and your partner offers to do the dinner dishes. The removal of this chore increases the likelihood that you will again mention your homework the next time it's your turn to do the dishes.	 © ferrantraite/iStockphoto
	You study hard and receive a good grade on your psychology exam. The addition of the good grade makes it more likely that you'll study hard for future exams.	You're allowed to skip the final exam because you did so well on your unit exams. The removal of the final exam makes it more likely that you'll work hard to do well on unit exams in the future.	

We admit that this terminology is very confusing because positive normally means something "good" and negative generally means something "bad." But recall that Skinner cautioned us to avoid subjective terms like good and bad, or pleasant and unpleasant because they are not external and directly observable. Instead, he used *positive* and *negative* in line with other scientific terminology. You'll find this section much easier if you always remember that "positive" is simply adding something [+], and "negative" is taking something away [–].

As with reinforcement, there are two kinds of punishers—primary and secondary. A **primary punisher** is any unlearned, innate stimulus, such as hunger or thirst, that punishes a response and thus decreases the probability that it will recur. In contrast, a **secondary punisher** is any learned stimulus, such as poor grades or a parking ticket, that punishes a response and thus decreases the probability that it will recur.

Primary punisher Any unlearned, innate stimulus, such as hunger or thirst, that punishes a response and thus decreases the probability that it will recur.

Secondary punisher Any learned stimulus, such as poor grades or a parking ticket, that punishes a response and thus decreases the probability that it will recur.

Positive punishment A process by which adding (or presenting) a stimulus following a response decreases the likelihood that the response will be repeated.

Negative punishment A process by which taking away (or removing) a stimulus following a response decreases the likelihood that the response will be repeated.

Also, like in reinforcement, there are two kinds of punishment—positive and negative. **Positive punishment** is a process by which adding (or presenting) a stimulus following a response decreases the likelihood that the response will be repeated. **Negative punishment** is a process by which taking away (or removing) a stimulus following a response decreases the likelihood that the response will be repeated (**Table 6.3**).

At this point, it's also very important to emphasize that negative reinforcement is NOT punishment. In fact, the two concepts are actually the complete opposite of one another. Reinforcement (both positive and negative) *increases* a behavior, whereas punishment (both positive and negative) *decreases* a behavior. (To check your understanding of the principles of both reinforcement and punishment, see **Figure 6.7**.)

Problems with Punishment

As you've seen, punishment is a tricky concept that's difficult to use appropriately and effectively. We often think we're punishing, yet the behaviors continue. Similarly, we too often mistakenly think we're reinforcing when we're actually punishing. The key thing to remember is that punishment, by definition, is a process that adds or takes away something, which causes a behavior to decrease. If the behavior does not decrease, it's NOT punishment!

In addition to these problems with punishment, to be effective it should always be *clear, direct, immediate*, and *consistent*. However, this is extremely hard to do. Police officers cannot stop all drivers each and every time they speed. And parents can't scold a child each time he or she curses.

TABLE 6.3 How Punishment Decreases (or Weakens) Behavior — **Real** World **Psychology**

	POSITIVE PUNISHMENT Stimulus added (+) and behavior decreases (or weakens)	**NEGATIVE PUNISHMENT** Stimulus taken away (–) and behavior decreases (or weakens)
PRIMARY PUNISHERS *Unlearned, innate stimuli that punish and decrease the probability of a response*	You must run four extra laps at soccer practice because you were late. Adding the four extra laps makes it less likely that you'll be late for soccer practice in the future. You forget to apply sunscreen, and as a consequence you later suffer a painful sunburn. The addition of the sunburn makes it less likely that you'll forget to apply sunscreen in the future.	You lose sleep for several nights "cramming" for your final exams. The loss of sleep makes it less likely that you'll try last-minute "cramming" for your future final exams. A hungry child is denied dessert because she refused to eat her dinner. The removal of the dessert option decreases the likelihood of the child refusing to eat her dinner in the future.
SECONDARY PUNISHERS *Learned stimuli that punish and decrease the probability of a response*	You text on your cell phone while driving, and receive a ticket. The addition of the ticket for texting makes it less likely you will text while driving in the future. You study hard for your psychology exam, and still receive a low grade. The addition of the low grade after studying hard decreases the likelihood that you will study hard for future exams.	A parent takes away a teen's cell phone following a poor report card. The removal of the phone makes it less likely that the teen will earn poor grades in the future. You argue aggressively with your friend, and he or she goes home. The removal of your friend's presence decreases the likelihood that you'll argue aggressively in the future.

© Fertnig/iStockphoto

Arcady/Shutterstock

FIGURE 6.7 **Using the "Skinner box" for both reinforcement and punishment** To test his behavioral theories, Skinner created an operant conditioning chamber, popularly known as a "Skinner box." Using this device, experimenters can teach subjects (like rats or pigeons) to perform specific behaviors, such as pressing a lever or pecking at a disk, in response to specific signals, such as a light or sound. In many experiments, the subject's responses also are mechanically recorded. Do you see how this highly controlled environment helps reduce potential experimental errors?

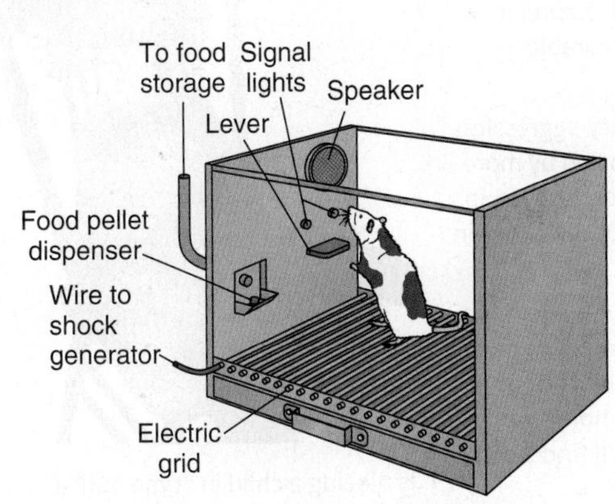

a. In Skinner's basic experimental design, an animal (such as a rat) could press a lever and food pellets or shocks (administered through an electric grid on the cage floor) could be used to administer reinforcement or punishment.

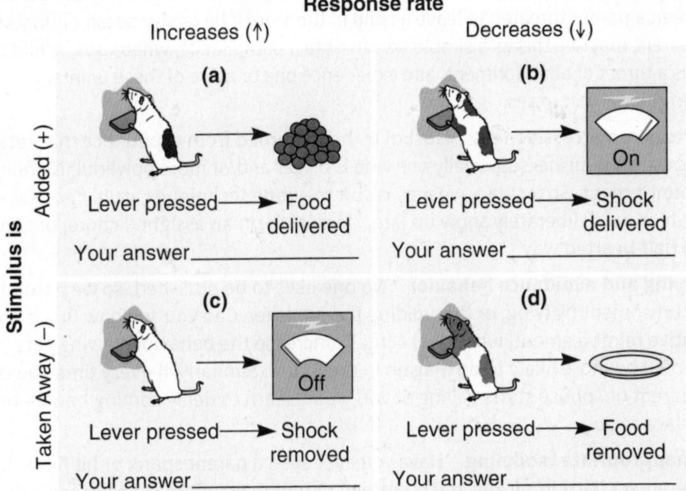

b. Use the blank lines in the four boxes below to fill in the label of the correct learning principle—*positive reinforcement, negative reinforcement, positive punishment,* or *negative punishment.*

Answers: (a) positive reinforcement, (b) positive punishment, (c) negative reinforcement, (d) negative punishment

Don't worry. Psychologists recognize that there are situations when punishment is necessary, such as when a child takes something that doesn't belong to him or her. However, even in limited circumstances like this, it can still have at least seven important drawbacks (**Table 6.4**).

After considering all these potential problems with punishment, you may be feeling a bit overwhelmed and wondering what to do instead. The most important reminder is that punishment teaches us *what not to do*, whereas reinforcement teaches us *what to do*. For specific tips on the effective use of both reinforcement and punishment, see the following **Real World Psychology**.

Real World **Psychology**—Understanding the World

Effective Use of Reinforcement and Punishment

These four suggestions can be helpful for those who are managing employees, raising children, or in any situation in which you're attempting to change another's behavior.

1. **Provide clear directions and feedback.** Have you noticed how frustrating it is when a boss (or an instructor) asks you to do something, but doesn't give you clear directions or helpful feedback on your work? When using either reinforcement or punishment, be sure to provide these, along with a sample or demonstration of the desired response. We all need to know precisely what to do, as well as what NOT to do.
2. **Use appropriate timing and order of presentation.** Reinforcers and punishers should be presented as close in time to the response as possible. If you're a manager, don't offer your staff a large party at the end of the year if they reach a significant goal. Instead, reward them with immediate compliments and small bonuses. Similarly, if your child hits another child, it's best to immediately correct him or her by explaining in no uncertain terms that "hitting is not allowed." In short, reinforcement and punishment should be applied as soon as possible, and always delivered *after* the behavior, never before!
3. **Be consistent.** To be effective, both reinforcement and punishment must be consistent. Have you noticed how some children or even workers get out of difficult assignments and gain special favors because they're constantly complaining or begging? As mentioned earlier, parents often start out saying "no" to a child whining for candy, but ultimately give in. Why? By giving in, the begging and/or complaining are removed, and the parent is *negatively reinforced*. At the same time, the child is *positively reinforced* because his or her begging and whining pay off! Can you see why these behaviors typically escalate and become even more resistant to extinction?
4. **Combine key learning principles.** The overall best method for changing behavior seems to be a combination of the major principles: Reinforce appropriate behavior, extinguish inappropriate behavior, and save punishment for the most extreme cases (such as a child hitting another child, or one employee abusing another).

TABLE 6.4 Potential Side Effects of Punishment

1. **Undesirable emotional responses** For the recipient, punishment often leads to fear, anxiety, frustration, anger, and hostility—obviously, not the responses most punishers intend. For example, modern parents generally disapprove of physical punishment. But how often have you seen a parent threaten to leave a child in the store if he or she doesn't hurry and catch up? The parent may see this as a simple way to obtain compliance, whereas the child may interpret it as a threat of abandonment, and experience one or more of these unintended, undesirable emotional responses.
2. **Passive aggressiveness** Most of us have learned from experience that retaliatory aggression toward a punisher (especially one who is bigger and/or more powerful) is often followed by more punishment. So instead, we may resort to subtle techniques, called *passive aggressiveness*, in which we deliberately show up late, "forget" to do an assigned chore, or complete the chore in a half-hearted way.
3. **Lying and avoidance behavior** No one likes to be punished, so we naturally try to avoid the punishment by lying, or by avoiding the punisher. Can you see how this is an example of negative reinforcement, which will actually increase the behavior? If lying gets you out of trouble, you'll be more likely to do it again in the future. Similarly, if every time you come home, your parent or spouse starts yelling at you, you'll learn to delay coming home—or you'll find another place to go.
4. **Inappropriate modeling** Have you ever seen a parent spank or hit his or her child for hitting another child? Ironically, the punishing parent may unintentionally serve as a "model" for the same behavior he or she is attempting to stop.
5. **Temporary suppression versus elimination** Punishment generally suppresses the behavior only temporarily, while the punisher is nearby. In addition, the recipient only learns what NOT to do, but not necessarily what he or she SHOULD do.
6. **Learned helplessness** Research shows that nonhuman animals will fail to learn an escape response after numerous repeated failures in the past. Do you see how this phenomenon, known as *learned helplessness*, might explain, in part, why some people stay in abusive relationships? Or why some students, who've experienced many failures in academic settings, might passively accept punishingly low grades, and/or engage in self-defeating behaviors, such as procrastination or minimal effort responses?
7. **Inappropriate rewards and escalation** Because punishment often produces a decrease in undesired behavior, at least for he moment, the punisher is in effect rewarded for applying punishment. To make matters worse, a vicious cycle may be established in which both the punisher and recipient are reinforced—the punisher for punishing, and the recipient for being fearful and submissive. This side effect may partially explain the escalation of violence in domestic abuse and bullying.

Real World Psychology

Cynthia Dopkin/Science Source Images

Is placing a child in "time out" a form of positive or negative punishment?

Answer: It depends on the circumstances and the individual. This type of negative punishment ("time out") is often considered more ethical than positive punishment. And it's often used by parents and preschool teachers as a consequence for unwanted behavior. It does remove the child from what the punisher considers a pleasurable environment, and allows him or her quiet time to think about the situation. However, if the child was acting out to gain attention, being placed in a special chair may be unintentionally reinforcing the very behavior the punisher is trying to decrease.

Q Think Critically

Using one or more of these seven side effects of punishment, answer the following questions:

1. **Why do you think roommates, children, and spouses refuse to load the dishwasher despite repeated nagging?**
2. **Why do drivers quickly slow down when they see a police car following behind, and then quickly resume speeding once the police officer is out of sight?**

Sources: Besemer et al., 2016; Lapré & Marsee, 2016; Miller et al., 2012; Oswald et al., 2015; Pear, 2016; Seligman & Maier, 1967; Walker & Gresham, 2016.

Principles of Operant Conditioning

Earlier, we discussed the six principles of classical conditioning. In this section, we explore six principles of operant conditioning: *acquisition, generalization, discrimination, extinction, shaping*, and *schedules of reinforcement*. (Note that the first four of these principles are very similar to those in classical conditioning, except that in classical conditioning the response is involuntary, whereas it is voluntary in operant conditioning.)

Acquisition (in operant conditioning) Learning occurs (is acquired) when an organism voluntarily links a response with a consequence, such as a reward.

1. **Acquisition** Recall that *acquisition (in classical conditioning)* refers to learning that occurs (is acquired) when an organism involuntarily links a neutral stimulus (NS) with an unconditioned stimulus (US). This acquisition then elicits the conditioned response (CR) and/or conditioned emotional response (CER). However, during **acquisition (in operant conditioning)**, learning occurs (is acquired) when an organism voluntarily links a response with a consequence, such as a reward.

2. **Generalization** *Generalization (in classical conditioning)* occurs when the CR is involuntarily elicited not only by the CS, but also by stimuli similar to the CS. In comparison, **generalization (in operant conditioning)** refers to voluntarily responding to a new stimulus, as if it is the original, previously conditioned stimulus (CS). A pigeon that's been trained to peck at a green light, might also peck at a red light. And, a young child who is rewarded for calling her father "Daddy," might generalize and call all men "Daddy." [Study tip: Note that in classical conditioning the CR is *involuntarily elicited*, whereas in operant conditioning the CR is a *voluntary response*.]

Generalization (in operant conditioning) Voluntarily responding to a new stimulus as if it were the original, previously conditioned stimulus (CS); the opposite of discrimination.

3. **Discrimination** *Discrimination (in classical conditioning)* refers to the learned ability to involuntarily distinguish (discriminate) between stimuli that differ from the CS. Likewise, **discrimination (in operant conditioning)** refers to the learned ability to distinguish (discriminate) between similar stimuli based on whether the response to the stimuli is reinforced or punished, and then to voluntarily respond accordingly. A pigeon might be punished after pecking at a green light, and not for pecking at a red light. As a result, it would quickly learn to only peck at red, and to stop pecking at green. Similarly, a child who is only reinforced for calling her father "Daddy," will quickly learn to stop calling all men "Daddy."

Discrimination (in operant conditioning) A learned ability to distinguish (discriminate) between similar stimuli based on whether the response to the stimuli is reinforced or punished, and then to voluntarily respond accordingly; the opposite of generalization.

4. **Extinction** Recall that *extinction (in classical conditioning)* involves a gradual diminishing of the conditioned response (CR) when the unconditioned stimulus (US) is withheld or removed. Similarly, **extinction (in operant conditioning)** refers to a gradual diminishing of a response when it is no longer reinforced. Skinner quickly taught pigeons to peck at a certain stimulus using food as a reward (Bouton & Todd, 2014; van den Akker et al., 2015). However, once the reinforcement stopped, the pigeons quickly stopped pecking. How does this apply to human behavior? If a local restaurant stops serving our favorite dishes, we'll soon stop going to that restaurant. Similarly, if we routinely ignore compliments or kisses from a long-term partner, he or she may soon stop giving them.

Extinction (in operant conditioning) The gradual diminishing of a conditioned response when it is no longer reinforced.

5. **Shaping** How do seals in zoos and amusement parks learn how to balance beach balls on their noses, or how to clap their flippers together on command from the trainers? For new and complex behaviors such as these, which aren't likely to occur naturally, **shaping** is the key. Skinner believed that shaping, or *rewarding successive approximations*, explains a variety of abilities that each of us possesses, from eating with a fork, to playing a musical instrument. Parents, athletic coaches, teachers, therapists, and animal trainers all use shaping techniques (Armstrong et al., 2014; Pear, 2016). See **Figure 6.8**.

Shaping Reinforcement is delivered for successive approximations of the desired response.

Continuous reinforcement Every correct response is reinforced.

Partial (intermittent) reinforcement Some, but not all, correct responses are reinforced.

6. **Schedules of Reinforcement** Now that we've discussed how we learn complex behaviors through shaping, you may want to know how to maintain them. When Skinner was training his animals, he found that learning was most rapid if the correct response was reinforced every time it occurred—a pattern called **continuous reinforcement**.

Although most effective during the initial training/ learning phase, continuous reinforcement unfortunately also leads to rapid *extinction*—the gradual diminishing of a response when it is no longer reinforced. Furthermore, in the real world, continuous reinforcement is generally not practical or economical. When teaching our children, we can't say, "Good job! You brushed your teeth!" every morning for the rest of their lives. As an employer, we can't give a bonus for every task our employees accomplish. For pigeons in the wild, and people in the real world, behaviors are almost always reinforced only occasionally and unpredictably—a pattern called **partial (or intermittent) reinforcement**.

Ron Cohn/The Gorilla Foundation

FIGURE 6.8 Shaping in action How do gorillas learn to have their teeth brushed? Zookeepers use simple shaping techniques: they first place the toothbrush at a safe distance; then bring it closer so they can hold it near the gorilla. Next, they reward the gorilla with grapes, apples, or popcorn if it opens its mouth while the toothbrush is near. Finally, they reward it again if it allows brushing (Wallan, 2015).

Given the impracticality, and near impossibility, of continuous reinforcement, let's focus on the good news regarding

FIGURE 6.9 Gambling—a partial schedule of reinforcement Gambling should be a punishing situation, and easily extinguished, because gamblers generally lose far more than they win. However, the fact that they occasionally, and unpredictably, win keeps them "hanging in there." In addition to this dangerous *partial schedule of reinforcement*, which is highly resistant to extinction, some research
[Q3] demonstrates that pathological gamblers are less able to make an association between negative events (such as losing lots of money), and the stimuli that cause those events (such as gambling; Stange et al., 2016; Templeton et al., 2015). As a critical thinker, can you see how this inability to see connections between losses and gambling might also be an example of the *confirmation* bias (discussed in Chapters 1 and 8)? Most gamblers are far more likely to note and remember their wins—and ignore their losses.

Blend Images / Getty Images, Inc.

Schedules of reinforcement Specific patterns of reinforcement (either fixed or variable) that determine when a behavior will be reinforced.

Fixed ratio (FR) schedule A reinforcer is delivered for the first response made after a fixed number of responses.

Variable ratio (VR) schedule A reinforcer is delivered for the first response made after a variable number of responses whose average is predetermined.

Fixed interval (FI) schedule A reinforcer is delivered for the first response made after a fixed period of time.

partially reinforced behaviors—they're highly resistant to extinction. Skinner found that pigeons that were reinforced on a continuous schedule would continue pecking approximately 100 times after food was removed completely—indicating extinction. In contrast, pigeons reinforced on a partial schedule continued to peck thousands of times (Skinner, 1956). Moving from pigeons to people, consider the human behavior of persistent gambling (**Figure 6.9**).

When using partial reinforcement, it's also important to note that some partial **schedules of reinforcement** are better suited for maintaining or changing behavior than others (Craig et al., 2014; Jessel & Borrero, 2014; Thrailkill & Bouton, 2015). There are four schedules—**fixed ratio (FR), variable ratio (VR), fixed interval (FI),** and **variable interval(VI). Table 6.5** defines these terms, compares their respective response rates, and provides examples. Note that in general, ratio schedules consistently elicit higher response rates than

TABLE 6.5 Four Schedules of Partial (Intermittent) Reinforcement **Real** World **Psychology**

	DEFINITIONS	RESPONSE RATES	EXAMPLES
RATIO SCHEDULES (RESPONSE BASED)			
Fixed ratio (FR)	Reinforcement occurs after a fixed, predetermined number of responses	Relatively high rate of response, but a brief drop-off just after reinforcement	You receive a free flight from your frequent flyer program after accumulating a given number of flight miles.
Variable ratio (VR)	Reinforcement occurs after a varying number of responses	Highest response rate, no pause after reinforcement; variability also makes it resistant to extinction	Slot machines are designed to pay out after an average number of responses (maybe every 10 times), but any one machine may pay out on the first responses, then seventh, then the twentieth.
INTERVAL SCHEDULES (TIME BASED)			
Fixed Interval (FI)	Reinforcement occurs after the first response, following a fixed period (interval) of time	Lowest response rate, responses increase near the time for the next reinforcement, but drop off after reinforcement and during intervals	You receive a monthly paycheck. Health inspectors visit a restaurant every 6 months.
Variable interval (VI)	Reinforcement occurs after the first response, following varying periods (intervals) of time	Relatively low, but steady, response rates because respondents cannot predict when reward will come; variability also makes it resistant to extinction	Your professor gives pop quizzes at random times throughout the course. A dog receives a treat if he stays in a sit position for a variable, unpredictable length of time.

interval schedules because the intervals are more predictable. In addition, variable schedules generally produce higher response rates than fixed schedules because schedules are more predictable. Therefore, do you see why variable ratios (VRs) elicit the highest response rate, whereas fixed intervals (FIs) produce the lowest?

How do we know which schedule to choose? The type of partial schedule selected depends on the type of behavior being studied, and on the speed of learning desired (Lubar, 2015; Pear, 2016; Snider et al., 2016). For example, suppose you want to teach your dog to sit. First, you could reinforce your dog with a cookie every time he sits (continuous reinforcement). To make his training more resistant to extinction, you then could switch to a partial reinforcement schedule. Using the *fixed ratio* schedule, you would offer a cookie only after your dog sits a certain number of times. As you can see in **Figure 6.10**, a fixed ratio leads to the highest overall response rate. But each of the four types of partial schedules has different advantages and disadvantages (see again Table 6.5).

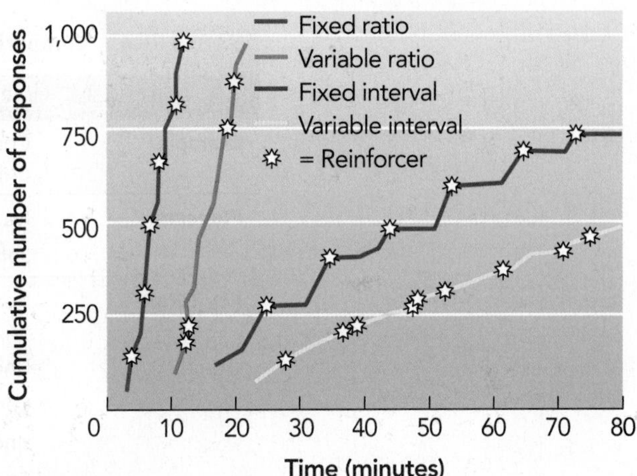

FIGURE 6.10 Which schedule is best? Each of the different schedules of *reinforcement* produces its own unique pattern of response. The best schedule depends on the specific task—see Table 6.5. (The "stars" on the lines represent the delivery of a reinforcer.) (Adapted from Skinner, 1961.)

Before going on, **Figure 6.11** offers even more examples of how operant conditioning applies to your everyday life. In addition, if you're feeling a bit overwhelmed with all the terms and concepts for both classical and operant conditioning, carefully study the summary provided in **Table 6.6**.

Variable interval (VI) schedule A reinforcer is delivered for the first response made after a variable period of time whose average is predetermined.

FIGURE 6.11 Operant conditioning in everyday life Reinforcement and punishment shape behavior in many aspects of our lives.

Real World Psychology

© Anderw Walters /Alamy Stock Photo

a. Prejudice and discrimination Although prejudice and discrimination show up early in life, children are not born believing others are inferior. How might posters like this one discourage children from developing (and adults from perpetuating) prejudice and discrimination?

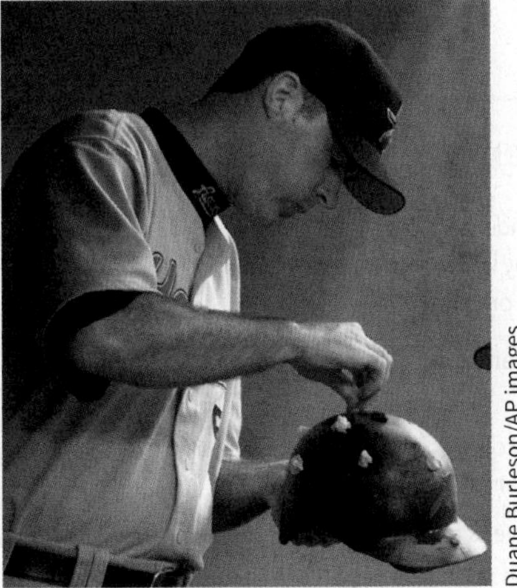

Duane Burleson/AP images

b. Superstition Like prejudice and discrimination, we are not born being superstitious. These attitudes are learned—partly through operant conditioning. Knocking on wood for good fortune, a bride wearing "something old" at her wedding, or this baseball player placing gum on his helmet are all superstitious behaviors that generally develop from accidental reinforcement. For example, the baseball player might have once placed his gum on his helmet and then hit a home run. He then associated the gum with winning and continued the practice for all later games.

© Bonnie Kamin/PhotoEdit-All rights reserved

c. Biofeedback Biofeedback relies on operant conditioning to treat ailments such as anxiety and chronic pain. For example, chronic pain patients are sometimes connected to electrodes and watch a monitor screen with a series of flashing lights, or listen to different beeps, which display changes in their internal bodily functions. The patients then use the machine's "feedback," flashing lights or beeps, to gauge their progress as they try various relaxation strategies to receive corresponding relief from the pain of muscle tension.

TABLE 6.6 Comparing Classical and Operant Conditioning

	CLASSICAL CONDITIONING	OPERANT CONDITIONING
Example	Cringing at the sound of a dentist's drill	A baby cries and you pick her up
Pioneers	Ivan Pavlov John B. Watson	Edward Thorndike B. F. Skinner
Key Terms	Neutral stimulus (NS) Unconditioned stimulus (US) Conditioned stimulus (CS) Unconditioned response (UR) Conditioned response (CR) Conditioned emotional response (CER)	Reinforcers and punishers (primary/secondary) Reinforcement (positive/negative) Punishment (positive/negative) Superstition Shaping Schedules of reinforcement (continuous/partial)
Key Principles and Major Similarities	Acquisition Generalization Discrimination Extinction Spontaneous recovery Higher-order conditioning	Acquisition Generalization Discrimination Extinction Schedules of reinforcement Shaping
Major Differences	Passive/involuntary response NS presented *before* the US	Active/voluntary response Consequences presented *after* the behavior

Retrieval Practice 6.2 | Operant Conditioning

SELF-TEST Completing this self-test, and then checking your answers by clicking on the answer button or by looking in Appendix B, will provide immediate feedback and helpful practice for exams.

1. Learning in which voluntary responses are controlled by their consequences is called _____.
   a. self-efficacy **b.** operant conditioning
   c. classical conditioning **d.** involuntary pairing
2. An employer who gives his or her employees a cash bonus after they've done a good job is an example of _____.
   a. positive reinforcement **b.** incremental conditioning
   c. classical conditioning **d.** bribery
3. _____ reinforcers normally satisfy an unlearned biological need.
   a. Positive **b.** Negative
   c. Primary **d.** none of these options
4. The overall best method for changing behavior is to _____.
   a. reinforce appropriate behavior
   b. extinguish inappropriate behavior
   c. save punishment for extreme cases
   d. all of these options
5. Gamblers become addicted partially because of a _____.
   a. previously generalized response discrimination
   b. previously extinguished response recovery
   c. partial (intermittent) reinforcement
   d. behavior being learned and not conditioned

Think Critically

1. You observe a parent yelling "No!" to his or her child who is screaming for candy in a supermarket. Given what you've learned about operant conditioning, can you predict how both the parent and the child will respond in similar future situations?
2. Can you think of a better alternative to yelling "No!"?

Real World Psychology

Can offering cash incentives and gift cards to smokers actually help them to quit?

Why do gamblers have such trouble quitting, even when they continue to lose money?

Blend Images/Getty Images, Inc.

HINT: LOOK IN THE MARGIN FOR **[Q2]** AND **[Q3]**

6.3 Cognitive-Social Learning

LEARNING OBJECTIVES

Retrieval Practice While reading the upcoming sections, respond to each Learning Objective in your own words.

Summarize the key terms and findings in the cognitive-social theory of learning.

- **Describe** insight learning, cognitive maps, and latent learning.
- **Discuss** observational learning and Bandura's four key factors.

So far, we have examined learning processes that involve associations between a stimulus and an observable behavior—the key to both classical and operant conditioning. Although some behaviorists believe that almost all learning can be explained in such stimulus–response terms, cognitive psychologists disagree. **Cognitive-social learning theory** (also called cognitive-social learning or cognitive-behavioral theory) incorporates the general concepts of conditioning. But rather than relying on a simple S–R (stimulus and response) model, this theory emphasizes the interpretation or thinking that occurs within the organism: S–O–R (stimulus–organism–response).

Cognitive-social learning theory A theory that emphasizes the roles of thinking and social learning.

According to this view, humans have attitudes, beliefs, expectations, motivations, and emotions that affect learning. Furthermore, humans and many nonhuman animals also are social creatures that are capable of learning new behaviors through the observation and imitation of others. In this section, we first look at insight and latent learning, followed by observational learning.

Insight and Latent Learning

Insight A sudden understanding or realization of how a problem can be solved.

Cognitive map A mental image of a three-dimensional space that an organism has navigated.

Latent learning Hidden learning that exists without behavioral signs.

Early behaviorists likened the mind to a "black box" whose workings could not be observed directly. German psychologist Wolfgang Köhler (1887–1967) wanted to look inside the box. He believed that there was more to learning—especially learning to solve a complex problem—than responding to stimuli in a trial-and-error fashion.

In one of a series of experiments, Köhler placed a banana just outside the reach of a caged chimpanzee. To reach the banana, the chimp had to use a stick placed near the cage to extend its reach. Köhler noticed that the chimp did not solve the problem in a random trial-and-error fashion. Instead, he seemed to sit and think about the situation for a while. Then, in a flash of **insight**, the chimp picked up the stick and maneuvered the banana to within its grasp (Köhler, 1925). Köhler called this *insight learning* because some internal mental event, which he could only describe as "insight," went on between the presentation of the banana and the use of the stick to retrieve it. (See **Figure 6.12** for another example of how Köhler's chimps solved a similar "out-of-reach banana" problem.)

FIGURE 6.12 Cognitive-social learning In a second Köhler experiment, chimpanzees were placed in a room with several scattered boxes, none of which was high enough to enable them to reach the banana. They initially ran around and unproductively jumped for the banana. Then, all of a sudden, they saw the solution—they stacked the boxes and used them to climb up and grab the banana! (Also, note how the chimp in the background is engaged in observational learning, our next topic.)

Like Köhler, Edward C. Tolman (1898–1956) believed that previous researchers underestimated human and nonhuman animals' cognitive processes and cognitive learning. He noted that, when allowed to roam aimlessly in an experimental maze with no food reward at the end, rats seemed to develop a **cognitive map**, or mental representation of the maze.

To further test the idea of cognitive learning, Tolman allowed one group of rats to aimlessly explore a maze, with no reinforcement. A second group was reinforced with food whenever they reached the end of the maze. The third group was not rewarded during the first 10 days of the trial, but starting on day 11, they found food at the end of the maze.

As expected from simple operant conditioning, the first and third groups were slow to learn the maze, whereas the second group, which had reinforcement, showed fast, steady improvement. However, when the third group started receiving reinforcement (on the 11th day), their learning quickly caught up to the group that had been reinforced every time (Tolman & Honzik, 1930). This showed that the nonreinforced rats had been thinking and building cognitive maps of the area during their aimless wandering and that their **latent learning** only showed up when there was a reason to display it (the food reward).

Cognitive maps and latent learning are not limited to rats. For example, a chipmunk will pay little attention to a new log in its territory (after initially checking it for food). When a predator comes along, however, the chipmunk heads directly for and hides beneath the log. Recent

Ty Milford/Masterfile

FIGURE 6.13 Cognitive maps in humans This young woman rides through her neighborhood for fun, without a specific destination. However, she is developing her own internal cognitive maps, and she could probably easily return to the local park even though she might not be able to give specific directions. Can you think of examples of similar cognitive maps from your own life?

experiments provide additional clear evidence of latent learning and the existence of internal, cognitive maps in both human and nonhuman animals (Brunyé et al., 2015; Geronazzo et al., 2016; Leising et al., 2015). See **Figure 6.13**. Do you remember your first visit to your college campus? You probably just wandered around checking out the various buildings, without realizing you were "latent learning" and building your own "cognitive maps." This exploration undoubtedly came in handy when you later needed to find your classes and the cafeteria!

Observational Learning

In addition to classical and operant conditioning and cognitive processes (such as insight and latent learning), we learn many things through **observational learning**, which is also called *imitation* or *modeling*. From birth to death, observational learning is very important to our biological, psychological, and social survival (the *biopsychosocial model*). Watching others helps us avoid dangerous stimuli in our environment, teaches us how to think and feel, and shows us how to act and interact socially (Askew et al., 2016; Pauen & Hoehl, 2015; Pear, 2016).

For example, toddlers typically go through a picky eating phase, but research shows that toddlers who watched their parents eating a novel food were far more likely to try that food than toddlers who were only repeatedly prompted by parents (Edelson et al., 2016). Unfortunately, observational learning also may lead to negative outcomes. Research finds that even very young toddlers will show a clear preference for looking at average- versus obese-sized figures (Ruffman et al., 2016). Noting that the toddlers' responses were correlated with their mothers' anti-fat attitudes, and were unrelated to [Q4] parental BMI or education, or the child's television viewing time, the researchers concluded that the toddlers' prejudices most likely resulted from modeling and observational learning. A similar example of bad modeling may come from research on math-anxious parents, who help with their child's math homework (see photo). This study found that the children of these parents actually learn less math over a school year, and are more likely to develop math anxiety themselves (Maloney et al., 2015).

golero/Getty Images

Observational learning The learning of new behaviors or information by watching and imitating others (also known as social learning or modeling).

Much of our knowledge about the power of observational learning initially came from the work of Albert Bandura and his colleagues (Bandura, 2011; Bandura et al., 1961; Bandura & Walters, 1963). Wanting to know whether children learn to be aggressive by watching others be aggressive, Bandura and his colleagues set up several experiments, in which children watched a live or televised adult model punch, throw, and hit a large inflated Bobo doll (**Figure 6.14** top).

Later, the children were allowed to play in the same room with the same Bobo doll. As Bandura hypothesized, children who had watched the live or televised aggressive model were much more aggressive with the Bobo doll than children who had not seen the modeled aggression (**Figure 6.14** bottom). In other words, "Monkey see, monkey do."

Thanks to the Bobo doll studies and his other experiments, Bandura established that observational learning requires at least four separate processes: *attention*, *retention*, *reproduction*, and *motivation* (**Figure 6.15**).

Albert Bandura

Albert Bandura

FIGURE 6.14 Bandura's Bobo doll study

Cognitive-Social Learning and Everyday Life

We use cognitive-social learning in many ways in our everyday lives, yet one of the most powerful examples is frequently overlooked—*media influences*. Experimental and correlational research clearly show that when we watch television, go to movies, and read books (see photo), magazines, or websites that portray people of color, women, and other groups in demeaning and stereotypical roles, we often learn to expect these behaviors and to accept them as "natural." Exposure of this kind initiates and reinforces the learning of prejudice (Dill & Thill, 2007; Scharrer & Ramasubramanian, 2015; van der Pligt & Vliek, 2016).

In addition to prejudice and stereotypes, watching popular media also teaches us what to eat, what toys to buy, what homes and clothes are most fashionable, and what constitutes "the good life." When a TV commercial shows children enjoying a particular cereal, and beaming at their mom in gratitude (and mom is smiling back), both children and parents in the audience are participating in a form of observational learning. They learn that they, too, will be rewarded for buying the advertised brand (with happy children). The good news is that research has found that media also may offer several benefits to viewers (see **PositivePsych**).

FIGURE 6.15 Bandura's four key factors in observational learning

A child wanting to become a premier ballerina, or you if you wanting to learn to paint, ski, or play a musical instrument, would need to incorporate these four factors to maximize learning.

a. Attention Observational learning requires attention. This is why teachers insist on having students watch their demonstrations.

b. Retention To learn new behaviors, we need to carefully note and remember the model's directions and demonstrations.

c. Reproduction Observational learning requires that we imitate the model.

Erik Isakson/Getty Images, Inc.

d. Motivation We are more likely to repeat a modeled behavior if the model is reinforced for the behavior (for example, with applause or other recognition).

PP PositivePsych

The Impressive Powers of Prosocial Media

Parents, educators, and politicians have long complained about media portrayals of teenage sexuality, and many teens are transfixed by reality television shows featuring pregnant teenagers, such as "16 and Pregnant" and "Teen Mom." But could these programs, which *accurately* portray the realities of teen pregnancy, have a positive effect on adolescent sexual behavior? To answer this, and other questions, researchers examined national teenage birth rates and collected data from Nielsen ratings of these programs, along with measurements of Google and Twitter searches conducted by viewers (Levine & Kearney, 2014). Surprising to some, the results showed that reality television shows featuring pregnant teenagers led to an estimated 5.7% decline in teen births in the 18 months following the reality shows' first broadcast!

Jupiter Images/Getty Images

Further good news regarding prosocial media comes from a recent cross-cultural study that tested levels of empathy and helpfulness in thousands of adolescents and young adults in seven different countries (Australia, China, Croatia, Germany, Japan, Romania and the United States). Happily, they found that greater exposure to *prosocial media*—meaning video games, movies, or TV programs showing helpful, caring and cooperative behaviors—led to higher levels of helping behavior among the viewers (Prot et al., 2014).

Unfortunately, the popular media also may lead to negative effects. Starting at a young age, the media is known to strongly influence our ideal body image (e.g., Harriger et al., 2010). See the following **PsychScience**.

PS PsychScience

Can Television Exposure Change Body Size Preference?

How do media images of women's bodies influence preferences for particular body shapes and sizes? To examine this important question, researchers compared preferences for different body sizes in men and women living in three distinct parts of Nicaragua (Boothroyd et al., 2016). One group was living in an urban area, with regular access to most forms of media, whereas the second group resided in a village with only television access. The third group was living in a remote area with little access to electricity, and hence low rates of any media viewing. Participants in each of the three areas were shown images of women's bodies, like those on the right, that varied on degree of thinness, and were then asked to rate their attractiveness on a scale of 1 to 5.

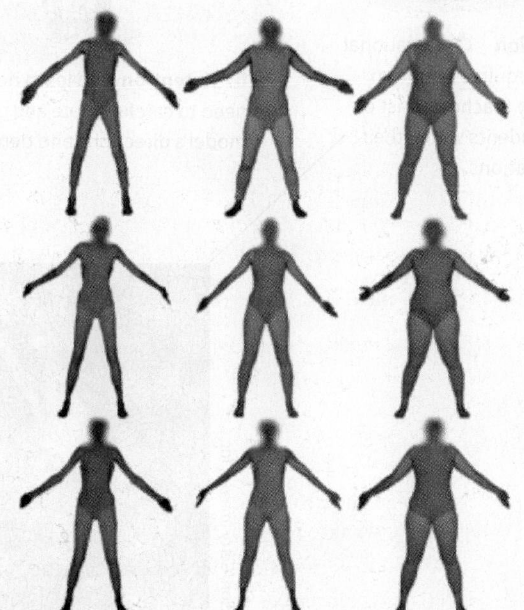

Can you predict their findings? As the researchers hypothesized, people living in the village with little access to media rated the thinner female bodies as the least attractive, whereas those living in the urban area with more media exposure rated the thinner female bodies as most attractive. Moreover, rates of dieting by women were in line with the participants' degree of exposure to media. Those living in urban areas with regular media access reported the strongest desire to lose weight, whereas women living in the area without regular exposure to television showed the least. These findings suggest that the thin ideal so commonly shown in the media may change both men's and women's beliefs about what is considered attractive in a given culture.

Why do you think the researchers limited their study to Nicaragua? Can you see how it would be difficult to find areas in more developed nations that are relatively free of media influences? How might this type of maladaptive observational learning contribute to body dissatisfaction, excessive dieting, and eating disorders, such as bulimia and anorexia (Chapter 10)?

Research Challenge

1. Based on the information provided, did this study (Boothroyd et al., 2016) use descriptive, correlational, and/or experimental research?
2. If you chose:
   - *descriptive research*, is this a naturalistic observation, survey/interview, case study, and/or archival research?
   - *correlational research*, is this a positive, negative, or zero correlation?
   - *experimental research*, label the IV, DV, experimental group(s), and control group.
   - both *descriptive* and *correlational*, answer the corresponding questions for both.

Check your answers by clicking on the answer button or by looking in Appendix B.

Note: The information provided in this study is admittedly limited, but the level of detail is similar to what is presented in most text books and public reports of research findings. Answering these questions, and then comparing your answers to those provided, will help you become a better critical thinker and consumer of scientific research.

At risk of leaving you with the impression that observational learning is primarily negative, we'd like to end on a more positive note. The following **Psychology and You** provides a quick, helpful way to review the three major forms of learning, while also improving your student success skills.

Psychology and You—Understanding Yourself

Using Learning Principles to Succeed in College

Having studied the principles of classical, operant, and cognitive-social learning, see if you can apply this new information to your overall educational goals.

1. **Classical conditioning** If you're overly anxious when taking exams, and you can see that this might be a personal CER, describe how you could use the principle of extinction to weaken this response.
2. **Operant conditioning** List three ways you can positively reinforce yourself for studying, completing assignments, and attending class.
3. **Cognitive-social learning** Discuss with friends what they do to succeed in college classes, and how participating in club and campus activities can reinforce your commitment to education.

Retrieval Practice 6.3 | Cognitive-Social Learning

SELF-TEST Completing this self-test, and then checking your answers by clicking on the answer button or by looking in Appendix B, will provide immediate feedback and helpful practice for exams.

1. _____ emphasizes the roles of thinking and social learning.
   a. Classical conditioning **b.** Operant conditioning
   c. Patent learning **d.** Cognitive-social learning theory
2. Insight is _____.
   a. based on unconscious classical conditioning
   b. an innate human reflex
   c. a sudden flash of understanding
   d. an artifact of operant conditioning
3. When walking to your psychology class, you note that the path you normally take is blocked for construction, so you quickly choose an alternate route. This demonstrates that you've developed _____ of your campus.
   a. a neural map **b.** insight into the layout
   c. a cognitive map **d.** none of these options
4. Latent learning occurs without being rewarded and _____.
   a. remains hidden until a future time when it is needed
   b. is easily extinguished
   c. serves as a discriminative stimuli
   d. has been found only in nonhuman species
5. Bandura's observational learning studies focused on how _____.
   a. rats learn cognitive maps through exploration
   b. children learn aggressive behaviors by observing aggressive models
   c. cats learn problem solving through trial and error
   d. chimpanzees learn problem solving through reasoning

Think Critically

1. What are some examples of how insight learning has benefited you in your life?
2. Are there instances in which observational learning has worked to your advantage?

Real World Psychology

Can children learn anti-fat prejudice and math anxiety from their parents?

golero/Getty Images

HINT: LOOK IN THE MARGIN FOR **[Q4]**

6.4 Biology of Learning

LEARNING OBJECTIVES

Retrieval Practice While reading the upcoming sections, respond to each Learning Objective in your own words.

Review the biological factors in learning.

- **Explain** how learning changes our brains.
- **Describe** how experiences and enriched environments affect our brains.
- **Discuss** the importance of mirror neurons.
- **Summarize** the role of evolution in learning.

Now that we've discussed how we learn through classical conditioning, operant conditioning, and cognitive-social learning, we need to explore the key biological factors in all forms of learning. In this section, we will examine both neurological and evolutionary influences on learning.

FIGURE 6.16 How our brains respond to reinforcement versus punishment

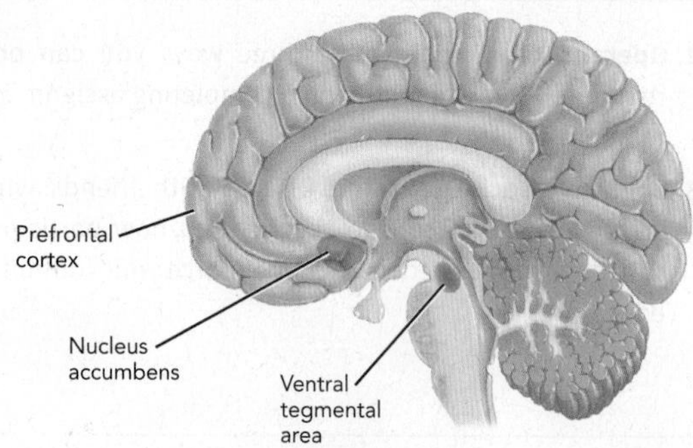

a. Learning from reinforcement primarily involves sections of the ventral tegmental area, nucleus accumbens, and prefrontal cortex.

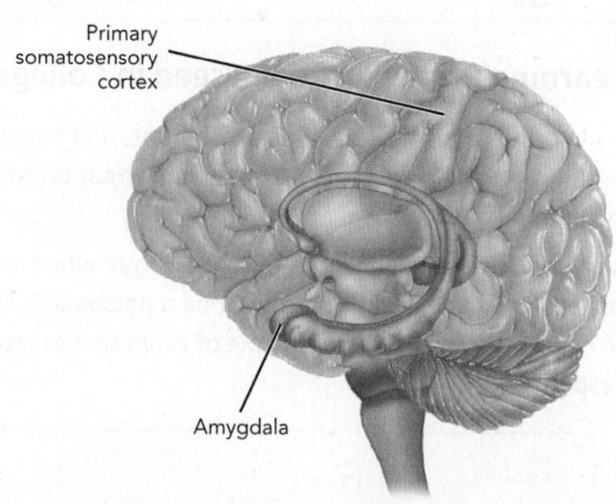

b. Learning from punishment involves some of the same brain regions as in reinforcement, but the amygdala and primary somatosensory cortex are particularly responsive, due to their role in fear and pain.

Neuroscience and Learning

Each time we learn something, either consciously or unconsciously, that experience creates new synaptic connections and alterations in a wide network of our brain's structures, including the cortex, cerebellum, hippocampus, hypothalamus, thalamus, and amygdala. Interestingly, it appears that somewhat different areas of our brains respond to reinforcement and punishment (Jean-Richard-Dit-Bressel & McNally, 2015; Matsumoto & Hikosaka, 2009; Ollmann et al., 2015). (See **Figure 6.16**.)

Evidence that learning changes brain structure first emerged in the 1960s, from studies of animals raised in *enriched* versus *deprived* environments. Compared with rats raised in a stimulus-poor environment, those raised in a colorful, stimulating "rat Disneyland" had a thicker cortex, increased nerve growth factor (NGF), more fully developed synapses, more dendritic branching, and improved performance on many tests of learning and memory (Ahlbeck et al., 2016; Hong et al., 2016; Lima et al., 2014).

Admittedly, it is a big leap from rats to humans, but research suggests that the human brain also responds to environmental conditions (**Figure 6.17**). For example, older adults who are exposed to stimulating environments generally perform better on intellectual

FIGURE 6.17 Environmental enrichment and the brain **Real** World **Psychology**

Given that environmental conditions play such an important role in enabling learning, can you see why it's so important to a child's brain development that he or she has the opportunity to attend classrooms, like the one on the left, which is filled with stimulating toys, games, and books? Similarly, how might an "enriched" cage environment, like the one on the right, encourage brain growth in rats and mice?

Photo Disc Green/Getty Images

Top-Pet-Pics/Alamy

and perceptual tasks than those in restricted environments (Petrosini et al., 2013; Rohlfs Domínguez, 2014; Schaeffer et al., 2014). Similarly, babies who spend their early weeks and months of life in an orphanage, and receive little or no one-on-one care or attention, show deficits in the cortex of the brain, indicating that early environmental conditions may have a lasting impact on cognitive development (Moutsiana et al., 2015; Nelson et al., 2014; Schoenmaker et al., 2014). The good news, however, is that children who are initially placed in an orphanage but later move on to foster care—where they receive more individual attention—show some improvements in brain development.

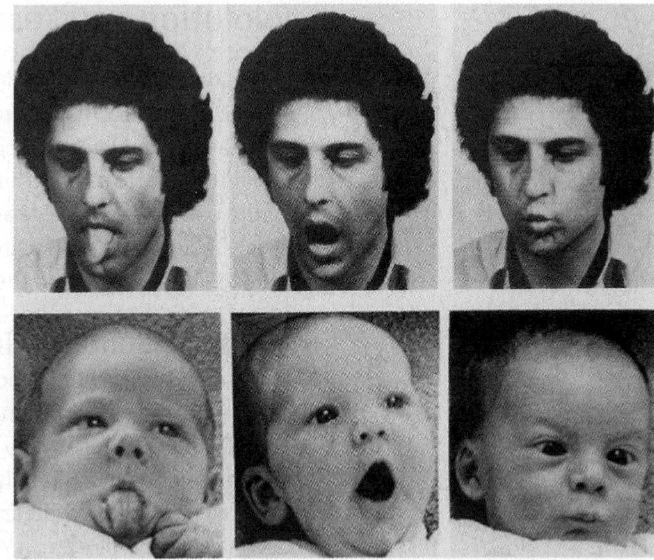

From: A.N. Meltzoff & M.K. Moore, "Imitation of facial and manual gestures by human neonates." Science, 1977, 198, 75–78.

FIGURE 6.18 Infant imitation—evidence of mirror neurons? In a series of well-known studies, Andrew Meltzoff and M. Keith Moore (1977, 1985, 1994) found that newborns could easily imitate such facial movements as tongue protrusion, mouth opening, and lip pursing.

Mirror Neurons Recent research has identified another neurological influence on learning processes, particularly imitation and observational learning. When an adult models a facial expression, even very young infants will immediately respond with a similar expression (Figure 6.18). At 9 months, infants will imitate facial actions a full day after first seeing them (Heimann & Meltzoff, 1996).

How can newborn infants so quickly imitate the facial expressions of others? Using fMRIs and other brain-imaging techniques, researchers have identified specific **mirror neurons** believed to be responsible for human empathy and imitation (Ahlsén, 2008; Fox et al., 2016; Lim & Okuno, 2015). When we see another person in pain, one reason we empathize and "share their pain," while seemingly unconsciously imitating their facial expressions, may be that our mirror neurons are firing.

Mirror neurons Neurons that fire (or are activated) when an action is performed, as well as when observing the actions or emotions of another; believed to be responsible for empathy, imitation, language, and the deficits of some mental disorders.

Mirror neurons were first discovered by neuroscientists who implanted wires in the brains of monkeys to monitor areas involved in planning and carrying out movement (Ferrari et al., 2005; Rizzolatti, 2014; Rizzolatti et al., 1996, 2008). When these monkeys moved and grasped an object, specific neurons fired, but they also fired when the monkeys simply observed another monkey performing the same or similar tasks.

Real World **Psychology**—Understanding the World

Mirror Neurons

Have you noticed how spectators at an athletic event sometimes slightly move their arms or legs in synchrony with the athletes? Mirror neurons may be the underlying biological mechanism for this imitation. Deficiencies in these neurons also might help explain the emotional deficits of children and adults with autism or schizophrenia, who often misunderstand the verbal and nonverbal cues of others (Alaerts et al., 2015; Brown et al., 2016; van der Weiden et al., 2015).

Carlos E. Santa Maria/Shutterstock

Scientists are excited about the promising links between mirror neurons and the thoughts, feelings, and actions of both humans and nonhumans. But we do not yet know the full extent of the influence of mirror neurons, nor do we know how they develop. However, we do appreciate that, thanks to our mirror neurons, we're born prepared to imitate, and imitation is essential to survival in our complex, highly developed social world.

Evolution and Learning

In addition to being born with brains that adapt and change with learning, humans and other animals are also born with various innate reflexes and instincts that help ensure their survival. However, these evolutionary responses are inherently inflexible, whereas learning allows us to more flexibly respond to complex environmental cues, such as spoken words and written symbols, which in turn enable us to survive and prosper in a constantly changing world. As we've seen, learning even enables nonhuman animals to be classically conditioned to salivate to tones and operantly conditioned to perform a variety of novel behaviors, such as a seal balancing a ball on its nose.

Taste aversion A classically conditioned dislike for, and avoidance of, a specific food whose ingestion is followed by illness.

Classical Conditioning Evolutionary and learning theorists initially believed that the fundamental laws of conditioning would apply to almost all species and all behaviors. However, researchers have discovered that some associations are much more readily learned than others. For example, when a food or drink is associated with nausea or vomiting, that particular food or drink more readily becomes a conditioned stimulus (CS) that triggers a conditioned **taste aversion**. Like other classically conditioned responses, taste aversions develop involuntarily (see **Psychology and You**).

Psychology and You—Understanding Yourself

Taste Aversion

Years ago, a young woman named Rebecca unsuspectingly bit into a Butterfinger candy bar filled with small, wiggling maggots. Horrified, she ran gagging and screaming to the bathroom.

© robtek/iStockphoto

Think Critically

1. After many years, Rebecca still feels nauseated when she even sees a Butterfinger candy bar. Can you use the term "discrimination" to explain why she doesn't feel similarly nauseated by the sight of a Snickers candy bar?
2. Under what conditions would a taste aversion be evolutionarily maladaptive?

The initial discovery of taste aversions is credited to psychologists John Garcia and his colleague Robert Koelling (1966). They produced a taste aversion in lab rats by pairing sweetened water (NS) and a shock (US), which produced nausea (UR). After being conditioned and then recovering from the illness, the rats refused to drink the sweetened water (CS) because of the conditioned taste aversion. Remarkably, however, Garcia and Koelling also discovered that only certain stimuli could produce aversions. Their rats developed aversions to tastes but not to sights or sounds.

Taste aversion illustrates an important evolutionary process. Being biologically prepared to quickly associate nausea with food or drink is obviously adaptive because it helps us avoid that specific food or drink, and similar ones, in the future (Buss, 2015; Goldfinch, 2015; Swami, 2011).

Similarly, perhaps because of the more "primitive" evolutionary threat posed by snakes, darkness, spiders, and heights, people tend to more easily develop phobias of these stimuli, compared to guns, knives, and electrical outlets. Research also shows that both adults and very young children have an innate ability to very quickly identify the presence of a snake, whereas they are less able to quickly identify other (non-life-threatening) objects, including a caterpillar, flower, or toad (see photo) (LoBue & DeLoache, 2008; Mallan et al., 2013; Young et al., 2012). We [Q5] apparently inherit a built-in (innate) readiness to form associations between certain stimuli and responses—but not others. This is known as **biological preparedness**.

© Amwu/iStockphoto

Biological preparedness The built-in (innate) readiness to form associations between certain stimuli and responses.

Operant Conditioning As we've just seen, there are biological, evolutionary limits on classical conditioning. The same is true in operant conditioning. Just as Garcia and Koelling couldn't produce noise–nausea associations, other researchers have found that an animal's natural behavior pattern can interfere with the learning of certain operant responses. For example, early researchers tried to teach a chicken to play a modified form of baseball (Breland & Breland, 1961). Through shaping and reinforcement, the chicken first learned to pull a loop that activated a swinging bat

7.1 The Nature of Memory

LEARNING OBJECTIVES

Retrieval Practice While reading the upcoming sections, respond to each Learning Objective in your own words.

Summarize the key factors, research findings, and major models of memory.

- **Define** memory and its constructive process.
- **Discuss** the two major memory models.
- **Explain** the function and process of sensory memory.
- **Review** the core principles of short-term memory (STM) and how it compares to working memory.
- **Describe** the core features, functions, and various types of long-term memory (LTM), and how to improve it.

Memory is learning that persists over time. It allows us to learn from our experiences and to adapt to ever-changing environments. Without it, we would have no past or future. Yet our memories are highly fallible. Although some people think of memory as a gigantic library, or an automatic video recorder, our memories are not exact recordings of events. Instead, memory is highly *selective* (Baddeley et al., 2015; Chen & Wyble, 2015; Matlin & Farmer, 2016). As discussed in Chapter 5, we only pay attention to, and remember, a small fraction of the information we're exposed to each day. Perhaps most important, memory is a **constructive process** through which we actively organize and shape information as it is being encoded, stored, and retrieved (Herriot, 2014; Karanian & Slotnick, 2015; Robins, 2016). As expected, this construction often leads to serious errors and biases, which we'll discuss throughout the chapter. Would you like personal proof of the constructive nature of your own memory? See the following **Psychology and You.**

Memory The persistence of learning over time; process by which information is encoded, stored, and retrieved.

Constructive process The process of organizing and shaping information during encoding, storage, and retrieval of memories.

Psychology and You—Understanding Yourself

A Personal Memory Test

Carefully read through all the words in the following list.

Sour	Chocolate	Pie	Bitter
Nice	Heart	Honey	Good
Honey	Cake	Candy	Taste
Artichoke	Tart	Sugar	Tooth

Now cover the list and write down all the words you remember.

Scoring:

15 to 16 words = excellent
10 to 14 words = average
5 to 9 words = below average
4 or fewer words = you might need a nap

How did you do? Did you recall seeing the words "sour" and "tooth"? Most students do, and it's a good example of the *serial-position effect*—the first and last words in the list are more easily remembered than those in the middle. Did you remember the word "artichoke" and "honey"? If you recalled "artichoke," it illustrates the power of *distinctiveness*, whereas if you remembered seeing "honey" it's because it was repeated two times. Both of these examples demonstrate how distinctive and/or repeated material are more easily encoded, stored, and recalled. Finally, did you see the word "*sweet*"? If so, look back over the list. That word is not there, yet most students commonly report seeing it. Why? As mentioned above, memory is not a faithful duplicate of an event; it is a *constructive process.* We actively shape and build on information as it is encoded and retrieved.

Think Critically

1. Other than this example of seeing the word "sweet," can you think of another example in which you may have created a false memory?
2. How might constructive memories create misunderstandings at work, and in our everyday relationships?

Memory Models

To understand memory (and its constructive nature), you need a model of how it operates. Over the years, psychologists have developed numerous models for memory, and we'll focus on the two most important ones.

Encoding, storage, and retrieval (ESR) model A memory model that involves three processes: *encoding* (getting information in), *storage* (retaining information for future use), and *retrieval* (recovering information).

Encoding, Storage, and Retrieval (ESR) Model

According to the **encoding, storage**, and **retrieval (ESR) model**, the barrage of information that we encounter every day goes through three basic operations: *encoding, storage*, and *retrieval*. Each of these processes represents a different function that is closely analogous to the parts and functions of a computer (**Process Diagram 7.1**).

STOP! This Process Diagram contains essential information NOT found elsewhere in the text, which is likely to appear on quizzes and exams. Be sure to study it CAREFULLY!

PROCESS DIAGRAM 7.1 Encoding, Storage, and Retrieval (ESR) Model vs. a Computer

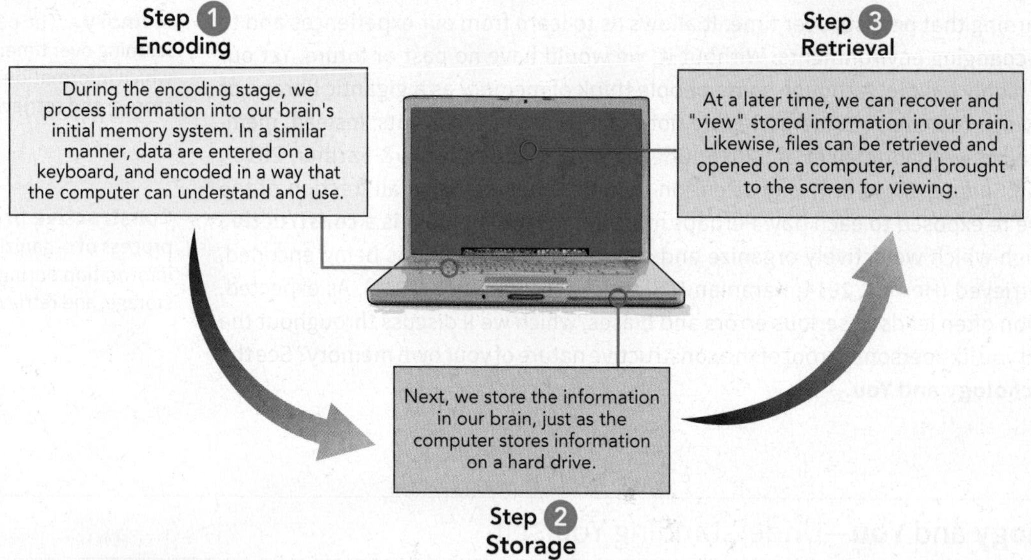

Step 1
Encoding
During the encoding stage, we process information into our brain's initial memory system. In a similar manner, data are entered on a keyboard, and encoded in a way that the computer can understand and use.
Step 3
Retrieval
At a later time, we can recover and "view" stored information in our brain. Likewise, files can be retrieved and opened on a computer, and brought to the screen for viewing.
Next, we store the information in our brain, just as the computer stores information on a hard drive.
Step 2
Storage

Encoding The first step of the ESR memory model; process of moving sensory information into memory storage.

Levels of processing A continuum of memory processing ranging from shallow to intermediate to deep, with deeper processing leading to improved encoding, storage, and retrieval.

To input data into a computer, you begin by typing letters and numbers on the keyboard. The computer then translates these keystrokes into its own electronic language. In a roughly similar fashion, our brains **encode** sensory information (sound, visual images, and other senses) into a neural code (language) it can understand and use.

Given that careful encoding is critical to being a good student and in almost all parts of life, let's examine it carefully. To successfully encode, the first step is to use *selective attention* (Chapters 4 and 5), and deliberately focus our attention on information that we want to remember. Next, we need to use a ***deep level of processing*** to successfully encode (Craik & Lockhart, 1972; Craik & Tulving, 1975; Dinsmore & Alexander, 2016). The term "levels of processing" refers to a continuum ranging from shallow to intermediate to deep, with deeper processing leading to improved encoding, storage, and retrieval. The most efficient way to deep process is to link the new material to other previously learned material. This is why your instructors (and we the authors of this text) use so many analogies and metaphors to introduce new material. For example, we created Process Diagram 7.1 to clarify that the ESR model of memory is analogous to the workings of a computer because we know that most of our readers have previous knowledge about the basic functions of computers. In addition to creating your own analogies, you can deeply process new information by putting it into your own words and/or talking about it with others.

Before going on, have you ever wondered why college instructors so often object to students using their smart phones during class lectures? It's primarily because instructors know that this type of distraction seriously interferes with selective attention and a deeper level of processing. But what about other activities like taking pictures during important events? Does being a photographer have similar negative effects? See the following **PsychScience**.

PS PsychScience

Can Taking Photos Impair Our Memories?

Researchers interested in this and related questions set up two studies using participants who were led on a guided tour of an art museum (Henkel, 2014). During the tour participants were asked to take note of certain objects, either by photographing them or by simply observing them. The next day their memory for the specific objects was tested. As you may have suspected, participants were less accurate in recognizing the objects they had photographed, and weren't able to answer as many questions about the objects' details, compared to those they had only observed.

However, when participants were asked to zoom in and photograph a specific part of the object, their subsequent recognition and detail memory was not impaired. Furthermore, participants' memories for features that were NOT zoomed in on were just as strong as memory for features that were zoomed in on. Can you see how this finding suggests that the selective attention and deeper levels of processing engaged by this focused activity improve overall encoding, and may eliminate the photo-taking-impairment effect?

This research has important implications. Given that it's difficult to always be paying full focused attention, we need to keep in mind that while we're mindlessly taking numerous "selfies" and other photos we may encode fewer details. This means that taking photos the whole time we're on vacation or during a child's dance recital may not only interfere with our full enjoyment of the event, but our actual memories of those special occasions as well! (Study Tip: While reading this and other college texts and/or listening to lectures, you can improve your learning and memory by consciously directing your brain to pay focused, selective attention to important details. You can also process the material at a deeper level by "zooming in" on important details.)

Owen Franken/Getty Images

Research Challenge

1. Based on the information provided, did this study (Henkel, 2014) use descriptive, correlational, and/or experimental research?
2. If you chose:
   - *descriptive research*, is this a naturalistic observation, survey/interview, case study, and/or archival research?
   - *correlational research*, is this a positive, negative, or zero correlation?
   - *experimental research*, label the IV, DV, experimental group(s), and control group.
   - both *descriptive* and *correlational*, answer the corresponding questions for both.

Check your answers by clicking on the answer button or by looking in Appendix B.

Note: The information provided in this study is admittedly limited, but the level of detail is similar to what is presented in most text books and public reports of research findings. Answering these questions, and then comparing your answers to those provided, will help you become a better critical thinker and consumer of scientific research.

Once information is *encoded*, it must be **stored**. Computer information is normally stored on a flash drive or hard drive, whereas human information is stored in our brains.

Finally, information must be **retrieved**, or taken out of storage. We retrieve stored information by going to files on our computer or to "files" in our brains. Keep this model in mind. To do well in college, or almost any other pursuit, you must successfully encode, store and retrieve a large amount of facts and concepts. Throughout this chapter, we'll discuss ways to improve your memory during each of these steps.

Storage The second step of the ESR memory model; retention of encoded information over time.

Retrieval The third step of the ESR memory model; recovery of information from memory storage.

Three-Stage Memory Model

Since the late 1960s, the most highly researched and widely used memory model has been the **three-stage memory model** (Atkinson & Shiffrin, 1968; Eichenbaum, 2013; Li, 2016). It remains the leading paradigm in memory research because it offers a convenient way to organize the major findings. Like the previous ESR model, the three-stage memory model has been compared to a computer, with an input, process, and output. However, unlike the ESR model, the three different storage "boxes," or memory stages all store and process information, but each has a different purpose, duration, and capacity (**Process Diagram 7.2**). Let's discuss each stage in more detail.

Three-stage memory model A memory model based on the passage of information through three stages (sensory, short-term, and long-term memory).

STOP! This Process Diagram contains essential information NOT found elsewhere in the text, which is likely to appear on quizzes and exams. Be sure to study it CAREFULLY!

PROCESS DIAGRAM 7.2 The Traditional Three-Stage Memory Model Each "box" represents a separate memory storage system that differs in purpose, duration, and capacity. When information is not transferred from sensory memory or short-term memory, it is assumed to be lost. Information stored in long-term memory can be retrieved, and send back to short-term memory for use.

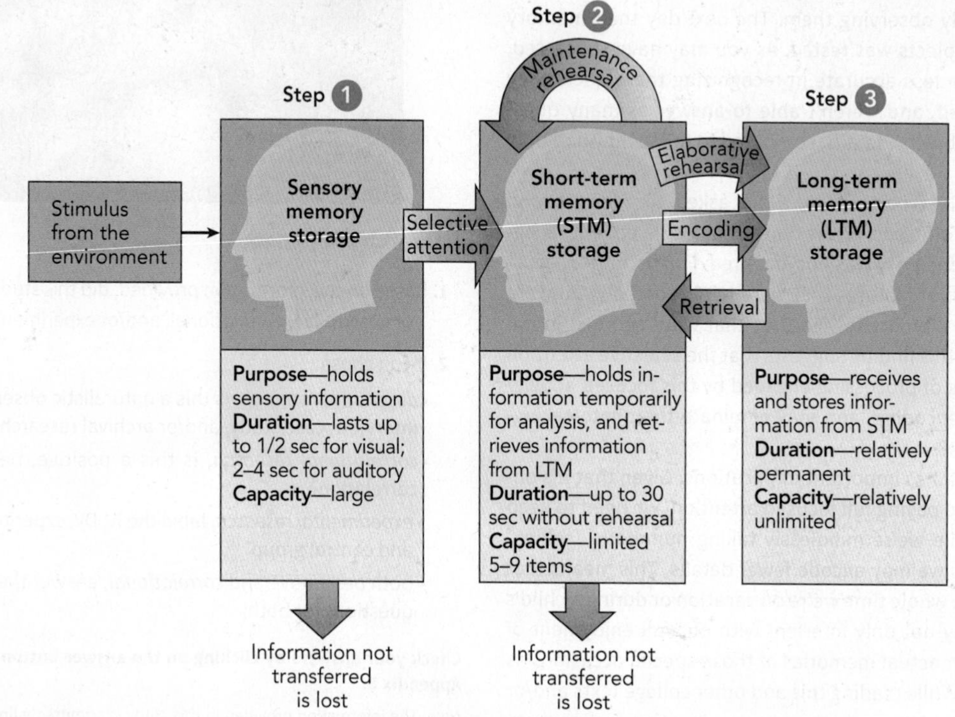

Sensory Memory

Sensory memory The initial memory stage, which holds sensory information; it has relatively large capacity, but the duration is only a few seconds.

Everything we see, hear, touch, taste, and smell must first enter our **sensory memory**. Once it's entered, the information remains in sensory memory just long enough for our brains to locate relevant bits of data and transfer it on to the next stage of memory. For visual information, known as *iconic memory*, the visual image (icon) stays in sensory memory only about one-half a second before it rapidly fades away.

In an early study of iconic sensory memory, George Sperling (1960) flashed an arrangement of 12 letters like the ones in **Figure 7.1** for 1/20 of a second. Most people, he found, could recall only 4 or 5 of the letters. But when instructed to report just the top, middle, or bottom row, depending on whether they heard a high, medium, or low tone, they reported almost all the letters correctly. Apparently, all 12 letters are held in sensory memory right after they are viewed, but only those that are immediately attended to are noted and processed.

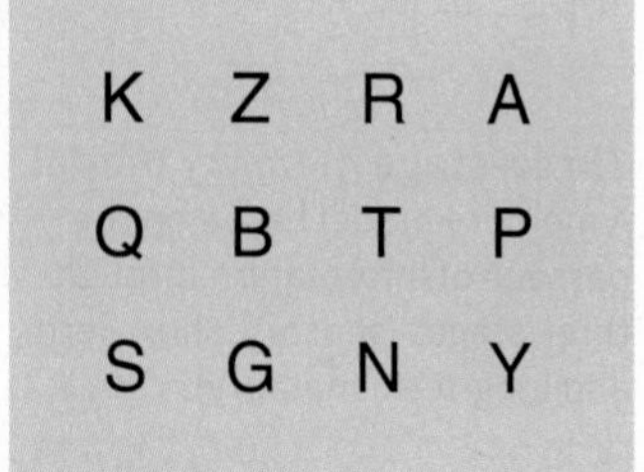

FIGURE 7.1 Sperling's test for iconic memory

Like the fleeting visual images in iconic memory, auditory stimuli (what we hear) is temporary, but a weaker "echo," or *echoic memory*, of this auditory input lingers for up to four seconds (Erviti et al., 2015; Kojima et al., 2014; Neisser, 1967). Why are visual and auditory memories so fleeting? We cannot process all incoming stimuli, so lower brain centers need only a few seconds to "decide" if the information is important enough to promote to conscious awareness (**Figure 7.2**).

Early researchers believed that sensory memory had an unlimited capacity. However, later research suggests that sensory memory does have limits and that stored images are fuzzier than once thought (Cohen, 2014; Franconeri et al., 2013; Howes & O'Shea, 2014.)

FIGURE 7.2 Demonstrating iconic and echoic memories

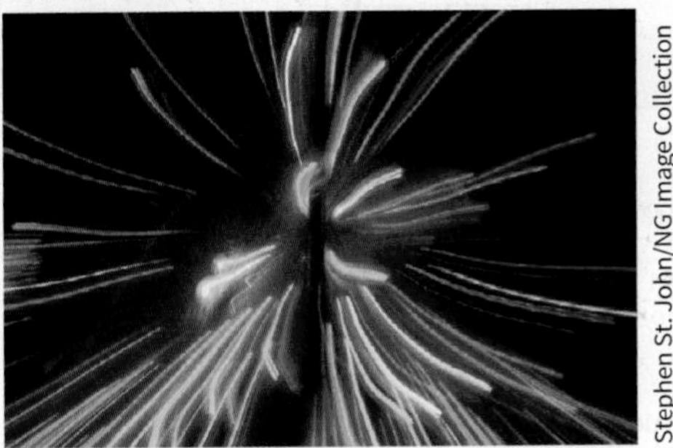

Stephen St. John/NG Image Collection

a. Visual images—iconic memory
To demonstrate the duration of visual memory, or *iconic memory*, swing a flashlight in a dark room. Because the image, or icon, lingers for a fraction of a second after the flashlight is moved, you see the light as a continuous stream, as in this photo, rather than as a succession of individual points.

Blue Jean Images/Getty Images

b. Auditory stimuli—echoic memory
Think back to a time when someone asked you a question while you were deeply absorbed in a task. Did you ask "What?" and then immediately answer without hearing a repeat of the question? Now you know why. A weaker "echo" (echoic memory) of auditory information is available for up to four seconds.

Short-Term Memory (STM)

The second stage of memory processing, **short-term memory (STM)**, temporarily stores and processes sensory stimuli. If the information is judged to be important, STM organizes and sends it along to long-term memory (LTM)—otherwise, information decays and is lost. STM also retrieves stored memories from LTM.

Short-term memory (STM) The second memory stage, which temporarily stores sensory information and sends and receives information to and from long-term memory (LTM); its capacity is limited to five to nine items, and it has a duration of about 30 seconds.

Chunking A memory technique involving grouping separate pieces of information into larger, more manageable units (or chunks).

Maintenance rehearsal The act of repeating information over and over to maintain it in short-term memory (STM).

Improving Your STM The capacity of STM is limited to 5 to 9 bits of information and the duration to less than 30 seconds (Bankó & Vidnyánsky, 2010; Nairne & Neath, 2013). To extend the *capacity* of STM, you can use a technique called **chunking**, which involves grouping separate pieces of information into larger, more manageable units (Gilbert et al., 2015; Miller, 1956; Portrat et al., 2016). Have you noticed that your credit card, social security, and telephone numbers are almost always grouped into three or four distinct units (sometimes separated by hyphens)? The reason is that it's easier to remember numbers in chunks rather than as a string of single digits.

Chunking even helps in football. What do you see when you observe this arrangement of players from a page of a sports playbook (**Figure 7.3**)? To the inexpert eye, it looks like a random assembly of lines and arrows, and a naive person generally would have little or no understanding or appreciation of the cognitive skills required in football. But experienced players and seasoned fans generally recognize many or all of the standard plays. To them, the scattered lines form meaningful patterns—classic arrangements that recur often. Just as you group the letters of this sentence into meaningful words and remember them long enough to understand the meaning of the sentence, expert football players group the different football plays into easily recalled patterns (or chunks).

You can also extend the *duration* of your STM almost indefinitely by consciously "juggling" the information—a process called **maintenance rehearsal**. You are using maintenance rehearsal when you look up a phone number and repeat it over and over until you key in the number.

In addition, people who are good at remembering names know how to take advantage of maintenance rehearsal. They repeat the name of each person they meet, aloud or silently, to keep it active in STM. They also make sure that other thoughts (such as their plans for what to say next) don't intrude.

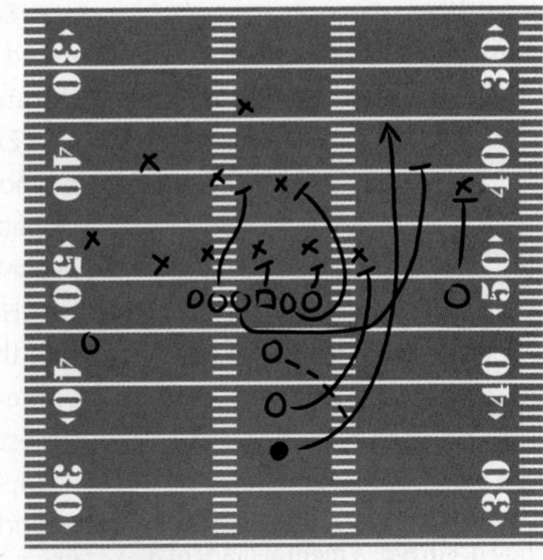

FIGURE 7.3 Chunking in football

Working Memory As you can see in **Figure 7.4**, short-term memory is more than just a passive, temporary "holding area." Given that active processing of information

FIGURE 7.4 How working memory might work Given that short-term memory (STM) is active, or *working*, it helps to picture STM as a "workbench," with a "worker" at the bench who selectively attends to certain sensory information, in addition to sending and retrieving material to and from long-term memory (LTM). The worker also manipulates the incoming, transferred, and retrieved information. Note the various "tools" the "worker" uses during the three stages of processing.

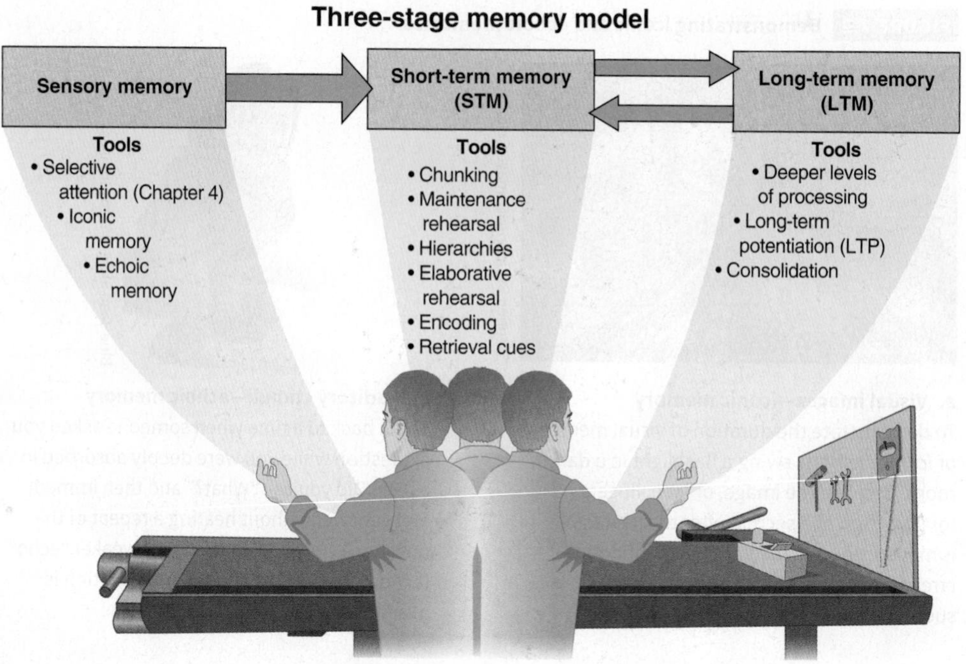

Working memory A newer understanding of short-term memory (STM) that emphasizes the active processing of information.

PhotoObjects.net/Getty Images

Long-term memory (LTM) The third stage of memory, which stores information for long periods of time; the capacity is virtually limitless, and the duration is relatively permanent.

Explicit/declarative memory A subsystem within long-term memory (LTM) that involves conscious, easily described (declared) memories; consists of semantic memories (facts) and episodic memories (personal experiences).

Semantic memory A subsystem of long-term memory (LTM) that stores general knowledge; a mental encyclopedia or dictionary.

Episodic memory A subsystem of long-term memory (LTM) that stores autobiographical events and the contexts in which they occurred; a mental diary of a person's life.

occurs in STM, many researchers prefer the term **working memory** (Baddeley, 1992, 2007; Radvansky & Ascraft, 2016). All our conscious thinking occurs in this "working memory," and the manipulation of information that occurs here helps explain some of the memory errors and false constructions described in this chapter.

For example, researchers have found that people who play action video games (like those in the photo) show higher levels of visual, working memory capacity than those who play a control (non-action) video game (Blacker et al., 2014). This suggests that certain types of video games may provide mental training exercises that boost particular types of memory. [Q1]

Long-Term Memory (LTM)

Once information has been transferred from STM, it is organized and integrated with other information in **long-term memory (LTM)**. LTM serves as a storehouse for information that must be kept for long periods. When we need the information, it is sent back to STM for our conscious use. Compared with sensory memory and short-term memory, long-term memory has relatively unlimited *capacity* and *duration* (Eichenbaum, 2013). But, just as with any other possession, the better we label and arrange our memories, the more readily we'll be able to retrieve them.

How do we store the vast amount of information we collect over a lifetime? Several types of LTM exist (**Figure 7.5**).

Explicit/declarative memory refers to intentional learning or conscious knowledge. If asked to remember your phone number or your mother's name, you can easily state (*declare*) the answers directly (*explicitly*).

Explicit/declarative memory can be further subdivided into two parts. **Semantic memory** is memory for general knowledge, rules, events, facts, and specific information. It is our mental encyclopedia. In contrast, **episodic memory** is like a mental diary. It records the major events (*episodes*) in our lives. Some of our episodic memories are short-lived, whereas others can last a lifetime.

Have you ever wondered why most adults can recall almost nothing of the years before they reached age 3? Research suggests that a concept of self, sufficient language development, and growth of the frontal lobes of the cortex (along with other structures) may be necessary for us to encode and retrieve early events many years later (Bauer & Larkina, 2014; Feldman, 2014; Pathman & Bauer, 2013). Interestingly, older adults describe their most important memories as occurring between the ages of 17 and 24, in part because many major life transitions—such as getting married, attending college, starting a first job, and having children—happen during this period of time (Steiner et al., 2014). Contrary to stereotypes about

FIGURE 7.5 LTM is divided and subdivided into various types

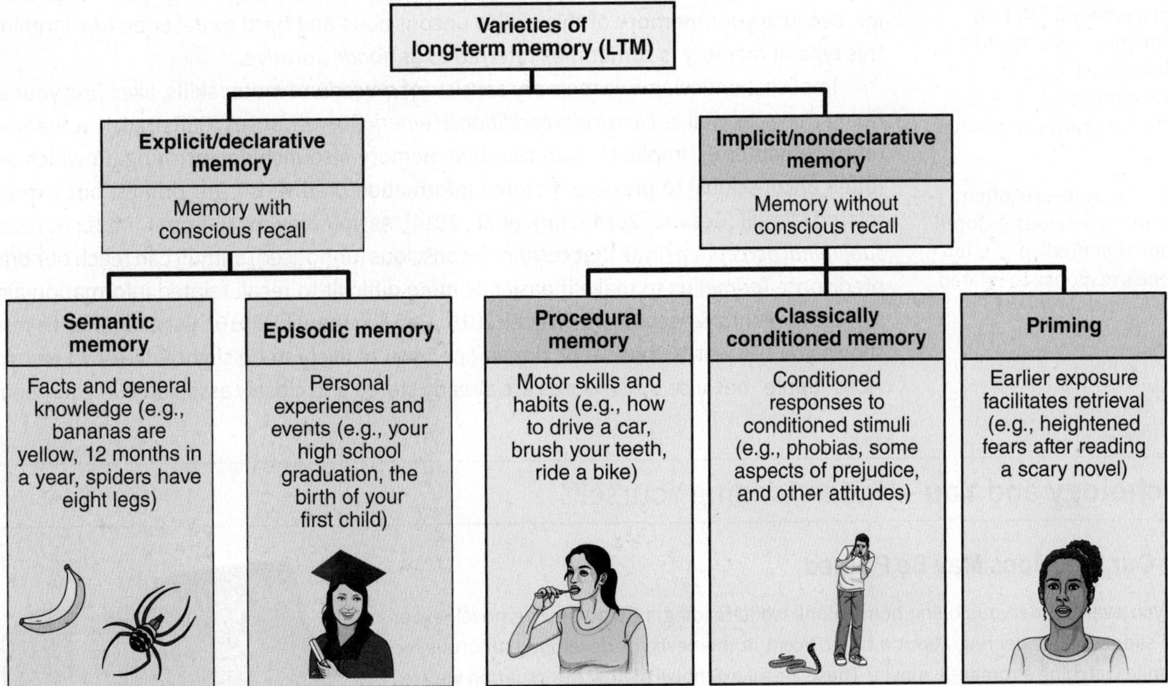

Age-related positivity effect The relative preference in older adults for positive over negative information in attention and memory.

the "grumpy old people," psychological research consistently finds an increase in happiness and well-being as we grow older (Kern et al., 2014; Riediger & Luong, 2016; Sutin et al., 2013). Why? See the **PositivePsych** feature.

PP PositivePsych

Memory and Age-Related Happiness

Why are older people generally happier than the young? Research finds that they tend to have stronger relationships, to value their time more than money, and to become more selective with their time and friendships as they age (Birditt & Newton, 2016; Vaillant, 2012; Whillans et al., 2016). In addition, according to the **age-related positivity effect** older adults generally prefer and pay more sustained attention to positive versus negative information. They also remember more positive than negative events (Carstensen, 1993, 2006; English & Carstensen, 2015; Mikels & Shuster, 2016).

To test possible neural changes underlying this positive attention and memory bias, researchers asked both younger adults (ages 19-31) and older adults (ages 61-80) to look at a series of photographs with positive and negative themes, such as a skier winning a race, or a wounded soldier, and to remember as much as they could about the photographs (Addis et al., 2010). While participants viewed these images, researchers measured their brain activity through the use of functional magnetic resonance imaging (fMRI) scans (Chapter 2). Surprisingly, they found no difference between brain activity in the encoding of information among younger and older adults while watching the negative images. However, when viewing the positive images, areas of older adults' brains that process emotions (the amygdala and the ventromedial prefrontal cortex) directly affected the

Rolf Bruderer/Blend Images/Getty Images

hippocampus. (As you recall, the hippocampus is responsible for encoding and storage of memories.) In contrast, in the younger adults' brains, the thalamus (a "simple" relay station) had a bigger influence on the hippocampus. This suggests that older adults may be better at sustaining attention on positive information, and remembering more good times, because brain regions that process positive emotions are instructing the hippocampus to "remember this."

Think Critically

1. Can you think of possible reasons why our brains become more alert to positive information as we age?
2. How might this information be used to increase your own level of happiness? (Tip: As emphasized throughout this text, we have considerable control over our brains—at almost any age. Therefore, we can use this control to deliberately focus on positive information and events, while avoiding the negative!)

Implicit/nondeclarative memory A subsystem within long-term memory (LTM) that contains memories independent of conscious recall; consists of procedural motor skills, priming, and simple classically conditioned responses.

Priming An exposure (often unconscious) to previously stored information that predisposes (or primes) one's response to related stimuli.

Implicit/nondeclarative memory refers to unintentional learning or unconscious knowledge. Try telling someone how you tie your shoelaces without demonstrating the actual behavior. Because your memory of this skill is unconscious and hard to describe (*declare*) in words, this type of memory is sometimes referred to as *nondeclarative*.

Implicit/nondeclarative memory consists of *procedural* motor skills, like tying your shoes or riding a bike, as well as *classically conditioned emotional* responses (CERs), such as fears and prejudices (Chapter 6). Implicit/nondeclarative memory also includes **priming**, in which exposure (often unconscious) to previously stored information predisposes (or primes) one's response to related stimuli (Cesario, 2014; Clark et al., 2014). As you may recall from Chapter 4, research on *subliminal perception* finds that certain unconscious (unnoticed) stimuli can reach our brains and predispose (*prime*) us to make it easier or more difficult to recall related information already in storage (Loebnitz & Aschemann-Witzel, 2016; Xiao & Yamauchi, 2016). For example, if a researcher shows you the words "red" and "fire engine," you're likely to be slightly faster to recognize the word "apple" because those words are already stored and closely associated in your memory.

Psychology and You—Understanding Yourself

How Our Emotions May Be Primed

Have you ever felt nervous being home alone while reading a Stephen King novel, experienced sadness after hearing about a tragic event in the news, or developed amorous feelings while watching a romantic movie? These are all examples of how the situation we are in may influence our mood, in conscious or unconscious ways. Given this new insight into how priming can "set you up" for certain emotions, can you see how those who haven't studied psychology might be more likely to mislabel or overreact to their feelings?

© CBW/Alamy Inc.

Improving Your LTM

There are several ways we can improve long-term memory. These include *organization*, *rehearsal* (or *repetition*), and *retrieval*.

Organization

To successfully encode information for LTM, we need to *organize* material into hierarchies. This means arranging a number of related items into broad categories that we further divide and subdivide. (This organizational strategy for LTM is similar to the strategy of chunking material in STM.) For instance, by grouping small subsets of ideas together (as subheadings under larger, main headings and within diagrams, tables, and so on), we hope to make the material in this book more understandable and *memorable*.

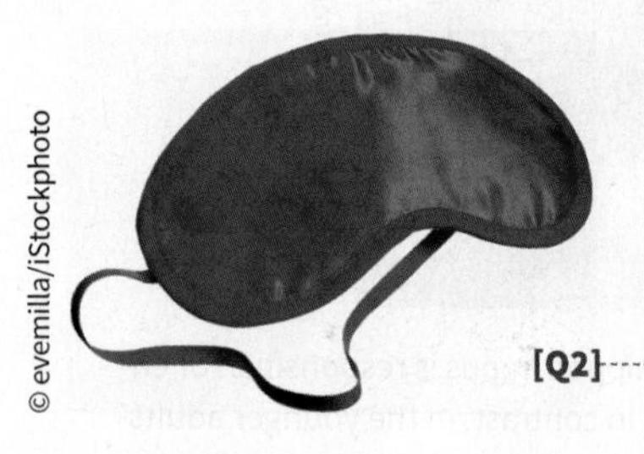
© evemilla/iStockphoto

[Q2]

Admittedly, organization takes time and work. But you'll be happy to know that some memory organization and filing is done automatically while you sleep or nap (Adi-Japha & Karni, 2016; Cona et al., 2014; Nielsen et al., 2015). In fact, people who rest and close their eyes for as little as 10 minutes (see the photo) show greater memory for details of a story they've just heard (Dewar et al., 2012). Unfortunately, despite claims to the contrary, research shows that we can't recruit our sleeping hours to memorize new material, such as a foreign language.

Rehearsal

Like organization, *rehearsal* improves encoding for both STM and LTM. If you need to hold information in STM for longer than 30 seconds, you can simply keep repeating it (maintenance rehearsal). But storage in LTM requires *deeper levels of processing*, called **elaborative rehearsal**.

Elaborative rehearsal A process of forming numerous connections of new information to material already stored in long-term memory (LTM); process of storing information that results in more durable, lasting memories.

The immediate goal of elaborative rehearsal is to *understand*—not to memorize. Fortunately, this attempt to understand is one of the best ways to encode new information into long-term memory.

This type of rehearsal involves forming a number of different connections of new material, and linking them to previously stored information. It's obviously easier to remember something if we associate it with something we already know. This is why we use so many analogies in this text. For example, earlier we compared the encoding, storage, and retrieval (ECR) model of memory to the workings of a computer, knowing that most of our readers are relatively familiar with computers.

Elaborative rehearsal was first proposed by Craik and Lockhart (1972) in their *levels of processing* model of memory. As discussed earlier, the term refers to the fact that we process our memories on a continuum from shallow, to intermediate, to deep, and that deep levels of processing result in improved encoding, storage, and retrieval. How does this apply to your everyday life? An interesting study found that students who took notes on laptops performed worse on conceptual questions than students who took notes on paper (Mueller & Oppenheimer, 2014). Why? The researchers suggested that students who take notes using a laptop tend to just transcribe lectures verbatim (*shallow processing*), rather than reframing lecture material in their own words (*deeper processing*). (Additional tips for improving elaborative rehearsal, and deeper levels of processing, are provided in the following **Psychology and You**.)

Psychology and You—Understanding Yourself

Improving Elaborative Rehearsal

Think about the other students in your college classes. Have you noticed that older students often tend to get better grades? This is, in part, because they've lived longer and can tap into a greater wealth of previously stored material. If you're a younger student (or an older student just returning to college), you can learn to process information at a deeper level and build your elaborative rehearsal skills by:

- ***Expanding (or elaborating on) the information*** The more you elaborate, or try to understand something, the more likely you are to remember it. For example, people who have a chance to reflect on a task show better learning/memory than those who don't (Schlichting & Preston, 2014). This study has clear implications teachers. Asking students to reflect on what they've just learned helps prompt them to remember that information better. As a student, you can discuss the major points of a lecture with your study group or practice repeating or reading something aloud. It's another form of *elaborative rehearsal* (Lafleur & Boucher, 2015).
- ***Linking new information to yourself*** All humans think about, and store memories, about themselves many times each day. Therefore, creating links between new information and our own experiences, beliefs, and memories will naturally lead to easier, and more lasting, memories. In addition to applying new information to your personal life, which is known as the *self-reference effect,* research shows that *visual imagery* (such as the numerous figures, photos and tables we've added to this text, and the personal images you create while listening to lectures or reading this text) greatly improves LTM and decreases forgetting (Collins et al., 2014; Leblond et al., 2016; Paivio, 1995).
- ***Finding meaningfulness*** When studying new terms in this book and other college textbooks, try to find meaning. For example, if you want to add the term *iconic memory* to your LTM, ask yourself, "What does the word *iconic* mean"? By looking it up on your smart phone, you'll discover that it comes from the Greek word for "image" or "likeness," which adds meaning to the word and thereby increases your retention. Similarly, when you meet people at a party, don't just maintenance-rehearse their name. Ask about their favorite TV shows, their career plans, political beliefs, or anything else that requires deeper analysis. You'll be much more likely to remember their names.

Retrieval Finally, effective *retrieval* is critical to improving long-term memory. There are two types of **retrieval cues** (**Figure 7.6**). *Specific* cues require you only to *recognize* the correct response. *General* cues require you to *recall* previously learned material by searching through all possible matches in LTM—a much more difficult task.

Retrieval cues A prompt or stimulus that aids recall or retrieval of a stored piece of information from long-term memory (LTM).

Real World Psychology—Understanding the World

The Power of Retrieval Cues

Whether cues require recall or only recognition is not all that matters. Imagine that while house hunting, you walk into a stranger's kitchen and are greeted with the unmistakable smell of freshly baked bread. Instantly, the aroma transports you to your grandmother's kitchen, where you spent many childhood afternoons doing your homework. You find yourself suddenly thinking of the mental shortcuts your grandmother taught you to help you learn your multiplication tables. You hadn't thought about these little tricks for years, but somehow a whiff of baking bread brought them back to you. Why?

In this imagined baking bread episode, you have stumbled upon the **encoding-specificity principle** (Tulving & Thompson, 1973). In most cases, we're able to remember better when we attempt to recall information in the *same* context in which we learned it (Gao et al., 2016; Grzybowski et al., 2014; Unsworth et al., 2012). Have you noticed that you tend to do better on exams when

Encoding-specificity principle The principle that retrieval of information is improved if cues received at the time of recall are consistent with those present at the time of encoding.

FIGURE 7.6 Retrieval cues and recall versus recognition Can you *recall*, in order, the names of the planets in our solar system? If not, it's probably because recall, like questions on an essay exam, requires retrieval using only general, nonspecific cues—like naming the planets. In contrast, a *recognition* task only requires you to identify the correct response, like a multiple-choice exam. Note how much easier it is to recognize the names of the planets when you're provided a specific retrieval cue, in this case the first three letters of each planet: Mer-, Ven-, Ear-, Mar-, Jup-, Sat-, Ura-, Nep-, Plu-. (Note that in 2006, Pluto was officially declassified as a planet and is now considered a "dwarf planet.")

Antonio M. Rosario/Photographer's Choice/Getty Images

you take them in the same seat and classroom in which you originally studied the material? This happens because the matching location acts as a retrieval cue for the information.

People also remember information better if their moods during learning and retrieval match (Forgas & Eich, 2013; Rokke & Lystad, 2014). This phenomenon, called *mood congruence*, occurs because a given mood tends to evoke memories that are consistent with that mood. When you're sad (or happy or angry), you're more likely to remember events and circumstances from other times when you were sad (or happy or angry).

In addition, memory retrieval is most effective when we are in the same state of consciousness as we were in when the memory was formed. For example, people who are intoxicated will better remember events that happened in a previous drunken state, compared to when they are sober. This is called *state-dependent retrieval* or *state dependent memory* (Hunt & Barnet, 2016; Jafari-Sabet et al., 2014; Zarrindast et al., 2014).

Mnemonic A strategy device that uses familiar information during the encoding of new information to enhance later recall.

One final trick for giving your recall a boost is to use **mnemonic** devices to encode items in a special way (see the following **Psychology and You**). However, these devices take practice and time, and some students find that they get better results using the other well-researched principles discussed throughout this chapter.

Psychology and You—Understanding Yourself

Improving Your Memory Using Mnemonic Devices

These three mnemonics improve memory by tagging information to physical locations (*method of loci*), organizing information into main and subsidiary topics (an *outline*), and using familiar information to remember the unfamiliar (*acronyms*).

a. Method of loci

Greek and Roman orators developed the *method of loci* to keep track of the many parts of their long speeches. Orators would imagine the parts of their speeches attached to places in a courtyard. For example, if an opening point in a speech was the concept of *justice*, they might visualize a courthouse placed in the back corner of their garden. Continuing this imaginary garden walk, the second point the orator might make would be about the prison system, and the third would be a set of scales, symbolizing the need for balance in government.

b. Outline organization

When listening to lectures and/or reading this text, draw a vertical line approximately 3 inches from the left margin of your notebook paper. Write main headings from the chapter outline to the left of the line and add specific details and examples from the lecture or text on the right, as in this example:

Outline	Details and Examples from Lecture and Text
1. Nature of Memory	______
a. Memory Models	______
b. Sensory Memory	______
c. Short-Term Memory (STM)	______

c. Acronyms

To use the *acronym method*, create a new code word from the first letters of the items you want to remember. For example, to recall the names of the Great Lakes, think of *HOMES* on a *great lake* (Huron, Ontario, Michigan, Erie, Superior). Visualizing homes on each lake also helps you remember the acronym of *homes*.

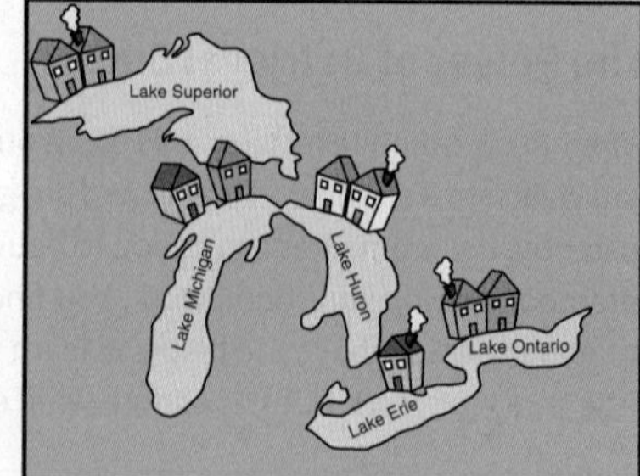

Think Critically

1. How could you use the method of loci to remember several items on your grocery shopping list?
2. How would you use the acronym method to remember the names of the last seven presidents of the United States?

Retrieval Practice 7.1 | The Nature of Memory

SELF-TEST Completing this self-test, and then checking your answers by clicking on the answer button or by looking in Appendix B, will provide immediate feedback and helpful practice for exams.

1. According to the ESR model, memory is a process that can be compared to the workings of ____.
   a. a board of executives **b.** a flashbulb memory
   c. redintegration **d.** a computer
2. Information in ____ lasts only a few seconds or less and has a relatively large (but not unlimited) storage capacity.
   a. perceptual processes **b.** working memory
   c. short-term storage **d.** sensory memory
3. ____ is the process of grouping separate pieces of information into a single unit.
   a. Chunking **b.** Collecting
   c. Conflation **d.** Dual-coding
4. In answering this question, the correct multiple-choice option may serve as a ____ for recalling accurate information from your long-term memory.
   a. specificity code **b.** retrieval cue
   c. priming pump **d.** flashbulb stimulus
5. The encoding-specificity principle says that information retrieval is improved when ____.
   a. both maintenance and elaborative rehearsal are used
   b. reverberating circuits consolidate information
   c. conditions of recovery are similar to encoding conditions
   d. long-term potentiation is accessed

Think Critically

1. What are some of the possible advantages and disadvantages of memory being a constructive process?
2. If you were forced to lose one type of memory—sensory, short-term, or long-term—which would you select? Why?

© evemilla/iStockphoto PhotoObjects.net/Getty Images

Real World Psychology

Do video game players have better working-memory skills?

How can taking a nap improve your memory?

HINT: LOOK IN THE MARGIN FOR **[Q1]** AND **[Q2]**

7.2 Forgetting

LEARNING OBJECTIVES

Retrieval Practice While reading the upcoming sections, respond to each Learning Objective in your own words.

Review the research, key theories, and important factors in forgetting.

- **Describe** Ebbinghaus's research on learning and forgetting.
- **Review** the five key theories of forgetting.
- **Identify** three key factors involved in forgetting.

We've all had numerous experiences with *forgetting*—the inability to remember information that was previously available. We misplace our keys, forget the name of a familiar person, and even miss important exams! Although forgetting can be annoying and sometimes even catastrophic, it's generally adaptive. If we remembered everything we ever saw, heard, or read, our minds would be overwhelmed with useless information.

Ebbinghaus's Forgetting Curve

Psychologists have long been interested in how and why we forget. Hermann Ebbinghaus first introduced the experimental study of learning and forgetting in 1885. As you can see in **Figure 7.7**, his research revealed that forgetting occurs soon after we learn something, and then gradually tapers off (Ebbinghaus, 1885).

If this dramatic "curve of forgetting" discourages you from studying, keep in mind that meaningful material is much more memorable than Ebbinghaus's nonsense syllables. Furthermore, after some time had passed and Ebbinghaus thought he had completely forgotten the material, he discovered that *relearning* it took less time than the initial learning took. Similarly,

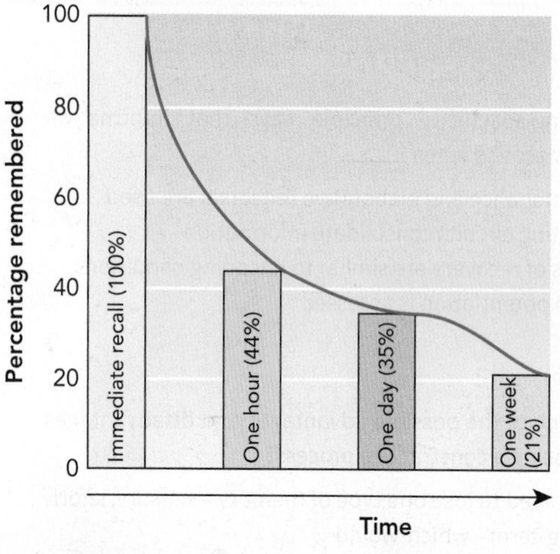

FIGURE 7.7 How quickly we forget Using himself as a research participant, Ebbinghaus calculated how long it took to learn a list of three-letter *nonsense syllables*, such as *SIB* and *RAL*. He found that one hour after he knew a list perfectly, he remembered only 44% of the syllables. A day later, he recalled 35%, and a week later only 21%.

Retroactive interference A memory problem that occurs when new information disrupts (*interferes* with) the recall of old, "retro" information; backward-acting interference.

Proactive interference A memory problem that occurs when old information disrupts (*interferes* with) the recall of new information; forward-acting interference.

if your college requires you to repeat some of the math or foreign language courses you took in high school, you'll be happily surprised by how much you recall and how much easier it is to relearn the information the second time around.

Theories of Forgetting

As mentioned earlier, the ability to forget is essential to the proper functioning of memory, and psychologists have developed several theories to explain why forgetting occurs (**Figure 7.8**): *decay*, *interference*, *motivated forgetting*, *encoding failure*, and *retrieval failure*. Each theory focuses on a different stage of the memory process or a particular type of problem in processing information.

In *decay theory*, memory is processed and stored in a physical form—for example, in a network of neurons. Connections between neurons probably deteriorate over time, leading to forgetting. This theory explains why skills and memory degrade if they go unused ("use it or lose it").

According to *interference theory*, forgetting is caused by two competing memories, particularly memories with similar qualities. At least two types of interference exist: *retroactive* and *proactive* (**Figure 7.9**). When new information disrupts (*interferes* with) the recall of old, "retro" information, it is called **retroactive interference** (acting backward in time). Learning your new home address may cause you to forget your old home address (prior, "retro," information is forgotten). Conversely, when old information disrupts (*interferes* with) the recall of NEW information, it is called **proactive interference** (acting forward in time). Old information (like the Spanish you learned in high school) may interfere with your ability to learn and remember material from your new college course in French.

Motivated forgetting theory is based on the idea that we forget some information for a reason. According to Freudian theory, people forget unpleasant or anxiety-producing information, either consciously or unconsciously, such as the box of cookies you ate last night. Interestingly, people who just finish a marathon race often rate the intensity and unpleasantness of their pain about a 5.5 on a scale of 1 to 10. However, when you ask these same people

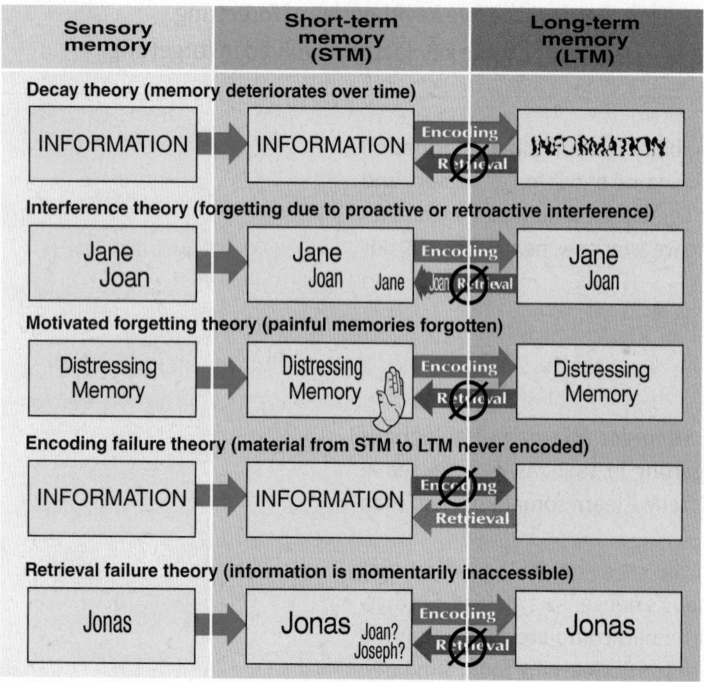

Mick Stevens/The New Yorker Collection/www.cartoonbank.com

FIGURE 7.8 Theories of forgetting Which of these five theories of forgetting best applies to this cartoon?

Note: If you want to remember these five theories, think of how forgetting involves memories that grow "dimmer," and note that the first letter of each theory has almost the same spelling—D-I-M-E-R.

FIGURE 7.9 **Retroactive interference and proactive interference**

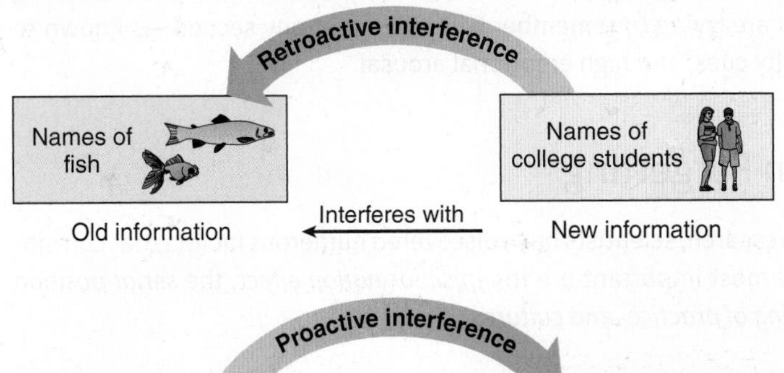

a. Retroactive (backward-acting) **interference** occurs when new information interferes with old information. This example comes from a story about an absent-minded ichthyology professor (fish specialist) who refused to learn the name of his college students. Asked why, he said, "Every time I learn a student's name, I forget the name of a fish!"

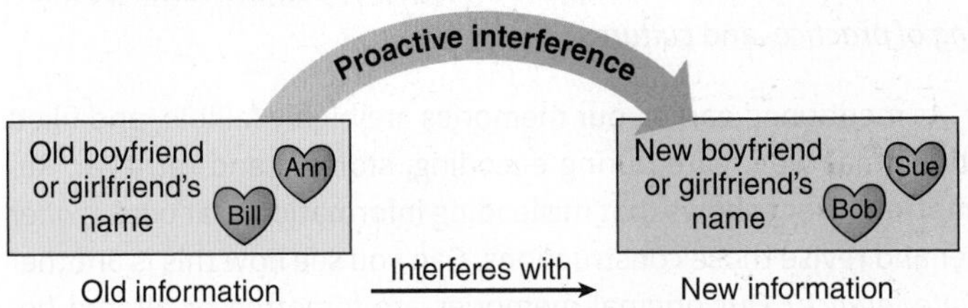

b. Proactive (forward-acting) **interference** occurs when old information interferes with new information. Have you ever been in trouble because you used an old partner's name to refer to your new partner? You now have a guilt-free explanation—proactive interference.

3 to 6 months later to report how they felt after the race, they've forgotten the pain, and guess that it was about a 3 (Babel, 2016). Do you see how the runners probably enjoyed the overall experience of the event and are motivated to forget the pain? Furthermore, this motivated forgetting theory may help explain why all children aren't only children—mothers tend to forget the actual pain of childbirth!

In *encoding failure theory*, our sensory memory receives the information and passes it to STM. But during STM, we may overlook precise details, and may not fully encode it, which would result in a failure to pass along a complete memory for proper storage in LTM (see the following **Psychology and You** feature).

Psychology and You—Understanding Yourself

Test Yourself | Can You Identify the Actual Apple Logo?

If you want a simple (but fascinating) example of encoding failure, try to identify which of the six examples shown on the right is the closest match for the actual Apple logo. Despite having seen the Apple logo thousands of times in our lives, most of us have difficulty recognizing the details. In fact, the Apple logo has several, easily distinguishing characteristics (the size of the bite, the direction the stem faces, the curve at the bottom of the Apple, and so on). Furthermore, this logo, like all others, was carefully designed to be memorable and distinctive, in order to increase consumer sales and brand loyalty. However, in a recent study with 85 undergraduates fewer than half of all participants correctly identified the logo. Even more surprising, only one student was able to correctly reproduce this logo when asked to draw it on a blank sheet of paper. Ironically, participants indicated HIGH levels of confidence for both their recognition and recall abilities (Blake et al., 2015).

How does this apply to your everyday life? Have you ever taken an exam and felt fairly confident that you did well, yet later received a low score? Most participants in this study felt similarly confident that they could easily identify the correct Apple logo. However, in both cases—identifying logos or taking exams–we may fail to succeed because we don't encode the fine details, and pass them along for storage in our LTM. Why is it important to remember how you did on this logo identification when studying for exams? Just as most people cannot identify the correct logo because of encoding failure, you may not recognize correct answers on a multiple-choice exam, or recall the important details required for an essay exam, because you failed to carefully study and encode important details from your textbooks. Keep in mind that you simply can't read a textbook like you casually read articles on the Internet or a novel. You must slow down and encode the details.

Answers: For copyright reasons, the researchers could not show the actual Apple logo, so none of the choices exactly matches the real logo. However, the bottom, middle figure was considered by the researchers to be the *closest* to the actual logo, which has the leaf facing the opposite way.

Tip-of-the-tongue (TOT) phenomenon A strong, confident feeling of knowing something, while not being able to retrieve it at the moment.

According to *retrieval failure theory*, memories stored in LTM aren't forgotten. They're just momentarily inaccessible. For example, the **tip-of-the-tongue (TOT) phenomenon**—the feeling that a word or an event you are trying to remember will pop out at any second—is known to result from interference, faulty cues, and high emotional arousal.

Factors Involved in Forgetting

Misinformation effect A memory error resulting from misleading information being presented after an event, which alters memories of the event itself.

Serial-position effect A characteristic of memory retrieval in which information at the beginning and end of a series is remembered better than material in the middle.

Since Ebbinghaus's original research, scientists have discovered numerous factors that contribute to forgetting. Five of the most important are the *misinformation effect*, the *serial-position effect*, *source amnesia*, *spacing of practice*, and *culture*.

1. **Misinformation Effect** As mentioned earlier, our memories are highly fallible, and filled with personal constructions that we create during encoding, storage, and retrieval. Research on the **misinformation effect** shows that misleading information that occurs *after an event* may further alter and revise those constructions. Can you see how this is another example of *retroactive interference*? Our original memories are forgotten or altered because of misleading, post-event information.

   For instance, participants in one study completed an interview in one room and then answered questions about it in another room (Morgan et al., 2013). Participants who received neutral questions like, "Was there a telephone in the room?" answered accurately for the most part, making errors on only 10% of the interview questions. However, other participants were asked questions such as, "What color was the telephone?" which falsely implied that there had been a telephone in the room. Of these respondents, 98% "remembered" a telephone. Other experiments have created false memories by showing participants doctored photos of themselves taking a completely fictitious hot-air balloon ride, or by asking participants to simply imagine an event, such as having a nurse remove a skin sample from their finger. In these and similar cases, a large number of participants later believed that the misleading information was correct, and that the fictitious or imagined events actually occurred (Kaplan et al., 2016; Kirk et al., 2015; Takarangi et al., 2016).

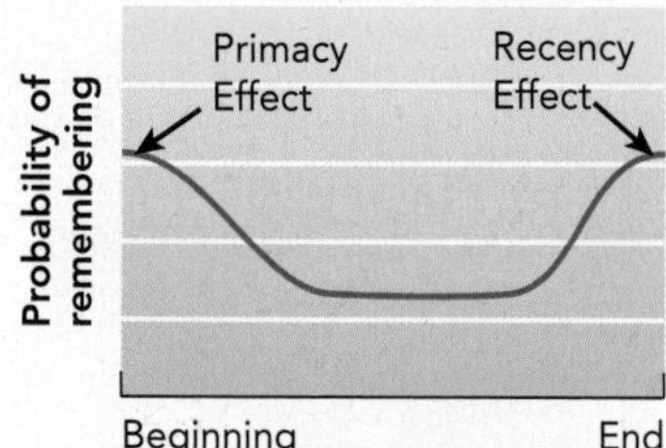

FIGURE 7.10 The serial-position effect When we try to recall a list of similar items, we tend to remember the first and last items best. Can you see how you can use this information to improve your chances for employment success? If a potential employer calls you to set up an interview, you can increase their memory of you (and your application) by asking to be either the first (*primacy effect*) or last (*recency effect*) candidate.

2. **Serial-Position Effect** Stop for a moment, and write down the names of all the U.S. presidents that you can immediately recall. How did you do? Research shows that most people recall presidents from the beginning of history (e.g., Washington, Adams, Jefferson), and the more recent (e.g., Clinton, Bush, Obama). This is known as the **serial-position effect** (**Figure 7.10**). We tend to recall items at the beginning (*primacy effect*) and the end (*recency effect*) better than those in the middle of the list. And when we do remember presidents in the middle, like President Abraham Lincoln, it's normally because they are associated with significant events, such as Lincoln and the Civil War. [Q3]

3. **Source Amnesia** Each day we read, hear, and process an enormous amount of information, and it's easy to get confused about how we learned who said what to whom, and in what context. Forgetting the origin of a previously stored memory is known

Real World Psychology—Understanding the World

The High Price of Forgetting

In 2015, Brian Williams was removed from his NBC news anchor position following allegations that he had misrepresented his own involvement in various wars and current events that he had covered. In particular, he implied that he faced far more dangerous circumstances than in reality he had. He later apologized to viewers, noting "I made a mistake in recalling the events of 12 years ago." Based on your knowledge of psychology from this chapter, what factors may have contributed to his memory errors?

Ray Tamarra/FilmMagic/Getty Images

© Maciej Dakowicz/Alamy Stock Photo

FIGURE 7.11 Source amnesia and negative political ads Think back to a recent political election. What type of television advertisements most readily come to mind? Research shows that we're more likely to recall ads that rely on creating negative feelings about one of the candidates. They stick in our memory even if we initially have negative feelings about them (Lariscy & Tinkham, 1999). In addition, over time the negative "facts" stay in our memory, and we forget the source—*source amnesia*! The good news for politicians, and in your personal life, is that direct rebuttals of negative ads are generally effective and do not backfire (Weeks & Garrett, 2014).

as **source amnesia** (Ferrie, 2015; Leichtman, 2006; Paterson et al., 2011). (See **Figure 7.11.**)

4. **Spacing of practice** Have you heard about the recent software programs and websites, such as *Lumosity*, that are heavily promoted on the Internet and television ads? They promise to dramatically decrease forgetting and improve our memory, while revolutionizing the way we learn (Schroers, 2014; Weir, 2014). Interestingly, most of these "new" programs are based on the older, well-established principle of **distributed practice**, in which studying or practice is broken up into a number of short sessions spaced out over time to allow numerous opportunities for "drill and practice." As you first discovered in the *Strategies for Student Success* at the end of Chapter 1, this type of spaced learning is widely recognized as one of the very best tools for learning and grade improvement (Dunlosky et al., 2013; Küpper-Tetzel, 2014; Mettler et al., 2016). In response to these research findings on the superiority of distributed practice, we've built in numerous opportunities for distributed practice and *self-tests* throughout this text. Unfortunately, many students do the exact opposite! They put off studying and believe they're better off using **massed practice** or "cramming" right before an exam, which is proven to be far less effective than distributed practice.

5. **Culture** Finally, as illustrated in **Figure 7.12**, cultural factors can play a role in memory and how well people remember what they have learned (Gutchess & Huff, 2016; Wang, 2011).

Source amnesia A memory error caused by forgetting the origin of a previously stored memory; also called source confusion or source misattribution.

Distributed practice A learning strategy in which studying or practice is broken up into a number of short sessions over a period of time; also known as spaced repetition.

Massed practice A study technique in which time spent learning is grouped (or massed) into long, unbroken intervals; also called cramming.

(c) Ferdinando Scianna/MagnumPhotos, Inc.

FIGURE 7.12 Culture and memory In many societies, tribal leaders pass down vital information through orally related stories. As a result, children living in these cultures have better memories for information that is related through stories than do other children.

Retrieval Practice 7.2 | Forgetting

SELF-TEST Completing this self-test, and then checking your answers by clicking on the answer button or by looking in Appendix B, will provide immediate feedback and helpful practice for exams.

1. According to the ____ theory of forgetting, memory is processed and stored in a physical form, and connections between neurons probably deteriorate over time.
   a. decay **b.** interference
   c. motivated forgetting **d.** retrieval failure
2. The ____ theory suggests that forgetting is caused by two competing memories, particularly memories with similar qualities.
   a. decay **b.** interference
   c. motivated forgetting **d.** encoding failure
3. The ____ effect suggests that people will recall information presented at the beginning and end of a list better than information from the middle of a list.
   a. recency **b.** latency
   c. serial position **d.** primacy
4. Distributed practice is a learning technique in which ____.
   a. students are distributed (spaced) equally throughout the room
   b. learning periods are broken up into a number of short sessions over a period of time
   c. learning decays faster than it can be distributed
   d. several students study together, distributing various subjects according to their individual strengths
5. Which of the following is *not* one of the key factors that contribute to forgetting outlined in the text?
   a. misinformation effect **b.** serial-position effect
   c. consolidation **d.** source amnesia

Think Critically

1. Briefly describe an example from your own life of source amnesia.
2. Why might advertisers of shoddy services or products benefit from channel surfing, especially if the television viewer is skipping from news programs to cable talk shows to infomercials?

Real World Psychology

Why do we remember President Lincoln better than President Truman?

W.F. Crummer/ Library of Congress

Chase-Statler/ Library of Congress

HINT: LOOK IN THE MARGIN FOR **[Q3]**

7.3 Biological Bases of Memory

LEARNING OBJECTIVES

Retrieval Practice While reading the upcoming sections, respond to each Learning Objective in your own words.

Summarize the biological factors involved in memory.

- **Describe** the synaptic and neurotransmitter changes that occur when we learn and remember.
- **Explain** how emotional arousal affects memory.
- **Identify** the major areas of the brain involved in memory storage.
- **Discuss** the biological factors in memory loss.

So far we have explored the nature of memory and the various models of how it is organized. We've also examined the various factors involved in forgetting. In this section, we'll explore the biological bases of memory—the synaptic and neurotransmitter changes, the effects of emotional arousal, where memories are stored, and the biological factors in memory loss.

Synaptic and Neurotransmitter Changes

In Chapters 2 and 6, we discussed how learning and memory modify our brains' neural networks. For instance, when learning to play a sport like tennis repeated practice builds specific neural pathways that make it progressively easier for you to get the ball over the net. These same pathways later enable you to remember how to play the game the next time you go out onto the tennis court.

Long-term potentiation (LTP) A long-lasting increase in neural sensitivity; a biological mechanism for learning and memory.

How do these changes, called **long-term potentiation (LTP)**, occur? They happen in at least two ways. First, early research with rats raised in enriched environments found that repeated stimulation of a synapse strengthens it by causing the dendrites to grow more spines (Rosenzweig et al., 1972). This repeated stimulation further results in more synapses and receptor sites, along with increased sensitivity.

Second, when learning and memory occur, there is a measurable change in the amount of neurotransmitter released, which thereby increases the neuron's efficiency in message transmission. Research with *Aplysia* (sea slugs) clearly demonstrates this effect (**Figure 7.13**).

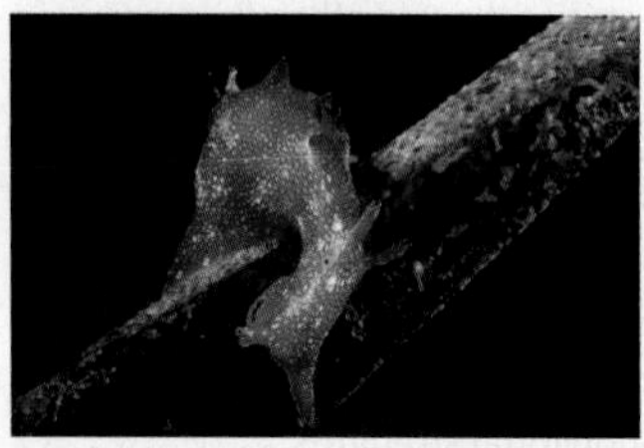

© Wolfgang Pölzer/Alamy Inc.

FIGURE 7.13 How does a sea slug learn and remember? After repeated squirting with water, followed by a mild shock, the sea slug, Aplysia, releases more neurotransmitters at certain synapses. These synapses then become more efficient at transmitting signals that allow the slug to withdraw its gills when squirted. As a critical thinker, can you explain why this ability might provide an evolutionary advantage?

Further evidence comes from research with genetically engineered "smart mice," which have extra receptors for a neurotransmitter named NMDA (N-methyl-d-aspartate). These mice perform significantly better on memory tasks than do normal mice (Lin et al., 2014; Plattner et al., 2014; Tsien, 2000).

Although it is difficult to generalize from sea slugs and mice, research on long-term potentiation (LTP) in humans supports the idea that LTP is one of the major biological mechanisms underlying learning and memory (Baddeley et al., 2015; Camera et al., 2016; Panja & Bramham, 2014).

Emotional Arousal and Memory

When stressed or excited, we naturally produce neurotransmitters and hormones that arouse the body, such as *epinephrine* and *cortisol* (Chapter 3). These chemicals also affect the amygdala (a brain structure involved in emotion), and other brain areas, such as the hippocampus and cerebral cortex (parts of the brain that are important for memory). Research has shown that these chemicals can interfere with, as well as enhance, how we encode, store, and retrieve our memories (Conway, 2015; Emilien & Durlach, 2015; Quas et al., 2016).

© morrbyte/iStockphoto

Interestingly, some research suggests that exposure to pornography can disrupt memory (see the photo). Researchers in one study asked men to view a series of both pornographic and nonpornographic images and judge whether they had previously seen each image (Laier et al., 2013). Men who saw the nonsexual images gave 80% correct answers, whereas men who saw the pornographic images gave only 67% correct answers. Can you see how sexual arousal interferes with working memory and how it may help explain these findings? [Q4]

On the other hand, emotional arousal can sometimes lead to memory enhancement, as shown by **flashbulb memories (FBMs)**—vivid, detailed, and near-permanent memories of emotionally significant moments or events (Brown & Kulik, 1977). During important historical, public, or autobiographical events, such as the 9/11 attack, the musician Prince's death, or other personally memorable occasions, it appears that our minds automatically create FBMs. We tend to remember incredible details, such as where we were, what was going on, and how we and others were feeling and reacting at that moment in time. And these memories are long lasting. In fact, researchers have found that people have retained their FBMs of the 9/11 attack for as long as 10 years, and that their confidence in these memories has remained high (Hirst et al., 2015). We also sometimes create uniquely personal (and happy) FBMs (see **Psychology and You**).

Flashbulb memory (FBM) A vivid, detailed, and near-permanent memory of an emotionally significant moment or event; memory resulting from a form of automatic encoding, storage, and later retrieval.

Psychology and You—Understanding Yourself

Common FBMs

Why do most people clearly remember their college graduations and wedding ceremonies, as shown in this photo of your author, Catherine Sanderson and her husband, on their wedding day? Due to the extraordinary level of emotionality that most of us experience during these happy occasions, we tend to automatically create detailed, long-lasting memories of our thoughts, feelings, and actions during these exciting and momentous events.

Catherine Sanderson and Bart Hollander

Thinking Critically

1. Do your personal memories of highly emotional events fit with what flashbulb memory (FBM) research suggests?
2. Despite documented errors with FBMs, most people are very confident in their personal accuracy. What problems might result from this overconfidence?

How does this happen? It's as if our brains command us to take "flash pictures" of these highly emotional events in order for us to "pay attention, learn, and remember." As we've just seen, a flood of neurotransmitters and hormones helps create strong, immediate memories. Furthermore, as discussed in Chapter 3, the flood of the hormone cortisol that happens during traumatic events has been studied as a contributor to long-lasting memories and, sadly, to PTSD (Drexler et al., 2015). In addition to these chemical changes, we actively replay these memories in our minds again and again, which further encourages stronger and more lasting memories (**Figure 7.14**).

Jupiterimages/Getty Images

FIGURE 7.14 A negative (and thankfully uncommon) FBM Researchers recently examined memory in passengers involved in a potentially life-threatening near plane crash of Air Transit (AT) Flight 236. The plane ran out of fuel over the Atlantic Ocean and thankfully glided safely to an island military base (McKinnon et al., 2015). Although no one was seriously hurt, virtually everyone experienced severe anxiety for the 25 minutes spent preparing to ditch at sea. This near accident occurred in 2001, and the research on their memory of the event was conducted in 2014. Despite the long passage of time, these passengers showed enhanced episodic recall of the event, including details like the oxygen masks coming down, jumping down the slide, and putting on life jackets.

Keep in mind that research shows that our FBMs for specific details, particularly the time and place the emotional event occurred, are fairly accurate (Rimmele et al., 2012). However, these FBMs suffer the same alterations and decay as all other forms of memory. They're NOT perfect recordings of events (Hirst et al., 2015; Lanciano et al., 2010; Schmidt, 2012). For instance, President George W. Bush's memory for how he heard the news of the September 11, 2001 attacks contained several errors (Greenberg, 2004). Similarly, shortly after the death of Michael Jackson, researchers asked participants to report on their FBMs and other reactions to the news of his death. When these same people were interviewed again 18 months later, researchers found that despite several discrepancies in their memories, confidence in their personal accuracy remained high (Day & Ross, 2014).

In sum, FBMs, like other forms of memory, are subject to alterations. What separates them from ordinary, everyday memories is their vividness and our subjective confidence in their accuracy. But confidence is not the same as accuracy—an important point we'll return to in the last part of this chapter. In addition, we all need to remember that our memory processes are sometimes impaired during high emotional arousal (see the **Real World Psychology** feature).

Real World **Psychology**—Understanding the World

How Emotional Arousal May Threaten Our Survival!

Chris Clor/Getty Images

News reports are filled with stories of people becoming dangerously confused during fires or other emergencies because they panic and forget important survival tips, such as the closest exit routes. Can you see why airlines and fire departments routinely provide safety and evacuation drills, or why it's dangerous to drive when we're arguing with a loved one, or to discipline our children when we're very angry? Recognizing that we're sometimes "not in our right minds" during times of high emotional arousal may save our lives—and our relationships!

Where Are Memories Located?

Early memory researchers believed that memory was *localized*, or stored in a particular brain area. Later research suggests that, in fact, memory tends to be localized not in a single area but in many separate areas throughout the brain (**Figure 7.15**).

Today, research techniques are so advanced that we can identify specific brain areas that are activated or changed during memory processes by using functional magnetic resonance imaging (fMRI) brain scans. For example, the brain activity of the previously mentioned passengers of the near crash of Air Transit (AT) Flight 236 was monitored using fMRIs to locate areas of the brain responsible for storing memories of the crash (Palombo et al., 2015). The survivors were shown videos of the AT disaster, the September 11, 2001 attack, and a comparatively nonemotional (neutral) event. The fMRI scans showed that traumatic memory enhancement was associated with activation in the amygdala, medial temporal lobe, anterior and posterior midline, and visual cortex in these passengers. This pattern was not observed in a comparison group of nontraumatized individuals who were also scanned.

The Biology of Memory Loss

So far in this section, we've discussed the neuronal and synaptic changes that occur when we learn and remember, how emotional arousal affects memory, and the major brain areas

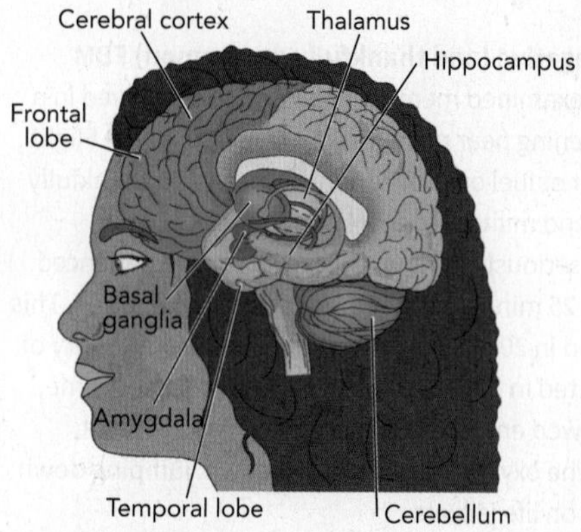

AREA OF THE BRAIN	EFFECTS ON MEMORY
Amygdala	Emotional memories
Basal ganglia and cerebellum	Creation and storage of basic memory and implicit/nondeclarative LTM (such as skills, habits, and simple classically conditioned responses)
Hippocampal formation (hippocampus and surrounding area)	Explicit/declarative and implicit/nondeclarative LTM, as well as sequences of events
Thalamus	Formation of new memories and spatial and working memory; implicit/nondeclarative and explicit/declarative LTM
Cerebral cortex	Encoding, storage, and retrieval of explicit/declarative and implicit/nondeclarative LTM

Source: Baddeley et al., 2015; Emilien & Durlach, 2015; Furuya et al., 2014; Garrett, 2015; Hara et al., 2014; McCormick et al., 2015; Radvansky & Ashcraft, 2016; Yamazaki et al., 2015.

Think Critically

1. What effect might damage to the amygdala have on a person's relationships with others?
2. How might damage to your thalamus affect your day-to-day functioning?

FIGURE 7.15 **The brain and memory** Note the location and names of the major areas of the brain responsible for encoding, storage, and retrieval of memories.

involved in memory activation and storage. Now we will explore how injury and disease affect our memory processes.

Traumatic Brain Injury (TBI) One of the leading causes of neurological disorders—including memory loss—among young U.S. men and women between the ages of 15 and 25 is *traumatic brain injury* (TBI). These injuries most commonly result from car accidents, falls, blows, and gunshot wounds.

TBI happens when the skull suddenly collides with another object. Compression, twisting, and distortion of the brain inside the skull all cause serious and sometimes permanent damage to the brain. The frontal and temporal lobes often take the heaviest hit because they directly collide with the bony ridges inside the skull.

One of the most troubling, and controversial, causes of TBIs is severe or repeated blows to the head during sports participation (CDC, 2016; Pearce et al., 2015; Solomon & Zuckerman, 2015). Both professional and nonprofessional athletes frequently experience *concussions*, a form of TBI, and multiple concussions can lead to *chronic traumatic encephalopathy (CTE)*. Sadly, the frequency of sports-related brain injuries may have been grossly underestimated (Baugh et al., 2015), and a growing body of research connects these multiple brain injuries to diseases and disorders like Alzheimer's, depression, and even suicide (see **Real World Psychology**).

Real World Psychology—Understanding the World

Professional Sports and Brain Damage

Junior Seau (photo on the left) was a famous, 10-time all-pro linebacker in the National Football League (NFL), who died as a result of suicide in 2012—at the age of 43. Experts later concluded that Seau suffered from chronic traumatic encephalopathy (CTE), a serious neurological disease linked to concussions—and to similar deaths of other sports players (CDC, 2016; Park, 2016; Pearce et al., 2015). Due to his personal concerns over concussions, San Francisco 49ers (NFL) linebacker Chris Borland, one of the league's top rookies (photo on the right), quit playing in 2015—despite being in the prime of his athletic career.

Al Bello/Getty Images

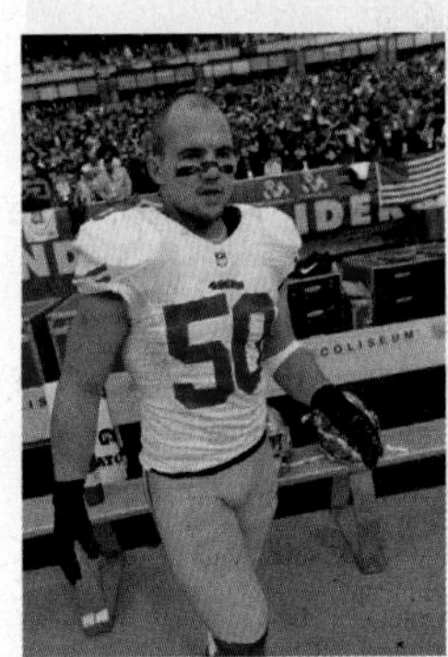

Michael Zagaris/San Francisco 49ers/Getty Images, Inc.

Amnesia Now that we know a little more about brain injuries and how they cause memory loss (or amnesia), let's examine the general topic of *amnesia.* It's important to note that being completely amnesic about your past and not knowing who you are is a common plot in movies and television. However, real-life amnesia generally doesn't cause a specific loss of self-identity. Instead, the individual typically has trouble retrieving more widespread and general old memories or forming new ones. These two forms of amnesia are called *retrograde* and *anterograde* (**Figure 7.16**).

FIGURE 7.16 Two types of amnesia

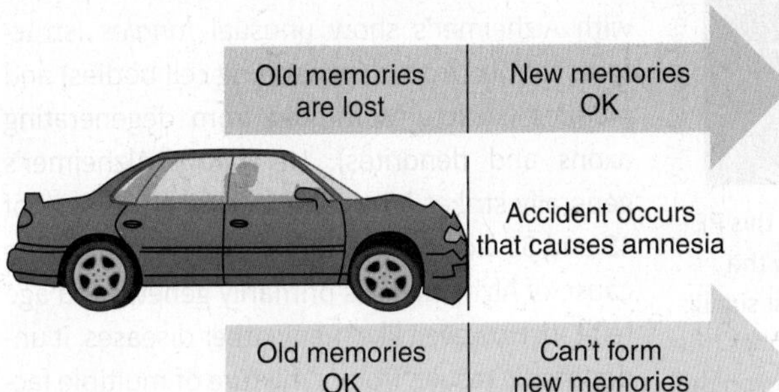

A Retrograde amnesia
After an accident or other brain injury, individuals with *retrograde amnesia* have no trouble forming new memories, but they do experience *amnesia* (loss of memories) for segments of the past–old, "retro" memories are lost.

B Anterograde amnesia
In contrast, people with *anterograde amnesia* have no trouble recovering old memories, but they do experience *amnesia* (cannot form new memories) after an accident or other brain injury.

Retrograde amnesia The inability to retrieve information from the past; backward-acting amnesia.

Consolidation The process by which LTM memories become stable in the brain; neural changes that take place when a memory is formed.

Anterograde amnesia The inability to form new memories; forward-acting amnesia.

© Duncan Williams/Icon SMI/Corbis

Pat Summit, coach of the Tennessee Lady Vols basketball team from 1974 until 2012 and the winningest college basketball coach of all time, announced in 2011 that she had early-stage Alzheimer's disease (AD). She later died from complications of the disease in 2016.

In **retrograde amnesia** (acting backward in time), the person has no memory (is amnesic) for events that occurred *before* the brain injury because those memories were never stored in LTM. However, the same person has no trouble remembering things that happened after the injury. As the name implies, only the old, "retro," memories are lost.

What causes retrograde amnesia? In cases where the individual is only amnesic for the events right before the brain injury, the cause may be a failure of consolidation. We learned earlier that during long-term potentiation (LTP), our neurons change to accommodate new learning. In addition, we know that it takes a certain amount of time for these neural changes to become fixed and stable in long-term memory, a process known as **consolidation**. Like heavy rain on wet cement, the brain injury "wipes away" unstable memories because the cement has not had time to harden (*retrograde amnesia*).

In contrast to retrograde amnesia, in which people lose memories for events *before* a brain injury, some people lose memory for events that occur *after* a brain injury, which is called **anterograde amnesia** (acting forward in time). This type of amnesia generally results from a surgical injury or from diseases, such as chronic alcoholism or senile dementia—a form of severe mental deterioration in old age. Continuing our analogy with cement, anterograde amnesia would be like having permanently hardened cement, which prevents the laying down of new memories.

Keep in mind that retrograde amnesia is normally temporary and somewhat common, such as what happens to football players after a head injury. In contrast, anterograde amnesia is relatively rare and most often permanent. However, patients often show surprising abilities to learn and remember procedural motor skills, such as mowing a lawn. Also note that some individuals have both forms of amnesia. For example, H.M. (the man introduced in the chapter opener) had anterograde amnesia, as well as mild memory loss for events in his life that happened the year or two before the operation (retrograde amnesia) (Annese et al., 2014; Corkin, 2013; Mauguière & Corkin, 2015).

Alzheimer's Disease (AD)

Like TBIs that can cause amnesia, various diseases can alter the physiology of the brain and nervous system, and thereby disrupt memory processes. For example, *Alzheimer's disease* (*AD*) is a progressive mental deterioration that occurs most commonly in old age (**Figure 7.17**). The most noticeable early symptoms are disturbances in memory, which become progressively worse until, in the final stages, the person fails to recognize loved ones, needs total nursing care, and ultimately dies (see photo of Pat Summit).

FIGURE 7.17 The effect of Alzheimer's disease (AD) on the brain

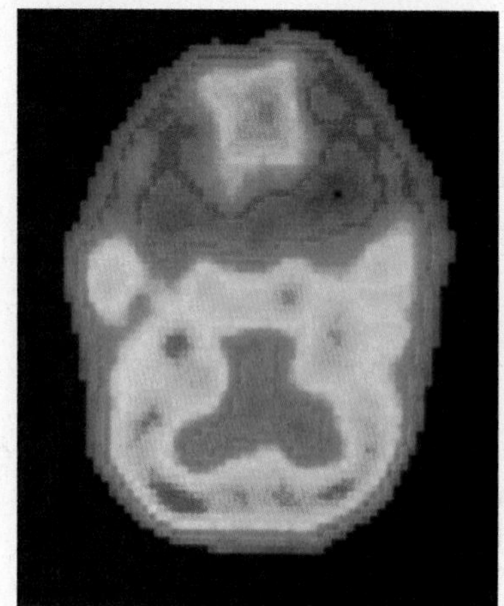

Science Source/Photo Researchers

a. Normal brain

In this PET scan of a normal brain, note the high amount of the red and yellow color (signs of brain activity).

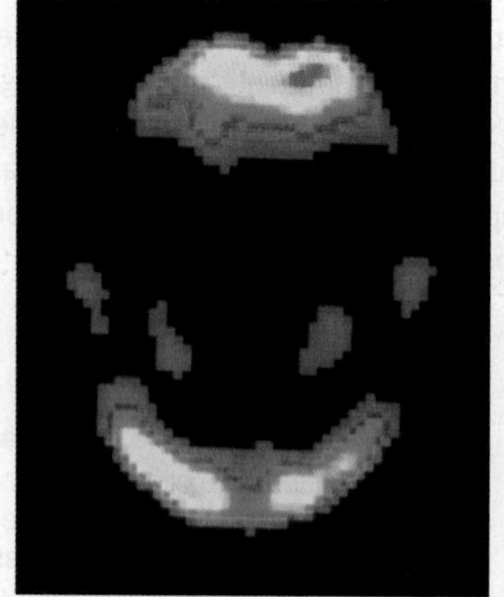

Science Source/Photo Researchers

b. Brain of a person with AD In this PET scan of a person with AD, note how the reduced activity in the brain is most significant in the temporal and parietal lobes (the mostly black areas in the center and on the sides of this AD patient's brain). These are the key areas for storing memories.

Alzheimer's does not attack all types of memory equally. A hallmark of the disease is an extreme decrease in *explicit/declarative memory*—failing to recall facts, information, and personal life experiences (Howes & O'Shea, 2014; Müller et al., 2014; Redondo et al., 2015). However, those who suffer from AD still retain some *implicit/nondeclarative* memories, such as simple classically conditioned responses and procedural tasks like brushing their teeth.

What causes AD? Brain autopsies of people with Alzheimer's show unusual *tangles* (structures formed from degenerating cell bodies) and *plaques* (structures formed from degenerating axons and dendrites). Hereditary Alzheimer's generally strikes its victims between the ages of 45 and 55 (see photo). Some experts believe the cause of Alzheimer's is primarily genetic and age related. However, like many other diseases, it undoubtedly results from a mixture of multiple factors (Guekht, 2016; Kumar et al., 2016; Tousseyn et al., 2015).

Understanding Repressed Memories Creating false memories may be somewhat common, but can we recover true memories that are buried in childhood? There is a great deal of debate regarding this question (Boag, 2012; Brodsky & Gutheil, 2016; Kaplan et al., 2016). *Repression* is the supposed unconscious coping mechanism by which we prevent anxiety-provoking thoughts from reaching consciousness. According to some research, repressed memories are *actively* and *consciously* "forgotten" in an effort to avoid the pain of their retrieval (Anderson et al., 2004; Boag, 2012). Can you see how in this case repression might be a form of motivated forgetting, which we discussed earlier? Others suggest that some memories are so painful that they exist only in an *unconscious* corner of the mind, making them inaccessible to the individual (Haaken, 2010; Mancia & Baggott, 2008). In these cases, therapy supposedly would be necessary to unlock the hidden memories.

Repression is a complex and controversial topic in psychology. No one doubts that some memories are forgotten and later recovered. What some question is the idea that *repressed memories* of painful experiences (especially childhood sexual abuse) are stored in the unconscious mind, especially since these memories may play a role in important judicial processes (Howe & Knott, 2015; Lampinen & Beike, 2015; Loftus & Cahill, 2007).

Critics suggest that most people who have witnessed or experienced a violent crime or have survived childhood sexual abuse have intense, persistent memories. They have trouble *forgetting*, not remembering. Other critics wonder whether therapists sometimes inadvertently create false memories in their clients during therapy. In this case, if a clinician even suggests the possibility of abuse, the client's own *constructive processes* may lead him or her to create a false memory. The client also might start to incorporate portrayals of abuse from movies and books into his or her own memory, forgetting their original sources (a form of *source amnesia*), and eventually coming to see them as reliable.

This is not to say that all psychotherapy clients who recover memories of sexual abuse (or other painful incidents) have invented those memories. For example, some research suggests that children may remember experiencing sexual abuse but not understand or recognize those behaviors as abuse until adulthood (McNally, 2012).

Unfortunately, the repressed memory debate is hotly contested. The stakes are high because lawsuits and criminal prosecutions of sexual abuse are sometimes based on recovered memories of childhood sexual abuse. However, the so-called, "memory wars" may be getting less heated. Comparing attitudes in the 1990s to today, researchers found less belief in repressed memories among mainstream psychologists, as well as among undergraduates with greater critical-thinking abilities (Patihis et al., 2014).

In short, while the debate over repressed memories continues, we must be careful not to ridicule or condemn people who recover true memories of abuse. In the same spirit, we must protect innocent people from wrongful accusations that come from false memories. Hopefully, with continued research (and perhaps new technology) we may someday better protect the interests of both the victim and the accused.

To close on another encouraging note, we're providing a final, brief section that summarizes the key tips for memory improvement. One of the many beauties of our human brain is that we can recognize the limits and problems of memory, and then develop appropriate coping mechanisms. Just as our ancestors domesticated wild horses and cattle to overcome the physical limits of the human body, we can develop similar approaches to improve our mental limits—especially those responsible for fine detail.

Memory Improvement—Strategies for Student Success

The following TEN TIPS for memory improvement were discussed earlier in this chapter, and in the *Strategies for Student Success* at the end of Chapter 1. They're all research based and particularly helpful for increasing college success and reducing wasted time. Given that the three key steps in memory are *encoding, storage,* and *retrieval* (the ESR model), we've arranged these tips accordingly. To get the maximum benefits, first read through the list placing a check mark ✓ in the blank space next to items you're currently using, a + mark by the tips you want to add, and a − mark by those strategies you don't plan to try. After adding the new skills to your daily study habits, look back and reconsider those items with a – mark. We'd like to hear how these strategies work out for you (casanderson@amherst.edu, khuffman@palomar.edu.).

ENCODING As discussed earlier, the first step in memory is successful *encoding*. To improve your study skills and exam performance, try these encoding tips:

- ______ *Pay attention and reduce interference.* When you really want to remember something, you must *selectively attend* to the information you want to successfully encode, and ignore distractions. During class, focus on the instructor, and sit away from distracting people or views outside. When studying, choose a place with minimal interferences. Also, recall from earlier chapters that *multitasking,* while studying or listening to lectures, greatly increases interference, and reduces your ability to pay attention.
- ______ *Strive for a deeper level of processing.* Some students try to study important terms or concepts by highlighting, rereading, or simply repeating the information over and over to themselves. As you recall from Chapter 1, highlighting and rereading are the LEAST effective study techniques. While repeating information (maintenance rehearsal) does extend the duration of STM beyond the normal limits of about 30 seconds, this type of rehearsal, highlighting, and rereading are all forms of *shallow processing*. They're not efficient for LTM or for preparing for exams. If you want to effectively encode (and later successfully retrieve) information, you need a deeper level of processing, which involves active reading and taking notes. Another way to deeply process is *elaborative* rehearsal, which involves thinking about the material, and relating it to other previously stored information. Hopefully, you've noticed that we formally define each key term immediately in the text, and generally give a brief explanation with one or two examples for each term. While studying this text, use these tools to help your elaborative rehearsal—and insure a deeper level of processing. In addition, try making up your own examples. The more elaborate the encoding of information, the more memorable it will become.
- ______ *Counteract the serial-position effect.* Because we tend to remember information that occurs at the beginning or end of a sequence, spend extra time with information in the middle. When reading or reviewing the text, start at different places—sometimes at the second section, sometimes at the fourth.

STORAGE The second step in successful memory is *storage*. The best way to create an effective storage system, in either your brain or your computer, is through logical filing and good organization. Try these two helpful tips:

- ______ *Use chunking.* Although the storage capacity of STM is only around five to nine items, you can expand it by chunking information into groups. For example, if you need to remember a 12 digit number, try grouping it into four groups of three numbers.
- ______ *Create hierarchies.* An efficient way to organize and store a large body of information is to create hierarchies, which involves grouping concepts from most general to most specific. Chapter outlines, and the tables and figures in this text, are examples of hierarchies. Be sure to study them carefully—and make up your own versions whenever possible.

RETRIEVAL The third and final stage of successful memory is *retrieval*. As you know, your grades in most courses are primarily determined by some form of quizzing or exams, both of which rely exclusively on retrieval. Here are five tips for improving retrieval:

- ______ *Practice testing.* Recall from Chapter 1 that research clearly shows that practice testing is one of the very best ways to improve your retrieval—and course grades (Aziz et al., 2014; Bourne & Healy, 2014; Dunlosky et al., 2013). Taking tests is not a favorite pastime for most people. However, if you think of it as "practice," then it becomes more attractive and logical. Just as we all need to practice our skateboarding tricks, golf swing, or dance routine, we need to practice testing ourselves—BEFORE any exam. This is why we provide so many self-testing options within this text (e.g., the learning objectives questions that start each section, the self-tests at the end of each major heading, and the key term review at the end of each chapter). We also offer numerous additional free tests on our website. Be sure to take advantage of these options.

- _____ *Distribute your practice.* In addition to practice testing, the next best way to improve your memory is through distributed practice. Researchers have found that we encode, store, and retrieve information better when our study sessions are distributed (or spaced out) over time (Dunlosky et al., 2013; Kang et al., 2014; Kornmeier et al., 2014). Although *massed practice* (cramming) can produce speedy, short-term learning, it's far less effective than distributed practice. There are at least two other major problems with staying up late or "pulling an all-nighter" to cram for exams: (1) Being drowsy while studying or taking an exam negatively affects overall performance, and (2) during sleep we process and store most of the new information we acquired when awake (Chapter 5).
- _____ *Remember the encoding specificity principle.* When we form memories, we store them with links to the way we thought about them at the time. Therefore, the closer the retrieval cues are to the original encoding situation, the better the retrieval. Because you encode a lot of material during class time, avoid "early takes" or makeup exams, which are generally scheduled in other classrooms. The *context* will be different, and your retrieval may suffer. Similarly, when you take a test, try to reinstate the same psychological and physiological state that you were in when you originally learned the material. According to the *mood congruence* effect, you will recall more if the mood of your test taking matches the mood of the original learning. Similarly, in line with the *state-dependent memory* research, if you normally drink coffee while studying, you might want to drink it again right before your exam.
- _____ *Employ self-monitoring.* When studying a text, you should periodically stop and test your understanding of the material using the built-in self-testing throughout each chapter. This type of self-monitoring is a common strategy of successful students. Even when you are studying a single sentence, you need to monitor your understanding. Furthermore, poor readers tend to read at the same speed for both easy and difficult material. Good readers (and more successful students) tend to monitor themselves and they slow down or repeat difficult material. Keep in mind that if you evaluate your learning only while you're reading the material, you may overestimate your understanding (because the information is still in STM). However, if you delay for at least a few minutes, and then test your understanding, your evaluation will be more accurate.
- _____ *Overlearn.* Successful students know that the best way to ensure their full understanding of material (and success on an exam) is through *overlearning*—studying information even after you think you already know it. Don't just study until you *think* you know it. Work hard until you *know* you know it!

A Final Word As we've seen throughout this chapter, our memories are remarkable—yet highly fickle. Recognizing our commonly shared frailties of memory will make us better jurors in the courtroom, more informed consumers, and more thoughtful, open-minded parents, teachers, students, and friends. Unfortunately, sometimes our memories are better than we would like. Traumatic, and extremely emotional, memories can persist even when we would very much like to forget. Though painful, these memories can sometimes provide important insights. As Elizabeth Loftus suggests in a letter to her deceased mother:

> *I thought then [as a 14-year-old] that eventually I would get over your death. I know today that I won't. But I've decided to accept that truth. What does it matter if I don't get over you? Who says I have to? David and Robert still tease me: "Don't say the M word or Beth will cry." So what if the word mother affects me this way? Who says I have to fix this? Besides, I'm too busy (Loftus, 2002, p. 70).*

Retrieval Practice 7.4 | Memory Distortions and Improvement

SELF-TEST Completing this self-test, and then checking your answers by clicking on the answer button or by looking in Appendix B, will provide immediate feedback and helpful practice for exams.

1. Problems with eyewitness recollections are so well established and important that judges now _____.
   - **a.** allow expert testimony on the unreliability of eyewitness testimony
   - **b.** routinely instruct jurors on the limits and unreliability of eyewitness recollections
   - **c.** both the above
   - **d.** none of the above
2. Researchers have demonstrated that it is _____ to create false memories.
   - **a.** relatively easy **b.** rarely possible
   - **c.** moderately difficult **d.** never possible
3. Dave was told the same childhood story of his father saving his neighbor from a fire so many times that he is now sure it is true, but all the evidence proves it never happened. This is an example of _____.
   - **a.** a repressed memory **b.** deluded childhood fantasies
   - **c.** a false memory **d.** early-onset juvenile dementia
4. _____ memories are related to anxiety-provoking thoughts or events that are supposedly prevented from reaching consciousness.
   - **a.** Suppressed **b.** Flashbulb
   - **c.** Flashback **d.** Repressed
5. To improve your encoding, you should _____.
   - **a.** pay attention and reduce interference
   - **b.** strive for a deeper level of processing
   - **c.** counteract the serial-position effect
   - **d.** all of these options

Think Critically

1. As an eyewitness to a crime, how could you use information in this chapter to improve your memory for specific details?
2. If you were a juror, what would you say to the other jurors about the reliability of eyewitness testimony?

Real World Psychology

Could someone falsely convince you as an adult that you committed a serious crime as a teenager?

Diverse Images/ Getty Images

HINT: LOOK IN THE MARGIN FOR **[Q5]**

Summary

7.1 The Nature of Memory 175

- **Memory** is an internal representation of some prior event or experience. It's also a **constructive process** that organizes and shapes information as it's being processed, stored, and retrieved.
- Major perspectives on memory include the **encoding, storage**, and **retrieval (ESR) model**, and the **three-stage memory model**, which proposes that information is stored and processed in **sensory memory**, **short-term memory (STM)**, and **long-term memory (LTM)**. Each stage differs in its purpose, duration, and capacity.
- Sensory memory has a relatively large capacity, but the duration is only for a few seconds. Visual sensory memory (**iconic memory**) only holds for about one-half of a second, whereas auditory sensory memory (**echoic memory**) lasts for up to 4 seconds.
- Short-term memory (STM) has a limited capacity and duration. Material is retained for as long as 30 seconds, but it's limited to 5 to 9 bits of information.
- **Chunking** and **maintenance rehearsal** improve STM's duration and capacity. Researchers now call the active processing of STM **working memory**.
- **LTM** is an almost unlimited storehouse for information that must be kept for long periods. The two major types of LTM are **explicit/declarative memory** and **implicit/nondeclarative memory**. Organization and **elaborative rehearsal** improve encoding. **Retrieval cues** help stimulate retrieval of information from LTM. According to the **encoding-specificity principle**, retrieval is improved when conditions of recovery are similar to encoding conditions.

7.2 Forgetting 185

- Early research by Ebbinghaus showed that we tend to forget newly learned information quickly, but we relearn the information more readily the second time.
- Researchers have proposed five major theories to explain forgetting—decay. **retroactive** and **proactive interference**, motivated forgetting, encoding failure, and retrieval failure. The **tip-of-the-tongue phenomenon** is an example of the retrieval failure theory.
- There are several major factors that help explain why we forget: the **misinformation effect**, the **serial-position effect**, **source amnesia**, spacing of practice, and culture.

7.3 Biological Bases of Memory 190

- Learning modifies the brain's neural networks through **long-term potentiation (LTP)**, strengthening particular synapses and affecting the ability of neurons to release their neurotransmitters.
- Emotional arousal increases neurotransmitters and hormones that affect several parts of the brain. Heightened arousal also can increase the encoding and storage of new information and the formation of **flashbulb memories (FBMs)**.

• Research using advanced techniques, such as the fMRI, has indicated that several brain regions are involved in encoding, storing, and retrieving memories.

• Traumatic brain injuries and disease, such as Alzheimer's disease (AD), can cause memory loss. Two major types of amnesia are **retrograde** and **anterograde amnesia**. The lack of **consolidation** may help explain retrograde amnesia.

7.4 Memory Distortions and Improvement 195

• People shape, rearrange, and distort their memories in order to create logic, consistency, and efficiency. Despite all their problems and biases, our memories are normally fairly accurate and usually serve us well.

• When memory errors occur in the context of the criminal justice system, they can have serious legal and social consequences. Problems with eyewitness testimony are so well established that judges often allow expert testimony on the unreliability of eyewitnesses.

• False memories are well-established phenomenon, which are relatively common and easy to create. However, memory repression (especially of childhood sexual abuse) is a complex and controversial topic.

• How can we improve our memory? Under *encoding*, pay attention and reduce interference, strive for a deeper level of processing, and counteract the serial-position effect. During *storage*, use chunking and hierarchies. During *retrieval*, practice test taking (in-text quizzes, web site quizzes, etc.), distribute vs. massed practice, remember the encoding specificity principle, and, finally, employ self-monitoring and overlearning.

Applying **Real** World **Psychology**

We began this chapter with five intriguing Real World Psychology questions, and you were asked to revisit these questions at the end of each section. Questions like these have an important and lasting impact on all of our lives. See if you can answer these additional critical thinking questions related to real world examples.

1. Many people think they can perfectly recall elaborate memories about how they felt or what they said when they first learned about devastating events, like the Boston Marathon bombings. What do you recall about this particular event? Do your memories fit with what flashbulb memory (FBM) research suggests?
2. Despite documented errors with FBMs, most people are very confident in their personal accuracy. What problems might result from this overconfidence?
3. Human memory is often compared to the workings of a computer. Based on your own experience, what are the advantages and limits of this comparison?
4. Amnesia is a common theme for Hollywood movies and television. How might these portrayals, which are often inaccurate, negatively influence the public's perception?

Boston Globe/Getty Images

5. What memory improvement techniques described in this chapter have you found to be helpful in your everyday life? What new strategies do you plan to try?

Key Terms

Retrieval Practice Write a definition for each term before turning back to the referenced page to check your answer.

- age-related positivity effect 181
- anterograde amnesia 194
- chunking 179
- consolidation 194
- constructive process 175
- distributed practice 189
- elaborative rehearsal 182
- encoding 176
- encoding-specificity principle 183
- encoding, storage, and retrieval (ESR) model 176
- episodic memory 180
- explicit/declarative memory 180
- flashbulb memory (FBM) 191
- implicit/nondeclarative memory 182
- levels of processing 176
- long-term memory (LTM) 180
- long-term potentiation (LTP) 190
- maintenance rehearsal 179
- massed practice 189
- memory 175
- misinformation effect 188
- mnemonic 184
- priming 182
- proactive interference 186
- retrieval 177
- retrieval cue 183
- retroactive interference 186
- retrograde amnesia 194
- semantic memory 180
- sensory memory 178
- serial-position effect 188
- short-term memory (STM) 179
- source amnesia 189
- storage 177
- three-stage memory model 177
- tip-of-the-tongue (TOT) phenomenon 188
- working memory 180

© ericsphotography/iStockphoto

Thinking, Language, and Intelligence

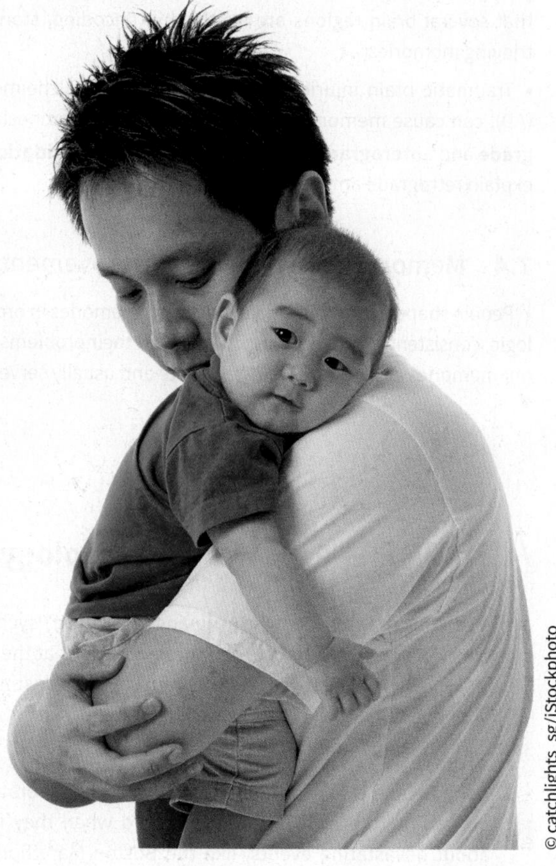
© catchlights_sg/iStockphoto

Real World Psychology

Things you'll learn in Chapter 8

[Q1] Why might some medical treatments be judged as more effective than they really are?

[Q2] Can outdoor activities or simply taking a walk improve your creativity?

[Q3] Does speaking multiple languages make you smarter?

[Q4] Do babies begin to learn language even before they are born?

[Q5] Can personal traits and character strengths be better predictors of achievement than IQ?

[Q6] Will watching TV dramas increase your emotional intelligence?

Throughout the chapter, margin icons for Q1–Q6 indicate where the text addresses these questions.

CHAPTER OUTLINE

Chapter Overview

Intellectual growth should commence at birth and cease only at death.

—Albert Einstein

You've undoubtedly heard of Albert Einstein, the German-born physicist who developed the theory of relativity and the well-known equation $E = mc^2$, which foreshadowed the development of nuclear power. But did you know that, as a young child Einstein, spoke so rarely and slowly that his parents feared that something was seriously wrong with him? Their concerns were obviously unfounded. Einstein is considered to be a true genius—one of the smartest people of all time—and we now know that many brilliant people were "late talkers" in childhood.

In this chapter, we focus on thinking, language, and intelligence—each of which was central to Einstein's achievements. These topics are also key to understanding how we think about, describe, and successfully navigate the world around us. As you can see, these three abilities are closely related, which explains why they're traditionally combined into one chapter—thinking, language, and intelligence. We begin with an exploration of the mental processes involved in thinking, problem solving, and creativity. Then we look at the world of language—its components, interrelationship with thinking, how it develops, and whether or not non-human animals use true language. We close with the definition and measurement of intelligence, and the controversies that surround it.

8.1 Thinking

LEARNING OBJECTIVES

Retrieval Practice While reading the upcoming sections, respond to each Learning Objective in your own words.

Summarize thinking, cognition, problem solving, and creativity.

- **Explain** cognitive building blocks and how they affect thinking.
- **Describe** the three stages of problem solving, including algorithms and heuristics.
- **Review** the five potential barriers to problem solving.
- **Identify** creativity and its major characteristics.

If you go on to major in psychology, you'll discover that researchers often group thinking, language, and intelligence under the larger umbrella of **cognition**, the mental activities of acquiring, storing, retrieving, and using knowledge (Groome et al., 2014; Matlin, 2016). We also technically, we discuss cognition throughout this text (for example, in chapters on sensation and perception, consciousness, learning, and memory). However, in this section we limit our discussion to *thinking*—what it is and where it's located.

Cognition The mental activities involved in acquiring, storing, retrieving, and using knowledge.

Every time we take in information and mentally act on it, we're thinking. These thought processes are both localized and distributed throughout our brains in networks of neurons. For example, during decision making, our brains are most active in the *prefrontal cortex*. This region associates complex ideas; makes plans; forms, initiates, and allocates attention; and supports multitasking. In addition to the localization of thinking processes, the prefrontal cortex links to other areas of the brain, such as the limbic system (Chapter 2), to synthesize information from several senses (Haas et al., 2015; Schmitgen et al., 2016; Viviani et al., 2015). Now that we know where thinking occurs, we need to discuss its basic components.

Cognitive Building Blocks

Imagine yourself lying, relaxed, in the warm, gritty sand on an ocean beach. Do you see palms swaying in the wind? Can you smell the salty sea and taste the dried salt on your lips? Can you hear children playing in the surf? What you've just created is a *mental image*, a mental representation of a previously stored sensory experience, which includes visual, auditory, olfactory, tactile, motor, and gustatory imagery (McKellar, 1972). We all have a mental space where we visualize and manipulate our sensory images (Laeng et al., 2014; Naselaris et al., 2015). Interestingly, research shows that when we create mental images and thoughts about "healthy foods," we tend to consider them less filling and actually order larger portions and eat more (Suher et al., 2016)!

In addition to mental images, our thinking includes forming *concepts*, or mental representations of a group or category (Burdett & Barrett, 2016; Lagarde et al., 2015; Pape et al., 2015). Concepts can be concrete (like car and concert) or abstract (like intelligence and beauty). They are essential to thinking and communication because they simplify and organize information. Normally, when you see a new object or encounter a new situation, you relate it to your existing conceptual structure and categorize it according to where it fits. For example, if you see a metal box with four wheels driving on the highway, you know it is a car, even if you've never seen that particular model before. How do we learn concepts? They

a. Prototypes

Stephen St. John/NG Image Collection

b. Artificial concepts

Gordon Wiltsie/NG Image Collection

c. Hierarchies

Higher-order concept	Animal			
Basic-level concept	Bird		Dog	
Lower-order concept	Robin	Penguin	Boxer	Poodle

FIGURE 8.1 Concepts When learning concepts, we most often use prototypes, artificial concepts, and hierarchies to simplify and categorize information. For example, when we encounter a bird, we fit it into our existing concept of a bird.

develop through the environmental interactions of three major building blocks—prototypes, artificial concepts, and hierarchies (Ferguson & Casasola, 2015; McDaniel et al., 2014).

- **Prototypes** When initially learning about the world, a young child develops a general, natural concept based on a typical representative, or **prototype** (**Figure 8.1a**), of *bird* after a parent points out a number of examples. Once the child develops the prototype of a *bird*, he or she then is able to quickly classify all flying animals, such as this robin, correctly.
- **Artificial concepts** We create *artificial* (or formal) *concepts* (**Figure 8.1b**) from logical rules or definitions. When an example doesn't quite fit the prototype, like a penguin, we must review our artificial concept of a bird: warm-blooded animals that fly, have wings and beaks, and lay eggs. Although this penguin doesn't fly, it has wings, a beak, and lays eggs. So it must be a bird.
- **Hierarchies** Creating *hierarchies*, or subcategories within broader concepts, helps us master new material more quickly and easily (**Figure 8.1c**). Note, however, that we tend to begin with basic-level concepts (the middle row on the diagram) when we first learn something (Rosch, 1978). For example, a child develops the basic-level concept for *bird* before learning the higher-order concept *animal* or the lower-order concept *robin*.

Problem Solving

Many years ago in Los Angeles, a 12-foot-high tractor-trailer reportedly got stuck under a bridge that was 6 inches too low. After hours of towing, tugging, and pushing, the police and transportation workers were stumped. Then a young boy happened by and asked, "Why don't you let some air out of the tires?" It was a simple, creative suggestion—and it worked.

Our lives are filled with problems—some simple, some difficult. In all cases, problem solving requires moving from a given state (the problem) to a goal state (the solution), a process that usually has three steps: *preparation*, *production*, and *evaluation* (Bourne et al., 1979).

Note in **Process Diagram 8.1** that during the preparation stage, we identify and separate relevant from irrelevant facts, and define the ultimate goal. Then, during the production stage, we generate possible solutions, called hypotheses, by using *algorithms* and *heuristics*. **Algorithms** are logical, step-by-step procedures that if followed correctly will always lead to an eventual solution. But they are not practical in many situations. **Heuristics**, or simplified rules based on experience, are much faster but do not guarantee a solution. Finally, during the evaluation stage we judge the hypotheses generated during the production stage against the criteria established in the preparation stage. See the following **Psychology and You** for sample problem-solving heuristics, and how they might apply to your current or future career.

Prototype A mental image or best example that embodies the most typical features of a concept or category.

Algorithm A logical, step-by-step procedure that, if followed correctly, will always eventually solve the problem.

Heuristic An educated guess, or "rule of thumb," often used as a shortcut for problem solving; does not guarantee a solution to a problem but does narrow the alternatives.

Psychology and You—Understanding Yourself

Problem Solving and Your Career

Considering your immediate goal to graduate from college, and your long-term career plans, you obviously can't try all possible options using *algorithms* to solve these problems. Instead, the three heuristics presented in **Table 8.1** may help focus your search and desired outcomes.

STOP! This Process Diagram contains essential information NOT found elsewhere in the text, which is likely to appear on quizzes and exams. Be sure to study it CAREFULLY!

PROCESS DIAGRAM 8.1 **Three Steps to the Goal** There are three stages of problem solving that help you attain a goal, such as moving to a new home.

1 Preparation
Begin by clarifying the problem using these three steps in preparation.

- Define the ultimate goal.

Move to a new home close to work.

- Outline your limits and/or desires.

✓ Must allow pets.
✓ Must be close enough to walk.
✓ I prefer a house to an apartment building.
✓ Fireplaces are nice.

- Separate the negotiable from the nonnegotiable.

✓ Must allow pets.
✓ Must be close enough to walk.
* I prefer a house to an apartment building.
* Fireplaces are nice.

2 Production
Next, test your possible paths and solutions with one or both of these methods.

- Use an **algorithm**, a logical step-by-step procedure that, if followed correctly, will eventually solve the problem. But algorithms may take a long time—especially for complex problems.

Look at every ad in the paper and call all of those that allow pets.

- Use a **heuristic**, a simple rule for problem solving that does not guarantee a solution, but offers a likely shortcut to it.

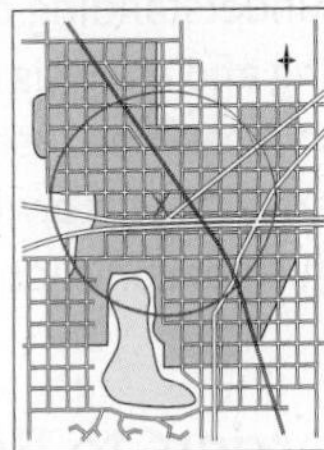

Work backwards from the solution—start by drawing a 1-mile radius around work to narrow the search.

3 Evaluation
Did your possible solutions solve the problem?

- If no, then you must return to the production and/or preparation stages.
- If yes, then take action to achieve your goal.

TABLE 8.1 Three Problem-Solving Heuristics and Your Career

PROBLEM-SOLVING HEURISTICS	DESCRIPTION	EXAMPLE
Working backward	Starts with the solution, a known condition, and works backward through the problem. Once the search has revealed the steps to be taken, the problem is solved.	Deciding you want to be an experimental psychologist, you ask your psychology professor to recommend graduate programs at various colleges and universities. Then you contact these institutions for information on their academic requirements and admission policies. Next, you adapt your current college courses to fit those institutional requirements and policies.
Means-end analysis	Problem solver determines what measures would reduce the difference between the existing, given state and the end goal. Once the means to reach the goal are determined, the problem is solved.	You know you need a high GPA to get into a good graduate school for experimental psychology. Therefore, you ask your professors for study suggestions, and interview several "A" students to compare their study habits to your own. You then determine the specific means (the number of hours and study techniques) required to meet your end goal of a high GPA.
Creating subgoals	Large, complex problems are broken down into a series of small subgoals. These subgoals then serve as a series of stepping stones, which can be taken one at a time to reach the end goal.	Getting a good grade in many college courses requires subgoals, like writing a successful term paper. To do this, you first choose a topic, and then go to the library and Internet to locate information related to that topic. Once you have the information, you organize it, create an outline, write the paper, review the paper, rewrite, rewrite again, and then submit the final paper, on or before the due date.

Mental set A fixed-thinking approach to problem solving that only sees solutions that have worked in the past.

Functional fixedness A barrier to problem solving that comes from thinking about objects as functioning only in their usual or customary way.

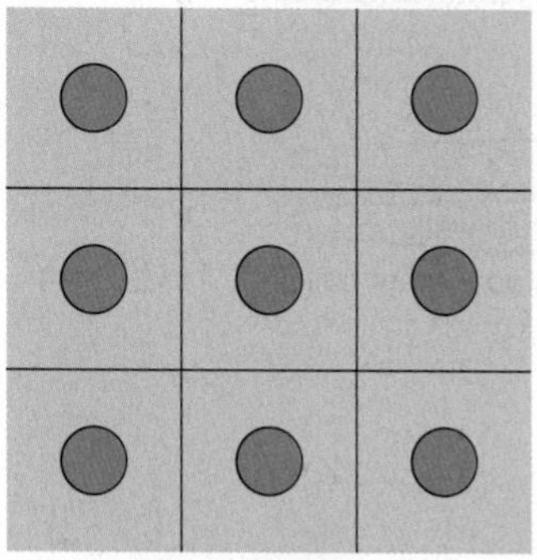

FIGURE 8.2 The nine-dot problem Can you connect all nine dots without lifting your pencil or using more than four lines? If not, the reason may be that you're trying to use *mental sets*—problem-solving strategies that have worked well for you in the past. Try "thinking outside the box" and then compare your answer to the solution presented at the end of the chapter.

In addition, we sometimes solve problems with a sudden flash of *insight*, like Köhler's chimps that stacked boxes to reach the bananas (Chapter 6). Keep in mind that these "aha" moments and sudden understanding often lead to more accurate solutions than those found through logical reasoning and analysis (Salvi et al., 2016). However, insight is somewhat unconscious and automatic so it can't be rushed. When stumped on a problem it sometimes helps to mentally set our problem aside for a while, in an *incubation period*, and the solution may then come to mind without further conscious thought.

Five Potential Barriers to Problem Solving

As we've just seen, algorithms, heuristics, and insight all help us solve problems in our daily life. In this section, we'll discuss five potential barriers to effective problem solving. Why do we say "potential"? It's because most of these factors have both positive and negative influences.

1. ***Mental sets*** Why are some problems so difficult to solve? The reason may be that we often stick to problem-solving strategies that have worked in the past, called **mental sets**, rather than trying new, possibly more effective ones (**Figure 8.2**).
2. ***Functional fixedness*** We also sometimes fail to see solutions to our problems because we tend to view objects as functioning only in the usual or customary way—a phenomenon known as **functional fixedness** (Chrysikou et al., 2016; Ness, 2015; Wright et al., 2015). When a child uses sofa cushions to build a fort, or you use a table knife instead of a screwdriver to tighten a screw, you both have successfully avoided functional fixedness. Similarly, the individual who discovered a way to retrofit diesel engines to allow them to use discarded restaurant oil as fuel also overcame functional fixedness—and may become very wealthy! For practice with functional fixedness, see **Figure 8.3**.

FIGURE 8.3 Overcoming functional fixedness Using only these supplies, can you mount the candle on a wall so that it can be lit in the normal way and without toppling over? The solution is at the end of the chapter.

3. ***Availability heuristic*** During every summer, we see repeated programs and "BREAKING NEWS" reports about shark attacks on unsuspecting swimmers, which lead viewers to a mistaken perception that such attacks are highly likely. In reality, ocean-goers are 1,817 times more likely to drown than to die from a shark attack! How might this type of media coverage also increase prejudice against certain groups, such as viewing all Muslims as terrorists, or create unrealistic fears from recent Zika or Ebola virus outbreaks (see **Figure 8.4**)? These are just some of the many examples of the **availability heuristic**, in which we take a mental shortcut, and make estimates of the frequency or likelihood of an event based on information that is most readily *available* in our memories. In other words, we give greater credence to information and examples that readily spring to mind (Mase et al., 2015; Tversky & Kahneman, 1974, 1993).

Mike Marsland/Getty Images

FIGURE 8.4 The availability heuristic in action Do you remember the intense fears of the Ebola virus in 2014? We all might have been less fearful if we'd known that fewer people in the United States have died from Ebola than have been married to Kim Kardashian!

Availability heuristic A cognitive strategy (or shortcut) that estimates the frequency or likelihood of an event based on information that is readily available in our memory.

Representativeness heuristic A cognitive strategy (or shortcut) that involves making judgments based on how well something matches (represents) an existing prototype or stereotype.

Confirmation bias The tendency to prefer information that confirms our preexisting positions or beliefs and to ignore or discount contradictory evidence; also known as remembering the 'hits' and ignoring the 'misses.'

4. ***Representativeness heuristic*** Have you ever been walking in the woods, and immediately froze or jumped away because you thought you saw a dangerous snake, when in fact it was just a twisted stick on the ground? If so, this would be an example of the **representativeness heuristic**, in which we estimate the probability of an event based on how well something matches (or *represents*) an existing prototype or stereotype in our minds (Bernard et al., 2016; Lien & Yuan, 2015; Peteros & Maleyeff, 2015). We all have a prototype of a snake in our mind and the twisted stick matches this prototype, which explains why this is also an example of the *availability heuristic*. While walking in the woods, you're primed to look out for snakes, and the sight of the twisted stick brought immediate images of a snake to your mind.

5. ***Confirmation bias*** Are you wondering why the U.S. Congress can't seem to solve serious national problems, like our deteriorating bridges and highways? Or why we can't resolve ongoing disputes with our roommates or spouses? It may be that we too often seek confirmation for our preexisting positions or beliefs and tend to ignore or discount contradictory evidence. As discussed in Chapters 1 and 4, this type of faulty thinking and barrier to problem solving is known as the **confirmation bias** (Knobloch-Westerwick et al., 2015; Nickerson, 1998; Webb et al., 2016). Can you also see how once we take a firm position or form a strong belief we typically become defensive and less open to new information? To make matters worse, the confirmation bias is closely related to what's called *belief perseverance*—our tendency to stick to our positions and beliefs even when we acknowledge the contrary information. Real-world examples of the confirmation bias (coupled with belief perseverance) are all around us—people who believe (or don't believe) that climate change is caused by human factors, that gun control can (or cannot) save lives, and that immigration helps (or hurts) our economy.

Like gamblers who keep putting coins into slot machines, we all have preexisting beliefs and biases that may lead us to focus only on our "hits" and ignore our "misses," officially known as confirmation biases. These biases lead to consequences ranging from small (see the following **Real World Psychology** feature) to the catastrophic (the U.S. war against Iraq based on the belief in weapons of mass destruction). There's even clear scientific research on how this bias operates in the medical field. For instance, researchers in one study examined the reported treatment outcomes in existing medical research records (Hrobjartsson et al., 2013). In some of these studies, the person who evaluated the effectiveness of specific medical treatments did not know whether the patient received a particular treatment or a placebo (they were "blind" to the condition). (See Chapter 1.) In other cases, however, the researcher who evaluated the treatment was aware of which treatment each patient received. Can you guess their findings? "Aware" evaluators judged the treatments to be more effective than the "non-aware" evaluators. Do you understand why? Medical doctors, therapists, and others who treat our ailments all have preexisting beliefs based on their professional training and clinical experience (see the photo).
[Q1] Unfortunately, once they develop a preferred treatment, they may only seek confirmatory evidence of their preexisting beliefs. As a result of this type of observer bias, certain treatments may be judged as being more effective than they actually are, and possibly better options will be ignored.

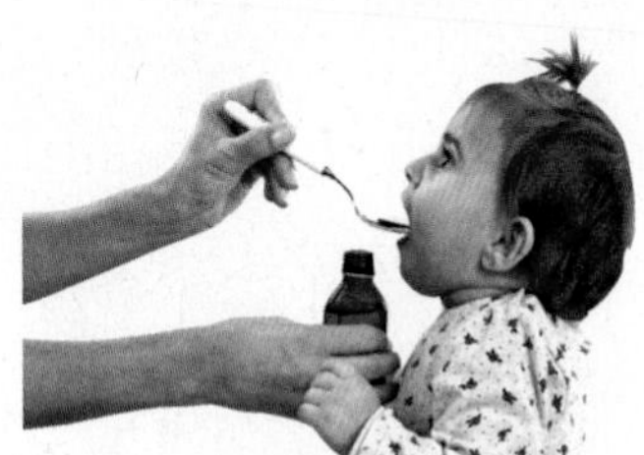

© Mehmet Hilmi Barcin/iStockphoto

Real World Psychology—Understanding the World

Sports Fans and Superstitious Beliefs

Have you heard of the *Sports Illustrated* magazine's "cover jinx"? The belief is that once a team or person appears on the cover of this magazine, something bad will soon befall them. For example, Oklahoma Sooners guard Buddy Hield appeared on the cover hyping Oklahoma's appearance in the 2016 NCAA Basketball Tournament. However, the Sooners were later blown out by the Villanova Wildcats 95-51 as Hield was held to just nine points. Similarly, the previously undefeated Notre Dame football team was on the cover and then lost the National Championship Game in 2013. Can you see how this is another example of the confirmation bias? Those who believe in the "jinx" might tend to look for examples to support it but fail to see examples that don't? Consider the fact that New York Yankees and Michael Jordan have had the most covers by a team and individual, respectively; and their exceptional winning histories were anything but "jinxed."

Strategies for Better Problem Solving Are you feeling overwhelmed with all these potential barriers to problem solving? If so, keep in mind that some of these cognitive strategies, such as the availability and representativeness heuristics, provide mental shortcuts that are generally far more likely to help than to hurt us (Pohl et al., 2013). They allow immediate "inferences that are fast, frugal, and accurate" (Todd & Gigerenzer, 2000, p. 736). If you note that several houses on your street have safety bars on their windows, you might be motivated to add your own safety bars, and thereby decrease your chances of being burglarized. Likewise, if you're hiking in an area with dangerous snakes, and you see a twisted stick on the ground, it's smart to initially freeze or jump away. When faced with an immediate decision, we often don't have time to investigate all the options. We need to make quick decisions based on the currently available information.

To see how all of this applies to your own personal life, think about the critical decisions surrounding choosing a college major and your future career. Imagine yourself as someone who once dreamed of becoming a physician or other highly competitive profession, but gave up this dream because of your low college entrance exam scores. Do you see how having a negative *mental set* that you just can't do well on exams might have created a self-fulfilling prophecy? Or how focusing on those low entrance exam scores (possible *functional fixedness*) may have blocked you from seeing other alternatives to becoming a physician? And how the *availability* and *representative heuristics* may have provided ready images and prototypes of future failures in the college courses required to be a physician. Finally, if you are someone who has decided NOT to pursue your career dream, did you fall victim to the *confirmation bias,* and only look for information that confirmed that decision (e.g., the hard work and high cost of all those years of medical training), while simultaneously ignoring or discounting the contradictory evidence (e.g., the high salary, job security, and job satisfaction) of that occupation?

In short, if you're questioning your ability to be a physician, or any other profession, because of these and other potential barriers, be sure to critically reevaluate your concerns and consider all your options. Also, be sure to talk to successful people in your desired career. You'll undoubtedly discover that personal traits, and character strengths, like self-control, motivation, perseverance, and having a growth mindset, are generally better predictors of achievement than college entrance exams or high IQ scores (Chua & Rubenfeld, 2014; Dweck, 2007; Mischel, 2014; Rattan et al., 2015).

Creativity

Everyone exhibits a certain amount of creativity in some aspects of life. Even when doing ordinary tasks, like planning an afternoon of errands, you are being somewhat creative. Similarly, if you've ever used a plastic garbage bag as a temporary rain jacket, or placed a thick, college textbook on a chair as a booster seat for a child, you've found creative solutions to problems.

TABLE 8.2 Three Elements of Creative Thinking

	EXPLANATIONS	NIKOLA TESLA EXAMPLES
Originality	Seeing unique or different solutions to a problem	After noting the limitations of Thomas Edison's direct current (DC) transmission system, Tesla devised a means of transmitting power via an alternating current (AC), which greatly reduced power loss over long distances.
Fluency	Generating a large number of possible solutions	Tesla developed numerous alternating current (AC) systems, including generators, motors, and transformers.
Flexibility	Shifting with ease from one type of problem-solving strategy to another	Tesla was a prolific inventor who held over 300 patents worldwide. He played a key role in developing florescent bulbs, neon signs, X-rays, the radio, lasers, remote controls, robotics, and even the technology used in modern cell phones.

Think Critically

1. Can you identify which of the three characteristics of creativity (originality, fluency, or flexibility) best explains your personal experiences with being creative?
2. Creativity is usually associated with art, poetry, and the like. What are other areas in which creativity should be highly valued?

How would psychologists operationally define creativity? Conceptions of creativity are obviously personal and influenced by culture, but most agree that a creative solution or performance generally produces original, appropriate, and valued outcomes in a novel way. Three characteristics are generally associated with **creativity**: *originality*, *fluency*, and *flexibility*. Nikola Tesla and his numerous technological developments offers a prime example of each of these characteristics (**Table 8.2**).

How do we measure creativity? Most tests focus on **divergent thinking**, a type of thinking in which we develop many possibilities from a single starting point (Baer, 2013; van de Kamp et al., 2015). In contrast to **convergent thinking**, which seeks the single-best solution to a problem, divergent thinking is open-ended and focused on generating multiple, novel solutions. For example, when assigned a research paper, many students have trouble coming up with something on their own. They're thinking "inside the box" when they focus on the specific problem of completing the assignment in a way that will please the professor. This is convergent thinking. Instead, most professors want to develop creative, divergent thinking and encourage (force?) their students to dig deeper to come up with their own unique ideas.

Psychologists have developed several methods to test for divergent thinking. For example, the Unusual Uses Test requires you to think of as many uses as possible for an object, such as a brick. In the Anagrams Test, you're asked to reorder the letters in a word to make as many new words as possible. To test your overall creativity, try the activities in the following **Psychology and You** feature.

Creativity The ability to produce original, appropriate, and valued outcomes in a novel way; consists of three characteristics—originality, fluency, and flexibility.

Divergent thinking A type of thinking that produces many solutions to the same problem.

Convergent thinking A type of thinking that seeks the single best solution to a problem.

Psychology and You—Understanding Yourself

Test Yourself | Are You Creative?

- Find 10 coins and arrange them in the configuration shown here. By moving only 2 coins, form two rows that each contains 6 coins. The solution is at the end of the chapter.
- In five minutes, see how many words you can make using the letters in the word *hippopotamus*.
- In five minutes, list all the things you can do with a paper clip.

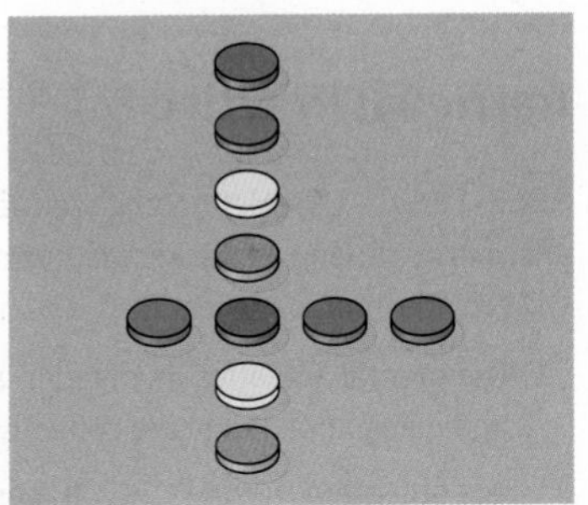

BJI/Blue Jean Images/Getty Images

[Q2]

How can we increase general creativity? For children, outdoor activities—such as climbing, jumping, and exploring—have a positive effect (Brussoni et al., 2015). Why? One reason might be that unstructured free play time (both indoors and outdoors) helps children to feel, express, regulate, and think about their own and others' emotions (Russ, 2014; Russ & Wallace, 2013). In addition to outdoor activities and free play time for both children and adults (see the photo), did you know that even taking a simple walk will increase creativity? Researchers asked participants to think about alternative ways for using a common object (Oppezzo & Schwartz, 2014). For example, for the word "button," a person might say "as a doorknob on a dollhouse." Half the participants did this task while sitting at a desk facing a blank wall, whereas the other half did it while walking on a treadmill facing a blank wall. Next, researchers repeated the study with participants walking outside, and in both conditions the walkers outperformed the sitters in creativity.

What are the obvious take home messages? The next time you need to be creative, take a walk! If you're a parent, can you see why this research on the value of outdoor activities and free play time is particularly important given the increasing pressure on parents and schools to emphasize science, math, and structured activities? Play appears to build the skills essential to success in the arts, entrepreneurship, and even fields like science and engineering. Researchers also suggest that because it allows safe practice for skills necessary for adult activities, play provides an evolutionary advantage to both human and nonhuman animals (Bateson & Martin, 2013; Tsai, 2015).

If you'd like further suggestions for increasing your own creativity, researchers have found that it requires the coming together of at least seven interrelated resources, as shown in **Table 8.3**. Can you think of ways to apply some or all of this information to your own life?

TABLE 8.3 Resources of Creative People

Affective processes	Emotional intelligence and joy in creative expression
Intellectual ability	Enough intelligence to see problems in a new light
Knowledge	Sufficient basic knowledge of the problem to effectively evaluate possible solutions
Thinking style	Novel ideas, divergent thinking, and ability to distinguish between the worthy and worthless
Personality	Conscientiousness, openness, and willingness to grow and change, take risks, and work to overcome obstacles
Motivation	Sufficient motivation to accomplish the task and more internal than external motivation
Environment	An environment that supports creativity

Which of these 7 resources do you think best explains Lady Gaga's phenomenal success? Interestingly, research shows that audiences like art more when they perceive the artist as eccentric—which certainly applies to Lady Gaga (Van Tilburg & Igou, 2014)!

Michael Travis/Corbis

Sources: Chrysikou et al., 2016; Li et al., 2015; Sternberg, 2014, 2015; van de kamp et al., 2015.

Retrieval Practice 8.1 | Thinking

SELF-TEST Completing this self-test, and then checking your answers by clicking on the answer button or by looking in Appendix B, will provide immediate feedback and helpful practice for exams.

1. The mental activities involved in acquiring, storing, retrieving, and using knowledge are collectively known as ____.

a. perception **b.** consciousness
c. cognition **d.** awareness

2. ____ is a logical step-by-step procedure that, if followed, will always eventually solve the problem.

a. An algorithm
b. A problem-solving set
c. A heuristic
d. Brainstorming

3. Rosa is shopping in a new supermarket and wants to find a standard type of mustard. Which problem-solving strategy would be most efficient?

   a. algorithm b. heuristic
   c. instinct d. mental set

4. _____ is a fixed-thinking approach to problem solving that only sees solutions that have worked in the past.

   a. Problem-solving set b. Functional fixedness
   c. Mental set d. Incubation

5. _____ is the ability to produce original, appropriate, and valued outcomes in a novel way.

   a. Problem solving b. Functional flexibility
   c. Incubation d. Creativity

Think Critically

1. During problem solving, do you use primarily algorithms or heuristics? What are the advantages of each?
2. Would you prefer to be highly creative or highly intelligent? Why?

Real World **Psychology**

Why might some medical treatments be judged as more effective than they really are?

Can outdoor activities or simply taking a walk improve your creativity?

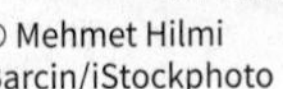

© Mehmet Hilmi Barcin/iStockphoto

BJI/Blue Jean Images/Getty Images

HINT: LOOK IN THE MARGIN FOR **[Q1]** AND **[Q2]**

8.2 Language

LEARNING OBJECTIVES

Retrieval Practice While reading the upcoming sections, respond to each Learning Objective in your own words.

Summarize the key characteristics and theories of language, and human versus nonhuman language.

- **Identify** language and its major building blocks.
- **Describe** the prominent theories of language and thinking, and how they interact.
- **Discuss** the major stages of language development, including the language acquisition device (LAD).
- **Review** the evidence and controversy surrounding nonhuman animals' acquisition and use of language.

Using **language** enables us to mentally manipulate symbols, thereby expanding our thinking. Whether it's spoken, written, or signed, language also allows us to communicate our thoughts, ideas, and feelings (Harley, 2014; Jandt, 2016).

Language A form of communication using sounds or symbols combined according to specified rules.

Language Characteristics

To produce language, we first build words using **phonemes** [FO-neems] and **morphemes** [MOR-feems]. Then we string words into sentences using rules of **grammar**, such as *syntax* and *semantics* (**Figure 8.5**).

Phoneme The smallest basic unit of speech or sound in any given language.

Morpheme The smallest meaningful unit of language; formed from a combination of phonemes.

Grammar The set of rules (syntax and semantics) governing the use and structure of language.

What happens in our brains when we produce and comprehend language? Language, like our thought processes, is both localized and distributed throughout our brains (**Figure 8.6**). For example, the amygdala is active when we engage in a special type of language—cursing or swearing. Why? Recall from Chapter 2 that the amygdala is linked to emotions, especially fear and rage. So it's logical that the brain regions activated by swearing or hearing swear words would be the same as those for fear and aggression.

As shown in Figure 8.6, additional parts of the brain are involved in language, including *Broca's area* (which is responsible for speech generation) and *Wernicke's area* (which controls language comprehension). Keep in mind that several additional areas, not shown on this figure, of the brain are activated during different types of language generation and listening.

How do we know which parts of the brain are involved with language? Scientists can track brain activity through a colored *positron emission tomography (PET) scan*. Injection of the radioactive isotope oxygen-15 into the bloodstream of the participant makes areas of the brain with high metabolic activity "light up" in red and orange on the scan (**Figure 8.7**).

FIGURE 8.5 **The three major building blocks of language**

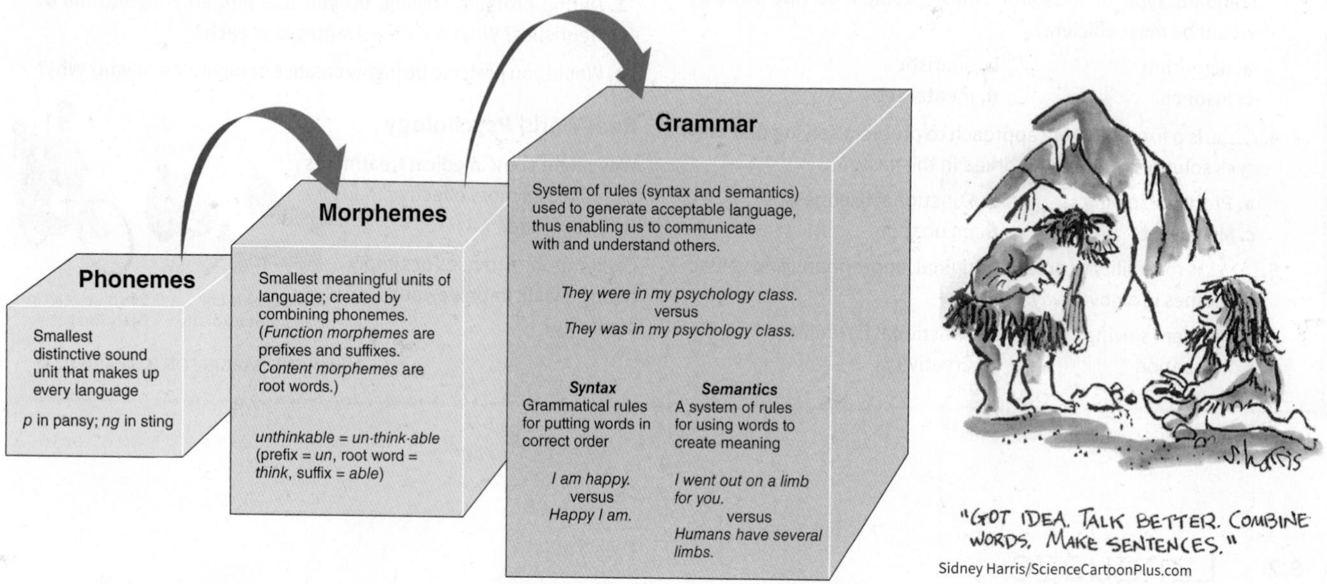

Phonemes
Smallest distinctive sound unit that makes up every language
p in pansy; ng in sting
Morphemes
Smallest meaningful units of language; created by combining phonemes. (Function morphemes are prefixes and suffixes. Content morphemes are root words.)
unthinkable = un-think-able (prefix = un, root word = think, suffix = able)
Grammar
System of rules (syntax and semantics) used to generate acceptable language, thus enabling us to communicate with and understand others.
They were in my psychology class. versus They was in my psychology class.
Syntax
Grammatical rules for putting words in correct order
I am happy. versus Happy I am.
Semantics
A system of rules for using words to create meaning
I went out on a limb for you. versus Humans have several limbs.
S. Harris
"GOT IDEA. TALK BETTER. COMBINE WORDS. MAKE SENTENCES."

Sidney Harris/ScienceCartoonPlus.com

Language Theories

Does the fact that you speak English instead of German—or Chinese instead of Swahili—determine how you reason, think, and perceive the world? Linguist Benjamin Whorf (1956) believed so. As evidence for his *linguistic relativity hypothesis*, Whorf offered a now classic example: Because Inuits (previously known as Eskimos) supposedly have many words for snow (*apikak* for "first snow falling," *pukak* for "snow for drinking water," and so on), they can reportedly perceive and think about snow differently from English speakers, who have only one word—*snow*.

Though intriguing, Whorf's hypothesis has not fared well. He apparently exaggerated the number of Inuit words for snow (Pullum, 1991) and ignored the fact that English speakers have a number of terms to describe various forms of snow, such as *slush*, *sleet*, *hard pack*, and *powder*. Other research has directly contradicted Whorf's theory. For example, Eleanor Rosch (1973) found that although people of the Dani tribe in New Guinea possess only two color names—one indicating cool, dark colors, and the other describing warm, bright colors—they discriminate among multiple hues as well as English speakers do.

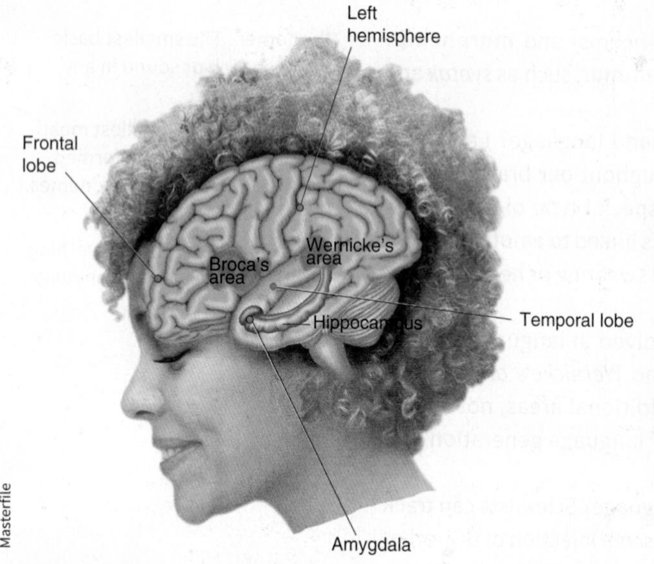

Masterfile

FIGURE 8.6 **Language and the brain**

Whorf apparently was mistaken in his belief that language *determines* thought. But there is no doubt that language *influences* thought (Bylund & Athanasopoulos, 2015; Yang, 2016; Zhong et al., 2015). People who speak multiple languages report that the language they're currently using affects their sense of self and how they think about events (Berry et al., 2011; Lai & Narasimhan, 2015). For example, people who speak both Chinese and English report that they tend to conform to Chinese cultural norms when speaking Chinese and to Western norms when speaking English. [Q3] Interestingly, research shows that speaking multiple languages, and even just learning one new language, offers a wide range of benefits that might make you smarter, including increased attention, better communication skills, and more gray matter in key brain regions (Bak et al., 2016; Bialystok & Craik, 2010; Fan et al., 2015; Olulade et al., 2016). For additional insights on language effects, see the following **Real World Psychology** and **PsychScience** features.

FIGURE 8.7 **Using PET scans to study language and the brain**

WDCN/Univ. College London/Photo Researchers

a. Language generated in the frontal lobe (center left) has its cognition checked in the temporal lobe (lower right).

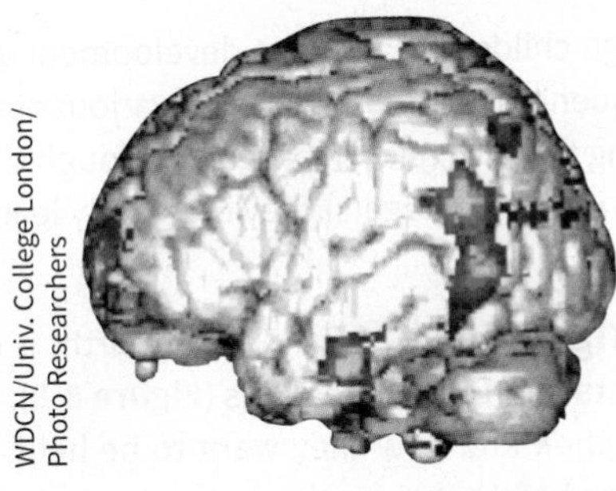

WDCN/Univ. College London/Photo Researchers

b. Working out the meaning of heard words makes areas of the temporal lobe light up.

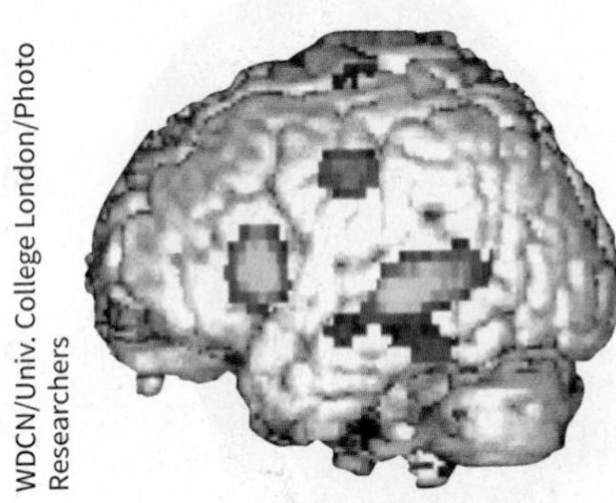

WDCN/Univ. College London/Photo Researchers

c. Repeating words increases activity in Broca's area and Wernicke's area, as well as a motor region responsible for pronouncing words (reddish area at the top).

Real World Psychology—Understanding the World

Language Distortions

Our words clearly influence the thinking of those who hear them. That's why companies avoid *firing* employees. Instead, employees are *outplaced* or *nonrenewed*. And, the military uses terms like *preemptive strike* to cover the fact that they attacked first and *tactical redeployment* to refer to a retreat. Similarly, the dentist who shot the African lion, known as Cecil, apologized for this act by saying, "I had no idea the lion I took was a known, local favorite." But he didn't "take" the lion. He killed it!

CAMERA PRESS/Villiers Steyn/Gallo Images/Redux Pictures

PS PsychScience

The Power of Words

Monika Adamczyk/Getty Images

Did you know that simply talking about helping others makes a person seem warm and leads to social approval? This real-world study examined 124 million words spoken in the House of Representatives by members of the U.S. Congress between 1996 and 2014 (Frimer et al., 2015). The researchers were looking for use of prosocial language and they found a strong link between the declining use of prosocial language and the public's disapproval of Congress 6 months later. This suggests that today's record-low levels of public approval of the U.S. Congress may, in part, be a product of declining use of prosocial language. Can you see how both government officials, and we as individuals, might gain greater social approval by talking more about cooperation and helping others?

Speaking of the power of words, a different set of researchers approached small children (ages 3 to 6), and in one condition, helping was referred to as a verb, such as, "Some children choose to help." In the second group, helping was referred to as a noun, such as, "Some children choose to be helpers" (Bryan et al., 2014). The children then began playing with toys. While they were playing, the researcher interrupted and offered four distinct opportunities for the children to provide help—to pick up a mess, open a container, put away toys, and pick up crayons that had spilled on the floor. Can you predict what they found? Children who heard the *noun* wording (helpers) helped significantly more than children who heard the *verb* wording (help).

Research Challenge

1. Based on the information provided, did this second study (Bryan et al., 2014) use descriptive, correlational, and/or experimental research?
2. If you chose:
   - *descriptive research*, is this a naturalistic observation, survey/interview, case study, and/or archival research?
   - *correlational research*, is this a positive, negative, or zero correlation?
   - *experimental research*, label the IV, DV, experimental group(s), and control group.
   - both *descriptive* and *correlational*, answer the corresponding questions for both.

Check your answers by clicking on the answer button or by looking in Appendix B.

Note: The information provided in this study is admittedly limited, but the level of detail is similar to what is presented in most textbooks and public reports of research findings. Answering these questions, and then comparing your answers to those provided, will help you become a better critical thinker and consumer of scientific research.

Language Development

Although children's language development varies in timing, virtually all children follow a similar sequence (see **Table 8.4**). The various stages within this table are believed to be universal, meaning that all children progress through similar stages regardless of the culture they're born into, or what language(s) they ultimately learn to speak.

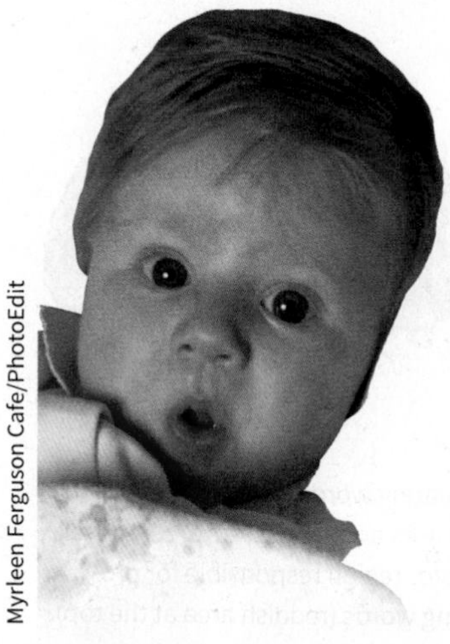

Myrleen Ferguson Cafe/PhotoEdit

FIGURE 8.8 Can you identify this emotion? Infants as young as 2.5 months can nonverbally express emotions, such as joy, surprise, or anger.

Prelinguistic Stage From birth, a child communicates through facial expressions, eye contact, and body gestures (**Figure 8.8**). Babies only hours old begin to "teach" their caregivers when and how they want to be held, fed, and played with. Babies even start to learn language before they are born. For example, researchers in one study played sounds from two different languages—English and Swedish—for babies at hospitals in both the United States and Sweden shortly after birth (Moon et al., 2013). These babies were given special pacifiers that were hooked up to a computer, and the more times they sucked on the pacifier, the more [Q4] times they heard the vowels. Half the babies heard sounds from the language they'd been exposed to in utero, whereas the others heard vowels from a different language. In both countries, the babies who heard the foreign vowels sucked more frequently than those who heard sounds from their native language, suggesting that babies have already become familiar—through listening to their mother's voice—with the sounds in their native language and are now more interested in hearing novel sounds!

TABLE 8.4 Language Acquisition

	Features	Examples
BIRTH TO 12 MONTHS		
Jaimie Duplass/iStockphoto	Crying (reflexive in newborns) becomes more purposeful	hunger cry, anger cry, and pain cry
	Cooing (vowel-like sounds) at 2–3 months	"ooooh," "aaaah"
	Babbling (consonants added) at 4–6 months	"bahbahbah," "dahdahdah"
12 MONTHS TO 2 YEARS		
iStockphoto	Babbling resembles language of the environment, and child understands that sounds relate to meaning	"Mama," "Da Da"
	Speech consists of one-word utterances	"Juice," "Up"
	Expressive ability more than doubles once words are joined into short phrases	"Daddy milk," "no night-night!"
	Overextension (using words to include objects that do not fit the word's meaning)	all men = "Daddy," all furry animals = "doggy"
2 YEARS TO 5 YEARS		
© kate_sept2004/iStockphoto	Telegraphic speech (like telegrams, omits nonessential connecting words)	"Me want cookie" "Grandma go bye-bye?"
	Vocabulary increases at a phenomenal rate	
	Child acquires a wide variety of grammar rules	adding *-ed* for past tense, adding s to form plurals
	Overgeneralization (applying basic rules of grammar even to cases that are exceptions to the rule)	"I goed to the zoo" "Two mans"

Note: Are you having difficulty differentiating between overextension and overgeneralization? Remember the g in overgeneralize as a cue that this term applies to problems with grammar.

Linguistic Stage After the prelinguistic stage, infants quickly move toward full language acquisition (see again Table 8.4). By age 5, most children have mastered basic grammar and typically use about 2,000 words (a level of mastery considered adequate for getting by in any given culture). Past this point, vocabulary and grammar gradually improve throughout life (Levey, 2014; Oller et al., 2014).

Theories of Language Development Some theorists believe that language capability is innate, primarily a matter of maturation. Noam Chomsky (1968, 1980) suggests that children are "prewired" with a neurological ability within the brain, known as a **language acquisition device (LAD)**, that enables them to analyze language and to extract the basic rules of grammar. This mechanism needs only minimal exposure to adult speech to unlock its potential. As evidence for this *nativist position*, Chomsky observes that children everywhere progress through the same stages of language development at about the same ages. He also notes that babbling is the same in all languages and that deaf babies babble just like hearing babies.

Language acquisition device (LAD) According to Chomsky, an innate mechanism within the brain, which enables a child to analyze language and extract the basic rules of grammar.

Nurturists argue that the nativist position doesn't fully explain individual differences in language development. They hold that children learn language through a complex system of rewards, punishments, and imitation. For example, parents smile and encourage any vocalizations from a very young infant. Later, they respond even more enthusiastically when the infant babbles "mama" or "dada." In this way, parents unknowingly use *shaping* (Chapter 6) to help babies learn language. Unfortunately, as discussed in the following **PositivePsych**, researchers have found a wide variability in how much parents talk or read to their children, and that this difference leads to serious gaps in the children's language development skills.

PP PositivePsych

Why Talk or Read to Babies?

Have you seen the TV public service ads emphasizing talking and reading to babies and toddlers? Did you know that the words and amount of talking babies hear (or don't hear) from their caregivers plays a fundamental role in helping them develop their critical language skills? To identify the specific factors that influence such language acquisition, researchers examined babies living in one of two communities—either a relatively wealthy college town or a low-income nearby area (Fernald et al., 2013). They found that caregivers from wealthier communities talk to their children much more frequently, which gives them a chance to learn new words and to form better vocabularies. A similar study reported that low-income children hear lower quantity and quality of words, which impacts their language expression ability (Hirsh-Pasek et al., 2015). Recognizing the importance of talking to babies, an enterprising company recently developed a word-tracking device, called Starling, that parents attach to their babies to record the number of verbal exchanges with their child (Ockerman, 2016).

In addition to talking, research has revealed numerous benefits of reading to babies and toddlers. For example, reading books is particularly important because they contain more unique words than children hear in everyday speech (Montag et al., 2015). Interestingly, other research shows that reading activates important areas of the child's brain (Hutton et al., 2015)! Using fMRI scans of brain activity in 3- to 5-year-old children as they listened to age-appropriate stories, the researchers found that children whose parents reported more reading at home and more books in the home showed significantly greater activation of the parietal-temporal-occipital association cortex, which is responsible for integrating sound and visual stimulation. Even though these children in the fMRI scanner were just listening to a story and could not see any pictures, they were actively integrating the sound of the words and imagining what they are hearing about. The greater levels of brain activation in children who are read to more often and have more books at home suggests that they gain more practice in developing visual images, which helps in overall language acquisition.

Hero Images/Getty Images

Can Human Animals Talk with Nonhuman Animals?

Without question, nonhuman animals communicate. They regularly send warnings, signal sexual interest, share locations of food sources, and so on. But can nonhuman animals master the complexity of human language? Since the 1930s, many language studies have attempted to answer this question by probing the language abilities of chimpanzees, gorillas, and other animals (Hoeschele & Fitch, 2016; Scott-Phillips, 2015; Zuberbühler, 2015).

One of the most successful early studies was conducted by Beatrice and Allen Gardner (1969), who recognized chimpanzees' manual dexterity and ability to imitate gestures. The Gardners used American Sign Language (ASL) with a chimp named Washoe. By the time Washoe was 4 years old, she had learned 132 signs and was able to combine them into simple sentences such as "Hurry, gimme toothbrush" and "Please tickle more." The famous gorilla Koko also uses ASL to communicate; she reportedly uses more than 1,000 signs (**Figure 8.9**).

In another well-known study, a chimp named Lana learned to use symbols on a computer to get things she wanted, such as food, a drink, and a tickle from her trainers, and to have her curtains opened (Rumbaugh et al., 1974). See **Figure 8.10**.

"ALTHOUGH HUMANS MAKE SOUNDS WITH THEIR MOUTHS AND OCCASIONALLY LOOK AT EACH OTHER, THERE IS NO SOLID EVIDENCE THAT THEY ACTUALLY COMMUNICATE WITH EACH OTHER."

Sidney Harris/ScienceCartoonPlus.com

Dolphins also are often the subject of interesting language research (see cartoon) (Kuczaj et al., 2015; Pack, 2015). Communication with dolphins is typically conducted with hand signals or audible commands transmitted through an underwater speaker system. In one typical study, trainers gave dolphins commands made up of two- to five-word sentences, such as "Big ball—square—return," which meant that they should go get the big ball, put it in the floating square, and return to the trainer (Herman et al., 1984). By varying the syntax (for example, the order of the words) and specific content of the commands, the researchers showed that dolphins are sensitive to these aspects of language.

Scientists disagree about how to interpret the findings on chimps, apes, and dolphins. Most believe nonhuman animals definitely communicate, but that they're not using true language because they don't convey subtle meanings, use language creatively, or communicate at an abstract level.

Ron Cohn/Gorilla Foundation/Koko.org

FIGURE 8.9 **Signing** According to her teacher, Penny Patterson, Koko has used ASL to converse with others, talk to herself, joke, express preferences, and even lie (Linden, 1993; Patterson, 2002).

Michael Nichols/NG Image Collection

FIGURE 8.10 **Computer-aided communication** Apes lack the necessary anatomical structures to vocalize the way humans do. For this reason, language research with chimps and gorillas has focused on teaching the animals to use sign language or to "speak" by pointing to symbols on a keyboard. Do you think this amounts to using language the same way humans do?

Other critics propose that these animals do not truly understand language, but are simply operantly conditioned (Chapter 6) to imitate symbols to receive rewards. Finally, many language scientists contend that data regarding animal language has not always been well documented (Beran et al., 2014; Savage-Rumbaugh, 1990; Terrace, 1979).

Proponents of animal language respond that apes can use language creatively and have even coined some words of their own. For example, Koko supposedly signed "finger bracelet" to describe a ring and "eye hat" to describe a mask (Patterson & Linden, 1981). Proponents also argue that, as demonstrated by the dolphin studies, animals can be taught to understand basic rules of sentence structure. As you can see, the jury is still out on whether nonhuman animals use "true" language or not. Stay tuned!

Retrieval Practice 8.2 | Language

SELF-TEST Completing this self-test, and then checking your answers by clicking on the answer button or by looking in Appendix B, will provide immediate feedback and helpful practice for exams.

1. _____ is the set of rules (syntax and semantics) that govern the use and structure of language.

a. Syntax **b.** Semantics
c. Pragmatics **d.** Grammar

2. Which rule of English is violated by this sentence? *The girl Anne is.*

a. deep structure **b.** phonemic structure
c. semantics **d.** syntax

3. "I goed to the zoo" and "I hurt my foots" are examples of _____.

a. prelinguistic verbalizations **b.** overexposure to adult "baby talk"
c. overgeneralization **d.** Noam Chomsky's theory of language acquisition

4. According to Chomsky, the innate mechanism that enables a child to analyze language is known as a(n) _____.

a. telegraphic understanding device (TUD) **b.** language acquisition device (LAD)
c. language and grammar translator (LGT) **d.** overgeneralized neural net (ONN)

5. Some researchers believe nonhuman animals are not using true language because they don't _____.

a. convey subtle meanings
b. use language creatively
c. communicate at an abstract level
d. all of these options

Think Critically

1. Describe a personal example of language influencing your thinking.

2. Review the evidence that nonhuman animals are able to learn and use language. Do you think apes and dolphins have true language? Why or why not?

Real World Psychology

Do babies begin to learn language even before they are born?

Does speaking multiple languages make you smarter?

© merrill/iStockphoto

HINT: LOOK IN THE MARGIN FOR **[Q3]** AND **[Q4]**

8.3 Intelligence

LEARNING OBJECTIVES

Retrieval Practice While reading the upcoming sections, respond to each Learning Objective in your own words.

Review the definition and measurement of intelligence, and the factors that influence it.

- **Define** intelligence.
- **Compare** the different forms and theories of intelligence.
- **Describe** how intelligence is measured, and the groups that fall at the extremes.

Many people equate intelligence with "book smarts." For others, the definition of intelligence depends on the characteristics and skills that are valued in a particular social group or culture (Goldstein et al., 2015; Plucker & Esping, 2014; Suzuki et al., 2014). For example, the Mandarin word that corresponds most closely to the word *intelligence* is a character meaning "good brain and talented" (Matsumoto, 2000). In other cultures, intelligence is associated with traits like imitation, effort, and social responsibility (Keats, 1982). An experiment carried out in seven countries even found that smiling versus non-smiling affected judgments of intelligence (Krys et al., 2014).

Interestingly, German respondents perceived smiling individuals as being more intelligent, whereas Chinese participants judged smilers as less intelligent.

Even among Western psychologists there is considerable debate over the definition of intelligence. In this discussion, we rely on a formal definition of **intelligence**—*the global capacity to think rationally, act purposefully, profit from experience, and deal effectively with the environment* (Wechsler, 1944, 1977).

Intelligence The global capacity to think rationally, act purposefully, profit from experience, and deal effectively with the environment.

The Nature of Intelligence

In the 1920s, British psychologist Charles Spearman first observed that high scores on separate tests of mental abilities tend to correlate with each other. Spearman (1923) thus proposed that intelligence is a single factor, which he termed **general intelligence (*g*)**. He believed that *g* underlies all intellectual behavior, including reasoning, solving problems, and performing well in all areas of cognition. Spearman's work laid the foundations for today's standardized intelligence tests (Bouchard, 2014; Cooper, 2015; Woodley of Menie & Madison, 2015).

General intelligence (*g*) Spearman's term for a common skill set that underlies all intellectual behavior.

About a decade later, L. L. Thurstone (1938) proposed 7 primary mental abilities: verbal comprehension, word fluency, numerical fluency, spatial visualization, associative memory, perceptual speed, and reasoning. J. P. Guilford (1967) later expanded this number, proposing that as many as 120 factors are involved in the structure of intelligence.

Around the same time, Raymond Cattell (1963, 1971) reanalyzed Thurstone's data and argued against the idea of multiple intelligences. He believed that two subtypes of g exist:

- **Fluid intelligence (*gf*)** refers to the ability to think speedily and abstractly, and to solve novel problems. Fluid intelligence is relatively independent of education and experience, and like most biological capacities, it declines with age (Gazes et al., 2016; Gerstorf et al., 2015; Klein et al., 2015).
- **Crystallized intelligence (*gc*)** refers to the store of knowledge and skills gained through experience and education (Santos, 2016; Sternberg, 2014, 2015). Crystallized intelligence tends to increase over the life span.

Fluid intelligence (*gf*) The ability to think speedily and abstractly, and to solve novel problems; *gf* tends to decrease over the life span.

Crystallized intelligence (*gc*) The store of knowledge and skills gained through experience and education; *gc* tends to increase over the life span.

Measuring Intelligence

Different IQ tests approach the measurement of intelligence from different perspectives. However, most are designed to predict grades in school. Let's look at the most commonly used IQ tests.

The *Stanford-Binet Intelligence Scale* is loosely based on the first IQ tests developed in France around the turn of the twentieth century by Alfred Binet. In the United States, Lewis Terman (1916) developed the Stanford-Binet (at Stanford University) to test the intellectual ability of U.S.-born children ages 3 to 16. The test is revised periodically—most recently in 2003. The test is administered individually and consists of such tasks as copying geometric designs, identifying similarities, and repeating number sequences.

After administering the individual test to a large number of people, researchers discovered that their scores typically are distributed in a **normal distribution** that forms a symmetrical, bell-shaped curve (**Figure 8.11**). This means that a majority of the scores fall in the middle of the curve and a few scores fall on the extremes. In addition to intelligence, measurements on many physical traits, like height and weight, also create a similar "bell curve" normal distribution.

Normal distribution A statistical term used to describe how traits are distributed within a population; IQ scores usually form a symmetrical, bell-shaped curve, with most scores falling near the average, and fewer scores near the extremes.

In the original version of the Stanford-Binet, results were expressed in terms of a **mental age (MA)**, which refers to an individual's level of mental development relative to that of others. For example, if a 7-year-old's score equaled that of an average 8-year-old, the child was considered to have a mental age of 8. To determine the child's **intelligence quotient (IQ)**, mental age was divided by the child's chronological age (actual age in years) and multiplied by 100.

Mental age (MA) An individual's level of mental development relative to that of others; mental age was initially used in comparison to chronological age (CA) to calculate IQ.

Intelligence quotient (IQ) An index of intelligence initially derived from standardized tests, which is computed by dividing mental age (MA) by chronological age (CA) and then multiplying by 100; now derived by comparing individual scores with the scores of others of the same age.

The most widely used intelligence test today, the *Wechsler Adult Intelligence Scale (WAIS)*, was developed by David Wechsler in the early 1900s. He later created a similar test for school-aged children. Like the Stanford-Binet, Wechsler's tests yield an overall intelligence score, in addition to separate index scores related to four specific areas: verbal comprehension, perceptual reasoning, working memory, and processing speed. See **Figure 8.12** for samples of the Wechsler's perceptual reasoning test items.

Today, most intelligence test scores are expressed as a comparison of a single person's score to a national sample of similar-aged people (see again Figure 8.11). Even though the actual IQ is no longer calculated using the original formula comparing mental and chronological ages, the term *IQ* remains as a shorthand expression for intelligence test scores.

What makes a good test? How are the tests developed by Binet and Wechsler any better than those published in popular magazines and presented on television programs? To be scientifically acceptable, all psychological tests must fulfill three basic requirements (Dombrowski, 2015; Jackson, 2016; Suzuki et al., 2014):

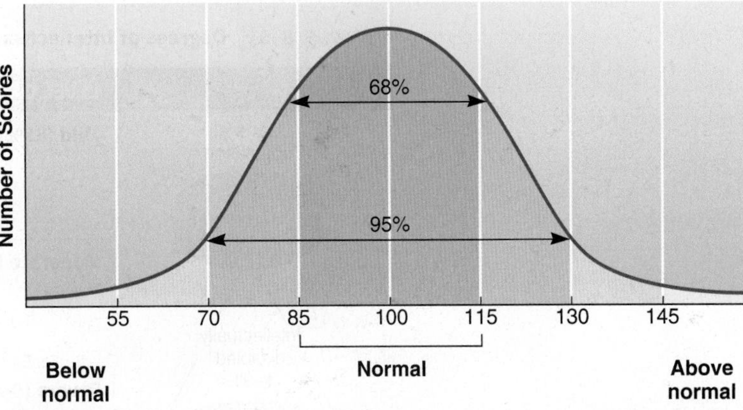

FIGURE 8.11 The normal distribution (bell curve) of scores on intelligence tests The term "bell curve" refers to the fact that the graph used to depict the normal distribution of scores (shown here) is shaped like a bell. The highest point at the top of the bell represents the most likely, probable score (100 points), whereas all the other scores are equally distributed around this center point. Note that 68% of people score 15 points above or below the national average, which is 100 points.

- **Standardization** in intelligence tests (as well as personality, aptitude, and most other tests) involves following a certain set of uniform procedures when administering a test. First, every test must have *norms*, or average scores, developed by giving the test to a representative sample of people (a diverse group of people who resemble those for whom the test is intended). Second, testing procedures must be standardized. All test takers must be given the same instructions, questions, and time limits, and all test administrators must follow the same objective score standards.
- **Reliability** is usually determined by retesting participants to see whether their test scores change significantly. Retesting can be done via the *test–retest method*, in which participants' scores on two separate administrations of the same test are compared, or via the *split-half method*, which splits a test into two equivalent parts (such as odd and even questions) and determines the degree of similarity between the two halves.
- **Validity** is the ability of a test to measure what it is designed to measure. The most important type of validity is *criterion-related validity*, or the accuracy with which test scores can be used to predict another variable of interest (known as the criterion). Criterion-related validity is expressed as the *correlation* (Chapter 1) between the test score and

Standardization A set of uniform procedures for administering and scoring a test; also, establishing norms by comparison with scores of a pretested group.

Reliability The degree to which a test produces similar scores each time it is used; stability or consistency of the scores produced by an instrument.

Validity The degree to which a test measures what it is intended to measure.

FIGURE 8.12 Items similar to those on the Wechsler adult intelligence scale (WAIS) These simulated items resemble those found in the Wechsler Adult Intelligence Scale, Fourth Edition (WAIS-IV). Previous editions of the WAIS included sections, such as Picture Arrangement, Block Design, and Object Assembly, which were dropped to increase reliability and user friendliness. WAIS-IV also takes less time to administer and the results show smaller differences based on level of education or racial/ethnic group membership. *Source*: Based on simulated items from the Wechsler Adult Intelligence Scale, Fourth Edition (WAIS-IV).

a. Visual Puzzles The test administrator asks: "Which three pieces go together to make this puzzle?"

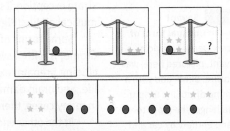

b. Figure Weights The test administrator asks: "Which one of these works to balance the scale?"

TABLE 8.5 Degrees of Intellectual Disability

General population

Intellectually disabled 1–3%

85% Mild

1–2% Profound

3–4% Severe

10% Moderate

LEVEL OF DISABILITY	IQ SCORES	CHARACTERISTICS
Mild (85%)	50–70	Usually able to become self-sufficient; may marry, have families, and secure full-time jobs in low-skilled occupations
Moderate (10%)	35–49	Generally able to perform simple, low-skilled tasks; may contribute to a certain extent to their livelihood
Severe (3–4%)	20–34	Generally able to follow daily routines, but needs supervision; with training, may learn basic communication skills
Profound (1–2%)	below 20	Generally able to perform only the most rudimentary behaviors, such as walking, feeding themselves, and saying a few phrases

the criterion. If two variables are highly correlated, then one can be used to predict the other. Thus, if a test is valid, its scores will be useful in predicting an individual's behavior in some other specified situation. One example is using intelligence test scores to predict grades in college.

Do you see why a test that is standardized and reliable but not valid is worthless? For example, a test for skin sensitivity may be easy to standardize (the instructions specify exactly how to apply the test agent), and it may be reliable (similar results are obtained on each retest). But it certainly would not be valid for predicting college grades.

Extremes in Intelligence

One of the best methods for judging the validity of a test is to compare people who score at the extremes. Despite the uncertainties discussed in the previous section, intelligence tests provide one of the major criteria for assessing mental ability at the extremes—specifically, for diagnosing *intellectual disability* and *mental giftedness*.

The clinical label *intellectually disabled* (previously referred to as *mentally retarded*) is applied when someone has significant deficits in general mental abilities, such as reasoning, problem solving, and academic learning. These deficits may also result in impairments of adaptive functioning including communication, social participation, and personal independence (American Psychiatric Association, 2013; Kumin, 2015).

Fewer than 3% of people are classified as having an intellectual disability (see **Table 8.5**). Of this group, 85% have only mild intellectual disability, and many become self-supporting, integrated members of society. Furthermore, people can score low on some measures of intelligence and still be average or even gifted in others (Miller et al., 2016; Treffert, 2014; Werner & Roth, 2014). The most dramatic examples are people with *savant syndrome*. People with savant syndrome generally score very low on IQ tests (usually between 40 and 70), yet they demonstrate exceptional skills or brilliance in specific areas, such as rapid calculation, art, memory, or musical ability (**Figure 8.13**).

© Justin Sutcliffe/Redux Pictures

FIGURE 8.13 Savant syndrome—an unusual form of intelligence Derek Paravicini, a musical savant, pictured here, was born premature, blind, and with a severe learning disability. In spite of these challenges, he plays the concert piano entirely by ear and has a repertoire of thousands of memorized pieces.

Some forms of intellectual disability stem from genetic abnormalities, such as Down syndrome, fragile-X syndrome, and phenylketonuria (PKU). Other causes are environmental, including prenatal exposure to alcohol and other drugs, extreme deprivation or neglect in early life, and brain damage from physical trauma, such as car accidents or sports injuries. However, in many cases, there is no known cause of the intellectual disability.

At the other end of the intelligence spectrum are people with especially high IQs (typically defined as being in the top 1 or 2%). In the early 1900s, Lewis Terman identified 1,500 gifted children—affectionately nicknamed the "Termites"—with IQs of 140 or higher (Terman, 1925). He and his colleagues then tracked their progress through adulthood. The number who became highly successful professionals was many times the number a random group would have produced (Kreger Silverman, 2013; Plucker & Esping, 2014; Terman, 1954). Those who were most successful tended to have extraordinary motivation, and they typically had someone at home or school who was especially encouraging (Goleman, 1980). Unfortunately, some of his so-called "Termites" became alcoholics, got divorced, and died as a result of suicide (Campbell & Feng, 2011; Leslie, 2000; Terman, 1954). In sum, a high IQ is no guarantee of success in every endeavor. As shown by the "Termites" study and the problem-solving research mentioned earlier, personal traits and character strengths, like self-control, motivation, and perseverance, may be the strongest predictors of overall achievement and well-being. Having a *growth-mindset,* the belief that intelligence can be developed over time, is particularly important to intellectual achievement (Dweck, 2007; Mischel, 2014; Rattan et al., 2015). [Q5]

Retrieval Practice 8.3 | Intelligence

SELF-TEST Completing this self-test, and then checking your answers by clicking on the answer button or by looking in Appendix B, will provide immediate feedback and helpful practice for exams.

1. The formal definition of intelligence stresses the global capacity to _____.
   a. successfully adapt to and perform well within relationships, in school, and on the job
   b. read, write, and do computations at home and at work
   c. perform verbally and physically within the environment
   d. think rationally, act purposefully, profit from experience, and deal effectively with the environment
2. The store of knowledge and skills gained through experience and education is known as _____ intelligence.
   a. crystallized **b.** fluid
   c. general **d.** specific
3. Which is the most widely used intelligence test?
   a. Wechsler Intelligence Scale for Children
   b. Wechsler Adult Intelligence Scale
   c. Stanford-Binet Intelligence Scale
   d. Binet-Terman Intelligence Scale
4. If a test gives you the same score each time you take it, that test would be _____.
   a. reliable **b.** valid
   c. standardized **d.** none of these options
5. Validity refers to the ability of a test to _____.
   a. return the same score on separate administrations of the test
   b. measure what it is designed to measure
   c. avoid discrimination between different cultural groups
   d. give a standard deviation of scores

Think Critically

1. Do you believe IQ tests are more reliable than valid? Explain.
2. Do you think IQ tests are culturally biased? Why or why not?

Real World Psychology

Can personal traits and character strengths be better predictors of achievement than IQ?

Andersen Ross/Getty Images

HINT: LOOK IN THE MARGIN FOR **[Q5]**

8.4 Intelligence Controversies

LEARNING OBJECTIVES

Retrieval Practice While reading the upcoming sections, respond to each Learning Objective in your own words.

Review the major controversies surrounding intelligence.

- **Discuss** the relative contributions of nature and nurture to IQ.
- **Describe** how and why groups differ in mental ability tests.
- **Identify** the various theories and controversies over multiple intelligences.

Psychologists have long debated several important questions related to intelligence: Is IQ mostly inherited or is it molded by our environment? Do men and women or racial and ethnic groups differ in mental abilities? If so, how and why? Is intelligence a general ability or a number of specific talents and aptitudes?

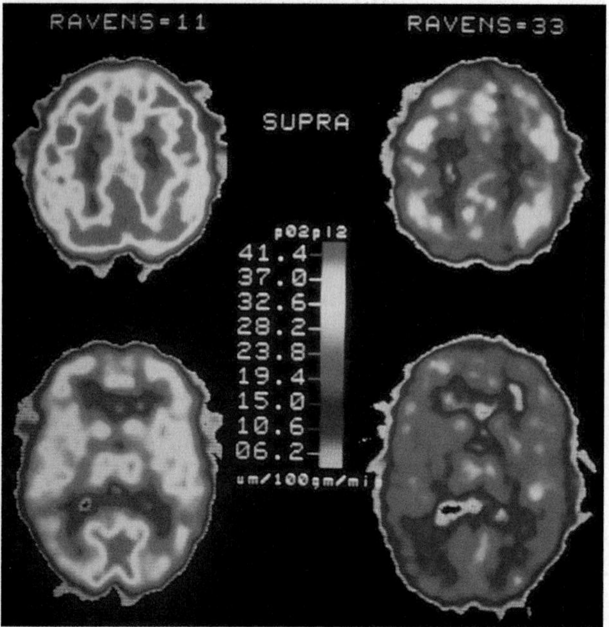

Courtesy Richard J. Haier, University of California-Irvine

FIGURE 8.14 Do intelligent brains work more efficiently? In PET scan images, red and yellow indicate more activity in relevant brain areas. Note how during problem-solving tasks, low-IQ brains (left) show more activity than high-IQ brains (right). This research suggests that lower-IQ brains actually work harder, although less efficiently, than higher-IQ brains.

Nature, Nurture, and IQ

How is brain functioning related to intelligence? What factors—environmental or hereditary—influence an individual's intelligence? These specific questions, and the controversies surrounding them, are discussed in this section.

The Brain's Influence on Intelligence A basic tenet of neuroscience is that all mental activity (including intelligence) results from neural activity in the brain. Most recent research on the biology of intelligence has focused on brain functioning. For example, neuroscientists have found that people who score highest on intelligence tests also respond more quickly on tasks requiring perceptual judgments (Hofman, 2015; Sternberg, 2014, 2015; Wagner et al., 2014).

In addition to a faster response time, research using positron emission tomography (PET) scans to measure brain activity (Chapter 2) suggests that intelligent brains work smarter, or more efficiently, than less-intelligent brains (Jung & Haier, 2007; Neubauer et al., 2004; Posthuma et al., 2001). See **Figure 8.14**.

Does size matter? It makes logical sense that bigger brains would be smarter. In fact, imaging studies have found a significant correlation between brain size (adjusted for body size) and intelligence (Bouchard, 2014; Moller & Erritzoe, 2014). Interestingly, some animals, such as whales and dolphins, do have larger brains than humans. However, our brains are larger relative to our body size. Surprisingly, Albert Einstein's brain was no larger than normal (Witelson et al., 1999). In fact, some of Einstein's brain areas were actually smaller than average, but the area responsible for processing mathematical and spatial information was 15% larger than average.

Genetic and Environmental Influences on Intelligence Similarities in intelligence between family members are due to a combination of hereditary (shared genetic material) and environmental factors (similar living arrangements and experiences). Researchers who are interested in the role of heredity in intelligence often focus on identical (monozygotic) twins because they share 100% of their genetic material, as shown in **Figure 8.15**. For example, the long-running Minnesota Study of Twins, an investigation of identical twins raised in different homes, and reunited only as adults, found that genetic factors appear to play a surprisingly large role in the IQ scores of identical twins (Bouchard, 2014; Rushton & Jensen, 2010).

In contrast, those who emphasize the environmental influences on intelligence would say that these twin study results are not conclusive. Adoption agencies tend to look for similar criteria in their choice of adoptive parents. Therefore, the homes of these "reared apart" twins were actually quite similar. In addition, these twins shared the same 9-month prenatal environment, which might have influenced their brain development and intelligence (Felson, 2014; White et al., 2002).

Additional evidence of the environmental influences on intelligence comes from studies of the multiple effects of abuse and neglect in childhood (see the **Real World Psychology** feature), as well as from

FIGURE 8.15 Genetic and environmental influences on IQ Note the higher correlations between identical twins' IQ test scores compared to correlations between all other pairs. Genes no doubt play a significant role in intelligence, but these effects are difficult to separate from environmental influences. (Based on Bouchard, 2014; Bouchard & McGue, 1981; Plomin & Deary, 2015.)

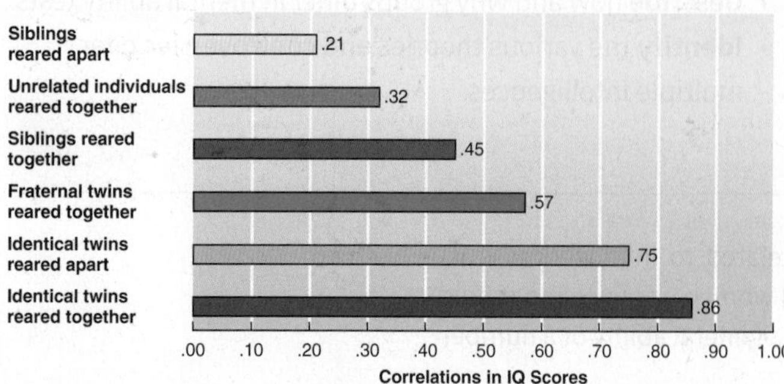

PhotoDisc, Inc./Getty Images

brain scans of children who are seriously neglected (**Figure 8.16**). Likewise, early malnutrition, which affects over 113 million children worldwide, can retard a child's intellectual development, curiosity, and motivation for learning (Peter et al., 2016; Schoenmaker et al., 2015; Venables & Raine, 2016). Interestingly, research has also found a measurable difference in the gray matter volume in the brains of only versus non-only children, which further supports the importance of the family environmental factors (Yang et al., 2016).

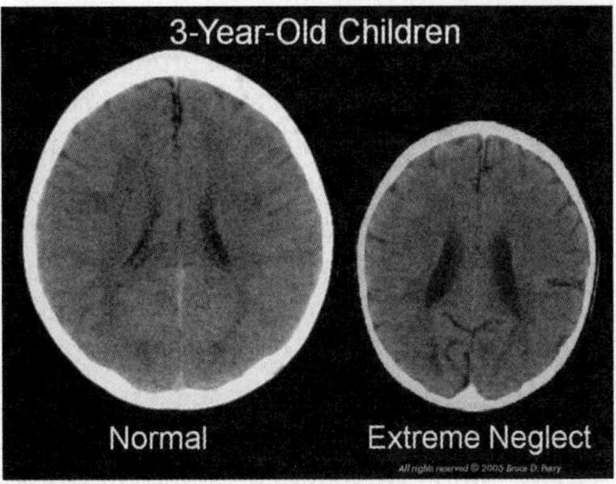
3-Year-Old Children
Normal
Extreme Neglect

FIGURE 8.16 **Neglect and IQ** These images illustrate the negative impact of neglect on the developing brain. The brain on the left is from a normal developing child, whose brain size is in the 50th percentile. The brain on the right is from a child suffering from severe sensory deprivation neglect, whose brain size is in the lowest third percentile.

Source: Photo supplied with kind permission from Springer Science+Business Media: Perry, B.D. Childhood experience and the expression of genetic potential: what childhood neglect tells us about nature and nurture Brain and Mind 3: 79-100, 2002.

Real World **Psychology**—Understanding the World

Multiple Sad Effects of Neglect and Abuse

In addition to permanent brain changes, children who lack reliable care and stable attachment, or who experience deliberate abuse in the first few years of life, show not only lower intelligence but also less empathy for others and a greater vulnerability to later substance abuse and addiction (Luby et al., 2012). In contrast, children who are enrolled in high-quality preschool programs and are regularly read to by their parents show increases in IQ. These studies provide further evidence that the environment, for better or worse, has a major impact (Protzko et al., 2013).

Twin Design/Shutterstock

In short, genetics and environment both play interacting and inseparable roles. Intelligence is like a rubber band. Heredity equips each of us with innate intellectual capabilities (our personal rubber band). But our environment helps deteriorate or stretch this band, which significantly influences whether or not we reach our full intellectual potential.

Group Differences in IQ Scores

As we've just seen, intelligence in general does show a high degree of heritability. However, it's VERY important to recognize that heritability cannot explain *between*-group differences! Note the overall difference between the average height of plants on the left and those on the right in **Figure 8.17**. Just as we cannot say that the difference *between* these two groups of plants is due to heredity, we similarly cannot say that differences in IQ *between* any two groups of people are due to heredity.

Note also the considerable variation in height *within* the group of plants on the left and those *within* the group on the right. Just as some plants are taller than others, there are individuals who score high on IQ tests and others who score low. Always remember that the greatest differences in IQ scores occur when we compare individuals *within* groups—not *between* groups.

What about the widely publicized differences between the sexes, such as those in verbal and math skills? Research using brain scans, autopsies, and volumetric measurements has found several sex differences in the brains of men and women (**Figure 8.18**). For example, two areas in the frontal and temporal lobes, associated with language skills, are generally larger in women than in men. In contrast, a region in the parietal lobes, correlated with manipulating spatial relationships and mathematical abilities, is typically larger in men than in women (Garrett, 2015; Ingalhalikar et al., 2014). **Table 8.6** illustrates the tasks researchers have used to demonstrate these and other sex differences.

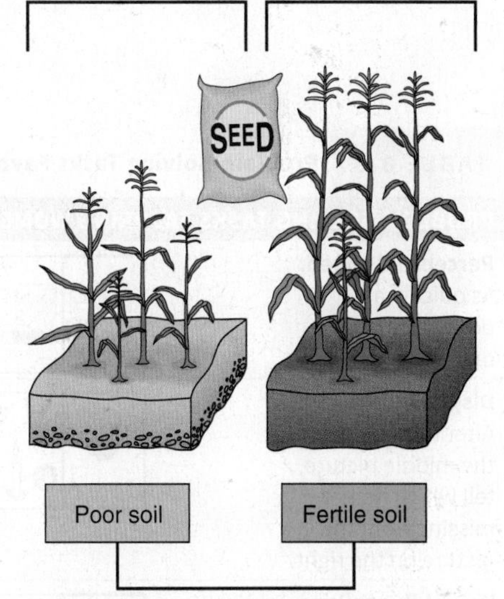
Differences *within* groups are due almost entirely to genetics (the seed).
SEED
Poor soil
Fertile soil
Differences *between* groups are due almost *entirely* to environment (the soil).

FIGURE 8.17 **Genetics versus environment** Note that even when you begin with the same package of seeds (genetic inheritance), the average height of corn plants in the fertile soil will be greater than the average height of corn plants in the poor soil (environmental influences). Therefore, no valid or logical conclusions can be drawn about the overall genetic differences between the two groups of plants because the two environments (soil) are so different. Similar logic must be applied to intelligence scores between groups.

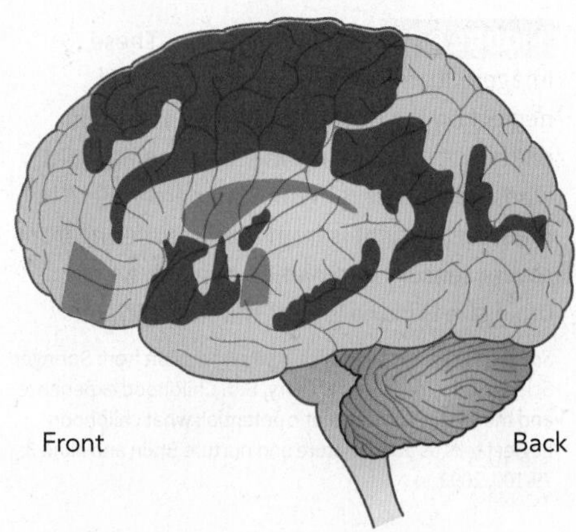

FIGURE 8.18 Brain sex differences Note that the areas in purple are, on average, larger in women, whereas the areas in green are, on average, larger in men.

How do we explain this? Evolutionary psychologies often suggest that sex differences like these may be the product of gradual genetic adaptations (Buss, 2015; Ingalhalikar et al., 2014). In ancient societies, men were most often the "hunters," while women were almost always the "gatherers." Therefore, the male's superiority on many spatial tasks and target-directed motor skills (see again Table 8.6) reportedly have evolved from the adaptive demands of hunting, whereas activities such as food gathering, childrearing, and domestic tool construction and manipulation may have contributed to the female's language superiority and fine motor coordination.

Some critics, however, suggest that evolution progresses much too slowly to account for this type of behavioral adaptation. Furthermore, there is wide cross-cultural variability in gender differences, and explanations of these differences are difficult to test scientifically (Halpern, 2014; Miller & Halpern, 2014; Newcombe, 2010). Other research has found that simply having both women and men play action-packed video games for a few short weeks almost completely removes the previously reported gender role differences in some spatial tasks (Feng et al., 2007).

In addition to possible gender differences in verbal and math skills, there is an ongoing debate in our country over the reported differences in IQ scores between various ethnic groups. Unfortunately, some of the strongest proponents of the "heritability of intelligence" argument seem to ignore the "fertile soil" background of the groups who score highest on IQ tests. As an open-minded, critical thinker, carefully consider these important research findings:

- Environmental and cultural factors may override genetic potential and later affect IQ test scores. Like plants that come from similar seeds, but are placed in poor versus enriched soil, children of color are more likely to grow up in stressful, lower socioeconomic conditions, which may hamper their true intellectual potential. Furthermore, in some ethnic groups

TABLE 8.6 Problem-Solving Tasks Favoring Women and Men

PROBLEM-SOLVING TASKS FAVORING WOMEN		PROBLEM-SOLVING TASK FAVORING MEN	
Perceptual speed: As quickly as possible, identify matching items.		**Spatial tasks:** Mentally rotate the 3-D object to identify its match.	
Displaced objects: After looking at the middle picture, tell which item is missing from the picture on the right.		**Spatial tasks:** Mentally manipulate the folded paper to tell where the holes will falls when it is unfolded.	
Verbal fluency: List words that begin with the same letter.	B - - - Bat, big, bike, bang, bark, bank, bring, brand, broom, bright, brook, bug, buddy, bunk	**Target-directed motor skills:** Hit the bull's eye.	
Precision manual tasks: Place the pegs in the holes as quickly as possible.		**Disembedding tests:** Find the simple shape on the left in the more complex figures.	
Mathematical calculation: Compute the answer.	72 $6\ (18+4)-78+{}^{36}/_{2}$	**Mathematical reasoning:** What is the answer?	$5\ {}^{1}/_{2}$ If you bicycle 24 miles a day, how many days will it take to travel 132 miles?

Digital Vision/Getty Images

FIGURE 8.21 **How do we develop emotional intelligence?** The mother in this photo appears to be empathizing with her young daughter and helping her to recognize and manage her own emotions. According to Goleman, this type of modeling and instruction is vital to the development of emotional intelligence.

Think Critically

1. Should preschools and elementary schools be required to teach children emotional intelligence? Why or why not?
2. What is the role of emotional intelligence (EI) in business? Should it be a factor in hiring and promotions? What might be the advantages and drawbacks if it did?

Psychology and You—Understanding Yourself

Optimizing Your Well-Being

© Yuri/iStockphoto

In Chapter 1, we introduced you to the field of *positive psychology*—the scientific study of optimal human functioning. One of the key researchers in this area, Martin Seligman, believes optimal well-being results from five core factors: *Positive emotion*, *Engagement*, *Relationships*, *Meaning*, and *Accomplishment* (PERMA). To learn more about positive psychology and these five factors, while also gaining invaluable personal insights, visit Dr. Seligman's home page. While there, be sure to complete one or more of the free, scientifically validated surveys: www.authentichappiness.sas.upenn.edu.

Retrieval Practice 8.4 | Intelligence Controversies

SELF-TEST Completing this self-test, and then checking your answers by clicking on the answer button or by looking in Appendix B, will provide immediate feedback and helpful practice for exams.

1. Does brain size matter?
   - **a.** Yes; some animals, such as whales and dolphins, have larger brains than humans, but our brains are larger relative to our body size.
   - **b.** Yes; brain-imaging studies have found a significant correlation between brain size (adjusted for body size) and intelligence.
   - **c.** No; men have larger brains but both sexes have similar IQs.
   - **d.** Yes, all of these options are true.
2. Which of the following persons would be most likely to have similar IQ test scores?
   - **a.** identical twins raised apart
   - **b.** identical twins raised together
   - **c.** fraternal twins raised apart
   - **d.** brothers and sisters from the same parents
3. By examining identical twins raised in different homes and reunited only as adults, _____ found that genetic factors appear to play a surprisingly large role in the IQ scores of identical twins.
   - **a.** the Minnesota Study of Twins
   - **b.** Lewis Terman's "Termites" research
   - **c.** the Stanford-Binet Intelligence Studies
   - **d.** David Wechsler's research
4. Howard Gardner proposed a theory of _____.
   - **a.** language development
   - **b.** fluid and crystallized intelligence
   - **c.** culture specificity intelligence
   - **d.** multiple intelligences
5. Awareness of a negative stereotype that affects oneself and may lead to impairment in performance is known as _____.
   - **a.** Flynn effect
   - **b.** "Obama effect"
   - **c.** bell curve
   - **d.** stereotype threat

Think Critically

1. Do you believe IQ tests are biased against certain groups? Why or why not?
2. How would someone with exceptionally low or high emotional intelligence behave?

Real World Psychology

Will watching TV dramas increase your emotional intelligence?

Moviestore collection Ltd/ Alamy Stock Photo

HINT: LOOK IN THE MARGIN FOR **[Q6]**

Summary

8.1 Thinking 205

- Thinking is a central aspect of **cognition**. Thought processes are distributed throughout the brain in neural networks. Mental images and **concepts** aid our thought processes. There are three major building blocks for concepts—**prototypes**, artificial concepts, and hierarchies.
- **Problem solving** usually has three steps: *preparation*, *production*, and *evaluation*. **Algorithms** are logical step-by-step procedures that eventually solve the problem. **Heuristics** are a cognitive strategy, or "rule of thumb," for problem solving.
- Barriers to problem solving include **mental set, functional fixedness, availability heuristic, representativeness heuristic**, and **confirmation bias**.
- **Creativity** is the ability to produce original, appropriate, and valued outcomes in a novel way. Creative thinking involves *originality, fluency*, and *flexibility.* Tests of creativity usually focus on **divergent thinking**, which involves generating as many alternatives or ideas as possible. In contrast, **convergent thinking**—or conventional thinking—works toward a single correct answer.

8.2 Language 213

- **Language** supports thinking and enables us to communicate. To produce language, we use **phonemes, morphemes**, and **grammar** (syntax and semantics). Several different parts of our brains are involved in producing and listening to language.
- According to Whorf's *linguistic relativity hypothesis*, language determines thought. Generally, this hypothesis is not supported, but it's clear that language does strongly influence thought.
- Children communicate nonverbally from birth. Their language development proceeds in stages: *prelinguistic*, which includes crying, cooing, and babbling, and *linguistic*, which includes single utterances, telegraphic speech, and acquisition of the basic rules of grammar.
- According to nativists, like Chomsky, humans are "prewired" with a **language acquisition device (LAD)** that enables language development, with minimal environmental input. Nurturists hold that children learn language through rewards, punishments, and imitation. Most psychologists hold an intermediate, interactionist view.
- Research with chimpanzees, gorillas, and dolphins suggests that these animals can learn and use basic rules of language. However, critics suggest nonhuman animal language is less complex, less creative, and not as rule laden as human language.

8.3 Intelligence 219

- There is considerable debate over the meaning of **intelligence**. But it's commonly defined by psychologists as the global capacity to think rationally, act purposefully, profit from experience, and deal effectively with the environment.
- Spearman proposed that intelligence is a single factor, which he termed **general intelligence (g)**. Thurstone and Guilford argued that intelligence included numerous distinct abilities. Cattell proposed two subtypes of *g*: **fluid intelligence (gf)** and **crystallized intelligence (gc)**.
- Early intelligence tests computed a person's **mental age (MA)** to arrive at an **intelligence quotient (IQ)**. Today, two of the most widely used intelligence tests are the *Stanford-Binet Intelligence Scale* and the *Wechsler Adult Intelligence Scale (WAIS)*. Intelligence tests commonly compare the performance of an individual with other individuals of the same age. The distribution of these test scores typically result in a **normal distribution** in a symmetrical, bell-shaped curve.
- To be scientifically acceptable, all psychological tests must fulfill three basic requirements: **standardization, reliability**, and **validity**.
- Intelligence tests provide one of the major criteria for assessing **intellectual disability** and **mental giftedness**, both of which exist on a continuum. Studies of people who are intellectually gifted found that they had more intellectual opportunities and tended to excel professionally. However, a high IQ does not guarantee success in every endeavor.

8.4 Intelligence Controversies 223

- Most recent research suggests that both nature and nurture are interacting influences on intelligence. Research on the biology of intelligence has focused on brain functioning, not size, and it indicates that intelligent people's brains respond especially quickly and efficiently.
- In answer to the questions of group differences and how gender and/or ethnicity affect IQ, heredity and the environment are always interacting, inseparable factors.
- Rather than a single *g* factor of intelligence, many contemporary cognitive theorists, including Gardner and Sternberg, believe that intelligence is a collection of many separate specific abilities. Goleman believes that **emotional intelligence (EI)**, the ability to empathize and manage our emotions and relationships, is just as important as any other kind of intelligence.

Applying Real World Psychology

We began this chapter with six intriguing Real World Psychology questions, and you were asked to revisit these questions at the end of each section. Questions like these have an important and lasting impact on all of our lives. See if you can answer these additional critical thinking questions related to real world examples.

T.K. Wanstal/The Image Works

1. Jerry Levy and Mark Newman, the two men shown in this photo, are identical twins who were separated at birth and first met as adults at a firefighter's convention. Research shows that IQ tends to be highly correlated for identical twins, but do you believe identical twins share a special connectedness? Why or why not?
2. Does the brothers' choosing the same uncommon profession seem like a case of special "twin-telepathy"? If so, how might *confirmation bias* contribute to the perception of twin-telepathy?
3. Would you prefer to be high in emotional intelligence or high in musical intelligence? Why?
4. How might being bilingual or multilingual be more of an asset in business than having a high IQ?
5. Which of the barriers to problem solving described in this chapter are the biggest problems for you? How will you work to overcome them?

Key Terms

Retrieval Practice Write your own definition for each term before turning back to the referenced page to check your answer.

Solutions

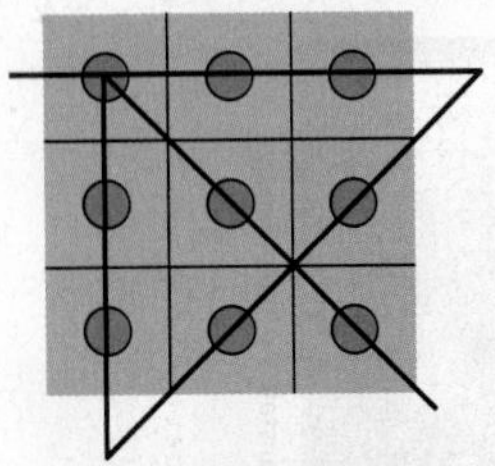

Nine-dot problem solution

People find this puzzle difficult because they see the arrangement of dots as a square—a mental set that limits possible solutions.

Candle problem solution

Use the tacks to mount the matchbox tray to the wall. Light the candle and use some melted wax to mount the candle to the matchbox.

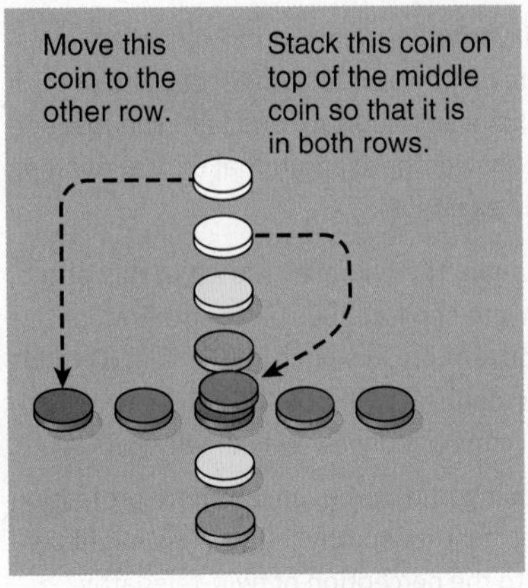
Move this coin to the other row.
Stack this coin on top of the middle coin so that it is in both rows.

Coin problem solution

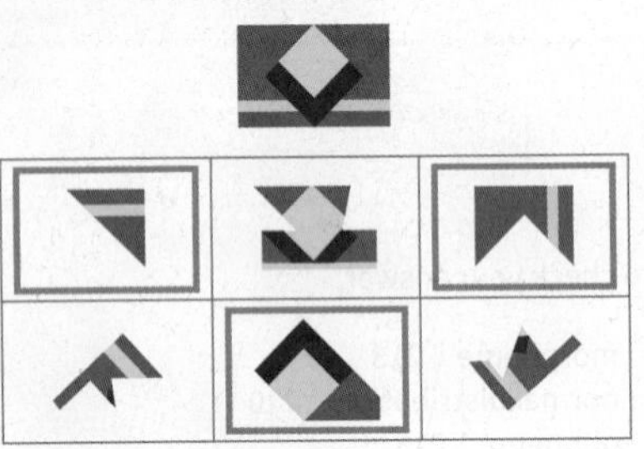

Ⓐ "Which three pieces go together to make this puzzle?"

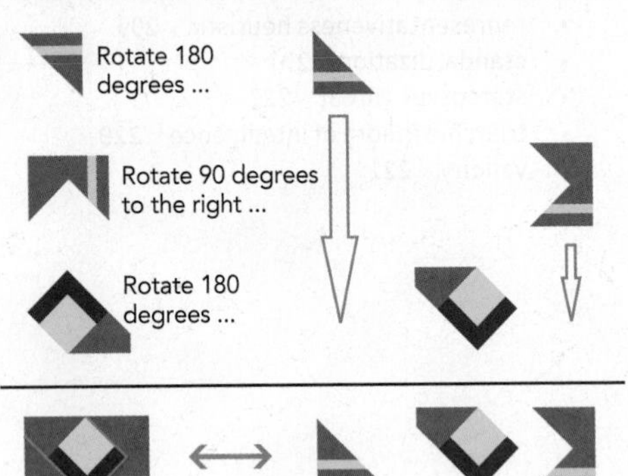
Rotate 180 degrees ...
Rotate 90 degrees to the right ...
Rotate 180 degrees ...

Wechsler Adult Intelligence Scale solution

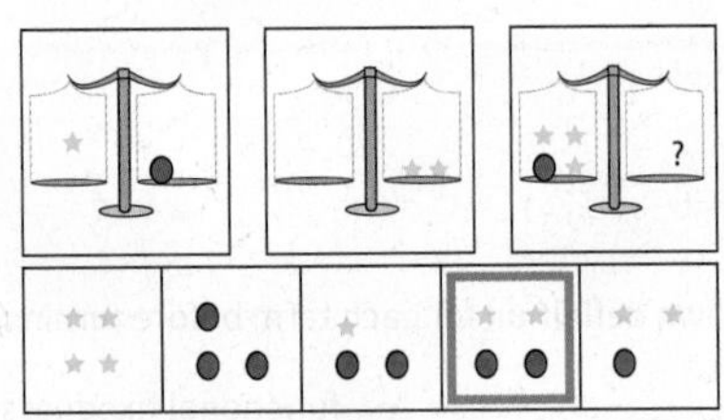

Ⓑ "Which one of these works to balance the scale?"

From the middle image, we deduce an empty scale would be out of balance, since we need two stars added to the right just to be in balance.

From the first image, since we know that the scale is two stars heavy on the left, if adding one star to the already heavier left side balances with one ball, a ball must equal three stars!

The final image shows three stars and one ball on the left. To balance on the right, we match what is shown on the left AND ADD two stars since we know the scale, by itself, is two stars heavy on the left.

Therefore we need one ball and five stars to balance. But that is NOT one of the answers! But we know one ball equals three stars. Looking at the possible answers, we see that two stars and two balls (1+1+3+3=8 stars) is the same as one ball and five stars (3+1+1+1+1+1=8 stars)—and that is the answer!

© jfairone/iStockphoto

CHAPTER **9**

Life Span Development

© Pojoslaw/Shutterstock

Real World **Psychology**

Things you'll learn in Chapter 9

[Q1] Why are young people more supportive of gay marriage than older adults?

[Q2] Does prenatal exposure to smoke increase the risk of obesity later in life?

[Q3] Why do teenagers sleep so much?

[Q4] Do babies learn faster when they're sitting up than when they're lying down?

[Q5] Does the taking and posting of self-portraits ("selfies") increase narcissism?

[Q6] Do today's college students want women to propose marriage?

Throughout the chapter, margin icons for Q1–Q6 indicate where the text addresses these questions.

CHAPTER OUTLINE

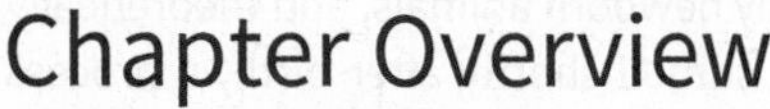

Chapter Overview

Are you one of the lucky ones who grew up with loving parents who documented every stage of your development with photos, videos, and/or journals—starting with your birth, first smile, first day of school, and all the way to your high school graduation? If so, you have a head start on the material in this chapter. As you might expect, studying development across the entire life span is a monumental task, so we've organized this chapter into three major sections—*physical*, *cognitive*, and *social-emotional development*. Before we begin, we need to briefly examine the research issues and methods psychologists use to study development.

9.1 Studying Development

LEARNING OBJECTIVES

Retrieval Practice While reading the upcoming sections, respond to each Learning Objective in your own words.

Review developmental psychology's theoretical issues and key research approaches.

- **Define** developmental psychology.
- **Discuss** the three key theoretical issues in developmental psychology.
- **Contrast** the cross-sectional research design with the longitudinal research design.

Developmental psychology The study of age-related behavior and mental processes from conception to death.

Critical period A specific time during which an organism must experience certain stimuli in order to develop properly in the future.

Imprinting The process by which attachments are formed during critical periods in early life.

REUTERS/Roger Schneider/Corbis

FIGURE 9.1 Critical periods and imprinting Some animals, like these baby cranes, simply attach to, or imprint on, the first large, moving object they see—in this case, French pilot Christian Moullec, who raised the cranes from birth.

Just as some parents carefully document their child's progress throughout his or her life, the field of **developmental psychology** studies growth and change throughout the eight major stages of life—from conception to death, or "womb to tomb" (**Table 9.1**). These studies have led to three key theoretical issues.

Theoretical Issues

Almost every area of research in human development frames questions around three major issues:

1. **Nature or nurture?** How do both genetics (nature) and life experiences (nurture) influence development? According to the *nature position*, development is largely governed by automatic, genetically predetermined signals in a process known as *maturation*. Just as a flower unfolds in accord with its genetic blueprint, humans crawl before we walk, and walk before we run.

   In addition, naturists believe there are **critical periods**, or windows of opportunity, that occur early in life when exposure to certain stimuli or experiences is necessary for proper development. For example, many newborn animals, and theoretically humans, form rigid attachments to particular stimuli shortly after birth, a process called **imprinting** (**Figure 9.1**).

   Human children may also have critical periods for normal development. For example, when doctors operate on infants who are born with *cataracts*, a condition in which the eye's lens is cloudy and distorts vision, they're able to see much better than if they're operated on after the age of 8. In addition, research has shown that appropriate social interaction with adults in the first few weeks of life is essential for creating normal cognitive and social development (Berger, 2015; Harker et al., 2016; Mermelshtine & Barnes, 2016). Sadly, a study of both Israeli and Palestinian children found that exposure to serious military/political violence at age 8 is associated with more aggressive behavior later

TABLE 9.1 Life Span Development

STAGE	APPROXIMATE AGE
Prenatal	Conception to birth
Infancy	Birth to 18 months
Early childhood	18 months to 6 years
Middle childhood	6 to 12 years
Adolescence	12 to 20 years
Young adulthood	20 to 45 years
Middle adulthood	45 to 60 years
Late adulthood	60 years to death

on, whereas witnessing such violence at later ages doesn't lead to such aggression (Boxer et al., 2013). These and other similar studies provide further evidence for critical periods—at least in the early years (see **PsychScience**).

2. **Stages or continuity?** Some developmental psychologists suggest that development generally occurs in *stages* that are discrete and qualitatively different from one to another, whereas others believe it follows a *continuous pattern*, with gradual, but steady and quantitative (measurable) changes (**Figure 9.2**).
3. **Stability or change?** Which of our traits are stable and present throughout our life span, and what aspects will change? Psychologists who emphasize *stability* hold that measurements of personality taken during childhood are important predictors of adult personality; those who emphasize *change* disagree.

FIGURE 9.2 **Stages versus continuity in development** There is an ongoing debate about whether development is better characterized by discrete stages or by gradual, continuous development.

a. Stage theorists think development results from discrete, qualitative changes.

b. Continuity theorists believe development results from gradual, quantitative (incremental) changes.

Which of these positions is most correct? Psychologists generally do not take a hard line either way. Rather, they prefer an interactionist perspective and/or the biopsychosocial model. For instance, in the nature-versus-nurture debate, psychologists agree that development emerges from unique genetic predispositions *and* environmental experiences (Auger, 2016; Cavanaugh & Blanchard-Fields, 2015; Gallagher & Jones, 2016).

PS PsychScience

Deprivation and Development

What happens if a child is deprived of appropriate stimulation during a critical period of development? Consider the story of Genie, the so-called "wild child." From the time she was 20 months old until authorities rescued her at age 13, Genie was locked alone in a tiny, windowless room. By day, she sat naked and tied to a child's toilet with nothing to do and no one to talk to. At night, she was immobilized in a kind of straitjacket and "caged" in a covered crib. Genie's abusive father forbade anyone to speak to her for those 13 years. If Genie made noise, her father beat her while he barked and growled like a dog.

Genie's tale is a heartbreaking account of the lasting scars from a disastrous childhood. In the years after her rescue, Genie spent thousands of hours receiving special training, and by age 19 she could use public transportation and was adapting well to special classes at school. Genie was far from normal, however. Her intelligence scores were still close to the cutoff for intellectual disability. And although linguists and psychologists worked with her for many years, she was never able to master grammatical structure, and was limited to sentences like "Genie go" (Rymer, 1993).

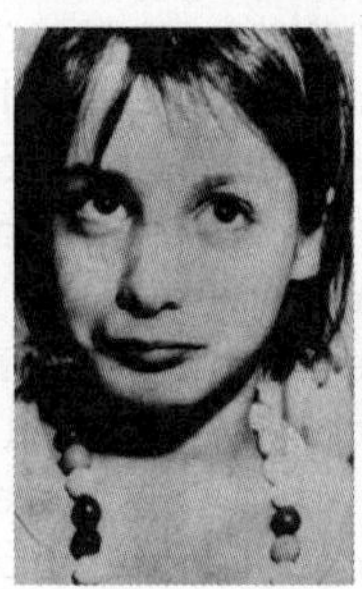

AP/Wide World Photos

These findings suggest that because of her extreme childhood isolation and abuse, Genie, like other seriously neglected or environmentally isolated children, missed a necessary critical period for language development (Curtiss, 1977; Raaska et al., 2013; Sylvestre & Mérette, 2010). To make matters worse, she was also subjected to a series of foster home placements, some of which were emotionally and physically abusive. According to the latest information, Genie now lives in a privately run facility for mentally underdeveloped adults (James, 2008).

Research Challenge

1. Based on the information provided, did this study (Rymer, 1993) use descriptive, correlational, and/or experimental research?
2. If you chose:
   - *descriptive research*, is this a naturalistic observation, survey/interview, case study, and/or archival research?
   - *correlational research*, is this a positive, negative, or zero correlation?
   - *experimental research*, label the IV, DV, experimental group(s), and control group.
   - both *descriptive* and *correlational*, answer the corresponding questions for both.

Check your answers by clicking on the answer button or by looking in Appendix B.

Note: The information provided in this study is admittedly limited, but the level of detail is similar to what is presented in most textbooks and public reports of research findings. Answering these questions, and then comparing your answers to those provided, will help you become a better critical thinker and consumer of scientific research.

FIGURE 9.3 Cross-sectional versus longitudinal research To study development, psychologists may use a cross-sectional research design, a longitudinal research design, or both.

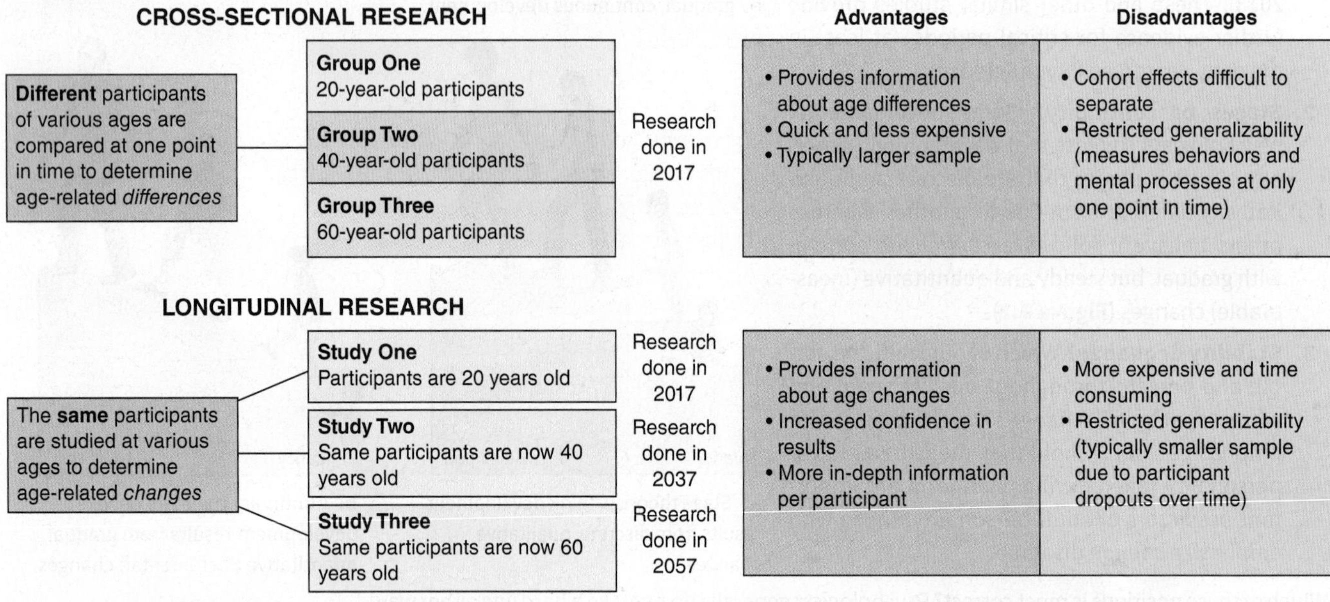

Research Approaches

Cross-sectional design In developmental psychology, a research technique that measures individuals of various ages at one point in time and provides information about age differences.

Longitudinal design In developmental psychology, a research design that measures individuals over an extended period and gives information about age changes.

To answer these three controversies and other questions, developmental psychologists typically use all the research methods discussed in Chapter 1. To study the entire human life span, they also need two additional techniques—*cross-sectional* and *longitudinal* (**Figure 9.3**).

The **cross-sectional design** measures individuals of various ages at a single point in time to provide information about age differences. For example, one cross-sectional study studied women in three different age groups (ages 22–34, 35–49, and 50–65) to examine whether body weight dissatisfaction changes with age (Siegel, 2010). Unfortunately, female body dissatisfaction appears to be quite stable—and relatively high—across the life span.

In contrast, a **longitudinal design** takes repeated measures of one person or a group of same-aged people over a long period of time to see how the individual or the group changes over time. For example, a group of developmental researchers wondered if peer ratings of personality taken during childhood might be better predictors of later adult personality than self-ratings (Martin-Storey et al., 2012). They first asked grade school children in 1976–1978 to rate themselves and their peers on several personality factors, such as likeability, aggression, and social withdrawal. In 1999-2003, the researchers returned and asked the same participants, now in mid-adulthood, to complete a second series of personality tests. As hypothesized, the peer ratings were better than self-ratings in predicting adult personality. Does this finding surprise you? If so, try contacting some of your childhood peers and then compare notes on how you remember one another's personality as children and now as adults.

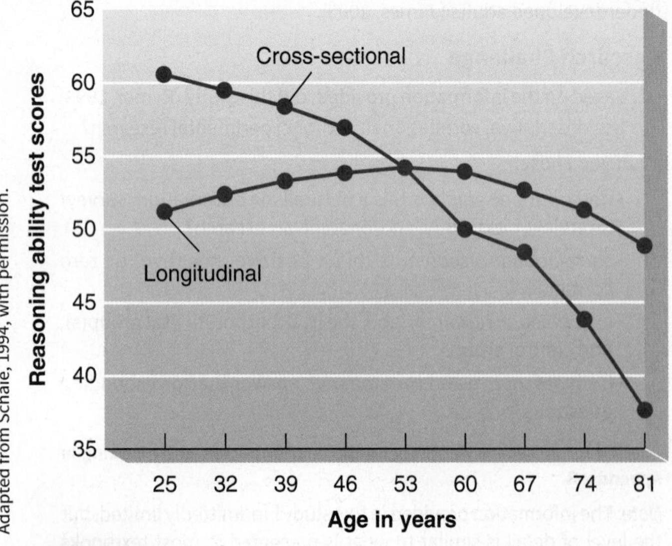

FIGURE 9.4 Which results are true? Cross-sectional studies have shown that reasoning and intelligence reach their peak in early adulthood and then gradually decline. In contrast, longitudinal studies have found that a marked decline does not begin until about age 60.

Now that you have a better idea of these two types of research, if you were a developmental psychologist interested in studying intelligence in adults, which design would you choose—cross-sectional or longitudinal? Before you decide, note the different research results shown in **Figure 9.4**.

Why do the two methods show such different results? Cross-sectional studies sometimes confuse genuine age differences with *cohort effects*—differences that result from specific histories of the age group studied. As shown in the top line in Figure 9.4, the 81-year-olds measured by the cross-sectional design have dramatically lower scores than the 25-year-olds. But is this due to aging, or perhaps to broad environmental differences, such as less formal education or poorer nutrition?

Paul Faith/Getty Images

A prime example of possible environmental effects on cross-sectional studies is the recent survey of attitudes towards gay marriage that found young people are much more in favor of gay marriage than older people (Pew Research Center, 2016). So, does this mean that people
[Q1] grow more opposed to gay marriage as they age? Probably not. These differences are most likely a reflection of cohort and generational effects. Young people today are generally more liberal and positive toward different sexual orientations, and therefore more likely to support gay marriage (see the photo). They'll also probably maintain their current attitudes as they age.

The key thing to remember is that because the different age groups, called *cohorts*, grew up in different historical periods, the results may not apply to people growing up at other times. With the cross-sectional design, age effects and cohort effects are sometimes inextricably tangled. (As a critical thinker, can you see how *cohort effects* are a unique research problem for cross-cultural studies, just as the *third-variable problem* poses a unique threat to correlational studies—discussed in Chapter 1?)

Longitudinal studies have their own share of limits and disadvantages. They are expensive in terms of time and money, and it is difficult for us to generalize their results. Because participants often drop out or move away during the extended test period, the experimenter may end up with a self-selected sample that differs from the general population in important ways. Each method of research has strengths and weaknesses (as you recall from the right-hand side of Figure 9.3). Keep these differences in mind when you read the findings of developmental research.

Before we go on, it's important to point out that modern researchers sometimes combine both cross-sectional and longitudinal designs into one study. For example, in Chapter 1, we discussed a study that examined whether well-being decreases with age (Sutin et al., 2013). When these researchers examined their combined cross-sectional and longitudinal data from two independent samples taken over 30 years, they initially found that well-being *declined* with age. However, when they then controlled for the fact that older cohorts started out with lower levels of well-being, they found that all the cohorts *increased* rather than decreased in well-being with age. The reversal in findings was explained by the fact that the older group of people had experienced instances of major turmoil in their younger years, including America's Great Depression during the 1930s. This means that this group started out with lower levels of well-being. Sadly, they apparently maintained these attitudes into their later years, compared to those who grew up during more prosperous times.

Why is this combination of two research designs important? It offers a more accurate and positive view of well-being in old age than what was indicated in either the cross-sectional design or the longitudinal design. It also suggests some troubling possibilities for today's young adults who are entering a stagnant workforce and high unemployment. As the study's authors say, this "economic turmoil may impede [their] psychological, as well as financial, growth even decades after times get better" (Sutin et al., 2013, p. 384). If you're one of these young adults, you'll be happy to hear that there's some very encouraging research showing that individuals who enter their teens and early 20s during a recession are less narcissistic than those who come of age in more prosperous times (Bianchi, 2014, 2015). In fact, CEOs who were in their teens and early 20s during bad economic times later paid themselves less compared to other top executives. The following **Psychology and You** offers even more good news for all ages.

Psychology and You—Understanding Yourself

Want to be Happier? Grow Older!

As just discussed here and in Chapters 1 and 7, researchers have found an increase in happiness and overall well-being as we grow older (Kern et al., 2014; Riediger & Luong, 2016; Sutin et al., 2013). Why? One interesting possibility comes from research showing that older adults tend to prefer and pay more sustained attention to positive over negative information (Carstensen, 1993, 2006; Livingstone & Isaacowitz, 2016; Reed et al., 2014). Further research finds that this *age-related positivity effect* may even increase immune functioning, overall healthy aging, and life satisfaction (Kalokerinos et al., 2014; Mikels & Shuster, 2016).

Interestingly, younger people tend to shown an opposite approach—preferring negative over positive information and events. Can you see how this might help explain why the college years can feel so painful and troublesome in your 20s, while in later years they might be remembered as "the best years of your life?" It appears that older adults have developed greater emotional regulation, and that they deliberately focus their attention and memory in a positive direction.

How can we use this information to improve our life regardless of age? In addition to deliberately focusing on positive information, research shows that practicing *gratitude exercises* can increase our well-being, happiness, and life satisfaction (Chaves et al., 2016; Israel-Cohen et al., 2015; Watkins et al., 2015). Simple examples of these exercises include creating a list of things we're grateful for, keeping a daily gratitude list of the top three things that we're grateful for, and writing letters to and/or visiting people who have had a positive impact on our lives.

Westend61/Getty Images

Retrieval Practice 9.1 | Studying Development

SELF-TEST Completing this self-test, and then checking your answers by clicking on the answer button or by looking in Appendix B, will provide immediate feedback and helpful practice for exams.

1. _____ studies age-related changes in behavior and mental processes from conception to death.
   a. Thanatology
   b. Teratogenology
   c. Human development
   d. Developmental psychology
2. _____ is governed by automatic, genetically predetermined signals.
   a. The cohort effect
   b. Secondary aging
   c. Thanatology
   d. Maturation
3. A specific time during which an organism must experience certain stimuli in order to develop properly in the future is known as _____.
   a. the cohort years
   b. a critical period
   c. the thanatology phase
   d. maturation
4. What three major questions are studied in developmental psychology?
   a. nature versus nurture, stages versus continuity, and stability versus change
   b. nature versus nurture, "chunking" versus continuity, and instability versus change
   c. nature versus nurture, stages versus continuity, and stagnation versus instability
   d. none of these options
5. _____ studies are the most time-efficient method, whereas _____ studies provide the most in-depth information per participant.
   a. Latitudinal; longitudinal
   b. Neo-gerontology; longitudinal
   c. Cross-sectional; longitudinal
   d. Class-racial; longitudinal

Think Critically

1. Which of the three important debates or questions in developmental psychology do you find most valuable? Why?
2. Based on what you have learned about critical periods, can you think of a circumstance in your own development, or that of your friends, when a critical period might have been disrupted or lost?

Real World Psychology

Why are young people more supportive of gay marriage than older adults?

Paul Faith/Getty Images

HINT: LOOK IN THE MARGIN FOR **[Q1]**

9.2 Physical Development

LEARNING OBJECTIVES

Retrieval Practice While reading the upcoming sections, respond to each Learning Objective in your own words.

Summarize the major physical changes that occur throughout our life span.

- **Discuss** how genetic material passes from one generation to the next.
- **Identify** the three phases of prenatal physical development.
- **Summarize** physical development during early childhood.
- **Describe** the physical changes that occur during adolescence and adulthood.

After studying the photos of your two authors as they've aged over the life span (**Figure 9.5**), or after reviewing your own similar photos, you may be amused and surprised by all the dramatic changes in physical appearance. But have you stopped to appreciate the incredible underlying process that

FIGURE 9.5 Changes in physical development over the life span As this series of photos of your two textbook authors show, physical changes occur throughout our lives. Our cognitive, social, and emotional processes, as well as our personalities also are continually changing, but the changes aren't as visible. (The top row is Catherine Sanderson at ages 1, 5, 10, 30. The bottom row is Karen Huffman at ages 1, 4, 10, 30 and 60.)

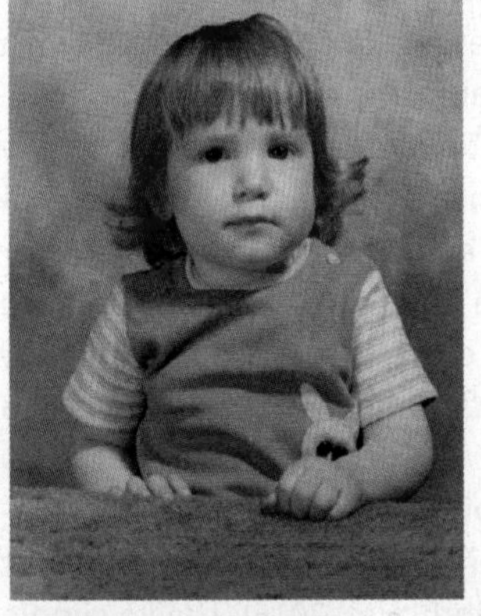

Courtesy of Catherine Sanderson

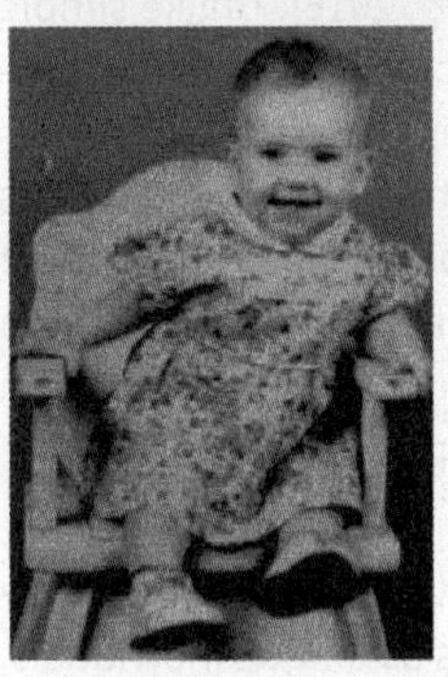

Courtesy of Karen Huffman

transforms all of us from birth to death? In this section, we will explore the fascinating processes of physical development from conception through childhood, adolescence, and adulthood.

Prenatal Development

At the moment of your conception, your biological mother and father each contributed 23 **chromosomes**, which are threadlike, linear strands of **DNA** (deoxyribonucleic acid) encoded with their **genes** (**Figure 9.6**). Interestingly, DNA of all humans (except identical twins) has unique, distinguishing features, much like the details on our fingerprints. This uniqueness is commonly used in forensics to exclude or identify criminal suspects. In addition, DNA analysis is often used for genetic testing during prenatal development to identify existing or potential future disorders.

Chromosome A threadlike molecule of DNA (deoxyribonucleic acid) that carries genetic information.

DNA The main constituent of chromosomes found in all living organisms, which transmits hereditary characteristics from parents to children; short for *deoxyribonucleic acid*.

Gene A segment of DNA (deoxyribonucleic acid) that occupies a specific place on a particular chromosome, and carries the code for hereditary transmission.

FIGURE 9.6 Conception and your hereditary code

A Before Conception Millions of sperm are released when a man ejaculates into a woman's vagina, but only a few hundred sperm survive the arduous trip up to the egg.

B Conception Although a joint effort is required to break through the outer coating, only one sperm will actually fertilize the egg. At the moment of conception, a father's sperm and a mother's egg each contribute 23 chromosomes, for a total of 46.

C Cell Nucleus Each cell in the human body (except red blood cells) contains a nucleus.

D Chromosomes Each cell nucleus contains 46 chromosomes, which are threadlike molecules of DNA (deoxyribonucleic acid).

E DNA and Genes Each DNA molecule contains thousands of genes, which are the most basic units of heredity.

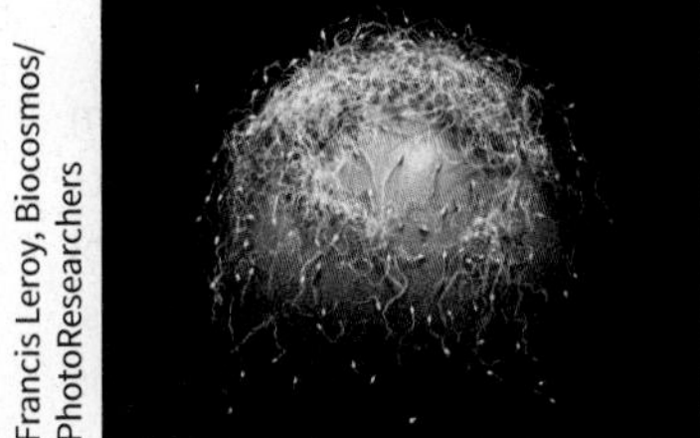

Francis Leroy, Biocosmos/PhotoResearchers

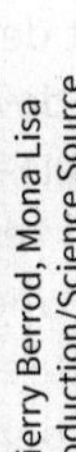

Thierry Berrod, Mona Lisa Production/Science Source

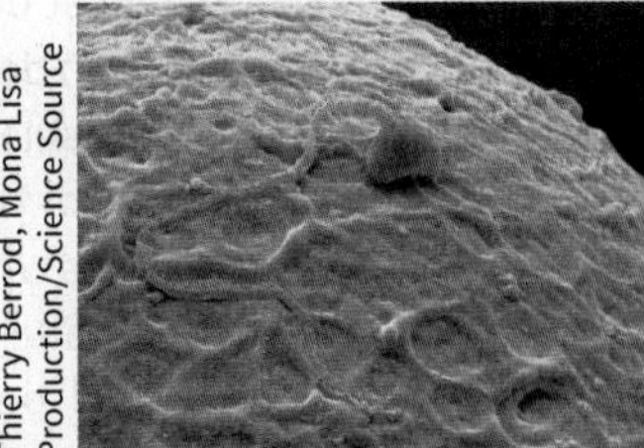

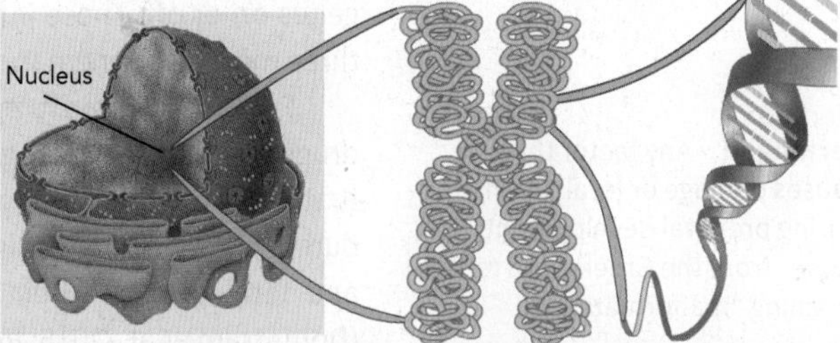

Note that *genes* are the basic building blocks of our entire biological inheritance (Garrett, 2015; Scherman, 2014). Each of our human characteristics and behaviors is related to the presence or absence of particular genes that control the transmission of traits. In some traits, such as blood type, a single pair of genes (one from each parent) determines what characteristics we will possess. When two genes for a given trait conflict, the outcome depends on whether the gene is *dominant* or *recessive*. A dominant gene reveals its trait whenever the gene is present. In contrast, the gene for a recessive trait is normally expressed only if the other gene in the pair is also recessive.

Unfortunately, there are numerous myths and misconceptions about traits supposedly genetically *determined* by dominant genes. For example, we once assumed that characteristics such as eye color, hair color, and height were the result of either one dominant gene, or two paired recessive genes. But modern geneticists now believe that these characteristics are *polygenic*, meaning they are controlled by multiple genes. One of the major goals of the new field of **behavioral genetics**, which studies the interplay of heredity and the environment, is to identify and study these polygenic traits.

Behavioral genetics The study of the relative effects of heredity and the environment on behavior and mental processes.

Epigenetics The study of how non-genetic factors, such as age, environment, lifestyle, or disease, affect how (and if) genes are expressed; "epi" means "above" or "outside of."

Another new and related field of research, known as **epigenetics**, studies how non-genetic factors can dramatically affect how (and if) inherited genes are expressed throughout our lives (Brody et al., 2016; Iakoubov et al., 2015; Wallack & Thornburg, 2016). Unlike simple genetic transmission, which is based on changes in the DNA sequence, changes in gene expression can have other causes, such as age, environment, lifestyle, or disease. (The term "epi" means "above" or "outside of.") In other words, nurture can shape nature! Epigenetic factors can switch genes "ON" or "OFF." For example, epigenetic factors like malnutrition or childhood abuse can prevent a child from reaching his or her full potential genetic height or maximum genetic intelligence (Denholm et al., 2013; Venable & Raine, 2016). The good news is that with environmental changes even identical twins are not destined to develop the same diseases.

Three Stages of Prenatal Development

Now that we've discussed the general principles of how our genes and our environment interact to form us as unique individuals, let's go back to the moment of your conception. At that point in time, you were a single cell barely 1/175 of an inch in diameter—smaller than the period at the end of this sentence. This new cell, called a *zygote*, then began a process of rapid cell division that resulted in a multimillion-celled infant (you) some nine months later.

Germinal period The first stage of prenatal development, beginning with ovulation and followed by conception and implantation in the uterus; the first two weeks of pregnancy.

Embryonic period The second stage of prenatal development, which begins after uterine implantation and lasts through the eighth week.

Fetal period The third, and final, stage of prenatal development (eight weeks to birth).

The vast changes that occur during the nine months of a full-term pregnancy are usually divided into three stages: the **germinal period**, **embryonic period**, and **fetal period** (**Process Diagram 9.1**). Prenatal growth and growth during the first few years after birth are both *proximodistal* (near to far), which means that the innermost parts of the body develop before the outermost parts. Thus, a fetus's arms develop before its hands and fingers. Development at this stage also proceeds *cephalocaudally* (head to tail)—a fetus's head is disproportionately large compared with the lower part of its body. Can you see how these two terms—proximodistal and cephalocaudal—help explain why an infant can lift its head before it can lift its arms and lift its arms before lifting its legs?

Hazards to Prenatal Development

As you recall, human development begins with the genes we inherit from our biological parents, and epigenetic factors, like age, lifestyle, and diseases, can dramatically affect how (and if) these inherited genes are expressed. For example, during pregnancy the *placenta* connects the fetus to the mother's uterus and serves as the link for delivery of food and excretion of wastes. Moreover, it screens out some, but not all, harmful substances. As you can see in **Table 9.2**, environmental hazards such as X-rays and toxic waste, drugs, and diseases can still cross the placental barrier and have an *epigenetic effect*—meaning they leave a chemical mark on the DNA that abnormally switches the fetus's genes on or off. These influences generally have the most devastating effects during the first three months of pregnancy, making this a *critical period* in development.

Teratogen Any factor that causes damage or fetal death during prenatal development; comes from the Greek word *teras*, meaning "malformation."

Perhaps the most important—and generally avoidable—danger to a fetus comes from drugs, both legal and illegal. Nicotine and alcohol are major **teratogens**, environmental agents that cause damage during prenatal development. Mothers who smoke tobacco or drink alcohol during pregnancy have significantly higher rates of premature births, low-birth-weight infants, and fetal deaths. Their children also show increased behavior and cognitive problems (Doulatram et al., 2015; Roozen et al., 2016).

STOP! This Process Diagram contains essential information NOT found elsewhere in the text, which is likely to appear on quizzes and exams. Be sure to study it CAREFULLY!

PROCESS DIAGRAM 9.1 Prenatal Development

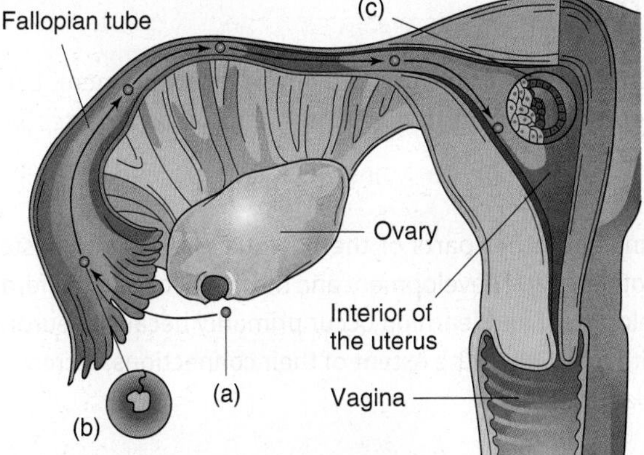

1. Germinal period: From conception to implantation
After discharge from either the left or right ovary (a), the ovum travels to the opening of the fallopian tube.

If fertilization occurs (b), it normally takes place in the first third of the fallopian tube. The fertilized ovum is referred to as a zygote.

When the zygote reaches the uterus, it implants itself in the wall of the uterus (c) and begins to grow tendril-like structures that intertwine with the rich supply of blood vessels located there. After implantation, the organism is known as an embryo.

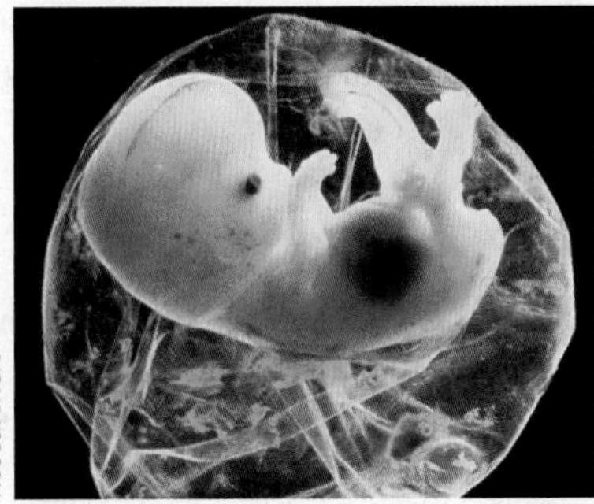

Biophoto Associates/Photo Researchers

2. Embryonic period: From implantation to eight weeks
At eight weeks, the major organ systems have become well differentiated. Note that at this stage, the head grows at a faster rate than other parts of the body.

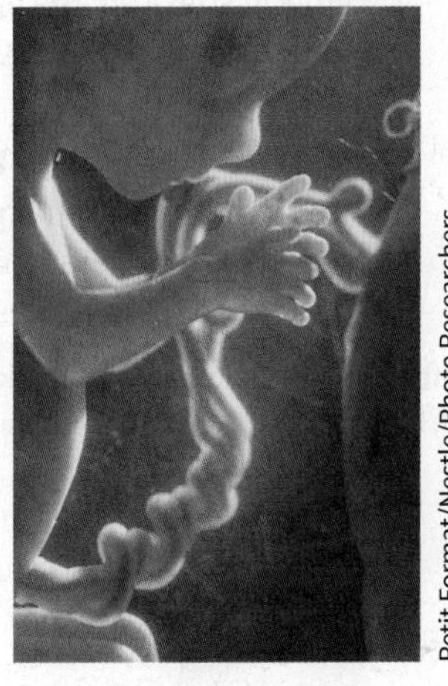

Petit Format/Nestle/Photo Researchers

3. Fetal period: From eight weeks to birth
After the eighth week, and until the moment of birth, the embryo is called a fetus. At four months, all the actual body parts and organs are established. The fetal stage is primarily a time for increased growth and "fine detailing."

As you can see in **Figure 9.7**, heavy maternal drinking may lead to a cluster of serious abnormalities called *fetal alcohol spectrum disorders (FASD).* The most severe form of this disorder is known as *fetal alcohol syndrome (FAS).* Recent research suggests that alcohol may leave chemical marks on DNA that abnormally turn off or on specific genes (Mason & Zhou, 2015). Tobacco might have a similar epigenetic effect. For example, children whose mothers smoked during pregnancy are more likely to be obese as adolescents, perhaps because in-utero exposure to nicotine changes a part of the brain that increases a preference for fatty foods (Haghighi et al., 2013, 2014). **[Q2]**

The pregnant mother obviously plays a primary role in prenatal development because her nutrition, her health, and almost everything she ingests can cross the placental barrier (a better term might be placental sieve). However, the father also plays a role. A father's smoking can pollute the air

TABLE 9.2 Sample Prenatal Environmental Conditions That Endanger a Child

MATERNAL FACTORS	POSSIBLE EFFECTS ON EMBRYO, FETUS, NEWBORN, OR YOUNG CHILD
Malnutrition	Low birth weight, malformations, less developed brain, greater vulnerability to disease
Exposure to: Environmental toxins, X-rays, excessive stress	Low birth weight, malformations, cancer, hyperactivity, irritability, feeding difficulties
Legal and illegal drugs: Certain prescription drugs, alcohol, nicotine, cocaine, methamphetamine	Inhibition of bone growth, hearing loss, low birth weight, fetal alcohol spectrum disorders (FASD), intellectual disability, attention deficits in childhood, death
Diseases: Heart and thyroid disease, diabetes, asthma, infectious diseases	Blindness, deafness, intellectual disability, heart and other malformations, brain infection, spontaneous abortion, premature birth, low birth weight, death

Sources: CDC, 2016; Doulatram et al., 2015; Maisto et al., 2015; Roozen et al., 2016.

Andy Levin/Science Source

FIGURE 9.7 Fetal alcohol spectrum disorders (FASD) Prenatal exposure to alcohol can result in FASD, and it's most severe form is called *fetal alcohol syndrome (FAS)*, including facial abnormalities and stunted growth. But the most disabling features of FAS are brain damage and neurobehavioral problems, ranging from hyperactivity and learning disabilities to intellectual disability, depression, and psychoses (CDC, 2016; Doulatram et al., 2015; Roozen et al., 2016).

the mother breathes—an epigenetic environmental factor. Genetically, the father can transmit heritable diseases, and alcohol, opiates, cocaine, various gases, lead, pesticides, and industrial chemicals can all damage sperm (Finegersh et al., 2015; Ji et al., 2013; Vassoler et al., 2014). Likewise, children of older fathers may be at higher risk of a range of mental difficulties, including attention deficits, bipolar disorder, autism, and schizophrenia (D'Onofrio et al., 2014; McGrath et al., 2014).

Early Childhood Development

Like the prenatal period, early childhood is a similar time of rapid physical development. Let's explore three key areas of change in early childhood: *brain*, *motor*, and *sensory/perceptual development*.

Brain Development Our brains and other parts of the nervous system grow faster than any other part of the body during both prenatal development and the first two years of life, as illustrated in **Figure 9.8**. This brain development and learning occur primarily because neurons grow in size. Also, the number of dendrites, as well as the extent of their connections, increases (Bornstein et al., 2014; Garrett, 2015; Swaab, 2014).

Motor Development Compared to the hidden, internal changes in brain development, the orderly emergence of active movement skills, known as *motor development*, is easily observed and measured. A newborn's first motor abilities are limited to *reflexes*, or involuntary

FIGURE 9.8 Brain development The brain undergoes dramatic changes from conception through the first few years of life. Keep in mind, however, that our brains continue to change and develop throughout our life span.

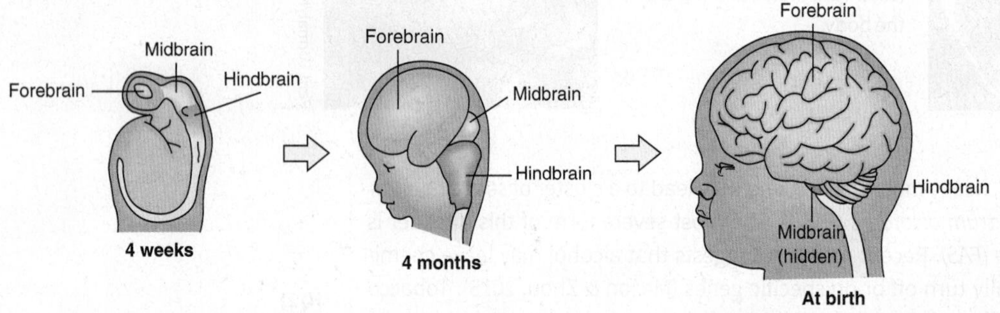

a. Prenatal brain development Recall from Chapter 2 that the human brain is divided into three major sections—the forebrain, midbrain, and hindbrain. Note how at three weeks after conception these three brain sections are one long neural tube, which later becomes the brain and spinal cord.

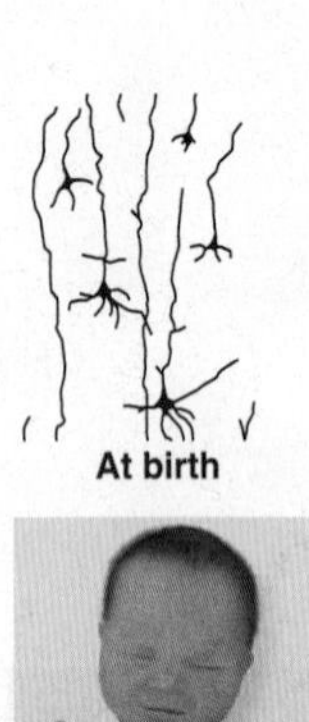

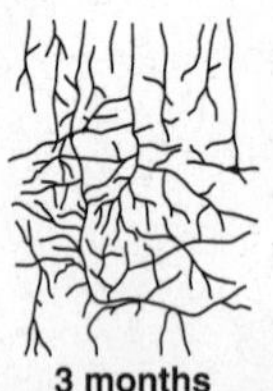

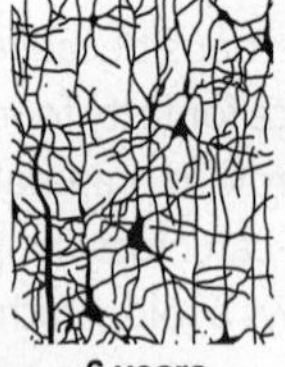

b. Brain growth during the first 14 years As infants learn and develop, synaptic connections between active neurons strengthen, and dendritic connections become more elaborate. Synaptic pruning (reduction of unused synapses) helps support this process. Myelination, the accumulation of fatty tissue coating the axons of nerve cells, continues until early adulthood.

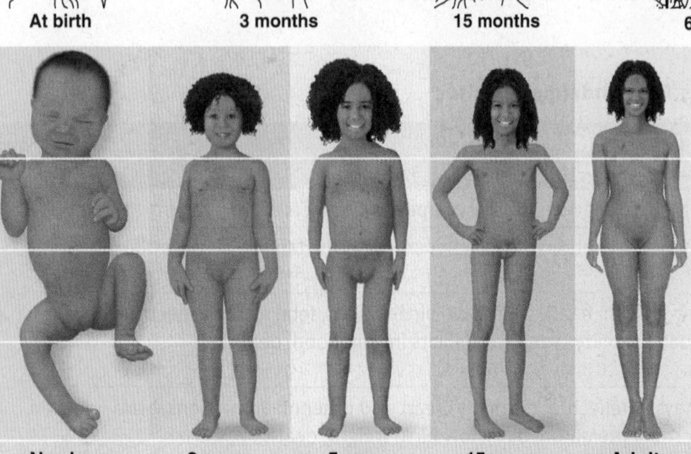

c. Brain and body changes over our life span There are dramatic changes in our brains and body proportions as we grow older. At birth, our head was one-fourth our total body's size, whereas in adulthood, our head is one-eighth.

responses to stimulation (Chapter 2). For example, the rooting reflex occurs when something touches a baby's cheek: The infant will automatically turn its head, open its mouth, and root for a nipple.

In addition to simple reflexes, the infant soon begins to show voluntary control over the movement of various body parts (**Figure 9.9**). Thus, a helpless newborn, who cannot even lift her head, is soon transformed into an active toddler capable of crawling, walking, and climbing. In fact, babies are highly motivated to begin walking because they can move faster than when crawling, and they get better with practice (Adolph & Berger, 2012; Berger, 2015). Keep in mind that motor development is largely due to natural maturation, but, like brain development, it can be affected by environmental influences, such as disease and neglect.

Certain cultural differences in childrearing also can explain some accelerated or delayed onset ages of major physical milestones, such as walking and crawling. For example, in some regions of Africa, the Caribbean, and India, caregivers vigorously massage and exercise infants as part of daily bathing routines, stretching infants' limbs, tossing them into the air, and propping them into sitting and walking positions (Karasik et al., 2010; Super & Harkness, 2015). Infants who receive massage and exercise begin sitting and walking at earlier ages than infants who do not. Similarly, the relatively recent practice in the United States of putting infants to sleep on their backs rather than their stomachs has resulted in delayed onset of crawling.

FIGURE 9.9 Milestones in motor development The acquisition and progression of motor skills, from chin up to walking up steps, is generally the same for all children, but the environment and personal experiences also play a role. In short, each child will follow his or her own personal timetable (Adolph & Berger, 2012; Berger, 2015).

Sensory and Perceptual Development At birth, and during the final trimester of pregnancy, the developing child's senses are quite advanced (Bardi et al., 2014; Levine & Munsch, 2014; NIH, 2016). For example, research shows that a newborn infant prefers his or her mother's voice, providing evidence that the developing fetus can hear sounds outside the mother's body (Lee & Kisilevsky, 2014; Von Hofsten, 2013). This raises the interesting possibility of fetal learning, and some have advocated special stimulation for the fetus as a way of increasing intelligence, creativity, and general alertness (Jarvis, 2014; Van de Carr & Lehrer, 1997).

In addition, a newborn can smell most odors and distinguish between sweet, salty, and bitter tastes. Breast-fed newborns also recognize the odor of their mother's milk compared to other mother's milk, formula, and other substances (Allam et al., 2010; Nishitani et al., 2009). Similarly, the newborn's sense of touch and pain is highly developed, as evidenced by reactions to circumcision and to heel pricks for blood testing, and by the fact that their pain reactions are lessened by the smell of their own mother's milk (Nishitani et al., 2009; Rodkey & Riddell, 2013; Vinall & Grunau, 2014).

The newborn's sense of vision, however, is poorly developed. At birth, an infant is estimated to have vision between 20/200 and 20/600 (Haith & Benson, 1998). Imagine what the infant's visual life is like: The level of detail you see at 200 or 600 feet (if you have 20/20 vision) is what an infant sees at 20 feet. Within the first few months, vision quickly improves, and by 6 months it is 20/100 or better. At 2 years, visual acuity is nearly at the adult level of 20/20 (Courage & Adams, 1990).

John Miles/The Image Bank/Getty Images, Inc.

FIGURE 9.10 Ready for responsibility? Adolescence is not a universal concept. Unlike the United States and other Western nations, some non-industrialized countries have no need for a slow transition from childhood to adulthood; children simply assume adult responsibilities as soon as possible.

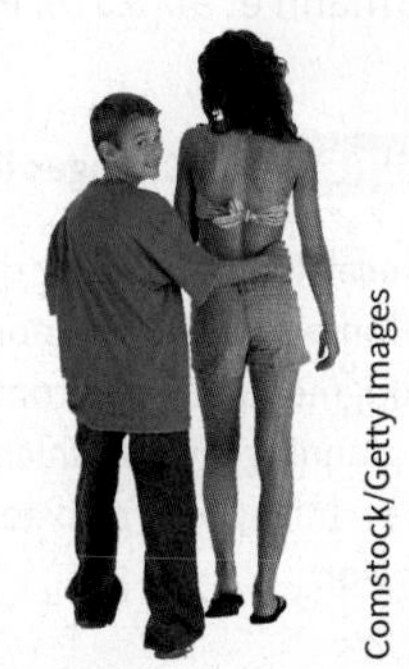

Comstock/Getty Images

FIGURE 9.11 Adolescent growth spurt Note the gender differences in height gain during puberty. Most girls are about two years ahead of boys in their growth spurt and are therefore taller than most boys between the ages of 10 and 14.

Adolescence

Adolescence is the loosely defined transition period of development between childhood and adulthood. In the United States, it roughly corresponds to the teenage years. However, the concept of adolescence and its meaning vary greatly across cultures (**Figure 9.10**).

Adolescence officially begins with **puberty**, the period of time when we mature sexually and become capable of reproduction. And one of the clearest and most dramatic physical signs of puberty is the *growth spurt*, which is characterized by rapid increases in height, weight, and skeletal growth (**Figure 9.11**) and by significant changes in reproductive structures and sexual

Puberty The biological changes during adolescence that lead to sexual maturation and the ability to reproduce.

characteristics. Maturation and hormone secretion cause rapid development of the ovaries, uterus, and vagina, and the onset of menstruation (*menarche*) in the adolescent female. In the adolescent male, the testes, scrotum, and penis develop, and he experiences his first ejaculation (*spermarche*). The testes and ovaries produce hormones that lead to the development of secondary sex characteristics, such as the growth of pubic hair, deepening of the voice and growth of facial hair in men, and growth of breasts in women (**Figure 9.12**). Do you recall how changes in height and weight, breast development and menstruation for girls, and a deepening voice and beard growth for boys were such important milestones for you and your adolescent peers?

Real World **Psychology**—Understanding the World

Puberty and Oversleeping

[Q3] Have you ever wondered why teenagers seem to sleep so much? Researchers have found that puberty is triggered by changes in the brain, including the release of certain hormones, which occur only during periods of *deep sleep* (D'Ambrosio & Redline, 2014; Shaw et al., 2012). This finding suggests that getting adequate, deep (slow-wave) sleep (see Chapter 5) during adolescence is an essential part of activating the reproductive system. Can you see why the increasing number of sleep problems in adolescents is a cause for concern, and why parents should actually be encouraging "oversleeping" in their teenagers?

The Teenage Brain As you recall, our brains and other parts of the nervous system grow faster than any other part of our bodies during both prenatal development and the first 2 years of life. In contrast to the rapid synaptic growth experienced in the earlier years, the adolescent's brain actively destroys (prunes) unneeded connections. Although it may seem counterintuitive, this pruning actually improves brain functioning by making the remaining connections between neurons more efficient. Interestingly, full maturity of the frontal lobes is not accomplished until the mid-twenties (**Figure 9.13**). Do you recall your teenage years as a time of exaggerated self-consciousness, feelings of special uniqueness, and risky behaviors? Psychologists now believe these effects may be largely due to your less-than-fully-developed frontal lobes (Casey et al., 2014; Fuhrmann et al., 2015; Pokhrel et al., 2013)!

FIGURE 9.12 Secondary sex characteristics Complex physical changes in puberty primarily result from hormones secreted from the ovaries and testes, the pituitary gland in the brain, and the adrenal glands near the kidneys.

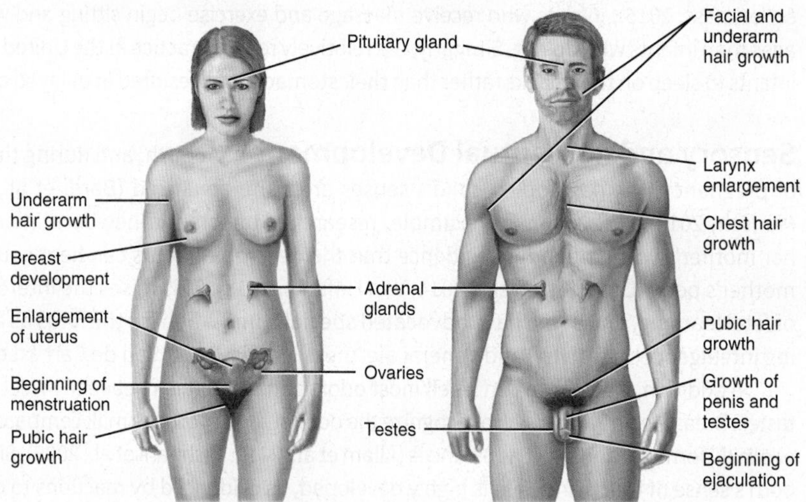

FIGURE 9.13 Changes in the brain

a. Recall from Chapter 2 that the frontal lobes are responsible for judgment, impulse control, and planning ahead, which may explain this type of risky teenage behavior.

b. During early childhood (ages 3–6), the frontal lobes experience a significant increase in the connections between neurons, which helps explain a child's rapid cognitive growth.

c. This rapid synaptic growth shifts to the temporal and parietal lobes during the ages of 7 to 15, which corresponds to their significant increases in language and motor skills.

d. During ages 16-20, synaptic pruning of unused connections in the frontal lobes, leads to increased brain efficiency, but full frontal lobe maturity only occurs in the mid-20s.

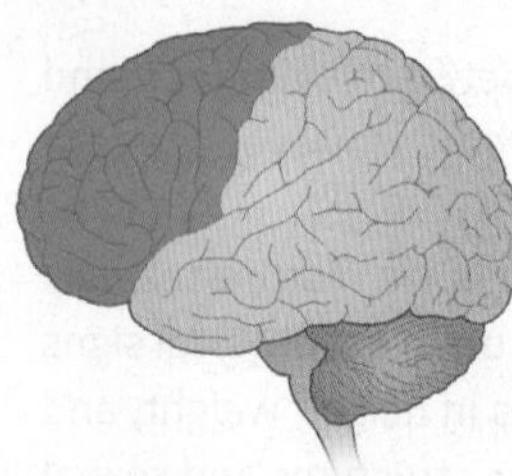

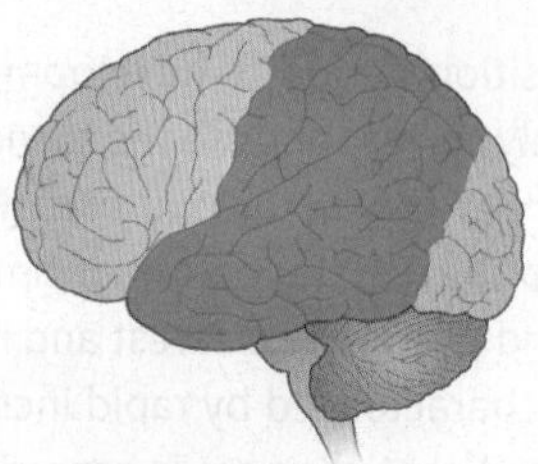

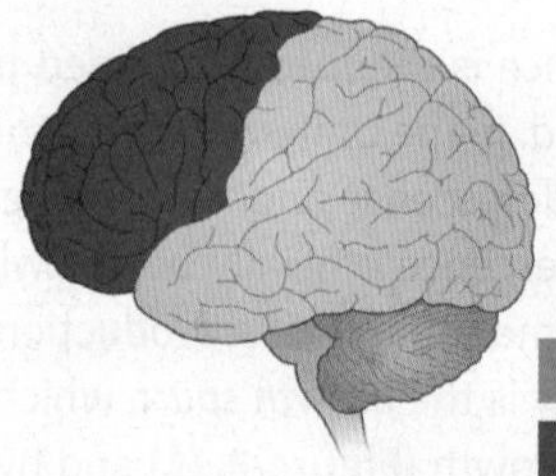

Adulthood

When does adulthood begin? In Western cultures, many define it as beginning after high school or college graduation, whereas others mark it as when we get our first stable job and become self-sufficient. Adulthood is typically divided into at least three periods: emerging/young adulthood (ages 20–45), middle adulthood (ages 45–60), and late adulthood (ages 60 to death).

Emerging/Young Adulthood

Although young adulthood is generally considered to begin at age 20, many developmental psychologists have added a new term, **emerging adulthood**, to refer to the time from the end of adolescence to the young-adult stage, approximately ages 18–25. This stage, which is found primarily in modern cultures, is characterized by the search for a stable job, self-sufficiency, and/or marriage and parenthood, along with five distinguishing features (Arnett, 2000, 2015; Munsey, 2006; Newman & Newman, 2015):

Emerging adulthood The age period from approximately 18–25 in which individuals in modern cultures have left the dependency of childhood, but not yet assumed adult responsibilities.

1. *Identity exploration*—young people decide who they are and what they want out of life.
2. *Instability*—a time marked by multiple changes in residence and relationships.
3. *Self-focus*—freed from social obligations and commitments to others, young people at this stage are focused on what they want and need before constraints of marriage, children, and career.
4. *Feeling in-between*—although taking responsibility for themselves, they still feel in the middle between adolescence and adulthood.
5. *Age of possibilities*—a time of optimism and belief that their lives will be better than their parents.

During this time period, some individuals experience modest physical increases in height and muscular development, and most of us find this to be a time of maximum strength, sharp senses, and overall stamina. However, a decline in strength and speed becomes noticeable in the 30s, and our hearing starts to decline as early as our late teens.

Middle Adulthood

Many physical changes during young adulthood happen so slowly that most people don't notice them until they enter their late 30s or early 40s. For example, around the age of 40, we first experience difficulty in seeing things close up and after dark, a thinning and graying of our hair, wrinkling of our skin, and a gradual loss in height coupled with weight gain (Landsberg et al., 2013; Saxon et al., 2014).

For women between ages 45–55, *menopause*, the cessation of the menstrual cycle, is the second most important life milestone in physical development. The decreased production of estrogen (the dominant female hormone) produces certain physical changes, including decreases in some types of cognitive and memory skills (Doty et al., 2015; Hussain et al., 2014; Pines, 2014). However, the popular belief that menopause (or "the change of life") causes serious psychological mood swings is not supported by current research. In fact, younger women are more likely to report irritability and mood swings, whereas women at midlife generally report positive reactions to aging, and the end of the menstrual cycle. They're also less likely to have negative experiences such as headaches (Sievert et al., 2007; Sugar et al., 2014).

In contrast to women, men experience a more gradual decline in hormone levels, and most men can father children until their 70s or 80s. Physical changes such as unexpected weight gain, decline in sexual responsiveness, loss of muscle strength, and graying or loss of hair may lead some men (and women as well) to feel depressed and to question their life progress. They often see these alterations as a biological signal of aging and mortality. Such physical and psychological changes in men are generally referred to as the *male climacteric* (or *andropause*). However, the popular belief that almost all men (and some women) go through a deeply disruptive midlife crisis, experiencing serious dissatisfaction with their work and personal relationships, is largely a myth.

Late Adulthood After middle age, most physical changes in development are gradual and occur in the heart and arteries, and in the sensory receptors. Cardiac output (the volume of blood pumped by the heart each minute) decreases, whereas blood pressure increases, due to the thickening and stiffening of arterial walls. Visual acuity and depth perception decline, hearing acuity lessens (especially for high-frequency sounds), smell sensitivity decreases, and some decline in cognitive and memory skills occurs (Dupuis et al., 2015; Fletcher & Rapp, 2013; Newman & Newman, 2015).

Why do we go through so many physical changes? What causes us to age and die? Setting aside aging and deaths resulting from disease, abuse, or neglect, known as *secondary aging*, let's focus on *primary aging* (gradual, inevitable age-related changes in physical and mental processes).

According to *cellular-clock theory*, primary aging is genetically controlled. Once the ovum is fertilized, the program for aging and death is set and begins to run. Researcher Leonard Hayflick (1965, 1996) found that human cells seem to have a built-in life span. After about 100 doublings of laboratory-cultured cells, they cease to divide. Based on this limited number of cell divisions, Hayflick suggests that we humans have a maximum life span of about 120 years—we reach the *Hayflick limit*. Why? One answer may be that small structures on the tips of our chromosomes, called *telomeres*, shorten each time a cell divides. After about 100 replications, the telomeres are too short and the cells can no longer divide (Broer et al., 2013; Hayashi et al., 2015; Rode et al., 2015).

The second major explanation of primary aging is *wear-and-tear theory*. Like any machine, repeated use and abuse of our organs and cell tissues cause our human bodies to simply wear out over time.

Late Adulthood Brain What about changes in the brain in later years? The public and most researchers long believed aging was inevitably accompanied by declining cognitive abilities and widespread death of neurons in the brain. Although this decline does happen with degenerative disorders like Alzheimer's disease (AD), it is no longer believed to be an inevitable part of normal aging (Hillier & Barrow, 2011; Whitbourne & Whitbourne, 2014). Furthermore, age-related cognitive problems are not on a continuum with AD. That is, normal forgetfulness does not mean that serious dementia is around the corner.

Aging does seem to take its toll on the *speed* of information processing (Chapter 7). Decreased speed of processing may reflect problems with *encoding* (putting information into long-term storage) and *retrieval* (getting information out of storage). If memory is like a filing system, older people may have more filing cabinets, and it may take them longer to initially file and later retrieve information. Although mental speed declines with age, general information processing and much of memory ability are largely unaffected by the aging process (Carey, 2014; Ramscar et al., 2014; Whitbourne & Whitbourne, 2014). Despite their concerns about "keeping up with 18-year-olds," older returning students often do as well or better than their younger counterparts in college classes.

This superior performance by older adult students may be due, in part, to their generally greater academic motivation, but it also reflects the importance of prior knowledge. Cognitive psychologists have clearly demonstrated that the more people know, the easier it is for them to lay down new memories (Goldstein, 2014; Matlin, 2016). Older students, for instance, generally find this chapter on development easier to master than younger students. Their interactions with children and greater, accumulated knowledge about life changes create a framework upon which to hang new information. In short, the more you know, the more you can learn. Thus, more education and having an intellectually challenging life may help you stay mentally sharp in your later years—another good reason for going to college and engaging in life-long learning (Branco et al., 2014; Huang & Zhou, 2013; Sobral et al., 2015).

Ageism A form of prejudice or discrimination based on physical age; similar to racism and sexism in its negative stereotypes.

Unfortunately, television, magazines, movies, and advertisements generally portray aging as a time of balding and graying hair, sagging body parts, poor vision, hearing loss, and, of course, no sex life. Can you see how our personal fears of aging and death, combined with these negative media portrayals, contribute to our society's widespread **ageism**–

prejudice and discrimination based on physical age (Lamont et al., 2015; West, 2015)? Sadly, a recent study found that older adults who reported discrimination based on their age had significantly lower physical and emotional health, and greater declines in health, than those who did not report such discrimination (Sutin et al., 2015). The good news is that advertisers have noted the large number of aging baby boomers, and are now producing ads with a more positive and accurate portrayal of aging as a time of vigor, interest, and productivity. See the following **Real World Psychology**.

Real World **Psychology**—Understanding the World

Achievement in Later Years

Our cognitive abilities generally grow and improve throughout our life span, as demonstrated by the achievements of people like Justices Ruth Bader Ginsburg and Antonin Scalia of the U.S. Supreme Court. Justice Scalia served from 1986 until his death in 2016, just shy of his 80th birthday. For decades Justice Scalia was the leading conservative voice on the Court. In her younger years, Justice Ginsburg worked tirelessly as a staunch courtroom advocate. Now in her 80s, she serves as a leading liberal voice on the Supreme Court.

Fun Fact: Despite their diametrically opposed political and legal philosophies, Justice Scalia and Justice Ginsburg had a great deal of mutual respect for one another and were known to be very close friends.

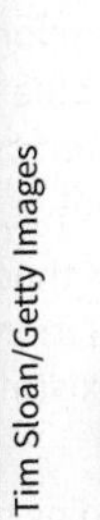

Tim Sloan/Getty Images

Mark Wilson/Getty Images

Retrieval Practice 9.2 | Physical Development

SELF-TEST Completing this self-test, and then checking your answers by clicking on the answer button or by looking in Appendix B, will provide immediate feedback and helpful practice for exams.

1. Behavioral genetics is the study of the relative effects of _____ on behavior and mental processes.

a. DNA and genetics
b. natural selection and adaptation
c. genetics and natural selection
d. heredity and environment

2. Teratogens are _____.

a. maternal defects that cause damage during neo-natal development.
b. factors that cause damage during prenatal development.
c. popular children's toys that studies have shown cause damage during early childhood development.
d. environmental diseases that cause damage during early childhood development.

3. The _____ is the first stage of prenatal development, which begins with conception and ends with implantation in the uterus (the first two weeks).

a. embryonic period
b. germinal period
c. critical period
d. none of these options

4. The clearest and most physical sign of puberty is the _____, characterized by rapid increases in height, weight, and skeletal growth.

a. menses
b. spermarche
c. growth spurt
d. age of fertility

5. Some employers are reluctant to hire older workers (50 years of age and older) because of a generalized belief that they are sickly and will take too much time off. This is an example of _____.

a. discrimination
b. prejudice
c. ageism
d. all of these options

Think Critically

1. If a mother knowingly ingests a quantity of alcohol, which causes her child to develop fetal alcohol syndrome (FAS), is she guilty of child abuse? Why or why not?

2. Based on what you have learned about development during late adulthood, do you think this period is inevitably a time of physical and mental decline? Why or why not?

Real World **Psychology**

Does prenatal exposure to smoke increase the risk of obesity later in life?

© milosluz/iStockphoto

Why do teenagers sleep so much?

Elenathewise/iStockphoto

HINT: LOOK IN THE MARGIN FOR **[Q2]** AND **[Q3]**

9.3 Cognitive Development

LEARNING OBJECTIVES

Retrieval Practice While reading the upcoming sections, respond to each Learning Objective in your own words.

Summarize the major theories of cognitive development and how cognition changes over the life span.

- **Explain** the roles of schemas, assimilation, and accommodation in cognitive development.
- **Describe** the major characteristics of Piaget's four stages of cognitive development.
- **Compare** Piaget's theory of cognitive development to Vygotsky's.

Schema A Piagetian term for a cognitive framework, or "blueprint," formed through interaction with an object or event.

Assimilation In Piaget's theory, the incorporation (assimilation) of new information into existing schemas.

Accommodation According to Piaget, the process of adjusting (accommodating) existing schemas to incorporate new information.

Just as a child's body and physical abilities change, his or her way of knowing and perceiving the world also grows and changes. Jean Piaget [pee-ah-ZHAY] provided some of the first great demonstrations of how children develop thinking and reasoning abilities (Piaget, 1952). He showed that an infant begins at a cognitively "primitive" level and that intellectual growth progresses in distinct stages, motivated by an innate need to know.

To appreciate Piaget's contributions, we need to consider three major concepts: schemas, assimilation, and accommodation. **Schemas** are the most basic units of intellect. They act as patterns that organize our interactions with the environment, like an architect's drawings or a builder's blueprints. For most of us, a common, shared schema for a car would likely be "a moving object with wheels and seats for passengers." However, we also develop unique schemas based on differing life experiences (see the **Psychology and You** feature).

Psychology and You—Understanding Yourself

Test Yourself | Do You Have an Artistic Schema?

Study the "impossible figure" to the right, and then try drawing this figure without tracing it. Students with artistic training generally find it relatively easy to reproduce, whereas the rest of us find it very hard or "impossible." This is because we lack the necessary artistic schema and cannot assimilate what we see. With practice and training, we could accommodate the new information and easily draw the figure.

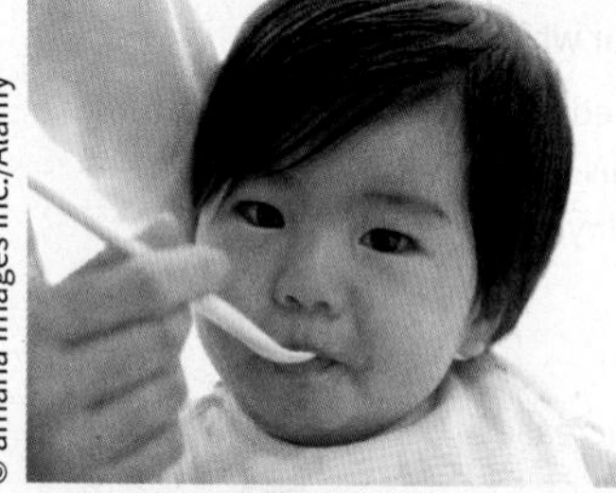

© amana images inc./Alamy

FIGURE 9.14 Accommodation When feeding from a spoon, infants initially try to suck on the spoon—an example of assimilation. However, when that doesn't work, they learn to shape their lips around the spoon and pull the food into their mouths—an example of accommodation.

In the first few weeks of life, the infant apparently has several *schemas* based on the innate reflexes of sucking, grasping, and so on. These schemas are primarily motor and may be little more than stimulus-and-response mechanisms (for example, the nipple is presented, and the baby sucks). Soon, other schemas emerge. The infant develops a more detailed schema for eating solid food, a different schema for the concepts of "mother" and "father," and so on.

Assimilation and *accommodation* are the two major processes by which schemas grow and change over time. **Assimilation** is the process of absorbing new information into existing schemas. For instance, infants use their sucking schema not only in sucking nipples, but also in sucking blankets and fingers. In **accommodation**, existing ideas are modified to fit new information. Accommodation generally occurs when new information or stimuli cannot be assimilated. New schemas are developed or old schemas are changed to better fit with the new information. An infant's first attempt to eat solid food with a spoon is a good example of accommodation (**Figure 9.14**).

Interestingly, researchers in one study found that babies who sat upright in infant seats while they explored different objects were much better at distinguishing between those objects than babies who were lying down while they explored (Woods & Wilcox, 2013). Although the researchers weren't exactly sure why sitting up helped babies learn more about [Q4]

Psychology and You—Understanding Yourself

Reliving Your Own Adolescent Egocentrism

Do these descriptions of the imaginary audience and personal fable ring true for you? If so, do you now understand how these beliefs might help explain some of the problems and challenges you faced in adolescence? As implied in this photo, many teens have difficulty accepting comfort and support from parents due to their belief that no one has ever felt or experienced what they have. One young woman remembered being very upset in middle school when her mother tried to comfort her over the loss of an important relationship. "I felt like she couldn't possibly know how it felt—no one could. I couldn't believe that anyone had ever suffered like this or that things would ever get better." Best advice for parents? Have patience and be comforting and reassuring. Teenagers whose parents use harsh verbal discipline (yelling or making serious threats) show more symptoms of depression and more behavior problems (lying, trouble in school, fighting with peers) (Wang & Kenny, 2014).

© fstop123/iStockphoto

Vygotsky Versus Piaget

As influential as Piaget's account of cognitive development has been, there are other important theories, and criticisms of Piaget, to consider. For example, Russian psychologist Lev Vygotsky emphasized the sociocultural influences on a child's cognitive development, rather than Piaget's internal schemas (Vygotsky, 1962). According to Vygotsky, children construct knowledge through their culture, language, and collaborative social interactions with more experienced thinkers (Mahn & John-Steiner, 2013; Scott, 2015; Yasnitsky, 2015). Unlike Piaget, Vygotsky believed that adults play an important instructor role in development and that this instruction is particularly helpful when it falls within a child's **zone of proximal development (ZPD)**, described in **Figure 9.16**.

Zone of proximal development (ZPD) Vygotsky's concept of the difference between what children can accomplish on their own and what they can accomplish with the help of others who are more competent.

Having briefly discussed Vygotsky's alternative theory, let's consider two major criticisms of Piaget—*underestimated abilities* and *underestimated genetic and cultural influences*. Research shows that Piaget may have underestimated young children's cognitive development. As we discussed earlier, infants develop concepts like object permanence at a much earlier age than Piaget suggested. In addition, Piaget believed that infancy and early childhood were a time of extreme egocentrism, in which children have little or no understanding of the perspective of others. However, research finds that empathy develops at a relatively young age (**Figure 9.17**).

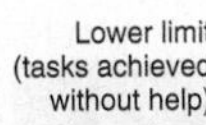

© omgimages/iStockphoto

FIGURE 9.16 Vygotsky's zone of proximal development (ZPD) Have you heard of "instructional scaffolding"? This term refers to providing support during the learning process that is tailored to the needs of the student. Vygotsky was one of the first to apply the general idea of scaffolding to early cognitive development. He proposed that the most effective teaching focuses on tasks between those a learner can do without help (the lower limit) and those he or she cannot do even with help (the upper limit). In this middle, *zone of proximal development (ZPD)*, tasks and skills can be "stretched" to higher levels with the guidance and encouragement of a more knowledgeable person.

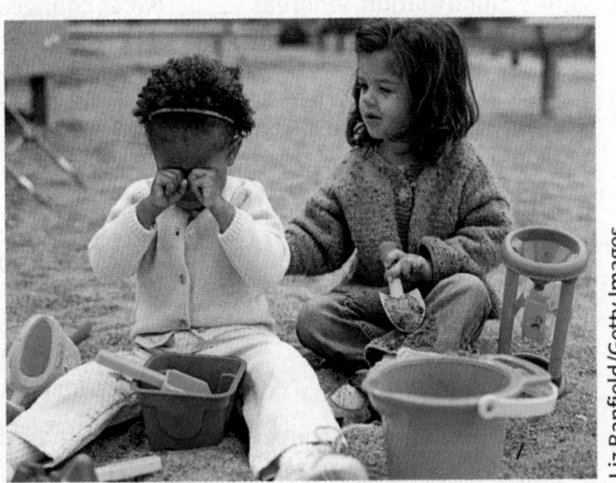

Liz Banfield/Getty Images

FIGURE 9.17 Are preoperational children always egocentric? Some toddlers and preschoolers clearly demonstrate empathy for other people. How does this ability to take another's perspective contradict Piaget's beliefs about egocentrism in very young children?

For example, even newborn babies tend to cry in response to the cry of another baby (Diego & Jones, 2007; Geangu et al., 2010). Also, preschoolers will adapt their speech by using shorter, simpler expressions when talking to 2-year-olds as compared to talking with adults.

Piaget's model, like other stage theories, has also been criticized for not sufficiently taking into account genetic and cultural differences (Newman & Newman, 2015; Shweder, 2011). During Piaget's time, the genetic influences on cognitive abilities were poorly understood, but as in the case of epigenetics, there has been a rapid explosion of information in this field in the last few years. In addition, formal education and specific cultural experiences can significantly affect cognitive development. Consider the following example from a researcher attempting to test the formal operational skills of a farmer in Liberia (Scribner, 1977):

RESEARCHER: All Kpelle men are rice farmers. Mr. Smith is not a rice farmer. Is he a Kpelle man?

KPELLE FARMER: I don't know the man. I have not laid eyes on the man myself.

Instead of reasoning in the "logical" way of Piaget's formal operational stage, the Kpelle farmer reasoned according to his specific cultural and educational training, which apparently emphasized personal knowledge. Not knowing Mr. Smith, the Kpelle farmer did not feel qualified to comment on him. Thus, Piaget's theory may have underestimated the effect of culture on a person's cognitive functioning.

Despite criticisms, however, Piaget's contributions to psychology are enormous. As one scholar put it, "assessing the impact of Piaget on developmental psychology is like assessing the impact of Shakespeare on English literature or Aristotle on philosophy—impossible" (Beilin, 1992, p. 191).

Retrieval Practice 9.3 | Cognitive Development

SELF-TEST Completing this self-test, and then checking your answers by clicking on the answer button or by looking in Appendix B, will provide immediate feedback and helpful practice for exams.

1. _____ was one of the first scientists to demonstrate that a child's intellect is fundamentally different from that of an adult's.

a. Baumrind **b.** Beck
c. Piaget **d.** Elkind

2. _____ occurs when existing schemas are used to absorb new information, whereas _____ makes changes and modifications to the schemas.

a. Adaptation; accommodation
b. Adaptation; reversibility
c. Egocentrism; postschematization
d. Assimilation; accommodation

3. A child who believes that trees have feelings is probably in the _____ stage of development.

a. sensorimotor **b.** preoperational
c. egocentric **d.** concrete operational

4. The ability to think abstractly and hypothetically occurs in Piaget's _____ stage.

a. egocentric **b.** postoperational
c. formal operational **d.** concrete operational

5. In Vygotsky's theory of cognitive development, the area between what children can accomplish on their own and what they can accomplish with the help of others who are more competent is called the _____.

a. concrete operational area **b.** postoperational zone
c. formal operational limits **d.** zone of proximal development

Think Critically

1. Piaget's theory states that all children progress through all the discrete stages of cognitive development in order and without skipping any. Do you agree with this theory? Do you know any children who seem to contradict this theory?

2. Based on what you've learned about schemas, what are some new schemas you've developed as part of your transition from high school to college?

Real World Psychology

Do babies learn faster when they're sitting up than when they're lying down?

Does the taking and posting of self-portraits ("selfies") increase narcissism?

© jfairone / iStockphoto

antoniodiaz/Shutterstock

HINT: LOOK IN THE MARGIN FOR **[Q4]** AND **[Q5]**

9.4 Social-Emotional Development

LEARNING OBJECTIVES

Retrieval Practice While reading the upcoming sections, respond to each Learning Objective in your own words.

Summarize how social-emotional factors affect development across the life span.

- **Review** attachment and the four key parenting styles.
- **Describe** Kohlberg's theory of moral development.
- **Review** Thomas and Chess's temperament theory.
- **Summarize** Erikson's eight psychosocial stages of development.
- **Explain** how sex and gender affect development.

In addition to physical and cognitive development, developmental psychologists study the way social and emotional factors affect development over the life span. In this section, we focus on *attachment*, *parenting styles*, *moral reasoning*, *personality*, *sex*, and *gender*.

Attachment

An infant arrives in the world with a multitude of behaviors that encourage a strong bond of **attachment** with primary caregivers. Returning to our earlier discussion of the nature–nurture controversy, researchers who advocate the nativist, or innate, position suggest that newborn infants are biologically equipped with verbal and nonverbal behaviors (such as crying, clinging, and smiling) and imprinting ("following") behaviors (such as crawling and walking after the caregiver) that elicit instinctive nurturing responses from the caregiver (Bowlby, 1969, 1989, 2000).

Attachment A strong emotional bond with special others that endures over time.

Studies have found numerous benefits to a child's good attachment, including lower levels of aggressive behavior, fewer sleep problems, and less social withdrawal (Ding et al., 2014). But as was the sad case of Genie, discussed at the start of this chapter, some children never form appropriate, loving attachments. What happens to these children? Researchers have investigated this question in two ways: They have looked at children and adults who spent their early years in institutions without the stimulation and love of a regular caregiver, as well as those who lived at home but were physically isolated under abusive conditions.

Tragically, infants raised in impersonal or abusive surroundings suffer from a number of problems. They seldom cry, coo, or babble; they become rigid when picked up; and they have few language skills. As for their social-emotional development, they tend to form shallow or anxious relationships. Some appear forlorn, withdrawn, and uninterested in their caretakers, whereas others seem insatiable in their need for affection. They also tend to show intellectual, physical, and perceptual deficiencies, along with increased susceptibility to infection, and neurotic "rocking" and isolation behaviors. There are even cases where healthy babies who were well-fed and kept in clean diapers—but seldom held or stimulated—actually died from lack of attachment (Bowlby, 2000; Duniec & Raz, 2011; Spitz & Wolf, 1946). Some research suggests that childhood emotional abuse and neglect is as harmful, in terms of long-term mental problems, as physical and sexual abuse (Spinazzola et al., 2014).

Nina Leen/Time Life Pictures/Getty Images

FIGURE 9.18 Harlow's study and contact comfort Although Harlow's studies of attachment in infant monkeys would be considered unethical today, it did clearly demonstrate that *touch*, and not *feeding*, is crucial to attachment.

Touch Harry Harlow and his colleagues (1950, 1971) also investigated the variables that might affect attachment. They created two types of wire-framed surrogate (substitute) "mother" monkeys: one covered by soft terry cloth and one left uncovered (**Figure 9.18**). The infant monkeys were fed by either the cloth or the wire mother, but they otherwise had access to both mothers. The researchers found that regardless of which surrogate was feeding them, the infant monkeys overwhelmingly preferred the soft, cloth surrogate–even when the wire surrogate was the one providing the food. In addition, monkeys "reared" by a cloth mother clung frequently to the soft material of their surrogate mother and developed greater emotional security and curiosity than did monkeys assigned to the wire mother.

Thanks in part to Harlow's research, psychologists discovered that *contact comfort*, the pleasurable, tactile sensations provided by a soft and cuddly "parent," is one of the most important variables in attachment (**Figure 9.19**). Further support comes from a study described in Chapter 4, which explains why hospitals now encourage premature babies to receive "kangaroo care," in which babies have skin-to-skin contact with a parent (Head, 2014; Metgud & Honap, 2015). For more information on how touch affects us—even as adults—see the following **PositivePsych**.

PP PositivePsych

Adults Need Hugs Too!

As we've just seen, contact comfort is critical for the physical and mental well-being of both monkeys and human infants. But did you know that the touch of others is an invaluable and important asset throughout our life span? Human touch has been repeatedly shown to be an effective way to solicit and provide social support (e.g., Robinson et al., 2015). It also can reduce the perception of pain, heart rate and blood pressure, and increase levels of oxytocin. Sadly, elderly nursing home residents and others often feel unwanted and their unsatisfied desire for social touch can lead to "touch hunger" (Ben-Zeév, 2014; Gallace & Spence, 2010; Rydé & Hjelm, 2016; Uvnäs-Moberg et al., 2015). Even something as simple as a hand massage can reduce disruptive behaviors in patients with dementia (Fu et al., 2013).

Hugs appear to be a particularly effective way of touching. In fact, people who get more frequent hugs are even less susceptible to infection and experience less severe illness symptoms (Cohen et al., 2015). In this study involving 404 healthy adults, perceived support was first assessed by a questionnaire, and frequencies of interpersonal conflicts and receiving hugs were derived from telephone interviews conducted on 14 consecutive evenings. Then, the participants were intentionally exposed to a common cold virus and monitored in quarantine to assess infection and signs of illness. The results showed that perceived social support reduced the risk of infection associated with experiencing conflicts. Hugs were responsible for one-third of the protective effect of social support. Among infected participants, greater perceived social support and more frequent hugs both resulted in less severe illness symptoms whether or not they experienced conflicts. Why? The researchers in this study suggest that a hug by a trusted person may act as an effective means of conveying support and that increasing the frequency of hugs might be an effective means of reducing the deleterious effects of stress.

Roberto Westbrook/Getty Images

Marili Forastieri/Digital Vision/Getty Images

FIGURE 9.19 The power of touch Parents around the world tend to kiss, nuzzle, comfort, and respond to their children with lots of physical contact, which points out its vital role in infant development. It also provides support for the biological, nature argument for attachment.

Ainsworth's Levels of Attachment Although physical contact between caregiver and child appears to be an innate, biological part of attachment, Mary Ainsworth and her colleagues (1967, 1978) discovered several interesting differences in the type and level of human attachment (**Figure 9.20**). For example, infants with a secure attachment style generally had caregivers who were sensitive and responsive to their signals of distress, happiness, and fatigue. In contrast, anxious/avoidant infants had caregivers who were aloof and distant, and anxious/ambivalent infants had inconsistent caregivers, who alternated between strong affection and indifference. Caregivers of disorganized/disoriented infants tended to be abusive or neglectful (Ainsworth, 1967; Ainsworth et al., 1978; Zeanah & Gleason, 2015).

As a critical thinker, can you offer additional explanations for attachment, other than differences in caregivers? What about differences in the infants themselves? Researchers have found that the temperament of the child does play an important role. An infant who is highly anxious and avoidant might not accept or respond to a caregiver's attempts to comfort and soothe. In addition, children and their parents share genetic tendencies and attachment patterns may reflect these shared genes. Finally, critics have suggested that Ainsworth's research does not account for cultural variations, such as cultures that encourage infants to develop attachments to multiple caregivers (Rothbaum et al., 2007; van IJzendoorn & Bakermans-Kranenburg, 2010).

Attachment Styles in Adulthood In addition to finding varying levels of infant attachment to parents, researchers have examined adult attachment patterns independent of their earlier infant patterns, with several interesting and/or troublesome results. For example,

FIGURE 9.20 Research on infant attachment For most children, parents are the earliest and most important factor in social development, and the attachment between parent and child is of particular interest to developmental psychologists.

1. After mother and baby spend some time in the experimental room, a stranger enters.

2. The mother then leaves the baby alone with the stranger.

3. The mother returns, and the stranger leaves.

4. The mother leaves, and the baby is alone until the stranger returns.

5. Once again, the mother returns, and the stranger leaves.

a. Strange situation procedure
Mary Ainsworth and her colleagues (1967, 2010) found significant differences in the typical levels of attachment between infants and their mothers using a technique called the strange situation procedure, in which they observed how infants responded to the presence or absence of their mother and a stranger.

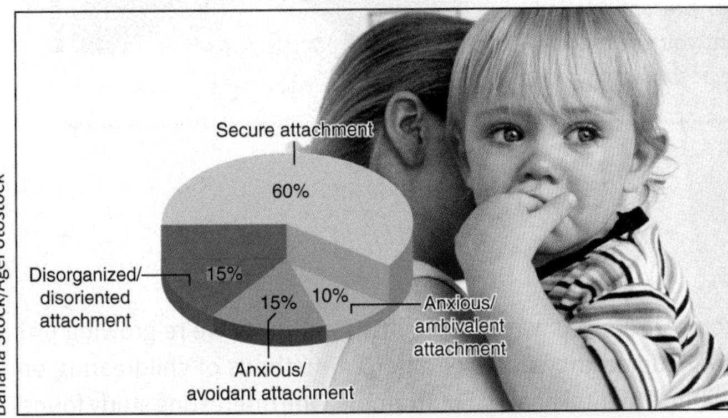

Secure Infant seeks closeness with mother when stranger enters. Uses her as a safe base from which to explore, shows moderate distress on separation from her, and is happy when she returns.	
Anxious/ambivalent Infant becomes very upset when mother leaves the room and shows mixed emotions when she returns.	
Anxious/avoidant Infant does not seek closeness or contact with the mother and shows little emotion when the mother departs or returns.	
Disorganized/disoriented Infant exhibits avoidant or ambivalent attachment, often seeming either confused or apprehensive in the presence of the mother.	

b. Degrees of attachment
Using the strange situation procedure, Ainsworth found that children could be divided into three groups: *Secure, anxious/avoidant, and anxious/ambivalent*. Later, psychologist Mary Main added a fourth category, *disorganized/disoriented* (Main & Solomon, 1986, 1990).

a secure attachment pattern is associated with higher subjective well-being (SWB), whereas adolescents and young adults with avoidant and anxious attachment patterns show more depressive symptoms (Desrosiers et al., 2014; Galinha et al., 2014). Another study found an association between pathological jealousy and the anxious/ambivalent style of attachment (Costa et al., 2015).

Researchers also looked at how varying types of attachment as infants might shape our later adult styles of romantic love (Fraley & Roisman, 2015; Salzman et al., 2014; Sprecher & Fehr, 2011). If we developed a secure, anxious/ambivalent, anxious/avoidant, or disorganized/disoriented style as infants, we tend to follow these same patterns in our adult approach to intimacy and affection. For example, young adults who experienced either unresponsive or overintrusive parenting during childhood are more likely to avoid committed romantic relationships as adults (Dekel & Farber, 2012). You can check your own romantic attachment style in the following **Psychology and You** feature. However, keep in mind that it's always risky to infer causation from correlation (see Chapter 1). Even if early attachment experiences are correlated with our later relationships, they do not determine them. Throughout life, we can learn new social skills and different approaches to all our relationships.

Psychology and You—Understanding Yourself

Test Yourself | What's Your Romantic Attachment Style?

Thinking of your current and past romantic relationships, place a check next to the statement that best describes your feelings about relationships.

_____ **1.** *I find it relatively easy to get close to others and am comfortable depending on them and having them depend on me. I don't often worry about being abandoned or about someone getting too close.*

_____ **2.** *I am somewhat uncomfortable being close. I find it difficult to trust partners completely or to allow myself to depend on them. I am nervous when anyone gets close, and love partners often want me to be more intimate than is comfortable for me.*

_____ **3.** *I find that others are reluctant to get as close as I would like. I often worry that my partner doesn't really love me or won't stay with me. I want to merge completely with another person, and this desire sometimes scares people away.*

According to research, 55% of adults agree with item 1 (secure attachment), 25% choose number 2 (anxious/avoidant attachment), and 20% choose item 3 (anxious/ambivalent attachment) (adapted from Fraley & Shaver, 1997; Hazan & Shaver, 1987). Note that the percentages for these adult attachment styles do not perfectly match those in Figure 9.20b, partly because the disorganized/disoriented attachment pattern was not included in this measurement of adult romantic attachments.

Think Critically

1. Do your responses as an adult match your childhood attachment experiences?
2. Does your romantic attachment style negatively affect your present relationship? If so, how might you use this new information to make positive changes?

© GlobalStock/iStockphoto

Parenting Styles

How much of our personality comes from the way our parents treat us as we're growing up? Researchers since the 1920s have studied the effects of different methods of childrearing on children's behavior, development, and mental health. For example, one interesting study found that teenagers whose parents used a controlling style—such as withholding love or creating feelings of guilt—later have more difficulty working out conflicts with friends and romantic partners (Oudekerk et al., 2015).

Other studies by Diana Baumrind (1980, 2013) found that parenting styles could be reliably divided into four broad patterns—*permissive-neglectful, permissive-indulgent, authoritarian,* and *authoritative*—which can be differentiated by their degree of *control/demandingness* (*C*) and *warmth/responsiveness* (*W*) (**Table 9.3**).

As you might expect, authoritative parenting, which encourages independence but still places controls and limits on behavior, is generally the most beneficial for both parents and children (Gherasim et al., 2016; Gouveia et al., 2016; Rodriguez et al., 2015). Sadly, research has found a link between permissive parenting and college students' sense of "academic entitlement," which in turn is associated with more perceived stress and poorer mental health among college students (Barton & Hirsh, 2016). Furthermore, authoritarian parenting by mothers and fathers is linked with increased behavior problems (Tavassolie et al., 2016).

What about the father's parenting style? Until recently, the father's role in discipline and child care was largely ignored. But fathers in Western countries have begun to take a more active role in child-rearing, and there has been a corresponding increase in research. From these studies, we now know that children do best with authoritative dads, who are absorbed with, excited about, and responsive to their children. It's important to note that children do best when parents share the same, consistent parenting styles, but mothers and fathers often differ in their approaches, and research shows that such differences increase marital conflict and child behavior problems (Tavassolie et al., 2016).

TABLE 9.3 Parenting Styles **Real World Psychology**

PARENTING STYLE	DESCRIPTION	EXAMPLE	EFFECT ON CHILDREN
Permissive-neglectful (low C, low W)	Parents make few demands, with little structure or monitoring (low C). They also show little interest or emotional support; may be actively rejecting (low W).	"I don't care about you—or what you do."	Children tend to have poor social skills, and little self-control (being overly demanding and disobedient).
Permissive-indulgent (low C, high W)	Parents set few limits or demands (low C), but are highly involved and emotionally connected (high W).	"I care about you—and you're free to do what you like!"	Children often fail to learn respect for others, and tend to be impulsive, immature, and out of control.
Authoritarian (high C, low W)	Parents are rigid and punitive (high C), but low on warmth and responsiveness (low W).	"I don't care what you want. Just do it my way, or else!"	Children tend to be easily upset, moody, aggressive, and often fail to learn good communication skills.
Authoritative (high C, high W)	Parents generally set and enforce firm limits (high C), while being highly involved, tender, and emotionally supportive high W).	"I really care about you, but there are rules, and you need to be responsible."	Children become self-reliant, self-controlled, high achieving, and emotionally well adjusted; also seem more content, goal oriented, friendly, and socially competent.

Note: The last two parenting styles (authoritarian and authoritative) are very similar. An easy way to remember is to notice the two Rs in authoRitaRian, and imagine a Rigid Ruler. Then note the last two Ts in authoriTaTive, and picture a Tender Teacher.

Sources: Baumrind, 2013; Berger, 2015; Bornstein et al., 2014; Topham et al., 2011.

Moral Development

In Europe, a cancer-ridden woman was near death, but an expensive drug existed that might save her. The woman's husband, Heinz, begged the druggist to sell the drug cheaper or to let him pay later. But he refused. Heinz became desperate and broke into the druggist's store and stole it. (Adapted from Kohlberg, 1964, pp. 18–19)

Was Heinz right to steal the drug? What do you consider moral behavior? Is morality "in the eye of the beholder," or are there universal moral truths and principles? Whatever your answer, your ability to think, reason, and respond to Heinz's dilemma may demonstrate your current level of moral development.

One of the most influential researchers in moral development was Lawrence Kohlberg (1927–1987). He presented what he called "moral stories" like the Heinz dilemma to people of all ages, not to see whether they judged Heinz right or wrong but to examine the reasons they gave for their decisions. On the basis of his findings, Kohlberg (1964, 1984) developed a model of moral development, with three broad levels each composed of two distinct stages (**Process Diagram 9.3**). Individuals at each stage and level may or may not support Heinz's stealing of the drug, but their reasoning changes from level to level. At the first, *precoventional level*, morality is self-centered and based on rewards, punishments, and exchange of favors. In contrast, during the second, *conventional level*, moral judgments are based on compliance with the rules and values of society. And, at the third, *postconventional level,* individuals develop personal standards for right and wrong. They define morality in terms of abstract principles and values that apply to all situations and societies.

Assessing Kohlberg's Theory

Kohlberg's ideas have led to considerable research on how we think about moral issues. But his theories have been the focus of three major areas of criticism:

1. *Moral reasoning versus behavior* Are people who achieve higher stages on Kohlberg's scale really more moral than others? Or do they just "talk a good game"?

   Some researchers have shown that a person's sense of moral identity, meaning the use of moral principles to define oneself, is often a good predictor of his or her behavior in real-world situations (Johnston et al., 2013; Stets & Carter, 2012). But others have found that situational factors are better predictors of moral behavior (Bandura, 1989, 2008; Frimer et al., 2014; Noval & Stahl, 2015). For example, research participants are more likely to steal when they are told the money comes from a large company rather than from individuals

STOP! This Process Diagram contains essential information NOT found elsewhere in the text, which is likely to appear on quizzes and exams. Be sure to study it CAREFULLY!

PROCESS DIAGRAM 9.3 **Kohlberg's Stages of Moral Development**

Step 1: Preconventional Level Morality is based on rewards, punishment, and exchange of favors.

Step 2: Conventional Level Moral judgments are based on compliance with the rules and values of society.

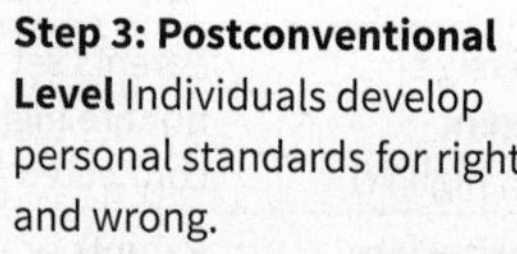

Step 3: Postconventional Level Individuals develop personal standards for right and wrong.

PRECONVENTIONAL LEVEL

(Stages 1 and 2—birth to adolescence) Moral judgment is *self-centered*. What is right is what one can get away with, or what is personally satisfying.

1 Punishment-obedience orientation

Focus is on self-interest—obedience to authority and avoidance of punishment. Because children at this stage have difficulty considering another's point of view, they ignore people's intentions.

2 Instrumental-exchange orientation

Children become aware of others' perspectives, but their morality is based on reciprocity—an equal exchange of favors.

CONVENTIONAL LEVEL

(Stages 3 and 4—adolescence to young adulthood) Moral reasoning is *other-centered*. Conventional societal rules are accepted because they help ensure the social order.

3 Good-child orientation

Primary moral concern is being nice and gaining approval; judges others by their intentions—"His heart was in the right place."

4 Law-and-order orientation

Morality based on a larger perspective—societal laws. Understanding that if everyone violated laws, even with good intentions, there would be chaos.

POSTCONVENTIONAL LEVEL

(Stages 5 and 6—adulthood) Moral judgments based on *personal standards for right and wrong*. Morality is defined in terms of abstract principles and values that apply to all situations and societies.

5 Social-contract orientation

Appreciation for the underlying purposes served by laws. Societal laws are obeyed because of the "social contract," but they can be morally disobeyed if they fail to express the will of the majority or fail to maximize social welfare.

6 Universal-ethics orientation

"Right" is determined by universal ethical principles (e.g., nonviolence, human dignity, freedom) that moral authorities might view as compelling or fair. These principles apply whether or not they conform to existing laws.

Sources: Based on Kohlberg, L. "Stage and Sequence: The Cognitive Developmental Approach to Socialization," in D. A. Goslin, The handbook of socialization theory and research. Chicago: Rand McNally, 1969, p. 376 (Table 6.2).

(Greenberg, 2002). And both men and women tell more sexual lies during casual relationships than during close relationships (Williams, 2001).

2. *Cultural differences* Some studies confirm that children from a variety of cultures generally follow Kohlberg's model and progress sequentially from his first level, the *preconventional*, to his second, the *conventional* (Rest et al., 1999; Snarey, 1995). However, other studies find differences among cultures (Csordas, 2014; Vozzola, 2014). For example, cross-cultural comparisons of responses to Heinz's moral dilemma show that Europeans and Americans tend to consider whether they like or identify with the victim in questions of morality. In contrast, Hindu Indians consider social responsibility and personal concerns two separate

issues (Miller & Bersoff, 1998). Researchers suggest that the difference reflects the Indians' broader sense of social responsibility.

Furthermore, in India, Papua New Guinea, and China, as well as in Israeli kibbutzim, people don't choose between the rights of the individual and the rights of society (as the top levels of Kohlberg's model require). Instead, most people seek a compromise solution that accommodates both interests (Killen & Hart, 1999; Miller & Bersoff, 1998). Thus, Kohlberg's standard for judging the highest level of morality (the postconventional) may be more applicable to cultures that value individualism over community and interpersonal relationships.

3. *Possible gender bias* Researcher Carol Gilligan criticized Kohlberg's model because on his scale, women often tend to be classified at a lower level of moral reasoning than men. She suggested that this difference occurred because Kohlberg's theory emphasizes values more often held by men, such as rationality and independence, while de-emphasizing common female values, such as concern for others and belonging (Gilligan, 1977, 1993; Kracher & Marble, 2008). However, most follow-up studies of Gilligan's specific theory have found few, if any, gender differences (Friesdorf et al., 2015; Gibbs, 2014).

Real World **Psychology**—Understanding the World

Morality—Personal Trait or the Situation?

Which do you believe is the better predictor of moral behavior—the person or the situation? You've undoubtedly seen this dilemma when students are faced with a choice to cheat on an exam or shoplift. How about the case of Lance Armstrong, who chose to use performance-enhancing drugs in sports competition? Was it the situation or his personal morality that most influenced his behavior?

Ragnar Singsaas/Getty Images

Personality Development

As an infant, did you lie quietly and seem oblivious to loud noises? Or did you tend to kick and scream and respond immediately to every sound? Did you respond warmly to people, or did you fuss, fret, and withdraw? Your answers to these questions help determine what developmental psychologists call your **temperament**, an individual's innate disposition, behavioral style, and characteristic emotional response.

Temperament An individual's characteristic manner and intensity of emotional response.

Thomas and Chess's Temperament Theory One of the earliest and most influential theories regarding temperament came from the work of psychiatrists Alexander Thomas and Stella Chess (Thomas & Chess, 1977, 1987). Thomas and Chess found that approximately 65% of the babies they observed could be reliably separated into three categories:

1. ***Easy children*** These infants were happy most of the time, relaxed and agreeable, and adjusted easily to new situations (approximately 40%).
2. ***Difficult children*** Infants in this group were moody, easily frustrated, tense, and overreactive to most situations (approximately 10%).
3. ***Slow-to-warm-up children*** These infants showed mild responses, were somewhat shy and withdrawn, and needed time to adjust to new experiences or people (approximately 15%).

Follow-up studies have found that certain aspects of these temperament styles tend to be consistent and enduring throughout childhood and even adulthood (Bates et al., 2014; Sayal et al., 2014). But that is not to say every shy, cautious infant ends up a shy adult. Many events take place between infancy and adulthood that shape an individual's development. Moreover, culture can also influence infant temperament. One recent study found that Dutch babies tend to be happier and easier to soothe, whereas babies born in the United States are typically more active and vocal (Sung et al., 2015). These temperament differences are thought to reflect cultural differences in parenting styles and values.

One of the most influential factors in early personality development is *goodness of fit* between a child's nature, parental behaviors, and the social and environmental setting (Mahoney, 2011; Seifer et al., 2014). For example, a slow-to-warm-up child does best if allowed time to adjust to new situations. Similarly, a difficult child thrives in a structured, understanding environment but not in an inconsistent, intolerant home. Alexander Thomas, the pioneer of temperament research, thinks parents should work with their child's temperament rather than trying to change it. Can you see how this idea of goodness of fit is yet another example of how nature and nurture interact?

Psychosocial stages Erikson's theory that identifies eight developmental stages, each involving a crisis that must be successfully resolved for proper future development.

Erikson's Psychosocial Theory

Like Piaget and Kohlberg, Erik Erikson developed a stage theory of development. He identified eight **psychosocial stages** of social development, with each stage marked by a "psychosocial" crisis or conflict that must be successfully resolved for proper future development (**Figure 9.21**).

The name for each psychosocial stage reflects the specific crisis encountered at that stage and two possible outcomes. The crisis or task of most young adults is *intimacy versus isolation*. This age group's developmental challenge is establishing deep, meaningful relations with others. Those who don't meet this challenge risk social isolation. Erikson believed that the more successfully we overcome each psychosocial crisis, the better chance we have to develop in a healthy manner (Erikson, 1950).

Many psychologists agree with Erikson's general idea that psychosocial crises, which are based on interpersonal and environmental interactions, do contribute to personality development (Marcia & Josselson, 2013; Svetina, 2014). However, Erikson also has his critics (Arnett, 2015; Spano et al., 2010). Some evidence now suggests that people may approach these valued life tasks at different ages, and potentially in different orders. Furthermore, identity development often continues through the late 20s, and is not simply a task approached by adolescents (Carlsson et al., 2015). In addition, Erikson's psychosocial stages are difficult to test scientifically, and the labels he used to describe the eight stages may not be entirely appropriate cross-culturally. For example, in individualistic cultures, *autonomy* is highly preferable to *shame and doubt*. But in collectivist cultures, the preferred resolution might be *dependence* or *merging relations* (Berry et al., 2011).

Despite their limits, Erikson's stages have greatly contributed to the study of North American and European psychosocial development. Also, by suggesting that development continues past adolescence, Erikson's theory has encouraged ongoing research and theory development across the life span.

Sex and Gender Influences on Development

Imagine for a moment what your life would be like if you were a member of the other sex. Would you think differently? Would you be more or less sociable and outgoing? Would your career plans or friendship patterns change? In this section, we will explore how our development is affected by *sex* (a biological characteristic determined at the moment of conception), **gender** (psychological and sociocultural meanings added to biological maleness or femaleness), **gender roles** (societal expectations for "appropriate" male and female thoughts, feelings, and actions), and *cultural differences*.

Gender A psychological and sociocultural phenomenon referring to learned, sex-related thoughts, feelings, and actions of men and women.

Gender roles A set of learned, societal expectations for thoughts, feelings, and actions considered "appropriate" for men and women, and expressed publicly by the individual.

Sex and Gender Differences

Physical anatomy is the most obvious biological sex difference between men and women. In addition to biological sex differences, scientists have noted numerous gender differences that affect our cognitive and personality development (**Table 9.4**). Keep in mind that these variations are statistically small, however, and represent few meaningful differences.

Gender-Role Development

By age 2, children are well aware of gender roles. From parents and other social forces, they quickly learn that boys "should" be strong, independent, aggressive, dominant, and achieving, whereas girls "should" be soft, dependent, passive, emotional, and "naturally" interested in children. Unfortunately, such expectations and stereotypes for how women and men should think, feel, or act may seriously limit both sexes in their choice of friendships, activities, and career goals (Best & Bush, 2016; Gianettoni & Guilley, 2016; Latu & Schmid Mast, 2016).

FIGURE 9.21 Erikson's eight stages of psychosocial development
Erikson identified eight stages of development, each of which is associated with its own unique psychosocial crisis.

Steve Raymer/NG Image Collection

1 Trust versus mistrust (birth–age 1)
Infants learn to *trust* or *mistrust* their caregivers and the world based on whether or not their needs—such as food, affection, safety—are met.

Prof. Karen Huffman

2 Autonomy versus shame and doubt (ages 1–3)
Toddlers start to assert their sense of independence (*autonomy*). If caregivers encourage this self-sufficiency, the toddler will learn to be independent versus feeling *shame* and *doubt*.

Dynamic Graphics, Inc./Creatas

3 Initiative versus guilt (ages 3–6)
Preschoolers learn to *initiate* activities and develop self-confidence and a sense of social responsibility. If not, they feel irresponsible, anxious, and *guilty*.

PhotoDisc/Getty Images, Inc.

4 Industry versus inferiority (ages 6–12)
Elementary school-aged children who succeed in learning new, productive life skills develop a sense of pride and competence (industry). Those who fail to develop these skills feel inadequate and unproductive (*inferior*).

Randy Olson/NG Image Collection

5 Identity versus role confusion (ages 12–20)
Adolescents develop a coherent and stable self-definition (identity) by exploring many roles and deciding who or what they want to be in terms of career, attitudes, and so on. Failure to resolve this *identity crisis* may lead to apathy, withdrawal, and/or *role confusion*.

Pablo Corral Vega/NG Image Collection

6 Intimacy versus isolation (early adulthood)
Young adults form lasting, meaningful ships that help them develop a sense of connectedness and *intimacy* with others. If not, they become psychologically *isolated*.

IT Stock

7 Generativity versus stagnation (middle adulthood)
The challenge for middle-aged adults is in nurturing the young, and making contributions to society through their work, family, or community activities. Failing to meet this challenge leads to self-indulgence and a sense of *stagnation*.

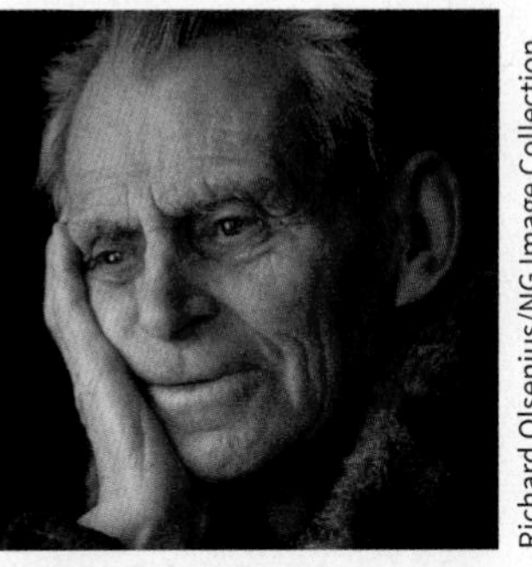

Richard Olsenius/NG Image Collection

8 Ego integrity versus despair (late adulthood)
During this stage, older adults reflect on their past. If this reflection reveals a life well-spent, the person experiences self-acceptance and satisfaction (*ego integrity*). If not, he or she experiences regret and deep dissatisfaction (*despair*).

TABLE 9.4 Research-Supported Sex and Gender Differences

BEHAVIOR	MORE OFTEN SHOWN BY MEN	MORE OFTEN SHOWN BY WOMEN
Sexual	• Begin masturbating sooner in life cycle and higher overall occurrence rates • Start sexual life earlier and have first orgasm through masturbation • More likely to recognize their own sexual arousal • More orgasm consistency with sexual partner	• Begin masturbating later in life cycle and lower overall occurrence rates • Start sexual life later and have first orgasm from partner stimulation • Less likely to recognize their own sexual arousal • Less orgasm consistency with sexual partner
Touching	• Touched, kissed, and cuddled less by parents • Less physical contact with other men and respond more negatively to being touched • More likely to initiate both casual and intimate touch with sexual partner	• Touched, kissed, and cuddled more by parents • More physical contact with other women and respond more positively to being touched • Less likely to initiate either casual or intimate touch with sexual partner
Friendship	• Larger number of friends and express friendship by shared activities	• Smaller number of friends and express friendship by shared communication about self
Personality	• More aggressive from a very early age • More self-confident of future success • Attribute success to internal factors and failures to external factors • Achievement more task oriented; motives are mastery and competition • More self-validating • Higher self-esteem	• Less aggressive from a very early age • Less self-confident of future success • Attribute success to external factors and failures to internal factors • Achievement more socially directed, with emphasis on self-improvement • More dependent on others for validation • Lower self-esteem
Cognitive abilities	• Slightly superior in math and visuospatial skills	• Slightly superior in verbal skills

Sources: Carroll, 2016; Chaplin, 2015; Eagly, 2015; Forgasz et al., 2015; Hofstede et al., 2015; Schmitt, 2015.

The existence of similar gender roles in many cultures suggests that evolution and biology may play a role in their formation. However, most research emphasizes two major psychosocial theories of gender-role development: *social learning* and *cognitive developmental* (**Figure 9.22**).

Social-learning theorists emphasize the power of the immediate situation and observable behaviors on gender-role development. Girls learn how to be "feminine," and boys learn how to be "masculine" in two major ways: (1) They receive rewards or punishments for specific gender-role behaviors, and (2) they watch and imitate the behavior of others, particularly their same-sex parent (Bandura, 1989, 2008; Risman & Davis, 2013). A boy who puts on his father's tie or baseball cap wins big, indulgent smiles from his parents. But what would happen if he put on his mother's nightgown or lipstick? Parents, teachers, and friends generally reward or punish behaviors according to traditional gender-role expectations. Thus, a child "socially learns" what it means to be male or female.

According to the *cognitive-developmental theory*, social learning is part of gender-role development, but it's much more than a passive process of receiving rewards or punishments and modeling others. Instead, cognitive developmentalists argue that children actively observe,

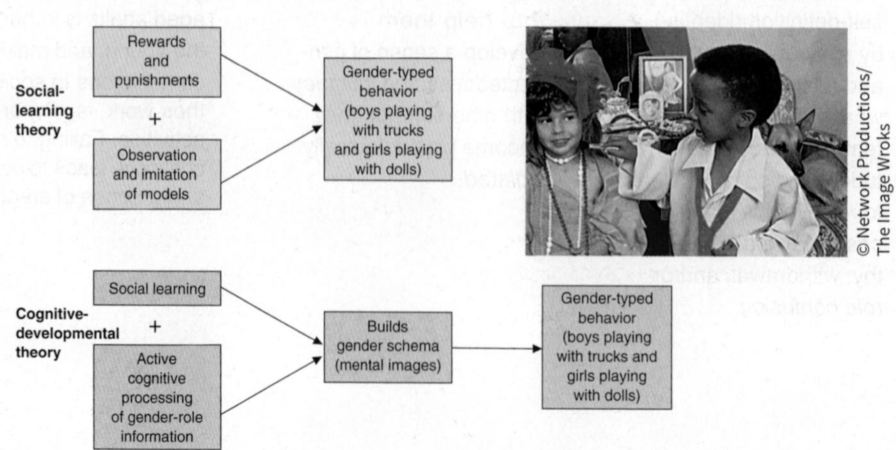

FIGURE 9.22 Gender-role development Social-learning theory focuses on a child's passive process of learning about gender through observation, rewards, and punishments, whereas cognitive-developmental theory emphasizes a child's active role in building a gender schema.

for fattening foods, and we've become accustomed to "supersized" cheeseburgers, "Big Gulp" drinks, and huge servings of dessert (Almiron-Roig et al., 2015; Fast et al., 2015; Folkvord et al., 2016). Moreover, we've been taught that we should eat three meals a day, whether we're hungry or not; that "tasty" food requires lots of salt, sugar, and fat; and that food is an essential part of the workplace and almost all social gatherings (**Figure 10.8**).

What about those people who can seemingly eat anything they want and still not add pounds? This may be a result of their ability to burn calories more effectively in the process of thermogenesis, a higher metabolic rate, and other possible individual and environmental factors (Pérusse et al., 2014; van Dongen et al., 2015; Zhou et al., 2015). In addition, researchers have isolated a large number of genes that contribute to normal and abnormal weight (Albuquerque et al., 2015; Dubois et al., 2016; van Dijk et al., 2015).

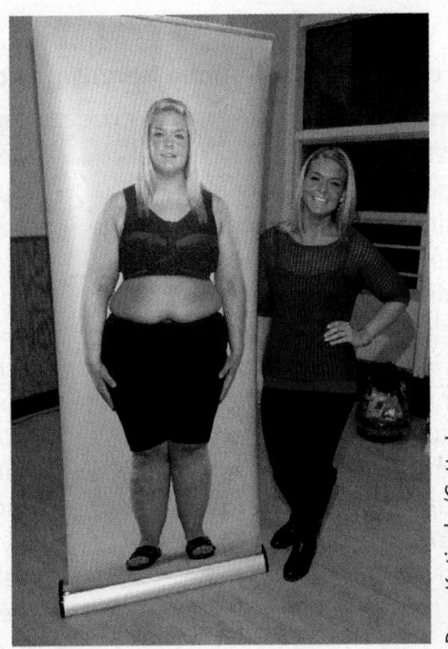

Dave Kotinsky/Getty Images

Christian Thomas/Getty Images

FIGURE 10.8 A fattening environment **Real** World **Psychology**

One of the most popular television programs, *The Biggest Loser*, shows how difficult it is for contestants to lose weight. Even more difficult, and seldom shown, is how hard it is to maintain weight loss. To make it permanent, we need to make lasting lifestyle changes regarding exercise and the amount and types of foods we eat and when we eat them. Can you see how our everyday environments, such as in the workplace shown here, might make it harder for a person who wants to make healthier lifestyle changes?

The good news is that one of these identified genes may provide a potential genetic explanation for why some people overeat and run a greater risk for obesity. For example, research finds that people who carry variants of the FTO gene don't feel full after eating and overeat because they have higher blood levels of ghrelin—a known hunger-producing hormone (Hess & Brüning, 2014; King et al., 2015; van Name et al., 2015). The good news is that ghrelin can be reduced by engaging in exercise and eating a high-protein diet (Bailey et al., 2015; Martins et al., 2014; Williams, 2013). But the researchers cautioned that more research is needed, and that human appetite and obesity are undoubtedly more complex than a single hormone. In addition, this focus on genes should not encourage people to feel helpless against obesity.

Eating Disorders

The three major eating disorders—*anorexia nervosa, bulimia nervosa*, and *binge-eating disorder*—are found in all ethnicities, socioeconomic classes, and both sexes. However, they are more common in women (American Psychiatric Association, 2013; Bohon, 2015; Eddy et al., 2016). **Anorexia nervosa** is characterized by an overwhelming fear of becoming obese, a need for control, the use of dangerous weight-loss measures, and a body image that is so distorted that even a skeletal, emaciated body is perceived as fat. The resulting extreme malnutrition often leads to osteoporosis, bone fractures, interruption of menstruation in women, and loss of brain tissue. A recent study suggests that anorexia is linked with particular brain activation patterns—such as the part of the brain linked with automatic responding (Foerde et al., 2015). This means that anorexic people may make food decisions based on habit (e.g., I only eat low fat foods), and not on reward centers, as do healthy people. Do you see how this might help explain why anorexics have such difficulty changing their behavior?

Anorexia nervosa An eating disorder characterized by an obsessive fear of obesity, a need for control, self-imposed starvation, and a severe loss of weight.

Occasionally, a person suffering from anorexia nervosa succumbs to the desire to eat and gorges on food, then vomits or takes laxatives. However, this type of bingeing and purging is more characteristic of **bulimia nervosa**. Individuals with bulimia go on recurrent eating binges and then purge by self-induced vomiting or the use of laxatives. They often show impulsivity in other areas, sometimes engaging in excessive shopping, alcohol abuse, or petty shoplifting (Buckholdt et al., 2015; Pearson et al., 2015; Slane et al., 2014). The vomiting associated with bulimia nervosa causes severe damage to the teeth, throat, and stomach. It also leads to cardiac arrhythmia, metabolic deficiencies, and serious digestive disorders.

Bulimia nervosa An eating disorder characterized by recurrent episodes of consuming large quantities of food (bingeing), followed by self-induced vomiting or laxative use (purging).

Binge-eating disorder An eating disorder characterized by recurrent episodes of consuming large amounts of food (bingeing), but not followed by purge behaviors.

Note that bulimia is similar to but not the same as **binge-eating disorder**. This disorder involves recurrent episodes of consuming large amounts of food in a discrete period of time,

TABLE 10.2 Symptoms of Anorexia Nervosa, Bulimia Nervosa, and Binge-Eating Disorder

ANOREXIA NERVOSA	BULIMIA NERVOSA	BINGE-EATING DISORDER
• Weight less than 85% of normal for age and height • Intense fear of gaining weight, even when underweight • Persistent behavior to avoid weight gain • Distorted body image, denial of seriousness of weight loss	• Repeated episodes of binge eating, consuming unusually large amounts of food in a short period of time • Feeling out of control over eating during the binge episode • Purging behaviors after eating, including vomiting, use of laxatives, or other medications, and/or excessive exercise • Alternating between overeating and fasting	• Repeated episodes of binge eating, consuming unusually large amounts of food in a short period of time • Feeling out of control over eating during the binge episode • Eating much more rapidly than normal, eating large amounts when not feeling physically hungry • Feelings ashamed and guilty after bingeing • No compensatory purging behaviors, such as vomiting, laxatives, and/or excessive exercise

Many celebrities, like Lady Gaga, have publicly shared their battles with eating disorders. But does this type of publicity increase or decrease the chance that their fans will suffer similar problems?

Chris Wolf/Getty Images

while feeling a lack of control over eating. However, the individual does not try to purge (American Psychiatric Association, 2013; Amianto et al., 2015). Individuals with binge-eating disorder generally eat more rapidly than normal, eat until they are uncomfortably full and eat when not feeling physically hungry. They also tend to eat alone because of embarrassment at the large quantities they are consuming, and they feel disgusted, depressed, or very guilty after bingeing.

There are many suspected causes of anorexia nervosa, bulimia nervosa, and binge-eating disorder. Some theories focus on physical causes, such as hypothalamic disorders, low levels of various neurotransmitters, and genetic or hormonal disorders. Other theories emphasize psychosocial factors, such as a need for perfection, a perceived loss of control, teasing about body weight, destructive thought patterns, depression, dysfunctional families, distorted body image, and emotional or sexual abuse (e.g., American Psychiatric Association, 2013; Brauhardt et al., 2014; Schneider, 2015). Interestingly, studies have found that women who frequently use social media are at greater risk of showing disordered eating. Apparently, browsing sites like Facebook leads to more body dissatisfaction. Women who compare their own photos with those of their friends, and women who over-value receiving comments and "likes" on their status updates, are at particular risk of eating disorders (Mabe et al., 2014).

Culture and ethnicity also play important roles in eating disorders (Lähteenmäki et al., 2014; Smart & Tsong, 2014). For instance, U.S. Blacks report fewer overall eating disorders and greater satisfaction with their bodies than other U.S. groups. Regardless of the causes of these eating disorders, it's important to recognize the symptoms of anorexia, bulimia, and binge-eating disorder (**Table 10.2**) and to seek therapy if the symptoms apply to you. The key point to remember is that all eating disorders are serious and chronic conditions that require treatment. In fact, some studies find that they have the highest mortality rates of all mental illnesses (Goldberg et al., 2015; Zerwas et al., 2015).

Achievement Motivation

Achievement motivation The desire to excel, especially in competition with others.

Do you wonder what motivates Olympic athletes to work so hard for a gold medal? What about someone like Oprah Winfrey, famous television star, thriving businesswoman, and generous philanthropist? Or Mark Zuckerberg, cofounder of Facebook? The key to understanding what motivates high-achieving individuals lies in what psychologist Henry Murray (1938) identified as a high need for achievement (nAch), or **achievement motivation**. See the following **Psychology and You**.

Psychology and You—Understanding Yourself

Test Yourself/Need for Achievement (nAch)

Researchers have identified at least six traits that distinguish people with a high nAch (Harwood et al., 2015; McClelland, 1958, 1993; Mokrova et al., 2013; Schunk & Zimmerman, 2013; Stadler, 2016). Place a check mark next to each trait that applies to you or to ones that you may want to work to develop:

- ______ *Preference for moderately difficult tasks* People high in nAch avoid tasks that are too easy because they offer little challenge or satisfaction. They also avoid extremely difficult tasks because the probability of success is too low.
- ______ *Competitiveness* High-achievement-oriented people are more attracted to careers and tasks that involve competition and an opportunity to excel.
- ______ *Preference for clear goals with competent feedback* High-achievement oriented people tend to prefer tasks with clear outcomes and situations in which they can receive feedback on their performance. Likewise, they prefer criticism from a harsh but competent evaluator to criticism from one who is friendlier but less competent.
- ______ *Self-regulation and personal responsibility* High-achievement oriented people purposefully control their thoughts and behaviors to attain their goals. In addition, they prefer being personally responsible for a project so that they can feel satisfied when the task is well done.
- ______ *Mental toughness and persistence* High-achievement oriented people have a mindset that allows them to persevere through difficult circumstances. It includes attributes like sacrifice and self-denial, which helps them maintain concentration and motivation when things aren't going well.
- ______ *More accomplished* People who have high nAch scores do better than others on exams, earn better grades in school, and excel in their chosen professions.

In addition to these six individual personality traits associated with nAch, researchers have found that highly motivated children tend to have parents who encourage independence and frequently reward successes (Aunola et al., 2013; Katz et al., 2011; Pomerantz & Kempner, 2013). In fact, children's motivation for academic success—along with their study skills—are better predictors of long-term math achievement than IQ (Murayama et al., 2012).

Our cultural values also affect achievement needs (Chi, 2013; Greenfield & Quiroz, 2013; Xu & Barnes, 2011). In fact, a study of 13,000 identical and fraternal twins from six different countries found that academic motivation (enjoyment of reading, math, science, etc.) is determined about half by these types of environmental experiences, with the other half being governed by genetics (Kovas et al., 2015).

Given that we have little control over our childhood or culture, it's important to know that [Q3] achievement is largely under our control—through a *growth mindset* and *grit*. Psychologist Carol Dweck (2007, 2012) suggests that having a **growth mindset** is the key to achievement. People like Michael Jordan believe that their abilities can change and grow through their own effort (see the photo). In contrast, those with a *fixed mindset* believe the opposite—that their abilities are fixed and set in stone! In addition to a growth mindset, research has shown that **grit** (perseverance and passion for long-term goals) is one of the most significant predictors of success—in both work and academic settings (Datu et al., 2016; Duckworth et al., 2007; Suzuk et al., 2015). Can you see how this research shows that through your own beliefs (a growth mindset) and personal efforts (grit) you too can be a high achiever? As you've discovered throughout this text, humans have a great capacity to change, adapt, and grow.

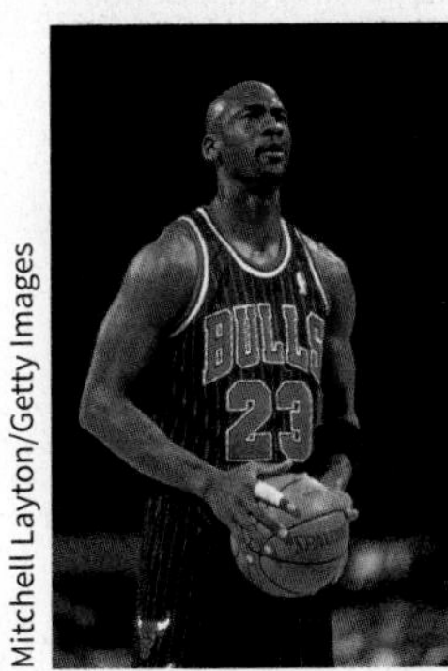

Mitchell Layton/Getty Images

Michael Jordan
According to the NBA, Michael Jordan ranks as the greatest basketball player of all time (All Time League Leaders, 2016). Psychological research suggests that his achievements reflect a growth mindset and true grit!

Growth mindset A psychological term referring to a self-perception or set of beliefs about abilities and the potential to change.

Grit A psychological term referring perseverance and passion in the pursuit of long-term goals.

Extrinsic motivation A type of motivation for a task or activity based on external incentives, such as rewards and punishments.

Intrinsic motivation A type of motivation for a task or activity based on internal incentives, such as enjoyment and personal satisfaction.

Extrinsic Versus Intrinsic Motivation

Have you ever noticed that for all the money and glory they receive, professional athletes often don't look like they're enjoying themselves very much? What's the problem? Why don't they appreciate how lucky they are to be able to make a living by playing games?

One way psychologists attempt to answer questions about motivation is by distinguishing between **extrinsic motivation**, based on external rewards or punishments, and **intrinsic motivation**, based on internal, personal satisfaction from a task or activity (Deci & Moller, 2005; Ryan & Deci, 2013). When we perform a task for no ulterior purpose, we use internal, personal reasons ("I like it"; "It's fun"). But when extrinsic rewards are added, the explanation shifts to external, impersonal reasons ("I did it for the money"; "I did it to please my parents"). This shift often decreases enjoyment and hampers performance. This is as true for professional athletes as it is for anyone else.

FIGURE 10.9 **How extrinsic rewards can sometimes be motivating**

Controlling reward

School gives every student a small reward for attendance → *Student is extrinsically motivated*: "I'll attend school if I get the reward."

Approval reward
Parents:
"We'll be very happy if you get A's like our neighbor's boy."
Student is extrinsically motivated:
"I'll get good grades to get their approval."

a. If extrinsic rewards are used to control, or gain approval, they generally decrease motivation. For example, when schools pay all students for simple attendance, or when parents give children approval or privileges for achieving good grades, they may unintentionally decrease the children's school attendance and good grades.

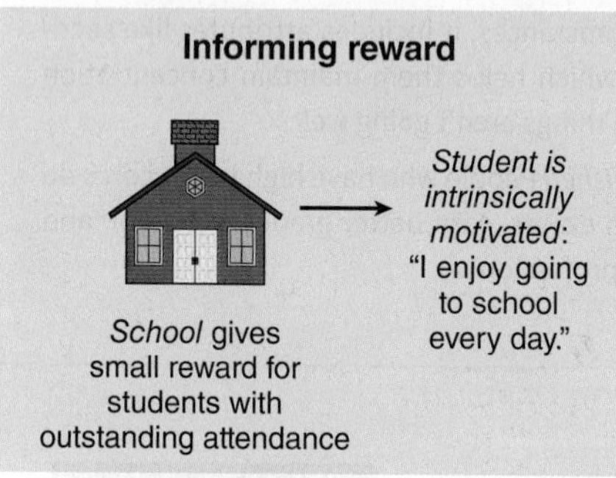
Informing reward
School gives small reward for students with outstanding attendance
Student is intrinsically motivated:
"I enjoy going to school every day."

"No strings" treat
Parents:
"We want to surprise you with a special treat for your good grades."
Student is intrinsically motivated:
"I like getting good grades."

b. Extrinsic rewards can be motivating if they are used to inform, and the reward has "no strings" attached. For instance, when a small reward is provided for outstanding attendance, or a surprise treat is offered for good grades, it may increase both motivation and enjoyment.

A classic experiment demonstrating this effect was conducted with preschool children who liked to draw (Lepper et al., 1973). These researchers found that children who were given paper and markers, and promised a reward for their drawings, were subsequently less interested in drawing than children who were not given a reward, or who were given an unexpected reward for their pictures when they were done. Likewise, a decade-long study of over 10,000 West Point cadets found that those who were motivated to pursue a military career for internal reasons, such as personal ambition, were more likely to receive early career promotions than those who attended a military academy for external reasons, such as family expectations (Wrzesniewski et al., 2014).

As it turns out, however, there is considerable controversy over individual differences in what motivates someone, and under what conditions giving external, extrinsic rewards increases or decreases motivation (Deci & Ryan, 1985, 2012; Koo et al., 2015; Pope & Harvey, 2015). Furthermore, research shows that not all extrinsic motivation is bad. A study of elementary school students, who were simply mailed books weekly during the summer, or mailed books along with a reading incentive, or assigned to a control group with no books or incentives, found that students who were initially more motivated to read were also more responsive to incentives (Guryan et al., 2015). As you can see in **Figure 10.9**, extrinsic rewards with "no strings attached" can actually increase motivation.

How does this apply to you and your everyday life? As a college student facing many high-stakes exams, have you noticed how often professors try to motivate their students with "scare tactics," such as frequently reminding you of how your overall GPA and/or scores on certain exams may be critical for entry into desirable jobs or for admittance to graduate programs? Does this type of extrinsic motivation help or hurt your motivation? One study found that when instructors use extrinsic consequences, such as fear tactics, as motivational tools, their students' intrinsic motivation and exam scores decrease (Putwain & Remedios, 2014). In fact, fear of failure may be one of the greatest detriments to intrinsic motivation (Covington & Müeller, 2001; Ma et al., 2014; Martin & Marsh, 2006).

What should teachers and students do instead? Rather than emphasizing high exam scores or overall GPA, researchers recommend focusing on specific behaviors required to avoid failure and attain success. In other words, as a student you can focus on improving your overall study techniques and test taking skills. See again the *Strategies for Student Success* at the end of Chapter 1. For additional help, check with your professor and/or your college counseling center. For help with increasing your overall motivation, see the following **Psychology and You**.

whether we are sad, happy, or mad? Positron emission tomography (PET) scans of the brain do show subtle differences in the overall physical arousal with basic emotions, such as happiness, fear, and anger (Levenson, 1992, 2007; Werner et al., 2007). But most people are not aware of these slight variations. Thus, there must be other explanations for how we experience emotion.

The *Cannon–Bard theory* (that arousal and emotions occur simultaneously and that all emotions are physiologically similar) has received some experimental support. Recall from our earlier discussion that victims of spinal cord damage still experience emotions—often more intensely than before their injuries. Instead of the thalamus, however, other research shows that it is the limbic system, hypothalamus, and prefrontal cortex that are activated in emotional experience (Junque, 2015; LeDoux, 2007; Schulze et al., 2016).

As mentioned earlier, research on the *facial-feedback hypothesis* has found a distinctive physiological response for basic emotions such as fear, sadness, and anger—thus partially confirming James–Lange's initial position. Facial feedback does seem to contribute to the intensity of our subjective emotional experience and our overall moods. So, if you want to change a bad mood or intensify a particularly good emotion, adopt the appropriate facial expression. Try smiling when you're sad and expanding your smiles when you're happy.

Finally, Schachter and Singer's *two-factor theory* emphasizes the importance of cognitive labels in emotions. But research shows that some neural pathways involved in emotion bypass the cortex and go directly to the limbic system. Recall our earlier example of jumping at the sight of a supposed snake and then a second later using the cortex to interpret what it was. This and other evidence suggest that emotions can take place without conscious cognitive processes. Thus, emotion is not simply the labeling of arousal.

In sum, certain basic emotions are associated with subtle differences in arousal. These differences can be produced by changes in facial expressions or by organs controlling the autonomic nervous system. In addition, "simple" emotions (fear and anger) do not initially require conscious cognitive processes. This allows a quick, automatic emotional response that can later be modified by cortical processes. On the other hand, "complex" emotions (jealousy, grief, depression, embarrassment, love) seem to require more extensive cognitive processes.

Retrieval Practice 10.3 | Components and Theories of Emotion

SELF-TEST Completing this self-test, and then checking your answers by clicking on the answer button or by looking in Appendix B, will provide immediate feedback and helpful practice for exams.

1. The three components of emotion are ____.

a. cognitive, biological, and behavioral
b. perceiving, thinking, and acting
c. positive, negative, and neutral
d. active/passive, positive/negative, and direct/ indirect

2. You feel anxious because you are sweating and your heart is beating rapidly. This statement illustrates the ____ theory of emotion.

a. two-factor **b.** James-Lange
c. Cannon-Bard **d.** physiological feedback

3. According to the ____, arousal and emotions occur separately but simultaneously.

a. Cannon-Bard theory
b. James-Lange theory
c. facial-feedback hypothesis
d. two-factor theory

4. Schacter and Singer's two factor theory emphasizes the ____ component of emotion.

a. stimulus-response **b.** physiological
c. behavioral-imitation **d.** cognitive

5. You grin broadly while your best friend tells you she was just accepted to medical school. The facial-feedback hypothesis predicts that you will feel ____.

a. happy
b. envious
c. angry
d. all of these emotions

Think Critically

1. If you were going on a date with someone or applying for an important job, how might you use the three key theories of emotion to increase the chances that things will go well?

2. Why do you think people around the world experience and express the same basic emotions, and what evolutionary advantages might help explain these similarities?

Real World Psychology

Can airport security agents increase their effectiveness by simply talking to passengers?

© Jim West/Alamy Stock Photo

HINT: LOOK IN THE MARGIN FOR **[Q5]**

10.4 Experiencing Emotions

LEARNING OBJECTIVES

Retrieval Practice While reading the upcoming sections, respond to each Learning Objective in your own words.

Review how emotions affect behavior.

- **Describe** the role of culture and evolution on emotion.
- **Summarize** the problems with using polygraph testing as a lie detector.
- **Discuss** the major components of happiness.

How do culture and evolution affect our emotions? Is the polygraph an effective way to detect lies? Why are some people happier than others? Can romantic love survive long-distance relationships? These are just a few of the questions, topics, and emotional experiences we'll explore in this section.

Culture and Evolution

Are emotions the same across all cultures? Given the seemingly vast array of emotions within our own culture, it may surprise you to learn that some researchers believe that all our feelings can be condensed into 6 to 12 culturally universal emotions (**Table 10.4**). These researchers hold that other emotions, such as love, are simply combinations of primary emotions with variations in intensity. As you can see in Table 10.4, most of these emotions are present in early infancy.

However, more recent research suggests that this previous list of basic emotions could be combined and reduced to just four: *happy, sad, afraid/surprised,* and *angry/disgusted* (Jack et al., 2014). Regardless of the exact number, researchers tend to agree that across cultures, the facial expression of emotions, such as a smile, is recognized by all as a sign of pleasure, whereas a frown is recognized as a sign of displeasure.

From an evolutionary perspective, the idea of universal facial expressions makes adaptive sense because such expressions signal others about our current emotional state (Awasthi & Mandal, 2015; Ekman & Keltner, 1997; Hwang & Matsumoto, 2015). Charles Darwin first advanced the evolutionary theory of emotion in 1872. He proposed that expression of emotions evolved in different species as a part of survival and natural selection. For example, expressions of fear help other human and nonhuman animals avoid danger, whereas expressions of anger and aggression are useful when fighting for mates or resources. Modern evolutionary theory suggests that basic emotions originate in the *limbic system*. Given that higher brain areas like the cortex developed later than the subcortical limbic system, evolutionary theory proposes that basic emotions evolved before thought.

Studies with infants provide further support for an evolutionary basis for emotions. For example, infants only a few hours old show distinct expressions of emotion that closely match adult facial expressions, and by the age of 7 months they can reliably interpret and recognize emotional information across both face and voice (Cole & Moore, 2015; Jessen & Grossman, 2015; Meltzoff & Moore, 1977, 1994). And all infants, even those who are born deaf and blind, show similar facial expressions in similar situations (Denmark et al., 2014; Field et al., 1982; Gelder et al., 2006). In addition, a study showed that families may have characteristic facial expressions, shared even by family members who have been blind from birth (Peleg et al., 2006). This collective evidence points to a strong biological, evolutionary basis for emotional expression and decoding.

© David J. Green - lifestyle themes/Alamy Stock Photo

In contrast to the evolutionary approach, other research has shown that our emotions are sometimes contagious! To test the hypothesis that certain emotions might spread through social media (see the photo), researchers first evaluated both positive and negative [Q6] emotions conveyed in Facebook posts (Coviello et al., 2014). Then, they compared the frequency of these emotional expressions to the amount of rainfall in each poster's city. As you

TABLE 10.4 Sample Basic Emotions

(Note the strong similarities among the four lists.)

CARROLL IZARD	PAUL EKMAN AND WALLACE FRIESEN	SILVAN TOMKINS	ROBERT PLUTCHIK
Fear	Fear	Fear	Fear
Anger	Anger	Anger	Anger
Disgust	Disgust	Disgust	Disgust
Surprise	Surprise	Surprise	Surprise
Joy	Happiness	Enjoyment	Joy
Shame	—	Shame	—
Contempt	Contempt	Contempt	—
Sadness	Sadness	—	Sadness
Interest	—	Interest	Anticipation
Guilt	—	—	—
—	—	—	Acceptance
—	—	Distress	—

Test Yourself

Using this list of emotions, try to identify the specific emotion reflected in each of the six infant faces.

Vladimir Godnik/beyond fotomedia/Getty Images

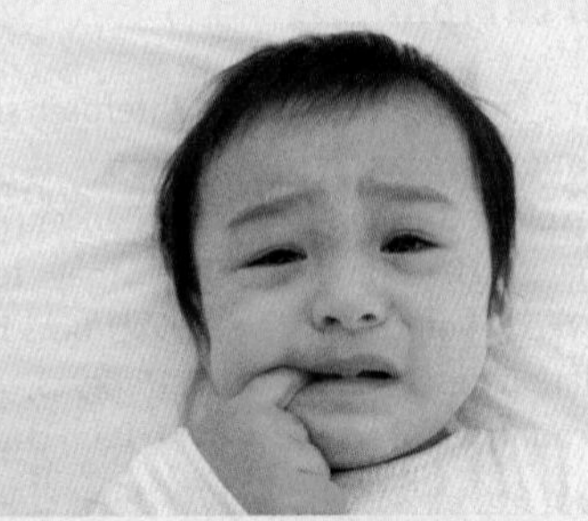
ICHIRO/Getty Images

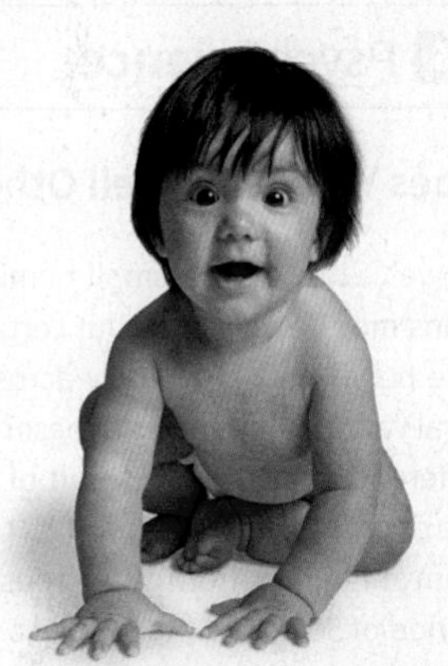
John Lund/Annabelle Breakey/Getty Images

arnoaltix/Getty Images

© Flashon Studio/Shutterstock

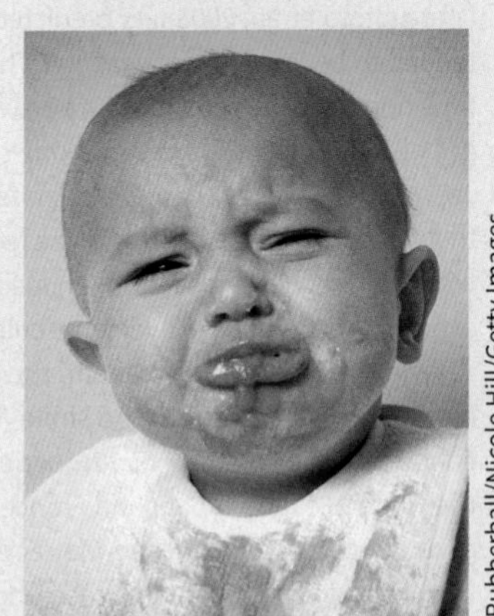
Rubberball/Nicole Hill/Getty Images

Answers: From left to right (top row) = fear, sadness, surprise (bottom row) = anger, joy/happiness, disgust.

might expect, people tend to post more negative emotions, and fewer positive emotions, on rainy days. In fact, in a large population, such as New York City, a rainy day leads to an additional 1500 negative posts compared to on a non-rainy day. [Q6] The researchers then examined how one person's Facebook post could impact the mood expressions posted by their friends

FIGURE 10.18 Can you identify these emotions? Most people easily recognize the emotional expression of happiness, such as the two women in the photo on the left. However, on occasion, our facial expressions don't seem to match our presumed emotions, as is the case in the photo on the right. In this case, the obviously happy skier is wiping away tears after winning gold in the 2014 Olympics, and he looks sad rather than happy.

DigitalVision/Getty Images

Odd Anderson/Getty Images

living in other cities. They found that having a friend post something negative on Facebook increases the probability of a person writing a negative post themselves, and decreases the likelihood of a positive post. [Q6]

In addition, emotions are much more complex than originally thought (Gendron et al., 2014; Hsu, 2016; Hwang & Matsumoto, 2015). For example, although we may all share similar facial expressions for some emotions, each culture has its own *display rules* (see **Real World Psychology** feature) that govern how, when, and where to express them (Allen et al., 2014; Ekman, 1993, 2004; Hess & Hareli, 2015). In addition to culture, gender, family background, norms, and individual differences affect our emotions and their expression (**Figure 10.18**). As you'll see in the following **PsychScience**, even a nation's historical pattern of migration may have an emotional effect.

PS PsychScience

Does Your Smile Tell Others Where You're From?

As we've just seen, a small number of emotions and facial expressions may be universal, but certain aspects of emotionally expressive behaviors vary widely across culture. What explains this cultural variance in expressiveness? A recent study suggests that some differences may be the result of *historical heterogeneity*—meaning the degree to which a country's present-day population descended from migration from numerous vs. few source countries over a period of 500 years (Rychlowska et al., 2015).

To test this hypothesis, the researchers carefully analyzed existing data on cultural rules for displaying emotions from 32 countries (Matsumoto et al., 2008). As predicted, countries with less migration tended to be less expressive. Why? The researchers suggest that over time homogeneous countries, those with less diversity, develop stronger display rules for how emotions should be openly expressed. In Japan, for instance, when subordinates are upset around their bosses they're more likely to conceal these feelings with smiles. For countries with a more diverse past, though, people need to beef up their facial expressions, perhaps to overcome cultural and language barriers.

In their follow-up research, the team zeroed in on a particular kind of facial expression: the smile (Rychlowska et al., 2015). They conducted a new study of 726 people in nine countries, including the United States, Japan, and France. Here again, participants were asked to complete a questionnaire regarding cultural rules for emotional expression. But in this case, they were asked to consider what constituted a good reason for someone else to smile, such as he or she "is a happy person," "wants to sell you something," and "feels inferior to you." The participants rated each reason to smile on a scale from strongly disagree to strongly agree.

The researchers then compared the results for each country with their migration numbers. In further support of their initial hypothesis, countries with less migration and less diversity thought smiles were related to the social hierarchy—people smile because they "feel inferior to you." In contrast, countries with greater and more diverse immigration over the past 500 years were more likely to interpret smiles as friendly gestures.

Westend61/Getty Images

Can you now see how your smile may tell others where you're from? If you smile more to strangers, you're more likely to be from countries with a history of numerous immigrants from various areas—such as the United States—compared to others who come from nations with fewer immigrants.

Research Challenge

1. Based on the information provided, did the researchers in these two studies (Rychlowska et al., 2015) use descriptive, correlational, and/or experimental research?
2. If you chose:
   - *descriptive research*, is this a naturalistic observation, survey/interview, case study, and/or archival research?
   - *correlational research*, is this a positive, negative, or zero correlation?
   - *experimental research*, label the IV, DV, experimental group(s), and control group.
   - both *descriptive* and *correlational*, answer the corresponding questions for both.

Check your answers by clicking on the answer button or by looking in Appendix B.

Note: The information provided in this study is admittedly limited, but the level of details is similar to what is presented in most text books and public reports of research findings. Answering these questions, and then comparing your answers to those provided, will help you become a better critical thinker and consumer of scientific research.

Real World Psychology—Understanding the World

Understanding Display Rules for Emotions

How do we learn our culture's display rules? Parents and other adults pass along their culture's specific emotional *display rules* to children by responding negatively or ignoring some emotions and being supportive and sympathetic to others. Public physical contact is also governed by display rules. Did you know that Americans, Europeans, and Asians are less likely than people in other cultures to touch one another, and that only the closest family members and friends might hug in greeting or farewell? In contrast, Latin Americans and Middle Easterners often kiss, embrace, and hold hands as a sign of casual friendship (Axtell, 2007). In fact, some Middle Eastern men commonly greet one another with a kiss (as shown in the photo). Can you imagine this same behavior among men in the U.S., who generally just shake hands, or pat one another's shoulders? Keep these cultural differences in mind when you're traveling. The "thumbs up" gesture is widely used in America to mean everything is okay, or the desire to hitch a ride. However in many Middle Eastern countries, the same gesture is similar to an American's raised middle finger!

Behrouz Mehri/AFP/Getty Images

The Polygraph as a Lie Detector

We've discussed the way emotions are affected by culture and evolution. Now we turn our attention to one of the hottest, and most controversial, topics in emotion research—the **polygraph**.

Polygraph An instrument that measures sympathetic arousal (heart rate, respiration rate, blood pressure, and skin conductivity) to detect emotional arousal, which in turn supposedly reflects lying versus truthfulness.

The polygraph is a machine that measures physiological indicators (such as heart rate and blood pressure) to detect emotional arousal, which supposedly reflects whether or not you are lying. Traditional polygraph tests are based on the assumption that when people lie, they feel stressed, and that this stress can be measured. As you can see in **Figure 10.19**, during a polygraph test multiple (poly) signals from special sensors assess four major indicators of stress and autonomic arousal: heart rate (pulse), blood pressure, respiration (breathing) rate, and perspiration (or skin conductivity). If the participant's bodily responses significantly increase when responding to key questions, the examiner will infer that the participant is lying (Granhag et al., 2015; Tomash & Reed, 2013).

Can you imagine what problems might be associated with the polygraph? First, many people become stressed even when telling the truth, whereas others can conceal their stress, and remain calm when deliberately lying. Second, emotions cause physiological arousal, and a polygraph

FIGURE 10.19 Polygraph testing Real World Psychology

Polygraph testing is based on the assumption that when we lie, we feel guilty, fearful, or anxious.

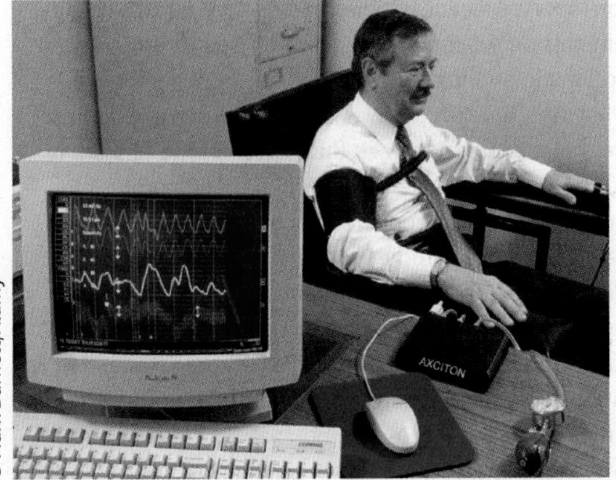

© Mark Burnett/Alamy

a. During a standard polygraph test, a band around the person's chest measures breathing rate, a cuff monitors blood pressure, and finger electrodes measure sweating, or galvanic skin response (GSR).

b. Note how the GSR rises sharply in response to the question, "Have you ever taken money from this bank?"

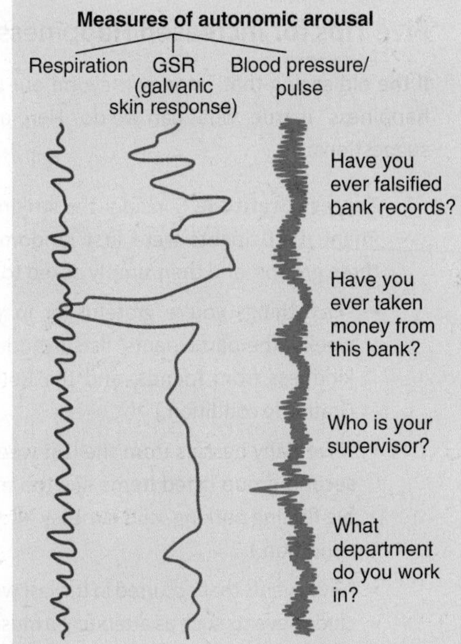

cannot tell which emotion is being felt (anxiety, irritation, excitement, or any other emotion). For this reason, some have suggested the polygraph should be relabeled as an "arousal detector." The third, and perhaps most important, problem is one of questionable accuracy. In fact, people can be trained to beat a lie detector (Kaste, 2015; Wollan, 2015). When asked a general, control question ("Where do you live?"), participants wishing to mislead the examiner can artificially raise their arousal levels by imagining their worst fears (being burned to death or buried alive). Then when asked relevant/guilty knowledge questions ("Did you rob the bank?"), they can calm themselves by practicing meditation tricks (imagining themselves relaxing on a beach).

In response to these and other problems, countless research hours and millions of dollars have been spent on new and improved lie-detection techniques. Although most people (and many police officers) believe that nonverbal cues—such as gaze aversion and increased movement—are indicative of deception, there is limited support for these beliefs (Bogaard et al., 2016). As we discovered earlier with the airport security research, talking to passengers increases detection of dishonesty and certain verbal cues can detect lying. For example, liars tend to tell less coherent stories and are less likely to make spontaneous corrections to their stories (Vrij et al., 2010). Perhaps the most promising method for lie detection is the use of brain scans, like *functional magnetic resonance imaging (fMRI)* (Farah et al., 2014; Jiang et al., 2015). Unfortunately, each of these new lie-detection techniques has potential problems. Furthermore, researchers have questioned their reliability and validity, and civil libertarians and judicial scholars raise doubts about their ethics and legality (Kaste, 2015; Lilienfeld et al., 2015; Roskey, 2013). While research on improved methods for lie detection continues, note that most courts do not accept polygraph test results, laws have been passed to restrict their use, and we should remain skeptical of their ability to detect guilt or innocence (Granhag et al., 2015; Handler et al., 2013; Tomash & Reed, 2013).

The Psychology of Happiness

What emotion is most important for your overall life satisfaction? If you said "happiness," you're on the right track. Although some people do report wanting to be wealthy, research around the world repeatedly finds that once we have enough money to meet our basic needs for comfort and security, additional funds fail to significantly increase our level of happiness (Diener & Biswas-Diener, 2002, 2008; Diener et al., 2015; Kushlev et al., 2015; Whillans et al., 2016). In short, more is not always better (see **Psychology and You**).

Psychology and You—Understanding Yourself

Five Tips for Increased Happiness

If the old saying that "money (beyond our basic needs) can't buy happiness" is true, what can we do? Here are five research-based suggestions:

1. **Express Gratitude** Consider the striking effects of this experiment. Participants were first randomly assigned to one of three groups, and then simply asked to write down:
   - "Five things you're grateful for in your life over the last week." The participants' lists included such things as God, kindness from friends, and the Rolling Stones. (Group 1: Gratitude condition.)
   - "Five daily hassles from the last week." Participants in this second group listed items like too many bills to pay, trouble finding parking, and a messy kitchen. (Group 2: Hassles condition.)
   - "Five events that occurred in the last week." This group's list included events such as attending a music festival, learning CPR, and cleaning out a closet. (Group 3: Events condition.)

   Before the experiment started, all participants kept daily journals recording their moods, physical health and general attitudes, which the researchers later used to compare how people in these three groups changed over time (Emmons & McCullough, 2003).

   As you might have expected, participants in the gratitude condition reported feeling happier. In fact, they were 25% happier from this very simple assignment! Likewise, they were more optimistic about the future and felt better about their lives. What was unexpected was that this group did almost 1.5 hours more exercise a week than those in the hassles or events condition, and had fewer symptoms of illness.

   Further evidence of a positive link between gratitude and happiness comes from studies showing that developing and expressing gratitude are linked with reduced cardiac risk, depression and anxiety symptoms, as well as with improved relationships with others and a less critical and more compassionate relationship with yourself (Mills et al., 2015; Petrocchi & Couyoumdjian, 2016). Keep in mind that your everyday expressions of gratitude can be very small. Simply thanking people who have helped us or given us good service at a restaurant, or writing down three things we are grateful for each night before going to bed, can have a substantial positive impact on our well-being, happiness, and life satisfaction.

2. **Change Your Behavior** As you discovered in Chapters 3 and 5, getting enough exercise, sleep, and spending time in nature all help make us feel better (Bell et al., 2015; Song et al., 2016; Wassing et al., 2016). Surprisingly, research shows that simply reading a book you love increases happiness (Berns et al., 2013). Reading apparently helps us feel connected to characters in a book, which in turn helps us feel connected with other people. Reading also can increase positive feelings, especially if the book inspires you to think about your own life in a new way, or to take action towards reaching your own goals. So, grab a book you find personally enjoyable (not one you "should read"). Then make a point of reading every day—a few minutes before bed, on a lunch break, or during your daily commute on public transportation.

   Another easy behavioral change that will increase your happiness is to act happy! Research shows that just changing your voice to a happier tone actually increases happiness (Aucouturier et al., 2016). In addition, as you discovered earlier in this chapter with the facial-feedback hypothesis, simply holding a pencil between your teeth (to force a simulated smile) increases pleasant feelings.

3. **Spend Your Money and Time Wisely** People who spend money on life experiences—*doing things*—show greater enduring happiness than those who spend money buying material possessions—*having things*. Spending money on tickets to the "big game," a Broadway show, or a fabulous trip is a great way to increase happiness. On the other hand, the pleasure we get from spending money on an expensive car, watch, or shoes is limited and momentary.

   Why? One factor is anticipation. It's more enjoyable to anticipate experiences than to anticipate acquiring possessions. The pleasure we get from looking forward to a two week trip is substantially greater than the pleasure we get from anticipating buying a new car. Another explanation is that we're far more likely to share experiences with others, whereas we generally acquire material possessions for solo use.

   A second way to spend your money wisely is to share it with others! Research shows that giving to others and performing acts of kindness and service are powerful ways to increase happiness (Lyubomirsky, 2008, 2013).

   Just as it's important to spend your money wisely, the same is true about your time. Given that the two are often interrelated, it's important to note that "money is simply something you trade your life energy for" (Robin et al., 2009). For example, if you're currently making $10 an hour and you're considering buying a new iPhone for $650, you need to calculate the real time/money cost. Are you willing to work 65 hours for that new phone? Really?

4. **Build and Maintain Close Relationships** As mentioned in Chapter 1, people who are happy tend to invest money, time and energy into having high-quality, close relationships (Diener & Tay, 2015; Galinha et al., 2016; Gander et al., 2016).

"All I want is a chance to prove money can't make me happy."

Patrick Hardin/CartoonStock

To examine how relationship quality affects happiness, researchers examined data from over 5,000 American adults, including information on the quality of their relationships with a spouse, family members and friends, as well as their rates of depression over a 10-year period (Teo et al., 2013). People with unhappy relationships were much more likely to develop depression, compared to those who were happily married or those who had other high quality relationships. In practical terms, this study reveals that one in seven adults with the lowest-quality relationships will become depressed compared to just one in 15 adults who have the highest quality relationships.

5. **Choose and Pursue Worthy Goals** This final tip for increasing happiness involves making a list of your most personally valuable and worthy goals, and the specific things you want to accomplish—daily and long-term. Note, however, that pursuing happiness (or money) for its own sake can backfire! Have you heard about people who win the lottery and later become less happy and satisfied? This type of **adaptation-level phenomenon** reflects the fact that we tend to judge a new situation or stimuli relative to a neutral level defined by our previous experiences with them. We win the lottery or get a new job with a higher income and naturally experience an initial surge of pleasure. We then adjust our neutral level higher, which, in turn, requires ever increasing improvements to gain a similar increase in happiness.

   In other words, happiness, like all emotions, is fleeting, and it's incredibly difficult to go backwards. This so-called *hedonic treadmill* shows us that the pleasures we acquire in all parts of our lives—money, material possessions, status, and even our relationships, can quickly become part of our everyday baseline and taken for granted—until they're taken away. Can you see how the previous tips on this list—expressing gratitude, changing your behavior, spending your time and money wisely, and building and maintaining close relationships—can help offset the dangers of this adaptation? For further tips on happiness, see the following **PositivePsych**.

Adaptation-level phenomenon A tendency to judge a new situation or stimuli relative to a neutral, "normal" level based on our previous experiences; we then adapt to this new level and it becomes the new "normal."

PP PositivePsych

Can Long-Distance Relationships Survive?

AvailableLight/Getty Images

One of the key ingredients to health and happiness is frequent physical contact within a satisfying romantic relationship. Yet, up to 75% of college students report having been in a long-distance romantic relationship (LDR), and over 3 million American spouses successfully live apart for a variety of reasons (cited in Borelli et al., 2015). How do these couples manage to survive (and even flourish) despite the relative lack of physical contact, reduced communication, and the financial burdens associated with being separated by large geographical distances? The answer may be that they practice what's called *relational savoring,* meaning sharing an experience that is shared with another person in an emotionally close relationship (Borelli et al., 2014). And "savoring" itself has been defined as the process of attending to, intensifying, and prolonging the positive emotions attached to experiences (Bryant & Veroff, 2007). In other words, paying close attention and relishing and delighting in experiences shared with our significant other.

Interested in the possibility that relational savoring in LDR couples might result in better emotional states and protection against relationship threats, researchers studied wives of military service members before and during their spouses' military deployment (Borelli et al., 2015). Participants were assigned to one of three groups. Wives in the neutral (control) condition were asked to think about and mentally replay their normal morning routine from the time they woke up until they left for work/school. In the *personal savoring* (experimental) condition, the wives were asked to focus and reflect on a personal positive experience. In the *relational savoring* (second experimental) condition, the wives were prompted to think about a positive experience with their partner when they felt especially "cherished, protected, or accepted."

In all conditions, participating wives not only reported on the details surrounding the experience, but also their thoughts and feelings. They were then asked to spend 2 minutes mentally reliving the event. Perhaps surprisingly, only the LDR participants who engaged in *relational savoring* showed increases in their positive emotions, decreases in their negative emotions, and increases in relationship satisfaction following a simulated relationship stressor task.

What's the important takeaway? If a brief laboratory experiment prompting LDR participants to engage in relational savoring can have such positive personal and relationship effects, think about how it could be applied to your own life. While practicing the gratitude exercises mentioned earlier, remind yourself to stop and "savor" those moments and memories of times you felt particularly cherished, protected, or accepted by your romantic partner.

Retrieval Practice 10.4 | Experiencing Emotions

SELF-TEST Completing this self-test, and then checking your answers by clicking on the answer button or by looking in Appendix B, will provide immediate feedback and helpful practice for exams.

1. According to evolutionary theory, basic emotions, like fear and anger, seem to originate in _____.

a. higher cortical areas of the brain
b. subtle changes in facial expressions
c. the limbic system
d. the interpretation of environmental stimuli

2. Cultural norms governing emotional expressions are called _____.

a. extrinsic guidelines
b. emotion regulators
c. display rules
d. none of these options

3. Which of the following is(are) recommended for increasing happiness?

a. Express gratitude.
b. Spend your money and time wisely.
c. Choose worthy goals.
d. All of these options.

4. The polygraph, or lie detector, measures primarily the _____ component of emotions.

a. physiological **b.** articulatory
c. cognitive **d.** subjective

5. Which of the following is TRUE about the polygraph?

a. It does in fact measure autonomic arousal.
b. It cannot tell which emotion is being felt.
c. People can be trained to beat a polygraph.
d. All of these options

Think Critically

1. How might differing cultural display rules explain why American tourists are often criticized by local residents for being "too loud and aggressive"?

2. After reading the section on polygraph tests, would you be willing to take a "lie detector" test if you were accused of a crime? Why or why not?

© David J. Green - lifestyle themes/ Alamy Stock Photo

Real World Psychology

Are our emotions contagious?

HINT: LOOK IN THE MARGIN FOR **[Q6]**

Summary

10.1 Theories of Motivation 271

- Biological theories of **motivation** emphasize **instincts**, drives (produced by the body's need for **homeostasis**), and arousal (the need for novelty, complexity, and stimulation).
- Psychological theories focus on the role of incentives, attributions, and expectancies in cognition.
- Maslow's **hierarchy of needs** theory takes a biopsychosocial approach. It prioritizes needs, with survival needs at the bottom and higher needs at the top.

10.2 Motivation and Behavior 276

- Both biological factors (the stomach, biochemistry, the brain) and psychosocial factors (stimulus cues and cultural conditioning) affect hunger and eating. These factors play a similar role in **obesity, anorexia nervosa, bulimia nervosa,** and **binge-eating disorder**.
- A high need for achievement (nAch), or **achievement motivation**, is generally learned in early childhood primarily through interactions with parents.
- Providing **extrinsic motivation** like money or praise for an intrinsically satisfying activity can undermine people's enjoyment and interest—their **intrinsic motivation**—for the activity. However, under the right conditions, extrinsic rewards can sometimes be motivational.
- The human motivation for sex is extremely strong. Masters and Johnson first studied and described the **sexual response cycle**, the series of physiological and sexual responses that occurs during sexual activity.
- Other sex research has focused on the roots of **sexual orientation**, and most studies suggest that genetics and biology play the dominant role. Sexual orientation remains a divisive issue, and gays, lesbians, bisexuals, and transgendered people often confront **sexual prejudice**.

10.3 Components and Theories of Emotion 286

- All **emotions** have three basic components: *biological arousal* (e.g., heart pounding), *cognitive* (thoughts, values, and expectations), and *behavioral expressions* (e.g., smiles, frowns, running). Studies of the biological component find that emotions involve a general, nonspecific arousal of the autonomic nervous system.
- According to the **James-Lange theory**, emotions follow from physiological changes. The **Cannon-Bard theory** suggests that emotions and physiological changes occur simultaneously. The **two-factor theory** suggests that emotions depend on two factors–physiological arousal and a cognitive labeling of that arousal.
- Each theory emphasizes different sequences or aspects of the three elements. According to the **facial-feedback hypothesis**, facial movements produce and/or intensify emotions. Other research emphasizes how different pathways in the brain trigger faster and slower emotional responses.

10.4 Experiencing Emotions 292

- Some researchers believe across all cultures people experience several basic, universal emotions, and that we express and recognize these emotions in essentially the same way. These findings and studies with infants support this evolutionary theory of emotion. However, other researchers question the existence of basic emotions, and note that *display rules* for emotional expression vary across cultures.
- **Polygraph** tests attempt to detect lying by measuring physiological signs of guilt, fear, and/or anxiety. Due to several problems with its underlying assumptions and accuracy, most courts do not accept polygraph test results, laws have been passed to restrict its use, and we should remain skeptical.
- Happiness is a popular topic in positive psychology, and it finds that money can only buy happiness up to a point. Once basic needs for comfort and security are met, more money is not necessarily better. Tips for increasing happiness include expressing gratitude, changing your behavior, spending your money and time wisely, building and maintaining close relationships, and choosing worthy goals.

Applying **Real** World **Psychology**

We began this chapter with six intriguing Real World Psychology questions, and you were asked to revisit these questions at the end of each section. Questions like these have an important and lasting impact on all of our lives. See if you can answer these additional critical thinking questions related to real world examples.

Tetra Images/SuperStock, Inc.

1. Nonhuman animals, like the kitten in this photo, sometimes display what we humans would label "curiosity." How might this trait be important for the survival and achievement of both human and nonhuman animals?
2. How do you think nonhuman animal motivation, like this kitten's, might differ from that of humans?
3. Think about your favorite hobbies or recreational activities (for example, riding your bike, watching TV, playing videogames). How would you explain these activities using the six theories of motivation (see Table 10.1, p. 274)?
4. Imagine yourself in a career as a health psychologist (Chapter 3). What type of public health efforts would you recommend to treat eating disorders?
5. Think back to a time when you felt very angry and upset over a misunderstanding with a special friend. Which of the three key components of emotion (biological, cognitive, or behavioral) best accounted for the intensity of your feelings? Which of the three major theories (the James-Lange, Cannon-Bard, or two-factor theory) best explains your overall emotional experience?
6. Do you believe people can (and should) control their emotions? Why or why not?

Key Terms

Retrieval Practice Write a definition for each term before turning back to the referenced page to check your answer.

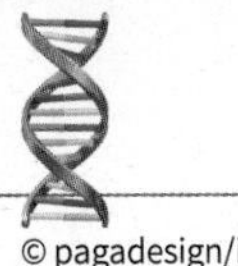
© pagadesign/iStockphoto

CHAPTER 11

Personality

© jonathandowney/iStockphoto

Real World Psychology

Things you'll learn in Chapter 11

[Q1] Are some people with highly negative attitudes toward gay people repressing their own sexual desires?

[Q2] Which personality traits are most important for your career and academic success?

[Q3] What parenting skills are also associated with increased marital satisfaction?

[Q4] Can spending time in a foreign country change your personality?

[Q5] Do our genes predict how much we will give to charity?

[Q6] Can social media postings be used to measure your personality?

Throughout the chapter, margin icons for Q1–Q6 indicate where the text addresses these questions.

CHAPTER OUTLINE

Chapter Overview

You have a strong need for other people to like and admire you. You tend to be critical of yourself. Although you have some personality weaknesses, you are generally able to compensate for them. At times, you have serious doubts about whether you have made the right decision or done the right thing.

—Adapted from Ulrich et al., 1963

Does this sound like you? A high percentage of research participants who read a similar personality description reported that the description was "very accurate"—even after they were informed that it was a *phony* horoscope (Hyman, 1981). Other research shows that about three-quarters of adults read newspaper horoscopes and that many of them believe astrological horoscopes were written especially for them (Sugarman et al., 2011; Wyman & Vyse, 2008).

Why are such spurious personality assessments so popular? One reason is that they seem to tap into our unique selves. Supporters of these horoscopes, however, ignore the fact that the traits they supposedly reveal are characteristics that almost everyone shares. Do you know anyone who doesn't "have a strong need for other people to like and admire" them? The traits in horoscopes are also generally flattering, or at least neutral.

Unlike the pseudopsychologies such as these newspaper horoscopes and Chinese fortune cookies, the descriptions presented by personality researchers are based on empirical studies. In this chapter, we first examine five leading theories of personality (psychoanalytic/psychodynamic, trait, humanistic, social-cognitive, and biological). We then discuss the tools and techniques psychologists have developed to measure, compare, and evaluate our individual personalities.

11.1 Psychoanalytic/Psychodynamic Theories

LEARNING OBJECTIVES

Retrieval Practice While reading the upcoming sections, respond to each Learning Objective in your own words.

Summarize the major concepts of psychoanalytic/ psychodynamic theories of personality.

- **Define** personality.
- **Review** the major concepts of Freud's psychoanalytic theory.
- **Compare** psychoanalytic and psychodynamic theories of personality.
- **Discuss** the major criticisms of psychoanalytic theories.

Personality Our unique and relatively stable pattern of thoughts, feelings, and actions.

Conscious In Freudian terms, thoughts or motives that a person is currently aware of or is remembering.

Preconscious Freud's term for thoughts, motives, or memories that exist just beneath the surface of awareness and can be called to consciousness when necessary.

Unconscious Freud's term for the reservoir of largely unacceptable thoughts, feelings, memories, and other information that lies beneath conscious awareness; in modern terms, subliminal processing that lies beneath the absolute threshold (Chapter 4)

Id According to Freud, the first personality structure that is present at birth, completely unconscious, and striving to meet basic drives, such as hunger, thirst, sex, and aggression; it operates on the pleasure principle.

Before discussing this first group of personality theorists, we need to provide a basic definition of **personality** as our *unique and relatively stable pattern of thoughts, feelings, and actions*. In other words, it describes how we are different from other people and what patterns of behavior are typical of us. We might qualify as an "extravert," for example, if we're talkative and outgoing most of the time. Or we may be described as "conscientious" if we're responsible and self-disciplined most of the time. (Keep in mind that *personality* is not the same as *character*, which refers to our ethics, morals, values, and integrity.)

Freud's Psychoanalytic Theory

One of the earliest theories of personality was Sigmund Freud's psychoanalytic perspective, which emphasized unconscious processes and unresolved past conflicts. Working from about 1890 until he died in 1939, Freud developed a theory of personality that has been one of the most influential—and controversial—theories in all of science (Bornstein & Huprich, 2015; Carducci, 2015; Cordón, 2012). Let's examine some of Freud's most basic and debatable concepts.

Levels of Consciousness Freud called the mind the "psyche" and asserted that it contains three *levels of consciousness*, or awareness: the **conscious**, the **preconscious**, and the **unconscious** (**Figure 11.1**). For Freud, the unconscious is all-important because it reportedly serves as a reservoir that stores our largely unacceptable thoughts, feelings, memories, and other information. It lies beneath our conscious awareness. However, it supposedly still has an enormous impact on our behavior—like the hidden part of the iceberg that sunk the ocean liner *Titanic*.

Although Freud never used the analogy himself, his levels of awareness are often compared to an iceberg:

- The tip of the iceberg would be analogous to the *conscious* mind, which is above the water and open to easy inspection.
- The *preconscious* mind (the area only shallowly submerged) contains information that can be viewed with a little extra effort.
- The large base of the iceberg is somewhat like the *unconscious*, completely hidden from personal inspection.

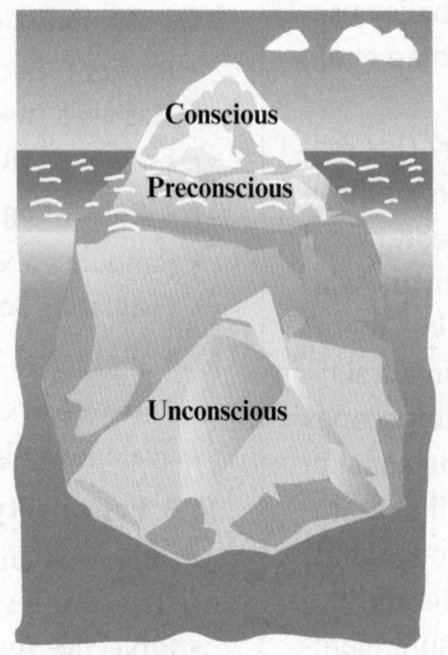

FIGURE 11.1 **Freud's three levels of consciousness**

Interestingly, because many of our unconscious thoughts and motives are unacceptable and threatening, Freud believed that they are normally *repressed* (held out of awareness)—unless they are unintentionally revealed by dreams or slips of the tongue, later called *Freudian slips* (**Figure 11.2**).

Personality Structure In addition to proposing that the mind functions at three levels of consciousness, Freud also believed personality was composed of three mental structures: the *id*, *ego*, and *superego* (**Figure 11.3**).

According to Freud, the **id** is the first personality structure that is present at birth, completely unconscious, and striving to meet basic drives, such as hunger, thirst, sex, and aggression. It is immature, impulsive, and irrational. When its primitive drives build up, the id seeks immediate gratification—a concept known as the *pleasure principle*. In other words, the id is like a newborn baby: It wants what it wants when it wants it!

"Good morning, beheaded—uh, I mean beloved."

FIGURE 11.2 Freudian slips Freud believed that a small slip of the tongue (now known as a *Freudian slip*) can reflect unconscious feelings that we normally keep hidden.

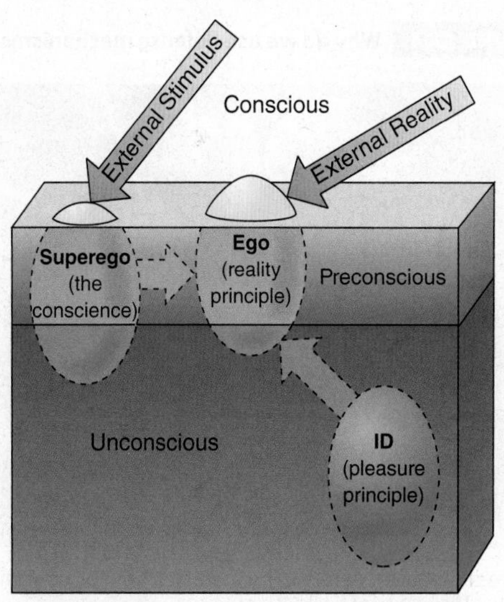

FIGURE 11.3 Freud's personality structure According to Freud, personality is composed of three structures—the id, ego, and superego. Note how the ego is primarily conscious and preconscious, whereas the id is entirely unconscious.

Freud further believed that the second personality structure, the **ego**, is the largely conscious, "executive" that deals with the demands of reality. It is responsible for planning, problem solving, reasoning, and controlling the potentially destructive energy of the id in ways that are compatible with the external world. Thus, the ego is responsible for delaying gratification when necessary. Contrary to the id's pleasure principle, the ego operates on the *reality principle* because it can understand and deal with objects and events in the real world.

Ego In Freud's theory, the second personality structure that is largely conscious, and the "executive," which deals with the demands of reality; it operates on the reality principle.

The final part of the psyche to develop is the **superego**, the third personality structure that serves as the center of morality. It provides internalized ideals and standards for judgment, and is often referred to as the "conscience."

Superego In Freud's theory, is the third personality structure that serves as the center of morality, providing internalized ideals and standards for judgment; often referred to as the "conscience."

Defense Mechanisms

As you might expect, the "morality" demands of the superego often conflict with the "infantile" needs and drives of the id. When the ego fails to satisfy both the id and the superego, anxiety slips into conscious awareness. Because anxiety is uncomfortable, Freud believed we avoid it through **defense mechanisms**, strategies the ego uses to reduce anxiety. Although defense mechanisms do help relieve the conflict-created anxiety, they distort reality and may increase self-deception (**Figure 11.4**). In addition to intellectualization and rationalization (shown in Figure 11.4), Freud identified several other defense mechanisms (**Table 11.1**).

Defense mechanisms Freud's term for the strategies the ego uses to reduce anxiety, which distort reality and may increase self-deception.

Psychosexual Stages

Although defense mechanisms are now an accepted part of modern psychology, other Freudian ideas are more controversial (Breger, 2014). For example, according to Freud, strong biological urges residing within the id push all children through five universal **psychosexual stages** (**Process Diagram 11.1**). The term *psychosexual* reflects Freud's belief that children experience sexual feelings from birth (in different forms from those experienced by adolescents and adults). Each of the five psychosexual stages is named for the type of sexual pleasure that supposedly characterizes the stage—for instance, the oral phase is named for the mouth, the key erogenous zone during infancy.

Psychosexual stages In Freudian theory, five developmental periods (oral, anal, phallic, latency, and genital) during which particular kinds of pleasures must be gratified if personality development is to proceed normally.

According to Freud, at each psychosexual stage the id's impulses and social demands come into conflict. Therefore, if a child's needs are not met, or are overindulged, at one particular stage, the child supposedly may *fixate,* and a part of his or her personality will remain stuck at that stage. Freud believed most individuals successfully pass through each of the five stages. But during stressful times, they may return (or *regress*) to an earlier stage in which prior needs were badly frustrated or overgratified.

FIGURE 11.4 **Why do we use defense mechanisms?**

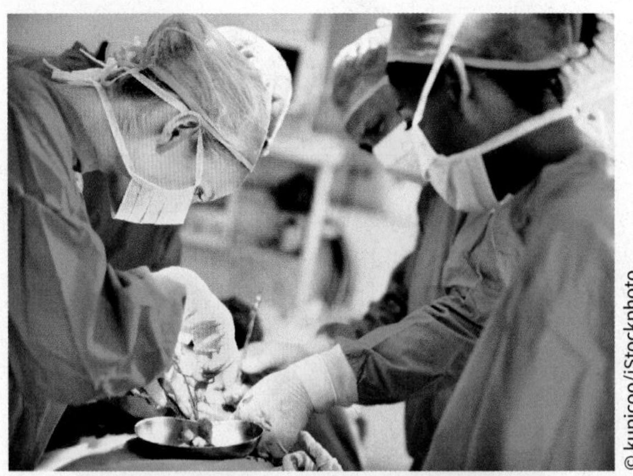

a. Freud believed defense mechanisms help us deal with unconscious conflicts, which explains why these physicians may *intellectualize* and distance themselves from the gruesome aspects of their work to avoid personal anxieties. Defense mechanisms can be healthy and helpful if we use them in moderation or on a temporary basis.

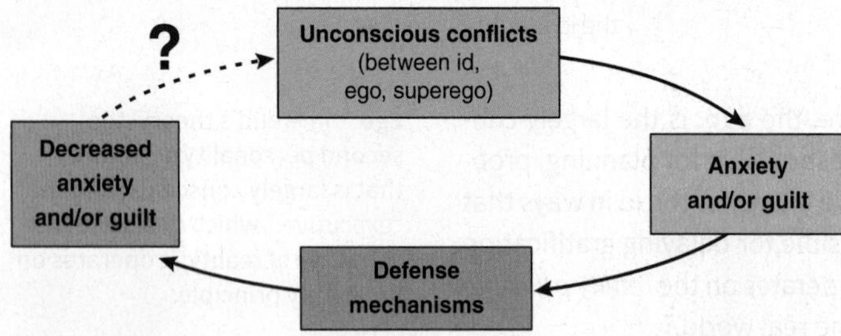

b. Unfortunately, defense mechanisms generally distort reality, and they create some of our most dangerous habits through a vicious self-reinforcing cycle. For example, an alcoholic who uses his paycheck to buy drinks may feel very guilty, but he can easily reduce this conflict by *rationalizing* that he deserves to relax and unwind with alcohol because he works so hard.

1. **Oral stage** (birth to 18 months) During this period, an infant receives satisfaction through sucking, eating, biting, and so on. Because the infant is highly dependent on parents and other caregivers to provide opportunities for oral gratification, fixation at this stage can easily occur. If caregivers overindulge an infant's oral needs, the child may fixate and as an adult become gullible ("swallowing" anything), dependent, and passive. The underindulged child, however, will develop into an aggressive, sadistic person who exploits others. According to Freud, orally fixated adults often orient their life around their mouth—overeating, becoming an alcoholic, smoking, or talking a great deal.
2. **Anal stage** (18 to 36 months) Once the child becomes a toddler, his or her erogenous zone shifts to the anus. The child supposedly receives satisfaction by having and retaining bowel movements. Because this is the time when most parents begin toilet training, the child's desire to control his or her own bowel movements often leads to strong conflict. Adults who are fixated at this stage, in Freud's view, may develop an *anal-retentive* personality and be highly controlled and compulsively neat. Or they may be very messy, disorderly, rebellious, and destructive—the so-called *anal-expulsive* personality.
3. **Phallic stage** (3 to 6 years) During the *phallic stage*, the major center of pleasure is the genitals. Masturbation and "playing doctor" with other children are common during this time. According to Freud, a 3- to 6-year-old boy also develops an unconscious sexual longing for his mother and jealousy and hatred for the rival father. This attraction creates a conflict

TABLE 11.1 **Sample Psychological Defense Mechanisms**

DEFENSE MECHANISM	DESCRIPTION	EXAMPLE
Repression	Preventing painful or unacceptable thoughts from entering consciousness	Forgetting the details of a tragic accident
Sublimation	Redirecting socially unacceptable impulses into acceptable activities	Redirecting aggressive impulses by becoming a professional fighter
Denial	Refusing to accept an unpleasant reality	Alcoholics refusing to admit their addiction
Rationalization	Creating a socially acceptable excuse to justify unacceptable behavior	Justifying cheating on an exam by saying "everyone else does it"
Intellectualization	Ignoring the emotional aspects of a painful experience by focusing on abstract thoughts, words, or ideas	Discussing your divorce without emotion while ignoring the hidden, underlying pain
Projection	Transferring unacceptable thoughts, motives, or impulses to others	Becoming unreasonably jealous of your mate while denying your own attraction to others
Reaction formation	Not acknowledging unacceptable impulses and overemphasizing their opposite	Promoting a petition against adult bookstores even though you are secretly fascinated by pornography
Regression	Reverting to immature ways of responding	Throwing a temper tantrum when a friend doesn't want to do what you'd like
Displacement	Redirecting impulses from the original source toward a less threatening person or object	Yelling at a coworker after being criticized by your boss

STOP! This Process Diagram contains essential information NOT found elsewhere in the text, which is likely to appear on quizzes and exams. Be sure to study it CAREFULLY!

PROCESS DIAGRAM 11.1 Freud's Five Psychosexual Stages of Development

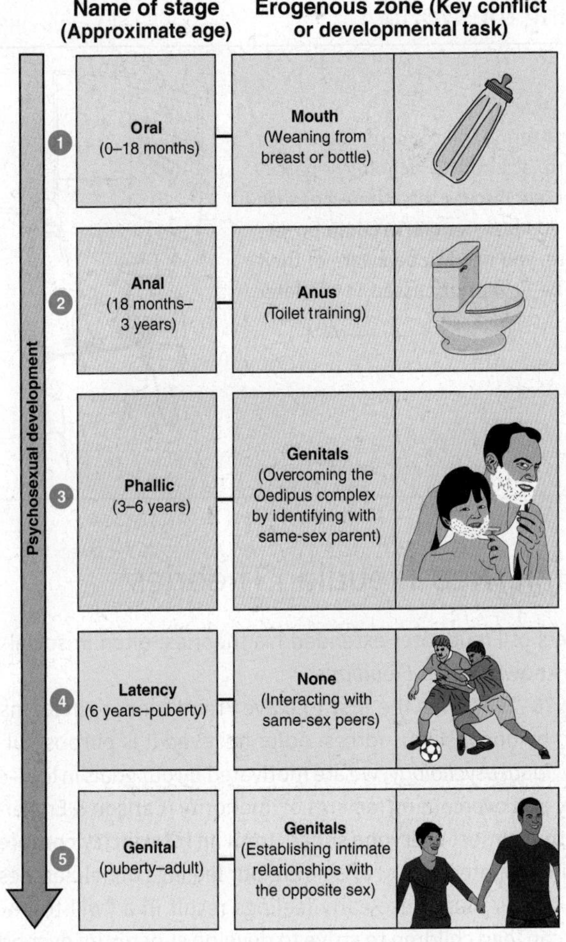

Name of stage (Approximate age)
Erogenous zone (Key conflict or developmental task)
Psychosexual development
1 Oral (0–18 months)
Mouth (Weaning from breast or bottle)
2 Anal (18 months–3 years)
Anus (Toilet training)
3 Phallic (3–6 years)
Genitals (Overcoming the Oedipus complex by identifying with same-sex parent)
4 Latency (6 years–puberty)
None (Interacting with same-sex peers)
5 Genital (puberty–adult)
Genitals (Establishing intimate relationships with the opposite sex)

Freud called the **Oedipus complex**, named after Oedipus, the legendary Greek king who unwittingly killed his father and married his mother. The young boy reportedly experiences guilt and fear of punishment from the rival father, perhaps by castration. The anxiety this produces is supposedly repressed into the unconscious, which leads to the development of the superego. The boy then identifies with his father and adopts the male gender role. If this stage is not resolved completely or positively, or the child fixates at this stage, Freud believed the boy grows up resenting his father and generalizes this feeling to all authority figures. What happens with little girls? Because a girl does not have a penis, she does not fear castration and fails to fully complete this stage and move on to successful identification with her mother. According to Freud, she develops *penis envy* and fails to develop an adequate superego, which Freud believed resulted in women being morally inferior to men. (You are undoubtedly surprised or outraged by this statement, but remember that Freud was a product of his times. Sexism was common at this point in history. And most modern psychodynamic theorists reject Freud's notion of penis envy, as we will see in the next section.)

Oedipus complex According to Freud, during the phallic stage (ages 3 to 6 years), a young boy develops a sexual attraction to his mother and rivalry with his father.

4. **Latency period** (6 years to puberty) Following the phallic stage, children supposedly repress sexual thoughts and engage in nonsexual activities, such as developing social and intellectual skills. The task of this stage is to develop successful interactions with same-sex peers and refine appropriate gender roles.

5. **Genital stage** (puberty to adulthood) With the beginning of adolescence, the genitals are again erogenous zones. Adolescents seek to fulfill their sexual desires through emotional attachment to members of the opposite sex. Unsuccessful outcomes at this stage lead to participation in sexual relationships based only on lustful desires, not on respect and commitment. For more information, see the following **Real World Psychology**.

Real World **Psychology**—Understanding the World

Freud and Modern Western Culture

Before going on, it's important to note that many of Freud's terms and concepts have been heavily criticized and are not widely accepted in modern, scientific psychology—particularly his psychosexual stages of development. However, we discuss them here because words, like *id, ego, superego, anal-retentive,* and *Oedipus complex*, remain in common, everyday usage and as a large part of our culture. Therefore, you need to be aware of their origin and their limited scientific credibility, which will be further discussed in the later evaluation section.

Wilbur Dawbarn/CartoonStock

Inferiority complex Adler's idea that feelings of inferiority develop from early childhood experiences of helplessness and incompetence.

Collective unconscious Jung's name for the deepest layer of the unconscious, which contains universal memories and archetypes shared by all people due to our common ancestral past.

Archetypes Jung's term for the collective, universal images and patterns, residing in the unconscious, that have symbolic meaning for all people.

Psychodynamic/Neo-Freudian Theories

Some initial followers of Freud later extended his theories, often in social and cultural directions. They became known as *neo-Freudians.*

Alfred Adler (1870–1937) was the first to leave Freud's inner circle. Instead of seeing behavior as motivated by unconscious forces, Adler believed it is purposeful and goal directed. According to his *individual psychology*, we are motivated by our goals in life—especially our goals of obtaining security and overcoming feelings of inferiority (Carlson & Englar-Carlson, 2013).

Adler believed that almost everyone suffers from an **inferiority complex**, or deep feelings of inadequacy and incompetence that arise from our feelings of helplessness as infants (Adler, 1927/1954). According to Adler, these early feelings result in a "will-to-power" that can take one of two paths. It can lead children to strive to develop superiority over others through dominance, aggression, or expressions of envy. Or, on a more positive note, it can encourage them to develop their full potential and creativity and to gain mastery and control of their lives (**Figure 11.5**).

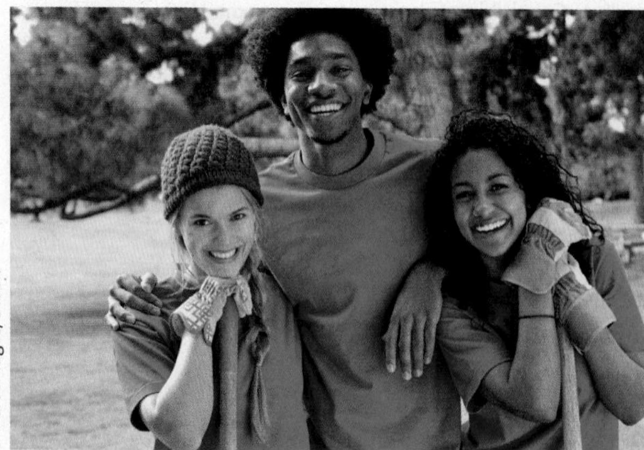

© Hero Images/Corbis

FIGURE 11.5 An upside to feelings of inferiority? Adler suggested that the will-to-power could be positively expressed through social interest—by identifying with others and cooperating with them for the social good. Can you explain how these volunteers might be fulfilling their will-to-power interest?

Another early Freud follower turned dissenter, Carl Jung [Yoong], developed *analytical psychology*. Like Freud, Jung (1875–1961) emphasized unconscious processes, but he believed that the unconscious contains positive and spiritual motives as well as sexual and aggressive forces.

Jung also thought that we have two forms of the unconscious mind: the personal unconscious and the collective unconscious. The *personal unconscious* is created from our individual experiences, whereas the **collective unconscious** is identical in each person and is inherited (Jung, 1933, 1936/1969). The collective unconscious consists of primitive images and patterns of thought, feeling, and behavior that Jung called **archetypes** (**Figure 11.6**).

Because of archetypal patterns in the collective unconscious, we supposedly perceive and react in certain predictable ways. One set of archetypes refers to gender roles (Chapter 9). Jung claimed that both males and females have patterns for feminine aspects of personality—*anima*—and masculine aspects of personality—

zookeepers, volunteers, researchers, and caretakers who knew the gorillas well to score each gorilla's personality. With these scorings, they reliably identified four distinct personality traits: *dominance*, *extraversion*, *neuroticism*, and *agreeableness* (Weiss et al., 2013).

Next, the researchers examined the association between levels of each of these personality traits and life expectancy. They found that gorillas scoring high on extraversion, which included behaviors such as sociability, activity, play, and curiosity, lived longer lives. This link was found in both male and female gorillas and across all the different types of environments in which this research was conducted.

What might explain this link? One possibility is that extraverted apes—just like extraverted people—develop stronger social networks, which helps increase survival and reduce stress. Can you think of other possible explanations?

Martin Harvey/Digital Vision/Getty Images

Research Challenge

1. Based on the information provided, did this study (Weiss et al., 2013) use descriptive, correlational, and/or experimental research?
2. If you chose:
   - *descriptive research*, is this a naturalistic observation, survey/interview, case study, and/or archival research?
   - *correlational research*, is this a positive, negative, or zero correlation?
   - *experimental research*, label the IV, DV, experimental group(s), and control group.
   - both *descriptive* and *correlational*, answer the corresponding questions for both.

Check your answers by clicking on the answer button or by looking in Appendix B.

Note: The information provided in this study is admittedly limited, but the level of detail is similar to what is presented in most textbooks and public reports of research findings. Answering these questions, and then comparing your answers to those provided, will help you become a better critical thinker and consumer of scientific research.

Evaluating Trait Theories

The five-factor model (FFM) is the first model to achieve the major goal of trait theory—to describe and organize personality characteristics using the smallest number of traits. Psychologist David Buss and his colleagues (1989, 2008) surveyed more than 10,000 men and women from 37 countries and found a surprising level of agreement in the characteristics that men and women value in a mate (**Table 11.2**). Note that both sexes tend to prefer mates with traits that closely match the FFM—dependability (conscientiousness), emotional stability (low neuroticism), pleasing disposition (agreeableness), and sociability (extraversion).

TABLE 11.2 Mate Preferences and the Five-Factor Model (FFM) — **Real World Psychology**

WHAT MEN MOST WANT IN A MATE	WHAT WOMEN MOST WANT IN A MATE
1. Mutual attraction—love	1. Mutual attraction—love
2. Dependable character	2. Dependable character
3. Emotional stability and maturity	3. Emotional stability and maturity
4. Pleasing disposition	4. Pleasing disposition
5. Good health	5. Education and intelligence
6. Education and intelligence	6. Sociability
7. Sociability	7. Good health
8. Desire for home and children	8. Desire for home and children
9. Refinement, neatness	9. Ambition and industriousness
10. Good looks	10. Refinement, neatness

© Michelle Marsan/Shutterstock

Source: Based on Buss et al., 1990.

Why is there such a high degree of shared preferences for certain personality traits? Scientists suggest that these traits may provide an evolutionary advantage to people who are more conscientious, extraverted, and agreeable—and less neurotic. For instance, people who are conscientious have better health, which is clearly advantageous (Israel et al., 2014). The evolutionary advantage is also confirmed by cross-cultural studies and comparative studies with dogs, chimpanzees, and other highly social species (e.g., Carlo et al., 2014; Gosling, 2008; Valchev et al., 2014).

In addition to having strong cross-cultural support, trait theories, like the FFM, allow us to predict real-life preferences and behaviors, such as our political attitudes, beliefs, and voting preferences, and even how much time we spend on Facebook (Bakker et al., 2016; Hart et al., 2015; Mondak & Canache, 2014). Furthermore, people who are extraverted have been found to prefer upbeat, energetic, and rhythmic types of music, such as rap and hip-hop. In contrast, people who are open to experience prefer complex, intense, and rebellious music, such as classical and rock (Langemeyer et al., 2012). As you might expect, personality may even affect your career choice and job satisfaction (see the following **Psychology and You**).

Psychology and You—Understanding Yourself

Matching Your Personality with Your Career

As mentioned earlier, the FFM traits of conscientiousness, agreeableness, and openness are clearly linked with job success. But what about other factors, such as the worker's job satisfaction? Do some personality characteristics make you better suited for certain jobs than others? According to psychologist John Holland's *personality-job-fit-theory*, a match (or "good fit") between our individual personality and our career choice is a major factor in determining job satisfaction (Holland, 1985, 1994). Research shows that a good fit between personality and occupation helps increase subjective well-being, job success, and job satisfaction. In other words, people tend to be happier and like their work when they're well matched to their jobs (Joeng et al., 2013; Perkmen & Sahin, 2013; Williamson et al., 2013). Check this table to see what job would be a good match for your personality.

PERSONALITY CHARACTERISTICS	HOLLAND PERSONALITY TYPE	MATCHING/CONGRUENT OCCUPATIONS
Shy, genuine, persistent, stable, conforming, practical	1. *Realistic:* Prefers physical activities that require skill, strength, and coordination	Mechanic, drill press operator, assembly-line worker, farmer
Analytical, original, curious, independent	2. *Investigative:* Prefers activities that involve thinking, organizing, and understanding	Biologist, economist, mathematician, news reporter
Sociable, friendly, cooperative, understanding	3. *Social:* Prefers activities that involve helping and developing others	Social worker, counselor, teacher, clinical psychologist
Conforming, efficient, practical, unimaginative, inflexible	4. *Conventional:* Prefers rule-regulated, orderly, and unambiguous activities	Accountant, bank teller, file clerk, manager
Imaginative, disorderly, idealistic, emotional, impractical	5. *Artistic:* Prefers ambiguous and unsystematic activities that allow creative expression	Painter, musician, writer, interior decorator
Self-confident, ambitious, energetic, domineering	6. *Enterprising:* Prefers verbal activities with opportunities to influence others and attain power	Lawyer, real estate agent, public relations specialist, small business manager

Source: Adapted and reproduced with special permission of the publisher, Psychological Assessment Resources, Inc., 16204 North Florida Avenue, Lutz, Florida 33549, from the *Dictionary of Holland Occupational Codes*, 3rd edition, by Gary D. Gottfredson, Ph.D., and John L. Holland, Ph.D., Copyright 1982, 1989, 1996. Further reproduction is prohibited without permission from PAR, Inc.

Despite their relative successes, critics argue that trait theories generally fail to consider situational determinants of personality or to offer sufficient explanations for why people develop specific traits (Chamorro-Premuzic, 2011; Cheung et al., 2011; Furguson et al., 2011). And although trait theories have shown personality to be fairly stable, they have failed to identify which characteristics last a lifetime and which are most likely to change (Carlo et al., 2014; Hosie et al., 2014; McCrae, 2011). Interestingly, research does show that certain stressful life events, such as being unemployed or experiencing natural disasters, can change our personalities (Boyce et al., 2015; Kandler et al., 2015; Milojev et al., 2014). Moreover, we can sometimes deliberately change our personalities if we have specific goals in mind (Hudson & Fraley, 2015). Would you like to be a more positive person and maybe change some parts of your own personality? See the **PositivePsych**.

PP PositivePsych

Can (and Should) We Improve Our Personality Traits?

Have you ever admired the personalities of others and wished you could be more like them? The good news is that many different types of positive traits can increase through training. In one study, researchers randomly divided 178 adults into three groups for a period of ten weeks (Proyer et al., 2013). One group focused on increasing the traits of "curiosity," "gratitude," "optimism," "humor" and "enthusiasm", another group focused on increasing the traits of "appreciation of beauty," "creativity," "kindness," "love of learning" and "foresight." The third group served as a control and did not complete any type of training. People in the two treatment groups completed brief exercises at some point each day, such as writing a thank you letter (to practice gratitude), or paying attention to things they found beautiful in the world (to train their appreciation of beauty). As predicted, findings revealed that people who focused on increasing positive traits, such as optimism and enthusiasm, indeed experienced greater life satisfaction at the end of the training sessions compared to those in the other two groups.

On the other hand, it's important to note that psychologists only *describe* personality traits. We don't advise on what traits *should be changed*. That's for you as an individual to decide. Moreover, personality traits (like "beauty") are largely in the "eye of the beholder." What traits some people decide is preferable over another depend on the group, culture, and history. For example, most people agree that Abraham Lincoln was perhaps one of the greatest U.S. presidents of all time. And some may consider Lady Gaga and Selena Gomez to be among the greatest musical talents in recent times. But did you know that all of these individuals are self-described as shy and introverted? After reading the previous section on introversion versus extraversion and our fast-paced, highly competitive society, you may think that it's better to be extraverted. But introverted people aren't necessarily "wallflower" social rejects. They have their own strengths and typically prefer being alone and quiet because they desire less stimulation. Keep in mind that almost all personality traits have both positive and negative characteristics. Furthermore, all our traits exist on a continuum and they often vary depending on the situation. No one is entirely extraverted nor always introverted. Some shy people can be very extraverted in small groups but introverted around people they don't know in large groups or parties.

Frederick M. Brown/Getty Images

Retrieval Practice 11.2 | Trait Theories

SELF-TEST Completing this self-test, and then checking your answers by clicking on the answer button or by looking in Appendix B, will provide immediate feedback and helpful practice for exams.

1. _____ is a statistical technique that groups large arrays of data into more basic units.

a. MMPI
b. FFM
c. Factor analysis
d. Regression analysis

2. What are the "Big Five" personality traits in the five-factor model?

a. conscientiousness, openness, extraversion, agreeableness, and neuroticism
b. shyness, conscientiousness, extraversion, agreeableness, and neuroticism
c. shyness, conscientiousness, introversion, agreeableness, and neuroticism
d. none of these options

3. People who score high in _____ are emotionally unstable and prone to insecurity, anxiety, guilt, worry, and moodiness.

a. openness
b. conscientiousness
c. extraversion
d. neuroticism

4. Trait theories of personality have been criticized for _____.

a. failing to explain why people develop specific traits
b. not including a large number of central traits
c. failing to identify which traits last and which are transient
d. not considering situational determinants of personality
e. all but one of these options

5. Which of the following is NOT associated with the trait theories of personality?

a. Cattell
b. Allport
c. Rorschach
d. Eysenck

Think Critically

1. After reading the descriptions for each of the Big Five personality dimensions, how well do you think they describe someone you know very well, can you predict how he or she might score on each of these traits?
2. Do you believe someone can change his or her core personality traits? Why or why not?

Real World **Psychology**

Which personality traits are most important for your career and academic success?

Kurhan/Shutterstock

HINT: LOOK IN THE MARGIN FOR **[Q2]**

11.3 Humanistic Theories

LEARNING OBJECTIVES

Retrieval Practice While reading the upcoming sections, respond to each Learning Objective in your own words.

Summarize the major concepts of humanistic theories of personality.

- **Discuss** the importance of self-actualization in humanistic theories.
- **Explain** why self-concept and unconditional positive regard are key aspects of in Roger's theory of personality.
- **Describe** how Maslow's hierarchy of needs affects personality.
- **Evaluate** the strengths and weaknesses of humanistic theories of personality.

Self-actualization The humanistic term for the inborn drive to realize our full potential and to develop all our talents and capabilities.

Self-concept The image of oneself that develops from interactions with significant others and life experiences.

Humanistic theories of personality emphasize each person's internal feelings, thoughts, and sense of basic worth. In contrast to Freud's generally negative view of human nature, humanists believe that people are naturally good (or, at worst, neutral) and that they possess a natural tendency toward **self-actualization**, the inborn drive to develop all their talents and capabilities.

According to this view, our personality and behavior depend on how we perceive and interpret the world, not on traits, unconscious impulses, or rewards and punishments. Humanistic psychology was developed largely by Carl Rogers and Abraham Maslow.

Rogers's Theory

To psychologist Carl Rogers (1902–1987), the most important component of personality is our **self-concept**, the way we see and feel about ourselves. Rogers emphasized that mental health and adjustment reflect the degree of overlap (congruence) between our perceived real and ideal selves (see the following **Psychology and You**). This self-perception is relatively stable over time and develops from our life experiences, particularly the feedback and perception of others.

Dear diary,
Sorry to bother you again.
LOW SELF-ESTEEM

Why do some people develop negative self-concepts and poor mental health, such as the man in the cartoon? Rogers believed that such outcomes generally result from early childhood experiences with parents and other adults who make their love and acceptance *conditional* and contingent on behaving in certain ways and expressing only certain feelings. Imagine being a child who is repeatedly told that your naturally occurring negative feelings and behaviors (which we all have) are totally unacceptable and unlovable. Can you see how your self-concept may become distorted? And why as an adult you might develop a shy, avoidant personality, always doubting the love and approval of others because they don't know "the real person hiding inside"?

Unconditional positive regard Rogers's term for love and acceptance with no "strings" (contingencies) attached.

To help children develop their fullest personality and life potential, Rogers cautioned that adults need to create an atmosphere of **unconditional positive regard**—love and acceptance with no "strings" (contingencies) attached (Feeney & Collins, 2015; Ray & Jayne, 2016; Schneider et al., 2015). Interestingly, parents who engage in responsive caregiving, a form of unconditional positive regard, also tend to show this same pattern of behavior toward their spouses, which in **[Q3]**

Psychology and You—Understanding Yourself

Measuring Your Personal Self-concept

Stop for a moment and briefly describe yourself as you'd *ideally* like to be and as how you *actually* are. Now draw two circles, labeled "real self" and "ideal self," depicting how much your two perceived selves overlap. According to Carl Rogers, if your real self and *ideal* self are nearly the same, with considerable overlap in the two circles, you have *congruence* between your two "selves" and a positive self-concept. Unfortunately, many people have experienced negative life events and feedback from others that have led to negative self-concepts. In Rogers's view, poor mental health and personality maladjustment develop from a mismatch, or *incongruence*, between our ideal and real selves.

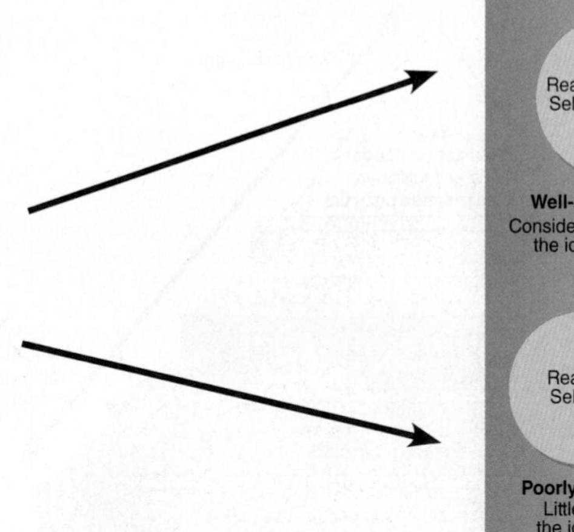

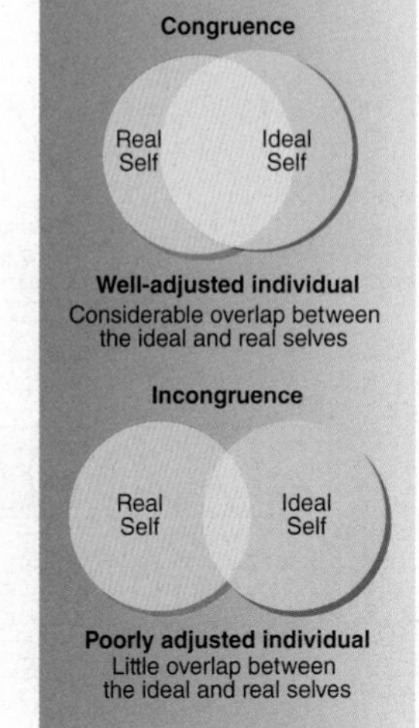

turn leads to higher levels of relationship satisfaction (Millings et al., 2013). This suggests that unconditional positive regard is important in all types of relationships. [Q3]

This is *not* to say that adults must approve of everything a child does. Rogers emphasizes that we must separate the value of the person from his or her behaviors—encouraging the person's innate positive nature, while discouraging destructive or hostile behaviors. Humanistic psychologists in general suggest that both children and adults must control their behavior so they can develop a healthy self-concept and satisfying relationships with others (**Figure 11.9**).

Maslow's Theory

Like Rogers, Abraham Maslow believed there is a basic goodness to human nature and a natural tendency toward *self-actualization*. Maslow saw personality development as a natural progression from lower to higher levels—a basic *hierarchy of needs* (Chapter 10). As newborns, we focus on physiological needs like hunger and thirst, and then as we grow and develop, we move on through four higher levels (**Figure 11.10**). Surveys from 123 countries found that people from around the world do share a focus on the same basic needs, and when those needs are met, they report higher levels of happiness (Tay & Diener, 2011).

According to Maslow, self-actualization is the inborn drive to develop all our talents and capacities. It requires understanding our own potential, accepting ourselves and others as unique individuals, and taking a problem-centered approach to life (Maslow, 1970). Self-actualization is an ongoing process of growth rather than an end product or accomplishment.

Maslow believed that only a few, rare individuals, such as Albert Einstein, Mohandas Gandhi, and Eleanor Roosevelt, become fully self-actualized. However, he saw self-actualization as part of every person's basic hierarchy of needs. (See Chapter 10 for more information about Maslow's theory.)

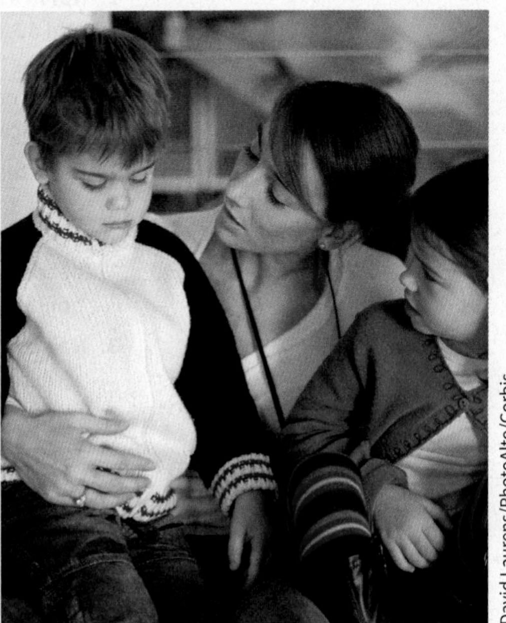

David Laurens/PhotoAlto/Corbis

FIGURE 11.9 Unconditional positive regard
In response to a child who is angry and hits his or her younger sibling, the parent acknowledges that it is the behavior that is unacceptable, and not the child: "I know you're angry with your sister, but we don't hit. And you won't be able to play with her for a while unless you control your anger."

Evaluating Humanistic Theories

Humanistic psychology was extremely popular during the 1960s and 1970s. It was seen as a refreshing new perspective on personality after the negative

FIGURE 11.10 Maslow's hierarchy of needs Although our natural movement is upward from physical needs toward the highest level, *self-actualization*, Maslow believed we sometimes "regress" toward a lower level—especially under stressful conditions. For example, during national disasters, people first rush to stockpile food and water (physiological needs) and then often clamor for a strong leader to take over, enforce the rules, and make things right (safety needs). See the photo.

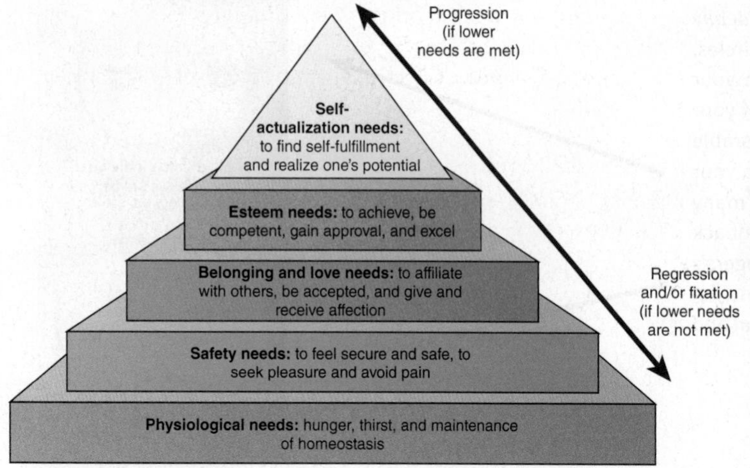

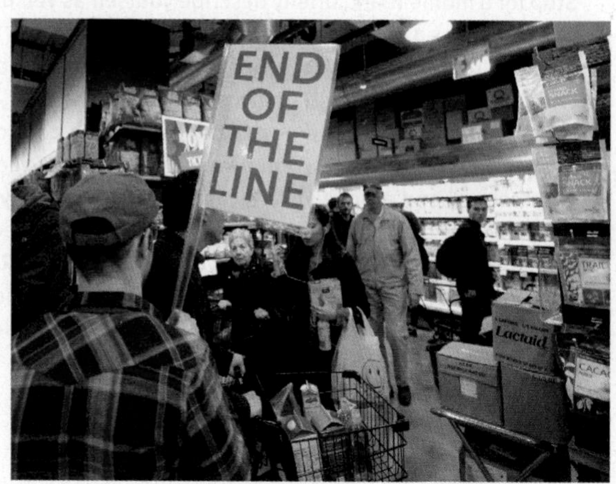

Timothy A Clary/AFP/Getty Images

determinism of the psychoanalytic approach and the mechanical nature of learning theories (Chapter 6). Although this early popularity has declined, humanistic theories have provided valuable insights that are useful for personal growth and self-understanding. They likewise play a major role in contemporary counseling and psychotherapy, as well as in modern childrearing, education, and managerial practices (Angus et al., 2015; DeRobertis, 2013; Schneider et al., 2015).

However, humanistic theories have been criticized (Berger, 2015; Henwood et al., 2014; Nolan, 2012) for the following:

1. **Naïve assumptions** Some critics suggest that humanistic theories are unduly optimistic and overlook the negative aspects of human nature. For example, critics have said that Hitler was "self-actualized," goal-driven, and believed he was fulfilling his potential. Furthermore, how would humanists explain deliberate mass genocide of large groups of people, horrific racist and terrorist attacks, and humankind's ongoing history of war and murder?
2. **Poor testability and inadequate evidence** Like many psychoanalytic terms and concepts, humanistic concepts such as unconditional positive regard and self-actualization are difficult to define operationally and to test scientifically. In addition, given that basic needs are often overlooked to pursue larger needs, such as hunger strikes to protest political conditions, how does that fit into Maslow's hierarchy of needs?
3. **Narrowness** Like trait theories, humanistic theories have been criticized for merely describing personality rather than explaining it. For example, where does the motivation for self-actualization come from? To say that it is an "inborn drive" doesn't satisfy those who favor using experimental research and scientific standards to study personality.

Retrieval Practice 11.3 | Humanistic Theories

SELF-TEST Completing this self-test, and then checking your answers by clicking on the answer button or by looking in Appendix B, will provide immediate feedback and helpful practice for exams.

1. The ______ approach emphasizes internal experiences, like feelings, thoughts, and the basic worth of the individual.

a. humanistic **b.** psychodynamic
c. personalistic **d.** motivational

2. Rogers suggested that ______ is necessary for a child to develop his or her fullest personality and life potential.

a. authoritative parenting
b. a challenging environment
c. unconditional positive regard
d. a friendly neighborhood

3. _____ believed in the basic goodness of individuals and their natural tendency toward self-actualization.

   a. Karen Horney **b.** Alfred Adler
   c. Abraham Maslow **d.** Carl Jung

4. To become self-actualized, we need to _____.

   a. understand our own potential
   b. accept ourselves and others as unique individuals
   c. take a problem-centered approach to life
   d. all of these options

5. A major criticism of humanistic psychology is that most of its concepts and assumptions _____.

   a. are invalid **b.** are unreliable
   c. are naive **d.** lack a theoretical foundation

Think Critically

1. Do you agree with Rogers that unconditional positive regard from parents is key to healthy personality development? Why or why not?
2. Thinking of the traits of a fully self-actualized person, can you identify someone who exhibits all or most of these qualities? Do you consider self-actualization a worthy goal? Why or why not?

Real World **Psychology**

What parenting skills are also associated with increased marital satisfaction?

© YouraPechkin/ iStockphoto

HINT: LOOK IN THE MARGIN FOR **[Q3]**

11.4 Social-Cognitive Theories

LEARNING OBJECTIVES

Retrieval Practice While reading the upcoming sections, respond to each Learning Objective in your own words.

Review the major concepts of social-cognitive theories of personality.

- **Explain** Bandura's and Rotter's approaches to personality.
- **Summarize** the strengths and weaknesses of the social-cognitive perspective on personality.

As you've just seen, psychoanalytic/psychodynamic, trait, and humanistic theories all tend to focus on internal, personal factors in personality development. In contrast, *social-cognitive* theories emphasize the influence of our *social* interpersonal interactions with the environment, along with our *cognitions*—our thoughts, feelings, expectations, and values.

Bandura's and Rotter's Approaches

Albert Bandura (see Chapter 6) has played a major role in reintroducing thought processes into personality theory. Cognition, or thought, is central to his concept of **self-efficacy**, which is very similar to our everyday notion of self-confidence (Bandura, 1997, 2012).

Self-efficacy Bandura's term for a person's learned expectation of success in a given situation; another term for self-confidence.

According to Bandura, if you have a strong sense of self-efficacy, you believe you can generally succeed and reach your goals, regardless of past failures and current obstacles. Your degree of self-efficacy will in turn affect which challenges you choose to accept and the effort you expend in reaching your goals (Bruning & Kauffman, 2016; Phan & Ngu, 2016). See **Psychology and You**.

How does self-efficacy affect personality? Bandura sees personality as being shaped by **reciprocal determinism**, which means that internal factors within the *person* (his or her personality, thoughts, expectations, etc.), the external *environment*, and his or her *behavior* all work as interacting (reciprocal) determinants of each other (**Figure 11.11**). Using Bandura's concept of self-efficacy, do you see how your own beliefs will affect how others respond to you and thereby influence your chance for success? Your belief ("I can succeed") will affect behaviors ("I'll work hard and ask for a promotion"), which in turn will affect the environment ("My employer recognized my efforts and promoted me").

Reciprocal determinism Bandura's belief that internal personal factors, the environment, and the individual's behavior all work as interacting (reciprocal) determinants of each other.

Julian Rotter's theory is similar to Bandura's in that it suggests that learning experiences create *cognitive expectancies* that guide behavior and influence the environment (Rotter, 1954, 1990). According to Rotter, your behavior or personality is determined by (1) what you expect to happen following a specific action and (2) the reinforcement value attached to specific outcomes.

Psychology and You—Understanding Yourself

Self-efficacy in Daily Life

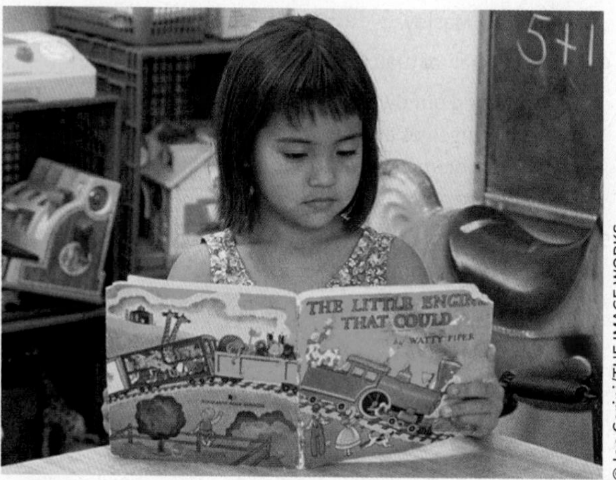

©Joe Carini/THE IMAGE WORKS

The classic-children's story *The Little Engine That Could* illustrates how we learn self-efficacy through our personal experiences with success. The little engine starts up a steep hill, saying, "I think I can, I think I can." After lots of hard work and perseverance, she ends up at the top of the hill and says, "I thought I could, I thought I could."

Bandura emphasized that self-efficacy is a *learned* expectation of success, but only in a given situation. It doesn't necessarily transfer to other circumstances. Bandura would suggest that the little engine's new-found self-efficacy will help her climb future hills. However, it wouldn't necessarily improve her overall speed or ability to turn sharp corners. Similarly, self-defense training significantly affects a woman's belief that she can improve her odds of escaping from or disabling a potential assailant or rapist. But it does not lead her to feel more capable in all areas of her life (Weitlauf et al., 2001).

How then can we transfer self-efficacy to other parts of our everyday life? If you've experienced success as an athlete, a parent, or even a videogame player, consider how the skills you've demonstrated in these areas can be transferred to your academic life. Instead of saying, "I just can't find time to study" or "I never do well on tests," remind yourself of how your ongoing success in athletics, parenting, or videogames has resulted from good time management, hours of practice, patience, hard work, and perseverance. Applying skills that are the same as or similar to skills you've successfully used before will help move you from "I can't" to "I think I can." And then when you get your first high grade in a difficult course, you can move on to "I know I can, I know I can!"

To understand your personality and behavior, Rotter used personality tests that measure your internal versus external *locus of control* (Chapter 3). Rotter's tests ask participants to respond to statements such as, "People get ahead in this world primarily by luck and connections rather than by hard work and perseverance" and "When someone doesn't like you, there is little you can do about it." As you may suspect, people with an external locus of control think the environment and external forces have primary control over their lives, whereas people with an *internal locus of control* think they can personally control events in their lives through their own efforts (**Figure 11.12**).

Evaluating Social-Cognitive Theories

The social-cognitive perspective holds several attractions. First, it offers testable, objective hypotheses and operationally defined terms, and it relies on

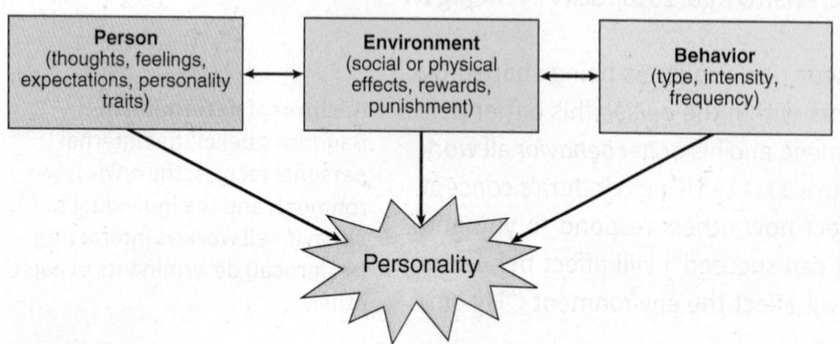

FIGURE 11.11 Bandura's theory of reciprocal determinism According to Albert Bandura, personality is determined by a three-way, reciprocal interaction of the internal characteristics of the person, the external environment, and the person's behavior.

"We're encouraging people to become involved in their own rescue."

FIGURE 11.12 Locus of control and achievement Despite this cartoon's humorous message, research does link a perception of control with higher achievement, greater life satisfaction, and better overall mental health (e.g., Albert & Dahling, 2016; Nowicki, 2016).

ViewStock/Getty Images

empirical data. Second, social-cognitive theories emphasize the role of cognitive processes in personality, and that both personality and situations predict behavior in real-world situations (Sherman et al., 2015). Relatedly, high school students who study abroad (thereby experiencing a change in environment) show greater changes in personality than those who do not (Hutteman
[Q4] et al., 2015). For instance, exchange students showed substantial increases in their self-esteem compared to those who stayed home (see the photo).

As we discussed earlier, there's a wealth of modern research connecting the Big Five personality traits to success in both work and academic settings, and these traits are closely related to the social-cognitive traits of self-efficacy and an internal locus of control. Furthermore, psychologist Carol Dweck has shown that our beliefs about our own abilities (*mindset*) influence how hard we try to achieve (see Chapter 10). For example, children who have a "fixed" mindset believe that intelligence is stable over time, so they aren't particularly motivated to try harder in school, since they believe such efforts won't really matter. In contrast, children who have a "growth" mindset believe that their efforts can make a difference, so they try harder in school, and, not surprisingly, perform better (Dweck, 2006, 2012; Yeager et al., 2016).

On the other hand, critics argue that social-cognitive theories focus too much on situational influences. They also suggest that this approach fails to adequately acknowledge the stability of personality, as well as sociocultural, emotional, and biological influences (Ahmetoglu & Chamorro-Premuzic, 2013; Berger, 2015; Cea & Barnes, 2015). One of the most influential studies on the potential stability of personality traits is the now classic "marshmallow test"—the lead researcher, Walter Mischel, was even a guest on the *Stephen Colbert* show. For more information, see the following **Real World Psychology**.

Real World **Psychology**—Understanding the World

The Stanford Marshmallow Test

Beginning in the early 1960s and 1970s, psychologist Walter Mischel and his colleagues conducted numerous experiments on *delayed gratification*, which is defined as "putting off a pleasurable experience in exchange for a larger but later reward." In their most famous study, they recruited over 600 children between the ages of 4 and 6, who attended a nursery school at Stanford University. Each child was led into a room, and seated alone at a table, with a very tempting marshmallow within easy reach (Mischel & Ebbesen, 1970). They were then told they could eat the marshmallow at any time, but if they waited for 15 minutes, they would get two marshmallows. The child was then left alone, while the researchers watched and recorded how long each child would wait before giving into temptation.

Can you imagine what happened? Some children immediately ate the marshmallow as soon as the researcher left the room. Others wiggled in their chairs, kicked at the table, stared at the marshmallow, smelled or petted the marshmallow, sang songs, and/or simply looked away—all in an attempt to resist temptation. Only a third of the children delayed gratification long enough to get the second marshmallow.

What makes this very simple research important is that the researchers continued to study the children for more than 40 years—with dramatic results! The amount of time the children were able to delay eating the first marshmallow, and wait for the second one (delayed gratification), was a significant predictor of who ended up with higher SAT scores, lower levels of substance abuse, lower likelihood of obesity, better responses to stress, greater academic performance and social skills as reported by their parents, and generally better scores in a range of other life measures (Caleza et al., 2016; Mischel, 1966, 2014; Mischel et al., 2011).

© Bill Aron/PhotoEdit

A final important thing to remember about this marshmallow study is that at every stage of our lives there will be numerous "marshmallows"—a fun party versus studying, an attractive new sexual partner versus our current one, a new car versus saving for retirement—that will potentially distract us from our long-term goals and personal best interests. The "simple" answer appears to be that when faced with important decisions we need to continually make mindful choices. If you'd like more information on the importance of self-control and delay of gratification with numerous practical applications, Mischel has written an entire book, *The Marshmallow Test* (Mischel, 2014).

Retrieval Practice 11.4 | Social-Cognitive Theories

SELF-TEST Completing this self-test, and then checking your answers by clicking on the answer button or by looking in Appendix B, will provide immediate feedback and helpful practice for exams.

1. According to Bandura, _____ relies on a person's belief about whether he or she can successfully engage in behaviors related to personal goals.
   a. self-actualization **b.** self-esteem
   c. self-efficacy **d.** self-congruence
2. Bandura's theory of _____ suggests that the person, behavior, and environment all interact to produce personality.
   a. self-actualization **b.** self-esteem maximization
   c. self-efficacy **d.** reciprocal determinism
3. _____ suggests that learning experiences create cognitive expectancies that guide behavior and influence the environment.
   a. Walter Mischel **b.** Julian Rotter
   c. Abraham Maslow **d.** Carl Sagan
4. According to Rotter, people with a(n) _____ believe the environment and external forces control events, whereas those with a(n) _____ believe in personal control.
   a. self-actualized personality; efficacy personality
   b. external locus of control; internal locus of control
   c. fatalistic view; humanistic opinion
   d. global locus of control; selfish locus of control
5. A criticism of the social-cognitive approach is that it focuses too much on _____ in understanding personality.
   a. scientific research
   b. unconscious forces
   c. situational influences
   d. expectancies

Think Critically

1. How would Bandura's social-cognitive concept of self-efficacy explain why bright students sometimes don't do well in college?
2. Do you have an internal or external locus of control? How might this affect your academic and lifetime achievement?

Real World Psychology

Can spending time in a foreign country change your personality?

ViewStock/Getty Images

HINT: LOOK IN THE MARGIN FOR **[Q4]**

11.5 Biological Theories

LEARNING OBJECTIVES

Retrieval Practice While reading the upcoming sections, respond to each Learning Objective in your own words.

Summarize the role that biology plays in personality.

- **Discuss** how brain structures, neurochemistry, and genetics influence personality.
- **Explain** the contributions and limitations of biological theories.
- **Describe** how the biopsychosocial model blends various approaches to personality.

In this section, we explore how biological factors influence our personalities. We conclude with a discussion of how all theories of personality ultimately interact in the *biopsychosocial model.*

Three Major Contributors to Personality

Hans Eysenck, the trait theorist mentioned earlier in the chapter, was one of the first to propose that personality traits are biologically based—at least in part. And modern research supports the theory that certain brain structures, neurochemistry, and genetics all may contribute to some personality characteristics. For example, how do we decide in the real world which risks are worth taking and which are not? Modern research using functional magnetic resonance imaging (fMRI) and other brain mapping techniques documents specific areas of the brain that correlate with trait impulsiveness and areas that differ between people with risk-averse versus risk-seeking personalities (Rass et al., 2016; Schilling et al., 2014).

Earlier research also found that increased electroencephalographic (EEG) activity in the left frontal lobes of the brain is associated with sociability (or extraversion), whereas greater EEG activity in the right frontal lobes is associated with shyness or introversion (Fishman & Ng, 2013; Tellegen, 1985).

A major limitation of research on brain structures and personality is the difficulty of identifying which structures are uniquely connected with particular personality traits. Neurochemistry seems to offer more precise data on how biology influences personality. For example, sensation seeking (Chapter 11) has consistently been linked with levels of monoamine oxidase (MAO), an enzyme that regulates levels of neurotransmitters such as dopamine (García et al., 2014; Zuckerman, 1994, 2004, 2014). Likewise, dopamine seems to be correlated with addictive personality traits, novelty seeking, and extraversion (Blum et al., 2013; Harris et al., 2015; Norbury & Husain, 2015; Schilling et al., 2014). See the following **Real World Psychology**.

Real World **Psychology**—Understanding the World

Biology's Impact on Personality

How can neurochemistry have such effects? Studies suggest that high-sensation seekers and extraverts tend to experience less physical arousal than introverts from the same stimulus (Fishman & Ng, 2013; Munoz & Anastassiou-Hadjicharalambous, 2011). Extraverts' low arousal apparently motivates them to seek out situations that will elevate their arousal. Moreover, it is believed that a higher arousal threshold is genetically transmitted. In other words, personality traits like sensation seeking and extraversion may be inherited. Our genes may also predict how we parent and even possible criminal behaviors, including arrest records (Armstrong et al., 2014; Klahr & Burt, 2014; van den Berg et al., 2016).

© FurmanAnna/iStockphoto

Personality and Behavioral Genetics This recognition that genetic factors have an important influence on personality has contributed to the relatively new field called *behavioral genetics,* which attempts to determine the extent to which behavioral differences among people are due to genetics as opposed to the environment (Chapter 9). One interesting study found that individuals with a "niceness gene" were more likely to report engaging in various types of prosocial behaviors, such as giving blood, volunteering, and donating to charitable organizations (Poulin et al., 2012). [Q5]

One way to measure genetic influences is to compare similarities in personality between identical twins and fraternal twins (see **Figure 11.13**). For example, studies of the five-factor model (FFM) suggest that genetic factors account for about 40 to 50% of personality traits (Bouchard, 1997, 2013; McCrae et al., 2010; Plomin et al., 2016).

In addition to conducting twin studies, researchers compare the personalities of parents with those of their biological children and their adopted children (see **Figure 11.14**). Studies of extraversion and neuroticism have found that parents' traits correlate moderately with those of their biological

FIGURE 11.13 **Identical versus fraternal twins**

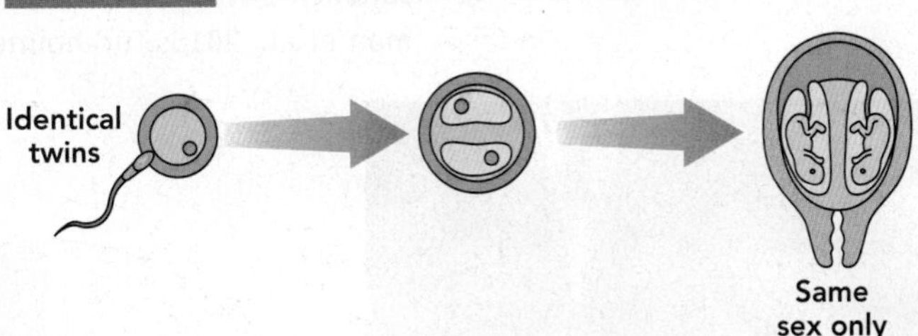

a. Identical (*monozygotic*—one egg) twins share 100% of the same genes because they develop from a single egg fertilized by a single sperm. They also share the same placenta, and are always the same sex.

b. Fraternal (*dizygotic*—two eggs) twins share, on average, 50% of their genes because they are formed when two separate sperm fertilize two separate eggs. Although they share the same general environment within the womb, they are no more genetically similar than non-twin siblings. They're simply nine-month "womb mates."

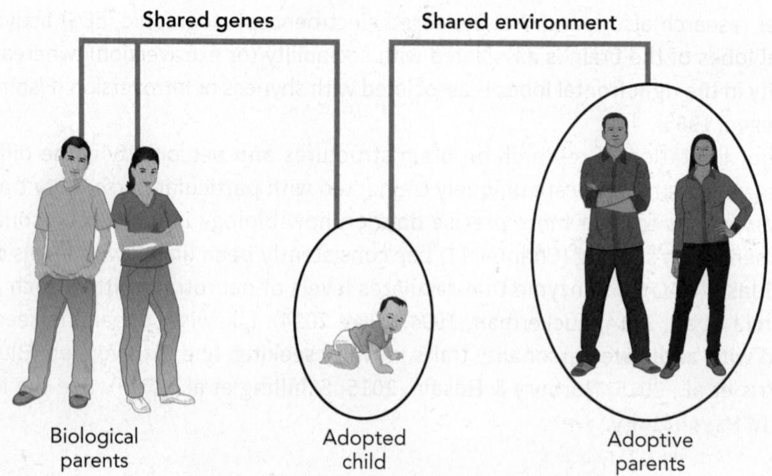

FIGURE 11.14 Adoption studies If adopted children are more like their biological family in some trait, then genetic factors probably had the greater influence. Conversely, if adopted children resemble their adopted family, even though they do not share similar genes, then environmental factors may predominate.

children and hardly at all with those of their adopted children (Bouchard, 1997; McCrae et al., 2000).

Evaluating Biological Theories

Modern research in biological theories has provided exciting insights, and established clear links between some personality traits and various brain areas, neurotransmitters, and/or genes. However, it's important to keep in mind that personality traits are never the result of a single biological process. For example, studies do show a strong inherited basis for personality, but researchers are careful not to overemphasize genetics (Cicchetti, 2016; Latzman et al., 2015; Turkheimer et al., 2014). Some believe the importance of the unshared environment—aspects of the environment that differ from one individual to another, even within a family—has been overlooked. Others fear that research on "genetic determinism" could be misused to "prove" that an ethnic or a racial group is inferior, that male dominance is natural, or that social progress is impossible.

In sum, there is no doubt that biological studies have produced valuable results. However, as is true for all the theories discussed in this chapter, no single personality theory explains everything we need to know about personality. Each theory offers different insights into how a person develops the distinctive set of characteristics we call "personality." That's why instead of adhering to any one theory, many psychologists believe in the *biopsychosocial approach*, or the idea that several factors—biological, psychological, and social—overlap in their contributions to personality (**Figure 11.15**).

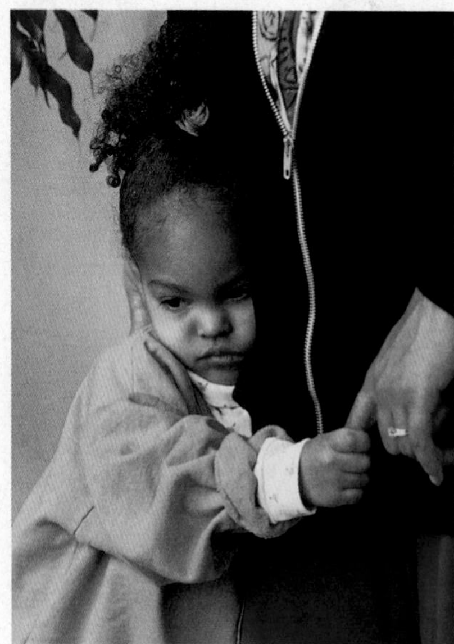
Rosanne Olson/Stone/Getty Images

FIGURE 11.15 Multiple influences on personality In addition to unknown factors, research has identified three other important influences on personality that might contribute to this child's apparent shyness.

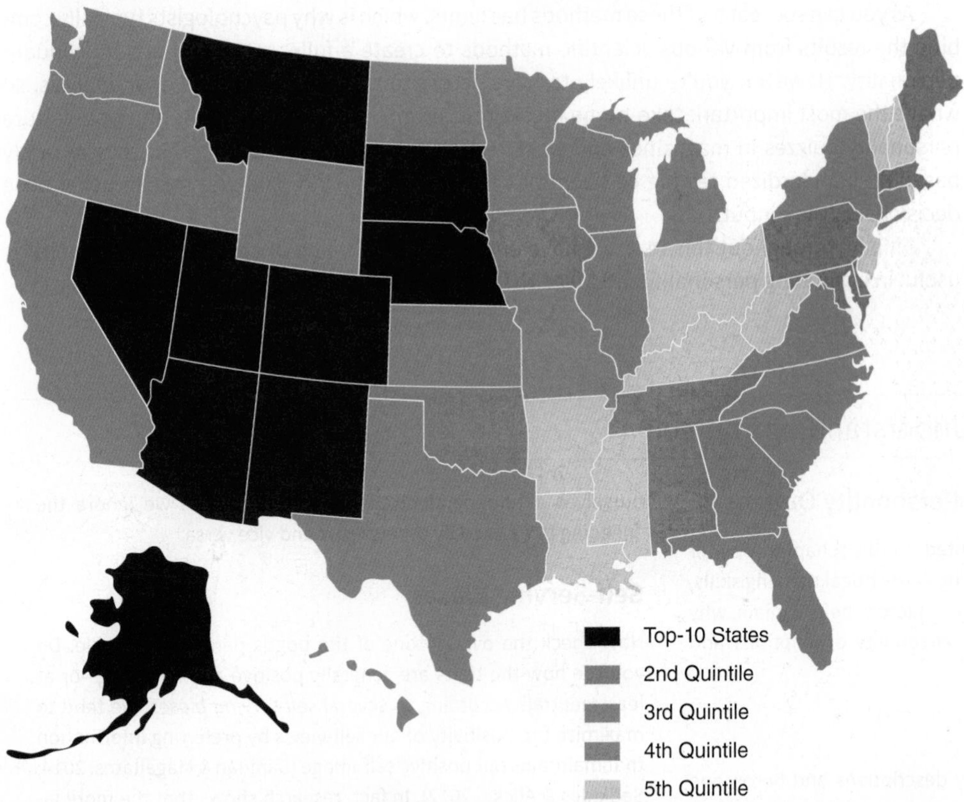

FIGURE 11.20 Entrepreneurship in the United States

with the outside world, reveals two distinct dimensions of personality—prosociality and industriousness—instead of the more widely accepted five personality traits (Gurven et al., 2013).

Differences in personality may also be seen in different parts of a single country (Rentfrow, 2014). For example, one study of over half a million people in the United States revealed regional differences in personality traits linked with entrepreneurial activity, defined as business-creation and self-employment rates (Obschonka et al., 2013). As you can see in **Figure 11.20**, certain regions are much more entrepreneurial than others. Why? The authors of the study suggested that the higher scores in the West, for example, might be a reflection of America's historical migration patterns of people moving from the East into the West (or from outside of America). They cite other research (e.g., Rentfrow et al., 2008) that suggests this selective migration may have had a lasting effect on personality due to the heritability of personality traits and the passing on of norms and values within the regions.

What do you think? How would you explain the differences? Can you see the overall value of expanding our study of personality from just looking at differences between individuals to examining regional differences, and how this expansion might increase our understanding of how personality is formed and its potential applications?

Projective Tests Although projective tests are extremely time-consuming to administer and interpret, their proponents suggest that because the method is unstructured, respondents may be more willing to talk honestly about sensitive topics. Critics point out, however, that the *reliability* and *validity* (Chapter 8) of projective tests is among the lowest of all tests of personality (Hartmann & Hartmann, 2014; Hunsley et al., 2015; Koocher et al., 2014). (Recall from Chapter 8 that reliability—the consistency of test results—and validity—whether the test actually measures what it was designed to measure—are the two most important criteria for a good test.)

As you can see, each of these methods has limits, which is why psychologists typically combine the results from various scientific methods to create a fuller picture of any individual's personality. However, you're unlikely to have access to this type of professional analysis, so what's the most important take-home message? Beware of pop-psych books and pop-culture personality quizzes in magazines and websites! They may be entertaining, but they're rarely based on standardized testing or scientific research of any kind, and you should never base decisions on their input.

Finally, throughout this text, we have emphasized the value of critical thinking, which is useful in evaluating personality tests (see the following **Psychology and You**).

Psychology and You—Understanding Yourself

What's Wrong with Pseudo-Personality Quizzes?

The personality horoscope presented in the chapter opener contains several logical fallacies. Using your critical thinking skills, can you see how the following three factors help explain why so many people believe in phony personality descriptions and predictions?

Barnum Effect

We often accept pseudo-personality descriptions and horoscope predictions because we think they are accurate. We tend to believe these tests have somehow tapped into our unique selves. In fact, they are ambiguous, broad statements that fit just about anyone (e.g., "You have a strong need for other people to like and admire you"). The existence of such generalities led to the term the *Barnum effect*, named for the legendary circus promoter P.T. Barnum, who said, "Always have a little something for everyone" (Wyman & Vyse, 2008).

Confirmation Bias

Look again at the introductory personality profile and count the number of times you agree with the statements. According to the *confirmation bias* (Chapter 8), we tend to notice and remember events that confirm our expectations and ignore those that are nonconfirming (Bhatia, 2014; Kukucka & Kassin, 2014). If we see ourselves as independent thinkers, for example, we ignore the "needing to be liked by others" part and vice versa.

Self-Serving Biases

Now check the overall tone of the bogus personality profile. Do you see how the traits are generally positive and flattering—or at least neutral? According to several *self-serving biases*, we tend to maximize the positivity of our self-views by preferring information that maintains our positive self-image (Sanjuán & Magallares, 2014; Sedkides & Alicke, 2012). In fact, research shows that the more favorable a personality description is, the more people believe it, and the more likely they are to believe it is personally unique (Guastello et al., 1989).

Taken together, these three logical fallacies help explain the common support for pop-psych personality tests and newspaper horoscopes. They offer something for everyone (*Barnum effect*). We pay attention only to what confirms our expectations (*confirmation bias*). And we like flattering descriptions (*self-serving biases*). You can test your understanding of these three biases in the following:

Think Critically

Using the information in this *Psychology and You* section, can you identify the two major fallacies in this cartoon?

Answer: self-serving biases and the Barnum effect.

Retrieval Practice 11.6 | Personality Assessment

SELF-TEST Completing this self-test, and then checking your answers by clicking on the answer button or by looking in Appendix B, will provide immediate feedback and helpful practice for exams.

1. In the 1800s, if you wanted to have your personality assessed, you would go to a phrenologist, who would determine your personality by studying/measuring ____.

a. projective tests **b.** ambiguous stimuli results
c. inkblot stain responses **d.** bumps on your head

2. The most widely researched and clinically used self-report personality test is the ____.

a. MMPI **b.** Rorschach Inkblot Test
c. TAT **d.** SVII

3. During a(n) ____, individuals are asked to respond to a standardized set of ambiguous stimuli.

a. projective test **b.** objective test
c. MMPI exam **d.** phrenology exam

4. The Rorschach Inkblot Test is an example of a(n) ____ test.

a. projective **b.** ambiguous stimuli
c. inkblot **d.** all these options

5. Two important criteria for evaluating the usefulness of tests used to assess personality are ____.

a. concurrence and prediction **b.** reliability and validity
c. consistency and correlation **d.** diagnosis and prognosis

Think Critically

1. Which method of personality assessment (interviews, behavioral observation, objective testing, or projective-testing) do you think is likely to be most informative? Can you think of circumstances in which one kind of assessment might be more effective than the others?

2. Why do you think objective personality tests like the MMPI are so popular and so widely used?

Real World **Psychology**

Can social media postings be used to measure your personality?

Stock Rocket/ Shutterstock

HINT: LOOK IN THE MARGIN FOR **[Q6]**

Summary

11.1 Psychoanalytic/Psychodynamic Theories 302

- **Personality** is defined as the unique and relatively stable patterns of thoughts, feelings, and actions.
- Freud, the founder of psychodynamic theory, believed that the mind contained three *levels of consciousness*: conscious, preconscious, and **unconscious**. He proposed that most psychological disorders originate from unconscious memories and instincts.
- Freud also asserted that personality was composed of the **id**, **ego**, and **superego**. When the ego fails to satisfy both the id and the superego, anxiety reportedly slips into conscious awareness, which triggers **defense mechanisms**.
- Freud believed that all children go through five **psychosexual stages**: oral, anal, phallic, latency, and genital. How specific conflicts at each of these stages are resolved is supposedly important to personality development.
- *Neo-Freudians* such as Adler, Jung, and Horney were influential followers of Freud who later rejected major aspects of Freudian theory. Adler emphasized the inferiority complex and the compensating will-to-power. Jung introduced the **collective unconscious** and **archetypes**. Horney stressed the importance of basic anxiety and refuted Freud's idea of penis envy, replacing it with power envy.

11.2 Trait Theories 308

- Allport believed that the best way to understand personality was to arrange a person's unique personality **traits** into a hierarchy. Cattell and Eysenck later reduced the list of possible personality traits using *factor analysis*.
- The **five-factor model (FFM)** clarified the *Big Five* major dimensions of **personality:** *openness*, *conscientiousness*, *extraversion*, *agreeableness*, and *neuroticism*.

11.3 Humanistic Theories 314

- Humanistic theories focus on internal experiences (thoughts and feelings) and the individual's **self-concept**.
- According to Rogers, mental health and self-esteem are related to the degree of congruence between our **self-concept** and life experiences. Rogers argued that poor mental health results when young children do not receive **unconditional positive regard** from caregivers.
- Maslow saw personality as the quest to fulfill basic physiological needs and to move toward the highest level of **self-actualization**.

11.4 Social-Cognitive Theories 317

- Social-cognitive theorists emphasize the importance of our interactions with the environment and how we interpret and respond to these external events.
- Cognition is central to Bandura's concept of **self-efficacy**. According to Bandura, self-efficacy affects which challenges we choose to accept and the effort we expend in reaching goals. His concept of **reciprocal**

determinism states that our self-efficacy beliefs also affect others' responses to us.

• Rotter's theory says that learning experiences create *cognitive expectancies* that guide behavior and influence the environment. Rotter believed that having an internal versus external *locus of control* affects personality and achievement.

11.5 Biological Theories 320

• Certain brain areas may contribute to personality. However, neurochemistry seems to offer more precise data on how biology influences personality. Research in *behavioral genetics* indicates that genetic factors also strongly influence personality.

• Instead of adhering to any one theory of personality, many psychologists believe in the biopsychosocial approach—the idea that several factors overlap in their contributions to personality.

11.6 Personality Assessment 323

• Psychologists use four basic methods to measure or assess personality: interviews, observations, objective tests, and projective techniques.

• **Objective personality tests** are widely used because we can administer them broadly and relatively quickly and evaluate them in a standardized fashion. To assess a range of personality traits, psychologists use multitrait inventories, such as the **MMPI**.

• **Projective tests** use unstructured stimuli that can be perceived in many ways. Projective tests, such as the **Rorschach Inkblot Test**, and the **Thematic Apperception Test (TAT)**, supposedly allow each person to project his or her own unconscious conflicts, psychological defenses, motives, and personality traits onto the test materials.

• The *Barnum effect*, *confirmation bias*, and the *self-serving* biases are the three most important fallacies of pseudo-personality tests.

Applying **Real** World **Psychology**

We began this chapter with six intriguing Real World Psychology questions, and you were asked to revisit these questions at the end of each section. Questions like these have an important and lasting impact on all of our lives. See if you can answer these additional critical thinking questions related to real world examples.

1. As first discussed in Chapter 9 and throughout this chapter, early childhood relationships, particularly between parent and child, are very important to our personality development and overall psychological health. According to the five psychosexual stages of development, how might Freud interpret this woman and her son's obvious attachment to one another? Can you think of an alternative, more logical, explanation for their attachment?
2. How would Rogers's emphasis on unconditional positive regard and Bandura's social-cognitive concept of self-efficacy relate to this mother's display of pleasure at her son's attempt to dry her hair?
3. Can you identify one or more defense mechanisms that you use in your life? If you find them to be unhealthy, what can you do to change them?

Cameron/Corbis Images

4. If you agree that self-actualization is a worthy goal, what are you doing to move in that direction?
5. Which theory of personality discussed in this chapter do you find most useful in understanding yourself and others? Why?

Key Terms

Retrieval Practice Write a definition for each term before turning back to the referenced page to check your answer.

- archetypes 306
- basic anxiety 307
- collective unconscious 306
- conscious 302
- defense mechanisms 303
- ego 303
- five-factor model (FFM) 309
- id 302
- inferiority complex 306
- Minnesota Multiphasic Personality Inventory (MMPI) 325
- Oedipus complex 305
- personality 302
- preconscious 302
- projective test 325
- psychosexual stages 303
- reciprocal determinism 317
- Rorschach Inkblot Test 325
- self-actualization 314
- self-concept 314
- self-efficacy 317
- superego 303
- Thematic Apperception Test (TAT) 325
- trait 309
- unconditional positive regard 314
- unconscious 302

© alexsl/iStockphoto

CHAPTER **12**

Psychological Disorders

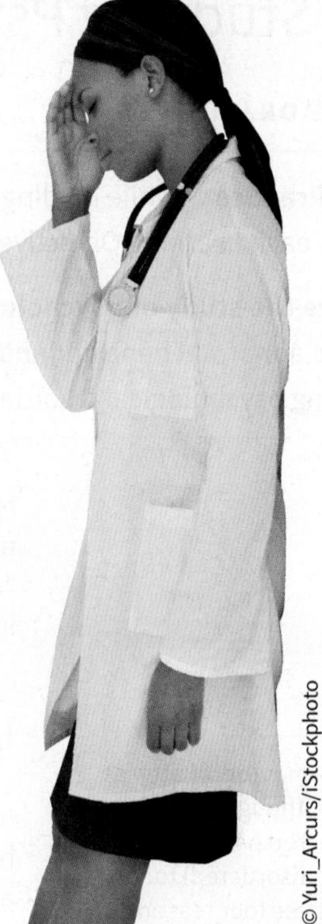

© Yuri_Arcurs/iStockphoto

Real World **Psychology**

Things you'll learn in Chapter 12

[Q1] How can media coverage of mass shootings create negative misperceptions about people with mental illness?

[Q2] What is the most "contagious" psychological disorder?

[Q3] Can Internet and cell phone use increase mental health problems?

[Q4] Are children who experience trauma at increased risk of developing schizophrenia later in life?

[Q5] How do changes in the brain help explain severe antisocial personality disorder?

[Q6] Are symptoms of depression in women more distressing, deserving of sympathy, and difficult to treat than the same signs in men?

Throughout the chapter, margin icons for Q1–Q6 indicate where the text addresses these questions.

Chapter Overview

Are you excited? Throughout history, psychological disorders have been the subject of intense fascination. Now, you finally get to read and study the part of psychology you've probably been waiting for from the very beginning! Hopefully, while reading this chapter you'll recognize how the earlier chapters have prepared you for a better understanding and appreciation of the complex issues surrounding abnormal behavior. We begin with a discussion of how psychological disorders are identified, explained, and classified. Then we explore six major categories of psychological disorders: anxiety disorders, depressive and bipolar disorders, schizophrenia, obsessive-compulsive disorder (OCD), and personality disorders. We close with a look at gender and cultural factors related to psychological disorders.

CHAPTER OUTLINE

12.1 Studying Psychological Disorders

LEARNING OBJECTIVES

Retrieval Practice While reading the upcoming sections, respond to each Learning Objective in your own words.

Summarize the study of psychological disorders.

- **Describe** abnormal behavior and the four criteria for identifying psychological disorders.
- **Explain** how perspectives on the causes of psychological disorders have changed throughout history.
- **Discuss** the pros and cons of the *Diagnostic and Statistical Manual of Mental Disorders (DSM).*

Most people agree that neither the artist who stays awake for 72 hours finishing a painting nor the shooter who kills 20 young school children is behaving normally. But what exactly is "normal"? How do we distinguish between eccentricity in the first case and abnormal behavior in the second?

Identifying and Explaining Psychological Disorders

Abnormal behavior Patterns of behaviors, thoughts, or emotions considered pathological (diseased or disordered) for one or more of these four reasons: deviance, dysfunction, distress, and/or danger.

As you can see, it's difficult to distinguish normal from abnormal behavior, and psychologists have struggled to create a precise definition. However, mental health professionals generally agree that **abnormal behavior** (or psychopathology) can be identified as patterns of behaviors, thoughts, or emotions considered pathological (diseased or disordered) for one or more of these four reasons: *deviance, dysfunction, distress,* and/or *danger* (**Figure 12.1**). Keep in

FIGURE 12.1 Four criteria for identifying abnormal behavior

sanjagrujic/Shutterstock

a. Deviance
Behaviors, thoughts, or emotions may be considered abnormal when they deviate from a society or culture's norms or values. For example, it's normal to be a bit concerned if friends are whispering, but abnormal if you're equally concerned when total strangers are whispering.

Ian West/Alamy

b. Dysfunction
When someone's dysfunction interferes with his or her daily functioning, such as drinking to the point that it interferes with holding a job, staying in school, or maintaining a relationship, it would be considered abnormal behavior.

Peter Dazeley/Photographer's Choice/Getty Image, Inc.

c. Distress
Behaviors, thoughts, or emotions that cause significant personal distress may qualify as abnormal. Self-abuse, serious relationship problems, and suicidal thoughts all indicate significant personal distress and unhappiness.

d. Danger
If someone's thoughts, emotions, or behaviors present a danger to self or others, such as engaging in road rage to the point of physical confrontation, it would be considered abnormal.

Digital Vision/Getty Images

TABLE 12.1 Common Myths About Mental Illness

Real World Psychology

- ***Myth: Mentally ill people are often dangerous and unpredictable.***

  Fact: Only a few disorders, such as some psychotic and antisocial personality disorders, are associated with violence. The stereotype that connects mental illness and violence persists because of prejudice, selective media attention, and negative portrayals in movies and on television.

- ***Myth: People with psychological disorders act in bizarre ways and are very different from normal people.***

  Fact: This is true for only a small minority of individuals and during a relatively brief portion of their lives. In fact, sometimes even mental health professionals find it difficult to distinguish normal from abnormal behaviors without formal screening.

- ***Myth: Psychological disorders are a sign of personal weakness.***

  Fact: Like all other illnesses, psychological disorders are a function of many factors, such as exposure to stress, genetic predispositions, a host of personal and sociocultural experiences, and family background. Mentally disturbed individuals can't be blamed for their illness any more than we blame people who develop cancer or other illnesses.

- ***Myth: A mentally ill person is only suited for low-level jobs and never fully recovers.***

  Fact: Once again, like all other illnesses, psychological disorders are complex, and their symptoms, severity, and prognoses differ for each individual. With therapy, the vast majority of those who are diagnosed as mentally ill eventually improve and lead normal, productive lives. Moreover, the extreme symptoms of some psychological disorders are generally only temporary. For example, U.S. President Abraham Lincoln, British Prime Minister Winston Churchill, scientist Isaac Newton, and other high achieving people all suffered from serious psychological disorders at various times throughout their careers.

© Ira Berger/Alamy Stock Photo

Is this behavior abnormal? Eccentric? Yes. Mentally disordered? Probably not.

Sources: Durand & Barlow, 2016; Lilienfeld et al., 2015; Metzl & MacLeish, 2015; National Alliance on Mental Health, 2015.

mind that abnormal behavior, like intelligence and creativity, is not composed of two discrete categories—"normal and "abnormal." Instead, mental health lies along a continuum, with people being unusually healthy at one end and extremely disturbed at the other (Kring et al., 2014; Sue et al., 2016).

When considering the four criteria for abnormal behavior, remember that no single criterion is adequate by itself. Furthermore, judgments of what is personally distressing, and what is deviant or dysfunctional, vary historically and cross-culturally. Perhaps the most important issue surrounding abnormal behavior is that the public generally overestimates the danger posed by those who suffer from psychological disorders, when in fact they are far more likely to be the *victims* of violence rather than the perpetrators. See **Table 12.1** for more about this and other myths of mental illness.

What causes abnormal behavior? Historically, evil spirits and witchcraft have been blamed (Shiraev, 2015; Sue et al., 2016; Walsh et al., 2014). Stone Age people, for example, believed that abnormal behavior stemmed from demonic possession; the "therapy" was to bore a hole in the skull so the evil spirit could escape, a process we call *trephining*. During the European Middle Ages, abnormal behavior was sometimes treated with *exorcism*, which was a religious or spiritual practice designed to evict the demons by making the troubled person's body inhospitable through lengthy prayers, fasting, and beatings. During the later Renaissance period (14th to the 17th century), many believed that some individuals chose to consort with the Devil. These supposed witches were often tortured, imprisoned for life, or executed (**Figure 12.2**).

Corbis Images

FIGURE 12.2 Witchcraft or mental illness? During the European Renaissance, some people, who may have been suffering from mental disorders, were accused of witchcraft and tortured or hung.

As the Renaissance ended, special mental hospitals called *asylums* began to appear in Europe. Initially designed to provide quiet retreats

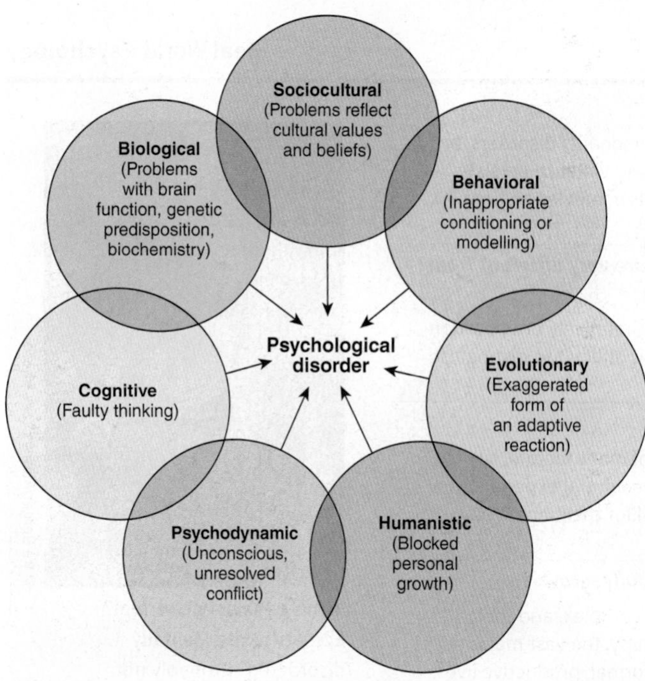

FIGURE 12.3 Seven psychological perspectives As you can see in this diagram, the seven major perspectives differ in their various explanations for the general causes of psychological disorders, but there is still considerable overlap.

from the world and to protect society, the asylums unfortunately became overcrowded, inhumane prisons (Radhika et al., 2015; Shiraev, 2015).

Improvement came in 1792, when Philippe Pinel, a French physician, was placed in charge of a Parisian asylum. Believing that inmates' behavior was caused by underlying physical illness, he insisted that they be unshackled and removed from their dark, unheated cells. Many inmates improved so dramatically that they could be released. Pinel's actions reflect the ideals of the modern *medical model*, which assumes that diseases (including mental illness) have physical causes that can be diagnosed, treated, and possibly cured and prevented. This medical model is the foundation of the branch of medicine, known as **psychiatry**, that deals with the diagnosis, treatment, and prevention of mental disorders.

In contrast, psychologists believe that focusing on "mental illness" overlooks important social and cultural factors, as well as our own personal thoughts, feelings, and actions that contribute to psychological disorders. Therefore, we take a multifaceted approach to explaining abnormal behavior, as shown in **Figure 12.3.**

Classifying Psychological Disorders

Psychiatry The branch of medicine that deals with the diagnosis, treatment, and prevention of mental disorders.

Diagnostic and Statistical Manual of Mental Disorders (DSM) A manual developed by the American Psychiatric Association that is used primarily to classify psychological disorders.

Neurosis An outmoded term and category dropped from the DSM, in which a person does not have signs of brain abnormalities and does not display grossly irrational thinking or violate basic norms but does experience subjective distress.

Psychosis A serious psychological disorder characterized by extreme mental disruption and defective or lost contact with reality.

Insanity The legal (not clinical) designation for a situation in which an individual cannot be held responsible for his or her actions or is incompetent to manage his or her own affairs because of mental illness.

In addition to identifying and explaining abnormal behavior, we need to classify those behaviors into specific categories. Why? Without a clear, reliable system for classifying the wide range of psychological disorders, scientific research on them would be almost impossible, and communication among mental health professionals would be seriously impaired. Fortunately, mental health specialists share a uniform classification system, the ***Diagnostic and Statistical Manual of Mental Disorders (DSM)***. This manual has been updated and revised several times, and the latest, fifth edition, was published in 2013 (American Psychiatric Association, 2013).

Each revision of the *DSM* has expanded the list of disorders and changed the descriptions and categories to reflect the latest in scientific research. For example, take the terms **neurosis** and **psychosis**. In previous editions of the *DSM*, the term *neurosis* reflected Freud's belief that all neurotic conditions arise from unconscious conflicts (Chapter 11). Now, conditions that were previously grouped under the heading *neurosis* have been formally studied and redistributed as separate categories. Unlike neurosis, the term *psychosis* is still listed in the current edition of the *DSM* because it remains useful for distinguishing the most severe psychological disorders, such as schizophrenia.

What about the term *insanity*? **Insanity** is a legal term indicating that a person cannot be held responsible for his or her actions or is incompetent to manage his or her own affairs because of mental illness. In the law, the definition of mental illness rests primarily on a person's inability to tell right from wrong (**Figure 12.4**). Bear in mind that the term "insanity" often appears in public conversations, but it's seldom used by psychologists. People suffer from specific psychological disorders–they're not "insane."

Understanding and Evaluating the DSM

To understand a disorder, we must first name and describe it. The *DSM* identifies and describes the symptoms of approximately 400 disorders, which are grouped into 22 categories (**Table 12.2**). Note that we focus on only the first 7 in this chapter (categories 8–14 are discussed in other chapters; 15–22 are beyond the scope of this book). Also, keep in mind

with **bipolar disorders**, however, rebound to the opposite state, known as *mania,* which is characterized by unreasonable elation and hyperactivity (**Figure 12.7**).

Bipolar disorder A psychological disorder characterized by repeated episodes of mania (unreasonable elation, often with hyperactivity) alternating with depression.

Real World **Psychology**—Understanding the World

Hollywood's Depiction of Bipolar Disorder

Did you know that the Oscar-nominated film *Silver Linings Playbook* was originally a gift from the director to his son, Matthew, who suffers from *bipolar disorder*? Viewers and mental health professionals, however, all agree that it's a gift for all because it casts a sensitive subject in a warmer light and helps offset the stigma so commonly associated with mental illness (Lopez, 2013).

During a manic episode, individuals often feel unusually "high" and optimistic, and experience unrealistically high self-esteem and grandiose beliefs about their abilities and powers. While mania feels good at first, it has serious and often dangerous side effects, such as becoming aggressive, and engaging in reckless behaviors, including inappropriate sexual activity, gambling away savings, giving away valuable possessions or going on wild spending sprees. In addition, they are often hyperactive and may not sleep for days at a time without becoming apparently fatigued. Thinking is faster than normal and can change abruptly to new topics, showing "rapid flight of ideas." Speech is also rapid ("pressured speech"), making it difficult for others to get a word in edgewise. A manic episode may last a few days or a few months, and it generally ends abruptly. The ensuing depressive episode generally lasts three times as long as the mania (Leigh, 2015; Ray, 2015).

The lifetime risk for bipolar disorder is low—between 0.5 and 1.6%—but it can be one of the most debilitating and lethal disorders. Due in part to the impulsivity associated with this disorder, the suicide rate is between 10 and 20% among sufferers (Depp et al., 2016; Ketter & Miller, 2015). Before going on, let's explore the link between bipolar disorder and creativity (see the following **PsychScience**).

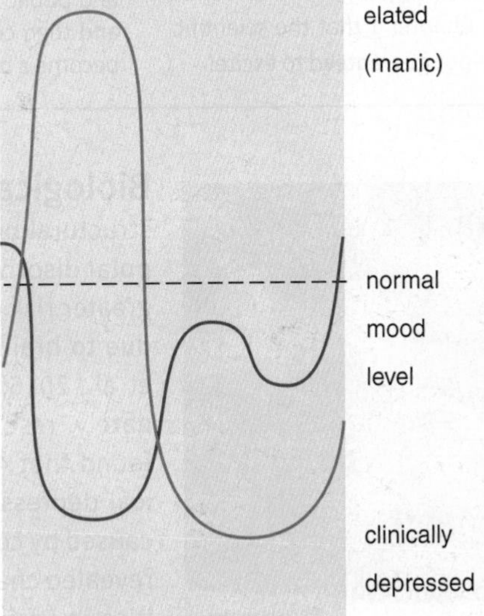

FIGURE 12.7 Depressive versus bipolar disorders If depressive disorders and bipolar disorders were depicted on a graph, they might look something like this. Remember that only in bipolar disorders do people experience manic episodes.

Explaining Depressive and Bipolar Disorders

As we've seen, depressive and bipolar disorders are characterized by extreme disturbances in emotional states. In this section, we will look at the biological and psychosocial factors that contribute to these disorders.

PS PsychScience

Creativity and Bipolar Disorder

What do you picture when you think of a creative genius? Thanks to movies, television, and novels, many people share the stereotypical image of an eccentric inventor or deranged artist, like the lead ballerina in the film *Black Swan*.

Is there an actual link between creativity and psychological disorders? Researchers interested in this question collected data from more than 1 million people, including their specific professions, whether they had ever been diagnosed and treated for a psychological disorder, and if so what type (Kyaga et al., 2012). Kyaga and his colleagues found that individuals in generally creative professions (scientific or artistic) were no more likely to suffer from investigated psychiatric disorders than those in other professions. However, bipolar disorder was significantly more common in artists and scientists, and particularly in authors.

What do you think? How would you explain this intriguing association between certain creative professions and bipolar disorder? Does the manic phase of bipolar disorder increase the energy levels of artists, scientists, and authors, giving them greater access to creative ideas than they would otherwise have? Or does it interfere with their overall output? Can you see how variables like choice of occupation might confound these results (Patra & Balhara, 2012)? As you'll discover later in this chapter, there is a strong genetic component in bipolar disorders. And, just as you are much more likely to enter a profession similar to that of your parents because of familiarity, access, and modeling, children of artists, scientists, and authors are more likely to choose similar professions—thus possibly explaining the link between creativity and mental illness.

If you find these questions fascinating and the lack of answers frustrating, you may be the perfect candidate for a career as a research psychologist. Recall from Chapter 1 that the scientific method is circular and never-ending—but guaranteed to excite!

© Fox Searchlight Pictures/Photofest

Research Challenge

1. Based on the information provided, did this study (Kyaga et al., 2012) use descriptive, correlational, and/or experimental research?
2. If you chose:
   - *descriptive research*, is this a naturalistic observation, survey/interview, case study, and/or archival research?
   - *correlational research*, is this a positive, negative, or zero correlation?
   - *experimental research*, label the IV, DV, experimental group(s), and control group.
   - both *descriptive* and *correlational* research, answer the corresponding questions for both

Check your answers by clicking on the answer button or by looking in Appendix B.

Note: The information provided in this study is admittedly limited, but the level of detail is similar to what is presented in most textbooks and public reports of research findings. Answering these questions, and then comparing your answers to those provided, will help you become a better critical thinker and consumer of scientific research.

Kent C. Horner/Getty Images

FIGURE 12.8 Brain damage and professional sports As discussed in Chapter 7, Junior Seau, who played in the NFL for 20 years, died by suicide from a gunshot wound to his chest in 2012 at the age of 43. Later studies concluded that he suffered from *chronic traumatic encephalopathy* (CTE), a form of concussion-related brain damage that has been found in numerous NFL players.

Biological Factors Recent research suggests that structural brain changes may contribute to depressive and bipolar disorders. For example, some professional athletes are at greater risk of developing such disorders as they age, possibly due to brain damage caused by repeated concussions (Bajwa et al., 2016; Broshek et al., 2015; Yang et al., 2015). Unfortunately, research on former professional football players has found that 41% show cognitive problems and 24% show clinical depression, which may result from neurological changes caused by concussions (Hart et al., 2013). Their brain scans also revealed changes in blood flow within the brain and abnormalities in various parts of the brain. Sadly, these changes may contribute to serious depression and increased risk of suicide (**Figure 12.8**).

Other research points to imbalances of neurotransmitters, including GABA, serotonin, norepinephrine, and dopamine, as possible causes of mood disorders (Artigas, 2015; Fakhoury, 2015; Yin et al., 2016). And both depressive disorders and bipolar disorders are sometimes treated with antidepressants, which affect the amount or functioning of these same neurotransmitters. Surprisingly, one small, recent study found that psilocybin, a hallucinogen from "magic" mushrooms, can help reduce the symptoms of depression (Mithoefer et al., 2016). Perhaps even more surprising, researchers have found that people who regularly ate fast food and commercially produced baked goods (such as croissants and doughnuts) were 51% more likely to develop depression later on (Sánchez-Villegas et al., 2011). Can you see how this may be the result of the chemicals in such foods leading to physiological changes in the brain and body?

As we've seen with the previous disorders, genetic research indicates that both depressive and bipolar disorders may be inherited (Antypa et al., 2016; Jacobs et al., 2015; Pandolfo et al., 2015). In contrast, research that takes an evolutionary perspective suggests that moderate depression may be a normal and healthy adaptive response to a very real loss, such as the death of a loved one, which helps us conserve energy and to step back and reassess our goals (Beck & Bredemeier, 2016; Neumann & Walter, 2015). And clinical, severe depression may just be an extreme version of this generally adaptive response.

Psychosocial Factors In contrast to the biological factors, psychosocial explanations of depression focus on environmental stressors, disturbances in the person's interpersonal relationships or self-concept, and any history of abuse or assault (Ege et al., 2015; Holshausen et al., 2016; Massing-Schaffer et al., 2015). The psychoanalytic explanation sees depression as the result of anger turned inward, or as the aftermath of experiencing a real or imagined loss, which is internalized as guilt, shame, self-hatred, and ultimately self-blame. The cognitive perspective explains depression as caused, at least in part, by negative thinking patterns, including a tendency to ruminate, or obsess, about problems (Arora et al., 2015; Yoon et al., 2014). The humanistic school says that depression results when a person demands perfection of him or herself or when positive growth is blocked (McCormack & Joseph, 2014; Short & Thomas, 2015).

According to the **learned helplessness** theory (Seligman, 1975, 2007), depression occurs when people (and other animals) become resigned to the idea that they are helpless to escape from a painful situation because of a history of repeated failures. For humans, learned helplessness may be particularly likely to trigger depression if the person attributes failure to causes that are internal ("my own weakness"), stable ("this weakness is long-standing and unchanging"), and global ("this weakness is a problem in lots of settings") (Barnum et al., 2013; Smalheiser et al., 2014; Travers et al., 2015).

Learned helplessness Seligman's term for a state of helplessness, or resignation, in which human or nonhuman animals fail to act to escape from a situation due to a history of repeated failures in the past.

[Q3] In addition to these and other psychological theories, several social factors may also contribute to the mood disorders. Perhaps most surprising is the finding that high Internet and cell phone use (see the photo) are linked with mental health problems, such as depression and anxiety (Panova & Lleras, 2016). This is particularly true when they're used to avoid negative experiences or feelings. However, no link was found if you're using them merely to escape boredom.

Axel Bueckert/Shutterstock

Before going on, please keep in mind that suicide is a major danger associated with both depressive disorder and bipolar disorder. Unfortunately, there are many suicide myths and misunderstandings (see **Table 12.3**) and many people who suffer with these disorders are so disturbed they lose contact with reality and may fail to recognize the danger signs or to seek help (see the **Psychology and You**). The following **Real World Psychology** also offers important information for both the sufferers and their family and friends.

On a slightly more positive note, research shows that one of the best ways to reduce suicides—although not depression—is to pass laws that limit access to handguns. Compared to states without such laws, those with background checks have a 53% lower gun suicide rate, those with mandated gun locks have a 68% lower gun suicide rate, and those with restrictions on open carry have a 42% lower gun suicide rate. Similarly, the longer the waiting period to buy a gun, the lower the gun suicide rate (Anestis et al., 2015; Metzl & MacLeish, 2015).

TABLE 12.3 Common Myths About Suicide

Real World Psychology

Because of the shame and secrecy surrounding suicide, there are many misconceptions and stereotypes. Can you correctly identify which of the following is true or false?

1. People who talk about suicide are less likely to actually complete it.
2. Suicide usually takes place with little or no warning.
3. Suicidal people are fully intent on dying.
4. Children of parents who attempt suicide are at greater risk of dying by suicide.
5. Suicidal people remain so forever.
6. Men are more likely than women to actually kill themselves by suicide.
7. When a suicidal person has been severely depressed, and seems to be "snapping out of it," the danger of suicide decreases substantially.
8. Only depressed people die by suicide.
9. Thinking about suicide is rare.
10. Asking a depressed person about suicide will push him or her over the edge, and cause a suicidal act that might not otherwise have occurred.

Now, compare your responses to the experts' answers and explanations:

1 and 2. **False** Up to three-quarters of those who take their own lives talk about it, and give warnings about their intentions beforehand. They may say, "If something happens to me, I want you to . . .," or "Life just isn't worth living." They also provide behavioral clues, such as giving away valued possessions, withdrawing from family and friends, and losing interest in favorite activities.

3. **False** Only about 3% to 5% of suicidal people truly intend to die. Most are just unsure about how to go on living. Unfortunately, they can't see their problems objectively enough to recognize alternative courses of action. They often gamble with death, arranging it so that fate or others will save them. However, once the suicidal crisis passes, they're generally grateful to be alive.
4. **True** Children of parents who attempt or die by suicide are at much greater risk of following in their footsteps. As Schneidman (1969) puts it, "The person who dies by suicide puts his psychological skeleton in the survivor's emotional closet" (p. 225).
5. **False** People who want to kill themselves are usually suicidal only for a limited period.
6. **True** Although women are much more likely to attempt suicide, men are far more likely to actually complete it. This is true because men generally use more effective and lethal methods, such as guns instead of pills.
7. **False** When people are first coming out of a depression, they are at greater risk because they now have the energy to actually die by suicide.
8. **False** Suicide rates are highest among people with major depressive disorders. However, suicide is also the leading cause of premature death in people who suffer from schizophrenia, and a major cause of death in people with anxiety disorders, and alcohol and other substance-related disorders. Furthermore, poor physical health, serious illness, loneliness, unemployment, and even natural disasters may push some people over the edge. Interestingly, people who work in careers that have great pressure for perfectionism—doctors, lawyers, architects, those in leadership roles—also are at elevated risk for perfectionism-related suicide.
9. **False** Estimates from various studies are that 40% to 80% of the general public has thought about attempting suicide at least once in their lives.
10. **False** Because society often considers suicide a terrible, shameful act, asking directly about it can give the person permission to talk. In fact, not asking is more likely to lead to further isolation and depression.

Sources: American Association of Suicidology, 2016; Birmaher & Brent, 2016; Lilienfeld et al., 2015; Minzenberg et al., 2014; Rebok et al, 2015; Suicide Basic Facts, 2015.

Psychology and You—Understanding Yourself

Test Yourself | Danger Signs for Suicide

Would you like a brief, informal self-test of your own symptoms of depression?
Answer the following questions, based on how you have been feeling over the past two weeks. Use a scale of 1 = at no time to 6 = all the time.

Have you felt low in spirits or sad?

Have you lost interest in your daily activities?

Have you felt lacking in energy and strength?

Have you felt less self-confident?

Have you had a bad conscience or feelings of guilt?

Have you felt that life wasn't worth living?

Have you had difficulty concentrating?

Have you felt very restless?

Have you felt subdued or slowed down?

Have you had trouble sleeping at night?

Have you suffered from a noticeably reduced or increased appetite?

Scoring: Higher numbers on this scale indicate higher levels of depression (Bech et al., 2011; Olsen et al., 2003). If you're currently feeling suicidal, seek help immediately!

© Bubbles Photolibrary/Alamy

The most important thing to remember is: **Suicide is a permanent response to what is generally a temporary problem! Don't ignore the warning signs. Get help fast!**

Real World Psychology—Understanding the World

What to Do If You Think Someone Is Suicidal

If you have a friend or loved one with serious depression, it may feel like you're walking through a minefield when you're attempting to comfort and help them. What do the experts suggest?

What NOT to Do:

- **Don't ignore the warning signs.** *(See again the Test Yourself)* Depression, like cancer or heart disease, is a critical, life-threatening brain disease. Knowing the signs of suicide risk can increase your confidence in how and when to intervene (Ramchand et al., 2016).
- **Don't equate suicide with "selfishness."** Just as we wouldn't say a drug addict and/or diabetic died because he or she lacked courage and were being selfish, we need to recognize the courage and strength of the chronically and deeply depressed who struggle each day NOT to die.
- **Don't be afraid to discuss suicide.** In a calm voice, ask the person a direct question, such as, "Are you thinking of hurting yourself?" Many people fear the topic of suicide because they think they might put that idea into the other person's head. As mentioned before, the reality is that virtually every adult knows what suicide is, and many have even considered it for themselves. Furthermore, people who are told "you can't be seriously considering suicide" often feel even more alone, become less likely to share their true feelings, and more likely to actually attempt it.
- **Don't abandon the person after the suicidal crisis has seemingly passed.** Depression and suicidal thoughts don't magically disappear. For many, the fight against depression is a painful, lifelong struggle, and your friend or loved one needs your ongoing support.

What To Do:

- **Stay with the person.** Encourage him or her to talk to you rather than to withdraw. Show the person that you care, but do not give false reassurances that "everything will be okay." If you feel like you can't handle the crisis by yourself, share your suspicions with parents, friends, or others who can help in a suicidal crisis. To save a life, you may have to betray a secret when someone confides in you.
- **Be Rogerian.** As mentioned in Chapters 11 and 13, Carl Rogers' four important qualities of communication (*empathy, unconditional positive regard, genuineness*, and *active listening*) are probably the best, and safest, approach for any situation—including talking with a depressed, suicidal person.
- **Find help fast!** If a friend or loved one mentions suicide, or if you believe he or she is considering it, get professional help fast! Most cities have walk-in centers that provide emergency counseling. Also, consider calling the police for emergency intervention, and/or the person's family, a therapist, the toll-free 7/24 hotline 1-800-SUICIDE, or 1-800-273-TALK.

Famous victims of suicide

Even people who enjoy enormous fame and financial success may be at risk for suicide, including well-known actors, comedians, and musicians, like Robin Williams (pictured here) and Kurt Cobain. Sadly, there are also tragic victims of suicide in other fields, such as professional athletes, like Olympic medalist Jeret Peterson, or football player Junior Seau; and influential writers or artists like Virginia Woolf, Ernest Hemingway, and Vincent van Gogh.

Retrieval Practice 12.3 | Depressive and Bipolar Disorders

SELF-TEST Completing this self-test, and then checking your answers by clicking on the answer button or by looking in Appendix B, will provide immediate feedback and helpful practice for exams.

1. A major difference between depressive disorder and bipolar disorder is that only in bipolar disorder do people have _____.
   - a. hallucinations or delusions
   - b. depression
   - c. manic episodes
   - d. a biochemical imbalance
2. Depressive and bipolar disorders are sometimes treated by _____ drugs, which affect the amount or functioning of norepinephrine, dopamine, and serotonin in the brain.
   - a. antidepressant
   - b. antipsychotics
   - c. mood congruence
   - d. none of these options
3. According to the theory known as _____, when faced with a painful situation from which there is no escape, animals and people enter a state of helplessness and resignation.
   - a. autonomic resignation
   - b. helpless resignation
   - c. resigned helplessness
   - d. learned helplessness
4. Which of the following is a myth about suicide?
   - a. People who talk about it are less likely to actually do it
   - b. Suicide usually occurs with little or no warning
   - c. Most people have never thought about suicide
   - d. all of these options
5. Internal, stable, and global attributions for failure or unpleasant circumstances are associated with _____ disorders.
   - a. anxiety
   - b. delusional
   - c. depressive
   - d. bipolar

Think Critically

1. Have you ever felt seriously depressed? How would you distinguish between "normal" depression and a serious depressive disorder?
2. Can you think of a personal example of how major depression served as a possible evolutionary advantage?

Real World Psychology

Can Internet and cell phone use increase mental health problems?

HINT: LOOK IN THE MARGIN FOR **[Q3]**

12.4 Schizophrenia

LEARNING OBJECTIVES

Retrieval Practice While reading the upcoming sections, respond to each Learning Objective in your own words.

Review how psychologists define, classify, and explain schizophrenia.

- **Identify** schizophrenia and its common characteristics.
- **Compare** the positive versus negative symptoms of schizophrenia.
- **Summarize** the biological and psychosocial factors that contribute to schizophrenia.

Imagine that your 17-year-old son's behavior has changed dramatically over the past few months. He has gone from being actively involved in sports and clubs to suddenly quitting all activities and refusing to go to school. He now talks to himself—mumbling and yelling out at times—and no longer regularly showers or washes his hair. Recently he announced, "The voices are telling me to jump out the window" (Kotowski, 2012).

Schizophrenia A group of severe psychological disorders involving major disturbances in perception, language, thought, emotion, and/or behavior.

This description is taken from the true case history of a patient who suffers from **schizophrenia**. As shown in this example and discussed in this section, people with schizophrenia have major disturbances in *perception* (seeing or hearing things that others don't), *language* (bizarre words and meanings), *thought* (impaired logic), *emotion* (exaggerated or blunted), and/or *behavior* (peculiar movements and social withdrawal). In addition, some may have serious problems caring for themselves, relating to others, and holding a job. The *DSM-5* places schizophrenia within the category of "schizophrenic spectrum and other psychotic disorders." Recall that psychosis refers to a serious loss of contact with reality. In extreme cases, the illness is so severe that it's considered a psychosis and treatment may require institutional or custodial care.

Schizophrenia is one of the most widespread and devastating psychological disorders. Approximately 1% of people in any given adult population will develop it in their lifetime, and approximately half of all people who are admitted to mental hospitals are diagnosed with this disorder (Brown & Lau, 2016; Castle & Buckley, 2015; Gottesman, 1991). Schizophrenia usually emerges between the late teens and the mid-30s and only rarely prior to adolescence or after age 45. It seems to be equally prevalent in men and women, but it's generally more severe and strikes earlier in men (Brown & Lau, 2016; Castle & Buckley, 2015; Silber, 2014; Zorrilla et al., 2015).

Many people confuse schizophrenia with dissociative identity disorder, which is sometimes referred to as *split* or *multiple personality disorder* (see the following **Real World Psychology**). *Schizophrenia* means "split mind," but when Eugen Bleuler coined the term in 1911, he was referring to the fragmenting of thought processes and emotions, not of personalities (Neale et al., 1983). As we discuss later in this chapter, dissociative identity disorder is popularly referred to as having a "split personality"—the rare and controversial condition of having more than one distinct personality.

Real World **Psychology**—Understanding the World

Do People with Schizophrenia Have Multiple Personalities?

As shown in this cartoon and in popular movies and television shows, schizophrenia is commonly confused with *multiple personality disorder* (now known as *dissociative identity disorder*, p. 353). This widespread error persists in part because of confusing terminology. Literally translated, *schizophrenia* means "split mind," referring to a split from reality that shows itself in disturbed perceptions, language, thought, emotions, and/or behavior.

In contrast, dissociative identity disorder (DID) refers to the condition in which two or more distinct personalities exist within the same person at different times. People with schizophrenia have only one personality.

Why does this matter? Confusing schizophrenia with multiple personalities is not only technically incorrect, it also trivializes the devastating effects of both disorders, which may include severe anxiety, social isolation, unemployment, homelessness, substance abuse, clinical depression, and even suicide (Joseph et al., 2015; Lasalvia et al., 2015; Lilienfeld et al., 2010, 2015).

"THANKS FOR CURING MY SCHIZOPHRENIA—WE'RE BOTH FINE NOW!"

Dave Parker/CartoonStock

Symptoms of Schizophrenia

Schizophrenia is a group of disorders characterized by a disturbance in one or more of the following areas: *perception*, *language*, *thought*, *affect* (emotions), and/or *behavior*.

Perception The senses of people with schizophrenia may be either enhanced or blunted. The filtering and selection processes that allow most people to concentrate on whatever they choose are impaired, and sensory stimulation is jumbled and distorted. People with schizophrenia may experience **hallucinations**—false, imaginary sensory perceptions that occur without external stimuli. Auditory hallucinations (hearing voices and sounds) is one of the most commonly noted and reported symptoms of schizophrenia.

Hallucination A false, imaginary sensory perception that occurs without an external, objective source, such as hearing voices that do not actually exist.

On rare occasions, people with schizophrenia hurt others in response to their distorted perceptions. But a person with schizophrenia is more likely to be self-destructive and suicidal than violent toward others.

Language and Thought For people with schizophrenia, words lose their usual meanings and associations, logic is impaired, and thoughts are disorganized and bizarre. When language and thought disturbances are mild, the individual jumps from topic to topic. With more severe disturbances, the person jumbles phrases and words together (into a "word salad") or creates artificial words. The most common—and frightening—thought disturbance experienced by people with schizophrenia is lack of contact with reality (psychosis).

Delusion A false or irrational belief maintained despite clear evidence to the contrary.

Delusions, false or irrational beliefs that are maintained despite clear evidence to the contrary, are also common in people with schizophrenia (see the cartoon). We all experience exaggerated thoughts from time to time, such as thinking a friend is trying to avoid us, but the delusions of schizophrenia are much more extreme. For example, if someone falsely believed that the postman who routinely delivered mail to his house every afternoon was a co-conspirator in a plot to kill him, it would likely qualify as a *delusion of persecution* or paranoia. In *delusions of grandeur*, people believe that they are someone very important, perhaps Jesus Christ or the Queen of England. In *delusions of control*, the person believes his or her thoughts or actions are being controlled by outside and/or alien forces— "the CIA is controlling my thoughts."

"That's the doctor who is treating me for paranoia. I don't trust him."

Emotion Changes in emotion usually occur in people with schizophrenia. In some cases, emotions are exaggerated and fluctuate rapidly. At other times, they become blunted. Some people with schizophrenia have *flattened affect*—almost no emotional response of any kind.

Behavior Disturbances in behavior may take the form of unusual actions that have special meaning to the sufferer. For example, one patient massaged his head repeatedly to "clear it" of unwanted thoughts. People with schizophrenia also may become *cataleptic* and assume a nearly immobile stance for an extended period.

Classifying Schizophrenia

For many years, researchers divided schizophrenia into five subtypes: *paranoid*, *catatonic*, *disorganized*, *undifferentiated*, and *residual*. Critics suggested that this system does not differentiate in terms of prognosis, cause, or response to treatment and that the undifferentiated type was merely a catchall for cases that are difficult to diagnose (Black & Grant, 2014; Castle & Buckley, 2015; Grossman & Walfish, 2014). For these reasons, researchers have proposed an alternative classification system:

1. **Positive schizophrenia symptoms** are additions to or exaggerations of normal functions. Delusions and hallucinations are examples of positive symptoms. (In this case, and as discussed in Chapter 6, "positive" means that "something is added," above and beyond normal levels.)

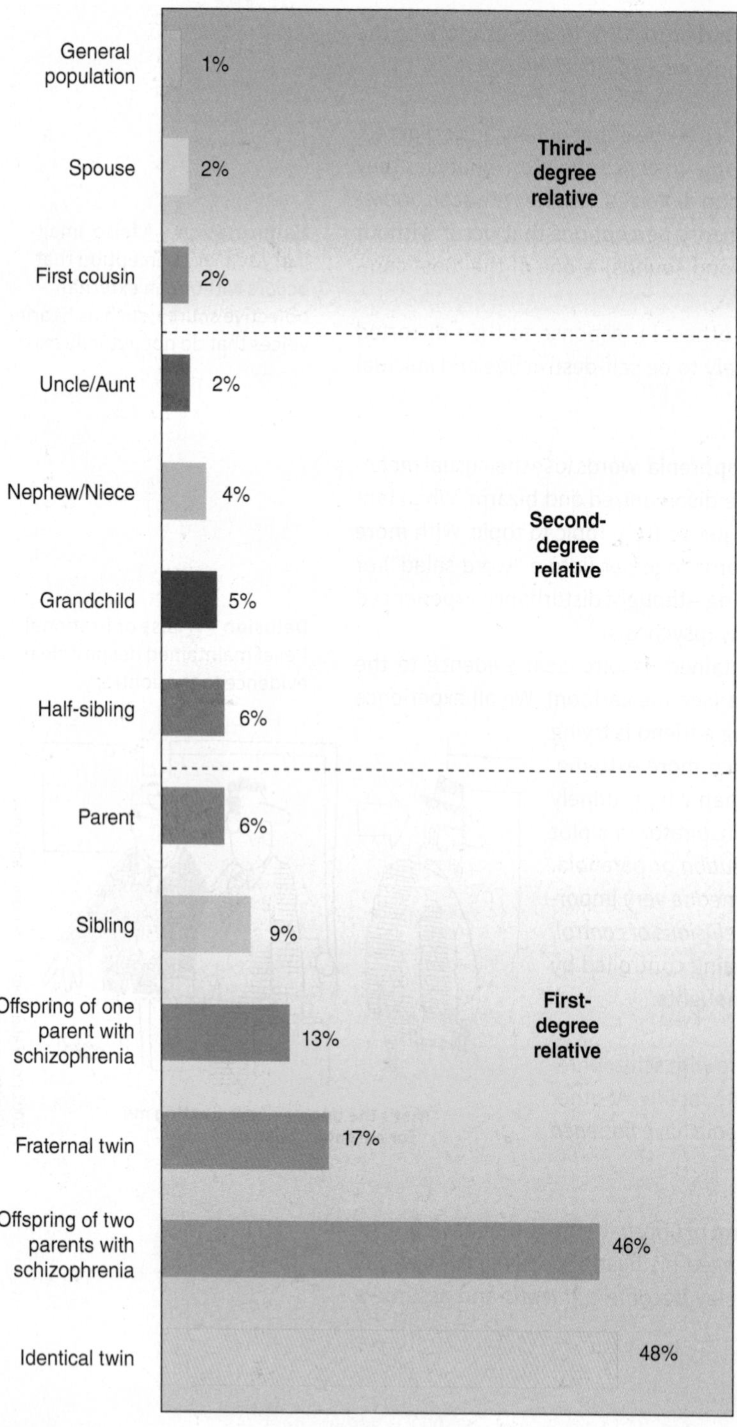

FIGURE 12.9 **Genetics and schizophrenia** As dramatically shown by this figure, the lifetime risk of developing schizophrenia is strongly linked with genetic inheritance. Is this a positive or negative correlation?

Answer: A positive correlation—the risk of developing schizophrenia increases as the genetic relatedness to an individual with schizophrenia increases.

2. **Negative schizophrenia symptoms** include the loss or absence of normal functions. Impaired attention, limited or toneless speech, flat or blunted affect, and social withdrawal are all classic negative symptoms of schizophrenia. (Recall again that "negative" is *not* the same as unpleasant or bad. It means that "something is taken away," and in this case daily functioning is "taken away" because it's so far below normal levels.)

Positive symptoms are more common when schizophrenia develops rapidly, whereas negative symptoms are more often found in slow-developing schizophrenia. Positive symptoms are associated with better adjustment before the onset and a better prognosis for recovery.

Explaining Schizophrenia

Because schizophrenia comes in many different forms, it probably has multiple biological and psychosocial bases. Let's look at biological contributions first.

Biological Factors

Most biological explanations of schizophrenia focus on genetics, neurotransmitters, and brain abnormalities:

- **Genetics** Current research indicates that the risk for schizophrenia increases with genetic similarity (Arnedo et al., 2015; Castellani et al., 2014; Gottesman, 1991). This means that people who share more genes with a person who has schizophrenia are more likely to develop the disorder (**Figure 12.9**).
- **Neurotransmitters** According to the *dopamine hypothesis*, overactivity of certain dopamine neurons in the brain causes some forms of schizophrenia (Gilani et al., 2014; Howes et al., 2015; Stopper & Floresco, 2015). This hypothesis is based on two observations. First, administering amphetamines increases the amount of dopamine and can produce (or worsen) some symptoms of schizophrenia, especially in people with a genetic predisposition to the disorder. Second, drugs that reduce dopamine activity in the brain reduce or eliminate some symptoms of schizophrenia.
- **Brain abnormalities** A third area of research in schizophrenia explores links to abnormalities in brain function and structure. Researchers have found larger cerebral ventricles (fluid-filled spaces in the brain) and right hemisphere dysfunction in some people with schizophrenia (Chakrabarty et al., 2014; Guo et al., 2015; Woodward & Heckers, 2015). Also, some people with chronic schizophrenia have a lower level of activity in specific areas of the brain (**Figure 12.10**).

Prenatal and Other Environmental Factors

Clearly, biological factors play a key role in schizophrenia. But the fact that the heritability of schizophrenia is only 48% even in

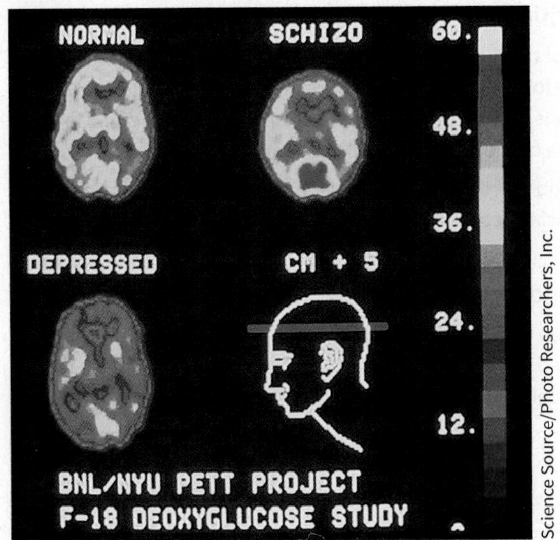

Science Source/Photo Researchers, Inc.

FIGURE 12.10 Brain activity in schizophrenia Using these positron emission tomography (PET) scans, compare the normal levels of brain activity (upper left) with those of a person with schizophrenia (upper right), and then with those of a person with depression (lower left). Warmer colors (reds, yellows) indicate increased brain activity, whereas cooler colors (blues and greens) indicate decreased activity.

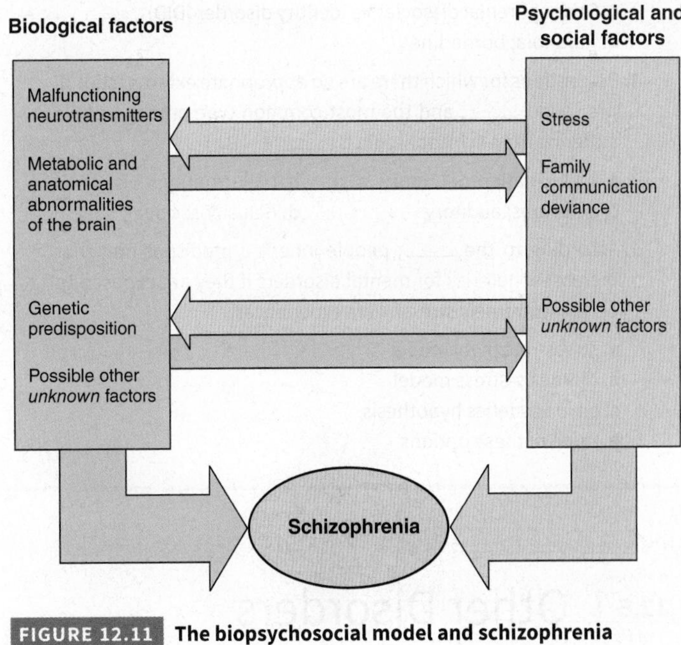

FIGURE 12.11 The biopsychosocial model and schizophrenia

identical twins—who share identical genes—tells us that nongenetic factors must contribute the remaining percentage. Furthermore, as we've seen throughout this text, *epigenetic* (meaning "in addition to genetic") factors often influence whether or not specific genes will be expressed.

If you're personally concerned about possibly developing schizophrenia, remember that with environmental changes even identical twins are not destined to develop the same diseases. And most psychologists believe there are several possible environmental and psychosocial contributors. For example, prenatal stress and viral infections, birth complications, low birth weight, immune responses, maternal malnutrition, and advanced paternal age are all suspected factors in the development of schizophrenia (Kneeland & Fatemi, 2013; Meyer, 2016; Webb, 2016).

According to the **diathesis-stress model** of schizophrenia, stress plays an essential role in triggering schizophrenic episodes in people with an inherited predisposition (or diathesis) toward the disease (Brown & Lau, 2016; Frau et al., 2015; Howes & Murray, 2014). In line with this model, children who experience severe trauma before age 16 are three times more likely than
[Q4] other people to develop schizophrenia (Bentall et al., 2012; DeRosse et al., 2014). People who experience stressful living environments, including poverty, unemployment, and crowding, are also at increased risk (Brown & Lau, 2016; Kirkbride et al., 2014; Sweeney et al., 2015).

Diathesis-stress model A hypothesis about the cause of certain disorders, such as schizophrenia, which suggests that people inherit a predisposition (or "diathesis") that increases their risk for psychological disorders when exposed to certain extremely stressful life experiences.

How should we evaluate the different theories about the causes of schizophrenia? Like virtually all psychological disorders, nature and nurture interact. Most scientists believe schizophrenia is probably the result of a combination of known and unknown interacting factors (**Figure 12.11**).

Retrieval Practice 12.4 | Schizophrenia

SELF-TEST Completing this self-test, and then checking your answers by clicking on the answer button or by looking in Appendix B, will provide immediate feedback and helpful practice for exams.

1. Major disturbances in perception, language, thought, emotion, and behavior may be diagnosed as ____.
   - **a.** schizophrenia
   - **b.** multiple dissociative disorder
   - **c.** borderline psychosis
   - **d.** neurotic psychosis

2. In extreme cases, schizophrenia is a form of ____, a term describing general lack of contact with reality.
   - **a.** multiple personality disorder
   - **b.** psychosis
   - **c.** borderline polar psychosis
   - **d.** all of these options

3. ____ refers to "split mind," whereas ____ refers to "split personality."
   - **a.** Psychosis; neurosis
   - **b.** Insanity; multiple personalities

c. Schizophrenia; dissociative identity disorder (DID)
d. Paranoia; borderline

4. Perceptions for which there are no appropriate external stimuli are called _____, and the most common type among people suffering from schizophrenia is _____.
   a. hallucinations; auditory
   b. hallucinations; visual
   c. delusions; auditory
   d. delusions; visual

5. According to the _____, people inherit a predisposition that increases their risk for mental disorders if they are exposed to certain extremely stressful life experiences.
   a. stress-reactivity model
   b. diathesis-stress model
   c. envirogenetics hypothesis
   d. none of these options

Think Critically

1. Most of the disorders discussed in this chapter have some evidence for a genetic predisposition. What would you tell a friend who has a family member with one of these disorders and fears that he or she might develop the same disorder?
2. What do you think are the most important biological and psychosocial factors that contribute to schizophrenia?

Real World **Psychology**

Are children who experience trauma at increased risk of developing schizophrenia later in life?

© IvonneW/ iStockphoto

HINT: LOOK IN THE MARGIN FOR **[Q4]**

12.5 Other Disorders

LEARNING OBJECTIVES

Retrieval Practice While reading the upcoming sections, respond to each Learning Objective in your own words.

Review the main features of obsessive-compulsive, dissociative, and personality disorders.

- **Identify** obsessive-compulsive disorder and its major symptoms.
- **Describe** dissociative disorders.
- **Discuss** personality disorders, including antisocial (ASPD) and borderline (BPD).

Having discussed anxiety disorders, mood disorders, and schizophrenia, we now explore three additional disorders: obsessive-compulsive, dissociative, and personality disorders.

Obsessive-Compulsive Disorder (OCD)

Obsessive-compulsive disorder (OCD) A psychological disorder characterized by persistent, unwanted, fearful thoughts (obsessions) and/or irresistible urges to perform repetitive and/or ritualized behaviors (compulsions).

Do you occasionally worry about whether or not you locked your doors and sometimes feel compelled to run back and check? Most people do. However, people with **obsessive compulsive disorder (OCD)** experience persistent, unwanted, fearful thoughts (obsessions) and/or irresistible urges to perform repetitive and/or ritualized behaviors (compulsions) to help relieve the anxiety created by the obsession. In adults, women are affected at a slightly higher rate than men, whereas men are more commonly affected in childhood (American Psychiatric Association, 2013).

Common examples of obsessions are fear of germs, fear of being hurt or of hurting others, and troubling religious or sexual thoughts. Examples of compulsions are repeatedly checking, counting, cleaning, washing all or specific body parts, or putting things in a certain order. As mentioned before, everyone worries and sometimes double-checks, but people with OCD have these thoughts and do these rituals for at least an hour or more each day, often longer (Berman et al., 2016; Essau & Ozer, 2015; Foa & Yadin, 2014).

Imagine what it would be like to worry so obsessively about germs that you compulsively wash your hands hundreds of times a day, until they are raw and bleeding. Most sufferers of OCD realize that their actions are senseless. But when they try to stop the behavior, they experience mounting anxiety, which is relieved only by giving in to the compulsions. Given that numerous biological and psychological factors contribute to OCD, it is most often treated with a combination of drugs and cognitive-behavior therapy (Emslie et al., 2016; Grant et al., 2014; Zilhão et al., 2015). See Chapter 13 and **Figure 12.12**.

Kevin Winter/Getty Images

FIGURE 12.12 Managing OCD Many celebrities suffer from OCD, including soccer star David Beckham, actors Megan Fox (pictured here) and Leonardo DiCaprio, and singer/actor Justin Timberlake. Fortunately, people can learn to manage the symptoms of OCD, through therapy and/or medication, and lead highly productive and fulfilling lives.

Image Source/Getty Images

FIGURE 12.13 Dissociation as an escape A common factor in dissociative disorders is the need to escape and cope with extreme stress (Spiegel et al., 2013). Imagine witnessing a loved one's death in a horrible car accident. Can you see how your mind might cope by blocking out all memory of the event?

Dissociative Disorders

If you've ever been daydreaming while driving home from your college campus, and then could not remember making one single turn, you may have experienced a normal form of *dissociation*, meaning a mild disconnection from your immediate surroundings.

The most dramatic extremes of this type of detachment are the **dissociative disorders**, characterized by a sudden break (*dissociation*) in conscious awareness, self-identity, and/or memory. Note that this is a disconnection or detachment from immediate surroundings, or from physical or emotional experience. It is very different from the loss of contact with reality seen in *psychosis* (**Figure 12.13**). There are several forms of dissociative disorders, including dissociative amnesia and dissociative identity disorder (DID). However, all are characterized by a splitting apart (a *dis-association*) of significant aspects of experience from memory or consciousness.

Dissociative disorder One of a group of psychological disorders characterized by a sudden break (*dissociation*) in conscious awareness, self-identity, and/or memory.

Dissociative identity disorder (DID) A psychological disorder characterized by the presence of two or more distinct personality systems (or identities) in the same individual; previously known as multiple personality disorder (MPD).

The most controversial, and least common, dissociative disorder is **dissociative identity disorder (DID)**—previously known as multiple personality disorder (MPD). An individual with this disorder has at least two separate and distinct personalities (or *identities*) in the same individual (**Figure 12.14**). Each personality has unique memories, behaviors, and social relationships. Transition from one personality to another occurs suddenly, and is often triggered by psychological stress (Chalavi et al, 2015; Spiegel & Simeon, 2015). Typically, there is a "core" personality, who has no knowledge or awareness of the alternate personalities, but is often aware of lost memories and lost periods of time. The disorder is diagnosed about equally among men and women (American Psychiatric Association, 2013).

DID is a controversial diagnosis. Some experts suggest that many cases are faked or result from false memories and/or an unconscious need to please a therapist (Dalenberg et al., 2014; Lilienfeld & Lynn, 2015; Lynn et al., 2016).

Stephen Dunn/Allsport/GettyImages.

FIGURE 12.14 A personal account of DID Herschel Walker, Pro Bowl NFL football player, Olympic bobsledder, and business and family man, now suggests that none of the people who played these roles were really he. They were his "alters," or alternate personalities. He has been diagnosed with the controversial diagnosis of *dissociative identity disorder (DID)*. Although some have suggested that the disorder helped him succeed as a professional athlete, it played havoc with his personal life. He's now in treatment and has written a book, *Breaking Free*, hoping to change the public's image of DID.

Personality Disorders

Personality disorder A psychological disorder characterized by chronic, inflexible, maladaptive personality traits, which cause significant impairment of social and occupational functioning.

Antisocial personality disorder (ASPD) A personality disorder characterized by egocentrism and a lack of conscience, remorse, or empathy for others.

What would happen if the characteristics of a personality were so inflexible and maladaptive that they significantly impaired someone's ability to function? This is what occurs with **personality disorders**. Several types of personality disorders are included in this category in the fifth edition of the *DSM*, but here we will focus on antisocial personality disorder (ASPD) and borderline personality disorder (BPD) (American Psychiatric Association, 2013).

Antisocial Personality Disorder (ASPD)

People with **antisocial personality disorder (ASPD)**—sometimes called *psychopaths* or *sociopaths*—are typically egocentric and exhibit a lack of conscience, remorse, or empathy for others. They're also manipulative, deceitful, and willing to use others for personal gain. These behaviors typically begin in childhood or early adolescence and continue through adulthood. They also lie so far outside the ethical and legal standards of society that many consider ASPD the most serious of all psychological disorders.

Unlike people with anxiety, mood disorders, and schizophrenia, those with this diagnosis feel little personal distress (and may not be motivated to change). Yet their maladaptive traits generally bring considerable harm and suffering to others (Cummings, 2015; Jones, 2016; Paris, 2015). Although serial killers are often seen as classic examples of people with ASPD, most people who have this disorder generally harm others in less dramatic ways—for example, as ruthless businesspeople and crooked politicians.

Unlike most other adults, individuals with ASPD act impulsively, without giving thought to the consequences. They are usually poised when confronted with their destructive behavior, and feel contempt for anyone they are able to manipulate. In addition, they typically change jobs and relationships suddenly, and often have a history of truancy from school or of being expelled for destructive behavior. People with antisocial personalities can be charming and persuasive, and they often have remarkably good insight into the needs and weaknesses of other people.

Twin and adoption studies suggest a possible genetic predisposition to ASPD (Dhamija et al., 2016; Kendler et al., 2015; Werner et al., 2015). Researchers also have found abnormally low autonomic activity during stress, right hemisphere abnormalities, reduced gray matter in the frontal lobes, and biochemical disturbances (Jiang et al., 2015; Kumari et al., 2014; Schiffer et al., 2014).

[Q5] For example, MRI brain scans of criminals currently in prison for violent crimes, such as rape, murder, or attempted murder, and showing little empathy and remorse for their crimes, reveal reduced gray matter volume in the prefrontal cortex (Gregory et al., 2012). (Recall from Chapter 2 that this is the area of the brain responsible for emotions, such as fear, empathy, and/or guilt.)

Evidence also exists for environmental or psychological causes. People with antisocial personality disorder often come from homes characterized by severely abusive parenting styles, emotional deprivation, harsh and inconsistent disciplinary practices, residential mobility, and antisocial parental behavior (Crego & Widiger, 2016; Dargis et al., 2016; Mok et al., 2016). Still other studies show a strong interaction between both heredity and environment (Haberstick et al., 2014; Paris, 2015; Trull et al., 2013).

Borderline Personality Disorder (BPD)

Mary's troubles first began in adolescence. She began to miss curfew, was frequently truant, and her grades declined sharply. Mary later became promiscuous and prostituted herself several times to get drug money . . . . She also quickly fell in love and overly idealized new friends. But when they quickly (and inevitably) disappointed her, she would angrily cast them aside. . . . Mary's problems, coupled with a preoccupation with inflicting pain on herself (by cutting and burning) and persistent thoughts of suicide, eventually led to her admittance to a psychiatric hospital at age 26 (Kring et al., 2010, pp 354–355).

Borderline personality disorder (BPD) A psychological disorder characterized by severe instability in emotions, relationships, and self-image, along with impulsive and self-destructive behaviors.

Mary's experiences are all classic symptoms of **borderline personality disorder (BPD)**. The core features of this disorder include a pervasive pattern of instability in emotions, relationships, and self-image, along with impulsive and self-destructive behaviors, such as truancy, promiscuity, drinking, gambling, and eating sprees. In addition, people with BPD may attempt suicide and sometimes engage in self-mutilating ("cutting") behaviors (Calati & Courtet, 2016; Crowell et al., 2016; Greenfield et al., 2015).

Those with BPD also tend to see themselves and everyone else in absolute terms—as either perfect or worthless. Constantly seeking reassurance from others, they may quickly erupt in anger at the slightest sign of disapproval. As you might expect, this disorder is typically marked by a long history of broken friendships, divorces, and lost jobs.

In short, people with this disorder appear to have a deep well of intense loneliness and a chronic fear of abandonment. Unfortunately, given their troublesome personality traits, friends, lovers, and even family members and therapists often do "abandon" them—thus creating a tragic self-fulfilling prophecy. Sadly, this disorder is among the most commonly diagnosed and functionally disabling of all psychological disorders (Arntz, 2015; Gunderson & Links, 2014; Rizvi & Salters-Pedneault, 2013). Originally, the term implied that the person was on the borderline between neurosis and schizophrenia, but the modern conceptualization no longer has this connotation. The good news is that BPD can be reliably diagnosed and it does respond to professional intervention—particularly in young people (Bateman & Fonagy, 2016; Gunderson & Links, 2014; Harley et al., 2016).

What causes BPD? Some research points to environmental factors, such as a childhood history of neglect, emotional deprivation, and/or physical, sexual, or emotional abuse (Chesin et al., 2015; Hunt et al., 2015; Vermetten & Spiegel, 2014). From a biological perspective, BPD also tends to run in families, and some data suggest that it is a result of impaired functioning of the brain's frontal lobes and limbic system, areas that control impulsive behaviors (Denny et al., 2016; Few et al., 2014; Stone, 2014). For example, research using neuroimaging reveals that people with BPD show more activity in parts of the brain associated with the experience of negative emotions, coupled with less activity in parts of the brain that help suppress negative emotion (Ruocco et al., 2013). As in almost all other psychological disorders, most researchers agree that BPD results from an interaction of biopsychosocial factors (Crego & Widiger, 2016; McMurran & Crawford, 2016; Stone, 2014).

Retrieval Practice 12.5 | Other Disorders

SELF-TEST Completing this self-test, and then checking your answers by clicking on the answer button or by looking in Appendix B, will provide immediate feedback and helpful practice for exams.

1. Repetitive, ritualistic behaviors, such as hand washing, counting, or putting things in order, are called a(n) ____.

a. obsessions **b.** compulsions
c. ruminations **d.** phobias

2. A disorder characterized by disturbances in conscious awareness, self-identity, and/or memory is known as a(n) ____.

a. dissociative disorder **b.** disoriented disorder
c. displacement disorder **d.** identity disorder

3. ____ is characterized by the presence of two or more separate and distinct personality systems in the same individual.

a. Multiple-personality dysfunction (MPD)
b. Disassociation disorder (DD)
c. Fictional-actor delusion (FAD)
d. Dissociative identity disorder (DID)

4. A serial killer would likely be diagnosed as a(n) ____ personality in the *Diagnostic and Statistical Manual (DSM)*.

a. dissociative disorder
b. antisocial personality disorder
c. multiple personality disorder
d. borderline psychosis

5. Instability in emotions, relationships, and self-image, along with impulsive and self-destructive behaviors, are characteristic of the ____ personality disorder.

a. manic depressive **b.** bipolar
c. borderline **d.** antisocial

Think Critically

1. How would you explain to others that schizophrenia is not the same as dissociative identity disorder (DID) (formerly called multiple personality disorder [MPD])?

2. Does the fact that research shows a genetic component to antisocial personality disorder change your opinion regarding the degree of guilt and responsibility of a mass-murdering terrorist after a vicious shooting spree?

Real World **Psychology**

How do changes in the brain help explain severe antisocial personality disorder?

© alexsl/ iStockphoto

HINT: LOOK IN THE MARGIN FOR **[Q5]**

12.6 Gender and Cultural Effects

LEARNING OBJECTIVES

Retrieval Practice While reading the upcoming sections, respond to each Learning Objective in your own words.

Summarize gender and cultural differences in psychological disorders.

- **Discuss** the possible gender differences in depression.
- **Explain** why it is difficult to directly compare psychological disorders, such as schizophrenia, across cultures.
- **Describe** how understanding culture-general symptoms and culture-bound disorders helps us overcome ethnocentrism in psychological disorders.

Among the Chippewa, Cree, and Montagnais-Naskapi Indians in Canada, there is a disorder called *windigo*—or *wiitiko*—*psychosis*, characterized by delusions and cannibalistic impulses. Believing they have been possessed by the spirit of a windigo, a cannibal giant with a heart and entrails of ice, victims become severely depressed (Faddiman, 1997). As the malady begins, the individual typically experiences loss of appetite, diarrhea, vomiting, and insomnia, and he or she may see people turning into beavers and other edible animals. In later stages, the victim becomes obsessed with cannibalistic thoughts and may even attack and kill loved ones in order to devour their flesh (Berreman, 1971; Thomason, 2014).

If you were a therapist, how would you treat this disorder? Does it fit neatly into any category of psychological disorders that we've just discussed? We began this chapter by discussing the complexities and problems with defining, identifying, and classifying abnormal behavior. Before we close, we need to add two additional confounding factors: gender and culture. In this section, we explore a few of the many ways in which men and women differ in their experience of abnormal behavior. We also look at cultural variations in abnormal behavior.

Gender Differences

When you picture someone suffering from depression, anxiety, alcoholism, or antisocial personality disorder, what is the gender of each person? Most people tend to visualize a woman for the first two and a man for the last two. There is some truth to these stereotypes.

Research has found many gender differences in the prevalence rates of various psychological disorders. Let's start with the well-established fact that around the world, the rate of severe depression for women is about double that for men (Navarro & Hurtado, 2015; Pérez & Gaviña, 2015; World Health Organization, 2011). Why is there such a striking gender difference?

Certain risk factors for depression (such as genetic predisposition, marital problems, pain, and medical illness) are common to both men and women. However, poverty is a well-known contributor to many psychological disorders, and women are far more likely than men to fall into the lowest socioeconomic groups. Women also experience more wage disparity and discrimination in the work force, sexual trauma, partner abuse, and chronic stress in their daily lives, which are all well-known contributing factors in depression (Doornbos et al., 2013; Jausoro Alzola & Marino, 2015; Platt et al., 2016).

To examine different expectations about depression as a function of gender, researchers in one study asked participants to read a story about a fictitious person (Kate in one version, Jack in the other). The story was exactly the same in both conditions and included the following information: "For the past two weeks, Kate/Jack has been feeling really down. S/he wakes up in the morning with a flat, heavy feeling that sticks with her/him all day. S/he isn't enjoying things the way s/he normally would. S/he finds it hard to concentrate on anything." Although all participants read the same story, those who read about Kate rated her symptoms as more distressing, deserving of sympathy, and difficult to treat (Swami et al., 2012). [Q6]

Research also suggests that some gender differences in depression may relate to the way women and men tend to internalize or externalize their emotions. Using structured interview techniques, researchers found that women ruminate more frequently than men, which means they are more likely to focus repetitively on their *internal* negative emotions and problems rather than engage in more external problem-solving strategies. In contrast, men tend to be more disinhibited and more likely to *externalize* their emotions and problems. (Kendler & Gardner, 2014; Rice et al., 2014).

Can you see how these gender differences in depression may result from misapplied gender roles? The most common symptoms of stereotypical depression, such as crying, low energy, dejected facial expressions, and withdrawal from social activities, are more socially acceptable for women than for men. In contrast, men in Western societies are typically socialized to suppress their emotions and to show their distress by acting out (being aggressive), acting impulsively (driving recklessly and committing petty crimes), and/or engaging in substance abuse. Given these differences in socialization and behaviors, combined with the fact that gender differences in depression are more pronounced in cultures with traditional gender roles, male depression may "simply" be expressed in less stereotypical ways, and therefore be underdiagnosed (Fields & Cochran, 2011; Pérez & Gaviña, 2015; Seedat et al., 2009). See the following **Psychology and You**.

Psychology and **You**—Understanding Yourself

Gender Strategies for Managing Depression

In order to prevent or reduce depression, women may benefit from learning better stress reduction and problem-focused coping strategies (Chapter 3). On the other hand, if it's true that men more often express their depression through impulsive, acting-out behaviors, then rewarding deliberate, planned behaviors over unintentional, spur-of-the moment ones may be helpful for treating some forms of male depression (Eaton et al., 2012).

© Piotr Marcinski/Shutterstock

Understanding the importance of genetic predispositions, external environmental factors (like poverty), and cognitive factors (like internalizing versus externalizing emotions and problems) may help mental health professionals better understand individual and gender-related differences in depression.

FIGURE 12.15 What is stressful?

David Alan Harvey/Magnum Photos, Inc.

a. Some stressors are culturally specific, such as feeling possessed by evil forces or being the victim of witchcraft.

Benelux/Zefa/Corbis

b. Other stressors are shared by many cultures, such as the unexpected death of a loved one or loss of a job (Al-Issa, 2000; Cechnicki et al., 2011; Ramsay et al., 2012).

Culture and Psychological Disorders

Individuals from different cultures experience psychological disorders in a variety of ways. For example, the reported incidence of schizophrenia varies in different cultures around the world. It is unclear whether these differences result from actual differences in prevalence of the disorder or from differences in definition, diagnosis, or reporting (Hsu, 2016; Luhrmann et al., 2015; McLean et al., 2014). The symptoms of schizophrenia also vary across cultures (Barnow & Balkir, 2013; Burns, 2013), as do the particular stressors that may trigger its onset (**Figure 12.15**).

Finally, despite the advanced treatment facilities and methods in industrialized nations, the prognosis for people with schizophrenia is sometimes better in nonindustrialized societies. The reason may be that the core symptoms of schizophrenia (poor rapport with others, incoherent speech, and so on) make it more difficult to survive in highly industrialized countries. In addition, in most industrialized nations families and other support groups are less likely to feel responsible for relatives and friends who have schizophrenia (Akyeampong et al., 2015; Burns et al., 2014; Eaton et al., 2012). On the other hand, some countries, such as Indonesia, still shackle and confine their mentally ill in filthy cells without basic human rights (Quiano, 2016).

TABLE 12.4 Culture-General Symptoms of Mental Health Difficulties

Nervous	Trouble sleeping	Low spirits
Weak all over	Personal worries	Restless
Feel apart, alone	Can't get along	Hot all over
Worry all the time	Can't do anything worthwhile	Nothing turns out right

Source: Brislin, 2000.

Avoiding Ethnocentrism

Most research on psychological disorders originates and is conducted primarily in Western cultures. Do you see how such a restricted sampling can limit our understanding of these disorders? And how this limited view could lead to an ethnocentric view—a view that one's own culture is "correct?"

Fortunately, cross-cultural researchers have devised ways to overcome these difficulties (Bernal et al., 2014; Hsu, 2016; Sue et al., 2016). For example, Robert Nishimoto (1988) has found several *culture-general symptoms* that are useful in diagnosing disorders across cultures (**Table 12.4**).

In addition, Nishimoto found several *culture-bound symptoms*, which are unique to different groups and generally only appear in one population. For example, Vietnamese and Chinese respondents report "fullness in head," Mexican respondents note "problems with [their] memory," and Anglo-American respondents report "shortness of breath" and "headaches." Apparently, people learn to express their problems in ways that are acceptable to others in the same culture (Brislin, 2000; Hsu, 2016; Shannon et al., 2015).

This division between culture-general and culture-bound symptoms also helps us better understand depression. Certain symptoms of depression (such as intense sadness, poor concentration, and low energy) seem to exist across all cultures (Walsh & Cross, 2013; World Health Organization, 2011). But there is evidence of some culture-bound symptoms. For example, feelings of guilt are found more often in North America and Europe than in other parts of the world. And in China, *somatization* (the conversion of depression into bodily complaints) occurs more frequently than it does in other parts of the world (Grover & Ghosh, 2014; Lim et al., 2011).

Just as there are culture-bound symptoms, researchers also have found culture-bound disorders (**Figure 12.16**). The earlier example of windigo psychosis, a disorder limited to a

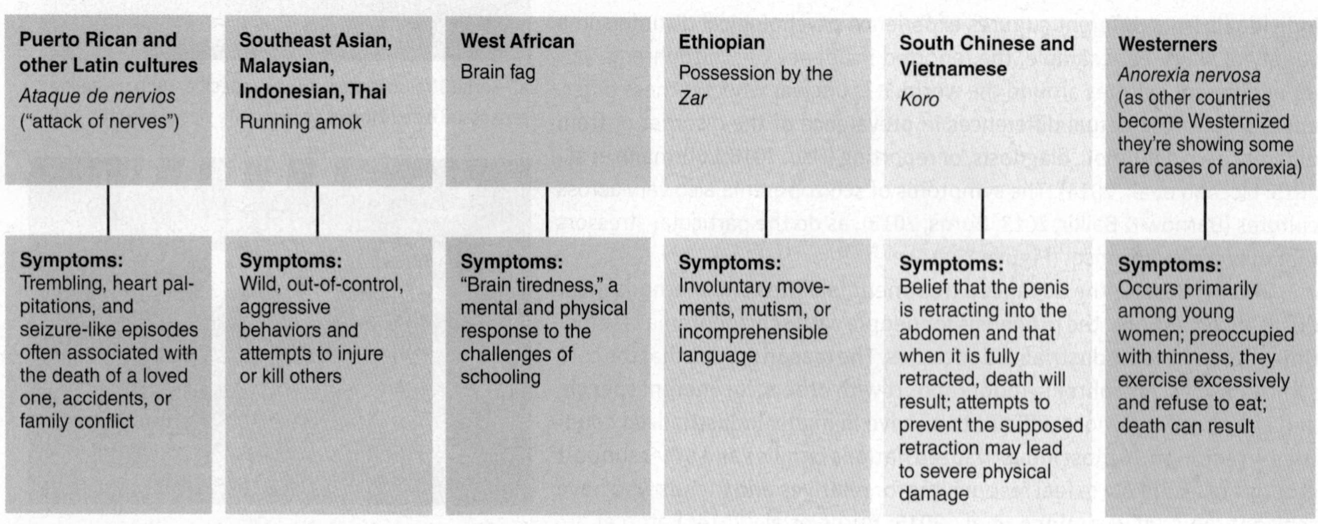

FIGURE 12.16 Culture-bound disorders Some disorders are fading as remote areas become more Westernized, whereas other disorders (such as anorexia nervosa) are spreading as other countries adopt Western values.

few groups of Canadian Indians, illustrates just such a case. Interestingly, the distinctions between many of the previously culture-bound and cultural-general symptoms and disorders may be disappearing as a result of globalization (Kato & Kanba, 2016; Ventriglio et al., 2016).

As you can see, culture has a strong affect on psychological disorders. Studying the similarities and differences across cultures can lead to better diagnosis and understanding. It also helps all of us avoid, or at least minimize, our ethnocentrism.

Before closing this chapter, we want to caution you that although it's tempting to use the information you've gained to diagnose yourself or others, only professionals are adequately trained to do so. If you're concerned about your own mental health or that of others, be sure to contact these professionals. In addition, the following **PositivePsych** explains how resilience offers an interesting, positive approach to mental health.

Resilience The ability to recover from or adapt effectively in the face of adversity.

PP PositivePsych

Resilience in Children and Adults

The bamboo that bends is stronger than the oak that resists.

—Japanese proverb

Children fortunate enough to grow up with days filled with play and discovery, nights that provide rest and security, and dedicated, loving parents usually turn out fine. But what about those who are raised in violent, impoverished, or neglectful situations? We all know that a troubled childhood creates significantly higher risks of serious psychological disorders, as well as physical, emotional, and behavioral problems. What is it about some children living in harsh circumstances that helps them survive and prosper — despite the odds?

The answer apparently is **resilience**—the ability to recover and adapt effectively in the face of adversity. Like bamboo that bends in strong winds, a resilient person flexes in response to hard times. Resilience has been studied throughout the world in a variety of situations, including homelessness, natural disasters, war, and family violence (e.g., Garmezy, 1983; Gibbons & Hickling, 2016; Gil-Rivas & Kilmer, 2016; Masten et al., 2014). And it is of particular interest to positive psychologists because it can teach us better ways to reduce risk, promote competence, and shift the course of development in more positive directions.

What characterizes a resilient child? Two pioneering researchers—Ann Masten and Douglas Coatsworth (1998)—identified several traits and the environmental circumstances that might account for the resilient child's success: (1) good intellectual functioning; (2) relationships with caring adults; and, as they grow older, (3) the ability to regulate their attention, emotions, and behavior. These traits obviously overlap. Good intellectual functioning, for example, may help resilient children solve problems or protect themselves from adverse conditions, as well as attract the interest of teachers who serve as nurturing adults. Their greater intellectual skills also may help them learn from their experiences and from the caring adults, so in later life they have better self-regulation skills.

Resiliency is not just a trait developed in childhood that helps us cope and compensate during difficult times. Adversity can even promote healthy development in adults (Konnikova, 2016). For example, a recent study examined how some people benefit even after experiencing an extraordinarily stressful event, such as a mass school shooting (Mancini et al., 2016). These researchers compared data in psychological adjustment, including anxiety and depression, in female students before the 2007 shooting at Virginia Tech (as part of an already ongoing study), and then again after the event. As you would expect, some students showed continued distress. But other students showed psychological improvement and resilience following these attacks, a phenomenon known as *posttraumatic growth*, which suggests that trauma can, at least at times, lead to positive outcomes (Tedeschi & Blevins, 2015; Zhou & Wu, 2016).

ZUMA Press, Inc./Alamy StockPhoto

What are the characteristics of adult resilience? According to psychologist George Bonanno (2012), a key component is *perception*. Do you perceive adversity as filled with meaning and an opportunity to grow and change? Or do you see it as devastating and uncontrollable. The good news is that we can develop a more resilient perception of adversity by cultivating the trait of *self-efficacy* and an *internal locus of control* (Chapter 11), as well as a more *optimistic, attributional style* (Chapter 14).

Before going on, it's important to recognize that this popular focus on resilience, when taken to extremes, may lead to a dangerous form of "blaming the victim." People who are homeless or mentally ill, as well as student activists protesting racism and sexism, have been blamed for lacking resilience, rather than properly questioning the large social policies that create and maintain these situations. While resilience is a useful concept and its skills can be developed, we must consider all the factors leading to adversity and avoid placing all the responsibility for survival on an individual's resiliency (Sehgal, 2015). Thinking back to the resilient child, Masten and Coatsworth remind us, "if we allow the prevalence of known risk factors for development to rise while resources for children fall, we can expect the competence of individual children and the human capital of the nation to suffer" (Masten & Coatsworth, 1998, p. 216).

Retrieval Practice 12.6 | Gender and Cultural Effects

SELF-TEST Completing this self-test, and then checking your answers by clicking on the answer button or by looking in Appendix B, will provide immediate feedback and helpful practice for exams.

1. When studying gender differences in mental health, researchers found that ____.
   - **a.** women ruminate more frequently than men
   - **b.** men tend to be more disinhibited and more likely to externalize their emotions and problems
   - **c.** men are typically socialized to suppress their emotions
   - **d.** all these options
2. Which of the following are examples of culture-general symptoms of mental health difficulties that are useful in diagnosing disorders across cultures?
   - **a.** trouble sleeping
   - **b.** worry all the time
   - **c.** can't get along
   - **d.** all of these options
3. Symptoms of mental illness that generally only appear in one population group are known as ____.
   - **a.** culture-bound symptoms
   - **b.** group specific disorders
   - **c.** group-think syndrome
   - **d.** culture-specific maladies
4. What disorder has the following symptoms: wild, out-of-control, aggressive behaviors and attempts to injure or kill others?
   - **a.** Brain fag
   - **b.** Running amok
   - **c.** Possession by the Zar
   - **d.** Koro
5. Somatization (the conversion of depression into bodily complaints) occurs more frequently in ____.
   - **a.** North and Central America
   - **b.** China
   - **c.** India
   - **d.** Europe

Think Critically

1. Culture clearly has strong effects on psychological disorders. How does this influence what you think about what is normal or abnormal?
2. As you've seen, some research suggests that depression in men is often overlooked because men are socialized to suppress their emotions and encouraged to express their distress by acting out, being impulsive, or engaging in substance abuse. Does this ring true with your own experiences and/or observations of others? If so, how might we change this situation?

Real World Psychology

Are symptoms of depression in women more distressing, deserving of sympathy, and difficult to treat than the same signs in men?

© Yuri_Arcurs/iStock

HINT: LOOK IN THE MARGIN FOR **[Q6]**

Summary

12.1 Studying Psychological Disorders 332

- **Abnormal behavior** is defined as patterns of behavior, thoughts, or emotions considered pathological for one or more of these four criteria: *deviance*, *dysfunction*, *distress*, and *danger*. Mental health exists on a continuum—not discrete categories of "normal" and "abnormal."
- Historically abnormal behavior was blamed on evil spirits and witchcraft. These beliefs were eventually replaced by the *medical model*, which in turn gave rise to the modern specialty of **psychiatry**. In contrast to the medical model, psychology offers a multifaceted approach to explaining abnormal behavior.
- The *Diagnostic and Statistical Manual of Mental Disorders (DSM)* provides detailed descriptions and classifications of psychological disorders. It also allows standardized diagnosis and improved communication among professionals and between professionals and patients.

12.2 Anxiety Disorders 337

- **Anxiety disorders** include **generalized anxiety disorder (GAD)**, **panic disorder**, and **phobias** (including agoraphobia, specific phobias, and social anxiety disorder).
- Psychological (faulty cognitions and maladaptive learning), biological (evolutionary and genetic predispositions, biochemical disturbances), and sociocultural (cultural pressures in industrialized nations) factors likely all contribute to anxiety. Classical and operant conditioning also can contribute to phobias.

12.3 Depressive and Bipolar Disorders 342

- Both depressive and bipolar disorders are characterized by extreme disturbances in emotional states. People suffering from **depressive disorders** may experience a lasting depressed mood without a clear trigger. In contrast, people with **bipolar disorder** alternate between periods of depression and mania (characterized by hyperactivity and poor judgment).
- Biological factors play a significant role in mood disorders. Psychosocial theories of depression focus on environmental stressors and disturbances in interpersonal relationships, thought processes, self-concept, and learning history, including **learned helplessness**.

12.4 Schizophrenia 348

- **Schizophrenia** is a group of disorders, each characterized by a disturbance in perception (including **hallucinations**), language, thought (including **delusions**), emotions, and/or behavior.
- In the past, researchers divided schizophrenia into multiple subtypes. More recently, researchers have proposed focusing instead on **positive schizophrenia symptoms** versus **negative schizophrenia symptoms**.

• Most biological theories of schizophrenia focus on genetics, neurotransmitters, and brain abnormalities. Psychologists believe that there are also at least two possible psychosocial contributors: stress and communication disorders in families.

12.5 Other Disorders 352

• **Obsessive-compulsive disorder (OCD)** involves persistent, unwanted, fearful thoughts (obsessions) and/or irresistible urges to perform an act or repeated rituals (compulsions), which help relieve the anxiety created by the obsession. Given that numerous biological and psychological factors contribute to OCD, it is most often treated with a combination of drugs and cognitive-behavior therapy (CBT).

• **Dissociative disorders** are characterized by a major loss of memory without a clear physical cause. A controversial, subtype of these disorders, **dissociative identity disorder (DID)**, involves the presence of two or more distinct personality systems in the same individual. Environmental variables appear to be the primary cause of dissociative disorders. Dissociation can be a form of escape from a past trauma.

• **Personality disorders** occur when inflexible, maladaptive personality traits cause significant impairment of social and occupational functioning. **Antisocial personality disorder** is a pattern of disregard for, and violation of, the rights of others. The most common personality disorder is **borderline personality disorder (BPD)**. Its core features are impulsivity and instability in mood, relationships, and self-image. Although some therapists have success with drug therapy and behavior therapy, the prognosis is not favorable.

12.6 Gender and Cultural Effects 356

• Men and women differ in their rates and experiences of abnormal behavior. For instance, in the case of depression, modern research suggests that the gender ratio differences may reflect an underlying predisposition toward internalizing or externalizing emotions and problems.

• People of different cultures experience psychological disorders in a variety of ways. For example, the reported incidence of schizophrenia varies in different cultures around the world, as do the disorder's symptoms, triggers, and prognosis.

• Some symptoms of psychological disorders, as well as some disorders themselves, are *culture general*, whereas others are *culture bound*.

Applying **Real** World **Psychology**

We began this chapter with six intriguing Real World Psychology questions, and you were asked to revisit these questions at the end of each section. Questions like these have an important and lasting impact on all of our lives. See if you can answer these additional critical thinking questions related to real world examples.

Jodi Cobb/NG Image Collection

1. Is this man's behavior abnormal? Which criteria for psychological disorders do his piercings and tattoos meet? Which do they not?
2. Can you think of any behavior *you* exhibit that might be considered abnormal if your own cultural norms were not taken into account?
3. We've all experienced anxiety. Which of the explanations described in this section do you feel best describes your personal experiences with it? Why?
4. Recall an experience you've had with depression. How was it similar to or different from what was discussed in the section on major depressive disorders?
5. In the section on schizophrenia, we pointed out that if one identical twin develops schizophrenia, there is a 48% chance that the other twin will do so as well. How does this high correlation support the diathesis-stress model?
6. Think about someone you know—a friend, a family member, or yourself—who suffers from one of the disorders described in this chapter. How does the information we've provided differ from or match what you've discovered from your own or others' experiences?

Key Terms

Retrieval Practice Write a definition for each term before turning back to the referenced page to check your answer.

- abnormal behavior 332
- antisocial personality disorder (ASPD) 354
- anxiety disorder 338
- bipolar disorder 343
- borderline personality disorder (BPD) 354
- comorbidity 335
- delusion 349
- depressive disorders 342
- *Diagnostic and Statistical Manual of Mental Disorders (DSM)* 334
- diathesis-stress model 351
- dissociative disorder 353
- dissociative identity disorder (DID) 353
- generalized anxiety disorder (GAD) 338
- hallucination 349
- insanity 334
- learned helplessness 345
- neurosis 334
- obsessive-compulsive disorder (OCD) 352
- panic disorder 339
- personality disorder 354
- phobia 339
- psychiatry 334
- psychosis 334
- schizophrenia 348

CHAPTER 13

© Okea/iStockphoto

Therapy

© tobkatrina/Shutterstock

Real World Psychology

Things you'll learn in Chapter 13

[Q1] Can changing your irrational thoughts and self-talk make you feel better about your body?

[Q2] How might accepting fears and worries rather than trying to eliminate them decrease PTSD?

[Q3] Could therapy help you hold a tarantula?

[Q4] Does simply watching other children play with dogs reduce dog phobias in young children?

[Q5] Do psychedelic drugs cause psychosis?

[Q6] Can therapy that is delivered over the telephone lead to lower levels of depression?

Throughout the chapter, margin icons for Q1–Q6 indicate where the text addresses these questions.

CHAPTER OUTLINE

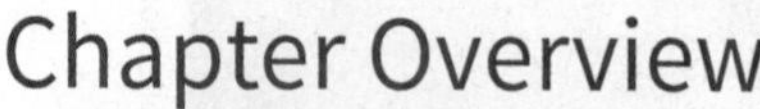

Chapter Overview

Throughout this text, we have emphasized the *science* of psychology, and this chapter is no exception. Now we'll explore how therapists apply this science during **psychotherapy** to help us improve our overall psychological functioning and adjustment to life, and to assist people suffering from one or more psychological disorders. Due to the common stereotype and stigma that therapy is only for deeply disturbed individuals, it's important to note that therapy provides an opportunity for everyone to have their specific problems addressed, as well as to learn better thinking, feeling, and behavioral skills useful in their everyday lives. In this chapter, we'll discuss the three major approaches to psychotherapy (**Figure 13.1**). Along the way we'll work to demystify and destigmatize its practice, and dispel some common myths (**Table 13.1**).

The chapter begins with what's known as the talk therapies, including psychoanalysis/psychodynamic, humanistic, and cognitive. Next we look at behavior therapies and the roles of classical conditioning, operant conditioning, and observational learning. Then we examine biomedical (or biological) therapies, including the topics of psychopharmacology, electroconvulsive therapy, and psychosurgery. Our final section looks at psychotherapy in perspective—its goals and effectiveness, its formats, and its cultural and gender issues.

Psychotherapy Any of a group of therapies used to treat psychological disorders and to improve psychological functioning and adjustment to life.

FIGURE 13.1 An overview of the three major approaches to therapy

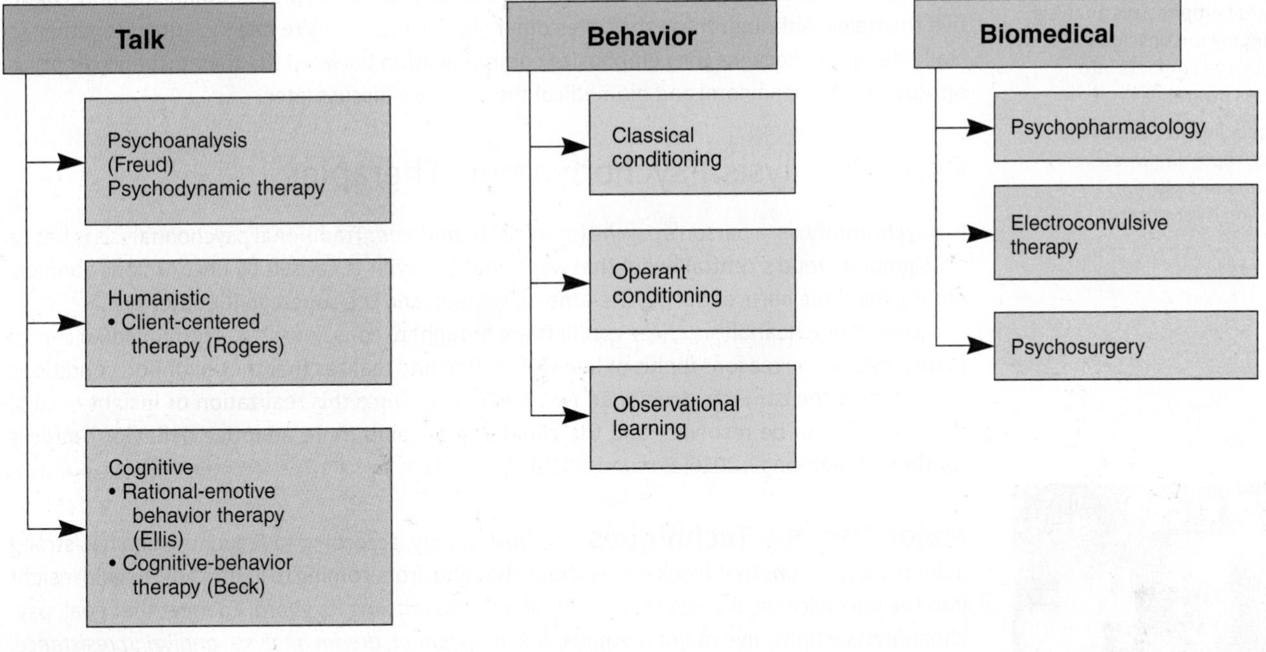

TABLE 13.1 Myths About Therapy

Real World **Psychology**

- ***Myth: There is one best therapy.***
  Fact: Many problems can be treated equally well with many different forms of therapy.
- ***Myth: Therapists can read your mind.***
  Fact: Good therapists often seem to have an uncanny ability to understand how their clients are feeling and to know when someone is trying to avoid certain topics. This is not due to any special mind-reading ability; it simply reflects their specialized training and daily experience working with troubled people.
- ***Myth: People who go to therapists are crazy or weak.***
  Fact: Most people seek counseling because of stress in their lives or because they realize that therapy can improve their level of functioning. It is difficult to be objective about our own problems. Seeking therapy is a sign of wisdom and personal strength.
- ***Myth: Only the rich can afford therapy.***
  Fact: Therapy can be expensive. But many clinics and therapists charge on a sliding scale, based on the client's income. Some insurance plans also cover psychological services.
- ***Myth: If I am taking meds, I don't need therapy.***
  Fact: Medications, such as antidepressants, are only one form of therapy. They can change brain chemistry, but they can't teach us to think, feel, or behave differently. Research suggests that a combination of drugs and psychotherapy may be best for some situations, whereas in other cases, psychotherapy or drug therapy alone may be most effective.

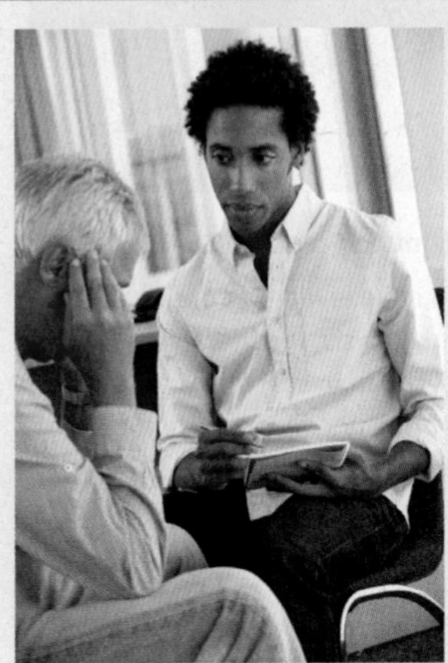

© Mark Bowden/iStockphoto

Sources: Hanscombe, 2015; Lilienfeld et al., 2010, 2015; Magnavita & Anchin, 2014; Seay & Sun, 2016.

13.1 Talk Therapies

LEARNING OBJECTIVES

Retrieval Practice While reading the upcoming sections, respond to each Learning Objective in your own words.

Review the three main forms of talk therapies.

- **Define** psychotherapy.
- **Describe** psychoanalysis and its core techniques and criticisms, along with modern psychodynamic therapies.
- **Discuss** humanistic therapies and their key techniques and evaluation.
- **Discuss** cognitive therapies and their core principles and evaluation.

Psychoanalysis A type of talk therapy, originated by Sigmund Freud, that emphasizes analysis and bringing unconscious thoughts and conflicts into conscious awareness.

Free association In psychoanalysis, reporting whatever comes to mind without monitoring its contents.

We begin our discussion of professional psychotherapy with traditional psychoanalysis and its modern counterpart, psychodynamic therapies. Then we explore humanistic and cognitive therapies. Although these therapies differ significantly, they're often grouped together as "talk therapies" because they emphasize communication between the therapist and client, as opposed to the behavioral and biomedical therapies we discuss later.

Psychoanalysis/Psychodynamic Therapies

In **psychoanalysis**, a person's *psyche* (or mind) is *analyzed*. Traditional psychoanalysis is based on Sigmund Freud's central belief that abnormal behavior is caused by unconscious conflicts among the three parts of the psyche—the id, the ego, and the superego (Chapter 11).

During psychoanalysis, these conflicts are brought to consciousness. The individual comes to understand the reasons for his or her dysfunction and realizes that the childhood conditions under which the conflicts developed no longer exist. Once this realization or insight occurs, the conflicts can be resolved, and the client can develop more adaptive behavior patterns (Barber & Solomonov, 2016; Bonomi, 2015).

© Hulton-Deutsch Collection/©Corbis

Sigmund Freud (1856–1939)

Freud believed that during psychoanalysis, the therapist's (or psychoanalyst's) major goal was to bring unconscious conflicts into consciousness.

Major Therapy Techniques

Unfortunately, according to Freud, the ego has strong *defense mechanisms* that block unconscious thoughts from coming to light. Thus, to gain insight into the unconscious, the ego must be "tricked" into relaxing its guard. To meet that goal, psychoanalysts employ five major methods: *free association*, *dream analysis*, *analyzing resistance*, *analyzing transference*, and *interpretation* (**Figure 13.2**).

Free Association According to Freud, when you let your mind wander and remove conscious censorship over thoughts—a process called **free association**—interesting and even bizarre connections seem to spring into awareness (see photo). Freud believed that the first thing to come to a patient's mind is often an important clue to what the person's unconscious wants to conceal. Having the client recline on a couch, with only the ceiling to look at, is believed to encourage free association (**Figure 13.3**).

Dream Analysis Recall from Chapter 5 that, according to Freud, our psychological defenses are lowered during sleep. Therefore, our forbidden desires and unconscious conflicts are supposedly more freely expressed during dreams. Even while dreaming, however, we recognize

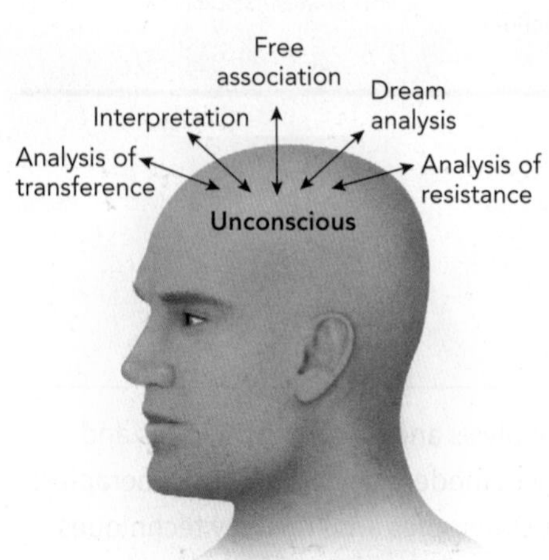

FIGURE 13.2 The five key techniques for psychoanalysis

S. Harris
"I'LL BARK, AND YOU BARK THE FIRST THING THAT COMES TO MIND."

S.Harris/CartoonStock

FIGURE 13.3 Freud's free association As shown in this popular cartoon, psychoanalysis is often portrayed as a client lying on a couch engaging in free association. Freud believed that this arrangement—with the client relaxed and the therapist out of his or her view—helps the client let down his or her defenses, making the unconscious more accessible.

these feelings and conflicts as unacceptable and must disguise them as images that have deeper symbolic meaning. Thus, using Freudian **dream analysis**, a dream of riding a horse or driving a car might be analyzed as just the surface description, or *manifest content*. In contrast, the hidden, underlying meaning, or *latent content*, might be analyzed as a desire for, or concern about, sexual intercourse.

Dream analysis In psychoanalysis, interpretation of the underlying true meaning of dreams to reveal unconscious processes.

Analysis of Resistance During free association or dream analysis, Freud found that clients often show an inability or unwillingness to discuss or reveal certain memories, thoughts, motives, or experiences. For example, if the client suddenly "forgets" what he or she was saying or completely changes the subject, it is the therapist's job to identify these possible cases of **resistance** and then help the client face his or her problems and learn to deal with them more realistically.

Resistance In psychoanalysis, the client's inability or unwillingness of a client to discuss or reveal certain memories, thoughts, motives, or experiences.

Analysis of Transference Freud believed that during psychoanalysis, clients disclose intimate feelings and memories, and the relationship between the therapist and client may become complex and emotionally charged. As a result, clients often apply, or *transfer*, some of their unresolved emotions and attitudes from past relationships onto the therapist. For example, a client might interact with the therapist as if the therapist were a lover or parent. The therapist uses this process of **transference** to help the client "relive" painful past relationships in a safe, therapeutic setting so that he or she can move on to healthier relationships.

Transference In psychoanalysis, the process by which a client attaches (transfers) to the therapist emotional reactions related to someone else in the client's life.

Interpretation The core of all psychoanalytic therapy is **interpretation**. During free association, dream analysis, resistance, and transference, the analyst listens closely and tries to find patterns and hidden conflicts. At the right time, the therapist explains or interprets the underlying meanings to the client.

Interpretation A psychoanalyst's explanation of a client's free associations, dreams, resistance, and transference; more generally, any statement by a therapist that presents a problem in a new way.

Evaluating Psychoanalysis As you can see, psychoanalysis is largely rooted in the assumption that repressed memories and unconscious conflicts actually exist. But, as we noted in Chapters 7 and 11, this assumption is the subject of heated, ongoing debate. Critics also point to two other problems with psychoanalysis (Grünbaum, 2015; Miltenberger, 2011; Ng et al., 2015):

- **Limited applicability** Psychoanalysis is time-consuming (often lasting several years with four to five sessions a week) and expensive. In addition, critics suggest that it applies only to a select group of highly motivated, articulate clients with less severe disorders and not to more complex disorders, such as schizophrenia.
- **Lack of scientific credibility** According to critics, it is difficult, if not impossible, to scientifically document the major tenets of psychoanalysis. How do we prove or disprove the existence of an unconscious mind or the meaning of unconscious conflicts and symbolic dream images?

Despite these criticisms, research shows that traditional psychoanalysis can be effective for those who have the time and money (Busch, 2014, 2015; Watkins, 2016).

Psychodynamic Therapies A modern derivative of Freudian psychoanalysis, **psychodynamic therapies**, includes both Freud's theories and those of his major followers—Carl Jung, Alfred Adler, Karen Horney, and Erik Erikson. In contrast to psychoanalysis, psychodynamic therapies are shorter and less intensive (once or twice a week versus several times a week and only for a few weeks or months versus years). Also, the client is treated face-to-face rather than reclining on a couch, and the therapist takes a more directive approach rather than waiting for unconscious memories and desires to slowly be uncovered.

Psychodynamic therapies A newer group of talk therapies that focuses on conscious processes and current problems; briefer, more directive, and more modern forms of psychoanalysis.

In addition, contemporary psychodynamic therapists focus less on unconscious, early-childhood roots of problems and more on conscious processes and current problems (Barber & Solomonov, 2016; Göttken et al., 2014; Short & Thomas, 2015). Such refinements have helped make treatments shorter, more available, and more effective for an increasing number of people. See **Figure 13.4** for one of the most popular modern forms of psychodynamic therapies.

© Wavebreak Media/Alamy StockPhoto

FIGURE 13.4 **Interpersonal therapy (IPT)** IPT, a variation of psychodynamic therapy, focuses on current relationships, with the goal of relieving immediate symptoms and teaching better ways to solve interpersonal problems. Research shows that it's effective for a variety of disorders, including depression, marital conflict, eating disorders, and drug addiction (Driessen et al., 2015; Normandin et al., 2015; Weitkamp et al., 2014).

Comstock/SUPERSTOCK

FIGURE 13.5 **Nurturing growth** Recall how you've felt when you've been with someone who considers you to be a worthy and good person with unlimited potential, a person who believes that your "real self" is unique and valuable. These are the feelings that are nurtured in humanistic therapy.

© Michael Rougier/Time & Life/Getty Images

Carl Rogers (1902–1987)

Humanistic therapies A group of talk therapies that emphasizes maximizing a client's inherent capacity for self-actualization by providing a nonjudgmental, accepting atmosphere.

Client-centered therapy A form of talk therapy, developed by Carl Rogers, that provides a warm, supportive atmosphere that encourages self-actualization and improves the client's self-concept; techniques include empathy, unconditional positive regard, genuineness, and active listening.

Empathy In Rogerian terms, a sensitive understanding and sharing of another's inner experience.

Unconditional positive regard Rogers's term for love and acceptance with no "strings" (conditions) attached.

Humanistic Therapies

In contrast to the psychoanalytic and psychodynamic focus on the unconscious, the humanistic approach emphasizes conscious processes and present versus past experiences. The name **humanistic therapies** reflects this focus on the human characteristics of a person's potential for self-actualization, free will, and self-awareness. Humanistic therapists assume that people with problems are suffering from a disruption of their normal growth potential and, hence, their self-concept. When obstacles are removed, the individual is free to become the self-accepting, self-actualized person everyone is capable of being (D'Souza & Gurin, 2016; Gelso et al., 2014; Schneider et al., 2015).

One of the best-known humanistic therapists is Carl Rogers (see photo), who developed an approach that encouraged people to actualize their potential and to relate to others in genuine ways. His approach is referred to as **client-centered therapy** (**Figure 13.5**). (Rogers used the term *client* because he believed the label *patient* implied that someone was sick or mentally ill rather than responsible and competent.)

Client-centered therapy, like psychoanalysis and psychodynamic therapies, explores thoughts and feelings as a way to obtain insight into the causes of behaviors. For Rogerian therapists, however, the focus is on providing an accepting atmosphere and encouraging healthy emotional experiences. Clients are responsible for discovering their own maladaptive patterns.

Major Therapy Techniques

Rogerian therapists create a therapeutic relationship by focusing on four important qualities of communication: *empathy*, *unconditional positive regard*, *genuineness*, and *active listening*.

Empathy

Using the technique of **empathy**, a sensitive understanding and sharing of another person's inner experience, therapists pay attention to body language and listen for subtle cues to help them understand the emotional experiences of clients. To further help clients explore their feelings, the therapist uses open-ended statements such as "You found that upsetting" or "You haven't been able to decide what to do about this" rather than asking questions or offering explanations.

Unconditional Positive Regard

Regardless of the clients' problems or behaviors, humanistic therapists offer them **unconditional positive regard**, a genuine caring and nonjudgmental attitude toward people based on their innate value as individuals. They avoid evaluative statements such as "That's good" and "You did the right thing" because such comments imply that the therapist is judging the client. Rogers believed that most of us receive conditional acceptance from our parents, teachers, and others, which leads to poor self-concepts and psychological disorders (**Figure 13.6**).

Genuineness Humanists believe that when therapists use **genuineness** and honestly share their thoughts and feelings with their clients, the clients will in turn develop self-trust and honest self-expression.

Active Listening Using **active listening**, which includes reflecting, paraphrasing, and clarifying what the client is saying, the clinician communicates that he or she is genuinely interested and paying close attention (see **Psychology and You**).

Pat Byrnes/The Cartoon Bank, Inc.

"Just remember, son, it doesn't matter whether you win or lose—unless you want Daddy's love."

FIGURE 13.6 Unconditional versus conditional positive regard According to Rogers, clients need to feel unconditionally accepted by their therapists in order to recognize and value their own emotions, thoughts, and behaviors. As this cartoon sarcastically implies, some parents withhold their love and acceptance unless the child lives up to their expectations.

Psychology and You—Understanding Yourself

Using Active Listening Personally and Professionally

If you want to try active listening in your personal life, keep in mind that to *reflect* is to hold a mirror in front of the person, enabling that person to see him- or herself. To *paraphrase* is to summarize in different words what the other person is saying. To *clarify* is to check that both the speaker and listener are on the same wavelength.

When a professional uses active listening, he or she might notice a client's furrowed brow and downcast eyes while he is discussing his military experiences and then might respond, "It sounds like you're angry with your situation and feeling pretty miserable right now." Can you see how this statement reflects the client's anger, paraphrases his complaint, and gives feedback to clarify the communication? This type of attentive, active listening is a relatively simple and well-documented technique that you can use to improve your communication with virtually anyone—professors, employers, friends, family, and especially your love partner.

© Mark Bowden/iStockphoto

Evaluating Humanistic Therapies Supporters say that there is empirical evidence for the efficacy of client-centered therapy, whereas critics argue that outcomes such as self-actualization and self-awareness are difficult to test scientifically. Furthermore, research on specific humanistic techniques has had mixed results (Cain et al., 2016; Erekson & Lambert, 2015; Schneider et al., 2015).

Cognitive Therapies

Cognitive therapies assume that faulty thoughts (cognitions) are the primary source for problems, and that our thoughts intervene between events and our reactions to them (Calkins et al., 2016; Clark, 2016; Evans, 2015).

Like psychoanalysts and humanists, cognitive therapists believe that exploring unexamined beliefs can produce insight into the reasons for disturbed thoughts, feelings, and behaviors. However, instead of believing that a change occurs because of insight, cognitive therapists suggest that *negative self-talk*, the unrealistic things a person tells himself or herself, is most important (Arora et al., 2015; Kross et al., 2014; Zourbanos et al., 2014). For example, research with women suffering from eating disorders found that changing a client's irrational thoughts
[Q1] and self-talk, such as "If I eat that cake, I will become fat instantly" or "I'll never have a dating relationship if I don't lose 20 pounds," resulted in their having fewer negative thoughts about their bodies (Bhatnagar et al., 2013).

Through a process called **cognitive restructuring**, clients learn to identify and dispute their irrational or maladaptive thought patterns. Do you see how if we first identify

Genuineness In Rogerian terms, being personally authentic and sincere; the awareness of one's true inner thoughts and feelings and the ability to share them honestly with others.

Active listening A communication technique that requires listening with total attention to what another is saying; techniques include reflecting, paraphrasing, and clarifying what the person says and means.

Cognitive therapies A group of talk therapies that focuses on changing faulty thought processes (cognitions); based on the assumption that thoughts intervene between events and reactions.

Cognitive restructuring A therapeutic process of learning to identify and dispute irrational or maladaptive thought patterns.

FIGURE 13.7 **Using cognitive restructuring to improve sales**

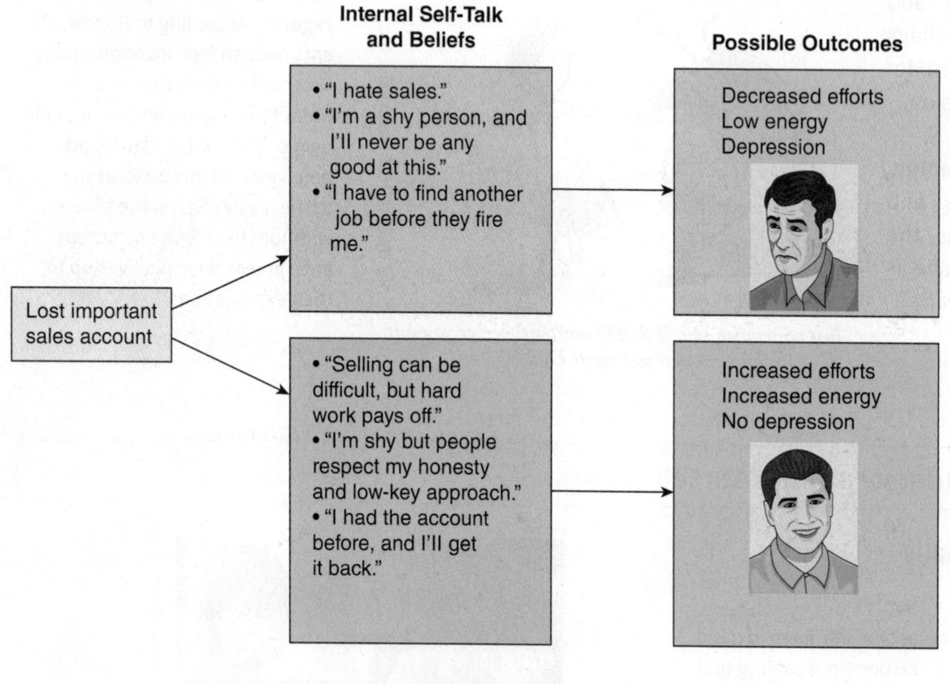
Internal Self-Talk and Beliefs
Possible Outcomes
Lost important sales account
• "I hate sales."
• "I'm a shy person, and I'll never be any good at this."
• "I have to find another job before they fire me."
Decreased efforts
Low energy
Depression
• "Selling can be difficult, but hard work pays off."
• "I'm shy but people respect my honesty and low-key approach."
• "I had the account before, and I'll get it back."
Increased efforts
Increased energy
No depression

Real World **Psychology**

a. Note how the negative interpretation and destructive self-talk leads to destructive and self-defeating outcomes.

b. Cognitive therapy teaches clients to challenge and change their negative beliefs and negative self-talk into positive ones, which, in turn, leads to more positive outcomes. Can you think of other situations in which such reinterpretation could be helpful?

our irrational thoughts, then we can logically challenge them, which in turn enables us to become more effective (**Figure 13.7**)?

Ellis's Rational-Emotive Behavior Therapy (REBT) One of the best-known cognitive therapists, Albert Ellis, suggested that irrational beliefs are the primary culprit in problem emotions and behaviors. He proposed that most people mistakenly believe they are unhappy or upset because of external, outside events, such as receiving a bad grade on an exam. Ellis suggested that, in reality, these negative emotions result from faulty interpretations and irrational beliefs (such as interpreting the bad grade as a sign of your incompetence and an indication that you'll never qualify for graduate school or a good job).

Rational-emotive behavior therapy (REBT) A form of talk therapy, developed by Albert Ellis, that focuses on eliminating negative emotional reactions through logic, confrontation, and examination of irrational beliefs.

To deal with these irrational beliefs, Ellis developed **rational-emotive behavior therapy (REBT)** (Cristea et al., 2016; Ellis & Ellis, 2011, 2014; Evans, 2015). (See **Process Diagram 13.1** and the following **Psychology and You**.)

Psychology and You—Understanding Yourself

Overcoming Irrational Misconceptions

Albert Ellis believed that people often require the help of a therapist to see through their defenses, and to challenge their self-defeating thoughts. For mild, everyday problems, our students have found that they can improve their own irrational beliefs and responses with the following suggestions:

1. **Identify and confront your belief system** Identify your irrational beliefs by asking yourself why you feel the particular emotions you do. Then, by confronting your thoughts and feelings, you can discover the irrational assumptions creating the problem consequences.
2. **Evaluate consequences** Rather than perpetuating negative emotions by assuming they must be experienced, focus on whether your reactions make you more effective and enable you to solve your problems. It's gratifying when people you cherish, love you in return. But if they don't, continuing to pursue them, or insisting that they must love you, will only be self-defeating.
3. **Practice effective ways of thinking and behaving** Imagine and rehearse thoughts and behaviors that are more effective, and outcomes that are more successful.

STOP! This Process Diagram contains essential information NOT found elsewhere in the text, which is likely to appear on quizzes and exams. Be sure to study it CAREFULLY!

PROCESS DIAGRAM 13.1 Ellis's Rational-Emotive Behavior Therapy (REBT) If you receive a poor performance evaluation at work, you might directly attribute your bad mood to the negative feedback. Psychologist Albert Ellis would argue that your self-talk ("I always mess up") between the event and the feeling is what actually upsets you. Furthermore, ruminating on all the other times you've "messed up" in your life maintains your negative emotional state and may even lead to anxiety disorders, depression, and other psychological disorders.

To treat these problems, Ellis developed an A–B–C–D approach: **A** stands for *activating event*, **B** the person's *belief system*, **C** the emotional *consequences*, and **D** the act of *disputing* erroneous beliefs. During therapy, Ellis helped his clients identify the A, B, C's underlying their irrational beliefs by actively arguing with, cajoling, and teasing them—sometimes in very blunt, confrontational language. Once clients recognized their self-defeating thoughts, he worked with them on how to *dispute* those beliefs and create and test out new, rational ones. These new beliefs then changed the maladaptive emotions—thus breaking the vicious cycle. (Note the arrow under D that goes backwards to B.)

Albert Ellis (1913–2007)

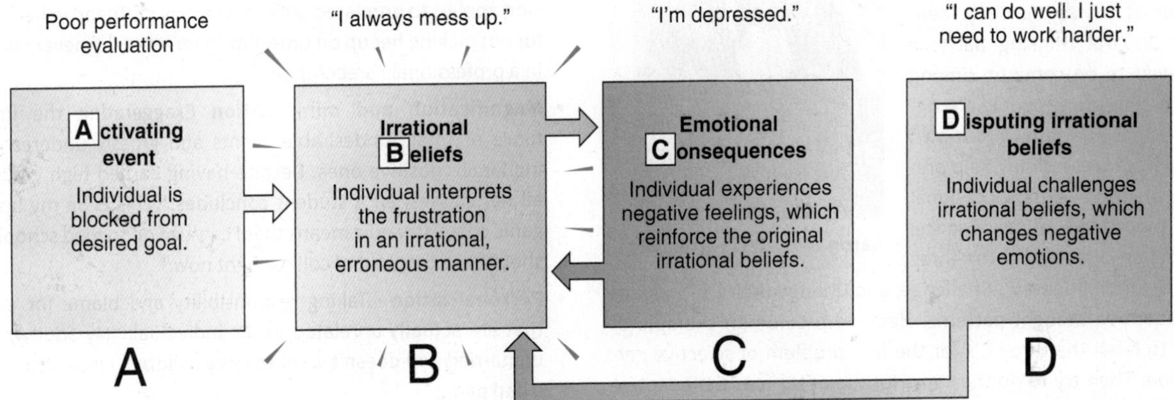
Poor performance evaluation
"I always mess up."
"I'm depressed."
"I can do well. I just need to work harder."
Activating event
Individual is blocked from desired goal.
Irrational Beliefs
Individual interprets the frustration in an irrational, erroneous manner.
Emotional Consequences
Individual experiences negative feelings, which reinforce the original irrational beliefs.
Disputing irrational beliefs
Individual challenges irrational beliefs, which changes negative emotions.
A
B
C
D

Beck's Cognitive-Behavior Therapy (CBT)

Another well-known cognitive therapist, Aaron Beck, also believes psychological problems result from illogical thinking and destructive self-talk (Beck, 1976, 2000; Beck & Dozois, 2014; Calkins et al., 2016). But Beck seeks to directly confront and change the behaviors associated with destructive cognitions. Beck's **cognitive-behavior therapy (CBT)** is designed to reduce *both* self-destructive thoughts *and* self-destructive behaviors.

Cognitive-behavior therapy (CBT) A type of therapy, developed by Aaron Beck, that combines cognitive therapy (changing faulty thinking) with behavior therapy (changing maladaptive behaviors).

Using cognitive-behavior therapy, clients are first taught to recognize and keep track of their thoughts. Next, the therapist trains the client to develop ways to test these automatic thoughts against reality. This approach helps depressed people discover that negative attitudes are largely a product of faulty thought processes.

At this point, Beck introduces the second phase of therapy—persuading the client to actively pursue pleasurable activities. Depressed individuals often lose motivation, even for experiences they used to find enjoyable. Simultaneously taking an active rather than a passive role and reconnecting with enjoyable experiences can help in recovering from depression (see the following **Psychology and You**).

One of the more modern forms of cognitive-behavior therapy (CBT) is *mindfulness-based cognitive therapy (MBCT)*. Using this approach, therapists help clients to become mindful of their streams of thoughts, including their fears, anxieties, and worries, at the very moments they're occurring and to *accept* such thoughts as mere events of the mind (Forkmann et al., 2016; Szabo et al., 2015). This newer form of CBT borrows heavily from a form of mindful meditation we discussed in Chapter 3. During MBCT, individuals are taught to pay attention

Howard Lipin/U-T San Diego/ ZUMAWire/Alamy Stock Photo

to the thoughts and feelings that flow through their minds and to accept such thoughts in a nonjudgmental way. To test the effectiveness of MBCT, 62 veterans suffering from PTSD were divided into two groups (Possemato et al., 2016). One group received the standard primary care, whereas the other received training in MBCT (see the photo). While both groups improved, those in the mindfulness group had significantly larger reductions in PTSD and depression, and maintained their gains in the 8-week follow up. Can you see how by accepting their fears and worries rather than trying to eliminate them, the veterans were less upset and affected by them? Mindfulness-based cognitive therapy been successfully applied to other psychological problems such as depression, personality disorders, and substance abuse (Dimidjian et al., 2016; Fortuna & Vallejo, 2015; Ottavi et al., 2016). [Q2]

Psychology and You—Understanding Yourself

A Cognitive Approach to Lifting Depression

One of the most successful applications of Beck's CBT is in the treatment of depression (Beck et al., 2012, 2015; Dobson, 2016; Hundt et al., 2016). Beck identified several thinking patterns believed to be common among depression-prone people. Recognizing these patterns in our own thought processes may help prevent or improve the occasional bad moods we all experience. Clients are first taught the three Cs—to Catch (identify), Challenge, and Change their irrational or maladaptive thought patterns. Here we provide an example of how to label the three C's for the first problem of *selective perception*. Then try to do the same for the other four maladaptive patterns.

Clem Murray/MCT/NewsCom

Aaron Beck (1921-present)

- **Selective perception** Focusing selectively on negative events while ignoring positive events. (*Catch the thought* = "Why am I the only person alone at this party?"; *Challenge it* = "I notice four other single people at this party"; *Change it* = "Being single has several advantages. I'll bet some of the couples are actually envying my freedom.")
- **Overgeneralization** Drawing sweeping, global, negative conclusions based on one incident, and then assuming that conclusion applies to unrelated areas of life. "My girlfriend yelled at me for not picking her up on time. I'm so forgetful. I'll never succeed in a professional career."
- **Magnification and minimization** Exaggerating the importance of small, undesirable events and grossly underestimating larger, positive ones. Despite having earned high grades in all her classes, an A student concludes: "This B on my last organic chemistry quiz means that I can't go on to med school, so I should just drop out of college right now."
- **Personalization** Taking responsibility and blame for events that are actually unrelated to the individual. "My adult child is unmarried and doesn't want to have children. I must have been a bad parent."
- **All-or-nothing thinking** Seeing things as black-or-white categories—where everything is either totally good or bad, right or wrong, a success or a failure. ("If I don't get straight A's, I'll never get a good job.")

Evaluating Cognitive Therapies

Cognitive therapies are highly effective treatments for depression, as well as anxiety disorders, bulimia nervosa, anger management, addiction, and even some symptoms of schizophrenia and insomnia (Hundt et al., 2016; Palermo et al., 2016; Sankar et al., 2015). However, both Beck and Ellis have been criticized for ignoring or denying the client's unconscious dynamics, overemphasizing rationality, and minimizing the importance of the client's past (Granillo et al., 2013; Hammack, 2003).

Other critics suggest that cognitive therapies are successful because they employ behavior techniques, not because they change the underlying cognitive structure (Bandura, 1969, 2008; Granillo et al., 2013; Walker & Lampropoulos, 2014). Imagine that you sought treatment for depression and learned to curb your all-or-nothing thinking, along with identifying activities and behaviors that lessened your depression. You can see why it's difficult to identify whether changing your cognitions or changing your behavior was the most significant therapeutic factor. But to clients who have benefited, it doesn't matter. CBT combines both, and it has a proven track record for lifting depression!

Retrieval Practice 13.1 | Talk Therapies

SELF-TEST Completing this self-test, and then checking your answers by clicking on the answer button or by looking in Appendix B, will provide immediate feedback and helpful practice for exams.

1. Psychoanalysis/psychodynamic, humanistic, and cognitive therapies are often grouped together as _____.
   a. talk therapies **b.** behavior therapies
   c. analytic therapies **d.** cognitive restructuring
2. The system of psychotherapy developed by Freud that seeks to bring unconscious conflicts into conscious awareness is known as _____.
   a. transference **b.** cognitive restructuring
   c. psychoanalysis **d.** the "hot seat" technique
3. A _____ therapist emphasizes the importance of empathy, unconditional positive regard, genuineness, and active listening.
   a. psychodynamic
   b. phenomenological behavior
   c. cognitive-behavior
   d. client-centered
4. According to rational-emotive behavior therapy (REBT), _____ often lead to depression and/or anxiety.
   a. unmet expectations
   b. stimulus events
   c. conditioning experiences
   d. irrational beliefs
5. Aaron Beck practices _____ therapy, which attempts to change not only destructive thoughts but the associated behaviors as well.
   a. psycho-behavior **b.** cognitive-behavior
   c. thinking-acting **d.** belief-behavior

Think Critically

1. Would you rather go to a therapist who uses modern psychodynamic therapy or one who practices traditional psychoanalysis? Why?
2. What is the significance of the term *client-centered therapy*?

© Gary Alvis/iStockphoto

Real World Psychology

Can changing your irrational thoughts and self-talk make you feel better about your body?

Howard Lipin/ U-T San Diego/ ZUMAWire/ Alamy Stock Photo

How might accepting fears and worries rather than trying to eliminate them decrease PTSD?

HINT: LOOK IN THE MARGIN FOR **[Q1]** AND **[Q2]**

13.2 Behavior Therapies

LEARNING OBJECTIVES

Retrieval Practice While reading the upcoming sections, respond to each Learning Objective in your own words.

Summarize the treatment techniques and criticisms of behavior therapies.

- **Describe** how classical conditioning is used in therapy.
- **Explore** how operant conditioning is used in therapy.
- **Explain** how observational learning is used in therapy.
- **Describe** two major criticisms of behavior therapies.

Behavior therapies A group of therapies that uses learning principles to reduce or eliminate maladaptive behaviors; techniques are based on classical and operant conditioning, along with observational learning.

The previously discussed talk therapies are often called "insight therapies" because they focus on self-awareness, but sometimes having insight into a problem does not automatically solve it. In **behavior therapies**, the focus is on the problem behavior itself rather than on any underlying causes (Duncan, 2014; Spiegler, 2016; Stoll & Brooks, 2015). Although the person's feelings and interpretations are not disregarded, they're also not emphasized. The therapist diagnoses the problem by listing maladaptive behaviors that occur and adaptive behaviors that are absent. The therapist then attempts to shift the balance of the two, drawing on the learning principles of *classical conditioning, operant conditioning,* and *observational learning* (Chapter 6).

SidneyHarris/ScienceCartoonsPlus.com

Classical Conditioning

Behavior therapists use the principles of classical conditioning to decrease maladaptive behaviors by creating new associations to replace the faulty ones (see the cartoon). We will explore two techniques based on these principles: *systematic desensitization* and *aversion therapy*.

Sitting behind the wheel of a nonmoving car in the driveway.

Driving along an empty, quiet street on a sunny day.

Driving along a busy street on a sunny day.

Driving on a busy expressway on a rainy night.

Amount of anxiety

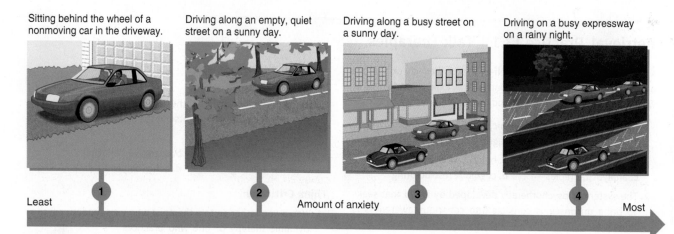

FIGURE 13.8 Systematic desensitization In systematic desensitization, the therapist and client together construct a *fear hierarchy*, a ranked listing of 10 or so related anxiety-arousing images—from the least fearful to the most. Then, while in a state of relaxation, the client mentally visualizes, or physically experiences, mildly anxiety-producing items at the lowest level of the hierarchy. After becoming comfortable with the mild stimulus, the client then works his or her way up to the most anxiety-producing items at the top. In sum, each progressive step on the fear hierarchy is repeatedly paired with relaxation, until the fear response or phobia is extinguished.

Systematic desensitization A behavior therapy technique in which a client is first asked to create a hierarchy of ordered fears and then taught to relax while gradually confronting the feared stimulus.

© Okea/iStockphoto

Aversion therapy A type of behavior therapy that pairs an aversive (unpleasant) stimulus with a maladaptive behavior in order to elicit a negative reaction to the target stimulus.

Recall from Chapter 6 that classical conditioning occurs when a neutral stimulus (NS) becomes associated with an unconditioned stimulus (US) to elicit a conditioned response (CR). Sometimes a classically conditioned fear response becomes so extreme that we call it a "phobia." To treat phobias, behavior therapists often use **systematic desensitization**, which begins with relaxation training, followed by imagining or directly experiencing various versions of a feared object or situation while remaining deeply relaxed (Schare et al., 2015; Tyner et al., 2016; Wolpe & Plaud, 1997). See **Figure 13.8** for a description of systematic desensitization useful for overcoming a driving phobia. Similarly, if you or a friend suffers from a spider phobia, you may be amazed to know that after just two or three hours of therapy, starting with simply looking at photos of spiders (see the photo), and then moving next to a tarantula in a glass aquarium, clients are able to eventually pet and hold the spider with their bare hands (Hauner et al., 2012)! [Q3]

How does relaxation training desensitize someone? Recall from Chapter 2 that the parasympathetic nerves control autonomic functions when we are relaxed. Because the opposing sympathetic nerves are dominant when we are anxious, it is physiologically impossible to be both relaxed and anxious at the same time. The key to success is teaching the client how to replace his or her fear response with relaxation when *exposed* to the fearful stimulus, which explains why these and related approaches are often referred to as *exposure therapies*. Modern virtual reality technology also uses systematic desensitization to expose clients to feared situations right in a therapist's office (**Figure 13.9**).

In contrast to systematic desensitization, **aversion therapy** uses classical conditioning techniques to create unpleasant (*aversive*) associations and responses rather than to extinguish them. People who engage in excessive drinking, for example, build up a number of pleasurable associations with alcohol. These pleasurable associations cannot always be prevented. Therefore, aversion therapy provides *negative associations* to compete with the pleasurable ones (**Figure 13.10**).

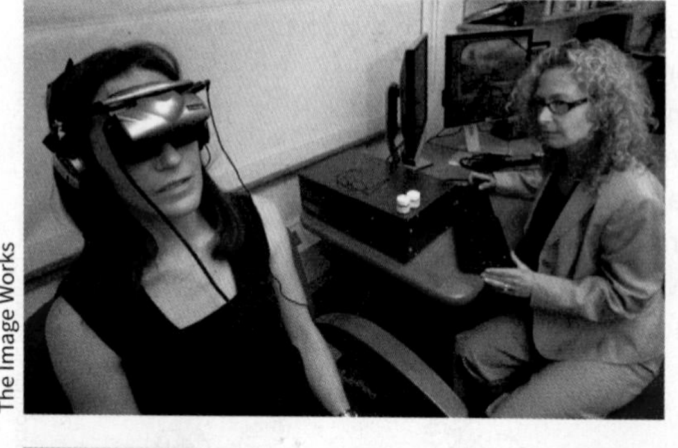

©Syracuse Newspapers/D.Lassman/ The Image Works

FIGURE 13.9 Virtual reality therapy Rather than use mental imaging or actual physical experiences of a fearful situation, virtual-reality headsets and data gloves allow a client with a fear of heights, for example, to have experiences ranging from climbing a stepladder all the way to standing on the edge of a tall building.

Operant Conditioning

As we discovered in Chapter 6, consequences are the heart of operant conditioning. Using a form of therapy called *behavior modification*, therapists provide reinforcement as a consequence for appropriate behaviors, and they withhold reinforcement for inappropriate behaviors. To develop complex

FIGURE 13.10 Aversion therapy The goal of aversion therapy is to create an undesirable, or *aversive*, response to a stimulus a person would like to avoid, such as alcohol.

1 During conditioning Someone who wants to stop drinking, for example, could take a drug called Antabuse that causes vomiting whenever alcohol enters the system.

2 After conditioning When the new connection between alcohol and nausea has been classically conditioned, engaging in the once desirable habit will cause an immediate aversive response.

behaviors, they often use *shaping*, which provides immediate rewards for successive approximations of the target behavior. Therapists have found this technique particularly successful in developing language skills in children with autism. First, the child is rewarded for connecting pictures or other devices with words; later, rewards are given only for using the pictures to communicate with others. This type of shaping can even be helpful if you suffer from the common problem of excessive shyness (see the following **Psychology and You**).

Psychology and You—Understanding Yourself

Overcoming Shyness

Shaping can help people acquire social skills and greater assertiveness. If you are painfully shy, for example, a clinician might first ask you to role-play simply saying hello to someone you find attractive. Then you might practice behaviors that gradually lead you to suggest a get-together or date. During such role-playing, or behavior rehearsal, the clinician gives you feedback and reinforcement for each successive step you take toward the end goal.

© DRB Images, LLC/iStockphoto

For clients in an inpatient treatment facility, adaptive behaviors can be taught or increased with techniques that provide immediate reinforcement in the form of tokens, which are objects or symbols that can be later exchanged for primary rewards, such as food, TV time, a private room, or outings. Clients might at first be given tokens for merely attending group therapy sessions. Later they will be rewarded only for actually participating in the sessions. Eventually, the tokens can be discontinued when the client receives the reinforcement of being helped by participation in the therapy sessions (Jowett Hirst et al., 2016; Mullen et al., 2015).

Modeling therapy A type of therapy characterized by watching and imitating models that demonstrate desirable behaviors.

Observational Learning

We all learn many things by observing others. Therapists use this principle in **modeling therapy**, in which clients are asked to observe and imitate appropriate models as they perform desired behaviors. For example, researchers successfully treated 4- and 5-year-old children with severe dog phobias by asking them first to watch other children play with dogs (see the photo), and then to
[Q4] gradually approach and get physically closer to the dogs themselves (May et al., 2013). When this type of therapy combines live modeling with direct and gradual practice, it is called *participant modeling*. This type of modeling is also effective in social skills training and assertiveness training (**Figure 13.11**).

© tobkatrina/Shutterstock

FIGURE 13.11 **Observational learning** During modeling therapy, a client might learn how to interview for a job by first watching the therapist role-play the part of the interviewee. The client then imitates the therapist's behavior and plays the same role. Over the course of several sessions, the client becomes gradually desensitized to the anxiety of interviews.

Digital Vision/Getty Images

Evaluating Behavior Therapies

Criticisms of behavior therapy fall into two major categories:

- **Generalizability** Critics argue that in the real world, clients are not consistently reinforced, and their newly acquired behaviors may disappear. To deal with this possibility, behavior therapists work to encourage clients to better recognize existing external real world rewards and to generate their own internal reinforcements, which they can then apply at their own discretion.
- **Ethics** Critics contend that it is unethical for one person to control another's behavior. Behaviorists, however, argue that rewards and punishments already control our behaviors. Behavior therapy actually increases our freedom by making these controls overt and by teaching people how to change their own behavior.

Despite these criticisms, behavior therapy is generally recognized as one of the most effective treatments for numerous problems, including phobias, obsessive-compulsive disorder, eating disorders, sexual dysfunctions, autism, intellectual disabilities, and delinquency (Cusack et al., 2016; Spiegler, 2016; Stoll & Brooks, 2015). For an immediate practical application of behavior therapy to your college life, see the following **Psychology and You**.

Psychology and You—Understanding Yourself

Test Yourself | Do You Have Test Anxiety?

Nearly everyone is somewhat anxious before an important exam. If you find this anxiety helpful and invigorating, skip this activity. On the other hand, if the days and evenings before a major exam are ruined by your anxiety and you sometimes "freeze up" while taking a test, try these tips, based on the three major forms of behavior therapy.

1. Classical Conditioning

This informal type of systematic desensitization will help decrease your feelings of anxiety:

Step 1: Review and practice the relaxation technique taught in Chapter 3.

Step 2: Create a 10-step "test-taking" hierarchy—starting with the least anxiety-arousing image (perhaps the day your instructor first mentions an upcoming exam) and ending with actually taking the exam.

Step 3: Beginning with the least-arousing image—say, hearing about the exam—picture yourself at each stage. While maintaining a calm, relaxed state, mentally work your way through all 10 steps. If you become anxious at any stage, stay there, repeating your relaxation technique until the anxiety diminishes.

Step 4: If you start to feel anxious the night before the exam, or even during the exam itself, remind yourself to relax. Take a few moments to shut your eyes and review how you worked through your hierarchy.

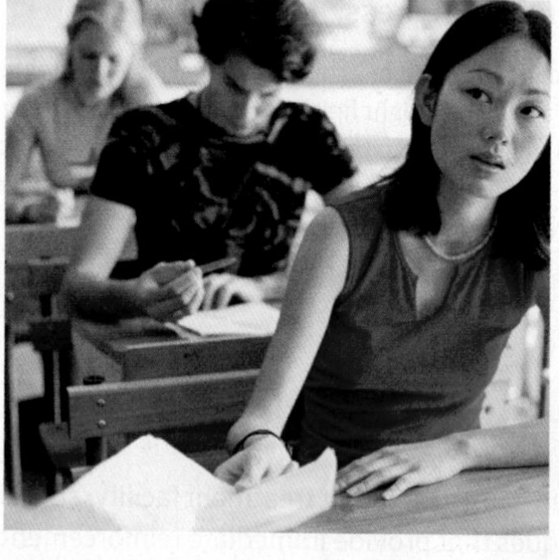

Stockbyte/Getty Images

2. Operant Conditioning

One of the best ways to avoid "freezing up" or "blanking out" on a test is to be fully prepared. To maximize your preparation, "shape" your behavior! Start small by answering the multiple-choice questions at the end of each major section of each chapter then check your answers by clicking on the answer button or by looking in Appendix B. Then move on to the longer self-grading quizzes that are available on our website, www.wiley.com/college/huffman. Following each of these "successive approximations," be sure to reward yourself in some way—call a friend, play with your children or pets, watch a video, or maybe check your Facebook page.

3. Observational Learning

Talk with your classmates who are getting good grades. Ask them for tips on how they prepare for exams and how they handle their own test anxieties. This type of modeling and observational learning can be very helpful—and it's a nice way to make friends.

Retrieval Practice 13.2 | Behavior Therapies

SELF-TEST Completing this self-test, and then checking your answers by clicking on the answer button or by looking in Appendix B, will provide immediate feedback and helpful practice for exams.

1. The main focus in behavior therapy is to increase _____ and decrease _____.

a. positive thoughts and feelings; negative thoughts and feelings
b. adaptive behaviors; maladaptive behaviors
c. coping resources; coping deficits
d. all these options

2. _____ pairs relaxation with a graduated hierarchy of anxiety-producing situations to extinguish the anxiety.

a. Modeling
b. Shaping
c. Systematic desensitization
d. Maslow's pyramid training

3. In behavior therapy, _____ techniques use shaping and tokens to increase adaptive behaviors.

a. classical conditioning **b.** modeling
c. social learning **d.** operant conditioning

4. In contrast to systematic desensitization, _____ uses classical conditioning techniques to create anxiety rather than prevent its arousal.

a. anxiety-modeling therapy
b. aversion therapy
c. anxiety therapy
d. subversion therapy

5. Asking clients with snake phobias to watch other (nonphobic) people handle snakes is an example of _____ therapy.

a. time out **b.** aversion
c. participative **d.** modeling

Think Critically

1. Imagine that you were going to use the principles of cognitive-behavioral therapy to change some aspect of your own thinking and behavior. If you'd like to quit smoking, or be more organized, how would you identify the faulty thinking perpetuating these behaviors and fears?

2. Once you've identified your faulty thinking patterns, what could you do to change your behavior?

3. Under what circumstances might behavior therapy be unethical?

© Okea/ iStockphoto

Real World Psychology

Could therapy help you hold a tarantula?

Does simply watching other children play with dogs reduce dog phobias in young children?

© tobkatrina/ Shutterstock

HINT: LOOK IN THE MARGIN FOR **[Q3]** AND **[Q4]**

13.3 Biomedical Therapies

LEARNING OBJECTIVES

Retrieval Practice While reading the upcoming sections, respond to each Learning Objective in your own words.

Review the types of biomedical therapies, and their risks and benefits.

- **Describe** biomedical therapies.
- **Identify** the major types of drugs used to treat psychological disorders.
- **Explain** what happens in electroconvulsive therapy and psychosurgery.
- **Summarize** the risks and benefits associated with biomedical therapies.

Some problem behaviors seem to be caused, at least in part, by chemical imbalances or disturbed nervous system functioning, and, as such, they can be treated with **biomedical therapies**. Psychiatrists or other medical personnel are generally the only ones who use biomedical (biological) therapies. However, in some states, licensed psychologists can prescribe certain medications, and they often work with clients receiving biomedical therapies. In this section, we will discuss three aspects of biomedical therapies: *psychopharmacology*, *electroconvulsive therapy* (*ECT*), and *psychosurgery*.

Biomedical therapies A group of therapies designed to alter brain functioning with biological or physical techniques, such as drugs, electroconvulsive therapy, and psychosurgery.

Psychopharmacology

Psychopharmacology The use of drugs to relieve or control the major symptoms of psychological disorders.

Since the 1950s, the field of **psychopharmacology** has effectively used drugs to relieve or control the major symptoms of psychological disorders. In some instances, using a psychotherapeutic drug is similar to administering insulin to people with diabetes, whose own bodies fail to manufacture enough. In other cases, drugs have been used to relieve or suppress the symptoms of psychological disturbances even when the underlying cause was not thought to be biological. As shown in **Table 13.2**, psychotherapeutic drugs are classified into four major categories: *antianxiety*, *antipsychotic*, *mood stabilizer*, and *antidepressant*.

How do the four categories differ? Antianxiety drugs generally create feelings of tranquility and relaxation, while also decreasing over-arousal in the brain. In contrast, antipsychotic drugs are designed to diminish or eliminate symptoms of psychosis, such as hallucinations. And mood-stabilizer drugs attempt to level off the emotional highs and lows of bipolar disorder. Interestingly, antidepressants were originally designed to lift depression—hence their name. However, they're now being successfully used in the treatment of some anxiety disorders, obsessive-compulsive disorder, posttraumatic stress disorder, and certain eating disorders.

How do drug treatments actually work? For most psychotherapeutic medications, including antidepressants, the best understood action of the drugs is to correct an imbalance in the

TABLE 13.2 Psychotherapeutic Drug Treatments for Psychological Disorders

	DESCRIPTION	EXAMPLES (TRADE NAMES)
Antianxiety Drugs Medications used to reduce anxiety, and decrease over-arousal in the brain; also known as anxiolytics or minor tranquilizers.	**Antianxiety drugs** lower the sympathetic activity of the brain—the crisis mode of operation—so that anxiety is diminished, and the person is calmer and less tense. Unfortunately, they're also potentially dangerous because they can reduce alertness, coordination, and reaction time. Moreover, they can have a synergistic (intensifying) effect with other drugs, which may lead to severe drug reaction—and even death.	Ativan Halcion Klonopin Librium Restoril Tranxene Valium Xanax
Antipsychotic Drugs Medications used to diminish or eliminate symptoms of psychosis; also known as neuroleptics or major tranquilizers.	**Antipsychotic drugs** reduce the agitated behaviors, hallucinations, delusions, and other symptoms associated with psychotic disorders, such as schizophrenia. Traditional antipsychotics work by decreasing activity at the dopamine receptors in the brain. A large number of clients markedly improve when treated with antipsychotic drugs.	Clozaril Geodon Invega Latuda Haldol Risperdal Seroquel Thorazine Zyprexa
Mood-Stabilizer Drugs Medications used to treat the combination of manic episodes and depression characteristics of bipolar disorders.	**Mood-stabilizer drugs** help steady mood swings, particularly for those suffering from bipolar disorder, a condition marked by extremes of both mania and depression. Because these drugs generally require up to three or four weeks to take effect, their primary use is in preventing future episodes, and helping to break the manic-depressive cycle.	Depakote Eskalith CR Lamictal Lithium Neurontin Tegretol Topamax Trileptal
Antidepressant Drugs Medications used to treat depression, some anxiety disorders, obsessive-compulsive disorder, posttraumatic stress disorder, and certain eating disorders (such as bulimia).	**Antidepressant drugs** are used primarily to reduce depression. There are several types of antidepressant drugs, including: *selective serotonin reuptake inhibitors (SNRIs), serotonin and norepinephrine reuptake inhibitors (SNRIs)*, norepinephrine and dopamine reuptake inhibitors (NDRIs), and *atypical antidepressants*. Each class of drugs affects neurochemical pathways in the brain in a slightly different way, increasing or decreasing the availability of certain chemicals. SSRIs (such as *Paxil* and *Prozac*) are by far the most commonly prescribed antidepressants. The atypical antidepressants are prescribed for those who fail to respond to, or experience undesirable side effects from, other antidepressants. It's important to note that it can take weeks or months for antidepressants to achieve their full effect.	Anafranil Celexa Cymbalta Effexor Elavil Lexapro Nardil Norpramin Parnate Paxil Pristiq Prozac Sarafem Tofranil Wellbutrin Zoloft

FIGURE 13.12 How antidepressants affect the brain Antidepressants are believed to work by increasing the availability of serotonin or norepinephrine, neurotransmitters that normally elevate mood and arousal. Shown here is the action of some of the most popular antidepressants—Prozac, Paxil, and other selective serotonin reuptake inhibitors (SSRIs).

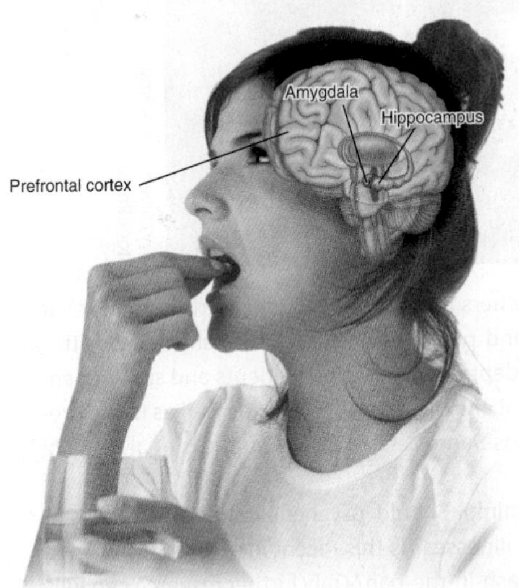

MedioImages/Photodisc/Getty Images, Inc.

a. Serotonin's effect on the brain
Some people with depression are believed to have lower levels of serotonin. Serotonin works in the prefrontal cortex, the hippocampus, and other parts of the brain to regulate mood, sleep, and appetite, among other things.

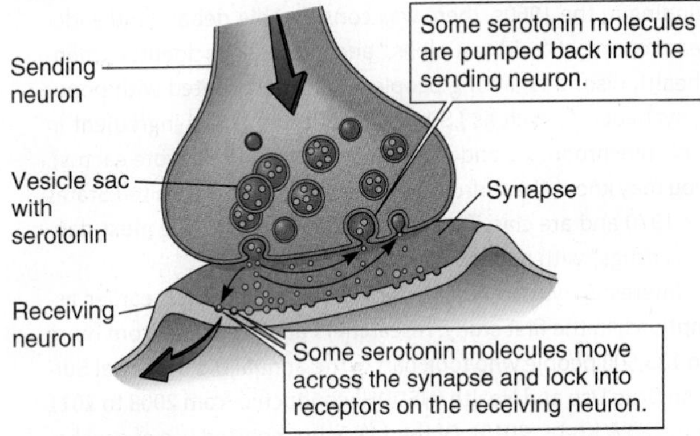

b. Normal neural transmission
Sending neurons normally release an excess of neurotransmitters, including serotonin. Some of the serotonin locks into receptors on the receiving neuron, but excess serotonin is pumped back into the sending neuron (called *reuptake*) for storage and reuse. If serotonin is reabsorbed too quickly, there is less available to the brain, which may result in depression.

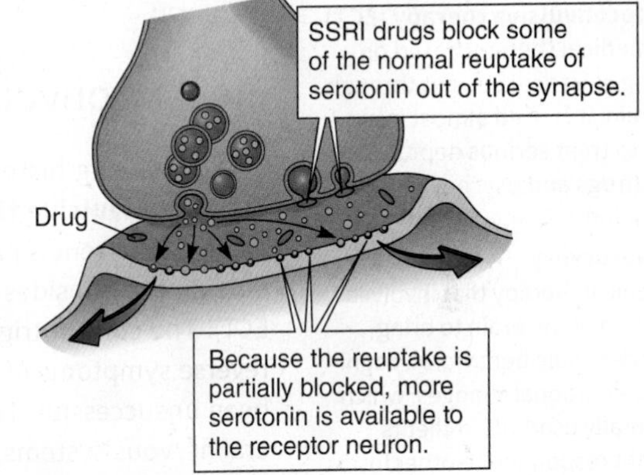

c. Partial blockage of reuptake by SSRIs
SSRIs, like Prozac, partially block the normal reuptake of excess serotonin, which leaves more serotonin molecules free to stimulate receptors on the receiving neuron. This increased neural transmission restores the normal balance of serotonin in the brain.

levels of neurotransmitters in the brain (**Figure 13.12**). Surprisingly, recent research has found that the drug *ketamine,* a dangerous date rape/party drug, called "Special K," also works to manage the symptoms of major depression, suicidal behaviors, and bipolar disorders. Widely known in the medical field for its anesthetic properties, ketamine changes the levels of brain neurotransmitters and appears to decrease thoughts of suicide because it targets parts of the brain responsible for executive and emotional processing (Lee et al., 2016). Due to its antisuicide effects, rapid onset, high efficacy, and good tolerability, ketamine shows promise as a potential treatment for depression and bipolar disorders (Kishimoto et al., 2016; Li et al., 2016; Reardon, 2015). However, it remains controversial due to the relative lack of empirical evidence, some serious side effects, and the potential for abuse (Zhang et al., 2016). For additional, intriguing (and controversial) psychotherapeutic drug research, see the following **Real World Psychology** feature.

In addition to correcting imbalances in the brain's neurotransmitters, other studies suggest that psychotherapeutic drugs, primarily antidepressants, may relieve depression and thoughts of suicide in three additional ways. They increase *neurogenesis,* the production of new neurons, or *synaptogenesis,* the production of new synapses, and/or they stimulate activity in various areas of the brain (Miller & Hen, 2015; Samuels et al., 2016; Walker et al., 2015).

Real World **Psychology**—Understanding the World

Do Psychedelic Drugs Cause Psychosis?

Beginning in the 1960s, there was considerable debate and widespread reports of "acid casualties," and increased incidents of mental health disorders among people who experimented with popular psychedelics, such as LSD, psilocybin (the active ingredient in "magic mushrooms"), and mescaline (found in the peyote cactus). As you may know, these drugs have been illegal in the United States since 1970 and are classified as schedule 1 drugs—"the most dangerous drugs" with no medicinal use.

Interestingly, two recent studies contradict these earlier assumptions. In the first study, researchers analyzed data from more than 135,000 people who took part in the annual U.S. National Survey on Drug Use and Health (NSDUH) conducted from 2008 to 2011 (Johansen & Krebs, 2015). Of the 14% who reported use of psyche-
[Q5] delics, the researchers found no increased risk of mental disorders, including schizophrenia, anxiety disorders, psychosis, depression, and suicide attempts. The second study, which analyzed 190,000 NSDUH respondents from 2008 to 2012, also found no link between psychedelic use and adverse mental health outcomes (Hendricks et al., 2015a). In fact, both studies suggested that psychedelic drug use may have produced lasting positive improvements in mental health. Other researchers have reviewed clinical trials, many that were double-blind and placebo-controlled, that showed positive relief of anxiety and depression in cancer patients and similar benefits with both alcohol and nicotine addiction, as well as in the prevention of suicide (dos Santos et al., 2016; Hendricks et al., 2015b; Nichols, 2016).

What do you think? Should psychedelics be used to treat physical and mental illnesses? Is this recent interest in psychedelics a flashback or a flash-in-the-pan? Only further research can fully answer these questions. (In the meantime, please remember that our inclusion of this research on psychedelics is not a recommendation for their use—either medically or recreationally.)

Electroconvulsive therapy (ECT) A biomedical therapy based on passing electrical current through the brain; it is used almost exclusively to treat serious depression when drugs and psychotherapy have failed.

Psychosurgery A form of biomedical therapy that involves alteration of the brain to bring about desirable behavioral, cognitive, or emotional changes, which is generally used when clients have not responded to other forms of treatment.

Electroconvulsive Therapy and Psychosurgery

There is a long history of using electrical stimulation to treat psychological disorders. In **electroconvulsive therapy (ECT)**, also known as electroshock therapy (EST), a moderate electrical current is passed through the brain. This can be done by placing electrodes on the outside of both sides of the head (bilateral ECT), or on only one side of the head (unilateral ECT). The current triggers a widespread firing of neurons, or brief seizures. ECT can quickly reverse symptoms of certain mental illnesses and often works when other treatments have been unsuccessful. The electric current produces many changes in the central and peripheral nervous systems, including activation of the autonomic nervous system, increased secretion of various hormones and neurotransmitters, and changes in the blood–brain barrier (**Figure 13.13**).

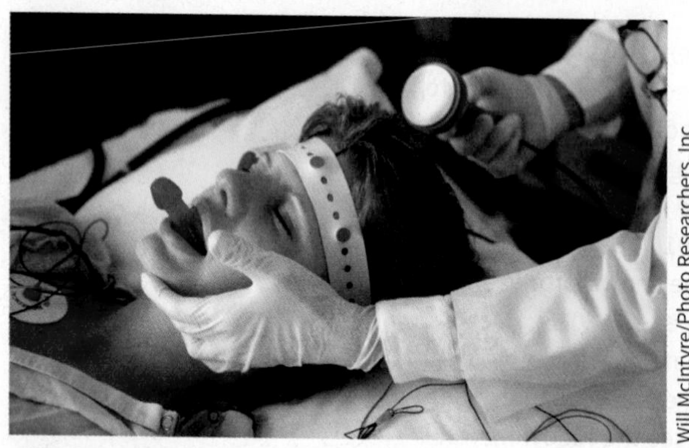

FIGURE 13.13 Electroconvulsive therapy (ECT) Modern ECT treatments are conducted with considerable safety precautions, including muscle-relaxant drugs that dramatically reduce muscle contractions, and medication to help clients sleep through the procedure. Note, however, that ECT is used less often today, and generally only when other treatments have failed, due to possibly serious side effects.

Despite not knowing exactly how ECT works, and the possibility that it may cause some short-term and long-term memory problems, the risks of untreated, severe depression are generally considered greater than the risks of ECT (Andrade et al., 2016; Berman & Prudic, 2013). Today it's used almost exclusively to treat serious depression when drugs and psychotherapy have failed, or in cases where rapid response is needed—as is the case with suicidal clients (Fligelman et al., 2016; Kellner et al., 2015; Vallejo-Torres et al., 2015).

The most extreme, and least used, biomedical therapy is **psychosurgery**—brain surgery performed to reduce serious debilitating psychological problems. Attempts to change disturbed thoughts, feelings, and behavior by altering the brain have a long history. In Roman times, for example, it was believed that a sword wound to the head could relieve insanity. In 1936, Portuguese neurologist Egaz Moniz first treated uncontrollable psychoses with a form of psychosurgery called a **lobotomy**, in which he cut the nerve fibers between the frontal lobes (where association areas for monitoring and planning behavior are found) and the thalamus and hypothalamus. Although these surgeries did reduce emotional outbursts and aggressiveness, some clients were left with debilitating brain damage.

Lobotomy An outmoded neurosurgical procedure for mental disorders, which involved cutting nerve pathways between the frontal lobes and the thalamus and hypothalamus.

Real World **Psychology**—Understanding the World

A Modern Alternative to Lobotomies

Two of the most notable examples of the damage from early lobotomies are Rosemary Kennedy, the sister of President John F. Kennedy, and Rose Williams, sister of American playwright Tennessee Williams. Both women were permanently incapacitated from lobotomies performed in the early 1940s. Thankfully, in the mid-1950s, when antipsychotic drugs came into use, psychosurgery virtually stopped.

Evaluating Biomedical Therapies

Like all other forms of therapy, biomedical therapies have both proponents and critics.

Psychopharmacology Drug therapy has been criticized on several grounds. First, although drugs may relieve symptoms for some people, they seldom provide cures and some individuals become physically dependent. In addition, psychiatric medications can cause a variety of side effects, ranging from mild fatigue to severe impairments in memory and movement.

It's important to note that drug therapy is more effective when combined with talk therapy. For example, researchers have examined whether children and teenagers experiencing clinical depression would benefit from receiving cognitive behavioral therapy (CBT) along with medication to treat this disorder. In one study, 75 youths (ages 8 to 17) received either an antidepressant alone, or an antidepressant along with CBT for 6 months (Kennard et al., 2014). Of those who received only the drug, 26.5% experienced depression, compared to only 9% of those who received the drug as well as CBT.

In modern times, psychotherapeutic drugs have led to revolutionary changes in mental health. Before the use of drugs, some patients were destined to spend a lifetime in psychiatric institutions. Today, most improve enough to return to their homes and lead successful lives—if they continue to take their medications to prevent relapse.

Repetitive transcranial magnetic stimulation (rTMS) A biomedical treatment that uses repeated magnetic field pulses targeted at specific areas of the brain.

ECT ECT currently serves as a valuable last-resort treatment for severe depression. However, similar benefits may be available through the latest advances in **repetitive transcranial magnetic stimulation (rTMS)**, which uses an electromagnetic coil placed on the scalp. Unlike ECT, which uses electricity to stimulate parts of the brain, rTMS uses magnetic pulses (**Figure 13.14**). To treat depression, the coil is usually placed over the prefrontal cortex, a region linked to deeper parts of the brain that regulate mood. Currently, rTMS's advantages over ECT are still unclear, but studies have shown marked improvement in depression, and clients experience fewer side effects (Bakker et al., 2015; Yadollahpour et al., 2016; Zhang et al., 2015).

Psychosurgery Given that all forms of psychosurgery are generally irreversible and potentially dangerous with serious or even fatal side effects, some critics say that it should be banned altogether. For these reasons, psychosurgery is considered experimental and remains a highly controversial treatment.

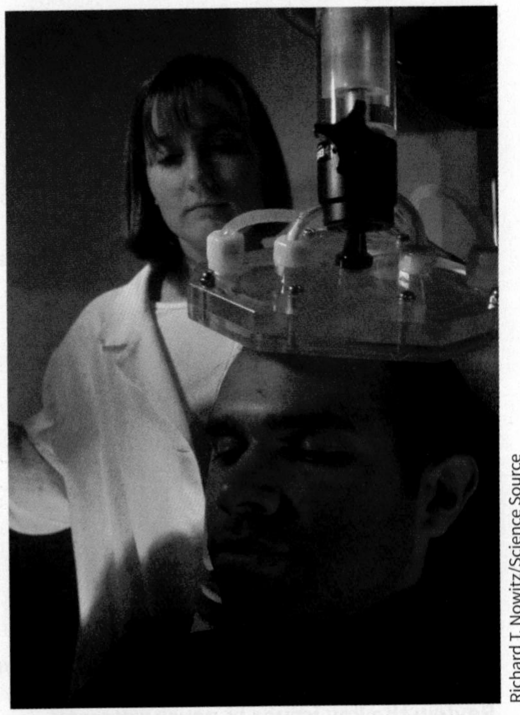

Richard T. Nowitz/Science Source

FIGURE 13.14 Repetitive transcranial magnetic stimulation (rTMS) Powerful electromagnets generate pulsed magnetic fields that are targeted at specific areas of the brain to treat depression.

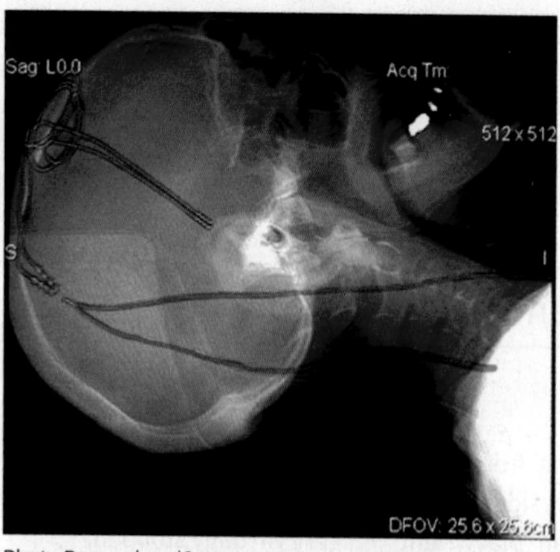

Photo Researchers/Getty Images

FIGURE 13.15 Deep brain stimulation (DBS) Stimulation from the implanted electrodes in the client's brain may bring relief to those suffering from Parkinson's disease, epilepsy, major depression, and other disorders.

Recently, psychiatrists have been experimenting with a much more limited and precise neurosurgical procedure called *deep brain stimulation (DBS)*. The surgeon drills two tiny holes into the skull, and implants electrodes in the area of the brain believed to be associated with a specific disorder (**Figure 13.15**). These electrodes are then connected to a "pacemaker" implanted in the chest or stomach that sends low-voltage electricity to the problem areas in the brain. Over time, this repeated stimulation can bring about significant improvement in Parkinson's disease, epilepsy, major depression, and other disorders (Fields, 2015; Kim et al., 2016; Lipsman et al., 2015). Research has also shown that clients who receive DBS along with antidepressants show lower rates of depression than those who receive either treatment alone (Brunoni et al., 2013).

Retrieval Practice 13.3 | Biomedical Therapies

SELF-TEST Completing this self-test, and then checking your answers by clicking on the answer button or by looking in Appendix B, will provide immediate feedback and helpful practice for exams.

1. The study of the effects of drugs on behavior and mental processes is known as ____.
   a. psychiatry **b.** psychoanalysis
   c. psychosurgery **d.** psychopharmacology
2. The effectiveness of antipsychotic drugs is thought to result primarily from decreasing activity at the ____ receptors.
   a. serotonin **b.** dopamine
   c. epinephrine **d.** all these options
3. In electroconvulsive therapy (ECT), ____.
   a. current is never applied to the left hemisphere
   b. seizures activate the central and peripheral nervous systems, stimulate hormone and neurotransmitter release, and change the blood–brain barrier
   c. convulsions are extremely painful and long lasting
   d. most clients receive hundreds of treatments because it is safer than in the past
4. ECT is used primarily to treat ____.
   a. phobias **b.** conduct disorders
   c. severe depression **d.** schizophrenia
5. The original form of psychosurgery developed by Egaz Moniz disconnected the ____ lobes from the thalamus and hypothalamus.
   a. occipital **b.** parietal
   c. temporal **d.** frontal

Think Critically

1. Are the potential benefits of psychopharmacology worth the risks? Is it ever ethical to force someone to take drugs to treat his or her mental illness?
2. If you, or someone you loved, were seriously depressed would you be in favor of ECT? Why or why not?

Real World Psychology

Do psychedelic drugs cause psychosis?

© Archive Image/Alamy StockPhoto

HINT: LOOK IN THE MARGIN FOR **[Q5]**

13.4 Psychotherapy in Perspective

LEARNING OBJECTIVES

Retrieval Practice While reading the upcoming sections, respond to each Learning Objective in your own words.

Review the key issues in psychotherapy.

- **Summarize** the goals and overall effectiveness of psychotherapy.
- **Describe** group, marital, family, and telehealth/electronic therapies.
- **Identify** the key cultural and gender issues important in therapy.
- **Summarize** the major career options for someone interested in becoming a therapist.

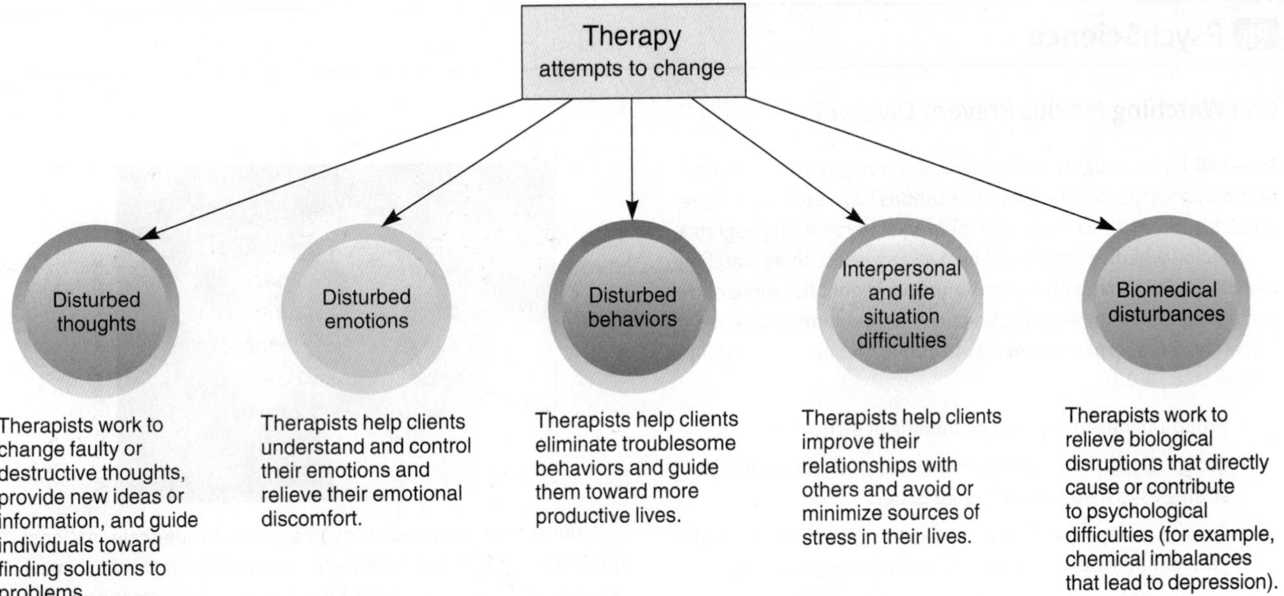

Therapy
attempts to change
Disturbed thoughts
Disturbed emotions
Disturbed behaviors
Interpersonal and life situation difficulties
Biomedical disturbances
Therapists work to change faulty or destructive thoughts, provide new ideas or information, and guide individuals toward finding solutions to problems.
Therapists help clients understand and control their emotions and relieve their emotional discomfort.
Therapists help clients eliminate troublesome behaviors and guide them toward more productive lives.
Therapists help clients improve their relationships with others and avoid or minimize sources of stress in their lives.
Therapists work to relieve biological disruptions that directly cause or contribute to psychological difficulties (for example, chemical imbalances that lead to depression).

FIGURE 13.16 **The five most common goals of therapy** Most therapies focus on one or more of these five goals. Can you identify which would be of most interest to psychodynamic, humanistic, cognitive, and behavioristic therapists?

It's currently estimated that there are more than 1,000 approaches to psychotherapy, and the number is continuing to rise (Gaudiano et al., 2015; Magnavita & Anchin, 2014). Given this high number, and wide variety of approaches, how would you choose one for yourself or someone you know? In the first part of this section, we discuss five goals common to all psychotherapies. Then we explore specific formats for therapy as well as considerations of culture and gender. Our aim is to help you synthesize the material in this chapter and put what you have learned about each of the major forms of therapy into a broader context.

Eclectic approach A perspective that combines elements of various therapies to find the most appropriate treatment; also known as integrative therapy.

Therapy Goals and Effectiveness

All major forms of therapy are designed to help the client in five specific areas (**Figure 13.16**).

Although most therapists work with clients in several of these areas, the emphasis varies according to the therapist's training and whether it is psychodynamic, cognitive, humanistic, behaviorist, or biomedical. Clinicians who regularly borrow freely from various theories are said to take an **eclectic approach**.

Does therapy work? After years of controlled studies and *meta-analysis*—a method of statistically combining and analyzing data from many studies—researchers have fairly clear evidence that it does. As you can see in **Figure 13.17**, early meta-analytic reviews combined studies of almost 25,000 people and found that the average person who received treatment was better off than 75% of the untreated control clients (Smith et al., 1980; Smith & Glass, 1977).

Studies also show that short-term treatments can sometimes be as effective as long-term treatments and that most therapies are equally effective for various disorders (Battino, 2015; Braakmann, 2015; Lilliengren et al., 2016). Even informal therapy techniques, like watching romantic comedies, have led to increased marital satisfaction (see **PsychScience**).

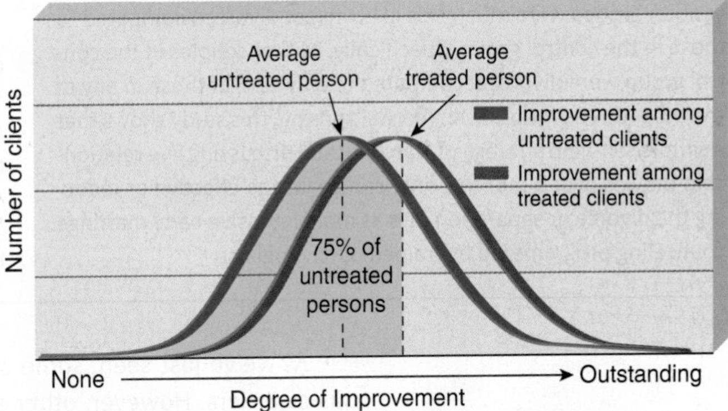

FIGURE 13.17 **Is therapy generally effective?** The average person who receives therapy is better off after it than a similar person who does not get treatment (Lilliengren et al., 2016; Smith et al., 1980; Smith & Glass, 1977). An analysis of more than 435 studies on the effectiveness of therapy for treating psychological disorders in children and adolescents revealed that therapy can lead to improvements in many different types of psychological disorders, including anxiety, autism, depression, disruptive behavior, eating problems, substance use, and traumatic stress (Chorpita et al., 2011).

PS PsychScience

Can Watching Movies Prevent Divorce?

As we all know, roughly half of all U.S. marriages end in divorce. Numerous secular and religious institutions have attempted to reduce this rate with various early marriage intervention programs. To examine whether simple self-help strategies, such as watching and discussing movies about relationships, might offer some of the same benefits as these professionally led intervention programs, researchers randomly assigned 174 couples to one of four groups (Rogge et al., 2013):

- Group 1 (control) received no training or instructions.
- Group 2 (conflict management) learned active listening strategies to help discuss heated issues.
- Group 3 (compassion and acceptance training) learned strategies for finding common ground and showing empathy.
- Group 4 (minimal intervention—movie and talk) attended a 10-minute lecture on relationship awareness and how watching couples in movies could help increase awareness of their own behaviors.

Following this initial assignment to groups, Group 1 received no training at all, but members of this group were similar to those in the three other groups in terms of age, education, ethnicity, relationship satisfaction, and other dimensions. Groups 2 and 3 attended weekly lectures, completed homework assignments, and met with a trained therapist periodically. In contrast, Group 4 only attended a 10-minute lecture, watched a romantic comedy, and then discussed 12 questions about the screen couple's interactions (such as, "Did they try using humor to keep things from getting nasty?"). They were then sent home with a list of 47 relationship-oriented movies and allowed to choose their favorite one to watch and discuss once a week for the next month.

The researchers then followed up with all couples 3 years later to see which of these approaches was most effective for preventing divorce. Much to their surprise, couples in all three of the intervention groups were much less likely to get divorced compared to those in the control group. Specifically, 24% of couples in the control group were divorced, compared to only 11% of those in any of the other three groups. Even more surprising, this study shows that a simple self-help strategy of watching and discussing five relationship movies over 1 month's time can be just as effective at reducing the divorce or separation rate as more intensive early marriage counseling programs led by trained psychologists.

MAD_Production / Shutterstock

Do you see how this study has exciting wide-scale, national applications? If "movie date night" can double as therapy, many U.S. couples might be saved from the very high emotional and financial costs of divorce. What about your own current or future relationships? If simply sharing and discussing a relationship movie now and then with your romantic partner might strengthen that relationship, why not try it? You can learn more about this study (and see a list of recommended movies with guided discussion questions) at: www.couples-research.com.

Research Challenge

1. Based on the information provided, did this study (Rogge et al., 2013) use descriptive, correlational, and/or experimental research?
2. If you chose:
   - *descriptive research*, is this a naturalistic observation, survey/interview, case study, and/or archival research?
   - *correlational research*, is this a positive, negative, or zero correlation?
   - *experimental research*, label the IV, DV, experimental group(s), and control group.
   - both *descriptive* and *correlational*, answer the corresponding questions for both.

Check your answers by clicking on the answer button or by looking in Appendix B.

Note: The information provided in this study is admittedly limited, but the level of detail is similar to what is presented in most textbooks and public reports of research findings. Answering these questions, and then comparing your answers to those provided, will help you become a better critical thinker and consumer of scientific research.

As we've just seen, some studies find that most therapies are equally effective for various disorders. However, other studies suggest that certain disorders are better treated with specific approaches. For example, anxiety disorders seem to respond best to exposure-based CBT, whereas symptoms of schizophrenia can be significantly relieved with medication (Bullis & Hofmann, 2016; Gillihan & Foa, 2016; Iglesias et al., 2016; Short & Thomas, 2015).

Finally, in recent years, the *empirically supported*, or *evidence-based practice* (*EBP*), *movement* has been gaining momentum because it seeks to identify which therapies have received the clearest research support for particular disorders (Gaudiano et al., 2015; Gray et al., 2015; Hamilton et al., 2016). Like all other movements, it has been criticized, but this type of empirically based research promises to be helpful for therapists and clients alike in their treatment decisions. For specific tips on finding a therapist for yourself or a loved one, see the following **Psychology and You**.

Psychology and **You**—Understanding Yourself

Choosing a Therapist

How do you find a good therapist for your specific needs? If you have the time (and money) to explore options, there are several steps you can take to find a therapist best suited to your specific goals. First, you might consult your psychology instructor, college counseling system, or family physician for specific referrals. In addition, most HMOs and health insurers provide lists of qualified professionals. Next, call the referred therapists and ask for an opportunity to discuss some questions. You could ask what their training was like, what approach they use, what their fees are, and whether they participate in your insurance plan.

Finding a therapist takes time and energy. If you need immediate help—you're having suicidal thoughts or are the victim of abuse—you should see if your community is one of the many that have medical hospital emergency services and telephone hotlines that provide counseling services on a 24-hour basis. In addition, most colleges and universities have counseling centers that provide immediate, short-term therapy to students free of charge.

Finally, if you're concerned about a friend or family member who might need therapy, you can follow the tips above to help locate a therapist and then possibly offer to go with him or her on their first appointment. If the individual refuses help and the problem affects you, it is often a good idea to seek therapy yourself. You will gain insights and skills that will help you deal with the situation more effectively.

For general help in locating a skilled therapist, identifying what types of initial questions to ask, learning how to gain the most benefits during therapy, and so on, consult the American Psychological Association (APA) website.

Think Critically

1. If you were looking for a therapist, would you want the therapist's gender to be the same as yours? Why or why not?
2. Do you think all insurance companies should be required to offer mental health coverage? Why or why not?

Therapy Formats

The therapies described earlier in this chapter are conducted primarily in a face-to-face, therapist-to-client format. In this section, we focus on several major alternatives: *group*, *family*, and *marital therapies*, which treat multiple individuals simultaneously, and *telehealth/electronic therapy*, which treats individuals via the Internet, e-mail, and/or smartphones.

Group Therapies In **group therapies**, multiple people meet together to work toward therapeutic goals. Typically, a group of 8 to 10 people meet with a therapist on a regular basis to talk about problems in their lives.

A variation on group therapy is the **self-help group**. Unlike other group approaches, self-help groups are not guided by a professional. They are simply circles of people who share a common problem, such as alcoholism, obesity, or breast cancer, and who meet to give and receive support. Programs such as Alcoholics Anonymous, Narcotics Anonymous, and Spenders Anonymous are examples of self-help groups. Although group members don't get the same level of individual attention found in one-on-one therapies, group and self-help therapies provide their own unique advantages (Bateganya et al., 2015; Castillo et al., 2016). They are far less expensive than one-on-one therapies and provide a broader base of social support. Group members also can learn from each other's experiences, share insights and coping strategies, and role-play social interactions together.

For example, researchers have studied group sessions in 12-step programs, like Alcoholics Anonymous, and they've found that people suffering from a combination of social anxiety disorders and substance abuse disorders, as well as recovering alcoholics, all show lower rates of relapse than those who don't participate in these self-help groups. This is particularly true if they also provide help to others (Pagano et al., 2013, 2015). In sum, research on self-help groups for alcoholism, obesity, and other disorders suggests that they can be very effective, either alone or in addition to individual psychotherapy (Kendra et al., 2015; McGillicuddy et al., 2015; O'Farrell et al., 2016). Keep in mind that therapists often recommend these alternative formats, such as group therapy, to their clients as an additional resource, while continuing their individual therapy.

Group therapies A form of therapy in which a number of people with similar concerns meet together to work toward therapeutic goals.

Self-help group A leaderless or non-professionally guided group in which members assist each other with a specific problem, as in Alcoholics Anonymous.

Marital and Family Therapies Given that a family or marriage is a system of interdependent parts, the problem of any one individual inevitably affects everyone. Therefore, all members are potential beneficiaries of therapy (Gunn et al., 2015; McGeorge et al., 2015; Smith,

© vgajic/iStockphoto

FIGURE 13.18 Family therapy Many families initially come into therapy believing that one member is the cause of all their problems. However, family therapists often find that this "identified client" is a scapegoat for deeper disturbances. How could changing ways of interacting within the family system promote the health of individual family members and the family as a whole?

2016). The line between family and marital or couples therapy is often blurred. Here, our discussion will focus on *family therapy*, in which the primary aim is to change maladaptive family interaction patterns (**Figure 13.18**). All members of the family attend therapy sessions, though at times the therapist may see family members individually or in twos or threes.

Family therapy is useful in treating a number of disorders and clinical problems. For example, the therapist can help families improve their communication styles and reframe their problems as a family issue versus an individual one. It can also be the most favorable setting for the treatment of adolescent substance abuse and eating disorders (Dodge, 2016; Horigian & Szapocnik, 2015; Kanbur & Harrison, 2016).

Telehealth/Electronic Therapy

Today millions of people are receiving advice and professional therapy in newer, electronic formats, such as the Internet, e-mail, virtual reality (VR), and interactive web-based conference systems such as Skype. This latest form of electronic therapy, often referred to as *telehealth*, allows clinicians to reach more clients and provide them with greater access to information regarding their specific problems (see the following **Real World Psychology** feature).

Real World **Psychology**—Understanding the World

Therapy—Is There an App for That?

Studies have long shown that therapy outcomes improve with increased client contact, and the electronic/telehealth format may be the easiest and most cost-effective way to increase this contact (Acierno et al., 2016; Bush et al., 2015; Gray et al., 2015). For example, when the effectiveness of cognitive behavioral therapy [Q6] delivered over the telephone was compared to the effectiveness of in-person visits for clients with major depressive disorder, researchers found that those who received phone therapy showed less improvement than those who received face-to-face therapy. However, the phone therapy clients were more likely to continue with therapy over time (Mohr et al., 2012).

© Doyeol Ahn/iStockphoto

Using electronic options such as the Internet and smartphones does provide alternatives to traditional one-on-one therapies, but, as you might expect, these unique approaches also raise concerns. Professional therapists fear, among other things, that without interstate and international licensing, or a governing body to regulate this type of therapy, there are no means to protect clients from unethical practices or incompetent therapists. What do you think? Would you be more likely to participate in therapy if it were offered via your smartphone, e-mail, or a website? Or is this too impersonal for you?

Cultural Issues in Therapy

The therapies described in this chapter are based on Western European and North American culture. Does this mean they are unique? Or do these psychotherapists accomplish some of the same things that, say, a native healer or shaman does? When we look at therapies in all cultures, we find that they have certain key features in common (Barnow & Balkir, 2013; Braakmann, 2015; Hall & Ibaraki, 2016):

- **Naming the problem** People often feel better just knowing that others experience the same problem and that the therapist has had experience with it.

- **Demonstrating the right qualities** Clients must feel that the therapist is caring, competent, approachable, and concerned with finding solutions to their problems.
- **Establishing credibility** Word-of-mouth testimonials and status symbols, such as diplomas on the wall, establish a therapist's credibility. A native healer may earn credibility by serving as an apprentice to a revered healer.
- **Placing the problem in a familiar framework** Some cultures believe evil spirits cause psychological disorders, so therapy is directed toward eliminating these spirits. Similarly, in cultures that emphasize the importance of early childhood experiences and the unconscious mind as the cause of mental disorders, therapy will be framed around these familiar issues.
- **Applying techniques to bring relief** In all cultures, therapy includes action. Either the client or the therapist must do something, and what the therapist does must fit the client's expectations—whether it is performing a ceremony to expel demons or talking with the client about his or her thoughts and feelings.
- **Meeting at a special time and place** The fact that therapy occurs outside the client's everyday experiences seems to be an important feature of all therapies.

Although there are basic similarities in therapies across cultures, there are also important differences. In the traditional Western European and North American model, the emphasis is on the client's self and on his or her having independence and control over his or her life—qualities that are highly valued in individualistic cultures. In collectivist cultures, however, the focus of therapy is on interdependence and the acceptance of life realities (Epstein et al., 2014; Lee et al., 2015; Seay & Sun, 2016). See the following **Real World Psychology**.

Real World **Psychology**—Understanding the World

Emphasizing Interdependence

In Japanese Naikan therapy, clients sit quietly from 5:30 a.m. to 9:00 p.m. for seven days and are visited by an interviewer every 90 minutes. During this time, they reflect on their relationships with others in order to discover personal guilt for having been ungrateful and troublesome and to develop gratitude toward those who have helped them (Itoh & Hikasa, 2014; Zhang et al., 2014).

Sky Bonillo/PhotoEdit

Not only does culture affect the types of therapy that are developed, but it also influences the perceptions of the therapist. What one culture considers abnormal behavior may be quite common—and even healthy—in others. For this reason, recognizing cultural differences is very important for building trust between therapists and clients and for effecting behavioral change (La Roche et al., 2015; Strauss et al., 2015; Weiler et al., 2015).

Gender and Therapy

In our individualistic Western culture, men and women present different needs and problems to therapists. Research has identified four unique concerns related to gender and psychotherapy (Moulding, 2016; O'Neil, 2015; Sáenz Herrero, 2015; Zerbe Enns et al., 2015):

1. **Rates of diagnosis and treatment of mental disorders** Women are diagnosed and treated for mental illness at a much higher rate than men. Are women "sicker" than men as a group, or are they just more willing to admit their problems? Or are the categories of illness biased against women? More research is needed to answer these questions.
2. **Stresses of poverty** Women are disproportionately likely to be poor. Poverty contributes to stress, which is directly related to many psychological disorders.

3. **Violence against women** Rape, incest, and sexual harassment—which are much more likely to happen to women than to men—may lead to depression, insomnia, posttraumatic stress disorder, eating disorders, and other problems.
4. **Stresses of multiple roles and gender-role conflict** Despite the many changes in gender roles in modern times, restrictive definitions of femininity and masculinity still limit both genders' well-being and human potential. Furthermore, most men and women today serve in many roles, as family members, students, wage earners, and so forth. The conflicting demands of their multiple roles often create special stresses unique to each gender.

Therapists must be sensitive to possible connections between clients' problems and their gender. Rather than just emphasizing drugs to relieve depression, it may be more appropriate for therapists to explore ways to relieve the stresses of multiple roles or poverty for both women and men. Can you see how helping a single parent identify parenting resources, such as play groups, parent support groups, and high-quality child care, might be just as effective at relieving depression as prescribing drugs? In the case of men, how might relieving loneliness or depression help decrease their greater problems with substance abuse and aggression?

If you've enjoyed this section on cultural and gender issues in therapy, as well as the earlier description of the various forms and formats of psychotherapy, you may be considering a possible career as a therapist. If so, see **Table 13.3**.

TABLE 13.3 Careers in Mental Health

Most colleges have counseling or career centers with numerous resources and trained staff to help you with your career choices. To give you an overview of the general field of psychotherapy, we've included a brief summary of the major types of mental health professionals, their degrees, required education beyond the bachelor's degree, job description, and type of training.

MAJOR TYPES OF MENTAL HEALTH PROFESSIONALS

Occupational Title	Degree	Nature of Training
Clinical psychologists	PhD (doctor of philosophy) PsyD (doctor of psychology)	Most clinical psychologists have a doctoral degree with training in research and clinical practice, and a supervised one-year internship in a psychiatric hospital or mental health facility. As clinicians, they work with client suffering from mental disorders, but many also work in colleges and universities as teachers and researchers, in addition to having their own private practice.
Counseling psychologists	MA (master of arts) PhD (doctor of philosophy) PsyD (doctor of psychology) EdD (doctor of education)	Counseling psychologists typically have a doctoral degree with training that focuses on less severe mental disorders, such as emotional, social, vocational, educational, and health-related concerns. In addition to providing psychotherapy, other career paths are open, such as teaching, research, and vocational counseling.
Pastoral counselor	None MA (master of arts) PhD (doctor of philosophy) DD (doctor of divinity)	Pastoral counselors combine spiritual advice and psychotherapy, and generally must hold a license and at least a master's or doctoral degree in their field of study. They typically work for counseling centers, churches, community programs, and hospitals.
Psychiatrists	MD (doctor of medicine)	After four years of medical school, an internship and residency in psychiatry are required, which includes supervised practice in psychotherapy techniques and biomedical therapies. In most states in the United States, psychiatrists, because they are M.D.s, are the only mental health specialists who can regularly prescribe drugs.
Psychiatric nurses	RN (registered nurse) MA (master of arts) PhD (doctor of philosophy)	Psychiatric nurses usually have a bachelor's or master's degree in nursing, followed by advanced training in the care of patients in hospital settings, and clients in mental health facilities.
Psychiatric social workers	MSW (master's in social work) DSW (doctor of social work) PhD (doctor of philosophy)	Psychiatric social workers usually have a master's degree in social work, followed by advanced training and experience in hospitals or outpatient settings working with people who have psychological problems.
School psychologists	MA (master of arts) PhD (doctor of philosophy) PsyD (doctor of psychology) EdD (doctor of education)	School psychologists generally begin with a bachelor's degree in psychology, followed by graduate training in psychological assessment and counseling for school-related issues and problems.

Before going on, we'd like to leave this chapter on a positive note. The psychotherapy techniques we've discussed are generally directed toward improving psychological disorders. However, psychologists are also committed to enhancing overall well-being and daily psychological functioning. In line with that, we offer the following **PositivePsych**.

Well-being therapy (WBT) A newer form of psychotherapy aimed at enhancing psychological well-being by focusing on personal growth and noticing and savoring the positive aspects of life.

PP PositivePsych

Protecting Your Mental Health

As you've seen throughout this text, psychology focuses on three major areas—*thoughts, feelings,* and *actions*. Therefore, to increase your everyday well-being and protect your mental health, consider the following research-based positive psychology tips for each area:

1. **Recognize and control your thoughts.** Would you like to be happier and more often in a great mood? You might start by reviewing and implementing the suggestions in the *PositivePsych* happiness section in Chapter 10. In addition, as discussed earlier, the 3 Cs of Beck's cognitive therapy (catching, challenging, and changing our faulty thought processes) are key to successful therapy—as well as in everyday life. Research also finds that having a positive view of the future and an optimistic, attributional style are important to mental health (Krok, 2015; Roepke & Seligman, 2016; Sachsenweger et al., 2015). Depressed people often suffer from a *depressive attribution style* of thinking, which means that they typically attribute negative events to internal, stable, and global causes. For example, "I failed because I'm unlucky, I have been throughout my life, and it affects all parts of my life." The good news is that social connections with others, which we discuss later in this list, can reduce this type of thinking (Cruwys et al., 2015).

   In addition, there is a wealth of research on the power of meditation in recognizing and gaining control of your thought processes. As discussed in Chapter 3, *mindfulness-based stress reduction (MBSR)* is linked with numerous health benefits, from better concentration and physical health to improved mental well-being (Mitchell & Heads, 2015; Sampaio et al, 2016; Thomas et al., 2016).

2. **Acknowledge and express your feelings.** Although we all have negative emotions and conflicts that often need to be acknowledged and resolved, as a general rule, recognizing and expressing your *positive* emotions, particularly feelings of *gratitude*, has been found to be an important avenue to mental health (see again Chapter 10's *PositivePsych* happiness feature). Noting what you're thankful for — from your significant other to catching the bus or subway before the doors close—will definitely improve your ability to cope with life's challenges. Being grateful also tends to increase your personal self-esteem and overall well-being (Lin, 2015).

   Interestingly, **well-being therapy (WBT)**, which focuses on personal growth and noticing and savoring the positive aspects of our lives, has been successful in promoting overall mental health, as well as in increasing resilience and sustained recovery from several psychological disorders (Nierenberg et al., 2016; Ruini & Fava, 2014).

Blend Images - Ariel Skelley/Getty Images

   Empathy is equally important. As you recall from our earlier discussion of Roger's client-centered therapy, empathy involves being a sensitive listener who understands and shares another's inner experience. The good news is that when you're being empathic, you're not only improving another person's self-acceptance and mental health, but also your own. In fact, providing emotional support (empathy) to another is more important than practical, instrumental support in increasing the provider's well-being (Morelli et al., 2015). In short, compassionate sharing of feelings and experiences benefits both parties. Perhaps because it helps all of us to feel accepted and less alone during life's inevitable ups and downs.

   Finally, *love for yourself* may be the most important emotional key to protecting your mental health. Self-care and self-compassion are not "selfish!" Self-compassion refers to a kind and nurturing attitude toward yourself, and research shows that it is positively linked with psychological flexibility and well-being (Homan, 2016; Marshall & Brockman, 2016). In other words, prioritize your well-being. When you're feeling frustrated and overwhelmed, allow yourself to say "no." Along with all the resources for coping mentioned in Chapter 3, keep in mind that "no" is a complete sentence. You don't have to explain your reasons for taking care of and loving yourself.

3. **Recognize and change your behaviors.** As discussed in several chapters of this text, "simply" eating the right food, getting enough exercise and sleep, and spending time in nature are all important to our well-being and may help protect our mental health (Bell et al., 2015; Song et al., 2016; Wassing et al., 2016). For example, research finds that even moderate exercise—20 to 30 minutes of walking a day—can prevent episodes of depression in the long term (Mammen & Faulkerner, 2013). Other research suggests that moderate exercise may be as helpful as psychotherapy or antidepressants (Craft & Perna, 2004).

   A second behavioral change that increases psychological health is to make someone else feel good. Studies show that volunteering and expressing kindness to others has a cyclical effect—doing a good deed for others makes them happier, which in turns makes you happier (Anik et al., 2011; Xi et al., 2016)! As previously mentioned, spending time in nature is important to mental health, but it also unexpectedly increases our willingness to help. In a very simple field experiment, confederates (people who were part of the experiment) accidentally dropped a glove while walking in an urban green park filled with large trees, lawns, and flowers (Guéguen & Stefan, 2016). Researchers found that passersby who saw the dropping of the glove after walking through the park were far more likely to help by picking up the glove than those who had not yet entered the park.

Perhaps the most important action you can take to protect your mental health is to enjoy and maintain your social connections. For example, research shows that people who feel more connected to others have lower rates of anxiety and depression (McLeigh, 2015). For this and many other reasons, we need to remind ourselves to spend as much time as possible with our friends and loved ones, whether it's going on vacation or just watching a movie together.

Retrieval Practice 13.4 | Psychotherapy in Perspective

SELF-TEST Completing this self-test, and then checking your answers by clicking on the answer button or by looking in Appendix B, will provide immediate feedback and helpful practice for exams.

1. When therapists combine techniques from various therapies, they are said to be using ____.

a. psychosynthetic therapy
b. biomedical therapy
c. managed care
d. an eclectic approach

2. A(n) ____ group does not have a professional leader, and members assist each other in coping with a specific problem.

a. self-help **b.** encounter
c. peer **d.** behavior

3. ____ treats the family as a unit, and members work together to solve problems.

a. Aversion therapy **b.** An encounter group
c. A self-help group **d.** Family therapy

4. Which of the following is *not* a culturally universal feature of therapy?

a. Naming the problem
b. Demonstrating the right qualities
c. Establishing rapport among family members
d. Placing the problem in a familiar framework

5. A Japanese therapy designed to help clients discover personal guilt for having been ungrateful and troublesome to others and to develop gratitude toward those who have helped them is known as ____.

a. Kyoto therapy **b.** Okado therapy
c. Naikan therapy **d.** Nissan therapy

Think Critically

1. Which of the universal characteristics of therapists do you believe is the most important? Why?

2. If a friend were having marital problems, how would you convince him or her to go to a marriage or family therapist, using information you've gained in this chapter?

Real World Psychology

Can therapy that is delivered over the telephone lead to lower levels of depression?

© mikered/iStockphoto

HINT: LOOK IN THE MARGIN FOR **[Q6]**

Summary

13.1 Talk Therapies 363

- **Psychotherapy** refers to techniques employed to improve psychological functioning and promote adjustment to life. There are three general approaches to therapy—*talk, behavior, and biomedical.*
- In **psychoanalysis**, the therapist seeks to Identify the patient's unconscious conflicts and to help the patient resolve them. The five major techniques of psychoanalysis are **free association, dream analysis, analysis of resistance, analysis of transference,** and **interpretation.**
- In modern **psychodynamic therapy**, treatment is briefer, and the therapist takes a more directive approach (and puts less emphasis on unconscious childhood memories) than in traditional psychoanalysis.
- **Humanistic therapy** seeks to maximize personal growth, encouraging people to actualize their potential and relate to others in genuine ways.
- Rogers's client-centered therapy **emphasizes empathy, unconditional positive regard, genuineness,** and **active listening.**
- **Cognitive therapy** focuses on faulty thought processes and beliefs to treat problem behaviors. Through insight into negative **self-talk** (the unrealistic things people say to themselves), the therapist can use **cognitive restructuring** to challenge and change destructive thoughts or inappropriate behaviors.
- Ellis's **rational-emotive behavior therapy (REBT)** focuses on eliminating negative emotional reactions through logic, confrontation, and examination of irrational beliefs. In comparison, Beck's **cognitive-behavior therapy (CBT)** combines cognitive therapy (including changing faulty thinking) with behavior therapy (changing maladaptive behaviors).

13.2 Behavior Therapies 371

- In **behavior therapy**, the focus is on the problem behavior itself rather than on any underlying causes. The therapist uses learning principles to change behavior.
- Classical conditioning techniques include **systematic desensitization** and **aversion therapy**.
- Operant conditioning techniques used to increase adaptive behaviors include *shaping* and *reinforcement*.
- In **modeling therapy**, clients observe and imitate others who are performing the desired behaviors.

13.3 Biomedical Therapies 375

- **Biomedical therapies** are based on the premise that chemical imbalances or disturbed nervous system functioning contributes to problem behaviors.
- **Psychopharmacology** is the most common form of biomedical therapy. Major classes of drugs used to treat psychological disorders are **antianxiety drugs**, **antipsychotic drugs**, **mood stabilizer drugs**, and **antidepressant drugs**.
- In **electroconvulsive therapy (ECT)**, an electrical current is passed through the brain, stimulating seizures that produce changes in the central and peripheral nervous systems. ECT is used primarily in cases of severe depression that do not respond to other treatments.
- In **repetitive transcranial magnetic stimulation (rTMS)**, powerful electromagnets generate pulsed magnetic fields that are targeted at specific areas of the brain to treat depression.
- The most extreme biomedical therapy is **psychosurgery**. *Lobotomy*, an older form of psychosurgery, is now outmoded, and often replaced with a more limited and precise surgical procedure called *deep brain stimulation* (*DBS*).

13.4 Psychotherapy in Perspective 380

- All major forms of therapy are designed to address disturbed thoughts, disturbed emotions, disturbed behaviors, interpersonal and life situation difficulties, and biomedical disturbances.
- Many therapists take an **eclectic approach** and combine techniques from various theories. Research indicates that, overall, therapy does work.
- In **group therapy**, multiple people meet together to work toward therapeutic goals. A variation is the **self-help group**, which is not guided by a professional. Therapists often refer their clients to group therapy and self-help groups in order to supplement individual therapy.
- In marital and family therapy, the aim is to change maladaptive patterns of interaction. Given that a marriage or family is a system of interdependent parts, all members are encouraged to attend all therapy sessions, however, the therapist may see members individually or in twos or threes.
- Telehealth/electronic therapy allows clinicians to reach more clients and provide greater access to information. But, there are concerns about licensing, regulations, and abuses.
- Therapies in all cultures share some common features, as well as important differences. Therapists must be sensitive and responsive to possible gender issues and cultural differences in order to build trust with clients and effect behavioral change.

Applying **Real** World **Psychology**

We began this chapter with six intriguing Real World Psychology questions, and you were asked to revisit these questions at the end of each section. Questions like these have an important and lasting impact on all of our lives. See if you can answer these additional critical thinking questions related to real world examples.

1. In the 2013 movie *Side Effects*, Rooney Mara and Channing Tatum portray a successful young couple, Emily and Martin, whose entire world falls apart when Emily's psychiatrist prescribes a new (fictional) psychoactive drug called Ablixa to treat her anxiety. The true *side effects* of the drug, as well as the underlying motivations and mental health of the main characters, are revealed only during the film's final scenes. How might this film contribute to negative stereotypes of psychotherapy and psychopharmacology?
2. Given that advertising for the fictional drug in this *Side Effects* movie closely matches the ads for actual psychoactive drugs, what special dangers and applications does widespread advertising for psychotherapeutic drugs pose for the real world?
3. Can you think of a Hollywood film that offers a positive portrayal of psychotherapy and/or psychopharmacology?
4. You undoubtedly had certain beliefs and ideas about therapy before reading this chapter. Has studying this chapter changed any of those beliefs and ideas?

Snap Stills/Rex Features/AP Photos

5. Which form of therapy described in this chapter do you personally find most appealing? Why?

Key Terms

Retrieval Practice Write a definition for each term before turning back to the referenced page to check your answer.

- active listening 367
- aversion therapy 372
- behavior therapies 371
- biomedical therapies 375
- client-centered therapy 366
- cognitive restructuring 367
- cognitive therapies 367
- cognitive-behavior therapy (CBT) 369
- dream analysis 364
- eclectic approach 381
- electroconvulsive therapy (ECT) 378
- empathy 366
- free association 364
- genuineness 367
- group therapies 383
- humanistic therapies 366
- interpretation 365
- lobotomy 379
- modeling therapy 373
- mood-stabilizer drugs 000
- psychoanalysis 364
- psychodynamic therapies 365
- psychopharmacology 375
- psychosurgery 378
- psychotherapy 362
- rational-emotive behavior therapy (REBT) 368
- repetitive transcranial magnetic stimulation (rTMS) 379
- resistance 365
- self-help group 383
- systematic desensitization 372
- transference 365
- unconditional positive regard 366
- well-being therapy (WBT) 387

CHAPTER **14**

Social Psychology

Real World **Psychology**

Things you'll learn in Chapter 14

[Q1] Why do athletes often blame their losses on bad officiating?

[Q2] How can taking a pain pill reduce attitude change?

[Q3] Can reading books about Harry Potter increase positive feelings toward gay people?

[Q4] If popular high-school students are anti-bullying and anti-drinking, does that reduce these behaviors among their peers?

[Q5] Why are we so surprised when our preferred presidential candidate loses?

[Q6] How does simple nearness (proximity) influence attraction?

Throughout the chapter, margin icons for Q1–Q6 indicate where the text addresses these questions.

CHAPTER OUTLINE

Chapter Overview

For many students and psychologists, your authors included, *social psychology* is the most exciting of all fields because it's about you and me and because almost everything we do is *social*! Unlike earlier chapters that focused on individual processes, like sensation and perception, memory, or personality, this chapter studies how large social forces, such as groups, social roles, and norms, bring out the best and worst in all of us. It is organized around three central themes: *social cognition*, *social influence*, and *social relations*. We begin with social cognition and the study of attributions, attitudes, and prejudice. Then we look at social influence, with the subtopics of conformity, obedience and group processes. We close with an examination of social relations, which includes aggression, altruism, and interpersonal attraction. Before reading on, check the misconceptions you may have about these topics in the following **Psychology and You**.

Psychology and You—Understanding Yourself

Test Yourself | How Much Do You Know About the Social World?

True or False?

_____ **1.** Flirting is a powerful way to increase your attractiveness to a potential mate.

_____ **2.** Persuasion is the most effective way to change attitudes.

_____ **3.** Groups generally make riskier or more conservative decisions than a single individual does.

_____ **4.** People wearing masks are more likely than unmasked individuals to engage in aggressive acts.

_____ **5.** Emphasizing gender differences may create and perpetuate prejudice.

_____ **6.** Substance abuse (particularly alcohol abuse) is a major factor in aggression.

_____ **7.** When people are alone, they are more likely to help another individual than when they are in a group.

_____ **8.** Looks are the primary factor in our initial feelings of attraction, liking, and love.

_____ **9.** Opposites attract.

_____ **10.** Romantic love generally starts to fade after 6 to 30 months.

Jason Stitt/Shutterstock

_____ **11.** Punching a pillow when you're angry can make you feel even more upset.

_____ **12.** Female named hurricanes are more deadly than those with male names.

Answers: Two of these statements are false. You'll find the answers within this chapter.

14.1 Social Cognition

LEARNING OBJECTIVES

Retrieval Practice While reading the upcoming sections, respond to each Learning Objective in your own words.

Review the field of social psychology and its largest subfield, social cognition.

- **Define** social psychology and social cognition.
- **Discuss** the attributional process and its errors, biases, and cultural factors.
- **Identify** attitudes and their three components.
- **Summarize** how attitudes are formed and changed.
- **Discuss** prejudice, its three components, and the factors that increase or decrease it.

Social psychology The branch of psychology that studies how others influence our thoughts, feelings, and actions.

Social psychology, one of the largest branches in the field of psychology, focuses on how other people influence our thoughts, feelings, and actions. In turn, one of its largest and most important subfields, *social cognition*, examines the way we think about and interpret ourselves and others (Mikulincer et al., 2015a; Smith et al., 2015). In this section, we will look at three of the most important topics in social cognition—*attributions, attitudes*, and *prejudice*.

Attributions

Have you ever been in a serious argument with a loved one—perhaps a parent, close friend, or romantic partner? If so, how did you react? Were you overwhelmed with feelings of anger? Did you attribute the fight to the other person's ugly, mean temper and consider ending the relationship? Or did you calm yourself with thoughts of how he or she is normally a rational person and therefore must be unusually upset by something that happened at work or elsewhere?

Can you see how these two alternative explanations, or **attributions**, for the causes of behavior or events can either destroy or maintain relationships? The study of attributions is a major topic in social cognition and social psychology. Everyone wants to understand and explain why people behave as they do and why events occur as they do. Humans are known to be the only reason-seeking animals! But social psychologists have discovered another explanation: Developing logical attributions for people's behavior makes us feel safer and more in control (Heider, 1958; Lindsay et al., 2015). Unfortunately, our attributions are frequently marred by several attributional biases and errors.

Loren Fishman/www.CartoonStock.com

FIGURE 14.1 Attribution in action One explanation for the FAE is that human personalities and behaviors are more salient or noticeable than situational factors. Do you see how studying this text and taking your college psychology course enriches your study of the "real world?" Now you also have a label to explain the joke behind this cartoon.

Attributional Errors and Biases

Think back to the example above. Do you recognize that attributing the fight to the bad character of the other person without considering possible situational factors, like pressures at work, may be the result of your own misguided biases in thinking? Suppose a new student joins your class and seems distant, cold, and uninterested in interaction. It's easy to conclude that she's unfriendly, and maybe even "stuck-up"—a dispositional (personality) attribution. If you later saw her in a one-to-one interaction with close friends, you might be surprised to find that she is very warm and friendly. In other words, her behavior apparently depends on the situation. This bias toward personal, dispositional factors rather than situational factors in our explanations for others' behavior is so common that it is called the **fundamental attribution error (FAE)** (Hooper et al., 2015; Moran et al., 2014; Ross, 1977).

Attribution The explanations we make about the causes of behaviors or events.

Fundamental attribution error (FAE) The tendency of observers to overestimate the influence of internal, dispositional factors on a person's behavior, while underestimating the impact of external, situational factors.

One reason for the FAE is that human personalities and behaviors are more salient or noticeable than situational factors. The **saliency bias** helps explain why people sometimes suggest that homeless people begging for money "should just go out and get a job"—a phenomenon also called "blaming the victim." (See **Figure 14.1**.)

Unlike the FAE, which commonly occurs when we're explaining others' behaviors, the **self-serving bias** refers to attributions (explanations) we make for our own behavior. In this case, we tend to favor internal (personality) attributions for our successes and external (situational) attributions for our failures. This bias is motivated by our desire to maintain positive self-esteem and a good public image (Sharma & Shakeel, 2015; Wiggin & Yalch, 2015). For example, students often take personal credit for doing well on an exam. If they fail a test, however, they tend to blame the instructor, the textbook, or the "tricky" questions. Similarly, elite Olympic athletes more often attribute their wins to internal (personal) causes, such as their skill and effort, while attributing their losses to external (situational) causes, such as bad equipment or poor officiating—see the photo (Aldridge & Islam, 2012; Mackinnon et al., 2015). [Q1]

© RTimages/iStockphoto

How do we explain the discrepancy between the attributions we make for ourselves and those we make for others? According to the **actor–observer effect** (Jones & Nisbett, 1971), when examining our own behaviors, we are the *actors* in the situation and know more about our own intentions and behaviors and naturally look to the environment for explanations: "I didn't tip the waiter because I got really bad service." In contrast, when explaining the behavior of others, we are *observing* the actors and therefore tend to blame the person, using a personality attribution: "She didn't tip the waiter because she's cheap" (**Figure 14.2**).

Saliency bias A type of attributional bias in which people tend to focus on the most noticeable (salient) factors when explaining the causes of behavior.

Self-serving bias The tendency to credit success to internal, personality factors, while blaming failure on external, situational factors.

Actor–observer effect The tendency to attribute other people's behavior to personality factors, while seeing our own behavior as caused by the situation.

Culture and Attributional Biases

Both the fundamental attribution error and the self-serving bias may depend in part on cultural factors (Cullen et al., 2015; Kastanakis & Voyer, 2014; Khandelwal et al., 2014). In highly individualistic cultures, like the United States, people are defined and understood as individual selves, largely responsible for their own successes and failures.

In contrast, people in collectivistic cultures, like China and Japan, are primarily defined as members of their social network, responsible for doing as others expect. Accordingly, they tend to be more aware of situational constraints on behavior, making the FAE less likely (Bond, 2015; Matsumoto & Juang, 2013; Tang et al., 2014).

FIGURE 14.2 The actor-observer effect We tend to explain our own behavior in terms of external factors (situational attributions) and others' behavior in terms of their internal characteristics (dispositional attributions).

Actor

Situational attribution

Focuses attention on external factors

"I don't even like drinking beer, but it's the best way to meet women."

Christine Schneider/©Corbis

Observer

Dispositional attribution

Focuses on the personality of the actor

"He seems to always have a beer in his hand; he must have a drinking problem."

The self-serving bias is also much less common in collectivistic cultures because self-esteem is related not to doing better than others but to fitting in with the group (Anedo, 2014; Berry et al., 2011; Morris, 2015). In Japan, for instance, the ideal person is aware of his or her shortcomings and continually works to overcome them—rather than thinking highly of himself or herself (Heine & Renshaw, 2002; Shand, 2013). Would you like to reduce your own attributional biases? See the following **Psychology and You**.

Psychology and You—Understanding Yourself

Reducing Attributional Biases

The key to making more accurate attributions begins with determining whether a given action stems mainly from personality factors, or from the external situation. Unfortunately, we too often focus on internal, dispositional (personality) factors. Why? We all naturally take cognitive shortcuts (Chapter 8), and we each tend to have unique and enduring personality traits (Chapter 11). To offset this often misguided preference for internal attributions, we can ask ourselves these four questions:

1. *Is the behavior unique or shared by others*? If a large, or increasing, number of people are engaging in the same behavior, such as rioting or homelessness, it's most likely the result of external, situational factors.
2. *Is the behavior stable or unstable?* If someone's behavior is relatively enduring and permanent, it may be correct to make a stable, personality attribution. However, before giving up on a friend who is often quick-tempered and volatile, we may want to consider his or her entire body of personality traits. If he or she is also generous, kind, and incredibly devoted, we could overlook these imperfections.
3. *Was the cause of the behavior controllable or uncontrollable?* Innocent victims of crime, like rape or robbery, are too often blamed for their misfortune because they shouldn't have "been in that part of town," "walking alone," and/or "dressed in expensive clothes." Obviously, these are inaccurate and unfair personality attributions, as well as examples of "blaming the victim."
4. *What would I do in the same situation?* Given our natural tendency toward *self-serving* biases and the *actor-observer effect,* if we conclude that we would behave in the same way, the behavior is most likely the result of external, situational factors.

In sum, given our natural tendency to make internal, personality attributions, we can improve our judgments of others by erring in the opposite direction—looking first for external causes. Furthermore, "giving others the benefit of the doubt" will not only help us avoid attributional errors, it may even save, or at least improve, our relationships.

Attitudes

Attitude The learned predisposition to respond positively or negatively to a particular object, person, or event.

When we observe and respond to the world around us, we are seldom completely neutral. Rather, our responses toward subjects as diverse as pizza, gun control, and abortion reflect our **attitudes**, which are *learned* predispositions to respond positively or negatively to a particular object, person, or event. Social psychologists generally agree that most attitudes have three ABC components: *Affect* (feelings), *Behavior* (actions), and *Cognitions* (thoughts/beliefs) (**Figure 14.3**).

Attitude Formation As mentioned, we tend to learn our attitudes, and this learning generally occurs from direct instruction, through personal experiences, or by watching others. In some cases, these sources may differ, depending on our gender. For example, researchers

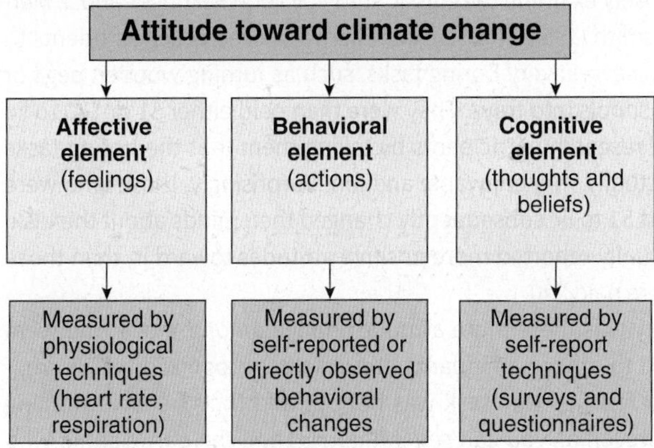

Tatiana Grozetskaya/Shutterstock

FIGURE 14.3 **Attitude formation** When social psychologists study attitudes, they measure each of the three ABC components: Affective, Behavioral, and Cognitive.

have found that teenage boys are more likely to learn sexual attitudes from media representations of sexual behavior, whereas teenage girls tend to learn their sexual attitudes from their mothers, as long as they feel close to their mothers (Vandenbosch & Eggermont, 2011).

Real World **Psychology**—Understanding the World

Health and Self-Image

Given the high prevalence of very thin women and lean, "ripped" men displayed on magazines, TV, and movies, it's easy to see why many people in our Western culture develop a shared preference for a certain, limited body type. Thankfully, research finds that just showing 100 women photographs of plus-size models (with a minimum clothing size of 16 and a BMI between 36 and 42) caused them to change their initial attitudes, which had been to prefer the thin ideal (Boothroyd et al., 2012). Can you see how ads that offer more realistic images, or the devastating effects of anorexia (like the two photos on the right), might improve the overall health and self-image of both men and women? Sadly, the model in the photo on the far right, Isabel Caro, died of anorexia at age 28.

JM5 WENN Photos/NewsCom

Agencia el Universal/El Universal de Mexico/NewsCom

Attitude Change Although attitudes begin to form in early childhood, they're obviously not permanent, a fact that advertisers and politicians know and exploit. As we've just seen in the study described in the **Real World Psychology** feature above, we can sometimes change attitudes through experiments. However, a much more common method is to make direct, persuasive appeals, such as in ads that say, "Friends Don't Let Friends Drive Drunk!"

Surprisingly, psychologists have identified an even more efficient strategy than persuasion. The strongest personal change comes when we notice contradictions between our thoughts, feelings, or actions—the three components of all attitudes. Such contradictions typically lead to a state of unpleasant psychological tension, known as **cognitive dissonance**. According to Leon Festinger's (1957) *cognitive disonance theory*, we all share a strong need for consistency among our thoughts, feelings, and actions, and when we notice inconsistencies we experience unpleasant dissonance. To relieve this discomfort we are highly motivated to change one or more of the three ABC components of our attitudes. For example, someone who is engaged to be married might notice a feeling of attraction to someone other than their intended spouse, and then might experience unpleasant tension from the contradiction (cognitive dissonance between their feelings of attraction and their belief that you should only feel that way about your spouse). To relieve the discomfort, they could break off the engagement, or, more appropriately, change their belief that feelings of attraction to others is normal and to be expected both before and after getting married.

Cognitive dissonance The unpleasant psychological tension we experience after noticing contradictions between our thoughts, feelings, and/or actions.

$1 Liars (Weak reason for lying)	→	High levels of cognitive dissonance	→	Large attitude change
$20 Liars (Strong reason for lying)	→	Low levels of cognitive dissonance	→	Little or no attitude change

FIGURE 14.4 Why cheap lies hurt more Note how lying for $20 creates less cognitive dissonance and less attitude change than lying for $1.

Given that cognitive dissonance is often an effective approach to attitude change in all our lives, it's important to fully understand it. Let's closely examine the classic study by Leon Festinger and J. Merrill Carlsmith (1959). These experimenters asked college students to perform several very boring tasks, such as turning wooden pegs or sorting spools into trays. They were then paid either $1 or $20 to lie to NEW research participants by telling them that the boring tasks were actually very enjoyable and fun. Surprisingly, those who were paid just $1 to lie subsequently changed their minds about the task, and actually reported more positive attitudes toward it, than those who were paid $20.

Why was there more attitude change among those who were paid only $1? All participants who lied to other participants presumably recognized the discrepancy between their initial beliefs and feelings (the task was boring) and their behavior (telling others it was enjoyable and fun). However, as you can see in **Figure 14.4**, the participants who were given insufficient monetary justification for lying (the $1 liars) apparently experienced greater *cognitive dissonance*. Therefore, to reduce their discomfort, they expressed more liking for the dull task, compared to those who received sufficient monetary justification (the $20 liars). This second group had little or no motivation to change their attitude—they lied for the money! (Note that in 1959, when the experiment was conducted, $20 would have been the economic equivalent of about $200 today.)

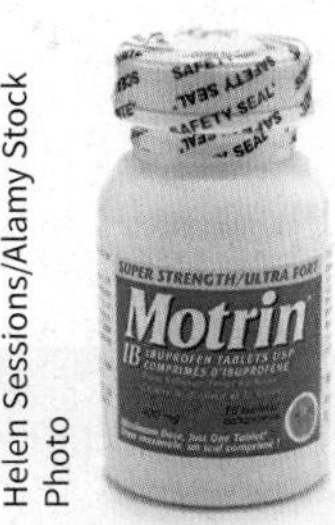

Helen Sessions/Alamy Stock Photo

Do you see the potential danger in how easily some participants in this classic study changed their thoughts and feelings about the boring task in order to match their behavior? Have you ever met someone whom you initially didn't like but you had to spend time with him or her and over time you actually began to like that person? Do you recognize how the initial discrepancy between your thoughts and feelings ("I'm an honest person but I'm pretending to like this person") might have led to cognitive dissonance, which in turn led to a change in your feelings?

Surprisingly, a clever experiment found that taking a simple pain killer, like the one in the photo, versus a placebo, can significantly reduce the amount of attitude change (DeWall et al., 2015). The acetaminophen reduced the individual's overall pain, including the discomfort
[Q2] created from *cognitive dissonance*, so the person was less motivated to change his or her attitude! One of our equally clever college students suggested that this experiment and cognitive dissonance theory might explain why everyone likes parties with lots of alcohol—it removes their sexual inhibitions! What do you think? Do you agree?

On a larger, national and international scale, consider how cognitive dissonance might help explain why military leaders keep sending troops to a seemingly endless war zone. They obviously can't change the actions that led to the initial loss of lives, so they may reduce their cognitive dissonance by replacing their previous cognitions (thoughts) that the loss of military lives is untenable, with a new cognition that the loss of military lives is justifiable because we're ultimately saving lives at home and/or in war-torn areas. Given the importance of this theory to your everyday life, be sure to carefully study **Process Diagram 14.1**.

Culture and Cognitive Dissonance

The experience of cognitive dissonance may depend on a distinctly Western way of thinking about and evaluating the self. As we mentioned earlier, people in Eastern cultures tend not to define themselves in terms of their individual accomplishments. For this reason, making a bad decision may not pose the same threat to self-esteem that it would in more individualistic cultures, such as the United States (Dessalles, 2011; Kokkoris & Kühnen, 2013; Na & Chan, 2015).

Prejudice

Prejudice A learned, unjustified negative attitude toward members of a particular group; it includes thoughts (stereotypes), feelings, and behavioral tendencies (discrimination).

I'm going to assume I'm a racist when I'm talking about a race that isn't mine because I don't know what that experience is like.

—Stephen Colbert

Prejudice, which literally means *prejudgment*, is a learned, unjustified negative attitude toward members of a particular group. Like all other attitudes, it's composed of three ABC

STOP! This Process Diagram contains essential information NOT found elsewhere in the text, which is likely to appear on quizzes and exams. Be sure to study it CAREFULLY!

PROCESS DIAGRAM 14.1 Understanding Cognitive Dissonance We've all noticed that people often say one thing, but do another. For example, why do some health professionals, who obviously know the dangers of smoking, continue to smoke?

1 When inconsistencies or conflicts exist between our thoughts, feelings, and actions, they can lead to strong feelings of psychological discomfort (*cognitive dissonance*).

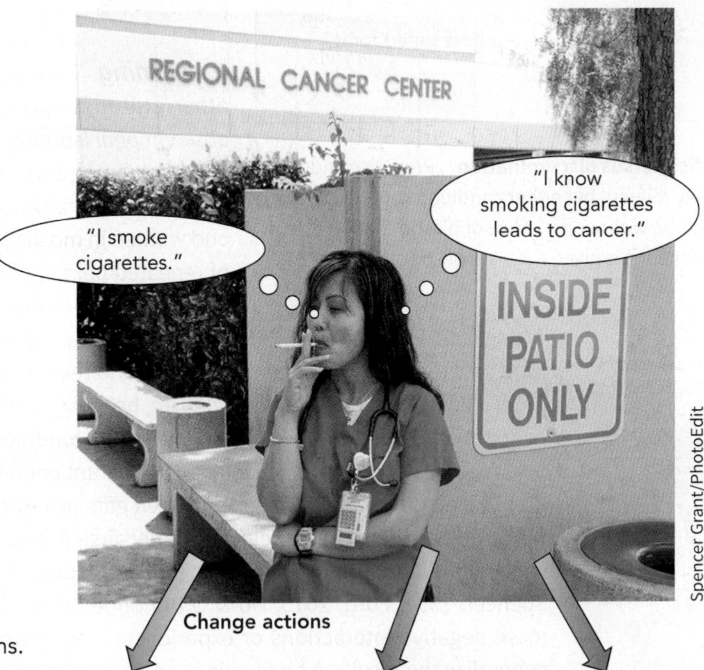
REGIONAL CANCER CENTER
"I smoke cigarettes."
"I know smoking cigarettes leads to cancer."
INSIDE PATIO ONLY
Spencer Grant/PhotoEdit

2 To reduce this cognitive dissonance, we are motivated to change our thoughts, feelings, and/or actions.

Change actions

Change thoughts and/or feelings

3a Changing actions, such as quitting smoking, can be hard to do.

"I don't smoke cigarettes any more."

3b If unable or unwilling to change their actions, individuals can use one or more of the four methods shown here to change their thoughts and/or feelings.

Change perceived importance of one of the conflicting cognitions: "Experiments showing that smoking causes cancer have only been done on animals."

Modify one or both of the conflicting cognitions or feelings: "I don't smoke that much." "I don't care if I die earlier. I love smoking!"

Add additional cognitions: "I only eat healthy foods, so I'm better protected from cancer."

Deny conflicting cognitions are related: "There's no real evidence linking cigarettes and cancer."

Overall Summary

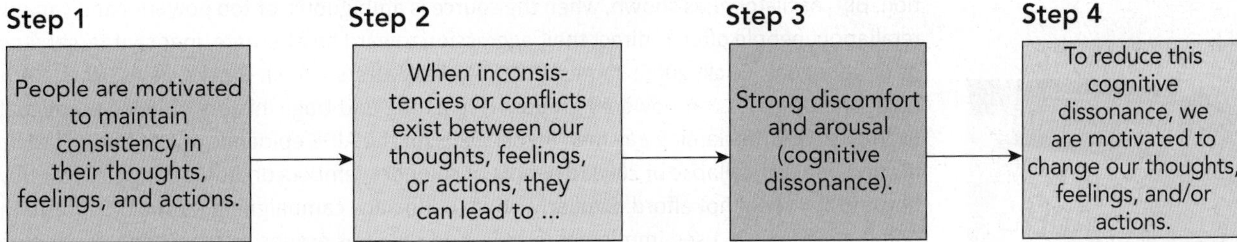
Step 1
People are motivated to maintain consistency in their thoughts, feelings, and actions.
Step 2
When inconsistencies or conflicts exist between our thoughts, feelings, or actions, they can lead to ...
Step 3
Strong discomfort and arousal (cognitive dissonance).
Step 4
To reduce this cognitive dissonance, we are motivated to change our thoughts, feelings, and/or actions.

elements: *Affective* (emotions about the group), *Behavioral* (**discrimination**—an unjustifiable, negative action directed toward members of a group), and *Cognitive* (**stereotypes**—overgeneralized beliefs about members of a group).

When we use the term *prejudice* here, we are referring to all three of these components. Note, though, that in everyday usage, *prejudice* often refers primarily to thoughts and feelings,

Discrimination An unjustifiable, negative action directed toward members of a group; also the behavioral component of prejudice.

Stereotypes The overgeneralized beliefs about members of a group; also the cognitive component of prejudice.

while *discrimination* is used to describe actions. When the terms are used in this way, they do not overlap completely, as shown in **Figure 14.5**.

	Prejudice: Yes	Prejudice: No
Discrimination: Yes	A person of color is *denied* a job because the owner of a business is prejudiced.	A person of color is *denied* a job because the owner of a business fears White customers won't buy from a person of color.
Discrimination: No	A person of color is *given* a job because the owner of a business hopes to attract a wider variety of customers.	A person of color is *given* a job because he or she is the best suited for it.

FIGURE 14.5 Prejudice versus discrimination Prejudice and discrimination are closely related, but either condition can exist without the other. The only situation without prejudice or discrimination in this example occurs when someone is given a job simply because he or she is the best candidate.

Common Sources of Prejudice

How does prejudice originate? Four commonly cited sources are *learning*, *limited resources*, *displaced aggression*, and *mental shortcuts* (**Figure 14.6**).

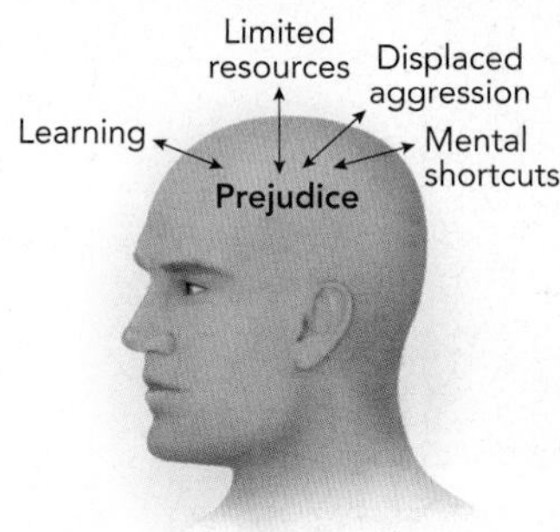

FIGURE 14.6 Which source best explains your own prejudices?

1. *Learning* People learn prejudice the same way they learn other attitudes—primarily through *classical conditioning* and *observational learning* (Chapter 6). For example, a form of classical conditioning and observational learning occurs after repeated exposure to negative, stereotypical portrayals of people of color and women in movies, magazines, TV, and the Internet. This type of repeated pairing of negative images with particular groups of people builds viewers' prejudice against those groups (Gattino & Tartaglia, 2015; Killen et al., 2015; Sigalow & Fox, 2014). Similarly, hearing parents, friends, and public figures express their prejudices creates and reinforces prejudice (Abolmaali et al., 2014; Brown, 2014; Miklikowska, 2015). *Ethnocentrism*, believing our own culture represents the norm or is superior to others, is another form of a classically conditioned or observationally learned prejudice.

We also develop prejudice through operant conditioning. For example, when people make prejudicial remarks or "jokes," they often gain attention and even approval from others. Sadly, denigrating others is also reinforcing because it boosts group cohesion among the initiators, while simultaneously fostering a negative disposition toward the targeted outgroup (Fein & Spencer, 1997; Ford, 2015; Ho & O'Donohoe, 2014). Furthermore, once someone has one or more negative interactions or experiences with members of a specific group, he or she may generalize the resulting bad feelings and prejudice to all members of that group.

2. *Limited Resources* A second source of prejudice is that in situations of limited resources prejudice pays off! Most of us understand that prejudice and discrimination exact a high price on their victims, but few appreciate the significant economic and political advantages they offer to the dominant group (Bonilla-Silva, 2016; Dreu et al., 2015; Wilkins et al., 2015). For example, the stereotype that people of color are inferior to Whites helps justify and perpetuate a social order in the United States in which White Americans hold disproportionate power and resources.

3. *Displaced Aggression* As a child, did you ever feel like hitting a sibling who was tormenting you? Frustration sometimes leads people to attack the perceived cause of that frustration. But, as history has shown, when the source is ambiguous, or too powerful and capable of retaliation, people often redirect their aggression toward an alternate, innocent target, known as a scapegoat (Glick, 2005; James, 2015; Media Matters, 2016). Blacks, Jews, Native Americans, and other less empowered groups have a long and tragic history of being scapegoated. Examples include blaming gay men in the 1980s for the AIDS epidemic or attributing the housing and banking collapse of 2008 to people of color or members of the working class for buying houses they could not afford. Similarly, some politicians campaigning for the U.S. presidential nomination in 2016 used immigrant, ethnic, and religious groups as scapegoats for numerous problems (**Figure 14.7**).

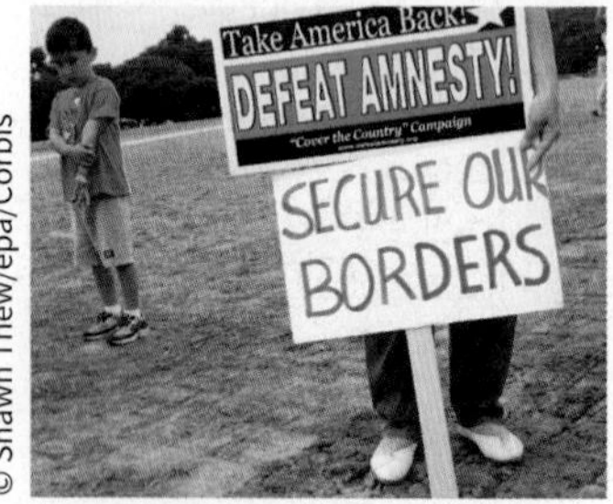

© Shawn Thew/epa/Corbis

FIGURE 14.7 Prejudice and immigration Can you identify which of the four sources of prejudice best explains this behavior?

4. *Mental Shortcuts* The fourth source of prejudice comes from everyday *mental shortcuts* that we create to simplify our complex social world (McFarlane, 2014; Prati et al., 2015). Stereotypes allow quick, helpful judgments about others, thereby freeing up mental resources for other activities. However, they also can lead to unforeseen, negative outcomes. For example, people use stereotypes as mental shortcuts when they create ingroups and outgroups. An *ingroup* is any category to which people see themselves as belonging; an *outgroup* is any other category. Research finds that ingroup members judge themselves more positively (as being more attractive, having better personalities, and more deserving of resources) compared with outgroup members—a phenomenon known as **ingroup favoritism** (Effron & Knowles, 2015; Hoogland et al., 2015; Sierksma et al., 2015). Members of the ingroup also tend to judge members of the outgroup as more alike and less diverse than members of their own group, a phenomenon aptly known as the **outgroup homogeneity effect** (Brewer, 2015; Kang & Lau, 2013; Ratner & Amodio, 2013). A danger of this erroneous belief is that when members of specific groups are not recognized as varied and complex individuals, it's easier to treat them in discriminatory ways.

Ingroup favoritism The tendency to judge members of the ingroup more positively than members of an outgroup.

Outgroup homogeneity effect The tendency to judge members of an outgroup as more alike and less diverse than members of the ingroup.

A sad example of the outgroup homogeneity effect occurs during wars and international conflicts. Viewing people on the other side as simply faceless enemies makes it easier to kill large numbers of soldiers and civilians. This type of dehumanization and facelessness also perpetuates our current high levels of fear and anxiety associated with terrorism (Greenwald & Pettigrew, 2014; Haslam, 2015; Lee et al., 2014).

Like all attitudes, prejudice can operate even without a person's conscious awareness or control—a process known as automatic bias, or **implicit bias** (Blair et al., 2015; Kubota & Phelps, 2016; Reuben et al., 2014). As you recall from Chapter 8, we naturally put things into groups or categories to help us make sense of the world around us. Unfortunately, the prototypes and hierarchies we develop are sometimes based on incorrect stereotypes of various groups that later lead to implicit biases. For example, researchers in one observational study found that bus drivers allowed Whites whose fare card didn't have enough money to ride for free 72% of the time, but allowed Blacks in the same situation to ride only 36% of the time (Mujcic & Frijters, 2013). A 2015 study (Lavy & Sand) found that teachers grade boys higher than girls (when names are known) on math tests, even when the girls outscore the boys on math tests when the tests are graded anonymously. Unfortunately, these teachers are underestimating girls' ability in math and overestimating boys' ability. On the other hand, comparable gender differences aren't seen for tests in other subjects, such as English and foreign language ability. Finally, a study of actual NFL games found that Black quarterbacks are more likely to be benched after making a mistake than White quarterbacks (Volz, 2016).

Implicit bias A hidden, automatic attitude that may guide behaviors independent of a person's awareness or control.

How do we identify our hidden, implicit biases? A common method is the *Implicit Association Test (IAT)*. You can "try this yourself" by going to: https://implicit.harvard.edu/implicit

Reducing Prejudice

As you can see in **Figure 14.8**, prejudice has a long, sad global history. The atrocities committed against the Jews and other groups during the Holocaust, as well as the current crises in the Middle East and Africa, offer stark reminders of the cost of human hatred. Within the United States, our history of slavery, current racial and gender disparities in employment, wealth, education, and healthcare, the current immigration

FIGURE 14.8 The high price of prejudice If pictures truly are "worth a thousand words," these photos speak volumes about the atrocities associated with prejudice: (a) the Holocaust, when millions of Jews, and other groups, were exterminated by the Nazis, (b) slavery in the United States, where millions of Africans were bought and sold as slaves, and (c) the 2016 nightclub shooting in Orlando, Florida, which left 49 people dead and 53 wounded, was a painful reminder of the ongoing dangers members of the LGBT community still face in modern America.

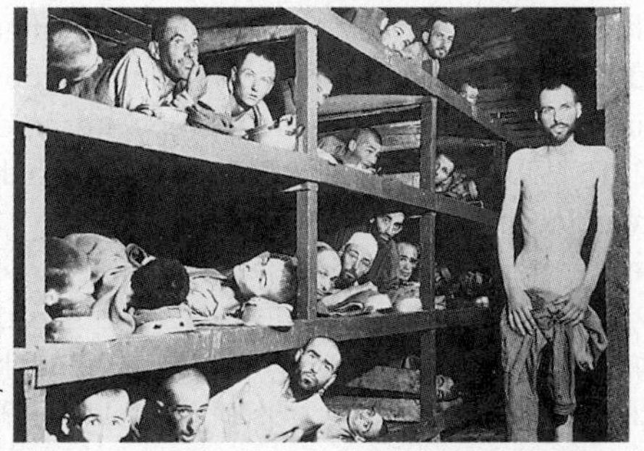
©AP/Wide World Photos
(a)

© North Wind Picture Archives/ The Image Works
(b)

Boston Globe/Getty Images, Inc.
(c)

FIGURE 14.9 How can we reduce prejudice? Do you recognize how the five approaches to combatting prejudice are at work in this simple game of tug-of-war? Similarly, how might large changes in social policy, such as school busing, integrated housing, and increased civil rights legislation, gradually change attitudes and eventually lead to decreased prejudice and discrimination?

controversy, and the stigma against mental illness (Chapters 12 and 13) all provide further troubling evidence of the ongoing costs of prejudice (Glaser, 2015; Jones & Corrigan, 2014; Marks et al., 2015).

What can we do to reduce and combat prejudice and discrimination? Five major approaches have been suggested: *cooperation with common goals*, *intergroup contact*, *cognitive retraining*, *cognitive dissonance*, and *empathy induction* (**Figure 14.9**).

1. *Cooperation with Common Goals* Research shows that one of the best ways to combat prejudice and discrimination is to encourage *cooperation* rather than *competition* (Kuchenbrandt et al., 2013; Price et al., 2013). Muzafer Sherif and his colleagues (1966, 1998) conducted an ingenious study to show the role of competition in promoting prejudice. The researchers artificially created strong feelings of ingroup and outgroup identification in a group of 11- and 12-year-old boys at a summer camp. They did this by physically separating the boys into different cabins and assigning different projects to each group, such as building a diving board or cooking out in the woods.

Once each group developed strong feelings of group identity and allegiance, the researchers set up a series of competitive games, including tug-of-war and touch football. They awarded desirable prizes to the winning teams. Because of this treatment, the groups began to pick fights, call each other names, and raid each other's camps. Researchers pointed to these behaviors as evidence of the experimentally produced prejudice.

The good news is that after using competition to create prejudice between the two groups, the researchers created "mini-crises" and tasks that required expertise, labor, and cooperation from both groups. Prizes were awarded to all and prejudice between the groups slowly began to dissipate. By the end of the camp, the earlier hostilities and *ingroup favoritism* had vanished. Sherif's study showed not only the importance of cooperation as opposed to competition but also the importance of *superordinate goals* (the "mini-crises") in reducing prejudice. Modern research agrees with Sherif's findings regarding the value of cooperation and common goals (Rutland & Killen, 2015; Sierksma et al., 2015; Zhang, 2015).

2. *Intergroup Contact* A second approach to reducing prejudice is to increase contact and positive experiences between groups (Dickter et al., 2015; Masciadrelli, 2014; Tropp & Page-Gould, 2015). However, as you just discovered with Sherif's study of the boys at the summer camp, contact can sometimes increase prejudice. Increasing contact works only under certain conditions that provide for *close interaction*, *interdependence* (superordinate goals that require cooperation), and *equal status*.

3. *Cognitive Retraining* Have you noticed that movies, television, and commercials still tend to emphasize gender differences—young boys are typically portrayed playing sports or computer games, whereas girls are more often shown putting on makeup or playing with dolls? Do you see how these repeated portrayals might increase and perpetuate gender stereotypes? Interestingly, cognitive retraining can help reduce this effect. For example, researchers in one study played specific tones while participants viewed counter-stereotypes, such as the word "math" being paired with a female face (Hu et al., 2015). Then, while the participants took a 90-minute nap, the researchers played the tones again to remind participants of these new pairings. This simple exercise led to lower rates of racial and sexual prejudice that lasted at least a week.

Another unique cognitive retraining approach, known as *racial colorblindness*, suggests that all people are fundamentally the same and that we should ignore racial and ethnic differences. In other words, just treat everyone as an individual. But others believe avoiding or ignoring racial/ethnic categories discounts serious racial/ethnic inequalities and thereby preserves the status quo (Babbitt et al., 2016; Bonilla-Silva, 2016). What do you think? Which approach do you think would lead to more equality and less prejudice and discrimination?

Finally, we can use cognitive retraining to reduce prejudice by encouraging people to selectively pay attention to *similarities* rather than *differences* between individuals and groups (Gaertner & Dovidio, 2014; Phillips & Ziller, 1997; West et al., 2014). Can you imagine what might happen if we didn't divide people into groups, such as people of color versus White (colorless?), Christian versus Muslim, or men versus women?

4. *Cognitive Dissonance* As you may recall from the previous section on attitudes, one of the most efficient methods to change an attitude is with *cognitive dissonance*, and prejudice is an attitude.

Each time we meet someone who does not conform to our prejudiced views, we experience dissonance—"I thought all gay men were effeminate. This guy is a deep-voiced professional athlete. I'm confused." To resolve the dissonance, we can maintain our stereotypes by saying, "This gay man is an exception to the rule." However, if we continue our contact with a large variety of gay men, or when the media includes numerous instances of non-stereotypical gay individuals, this "exception to the rule" defense eventually breaks down, the need for cognitive consistency rises, and attitude change (prejudice reduction) is likely to happen (Gawronski et al., 2012; Heitland & Bohner, 2010; Papageorgiou, 2013). See **Figure 14.10**.

5. *Empathy Induction* We've saved the best for last! Very surprising—and very encouraging—research has shown that we can successfully reduce prejudice by "simply" taking another's perspective—as demonstrated in the **PsychScience** (Boag & Carnelley, 2016; Broockman & Kalla, 2016; Prati et al., 2015). This type of *empathy induction* is further promoted by televised specials and Hollywood movies, like *42* and *Selma,* that help us understand and sympathize with the pressures and heroic struggles of Blacks to gain equal rights. Surprisingly, even just reading Harry Potter books appear to make people more tolerant (**Figure 14.11**).

© Kevin Winter/Getty Images

FIGURE 14.10 Breaking the "Gay barrier" Michael Sam (pictured here accepting the Arthur Ashe Courage Award) became the first openly gay National Football League draftee in 2014. In 2015, Sam signed a two-year contract with the Montreal Alouettes of the Canadian Football League–the first openly gay player in the CFL's history.

Godong/Alamy Stock Photo

FIGURE 14.11 Harry Potter reduces prejudice? A clever study found that high school students who had read more books in the Harry Potter series had more positive feelings toward gay people, and showed lower levels of prejudice towards immigrants (Vezzali et al., 2015). [Q3]

PS PsychScience

Can a 10-Minute Conversation Reduce Prejudice?

As we all know, advertising campaigns or even talking directly to people rarely, if ever, persuades people to change their attitudes—especially on sensitive topics like politics or prejudice. However, a recent study sent letters to 35,550 homes in the Miami area asking individuals to participate in a study for a small reward, which resulted in 1,825 volunteer participants (Broockman & Kalla, 2016). The researchers then sent 56 canvassers—some transgender, others not—to knock on the doors 501 of these participants to have a 10-minute conversation. Half of the canvassers talked about being transgender (meaning a person whose self identity does not conform to the sex they were assigned at birth). The other canvassers talked about recycling. In both cases, participants completed a survey before and after the conversation to measure their attitudes regarding transgender people. The effects were really remarkable. A 10-minute conversation with a random stranger led to decreases in *transphobia* greater than American's average decrease in homophobia from 1998 to 2012! And these effects lasted at least 3 months. Surprisingly, it didn't matter whether the interviewer was transgender or not.

What did matter, and why these researchers succeeded where most others have failed, is that they trained the canvassers in a new technique, called "deep canvassing." Rather than just presenting facts and talking "to" someone, the canvassers asked participants to recall and discuss their own personal experiences they had had with judgment or prejudice. Afterwards, they were encouraged to think about how their story related to those of transgender people. In short, this deep-canvassing technique is another form of *empathy induction*—encouraging active perspective taking, in turn, leads to reduced prejudice.

EdBockStock/Alamy StockPhoto

Can you see why this research has been widely cited in scientific journals and the mass media as being "groundbreaking," "monumentally important," and may lead to a new field of research on prejudice reduction (Bohannon, 2016; Resnick, 2016)? It's because deeply held attitudes, like prejudice, are notoriously difficult to change. And if it can work on something like transphobia, it might also be used to change public opinion about gay marriage, climate change, immigration, and other important topics. How can you use this in your own life if you want to change your own or others' attitudes? The first step would be recalling a similar personal experience and the accompanying painful emotions and reactions. Then encourage yourself and others to try to imagine the suffering of another group—such as that of gay and transgender people. As we've noted throughout this text, *empathy*, placing ourselves in the shoes of another, is key to better social relations in almost all parts of life.

Research Challenge

1. Based on the information provided, did this study (Broockman & Kalla, 2016) use descriptive, correlational, and/or experimental research?
2. If you chose:
   - *descriptive research*, is this a naturalistic observation, survey/interview, case study, and/or archival research?
   - *correlational research*, is this a positive, negative, or zero correlation?
   - *experimental research*, label the IV, DV, experimental group(s), and control group.
   - both *descriptive* and *correlational*, answer the corresponding questions for both.

Check your answers by clicking on the answer button or by looking in Appendix B.

NOTE: The information provided in this study is admittedly limited, but the level of detail is similar to what is presented in most text books and public reports of research findings. Answering these questions, and then comparing your answers to those provided, will help you become a better critical thinker and consumer of scientific research.

Retrieval Practice 14.1 | Social Cognition

SELF-TEST Completing this self-test, and then checking your answers by clicking on the answer button or by looking in Appendix B, will provide immediate feedback and helpful practice for exams.

1. The explanations we make about the causes of behaviors or events.
   a. impression management **b.** stereotaxic determination
   c. attributions **d.** person perception
2. The two major attribution mistakes we make are the _____ and the _____.
   a. fundamental attribution error; self-serving bias
   b. situational attributions; dispositional attributions
   c. actor bias; observer bias
   d. stereotypes; biases
3. Label the three components of attitudes.

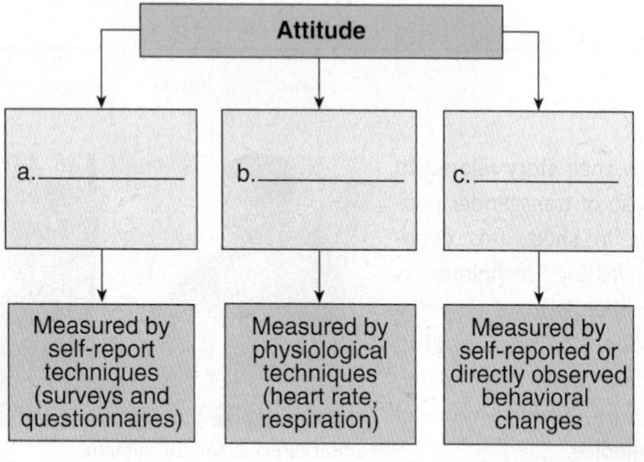

4. _____ is the cognitive component of prejudice.
   a. Harassment **b.** A stereotype
   c. Discrimination **d.** All of these options
5. Which of the following is an example of the outgroup homogeneity effect?
   a. "You don't belong here." **b.** "We are all alike."
   c. "You can't tell those people apart."
   d. All of these options.

Think Critically

1. Why do we tend to blame others for their misfortunes but deny responsibility for our own failures?
2. Have you ever changed a strongly held attitude? What caused you to do so?
3. Do you believe you are free of prejudice? After reading this chapter, which of the many factors that cause prejudice do you think is most important to change?

Real World **Psychology**

Why do athletes often blame their losses on bad officiating?

How can taking a pain pill reduce attitude change?

Can reading books about Harry Potter increase positive feelings toward gay people?

Helen Sessions/Alamy Stock Photo

© RTimages/iStockphoto

Godong/Alamy Stock Photo

HINT: LOOK IN THE MARGIN FOR **[Q1]**, **[Q2]**, AND **[Q3]**

14.2 Social Influence

LEARNING OBJECTIVES

Retrieval Practice While reading the upcoming sections, respond to each Learning Objective in your own words.

Review the main types of social influence.
- **Define** social influence.
- **Discuss** conformity and the factors that contribute to it.
- **Describe** obedience and the situational factors that increase it.
- **Explain** how group membership affects our behaviors and decision making.

In the previous section, we explored the way we think about and interpret ourselves and others through *social cognition*. We now focus on *social influence:* how situational factors and other people affect us. In this section, we explore three key topics—*conformity*, *obedience*, and *group processes*.

Conformity

Imagine that you have volunteered for a psychology experiment on visual perception. All participants are shown two cards. The first card has only a single vertical line on it, while the second card has three vertical lines of varying lengths. Your task is to determine which of the three lines on the second card (marked A, B, or C) is the same length as the single line on the first card (marked X).

X

A B C

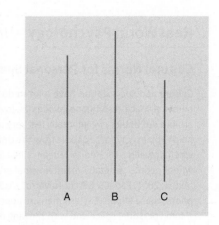

FIGURE 14.12 Solomon Asch's study of conformity Which line (A, B, or C) is most like line X? Could anyone convince you otherwise?

You are seated around a table with six other people, and everyone is called on in order. Because you are seated to the left of the seventh participant, you are always next to last to provide your answers. On the first two trials, everyone agrees on the correct line. However, on the third trial, your group is shown two cards like those in **Figure 14.12**. The first participant chooses line A as the closest in length to line X, an obvious wrong answer! When the second, third, fourth, and fifth participants also say line A, you really start to wonder: "What's going on here? Are they wrong, or am I?"

What do you think you would do at this point in the experiment? Would you stick with your convictions and say line B, regardless of what the others have answered? Or would you go along with the group? What you don't know is that the other six participants are actually *confederates* of the experimenter (that is, they're working with the experimenter and purposely giving wrong answers). Their incorrect responses were designed to test you and the other true participant's degree of **conformity**, which is defined as a change in thoughts, feelings, or actions because of real or imagined group pressure.

Conformity A change in thoughts, feelings, or actions because of real or imagined group pressure.

In the original version of this experiment, conducted by Solomon Asch, more than one-third of the participants conformed and agreed with the group's obviously incorrect choice (Asch, 1951). (Participants in a control group experienced no group pressure and almost always chose correctly.) Asch's study has been conducted in at least 17 countries, and the amount of conformity has varied depending upon factors such as age and personality (Mori et al., 2014; Tennen et al., 2013; Trautmann-Lengsfeld & Hermann 2014). Using a similar Asch research set up, researchers found that some participants were even willing to adjust their moral decisions when faced with social pressure (Kundu & Cummins, 2013).

Why are we so likely to conform? To the onlooker, conformity is often difficult to understand. Even the conformer sometimes has a hard time explaining his or her behavior. Let's look at three factors that drive conformity:

- **Normative social influence** Have you ever asked what others are wearing to a party, or copied your neighbor at a dinner party to make sure you picked up the right fork? One of the first reasons we conform is that we want to go along with group *norms*, which are expected behaviors generally adhered to by members of a group. We usually submit to this type of **normative social influence** out of our need for approval and acceptance by the group. Furthermore, conforming to group norms makes us feel good and it's often more adaptive to conform (Baldry & Pagliaro, 2014; Higgs, 2015; Oarga et al., 2015). (For an interesting example of everyday cultural norms, see the following **Real World Psychology** feature.)

Normative social influence A type of conforming based on the need to be liked, accepted, and approved of by others.

- **Informational social influence** Have you ever bought a specific product simply because of a friend's recommendation? In this case, you probably conformed not to gain your friend's approval, an example of normative social influence, but because you assumed that he or she had more information than you did, a case of **informational social influence**. Given

Informational social influence A type of conforming based on the need for information and direction.

Real World Psychology—Understanding the World

Cultural Norms for Personal Space

Culture and socialization have a lot to do with shaping norms for personal space. If someone invades the invisible "personal bubble" around our bodies, we generally feel very uncomfortable. This may help explain why some people from the United States feel awkward when traveling to Mediterranean and Latin American countries where people generally maintain smaller interpersonal distances (Axtell, 2007; Fadel & Garcia-Navarro, 2013). As you can see in this photo, these Middle Eastern men are apparently comfortable with a small personal space and with showing male-to-male affection.

Interestingly, children in our own Western culture also tend to stand very close to others until they are socialized to recognize and maintain greater personal distance. Furthermore, friends stand closer than strangers, women tend to stand closer than men, and violent prisoners prefer approximately three times as much personal space as nonviolent prisoners (Andersen, 2014; Axtell, 2007; Iachini et al., 2016).

If you'd like to experience the Western culture's norm for personal space, try this informal, *norm violation* exercise. Approach a fellow student on campus and ask for directions to the bookstore, library, or some other landmark. As you are talking, move toward the person until you invade his or her personal space. You should be close enough to almost touch toes. How does the person respond? How do you feel? Now repeat the process with another student. This time try standing 5 to 6 feet away while asking directions.

AFP/Getty Images, Inc.

Which procedure was most difficult for you? Most people think this will be a fun assignment. However, they often find it extremely difficult to willingly break unwritten cultural norms for personal space.

Think Critically

1. How might cultural differences in personal space help explain why U.S. travelers abroad are sometimes seen as being "too loud and brassy"?
2. Given that men and women have different norms for personal space, what effect might this have on their relationships?

that participants in Asch's experiment observed all the other participants giving unanimous decisions on the length of the lines, can you see how they may have conformed because they believed the others had more information than they did?

Reference groups Any group that individuals use as a standard for evaluating themselves.

- **Reference groups** The third major factor in conformity is the power of **reference groups**—people we most admire, like, and want to resemble. Attractive actors and popular sports stars are paid millions of dollars to endorse products because advertisers know that we want to be as cool as LeBron James or as beautiful as Natalie Portman (Arsena et al., 2014; Schulz, 2015). Of course, we also have more important reference groups in our lives—parents, friends, family members, teachers, religious leaders, and classmates—all of whom affect our willingness to conform. Interestingly, research shows that specific people (called "social referents") can have an outsized influence over others' attitudes and behaviors. For example, one study found that by encouraging a small set of popular high school students to take a public stance against typical forms of conflict, such as bullying, overall levels of conflict were reduced by an estimated 30% (Paluck et al., 2016). Similarly, popular high school students' attitudes about alcohol use (see the photo) have been shown to have a substantial influence on alcohol consumption by other students in their school (Teunissen et al., 2012). Surprisingly, popular peers who had *negative* attitudes toward alcohol use were even more influential in determining rates of teenage drinking than those with positive attitudes! [Q4]

© flubydust/iStockphoto

Obedience

Obedience The act of following direct commands, usually from an authority figure.

As we've seen, conformity means going along with the group. A second form of social influence, **obedience**, involves going along with direct commands, usually from someone in a position of authority. From very early childhood, we're socialized to respect and obey our parents, teachers, and other authority figures.

Conformity and obedience aren't always bad (**Figure 14.13**). In fact, we generally conform and obey most of the time because it's in our own best interests (and everyone else's) to do so. Like most other North Americans, we stand in line at a movie theatre instead of pushing ahead of others. This allows an orderly purchasing of tickets. Conformity and obedience allow social life to proceed with safety, order, and predictability.

However, on some occasions, it is important not to conform or obey. We don't want teenagers (or adults) engaging in risky sex or drug use just to be part of the crowd. And we don't want soldiers (or anyone else) mindlessly following orders just because they were told to do so by an authority figure. Recognizing and resisting destructive forms of obedience are particularly important to our society—and to social psychology. Let's start with an examination of a classic series of studies on obedience by Stanley Milgram (1963, 1974).

David McNew/Staff/Getty Images

FIGURE 14.13 Good reasons for conforming and obeying These people willingly obey the firefighters who order them to evacuate a building, and many lives are saved. What would happen to our everyday functioning if most people did not go along with the crowd or generally did not obey orders?

Imagine that you have responded to a newspaper ad seeking volunteers for a study on memory. At the Yale University laboratory, an experimenter explains to you and another participant that he is studying the effects of punishment on learning and memory. You are selected to play the role of the "teacher." The experimenter leads you into a room where he straps the other participant—the "learner"—into a chair. He applies electrode paste to the learner's wrist "to avoid blisters and burns" and attaches an electrode that is connected to a shock generator.

Next, you're led into an adjacent room and told to sit in front of this same shock generator, which is wired through the wall to the chair of the learner. (The setup for the experiment is illustrated in **Figure 14.14***.) The shock machine consists of 30 switches representing successively higher levels of shock, from 15 volts to 450 volts. Written labels appear below each group of switches, ranging from "Slight Shock" to "Danger: Severe Shock," all the way to "XXX." The experimenter explains that it is your job to teach the learner a list of word pairs and to punish any errors by administering a shock. With each wrong answer, you are to increase the shock by one level.*

You begin teaching the word pairs, but the learner's responses are often wrong. Before long, you are inflicting shocks that you can only assume must be extremely painful. After you administer 150 volts, the learner begins to protest: "Get me out of here . . . I refuse to go on."

You hesitate, and the experimenter tells you to continue. He insists that even if the learner refuses to answer, you must keep increasing the shock levels. But the other person is obviously in pain. What will you do?

The psychologist who designed this study, Stanley Milgram, was actually investigating not punishment and learning but obedience to authority: Would participants obey the experimenter's prompts and commands to shock another human being? In Milgram's public survey, fewer than 25% thought they would go beyond 150 volts. And no respondents predicted that they would go past the 300-volt level. Yet 65% of the teacher-participants in this series of studies obeyed completely—going all the way to the end of the scale (450 volts), even beyond the point when the "learner" (Milgram's confederate) stopped responding altogether.

Even Milgram was surprised by his results. Before the study began, he polled a group of psychiatrists, and they predicted that most

FIGURE 14.14 Milgram's study on obedience Under orders from an experimenter, would you, as "teacher," use this shock generator to shock a man (the "learner") who is screaming and begging to be released? Few people believe they would, but research shows otherwise.

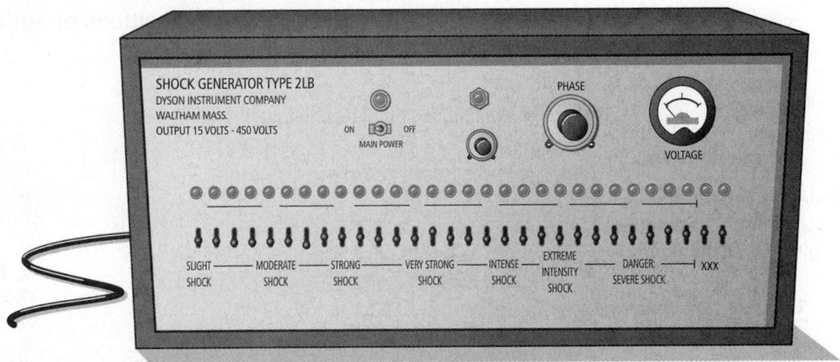

Milgram's Shock Generator

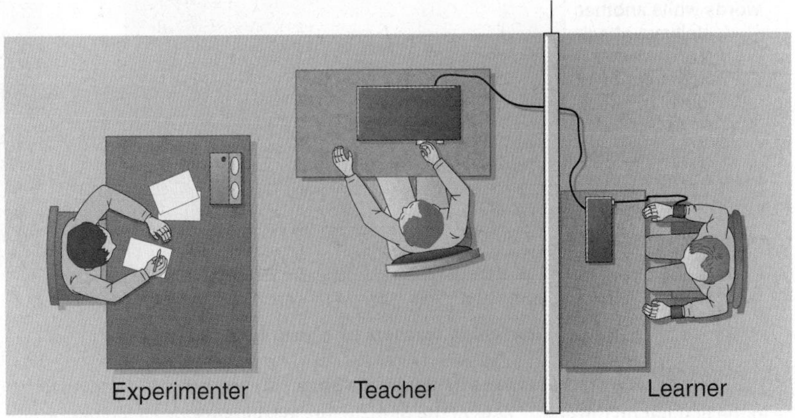

Experimental Set Up

people would refuse to go beyond 150 volts and that fewer than 1% of those tested would "go all the way." But, as Milgram discovered, 65% of his participants—men and women of all ages and from all walks of life—administered the highest voltage. The study has been partially replicated many times and in many other countries (Corti & Gillespie, 2015; Graupmann & Frey, 2014; Haslam et al., 2015a).

Note however that this research has been heavily criticized and Milgram's full, original setup could never be undertaken today due to ethical and moral considerations (Brannigan et al., 2015; Griggs & Whitehead, 2015). Deception is a necessary part of some research, but the degree of it in Milgram's research and the discomfort of the participants would never be allowed under today's research standards. In addition, recent reviews have revealed that Milgram failed to adequately debrief some participants, or to use a standard procedure for all participants—two research requirements discussed in Chapter 1. These findings raise serious concerns about the validity of Milgram's findings and the ethical treatment of his participants.

One final, important reminder: The *"learner" was an accomplice of the experimenter and only pretended to be shocked.* Milgram provided specific scripts that they followed at every stage of the experiment. In contrast, the "teachers" were true volunteers who believed they were administering real shocks. Although they suffered and protested, in the final analysis, most still obeyed.

Why did the teachers in Milgram's study obey the orders to shock a fellow participant, despite their moral objections? Are there specific circumstances that increase or decrease obedience? In a series of follow-up studies, Milgram found several important factors that influenced obedience: *legitimacy and closeness of the authority figure*, *remoteness of the victim*, *assignment of responsibility*, and *modeling or imitation of others* (Auzoult, 2015; Greenberg et al., 2015; Hollander, 2015; Reicher, 2014). See **Figure 14.15**.

In addition to the four factors that Milgram identified, researchers have discovered other important factors in obedience, including the following:

- **Socialization** Can you see how socialization might help explain many instances of mindless and sometimes destructive obedience? From an early age, we're all taught to listen to and respect people in positions of authority. In this case, participants in Milgram's study

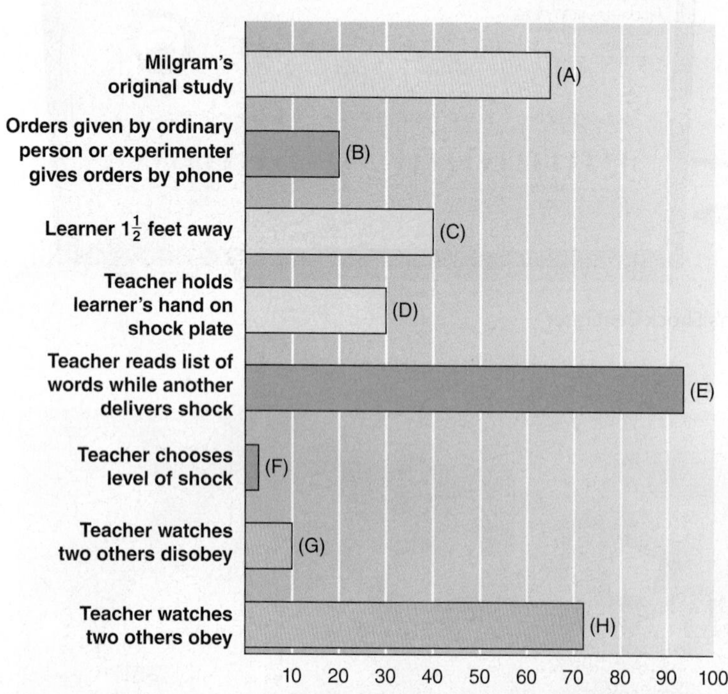

1. Legitimacy and closeness of the authority figure
When orders came from an ordinary person, and when the experimenter left the room and gave orders by phone, 20% of the teachers gave the full 450-volt shocks. (Bar B on graph.)

2. Remoteness of the victim
When the learner was only $1\frac{1}{2}$ feet away from the teacher, 40% of the teachers gave the highest level of shocks. Surprisingly, when the teacher had to actually hold the learner's hand on the shock plate, obedience was still 30%. (Bars C and D on graph.)

3. Assignment of responsibility
When the teacher simply read the list of words, while another delivered the shock, obedience jumped to almost 94%. However, when the teacher was responsible for choosing the level of shock, only 3% obeyed. (Bars E and F on graph.)

4. Modeling or imitating others
When teachers watched two other teachers refuse to shock the learner, only 10% gave the full 450-volt shocks. However, when they watched two other teachers obey, their obedience jumped to over 70% (Milgram, 1963, 1974). (Bars G and H on graph.)

FIGURE 14.15 Four factors that affect why we obey As you can see in the first bar on the graph, 65% of the participants in Milgram's early studies gave the learner the full 450-volt level of shocks. Note also how the color coding on the other bars on the graph (dark pink, yellow, green, and blue) corresponds to the four major conditions that either increased or decreased obedience to authority.

came into the research lab with a lifetime of socialization toward the value of scientific research and respect for the experimenter's authority. They couldn't suddenly step outside themselves and question the morality of this particular experimenter and his orders.

- **The foot-in-the-door technique** The step-wise actions in many obedience situations may help explain why so many people were willing to give the maximum shocks in Milgram's study. The initial mild level of shocks may have worked as a **foot-in-the-door technique**, in which a first, small request is used as a setup for later, larger requests. Once Milgram's participants complied with the initial request, they might have felt obligated to continue.

Foot-in-the-door technique A process in which an initial, small request is used as a setup for a later, larger request.

- **Adherence to ideologies** Some film critics and political commentators have suggested that popular movies like *American Sniper,* with their heavy emphasis on unwavering obedience to authority, might be encouraging a military ideology that justifies the wartime killing of others (e.g., Frangicetto, 2015). In support of this position, archival research on Milgram's original study (Haslam et al., 2015b) found that the "teachers" were actually happy to participate—in spite of the emotional stress. Why? The participants believed they were contributing to a valuable enterprise with virtuous goals. Do you agree with archival researchers who suggest that the major ethical problem with Milgram's study lies not with the stress generated for the "teachers," but with the ideology used to justify harming others?
- **Relaxed moral guard** One common intellectual illusion that hinders critical thinking about obedience is the belief that only evil people do evil things, or that evil announces itself. The experimenter in Milgram's study looked and acted like a reasonable person who was simply carrying out a research project. Because he was not seen as personally corrupt and evil, the participants' normal moral guard was down, which can maximize obedience. As philosopher Hannah Arendt has suggested, the horrifying thing about the Nazis was not that they were so deviant but that they were so "terrifyingly normal."

Real World **Psychology**—Understanding the World

A Model of Civil Disobedience

Although the forces underlying obedience can be loud and powerful, even one quiet, courageous, dissenting voice can make a difference. Perhaps the most beautiful and historically important example of just this type of bravery occurred in Alabama in 1955. Rosa Parks boarded a bus and, as expected in those times, obediently sat in the back section marked "Negroes." When the bus became crowded, the driver told her to give up her seat to a White man. Surprisingly for those days, Parks quietly but firmly refused and was eventually forced off the bus by police and arrested. This single act of disobedience was a major catalyst for the civil rights movement and the later repeal of Jim Crow laws in the South. Today, Rosa Parks's courageous stand also inspires the rest of us to carefully consider when it is appropriate and good to obey authorities and when we must resist unethical or dangerous demands.

© Bettmann/Corbis

Group Processes

Although we seldom recognize the power of group membership, social psychologists have identified several important ways that groups affect us.

Group Membership How do the roles that we play within groups affect our behavior? This question fascinated social psychologist Philip Zimbardo. In his famous study at Stanford University, 24 carefully screened, well-adjusted young college men were paid $15 a day for participating in a two-week simulation of prison life (Haney et al., 1978; Zimbardo, 1993).

The students were randomly assigned to the role of either prisoner or guard. Prisoners were "arrested," frisked, photographed, fingerprinted, and booked at the police station. They were then blindfolded and driven to the "Stanford Prison." There, they were given ID numbers, deloused, issued prison clothing (tight nylon caps, shapeless gowns, and no underwear), and locked in cells. Participants assigned to be guards were outfitted with official-looking uniforms,

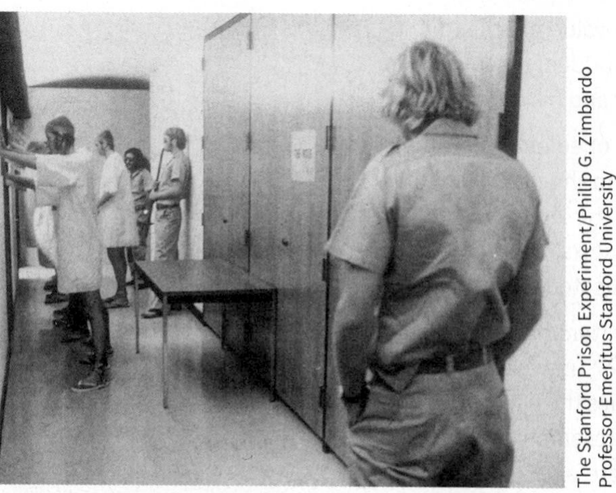

FIGURE 14.16 **Power corrupts** Zimbardo's prison study showed how the demands of roles and situations could produce dramatic changes in behavior in just a few days. Can you imagine what happens to prisoners during life imprisonment, six-year sentences, or even a few nights in jail?

official police nightsticks ("billy clubs"), and whistles, and they were given complete control.

Not even Zimbardo foresaw how the study would turn out. Although some guards were nicer to the prisoners than others, they all engaged in some abuse of power. The slightest disobedience was punished with degrading tasks or the loss of "privileges" (such as eating, sleeping, and washing). As demands increased and abuses began, the prisoners became passive and depressed. One prisoner fought back with a hunger strike, which ended with a forced feeding by the guards.

Four prisoners had to be released within the first four days because of severe psychological reactions. The study was stopped after only six days because of the alarming psychological changes in the participants.

Note that this was not a true experiment in that it lacked a control group, an operational definition, and clear measurements of the dependent variable (Chapter 1). However, it did provide valuable insights into the potential effects of roles on individual behavior (**Figure 14.16**). According to interviews conducted after the study, the students became so absorbed in their roles that they forgot they were participants in a psychology study (Zimbardo et al., 1977).

Deindividuation The reduced self-consciousness, inhibition, and personal responsibility that sometimes occurs in a group, particularly when the members feel anonymous.

Zimbardo's study also demonstrates **deindividuation**. To be deindividuated means that we feel less self-conscious, less inhibited, and less personally responsible as a member of a group than when we're alone. This is particularly true when we feel anonymous (see the following **Psychology and You**). Groups sometimes actively promote deindividuation by requiring members to wear uniforms, for example, as a way to increase allegiance and conformity.

Group Decision Making

We've just seen how group membership affects the way we think about ourselves, but how do groups affect our decisions? Are two heads truly better than one?

Most people assume that group decisions are more conservative, cautious, and middle-of-the-road than individual decisions. But is this true? Initial investigations indicated that after discussing an issue, people in groups actually supported riskier decisions than decisions they made as individuals before the discussion (Stoner, 1961). Subsequent research on this *risky-shift phenomenon*, however, shows that some groups support riskier decisions while others support more conservative decisions (Atanasov & Kunreuther, 2016; Liu & Latané, 1998; McGloin & Thomas, 2016).

Group polarization The tendency for the decisions and opinions of group members to become more extreme (either riskier or more conservative), depending on the members' initial dominant tendency.

How can we tell whether a given group's decision will be risky or conservative? A group's final decision depends primarily on its dominant *preexisting* tendencies. If the dominant initial position is risky, the final decision will be even riskier, and the reverse is true if the initial position is conservative—a process called **group polarization** (Davis & Mason, 2016; Keating et al., 2016; Mikulincer et al., 2015b).

What causes group polarization? It appears that as individuals interact and share their opinions, they pick up new and more persuasive information that supports their original

Psychology and You—Understanding Yourself

Lost in the Crowd

One of the most compelling explanations for deindividuation is the fact that the presence of others tends to increase arousal and feelings of anonymity, which is a powerful disinhibitor. As you can see in this photo, deindividuation can be healthy and positive when we're part of a happy, celebratory crowd. However, it also helps explain why vandalism seems to increase on Halloween (when people commonly wear masks), why cyberbullying occurs on the Internet, and why most crimes and riots occur at night—under the cover of darkness (Haines & Mann, 2011; Tang & Fox, 2016; Zimbardo, 2007). Can you imagine your own behavior changing under such conditions?

opinions, which may help explain why American politics have become so polarized in recent years (Gruzd & Roy, 2014; Suhay, 2015; Westfall et al., 2015). In addition, group polarization may explain how if we only interact and work with like-minded people, or only read newspapers and watch news programs that support our preexisting opinions, and talk politics only with those who agree with us, we're likely to become even more polarized. An interesting study in Washington, DC found that interns who worked in a partisan workplace became more polarized in their opinions than those who worked in less partisan environments (Jones, 2013).

Group polarization is also important within the legal system. Imagine yourself as a member of a jury (**Figure 14.17**). In an ideal world, attorneys from both sides would present the essential facts of the case. Then, after careful deliberation, each individual juror would move from his or her initially neutral position toward the defendant to a more extreme position—either conviction or acquittal. In a not-so-ideal world, the quality of legal arguments from opposing sides may not be equal, you and the other members of the jury may not be neutral at the start, and group polarization may cause most jurors to make riskier or more conservative judgments than they would have on their own.

Exactostock/SuperStock

FIGURE 14.17 Juries and group polarization When might group polarization be both a desirable and an undesirable part of jury deliberation?

A related phenomenon is **groupthink**, which occurs when maintaining harmony among group members becomes more important than making a good decision (Brodbeck & Guillaume, 2015; Janis, 1972; Jones et al., 2016). As you can see in **Figure 14.18**, there are many factors that explain groupthink, but the two most important might be the pressure for uniformity, and the

Groupthink The faulty decision making that occurs when maintaining group harmony becomes more important than making a good decision.

FIGURE 14.18 How groupthink occurs

Real World **Psychology**

a. The process of groupthink begins when group members feel a strong sense of cohesiveness and isolation from the judgments of qualified outsiders. Add a directive leader and little chance for debate, and we have the recipe for a potentially dangerous decision.

Blend Images - Jose Luis Pelaez Inc/Getty Images, Inc.

b. Few people realize that the decision to marry can be a form of groupthink. (Remember that a "group" can have as few as two members.) When planning a marriage, a couple may show symptoms of groupthink such as an illusion of invulnerability ("We're different—we won't ever get divorced"), collective rationalizations ("Two can live more cheaply than one"), shared stereotypes of the outgroup ("Couples with problems just don't know how to communicate"), and pressure on dissenters ("If you don't support our decision to marry, we don't want you at the wedding").

Groupthink

Antecedent Conditions

1 A highly cohesive group of decision makers
2 Insulation of the group from outside influences
3 A directive leader
4 Lack of procedures to ensure careful consideration of the pros and cons of alternative actions
5 High stress from external threats with little hope of finding a better solution than that favored by the leader

↓

Strong desire for group consensus—the groupthink tendency

↓

Symptoms of Groupthink

1 Illusion of invulnerability
2 Belief in the morality of the group
3 Collective rationalizations
4 Stereotypes of outgroups
5 Self-censorship of doubts and dissenting opinions
6 Illusion of unanimity
7 Direct pressure on dissenters

↓

Symptoms of Poor Decision Making

1 An incomplete survey of alternative courses of action
2 An incomplete survey of group objectives
3 Failure to examine risks of the preferred choice
4 Failure to reappraise rejected alternatives
5 Poor search for relevant information
6 Selective bias in processing information
7 Failure to develop contingency plans

↓

Low probability of successful outcome

unwillingness to hear dissenting information. Many highly publicized tragedies—from our failure to anticipate the attack on Pearl Harbor in 1941, to the terrorist attacks of September 11 and the subsequent war in Iraq—have been blamed on groupthink. Groupthink might also help explain why so few coaches or other staff members responded to allegations of child abuse by Jerry Sandusky, former assistant football coach at Penn State University.

How can we prevent, or at least minimize, groupthink? As a critical thinker, first study the list of the antecedent conditions and symptoms of groupthink provided in Figure 14.18, and then try generating your own ideas for possible solutions. For example, you might suggest that group leaders either absent themselves from discussions or remain impartial and silent. Second, you might suggest that group members should avoid isolation, should be encouraged to voice their dissenting opinions, and should seek advice and input from outside experts. A third option is to suggest that members should generate as many alternatives as possible and that they should vote by secret ballot versus a show of hands. Finally, you might suggest that group members should be reminded that they will be held responsible for their decisions, which will help offset the illusion of invulnerability, collective rationalizations, stereotypes, and so on.

Some of these recommendations for avoiding groupthink were carefully implemented in the decisions that led to the 2011 assassination raid on Osama bin Laden's compound. Before the final call, each member of President Obama's decision-making team was polled, and Vice President Joe Biden felt free to disagree (Landler, 2012). For an in-depth, fascinating look at groupthink, watch the classic 1957 film *Twelve Angry Men*.

Richard Ellis/Alamy Stock Photo

On a final, more personal level, can you see how spending time on social media, like Facebook, might increase both group polarization and groupthink? It's because we generally "friend" or "follow" people on social media who share our values and attitudes. And research has found that this limited information pool creates a type of "political bubble," in which we're more likely to post and read one-sided news stories and comments that we and our friends favor (Bakshy et al., 2015). Furthermore, researchers have found that people tend to "unfriend" those with different political views, which can become particularly common during heated political times, such as the 2016 U.S. elections—see the photo (John & Dvir-Gvirsman, 2015). Does this research also help explain why people become so upset when their preferred presidential candidate loses? Our restricted "political bubble" has created a misperception that virtually "everyone I know voted for him or her!" **[Q5]**

Retrieval Practice 14.2 | Social Influence

SELF-TEST Completing this self-test, and then checking your answers by clicking on the answer button or by looking in Appendix B, will provide immediate feedback and helpful practice for exams.

1. The act of changing thoughts, feelings, or actions as a result of real or imagined group pressure is called ____.
   - **a.** norm compliance
   - **b.** obedience
   - **c.** conformity
   - **d.** mob rule
2. What percentage of people in Milgram's original study were willing to give the highest level of shock (450 volts)?
   - **a.** 45 percent
   - **b.** 90 percent
   - **c.** 65 percent
   - **d.** 10 percent
3. Which of the following factors may contribute to destructive obedience?
   - **a.** remoteness of the victim
   - **b.** foot-in-the-door
   - **c.** socialization
   - **d.** all these options.
4. One of the most critical factors in deindividuation is ____.
   - **a.** loss of self-esteem
   - **b.** anonymity
   - **c.** identity diffusion
   - **d.** group cohesiveness
5. Faulty decision making that occurs when maintaining group harmony becomes more important than making a good decision is known as ____.
   - **a.** the risky-shift
   - **b.** group polarization
   - **c.** groupthink
   - **d.** destructive conformity

Think Critically

1. Explain how group membership has affected your own behavior and decision making.
2. How might Milgram's results relate to some aspects of modern warfare?
3. Have you ever done something wrong in a group that you would not have done if you were alone? What have you learned from this chapter that might help you avoid this behavior in the future?

Real World **Psychology**

If popular high-school students are anti-bullying and anti-drinking, does that reduce these behaviors among their peers?

Why are we so surprised when our preferred presidential candidate loses?

© flubydust/iStockphoto

Richard Ellis/Alamy Stock Photo

HINT: LOOK IN THE MARGIN FOR **[Q4]** AND **[Q5]**

14.3 Social Relations

LEARNING OBJECTIVES

Retrieval Practice While reading the upcoming sections, respond to each Learning Objective in your own words.

Summarize the influence of interpersonal relations.

- **Define** social relations.
- **Discuss** aggression and the factors that increase and decrease it.
- **Describe** altruism and the factors that increase and decrease it.
- **Identify** interpersonal attraction and love, along with the factors that affect them.

Kurt Lewin (1890–1947), often considered the "father of social psychology," was among the first people to suggest that all behavior results from interactions between the individual and the environment. In this final section, on *social relations*, we explore how we develop and are affected by interpersonal relations, including aggression, altruism, and interpersonal attraction.

Aggression

Why do people act aggressively? What exactly is aggression? When we intentionally try to inflict psychological or physical harm on another, psychologists define it as **aggression**. In this section, we explore its multiple causes and possible ways to reduce it.

Aggression Any behavior intended to cause psychological or physical harm to another individual.

Biological Explanations Because aggression has such a long history and is found in all cultures, some scientists believe that humans are instinctively aggressive (Buckholtz & Meyer-Lindenberg, 2015; Buss & Duntley, 2014; Peper et al., 2015). Most social psychologists, however, reject this "instinct" argument, but do accept the fact that biology plays a role. For example, twin studies suggest that some individuals are genetically predisposed to have hostile, irritable temperaments and to engage in aggressive acts (Lacourse et al., 2014; Rhee & Waldman, 2011). In addition, studies have linked brain injuries, the hormone testosterone and lowered levels of some neurotransmitters with aggressive behavior (Angus et al., 2016; Cristofori et al., 2016; Pfattheicher & Keller, 2014).

Psychosocial Explanations Substance abuse (particularly alcohol abuse) is a major factor in many forms of aggression (Abbey et al., 2014; Heinz et al., 2015; Kose et al., 2015). Similarly, aversive stimuli, such as loud noise, heat, pain, bullying, insults, and foul odors, also may increase aggression (Anderson, 2001; DeWall et al., 2013).

Real World Psychology—Understanding the World

Aggression in Sports

In June of 2014, Luis Suarez, a soccer player from Uruguay, bit an Italian soccer player on the shoulder during a heated World Cup match. Experts suggested that psychosocial factors, such as frustration, heat, and loud noise, may have contributed to this behavior.

Daniel Garcia/AFP/Getty Images

In addition, social-learning theory suggests that people raised in a culture with aggressive models will develop more aggressive responses (Farrell et al., 2014; Kirk & Hardy, 2014; Suzuki &

Lucas, 2015). For example, the United States has a high rate of violent crime, and there are widespread portrayals of violence on TV, the Internet, movies, and video games which may contribute to aggression in both children and adults (Breuer et al., 2015; Busching et al., 2015; Strasburger et al., 2014). Interestingly, psychologist Bryan Gibson and his colleagues are among the first to demonstrate experimentally that watching documentary-type reality TV shows, in which verbal and relational (e.g., bullying) aggression are prevalent, increases viewer aggression more than watching violent crime drama (Gibson et al., 2016). In short, reality TV programs are not just "harmless entertainment"—they do in fact increase physical aggression.

Keep in mind, however, that the research linking violent media and video games with increased aggression remains somewhat controversial (Ferguson, 2010, 2015; Hoffman, 2014), and the link between violent media and aggression appears to be at least a two-way street. Laboratory studies, correlational research, and cross-cultural studies have found both that exposure to violence increases aggressiveness and that aggressive individuals tend to seek out violent media and video games (Kalnin et al., 2011; Krahé, 2013; Qian et al., 2013).

Reducing Aggression How can we control or eliminate aggression? Some people suggest we should release aggressive impulses by engaging in harmless forms of aggression, such as exercising vigorously, punching a pillow, or watching competitive sports. But studies suggest that this type of *catharsis* doesn't really help and may only intensify the feeling (Bushman, 2002; Kuperstok, 2008; Seebauer et al., 2014).

A more effective approach is to introduce *incompatible responses*. Because certain emotional responses, such as empathy and humor, are incompatible with aggression, purposely making a joke or showing some sympathy for an opposing person's point of view can reduce anger and frustration (Baumeister & Bushman, 2014; Gottman, 2015; Maldonado et al., 2014).

Before going on, it's important to talk about the numerous sociocultural factors that contribute to aggression, including gender, developmental issues, and socioeconomic factors. In addition, the presence and use of guns greatly increases aggression, and firearm violence affects everyone—particularly those targeted by hate and prejudice (Frattaroli & Buggs, 2016; McDaniel & Belar, 2016; Williamson et al., 2014). Given that the rate of gun homicides in the United States remains substantially higher than in almost every other nation in the world, the American Psychological Association (APA) commissioned a panel of experts to investigate the best methods for preventing gun violence. Consider their three key recommendations:

Altruism Prosocial behaviors designed to help or benefit others.

Evolutionary theory of helping A theory suggesting that altruism is an instinctual behavior, which has evolved because it favors survival of the helper's genes.

1. *Primary (or universal) prevention* involves healthy development in the general population, such as teaching better social and communication skills to all ages.
2. *Secondary (or selective) prevention* consists of providing assistance for at-risk individuals, including mentoring programs and conflict-mediation services.
3. *Tertiary (or indicated) prevention* involves intensive services for individuals with a history of aggressive behavior, to prevent a recurrence or escalation of aggression, such as programs that rehabilitate juvenile offenders (American Psychological Association, 2013).

Mark Pardew/AP Images

FIGURE 14.19 An example of true altruism? A firefighter gives water to a koala during the devastating Black Saturday bushfires in Victoria, Australia, in 2009.

Altruism

After reading about all the problems with aggression, you will no doubt be relieved to discover that human beings also behave in positive ways. People help and support one another by donating blood, giving time and money to charities, aiding stranded motorists, and so on. **Altruism**, a form of *prosocial behavior*, consists of behaviors designed to help or benefit others (**Figure 14.19**).

When and Why Do We Help? There are three key approaches predicting when and why we help (**Figure 14.20**). The **evolutionary theory of helping** suggests that altruism is an instinctual behavior that has evolved because it favors survival of the helper's genes (Kurzban

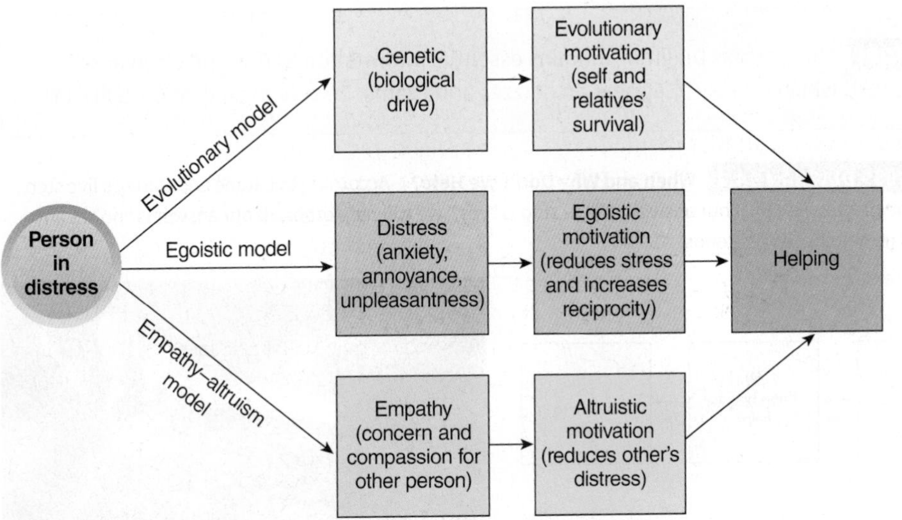

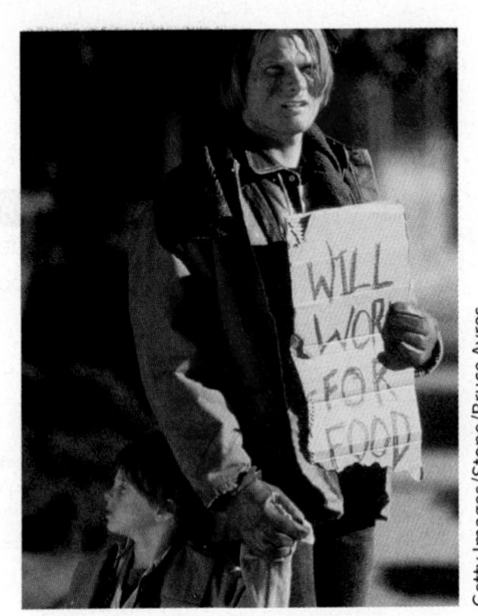

Getty Images/Stone/Bruce Ayres

FIGURE 14.20 Three models for helping altruism Which of the three models for helping shown in this figure do you think provides the best explanation for why someone might give food or money to the man in this photo?

et al., 2015; Richardson, 2015; Wilson, 2015). By helping our own biological child, or other relative, we increase the odds of our own genes' survival.

Other research suggests that altruism may actually be self-interest in disguise. According to this **egoistic model of helping**, we help others only because we hope for later reciprocation, because it makes us feel virtuous, or because it helps us avoid feeling distressed or guilty (Dickert et al., 2015; Schroeder & Graziano, 2015).

Egoistic model of helping A proposed explanation for helping that suggests we help because of anticipated gain—later reciprocation, increased self-esteem, or avoidance of distress and guilt.

Empathy–altruism hypothesis A proposed explanation for helping that suggests we help because of empathy for someone in need.

Opposing the evolutionary and egoistic models is the **empathy–altruism hypothesis** (Batson, 2014; Lebowitz & Dovidio, 2015; Lemmon & Wayne, 2014). This perspective holds that simply seeing or hearing of another person's suffering can create *empathy*—a subjective grasp of that person's feelings or experiences. And when we feel empathic toward another, we are motivated to help that person for his or her own sake. For example, middle school students who had been bullied are more likely to say that they would help another student who was being bullied (Batanova et al., 2014). The ability to empathize may even be innate. Research with newborn infants finds that they're more likely to cry, and become distressed, at the sound of another infant's cries, or after hearing the cries of an infant chimpanzee, but not to tape recordings of their own cries (Geangu et al., 2010; Hay, 1994; Laible & Karahuta, 2014).

Why Don't We Help?

In 1964, a young woman, Kitty Genovese, was brutally stabbed to death near her apartment building in New York City. The attack occurred about 3:00 A.M. and lasted for over half an hour. According to news reports at the time, 38 of her neighbors supposedly watched the repeated attacks, and heard her screams for help—yet no one came to her aid. Finally, one neighbor called the police, but it was too late. Kitty Genovese had died.

The story of Kitty Genovese's murder gained national attention, with many people attributing her neighbors' alleged lack of responsiveness to the callousness of big city dwellers—New York City residents, in particular. It's important to note, however, that later investigations found the early news reports to be filled with errors (Griggs, 2015; Seedman & Hellman, 2014).

Despite the inaccuracies, this case inspired psychologists John Darley and Bibb Latané (1968) to conduct a large number of studies investigating exactly when, where, and why we do or don't help our fellow human beings. They found that whether or not someone helps depends on a series of interconnected events and decisions: The potential helper must notice what is happening, interpret the event as an emergency, accept personal responsibility for helping, decide how to help, and then actually initiate the helping behavior (**Process Diagram 14.2**).

STOP! This Process Diagram contains essential information NOT found elsewhere in the text, which is likely to appear on quizzes and exams. Be sure to study it CAREFULLY!

PROCESS DIAGRAM 14.2 **When and Why Don't We Help?** According to Latané and Darley's five step decision process (1968), if our answer at each step is "yes," we will help others. If our answer is "no" at any point, the helping process ends.

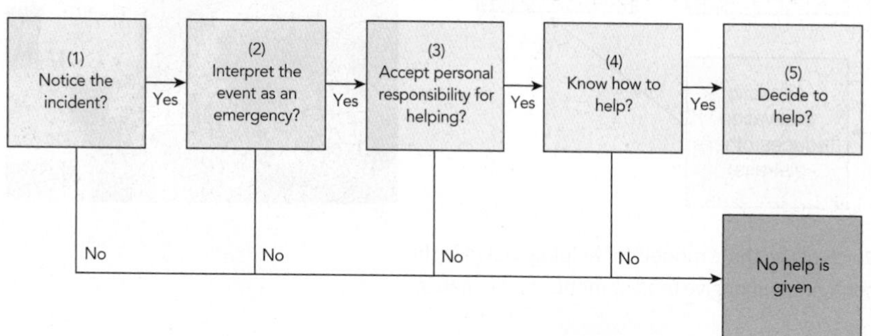

Sam Sarkis/Photodisc/Getty

How does this sequence explain television news reports and "caught on tape" situations in which people are robbed or attacked, and no one comes to their aid? Potential helpers must first notice the incident and interpret it as an emergency (Steps 1 and 2). However, the breakdown in the decision to help generally comes at the third stage—*accepting personal responsibility for helping*. In follow-up interviews, most onlookers report that they failed to intervene and accept responsibility because they were certain that someone must already have called for "official" help, such as the police or an ambulance. This so-called **bystander effect** is a well-known problem that affects our helping behavior.

Bystander effect A phenomenon in which the greater the number of bystanders, the less likely it is that any one individual will feel responsible for seeking help or giving aid to someone who is in need of help.

Diffusion of responsibility The dilution (diffusion) of personal responsibility for acting when others are present.

Why are we less likely to help when others are around? According to the principle of **diffusion of responsibility**, we assume the responsibility for acting is shared, or diffused, among all onlookers. In contrast, when we're the lone observer, we recognize that we have the sole responsibility for acting. As a critical thinker, can you see how *informational social influence*, which we discussed earlier, may also play a role? Given that people in a group monitor the behavior of others to determine how to behave, we often fail to act because we assume others have more information than we do. For a practical application of all these terms, see the following **Psychology and You**.

Psychology and You—Understanding Yourself

Saving Your Own Life!

In one of the earliest studies of the failure to interpret a situation as an emergency, participants were asked to complete a questionnaire, either alone or with others. While they were working, a large amount of smoke was pumped into the room through a wall vent to simulate an emergency. As you might expect, most of the participants working alone, about 75%, quickly reported the smoke. In contrast, fewer than 40% reported smelling smoke when three other participants were in the room, and only 10% reported the smoke when they were with passive participants who ignored the smoke (Latané & Darley, 1968). Keep this study in mind when you're in a true emergency situation. Do not simply rely on others for information. Make your own quick decisions to act. It may save your life!

© AndrewJohnson/iStockphoto

How Can We Promote Helping? Considering what we've just learned about the *bystander effect*, *diffusion of responsibility*, and *informational social influence*, the answers are to first clarify when help is needed, and then assign responsibility. For example, most parents teach their children to scream as loudly as they can if they're being abducted by a stranger. Given that children often scream, for a variety of reasons, can you see why this might not work? Instead, children should be taught to make eye contact with anyone who may be watching, and then to shout something like: "This isn't my parent. Help me!"

On the other hand, if you notice a situation in which it seems unclear whether someone needs help or not, simply ask: "Do you need help?" Note, however, that there are occasions when someone in desperate need of help can't verbally respond to questions, and we may need to take immediate action. For example, during the final stages of drowning (versus just distressed swimming), victims are trying so hard to inhale and stay afloat that they're unable to call or signal for help. (For more information on the *instinctive drowning response*, see http://mariovittone.com/2010/05/154/)

In addition to these personal tips for increasing altruism, highly publicized television programs, like ABC's "What Would You Do?" and "CNN Heroes," which honor and reward altruism, also increase helping. Enacting laws that protect helpers from legal liability, so-called "good Samaritan" laws, further encourages helping behavior. If you'd like more information on acts of true altruism, such as kidney donation, see **PositivePsych**.

PP PositivePsych

Would You Donate a Kidney to a Stranger?

In what is a particularly remarkable act of altruism, each year people donate one of their kidneys to strangers (people they aren't related to and don't know). They receive nothing in return, and generally experience serious pain and discomfort, along with a somewhat lengthy period of recovery. What prompts this type of generosity? Under what conditions would you donate a kidney to a stranger? Some research suggests that people who feel good about themselves overall are more likely to engage in other types of prosocial behavior, such as volunteering and giving money to charity, which might explain organ donation.

To examine this idea, researchers in the United States compared rates of kidney donations in different states with each state's overall level of well-being (Brethel-Haurwitz & Marsh, 2014). As predicted, states with higher rates of kidney donation tended to have higher rates of well-being. This finding held true even after the researchers took into account other factors that could explain this relationship, such as household income, age, education, religion, and mental and physical health.

PA images/Alamy Stock Photo

What do you think? Beyond giving a kidney while you're alive, are you registered as an organ donor upon your death? Given the thousands of people who die each year who are on waiting lists for donor organs, should we adopt policies like considering everyone to be a donor unless they officially "opt-out?" If you'd like more information on the facts and myths about organ donation, visit: http://www.americantransplantfoundation.org/about-transplant/facts-and-myths/

Interpersonal Attraction

What causes us to feel admiration, liking, friendship, intimacy, lust, or love? All these social experiences are reflections of *interpersonal attraction*, our positive feelings toward another. Psychologists have found three compelling factors in interpersonal attraction: *physical attractiveness*, *proximity*, and *similarity*. Each influences attraction in different ways.

Physical Attractiveness The way we look—including facial characteristics, body size and shape, and manner of dress—is one of the most important factors in our initial attraction, liking, or loving of others (Buss, 2003, 2011; Fletcher et al., 2014; Sprecher et al., 2015). In addition, attractive individuals are seen as more poised, interesting, cooperative, achieving, sociable, independent, intelligent, healthy, and sexually warm than unattractive people (Khan & Sutcliffe, 2014; Mattes & Milazzo, 2014; Sofer et al., 2015).

Interestingly, evolutionary psychologists have long argued that men prefer attractive women because youth and good looks generally indicate better health, sound genes, and high

FIGURE 14.21 Culture and attraction Which of these two women do you find most attractive? Both women appear healthy, but can you see how your cultural background might train you to prefer one look over the other?

fertility. Women also feel attracted to healthy-looking men, in addition to preferring men with maturity and resources. According to evolutionary theorists, this preference reflects the fact that mature men with more resources would be better providers, and the responsibility of rearing and nurturing children has historically fallen primarily on women's shoulders (Buss, 1989, 2011; Souza et al., 2016; Valentine et al., 2014).

However, as they say, beauty is also in "the eye of the beholder." What we judge as beautiful varies somewhat from era to era and culture to culture (**Figure 14.21**). For example, the Chinese once practiced foot binding because small feet were considered beautiful in women. All the toes except the big one were bent under a young girl's foot and into the sole. Tragically, the incredible pain and physical distortion made it almost impossible for her to walk. She also suffered chronic bleeding and frequent infections throughout her life (Dworkin, 1974). Even in modern times, cultural demands for attractiveness encourage an increasing number of men and women to undergo expensive, and often painful, surgery to *increase* the size of their eyes, breasts, lips, chest, penis, and buttocks. Ironically, they also use surgery to *decrease* the size of their nose, ears, chin, stomach, hips, and thighs.

So how do those of us who are not "superstar beautiful" manage to find mates—without these extreme measures? Research (and experience) shows that both sexes generally don't hold out for partners who are ideally attractive. Instead, according to the *matching hypothesis,* we tend to select partners whose physical attractiveness approximately matches our own (McClintock, 2014; Prichard et al., 2014; Regan, 1998, 2011). Furthermore, researchers have found human mating involves a host of mental skills and attributes, including charisma, humor, personality, intelligence, compassion, and even clever pick-up lines (Dillon et al., 2015; Watson et al., 2014).

Perhaps the least recognized, but one of the most effective, ways to increase attractiveness is through verbal and nonverbal flirting. While there are a multitude of ways to verbally flirt, the two most universally successful nonverbal methods for both sexes are *smiling* and *eye contact*. Why is flirting so important? It signals availability and romantic interest. Specifically, given that almost everyone fears rejection, flirting provides positive cues of your interest (Hall & Xing, 2015; Kurzban, 2014; Sprecher et al., 2015). If you'd like more tips and information on flirting, try these semi-scientific websites: http://www.sirc.org/publik/flirt.pdf http://theweek.com/articles/448643/how-flirt-according-science

Proximity Attraction also depends on the two people being in the same place at the same time. Thus, *proximity*, or geographic nearness, is another major factor in attraction—see the photo (Finkel et al., 2015; Greenberg et al., 2015; Sprecher et al., 2015). One examination of over 300,000 Facebook users found that even though people can have relationships with people throughout the world, the likelihood of a friendship decreases as distance between people increases (Nguyen & Szymanski, 2012). If you're wondering if this is a case of correlation being confused with causation, that's great! You're becoming an educated consumer of research and a good critical thinker. [Q6]

In fact, there is experimental evidence supporting a potentially causative link between proximity and attraction. For example, oxytocin, a naturally occurring bodily chemical, is known to be a key facilitator of interpersonal attraction and parental attachment (Goodson, 2013; Preckel et al., 2014; Weisman et al., 2012). In one very interesting experiment, the intranasal administration of oxytocin stimulated men in monogamous relationships, but not single ones, to keep a much greater distance between themselves and an attractive woman during a first encounter (Scheele et al., 2012). The researchers concluded that oxytocin may help maintain monogamous relationships by making men avoid close personal proximity to other women.

Why is proximity so important? It's largely due to *repeated exposure*. Just as familiar people become more physically attractive over time, repeated exposure also increases overall liking (**Figure 14.22**). This makes sense from an evolutionary point of view. Things we have seen before are less likely to pose a threat than novel stimuli (Kongthong et al., 2014; Monin, 2003; Yoshimoto et al., 2014). In addition, repeated exposure explains why modern advertisers tend to run highly redundant ad campaigns with familiar faces and jingles. In short, repeated exposure generally increases liking!

Bernhard Kuhmsted/Retna

FIGURE 14.22 Repeated exposure—why we hate photos of ourselves Research shows that we generally dislike our own photos, and prefer a reversed image of ourselves because it is the familiar face we're accustomed to seeing in the mirror. However, when presented with reversed and nonreversed photos, close friends prefer the nonreversed images (Mita et al., 1977). The photo on the left is the reversed image.

Similarity The major cementing factor for long-term relationships, whether liking or loving, is *similarity*. We tend to prefer, and stay with, people who are most like us—those who share our ethnic background, social class, interests, and attitudes (Brown & Brown, 2015; Sanbonmatsu et al., 2011; Watson et al., 2014). In other words, "birds of a feather flock together."

What about the old saying "opposites attract"? The term *opposites* here probably refers to personality traits rather than to social background or values. An attraction to a seemingly opposite person is more often based on the recognition that in one or two important personality traits, that person offers something we lack. In sum, lovers can enjoy some differences, but the more alike people are, the more both their loving and their liking endure.

The following **Psychology and You** feature offers a fun test of your understanding of the three factors in interpersonal attraction. Try it!

Psychology and You—Understanding Yourself

Test Yourself | Understanding Interpersonal Attraction

Based on your reading of this section, can you explain Kvack's love for the wooden dummy?

Answers: Research shows that similarity is the best predictor of long-term relationships. As shown here, however, many people ignore dissimilarities and hope that their chosen partner will change over time.

Loving Others It's easy to see why interpersonal attraction is a fundamental building block of our feelings about others. But how do we make sense of love? Why do we love some people and not others? Many people find the subject to be alternately mysterious, exhilarating, comforting—and even maddening. In this section, we explore four perspectives on love—*Sternberg's triangular theory*, his emphasis on *consummate love*, *romantic love*, and *companionate love*.

Robert Sternberg, a well-known researcher on creativity and intelligence (Chapter 8), produced a **triangular theory of love** (Sternberg, 1986, 1988, 2006). As you can see in **Figure 14.23**, his theory suggests that different types and stages of love result from three basic components:

- **Intimacy**—emotional closeness and connectedness, mutual trust, friendship, warmth, self-disclosure, and forming of "love maps."

Triangular theory of love Sternberg's theory that different stages and types of love result from three basic components—*intimacy*, *passion*, and *commitment*; Sternberg's consummate love is a combination of all three components.

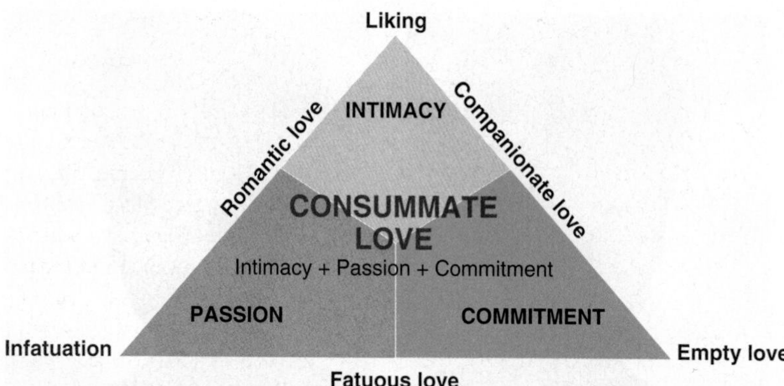

FIGURE 14.23 **Sternberg's triangular theory of love** According to Sternberg, we all experience various forms and stages of love, six of which are seen as being on the outside of the triangle. He proposes that only true *consummate love* is inside the triangle because it includes a healthy balance of intimacy, passion, and commitment. Note that the balance among these three components naturally shifts and changes over the course of a relationship, but relationships based on only one or two of these elements are generally less fulfilling and less likely to survive.

- **Passion—sexual** attraction and desirability, physical excitement, a state of intense longing to be with the other.
- **Commitment**—permanence and stability, the decision to stay in the relationship for the long haul, and the feelings of security that go with this intention.

For Sternberg, a healthy degree of all three components in both partners characterizes the fullest form of love, **consummate love**. Trouble occurs when one of the partners has a higher or lower need for one or more of the components. For example, if one partner has a much higher need for intimacy and the other partner has a stronger interest in passion, this lack of compatibility can be fatal to the relationship—unless the partners are willing to compromise and strike a mutually satisfying balance (Sternberg, 2014).

When you think of romantic love, do you imagine falling in love, a magical experience that puts you on cloud nine? **Romantic love**, which is an intense feeling of attraction to another in an erotic context, has intrigued people throughout history (Acevedo & Aron, 2014; Fehr, 2015; Gottman, 2015). Its intense joys and sorrows also have inspired countless poems, novels, movies, and songs around the world. A cross-cultural study by anthropologists William Jankowiak and Edward Fischer found romantic love in 147 of the 166 societies they studied. They concluded that "romantic love constitutes a human universal or, at the least, a near universal" (1992, p. 154).

Consummate love Sternberg's strongest and most enduring type of love, based on a balanced combination of intimacy, passion, and commitment.

Romantic love An intense feeling of attraction to another in an erotic context.

Romantic love may be almost universal, but even in the most devoted couples, the intense attraction and excitement of romantic love generally begin to fade 6 to 30 months after the relationship begins. However, as you can see in the two following **Psychology and You** features, companionate love can even be found online, and it tends to grow and evolve over time (Fehr et al., 2014; Hatfield & Rapson, 1996; Livingston, 1999). Why? Further research explains that **companionate love** is based on deep and lasting trust, caring, tolerance, and friendship, which slowly develops as couples grow and spend more time together. In contrast, romantic love is largely based on mystery and fantasy. People often fall in love with what they want another person to be—and these illusions usually fade with the realities of everyday living (Fletcher & Simpson, 2000; Levine, 2001).

Companionate love A type of strong and enduring love characterized by deep trust, caring, tolerance, and friendship.

Psychology and You—Understanding Yourself

Can You Find Lasting Love Via Online Dating?

To test this question, researchers conducted an on-line survey of over 19,000 Americans (Cacioppo et al., 2013). Participants were asked if they were currently married, if they had ever been divorced, and/or if they met their current or former spouse on-line. Those who were married also completed a measure of relationship satisfaction.

Researchers then compared divorce rates and marital satisfaction for those who met their spouse on-line versus not on-line. Interestingly, they found a higher level of marital satisfaction and a significantly lower divorce rate for those whose marriages started on-line versus those that started off-line. Can you think of topics from this or any other chapter in this text, or from your own life experiences, that might explain why relationships which start on-line may in fact be longer lasting and more satisfying than those that start in more traditional ways?

Psychology and You—Understanding Yourself

Love Over the Lifespan

How can we keep romantic love alive? One of the most constructive ways is to recognize its fragile nature and nurture it with carefully planned surprises, flirting, flattery, and special dinners and celebrations. In the long run, however, romantic love's most important function might be to keep us attached long enough to move on to the deeper and more enduring companionate love.

As you can see in the figure, romantic love is high in the beginning of a relationship, but it tends to diminish over time, with periodic resurgences, or "spikes." In contrast, companionate love usually steadily increases over time. One reason may be that satisfaction grows as we come to recognize the lasting value of companionship and intimacy (Gottman, 2011, 2015; Jacobs Bao & Lyubomirsky, 2013; Regan, 2011). One tip for maximizing companionate love is to overlook each other's faults. People are more satisfied with relationships when they have a somewhat idealized perception of their partner (Barelds & Dijkstra, 2011; Morry et al., 2014; Regan, 2011). This makes sense in light of research on cognitive dissonance (discussed earlier). Idealizing our mates allows us to believe we have a good deal—and thereby avoid any cognitive dissonance that might arise when we see an attractive alternative. As Benjamin Franklin wisely said, "Keep your eyes wide open before marriage, and half shut afterwards."

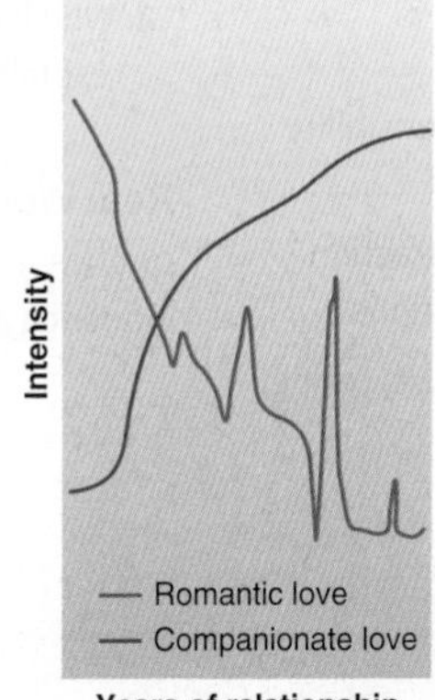

Sisse Brimberg & Cotton Coulson/NG Image Collection

Annie Griffiths Belt/NG Image Collection

Alaska Stock Images/NG Image Collection

Final Note As the authors of this text, and your tour guides through the fascinating world of psychology, we hope you've enjoyed the journey. For us, the key take-home message, which we hope you'll always remember, is that every human on this planet is an exclusive combination of a physical body, a complex system of mental processes, and large, sociocultural factors. Our deepest wish is that you'll make the most out of your own unique combination, and will apply what you've learned about yourself and others to improve your own life and the world around you.

Warmest regards,

Catherine A. Sanderson   Karen R. Huffman

Retrieval Practice 14.3 | Social Relations

SELF-TEST Completing this self-test, and then checking your answers by clicking on the answer button or by looking in Appendix B, will provide immediate feedback and helpful practice for exams.

1. One of the most effective ways to reduce aggression is to ____.

a. release aggressive impulses with catharsis
b. introduce incompatible responses
c. encourage competition
d. none of these options

2. Altruism refers to actions designed to help others when ____.

a. there is no obvious benefit to oneself
b. there is a benefit to the altruistic person

c. they have previously helped you
d. they are in a position to help you in the future

3. Onlookers to crimes sometimes fail to respond to cries for help because of the _____ phenomenon.
   a. empathy–altruism   b. egoistic model
   c. inhumanity of large cities   d. diffusion of responsibility
4. The positive feelings we have toward others is called _____.
   a. affective relations   b. interpersonal attraction
   c. interpersonal attitudes   d. affective connections
5. A strong and lasting love characterized by deep trust, caring, tolerance, and friendship called _____.
   a. companionate love   b. intimate love
   c. passionate love   d. all these options

Think Critically

1. Which of the major theories of aggression do you believe explains most acts of violence? Explain.
2. Which of the three major theories of helping do you find best explains why you tend to help others?

Real World Psychology

How does simple nearness (proximity) influence attraction?

© Gelpi JM/Shutter stock

HINT: LOOK IN THE MARGIN FOR **[Q6]**

Summary

14.1 Social Cognition 392

- **Social psychology** is the study of how other people influence our thoughts, feelings, and actions. **Social cognition**, the way we think about and interpret ourselves and others, relies on **attributions**, which help us explain behaviors and events. However, these attributions are frequently marred by the **fundamental attribution error (FAE)**, the **self-serving bias**, and the **actor observer effect**, some of which may depend in part on cultural factors.
- **Attitudes** have three ABC components: *affective*, *behavioral*, and *cognitive*. An efficient strategy for changing attitudes is to create **cognitive dissonance**.
- Like all other attitudes, **prejudice** includes three ABC components: *affective*, *behavioral*, and *cognitive*. Four commonly cited sources of prejudice are *learning*, *limited resources*, *displaced aggression*, and *mental shortcuts*.
- How can we overcome prejudice? There are five general approaches: *cooperation with common goals*, *intergroup contact*, *cognitive retraining*, *cognitive dissonance*, and *empathy induction*.

14.2 Social Influence 402

- **Conformity** involves changes in thoughts, feelings, or actions in response to real or imagined group pressure. People conform out of a desire for liking, acceptance, or approval (**normative social influence**), out of a need for more information and direction (**informational social influence**), and to match the behavior of those they like, admire, and want to be like (**reference group**).
- **Obedience** refers to following direct commands, usually from an authority figure. Milgram's study showed that a surprisingly large number of people obey orders even when they believe another human being is physically harmed.
- Milgram's research demonstrated the startling power of social situations to create obedience. Legitimacy and closeness of the authority figure, remoteness of the victim, assignment of responsibility, and modeling or imitation of others are the four major factors in obedience.
- The degree of deception and discomfort to which Milgram's participants were subjected raises serious ethical questions, and the same study would never be done today.
- To decrease destructive obedience, we need to reexamine *socialization*, the *foot-in-the-door* technique, and a *relaxed moral guard*.
- The roles we play within groups strongly affect our behavior, as Zimbardo's Stanford Prison experiment showed. Zimbardo's study also demonstrated **deindividuation**. In addition, as we interact with others, **group polarization** and **groupthink** tend to occur. Both processes may hinder effective decision making.

14.3 Social Relations 411

- **Aggression** is any behavior intended to cause psychological or physical harm to another. Several biological factors may help explain aggression, including genetic predisposition, aggression circuits in the brain, hormones, and neurotransmitters. Psychosocial explanations for aggression include substance abuse, aversive stimuli, media violence, and social learning.
- How can we reduce aggression? Releasing aggressive feelings through violent acts or watching violence (catharsis) is not an effective way to reduce aggression. Introducing incompatible responses (such as humor) and teaching social and communication skills are more efficient.
- **Altruism** refers to actions designed to help others with no obvious benefit to the helper. Evolutionary theory suggests that **altruism** is an evolved, instinctual behavior. Other research suggests that helping may actually be self-interest in disguise—the **egoistic model**. The **empathy–altruism hypothesis** proposes that although altruism is occasionally based on selfish motivations, it is sometimes truly selfless and motivated by empathy or concern for others.
- Latané and Darley found that in order for helping to occur, the potential helper must notice what is happening, interpret the event as an emergency, take personal responsibility for helping, know how to help, and then actually initiate the helping behavior.

- Psychologists have found at least three compelling factors in **interpersonal attraction:** physical attractiveness, proximity, and similarity. Sternberg suggests that **consummate love** depends on a healthy degree of intimacy, passion, and commitment. **Romantic love** is an intense feeling of attraction to another in an erotic context, whereas **companionate love** is a strong, enduring love characterized by deep trust, caring, tolerance, and friendship.

Applying **Real** World **Psychology**

We began this chapter with six intriguing Real World Psychology questions, and you were asked to revisit these questions at the end of each section. Questions like these have an important and lasting impact on all of our lives. See if you can answer these additional critical thinking questions related to real world examples.

1. What were the major social factors that contributed to Rosa Parks, pictured here, being willing to stand up against the bus driver who ordered her to give her seat to a White man? Does her model of disobedience encourage you to follow her example? Why or why not?
2. Can you think of an example from your own life, or from the life of one of your friends, in which attitudes did not match behavior? How might strong attitudes be a better predictor of actual behavior than weak ones?
3. In both Asch's conformity experiment and Milgram's study of obedience, the presence of another person greatly affected the behaviors of the research participants. How would you explain this?
4. Thinking about the most important romantic relationship in your life, explain how each of the major factors in interpersonal attraction—physical attractiveness, proximity, and similarity—affect this relationship.

William Philpott/Reuters/©Corbis

5. Imagine yourself with a career as a social psychologist. Which of the key factors discussed in this chapter would you be most and least interested in studying? Why?

Key Terms

Retrieval Practice Write a definition for each term before turning back to the referenced page to check your answer.

- actor–observer effect 393
- aggression 411
- altruism 412
- attitude 394
- attribution 393
- bystander effect 414
- cognitive dissonance 395
- companionate love 418
- conformity 403
- consummate love 418
- deindividuation 408
- diffusion of responsibility 414
- discrimination 397
- egoistic model of helping 413
- empathy–altruism hypothesis 413
- evolutionary theory of helping 412
- foot-in-the-door technique 407
- fundamental attribution error (FAE) 393
- group polarization 408
- groupthink 409
- Implicit bias 399
- Informational social influence 403
- ingroup favoritism 399
- normative social influence 403
- obedience 404
- outgroup homogeneity effect 399
- prejudice 396
- reference groups 404
- romantic love 418
- saliency bias 393
- self-serving bias 393
- social psychology 392
- stereotype 397
- triangular theory of love 417

Appendix A

Statistics and Psychology

We are constantly bombarded by numbers: "On sale for 30 percent off," "70 percent chance of rain," "9 out of 10 doctors recommend," "Your scores on the SAT were in the 75th percentile." Businesses and advertisers use numbers to convince us to buy their products. College admission officers use SAT percentile scores to help them decide whom to admit to their programs. And, as you've seen throughout this text, psychologists use numbers to support or refute psychological theories and demonstrate that certain behaviors are indeed the result of specific causal factors.

When we use numbers in these ways, we're all using statistics. **Statistics** is a branch of applied mathematics that uses numbers to describe and analyze information on a subject. If you're considering a major in psychology, you may be surprised to learn that a full course in statistics is generally required for this major. Why? Statistics make it possible for psychologists to quantify the information we obtain in our studies. We can then critically analyze and evaluate this information. Statistical analysis is imperative for researchers to describe, predict, or explain behavior. As you'll recall from the so-called "Bobo doll" study in Chapters 6 and 14, Albert Bandura (1973) proposed that watching violence on television causes aggressive behavior in children. In carefully controlled experiments, he gathered numerical information and analyzed it according to specific statistical methods. The statistical analysis helped him substantiate that the aggression of his participants and the aggressive acts they had seen on television were related, and that the relationship was not mere coincidence.

Statistics The branch of applied mathematics that deals with the collection, calculation, analysis, interpretation, and presentation of numerical facts or data.

Although statistics is a branch of applied mathematics, you don't have to be a math genius to understand it. Simple arithmetic is all we need for most of the calculations. For more complex statistics involving more complicated mathematics, computer programs are readily available. What is more important than learning the mathematical computations, however, is developing an understanding of when and why each type of statistic is used. The purpose of this appendix is to help you develop this understanding and to become a better consumer of the statistics that bombard us each day. In addition, we hope to increase your appreciation for the important role this form of math plays in the science of psychology.

Gathering and Organizing Data

Psychologists design their studies to facilitate gathering information about the factors they want to study. The information they obtain is known as *data* (data is plural; its singular is datum). When the data are gathered, they are generally in the form of numbers; if they aren't, they are converted to numbers. After they are gathered, the data must be organized in such a way that statistical analysis is possible. In the following section, we will examine the methods used to gather and organize information.

Variables

When studying a behavior, psychologists normally focus on one particular factor to determine whether it has an effect on the behavior. This factor is known as a *variable*, which is, in effect, anything that can assume more than one value (see Chapter 1). Height, weight, sex, eye color, and scores on an IQ test or a video game are all factors that can assume more than one value and are therefore variables. Some will vary between people, such as eye color, or may even vary within one person, such as scores on a video game (the same person might get 10,000 points on one try and only 800 on another). In contrast to a variable, anything that remains the same and does not vary is called a *constant*. If researchers use only women in their research, then sex is a constant, not a variable.

In nonexperimental studies, variables can be factors that are merely observed through naturalistic observation or case studies, or they can be factors about which people are questioned in a test or survey. In experimental studies, the two major types of variables are independent and dependent variables.

Independent variables are those that are manipulated by the experimenter. For example, suppose we were to conduct a study to determine whether the sex of the debater influences the outcome of a debate. In this study, one group of participants watches a videotape of a debate between a man arguing the "pro" side and a woman arguing the "con"; another group watches the same debate, but with the pro and con roles reversed. Note that in both cases, the debaters follow a prepared "pro" or "con" script. Also note that the form of the presentation viewed by each group (whether "pro" is argued by a man or a woman) is the independent variable because the experimenter manipulates the form of presentation seen by each group.

Another example might be a study to determine whether a particular drug has any effect on a manual dexterity task. To study this question, we would administer the drug to one group and no drug to another. The independent variable would be the amount of drug given (some or none).

The *dependent variable* is a factor that results from, or depends on, the independent variable. It is a measure of some outcome or, most commonly, a measure of the participants' behavior. In the debate example, each participant's choice of the winner of the debate would be the dependent variable. In the drug experiment, the dependent variable would be each participant's score on the manual dexterity task.

Frequency Distributions

After conducting a study and obtaining measures of the variable(s) being studied, psychologists need to organize the data in a meaningful way. **Table A.1** presents test scores from a Math Aptitude Test collected from 50 college students. This information is called *raw data* because there is no order to the numbers. They are presented as they were collected and are therefore "raw."

The lack of order in raw data makes them difficult to study. Thus, the first step in understanding the results of an experiment is to impose some order on the raw data. There are several ways to do this. One of the simplest is to create a *frequency distribution*, which shows the number of times a score or event occurs. Although frequency distributions are helpful in several ways, the major advantages are that they allow us to see the data in an organized manner and they make it easier to represent the data on a graph.

The simplest way to make a frequency distribution is to list all the possible test scores, then tally the number of people *(N)* who received those scores. **Table A.2** presents a frequency distribution using the raw data from Table A.1. As you can see, the data are now easier to read.

TABLE A.1 Math Aptitude Test Scores for 50 College Students

73	57	63	59	50
72	66	50	67	51
63	59	65	62	65
62	72	64	73	66
61	68	62	68	63
59	61	72	63	52
59	58	57	68	57
64	56	65	59	60
50	62	68	54	63
52	62	70	60	68

TABLE A.2 Frequency Distribution of 50 Students on Math Aptitude Test

SCORE	FREQUENCY	SCORE	FREQUENCY
73	2	61	2
72	3	60	2
71	0	59	5
70	1	58	1
69	0	57	3
68	5	56	1
67	1	55	0
66	2	54	1
65	3	53	0
64	2	52	2
63	5	51	1
62	5	50	3
			Total 50

This type of frequency distribution is practical when the number of possible scores is 50 or fewer. However, when there are more than 10 possible scores it can be even harder to make sense out of the frequency distribution than the raw data. This can be seen in **Table A.3**, which presents the hypothetical Psychology Aptitude Test scores for 50 students. Even though there are only 50 actual scores in this table, the number of possible scores ranges from a high of 1390 to a low of 400. If we included zero frequencies there would be 100 entries in a frequency distribution of this data, making the frequency distribution much more difficult to understand than the raw data. If there are more than 20 possible scores, therefore, a *group frequency distribution* is normally used.

In a *group frequency distribution,* individual scores are represented as members of a group of scores or as a range of scores (see **Table A.4**). These groups are called *class intervals*. Grouping these scores makes it much easier to make sense out of the distribution, as you can see from the relative ease in understanding Table A.4 as compared to Table A.3. Group frequency distributions are also easier to represent on a graph.

When graphing data from frequency distributions, the class intervals are typically represented along the *abscissa* (the horizontal or *x* axis). The frequency is represented along the *ordinate* (the vertical or *y* axis). Information can be graphed in the form of a bar graph, called a *histogram*, or in the form of a point or line graph, called a *polygon*. **Figure A.1** shows a

TABLE A.3 Psychology Aptitude Test Scores for 50 College Students

1350	750	530	540	750
1120	410	780	1020	430
720	1080	1110	770	610
1130	620	510	1160	630
640	1220	920	650	870
930	660	480	940	670
1070	950	680	450	990
690	1010	800	660	500
860	520	540	880	1090
580	730	570	560	740

TABLE A.4 Group Frequency Distribution of Psychology Aptitude Test Scores for 50 College Students

CLASS INTERVAL	FREQUENCY
1300–1390	1
1200–1290	1
1100–1190	4
1000–1090	5
900–990	5
800–890	4
700–790	7
600–690	10
500–590	9
400–490	4
Total	50

histogram presenting the data from Table A.4. Note that the class intervals are represented along the bottom line of the graph (the *x* axis) and the height of the bars indicates the frequency in each class interval. Now look at **Figure A.2**. The information presented here is exactly the same as that in Figure A.1 but is represented in the form of a polygon rather than a histogram. Can you see how both graphs illustrate the same information? Even though graphs like these are quite common today, we have found that many students have never been formally taught how to read graphs, which is the topic of our next section.

How to Read a Graph

Every graph has several major parts. The most important are the labels, the axes (the vertical and horizontal lines), and the points, lines, or bars. Find these parts in Figure A.1.

The first thing we should all notice when reading a graph is the labels because they tell what data are portrayed. Usually the data consist of the descriptive statistics, or the numbers used to measure the dependent variables. For example, in Figure A.1 the horizontal axis is labeled "Psychology Aptitude Test Scores," which is the dependent variable measure; the vertical axis is labeled "Frequency," which means the number of occurrences. If a graph is not labeled, as we sometimes see in TV commercials or magazine ads, it is useless and should be ignored. Even when a graph *is* labeled, the labels can be misleading. For example, if graph designers want to distort the information, they can elongate one of the axes. Thus, it is important to pay careful attention to the numbers as well as the words in graph labels.

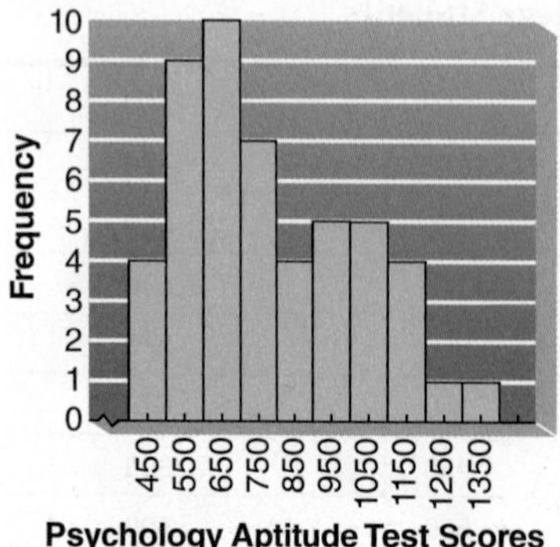

FIGURE A.1 A histogram illustrating the information found in Table A4

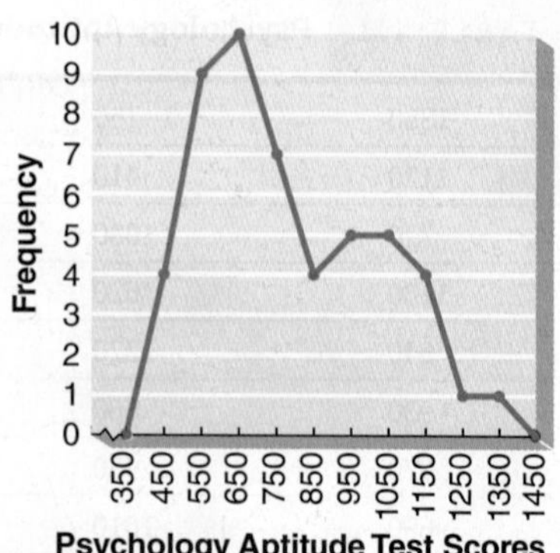

FIGURE A.2 A polygon illustrating the information found in Table A4

Next, we need to focus on the bars, points, or lines on the graph. In the case of histograms like the one in Figure A.1, each bar represents the class interval. The width of the bar stands for the width of the class interval, whereas the height of the bar stands for the frequency in that interval. Look at the third bar from the left in Figure A.1. This bar represents the interval "600 to 690 Psychology Aptitude Scores," which has a frequency of 10. Can you see how this directly corresponds to the same class interval in Table A.4? Graphs and tables are both merely alternate ways of illustrating information.

Reading point or line graphs is the same as reading a histogram. In a point graph, each point represents two numbers, one found along the horizontal axis and the other found along the vertical axis. A polygon is identical to a point graph except that it has lines connecting the points. Figure A.2 is an example of a polygon, where each point represents a class interval and is placed at the center of the interval and at the height corresponding to the frequency of that interval. To make the graph easier to read, the points are connected by straight lines.

Displaying the data in a frequency distribution or in a graph is much more useful than merely presenting raw data and can be especially helpful when researchers are trying to find relations between certain factors. However, as we explained earlier, if psychologists want to make precise predictions or explanations, we need to perform specific mathematical computations on the data. How we use these computations, or statistics, is the topic of our next section.

Uses of the Various Statistics

The statistics psychologists use in a study depend on whether they are trying to describe and predict behavior or explain it. When they use statistics to describe behavior, as in reporting the average score on the hypothetical Psychology Aptitude Test, they are using **descriptive statistics**. When they use them to explain behavior, as Bandura did in his study of children modeling aggressive behavior seen on TV, they are using **inferential statistics**.

Descriptive statistics Mathematical methods used to describe and summarize sets of data in a meaningful way.

Inferential statistics Mathematical procedures that provide a measure of confidence about how likely it is that a certain result appeared by chance.

Descriptive Statistics

Descriptive statistics are the numbers used to describe the dependent variable. They can be used to describe characteristics of a *population* (an entire group, such as all people living in the United States) or a *sample* (a part of a group, such as a randomly selected group of 25 students from a given college or university). The major descriptive statistics include measures of central tendency (mean, median, and mode), measures of variation (variance and standard deviation), and correlation.

Measures of Central Tendency Statistics indicating the center of the distribution are called *measures of central tendency,* which include the mean, median, and mode. They are all scores that are typical of the center of the distribution. The **mean** is the arithmetic average, and it is what most of us think of when we hear the word "average." The **median** is the middle score in a distribution—half the scores fall above it and half fall below it. The **mode** is the score that occurs most often.

Mean The arithmetic average of a distribution, which is obtained by adding the values of all the scores and dividing by the number of scores (N).

Median The halfway point in a set of data; half the scores fall above the median, and half fall below it.

Mode The score that occurs most frequently in a data set.

Mean What is your average exam score in your psychology class? What is the average yearly rainfall in your part of the country? What is the average reading test score in your city? When these types of questions ask for the average, they're generally asking for the "mean." The arithmetic *mean* is the weighted average of all the raw scores, which is computed by totaling all the raw scores and then dividing that total by the number of scores added together. In statistical computation, the mean is represented by an "X" with a bar above it ($\bar{X}$, pronounced "X bar"), each individual raw score by an "X," and the total number of scores by an "N." For example, if we wanted to compute the $\bar{X}$ of the raw statistics test scores in Table A.1, we would sum all the

TABLE A.5 Computation of the Mean for 10 IQ Scores

IQ SCORES X
143
127
116
98
85
107
106
98
104
116
$\Sigma X = 1100$
$\text{Mean} = \bar{X} = \dfrac{\Sigma X}{N} = \dfrac{1,100}{10} = 110$

X's (Σ, with Σ meaning sum) and divide by N (number of scores). In Table A.1, the sum of all the scores is equal to 3100 and there are 50 scores. Therefore, the mean of these scores is

$$\bar{X} = \frac{3100}{50} = 62$$

Table A.5 illustrates how to calculate the mean for 10 IQ scores.

Median The *median* is the middle score in the distribution once all the scores have been arranged in rank order. If *N* (the number of scores) is odd, then there actually is a middle score and that middle score is the median. When *N* is even, there are two middle scores and the median is the mean of those two scores. **Table A.6** shows the computation of the median for two different sets of scores, one set with 15 scores and one with 10.

Mode Of all the measures of central tendency, the easiest to compute is the *mode*, which is merely the most frequent score. It is computed by finding the score that occurs most often. Whereas there is always only one mean and only one median for each distribution, there can be more than one mode. **Table A.7** shows how to find the mode in a distribution with one mode (unimodal) and in a distribution with two modes (bimodal).

There are several advantages to each of these measures of central tendency, but in psychological research the mean is used most often.

Range A measure of the dispersion of scores between the highest and lowest scores.

Standard deviation A computed measure of how much scores in a sample differ from the mean of the sample.

Measures of Variation

When describing a distribution, it is not sufficient merely to give the central tendency; it is also necessary to give a *measure of variation*, which is a measure of the spread of the scores. By examining this **range**, or spread of scores, we can determine whether the scores are bunched around the middle or tend to extend away from the middle. **Figure A.3** shows three different distributions, all with the same mean but with different spreads of scores. You can see from this figure that, in order to describe these different distributions accurately, there must be some measures of the variation in their spread. The most widely used measure of variation is the **standard deviation**, which is represented by a lowercase s. The standard deviation is a standard measurement of how much the scores in a distribution deviate from the mean. The formula for the standard deviation is

$$s = \sqrt{\frac{\Sigma(X - \bar{X})^2}{N}}$$

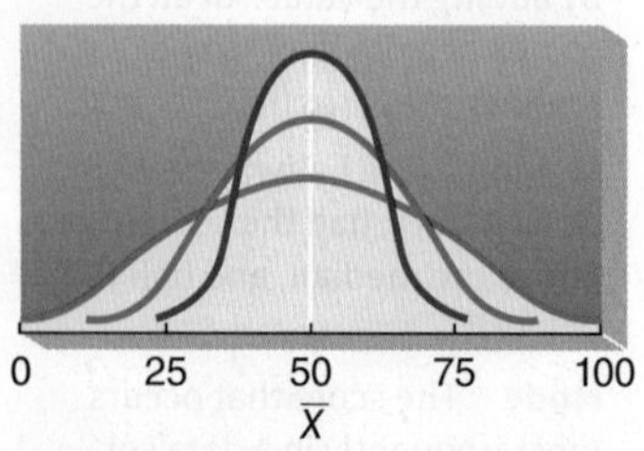

FIGURE A.3 Three distributions having the same mean but a different variability

TABLE A.6 Computation of the Median for Odd and Even Numbers of IQ Scores

IQ	IQ
139	137
130	135
121	121
116	116
107	108 ← middle score
101	106 ← middle score
98	105
96 ← middle score	101
84	98
83	97
82	N = 10
75	N is even
75	
68	
65	$\text{Median} = \frac{106 + 108}{2} = 107$
N = 15	
N is odd	

TABLE A.7 Finding the Mode for Two Different Distributions

IQ	IQ
139	139
138	138
125	125
116 ←	116 ←
116 ←	116 ←
116 ←	116 ←
107	107
100	98 ←
98	98 ←
98	98 ←
Mode = most frequent score	Mode = 116 and 98
Mode = 116	

Table A.8 illustrates how to compute the standard deviation.

Most distributions of psychological data are bell-shaped. That is, most of the scores are grouped around the mean, and the farther the scores are from the mean in either direction, the fewer the scores. Notice the bell shape of the distribution in Figure A.4. Distributions such

TABLE A.8 Computation of the Standard Deviation for 10 IQ Scores

IQ SCORES X	$X - \bar{X}$	$(X - \bar{X})^2$
143	33	1089
127	17	289
116	6	36
98	−12	144
85	−25	625
107	−3	9
106	−4	16
98	−12	144
104	−6	36
116	6	36
$\Sigma X = 1100$		$\Sigma(X - \bar{X})^2 = 2424$
Standard Deviation = s		
$= \sqrt{\frac{\Sigma(X - \bar{X})^2}{N}} = \sqrt{\frac{2424}{10}}$		
$= \sqrt{242.4} = 15.569$		

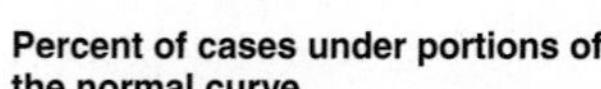

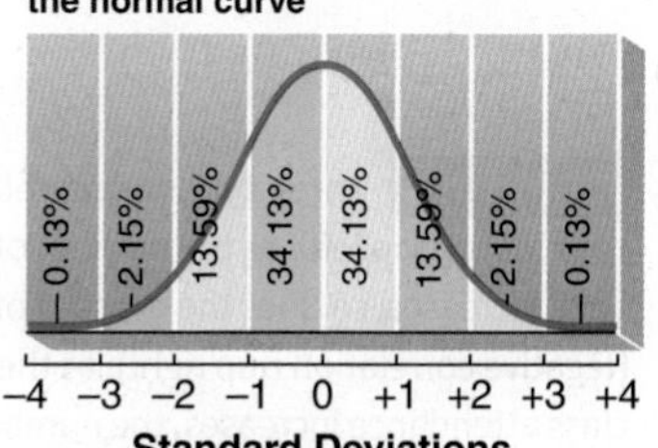

FIGURE A.4 A normal distribution forms a bell-shaped curve In a normal distribution, two-thirds of the scores lie between one standard deviation above and one standard deviation below the mean.

Normal distribution A symmetrical, bell-shaped curve that represents a set of data in which most scores occur in the middle of the possible range, with fewer and fewer scores near the extremes.

as this are called **normal distributions**. In normal distributions, as shown in Figure A.4, approximately two-thirds of the scores fall within a range that is one standard deviation below the mean to one standard deviation above the mean. For example, the Wechsler IQ tests (see Chapter 7) have a mean of 100 and a standard deviation of 15. This means that approximately two-thirds of the people taking these tests will have scores between 85 and 115.

Correlation

Suppose for a moment that you are sitting in the student union with a friend. To pass the time, you and your friend decide to play a game in which you try to guess the height of the next man who enters the union. The winner, the one whose guess is closest to the person's actual height, gets a piece of pie paid for by the loser. When it is your turn, what do you guess? If you're like most people, you'll probably try to estimate the mean of all the men in the union and use that as your guess. The mean is almost always our best guess when we have no other information.

Now let's change the game a little and add a friend who stands outside the union and weighs the next man who enters the union. If your friend texts you with the information that this man weighs 125 pounds, without seeing him would you still predict that he's of average height? Probably not. You'd most likely guess that he's below the mean. Why? Because you intuitively understand that there is a *correlation* (Chapter 1), a relationship, between height and weight, with tall people usually weighing more than short people. Given that 125 pounds is less than the average weight for men, you'll probably guess a less-than-average height. The statistic used to measure this type of relationship between two variables is called a correlation coefficient.

Correlation Coefficient

A *correlation coefficient* (Chapter 1) measures the relationship between two variables, such as height and weight or IQ and annual income. Given any two variables, there are three possible relationships between them: *positive, negative*, and *zero* (no relationship). A *positive relationship* exists when the two variables vary in the same direction (e.g., as height increases, weight normally also increases). A *negative relationship* occurs when the two variables vary in opposite directions (e.g., as temperatures go up, hot chocolate sales go down). There is a *zero* (no) *relationship* when the two variables vary totally independently of one another (e.g., there is no relationship between your height and the number of times you brush your teeth). **Figure A.5** illustrates these three types of correlations.

The computation and the formula for a correlation coefficient (correlation coefficient is delineated by the letter *"r"*) are shown in **Table A.9**. The correlation coefficient *(r)* always has a value between +1 and −1 (it is never greater than +1 and it is never smaller than −1). When *r* is close to +1, it signifies a high positive relationship between the two variables (as one variable goes up, the other variable also goes up). When *r* is close to −1, it signifies a high negative

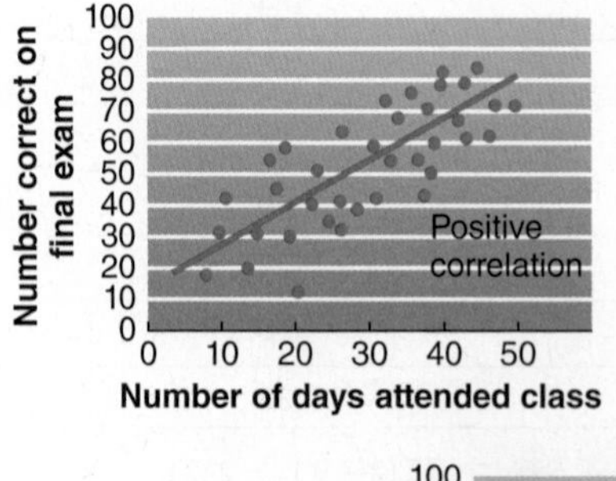

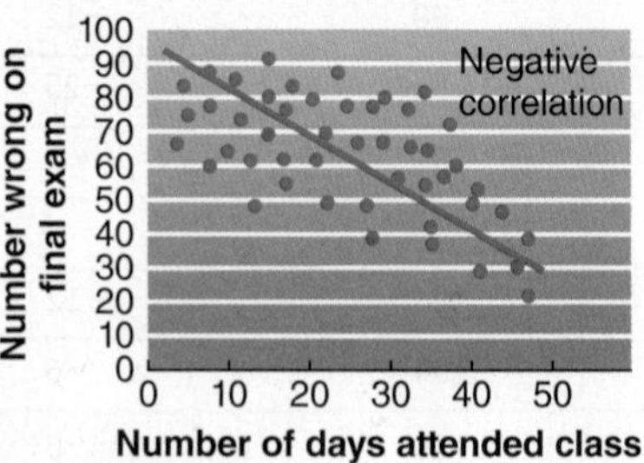

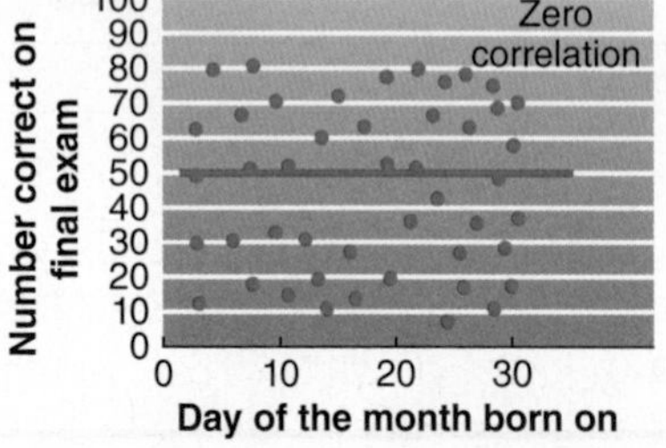

FIGURE A.5 Three types of correlation Positive correlation (top left): as the number of days of class attendance increases, so does the number of correct exam items. Negative correlation (top right): as the number of days of class attendance increases, the number of incorrect exam items decreases. Zero correlation (bottom): the day of the month on which one is born has no relationship to the number of correct exam items.

TABLE A.9 Computation of Correlation Coefficient Between Height and Weight for 10 Men

HEIGHT (INCHES)		WEIGHT (POUNDS)		
X	X^2	Y	Y^2	XY
73	5,329	210	44,100	15,330
64	4,096	133	17,689	8,512
65	4,225	128	16,384	8,320
70	4,900	156	24,336	10,920
74	5,476	189	35,721	13,986
68	4,624	145	21,025	9,860
67	4,489	145	21,025	9,715
72	5,184	166	27,556	11,952
76	5,776	199	37,601	15,124
71	5,041	159	25,281	11,289
Total = 700	49,140	1,630	272,718	115,008

$$r = \frac{N \cdot \Sigma XY - \Sigma X \cdot \Sigma Y}{\sqrt{[N \cdot \Sigma X^2 - (\Sigma X)^2} \sqrt{[N \cdot \Sigma Y^2 - (\Sigma Y)^2]}}$$

$$r = \frac{10 \cdot 115{,}008 - 700 \cdot 1{,}630}{\sqrt{[10 \cdot 49{,}140 - 700^2]} \sqrt{[10 \cdot 272{,}718 - 1{,}630^2]}}$$

$$r = 0.92$$

relationship between the two variables (as one variable goes up, the other variable goes down). When r is 0, there is no linear relationship between the two variables being measured.

Correlation coefficients can be quite helpful in making predictions. Bear in mind, however, that predictions are just that: *predictions.* They will have some error as long as the correlation coefficients on which they are based are not perfect (+1 or −1). Also, correlations cannot reveal any information regarding causation. Merely because two factors are correlated, it does not mean that one factor causes the other. Consider, for example, ice cream consumption and swimming pool use. These two variables are positively correlated with one another, in that as ice cream consumption increases, so does swimming pool use. But nobody would suggest that eating ice cream *causes* swimming, or vice versa. Similarly, just because LeBron James eats Wheaties and can do a slam dunk it does not mean that you will be able to do one if you eat the same breakfast. The only way to determine the *cause* of behavior is to conduct an experiment and analyze the results by using inferential statistics.

Inferential Statistics

Knowing the descriptive statistics associated with different distributions, such as the mean and standard deviation, can enable us to make comparisons between various distributions. By making these comparisons, we may be able to observe whether one variable is related to another or whether one variable has a causal effect on another. When we design an experiment specifically to measure causal effects between two or more variables, we use *inferential statistics* to analyze the data collected. Although there are many inferential statistics, the one we will discuss is the t-test, since it is the simplest.

T-Test Suppose we believe that drinking alcohol causes a person's reaction time to slow down. To test this hypothesis, we recruit 20 participants and separate them into two groups. We ask the participants in one group to drink a large glass of orange juice with one ounce of alcohol for every 100 pounds of body weight (e.g., a person weighing 150 pounds would get 1.5

TABLE A.10 Reaction Times in Milliseconds (MSEC) for Participants in Alcohol and no Alcohol Conditions and Computation of t

RT (MSEC) ALCOHOL X_1	RT (MSEC) NO ALCOHOL X_2
200	143
210	137
140	179
160	184
180	156
187	132
196	176
198	148
140	125
159	120
$SX_1 = 1{,}770$	$SX_2 = 1{,}500$
$N_1 = 10$	$N_2 = 10$
$\bar{X}_1 = 177$	$\bar{X}_2 = 150$
$s_1 = 24.25$	$s_2 = 21.86$
$\Sigma_{\bar{X}1} = \frac{S}{\sqrt{N_1 - 1}} = 8.08$	$\Sigma_{\bar{X}2} = \frac{S}{\sqrt{N_2 - 1}} = 7.29$
$S_{\bar{X}1-\bar{X}2} = \sqrt{S_{\bar{X}1}^2 + S_{\bar{X}2}^2} = \sqrt{8.08^2 + 7.29^2} = 10.88$	
$t = \frac{\bar{X}_1 - \bar{X}_2}{S_{\bar{X}1-\bar{X}2}} = \frac{177 - 150}{10.88} = 2.48$	
$t = 2.48, p < .05$	

ounces of alcohol). We ask the control group to drink an equivalent amount of orange juice with no alcohol added. Fifteen minutes after the drinks, we have each participant perform a reaction time test that consists of pushing a button as soon as a light is flashed. (The reaction time is the time between the onset of the light and the pressing of the button.) **Table A.10** shows the data from this hypothetical experiment. It is clear from the data that there is definitely a difference in the reaction times of the two groups: There is an obvious difference between the means. However, it is possible that this difference is due merely to chance. To determine whether the difference is real or due to chance, we can conduct a *t*-test. We have run a sample *t*-test in Table A.10.

The logic behind a *t*-test is relatively simple. In our experiment we have two samples. If each of these samples is from the *same* population (e.g., the population of all people, whether drunk or sober), then any difference between the samples will be due to chance. On the other hand, if the two samples are from *different* populations (e.g., the population of drunk individuals *and* the population of sober individuals), then the difference is a significant difference and not due to chance.

If there is a significant difference between the two samples, then the independent variable must have caused that difference. In our example, there is a significant difference between the alcohol and the no alcohol groups. We can tell this because *p* (the probability that this *t* value will occur by chance) is less than .05. To obtain the *p,* we need only look up the *t* value in a statistical table, which is found in any statistics book. In our example, because there is a significant difference between the groups, we can reasonably conclude that the alcohol did cause a slower reaction time.

A Final Word

In this brief Appendix A, we've discussed the major topics of how to gather and organize your data and the common uses of various statistics. For more information, consult a statistics textbook or an educational website, such as the following.

www.mathsisfun.com/dataonlinecourses.science.psu.edu/statprogram/review_of_basic_statistics
www.wikihow.com/Understand-and-Use-Basic-Statisticsawuch

On the other hand, you may be feeling overwhelmed and may not want more information. You might also be overly anxious and very concerned knowing that psychology majors need to take one or more full courses in statistics. If so, don't panic! Learning statistics is much like learning another language. You begin with the basic rules of "grammar," which in the case of statistics involves the use of symbols and notation. Later, you'll advance on to practice with conversation, which in statistics means hours of homework.

We recognize that doing homework and learning another language may not sound appealing to you at this time. However, it's important to know that a basic understanding of statistics is essential to conducting or interpreting research—and to becoming an informed, everyday consumer. Furthermore, "fluency" in the language of statistics will make you much more employable and could even earn you a higher salary.

Note that if you truly panic at the thought of studying statistics, or suffer from serious "math anxiety," your psychology instructor or college counselor can provide specific guidance and advice. In addition, the following website offers immediate options and self-help techniques: http://www.mathpower.com/

Appendix B

Answers to Self-test Retrieval Practice Questions and Research Challenges

Chapter 1 Introduction and Research Methods

Self-Test—1.1 Introducing Psychology (p. 10) 1. d. 2. a. 3. c. 4. a. 5. d. **Self-Test—1.2 The Science of Psychology (p. 15)** 1. b. 2. Step 1 = Observation and literature review, Step 2 = Testable hypothesis, Step 3 = Research design, Step 4 = Data collection and analysis, Step 5 = Publication, Step 6 = Theory development. 3. d. 4. b. 5. d. **Self-Test—1.3 Research Methods (p. 25)** 1. b. 2. b. 3. a. 4. c. 5. b. **Self-Test—1.4 Strategies for Student Success (p. 31)** 1. c. 2. Survey, Question, Read, Recite, Review, and write. 3. a. 4. a. 5. d. **Research Challenge (p. 25)** Question 1: Experimental. Question 2: IV = whether or not hooked up to "lie detector," DV = participants' reporting of particular behaviors. Experimental Group = participants supposedly hooked up to "lie detector." Control Group = participants not hooked up to "lie detector."

Chapter 2 Neuroscience and Biological Foundations

Self-Test—2.1 Neural and Hormonal Processes (p. 41) 1. c. 2. d. 3. c. 4. b. 5. c. **Self-Test—2.2 Nervous System Organization (p. 48)** 1. d. 2. a. 3. d. 4. c. 5. d. **Self-Test—2.3 A Tour Through the Brain (pp. 53–54)** 1. Refer to Figure 2.10. 2. b. 3. d. 4. c. 5. c. **Self-Test—2.4 The Cerebral Cortex (p. 60)** 1. Refer to Figure 2.16. 2. b. 3. d. 4. c. 5. c. **Research Challenge (p. 56)** Question 1: Descriptive. Question 2: Case study.

Chapter 3 Stress and Health Psychology

Self-Test—3.1 Understanding Stress (p. 72) 1. d. 2. c. 3. c. 4. b. 5. c. **Self-Test—3.2 Stress and Illness (p. 77)** 1. b. 2. d. 3. d. 4. b. 5. d. **Self-Test—3.3 Stress Management (p. 83)** 1. a. 2. d. 3. b. 4. d. 5. d. **Self-Test—3.4 Health Psychology (p. 87)** 1. d. 2. a. 3. a. 4. d. 5. c. **Research Challenge (p. 85)** Question 1: Descriptive and correlational. Question 2: Archival research and negative correlation: increased success winning elections is associated with a decreased life expectancy.

Chapter 4 Sensation and Perception

Self-Test—4.1 Understanding Sensation (p. 96) 1. b. 2. a. 3. c. 4. a. 5. b. **Self-Test—4.2 How We See and Hear (p. 103)** 1. Refer to Process Diagram 4.1. 2. c. 3. b. 4. Refer to Process Diagram 4.2. 5. c. **Self-Test—4.3 Our Other Important Senses (p. 108)** 1. c. 2. c. 3. d. 4. d. 5. b. **Self-Test—4.4 Understanding Perception (p. 117)** 1. c. 2. b. 3. a. 4. b. 5. b. **Research Challenge (p. 116)** Question 1: Both studies used experimental research techniques. Question 2: IV in both studies was the color of the shirt. DV (Study 1) = number of emails, DV (Study 2) = attractiveness and interest in dating/kissing/engaging in sexual activity. Experimental Group = participants wearing the color red. Control Group = participants wearing colors other than red.

Chapter 5 States of Consciousness

Self-Test—5.1 Understanding Consciousness (p. 122) 1. b. 2. a. 3. d. 4. b. 5. d. **Self-Test—5.2 Understanding Sleep and Dreams (p. 132)** 1. d. 2. c. 3. a. 4. a. 5. c. **Self-Test—5.3 Psychoactive Drugs (p. 139)** 1. a. 2. d. 3. a. 4. a. 5. c. **Self-Test—5.4 Meditation and Hypnosis (p. 143)** 1. d. 2. d. 3. b. 4. c. 5. b. **Research Challenge (p. 122)** Question 1: Experimental. Question 2: IV = four driving conditions (driving alone, speaking to a passenger, driving alone while talking on a cell phone to a person in a remote condition, driving alone while talking on a cell phone to a remote person who shared the view of the driver and what the driver could see). DV = drivers' performance. Experimental Group(s) = driving while speaking to a passenger alongside him or her in the simulator, driving alone while speaking on a hands-free cell phone to someone in a remote location, and driving alone while speaking on a hands-free cell phone to someone in a remote location (who could see the face of the driver and also observe the driving scene through a videophone). Control Group = driving alone.

Chapter 6 Learning

Self-Test—6.1 Classical Conditioning (pp. 152–153) 1. c. 2. c. 3. d. 4. d. 5. b. **Self-Test—6.2 Operant Conditioning (p. 162)** 1. b. 2. a. 3. c. 4. d. 5. c. **Self-Test—6.3 Cognitive-Social Learning (p. 167)** 1. d. 2. c. 3. c. 4. a. 5. b. **Self-Test—6.4 Biology of Learning (p. 171)** 1. c. 2. d. 3. b. 4. d. 5. c. **Research Challenge (p. 166)** Question 1: Both descriptive and correlational. Question 2: Descriptive = survey/interview. Correlation = positive. (Note that this study also has many elements of an experiment, but it lacks random assignment.)

Chapter 7 Memory

Self-Test—7.1 The Nature of Memory (p. 185) 1. d. 2. d. 3. a. 4. b. 5. c. **Self-Test—7.2 Forgetting (p. 189)** 1. a. 2. b. 3. c. 4. b. 5. c. **Self-Test—7.3 Biological Bases of Memory (p. 195)** 1. c. 2. d. 3. d. 4. c. 5. c. **Self-Test—7.4 Memory Distortions and Improvement (p. 202)** 1. c. 2. a. 3. c. 4. d. 5. d. **Research Challenge (p. 174)** Question 1: Experimental. Question 2: IV(s) = taking a general photograph, taking a zoomed-in photo, merely observing a museum object, DV = accuracy of memory for the object viewed or photographed. Experimental Group(s) = participants taking a general photograph, participants taking a zoomed-in photograph. Control Group = participants who simply observed the museum object.

Chapter 8 Thinking, Language, and Intelligence

Self-Test—8.1 Thinking (pp. 212–213) 1. c. 2. a. 3. b. 4. c. 5. d. **Self-Test—8.2 Language (p. 219)** 1. d. 2. d. 3. c. 4. b. 5. d. **Self-Test—8.3 Intelligence (p. 223)** 1. d. 2. a. 3. b. 4. a. 5. b. **Self-Test—8.4 Intelligence Controversies (p. 231)** 1. d . 2. b. 3. a. 4. d. 5. d. **Research Challenge (p. 215)** Question 1: Experimental. Question 2: IV = language used (noun or verb form of the word "help"), DV = degree of helping behavior by the children. Experimental Group(s) = children who heard the noun ("helpers"), children who heard the verb ("help"). Control Group = no "true" control group. As in many experiments, the researchers compared the two conditions and used random assignment.

Chapter 9 Life Span Development

Self-Test—9.1 Studying Development (p. 240) 1. d. 2. d. 3. b. 4. a. 5. c. **Self-Test—9.2 Physical Development (p. 249)** 1. d. 2. b. 3. b. 4. c. 5. d. **Self-Test—9.3 Cognitive Development (p. 256)** 1. c. 2. d 3. b. 4. c. 5. d. **Self-Test—9.4 Social-Emotional Development (pp. 267–268)** 1. a. 2. d. 3. c. 4. b. 5. d. **Research Challenge (p. 239)** Question 1: Descriptive. Question 2: Case study.

Chapter 10 Motivation and Emotion

Self-Test—10.1 Theories of Motivation (p. 275) 1. a. 2. d. 3. b. 4. d. 5. b. **Self-Test—10.2 Motivation and Behavior (p. 285)** 1. a. 2. c. 3. c. 4. d. 5. c. **Self-Test—10.3 Components and Theories of Emotion (p. 291)** 1. a. 2. b. 3. a. 4. d. 5. a. **Self-Test—10.4 Experiencing Emotions (p. 298)** 1. c. 2. c. 3. d. 4. a. 5. d. **Research Challenge (p. 294)** Question 1: Descriptive and correlational. Question 2: Study 1 = archival, positive correlation (less diversity correlated with less emotional expressiveness). Study 2 = survey/interview.

Chapter 11 Personality

Self-Test—11.1 Psychoanalytic/Psychodynamic Theories (p. 308) 1. d. 2. b. 3. d. 4. c. 5. c. **Self-Test—11.2 Trait Theories (pp. 313–314)** 1. c. 2. a. 3. d. 4. e. 5. c. **Self-Test—11.3 Humanistic Theories (pp. 316–317)** 1. a. 2. c. 3. c. 4. d. 5. c. **Self-Test—11.4 Social-Cognitive Theories (p. 320)** 1. c. 2. d. 3. b. 4. b. 5. c. **Self-Test—11.5 Biological Theories (p. 323)** 1. b. 2. d. 3. a. 4. d. 5. b. **Self-Test—11.6 Personality Assessment (p. 329)** 1. d. 2. a. 3. a. 4. d. 5. b. **Research Challenge (p. 311)** Question 1: Descriptive and correlational. Question 2: Descriptive = naturalistic observation. Correlational = positive (gorilla life expectancy was positively correlated with personality trait of extroversion).

Chapter 12 Psychological Disorders

Self-Test—12.1 Studying Psychological Disorders (p. 337) 1. c. 2. a. 3. b. 4. Refer to Figure 12.3. 5. d. **Self-Test—12.2 Anxiety Disorders (pp. 341–342)** 1. Refer to Figure 12. 5. 2. a. 3. c. 4. b. 5. c. **Self-Test—12.3 Depressive and Bipolar Disorders (p. 347)** 1. c. 2. a. 3. d. 4. d. 5. c. **Self-Test—12.4 Schizophrenia (pp. 351–352)** 1. a. 2. b. 3. c. 4. a. 5. b. **Self-Test—12.5 Other Disorders (p. 355)** 1. b. 2. a. 3. d. 4. b. 5. c. **Self-Test—12.6 Gender and Cultural Effects (p. 360)** 1. d. 2. d. 3. a. 4. b. 5. b. **Research Challenge (p. 344)** Question 1: Descriptive. 2. Survey/Interview.

Chapter 13 Therapy

Self-Test—13.1 Talk Therapies (p. 371) 1. a. 2. c. 3. d. 4. d. 5. b. **Self-Test—13.2 Behavior Therapies (p. 375)** 1. b. 2. c. 3. d. 4. b. 5. d. **Self-Test—13.3 Biomedical Therapies (p. 380)** 1. d. 2. b. 3. b. 4. c. 5. d. **Self-Test—13.4 Psychotherapy In Perspective (p. 388)** 1. d. 2. a. 3. d. 4. c. 5. c. **Research Challenge (p. 382)** Question 1: Experimental. Question 2: IV = varying amounts of training or instructions, including how to watch movies, DV = divorce rate after 3 years. Experimental Group(s) = the three "intervention" groups. Control Group = couples who received no training or instructions.

Chapter 14 Social Psychology

Self-Test—14.1 Social Cognition (p. 402) 1. c. 2. a. 3. Affect (feelings), Behavior (actions), and Cognitions (thoughts/beliefs). 4. b. 5. c. **Self-Test—14.2 Social Influence (p. 410)** 1. c. 2. c. 3. d. 4. b. 5. c. **Self-Test—14.3 Social Relations (pp. 419–420)** 1. b. 2. a. 3. d. 4. b. 5. a. **Research Challenge (p. 402)** Question 1: Experimental. Question 2: IV = topic discussed (transgendered or recycling), DV = reduction in transphobia. Experimental Group = those that discussed transgender issues. Control Group = those that discussed recycling.

Chapters 15 and 16 available separately upon request.

Chapter 15 Gender and Human Sexuality

Self-Test—15.1 Studying Human Sexuality (p. 425) 1. b. 2. d. 3. d. 4. b. 5. c. **Self-Test—15.2 Sexual Identity (p. 431)** 1. d. 2. d. 3. b. 4. a. 5. c. **Self-Test—15.3 Sex Problems (p. 440)** 1. d. 2. b. 3. d. 4. a. 5. c. **Self-Test—15.4 Sex and Modern Life (p. 448)** 1. d. 2. d. 3. c. 4. c. 5. b. **Research Challenge (p. 428)** Question 1: Descriptive. Question 2. Archival.

Chapter 16 Industrial/Organizational Psychology

Self-Test—16.1 Introducing I/O Psychology (p. 455) 1. b. 2. d. 3. a = Munsterberg. b = Taylor. c = Scott. 4. c. 5. c. **Self-Test—16.2 Management Perspective (p. 466)** 1. c. 2. b. 3. b. 4. d. 5. d. **Self-Test—16.3 Worker Perspective (p. 479)** 1. a. 2. d. 3. d. 4. a = goal. b = expectancy. c = equity. 5. d **Research Challenge (p. 470)** Question 1: Both descriptive and correlational. Question 2: Survey/archival and a positive correlation (higher "fearless dominance" rating equals higher presidential performance rating).

References

Abbey, A., Wegner, R., Woerner, J., Pegram, S. E., & Pierce, J. (2014). Review of survey and experimental research that examine the relationship between alcohol consumption and men's sexual aggression perpetration. *Trauma, Violence, & Abuse, 15,* 265–282. doi:10.1177/1524838014521031

Abolmaali, K., Ghafari, T., & Ajilchi, B. (2014). The prediction of high school girls' happiness based on their educational major and their mothers' gender stereotypes. *Advances in Applied Sociology, 4,* 121–127. doi:10.4236/aasoci.2014.44015.

Acevedo, B. P., & Aron, A. P. (2014). Romantic love, pair-bonding, and the dopaminergic reward system. In M. Mikulincer & P. R. Shaver (Eds.), *Mechanisms of social connection: From brain to group* (pp. 55–69). Washington, DC: American Psychological Association. doi: 10.1037/14250-004

Acierno, R., Gros, D. F., Ruggiero, K. J., Hernandez-Tejada, M. A., Knapp, R. G., Lejuez, C. W., . . . Tuerk, P. W. (2016). Behavioral activation and therapeutic exposure for posttraumatic stress disorder: A noninferiority trial of treatment delivered in person versus home-based telehealth. *Depression and Anxiety, 33,* 415–423. doi:10.1002/da.22476

Adachi, T., Fujino, H., Nakae, A., Mashimo, T., & Sasaki, J. (2014). A meta-analysis of hypnosis for chronic pain problems: A comparison between hypnosis, standard care, and other psychological interventions. *International Journal of Clinical and Experimental Hypnosis, 62,* 1–28. doi:10.1080/00207144.2013.841471

Adams, L. Y. (2015). *Workplace mental health: Manual for nurse managers.* New York, NY: Springer.

Adams, M. J., Majolo, B., Ostner, J., Schülke, O., De Marco, A., Thierry, B., . . . Weiss, A. (2015). Personality structure and social style in macaques. *Journal of Personality and Social Psychology, 109,* 338–353. http://dx.doi.org/10.1037/pspp0000041

Addis, D. R., Leclerc, C. M., Muscatell, K., & Kensinger, E. A. (2010). There are age-related changes in neural connectivity during the encoding of positive, but not negative, information. *Cortex, 46,* 425–433. http://doi.org/10.1016/j.cortex.2009.04.011

Adelmann, P. K., & Zajonc, R. B. (1989). Facial efference and the experience of emotion. *Annual Review of Psychology, 40,* 249–280.

Adi-Japha, E., & Karni, A. (2016). Time for considering constraints on procedural memory consolidation processes: Comment on Pan and Rickard (2015) with specific reference to developmental changes. *Psychological Bulletin, 142,* 568–571. http://dx.doi.org/10.1037/bul0000048

Adler, A. (1927/1954). *Understanding human nature.* New York, NY: Greenburg.

Adolph, K. E., & Berger, S. E. (2012). Physical and motor development. In M. H. Bornstein & M. E. Lamb (Eds.), *Cognitive development: An advanced textbook* (pp. 257–318). New York, NY: Psychology Press.

Adolph, K. E., Dretch, K. S., & LoBue, V. (2014). Fear of heights in infants? *Current Directions in Psychological Science, 23,* 60–66.

Ahlbeck Bergendahl, I., Salvanes, A. G. V., & Braithwaite, V. A. (2016). Determining the effects of duration and recency of exposure to environmental enrichment. *Applied Animal Behaviour Science, 176,* 163–169. doi:10.1016/j.applanim.2015.11.002

Ahlsén, E. (2008). Embodiment in communication—Aphasia, apraxia, and the possible role of mirroring and imitation. *Clinical Linguistics & Phonetics, 22,* 311–315.

Ahmetoglu, G., & Chamorro-Premuzic, T. (2013). *Psych 101.* New York, NY: Springer.

Ahrens, L. M., Mühlberger, A., Auli, P., & Wieser, M. J. (2015). Impaired visuocortical discrimination learning of socially conditioned stimuli in social anxiety. *Social Cognitive and Affective Neuroscience, 10,* 929–937. doi:10.1093/scan/nsu140

Ainsworth, M. D. S. (1967). *Infancy in Uganda: Infant care and the growth of love.* Baltimore, MD: Johns Hopkins University Press.

Ainsworth, M. D. S. (2010). Security and attachment. In R. Volpe (Ed.), *The secure child: Timeless lessons in parenting and childhood education* (pp. 43–53). Charlotte, NC: Information Age.

Ainsworth, M. D. S., Blehar, M., Waters, E., & Wall, S. (1978). *Patterns of attachment: Observations in the strange situation and at home.* Hillsdale, NJ: Erlbaum.

Aizer, A. A., Chen, M. H., McCarthy, E. P., Mendu, M. L., Koo, S., Wilhite, T. J., . . . Nguyen, P. L. (2013). Marital status and survival in patients with cancer. *Journal of Clinical Oncology, 31,* 3869–3876. doi:10.1200/JCO.2013.49.6489.

Akyeampong, E., Hill, A. G., & Kleinman, A. (Eds.). (2015). *The culture of mental illness and psychiatric practice in Africa.* Bloomington, IN: Indiana University Press.

Alaerts, K., Geerlings, F., Herremans, L., Swinnen, S. P., Verhoeven, J., Sunaert, S., & Wenderoth, N. (2015). Functional organization of the action observation network in autism: A graph theory approach. *PLoS ONE, 10:* e0137020.

Albert, M. A., & Dahling, J. J. (2016). Learning goal orientation and locus of control interact to predict academic self-concept and academic performance in college students. *Personality and Individual Differences, 97,* 245–248. http://dx.doi.org/10.1016/j.paid.2016.03.074

Albright, T. D. (2015). Perceiving. *Daedalus, 144,* 22–41. doi:10.1162/DAED_a_00315

Albuquerque, D., Stice, E., Rodríguez-López, R., Manco, L., & Nóbrega, C. (2015). Current review of genetics of human obesity: From molecular mechanisms to an evolutionary perspective. *Molecular Genetics and Genomics, 6,* 1–31. doi:10.1007/s00438-015-1015-9

Aldrich, D. P., & Meyer, M. A. (2015). Social capital and community resilience. *American Behavioral Scientist, 59,* 254–269. doi:10.1177/0002764214550299

Aldridge, L. J., & Islam, M. R. (2012). Cultural differences in athlete attributions for success and failure: The sports pages revisited. *International Journal of Psychology, 47,* 67–75.

Alenina, N., & Klempin, F. (2015). The role of serotonin in adult hippocampal neurogenesis. *Behavioural Brain Research, 277,* 49–57. doi:10.1016/j.bbr.2014.07.038

Al-Issa, I. (2000). Culture and mental illness in Algeria. In I. Al-Issa (Ed.), *Al-Junun: Mental illness in the Islamic world* (pp. 101–119). Madison, CT: International Universities Press.

Alladin, A. (2016). *Integrative CBT for anxiety disorders: An evidence-based approach to enhancing cognitive behavioural therapy with mindfulness and hypnotherapy.* Hoboken, NJ: Wiley. doi:10.1002/9781118509869

Allam, M. D.-E., Soussignan, R., Patris, B., Marlier, L., & Schaal, B. (2010). Long-lasting memory for an odor acquired at the mother's breast. *Developmental Science, 13,* 849–863.

Allan, N. P., Oglesby, M. E., Short, N. A., & Schmidt, N. B. (2016). Examining the panic attack specifier in social anxiety disorder. *Cognitive Behaviour Therapy, 45,* 177–181. http://dx.doi.org/10.1080/16506073.2015.1124447

Allen, J. A., Diefendorff, J. M., & Ma, Y. (2014). Differences in emotional labor across cultures: A comparison of Chinese and U.S. service workers. *Journal of Business and Psychology, 29,* 21–35. doi:10.1007/s10869-013-9288-7

Allport, G. W. (1937). *Personality: A psychological interpretation.* New York, NY: Holt, Rinehart and Winston.

Allport, G. W., & Odbert, H. S. (1936). Trait-names: A psycho-lexical study. *Psychological Monographs: General and Applied, 47,* 1–21.

All Time League Leaders. (2016). NBA.com. Retrieved from http://stats.nba.com/leaders/alltime/?ls=iref:nba:gnav

Almiron-Roig, E., Tsiountsioura, M., Lewis, H. B., Wu, J., Solis-Trapala, I., & Jebb, S. A. (2015). Large portion sizes increase bite size and eating rate in overweight women.

Physiology & Behavior, 139, 297–302. doi:10.1016/j.physbeh.2014.11.041

Alpár, A., Di Marzo, V., & Harkany, T. (2016). At the tip of an iceberg: Prenatal marijuana and its possible relation to neuropsychiatric outcome in the offspring. *Biological Psychiatry, 79,* e33–e45. http://dx.doi.org/10.1016/j.biopsych.2015.09.009

Alvarez, D. (2011). "I had to teach hard": Traumatic conditions and teachers in post-Katrina classrooms. *The High School Journal, 94,* 28–39.

American Association of Suicidology (2016). *Myths about suicide.* Retrieved from http://www.suicidology.org/about-aas/national-suicide-prevention-week/myth-fact

American Heart Association. (2013). *Statistical fact sheet: 2013 update.* Retrieved from http://www.heart.org/idc/groups/heart-public/@wcm/@sop/@smd/documents/downloadable/ucm_319588.pdf

American Psychiatric Association (2013). *Diagnostic and statistical manual of mental disorders* (5th ed.). Washington, DC: American Psychiatric Association.

American Psychological Association. (2009). Committee on Animal Research and Ethics (CARE) Annual Report 2009. http://www.apa.org/science/leadership/care/2009-report.aspx

American Psychological Association (2013). Gun violence: Prediction, prevention, and policy. Public and Member Communications, Public Affairs Office. Washington, DC: American Psychological Association. doi:10.1-37/e647302013-001

American Psychological Association. (2014). *Graduate study in psychology: 2014.* Washington, DC: American Psychological Association.

Amianto, F., Ottone, L., Abbate Daga, G., & Fassino, S. (2015). Binge-eating disorder diagnosis and treatment: A recap in front of DSM-5. *BMC Psychiatry, 15,* Article ID 70.

Andersen, P. A. (2014). Nonverbal immediacy in interpersonal communication. In A. W. Siegman & S. Feldman (Eds.), *Multichannel integrations of nonverbal behavior* (pp. 1–36). New York, NY: Psychology Press.

Anderson, C. A. (2001). Heat and violence. *Current Directions in Psychological Science, 10,* 33–38.

Anderson, M. C., Ochsner, K. N., Kuhl, B., Cooper, J., Robertson, E., Gabrieli, S. W., . . . Gabrieli, J. D. E. (2004). Neural systems underlying the suppression of unwanted memories. *Science, 303,* 232–235. doi:10.1126/science.1089504

Ando, J., Fujisawa, K. K., Shikishima, C., Hiraishi, K., Nozaki, M., Yamagata, S., . . . Ooki, S. (2013). Two cohort and three independent anonymous twin projects at the Keio Twin Research Center (KoTReC). *Twin Research & Human Genetics, 16,* 202–216. doi:10.1017/thg.2012.13

Andrade, C., Arumugham, S. S., & Thirthalli, J. (2016). Adverse effects of electroconvulsive therapy. *Psychiatric Clinics of North America, 39, 513–530.* http://dx.doi.org/10.1016/j.psc.2016.04.004

Andreassen, C. S., Torsheim, T., Brunborg, G. S., & Pallesen, S. (2012). Development of a Facebook addiction scale. *Psychological Reports, 110,* 501–517.

Anedo, A. O. (2014). Culture as a vehicle for studying individual differences. *Unizik Journal of Arts and Humanities, 12,* 104–125.

Anestis, M. D., Khazem, L. R., Law, K. C., Houtsma, C., LeTard, R., Moberg, F., & Martin, R. (2015). The association between state laws regulating handgun ownership and statewide suicide rates. *American Journal of Public Health, 105,* 2059–2067. doi:10.2105/AJPH.2014.302465

Angus, D. J., Schutter, D. J. L. G., Terburg, D., van Honk, J., & Harmon-Jones, E. (2016). A review of social neuroscience research on anger and aggression. In E. Harmon-Jones & M. Inzlicht (Eds.), *Social neuroscience: Biological approaches to social psychology* (pp. 223–246). New York, NY: Routledge/Taylor & Francis Group.

Angus, L., Watson, J. C., Elliott, R., Schneider, K., & Timulak, L. (2015). Humanistic psychotherapy research 1990–2015: From methodological innovation to evidence-supported treatment outcomes and beyond. *Psychotherapy Research, 25,* 330–347. doi:10.1080/10503307.2014.989290

Anicich, E. M., Swaab, R. I., & Galinsky, A. D. (2015). Hierarchical cultural values predict success and mortality in high-stakes teams. *Proceedings of the National Academy of Sciences of the United States of America, 112,* 1338–1343. doi:10.1073/pnas.1408800112

Anik, L., Aknin, L. B., Norton, M. I., & Dunn, E. W. (2011). Feeling good about giving: The benefits (and costs) of self-interested charitable behavior. In D. M. Oppenheimer & C. Y. Olivola (Eds.), *The science of giving: Experimental approaches to the study of charity* (pp. 3–13). New York, NY: Psychology Press.

Anisman, H. (2016). *Health psychology.* Thousand Oaks, CA: Sage.

Anker, J. J., Kushner, M. G., Thuras, P., Menk, J., & Unruh, A. S. (2016). Drinking to cope with negative emotions moderates alcohol use disorder treatment response in patients with co-occurring anxiety disorder. *Drug and Alcohol Dependence, 159,* 93–100. doi:10.1016/j.drugalcdep.2015.11.031

Annese, J., Schenker-Ahmed, N. M., Bartsch, H., Maechler, P., Sheh, C., Thomas, N., . . . Corkin, S. (2014). Postmortem examination of patient H.M.'s brain based on histological sectioning and digital 3D reconstruction. *Nature Communications, 5.* doi:10.1038/ncomms4122

Antes, A. L. (2016). Navigating the gray areas of scientific work: Questionable research practices and training in the responsible conduct of research. In A. Dade, L. Olafson, & S. M. DiBella (Eds.), *Implementing a comprehensive research compliance program: A handbook for research officers* (pp. 145–180). New York, NY: Springer.

Antunes, H. K., Leite, G. S., Lee, K. S., Barreto, A. T., Santos, R. V., Souza, H. S., . . . de Mello, M. T. (2016). Exercise deprivation increases negative mood in exercise-addicted subjects and modifies their biochemical markers. *Physiology & Behavior, 156,* 182–190. doi:10.1016/j.physbeh.2016.01.028

Antypa, N., Souery, D., Tomasini, M., Albani, D., Fusco, F., Mendlewicz, J., & Serretti, A. (2016). Clinical and genetic factors associated with suicide in mood disorder patients. *European Archives of Psychiatry and Clinical Neuroscience, 266,* 181–193. http://dx.doi.org/10.1007/s00406-015-0658-1

Anxiety and Depression Association of America. (2016). Facts and statistics. *ADAA.* Retrieved from https://www.adaa.org/about-adaa/press-room/facts-statistics

APA Congressional Briefing. (2015). APA congressional briefing highlights role of animal research in understanding human development. *Psychological Science Agenda, 29.* No Pagination Specified. doi:10.1037/e525222015-003

Aragona, M. (2015). Rethinking received views on the history of psychiatric nosology: Minor shifts, major continuities. In P. Zachar, D. S. Stoyanov, M. Aragona, & A. Jablensky (Eds.), *International perspectives in philosophy and psychiatry. Alternative perspectives on psychiatric validation* (pp. 27–46). New York, NY: Oxford University Press.

Arbona, C., & Jimenez, C. (2014). Minority stress, ethnic identity, and depression among Latino/a college students. *Journal of Counseling Psychology, 61,* 162–168. doi:10.1037/a0034914

Arca, M. (2015). Dyslipidemia and cardiovascular risk in obesity. In A. Lenzi, S. Migliaccio, & L. M. Donini (Eds.), *Multidisciplinary approach to obesity: From assessment to treatment* (pp. 121–130). Cham, CH: Springer. doi:10.1007/978-3-319-09045-0_12

Armstrong, K. H., Ogg, J. A., Sundman-Wheat, A. N., & Walsh, A. S. J. (2014). Evidence-based practices with children and their caregivers. In K. H. Armstrong, J. A. Ogg, A. N. Sundman-Wheat, & A. S. J. Walsh (Eds.), *Evidence-based interventions for children with challenging behavior* (pp. 51–110). New York, NY: Springer.

Armstrong, T. A., Boutwell, B. B., Flores, S., Symonds, M., Keller, S., & Gangitano, D. A. (2014). Monoamine oxidase A genotype, childhood adversity, and criminal behavior in an incarcerated sample. *Psychiatric Genetics, 24,* 164–171. doi:10.1097/YPG.0000000000000033

Arnal, P. J., Drogou, C., Sauvet, F., Regnauld, J., Dispersyn, G., Faraut, B., . . . Chennaoui, M. (2016). Effect of sleep extension on the subsequent testosterone, cortisol and prolactin responses to total sleep deprivation and recovery. *Journal of Neuroendocrinology, 28,* 1–9. http://dx.doi.org/10.1111/jne.12346

Arnedo, J., Svrakic, D. M., del Val, C., Romero-Zaliz, R., Hernández-Cuervo, H., Fanous, A. H., . . . Molecular Genetics of Schizophrenia Consortium. (2015). Uncovering the hidden risk architecture of the schizophrenias: Confirmation in three independent genome-wide association studies. *The American Journal of Psychiatry, 172,* 139–153. doi:10.1176/appi.ajp2014.14040435

Arnett, J. J. (2000). Emerging adulthood: A theory of development from the late teens through the twenties. *American Psychologist, 55,* 469–480.

Arnett, J. J. (2015). Identity development from adolescence to emerging adulthood: What we know and (especially) don't know. In K. C. McLean & M. Sved (Eds.), *The Oxford handbook of identity development* (pp. 53–64). New York, NY: Oxford University Press.

Arntz, A. (2015). Borderline personality disorder. In A. T. Beck, D. D. Davis, & A. Freeman (Eds.), *Cognitive therapy of personality disorders* (3rd ed., pp. 366–390). New York, NY: Guilford.

Aronson, J., Jannone, S., McGlone, M., & Johnson-Campbell, T. (2009). The Obama effect: An experimental test. *Journal of Experimental Social Psychology, 45,* 957–960. doi:10.1016/j. jesp.2009.05.006

Arora, P., Pössel, P., Barnard, A. D., Terjesen, M., Lai, B. S., Ehrlich, C. J., . . . Gogos, A. K. (2015). Cognitive interventions. In R. Flanagan, K. Allen, & E. Levine (Eds.), *Cognitive and behavioral interventions in the schools: Integrating theory and research into practice* (pp. 221–248). New York, NY: Springer. doi:10.100AC7/978-1-4939-1972-7

Arora, P., Pössel, P., Barnard, A. D., Terjesen, M., Lai, B. S., Ehrlich, C. J., . . . Gogos, A. K. (2015). Cognitive interventions. In R. Flanagan, K. Allen, & E. Levine (Eds.), *Cognitive and behavioral interventions in the schools: Integrating theory and research into practice* (pp. 221–248). New York, NY: Springer. doi:10.1007/978-1-4939-1972-7

Arsena, A., Silvera, D. H., & Pandelaere, M. (2014). Brand trait transference: When celebrity endorsers acquire brand personality traits. *Journal of Business Research, 67,* 1537–1543. doi:10.1016/j.jbusres.2014.01.011

Artigas, F. (2015). Developments in the field of antidepressants, where do we go now? *European Neuropsychopharmacology, 25,* 657–670. doi:10.1016/j.euroneuro.2013.04.013

Aruguete, M. S., & Hardy, P. M. (2016). Performance attributions of African American and White college students. *North American Journal of Psychology, 18,* 257–268.

Asch, S. E. (1951). Effects of group pressure upon the modification and distortion of judgment. In H. Guetzkow (Ed.), *Groups, leadership, and men: Research in human relations* (pp. 170–190). Pittsburgh, PA: Carnegie Press.

Ashrafioun, L., Pigeon, W. R., Conner, K. R., Leong, S. H., & Oslin, D. W. (2016). Prevalence and correlates of suicidal ideation and suicide attempts among veterans in primary care referred for a mental health evaluation. *Journal of Affective Disorders, 189,* 344–350. http://dx.doi.org/10.1016/j.jad.2015.09.014

Ashton, J. (2013, January 29). *10 cures for technostress.* Retrieved from http://readwrite.com/2013/01/29/10-cures-for-technostress#awesm=~oAYFmEMmcWejFE

Ashworth, D. K., Sletten, T. L., Junge, M., Simpson, K., Clarke, D., Cunnington, D., & Rajaratnam, S. M. W. (2015). A randomized controlled trial of cognitive behavioral therapy for insomnia: An effective treatment for comorbid insomnia and depression. *Journal of Counseling Psychology, 62,* 115–123. doi:10.1037/cou0000059

Askenasy, J. J. (2016). Low facing dreams. *Abnormal and Behavioral Psychology, 2,* 109. doi:10.4172/abp.1000109

Askew, C., Reynolds, G., Fielding-Smith, S., & Field, A. P. (2016). Inhibition of vicariously learned fear in children using positive modeling and prior exposure. *Journal of Abnormal Psychology, 125,* 279–291. doi:10.1037/abn0000131

Asl, S. S., Saifi, B., Sakhaie, A., Zargooshnia, S., & Mehdizadeh, M. (2015). Attenuation of ecstasy-induced neurotoxicity by N-acetylcysteine. *Metabolic Brain Disease, 30,* 171–181. doi:10.1007/s11011-014-9598-0

Atanasov, P. D., & Kunreuther, H. (2016). Cautious defection: Group representatives cooperate and risk less than individuals. *Journal of Behavioral Decision Making, 29,* 372–380. doi:10.1002/bdm.1880

Atkinson, R. C., & Shiffrin, R. M. (1968). Human memory: A proposed system and its control processes. In K. W. Spence & J. T. Spence (Eds.), *The psychology of learning and motivation* (Vol. 2, pp. 90–91). New York, NY: Academic Press.

Aucouturier, J.-J., Johansson, P., Hall, L., Segnini, R., Mercadié, L., & Watanabe, K. (2016). Covert digital manipulation of vocal emotion alter speakers' emotional states in a congruent direction. *Proceedings of the National Academy of Sciences of the United States of America, 113,* 948–953. doi:10.1073/pnas.1506552113

Au, E. W. M. (2015). Locus of control, self-efficacy, and the mediating effect of outcome control: Predicting course-level and global outcomes in an academic context. *Anxiety, Stress & Coping, 28,* 425–444. doi:10.1080/10615806.2014.976761

Auger, A. P. (2016). Genetic, epigenetic and gene-environment interactions: Impact on the pathogenesis of mental illnesses in women. In D. J. Castle & K. M. Abel (Eds.), *Comprehensive women's mental health* (pp. 45–54). New York, NY: Cambridge University Press.

Augustinack, J. C., van der Kouwe, A. J. W., Salat, D. H., Benner, T., Stevens, A. A., Annese, J., . . . Corkin, S. (2014). H.M.'s contributions to neuroscience: A review and autopsy studies. *Hippocampus, 24,* 1267–1286. http://dx.doi.org/10.1002/hipo.22354

Aunola, K., Viljaranta, J., Lehtinen, E., & Nurmi, J. E. (2013). The role of maternal support of competence, autonomy and relatedness in children's interests and mastery orientation. *Learning and Individual Differences, 25,* 171–177. doi:10.1016/j.lindif.2013.02.002

Auzoult, L. (2015). Autonomy and resistance to authority. *Swiss Journal of Psychology, 74,* 49–53. doi:10.1024/1421-0185/a000149

Avieli, H., Ben-David, S., & Levy, I. (2016). Predicting professional quality of life among professional and volunteer caregivers. *Psychological Trauma: Theory, Research, Practice, and Policy, 8,* 80–87. doi:10.1037/tra0000066

Awasthi, A., & Mandal, M. K. (2015). Facial expressions of emotions: Research perspectives. In M. K. Mandal & A. Awasthi (Eds.), *Understanding facial expressions in communication: Cross-cultural and multidisciplinary perspectives* (pp. 1–18). New York, NY: Springer. doi:10.1007/978-81-322-1934-7_1

Axtell, R. E. (2007). *Essential do's and taboos: The complete guide to international business and leisure travel.* Hoboken, NJ: Wiley.

Aziz, W., Wang, W., Kesaf, S., Mohamed, A. A., Fukazawa, Y., & Shigemoto, R. (2014). Distinct kinetics of synaptic structural plasticity, memory formation, and memory decay in massed and spaced learning. *Proceedings of the National Academy of Sciences of the United States of America, 11,* E194–E202. doi:10.1073/pnas.1303317110

Babbitt, L. G., Toosi, N. R., & Sommers, S. R. (2016). A broad and insidious appeal: Unpacking the reasons for endorsing racial color blindness. In H. A. Neville, M. E. Gallardo, & D. W. Sue (Eds.), *The myth of racial color blindness: Manifestations, dynamics, and impact* (pp. 53–68). Washington, DC: American Psychological Association. http://dx.doi.org/10.1037/14754-004

Babel, P. (2016). Memory of pain induced by physical exercise. *Memory, 24,* 548–559. doi:10.1080/09658211.2015.1023809.

Baddeley, A. D. (1992). Working memory. *Science, 255,* 556–559. doi:10.1126/science.1736359

Baddeley, A. D. (2007). *Working memory, thought, and action. Oxford psychology series.* New York, NY: Oxford University Press.

Baddeley, A. D., Eysenck, M. W., & Anderson, M. C. (2015). *Memory.* New York, NY: Psychology Press.

Baer, J. (2013). Teaching for creativity: Domains and divergent thinking, intrinsic motivation, and evaluation. In M. Banks Gregerson, H. T. Snyder, & J. C. Kaufman (Eds.), *Teaching creatively and teaching creativity* (pp. 175–181). New York, NY: Springer.

Bagby, R. M., Sellbom, M., Ayearst, L. E., Chmielewski, M. S., Anderson, J. L., & Quilty, L. C. (2014). Exploring the hierarchical structure of the MMPI-2-RF personality psychopathology five in psychiatric patient and university student samples. *Journal of Personality Assessment, 96,* 166–172. doi:10.1080/00223891.2013.825623

Bailey, D. P., Smith, L. R., Chrismas, B. C., Taylor, L., Stensel, D. J., Deighton, K., . . . Kerr, C. J. (2015). Appetite and gut hormone responses to moderate-intensity continuous exercise versus high-intensity interval exercise, in normoxic and hypoxic conditions. *Appetite, 89,* 237–245. doi:10.1016/j.appet.2015.02.019

Bailey, J. M., Vasey, P. L., Diamond, L M., Breedlove, S. M., Vilain, E., & Epprecht, M. (2016). Sexual orientation, controversy, and science. *Psychological Science in the Public Interest, 17,* 45–101. doi:10.1177/1529100616637616

Baillargeon, R., & DeVos, J. (1991). Object permanence in young infants: Further evidence. *Child Development, 62,* 1227–1246. doi:10.2307/1130803

Bajwa, N. M., Halavi, S., Hamer, M., Semple, B. D., Noble-Haeusslein, L. J., Baghchechi, M., . . . Obenaus, A. (2016). Mild concussion, but not moderate traumatic brain injury, is associated with long-term depression-like phenotype in mice. *PLoS ONE, 11:* e0146886. http://dx.doi.org/10.1371/journal.pone.0146886

Baker, S. (2015, January 3). Breaking the taboo: It's time to talk about mental health. *CNN Vital Signs.* http://www.cnn.com/search/?text=breaking+the+taboo+it%27s+-time+to+talk+about+mental+health+baker

Bakker, B. N., Klemmensen, R., Nørgaard, A. A., & Schumacher, G. (2016). Stay loyal or exit the party? How openness to experience and extroversion explain vote switching. *Political Psychology, 37,* 419–429. http://dx.doi.org/10.1111/pops.12257

Bakker, N., Shahab, S., Giacobbe, P., Blumberger, D. M., Daskalakis, Z. J., Kennedy, S. H., & Downar, J. (2015). rTMS of the dorsomedial prefrontal cortex for major depression: Safety, tolerability, effectiveness, and outcome predictors for 10 Hz versus intermittent theta-burst stimulation. *Brain Stimulation, 8,* 208–215. doi:10.1016/j.brs.2014.11.002

Bakou, A., Margiotoudi, K., Kouroupa, A., & Vatakis, A. (2014). Temporal and sensory experiences in the dreams of sighted and congenital blind individuals. *Procedia-Social and Behavioral Sciences, 126,* 188–189. doi:10.1016/j.sbspro.2014.02.364

Bakshy, E., Messing, S., & Adamic, L. A. (2015). Exposure to ideologically diverse news and opinion on Facebook. *Science, 348,* 1130–1132. doi:10.1126/science.aaa1160

Bak, T. H., Long, M. R., Vega-Mendoza, M., & Sorace, A. (2016). Novelty, challenge, and practice: The impact of intensive language learning on attentional functions. *Plos One,* 11: e0153485. doi:10.1371/journal.pone.0153485.

Baldry, A. C., & Pagliaro, S. (2014). Helping victims of intimate partner violence: The influence of group norms among lay people and the police. *Psychology of Violence, 4,* 334–347. doi:10.1037/a0034844

Bandura, A. (1969). *Principles of behavior modification.* New York, NY: Holt, Rinehart & Winston.

Bandura, A. (1989). Self-regulation of motivation and action through internal standards and goal systems. In L. A. Pervin (Ed.), *Goals concepts in personality and social psychology* (pp. 19–85). Hillsdale, NJ: Erlbaum.

Bandura, A. (1997). *Self-efficacy: The exercise of control.* New York, NY: Freeman.

Bandura, A. (2008). Reconstrual of "free will" from the agentic perspective of social cognitive theory. In J. Baer, J. C. Kaufman, & R. F. Baumeister (Eds.), *Are we free? Psychology and free will* (pp. 86–127). New York, NY: Oxford University Press.

Bandura, A. (2011). But what about that gigantic elephant in the room? In R. M. Arkin (Ed.), *Most underappreciated: 50 prominent social psychologists describe their most unloved work* (pp. 51–59). New York, NY: Oxford University Press.

Bandura, A. (2012). Social cognitive theory. In P. A. M. Van Lange, A. W. Kruglanski, & E. T. Higgins (Eds.), *Handbook of theories of social psychology* (Vol. 1, pp. 349–373). Thousand Oaks, CA: Sage.

Bandura, A., Ross, D., & Ross, S. (1961). Transmission of aggression through imitation of aggressive models. *Journal of Abnormal & Social Psychology, 63,* 575–582. doi:10.1037/h0045925

Bandura, A., & Walters, R. H. (1963). *Social learning and personality development.* New York, NY: Holt, Rinehart and Winston.

Banerjee, S. C., Greene, K., Yanovitzky, I., Bagdasarov, Z., Choi, S. Y., & Magsamen-Conrad, K. (2015). Adolescent egocentrism and indoor tanning: Is the relationship direct or mediated? *Journal of Youth Studies, 18,* 357–375. doi:10.1080/13676261.2014.963536

Bankó, É. M., & Vidnyánszky, Z. (2010). Retention interval affects visual short-term memory encoding. *Journal of Neurophysiology, 103,* 1425–1430. doi:10.1152/jn.00868.2009

Banks, J. B., Tartar, J. L., & Tamayo, B. A. (2015). Examining factors involved in stress-related working memory impairments: Independent or conditional effects? *Emotion, 15,* 827–836. http://dx.doi.org/10.1037/emo0000096

Baptista, J., Derakhshani, M., & Tressoldi, P. E. (2015). Explicit anomalous cognition: A review of the best evidence in Ganzfeld, forced choice, remote viewing and dream studies. In E. Cardeña, J. Palmer, & D. Marcusson-Clavertz (Eds.), *Parapsychology: A handbook for the 21st century* (pp. 192–214). Jefferson, NC: McFarland & Co.

Barber, J. P., & Solomonov, N. (2016). Psychodynamic theories. In J. C. Norcross, G. R. VandenBos, D. K. Freedheim, & Olatunji, B. O. (Eds.), *APA handbook of clinical psychology: Theory and research, Vol. 2* (pp. 53–77). Washington, DC: American Psychological Association. http://dx.doi.org/10.1037/14773-003

Bardi, L., Regolin, L., & Simion, F. (2014). The first time ever I saw your feet: Inversion effect in newborns' sensitivity to biological motion. *Developmental Psychology, 50,* 986–993. doi:10.1037/a0034678

Barelds, D. P. H., & Dijkstra, P. (2011). Positive illusions about a partner's personality and relationship quality. *Journal of Research in Personality, 45,* 37–43.

Bargh, J. A. (2014). Our unconscious mind. *Scientific American, 310,* 30–37.

Barnes, J. C., Boutwell, B. B., & Beaver, K. M. (2014). Genetic and nonshared environmental factors predict handgun ownership in early adulthood. *Death Studies, 38,* 156–164. doi:10.1080/07481187.2012.738769

Barnow, S., & Balkir, N. (Eds.). (2013). *Cultural variations in psychopathology: From research to practice.* Cambridge, MA: Hogrefe.

Barnum, S. E., Woody, M. L., & Gibb, B. E. (2013). Predicting changes in depressive symptoms from pregnancy to postpartum: The role of brooding rumination and negative inferential styles. *Cognitive Therapy and Research, 37,* 71–77.

Barrett, D., Sogolow, Z., Oh, A., Panton, J., Grayson, M., & Justiniano, M. (2014). Content of dreams from WWII POWs. *Imagination, Cognition and Personality, 33,* 193–204. doi:10.2190/IC.33.1-2.g

Barton, A. L., & Hirsch, J. K. (2016). Permissive parenting and mental health in college students: Mediating effects of academic entitlement. *Journal of American College Health, 64,* 1–8. http://dx.doi.org/10.1080/07448481.2015.1060597

Batanova, M., Espelage, D. L., & Rao, M. A. (2014). Early adolescents' willingness to intervene: What roles do attributions, affect, coping, and self-reported victimization play? *Journal of School Psychology, 52,* 279–293. doi:10.1016/j.jsp.2014.02.001

Bateganya, M. H., Amanyeiwe, U., Roxo, U., & Dong, M. (2015). Impact of support groups for people living with HIV on clinical outcomes: A systematic review of the literature. *Journal of Acquired Immune Deficiency Syndromes, 68,* S368–S374. doi:10.1097/QAI.0000000000000519

Bateman, A. W., & Fonagy, P. (2016). The role of mentalization in treatments for personality disorder. In W. J. Livesley, G. Dimaggio, & J. F. Clarkin (Eds.), *Integrated treatment for personality disorder: A modular approach* (pp. 148–172). New York, NY: Guilford Press.

Bates, J. E., Schermerhorn, A. C., & Petersen, I. T. (2014). Temperament concepts in developmental psychopathology. In M. Lewis & K. Rudolph (Eds.), *Handbook of developmental psychopathology* (pp. 311–329). New York, NY: Springer.

Bateson, P., & Martin, P. (2013). *Play, playfulness, creativity and innovation.* New York, NY: Cambridge University Press. doi:10.1017/CBO9781139057691

Batson, C. D. (2014). *The altruism question: Toward a social-psychological answer.* New York, NY: Psychology Press.

Battino, R. (2015). *When all else fails: Some new and some old tools for doing brief therapy.* Norwalk, CT: Crown.

Bauer, G., & Hämmig, O. (Eds.). (2014). *Bridging occupational, organizational, and public health: A transdisciplinary approach.* New York, NY: Springer.

Bauer, P. J., & Larkina, M. (2014). Childhood amnesia in the making: Different distributions of autobiographical memories in children and adults. *Journal of Experimental Psychology: General, 143,* 597–611. doi:10.1037/a0033307

Baugh, C. M., Kiernan, P. T., Kroshus, E., Daneshvar, D. H., Montenigro, P. H., McKee, A. C., & Stern, R. A. (2015). Frequency of head-impact-related outcomes by position in NCAA division 1 collegiate football players. *Journal of Neurotrauma, 32,* 314–326. doi:10.1089/neu.2014.3582

Baumeister, R. F., & Bushman, B. (2014). *Social psychology and human nature* (3rd ed.). Boston, MA: Cengage Learning.

Baum, M. J., & Cherry, J. A. (2015). Processing by the main olfactory system of chemosignals that facilitate mammalian reproduction. *Hormones and Behavior, 68,* 53–64. doi:10.1016/j.yhbeh.2014.06.003

Baumrind, D. (1980). New directions in socialization research. *American Psychologist, 35,* 639–652.

Baumrind, D. (2013). Authoritative parenting revisited: History and current status. In R. E. Larzelere, A. S. Morris, & A. W. Harrist (Eds.), *Authoritative parenting: Synthesizing nurturance and discipline for optimal child development* (pp. 11–34). Washington, DC: American Psychological Association.

Bech, P., Fava, M., Trivedi, M. H., Wisniewski, S. R., & Rush, A. J. (2011). Factor structure and dimensionality of the two depression scales in STAR*D using level 1 datasets. *Journal of Affective Disorders, 132,* 396–400.

Beck, A. T. (1976). *Cognitive therapy and the emotional disorders.* New York, NY: International Universities Press.

Beck, A. T. (2000). *Prisoners of hate.* New York, NY: Harper Perennial.

Beck, A. T., & Bredemeier, K. (2016). A unified model of depression: Integrating clinical, cognitive, biological, and evolutionary perspectives. *Clinical Psychological Science, 4,* 596–619. doi:10.1177/2167702616628523

Beck, A. T., & Dozois, D. J. A. (2014). *Cognitive theory and therapy: Past, present, and future.* New York, NY: Oxford University Press.

Beck, A. T., Freeman, A., & Davis, D. D. (2015). General principles and specialized techniques in cognitive therapy of personality disorders. In A. T. Beck, D. D. Davis, & A. Freeman (Eds.), *Cognitive therapy of personality disorders* (3rd ed., pp. 97–124). New York, NY: Guilford.

Beck, A. T., Haigh, E. A. P., & Baber, K. F. (2012). Biological underpinnings of the cognitive model of depression: A prototype for psychoanalytic research. *Psychoanalytic Review, 99,* 515–537.

Beebe, K. R. (2014). Hypnotherapy for labor and birth. *Nursing for Women's Health, 18,* 48–59. doi:10.1111/1751-486X.12093

Beilin, H. (1992). Piaget's enduring contribution to developmental psychology. *Developmental Psychology, 28,* 191–204.

Belkind-Gerson, J., Hotta, R., Whalen, M., Nayyar, N., Nagy, N., Cheng, L., . . . Dietrich, J. (2016). Engraftment of enteric neural progenitor cells into the injured adult brain. *BMC Neuroscience, 17,* Article 5. doi:10.1186/s12868-016-0238-y

Bell, S. L., Phoenix, C., Lovell, R., & Wheeler, B. W. (2015). Seeking everyday wellbeing: The coast as a therapeutic landscape. *Social Science & Medicine, 142,* 56–67. http://dx.doi.org/10.1016/j.socscimed.2015.08.011

Bem, D. J. (2011). Feeling the future: Experimental evidence for anomalous retroactive influences on cognition and affect. *Journal of Personality and Social Psychology, 100, 407–425.* doi:10.1037/a0021524

Bem, S. L. (1981). Gender schema theory: A cognitive account of sex typing. *Psychological Review, 88,* 354–364. doi:10.1037/0033-295X.88.4.354

Bem, S. L. (1993). *The lenses of gender: Transforming the debate on sexual inequality.* New Haven, CT: Yale University Press.

Benjamin, L. T., Cavell, T. A., & Shallenberger, W. R. (1984). Staying with initial answers on objective tests: Is it a myth? *Teaching of Psychology, 11,* 133–141.

Bennion, K. A., Steinmetz, K. R. M., Kensinger, E. A., & Payne, J. D. (2015). Sleep and cortisol interact to support memory consolidation. *Cerebral Cortex, 25,* 646–657. doi:10.1093/cercor/bht255

Ben-Porath, Y. S. (2013). Self-report inventories: Assessing personality and psychopathology. In J. R. Graham, J. A. Naglieri, & I. B. Weiner (Eds.), *Handbook of psychology, Vol. 10. Assessment psychology* (2nd ed., pp. 622–644). Hoboken, NJ: Wiley.

Benson, H. (2000). *The relaxation response.* New York, NY: HarperTorch.

Ben-Soussan, T. D., Piervincenzi, C., Venditti, S., Verdone, L., Caserta, M., & Carducci, F. (2015). Increased cerebellar volume and BDNF level following quadrato motor training. *Synapse, 69,* 1–6. doi:10.1002/syn.21787

Bentall, R. P., Wickham, S., Shevlin, M., & Varese, F. (2012). Do specific early-life adversities lead to specific symptoms of psychosis? A study from the 2007 The Adult Psychiatric Morbidity Survey. *Schizophrenia Bulletin, 38,* 734–740.

Benton, T. R., McDonnell, S. A., Thomas, N., Ross, D. F., & Honerkamp, N. (2014). On the admissibility of expert testimony on eyewitness identification: A legal and scientific evaluation. *Tennessee Journal of Law & Policy, 2,* 392. Retrieved from http:// trace.tennessee.edu/tjlp/vol2/iss3/3

Ben-Zeév, A. (2014). Why a lover's touch is so powerful. *Psychology Today.* Retrieved from https://www.psychologytoday.com/blog/in-the-name-love/201405/why-lovers-touch-is-so-powerful

Beran, M. J., Parrish, A. E., Perdue, B. M., & Washburn, D. A. (2014). Comparative cognition: Past, present, and future. *International Journal of Comparative Psychology, 27,* 3–30.

Berger, J. (2015). *Personality* (9th ed.). Stamford, CT: Cengage Learning.

Berger, K. S. (2015). *Developing person through childhood and adolescence* (10th ed.). New York, NY: Worth.

Berlyne, D. E. (1970). Novelty, complexity, and hedonic value. *Perception and Psychophysics, 8,* 279–286.

Berman, J., & Prudic, J. (2013). Electroconvulsive therapy. In J. J. Mann, P. J. McGrath, & S. P. Roose (Eds.), *Clinical handbook for the management of mood disorders* (pp. 311–324). New York, NY: Cambridge University Press. http://dx.doi.org/10.1017/CBO9781139175869.024

Berman, N. C., Elliott, C. M., & Wilhelm, S. (2016). Cognitive behavioral therapy for obsessive-compulsive disorder: Theory, assessment, and treatment. In T. J. Petersen, S. E. Sprich, & S. Wilhelm (Eds.), *The Massachusetts General Hospital handbook of cognitive behavioral therapy.* (pp. 105–115). Totowa, NJ: Humana Press. http://dx.doi.org/10.1007/978-1-4939-2605-3_8

Berman, S. M., Paz-Filho, G., Wong, M.-L., Kohno, M., Licinio, J., & London, E. D. (2013). Effects of leptin deficiency and replacement on cerebellar response to food-related cues. *The Cerebellum, 12,* 59–67. doi:10.1007/s12311-012-0360-z

Bernal, G., Cumba-Avilés, E., & Rodriguez-Quintana, N. (2014). Methodological challenges in research with ethnic, racial, and ethnocultural groups. In F. T. L. Leong, L. Comas-Díaz, G. C. Nagayama Hall, V. C. McLoyd,

& J. E. Trimble (Eds.), *APA handbook of multicultural psychology: Vol. 1. Theory and research* (pp. 105–123). Washington, DC: American Psychological Association. doi:10.1037/14189-006

Bernard, L. L. (1924). *Instinct.* New York, NY: Holt.

Bernard, S., Clément, F., & Mercier, H. (2016). Wishful thinking in preschoolers. *Journal of Experimental Child Psychology, 141,* 267–274. http://dx.doi.org/10.1016/j.jecp.2015.07.018

Berns, G. S., Blaine, K., Prietula, M. J., & Pye, B. E. (2013). Short- and long-term effects of a novel on connectivity in the brain. *Brain Connectivity, 3,* 590–600. http://doi.org/10.1089/brain.2013.0166

Berns, G. S., Brooks, A. M., & Spivak, M. (2015). Scent of the familiar: An fMRI study of canine brain responses to familiar and unfamiliar human and dog odors. *Behavioural Processes, 110,* 37–46. doi:10.1016/j.beproc.2014.02.011

Berreman, G. (1971). *Anthropology today.* Del Mar, CA: CRM.

Berry, J., Poortinga, Y., Breugelmans, S., Chasiotis, A., & Sam, D. (2011). *Cross-cultural psychology: Research and applications* (3rd ed.). Cambridge, UK: Cambridge University Press.

Besemer, S., Loeber, R., Hinshaw, S. P., & Pardini, D. A. (2016). Bidirectional associations between externalizing behavior problems and maladaptive parenting within parent-son dyads across childhood. *Journal of Abnormal Child Psychology.* No Pagination Specified. doi:10.1007/s10802-015-0124-6

Best, D. L., & Bush, C. D. (2016). Gender roles in childhood and adolescence. In U. P. Gielen & J. L. Roopnarine (Eds.), *Childhood and adolescence: Cross-cultural perspectives and applications* (2nd ed., pp. 209–239). Santa Barbara, CA: Praeger.

Best, M., Lawrence, N. S., Logan, G. D., McLaren, I. P. L., & Verbruggen, F. (2016). Should I stop or should I go? The role of associations and expectancies. *Journal of Experimental Psychology: Human Perception and Performance, 42,* 115–137. http://dx.doi.org/10.1037/xhp0000116

Bevan, J. L., Gomez, R., & Sparks, L. (2014). Disclosures about important life events on Facebook: Relationships with stress and quality of life. *Computers in Human Behavior, 39,* 246–253. http://dx.doi.org/10.1016/j.chb.2014.07.021

Bhatia, S. (2014). Confirmatory search and asymmetric dominance. *Journal of Behavioral Decision Making, 27,* 468–476. doi:10.1002/bdm.1824

Bhatnagar, K. A. C., Wisniewski, L., Solomon, M., & Heinberg, L. (2013). Effectiveness and feasibility of a cognitive-behavioral group intervention for body image disturbance in women with eating disorders. *Journal of Clinical Psychology, 69,* 1–13.

Bialystok, E., & Craik, F. I. M. (2010). Cognitive and linguistic processing in the bilingual mind. *Current Directions in Psychological Science, 19,* 19–23. doi:10.1177/0963721409358571

Bianchi, E. C. (2014). Entering adulthood in a recession tempers later narcissism. *Psychological Science, 25,* 1429–1437. doi:10.1177/0956797614532818

Bianchi, E. C. (2015). Assessing the robustness of the relationship between entering adulthood in a recession and narcissism. *Psychological Science, 26,* 537–538. doi:10.1177/0956797614568157

Bianchi, M. (Ed.). (2014). *Sleep deprivation and disease: Effects on the body, brain and behavior.* New York, NY: Springer.

Bick, J., Nguyen, V., Leng, L., Piecychna, M., Crowley, M. J., Bucala, R., . . . Grigorenko, E. L. (2015). Preliminary associations between childhood neglect, MIF, and cortisol: Potential pathways to long-term disease risk. *Developmental Psychobiology, 57,* 131–139. doi:10.1002/dev.21265

Biering, K., Andersen, J. H., Lund, T., & Hjollund, N. H. (2015). Psychosocial working environment and risk of adverse cardiac events in patients treated for coronary heart disease. *Journal of Occupational Rehabilitation, 25,* 770–775. http://dx.doi.org/10.1007/s10926-015-9585-2

Birditt, K. S., & Newton, N. J. (2016). Theories of social support and aging. In N. A. Pachana (Ed.), *Encyclopedia of gerontology* (pp. 1–7). New York, NY: Springer.

Birmaher, B., & Brent, D. A. (2016). Depressive and disruptive mood dysregulation disorders. In M. K. Dulcan (Ed.), *Dulcan's textbook of child and adolescent psychiatry* (2nd ed., pp. 245–276). Arlington, VA: American Psychiatric Publishing.

Blacha, C., Schmid, M. M., Gahr, M., Freudenmann, R. W., Plener, P. L., Finter, F., . . . Schönfeldt-Lecuona, C. (2013). Self-inflicted testicular amputation in first lysergic acid diethylamide use. *Journal of Addiction Medicine, 7,* 83–84.

Black, D. W., & Grant, J. E. (2014). *DSM-5 guidebook: The essential companion to the Diagnostic and Statistical Manual of Mental Disorders* (5th ed.). Arlington, VA: American Psychiatric Publishing.

Black, J., & Barnes, J. L. (2015). Fiction and social cognition: The effect of viewing award-winning television dramas on theory of mind. *Psychology of Aesthetics, Creativity, and the Arts, 9,* 423–429. http://dx.doi.org/10.1037/aca0000031

Blacker, K. J., Curby, K. M., Klobusicky, E., & Chein, J. M. (2014). Effects of action video game training on visual working memory. *Journal of Experimental Psychology: Human Perception and Performance, 40,* 1992–2004. doi:10.1037/a0037556

Blair, I. V., Dasgupta, N., & Glaser, J. (2015). Implicit attitudes. In M. Mikulincer, P. R. Shaver, E. Borgida, & J. A. Bargh (Eds.), *APA handbook of personality and social psychology, Vol. 1. Attitudes and social cognition* (pp. 665–691). Washington, DC: American Psychological Association. doi:10.1037/14341-021

Blake, A. B., Nazarian, M., & Castel, A. D. (2015). The Apple of the mind's eye: Everyday attention, metamemory, and reconstructive memory for the Apple logo. *The Quarterly Journal of Experimental Psychology, 68,* 858–865. doi:10.1080/17470218. 2014.1002798

Blanc, J., Bui, E., Mouchenik, Y., Derivois, D., & Birmes, P. (2015). Prevalence of post-traumatic stress disorder and depression in two groups of children one year after the January 2010 earthquake in Haiti. *Journal of Affective Disorders, 172,* 121–126. doi:10.1016/j.jad.2014.09.055

Blecha, P. (2004). *Taboo tunes: A history of banned bands and censored songs.* San Francisco, CA: Backbeat.

Bleske-Rechek, A., Morrison, K. M., & Heidtke, L. D. (2015). Causal inference from descriptions of experimental and non-experimental research: Public understanding of correlation-versus-causation. *The Journal of General Psychology, 142,* 48–70. doi:10.1080/00221309.2014.977216

Blum, K., Oscar-Berman, M., Barh, D., Giordano, J., & Gold, M. S. (2013). Dopamine genetics and function in food and substance abuse. *Journal of Genetic Syndromes & Gene Therapy, 4:* 1000121.

Blumberg, M. S. (2015). Developing sensorimotor systems in our sleep. *Current Directions in Psychological Science, 24,* 32–37. doi:10.1177/0963721414551362

Blume-Marcovici, A. (2010). Gender differences in dreams: Applications to dream work with male clients. *Dreaming, 20,* 199–210.

Blunden, S., & Galland, B. (2014). The complexities of defining optimal sleep: Empirical and theoretical considerations with a special emphasis on children. *Sleep Medicine Reviews, 18,* 371–378. doi:10.1016/j.smrv.2014.01.002

Boag, E. M., & Carnelley, K. B. (2016). Attachment and prejudice: The mediating role of empathy. *British Journal of Social Psychology, 55,* 337–356. http://dx.doi.org/10.1111/bjso.12132

Boag, S. (2012). *Freudian repression, the unconscious, and the dynamics of inhibition.* London, UK: Karnac.

Boergers, J., Gable, C. J., & Owens, J. A. (2014). Later school start time is associated with improved sleep and daytime functioning in adolescents. *Journal of Developmental & Behavioral Pediatrics, 35,* 11–17. doi:10.1097/DBP.0000000000000018

Bogaard, G., Meijer, E. H., Vrij, A., & Merckelbach, H. (2016) Strong, but wrong: Lay people's and police officers' beliefs about verbal and nonverbal cues to deception.

PLoS ONE, 11: e0156615. doi:10.1371/journal.pone.0156615

Bohannon, J. (2016, April 7). For real this time: Talking to people about gay and transgender issues can change their prejudices. *Science*. doi:10.1126/science.aaf9890

Bohon, C. (2015). Feeding and eating disorders. In L. W. Roberts & A. K. Louie (Eds.), *Study guide to DSM-5®* (pp. 233–250). Arlington, VA: American Psychiatric Publishing.

Bonanno, G. A. (2012). Uses and abuses of the resilience construct: Loss, trauma, and health-related adversities. *Social Science & Medicine, 74*, 753–756. http://dx.doi.org/10.1016/j.socscimed.2011.11.022

Bond, M. H. (Ed.). (2015). *Oxford handbook of Chinese psychology.* New York, NY: Oxford University Press.

Bonilla-Silva, E. (2016). Down the rabbit hole: Color-blind racism in Obamerica. In H. A. Neville, M. E. Gallardo, & D. W. Sue (Eds.), *The myth of racial color blindness: Manifestations, dynamics, and impact* (pp. 25–38). Washington, DC: American Psychological Association. http://dx.doi.org/10.1037/14754-002

Bonomi, C. (2015). *The cut and the building of psychoanalysis, Volume 1: Sigmund Freud and Emma Eckstein.* London and New York, NY: Routledge.

Boothroyd, L. G., Jucker, J. L., Thornborrow, T., Jamieson, M. A., Burt, D. M., Barton, R. A., . . . Tovée, M. J. (2016). Television exposure predicts body size ideals in rural Nicaragua. *British Journal of Psychology.* No Pagination Specified. doi:10.1111/bjop.12184

Boothroyd, L. G., Tovee, M. T., & Pollett, T. (2012). Mechanisms of change in body size preferences. *PLoS ONE, 7*: e48691.

Bootzin, R. R., Blank, E. & Peck, T. (2015). Sleeping well. In S J. Lynn, W. T. O'Donohue, & S. O. Lilienfeld (Eds.) *Health, happiness, and well-being: Better living through psychological science* (pp. 168–194). Thousand Oaks, CA: Sage.

Borelli, J. L., Rasmussen, H. F., Burkhart, M. L., & Sbarra, D. A. (2015). Relational savoring in long-distance romantic relationships. *Journal of Social and Personal Relationships, 32*, 1083–1108. doi:10.1177/0265407514558960

Borelli, J. L., Sbarra, D. A., Snavely, J. E., McMakin, D. L., Coffey, J. K., Ruiz, S. K., . . . Chung, S. Y. (2014). With or without you: Attachment avoidance predicts non-deployed spouses' reactions to relationship challenges during deployment. *Professional Psychology: Research and Practice, 45*, 478–487. http://dx.doi.org/10.1037/a0037780

Borghans, L., Golsteyn, B., Heckman, J., & Humphries, J. (2011). Identification problems in personality psychology (Report No. 16917). Retrieved from http://www. nber.org/papers/w16917

Bornstein, M. H., Arterberry, M. E., & Lamb, M. E. (2014). *Development in infancy: A contemporary introduction* (5th ed.). New York, NY: Psychology Press.

Bornstein, R. F. (2015). From surface to depth: Toward a more psychodynamically informed DSM-6. *Psychoanalytic Inquiry, 35*, 45–59. doi:10.1080/07351690.2015.987592

Bornstein, R. F., & Huprich, S. K. (2015). Prologue: Toward an empirically informed 21st-century psychoanalysis: Challenges and opportunities. *Psychoanalytic Inquiry, 35(Supp1)*, 2–4. http://dx.doi.org/10.1080/07351690.2014.987589

Botella, C., Bretón-López, J., Serrano, B., García-Palacios, A., Quero, S., & Baños, R. (2014). Treatment of flying phobia using virtual reality exposure with or without cognitive restructuring: Participants' preferences. *Revista de Psicopatología y Psicología Clínica, 19*, 157–169. doi:10.5944/rppc.vol.19.num.3.2014.13898

Bouazzaoui, B., Follenfant, A., Ric, F., Fay, S., Croizet, J.-C., Atzeni, T., & Taconnat, L. (2016). Ageing-related stereotypes in memory: When the beliefs come true. *Memory, 24*, 659–668. http://dx.doi.org/10.1080/09658211.2015.1040802

Bouchard, T. J. (2014). Genes, evolution and intelligence. *Behavior Genetics, 44*, 549–577. doi:10.1007/s10519-014-9646-x

Bouchard, T. J., Jr. (1997). The genetics of personality. In K. Blum & E. P. Noble (Eds.), *Handbook of psychiatric genetics* (pp. 273–296). Boca Raton, FL: CRC Press.

Bouchard, T. J., Jr. (2013). Genetic influence on human psychological traits. In S. M. Downes & E. Machery (Eds.), *Arguing about human nature: Contemporary debates. Arguing about philosophy* (pp. 139–144). New York, NY: Routledge/Taylor & Francis Group.

Bouchard, T. J., Jr., & McGue, M. (1981). Familial studies of intelligence: A review. *Science, 212*, 1055–1059. doi:10.1126/science.7195071

Boucher, K. L., Rydell, R. J., & Murphy, M. C. (2015). Forecasting the experience of stereotype threat for others. *Journal of Experimental Social Psychology, 58*, 56–62. doi:10.1016/j.jesp.2015.01.002

Bougard, C., Davenne, D., Espie, S., Moussay, S., & Léger, D. (2016). Sleepiness, attention and risk of accidents in powered two-wheelers. *Sleep Medicine Reviews, 25*, 40–51. doi:10.1016/j.smrv.2015.01.006

Boundy, E. O., Dastjerdi, R., Spiegelman, D., Fawzi, W. W., Missmer, S. A., Lieberman, E., . . . Chan, G. J. (2016). Kangaroo mother care and neonatal outcomes: A meta-analysis. *Pediatrics, 137*, 1–16. doi:10.1542/peds.2015-2238

Bourne, L. E., Dominowski, R. L., & Loftus, E. F. (1979). *Cognitive processes.* Englewood Cliffs, NJ: Prentice Hall.

Bourne, L. E., & Healy, A. F. (2014). What's this book all about? In L. E. Bourne & A. F. Healy (Eds.), *Train your mind for peak performance: A science-based approach for achieving your goals* (pp. 3–22). Washington, DC: American Psychological Association.

Bouton, M. E., & Todd, T. P. (2014). A fundamental role for context in instrumental learning and extinction. *Behavioural Processes, 104*, 13–19. doi:10.1016/j.beproc.2014.02.012

Bouvet, R., & Bonnefon, J.-F. (2015). Non-reflective thinkers are predisposed to attribute supernatural causation to uncanny experiences. *Personality and Social Psychology Bulletin, 41*, 955–961. http://dx.doi.org/10.1177/0146167215585728

Bowers, D., Dietz, J., & Jones, J. (2014). Assessment of emotion, mood and affect associated with neurologic disorders. In M. W. Parsons, T. A. Hammeke, & P. J. Snyder (Eds.), *Clinical neuropsychology: A pocket handbook for assessment* (3rd ed., pp. 633–658). Washington, DC: American Psychological Association. doi:10.1037/14339-027

Bowlby, J. (1969). *Attachment and loss: Vol. 1. Attachment.* New York, NY: Basic.

Bowlby, J. (1989). *Secure attachment.* New York, NY: Basic Books.

Bowlby, J. (2000). *Attachment.* New York, NY: Basic.

Boxer, P., Huesmann, L. R., Dubow, E. F., Landau, S. F., Gvirsman, S. D., Shikahi, K., & Ginges, J. (2013). Exposure to violence across the social ecosystem and the development of aggression: A test of ecological theory in the Israeli–Palestinian conflict. *Child Development, 84*, 163–177. doi:10.1111/j.1467-8624.2012.01848.x

Boyce, C. J., Wood, A. M., Daly, M., & Sedikides, C. (2015). Personality change following unemployment. *Journal of Applied Psychology, 100*, 991–1011. http://dx.doi.org/10.1037/a0038647

Braakmann, D. (2015). Historical paths in psychotherapy research. In O. C. G. Gelo, A. Pritz, & B. Rieken (Eds.), *Psychotherapy research: Foundations, process, and outcome* (pp. 39–65). Vienna, AT: Springer-Verlag Wien. doi:10.1007/978-3-7091-1382-0

Bradshaw, D. H., Chapman, C. R., Jacobson, R. C., & Donaldson, G. W. (2012). Effects of music engagement on responses to painful stimulation. *Clinical Journal of Pain, 28*, 418–427.

Branch, J. (2014, February 26). Brain trauma extends to the soccer field. *New York Times.* Retrieved from http://www.nytimes.com/2014/02/27/sports/soccer/researchers-find-brain-trauma-disease-in-a-soccer-player.html

Branco, L. D., Cotrena, C., Pereira, N., Kochhann, R., & Fonseca, R. P. (2014). Verbal and visuospatial executive functions in healthy elderly: The impact of education and frequency of reading and writing. *Dementia & Neuropsychologia, 8*, 155–161.

Brannigan, A., Nicholson, I., & Cherry, F. (2015). Introduction to the special issue:

Unplugging the Milgram machine. *Theory & Psychology, 25,* 551–563. http://dx.doi.org/10.1177/0959354315604408

Brannon, T. N., Markus, H. R., & Taylor, V. J. (2015). "Two souls, two thoughts," two self-schemas: Double consciousness can have positive academic consequences for African Americans. *Journal of Personality and Social Psychology, 108,* 586-609. http://dx.doi.org/10.1037/a0038992

Brauhardt, A., Rudolph, A., & Hilbert, A. (2014). Implicit cognitive processes in binge-eating disorder and obesity. *Journal of Behavior Therapy and Experimental Psychiatry, 45,* 285–290. doi:10.1016/j.jbtep.2014.01.001

Bredesen, D. E. (2014). Reversal of cognitive decline: A novel therapeutic program. *Aging, 6,* 707–717. PMCID:PMC4221920

Bredie, W. L. P., Tan, H. S. G., & Wendin, K. (2014). A comparative study on facially expressed emotions in response to basic tastes. *Chemosensory Perception, 7,* 1–9. doi:10.1007/s12078-014-9163-6

Breger, L. (2014). Psychopathia sexualis: Sexuality in old and new psychoanalysis. *Journal of Clinical Psychology, 70,* 147–159. doi:10.1002/jclp.22066

Breland, K., & Breland, M. (1961). The misbehavior of organisms. *American Psychologist, 16,* 681–684. doi:10.1037/h0040090

Brethel-Haurwitz, K. M., & Marsh, A. A. (2014). Geographical differences in subjective well-being predict extraordinary altruism. *Psychological Science, 25,* 762–771. doi:10.1177/0956797613516148

Breuer, J., Scharkow, M., & Quandt, T. (2015). Sore losers? A reexamination of the frustration-aggression hypothesis for colocated video game play. *Psychology of Popular Media Culture, 4,* 126–137. doi:10.1016/j.iheduc.2015.01.001

Brewer, M. B. (2015). Motivated entitativity: When we'd rather see the forest than the trees. In S. J. Stroessner & J. W. Sherman (Eds.), *Social perception from individuals to groups* (pp. 161–176). New York, NY: Psychology Press.

Brewer, N., Weber, N., Wootton, D., & Lindsay, D. D. (2012). Identifying the bad guy in a lineup using confidence judgments under deadline pressure. *Psychological Science, 23,* 1208–1214. doi:10.1177/0956797612441217

Brewer, T. L., & Collins, M. (2014). A review of clinical manifestations in adolescent and young adults after use of synthetic cannabinoids. *Journal for Specialists in Pediatric Nursing, 19,* 119–126. doi:10.1111/jspn.12057

Brislin, R. W. (2000). *Understanding culture's influence on behavior* (3rd ed.). Ft. Worth, TX: Harcourt.

Brodbeck, F. C., & Guillaume, Y. R. (2015). Effective decision making and problem solving in projects. In E. Bendoly, W. Van Wezel, & D. Bachrach (Eds.), *Applied psychology for project managers* (pp. 37–52). Berlin, DE: Springer.

Brodsky, S. L. & Gutheil, T. G. (2016). In S. L. Brodsky, & T. G. Gutheil (Eds.), *The expert expert witness: More maxims and guidelines for testifying in court* (2nd ed., pp. 156–159). Washington, DC: American Psychological Association. http://dx.doi.org/10.1037/14732-038

Brody, G. H., Yu, T., Chen, E., Beach, S. R. H., & Miller, G. E. (2016). Family-centered prevention ameliorates the longitudinal association between risky family processes and epigenetic aging. *Journal of Child Psychology and Psychiatry, 57,* 566–574. http://dx.doi.org/10.1111/jcpp.12495

Broer, L., Codd, V., Nyholt, D., Deelen, J., Mangino, M., Willemsen, G., . . . Boomsma, D. I. (2013). Meta-analysis of telomere length in 19,713 subjects reveals high heritability, stronger maternal inheritance and a paternal age effect. *European Journal of Human Genetics, 21,* 1163–1168. doi:10.1038/ejhg.2012.303

Broockman, D., & Kalla, J. (2016). Durably reducing transphobia: A field experiment on door-to-door canvassing. *Science, 353,* 220–224. doi:10.1126/science.aad9713

Brooks, S. (2015). Does personal social media usage affect efficiency and well-being? *Computers in Human Behavior, 46,* 26–37. http://dx.doi.org/10.1016/j.chb.2014.12.053

Broshek, D. K., De Marco, A. P., & Freeman, J. R. (2015). A review of post-concussion syndrome and psychological factors associated with concussion. *Brain Injury, 29,* 228–237. doi:10.3109/02699052.2014.974674

Brown, A. S., & Lau, F. S. (2016). A review of the epidemiology of schizophrenia. In M. V. Pletnikov, & J. Waddington (Eds.), *Modeling the psychopathological dimensions of schizophrenia: From molecules to behavior* (pp. 17–30). San Diego, CA: Elsevier Academic Press. http://dx.doi.org/10.1016/B978-0-12-800981-9.00002-X

Brown, C. S. (2014). *Parenting beyond blue & pink: How to raise your kids free of gender stereotypes.* New York, NY: Random House.

Brown, E., Gonzalez-Liencres, C., Tas, C., & Brüne, M. (2016). Reward modulates the mirror neuron system in schizophrenia: A study into the mu rhythm suppression, empathy, and mental state attribution. *Social Neuroscience, 11,* 175–186. doi:10.1080/17470919.2015.1053982

Brown, L. M., Frahm, K. A., & Bongar, B. (2013). Crisis intervention. In G. Stricker, T. A. Widiger, & I. B. Weiner (Eds.), *Handbook of psychology, Vol. 8. Clinical psychology* (2nd ed., pp. 408–430). Hoboken, NJ: Wiley.

Brown, M. A., & Brown, J. D. (2015). Self-enhancement biases, self-esteem, and ideal mate preferences. *Personality and Individual Differences, 74,* 61–65. doi:10.1016/j.paid.2014.09.039

Brown, R., & Kulik, J. (1977). Flashbulb memories. *Cognition, 5,* 73–99. doi:10.1016/0010-0277(77)90018-X

Brown, W. A. (2013). *The placebo effect in clinical practice.* New York, NY: Oxford University Press.

Bruning, R. H., & Kauffman, D. F. (2016). Self-efficacy beliefs and motivation in writing development. In C. A. MacArthur, S. Graham, & J. Fitzgerald (Eds.), *Handbook of writing research* (2nd ed., pp. 160–173). New York, NY: Guilford Press.

Brunoni, A. R., Valiengo, L., Baccaro, A., Zan.o, T. A., de Oliveira, J. F., Goulart, A., . . . Fregni, F. (2013). The sertraline vs electrical current therapy for treating depression clinical study: Results from a factorial, randomized, controlled trial. *JAMA Psychiatry, 70,* 383–391.

Bruns, G. L., & Carter, M. M. (2015). Ethnic differences in the effects of media on body image: The effects of priming with ethnically different or similar models. *Eating Behaviors, 17,* 33–36. doi:10.1016/j.eatbeh.2014.12.006

Brunyé, T., Burte, H., Houck, L. A., & Taylor, H. A. (2015). The map in our head is not oriented north: Evidence from a real-world environment. *PLoS ONE, 10*: e0135803.

Brussoni, M., Gibbons, R., Gray, C., Ishikawa, T., Sandseter, E. B. H., Bienenstock, A., . . . Tremblay, M. S. (2015). What is the relationship between risky outdoor play and health in children? A systematic review. *International Journal of Environmental Research and Public Health, 12,* 6423–6454. http://doi.org/10.3390/ijerph120606423

Bryan, C. J., Master, A., & Walton, G. M. (2014). "Helping" versus "being a helper": Invoking the self to increase helping in young children. *Child Development, 85,* 1836–1842. doi:10.1111/cdev.12244

Bryant, F. B., & Veroff J. (2007). *Savoring: A new model of positive experience.* Mahwah, NJ: Lawrence Erlbaum.

Bryant, N. B., & Gómez, R. L. (2015). The teen sleep loss epidemic: What can be done? *Translational Issues in Psychological Science, 1,* 116–125. doi:10.1037/tps0000020

Buchy, L., Cannon, T. D., Anticevic, A., Lyngberg, K., Cadenhead, K. S., Cornblatt, B. A., . . . Addington, J. (2015). Evaluating the impact of cannabis use on thalamic connectivity in youth at clinical high risk of psychosis. *BMC Psychiatry, 15,* Article 276.

Buckholdt, K. E., Parra, G. R., Anestis, M. D., Lavender, J. M., Jobe-Shields, L. E., Tull, M. T., & Gratz, K. L. (2015). Emotion regulation difficulties and maladaptive behaviors: Examination of deliberate self-harm, disordered eating, and substance misuse in two samples. *Cognitive Therapy and Research, 39,* 140–152. doi:10.1007/s10608-014-9655-3

Buckholtz, J. W., & Meyer-Lindenberg, A. (2015). Genetic perspectives on the neurochemistry of human aggression and violence. In T. Canli (Ed.), *The Oxford handbook of molecular psychology* (pp. 121–144). New York, NY:

Oxford University Press. doi:10.1093/oxfordhb/9780199753888.013.009

Buckingham, G., & MacDonald, A. (2016). The weight of expectation: Implicit, rather than explicit, prior expectations drive the size–weight illusion. *The Quarterly Journal of Experimental Psychology, 69,* 1831–1841. http://dx.doi.org/10.1080/17470218.2015.1100642

Buckley, T., Soo Hoo, S. Y., Fethney, J., Shaw, E., Hanson, P. S., & Tofler, G. H. (2015). Triggering of acute coronary occlusion by episodes of anger. *European Heart Journal: Acute Cardiovascular Care, 4,* 493–498. doi:10.1177/2048872615568969

Buckner, J. D., & Terlecki, M. A. (2016). Social anxiety and alcohol-related impairment: The mediational impact of solitary drinking. *Addictive Behaviors, 58,* 7–11. http://dx.doi.org/10.1016/j.addbeh.2016.02.006

Bui, D. C., & McDaniel, M. A. (2015). Enhancing learning during lecture note-taking using outlines and illustrative diagrams. *Journal of Applied Research in Memory and Cognition, 4,* 129–135. http://dx.doi.org/10.1016/j.jarmac.2015.03.002

Bujisic, M., Wu, L. L., Mattila, A., & Bilgihan, A. (2014). Not all smiles are created equal: Investigating the effects of display authenticity and service relationship on customer tipping behavior. *International Journal of Contemporary Hospitality Management, 26,* 293–306. doi:10.1108/IJCHM10-2012-0181

Bullis, J. R., & Hofmann, S. G. (2016). Adult anxiety and related disorders. In C. M. Nezu & A. M. Nezu (Eds.), *The Oxford handbook of cognitive and behavioral therapies* (pp. 291–311). New York, NY: Oxford University Press.

Burdett, E. R. R., & Barrett, J. L. (2016). The circle of life: A cross–cultural comparison of children's attribution of life–cycle traits. *British Journal of Developmental Psychology, 34,* 276–290. http://dx.doi.org/10.1111/bjdp.12131

Burke-Aaronson, A. C. (2015). Skin-to-skin care and breast-feeding in the perioperative suite. *MCN: The American Journal of Maternal/Child Nursing, 40,* 105–109. doi:10.1097/NMC.0000000000000113

Burns, J. K. (2013). The social determinants of schizophrenia: An African journey in social epidemiology. *Public Health Reviews, 34.* Retrieved from http://www.publichealthreviews.eu/upload/pdffiles/12/00_Burns.pdf

Burns, J. K., Tomita, A., & Kapadia, S. (2014). Income inequality and schizophrenia: Increased schizophrenia incidence in countries with high levels of income inequality. *International Journal of Social Psychiatry, 60,* 185–196. doi:10.1177/0020764013481426

Burri, A., Spector, T., & Rahman, Q. (2015). Common genetic factors among sexual orientation, gender nonconformity, and number of sex partners in female twins: Implications for the evolution of homosexuality. *Journal of Sexual Medicine, 12,* 1004–1011. doi:10.1111/jsm.12847

Busch, F. (2014). *Creating a psychoanalytic mind: A psychoanalytic method and theory.* New York, NY: Routledge/Taylor & Francis Group.

Busch, F. (2015). Our vital profession. *The International Journal of Psychoanalysis, 96,* 553–568. doi:10.1111/1745-8315.12349

Busching, R., Gentile, D. A., Krahé, B., Möller, I., Khoo, A., Walsh, D. A., & Anderson, C. A. (2015). Testing the reliability and validity of different measures of violent video game use in the United States, Singapore, and Germany. *Psychology of Popular Media Culture, 4,* 97–111. doi:10.1037/ppm0000004

Bushman, B. J. (2002). Does venting anger feed or extinguish the flame? Catharsis, rumination, distraction, anger and aggressive responding. *Personality & Social Psychology Bulletin, 28,* 724–731.

Bushman, B. J. (2016). *Aggression and violence: A social psychological perspective.* New York, NY: Psychology Press.

Bush, N. E., Dobscha, S. K., Crumpton, R., Denneson, L. M., Hoffman, J. E., Crain, A., . . . Kinn, J. T. (2015). A virtual hope box smartphone app as an accessory to therapy: Proof-of-concept in a clinical sample of veterans. *Suicide and Life-Threatening Behavior, 45,* 1–9. doi:10.1111/sltb.12103

Buss, D. M. (1989). Sex differences in human mate preferences: Evolutionary hypotheses tested in 37 cultures. *Behavioral and Brain Sciences, 12,* 1–49.

Buss, D. M. (2003). *The evolution of desire: Strategies of human mating.* New York, NY: Basic.

Buss, D. M. (2008). *The evolution of desire: Strategies of human mating* (4th ed.). New York, NY: Basic.

Buss, D. M. (2011). *Evolutionary psychology: The new science of the mind* (4th ed.). Upper Saddle River, NJ: Prentice-Hall.

Buss, D. M. (2015). *The handbook of evolutionary psychology* (2nd ed.). Hoboken, NJ: Wiley.

Buss, D. M., Abbott, M., Angleitner, A., Asherian, A., Biaggio, A., Blanco-Villasenor, A., . . . Yang, K.-S. (1990). International preferences in selecting mates: A study of 37 cultures. *Journal of Cross-Cultural Psychology, 21,* 5–47. doi:10.1177/0022022190211001

Buss, D. M., & Duntley, J. D. (2014). Intimate partner violence in evolutionary perspective. In T. K. Shackelford & R. D. Hansen (Eds.), *The evolution of violence* (pp. 1–21). New York, NY: Springer.

Butcher, J. N. (2000). Revising psychological tests: Lessons learned from the revision of the MMPI. *Psychological Assessment, 12,* 263–271.

Butcher, J. N. (2011). *A beginner's guide to the MMPI-2* (3rd ed.). Washington, DC: American Psychological Association.

Buxton, O. M., Cain, S. W., O'Connor, S. P., Porter, J. H., Duff y, J. F., Wang, W., . . . Shea, S. A. (2012). Adverse metabolic consequences in humans of prolonged sleep restriction combined with circadian disruption. *Science Translational Medicine, 4,* 129ra43. doi:10.1126/scitranslmed.3003200

Bylund, E., & Athanasopoulos, P. (2015). Televised Whorf: Cognitive restructuring in advanced foreign language learners as a function of audiovisual media exposure. *Modern Language Journal, 99,* 123–137. doi:10.1111/j.1540-4781.2015.12182.x

Cacioppo, J. T., Cacioppo, S., Gonzaga, G. C., Ogburn, E. L., & VanderWeele, T. J. (2013). Marital satisfaction and break-ups differ across on-line and off-line meeting venues. *Proceedings of the National Academy of Sciences of the United States of America, 110,* 10135–10140.

Cain, D. J., Keenan, K., & Rubin, S. (Eds.). (2016). *Humanistic psychotherapies: Handbook of research and practice* (2nd ed.). Washington, DC: American Psychological Association.

Caine, R. N., Caine, G., McClintic, C., & Klimek, K. J. (2016). *12 brain/mind learning principles in action: Teach for the development of higher-order thinking and executive function* (3rd ed.). Thousand Oaks, CA: Corwin Press.

Calati, R., & Courtet, P. (2016). Is psychotherapy effective for reducing suicide attempt and non-suicidal self-injury rates? Meta-analysis and meta-regression of literature data. *Journal of Psychiatric Research, 79,* 8–20. http://dx.doi.org/10.1016/j.jpsychires.2016.04.003

Calderwood, C., & Ackerman, P. L. (2016). The relative salience of daily and enduring influences on off-job reactions to work stress. *Stress and Health.* No Pagination Specified. http://dx.doi.org/10.1002/smi.2665

Caleza, C., Yãnez-Vico, R. M., Mendoza, A., & Iglesias-Linares, A. (2016). Childhood obesity and delayed gratification behavior: A systematic review of experimental studies. *The Journal of Pediatrics, 169,* 201–207. http://dx.doi.org/10.1016/j.jpeds.2015.10.008

Calkins, A. W., Park, J. M., Wilhelm, S., & Sprich, S. (2016). Basic principles and practice of cognitive behavioral therapy. In T. J. Petersen, S. Sprich, & S. Wilhelm (Eds.), *The Massachusetts General Hospital handbook of cognitive behavioral therapy* (pp. 5–14). New York, NY: Springer. doi:10.1007/978-1-4939-2605-3_2

Camera, D., Coleman, H. A., Parkington, H. C., Jenkins, T. A., Pow, D. V., Boase, N., . . . Poronnik, P. (2016). Learning, memory and long-term potentiation are altered in Nedd4 heterozygous mice. *Behavioural Brain Research, 303,* 176–181. http://dx.doi.org/10.1016/j.bbr.2016.01.054

Campbell, J. R., & Feng, A. X. (2011). Comparing adult productivity of American mathematics, physics, and chemistry Olympians with Terman's longitudinal study. *Roeper Review: A Journal on Gifted Education, 33,* 18–25. doi:10.1080/02783193.2011.530203

Campbell, L. F., Norcross, J. C., Vasquez, M. J. T., & Kaslow, N. J. (2013). Recognition of psychotherapy effectiveness: The APA resolution. *Psychotherapy, 50,* 98–101. doi:10.1037/a0031817

Campbell, M. C., Black, K. J., Weaver, P. M., Lugar, H. M., Videen, T. O., Tabbal, S. D., . . . Hershey, T. (2012). Mood response to deep brain stimulation of the subthalamic nucleus in Parkinson's Disease. *Journal of Neuropsychiatry and Clinical Neurosciences, 24,* 28–36. doi:10.1176/appi.neuropsych.11030060

Campbell, S. N., Zhang, C., Monte, L., Roe, A. D., Rice, K. C., Tach., Y., . . . Rissman, R. A. (2015). Increased tau phosphorylation and aggregation in the hippocampus of mice overexpressing corticotropin-releasing factor. *Journal of Alzheimer's Disease, 43,* 967–976.

Capodilupo, C. M., & Kim, S. (2014). Gender and race matter: The importance of considering intersections in Black women's body image. *Journal of Counseling Psychology, 61,* 37–49. doi:10.1037/a0034597

Cardoso, C., Ellenbogen, M. A., Serravalle, L., & Linnen, A-M. (2013). Stress-induced negative mood moderates the relation between oxytocin administration and trust: Evidence for the tend-and-befriend response to stress? *Psychoneuroendocrinology, 38,* 2800–2804. doi:10.1016/j.psyneuen.2013.05.006

Carducci, B. J. (2015). *Psychology of personality: Viewpoints, research, and applications* (3rd ed.). Hoboken, NJ: Wiley.

Carey, B. (2014, January 27). The older mind may just be a fuller mind. *New York Times.* Retrieved from http://newoldage.blogs.nytimes.com/2014/01/27/the-oldermind-may-just-be-a-fuller-mind/?action=click&contentCollection=U.S.&module=MostEmailed&version=Full®ion=Marginalia&src=me&pgtype=article

Carlo, G., Knight, G. P., Roesch, S. C., Opal, D., & Davis, A. (2014). Personality across cultures: A critical analysis of Big Five research and current directions. In F. T. L. Leong, L. Comas-Díaz, G. C. Nagayama Hall, V. C. McLoyd, & J. E. Trimble (Eds.), *APA handbook of multicultural psychology, Vol. 1. Theory and research* (pp. 285–298). Washington, DC: American Psychological Association. doi:10.1037/14189-015

Carlson, J. D., & Englar-Carlson, M. (2013). Adlerian therapy. In J. Frew & M. D. Spiegler (Eds.), *Contemporary psychotherapies for a diverse world* (1st rev. ed., pp. 87–129). New York, NY: Routledge.

Carlsson, J., Wängqvist, M., & Frisén, A. (2015). Identity development in the late twenties: A never ending story. *Developmental Psychology, 51,* 334–345. doi:10.1037/a0038745

Carmassi, C., Gesi, C., Simoncini, M., Favilla, L., Massimetti, G., Olivieri, M. C., . . . Dell'Osso, L. (2016). DSM-5 PTSD and posttraumatic stress spectrum in Italian emergency personnel: Correlations with work and social adjustment. *Neuropsychiatric Disease and Treatment,* Article *12,* 375–381.

Carpenter, G. S. J., Carpenter, T. P., Kimbrel, N. A., Flynn, E. J., Pennington, M. L., Cammarata, C., . . . Gulliver, S. B. (2015). Social support, stress, and suicidal ideation in professional firefighters. *American Journal of Health Behavior, 39,* 191–196. doi:10.5993/AJHB.39.2.5

Carroll, J. (2016). *Sexuality now: Embracing diversity* (5th ed.). Boston, MA: Cengage Learning.

Carskadon, M. A., Wolfson, A. R., Acebo, C., Tzischinsky, O., & Seifer, R. (1998). Adolescent sleep patterns, circadian timing, and sleepiness at a transition to early school days. *Sleep, 21,* 871–881.

Carstensen, L. L. (1993). Motivation for social contact across the life span: A theory of socioemotional selectivity. In J. E. Jacobs (Ed.), *Nebraska symposium on motivation, 1992: Developmental perspectives on motivation* (pp. 209–254). Lincoln, NE: University of Nebraska Press.

Carstensen, L. L. (2006). The influence of a sense of time on human development. *Science, 312,* 1913–1915. doi:10.1126/science.1127488

Carter, K. A., Hathaway, N. E., & Lettieri, C. F. (2014). Common sleep disorders in children. *American Family Physician, 89,* 368–377.

Cartwright, S., & Cooper, C. (2014). Towards organizational health: Stress, positive organizational behavior, and employee well-being. In G. F. Bauer & O. Hämmig (Eds.), *Bridging occupational, organizational, and public health: A transdisciplinary approach* (pp. 29–42). New York, NY: Springer.

Casey, B. J., Kosofsky, B. E., & Bhide, P. G. (2014). Teenage brains: Think different? *Developmental Neuroscience, 36.* doi:10.1159/isbn.978-3-318-02676-4

Cashel, M. L. (2016). What counselors should know about personality assessments. In I. Marini & M. A. Stebnicki (Eds.), *The professional counselor's desk reference* (2nd ed., pp. 299–303). New York, NY: Springer.

Castaldelli-Maia, J. M., Ventriglio, A., & Bhugra, D. (2016). Tobacco smoking: From 'glamour' to 'stigma.' A comprehensive review. *Psychiatry and Clinical Neurosciences, 70,* 24–33. doi.org/10.1111/pcn.12365

Castellani, C. A., Awamleh, Z., Melka, M. G., O'Reilly, R. L., & Singh, S. M. (2014). Copy number variation distribution in six monozygotic twin pairs discordant for schizophrenia. *Twin Research and Human Genetics, 17,* 108–120. doi:10.1017/thg.2014.6

Castillo, D. T., Chee, C. L., Nason, E., Keller, J., C'de Baca, J., Qualls, C., . . . Keane, T. M. (2016). Group-delivered cognitive/exposure therapy for PTSD in women veterans: A randomized controlled trial. *Psychological Trauma: Theory, Research, Practice, and Policy, 8,* 404–412. http://dx.doi.org/10.1037/tra0000111

Castle, D. J., & Buckley, P. F. (2015). *Schizophrenia* (2nd ed., rev. and updated). New York, NY: Oxford Psychiatry Library.

Castral, T. C., Warnock, F., dos Santos, C. B., Daré, M. F., Moreira, A. C., Antonini, S. R. R., & Scochi, C. G. S. (2015). Maternal mood and concordant maternal and infant salivary cortisol during heel lance while in kangaroo care. *European Journal of Pain, 19,* 429–438. doi:10.1002/ejp.566

Cattell, R. B. (1950). *Personality: A systematic, theoretical, and factual study.* New York, NY: McGraw-Hill.

Cattell, R. B. (1963). Theory of fluid and crystallized intelligence: A critical experiment. *Journal of Educational Psychology, 54,* 1–22.

Cattell, R. B. (1971). *Abilities: Their structure, growth, and action.* Boston, MA: Houghton Mifflin.

Cattell, R. B. (1990). Advances in Cattellian personality theory. In L. A. Pervin (Ed.), *Handbook of personality: Theory and research* (pp. 101–110). New York, NY: Guilford.

Cavanaugh, J., & Blanchard-Fields, F. (2015). *Adult development and aging.* Stamford, CT: Cengage Learning.

Cavazos-Rehg, P. A., Krauss, M. J., Spitznagel, E. L., Chaloupka, F. J., Schootman, M., Grucza, R. A., & Bierut, L. J. (2012). Associations between selected state laws and teenagers' drinking and driving behaviors. *Alcoholism: Clinical and Experimental Research, 36,* 1647–1652. doi:10.1111/j.1530-0277.2012.01764.x

CDC. (2016). A to Z: Before and during pregnancy. *Centers for Disease Control.* Retrieved from http://www.cdc.gov/ncbddd/index.html

CDC. (2016, February 18). 1 in 3 adults don't get enough sleep. *CDC Newsroom.* Retrieved from http://www.cdc.gov/media/releases/2016/p0215-enough-sleep.html

CDC. (2016). TBI: Get the facts. *Centers for Disease Control and Prevention.* Retrieved from http://www.cdc.gov/traumaticbraininjury/get_the_facts.html

Cea, N. F., & Barnes, G. E. (2015). The development of addiction-prone personality traits in biological and adoptive families. *Personality and Individual Differences, 82,* 107–113. doi:10.1016/j.paid.2015.02.035

Cechnicki, A., Hanuszkiewicz, I., Polczyk, R., & Bielańska, A. (2011). Prognostic value of duration of untreated psychosis in long-term outcome of schizophrenia. *Medical Science Monitor: International Medical Journal of Experimental and Clinical Research, 17*(5), CR277–CR283. http://doi.org/10.12659/MSM.881768

Centers for Disease Control. (2011). *Healthy weight—it's not a diet, it's a lifestyle!* Retrieved from: http://www.cdc.gov/healthyweight/assessing/bmi/adult_bmi/english_bmi_calculator/bmi_calculator.html

Centers for Disease Control and Prevention (2016). *Smoking and tobacco use.* Retrieved from http://www.cdc.gov/tobacco/data_statistics/fact_sheets/fast_facts/

Cesario, J. (2014). Priming, replication, and the hardest science. *Perspectives on Psychological Science, 9,* 40–48. doi:10.1177/1745691613513470

Chaby, L. E., Cavigelli, S. A., Hirrlinger, A. M., Caruso, M. J., & Braithwaite, V. A. (2015). Chronic unpredictable stress during adolescence causes long-term anxiety. *Behavioural Brain Research, 278,* 492–495. doi:10.1016/j.bbr. 2014.09.003

Chakrabarty, M., Sarkar, S., Chatterjee, A., Ghosal, M., Guha, P., & Deogaonkar, M. (2014). Metaphor comprehension deficit in schizophrenia with reference to the hypothesis of abnormal lateralization and right hemisphere dysfunction. *Language Sciences, 44,* 1–14. doi:10.1016/j.langsci.2014.01.002

Chalavi, S., Vissia, E. M., Giesen, M. E., Nijenhuis, E. R. S., Draijer, N., Cole, J. H., . . . Reinders, A. A. T. S. (2015). Abnormal hippocampal morphology in dissociative identity disorder and post-traumatic stress disorder correlates with childhood trauma and dissociative symptoms. *Human Brain Mapping, 36,* 1692–1704. doi:10.1002/hbm.22730

Chambers, A. M., & Payne, J. D. (2015). The memory function of sleep. In D. R. Addis, M. Barense, & A. Duarte (Eds.), *The Wiley handbook on the cognitive neuroscience of memory* (pp. 218–243). Hoboken, NJ: Wiley. http://dx.doi.org/10.1002/9781118332634.ch11

Chamorro-Premuzic, T. (2011). *Personality and individual differences.* Malden, MA: Blackwell.

Chance, P. (2014). *Learning and behavior* (7th ed.). Belmont, CA: Cengage Learning.

Chang, A.-M., Aeschbach, D., Duffy, J. F., & Czeisler, C. A. (2015). Evening use of light-emitting eReaders negatively affects sleep, circadian timing, and next-morning alertness. *Proceedings of the National Academy of Sciences of the United States of America, 112,* 1232–1237. doi:10.1073/pnas.1418490112

Chang, C.-Y. (2012). The survey research of kindergarten children's dreams. *Chinese Journal of Guidance and Counseling, 33,* 1–23.

Chang, E. C., & Kwon, P. (2014). Special issue on psychopathology in Asians and the DSM-5: Culture matters. *Asian Journal of Psychiatry, 7,* 66–67. doi:10.1016/j.ajp.2013.12.001

Chang, H. Y., Keyes, K. M., Mok, Y., Jung, K. J., Shin, Y.-J., & Jee, S. H. (2015). Depression as a risk factor for overall and hormone-related cancer: The Korean cancer prevention study. *Journal of Affective Disorders, 173,* 1–8. doi:10.1016/j. jad.2014.10.064

Chaplin, T. M. (2015). Gender and emotion expression: A developmental contextual perspective. *Emotion Review, 7,* 14–21.

Chapman, B., Fiscella, K., Duberstein, P., Kawachi, I., & Muennig, P. (2014). Measurement confounding affects the extent to which verbal IQ explains social gradients in mortality. *Journal of Epidemiology and Community Health, 68,* 728–733. doi:10.1136/jech-2013-203741

Charles, K. (2011). Retrieved from www.napier.ac.uk/media/Pages/NewsDetails.aspx?NewsID=187.

Charles, L. E., Fekedulegn, D., Landsbergis, P., Burchfiel, C. M., Baron, S., Kaufman, J. D., . . . Roux, A. V. D. (2014). Associations of work hours, job strain, and occupation with endothelial function: The Multi-Ethnic Study of Atherosclerosis (MESA). *Journal of Occupational and Environmental Medicine, 56,* 1153–1160. http://dx.doi.org/10.1097/JOM.0000000000000311

Charles, S. T., & Robinette, J. W. (2015). Emotion and emotion regulation. In P. A. Lichtenberg, B. T. Mast, B. D. Carpenter, & J. Loebach Wetherell (Eds.), *APA handbook of clinical geropsychology, Vol. 1. History and status of the field and perspectives on aging* (pp. 235–258). Washington, DC: American Psychological Association. doi:10.1037/14458-011

Chaves, C., Hervas, G., García, F. E., & Vazquez, C. (2016). Building life satisfaction through well-being dimensions: A longitudinal study in children with a life-threatening illness. *Journal of Happiness Studies, 17,* 1051–1067. http://dx.doi.org/10.1007/s10902-015-9631-y

Chen, A. C-H., Chang, R. Y-H., Besherat, A., & Baack, D. W. (2013). Who benefits from multiple brand celebrity endorsements? An experimental investigation. *Psychology & Marketing, 30,* 850–860. doi: 10.1002/mar.20650

Chen, H., & Wyble, B. (2015). Amnesia for object attributes: Failure to report attended information that had just reached conscious awareness. *Psychological Science, 26,* 203–210. doi: 10.1177/0956797614560648

Chen, S., Yao, N., Qian, M., & Lin, M. (2016). Attentional biases in high social anxiety using a flanker task. *Journal of Behavior Therapy and Experimental Psychiatry, 51,* 27–34. http://dx.doi.org/10.1016/j.jbtep.2015.12.002

Cheng, J. T., Tracy, J. L., Ho, S., & Henrich, J. (2016). Listen, follow me: Dynamic vocal signals of dominance predict emergent social rank in humans. *Journal of Experimental Psychology: General, 145,* 536–547. http://dx.doi.org/10.1037/xge0000166

Cherry, K. E., Sampson, L., Nezat, P. F., Cacamo, A., Marks, L. D., & Galea, S. (2015). Long-term psychological outcomes in older adults after disaster: Relationships to religiosity and social support. *Aging & Mental Health, 19,* 430–443. doi:10.1080/13607863.2014.941325

Chesin, M., Fertuck, E., Goodman, J., Lichenstein, S., & Stanley, B. (2015). The interaction between rejection sensitivity and emotional maltreatment in borderline personality disorder. *Psychopathology, 48,* 31–35. doi:10.1159/00036519

Cheung, F., van de Vijver, F., & Leong, F. (2011). Toward a new approach to the study of personality in culture. *American Psychologist, 66,* 593–603. doi:10.1037/a0022389

Chiesa, J. J., Duhart, J. M., Casiraghi, L. P., Paladino, N., Bussi, I. L., & Golombek, D. A. (2015). Effects of circadian disruption on physiology and pathology: From bench to clinic (and back). *Mechanisms of circadian systems in animals and their clinical relevance* (pp. 289–320). New York, NY: Springer. doi:10.1007/978-3-319-08945-4_15

Chi, L. (2013). Intergenerational transmission of educational attainment: Three levels of parent–child communication as mediators. *PsyCh Journal, 2,* 26–38. doi:10.1002/pchj.16

Chomsky, N. (1968). *Language and mind.* New York, NY: Harcourt, Brace, World.

Chomsky, N. (1980). *Rules and representations.* New York, NY: Columbia University Press.

Chorpita, B. F., Daleiden, E. L., Ebesutani, C., Young, J., Becker, K. D., Nakamura, B. J., . . . Starace, N. (2011). Evidence-based treatments for children and adolescents: An updated review of indicators of efficacy and effectiveness. *Clinical Psychology: Science and Practice, 18,* 154–172.

Christenfeld, N. J. S., & Mandler, G. (2013). Emotion. In D. K. Freedheim & I. B. Weiner (Eds.), *Handbook of psychology, Vol. 1. History of psychology* (2nd ed., pp. 177–197). Hoboken, NJ: Wiley.

Christian, J. B., Bourgeois, N. E., & Lowe, K. A. (2015). Cholesterol screening in US adults and awareness of high cholesterol among individuals with severe hypertriglyceridemia: National Health and Nutrition Examination Surveys 2001–2008. *Journal of Cardiovascular Nursing, 30,* 26–34. doi:10.1097/JCN.0000000000000101

Chrysikou, E. G., Motyka, K., Nigro, C., Yang, S.-I, & Thompson-Schill, S. L. (2016). Functional fixedness in creative thinking tasks depends on stimulus modality. *Psychology of Aesthetics, Creativity, and the Arts.* No Pagination Specified. http://dx.doi.org/10.1037/aca000005

Chua, A., & Rubenfeld, J. (2014). What drives success? *New York Times.* Retrieved from http://www.nytimes.com/2014/01/26/opinion/sunday/what-drives-success.html

Chucair-Elliott, A. J., Elliott, M. H., Cohen, A., & Carr, D. J. (2015). Corneal stem cells: A source of cell renewal with therapeutic potential. In M. Babizhayev, D. Wan-Cheng Li, A. Kasus-Jacobi, L. Žorić, & J. Alió (Eds.), *Studies on the cornea and lens* (pp. 99–113). New York, NY: Springer.

Cicchetti, D. (2016). Socioemotional, personality, and biological development: Illustrations from a multilevel developmental psychopathology perspective on child maltreatment. *Annual Review of Psychology, 67,* 187–211. http://dx.doi.org/10.1146/annurev-psych-122414-033259

Cirelli, L. K., Einarson, K. M., & Trainor, L. J. (2014). Interpersonal synchrony increases prosocial behavior in infants. *Developmental Science, 17,* 1003–1011. doi:10.1111/desc.12193

Clark, D. A. (2016). Finding the self in a cognitive behavioral perspective. In M. Kyrios, R. Moulding, G. Doron, S. S. Bhar, M. Nedeljkovic, & M. Mikulincer (Eds.), *The self in understanding and treating psychological disorders* (pp. 40–49). New York, NY: Cambridge University Press.

Clark, K. D., Quigley, N. R., & Stumpf, S. A. (2014). The influence of decision frames and vision priming on decision outcomes in work groups: Motivating stakeholder considerations. *Journal of Business Ethics, 120,* 27–38. doi:10.1007/s10551-013-1648-8

Clifford, K. (2015). Understanding a silent killer. *UTMB Health.* Retrieved from http://www.utmb.edu/impact-archive/article.aspx?IAID=1744

Cohen, A. B. (Ed.). (2014). *Culture reexamined: Broadening our understanding of social and evolutionary influences.* Washington, DC: American Psychological Association. doi:10.1037/14274-000

Cohen, A., & Israel, M. (2015). Exogenous control processes: Controlled and automatic. In J. G. W. Raaijmakers, A. H. Criss, R. L. Goldstone, R. M. Nosofsky, & M. Steyvers (Eds.), *Psychology Press festschrifts. Cognitive modeling in perception and memory: A festschrift for Richard M. Shiffrin* (pp. 16–34). New York, NY: Psychology Press

Cohen, C., Janicki-Deverts, D., Doyle, W. J., Miller, G. E., Frank, E., Rabin, B. S., & Turner, R. B. (2012). Chronic stress, glucocorticoid receptor resistance, inflammation, and disease risk. *Proceedings of the National Academy of Sciences of the United States of America, 109,* 5995–5999. doi:10.1073/pnas.1118355109

Cohen, J. A., Scheid, J., & Gerson, R. (2014). Transforming trajectories for traumatized children. *Journal of the American Academy of Child and Adolescent Psychiatry, 53,* 9–13. doi:10.1016/j.jaac.2013.10.004

Cohen, N., Margulies, D. S., Ashkenazi, S., Schaefer, A., Taubert, M., Henik, A., . . . Okon-Singer, H. (2016). Using executive control training to suppress amygdala reactivity to aversive information. *NeuroImage, 125,* 1022–1031. doi:10.1016/j.neuroimage.2015.10.069

Cohen, R. A. (2014). Mutual constraint of memory and attention. In R. A. Cohen (Ed.), *The neuropsychology of attention* (pp. 763–777). New York, NY: Springer. doi:10.1007/978-0-38772639-7_24

Cohen, S., Doyle, W. J., Turner, R. B., Alper, C. M., & Skoner, D. P. (2003). Sociability and susceptibility to the common cold. *Psychological Science, 14,* 389–395. doi:10.1111/1467-9280.01452

Cohen, S., Janicki-Deverts, D., Turner, R. B., & Doyle, W. J. (2015). Does hugging provide stress-buffering social support? A study of susceptibility to upper respiratory infection and illness. *Psychological Science, 26,* 135–147. http://doi.org/10.1177/0956797614559284

Cohn, M. A., Pietrucha, M. E., Saslow, L. R., Hult, J. R., & Moskowitz, J. T. (2014). An online positive affect skills intervention reduces depression in adults with type 2 diabetes. *The Journal of Positive Psychology, 9,* 523–534. doi:10.1080/17439760. 2014.920410

Cole, D. L. (1982). Psychology as a liberating art. *Teaching of Psychology,* 9, 23–26.

Cole, P. M., & Moore, G. A. (2015). About face! Infant facial expression of emotion. *Emotion Review, 7,* 116–120. doi:10.1177/1754073914554786

Collins, E. K., Mccabe, J. A., Hauptman, A. J., Meyers-Orr, B. M., & Stern, B. Z. (2014, August). Does picture generation enhance keyword mnemonic learning? Presented at American Psychological Association (APA) Annual Convention, Washington, DC. doi:10.1037/e544392014-001

Cona, F., Lacanna, M., & Ursino, M. (2014). A thalamo-cortical neural mass model for the simulation of brain rhythms during sleep. *Journal of Computational Neuroscience, 37,* 125–148. doi:10.1007/s10827-013-0493-1

Connelly, B. S., & Hülsheger, U. R. (2012). A narrower scope or a clearer lens of personality? Examining sources of observers' advantages over self-reports for predicting performance. *Journal of Personality, 80,* 603–631. doi:10.1111/j.14676494.2011.00744.x

Connelly, B. S., & Ones, D. S. (2010). Another perspective on personality: Meta-analytic integration of observers' accuracy and predictive validity. *Psychological Bulletin, 136,* 1092–1122. doi:10.1037/a0021212

Consedine, N. S., & Soto, J. A. (2014). Cultural considerations in health research: A psychological perspective. In F. T. L. Leong, L. Comas-Díaz, G. C. Nagayama Hall, V. C. McLoyd, & J. E. Trimble (Eds.), *APA handbook of multicultural psychology, Vol. 2: Applications and training* (pp. 119–132). Washington, DC: American Psychological Association. doi:10.1037/14187-007

Considering a Career. (2011). Becoming a health psychologist. *APA Division 38.* Retrieved from http://www.health-psych.org/AboutHowtoBecome.cfm

Conway, L. G., III, Houck, S. C., & Gornick, L. J. (2014). Regional differences in individualism and why they matter. In P. J. Rentfrow (Ed.), *Geographical psychology: Exploring the interaction of environment and behavior* (pp. 31–50). Washington, DC: American Psychological Association.

Conway, M. (2015). *Flashbulb memories.* New York, NY: Psychology Press.

Cooper, C. (2015). *Intelligence and human abilities: Structure, origins and applications* (2nd ed.). New York, NY: Routledge.

Cordeira, J. W., Felsted, J. A., Teillon, S., Daftary, S., Panessiti, M., Wirth, J., . . . Rios, M. (2014). Hypothalamic dysfunction of the thrombospondin receptor α2δ-1 underlies the overeating and obesity triggered by brain-derived neurotrophic factor deficiency. *Journal of Neuroscience, 34,* 554–565. doi:10.1523/JNEUROSCI.1572-13.2014

Cordón, L. (2012). *All things Freud: An encyclopedia of Freud's world* (Vols. 1–2). Santa Barbara, CA: Greenwood.

Corey, G. (2013). *Theory and practice of counseling and psychotherapy.* Belmont, CA: Wadsworth.

Corkin, S. (2013). *Permanent present tense: The unforgettable life of the amnesic patient, H. M.* New York, NY: Basic Books.

Correll, J., Park, B., Judd, C. M., & Wittenbrink, B. (2002). The police officer's dilemma: Using ethnicity to disambiguate potentially threatening individuals. *Journal of Personality & Social Psychology, 83,* 1314–1329.

Corr, P. J., & Cooper, A. J. (2016). The Reinforcement Sensitivity Theory of Personality Questionnaire (RST-PQ): Development and validation. *Psychological Assessment.* No Pagination Specified. http://dx.doi.org/10.1037/pas0000273

Corti, K., & Gillespie, A. (2015). Revisiting Milgram's cyranoid method: Experimenting with hybrid human agents. *The Journal of Social Psychology, 155,* 30–56. doi:10.1080/00224545.2014.959885

Costa, A. L., Sophia, E. C., Sanches, C., Tavares, H., & Zilberman, M. L. (2015). Pathological jealousy: Romantic relationship characteristics, emotional and personality aspects, and social adjustment. *Journal of Affective Disorders, 174,* 38–44. doi:10.1016/j.jad.2014.11.017

Costa, P. T., Jr., & McCrae, R. R. (2011). The five-factor model, five-factor theory, and interpersonal psychology. In L. M. Horowitz & S. Strack (Eds.), *Handbook of interpersonal psychology: Theory, research, assessment, and therapeutic interventions* (pp. 91–104). Hoboken, NJ: Wiley.

Cote, J., Clobert, J., Brodin, T., Fogarty, S., & Sih, A. (2014). Personality traits and spatial ecology in nonhuman animals. In P. J. Rentfrow (Ed.), *Geographical psychology: Exploring the interaction of environment and behavior* (pp. 89–112). Washington, DC: American Psychological Association. doi:10.1037/14272-006

Courage, M. L., & Adams, R. J. (1990). Visual acuity assessment from birth to three years using the acuity card procedures: Cross-sectional and longitudinal samples. *Optometry and Vision Science, 67,* 713–718.

Coviello, L., Sohn, Y., Kramer, A. D. I., Marlow, C., Franceschetti, M., Christakis, N. A., & Fowler, J. H. (2014). Detecting emotional contagion in massive social networks. *PLoS ONE, 9:* e90315. doi:10.1371/journal.pone.0090315

Covington, M. V., & Müeller, K. J. (2001). Intrinsic versus extrinsic motivation: An approach/avoidance reformulation. *Educational Psychology Review, 132,* 157–176.

Coyne, J. C., & Tennen, H. (2010). Positive psychology in cancer care: Bad science, exaggerated claims, and unproven medicine. *Annals of Behavioral Medicine, 39,* 16–26. doi: 10.1007/s12160-009-9154-z

Craft, L. L., & Perna, F. M. (2004). The benefits of exercise for the clinically depressed. *Primary Care Companion to The Journal of Clinical Psychiatry, 6,* 104–111.

Craig, A. R., Lattal, K. A., & Hall, E. G. (2014). Pausing as an operant: Choice and discriminated responding. *Journal of the Experimental Analysis of Behavior, 101,* 230–245. doi:10.1002/jeab.73

Craik, F. I., & Lockhart, R. S. (1972). Levels of processing: A framework for memory research. *Journal of Verbal Learning and Verbal Behavior, 11,* 671–684. doi:10.1016/S0022-5371(72)80001-X

Craik, F. I., & Tulving, E. (1975). Depth of processing and the retention of words in episodic memory. *Journal of Experimental Psychology: General, 104,* 268–294. doi:10.1037/0096-3445.104.3.268

Cranley, N. M., Cunningham, C. J. L., & Panda, M. (2016). Understanding time use, stress and recovery practices among early career physicians: An exploratory study. *Psychology, Health & Medicine, 21,* 362–367. http://dx.doi.org/10.1080/13548506.2015.1061675

Crego, C., & Widiger, T. A. (2016). Personality disorders. In J. E. Maddux & B. A. Winstead (Eds.), *Psychopathology: Foundations for a contemporary understanding* (4th ed., pp. 218–236). New York, NY: Routledge/Taylor & Francis Group.

Crescentini, C., Chittaro, L, Capurso, V., Sioni, R., & Fabbro, F. (2016). Psychological and physiological responses to stressful situations in immersive virtual reality: Differences between users who practice mindfulness meditation and controls. *Computers in Human Behavior, 59,* 304–316. http://dx.doi.org/10.1016/j.chb.2016.02.031

Creswell, J. D., Taren, A. A., Lindsay, E. K., Greco, C. M., Gianaros, P. J., Fairgrieve, A., . . . Gerris, J. L. (2016). Alterations in resting-state functional connectivity link mindfulness meditation with reduced Interleukin-6: A randomized controlled trial. *Biological Psychiatry, 80,* 53–61.

Cristea, I. A., Stefan, S., David, O., Mogoase, C., & Dobrean, A. (2016). *REBT in the treatment of anxiety disorders in children and adults.* Cham, CH: Springer International Publishing.

Cristofori, I., Zhong, W., Mandoske, V., Chau, A., Krueger, F., Strenziok, M., & Grafman, J. (2016). Brain regions influencing implicit violent attitudes: A lesion-mapping study. *The Journal of Neuroscience, 36,* 2757–2768. http://dx.doi.org/10.1523/JNEUROSCI.2975-15.2016

Crowell, S. E., Yaptangco, M., & Turner, S. L. (2016). Coercion, invalidation, and risk for self-injury and borderline personality traits. In T. J. Dishion & J. J. Snyder (Eds.), *The Oxford handbook of coercive relationship dynamics* (pp. 182–193). New York, NY: Oxford University Press.

Cruwys, T., South, E. I., Greenaway, K. H., & Haslam, S. A. (2015). Social identity reduces depression by fostering positive attributions. *Social Psychological and Personality Science, 6,* 65–74. http://dx.doi.org/10.1177/1948550614543309

Csordas, T. J. (2014). Afterword: Moral experience in anthropology. *Ethos, 42,* 139–152. doi:10.1111/etho.12043

Cullen, D., & Gotell, L. (2002). From orgasms to organizations: Maslow, women's sexuality and the gendered foundations of the needs hierarchy. *Gender, Work & Organization, 9,* 537–555.

Cullen, K. L., Gentry, W. A., & Yammarino, F. J. (2015). Biased self-perception tendencies: Self-enhancement/self-diminishment and leader derailment in individualistic and collectivistic cultures. *Applied Psychology, 64,* 161–207. doi:10.1111/apps.12026

Cummings, M. A. (2015). The neurobiology of psychopathy: Recent developments and new directions in research and treatment. *CNS Spectrums, 20,* 200–206. doi:10.1017/S1092852914000741.

Curtiss, S. (1977). *Genie: A psycholinguistic study of a modern-day "wild child."* New York, NY: Academic Press.

Cusack, K., Jonas, D. E., Forneris, C. A., Wines, C., Sonis, J., Middleton, J. C., . . . Gaynes, B. N. (2016). Psychological treatments for adults with posttraumatic stress disorder: A systematic review and meta-analysis. *Clinical Psychology Review, 43,* 128–141. doi:10.1016/j.cpr.2015.10.003

Cussen, V. A., & Mench, J. A. (2014). Personality predicts cognitive bias in captive psittacines, Amazona amazonica. *Animal Behaviour, 89,* 123–130. doi:10.1016/j. anbehav.2013.12.022

Cutler, B. L., & Kovera, M. B. (2013). Evaluation for eyewitness identification. In R. Roesch & P. A. Zapf (Eds.), *Best practices in forensic mental health assessment. Forensic assessments in criminal and civil law: A handbook for lawyers* (pp. 118–132). New York, NY: Oxford University Press.

Dalenberg, C. J., Brand, B. L., Loewenstein, R. J., Gleaves, D. H., Dorahy, M. J., Cardeña, E., . . . Spiegel, D. (2014). Reality versus fantasy: Reply to Lynn et al. (2014). *Psychological Bulletin, 140,* 911–920. doi:10.1037/a0036685

D'Ambrosio, C., & Redline, S. (2014). Sleep across the lifespan. In S. Redline & N. Berger (Eds.), *Impact of sleep and sleep disturbances on obesity and cancer* (pp. 1–23). New York, NY: Springer.

Dana, R. H. (2014). Personality tests and psychological science: Instruments, populations, practice. In F. T. L. Leong, L. Comas-Díaz, G. C. Nagayama Hall, V. C. McLoyd, & J. E. Trimble (Eds.), *APA handbook of multicultural psychology, Vol. 2. Applications and training* (pp. 181–196). Washington, DC: American Psychological Association. doi:10.1037/14187-011

Danner, F., & Phillips, B. (2008). Adolescent sleep, school start times, and teen motor vehicle crashes. *Journal of Clinical Sleep Medicine, 4,* 533–535.

Dargis, M., Newman, J., & Koenigs, M. (2016). Clarifying the link between childhood abuse history and psychopathic traits in adult criminal offenders. *Personality Disorders: Theory, Research, and Treatment, 7,* 221–228. http://dx.doi.org/10.1037/per0000147

Darley, J. M., & Latané, B. (1968). Bystander intervention in emergencies: Diffusion of responsibility. *Journal of Personality and Social Psychology, 8,* 377–383.

Darwin, C. (1859). The origin of species by means of natural selection; or the preservation of favoured races in the struggle for life. *Nature, 5,* 318–319. doi:10.1038/005318a0

Datu, J. A. D., Yuen, M., & Chen, G. (2016). Grit and determination: A review of literature with implications for theory and research. *Journal of Psychologists and Counsellors in Schools.* No Pagination Specified. http://dx.doi.org/10.1017/jgc.2016.2

Davidson, P., Carlsson, I., Jönsson, P., & Johansson, M. (2016). Sleep and the generalization of fear learning. *Journal of Sleep Research, 25,* 88–95. doi:10.1111/jsr.12339

David, S. P., McClure, J. B., & Swan, G. E. (2013). Nicotine dependence. In A. M. Nezu, C. M. Nezu, P. A. Geller, & I. B. Weiner (Eds.), *Handbook of psychology, Vol. 9. Health psychology* (2nd ed., pp. 149–181). Hoboken, NJ: Wiley.

Davies, M. S., Strickland, T. L., & Cao, M. (2014). Neuropsychological evaluation of culturally diverse populations. In F. T. L. Leong, L. Comas-Díaz, G. C. Nagayama Hall, V. C. McLoyd, & J. E. Trimble (Eds.), *APA handbook of multicultural psychology, Vol. 2: Applications and training* (pp. 231–251). Washington, DC: American Psychological Association. doi: 10.1037/14187-014

Davis, N. T., & Mason, L. (2016). Sorting and the split-ticket: Evidence from presidential and subpresidential elections. *Political Behavior, 38,* 337–354. http://dx.doi.org/10.1007/s11109-015-9315-7

Dawkins, R. (2016). *The selfish gene: 40th anniversary edition.* New York, NY: Oxford University Press.

Dawson, K. M., O'Brien, K. E., & Beehr, T. A. (2016). The role of hindrance stressors in the job demand–control–support model of occupational stress: A proposed theory revision.

Journal of Organizational Behavior, 37, 397–415. http://dx.doi.org/10.1002/job.2049

Day, M. V., & Ross, M. (2014). Predicting confidence in flashbulb memories. *Memory, 22,* 232–242. doi:10.1080/09658211.2013.778290

Dean, J. (2015). The most common mental health problem is "contagious." *PsyBlog.* Retrieved from http://www.spring.org.uk/2015/05/the-most-common-mental-health-problem-is-contagious.php

de Biase, S., Milioli, G., Grassi, A., Lorenzut, S., Parrino, L., & Gigli, G. L. (2014). Sleep hygiene. In G. Sergio, L. Nobili, & G. Costa (Eds.), *Sleepiness and human impact assessment* (pp. 289–295). New York, NY: Springer Milan.

de Bruijn, D. M., & de Graaf, I. M. (2016). The role of substance use in same-day intimate partner violence: A review of the literature. *Aggression and Violent Behavior, 27,* 142–151. doi:10.1016/j.avb.2016.02.010

De Castella, K., & Byrne, D. (2015, February 13). My intelligence may be more malleable than yours: The revised implicit theories of intelligence (self-theory) scale is a better predictor of achievement, motivation, and student disengagement. *European Journal of Psychology of Education, 30,* 245–267. doi:10.1007/s10212-015-0244-y

Deci, E. L., & Moller, A. C. (2005). The concept of competence: A starting place for understanding intrinsic motivation and self-determined extrinsic motivation. In A. J. Elliot & C. S. Dweck (Eds.), *Handbook of competence and motivation* (pp. 579–597). New York, NY: Guilford.

Deci, E. L., & Ryan, R. M. (1985). *Intrinsic motivation and self-determination in human behavior.* New York, NY: Plenum.

Deci, E. L., & Ryan, R. M. (2012). Self-determination theory. In P. A. M. Van Lange, A. W. Kruglanski, & E. T. Higgins (Eds.), *Handbook of theories of social psychology* (Vol. 1, pp. 416–436). Thousand Oaks, CA: Sage.

Deconinck, F. J. A., Smorenburg, A. R. P., Benham, A., Ledebt, A., Feltham, M. G., & Savelsbergh, G. J. P. (2015). Reflections on mirror therapy: A systematic review of the effect of mirror visual feedback on the brain. *Neurorehabilitation and Neural Repair, 29,* 349–361. http://dx.doi.org/10.1177/1545968314546134

Deeb, R., Judge, P., Peterson, E., Lin, J. C., & Yaremchuk, K. (2014). Snoring and carotid artery intima-media thickness. *The Laryngoscope, 124,* 1486–1491. doi:10.1002/lary.24527

Deer, T. R., Leong, M. S., & Ray, A. L. (Eds.). (2015). *Treatment of chronic pain by integrative approaches: The American Academy of Pain Medicine textbook on patient management.* New York, NY: Springer. doi:10.1007/978-1-4939-1821-8

Dekel, S., & Farber, B. A. (2012). Models of intimacy of securely and avoidantly attached young adults. *The Journal of Nervous and Mental Disease, 200,* 156–162. doi:10.1097/NMD.0b013e3182439702

Delahaij, R., & van Dam, K. (2016).Coping style development: The role of learning goal orientation and metacognitive awareness. *Personality and Individual Differences, 92,* 57–62. http://dx.doi.org/10.1016/j.paid.2015.12.012

Dement, W. C., & Wolpert, E. (1958). The relation of eye movements, bodily motility, and external stimuli to dream content. *Journal of Experimental Psychology, 53,* 543–553. doi:10.1037/h0040031

Denholm, R., Power, C., & Li, L. (2013). Adverse childhood experiences and child-to-adult height trajectories in the 1958 British birth cohort. *International Journal of Epidemiology, 42,* 1399–1409. doi:10.1093/ije/dyt169

Denmark, T., Atkinson, J., Campbell, R., & Swettenham, J. (2014). How do typically developing deaf children and deaf children with autism spectrum disorder use the face when comprehending emotional facial expressions in British sign language? *Journal of Autism and Developmental Disorders, 44,* 2584–2592. doi:10.1007/s10803-014-2130-x

Denny, B. T., Fan, J., Liu, X., Guerreri, S., Mayson, S. J., Rimsky, L., . . . Koenigsberg, H. W. (2016). Brain structural anomalies in borderline and avoidant personality disorder patients and their associations with disorder-specific symptoms. *Journal of Affective Disorders, 200,* 266–274. http://dx.doi.org/10.1016/j.jad.2016.04.053

Denovan, A., & Macaskill, A. (2016). Stress and subjective well-being among first year UK undergraduate students. *Journal of Happiness Studies.* No Pagination Specified. http://dx.doi.org/10.1007/s10902-016-9736-y

Depp, C. A., Moore, R. C., Dev, S. I., Mausbach, B. T., Eyler, L. T., & Granholm, E. L. (2016). The temporal course and clinical correlates of subjective impulsivity in bipolar disorder as revealed through ecological momentary assessment. *Journal of Affective Disorders, 193,* 145–150. http://dx.doi.org/10.1016/j.jad.2015.12.016

DeRobertis, E. M. (2013). Humanistic psychology: Alive in the 21st century? *Journal of Humanistic Psychology.* doi:10.1177/0022167812473369.

DeRosse, P., Nitzburg, G. C., Ikuta, T., Peters, B. D., Malhotra, A. K., & Szeszko, P. R. (2015). Evidence from structural and diffusion tensor imaging for frontotemporal deficits in psychometric schizotypy. *Schizophrenia Bulletin, 41,* 104–114. doi:10.1093/schbul/sbu150

DeRosse, P., Nitzburg, G. C., Kompancaril, B., & Malhotra, A. K. (2014). The relation between childhood maltreatment and psychosis in patients with schizophrenia and nonpsychiatric controls. *Schizophrenia Research, 155,* 66–71. doi:10.1016/j.schres.2014.03.009

DeSoto, K. A., & Roediger, H. L. (2014). Positive and negative correlations between confidence and accuracy for the same events in recognition of categorized lists. *Psychological Science, 25,* 781–788. doi:10.1177/0956797613516149

Desrosiers, A., Sipsma, H., Callands, T., Hansen, N., Divney, A., Magriples, U., & Kershaw, T. (2014). "Love hurts": Romantic attachment and depressive symptoms in pregnant adolescent and young adult couples. *Journal of Clinical Psychology, 70,* 95–106. doi:10.1002/jclp.21979

Dessalles, J. (2011). Sharing cognitive dissonance as a way to reach social harmony. *Social Science Information/Sur Les Sciences Sociales, 50,* 116–127. doi:10.1177/0539018410388835

de Tychey, C., Vandelet, E., Laurent, M., Lighezzolo-Alnot, J., Prudent, C., & Evrard, R. (2016). Child sexual abuse, baby gender, and intergenerational psychic transmission: An exploratory, projective psychoanalytic approach. *Psychoanalytic Review, 103,* 221–250. http://dx.doi.org/10.1521/prev.2016.103.2.221

de Waal, F. B. M., Smith Churchland, P., Pievani, T., & Parmigiani, S. (Eds.). (2014). *Evolved morality: The biology and philosophy of human conscience.* Leiden, Netherlands: E. J. Brill. http://dx.doi.org/10.1163/9789004263888

DeWall, C. N., Anderson, C. A., & Bushman, B. J. (2013). Aggression. In H. Tennen, J. Suls, & I. B. Weiner (Eds.), *Handbook of psychology, Vol. 5. Personality and social psychology* (2nd ed., pp. 449–466). Hoboken, NJ: Wiley.

DeWall, C. N., Chester, D. S., & White, D. S. (2015). Can acetaminophen reduce the pain of decision-making? *Journal of Experimental Social Psychology, 56,* 117–120. doi:10.1016/j.jesp.2014.09.006

Dewar, M., Alber, J., Butler, C., Cowan, N., & Della Sala, S. (2012). Brief wakeful resting boosts new memories over the long term. *Psychological Science, 23,* 955–960. doi:10.1177/0956797612441220

Deweese, M. M., Robinson, J. D., Cinciripini, P. M., & Versace, F. (2016). Conditioned cortical reactivity to cues predicting cigarette-related or pleasant images. *International Journal of Psychophysiology, 101,* 59–68. doi:10.1016/j.ijpsycho.2016.01.007

Dhamija, D., Tuvblad, C., & Baker, L. A. (2016). Behavioral genetics of the externalizing spectrum. In T. P. Beauchaine & S. P. Hinshaw (Eds.), *The Oxford handbook of externalizing spectrum disorders* (pp. 105–124). New York, NY: Oxford University Press.

Diaz, K. M., Boothill, J. N., Seals, S. R., Hooker, S. P., Sims, M., Dubbert, P. M., . . . Shimbo, D. (2016). Sedentary behavior and subclinical atherosclerosis in African Americans: Cross-sectional analysis of the Jackson heart study. *International Journal of Behavioral Nutrition and Physical Activity, 13,* 31. doi:10.1186/s12966-016-0349-y

Dibbets, P., van den Broek, A., & Evers, E. A. T. (2015). Fear conditioning and extinction in anxiety- and depression-prone persons. *Memory, 23,* 350–364. doi:10.1080/09658211.2014.88670

Dickert, S., Västfjäll, D., & Slovic, P. (2015). Neuroeconomics and dual information processes underlying charitable giving. In E. A. Wilhelms & V. F. Reyna (Eds.), *Neuroeconomics, judgment, and decision making* (pp. 181–199). New York, NY: Psychology Press.

Dickter, C. L., Gagnon, K. T., Gyurovski, I. I., & Brewington, B. S. (2015). Close contact with racial outgroup members moderates attentional allocation towards outgroup versus ingroup faces. *Group Processes & Intergroup Relations, 18,* 76–88. doi:10.1177/1368430214527854

Diego, M. A., & Jones, N. A. (2007). Neonatal antecedents for empathy. In T. Farrow & P. Woodruff (Eds.), *Empathy in mental illness* (pp. 145–167). New York, NY: Cambridge University Press.

Dieleman, G. C., Huizink, A. C., Tulen, J. H. M., Utens, E. M. W. J., & Tiemeier, H. (2016). Stress reactivity predicts symptom improvement in children with anxiety disorders. *Journal of Affective Disorders, 196,* 190–199. http://dx.doi.org/10.1016/j.jad.2016.02.022

Diener, E. & Biswas-Diener, R. (2002). Will money increase subjective well-being? A literature review and guide to needed research. *Social Indicators Research, 57,* 119–169.

Diener, E., & Biswas-Diener, R. (2008). *Happiness: Unlocking the mysteries of psychological wealth.* Hoboken, NJ: Blackwell Publishing. http://dx.doi.org/10.1002/9781444305159

Diener, E., Oishi, S., & Lucas, R. E. (2015). National accounts of subjective well-being. *American Psychologist, 70,* 234–242. http://dx.doi.org/10.1037/a0038899

Diener, E., & Tay, L. (2015). Subjective well-being and human welfare around the world as reflected in the Gallup World Poll. *International Journal of Psychology, 50,* 135–149. http://dx.doi.org/10.1002/ijop.12136

DiFeliceantonio, A. G., Mabrouk, O. S., Kennedy, R. T., & Berridge, K. C. (2012). Enkephalin surges in dorsal neostriatum as a signal to eat. *Current Biology, 22,* 1918–1924. doi:10.1016/j.cub. 2012.08.014

DiGrazia, J., McKelvey, K., Bollen, J., & Rojas, F. (2013). More tweets, more votes: Social media as a quantitative indicator of political behavior. *PLoS ONE, 8:* e79449. doi:10.1371/journal.pone.0079449

Dill, K. E., & Thill, K. P. (2007). Video game characters and the socialization of gender roles: Young people's perceptions mirror sexist media depictions. *Sex Roles, 57,* 851–864.

Dillon, H. M., Adair, L. E., Geher, G., Wang, Z., & Strouts, P. H. (2015). Playing smart: The mating game and mating intelligence. *Current Psychology,* 1–11. doi:10.1007/s12144-015-9309-y

Dillon, S. (2009, January 22). Study sees an Obama effect as lifting Black test-takers. *New York Times.* Retrieved from http://www.nytimes.com/2009/01/23/education/23gap.html

Dimidjian, S., Goodman, S. H., Felder, J. N., Gallop, R., Brown, A. P., & Beck, A. (2016). Staying well during pregnancy and the postpartum: A pilot randomized trial of mindfulness-based cognitive therapy for the prevention of depressive relapse/recurrence. *Journal of Consulting and Clinical Psychology, 84,* 134–145. http://dx.doi.org/10.1037/ccp0000068

Dingus, T. A., Guo, F., Lee, S., Antin, J. F., Perez, M., Buchanan-King, M., & Hankey, J. (2016). Driver crash risk factors and prevalence evaluation using naturalistic driving data. *Proceedings of the National Academy of Sciences of the United States of America, 113,* 2636–2641. doi:10.1073/pnas.1513271113

Ding, Y. H., Xu, X., Wang, Z. Y., Li, H. R., & Wang, W. P. (2014). The relation of infant attachment to attachment and cognitive and behavioural outcomes in early childhood. *Early Human Development, 90,* 459–464. doi:10.1016/j.earlhumdev.2014.06.004.

Dinsmore, D. L., & Alexander, P. A. (2016). A multidimensional investigation of deep-level and surface-level processing. *Journal of Experimental Education, 84,* 213–244. http://dx.doi.org/10.1080/00220973.2014.979126

Dirks-Linhorst, P. A. (2013). An analysis of Missouri's insanity acquittee population, 1980–2009: Differences within African American insanity acquittees. *Journal of Ethnicity in Criminal Justice, 11,* 44–70.

Dixon, R. W., Youssef, G. J., Hasking, P., Yücel, M., Jackson, A. C., & Dowling, N. A. (2016). The relationship between gambling attitudes, involvement, and problems in adolescence: Examining the moderating role of coping strategies and parenting styles. *Addictive Behaviors, 58,* 42–46. http://dx.doi.org/10.1016/j.addbeh.2016.02.011

Dobson, K. S. (2016). The efficacy of cognitive-behavioral therapy for depression: Reflections on a critical discussion. *Clinical Psychology: Science and Practice, 23,* 123–125. doi:10.1111/cpsp.12151

Dodge, E. (2016). Forty years of eating disorder–focused family therapy—The legacy of 'psychosomatic families'. *Advances in Eating Disorders, 4,* 219–227. http://dx.doi.org/10.1080/21662630.2015.1099452

Dolev-Cohen, M., & Barak, A. (2013). Adolescents' use of instant messaging as a means of emotional relief. *Computers in Human Behavior, 29,* 58–63.

Dombrowski, S. C. (2015). *Psychoeducational assessment and report writing.* New York, NY: Springer. doi:10.1007/978-1-4939-1911-6

Domhoff, G. W. (2003). *The scientific study of dreams: Neural networks, cognitive development, and content analysis.* Washington, DC: American Psychological Association.

Domhoff, G. W. (2010). Dream content is continuous with waking thought, based on preoccupations, concerns, and interests. *Sleep Medicine Clinics, 5,* 203–215.

D'Onofrio, B. M., Rickert, M. E., Frans, E., Kuja-Halkola, R., Almqvist, C., Sjolander, A., . . . Lichtenstein, P. (2014). Paternal age at childbearing and offspring psychiatric and academic morbidity. *JAMA Psychiatry, 71,* 432–438. doi:10.1001/jamapsychiatry.2013.4525

Donovan, C. L, Cobham, V., Waters, A. M., & Occhipinti, S. (2015). Intensive group-based CBT for child social phobia: A pilot study. *Behavior Therapy, 46,* 350–364. doi:10.1016/j.beth.2014.12.005

Doornbos, M. M., Zandee, G. L., DeGroot, J., & Warpinski, M. (2013). Desired mental health resources for urban, ethnically diverse, impoverished women struggling with anxiety and depression. *Qualitative Health Research, 23,* 78–92.

dos Santos, R. G., Osório , F. L., Crippa, J. A. S., Riba, J., Zuardi, A. W., & Hallak, J. E. C. (2016). Antidepressive, anxiolytic, and antiaddictive effects of ayahuasca, psilocybin and lysergic acid diethylamide (LSD): A systematic review of clinical trials published in the last 25 years: Antidepressive effects of ayahuasca, psilocybin and LSD. *Therapeutic Advances in Psychopharmacology, 6,* 193–213. doi:10.1177/2045125316638008

Doty, R. L., Tourbier, I., Ng, V., Neff , J., Armstrong, D., Battistini, M., . . . Sondheimer, S. J. (2015). Influences of hormone replacement therapy on olfactory and cognitive function in postmenopausal women. *Neurobiology of Aging, 36,* 2053–2059. doi:10.1016/j.neurobiolaging.2015.02.028

Doulatram, G., Raj, T. D., & Govindaraj, R. (2015). Pregnancy and substance abuse. In A. Kaye, N. Vadivelu, & R. Urman (Eds.). *Substance abuse* (pp. 453–494). New York, NY: Springer.

Draganich, C., & Erdal, K. (2014). Placebo sleep affects cognitive functioning. *Journal of Experimental Psychology: Learning, Memory, and Cognition, 40,* 857–864. doi:10.1037/a0035546

Dreu, C. K. W. D., Aaldering, H., & Saygi, Ö. (2015). Conflict and negotiation within and between groups. In M. Mikulincer, P. R. Shaver, J. F. Dovidio, & J. A. Simpson (Eds.), *APA handbook of personality and social psychology, Vol. 2. Group processes* (pp. 151–176). Washington, DC: American Psychological Association. doi:10.1037/14342-006

Drew, L. (2013). What is the point of sleep? *New Scientist, 217,* 38–39.

Drexler, S. M., Merz, C. J., Hamacher-Dang, T. C., Tegenthoff, M., & Wolf, O. T. (2015). Effects of cortisol on reconsolidation of reactivated fear memories. *Neuropsychopharmacology, 40,* 3036–3043. doi:10.1038/npp.2015.160.

Driessen, E., Van, H. L., Peen, J., Don, F. J., Kool, S., Westra, D., . . . Dekker, J. J. M. (2015). Therapist-rated outcomes in a randomized clinical trial comparing cognitive behavioral therapy and psychodynamic therapy for major depression. *Journal of Affective Disorders, 170,* 112–118. doi:10.1016/j.jad.2014.08.023

D'Souza, J., & Gurin, M. (2016). The universal significance of Maslow's concept of self-actualization. *The Humanistic Psychologist, 44,* 210–214. http://dx.doi.org/10.1037/hum0000027.

Dubois, L., Diasparra, M., Bogl, L. -H., Fontaine-Bisson, B., Bédard, B., Tremblay, R. E., . . . Boivin, M. (2016). Dietary intake at 9 years and subsequent body mass index in adolescent boys and girls: A study of monozygotic twin pairs. *Twin Research and Human Genetics, 19,* 47–59. http://dx.doi.org/10.1017/thg.2015.97

Duckworth, A. L., Peterson, C., Matthews, M. D., & Kelly, D. R. (2007). Grit: Perseverance and passion for long-term goals. *Journal of Personality and Social Psychology, 92,* 1087–1101. http://dx.doi.org/10.1037/0022-3514.92.6.1087

Duits, P., Cath, D. C., Lissek, S., Hox, J. J., Hamm, A. O., Engelhard, I. M., . . . Baas, J. M. P. (2015). Updated meta-analysis of classical fear conditioning in the anxiety disorders. *Depression and Anxiety, 32,* 239–253. doi:10.1002/da.22353

Dumfart, B., & Neubauer, A. C. (2016). Conscientiousness is the most powerful noncognitive predictor of school achievement in adolescents. *Journal of Individual Differences, 37,* 8–15. http://dx.doi.org/10.1027/1614-0001/a000182

Duncan, B. L. (2014). *On becoming a better therapist: Evidence-based practice one client at a time* (2nd ed.). Washington, DC: American Psychological Association. doi:10.1037/14392-000

Duniec, E., & Raz, M. (2011). Vitamins for the soul: John Bowlby's thesis of maternal deprivation, biomedical metaphors and the deficiency model of disease. *History of Psychiatry, 22,* 93–107.

Dunlosky, J., & Rawson, K. A. (2015). Do students use testing and feedback while learning? A focus on key concept definitions and learning to criterion. *Learning and Instruction, 39,* 32–44. doi:10.1016/j.learninstruc.2015.05.003

Dunlosky, J., Rawson, K. A., Marsh, E. J., Nathan, M. J., & Willingham, D. T. (2013). Improving students' learning with effective learning techniques: Promising directions from cognitive and educational psychology. *Psychological Science in the Public Interest, 14,* 4–58. doi:10.1177/1529100612453266

Dunne, F. J., Jaffar, K., & Hashmi, S. (2015). Legal highs—NOT so new and still growing in popularity. *British Journal of Medical Practitioners, 8,* a801.

Dunn, E. W., Aknin, L. B., & Norton, M. I. (2008). Spending money on others promotes happiness. *Science, 319,* 1687–1688. doi:10.1126/science.1150952

Dupuis, K., Pichora-Fuller, M. K., Chasteen, A. L., Marchuk, V., Singh, G., & Smith, S. L. (2015). Effects of hearing and vision impairments on the Montreal Cognitive Assessment. *Aging, Neuropsychology, and Cognition, 22,* 413–437. doi:10.1016/j.neurobiolaging.2015.02.028

Durand, V. M., & Barlow, D. H. (2016). *Essentials of abnormal psychology* (7th ed.). Boston, MA: Cengage Learning.

Durik, A. M., Shechter, O. G., Noh, M., Rozek, C. S., & Harackiewicz, J. M. (2015). What if I can't? Success expectancies moderate the effects of utility value information on situational interest and performance. *Motivation and Emotion, 39,* 104–118. doi:10.1007/s11031-014-9419-0

Dweck, C. (2007). *Mindset: The new psychology of success.* New York, NY: Ballantine.

Dweck, C. S. (2006). *Mindset: The new psychology of success.* New York, NY: Random House.

Dweck, C. S. (2012). *Mindset: How you can fulfill your potential.* Boston, MA: Little, Brown.

Dweck, C. S. (2012). Mindsets and human nature: Promoting change in the Middle East, the schoolyard, the racial divide, and willpower. *American Psychologist, 67,* 614–622. http://dx.doi.org/10.1037/a0029783

Dworkin, A. (1974). *Woman hating.* New York, NY: Dutton.

Eade, S., & Heaton, T. (2016, April 9). Dementia's links to minor trauma found in most contact sports. *Stuff.co.nz.* Retrieved from http://www.stuff.co.nz/sport/78615910/dementias-links-to-minor-trauma-found-in-most-contact-sports

Eagly, A. H. (2015). On comparing men and women. In V. Burr (Ed.), *Gender and psychology (Vol. I). Critical concepts in psychology* (pp. 168–176). New York, NY: Routledge/Taylor & Francis Group.

Eaton, N. R., Keyes, K. M., Krueger, R. F., Balsis, S., Skodol, A. E., Markon, K. E., . . . Hasin, D. S. (2012). An invariant dimensional liability model of gender differences in mental disorder prevalence: Evidence from a national sample. *Journal of Abnormal Psychology, 121,* 282–288.

Ebbinghaus, H. (1885). *Memory: A contribution to experimental psychology.* New York, NY: Dover Publications.

Eddy, K. T., Murray, H. B., & Le Grange, D. (2016). Eating and feeding disorders. In M. K. Dulcan (Ed.), *Dulcan's textbook of child and adolescent psychiatry* (2nd ed., pp. 435–460). Arlington, VA: American Psychiatric Publishing, Inc.

Edelson, L. R., Mokdad, C., & Martin, N. (2016). Prompts to eat novel and familiar fruits and vegetables in families with 1-3 year-old children: Relationships with food acceptance and intake. *Appetite, 99,* 138–148. doi:10.1016/j.appet.2016.01.015

Effron, D. A., & Knowles, E. D. (2015). Entitativity and intergroup bias: How belonging to a cohesive group allows people to express their prejudices. *Journal of Personality and Social Psychology, 108,* 234–253. doi:10.1037/pspa0000020

Ege, M. A., Messias, E., Thapa, P. B., & Krain, L. P. (2015). Adverse childhood experiences and geriatric depression: Results from the 2010 BRFSS. *The American Journal of Geriatric Psychiatry, 23,* 110–114. doi:10.1016/j.jagp.2014.08.014

Eggermont, J. J. (2015). The auditory cortex and tinnitus—A review of animal and human studies. *European Journal of Neuroscience, 41,* 665–676. doi:10.1111/ejn.12759

Ehrlich, K. B., Miller, G. E., Rohleder, N., & Adam, E. K. (2016). Trajectories of relationship stress and inflammatory processes in adolescence. *Development and Psychopathology, 28,* 127–138. http://dx.doi.org/10.1017/S0954579415000334

Eichenbaum, H. (2013). Memory systems. In R. J. Nelson, S. J. Y. Mizumori, & I. B. Weiner (Eds.), *Handbook of psychology, Vol. 3. Behavioral neuroscience* (2nd ed., pp. 551–573). Hoboken, NJ: Wiley.

Ekman, P. (1993). Facial expression and emotion. *American Psychologist, 48,* 384–392.

Ekman, P. (2004). *Emotions revealed: Recognizing faces and feelings to improve communication and emotional life.* Thousand Oaks, CA: Owl.

Ekman, P., & Keltner, D. (1997). Universal facial expressions of emotion: An old controversy and new findings. In U. C. Segerstrale & P. Molnar (Eds.), *Nonverbal communication: Where nature meets culture* (pp. 27–46). Mahwah, NJ: Erlbaum.

Elder, A. B. (2016). Experiences of older transgender and gender nonconforming adults in psychotherapy: A qualitative study. *Psychology of Sexual Orientation and Gender Diversity, 3,* 180–186. http://dx.doi.org/10.1037/sgd0000154

Eldred, S. M., & Eligon, J. (2016, May 10). Prince's doctor arrived with test results only to find him dead. *New York Times.* Retrieved from http://www.nytimes.com/2016/05/11/arts/music/princes-doctor-arrived-with-test-results-only-to-find-him-dead.html

Eley, T. C., McAdams, T. A., Rijsdijk, F. V., Lichtenstein, P., Narustye, J., Reiss, D., . . . Neiderhiser, J. M. (2015). The intergenerational transmission of anxiety: A children-of-twins study. *The American Journal of Psychiatry, 172,* 630–637. doi:10.1176/appi.ajp.2015.14070818

Eligon, J., Kovaleski, S. F., & Coscarelli, J. (2016, May 4). Prince's addiction and an intervention too late. *New York Times.* Retrieved from http://www.nytimes.com/2016/05/05/arts/music/friends-sought-help-for-princes-addiction-lawyer-says.html?_r=0

Elkind, D. (1967). Egocentrism in adolescence. *Child Development, 38,* 1025–1034.

Elkind, D. (2007). *The hurried child: Growing up too fast too soon* (25th anniversary ed.). Cambridge, MA: Da Capo.

Elliot, A. J., Neista Kayser, D., Greitemeyer, T., Lichtenfeld, S., Gramzow, R. H., Maier, M. A., & Liu, H. (2010). Red, rank, and romance in women viewing men. *Journal of Experimental Psychology: General, 139,* 399–417. doi: 10.1037/a0019689

Ellis, A., & Ellis, D. J. (2011). *Rational emotive behavior therapy.* Washington, DC: American Psychological Association.

Ellis, A., & Ellis, D. J. (2014). Rational emotive behavior therapy. In G. R. VandenBos, E. Meidenbauer, & J. Frank-McNeil (Eds.), *Psychotherapy theories and techniques: A reader* (pp. 289–298). Washington, DC: American Psychological Association. doi:10.1037/14295-031

Emilien, G., & Durlach, C. (2015). *Memory: Neuropsychological, imaging and psychopharmacological perspectives.* New York, NY: Psychology Press.

Emmons, R. A., & McCullough, M. E. (2003). Counting blessings versus burdens: An experimental investigation of gratitude and subjective well-being in daily life. *Journal of Personality and Social Psychology, 84,* 377–389. http://dx.doi.org/10.1037/0022-3514.84.2.377

Emslie, G. J., Croarkin, P., Chapman, M. R., & Mayes, T. L. (2016). Antidepressants. In M. K. Dulcan (Ed.), *Dulcan's textbook of child and adolescent psychiatry* (2nd ed., pp. 737–768). Arlington, VA: American Psychiatric Publishing, Inc.

English, T., & Carstensen, L. L. (2015). Does positivity operate when the stakes are high? Health status and decision making among older adults. *Psychology and Aging, 30,* 348–355. http://dx.doi.org/10.1037/a0039121

Epley, N., & Schroeder, J., (2014). Mistakenly seeking solitude. *Journal of Experimental Psychology: General, 143,* 1980–1999. doi:10.1037/a0037323

Epstein, N. B., Curtis, D. S., Edwards, E., Young, J. L., & Zheng, L. (2014). Therapy with families in China: Cultural factors influencing the therapeutic alliance and therapy goals. *Contemporary Family Therapy: An International Journal, 36,* 201–212. doi:10.1007/s10591-014-9302-x

Erekson, D. M., & Lambert, M. J. (2015). Client-centered therapy. *The Encyclopedia of Clinical Psychology,* 1–5. doi:10.1002/9781118625392.wbecp073

Erikson, E. (1950). *Childhood and society.* New York, NY: Norton.

Erviti, M., Semal, C., Wright, B. A., Amestoy, A., Bouvard, M. P., & Demany, L. (2015). A late-emerging auditory deficit in autism. *Neuropsychology, 29,* 454–462. doi:10.1037/neu0000162

Esch, T. (2014). The neurobiology of meditation and mindfulness. In S. Schmidt & H. Walach (Eds.), *Meditation—neuroscientific approaches and philosophical implications* (pp. 153–173). New York, NY: Springer. doi:10.1007/978-3-319-01634-4_9

Essau, C. A., & Ozer, B. U. (2015). Obsessive-compulsive disorder. In T. P. Gullotta, R. W. Plant, & M. A. Evans (Eds.), *Handbook of adolescent behavioral problems: Evidence-based approaches to prevention and treatment* (2nd ed., pp. 235–263). New York, NY: Springer. doi:10.1007/978-1-4899-7497-6

Essau, C. A., & Petermann, F. (Eds.). (2013). *Anxiety disorders in children and adolescents: Epidemiology, risk factors and treatment* (Vol. 4). New York, NY: Routledge.

Esteve, R., Marquina-Aponte, V., & Ramírez-Maestre, C. (2014). Postoperative pain in children: Association between anxiety sensitivity, pain catastrophizing, and female caregivers' responses to children's pain. *The Journal of Pain, 15,* 157–168. doi:10.1016/j.jpain.2013.10.007

Ethical Principles of Psychologists and Code of Conduct. (2016). In A.E. Kazdin (Ed.), *Methodological issues and strategies in clinical research* (4th ed., pp. 495–512). Washington, DC: American Psychological Association. doi:10.1037/14805-030

Evans, I. M. (2015). *How and why thoughts change: Foundations of cognitive psychotherapy.* New York, NY: Oxford University Press.

Eysenck, H. J. (1967). *The biological basis of personality.* Springfield, IL: Thomas.

Eysenck, H. J. (1990). Biological dimensions of personality. In L. A. Pervin (Ed.), *Handbook of personality: Theory and research* (pp. 244–276). New York, NY: Guilford.

Fabre, B., Grosman, H., Mazza, O., Nolazco, C., Machulsky, N. F., Mesch, V., . . . Berg, G. (2013). Relationship between cortisol, life events and metabolic syndrome in men. *Stress, 16,* 16–23. doi:10.3109/10253890.2012.676112.

Faddiman, A. (1997). *The spirit catches you and you fall down.* New York, NY: Straus & Giroux.

Fadel, L., & Garcia-Navarro, L. (2013). How different cultures handle personal space. *NPR.* Retrieved from http://www.npr.org/sections/codeswitch/2013/05/05/181126380/how-different-cultures-handle-personal-space

Fagelson, M., & Baguley, D. M. (2016). Influences of amplified music. In D. M. Baguley & M. Fagelson (Eds.), *Tinnitus: Clinical and research perspectives* (pp. 129–143). San Diego, CA: Plural Publishing.

Fahnehjelm, K. T., Törnquist, A. L., Olsson, M., Bäckström, I., Grönlund, M. A., & Winiarski, J. (2016). Cataract after allogeneic hematopoietic stem cell transplantation in childhood. *Acta Paediatrica, 105,* 82–89. doi:10.1111/apa.13173

Fakhoury, M. (2015). New insights into the neurobiological mechanisms of major depressive disorders. *General Hospital Psychiatry, 37,* 172–177. doi:10.1016/j.genhosppsych.2015.01.005

Falkner, A. L., & Lin, D. (2014). Recent advances in understanding the role of the hypothalamic circuit during aggression. *Frontiers in Systems Neuroscience, 8,* Article 168.

Fang, J., Prybutok, V., & Wen, C. (2016). Shirking behavior and socially desirable responding in online surveys: A cross-cultural study comparing Chinese and American samples. *Computers in Human Behavior, 54,* 310–317. doi:10.1016/j.chb.2015.08.019

Fan, H., Li, T.-F., Gong, N., & Wang, Y.-X. (2016). Shanzhiside methylester, the principle effective iridoid glycoside from the analgesic herb Lamiophlomis rotata, reduces neuropathic pain by stimulating spinal microglial β-endorphin expression. *Neuropharmacology, 101,* 98–109. doi:10.1016/j.neuropharm.2015.09.010

Fan, L. B., Blumenthal, J. A., Watkins, L. L., & Sherwood, A. (2015). Work and home stress: Associations with anxiety and depression symptoms. *Occupational Medicine, 65,* 110–116. doi:10.1093/occmed/kqu181

Fan, S. P., Liberman, Z., Keysar, B., & Kinzler, K. D. (2015). Early exposure to multilingual environment promotes effective communication. *Psychological Science,* 26, 1090-1097O. doi:10.1177/0956797615574699

Farah, M. J., Hutchinson, J. B., Phelps, E. A., & Wagner, A. D. (2014). Functional MRI-based lie detection: Scientific and societal challenges. *Nature Reviews Neuroscience, 15,* 123–131. doi:10.1038/nrn3665

Farooqui, A. A., & Manly, T. (2015). Anticipatory control through associative learning of subliminal relations: Invisible may be better than visible. *Psychological Science, 26,* 325–334. doi:10.1177/0956797614564191

Farrell, A. D., Mehari, K. R., Kramer-Kuhn, A., & Goncy, E. A. (2014). The impact of victimization and witnessing violence on physical aggression among high-risk adolescents. *Child Development, 85,* 1694–1710. doi:10.1111/cdev.12215

Fast, L. C., Harman, J. J., Maertens, J. A., Burnette, J. L., & Dreith, F. (2015). Creating a measure of portion control self-efficacy. *Eating Behaviors, 16,* 23–30. doi:10.1016/j.eatbeh.2014.10.009

Feeney, B. C., & Collins, N. L. (2015). A new look at social support: A theoretical perspective on thriving through relationships. *Personality and Social Psychology Review, 19,* 113–147. doi:10.1177/1088868314544222

Fehr, B. (2015). Love: Conceptualization and experience. In M. Mikulincer, P. R. Shaver, J. A. Simpson, & J. F. Dovidio (Eds.), *APA handbook of personality and social psychology, Vol. 3. Interpersonal relations* (pp. 495–522). Washington, DC: American Psychological Association. doi:10.1037/14344-018

Fehr, B., Harasymchuk, C., & Sprecher, S. (2014). Compassionate love in romantic relationships: A review and some new findings. *Journal of Social and Personal Relationships, 31,* 575–600. doi:10.1177/0265407514533768.

Fein, S., & Spencer, S. J. (1997). Prejudice as self-image maintenance: Affirming the self through derogating others. *Journal of Personality and Social Psychology, 73,* 31–44.

Feldman, R., Rosenthal, Z., & Eidelman, A. I. (2014). Maternal-preterm skin-to-skin contact enhances child physiologic organization and cognitive control across the first 10 years of life. *Biological Psychiatry, 75,* 56–64.

Feldman, S. (2014). *Development across a lifetime* (7th ed.). Essex, UK: Pearson.

Felleman, B. I., Stewart, D. G., Simpson, T. L., Heppner, P. S., & Kearney, D. J. (2016). Predictors of depression and PTSD treatment response among veterans participating in mindfulness-based stress reduction. *Mindfulness, 7,* 888–895. http://dx.doi.org/10.1007/s12671-016-0527-7

Felson, J. (2014). What can we learn from twin studies? A comprehensive evaluation of the equal environments assumption. *Social Science Research, 43,* 184–199. doi:10.1016/j.ssresearch.2013.10.004

Feng, J., Spence, I., & Pratt, J. (2007). Playing an action video game reduces gender differences in spatial cognition. *Psychological Science, 18,* 850–855. doi:10.1111/j.1467-9280.2007.01990.x

Ferguson, C. J. (2010). Violent crime research: An introduction. In C. J. Ferguson (Ed.), *Violent crime: Clinical and social implications* (pp. 3–18). Thousand Oaks, CA: Sage.

Ferguson, C. J. (2015). Does movie or video game violence predict societal violence? It depends on what you look at and when—Revised. *Journal of Communication, 65,* 193–212. doi:10.1111/jcom.12142

Ferguson, K. T., & Casasola, M. (2015). Are you an animal too? US and Malawian infants' categorization of plastic and wooden animal replicas. *Infancy, 20,* 189–207. doi:10.1111/infa.12069

Fernald, A., Marchman, V. A., & Weisleder, A. (2013). SES differences in language processing skill and vocabulary are evident at 18 months. *Developmental Science, 16,* 234–248. doi:10.1111/desc.12019

Ferrari, P. F., Rozzi, S., & Fogassi, L. (2005). Mirror neurons responding to observation of actions made with tools in monkey ventral pre-motor cortex. *Journal of Cognitive Neuroscience, 17,* 212–226.

Ferrie, A. (2015, April 4). Source amnesia and advertising. *The Consumer Psychologist.* Retrieved from http://www.theconsumerpsychologist.com/2015/04/04/sourceamnesia-and-advertising/

Festinger, L. (1957). *A theory of cognitive dissonance.* Stanford, CA: Stanford University Press.

Festinger, L. A., & Carlsmith, J. M. (1959). Cognitive consequences of forced compliance. *Journal of Abnormal and Social Psychology, 58,* 203–210.

Few, L. R., Grant, J. D., Trull, T. J., Statham, D. J., Martin, N. G., Lynskey, M. T., & Agrawal, A. (2014). Genetic variation in personality traits explains genetic overlap between borderline personality features and substance use disorders. *Addiction, 109,* 2118–2127. doi:10.1111/add.12690

Field, K. M., Woodson, R., Greenberg, R., & Cohen, D. (1982). Discrimination and imitation of facial expressions by neonates. *Science, 218,* 179–181. doi:10.1016/S0163-6383(83)90316-8

Fields, A., & Cochran, S. (2011). Men and depression: Current perspectives for health care professionals. *American Journal of Lifestyle Medicine, 5,* 92–100.

Fields, J. A. (2015). Effects of deep brain stimulation in movement disorders on cognition and behavior. In A. I. Tröster (Ed.), *Clinical neuropsychology and cognitive neurology of Parkinson's disease and other movement disorders* (pp. 332–375). New York, NY: Oxford University Press.

Fildes, A., van Jaarsveld, C. H., Llewellyn, C. H., Fisher, A., Cooke, L., & Wardle, J. (2014). Nature and nurture in children's food preferences. *The American Journal of Clinical Nutrition, 99,* 911–917. doi:10.3945/ajcn.113.077867

Finegersh, A., Rompala, G. R., Martin, D. I. K., & Homanics, G. E. (2015). Drinking beyond a lifetime: New and emerging insights into paternal alcohol exposure on subsequent generations. *Alcohol, 49,* 461–470. doi:10.1016/j.alcohol.2015.02.008

Finkel, E. J., Norton, M. I., Reis, H. T., Ariely, D., Caprariello, P. A., Eastwick, P. W., . . . Maniaci, M. R. (2015). When does familiarity promote versus undermine interpersonal attraction? A proposed integrative model from erstwhile adversaries. *Perspectives on Psychological Science, 10,* 3–19. doi:10.1177/1745691614561682

Fink, G. (2011). Stress controversies: Post-traumatic stress disorder, hippocampal volume, gastroduodenal ulceration. *Journal of Neuroendocrinology, 23,* 107–117. doi:10.1111/j.1365-2826.2010.02089.x

Finley, E. P., Bollinger, M., No.l, P. H., Amuan, M. E., Copeland, L. A., Pugh, J., . . . Pugh, M. J. V. (2015). A national cohort study of the association between the Polytrauma Clinical Triad and suicide-related behavior among US veterans who served in Iraq and Afghanistan. *American Journal of Public Health, 105,* 380–387. doi:10.2105/AJPH.2014.301957

Finn, J. A., Arbisi, P. A., Erbes, C. R., Polusny, M. A., & Thuras, P. (2014). The MMPI–2 restructured form personality psychopathology five scales: Bridging DSM-5 section 2 personality disorders and DSM-5 section 3 personality trait dimensions. *Journal of Personality Assessment, 96,* 173–184. doi:10.1080/00223891.2013.866569

Fisher, T. D. (2013). Gender roles and pressure to be truthful: The bogus pipeline modifies gender differences in sexual but not non-sexual behavior. *Sex Roles, 68,* 401–414. doi:10.1007/s11199-013-0266-3

Fishman, I., & Ng, R. (2013). Error-related brain activity in extraverts: Evidence for altered response monitoring in social context. *Biological Psychology, 93,* 225–230. doi:10.1016/j.biopsycho.2013.02.010

Fivush, R., Bohanek, J. G., Zaman, W., & Grapin, S. (2012). Gender differences in adolescents' autobiographical narratives. *Journal of Cognition and Development, 13,* 295–319. doi:10.1080/15248372.2011.590787

Fleming, R. W. (2014). Visual perception of materials and their properties. *Vision Research, 94,* 62–75.

Fletcher, B. R., & Rapp, P. R. (2013). Normal neurocognitive aging. In R. J. Nelson, S. J. Y. Mizumori, & I. B. Weiner (Eds.), *Handbook of psychology, Vol. 3. Behavioral neuroscience* (2nd ed., pp. 643–663). Hoboken, NJ: Wiley.

Fletcher, G. J., Kerr, P. S., Li, N. P., & Valentine, K. A. (2014). Predicting romantic interest and decisions in the very early stages of mate selection standards: Accuracy and sex differences. *Personality and Social Psychology Bulletin, 40,* 540–550. doi:10.1177/0146167213519481

Fletcher, G. J. O., & Simpson, J. A. (2000). Ideal standards in close relationships: Their structure and functions. *Current Directions in Psychological Science, 9,* 102–105.

Flett, G. L., Goldstein, A. L., Pechenkov, I. G., Nepon, T., & Wekerle, C. (2016). Antecedents, correlates, and consequences of feeling like you don't matter: Associations with maltreatment, loneliness, social anxiety, and the five-factor model. *Personality and Individual Differences, 92,* 52–56. http://dx.doi.org/10.1016/j.paid.2015.12.014

Fligelman, B., Pham, T., Bryson, E. O., Majeske, M., & Kellner, C. H. (2016). Resolution of acute suicidality after a single right unilateral electroconvulsive therapy. *The Journal of ECT, 32,* 71–72. http://dx.doi.org/10.1097/YCT.0000000000000258

Flores, G., Flores-Gómez, G. D., & de Jesús Gomez-Villalobos, M. (2016). Neuronal changes after chronic high blood pressure in animal models and its implication for vascular dementia. *Synapse, 70,* 198–205. doi:10.1002/syn.21887

Flor, H. (2013). Cultural influences on perceptions of pain. In S. Barnow & N. Balkir (Eds.), *Cultural variations in psychopathology: From research to practice* (pp. 173–183). Cambridge, MA: Hogrefe.

Flynn, J. R. (1987). Massive IQ gains in 14 nations: What IQ tests really measure. *Psychological Bulletin, 101,* 171–191. doi:10.1037/0033-2909.101.2.171

Flynn, J. R. (2010). Problems with IQ gains: The huge vocabulary gap. *Journal of Psychoeducational Assessment, 28,* 412–433. doi:10.1177/0734282910373342

Flynn, J., te Nijenhuis, J., & Metzen, D. (2014). The *g* beyond Spearman's *g*: Flynn's paradoxes resolved using four exploratory metaanalyses. *Intelligence, 44,* 1–10. doi:10.1016/j.intell.2014.01.009

Foa, E. B., & Yadin, E. (2014). Obsessive compulsive disorder. In L. Grossman & S. Walfish (Eds.), *Translating psychological research into practice* (pp. 225–231). New York, NY: Springer.

Foell, J., Bekrater-Bodmann, R., Diers, M., & Flor, H. (2014). Mirror therapy for phantom limb pain: Brain changes and the role of body representation. *European Journal of Pain, 18,* 729–739. doi:10.1002/j.1532-2149.2013.00433.x

Foerde, K., Steinglass, J., Shohamy, D., & Walsh, B. T. (2015). Neural mechanisms supporting maladaptive food choices in anorexia nervosa. *Nature Neuroscience, 18,* 1571–1573. http://doi.org/10.1038/nn.4136

Folkvord, F., Anschütz, D. J., & Buijzen, M. (2016). The association between BMI development among young children and (un)healthy food choices in response to food advertisements: A longitudinal study. *The International Journal of Behavioral Nutrition and Physical Activity, 13,* Article 16. http://dx.doi.org/10.1186/s12966-016-0340-7

Ford, T. E. (2015). The social consequences of disparagement humor: Introduction and overview. *Humor, 28,* 163–169. http://dx.doi.org/10.1515/humor-2015-0016

Forgas, J. P., & Eich, E. (2013). Affective influences on cognition: Mood congruence, mood dependence, and mood effects on processing strategies. In A. F. Healy, R. W. Proctor, & I. B. Weiner (Eds.), *Handbook of psychology, Vol. 4. Experimental psychology* (2nd ed., pp. 61–82). Hoboken, NJ: Wiley.

Forgasz, H., Leder, G., Mittelberg, D., Tan, H., & Murimo, A. (2015). Affect and gender. In B. Pepin & B. Roesken-Winter (Eds.), *Advances in mathematics education. From beliefs to dynamic affect systems in mathematics education: Exploring a mosaic of relationships and interactions* (pp. 245–268). New York, NY: Springer. http://dx.doi.org/10.1007/978-3-319-06808-4_12

Forkmann, T., Brakemeir, E.-L., Teismann, T., Schramm, E., & Michalak, J. (2016). The effects of mindfulness-based cognitive therapy and cognitive behavioral analysis system of psychotherapy added to treatment as usual on suicidal ideation in chronic depression: Results of a randomized-clinical trial. *Journal of Affective Disorders, 200,* 51–57. http://dx.doi.org/10.1016/j.jad.2016.01.047

Fortuna, L. R., & Vallejo, Z. (2015). *Treating co-occurring adolescent PTSD and addiction: Mindfulness-based cognitive therapy for adolescents with trauma and substance-abuse disorders.* Oakland, CA: Context Press/New Harbinger Publications.

Fouladi, D. B., Nassiri, P., Monazzam, E. M., Farahani, S., Hassanzadeh, G., & Hoseini, M. (2012). Industrial noise exposure and salivary cortisol in blue collar industrial workers. *Noise Health, 14,* 184–189.

Foulkes, D. (1993). Children's dreaming. In D. Foulkes & C. Cavallero (Eds.), *Dreaming as cognition* (pp. 114–132). New York, NY: Harvester Wheatsheaf.

Foulkes, D. (1999). *Children's dreaming and the development of consciousness.* Cambridge, MA: Harvard University Press.

Fox, J., & Moreland, J. J. (2015). The dark side of social networking sites: An exploration of the relational and psychological stressors associated with Facebook use and affordances. *Computers in Human Behavior, 45,* 168–176. doi:10.1016/j.chb.2014.11.083

Fox, N. A., Bakermans-Kranenburg, M. J., Yoo, K. H., Bowman, L. C., Cannon, E. N., Vanderwert, R. E., . . . van IJzendoorn, M. H. (2016). Assessing human mirror activity with EEG mu rhythm: A meta-analysis. *Psychological Bulletin, 142,* 291–313. doi:10.1037/bul0000031

Fraley, R. C., & Roisman, G. I. (2015). Early attachment experiences and romantic functioning: Developmental pathways, emerging issues, and future directions. In J. A. Simpson & W. S. Rholes (Eds.), *Attachment theory and research: New directions and emerging themes* (pp. 9–38). New York, NY: Guilford.

Fraley, R. C., & Shaver, P. R. (1997). Adult attachment and the suppression of unwanted thoughts. *Journal of Personality and Social Psychology, 73,* 1080–1091.

Francis, G. (2012). Too good to be true: Publication bias in two prominent studies from experimental psychology. *Psychonomic Bulletin & Review, 19,* 151–156. doi:10.3758/s13423-012-0227-9

François, M., Barde, S., Achamrah, N., Breton, J., do Rego, J.-C., Coëffier, M., . . . Fetissov, S. O. (2015). The number of preproghrelin mRNA expressing cells is increased in mice with activity-based anorexia. *Neuropeptides, 51,* 17–23. http://dx.doi.org/10.1016/j.npep.2015.04.003

Franconeri, S. L., Alvarez, G. A., & Cavanagh, P. (2013). Flexible cognitive resources: Competitive content maps for attention and memory. *Trends in Cognitive Sciences, 17,* 134–141. doi:10.1016/j.tics.2013.01.010

Frangicetto, T. (2015, May 22). American Sniper and the warrior cult. *Buck County Courier Times,* p. A9. Retrieved from http://www.buckscountycouriertimes.com/opinion/op-ed/american-sniper-and-the-warrior-cult/article_c9ec7de8-5f18-59dd-9300-c8f78603052f.html

Frattaroli, S., & Buggs, S. A. L. (2016). Decreasing gun violence: Social and public health interventions. In L. H. Gold & R. I. Simon (Eds.), *Gun violence and mental illness* (pp. 381–406). Arlington, VA: American Psychiatric Association.

Frau, R., Abbiati, F., Bini, V., Casti, A., Caruso, D., Devoto, P., & Bortolato, M. (2015). Targeting neurosteroid synthesis as a therapy for schizophrenia-related alterations induced by early psychosocial stress. *Schizophrenia Research, 168,* 640–658. doi:10.1016/j.schres.2015.04.044

Freedheim, D. K., & Weiner, I. B. (Eds.) (2013). *Handbook of Psychology, Volume 1, History of Psychology, 2nd Edition.* Hoboken, NJ: Wiley.

French, A. S., Sellier, M.-J., Moutaz, A. A., Guigue, A., Chabaud, M.-A., Reeb, P. D., . . . Marion-Poll, F. (2015). Dual mechanism for bitter avoidance in Drosophila. *The Journal of Neuroscience, 35,* 3990–4004. doi:10.1523/JNEUROSCI. 1312-14.2015

Frenda, S. J., Patihis, L., Loftus, E. F., Lewis, H. C., & Fenn, K. M. (2014). Sleep deprivation and false memories. *Psychological Science, 25,* 1674–1681. doi:10.1177/0956797614534694.

Friedman, M. J. (2015). The human stress response. In N. C. Bernardy & M. J. Friedman (Eds.), *A practical guide to PTSD treatment: Pharmacological and psychotherapeutic approaches* (pp. 9–19). Washington, DC: American Psychological Association. doi:10.1037/14522-002

Friesdorf, R., Conway, P., & Gawronski, B. (2015). Gender differences in responses to moral dilemmas: A process dissociation analysis. *Personality and Social Psychology Bulletin, 41,* 696–713. doi:10.1177/0146167215575731

Frimer, J. A., Aquino, K., Gebauer, J. E., Zhu, L. L., & Oakes, H. (2015). A decline in prosocial language helps explain public disapproval of the US Congress. *Proceedings of the National Academy of Sciences of the United States of America, 112,* 6591–6594. doi:10.1073/pnas.1500355112

Frimer, J. A., Schaefer, N. K., & Oakes, H. (2014). Moral actor, selfish agent. *Journal of Personality and Social Psychology, 106,* 790–802. doi:10.1037/a0036040

Fryer, R. G., Jr. (2010). Financial incentives and student achievement: Evidence from randomized trials. National Bureau of Economic Research, Working Paper No. 15898.

Fu, C. Y., Moyle, W., & Cooke, M. (2013). A randomised controlled trial of the use of aromatherapy and hand massage to reduce disruptive behaviour in people with dementia. *BMC Complementary and Alternative Medicine, 13,* Article 165. http://dx.doi.org/10.1155/2013/790792

Fuhrmann, D., Knoll, L. J., & Blakemore, S.-J. (2015). Adolescence as a sensitive period of brain development. *Trends in Cognitive Sciences, 19,* 558–566. http://dx.doi.org/10.1016/j.tics.2015.07.008

Furguson, E., Chamorro-Premuzic, T., Pickering, A., & Weiss, A. (2011). Five into one does go: A critique of the general factor of personality. In T. Chamorro-Premuzic, S. von Stumm, & A. Furnam (Eds.), *Wiley-Blackwell handbook of*

individual differences (pp. 162–186). Chichester, West Sussex, UK: Wiley-Blackwell.

Furuya, Y., Matsumoto, J., Hori, E., Boas, C. V., Tran, A. H., Shimada, Y., . . . Nishijo, H. (2014). Place-related neuronal activity in the monkey parahippocampal gyrus and hippocampal formation during virtual navigation. *Hippocampus, 24,* 113–130. doi:10.1002/hipo.22209

Fyhri, A., & Phillips, R. O. (2013). Emotional reactions to cycle helmet use. *Accident Analysis and Prevention, 50,* 59–63. doi:10.1016/j.aap.2012.03.027.

Gaertner, S. L., & Dovidio, J. F. (2014). *Reducing intergroup bias: The common ingroup identity model.* New York, NY: Routledge.

Gaetz, M., Weinberg, H., Rzempoluck, E., & Jantzen, K. J. (1998). Neural network classifications and correlational analysis of EEG and MEG activity accompanying spontaneous reversals of the Necker Cube. *Cognitive Brain Research, 6,* 335–346.

Gagnepain, P., Henson, R. N., & Anderson, M. C. (2014). Suppressing unwanted memories reduces their unconscious influence via targeted cortical inhibition. *Proceedings of the National Academy of Sciences of the United States of America, 111,* E1310–E1319. doi:10.1073/pnas.1311468111

Galinha, I. C., Garcia-Martín, M. A., Gomes, C., & Oishi, S. (2016). Criteria for happiness among people living in extreme poverty in Maputo, Mozambique. *International Perspectives in Psychology: Research, Practice, Consultation, 5,* 67–90. http://dx.doi.org/10.1037/ipp0000053

Galinha, I. C., Oishi, S., Pereira, C. R., Wirtz, D., & Esteves, F. (2014). Adult attachment, love styles, relationship experiences and subjective well-being: Cross-cultural and gender comparison between Americans, Portuguese, and Mozambicans. *Social Indicators Research, 119,* 823–852. doi:10.1007/s11205-013-0512-7

Galla, B. M., & Duckworth, A. L. (2015). More than resisting temptation: Beneficial habits mediate the relationship between self-control and positive life outcomes. *Journal of Personality and Social Psychology, 109,* 508–525. doi:10.1037/pspp0000026

Gallace, A. & Spence, C. (2010). The science of interpersonal touch: An overview. *Neuroscience & Biobehavioral Reviews, 34,* 246–259.

Gallagher, B. J. III, & Jones, B. J. (2016). Neglect and hereditary risk: Their relative contribution to schizophrenia with negative symptomatology. *International Journal of Social Psychiatry, 62,* 235–242. http://dx.doi.org/10.1177/0020764015623974

Gamble, T., & Walker, I. (2016). Wearing a bicycle helmet can increase risk taking and sensation seeking in adults. *Psychological Science, 27,* 289–294. http://dx.doi.org/10.1177/0956797615620784

Gander, F., Proyer, R. T., & Ruch, W. (2016). The subjective assessment of accomplishment and positive relationships: Initial validation and correlative and experimental evidence for their association with well-being. *Journal of Happiness Studies.* No Pagination Specified. http://dx.doi.org/10.1007/s10902-016-9751-z

Ganzer, F., Bröning, S., Kraft, S., Sack, P.-M., & Thomasius, R. (2016). Weighing the evidence: A systematic review on long-term neurocognitive effects of cannabis use in abstinent adolescents and adults. *Neuropsychology Review, 26,* 186–222. http://dx.doi.org/10.1007/s11065-016-9316-2

Gao, Y., Bai, C., Zheng, D., Li, C., Zhang, W., Li, M., . . . Ma, Y. (2016). Combination of melatonin and Wnt-4 promotes neural cell differentiation in bovine amniotic epithelial cells and recovery from spinal cord injury. *Journal of Pineal Research: Molecular, Biological, Physiological and Clinical Aspects of Melatonin, 60,* 303–312. doi:10.1111/jpi.12311

Gao, Z., Gao, Q., Tang, N., Shui, R., & Shen, M. (2016). Organization principles in visual working memory: Evidence from sequential stimulus display. *Cognition, 146,* 277–288. http://dx.doi.org/10.1016/j.cognition.2015.10.005

Garcia, J., & Koelling, R. A. (1966). Relation of cue to consequence in avoidance learning. *Psychonomic Science, 4,* 123–124.

García, L. F., Aluja, A., Fibla, J., & García, O. (2014). Association genetic study within the framework of Zuckerman's psychobiological personality model. *Personality and Individual Differences, 60,* S51.

Gardner, B., Phillips, L. A., & Judah, G. (2016). Habitual instigation and habitual execution: Definition, measurement, and effects on behaviour frequency. *British Journal of Health Psychology, 21,* 613–630. doi:10.1111/bjhp.12189

Gardner, H. (1983). *Frames of mind.* New York, NY: Basic.

Gardner, H. (2008). Who owns intelligence? *The Jossey-Bass reader on the brain and learning* (pp. 120–132). San Francisco, CA: Jossey-Bass.

Gardner, R. A., & Gardner, B. T. (1969). Teaching sign language to a chimpanzee. *Science, 165,* 664–672.

Gardstrom, S., & Sorel, S. (2015). Music therapy methods. In B. Wheeler (Ed.), *Music therapy handbook* (pp. 116–128). New York, NY: Guilford.

Garg, R., Levin, E., & Tremblay, L. (2016). Emotional intelligence: Impact on post-secondary academic achievement. *Social Psychology of Education.* No Pagination Specified. http://dx.doi.org/10.1007/s11218-016-9338-x

Garmezy, N. (1983). Stressors of childhood. In N. Garmezy & M. Rutter (Eds.), *Stress, coping, and development in children* (pp. 43–84). Baltimore, MD: Johns Hopkins University Press.

Garrett, B. (2015). *Brain and behavior: An introduction to biological psychology* (4th ed.). Thousand Oaks, CA: Sage.

Gaspar, J. G., Street, W. N., Windsor, M. B., Carbonari, R., Kaczmarski, H., Kramer, A. F., & Mathewson, K. E. (2014). Providing views of the driving scene to drivers' conversation partners mitigates cell-phone-related distraction. *Psychological Science, 25,* 2136–2146. doi:10.1177/0956797614549774

Gattino, S., & Tartaglia, S. (2015). The effect of television viewing on ethnic prejudice against immigrants: A study in the Italian context. *International Journal of Intercultural Relations, 44,* 46–52. doi:10.1016/j.ijintrel.2014.11.004

Gaudiano, B. A., Dalrymple, K. L., Weinstock, L. M., & Lohr, J. M. (2015). The science of psychotherapy: Developing, testing, and promoting evidence-based treatments. In S. O. Lilienfeld, S. J. Lynn, & J. M. Lohr (Eds.), *Science and pseudoscience in clinical psychology* (2nd ed., pp. 155–190). New York, NY: Guilford.

Gawronski, B., Brochu, P. M., Sritharan, R., & Strack, F. (2012). Cognitive consistency in prejudice-related belief systems: Integrating old-fashioned, modern, aversive, and implicit forms of prejudice. In B. Gawronski & F. Strack (Eds.), *Cognitive consistency: A fundamental principle in social cognition* (pp. 369–389). New York, NY: Guilford Press.

Gazes, Y., Bowman, F. D., Razlighi, Q. R., O'Shea, D., Stern, Y., & Habeck, C. (2016). White matter tract covariance patterns predict age-declining cognitive abilities. *NeuroImage, 125,* 53–60. http://dx.doi.org/10.1016/j.neuroimage.2015.10.016

Gazzaniga, M. S. (2009). The fictional self. In D. J. H. Mathews, H. Bok, & P. V. Rabins (Eds.), *Personal identity and fractured selves: Perspectives from philosophy, ethics, and neuroscience* (pp. 174–185). Baltimore, MD: Johns Hopkins University Press.

Geangu, E., Benga, O., Stahl, D., & Striano, T. (2010). Contagious crying beyond the first days of life. *Infant Behavior & Development, 33,* 279–288.

Geisinger, K. F., & McCormick, C. (2013). Testing and assessment in cross-cultural psychology. In J. R. Graham, J. A. Naglieri, & I. B. Weiner (Eds.), *Handbook of psychology, Vol. 10: Assessment psychology* (2nd ed., pp. 114–139). Hoboken, NJ: Wiley.

Gelder, B. D., Meeren, H. K., Righart, R. Stock, J. V., van de Riet, W. A., & Tamietto, M. (2006). Beyond the face: Exploring rapid influences of context on face processing. *Progress in Brain Research, 155,* 37–48.

Gelso, C. J., Nutt Williams, E., & Fretz, B. R. (2014). The third force: The humanistic-experiential approach. In C. J. Gelso, E. Nutt Williams, & B. R. Fretz (Eds.), *Counseling psychology* (3rd ed., pp. 357–391). Washington, DC: American Psychological Association. doi:10.1037/14378-013

Gendron, M., Roberson, D., van der Vyver, J. M., & Barrett, L. F. (2014). Perceptions of emotion from facial expressions are not culturally universal: Evidence from a remote culture. *Emotion, 14,* 251–262. doi:10.1037/a0036052

Gentile, D. A., Reimer, R. A., Nathanson, A. I., Walsh, D. A., & Eisenmann, J. C. (2014). Protective effects of parental monitoring of children's media use: A prospective study. *JAMA Pediatrics, 168,* 479–484. doi:10.1001/jamapediatrics.2014.146.

Geronazzo, M., Bedin, A., Brayda, L., Campus, C., & Avanzini, F. (2016). Interactive spatial sonification for non-visual exploration of virtual maps. *International Journal of Human-Computer Studies, 85,* 4–15. doi:10.1016/j.ijhcs.2015.08.004

Gerring, J. P., & Vasa, R. A. (2016). The Oxford handbook of head injury and externalizing behavior. In T. P. Beauchaine & S. P. Hinshaw (Eds.), *The Oxford handbook of externalizing spectrum disorders* (pp. 403–415). New York, NY: Oxford University Press.

Gerson, S. A., & Woodward, A. L. (2014). Learning from their own actions: The unique effect of producing actions on infants' action understanding. *Child Development, 85,* 264–277. http://dx.doi.org/10.1111/cdev.12115

Gerstorf, D., Hülür, G., Drewelies, J., Eibich, P., Duezel, S., Demuth, I., . . . Lindenberger, U. (2015). Secular changes in late-life cognition and well-being: Towards a long bright future with a short brisk ending? *Psychology and Aging, 30,* 301–310. doi:10.1037/pag0000016

Gherasim, L. R., Brumariu, L. E., & Alim, C. L. (2016). Parenting style and children's life satisfaction and depressive symptoms: Preliminary findings from Romania, France, and Russia. *Journal of Happiness Studies.* No Pagination Specified. http://dx.doi.org/10.1007/s10902-016-9754-9

Gianettoni, L., & Guilley, E. (2016). Sexism and the gendering of professional aspirations. In K. Faniko, F. Lorenzi-Cioldi, O. Sarrasin, & E. Mayor (Eds.), *Gender and social hierarchies: Perspectives from social psychology* (pp. 11–25). New York, NY: Routledge/Taylor & Francis.

Gibbons, S. W., & Hickling, E. J. (2016). Risk and resilience factors in combat military health care providers. In S. MacDermith Wadsworth & D. S. Riggs (Eds.), *War and family life. Risk and resilience in military and veteran families* (pp. 181–193). Cham, CH: Springer International Publishing. http://dx.doi.org/10.1007/978-3-319-21488-7_10

Gibbs, J. C. (2014). *Moral development and reality: Beyond the theories of Kohlberg, Hoffman, and Haidt* (3rd ed.). New York, NY: Oxford University Press.

Gibbs, N. (1995, October 2). The EQ factor. *Time,* 60–68.

Gibson, B., Thompson, J., Hou, B., & Bushman, B. J. (2016). Just harmless entertainment? Effects of surveillance reality TV on physical aggression. *Psychology of Popular Media Culture, 5,* 66–73. http://dx.doi.org/10.1037/ppm0000040

Gibson, E. J., & Walk, R. D. (1960). The visual cliff. *Scientific American, 202,* 67–71.

Gilani, A. I., Chohan, M. O., Inan, M., Schobel, S. A., Chaudhury, N. H., Paskewitz, S., . . . Moore, H. (2014). Interneuron precursor transplants in adult hippocampus reverse psychosis-relevant features in a mouse model of hippocampal disinhibition. *Proceedings of the National Academy of Sciences of the United States of America, 111,* 7450–7455. doi:10.1073/pnas.1316488111

Gilbert, A. C., Boucher, V. J., & Jemel, B. (2015). The perceptual chunking of speech: A demonstration using ERPs. *Brain Research, 1603,* 101–113. doi:10.1016/j.brainres.2015.01.032

Gilberti, M. (2016). Mental illness is no laughing matter. *U.S. News.* Retrieved from http://www.usnews.com/opinion/blogs/policy-dose/articles/2016-03-08/bernie-sanders-mentalhealth-joke-about-the-gop-isnt-funny

Gilbert, P. (2014). Practical and conceptual utility for the treatment and study of social anxiety disorder. In J. Weeks (Ed.), *The Wiley Blackwell handbook of social anxiety disorder* (pp. 24–52). Chichester, UK: Wiley-Blackwell.

Gilligan, C. (1977). In a different voice: Women's conception of morality. *Harvard Educational Review, 47,* 481–517.

Gilligan, C. (1993). Adolescent development reconsidered. In A. Garrod (Ed.), *Approaches to moral development: New research and emerging themes* (pp. 264–280). New York, NY: Teachers College Press.

Gillihan, S. J., & Foa, E. B. (2016). Exposure-based interventions for adult anxiety disorders, obsessive-compulsive disorder, and posttraumatic stress disorder. In C. M. Nezu & A. M. Nezu (Eds.), *The Oxford handbook of cognitive and behavioral therapies* (pp. 96–117). New York, NY: Oxford University Press.

Gil-Rivas, V., & Kilmer, R. P. (2016). Building community capacity and fostering disaster resilience. *Journal of Clinical Psychology.* No Pagination Specified. http://dx.doi.org/10.1002/jclp.22281

Giluk, T. L., & Postlethwaite, B. E. (2015). Big five personality and academic dishonesty: A meta-analytic review. *Personality and Individual Differences, 72,* 59–67. doi:10.1016/j.paid.2014.08.027

Ginzburg, H. M., & Bateman, D. J. (2008). New Orleans medical students post-Katrina—An assessment of psychopathology and anticipatory transference of resilience. *Psychiatric Annals, 38,* 145–156.

Glaser, J. (2015). *Suspect race: Causes and consequences of racial profiling.* New York, NY: Oxford University Press.

Glick, P. (2005). Choice of scapegoats. In J. F. Dovidio, P. Glick, & L. A. Rudman (Eds.), *On the nature of prejudice: Fifty years after Allport* (pp. 244–261). Malden, MA: Blackwell.

Goh, G. H., Mark, P. J., & Maloney, S. K. (2016). Altered energy intake and the amplitude of the body temperature rhythm are associated with changes in phase, but not amplitude, of clock gene expression in the rat suprachiasmatic nucleus in vivo. *Chronobiology International, 33,* 85–97. http://dx.doi.org/10.3109/07420528.2015.1112395

Goldberg, S., Werbeloff, N., Shelef, L., Fruchter, E., & Weiser, M. (2015). Risk of suicide among female adolescents with eating disorders: A longitudinal population-based study. *Eating and Weight Disorders—Studies on Anorexia, Bulimia and Obesity, 30,* 295–300. doi:10.1007/s40519-015-0176-1

Goldfinch, A. (2015). *Rethinking evolutionary psychology.* New York, NY: Palgrave Macmillan.

Goldstein, A. M., Morse, S. J., & Packer, I. K. (2013). Evaluation of criminal responsibility. In R. K. Otto & I. B. Weiner (Eds.), *Handbook of psychology, Vol. 11. Forensic psychology* (2nd ed., pp. 440–472). Hoboken, NJ: Wiley.

Goldstein, B. (2015). *Cognitive psychology: Connecting mind, research, and everyday experience* (4th ed.). Stamford, CT: Cengage Learning.

Goldstein, E. B. (2014). *Sensation and perception* (9th ed.). Belmont, CA: Cengage Learning.

Goldstein, E. G. (2014). *Cognitive psychology: Connecting mind, research, and everyday experience* (4th ed.). Belmont, CA: Cengage Learning.

Goldstein, R. B., Smith, S. M., Chou, S. P., Saha, T. D., Jung, J., Zhang, H., . . . Grant, B. F. (2106). The epidemiology of DSM-5 posttraumatic stress disorder in the United States: Results from the National Epidemiologic Survey on Alcohol and Related Conditions—III. *Social Psychiatry and Psychiatric Epidemiology.* No Pagination Specified. http://dx.doi.org/10.1007/s00127-016-1208-5

Goldstein, S., Princiotta, D., & Naglieri, J. A. (Eds.). (2015). *Handbook of intelligence: Evolutionary theory, historical perspective, and current concepts.* New York, NY: Springer. doi:10.1007/978-1-4939-1562-0

Goleman, D. (1980, February). 1,528 little geniuses and how they grew. *Psychology Today,* 28–53.

Goleman, D. (1995). *Emotional intelligence: Why it can matter more than IQ.* New York, NY: Bantam.

Goleman, D. (2000). *Working with emotional intelligence.* New York, NY: Bantam Doubleday.

Goleman, D. (2008). Leading resonant teams. In F. Hesselbein & A. Shrader (Eds.), *Leader to leader 2: Enduring insights on leadership from the Leader to Leader Institute's award-winning journal* (pp. 186–195). San Francisco, CA: Jossey-Bass.

Gonçalves, M., Amici, R., Lucas, R., Åkerstedt, T., Cirignotta, F., Horne, J., . . .

Grote, L. (2015). Sleepiness at the wheel across Europe: A survey of 19 countries. *Journal of Sleep Research, 24,* 242–253. doi:10.1111/jsr.12267

Gonyea, D., & Montanaro, D. (2015, June 19). Predictably, Democrats, Republicans don't agree on Charleston causes, solutions. *NPR.* Retrieved from http://www.npr.org/sections/itsallpolitics/2015/06/19/415747034/predictably-democratsrepublicans-dont-agree-on-charleston-causes-solutions

González, V. V., Navarro, V., Miguez, G., Betancourt, R., & Laborda, M. A. (2016). Preventing the recovery of extinguished ethanol tolerance. *Behavioural Processes, 124,* 141–148. doi:10.1016/j.beproc.2016.01.004

Goodson, J. L. (2013). Deconstructing sociality, social evolution and relevant nonapeptide functions. *Psychoneuroendocrinology, 38,* 465–478.

Goodwin, C. J. (2012). *A history of modern psychology* (4th ed.). Hoboken, NJ: Wiley.

Goodwin, J., & Goodwin, K. (2013). *Research in psychology: Methods and design* (7th ed). Hoboken, NJ: Wiley.

Gorges, J., & Göke, T. (2015). How do I know what I can do? Anticipating expectancy of success regarding novel academic tasks. *British Journal of Educational Psychology, 85,* 75–90. doi:10.1111/bjep.12064

Gosling, S. D. (2008). Personality in non-human animals. *Social and Personality Compass, 2,* 985–1001.

Gosling, S. D., & John, O. P. (1999). Personality dimensions in nonhuman animals: Across-species review. *Current Directions in Psychological Science, 8,* 69–75.

Gosling, S. D., Kwan, V. S. Y., & John, O. P. (2004). A dog's got personality: A cross-species comparative approach to personality judgments in dogs and humans. *Journal of Personality and Social Psychology, 85,* 1161–1169.

Gottesman, I. I. (1991). *Schizophrenia genesis: The origins of madness.* New York, NY: Freeman.

Göttken, T., White, L. O., Klein, A. M., & von Klitzing, K. (2014). Short-term psychoanalytic child therapy for anxious children: A pilot study. *Psychotherapy, 51,* 148–158. doi:10.1037/a0036026

Gottman, J. M. (2011). *The science of trust: Emotional attunement for couples.* New York, NY: Norton & Co.

Gottman, J. M. (2015). *Principia amoris: The new science of love.* New York, NY: Routledge/Taylor & Francis Group.

Gouveia, M. J., Carona, C., Canavarro, M. C., & Moreira, H. (2016). Self-compassion and dispositional mindfulness are associated with parenting styles and parenting stress: The mediating role of mindful parenting. *Mindfulness, 7,* 700–712. http://dx.doi.org/10.1007/s12671-016-0507-y

Goyal, M., Singh, S., Sibinga, E. M., Gould, N. F., Rowland-Seymour, A., Sharma, R., . . . Haythornthwaite, J. A. (2014). Meditation programs for psychological stress and well-being: A systematic review and meta-analysis. *JAMA Internal Medicine, 174,* 357–368. doi:10.1001/jamainternmed.2013.13018

Graber, R., Turner, R., & Madill, A. (2016). Best friends and better coping: Facilitating psychological resilience through boys' and girls' closest friendships. *British Journal of Psychology, 107,* 338–358. doi:10.1111/bjop.12135

Granger, N., Franklin, R. J., & Jeffery, N. D. (2014). Cell therapy for spinal cord injuries: What is really going on? *The Neuroscientist, 20,* 623–638. doi:10.1177/1073858413514635

Granhag, P. A., Vrij, A., & Verschuere, B. (Eds.). (2015). *Detecting deception: Current challenges and cognitive approaches.* Malden, MA: Wiley-Blackwell.

Granillo, M. T., Perron, B. E., Jarman, C., & Gutowski, S. M. (2013). Cognitive behavioral therapy with substance use disorders: Theory, evidence, and practice. In M. G. Vaughn & B. E. Perron (Eds.), *Social work practice in the addictions* (pp. 101–118). New York, NY: Springer.

Grant, J. E., Odlaug, B. L., & Schreiber, L. R. N. (2014). Pharmacotherapy for obsessive-compulsive and related disorders among adults. In E. A. Storch & D. McKay (Eds.), *Obsessive-compulsive disorder and its spectrum: A life-span approach* (pp. 317–343). Washington, DC: American Psychological Association. doi:10.1037/14323-016

Graupmann, V., & Frey, D. (2014). Bad examples: How thinking about blind obedience can induce responsibility and courage. *Peace and Conflict: Journal of Peace Psychology, 20,* 124–134. doi:10.1037/pac0000021

Gray, M. J., Hassija, C. M., Jaconis, M., Barrett, C., Zheng, P., Steinmetz, S., & James, T. (2015). Provision of evidence-based therapies to rural survivors of domestic violence and sexual assault via telehealth: Treatment outcomes and clinical training benefits. *Training and Education in Professional Psychology, 9,* 235–241. doi:10.1037/tep0000083

Gray, R., & Beilock, S. L. (2011). Hitting is contagious: Experience and action induction. *Journal of Experimental Psychology: Applied, 17,* 49-59. http://dx.doi.org/10.1037/a0022846

Gray, S. J., & Gallo, D. A. (2016). Paranormal psychic believers and skeptics: A large-scale test of the cognitive differences hypothesis. *Memory & Cognition, 44,* 242–261. http://dx.doi.org/10.3758/s13421-015-0563-x

Greenaway, K. H., Storrs, K. R., Philipp, M. C., Louis, W. R., Hornsey, M. J., & Vohs, K. D. (2015). Loss of control stimulates approach motivation. *Journal of Experimental Social Psychology, 56,* 235–241. doi:10.1016/j.jesp.2014.10.009

Greenberg, D. L. (2004). President Bush's false [flashbulb] memory of 9/11/01. *Applied Cognitive Psychology, 18,* 363–370. doi:10.1002/acp.1016

Greenberg, J. (2002). Who stole the money, and when? Individual and situational determinants of employee theft. *Organizational Behavior and Human Decision Processes, 89,* 985–1003.

Greenberg, J., Schmader, T., Arndt, J., & Landau, M. (2015). *Social psychology: The science of everyday life.* New York, NY: Worth.

Greene, J. (2016). *Thinking and language* (5th ed.). New York, NY: Routledge.

Greenfield, B., Henry, M., Lis, E., Slatkoff , J., Guil., J.-M., Dougherty, G., . . . de Castro, F. (2015). Correlates, stability and predictors of borderline personality disorder among previously suicidal youth. *European Child & Adolescent Psychiatry, 24,* 397–406. doi:10.1007/s00787-014-0589-9

Greenfield, P. M., & Quiroz, B. (2013). Context and culture in the socialization and development of personal achievement values: Comparing Latino immigrant families, European American families, and elementary school teachers. *Journal of Applied Developmental Psychology, 34,* 108–118. doi:10.1016/j.appdev.2012.11.002

Greenwald, A. G., & Pettigrew, T. F. (2014). With malice toward none and charity for some: Ingroup favoritism enables discrimination. *American Psychologist, 69,* 669–684. doi:10.1037/a0036056

Gregory, S., Fytche, D., Simmons, A., Kumari, V., Howard, M., Hodgins, S., & Blackwood, N. (2012). The antisocial brain: Psychopathy matters. *Archives of General Psychiatry, 69,* 962–972.

Griggs, R. A. (2015). Coverage of the Phineas Gage story in introductory psychology textbooks: Was Gage no longer Gage? *Teaching of Psychology, 42,* 195–202. doi:10.1177/0098628315587614

Griggs, R. A. (2015). The Kitty Genovese story in introductory psychology textbooks: Fifty years later. *Teaching of Psychology, 42,* 149–152. doi:10.1177/0098628315573138

Griggs, R. A., & Whitehead III, G. I. (2015). Coverage of recent criticisms of Milgram's obedience experiments in introductory social psychology textbooks. *Theory & Psychology, 25,* 564–580. http://dx.doi.org/10.1177/0959354315601231

Grimm, S., Pestke, K., Feeser, M., Aust, S., Weigand, A., Wang, J., . . . Bajbouj, M. (2014). Early life stress modulates oxytocin effects on limbic system during acute psychosocial stress. *Social Cognitive and Affective Neuroscience, 9,* 1828–1835. doi:10.1093/scan/nsu020

Groome, D., Brace, N., Edgar, G., Edgar, H., Eysenck, M., Manly, . . . Styles, E. (2014). *An introduction to cognitive psychology: Processes and disorders* (3rd ed.). New York, NY: Psychology Press.

Grossman, L., & Walfish, S. (Eds.). (2014). *Translating psychological research into practice.* New York, NY: Springer.

Grover, S., & Ghosh, A. (2014). Somatic symptom and related disorders in Asians and Asian Americans. *Asian Journal of Psychiatry, 7,* 77–79. doi:10.1016/j.ajp.2013.11.014

Grünbaum, A. (2015). Critique of psychoanalysis. In S. Boag, L. A. W. Brakel, & V. Talvitie (Eds.), *Philosophy, science, and psychoanalysis: A critical meeting* (pp. 1–36). London: Karnac Books.

Gruzd, A., & Roy, J. (2014). Investigating political polarization on Twitter: A Canadian perspective. *Policy & Internet, 6,* 28–45. doi:10.1002/1944-2866.POI354

Grzybowski, S. J., Wyczesany, M., & Kaiser, J. (2014). The influence of context on the processing of emotional and neutral adjectives–An ERP study. *Biological Psychology, 99,* 137–149. doi:10.1016/j.biopsycho.2014.01.002

Guardino, C. M., Schetter, C. D., Saxbe, D. E., Adam, E. K., Ramey, S. L., Shalowitz, M. U., & Community Child Health Network (2016). Diurnal salivary cortisol patterns prior to pregnancy predict infant birth weight. *Health Psychology, 35,* 625–633. http://dx.doi.org/10.1037/hea0000313

Guastello, S. J., Guastello, D. D., & Craft, L. L. (1989). Assessment of the Barnum effect in computer-based test interpretations. *Journal of Psychology: Interdisciplinary and Applied, 123,* 477–484. doi:10.1080/00223980.1989.10543001

Guéguen, N., & Jacob, C. (2014). Clothing color and tipping: Gentlemen patrons give more tips to waitresses with red clothes. *Journal of Hospitality & Tourism Research, 38,* 275–280. doi:10.1177/1096348012442546

Guéguen, N., & Stefan, J. (2016). "Green altruism": Short immersion in natural green environments and helping behavior. *Environment and Behavior, 48,* 324–342. http://dx.doi.org/10.1177/0013916514536576

Guekht, A. (2016). Dementia. In M. Mula (Ed.), *Neuropsychiatric symptoms of epilepsy* (pp. 235–254). Cham, CH: Springer International Publishing. http://dx.doi.org/10.1007/978-3-319-22159-5_14

Guilford, J. P. (1967). *The nature of human intelligence.* New York, NY: McGraw-Hill.

Gulliver, S. B., Zimering, R., Carpenter, G. S., Giardina, A., & Farrar, J. (2014). The psychological consequences of disaster. In P. Ouimette & J. P. Read (Eds.), *Trauma and substance abuse: Causes, consequences, and treatment of comorbid disorders* (2nd ed., pp. 125–141). Washington, DC: American Psychological Association. doi:10.1037/14273-007

Gumz, M. L. (Ed.). (2016). *Circadian clocks: Role in health and disease.* New York, NY: Springer Science + Business Media. http://dx.doi.org/10.1007/978-1-4939-3450-8

Gunderson, J. G., & Links, P. (2014). *Handbook of good psychiatric management for borderline personality disorder.* Arlington, VA: American Psychiatric Publishing.

Gunn, W. B., Jr., Haley, J., Prouty, A. M., & Robertson, J. (2015). Systemic approaches: Family therapy. In H. T. Prout & A. L. Fedewa (Eds.), *Counseling and psychotherapy with children and adolescents: Theory and practice for school and clinical settings* (5th ed., pp. 317–355). Hoboken, NJ: Wiley.

Guo, W., Song, Y., Liu, F., Zhang, Z., Zhang, J., Yu, M., . . . Zhao, J. (2015). Dissociation of functional and anatomical brain abnormalities in unaffected siblings of schizophrenia patients. *Clinical Neurophysiology, 126,* 927–932. doi:10.1016/j.clinph.2015.01.025

Gurven, M., von Rueden, C., Massenkoff, M., Kaplan, H., & Lero Vie, M. (2013). How universal is the big five? Testing the five-factor model of personality variation among forager-farmers in the Bolivian Amazon. *Journal of Personality and Social Psychology, 104,* 354–370. doi:10.1037/a0030841

Guryan, J., Kim, J. S., & Park, K. (2015). Motivation and incentives in education: Evidence from a summer reading experiment. National Bureau of Economic Research, Working Paper No. 20918.

Gutchess, A., & Huff, S. (2016). Cross-cultural differences in memory. In J. Y. Chiao, S. -C. Li, R. Seligman, & R. Turner (Eds.), *The Oxford handbook of cultural neuroscience. Oxford library of psychology* (pp. 155–169). New York, NY: Oxford University Press.

Guveli, H., Anuk, D., Oflaz, S., Guveli, M. E., Yildirim, N. K., Ozkan, M., & Ozkan, S. (2015). Oncology staff: Burnout, job satisfaction and coping with stress. *Psycho-Oncology, 24,* 926–931. doi:10.1002/pon.3743

Haaken, J. (2010). *Hard knocks: Domestic violence and the psychology of storytelling.* New York, NY: Routledge/Taylor & Francis Group.

Haas, B. W., Ishak, A., Anderson, I. W., & Filkowski, M. M. (2015). The tendency to trust is reflected in human brain structure. *NeuroImage, 107,* 175–181. doi:10.1016/j.neuroimage.2014.11.060

Haberstick, B. C., Lessem, J. M., Hewitt, J. K., Smolen, A., Hopfer, C. J., Halpern, C. T., . . . Harris, K. M. (2014). MAOA genotype, childhood maltreatment, and their interaction in the etiology of adult antisocial behaviors. *Biological Psychiatry, 75,* 25–30. doi:10.1038/sj.mp.4001851

Hackley, C. (2007). Marketing psychology and the hidden persuaders. *The Psychologist, 20,* 488–490.

Hagenberg, A., & Carpenter, D. C. (2014). Mirror visual feedback for phantom pain: International experience on modalities and side effects discussed by expert panel. A Delphi study. *PM&R, 6,* 708–715. doi:10.1016/j.pmrj.2014.01.005

Haghighi, A., Melka, M. G., Bernard, M., Abrahamowicz, M., Leonard, G. T., Richer, L., . . . Pausova, Z. (2014). Opioid receptor mu 1 gene, fat intake and obesity in adolescence. *Molecular Psychiatry, 19,* 63–68. doi:10.1038/mp.2012.179

Haghighi, A., Schwartz, D. H., Abrahamowicz, M., Leonard, G. T., Perron, M., Richer, L., . . . Pausova, Z. (2013). Prenatal exposure to maternal cigarette smoking, amygdala volume, and fat intake in adolescence. *JAMA Psychiatry, 70,* 98–105.

Haines, E. L., Deaux, K., & Lofaro, N. (2016). The times they are a-changing . . . or are they not? A comparison of gender stereotypes, 1983–2014. *Psychology of Women Quarterly, 40,* 353–363. doi:10.1177/0361684316634081

Haines, R., & Mann, J. (2011). A new perspective on de-individuation via computer-mediated communication. *European Journal of Information Systems, 20,* 156–167.

Hair, N. L., Hanson, J. L., Wolfe, B. L., & Pollak, S. D. (2015). Association of child poverty, brain development, and academic achievement. *JAMA Pediatrics, 169,* 822–829. doi:10.1001/jamapediatrics.2015.1475.

Haith, M. M., & Benson, J. B. (1998). Infant cognition. In W. Damon (Series Ed.) & D. Kuhn & R. S. Siegler (Vol. Eds.), *Handbook of child psychology: Vol. 2. Cognition, perception, and language* (5th ed., pp. 199–254). New York, NY: Wiley

Hajak, G., Lemme, K., & Zisapel, N. (2015). Lasting treatment effects in a postmarketing surveillance study of prolonged-release melatonin. *International Clinical Psychopharmacology, 30,* 36–42. doi:10.1097/YIC.0000000000000046

Halbesleben, J. R. B., Wheeler, A. R., & Paustian-Underdahl, S. C. (2013). The impact of furloughs on emotional exhaustion, self-rated performance, and recovery experiences. *Journal of Applied Psychology, 98,* 492–503. doi:10.1037/a0032242

Hall, E. V., & Livingston, R. W. (2012). The hubris penalty: Biased responses to "Celebration" displays of black football players. *Journal of Experimental Social Psychology, 48,* 899–904. doi:10.1016/j.jesp.2012.02.004

Hall, G. C. N., & Ibaraki, A. Y. (2016). Multicultural issues in cognitive-behavioral therapy: Cultural adaptations and goodness of fit. In C. M. Nezu & A. M. Nezu (Eds.), *The Oxford handbook of cognitive and behavioral therapies* (pp. 465–481). New York, NY: Oxford University Press.

Hall, J. A., & Xing, C. (2015). The verbal and nonverbal correlates of the five flirting styles. *Journal of Nonverbal Behavior, 39,* 41–68. doi:10.1007/s10919-014-0199-8

Hall, W., & Degenhardt, L. (2014). The adverse health effects of chronic cannabis use. *Drug Testing and Analysis, 6,* 39–45. doi:10.1002/dta.1506

Halpern, D. F. (2014). *Thought and knowledge: An introduction to critical thinking* (5th ed.). New York, NY: Psychology Press.

Halpern, D., Valenzuela, S., & Katz, J. E. (2016). "Selfie-ists" or "Narci-selfiers"?: A cross-lagged panel analysis of selfie taking and narcissism. *Personality and Individual Differences, 97*, 98–101. http://dx.doi.org/10.1016/j.paid.2016.03.019

Halpern, S. D., French, B., Small, D. S., Saulsgiver, K., Harhay, M. O., Audrain-McGovern, J., . . . Volpp, K. G. (2015). Randomized trial of four financial-incentive programs for smoking cessation. *New England Journal of Medicine, 372*, 2108-2117. doi:10.1056/NEJMoa1414293

Hamilton, J., Daleiden, E., & Youngstrom, E. (2016). Evidence-based practice. In M. K. Dulcan (Ed.), *Dulcan's textbook of child and adolescent psychiatry* (2nd ed., pp. 523–537). Arlington, VA: American Psychiatric Publishing, Inc.

Hammack, P. L. (2003). The question of cognitive therapy in a postmodern world. *Ethical Human Sciences and Services, 5*, 209–224.

Handler, M., Honts, C. R., & Nelson, R. (2013). Information gain of the directed lie screening test. *Polygraph, 42*, 192–202.

Haney, C., Banks, C., & Zimbardo, P. (1978). Interpersonal dynamics in a simulated prison. *International Journal of Criminology and Penology, 1*, 69–97.

Hanscombe, E. (2015). The real psychotherapist: An impossibility for film. In L. Huskinson & T. Waddell (Eds.), *Eavesdropping: The psychotherapist in film and television* (pp. 51–63). New York, NY: Routledge/Taylor & Francis Group.

Hara, Y., Yuk, F., Puri, R., Janssen, W. G., Rapp, P. R., & Morrison, J. H. (2014). Presynaptic mitochondrial morphology in monkey prefrontal cortex correlates with working memory and is improved with estrogen treatment. *Proceedings of the National Academy of Sciences of the United States of America, 111*, 486–491. doi:10.1073/pnas.1311310110

Harker, C. M., Ibañez, L. V., Nguyen, T. P., Messinger, D. S., & Stone, W. L. (2016). The effect of parenting style on social smiling in infants at high and low risk for ASD. *Journal of Autism and Developmental Disorders. 46*, 2399–2407. http://dx.doi.org/10.1007/s10803-016-2772-y

Harley, A., Kumar, D., & Agarwal, A. (2016). The common characteristics between infertility and recurrent pregnancy loss. In A. Bashiri, A. Harlev, & A. Agarwal (Eds.), *Recurrent pregnancy loss: Evidence-based evaluation, diagnosis and treatment* (pp. 143–152). New York, NY: Springer. doi:10.1007/978-3-319-27452-2_10

Harley, R., Eisner, L., Prairie, E., & Jacobo, M. (2016). Treatment of borderline personality disorder. In T. J. Petersen, S. E. Sprich, & S. Wilhelm (Eds.), *The Massachusetts General Hospital handbook of cognitive behavioral therapy* (pp. 227–242). Totowa, NJ: Humana Press. http://dx.doi.org/10.1007/978-1-4939-2605-3_17

Harley, T. A. (2014). *The psychology of language: From data to theory* (4th ed.). New York, NY: Psychology Press.

Harlow, H. F., Harlow, M. K., & Meyer, D. R. (1950). Learning motivated by a manipulation drive. *Journal of Experimental Psychology, 40*, 228–234.

Harlow, H. F., Harlow, M. K., & Suomi, S. J. (1971). From thought to therapy: Lessons from a primate laboratory. *American Scientist, 59*, 538–549.

Harlow, J. (1868). Recovery from the passage of an iron bar through the head. *Publications of the Massachusetts Medical Society, 2*, 237–246.

Harmon-Jones, E., & Harmon-Jones, C. (2015). Neural foundations of motivational orientations. In G. H. E. Gendolla, M. Tops, & S. L. Koole (Eds.), *Handbook of biobehavioral approaches to self-regulation* (pp. 175–187). New York, NY: Springer. doi:10.1007/978-1-4939-1236-0_12

Harriger, J. A., Calogero, R. M., Witherington, D. C., & Smith, J. E. (2010). Body size stereotyping and internalization of the thin ideal in preschool girls. *Sex Roles, 63*, 609–620. doi:10.1007/ s11199-010-9868-1

Harris, E., McNamara, P., & Durso, R. (2015). Novelty seeking in patients with right-versus left-onset Parkinson disease. *Cognitive and Behavioral Neurology, 28*, 11–16. doi:10.1097/WNN.0000000000000047.

Hart, J., Kraut, M. A., Womack, K. B., Strain, J., Didehbani, N., Bartze, E., . . . Cullum, C. M. (2013). Neuroimaging of cognitive dysfunction and depression in aging retired National Football League players: A cross-sectional study. *JAMA Neurology, 70*, 326–335.

Hart, J., Nailling, E., Bizer, G. Y., & Collins, C. K. (2015). Attachment theory as a framework for explaining engagement with Facebook. *Personality and Individual Differences, 77*, 33–40. doi:10.1016/j.paid.2014.12.016

Hartmann, E., & Hartmann, T. (2014). The impact of exposure to Internet-based information about the Rorschach and the MMPI-2 on psychiatric outpatients' ability to simulate mentally healthy test performance. *Journal of Personality Assessment, 99*, 432–444. doi:10.1080/00223891.2014.882342

Harwood, C. G., Keegan, R. J., Smith, J. M. J., & Raine, A. S. (2015). A systematic review of the intrapersonal correlates of motivational climate perceptions in sport and physical activity. *Psychology of Sport and Exercise, 18*, 9–25. http://dx.doi.org/10.1016/j.psychsport.2014.11.005

Haslam, N. (2015). Dehumanization and intergroup relations. In M. Mikulincer, P. R. Shaver, J. F. Dovidio, & J. A. Simpson (Eds.), *APA handbook of personality and social psychology, Vol. 2. Group processes* (pp. 295–314). Washington, DC: American Psychological Association. doi:10.1037/14342-011

Haslam, S. A., Reicher, S. D., & Millard, K. (2015a). Shock treatment: Using immersive digital realism to restage and re-examine Milgram's obedience to authority research. *PLoS ONE, 10*. doi:10.1371/journal.pone.0109015

Haslam, S. A., Reicher, S. D., Millard, K., & McDonald, R. (2015b). 'Happy to have been of service': The Yale archive as a window into the engaged followership of participants in Milgram's 'obedience' experiments. *British Journal of Social Psychology, 54*, 55–83. doi:10.1111/bjso.12074

Hatfield, E., & Rapson, R. L. (1996). *Love and sex: Cross-cultural perspectives.* Needham Heights, MA: Allyn & Bacon.

Hauner, K. K., Mineka, S., Voss, J. L., & Paller, K. A. (2012). Exposure therapy triggers lasting reorganization of neural fear processing. *Proceedings of the National Academy of Sciences of the United States of America, 109*, 9203–9208.

Hayashi, M. T., Cesare, A. J., Riversa, T., & Karlseder, J. (2015). Cell death during crisis is mediated by mitotic telomere deprotection. *Nature, 522*, 492–496. doi:10.1038/nature14513

Hay, D. F. (1994). Prosocial development. *Journal of Child Psychology and Psychiatry, 35*, 29–71.

Hayflick, L. (1965). The limited in vitro lifetime of human diploid cell strains. *Experimental Cell Research, 37*, 614–636. doi:10.1016/0014-4827(65)90211-9

Hayflick, L. (1996). *How and why we age.* New York, NY: Ballantine.

Hays, P. A. (2014). *LifeTools: Books for the general public. Creating well-being: Four steps to a happier, healthier life.* Washington, DC: American Psychological Association.

Hazan, C., & Shaver, P. (1987). Romantic love conceptualized as an attachment process. *Journal of Personality and Social Psychology, 52*, 511–524.

Head, L. M. (2014). The effect of kangaroo care on neurodevelopmental outcomes in preterm infants. *The Journal of Perinatal & Neonatal Nursing, 28*, 290–299. doi:10.1097/JPN.0000000000000062.

Heffner, K. L., Crean, H. F., & Kemp, J. E. (2016). Meditation programs for veterans with posttraumatic stress disorder: Aggregate findings from a multi-site evaluation. *Psychological Trauma: Theory, Research, Practice, and Policy, 18*, 365–374. http://dx.doi.org/10.1037/tra0000106

Heider, F. (1958). *The psychology of interpersonal relations.* Hoboken, NJ: Wiley.

Heimann, M., & Meltzoff, A. N. (1996). Deferred imitation in 9- and 14-month-old infants. *British Journal of Developmental Psychology, 14*, 55–64. doi:10.1111/j.2044-835X.1996.tb00693.x

Heine, S. J., & Renshaw, K. (2002). Inter-judge agreement, self-enhancement, and liking:

Cross-cultural divergences. *Personality and Social Psychology Bulletin, 28,* 578–587.

Heinz, A. J., Makin-Byrd, K., Blonigen, D. M., Reilly, P., & Timko, C. (2015). Aggressive behavior among military veterans in substance use disorder treatment: The roles of posttraumatic stress and impulsivity. *Journal of Substance Abuse Treatment, 50,* 59–66. doi:10.1016/j.jsat.2014.10.014

Heitland, K., & Bohner, G. (2010). Reducing prejudice via cognitive dissonance: Individual differences in preference for consistency moderate the effects of counter-attitudinal advocacy. *Social Influence, 5,* 164–181. http://dx.doi.org/10.1080/15534510903332261

Helbig-Lang, S., Rusch, S., & Lincoln, T. M. (2015). Emotion regulation difficulties in social anxiety disorder and their specific contributions to anxious responding. *Journal of Clinical Psychology, 71,* 241–249. doi:10.1002/jclp.22135

Hellström, P. M. (2013). Satiety signals and obesity. *Current Opinion in Gastroenterology, 29,* 222–227. doi:10.1097/MOG.0b013e32835d9ff8

Hendricks, P. S., Thorne, C. B., Clark, C. B., Coombs, D. W., & Johnson, M. W. (2015a). Classic psychedelic use is associated with reduced psychological distress and suicidality in the United States adult population. *Journal of Psychopharmacology, 29,* 280–288. doi:10.1177/0269881114565653

Hendricks, P. S., Johnson, M. W., & Griffiths, R. R. (2015b). Psilocybin, psychological distress, and suicidality. *Journal of Psychopharmacology, 29,* 1041–1043. doi:10.1177/0269881115598338

Henkel, L. A. (2014). Point and shoot memories: The influence of taking photos on memory for a museum tour. *Psychological Science, 25,* 396–402.

Henwood, B. F., Derejko, K.-S., Couture, J., & Padgett, D. K. (2014). Maslow and mental health recovery: A comparative study of homeless programs for adults with serious mental illness. *Administration and Policy in Mental Health and Mental Health Services Research, 42,* 220–228. doi:10.1007/s10488-014-0542-8

Herbert, H. S., Manjula, M., & Philip, M. (2013). Resilience and factors contributing to resilience among the offsprings of parents with schizophrenia. *Psychological Studies, 58,* 80–88. doi:10.1007/s12646-012-0168-4

Herbst, R. S., Hobin, J. A., & Gritz, E. R. (2014). AACR celebrates 50 years of tobacco research and policy. *Clinical Cancer Research, 20,* 1709–1718. doi:10.1158/1078-0432. CCR-14-0427

Herek, G. M., Gillis, J. R., & Cogan, J. C. (2015). Internalized stigma among sexual minority adults: Insights from a social psychological perspective. *Stigma and Health, 1,* 18–34. doi.10.1037/a0014672

Herisson, F. M., Waas, J. R., Fredriksson, R., Schiöth, H. B., Levine, A. S., & Olszewski, P. K. (2016). Oxytocin acting in the nucleus accumbens core decreases food intake. *Journal of Neuroendocrinology, 28.* No Pagination Specified.

Herman, A. I., DeVito, E. E., Jensen, K. P., & Sofuoglu, M. (2014). Pharmacogenetics of nicotine addiction: Role of dopamine. *Pharmacogenomics, 15,* 221–234. doi:10.2217/pgs.13.246

Herman, L. M., Richards, D. G., & Woltz, J. P. (1984). Comprehension of sentences by bottle-nosed dolphins. *Cognition, 16,* 129–139. doi:10.1016/0010-0277(84)90003-9

Hernandez, R., Kershaw, K. N., Siddique, J., Boehm, J. K., Kubzansky, L. D., Diez-Roux, A., . . . Lloyd-Jones, D. M. (2015). Optimism and cardiovascular health: Multi-ethnic study of atherosclerosis (MESA). *Health Behavior and Policy Review, 2,* 62–73. doi:10.14485/HBPR.2.1.6

Herriot, P. (2014). *Attributes of memory.* New York, NY: Psychology Press.

Hertel, G., Rauschenbach, C., Thielgen, M. M., & Krumm, S. (2015). Are older workers more active copers? Longitudinal effects of age-contingent coping on strain at work. *Journal of Organizational Behavior, 36,* 514–537. doi:10.1002/job.1995

Hess, M. E., & Brüning, J. C. (2014). The fat mass and obesity-associated (FTO) gene: Obesity and beyond? *Biochimica et Biophysica Acta (BBA)—Molecular Basis of Disease, 1842,* 2039–2047. doi:10.1016/j.bbadis.2014.01.017

Hess, U., & Hareli, S. (2015). The role of social context for the interpretation of emotional facial expressions. In M. Mandal & A. Awasthi (Eds.), *Understanding facial expressions in communication* (pp. 119–141). New Delhi, IN: Springer. doi:10.1007/978-81-322-1934-7_7

Higgs, S. (2015). Social norms and their influence on eating behaviours. *Appetite, 86,* 38–44. doi:10.1016/j.appet.2014.10.021

Hilgard, E. R. (1978). Hypnosis and consciousness. *Human Nature, 1,* 42–51.

Hilgard, E. R. (1992). Divided consciousness and dissociation. *Consciousness and Cognition, 1,* 16–31.

Hillier, S. M., & Barrow, G. M. (2011). *Aging, the individual, and society* (9th ed.). Belmont, CA: Cengage Learning.

Himes, S., Yanover, T., & Thompson, J. K. (2015). Eating disorders. In F. Andrasik, J. L. Goodie, & A. L. Peterson (Eds.), *Biopsychosocial assessment in clinical health psychology* (pp. 49–60). New York, NY: Guilford.

Hing, N., Lamont, M., Vitartas, P., & Fink. E. (2015). Sports bettors' responses to sports-embedded gambling promotions: Implications for compulsive consumption. *Journal of Business Research, 68,* 2057–2066. doi:10.1016/j.jbusres.2015.03.003

Hirsh-Pasek, K., Adamson, L., Bakeman, R., Golinkoff, R. M., Pace, A., Yust, P., & Suma, K. (2015). The contribution of early communication to low-income children's language success. *Psychological Science, 26,* 1071–1083.

Hirst, W., Phelps, E. A., Meksin, R., Vaidya, C. J., Johnson, M. K., Mitchell, K. J., . . . Olsson, A. (2015). A ten-year follow-up of a study of memory for the attack of September 11, 2001: Flashbulb memories and memories for flashbulb events. *Journal of Experimental Psychology: General, 144,* 604–623. doi:10.1037/xge0000055

Hively, K., & El-Alayli, A. (2014). "You throw like a girl": The effect of stereotype threat on women's athletic performance and gender stereotypes. *Psychology of Sport and Exercise, 15,* 48–55. doi:10.1016/j.psychsport.2013.09.001

Hobson, J. A. (1999). *Dreaming as delirium: How the brain goes out of its mind.* Cambridge, MA: MIT Press.

Hobson, J. A. (2005). In bed with Mark Solms? What a nightmare! A reply to Domhoff. *Dreaming, 15,* 21–29.

Hobson, J. A., & McCarley, R. W. (1977). The brain as a dream state generator: An activation-synthesis hypothesis of the dream process. *American Journal of Psychiatry, 134,* 1335–1348.

Hobson, J. A., Sangsanguan, S., Arantes, H., & Kahn, D. (2011). Dream logic—The inferential reasoning paradigm. *Dreaming, 21,* 1–15.

Hoeschele, M., & Fitch, W. T. (2016). Phonological perception by birds: Budgerigars can perceive lexical stress. *Animal Cognition, 19,* 643–654. http://dx.doi.org/10.1007/s10071-016-0968-3

Hoffman, A. J. (2014). Violent media games and aggression—Is it really time for a mea culpa? *American Psychologist, 69,* 305–306. doi:10.1037/a0035289

Hofman, M. A. (2015). Evolution of the human brain: From matter to mind. In S. Goldstein, D. Princiotta, & J. A. Naglieri (Eds.), *Handbook of intelligence: Evolutionary theory, historical perspective, and current concepts* (pp. 65–82). New York, NY: Springer. doi:10.1007/978-1-4939-1562-0

Hofstede, G. J., Dignum, F., Prada, R., Student, J., & Vanhée, L. (2015). Gender differences: The role of nature, nurture, social identity and self-organization. In *Multi-Agent-Based Simulation XV* (pp. 72–87). Cham, CH: Springer International Publishing.

Hogan, T. P. (2013). *Psychological testing: A practical introduction* (3rd ed.). Hoboken, NJ: Wiley.

Hole, J., Hirsch, M., Ball, E., & Meads, C. (2015). Music as an aid for postoperative recovery in adults: A systematic review and meta-analysis. *The Lancet*, 386, 1659–1671. doi:10.1016/S0140-6736(15)60169-6

Hollander, M. M. (2015). The repertoire of resistance: Non-compliance with directives in Milgram's 'obedience' experiments. *British Journal of Social Psychology, 54,* 425–444. doi:10.1111/bjso.12099

Holland, J. L. (1985). *Making vocational choices: A theory of vocational personalities* *and work environments* (2nd ed.). Englewood Cliffs, NJ: Prentice Hall.

Holland, J. L. (1994). *Self-directed search form R.* Lutz, FL: Psychological Assessment Resources.

Holman, E. A., Garfin, D. R., & Silver, R. C. (2014). Media's role in broadcasting acute stress following Boston Marathon bombings. *Proceedings of the National Academy of Sciences of the United States of America, 111,* 93–98. doi:10.1073/pnas.1316265110

Holmes, T. H., & Rahe, R. H. (1967). The Social Readjustment Rating Scale. *Journal of Psychosomatic Research, 11,* 213–218. doi: 10.1016/0022-3999(67)90010-4

Holshausen, K., Bowie, C. R., & Harkness, K. L. (2016). The relation of childhood maltreatment to psychotic symptoms in adolescents and young adults with depression. *Journal of Clinical Child and Adolescent Psychology, 45,* 241–247. http://dx.doi.org/10.1080/15374416.2014.952010

Homan, K. J. (2016). Self-compassion and psychological well-being in older adults. *Journal of Adult Development, 23,* 111–119. http://dx.doi.org/10.1007/s10804-016-9227-8

Ho, M., & O'Donohoe, S. (2014). Volunteer stereotypes, stigma, and relational identity projects. *European Journal of Marketing, 48,* 854–877. doi:10.1108/EJM-11-2011-0637

Hong, F.-Y., & Chiu, S.-L. (2016). Factors influencing Facebook usage and Facebook addictive tendency in university students: The role of online psychological and Facebook usage motivation. *Stress and Health, 32,* 117–127. doi:10.1002/smi.2585

Hong, S. L., Estrada-Sánchez, A. M., Barton, S. J., & Rebec, G. V. (2016). Early exposure to dynamic environments alters patterns of motor exploration throughout the lifespan. *Behavioural Brain Research, 302,* 81–87. doi:10.1016/j.bbr.2016.01.007

Hoogland, C. E., Ryan Schurtz, D., Cooper, C. M., Combs, D. J. Y., Brown, E. G., & Smith, R. H. (2015). The joy of pain and the pain of joy: In-group identification predicts schadenfreude and gluckschmerz following rival groups' fortunes. *Motivation and Emotion, 39,* 260–281. doi:10.1007/s11031-014-9447-9

Hoogwegt, M. T., Versteeg, H., Hansen, T. B., Thygesen, L. C., Pedersen, S. S., & Zwisler, A.- D. (2013). Exercise mediates the association between positive affect and 5-year mortality in patients with ischemic heart disease. *Circulation: Cardiovascular Quality and Outcomes, 6,* 559–566. doi:10.1161/CIRCOUTCOMES.113.000158

Hooper, N., Erdogan, A., Keen, G., Lawton, K., & McHugh, L. (2015). Perspective taking reduces the fundamental attribution error. *Journal of Contextual Behavioral Science, 4,* 69–72. doi:10.1016/j.jcbs.2015.02.002

Hope, A. E., & Sugarman, L. I. (2015). Orienting hypnosis. *American Journal of Clinical Hypnosis, 57,* 212–229. doi:10.1080/00029157.2014.976787

Hoppe, A. (2011). Psychosocial working conditions and well-being among immigrant and German low-wage workers. *Journal of Occupational Health Psychology, 16,* 187–201. http://dx.doi.org/10.1037/a0021728

Horigian, V. E., & Szapocznik, J. (2015). Brief strategic family therapy: Thirty-five years of interplay among theory, research, and practice in adolescent behavior problems. In L. M. Scheier (Ed.), *Handbook of adolescent drug use prevention: Research, intervention strategies, and practice* (pp. 249–265). Washington, DC: American Psychological Association. doi:10.1037/14550-015

Hori, H., Koga, N., Hidese, S., Nagashima, A., Kim, Y., Higuchi, T., & Kunugi, H. (2016). 24-h activity rhythm and sleep in depressed outpatients. *Journal of Psychiatric Research, 77,* 27–34. http://dx.doi.org/10.1016/j.jpsychires.2016.02.022

Horney, K. (1939). *New ways in psychoanalysis.* New York, NY: International Universities Press.

Horney, K. (1945). *Our inner conflicts: A constructive theory of neurosis.* New York, NY: Norton.

Horta, B. L., Loret de Mola, C., & Victora, C. G. (2015). Breastfeeding and intelligence: A systematic review and meta-analysis. *Acta Paediatrica, 104,* 14–19. doi:10.1111/apa.13139

Horwath, E., & Gould, F. (2011). Epidemiology of anxiety disorders. In M. Tsuang, M. Tohen, & P. Jones (Eds.), *Textbook in psychiatric epidemiology* (3rd ed., pp. 311–328). Hoboken, NJ: Wiley.

Hosie, J., Gilbert, F., Simpson, K., & Daffern, M. (2014). An examination of the relationship between personality and aggression using the general aggression and five factor models. *Aggressive Behavior, 40,* 189–196. doi:10.1002/ab.21510

Hou, G., Xiong, W., Wang, M., Chen, X., & Yuan, T. (2014). Chronic stress influences sexual motivation and causes damage to testicular cells in male rats. *Journal of Sexual Medicine, 11,* 653–663. doi:10.1111/jsm.12416

Howard, M. E., Jackson, M. L., Berlowitz, D., O'Donoghue, F., Swann, P., Westlake, J., . . . Pierce, R. J. (2014). Specific sleepiness symptoms are indicators of performance impairment during sleep deprivation. *Accident Analysis and Prevention, 62,* 1–8. doi:10.1016/j.aap.2013.09.003

Howell, J. A., McEvoy, P. M., Grafton, B., Macleod, C., Kane, R. T., **Anderson, R. A., & Egan, S. J.** (2016). Selective attention in perfectionism: Dissociating valence from perfectionism-relevance. *Journal of Behavior Therapy and Experimental Psychiatry, 51,* 100–108. http://dx.doi.org/10.1016/j.jbtep.2016.01.004

Howe, M. L., & Knott, L. M. (2015). The fallibility of memory in judicial processes: Lessons from the past and their modern consequences. *Memory, 23,* 633–656. doi:10.1080/09658211.2015.1010709

Howes, M. B., & O'Shea, G. (2014). *Human memory: A constructivist view.* San Diego, CA: Elsevier.

Howes, O. D., & Murray, R. M. (2014). Schizophrenia: An integrated socio-developmental-cognitive model. *The Lancet, 383,* 1677–1687. doi:10.1016/S0140-6736(13)62036-X

Howes, O., McCutcheon, R., & Stone, J. (2015). Glutamate and dopamine in schizophrenia: An update for the 21st century. *Journal of Psychopharmacology, 29,* 97–115. doi:10.1177/0269881114563634

Hrobjartsson, A., Ravaud, P., Tendal, B., Thomsen, A. S. S., Boutron, I., Emanuelsson, F., . . . Brorson, S. (2013). Observer bias in randomized clinical trials with measurement scale outcomes: A systematic review of trials with both blinded and nonblinded assessors. *Canadian Medical Association Journal, 185,* E201–E211. doi:10.1503/cmaj.120744

Hsiao, S. S., & Gomez-Ramirez, M. (2013). Neural mechanisms of tactile perception. In R. J. Nelson, S. J. Y. Mizumori, & I. B. Weiner (Eds.), *Handbook of psychology, Vol. 3. Behavioral neuroscience* (2nd ed., pp. 206–239). Hoboken, NJ: Wiley.

Hsu, S. (2016). Motivation and emotions: What guides our behavior? In C. Tien-Lun Sun (Ed.), *Psychology in Asia: An introduction* (pp. 211–249). Boston, MA: Cengage Learning.

Hsu, S. (2016). Psychological disorders. In C. Tien-Lun Sun (Ed.), *Psychology in Asia: An introduction* (pp. 349–394). Boston, MA: Cengage Learning.

Huang, W., & Zhou, Y. (2013). Effects of education on cognition at older ages: Evidence from China's Great Famine. *Social Science & Medicine, 98,* 54–62. doi:10.1016/j.socscimed.2013.08.021

Huang, Y., Xu, S., Hua, J., Zhu, D., Liu, C., Hu, Y., . . . Xu, D. (2015). Association between job strain and risk of incident stroke: A meta-analysis. *Neurology, 85,* 1648–1654. http://dx.doi.org/10.1212/WNL.0000000000002098

Huber, A., Lui, F., Duzzi, D., Pagnoni, G., & Porro, C. A. (2014). Structural and functional cerebral correlates of hypnotic suggestibility. *PLoS ONE, 9,* 1–6. doi:10.1371/journal.pone.0093187

Hudson, H. M., Gallant-Shean, M. B., & Hirsch, A. R. (2015). Chemesthesis, thermogenesis, and nutrition. In A. Hirsch (Ed.), *Nutrition and sensation* (pp. 175–192). Boca Raton, FL: Taylor & Francis.

Hudson, N. W., & Fraley, R. C. (2015). Volitional personality trait change: Can people choose to change their personality traits? *Journal of Personality and Social Psychology, 109,* 490–507.

Hughes, J. M., Alo, J., Krieger, K., & O'Leary, L. M. (2016). Emergence of internal and external motivations to respond without prejudice in White children. *Group Processes & Intergroup Relations,* 19, 202–216. doi:10. 1177/1368430215603457

Hull, C. (1952). *A behavior system.* New Haven, CT: Yale University Press.

Humes, K., & Hogan, H. (2015). Do current race and ethnicity concepts reflect a changing America? In R. Bangs & L. E. Davis (Eds.), *Race and social problems: Restructuring inequality* (pp. 15–38). New York, NY: Springer. doi: 10.1007/978-1-4939-0863-9_2

Hundt, N. E., Calleo, J. S., Williams, W., & Cully, J. A. (2016). Does using cognitive-behavioural therapy skills predict improvements in depression? *Psychology and Psychotherapy: Theory, Research, and Practice, 89,* 235–238. doi:10.1111/papt.12065

Hunsley, J., Lee, C. M., Wood, J. M., & Taylor, W. (2015). Controversial and questionable assessment techniques. In S. O. Lilienfeld, S. J. Gould, & J. M. Lohr (Eds.), *Science and pseudoscience in clinical psychology* (2nd ed., pp. 42–82). New York, NY: Guilford.

Hunt, E., Bornovalova, M. A., & Patrick, C. J. (2015). Genetic and environmental overlap between borderline personality disorder traits and psychopathy: Evidence for promotive effects of factor 2 and protective effects of factor 1. *Psychological Medicine, 45,* 1471–1481. doi:10.1017/S003329171400260

Hunt, P. S., & Barnet, R. C. (2016). Adolescent and adult rats differ in the amnesic effects of acute ethanol in two hippocampus-dependent tasks: Trace and contextual fear conditioning. *Behavioural Brain Research, 298(Part A),* 78–87. http://dx.doi.org/10.1016/j.bbr.2015.06.046

Hussain, D., Shams, W. M., & Brake, W. G. (2014). Estrogen and memory system bias in females across the lifespan. *Translational Neuroscience, 5,* 35–50. doi:10.2478/s13380-014-0209-7

Hutteman, R., Nestler, S., Wagner, J., Egloff, B. & Back, M. D. (2015). Wherever I may roam: Processes of self-esteem development from adolescence to emerging adulthood in the context of international student exchange. *Journal of Personality and Social Psychology, 108,* 767–783.

Hutton, J. S., Horowitz-Kraus, T., Mendelsohn, A. L., DeWitt, T., Holland, S. K., & the C-MIND Authorship Consortium. (2015). Home reading environment and brain activation in preschool children listening to stories. *Pediatrics, 136,* 466–478. doi:10.1542/peds. 2015-0359

Hu, X., Antony, J. W., Creery, J. D., Vargas, I. M., Bodenhausen, G. V., & Paller, K. A. (2015). Unlearning implicit social biases during sleep. *Science, 348,* 1013–1015. doi:10.1126/science. aaa3841

Hu, X., & Kaplan, S. (2015). The effects of unconsciously derived affect on task satisfaction and performance. *Journal of Business and Psychology, 30,* 119–135. doi:10.1007/s10869-013-9331-8

Hwang, H., & Matsumoto, D. (2015). Evidence for the universality of facial expressions of emotion. In M. K. Mandal & A. Awasthi (Eds.), *Understanding facial expressions in communication: Cross-cultural and multidisciplinary perspectives* (pp. 41–56). New York, NY: Springer. doi:10.1007/978-81-322-1934-7_3

Hyman, R. (1981). Cold reading: How to convince strangers that you know all about them. In K. Fraizer (Ed.), *Paranormal borderlands of science* (pp. 232–244). Buffalo, NY: Prometheus.

Hyman, R. (1996). The evidence for psychic functioning: Claims vs. reality. *Skeptical Inquirer, 20,* 24–26.

Iachini, T., Coello, Y., Frassinetti, F., Senese, V. P., Galante, F., & Ruggiero, G. (2016). Peripersonal and interpersonal space in virtual and real environments: Effects of gender and age. *Journal of Environmental Psychology, 45,* 154–164. http://dx.doi.org/10.1016/j.jenvp.2016.01.004

Iakoubov, L., Mossakowska, M., Szwed, M., & Puzianowska-Kuznicka, M. (2015). A common copy number variation polymorphism in the CNTNAP2 gene: Sexual dimorphism in association with healthy aging and disease. *Gerontology, 61,* 24–31. doi:10.1159/000363320

Iglesias, A., & Iglesias, A. (2014). Hypnosis aided fixed role therapy for social phobia: A case report. *American Journal of Clinical Hypnosis, 56,* 405–412. doi:10.1080/00029157. 2013.808166

Iglesias, C., Sáiz, P. A., García-Portilla, P., & Bobes, J. (2016). Antipsychotics. In P. Courtet (Ed.), *Understanding suicide: From diagnosis to personalized treatment* (pp. 313–327). Cham, CH: Springer International Publishing.

Iliff, J. J., Wang, M., Liao, Y., Plogg, B. A., Peng, W., Gundersen, G. A., . . . Nedergaard, M. (2012). A paravascular pathway facilitates CSF flow through the brain parenchyma and the clearance of interstitial solutes, including amyloid ⊠. *Science Translational Medicine, 4,* 147ra111. doi:10.1126/scitranslmed.3003748

Ingalhalikar, M., Smith, A., Parker, D., Satterthwaite, T. D., Elliott, M. A., Ruparel, K., . . . Verma, R. (2014). Sex differences in the structural connectome of the human brain. *Proceedings of the National Academy of Sciences of the United States of America, 111,* 823–828. doi:10.1073/pnas.1316909110

Institute for Laboratory Animal Research (ILAR). (2009). Home page. Retrieved from http://dels.nas.edu/ilar_n/ilarhome/

Israel-Cohen, Y., Uzefovsky, F., Kashy-Rosenbaum, G., & Kaplan, O. (2015). Gratitude and PTSD symptoms among Israeli youth exposed to missile attacks: Examining the mediation of positive and negative affect and life satisfaction. *The Journal of Positive Psychology, 10,* 99–106. doi:1080/17439760.2014.927910

Israel, S., Moffitt, T. E., Belsky, D. W., Hancox, R. J., Poulton, R., Roberts, B., . . . Caspi, A. (2014). Translating personality psychology to help personalize preventive medicine for young adult patients. *Journal of Personality and Social Psychology, 106,* 484–498. doi:10.1037/a0035687

Itoh, K., & Hikasa, M. (2014). Focusing and Naikan, a uniquely Japanese way of therapy. In G. Madison (Ed.), *Emerging practice in focusing-oriented psychotherapy: Innovative theory and applications* (pp. 112–125). London, UK: Jessica Kingsley.

Ivanenko, A., & Johnson, K. P. (2016). Sleep disorders. In M. K. Dulcan (Ed.), *Dulcan's textbook of child and adolescent psychiatry* (2nd ed., pp. 495–519). Arlington, VA: American Psychiatric Publishing. http://dx.doi.org/10.1176/appi.books.9781615370306.md23

Iwanicki, S., & Lehmann, J. (2015). Behavioral and trait rating assessments of personality in common marmosets (*Callithrix jacchus*). *Journal of Comparative Psychology, 129,* 205–217. http://dx.doi.org/10.1037/a0039318

Jack, A. I., Boyatzis, R. E., Khawaja, M. S., Passarelli, A. M., & Leckie, R. L. (2013). Visioning in the brain: An fMRI study of inspirational coaching and mentoring. *Social Neuroscience, 8,* 369–384. doi:10.1080/17470919.2013.808259.

Jack, R. E., Garrod, O. G. B., & Schyns, P. G. (2014). Dynamic facial expressions of emotion transmit an evolving hierarchy of signals over time. *Current Biology, 24,* 187–192. doi:10.1016/j.cub.2013.11.064

Jackson, S. (2016). *Research methods and statistics: A critical thinking approach* (5th ed.). Boston, MA: Cengage Learning.

Jacob, K. S. (2014). DSM-5 and culture: The need to move towards a shared model of care within a more equal patient–physician partnership. *Asian Journal of Psychiatry, 7,* 89–91. doi:10.1016/j. ajp.2013.11.012

Jacobs Bao, K., & Lyubomirsky, S. (2013). Making it last: Combating hedonic adaptation in romantic relationships. *The Journal of Positive Psychology, 8,* 196–206.

Jacobs, R. H., Orr, J. L., Gowins, J. R., Forbes, E. E., & Langenecker, S. A. (2015). Biomarkers of intergenerational risk for depression: A review of mechanisms in longitudinal high-risk (LHR) studies. *Journal of Affective Disorders, 175,* 494–506. doi:10. 1016/j.jad.2015.01.038

Jafari-Sabet, M., Khodadadnejad, M. A., Ghoraba, S., & Ataee, R. (2014). Nitric oxide in the dorsal hippocampal area is involved on muscimol state-dependent memory in the step-down passive avoidance test. *Pharmacology Biochemistry and Behavior, 117,* 137–143. doi:10.1016/j.pbb.2013.12.010

James, S. D. (2008, May 7). Wild child speechless after tortured life. *ABC News.* Retrieved from http://abcnews.go.com/Health/story?id54804490&page51

James, W. (1890). *The principles of psychology* (Vol. 2). New York, NY: Holt.

James, Z. (2015). Hate crimes against Gypsies, Travellers and Roma in Europe. In N. Hall, A. Corb, P. Giannasi, & J. G. D. Grieve (Eds.), *The Routledge international handbook on hate crime* (pp. 237–248). New York, NY: Routledge/ Taylor & Francis Group.

Jandt, F. (2016). *An introduction to intercultural communication: Identities in a global community* (8th ed.). Thousand Oaks, CA: Sage.

Janis, I. L. (1972). *Victims of groupthink: A psychological study of foreign-policy decisions and fiascoes.* Boston, MA: Houghton Mifflin.

Jankowiak, W., & Fischer, E. (1992). Cross-cultural perspective on romantic love. *Ethnology, 31,* 149–155.

Jaremka, L. M., Glaser, R., Loving, T. J., Malarkey, W. B., Stowell, J. R., & Kiecolt-Glaser, J. K. (2013). Attachment anxiety is linked to alterations in cortisol production and cellular immunity. *Psychological Science, 24,* 272–279. doi:10.1177/0956797612452571

Jarvis, J. (2014). Auditory and neuronal fetal environment factors impacting early learning development. *International Journal of Childbirth Education, 29,* 27–31.

Jausoro Alzola, K., & Marino, M. (2015). Women's mental health around the world: Education, poverty, discrimination and violence, and political aspects. In M. Sáenz-Herrero (Ed.), *Psychopathology in women: Incorporating gender perspective into descriptive psychopathology* (pp. 3–24). Cham, CH: Springer International Publishing. doi:10.1007/978-3-319-05870-2

Jean-Richard-Dit-Bressel, P., & McNally, G. P. (2015). The role of the basolateral amygdala in punishment. *Learning & Memory, 22,* 128–137. doi:10.1101/lm.035907.114

Jessel, J., & Borrero, J. C. (2014). A laboratory comparison of two variations of differential-reinforcement-of-low-rate procedures. *Journal of Applied Behavior Analysis, 47,* 314–324. doi:10.1002/jaba.114

Jessen, S., & Grossmann, T. (2015). Neural signatures of conscious and unconscious emotional face processing in human infants. *Cortex, 64,* 260–270. doi:10.1016/j.cortex.2014.11.007

Jiang, W., Liao, J., Liu, H., Huang, R., Li, Y., & Wang, W. (2015). [Brain structure analysis for patients with antisocial personality disorder by MRI]. Zhong nan da xue xue bao. Yi xue ban=Journal of Central South University. *Medical Sciences, 40,* 123–128. doi:10.11817/j.issn.1672-7347.2015.02.002

Jiang, W., Liu, H., Zeng, L., Liao, J., Shen, H., Luo, A., . . . Wang, W. (2015). Decoding the processing of lying using functional connectivity MRI. *Behavioral and Brain Functions: BBF,* 11:1. doi:10.1186/s12993-014-0046-4

Jiang, W., Zhao, F., Guderley, N., & Manchaiah, V. (2016). Daily music exposure dose and hearing problems using personal listening devices in adolescents and young adults: A systematic review. *International Journal of Audiology, 55,* 197–205. http://dx.doi.org/10.3109/14992027.2015.1122237

Ji, G., Yan, L., Liu, W., Qu, J., & Gu, A. (2013). OGG1 Ser326Cys polymorphism interacts with cigarette smoking to increase oxidative DNA damage in human sperm and the risk of male infertility. *Toxicology Letters, 218,* 144–149. doi:10.1016/j.toxlet.2013.01.017

Jobin, J., Wrosch, C., & Scheier, M. F. (2014). Associations between dispositional optimism and diurnal cortisol in a community sample: When stress is perceived as higher than normal. *Health Psychology, 33,* 382–391.

Joeng, J. R., Turner, S. L., & Lee, K. H. (2013). South Korean college students' Holland Types and career compromise processes. *The Career Development Quarterly, 61,* 64–73. doi:10.1002/j.2161-0045.2013.00036.x

Johansen, P. -O., & Krebs, T. S. (2015). Psychedelics not linked to mental health problems or suicidal behavior: A population study. *Journal of Psychopharmacology, 29,* 270–279. doi:10.1177/0269881114568039

John, N. A., & Dvir-Gvirsman, S. (2015). "I don't like you any more": Facebook unfriending by Israelis during the Israel–Gaza conflict of 2014. *Journal of Communication, 65,* 953–974. doi:10.1111/jcom.12188

John, P., & Pineño, O. (2015). Biological significance in human causal learning. *Psi Chi Journal of Psychological Research, 20,* 65–72.

Johns, B., & Jones, M. N. (2015). Generating structure from experience: A retrieval-based model of language processing. *Canadian Journal of Experimental Psychology/Revue canadienne de psychologieexperimentale, 69,* 233–251. doi:10.1037/cep0000053

Johnston, M. E., Sherman, A., & Grusec, J. E. (2013). Predicting moral outrage and religiosity with an implicit measure of moral identity. *Journal of Research in Personality, 47,* 209–217. doi:10.1016/j.jrp.2013.01.006

Jones, A., Lankshear, A., & Kelly, D. (2016). Giving voice to quality and safety matters at board level: A qualitative study of the experiences of executive nurses working in England and Wales. *International Journal of Nursing Studies, 59,* 169–176. http://dx.doi.org/10.1016/j.ijnurstu.2016.04.007

Jones, D. A. (2013). The polarizing effect of a partisan workplace. *PS: Political Science and Politics, 46,* 67–73. doi:10.1017/S1049096512001254

Jones, D. W. (2016). *Disordered personalities and crime: An analysis of the history of moral insanity.* New York, NY: Routledge/Taylor & Francis Group.

Jones, E. E., & Nisbett, R. E. (1971). *The actor and the observer: Divergent perceptions of the causes of behavior.* Morristown, NJ: General Learning.

Jones, N., & Corrigan, P. W. (2014). Understanding stigma. In P. W. Corrigan (Ed.), *The stigma of disease and disability: Understanding causes and overcoming injustices* (pp. 9–34). Washington, DC: American Psychological Association. doi:10.1037/14297-002

Jones, S. G., & Benca, R. M. (2013). Sleep and biological rhythms. In R. J. Nelson, S. J. Y. Mizumori, & I. B. Weiner (Eds.), *Handbook of psychology, Vol. 3. Behavioral neuroscience* (2nd ed., pp. 365–394). Hoboken, NJ: Wiley.

Joo, Y. J., Lim, K. Y., & Kim, N. H. (2016). The effects of secondary teachers' technostress on the intention to use technology in South Korea. *Computers & Education, 95,* 114–122. http://dx.doi.org/10.1016/j.compedu.2015.12.004

Joseph, A. J., Tandon, N., Yang, L. H., Duckworth, K., Torous, J., Seidman, L. J., & Keshavan, M. S. (2015). #Schizophrenia: Use and misuse on Twitter. *Schizophrenia Research, 165,* 111–115. doi:10.1016/j.schres.2015.04.009

Joseph, N. T., Matthews, K. A., & Myers, H. F. (2014). Conceptualizing health consequences of Hurricane Katrina from the perspective of socioeconomic status decline. *Health Psychology, 33,* 139–146. doi:10.1037/a0031661

Jouffre, S. (2015). Power modulates over-reliance on false cardiac arousal when judging target attractiveness: The powerful are more centered on their own false arousal than the powerless. *Personality and Social Psychology Bulletin, 41,* 116–126. doi:10.1177/0146167214559718

Jouhanneau, M., Cornilleau, F., & Keller, M. (2014). Peripubertal exposure to male odors influences female puberty and adult expression of male-directed odor preference in mice. *Hormones and Behavior, 65,* 128–133. doi:10.1016/j.yhbeh.2013.12.006

Jowett Hirst, E. S., Dozier, C. L., & Payne, S. W. (2016). Efficacy of and preference for reinforcement and response cost in token economies. *Journal of Applied Behavior Analysis, 49,* 329–345. doi:10.1002/jaba.294

Jung, C. G. (1933). *Modern man in search of a soul.* New York, NY: Harcourt Brace.

Jung, C. G. (1936/1969). The concept of collective unconscious. In *Collected Works* (Vol. 9, Part 1). Princeton, NJ: Princeton University Press. (Original work published 1936.)

Jung, R. E., & Haier, R. J. (2007). The Parieto-Frontal Integration Theory (P-FIT) of intelligence: Converging neuroimaging evidence. *Behavioral and Brain Sciences, 30,* 135–154. doi:10.1017/S0140525X07001185

Jung, S. H., Wang, Y., Kim, T., Tarr, A., Reader, B., Powell, N., & Sheridan, J. F. (2015). Molecular mechanisms of repeated social defeat-induced glucocorticoid resistance: Role of microrna. *Brain, Behavior, and Immunity, 44,* 195–206. doi:10.1016/j.bbi.2014.09.015

Junque, C. (2015). Structural and functional neuroimaging of cognition and emotion in Parkinson's disease. In A. I. Tröster (Ed.), *Clinical neuropsychology and cognitive neurology of Parkinson's disease and other movement disorders* (pp. 148–178). New York, NY: Oxford.

Kalnin, A. J., Edwards, C. R., Wang, Y., Kronenberger, W. G., Hummer, T. A., Mosier, K. M., . . . Mathews, V. P. (2011). The interacting role of media violence exposure and aggressive–disruptive behavior in adolescent brain activation during an emotional Stroop task. *Psychiatry Research: Neuroimaging, 192,* 12–19.

Kalokerinos, E. K., von Hippel, W., Henry, J. D., & Trivers, R. (2014). The aging positivity effect and immune function: Positivity in recall predicts higher CD4 counts and lower CD4 activation. *Psychology and Aging, 29,* 636–641. doi:10.1037/a0037452

Kanbur, N., & Harrison, A. (2016). Co-occurrence of substance use and eating disorders: An approach to the adolescent patient in the context of family centered care. A literature review. *Substance Use & Misuse, 51,* 853–860. http://dx.doi.org/10.3109/10826084.2016.1155614

Kandler, C., Kornadt, A. E., Hagemeyer, B., & Neyer, F. J. (2015). Patterns and sources of personality development in old age. *Journal of Personality and Social Psychology, 109,* 175–191. http://dx.doi.org/10.1037/pspp0000028

Kang, S. H., Lindsey, R. V., Mozer, M. C., & Pashler, H. (2014). Retrieval practice over the long term: Should spacing be expanding or equal-interval? *Psychonomic Bulletin & Review, 21,* 1544–1550. doi:10.3758/s13423-014-0636-z

Kang, S.-M., & Lau, A. S. (2013). Revisiting the out-group advantage in emotion recognition in a multicultural society: Further evidence for the in-group advantage. *Emotion, 13,* 203–215.

Kapexhiu, K. (2015). Repetition and content implications in advertising wear out: A practitioner's view. *Advances in Social Sciences Research Journal, 2,* 204–209. doi:10.14738/assrj.210.1513

Kaplan, R. L., Van Damme, I., Levine, L. J., & Loftus, E. F. (2016). Emotion and false memory. *Emotion Review, 8,* 8–13. http://dx.doi.org/10.1177/1754073915601228

Karanian, J. M., & Slotnick, S. D. (2015). Memory for shape reactivates the lateral occipital complex. *Brain Research, 1603,* 124–132. doi:10.1016/j.brainres.2015.01.024

Karasik, L. B., Adolph, K. E., Tamis-LeMonda, C. S., Bornstein, M. H. (2010). WEIRD walking: Cross-cultural research on motor development. *Behavioral and Brain Sciences, 33,* 95–96. doi:10.1017/S0140525X10000117

Kastanakis, M. N., & Voyer, B. G. (2014). The effect of culture on perception and cognition: A conceptual framework. *Journal of Business Research, 67,* 425–433. doi:10.1016/j.jbusres.2013.03.028

Kaste, M. (2015, January 2). Trial of polygraph critic renews debate over tests' accuracy. *NPR.* Retrieved from http://www.npr.org/2015/01/02/371925732/trialof-polygraph-critic-renews-debate-over-tests-accuracy

Kato, T., & Kanba, S. (2016). Boundless syndromes in modern society: An interconnected world producing novel psychopathology in the 21st century. *Psychiatry and Clinical Neurosciences, 70,* 1–2. http://dx.doi.org/10.1111/pcn.12368

Katz, I., Kaplan, A., & Buzukashvily, T. (2011). The role of parents' motivation in students' autonomous motivation for doing homework. *Learning and Individual Differences, 21,* 376–386. doi:10.1016/j.lindif.2011.04.001

Kaye, L. K., & Pennington, C. R. (2016). "Girls can't play": The effects of stereotype threat on females' gaming performance. *Computers in Human Behavior, 59,* 202–209. http://dx.doi.org/10.1016/j.chb.2016.02.020

Kearney, M. S., & Levine, P. B. (2015). Media influences on social outcomes: The impact of MTV's *16 and Pregnant* on teen childbearing. *American Economic Review, 105,* 3597–3632. doi:10.1257/aer.20140012

Keating, J., Van Boven, L., & Judd, C. M. (2016). Partisan underestimation of the polarizing influence of group discussion. *Journal of Experimental Social Psychology, 65,* 52–58. http://dx.doi.org/10.1016/j.jesp.2016.03.002

Keats, D. M. (1982). Cultural bases of concepts of intelligence: A Chinese versus Australian comparison. In P. Sukontasarp, N. Yongsiri, P. Intasuwan, N. Jotiban, & C. Suvannathat (Eds.), *Proceedings of the second Asian workshop on child and adolescent development* (pp. 67–75). Bangkok, TH: Burapasilpa Press.

Keller, S. M., & Tuerk, P. W. (2016). Evidence-based psychotherapy (EBP) non-initiation among veterans offered an EBP for post-traumatic stress disorder. *Psychological Services, 13,* 42–48. http://dx.doi.org/10.1037/ser0000064

Kellner, C. H., Kaicher, D. C., Banerjee, H., Knapp, R. G., Shapiro, R. J., Briggs, M. C., . . . Liebman, L. S. (2015). Depression severity in electroconvulsive therapy (ECT) versus pharmacotherapy trials. *The Journal of ECT, 31,* 31–33. doi:10.1097/YCT.0000000000000135

Kemp, A. H., Krygier, J., & Harmon-Jones, E. (2015). Neuroscientific perspectives of emotion. In R. A. Calvo, S. K. D'Mello, J. Gratch, & A. Kappas (Eds.), *The Oxford handbook of affective computing* (pp. 38–53). New York, NY: Oxford. doi:10.1093/oxfordhb/9780199942237.013.016

Kendler, K. S., & Gardner, C. O. (2014). Sex differences in the pathways to major depression: A study of opposite-sex twin pairs. *American Journal of Psychiatry, 171,* 426–435. doi:10.1176/appi.ajp.2013.13101375

Kendler, K. S., Maes, H. H., Lönn, S. L., Morris, N. A., Lichtenstein, P., Sundquist, J., & Sundquist, K. (2015). A Swedish national twin study of criminal behavior and its violent, white-collar and property subtypes. *Psychological Medicine, 45,* 2253–2262. doi:10.1017/S0033291714002098.

Kendra, M. S., Weingardt, K. R., Cucciare, M. A., & Timko, C. (2015). Satisfaction with substance use treatment and 12-step groups predicts outcomes. *Addictive Behaviors, 40,* 27–32. doi:10.1016/j.addbeh.2014.08.003

Kendzerska, T., Mollayeva, T., Gershon, A. S., Leung, R. S., Hawker, G., & Tomlinson, G. (2014). Untreated obstructive sleep apnea and the risk for serious long-term adverse outcomes: A systematic review. *Sleep Medicine Reviews, 18,* 49–59. doi:10.1016/j.smrv.2013.01.003

Kendzor, D. E., Businelle, M. S., Poonawalla, I. B., Cuate, E. L., Kesh, A., Rios, D. M., & Balis, D. S. (2015). Financial incentives for abstinence among socioeconomically disadvantaged individuals in smoking cessation treatment. *American Journal of Public Health, 105,* 1198–1205. doi:10.2105/AJPH.2014.302102

Kennard, B. D., Emslie, G. J., Mayes, T. L., Nakonezny, P. A., Jones, J. M., Foxwell, A. A., & King, J. (2014). Sequential treatment with fluoxetine and relapse-prevention CBT to improve outcomes in pediatric depression. *The American Journal of Psychiatry, 171,* 1083–1090.

Kepner, T. (2016, May 23). Tony Gwynn's family sues tobacco industry, seeking recourse over fatal habit. *New York Times.* Retrieved from http://www.nytimes.com/2016/05/24/sports/baseball/tony-gwynn-family-sues-to-bacco-altria-death.html

Kern, M. L., Eichstaedt, J. C., Schwartz, H. A., Park, G., Ungar, L. H., Stillwell, D. J., . . . Seligman, M. E. P. (2014). From "Sooo excited!!!" to "So proud": Using language to study development. *Developmental Psychology, 50,* 178–188. doi:10.1037/a0035048

Kerr, D. C. R., Washburn, I. J., Morris, M. K., Lewis, K. A. G., & Tiberio, S. S. (2015). Event-level associations of marijuana and heavy alcohol use with intercourse and condom use. *Journal of Studies on Alcohol and Drugs, 76,* 733–737.

Kershaw, K. N., Lewis, T. T., Roux, A. V. D., Jenny, N. S., Liu, K., Penedo, F. J., & Carnethon, M. R. (2016). Self-reported experiences of discrimination and inflammation among men and women: The multi-ethnic study of atherosclerosis. *Health Psychology, 35,* 343–350. http://dx.doi.org/10.1037/hea0000331

Ketter, T. A., & Miller, S. (2015). Bipolar and related disorders. In L. W. Roberts & A. K. Louie (Eds.), *Study guide to DSM-5®* (pp. 99–111). Arlington, VA: American Psychiatric Publishing.

Khandelwal, K., Dhillon, M., Akalamkam, K., & Papneja, D. (2014). The ultimate attribution error: Does it transcend conflict? The case of Muslim adolescents in Kashmir and Delhi. *Psychological Studies, 59,* 427–435. doi:10.1007/s12646-014-0240-3

Khan, R. F., & Sutcliffe, A. (2014). Attractive agents are more persuasive. *International Journal of Human–Computer Interaction, 30,* 142–150. doi:10.1080/10447318.2013.839904

Killen, M., & Hart, D. (1999). *Morality in everyday life: Developmental perspectives.* New York, NY: Cambridge University Press.

Killen, M., Hitti, A., & Mulvey, K. L. (2015). Social development and intergroup relations. In M. Mikulincer, P. R. Shaver, J. F. Dovidio, & J. A. Simpson (Eds.), *APA handbook of personality and social psychology, Vol. 2. Group processes* (pp. 177–201). Washington, DC: American Psychological Association. doi:10.1037/14342-007

Kilpatrick, L. A., Suyenobu, B. Y., Smith, S. R., Bueller, J. A., Goodman, T., Creswell, J. D., . . . Naliboff, B. D. (2011). Impact of mindfulness-based stress reduction training on intrinsic brain connectivity. *NeuroImage, 56,* 290–298.

Kim, H. K., Nunes, P. V., Oliveira, K. C., Young, L. T., & Lafer, B. (2016). Neuropathological relationship between major depression and dementia: A hypothetical model and review. *Progress in Neuro-Psychopharmacology & Biological Psychiatry, 67,* 51–57. doi:10.1016/j.pnpbp.2016.01.008

Kim, J. H., Son, Y. D., Kim, J. H., Choi, E. J., Lee, S. Y., Lee, J. E., . . . Kim, Y. B. (2015). Serotonin transporter availability in thalamic subregions in schizophrenia: A study using 7.0-T MRI with [11 C] DASB high-resolution PET. *Psychiatry Research: Neuroimaging, 231,* 50–57. doi:10.1016/j.pscychresns.2014.10.022

Kim, P., Strathearn, L., & Swain, J. E. (2016). The maternal brain and its plasticity in humans. *Hormones and Behavior, 77,* 113–123. doi:10.1016/j.yhbeh.2015.08.001

Kim, Y.-K., Na, K.-S., Myint, A.-M., & Leonard, B. E. (2016). The role of pro-inflammatory cytokines in neuroinflammation, neurogenesis and the neuroendocrine system in major depression. *Progress in Neuro-Psychopharmacology & Biological Psychiatry, 64,* 277–284. http://dx.doi.org/10.1016/j.pnpbp.2015.06.008

Kim, Y., Morath, B., Hu, C., Byrne, L. K., Sutor, S. L., Frye, M. A., & Tye, S. J. (2016). Antidepressant actions of lateral habenula deep brain stimulation differentially correlate with CaMKII/GSK3/AMPK signaling locally and in the infralimbic cortex. *Behavioural Brain Research, 306,* 170–177. http://dx.doi.org/10.1016/j.bbr.2016.02.039

King, J. A., Garnham, J. O., Jackson, A. P., Kelly, B. M., Xenophontos, S., & Nimmo, M. A. (2015). Appetite-regulatory hormone responses on the day following a prolonged bout of moderate-intensity exercise. *Physiology & Behavior, 141,* 23–31. doi:10.1016/j.physbeh.2014.12.050

Kirisci, L., Tarter, R., Ridenour, T., Zhai, Z. W., Fishbein, D., Reynolds, M., & Vanyukov, M. (2013). Age of alcohol and cannabis use onset mediates the association of transmissible risk in childhood and development of alcohol and cannabis disorders: Evidence for common liability. *Experimental and Clinical Psychopharmacology, 21,* 38–45.

Kirkbride, J. B., Jones, P. B., Ullrich, S., & Coid, J. W. (2014). Social deprivation, inequality, and the neighborhood-level incidence of psychotic syndromes in East London. *Schizophrenia Bulletin, 40,* 169–180. doi:10.1093/schbul/sbs151

Kirk, D. S., & Hardy, M. (2014). The acute and enduring consequences of exposure to violence on youth mental health and aggression. *Justice Quarterly, 31,* 539–567. doi:10.1080/07418825.2012.737471

Kirk, E., Gurney, D., Edwards, R., & Dodimead, C. (2015). Handmade memories: The robustness of the gestural misinformation effect in children's eyewitness interviews. *Journal of Nonverbal Behavior, 39,* 259–273. doi:10.1007/s10919-015-0210-z

Kishimoto, T., Chawla, J. M., Hagi, K., Zarate, C. A., Kane, J. M., Bauer, M., & Correll, C. U. (2016). Single-dose infusion ketamine and non-ketamine n-methyl-d-aspartate receptor antagonists for unipolar and bipolar depression: A meta-analysis of efficacy, safety and time trajectories. *Psychological Medicine, 46,* 1459–1472. http://dx.doi.org/10.1017/S0033291716000064

Kite, M. E. (2013). Teaching about race and ethnicity. In D. S. Dunn, R. A. R. Gurung, K. Z. Naufel, & J. H. Wilson (Eds.), *Controversy in the psychology classroom: Using hot topics to foster critical thinking* (pp. 169–184). Washington, DC: American Psychological Association.

Kivimäki, M., Nyberg, S. J., Batty, G. D., Fransson, E. I., Heikkila, K., Alfredsson, L., . . . Theorell, T. (2012). Job strain as a risk factor for coronary heart disease: A collaborative metaanalysis of individual participant data. *Lancet, 380,* 1491–1497. doi:10.1016/S0140-6736(12)60994-5

Klahr, A. M., & Burt, S. A. (2014). Elucidating the etiology of individual differences in parenting: A meta-analysis of behavioral genetic research. *Psychological Bulletin, 140,* 544–586. doi:10.1037/a0034205

Klauer, S. G., Guo, F., Simons-Morton, B. G., Ouimet, M. C., Lee, S. E., & Dingus, T. A. (2014). Distracted driving and risk of road crashes among novice and experienced drivers. *New England Journal of Medicine, 370,* 54–59. doi:10.1056/NEJMsa1204142

Klein, R. M., Dilchert, S., Ones, D. S., & Dages, K. D. (2015). Cognitive predictors and age-based adverse impact among business executives. *Journal of Applied Psychology, 100,* 1497–1510. doi:10.1037/a0038991

Klink, M. (Ed.). (2014). *Interaction of immune and cancer cells.* Vienna, AT: Springer.

Kneeland, R. E., & Fatemi, S. H. (2013). Viral infection, inflammation and schizophrenia. *Progress in Neuro-Psychopharmacology & Biological Psychiatry, 42,* 35–48. http://doi.org/10.1016/j.pnpbp.2012.02.001

Knobloch-Westerwick, S., Mothes, C., Johnson, B. K., Westerwick, A., & Donsbach, W. (2015). Political online information searching in Germany and the United States: Confirmation bias, source credibility, and attitude impacts. *Journal of Communication, 65,* 489–511. doi:10.1111/jcom.12154

Knutson, K. L. (2012). Does inadequate sleep play a role in vulnerability to obesity? *American Journal of Human Biology, 24,* 361–371.

Kohlberg, L. (1964). Development of moral character and moral behavior. In L. W. Hoffman & M. L. Hoffman (Eds.), *Review of child development research* (Vol. 1, pp. 381–431). New York, NY: Sage.

Kohlberg, L. (1984). *The psychology of moral development: Essays on moral development* (Vol. 2). San Francisco, CA: Harper & Row.

Köhler, W. (1925). *The mentality of apes.* New York, NY: Harcourt Brace Jovanovich.

Kojima, T., Karino, S., Yumoto, M., & Funayama, M. (2014). A stroke patient with impairment of auditory sensory (echoic) memory. *Neurocase, 20,* 133–143. doi:10.1080/13554794.2012.732091

Kokkoris, M. D., & Kühnen, U. (2013). Choice and dissonance in a European cultural context: The case of Western and Eastern Europeans. *International Journal of Psychology, 48,* 1260–1266. doi:10.1080/00207594.2013.766746

Kokolus, K., Spangler, H., Povinelli, B., Farren, M., Lee, K., & Repasky, E. (2014). Stressful presentations: Mild chronic cold stress in mice influences baseline properties of dendritic cells. *Frontiers in Immunology, 5,* 23. doi:10.3389/fimmu.2014.00023

Kongthong, N., Minami, T., & Nakauchi, S. (2014). Gamma oscillations distinguish mere exposure from other likability effects. *Neuropsychologia, 54,* 129–138. doi:10.1016/j.neuropsychologia.2013.12.021

Konnikova, M. (2014, Jan. 14). Goodnight. Sleep clean. *New York Times.* Retrieved from http://www.nytimes.com/2014/01/12/opinion/sunday/goodnight-sleep-clean. html?nl=todaysheadlines&emc=edit_th_20140112&_r=0

Konnikova, M. (2016, February 11). How people learn to become resilient. *The New Yorker.* Retrieved from http://www.newyorker.com/science/maria-konnikova/the-secret-formula-for-resilience

Koo, C., Chung, N., & Nam, K. (2015). Assessing the impact of intrinsic and extrinsic motivators on smart green IT device use: Reference group perspectives. *International Journal of Information Management, 35,* 64–79. doi:10.1016/j.ijinfomgt.2014.10.001

Koocher, G. P., McMann, M. R., Stout, A. O., & Norcross, J. C. (2014). Discredited assessment and treatment methods used with children and adolescents: A Delphi Poll. *Journal of Clinical Child & Adolescent Psychology, 25,* 1–8. doi:10.1080/15374416. 2014.895941

Kornmeier, J., Spitzer, M., & Sosic-Vasic, Z. (2014). Very similar spacing-effect patterns in very different learning/practice domains. *PLoS ONE, 9,* 1–11. doi:10.1371/journal.pone.0090656

Kose, S., Steinberg, J. L., Moeller, F. G., Gowin, J. L., Zuniga, E., Kamdar, Z. N., . . . Lane, S. D. (2015). Neural correlates of impulsive aggressive behavior in subjects with a history of alcohol dependence. *Behavioral Neuroscience, 129,* 183–196. doi:10.1037/bne0000038.

Kosinski, M., Stillwell, D., & Graepel, T. (2013). Private traits and attributes are predictable from digital records of human behavior. *Proceedings of the National Academy of Sciences of the United States of America, 110,* 5802–5805. doi:10.1073/pnas.1218772110

Kotagal, S., & Kumar, S. (2013). Childhood onset narcolepsy cataplexy-more than just a sleep disorder. *Sleep, 36,* 161–162.

Kotowski, A. (2012). Case study: A young male with auditory hallucinations in paranoid schizophrenia. *International Journal of Nursing Knowledge, 23,* 41–44.

Kovas, Y., Garon-Carrier, G., Boivin, M., Petrill, S. A., Plomin, R., Malykh, S. B., . . . Vitaro, F. (2015). Why children differ in motivation to learn: Insights from over 13,000 twins from 6 countries. *Personality and Individual Differences, 80,* 51–63. http://doi.org/10.1016/j.paid.2015.02.006

Kracher, B., & Marble, R. P. (2008). The significance of gender in predicting the cognitive moral development of business practitioners using the Socioemotional Reflection Objective Measure. *Journal of Business Ethics, 78,* 503–526.

Kraft, T. L., & Pressman, S. D. (2012). Grin and bear it: The influence of manipulated positive facial expression on the stress response. *Psychological Science, 23,* 1372–1378. doi:10.1177/0956797612445312

Krahé, B. (2013). *The social psychology of aggression* (2nd ed.). New York, NY: Psychology Press.

Kreger Silverman, L. (2013). *Psych 101: Giftedness 101.* New York, NY: Springer.

Kreitz, C., Furley, P., Simons, D., & Memmert, D. (2016). Does working memory capacity predict cross-modally induced failures of awareness? *Consciousness and Cognition: An International Journal, 39,* 18–27. http://dx.doi.org/10.1016/j.concog.2015.11.010

Kress, T., Aviles, C., Taylor, C., & Winchell, M. (2011). Individual/collective human needs: (Re) theorizing Maslow using critical, sociocultural, feminist, and indigenous lenses. In C. Malott & B. Porfilio (Eds.), *Critical pedagogy in the twenty-first century: A new generation of scholars* (pp. 135–157). Charlotte, NC: Information Age.

Kress, V. E., Hoffman, R. M., Adamson, N., & Eriksen, K. (2013). Informed consent, confidentiality, and diagnosing: Ethical guidelines for counselor practice. *Journal of Mental Health Counseling, 35,* 15–28. Retrieved from http://essential.metapress.com/content/5q82020u18r46007/

Kring, A. M., Johnson, S. L., Davison, G. C., & Neale, J. M. (2014). *Abnormal psychology* (13th ed.). Hoboken, NJ: Wiley.

Krishna, G. (1999). *The dawn of a new science.* Los Angeles, CA: Institute for Consciousness Research.

Krok, D. (2015). The mediating role of optimism in the relations between sense of coherence, subjective and psychological well-being among late adolescents. *Personality and Individual Differences, 85,* 134–139. http://dx.doi.org/10.1016/j.paid.2015.05.006

Kross, E., Bruehlman-Senecal, E., Park, J., Burson, A., Dougherty, A., Shablack, H., . . . Ayduk, O. (2014). Self-talk as a regulatory mechanism: How you do it matters. *Journal of Personality and Social Psychology, 106,* 304–324. doi:10.1037/a0035173

Kross, E., Verduyn, P., Demiralp, E., Park, J., Lee, D. S., Lin, N., . . . Ybarra, O. (2013). Facebook use predicts declines in subjective well-being in young adults. *PLoS ONE, 8:* e69841. doi:10.1371/journal.pone.0069841

Krug, H. E., Bert, J. S., Dorman, C. W., Frizelle, S. P., Funkenbusch, S. C., & Mahowald, M. L. (2015). Substance p expression in the murine lumbar dorsal root ganglia: Effect of chronic inflammatory arthritis knee pain and treatment with IA vanilloids. *Osteoarthritis and Cartilage, 23,* A358–A359. doi:10.1016/j.joca.2015.02.661

Krumhuber, E. G., Likowski, K. U., & Weyers, P. (2014). Facial mimicry of spontaneous and deliberate Duchenne and non-Duchenne smiles. *Journal of Nonverbal Behavior, 38,* 1–11. doi:10.1007/s10919-013-0167-8

Krys, K., Hansen, K., Xing, C., Szarota, P., & Yang, M. M. (2014). Do only fools smile at strangers? Cultural differences in social perception of intelligence of smiling individuals. *Journal of Cross-Cultural Psychology, 45,* 314–321. doi:10.1177/0022022113513922

Ksiazkiewicz, A., Ludeke, S., & Krueger, R. (2016). The role of cognitive style in the link between genes and political ideology. *Political Psychology.* No Pagination Specified. doi:10.1111/pops.12318

Kubera, K. M., Sambataro, F., Vasic, N., Wolf, N. D., Frasch, K., Hirjak, D., . . . Wolf, R. C. (2014). Source-based morphometry of gray matter volume in patients with schizophrenia who have persistent auditory verbal hallucinations. *Progress in Neuro-Psychopharmacology and Biological Psychiatry, 50,* 102–109. doi:10.1016/j.pnpbp.2013.11.015

Kubiak, T., Vögele, C., Siering, M., Schiel, R., & Weber, H. (2008). Daily hassles and emotional eating in obese adolescents under restricted dietary conditions—The role of ruminative thinking. *Appetite, 51,* 206–209. doi:10.1016/j.appet.2008.01.008

Kubota, J. T., & Phelps, E. A. (2016). Insights from functional magnetic resonance imaging research on race. In T. D. Nelson (Ed.), *Handbook of prejudice, stereotyping, and discrimination* (2nd ed., pp. 299–312). New York, NY: Psychology Press.

Kuchenbrandt, D., Eyssel, F., & Seidel, S. K. (2013). Cooperation makes it happen: Imagined intergroup cooperation enhances the positive effects of imagined contact. *Group Processes & Intergroup Relations, 16,* 636–648. doi:10.1177/1368430212470172

Kuczaj, S. A., Frick, E. E., Jones, B. L., Lea, J. S. E., Beecham, D., & Schnöller, F. (2015). Underwater observations of dolphin reactions to a distressed conspecific. *Learning & Behavior, 43,* 289–300. doi:10.3758/s13420-015-0179-9

Kühn, S., Gleich, T., Lorenz, R. C., Lindenberger, U., & Gallinat, J. (2014). Playing Super Mario induces structural brain plasticity: Gray matter changes resulting from training with a commercial video game. *Molecular Psychiatry, 19,* 265–271. doi:10.1038/mp.2013.120

Kukucka, J., & Kassin, S. M. (2014). Do confessions taint perceptions of handwriting evidence? An empirical test of the forensic confirmation bias. *Law and Human Behavior, 38,* 256–270. doi:10.1037/lhb0000066

Kumar, D. K. V., Choi, S. H., Washicosky, K. J., Eimer, W. A., Tucker, S., Ghofrani, J., . . . Moir, R. D. (2016). Amyloid-β peptide protects against microbial infection in mouse and worm models of Alzheimer's disease. *Science Translational Medicine, 8,* 340–372. doi:10.1126/scitranslmed.aaf1059

Kumari, V., Uddin, S., Premkumar, P., Young, S., Gudjonsson, G. H., Raghuvanshi, S., . . . Das, M. (2014). Lower anterior cingulate volume in seriously violent men with antisocial personality disorder or schizophrenia and a history of childhood abuse. *Australian and New Zealand Journal of Psychiatry, 48,* 153–161. doi:10.1177/0004867413512690

Kumin, L. (2015). Intellectual disability. In M. R. Kerins (Ed.), *Child and adolescent communication disorders: Organic and neurogenic bases* (pp. 99–151). San Diego, CA: Plural.

Kundu, P., & Cummins, D. D. (2013). Morality and conformity: The Asch paradigm applied to moral decisions. *Social Influence, 8,* 268–279. http://dx.doi.org/10.1080/15534510.2012.727767

Kunze, A. E., Arntz, A., & Kindt, M. (2015). Fear conditioning with film clips: A complex associative learning paradigm. *Journal of Behavior Therapy and Experimental Psychiatry, 47,* 42–50. doi:10.1016/j.jbtep.2014.11.007

Kuperstok, N. (2008). Effects of exposure to differentiated aggressive films, equated for levels of interest and excitation, and the vicarious hostility catharsis hypothesis. *Dissertation Abstracts International: Section B: The Sciences and Engineering, 68,* 4806.

Küpper-Tetzel, C. E. (2014). Understanding the distributed practice effect: Strong effects on weak theoretical grounds. *ZeitschriftfürPsychologie, 222,* 71–81. doi:10.1027/2151-2604/a000168

Kurth, F., MacKenzie-Graham, A., Toga, A. W., & Luders, E. (2014). Shifting brain asymmetry: The link between meditation and structural lateralization. *Social Cognitive and Affective Neuroscience, 10,* 55–61. doi:10.1093/scan/nsu029

Kurzban, R. (2014). Covert sexual signaling: Human flirtation and implications for other social species. *Evolutionary Psychology, 12,* 549–569.

Kurzban, R., Burton-Chellew, M. N., & West, S. A. (2015). The evolution of altruism in humans. *Annual Review of Psychology, 66,* 575–599. doi:10.1146/annurev-psych-010814-015355

Kushlev, K., & Dunn, E. W. (2015). Checking email less frequently reduces stress. *Computers in Human Behavior, 43,* 220–228. doi:10.1016/j.chb.2014.11.005

Kushlev, K., Dunn, E. W., & Lucan, R. E. (2015). Higher income is associated with less daily sadness but not more daily happiness. *Social Psychological and Personality Science, 6,* 483–489. http://dx.doi.org/10.1177/1948550614568161

Kyaga, S., Landén, M., Boman, M., Hultman, C. M., Långström, N., & Lichtenstein, P. (2012). Mental illness, suicide and creativity: 40-year prospective total population study. *Journal of Psychiatric Research, 47,* 83–90.

LaBrie, J. W., Kenney, S. R., Napper, L. E., & Miller, K. (2014). Impulsivity and alcohol-related risk among college students: Examining urgency, sensation seeking and the moderating influence of beliefs about alcohol's role in the college experience. *Addictive Behaviors, 39,* 159–164. doi:10.1016/j.addbeh.2013.09.018

Lacourse, E., Boivin, M., Brendgen, M., Petitclerc, A., Girard, A., Vitaro, F., . . . Tremblay, R. E. (2014). A longitudinal twin study of physical aggression during early childhood: Evidence for a developmentally dynamic genome. *Psychological Medicine, 44,* 2617–2627. doi:10.1017/S0033291713003218

Laeng, B., Bloem, I. M., D'Ascenzo, S., & Tommasi, L. (2014). Scrutinizing visual images: The role of gaze in mental imagery and memory. *Cognition, 131,* 263–283. doi:10.1016/j.cognition.2014.01.003

Lafleur, A., & Boucher, V. J. (2015). The ecology of self-monitoring effects on memory of verbal productions: Does speaking to someone make a difference? *Consciousness and Cognition, 36,* 139–146. doi:10.1016/j.concog.2015.06.015

Lagarde, J., Valabrègue, R., Corvol, J.-C., Garcin, B., Volle, E., Le Ber, I., . . . Levy, R. (2015). Why do patients with neurodegenerative frontal syndrome fail to answer: 'In what way are an orange and a banana alike'? *Brain: A Journal of Neurology,* 138, 456–471. doi:10.1093/brain/awu359

Lähteenmäki, S., Saarni, S., Suokas, J., Saarni, S., Perälä, J., Lönnqvist, J., & Suvisaari, J. (2014). Prevalence and correlates of eating disorders among young adults in Finland. *Nordic Journal of Psychiatry, 68,* 196–203. doi:10.3109/08039488.2013.797021

Laible, D., & Karahuta, E. (2014). Prosocial behaviors in early childhood. In L. M. Padilla-Walker & G. Carlo (Eds.), *Prosocial development: A multidimensional approach* (pp. 350–366). Oxford, UK: Oxford University Press.

Laier, C., Schulte, F. P., & Brand, M. (2013). Pornographic picture processing interferes with working memory performance. *Journal of Sex Research, 50,* 642-652. doi:10.1080/00224499.2012.716873.

Lai, V. T., & Narasimhan, B. (2015). Verb representation and thinking-for-speaking effects in Spanish-English bilinguals. In R. G. de Almeida & C. Manouilidou (Eds.), *Cognitive science perspectives on verb representation and processing* (pp. 235–256). Cham, CH: Springer. doi:10.1007/978-3-319-10112-5_11

Lamer, S. A., Reeves, S. L., & Weisbuch, M. (2015). The nonverbal environment of self-esteem: Interactive effects of facial-expression and eye-gaze on perceivers' self-evaluations. *Journal of Experimental Social Psychology, 56,* 130–138. doi:10.1016/j.jesp.2014.09.010

Lamont, P. (2013). *Extraordinary beliefs: A historical approach to a psychological problem.* New York, NY: Cambridge University Press.

Lamont, R. A., Swift, H. J., & Abrams, D. (2015). Ageism: A review and meta-analysis of age-based stereotype threat: Negative stereotypes, not facts, do the damage. *Psychology and Aging, 30,* 180–193. doi:10.1037/a0038586

Lampinen, J. M., & Beike, D. R. (2015). *Memory 101. The psych 101 series.* New York, NY: Springer.

Lanciano, T., Curci, A., & Semin, G. R. (2010). The emotional and reconstructive determinants of emotional memories: An experimental approach to flashbulb memory investigation. *Memory, 18,* 473–485.

Landeira-Fernandez, J. (2015). Participation of NMDA receptors in the lateral hypothalamus in gastric erosion induced by cold-water restraint. *Physiology & Behavior, 140,* 209–214. doi:10.1016/j.physbeh.2014.12.038

Landicho, L. C., Cabanig, M. C. A., Cortes, M. S. F., & Villamor, B. J. G. (2014). Egocentrism and risk-taking among adolescents. *Asia Pacific Journal of Multidisciplinary Research, 2,* 132–142.

Landler, M. (2012). From Biden, a vivid account of Bin Laden decision. *New York Times.* Retrieved from http://thecaucus.blogs.nytimes.com/2012/01/30/from-biden-avivid-account-of-bin-laden-decision/

Landsberg, L., Aronne, L. J., Beilin, L. J., Burke, V., Igel, L. I., Lloyd-Jones, D., & Sowers, J. (2013). Obesity-related hypertension: Pathogenesis, cardiovascular risk, and treatment—A position paper of the Obesity Society and the American Society of Hypertension. *Obesity, 21,* 8–24. doi:10.1002/oby.20181

Langer, S. L., Romano, J. M., Mancl, L., & Levy, R. L. (2014). Parental catastrophizing partially mediates the association between parent-reported child pain behavior and parental protective responses. *Pain Research and Treatment, 2014,* Article ID 751097. doi:10.1155/2014/751097

Langmeyer, A., Guglhör-Rudan, A., & Tarnai, C. (2012). What do music preferences reveal about personality? A cross-cultural replication using self-ratings and ratings of music samples. *Journal of Individual Differences, 33,* 119–130.

Langston, W., & Hubbard, T. (2014). The effects of prior belief, expectations, and experience on belief in ghosts. *Abstracts of the 55th Psychonomic Society Annual Meeting, Volume 19.* http://dx.doi.org/10.1037/e528942014-335

Långström, N., Rahman, Q., Carlström, E., & Lichtenstein, P. (2010). Genetic and environmental effects on same-sex sexual behavior: A population study of twins in Sweden. *Archives of Sexual Behavior, 39,* 75–80.

Lapré, G., & Marsee, M. A. (2016). The role of race in the association between corporal punishment and externalizing problems: Does punishment severity matter? *Journal of Child and Family Studies, 25,* 432-441. doi:10.1007/s10826-015-0250-3

Lariscy, R. A. W., & Tinkham, S. F. (1999). The sleeper effect and negative political advertising. *Journal of Advertising, 28,* 13–30.

La Roche, M. J., Davis, T. M., & D'Angelo, E. (2015). Challenges in developing acultural evidence-based psychotherapy in the USA: Suggestions for international studies. *Australian Psychologist, 50,* 95–101. doi:10.1111/ap.12085

Larzelere, M. M., & Campbell, J. S. (2016). Disordered sleep. In M. A. Burg & O. Oyama (Eds.), *The behavioral health specialist in primary care: Skills for integrated practice* (pp. 161–183). New York, NY: Springer.

Lasalvia, A., Penta, E., Sartorius, N., & Henderson, S. (2015). Should the label "schizophrenia" be abandoned? *Schizophrenia Research, 162,* 276–284. doi:10.1016/j.schres.2015.01.031

Lasnier, G. (2013). Popping the question is his job. *Newscenter.* Retrieved from http://news.ucsc.edu/2013/01/marriage-traditions.html

Latané, B., & Darley, J. M. (1968). Group inhibition of bystander intervention in emergencies. *Journal of Personality and Social Psychology, 10,* 215–221.

Latu, I., & Schmid Mast, M. (2016). The effects of stereotypes of women's performance in male-dominated hierarchies: Stereotype threat activation and reduction through role models. In K. Faniko, F. Lorenzi-Cioldi, O. Sarrasin, & E. Mayor (Eds.), *Gender and social hierarchies:*

Perspectives from social psychology (pp. 75–87). New York, NY: Routledge/Taylor & Francis.

Latzman, R. D., Freeman, H. D., Schapiro, S. J., & Hopkins, W. D. (2015). The contribution of genetics and early rearing experiences to hierarchical personality dimensions in chimpanzees (Pan troglodytes). *Journal of Personality and Social Psychology, 109,* 889–900. doi:10.1037/pspp0000040

Lavie, L. (2015). Oxidative stress in obstructive sleep apnea and intermittent hypoxia—Revisited—The bad ugly and good: Implications to the heart and brain. *Sleep Medicine Reviews, 20,* 27–45. doi:10.1016/j.smrv.2014.07.003

LaVoie, N., Lee, Y.-C., & Parker, J. (2016). Preliminary research developing a theory of cell phone distraction and social relationships. *Accident Analysis and Prevention, 86,* 155–160. http://dx.doi.org/10.1016/j.aap.2015.10.023

Lavy, V., & Sand, E. (2015). On the origins of gender human capital gaps: Short and long term consequences of teachers' stereotypical biases. National Bureau of Economic Research, Working Paper No. w20909.

Leaper, C. (2013). Gender development during childhood. In P. D. Zelazo (Ed.), *Oxford handbook of developmental psychology* (pp. 327–377). New York, NY: Oxford University Press.

Lease, H., Hendrie, G. A., Poelman, A. A. M., Delahunty, C., & Cox, D. N. (2016). A Sensory-Diet database: A tool to characterise the sensory qualities of diets. *Food Quality and Preference, 49,* 20–32. http://dx.doi.org/10.1016/j.foodqual.2015.11.010

Lea, T., de Wit, J., & Reynolds, R. (2014). Minority stress in lesbian, gay, and bisexual young adults in Australia: Associations with psychological distress, suicidality, and substance use. *Archives of Sexual Behavior, 43,* 1571–1578. http://dx.doi.org/10.1007/s10508-014-0266-6

Leblond, M., Laisney, M., Lamidey, V., Egret, S., de La Sayette, V., Chételat, G., . . . Eustache, F. (2016). Self-reference effect on memory in healthy aging, mild cognitive impairment and Alzheimer's disease: Influence of identity valence. *Cortex, 74,* 177–190. http://dx.doi.org/10.1016/j.cortex.2015.10.017

Lebowitz, M. S., & Dovidio, J. F. (2015). Implications of emotion regulation strategies for empathic concern, social attitudes, and helping behavior. *Emotion, 15,* 187–194. doi:10.1037/a0038820

LeDoux, J. E. (1996). *The emotional brain: The mysterious underpinnings of emotional life.* New York, NY: Simon & Schuster.

LeDoux, J. E. (1998). *The emotional brain.* New York, NY: Simon & Schuster.

LeDoux, J. E. (2007). Emotional memory. *Scholarpedia, 2,* 180. doi:10.4249/scholarpedia.1806

LeDoux, J. E. (2014). Coming to terms with fear. *Proceedings of the National Academy of Sciences of the United States of America, 111,* 2871–2878. doi:10.1073/pnas.1400335111

Lee, G. Y., & Kisilevsky, B. S. (2014). Fetuses respond to father's voice but prefer mother's voice after birth. *Developmental Psychobiology, 56,* 1–11. doi:10.1002/dev.21084

Lee, H. S., Jung, H. S., & Sumner, A. (2015). A cross-cultural analysis of perception on ageist attitudes between Korean and American social work students. *Korean Social Science Journal, 42,* 25–37. doi:10.1007/s10591-015-9337-7

Lee, M. L., Howard, M. E., Horrey, W. J., Liang, Y., Anderson, C., Shreeve, M. S., . . . Czeisler, C. A. (2016a). High risk of near-crash driving events following night-shift work. *Proceedings of the National Academy of Sciences of the United States of America, 113,* 176–181. doi:10.1073/pnas.1510383112

Lee, T. L., Gelfand, M. J., & Kashima, Y. (2014). The serial reproduction of conflict: Third parties escalate conflict through communication biases. *Journal of Experimental Social Psychology, 54,* 68–72. doi:10.1016/j.jesp.2014.04.006

Lee, Y., Syeda, K., Maruschak, N. A., Cha, D. S., Mansur, R. B., Wium-Andersen, I. K., . . . McIntyre, R. S. (2016). A new perspective on the anti-suicide effects with ketamine treatment: A procognitive effect. *Journal of Clinical Psychopharmacology, 36,* 50–56. http://dx.doi.org/10.1097/JCP.0000000000000441

Legarreta, M., Graham, J., North, L., Bueler, C. E., McGlade, E., & Yurgelun-Todd, D. (2015). DSM-5 posttraumatic stress disorder symptoms associated with suicide behaviors in veterans. *Psychological Trauma: Theory, Research, Practice, and Policy, 7,* 277–285. doi:10.1037/tra0000026

Lehr, D. (2009). *The fence: A police cover-up along Boston's racial divide.* New York, NY: HarperCollins.

Leichtman, M. D. (2006). Cultural and maturational influences on long-term event memory. In L. Balter & C. S. Tamis-LeMonda (Eds.), *Child psychology: A handbook of contemporary issues* (2nd ed., pp. 565–589). New York, NY: Psychology Press.

Leigh, H. (2015). Affect, mood, emotions: Depressive disorders and bipolar and related disorders. In H. Leigh & J. Strltzer (Eds.), *Handbook of consultation-liaison psychiatry* (2nd ed., pp. 225–235). New York, NY: Springer. doi:10.1007/978-3-319-11005-9

Leising, K. J., Wong, J., & Blaisdell, A. P. (2015). Extinction and spontaneous recovery of spatial behavior in pigeons. *Journal of Experimental Psychology: Animal Learning and Cognition, 41,* 371–377. doi:10.1037/xan0000076

Lemmon, G., & Wayne, S. J. (2014). Underlying motives of organizational citizenship behavior comparing egoistic and altruistic motivations. *Journal of Leadership & Organizational Studies, 22,* 129–148. doi:10.1177/1548051814535638.

Lemogne, C., Schuster, J-P., Levenstein, S., Melchior, M., Nabi, H., Ducimetière, P., . . . Consoli, S. M. (2015). Hostility and the risk of peptic ulcer in the GAZEL cohort. *Health Psychology, 34,* 181–185. doi:10.1037/hea0000129

Lepper, M. R., Greene, D., & Nisbett, R. E. (1973). Undermining children's intrinsic interest with extrinsic rewards: A test of the overjustification hypothesis. *Journal of Personality and Social Psychology, 28,* 129–137.

Leslie, M. (2000, July/August). The vexing legacy of Lewis Terman. *Stanford Magazine.* Retrieved from http://www.stanfordalumni.org/news/magazine/2000/julaug/articles/terman.html

LeVay, S. (2003). Queer science: The use and abuse of research into homosexuality. *Archives of Sexual Behavior, 32,* 187–189.

LeVay, S. (2012). *Gay, straight, and the reason why: The science of sexual orientation.* New York, NY: Oxford.

Levenson, R. W. (1992). Autonomic nervous system differences among emotions. *Psychological Science, 3,* 23–27.

Levenson, R. W. (2007). Emotion elicitation with neurological patients. In J. A. Coan & J. B. Allen (Eds.), *Handbook of emotion elicitation and assessment* (pp. 158–168). Oxford, UK: Oxford.

Levey, S. (2014). *Introduction to language development.* San Diego, CA: Plural.

Levine, J. R. (2001). *Why do fools fall in love: Experiencing the magic, mystery, and meaning of successful relationships.* New York, NY: Jossey-Bass.

Levine, L., & Munsch, J. (2014). *Child development: An active learning approach.* Thousand Oaks, CA: Sage.

Levine, P. A. (2015). *Trauma and memory: Brain and body in a search for the living past.* New York, NY: North Atlantic.

Levinthal, S. F. (2016). *Drugs, behavior, and modern society* (8th ed.). Upper Saddle River, NJ: Pearson.

Lewin, K. (1951). *Field theory in social science.* Upper Saddle River, NJ: Pearson.

Liang, H.-L. (2015). Are you tired? Spillover and crossover effects of emotional exhaustion on the family domain. *Asian Journal of Social Psychology, 18,* 22–32. http://dx.doi.org/10.1111/ajsp.12075

Li, C.-T., Chen, M.-H., Lin, W.-C., Hong, C.-J., Yang, B.-H., Liu, R.-S., . . . Su, T.-P. (2016). The effects of low-dose ketamine on the prefrontal cortex and amygdala in treatment-resistant depression: A randomized controlled study. *Human Brain Mapping, 37,* 1080–1090. http://dx.doi.org/10.1002/hbm.23085

Lien, J. W., & Yuan, J. (2015). The cross-sectional "Gambler's Fallacy": Set representativeness in lottery number choices. *Journal of Economic Behavior & Organization, 109,* 163–172. doi:10.1016/j.jebo.2014.10.011

Lilienfeld, S. O., & Lynn, S. J. (2015). Dissociative identity disorder: A contemporary scientific perspective. In S. O. Lilienfeld, S. J.

Lynn, & J. M. Lohr (Eds.), *Science and pseudoscience in clinical psychology* (2nd ed., pp. 113–152). New York, NY: Guilford.

Lilienfeld, S. O., Lynn, S. J., & Ammirati, R. J. (2015). Science versus pseudoscience. *The Encyclopedia of Clinical Psychology,* 1–7. Hoboken, NJ: Wiley. doi:10.1002/9781118625392.wbecp572

Lilienfeld, S. O., Lynn, S. J., Ruscio, J., & Beyerstein, B. L. (2010). *50 great myths of popular psychology: Shattering widespread misconceptions about human behavior.* Malden, MA: Wiley-Blackwell.

Lilliengren, P., Johansson, R., Lindqvist, K., Mechler, J., & Andersson, G. (2016). Efficacy of experiential dynamic therapy for psychiatric conditions: A meta-analysis of randomized controlled trials. *Psychotherapy, 53,* 90–104. http://dx.doi.org/10.1037/pst0000024

Lima, A. S., Silva, K., Padovan, C. M., Almeida, S. S., & Hebihara Fukuda, M. T. (2014). Memory, learning, and participation of the cholinergic system in young rats exposed to environmental enrichment. *Behavioural Brain Research, 259,* 247–252. doi:10.1016/j.bbr.2013.10.046

Lim, A., & Okuno, H. G. (2015). A recipe for empathy: Integrating the mirror system, insula, somatosensory cortex and motherese. *International Journal of Social Robotics, 7,* 35–49. doi:10.1007/s12369-014-0262-y

Lim, D., Condon, P., & DeSteno, D. (2015). Mindfulness and compassion: An examination of mechanism and scalability. *PLoS ONE, 10*: e0118221. doi:10.1371/journal.pone.0118221

Lim, L., Chang, W., Yu, X., Chiu, H., Chong, M., & Kua, E. (2011). Depression in Chinese elderly populations. *Asia-Pacific Psychiatry, 3,* 46–53.

Lin, C.-C. (2015). Self-esteem mediates the relationship between dispositional gratitude and well-being. *Personality and Individual Differences, 85,* 145–148. http://dx.doi.org/10.1016/j.paid.2015.04.045

Lin, C.-S., Hsieh, J.-C., Yeh, T.-C., Lee, S.-Y., & Niddam, D. M. (2013). Functional dissociation within insular cortex: The effect of pre-stimulus anxiety on pain. *Brain Research, 1493,* 40–47. doi:10.1016/j.brainres.2012.11.035

Linden, E. (1993, March 22). Can animals think? *Time,* pp. 54–61.

Lindner, I., & Henkel, L. A. (2015). Confusing what you heard with what you did: False action-memories from auditory cues. *Psychonomic Bulletin & Review, 22,* 1791–1797. doi:10.3758/s13423-015-0837-0

Lindsay, D. S., Yonelinas, A. P., & Roediger, H. L., II (Eds.). (2015). *Remembering: Attributions, processes, and control in human memory: Essays in honor of Larry Jacoby* (C. M. Kelley, Trans.). New York, NY: Psychology Press.

Lin, N., Pan, X.-D., Chen, A.-Q., Zhu, Y.-G., Wu, M., Zhang, J., & Chen, X.-C. (2014). Tripchlorolide improves age-associated cognitive deficits by reversing hippocampal synaptic plasticity impairment and NMDA receptor dysfunction in SAMP8 mice. *Behavioural Brain Research, 258,* 8–18. doi:10.1016/j.bbr.2013.10.010

Lippa, R. A. (2016). Biological influences on masculinity. In Y. J. Wong & S. R. Wester (Eds.), *APA handbook of men and masculinities* (pp. 187–209). Washington, DC: American Psychological Association. doi:10.1037/14594-009

Lipsman, N., Giacobbe, P., & Lozano, A. M. (2015). Deep brain stimulation for the management of treatment-refractory major depressive disorder. In B. Sun & A. De Salles (Eds.), *Neurosurgical treatments for psychiatric disorders* (pp. 95–104). New York, NY: Springer. doi:10.1007/978-94-017-9576-0

Littlewood, D. L., Gooding, P. A., Panagioti, M., & Kyle, S. D. (2016). Nightmares and suicide in posttraumatic stress disorder: The mediating role of defeat, entrapment, and hopelessness. *Journal of Clinical Sleep Medicine, 12,* 393–399. http://dx.doi.org/10.5664/jcsm.5592

Liu, H. (2009). Till death do us part: Marital status and US mortality trends, 1986–2000. *Journal of Marriage and Family, 71,* 1158–1173. doi:10.1111/ j.1741-3737.2009.00661.x

Liu, J. H., & Latané, B. (1998). Extremitization of attitudes: Does thought- and discussion-induced polarization cumulate? *Basic and Applied Social Psychology, 20,* 103–110.

Liu, L., Preotiuc-Pietro, D., Samani, Z. R., Moghaddam, M. E., & Ungar, L. (2016). Analyzing personality through social media profile picture choice. *AAAI Digital Library.* Retrieved from https://sites.sas.upenn.edu/danielpr/publications/analyzing-personality-through-social-media-profile-picture-choice

Livingstone, K. M., & Isaacowitz, D. M. (2016). Age differences in use and effectiveness of positivity in emotion regulation: The sample case of attention. In A. D. Ong & C. E. Löckenhoff (Eds.), *Emotion, aging, and health. Bronfenbrenner series on the ecology of human development* (pp. 31–48). Washington, DC: American Psychological Association. http://dx.doi.org/10.1037/14857-003

Livingston, J. A. (1999). Something old and something new: Love, creativity, and the enduring relationship. *Bulletin of the Menninger Clinic, 63,* 40–52.

Li, W., Li, X., Huang, L., Kong, X., Yang, W., Wei, D., . . . Liu, J. (2015). Brain structure links trait creativity to openness to experience. *Social Cognitive and Affective Neuroscience, 10,* 191–198. doi:10.1093/scan/nsu041

Li, W. O. (2016). Consciousness: How we perceive and become aware of our world. In C. Tien-Lun Sun (Ed.), *Psychology in Asia: An introduction* (pp. 127–173). Boston, MA: Cengage Learning.

Li, W. O. (2016). Learning and memory: How do we learn and retain new knowledge? In C. Tien-Lun Sun (Ed.), *Psychology in Asia: An introduction* (pp. 175–210). Boston, MA: Cengage Learning.

Li, X., Semenova, S., D'Souza, M. S., Stoker, A. K., & Markou, A. (2014). Involvement of glutamatergic and GABAergic systems in nicotine dependence: Implications for novel pharmacotherapies for smoking cessation. *Neuropharmacology, 76,* 554–565. doi:10.1016/j.neuropharm.2013.05.042

LoBue, V. (2013). What are we so afraid of? How early attention shapes our most common fears. *Child Development Perspectives, 7,* 38–42. doi:10.1111/cdep.12012

LoBue, V., & DeLoache, J. S. (2008). Detecting the snake in the grass: Attention to fear-relevant stimuli by adults and young children. *Psychological Science, 19,* 284–289. doi:10.1111/j.1467-9280.2008.02081.x

Loebnitz, N., & Aschemann-Witzel, J. (2016). Communicating organic food quality in China: Consumer perceptions of organic products and the effect of environmental value priming. *Food Quality and Preference, 50,* 102–108. http://dx.doi.org/10.1016/j.foodqual.2016.02.003

Loflin, M., & Earleywine, M. (2015). The case for medical marijuana: An issue of relief. *Drug and Alcohol Dependence, 149,* 293–297. doi:10.1016/j.drugalcdep.2015.01.006

Loftus, E. (2002, May/June). My story: Dear mother. *Psychology Today,* 67–70.

Loftus, E. F. (1993). Psychologists in the eyewitness world. *American Psychologist, 48,* 550–552. doi:10.1037/0003-066X.48.5.550

Loftus, E. F. (2010). Afterword: Why parapsychology is not yet ready for prime time. In S. Krippner & H. L. Friedman (Eds.), *Debating psychic experience: Human potential or human illusion?* (pp. 211–214). Santa Barbara, CA: Praeger/ABC-CLIO.

Loftus, E. F. (2011). How I got started: From semantic memory to expert testimony. *Applied Cognitive Psychology, 25,* 347–348. doi:10.1002/acp.1769

Loftus, E. F., & Cahill, L. (2007). Memory distortion from misattribution to rich false memory. In J. S. Nairne (Ed.), *The foundations of remembering: Essays in honor of Henry L. Roediger, III* (pp. 413–425). New York, NY: Psychology Press.

Lohr, J. B., Palmer, B. W., Eidt, C. A., Aailabovina, S., Mausbach, B. T., Wolkowitz, O. M., . . . Jeste, D. V. (2015). Is post-traumatic stress disorder associated with premature senescence? A review of the literature. *The American Journal of Geriatric Psychiatry, 23,* 709–726. http://dx.doi.org/10.1016/j.jagp.2015.04.001

Lohse, M., Garrido, L., Driver, J., Dolan, R. J., Duchaine, B. C., & Furl, N. (2016). Effective connectivity from early visual cortex to posterior occipitotemporal face areas supports face selectivity and predicts developmental prosopagnosia. *The Journal of Neuroscience, 36,* 3821–3828. http://dx.doi.org/10.1523/JNEUROSCI.3621-15.2016

Lopez, K. (2013). "Silver Linings" hits close to home for director Russell. Retrieved from http://www.usatoday.com/story/news/nation/2013/02/08/silver-lining-playbook-mental-illness/1891065/

Lopez, S., Pedrotti, J., & Snyder, C. (2015). *Positive psychology: The scientific and practical explorations of human strengths* (3rd ed.). Thousand Oaks, CA: Sage.

Louie, A. K., & Roberts, L. W. (2015). Anxiety disorders. In L. W. Roberts & A. K. Louie (Eds.), *Study guide to DSM-5®* (pp. 137–153). Arlington, VA: American Psychiatric Publishing.

Loving, T. J., & Sbarra, D. A. (2015). Relationships and health. In M. Mikulincer, P. R. Shaver, J. A. Simpson, & J. F. Dovidio (Eds.), *APA handbooks in psychology. APA handbook of personality and social psychology, Vol. 3. Interpersonal relations* (pp. 151–176). Washington, DC: American Psychological Association. doi:10.1037/14344-006

Lubar, J. F. (2015). Optimal procedures in Z-score neurofeedback: Strategies for maximizing learning for surface and LORETA neurofeedback. In R. W. Thatcher & J. F. Lubar (Eds.), *Z score neurofeedback: Clinical applications* (pp. 41–58). San Diego, CA: Elsevier. doi:10.1016/B978-0-12-801291-8.00003-0

Luby, J. L., Barch, D. M., Belden, A., Gaffrey, M. S., Tillman, R., Babb, C., . . . Botteron, K. N. (2012). Maternal support in early childhood predicts larger hippocampal volumes at school age. *Proceedings of the National Academy of Sciences of the United States of America, 109,* 2854–2859.

Lu, C.-Q., Lu, J. J., Du, D.-Y., & Brough, P. (2016). Crossover effects of work-family conflict among Chinese couples. *Journal of Managerial Psychology, 31,* 235–250. http://dx.doi.org/10.1108/JMP-09-2012-0283

Lu, H.-C., & Mackie, K. (2016). An introduction to the endogenous cannabinoid system. *Biological Psychiatry, 79,* 516–525. http://dx.doi.org/10.1016/j.biopsych.2015.07.028

Luhrmann, T. M., Padmavati, R., Tharoor, H., & Osei, A. (2015). Differences in voice-hearing experiences of people with psychosis in the USA, India and Ghana: Interview-based study. *The British Journal of Psychiatry, 206,* 41–44. doi:10.1192/bjp.bp.113.139048

Luo, S., Monterosso, J. R., Sarpelleh, K., & Page, K. A. (2015). Differential effects of fructose versus glucose on brain and appetitive responses to food cues and decisions for food rewards. *Proceedings of the National Academy of Sciences of the United States of America, 112,* 6509–6514. http://doi.org/10.1073/pnas.1503358112

Lynn, S. J., Krackow, E., Loftus, E. F., Locke, T. G., & Lillienfeld, S. O. (2015). Constructing the past: Problematic memory recovery techniques in psychotherapy. In S. O. Lilienfeld, S. J. Lynn, & J. M. Lohr (Eds.), *Science and pseudoscience in clinical psychology* (2nd ed., pp. 210–244). New York, NY: Guilford.

Lynn, S. J., Lilienfeld, S. O., Merckelbach, H., Maxwell, R., Baltman, J., & Giesbrecht, T. (2016). Dissociative disorders. In J. E. Maddux & B. A. Winstead (Eds.), *Psychopathology: Foundations for a contemporary understanding* (4th ed., pp. 298–317). New York, NY: Routledge/Taylor & Francis Group.

Lysiak, M. (2015, June 19). Charleston massacre: Mental illness common thread for mass shootings. *Newsweek.* Retrieved from http://www.newsweek.com/charleston-massacre-mental-illness-common-thread-mass-shootings-344789

Lyubomirsky, S. (2008). *The how of happiness: A scientific approach to getting the life you want.* New York, NY: Penguin Press.

Lyubomirsky, S. (2013). *The myths of happiness: What should make you happy, but doesn't, what shouldn't make you happy, but does.* New York, NY: Penguin Press.

Maack, D. J., Buchanan, E., & Young, J. (2015). Development and psychometric investigation of an inventory to assess fight, flight, freeze tendencies: The Fight, Flight, Freeze Questionnaire. *Cognitive Behaviour Therapy, 44,* 117–127. http://dx.doi.org/10.1080/16506073.2014.972443

Mabe, A. G., Forney, K. J., & Keel, P. K. (2014). Do you "like" my photo? Facebook use maintains eating disorder risk. *International Journal of Eating Disorders, 47,* 516–523. doi:10.1002/eat.22254

Mackinnon, S. P., Smith, S. M., & Carter-Rogers, K. (2015). Multidimensional self-esteem and test derogation after negative feedback. *Canadian Journal of Behavioural Science/Revue Canadienne des Sciences du Comportement, 47,* 123–126. doi:10.1037/a0038364

Macmillan, M. B. (2000). *An odd kind of fame: Stories of Phineas Gage.* Cambridge, MA: MIT Press.

Macmillan, M., & Lena, M. L. (2010). Rehabilitating Phineas Gage. *Neuropsychological Rehabilitation, 20,* 641–658. doi:10.1080/09602011003760527

Madden, K., Middleton, P., Cyna, A. M., Matthewson, M., & Jones, L. (2012). Hypnosis for pain management during labour and childbirth. *Cochrane Database of Systematic Reviews, 11.* doi:10.1002/14651858.CD009356

Maggi, R., Zasso, J., & Conti, L. (2015). Neurodevelopmental origin and adult neurogenesis of the neuroendocrine hypothalamus. *Frontiers in Cellular Neuroscience, 8,* 440. doi:10.3389/fncel.2014.00440

Maggi, S., Busetto, L., Noale, M., Limongi, F., & Crepaldi, G. (2015). Obesity: Definition and epidemiology. In A. Lenzi, S. Migliaccio, & L. M. Donini (Eds.), *Multidisciplinary approach to obesity: From assessment to treatment* (pp. 31–39). New York, NY: Springer. doi:10.1007/978-3-319-09045-0_3

Magnavita, J. J., & Anchin, J. C. (2014). *Unifying psychotherapy: Principles, methods, and evidence from clinical science.* New York, NY: Springer.

Maher, J. P., & Conroy, D. E. (2016). A dual-process model of older adults' sedentary behavior. *Health Psychology, 35,* 262–272. http://dx.doi.org/10.1037/hea0000300

Mahn, H., & John-Steiner, V. (2013). Vygotsky and sociocultural approaches to teaching and learning. In W. M. Reynolds, G. E. Miller, & I. B. Weiner (Eds.), *Handbook of psychology, Vol. 7. Educational psychology* (2nd ed., pp. 117–145). Hoboken, NJ: Wiley.

Mahoney, A. (2011). Goodness of fit: The challenge of parenting gifted children. In J. L. Jolly, D. J. Treffinger, T. F. Inman, & J. F. Smutny (Eds.), *Parenting gifted children: The authoritative guide from the National Association for Gifted Children* (pp. 539–545). Waco, TX: Prufrock.

Maier, C., Laumer, S., Weinert, C., & Weitzel, T. (2015). The effects of technostress and switching stress on discontinued use of social networking services: A study of Facebook use. *Information Systems Journal, 25,* 275–308. doi:10.1111/isj.12068

Main, M., & Solomon, J. (1986). Discovery of an insecure-disorganized attachment pattern. In T. Brazelton & M. W. Yogman (Eds.), *Affective development in infancy* (pp. 95–124). Westport, CT: Ablex.

Main, M., & Solomon, J. (1990). Procedures for identifying infants as disorganized/disoriented during the Ainsworth Strange Situation. In M. T. Greenberg, D. Cicchetti, & E. M. Cummings (Eds.), *Attachment in the preschool years: Theory, research, and intervention* (pp. 121–160). Chicago, IL: University of Chicago Press.

Maisto, S. A., Galizio, M., & Connors, G. J. (2015). *Drug use and abuse* (7th ed.). Boston, MA: Cengage Learning.

Major, B., Spencer, S., Schmader, T., Wolfe, C., & Crocker, J. (1998). Coping with negative stereotypes about intellectual performance: The role of psychological disengagement. *Personality & Social Psychology Bulletin, 24,* 34–50.

Makinodan, M., Rosen, K. M., Ito, S., & Corfas, G. (2012). A critical period for social experience-dependent oligodendrocyte maturation and myelination. *Science, 337,* 1357–1360. doi:10.1126/science.1220845.

Maldonado, R. C., DiLillo, D., & Hoffman, L. (2014). Can college students use emotion regulation strategies to alter intimate partner aggression-risk behaviors? An examination using I3 Theory. *Psychology of Violence, 5,* 46–55. doi:10.1037/a0035454

Malgady, R. G., Castagno, R. M., & Cardinale, J. A. (2014). Clinical tests and assessment: Ethnocultural and linguistic bias in mental health evaluation of Latinos. In F. T. L. Leong, L. Comas-Díaz, G. C. Nagayama Hall, V. C. McLoyd, & J. E. Trimble (Eds.), *APA handbook of multicultural psychology, Vol.2. Applications and training* (pp. 165–179). Washington, DC:

American Psychological Association. doi:10.1037/14187-010

Malinowski, J., & Horton, C. L. (2014). Evidence for the preferential incorporation of emotional waking-life experiences into dreams. *Dreaming, 24,* 18–31. doi:10.1037/a0036017

Mallan, K. M., Lipp, O. V., & Cochrane, B. (2013). Slithering snakes, angry men and out-group members: What and whom are we evolved to fear? *Cognition and Emotion, 27,* 1168–1180. doi:10.1080/02699931.2013.778195

Mallya, S., & Fiocco, A. J. (2016). Effects of mindfulness training on cognition and well-being in healthy older adults. *Mindfulness, 7,* 453–465. http://dx.doi.org/10.1007/s12671-015-0468-6

Maloney, E. A., Gunderson, E. A., Levine, S. C., & Beilock, S. L. (2015). Intergenerational effects of parents' math anxiety on children's math achievement and anxiety. *Psychological Science, 26,* 1480–1488. doi:10.1177/0956797615592630.

Mammen, G., & Faulkner, G. (2013). Physical activity and the prevention of depression: A systematic review of prospective studies. *American Journal of Preventive Medicine, 45,* 649–657. doi:10.1016/j.amepre.2013.08.001.

Mancia, M., & Baggott, J. (2008). The early unrepressed unconscious in relation to Matte-Blanco's thought. *International Forum of Psychoanalysis, 17,* 201–212. doi:10.1080/08037060701676359

Mancini, A. D., Littleton, H. L., & Grills, A. E. (2016). Can people benefit from acute stress? Social support, psychological improvement, and resilience after the Virginia Tech campus shootings. *Clinical Psychological Science, 4,* 401–417. doi:10.1177/2167702615601001

Manstead, A. S. R., & Parkinson, B. (2015). Emotion theories. In B. Gawronski & G. V. Bodenhausen (Eds.), *Theory and explanation in social psychology* (pp. 84–107). New York, NY: Guilford.

Maples-Keller, J. L., Berke, D. S., Few, L. R., & Miller, J. D. (2016). A review of sensation seeking and its empirical correlates: Dark, bright, and neutral hues. In V. Zeigler-Hill & D. K. Marcus (Eds.), *The dark side of personality: Science and practice in social, personality, and clinical psychology* (pp. 137–156). Washington, DC: American Psychological Association. http://dx.doi.org/10.1037/14854-008

Ma, Q., Jin, J., Meng, L., & Shen, Q. (2014). The dark side of monetary incentive: How does extrinsic reward crowd out intrinsic motivation. *NeuroReport: For Rapid Communication of Neuroscience Research, 25,* 194–198. doi:10.1097/WNR.0000000000000113

Marchant, J. (2016). *Cure: A journey into the science of mind over body.* New York, NY: Crown.

Marcia, J., & Josselson, R. (2013). Eriksonian personality research and its implications for psychotherapy. *Journal of Personality, 81,* 617–629. doi:10.1111/jopy.12014

Marczinski, C. A. (2014). *Drug use, misuse, and abuse.* Hoboken, NJ: Wiley.

Market Opinion Research International (MORI). (2005, January). *Use of animals in medical research for coalition for medical progress.* London, UK: Author.

Marks, A. K., Ejesi, K., McCullough, M. B., & Coll, C. G. (2015). Developmental implications of discrimination. *Handbook of Child Psychology and Developmental Science, 3,* 1–42. doi:10.1002/9781118963418.childpsy309

Marshall, E.-J., & Brockman, R. N. (2016). The relationships between psychological flexibility, self-compassion, and emotional well-being. *Journal of Cognitive Psychotherapy, 30,* 60–72. http://dx.doi.org/10.1891/0889-8391.30.1.60

Martin, A. J., & Marsh, H. W. (2006). Academic resilience and its psychological and educational correlates: A construct validity approach. *Psychology in the Schools, 43,* 267–281.

Martínez-Hernáez, A., Carceller-Maicas, N., DiGiacomo, S. M., & Ariste, S. (2016). Social support and gender differences in coping with depression among emerging adults: A mixed-methods study. *Child and Adolescent Psychiatry and Mental Health, 10,* Article 2. http://dx.doi.org/10.1186/s13034-015-0088-x

Martins, C., Stensvold, D., Finlayson, G., Holst, J., Wisloff, U., Kulseng, B., . . . King, N. A. (2014). Effect of moderate- and high-intensity acute exercise on appetite in obese individuals. *Medicine and Science in Sports and Exercise, 47,* 40–48. doi:10.1249/MSS.0000000000000372

Martin-Storey, A., Serbin, L. A., Stack, D. M., Ledingham, J. E., & Schwartzman, A. E. (2012). Self and peer perceptions of childhood aggression, social withdrawal and likeability predict adult personality factors: A prospective longitudinal study. *Personality and Individual Differences, 53,* 843–848. doi:10.1016/j.paid.2012.06.018

Marx, D. M., Ko, S. J., & Friedman, R. A. (2009). The "Obama effect": How a salient role model reduces race-based performance differences. *Journal of Experimental Social Psychology, 45,* 953–956. doi:10.1016/j.jesp.2009.03.012

Masciadrelli, B. P. (2014). "I learned that the aging population isn't that much different from me": The final outcomes of a Gero-Ed BEL project. *Journal of Gerontological Social Work, 57,* 24–36.

Mase, A. S., Cho, H., & Prokopy, L. S. (2015). Enhancing the Social Amplification of Risk Framework (SARF) by exploring trust, the availability heuristic, and agricultural advisors' belief in climate change. *Journal of Environmental Psychology, 41,* 166–176. doi:10.1016/j.jenvp.2014.12.004

Maslow, A. H. (1954). *Motivation and personality.* New York, NY: Harper & Row.

Maslow, A. H. (1970). *Motivation and personality.* New York, NY: Harper & Row.

Maslow, A. H. (1999). *Toward a psychology of being* (3rd ed.). New York, NY: Wiley.

Mason, S., & Zhou, F. C. (2015). Editorial: Genetics and epigenetics of fetal alcohol spectrum disorders. *Frontiers in Genetics, 6,* 146. doi:10.3389/fgene.2015.00146

Massing-Schaffer, M., Liu, R. T., Kraines, M. A., Choi, J. Y., & Alloy, L. B. (2015). Elucidating the relation between childhood emotional abuse and depressive symptoms in adulthood: The mediating role of maladaptive interpersonal processes. *Personality and Individual Differences, 74,* 106–111. doi:10.1016/j.paid.2014.09.045

Masten, A. S., & Coatsworth, J. D. (1998). The development of competence in favorable and unfavorable environments: Lessons from research on successful children. *American Psychologist, 53,* 205–220. http://dx.doi.org/10.1037/0003-066X.53.2.205

Masten, A. S., Cutuli, J. J., Herbers, J. E., Hinz, E., Obradović, J., & Wenzel, A. J. (2014). Academic risk and resilience in the context of homelessness. *Child Development Perspectives, 8,* 201–206. http://dx.doi.org/10.1111/cdep.12088

Master, A., Cheryan, S., & Meltzoff, A. N. (2016). Computing whether she belongs: Stereotypes undermine girls' interest and sense of belonging in computer science. *Journal of Educational Psychology, 108,* 424–437. http://dx.doi.org/10.1037/edu0000061

Master, S. L., Eisenberger, N. I., Taylor S. E., Naliboff, B. D., Shirinyan, D., & Lieberman, M. D. (2009). A picture's worth: Partner photographs reduce experimentally induced pain. *Psychological Science, 20,* 1316–1318. doi:10.1111/j.1467-9280.2009.02444.x

Masters, W. H., & Johnson, V. E. (1966). *Human sexual response.* Boston, MA: Little, Brown.

Mathes, J., Schredl, M., & Göritz, A. S. (2014). Frequency of typical dream themes in most recent dreams: An online study. *Dreaming, 24,* 57–66. doi:10.1037/a0035857

Matlin, M. W. (2016). *Cognition* (9th ed.). Hoboken, NJ: Wiley.

Matlin, M. W., & Farmer, T. A. (2016). *Cognition* (9th ed.). Hoboken, NJ: Wiley.

Matsumoto, D. (2000). *Culture and psychology: People around the world.* Belmont, CA: Cengage Learning.

Matsumoto, D., & Juang, L. (2013). *Culture and psychology* (5th ed.). Belmont, CA: Cengage Learning.

Matsumoto, D., Yoo, S. H., & Fontaine, J. (2008). Mapping expressive differences around the world: The relationship between emotional display rules and individualism versus collectivism. *Journal of Cross-Cultural Psychology, 39,* 55–74. doi:10.1177/0022022107311854

Matsumoto, M., & Hikosaka, O. (2009). Two types of dopamine neurons distinctly convey positive and negative emotional signals. *Nature, 459,* 837–841. doi:10.1038/nature08028

Mattes, K., & Milazzo, C. (2014). Pretty faces, marginal races: Predicting election outcomes using trait assessments of British parliamentary candidates. *Electoral Studies, 34,* 177–189. doi:10.1016/j.electstud.2013.11.004

Mauguière, F., & Corkin, S. (2015). H.M. never again! An analysis of H. M.'s epilepsy and treatment. *Revue Neurologique, 171,* 273–281. http://dx.doi.org/10.1016/j.neurol.2015.01.002

Maule, J., Witzel, C., & Franklin, A. (2014). Getting the gist of multiple hues: Metric and categorical effects on ensemble perception of hue. *Journal of the Optical Society of America, 31,* A93–A102. doi:10.1364/JOSAA.31.000A93

May, A. C., Rudy, B. M., Davis, T. E., & Matson, J. L. (2013). Evidence-based behavioral treatment of dog phobia with young children: Two case examples. *Behavior Modification, 37,* 143–160.

Mayordomo-Rodríguez, T., Meléndez-Moral, J. C., Viguer-Segui, P., & Sales-Galán, A. (2015). Coping strategies as predictors of well-being in youth adult. *Social Indicators Research, 122,* 479–489. doi:10.1007/s11205-014-0689-4

Mazandarani, A., Aguilar-Vafaie, M. E., & Domhoff, G. (2013). Content analysis of Iranian college students' dreams: Comparison with American data. *Dreaming, 23,* 163–174. doi:10.1037/ a0032352

McCarthy, M. M., Pickett, L. A., vanRyzin, J. W., & Kight, K. (2015). Surprising origins of sex differences in the brain. *Hormones & Behavior, 76,* 3–10. doi:10.1016/j.yhbeh.2015.04.013

McClelland, D. C. (1958). Risk-taking in children with high and low need for achievement. In J. W. Atkinson (Ed.), *Motives in fantasy, action, and society* (pp. 306–321). Princeton, NJ: Van Nostrand.

McClelland, D. C. (1993). Intelligence is not the best predictor of job performance. *Current Directions in Psychological Science, 2,* 5–6.

McClintock, E. A. (2014). Beauty and status: The illusion of exchange in partner selection? *American Sociological Review, 79,* 575–604. doi:10.1177/0003122414536391.

McCormack, L., & Joseph, S. (2014). Psychological growth in aging Vietnam veterans: Redefining shame and betrayal. *Journal of Humanistic Psychology, 54,* 336–355. doi:10.1177/0022167813501393

McCormick, D. A., McGinley, M. J., & Salkoff, D. B. (2015). Brain state dependent activity in the cortex and thalamus. *Current Opinion in Neurobiology, 31,* 133–140. doi:10.1016/j.conb.2014.10.003

McCrae, R. (2011). Cross-cultural research on the five-factor model of personality. *Online Readings in Psychology and Culture, Unit 4.* Retrieved from http://scholarworks. gvsu.edu/orpc/vol4/iss4/1

McCrae, R. R., & Costa, P. T., Jr. (2013). Introduction to the empirical and theoretical status of the five-factor model of personality traits. In T. A. Widiger & P. T. Costa, Jr. (Eds.), *Personality disorders and the five-factor model of personality* (3rd ed., pp. 15–27). Washington, DC: American Psychological Association.

McCrae, R. R., Costa, P. T., Jr., Martin, T. A., Oryol, V. E., Rukavishnikov, A. A., Senin, I. G., . . . Urbánek, T. (2004). Consensual validation of personality traits across cultures. *Journal of Research in Personality, 38,* 179–201.

McCrae, R. R., Costa, P. T., Jr., Ostendorf, F., Angleitner, A., Hřebíčková, M., Avia, M. D., . . . Smith, P. B. (2000). Nature over nurture: Temperament, personality, and life span development. *Journal of Personality and Social Psychology, 78,* 173–186. doi:10.1037/0022-3514.78.1.173

McCrae, R. R., Scally, M., Terracciano, A., Abecasis, G. R., & Costa, P. T. Jr. (2010). An alternative to the search for single polymorphisms: Toward molecular personality scales for the five-factor model. *Journal of Personality and Social Psychology, 99,* 1014–1024. http://dx.doi.org/10.1037/a0020964

McDaniel, M. A., Cahill, M. J., Robbins, M., & Wiener, C. (2014). Individual differences in learning and transfer: Stable tendencies for learning exemplars versus abstracting rules. *Journal of Experimental Psychology: General, 143,* 668–693. doi:10.1037/a0032963

McDaniel, S. H., & Belar, C. D. (2016). Firearm violence prevention is a human rights issue. *APA Public Interest Directorate.* Retrieved from https://psychologybenefits.org/2016/06/27/firearm-violence-prevention-is-a-human-rights-issue/

McDougall, D. (2013). Applying single-case design innovations to research in sport and exercise psychology. *Journal of Applied Sport Psychology, 25,* 33–45. doi:10.1080/10413200.2012.720640

McDougall, W. (1908). *Social psychology.* New York, NY: Putnam's Sons.

McFarlane, D. A. (2014). A positive theory of stereotyping and stereotypes: Is stereotyping useful? *Journal of Studies in Social Sciences, 8,* 140–163.

McGeorge, C. R., Carlson, T. S., & Wetchler, J. L. (2015). The history of marriage and family therapy. In J. L. Wetchler & L. L. Hecker (Eds.), *An introduction to marriage and family therapy* (2nd ed., pp. 3–42). New York, NY: Routledge/Taylor & Francis Group.

McGillicuddy, N. B., Rychtarik, R. G., & Papandonatos, G. D. (2015). Skill training versus 12-step facilitation for parents of substance-abusing teens. *Journal of Substance Abuse Treatment, 50,* 11–17. doi:10.1016/j.jsat.2014.09.006

McGinty, E., Webster, D., & Barry, C. (2013). Effects of news media messages about mass shootings on attitudes toward persons with serious mental illness and public support for gun control policies. *American Journal of Psychiatry, 170,* 494–501.

McGlinchey, E. L. (2015). Sleep and adolescents. In K. A. Babson & M. T. Feldner (Eds.), *Sleep and affect: Assessment, theory, and clinical implications* (pp. 421–439). San Diego, CA: Elsevier.

McGloin, J. M., & Thomas, K. J. (2016). Incentives for collective deviance: Group size and changes in perceived risk, cost, and reward. *Criminology, 54,* 459–486. http://dx.doi.org/10.1111/1745-9125.12111

McGrath, J. J., Petersen, L., Agerbo, E., Mors, O., Mortensen, P. B., & Pedersen, C. B. (2014). A comprehensive assessment of parental age and psychiatric disorders. *JAMA Psychiatry, 71,* 301–309. doi:10.1001/jamapsychiatry.2013.4081

McKee, A. C., Daneshvar, D. H., Alvarez, V. E., & Stein, T. D. (2014). The neuropathology of sport. *Acta Neuropathologica, 127,* 29–51. doi:10.1007/s00401-013-1230-6

McKee, A. C., Stein, T. D., Nowinski, C. J., Stern, R. A., Daneshvar, D. H., Alvarez, V. E., . . . Cantu, R. C. (2013). The spectrum of disease in chronic traumatic encephalopathy. *Brain: A Journal of Neurology, 136,* 43–64. doi:10.1093/brain/aws307

McKellar, P. (1972). Imagery from the standpoint of introspection. In P. W. Sheehan (Ed.), *The function and nature of imagery* (pp. 36–61). New York, NY: Academic Press.

McKim, D. B., Niraula, A., Tarr, A. J., Wohleb, E. S., Sheridan, J. F., & Godbout, J. P. (2016). Neuroinflammatory dynamics underlie memory impairments after repeated social defeat. *The Journal of Neuroscience, 36,* 2590–2604. doi:10.1523/JNEUROSCI.2394-15.2016

McKinnon, M. C., Palombo, D. J., Nazarov, A., Kumar, N., Khuu, W., & Levine, B. (2015). Threat of death and autobiographical memory: A study of passengers from flight AT236. *Clinical Psychological Science, 3,* 487–502. doi:10.1177/2167702614542280

McLean, C. P., Su, Y. J., & Foa, E. B. (2015). Mechanisms of symptom reduction in a combined treatment for comorbid posttraumatic stress disorder and alcohol dependence. *Journal of Consulting and Clinical Psychology, 83,* 655–661. doi:10.1037/ccp0000024

McLean, D., Thara, R., John, S., Barrett, R., Loa, P., McGrath, J., & Mowry, B. (2014). DSM-IV "criterion A" schizophrenia symptoms across ethnically different populations: Evidence for differing psychotic symptom content or structural organization? *Culture, Medicine and Psychiatry, 38,* 406–426. doi:10.1007/s11013-014-9385-8

McLeigh, J. D. (2015). Creating conditions that promote trust and participation by young people . . . And why it matters. *American Journal of Orthopsychiatry, 85*, S67–S69. http://dx.doi.org/10.1037/ort0000134

McMurran, M., & Crawford, M. J. (2016). Personality disorders. In C. M. Nezu & A. M. Nezu (Eds.), *The Oxford handbook of cognitive and behavioral therapies* (pp. 438–461). New York, NY: Oxford University Press.

McNally, R. J. (2012). Searching for repressed memory. *Nebraska Symposium on Motivation, 58,* 121–147. doi:10.1007/978-1-4614-1195-6_4

Meaidi, A., Jennum, P., Ptito, M., & Kupers, R. (2014). The sensory construction of dreams and nightmare frequency in congenitally blind and late blind individuals. *Sleep Medicine, 15,* 586–595. doi:10.1016/j.sleep.2013.12.008

Media Matters. (2016). Tavis Smiley blasts "political sycophants" for "scapegoating" Black lives matter. *The Place for Politics*. Retrieved from http://www.mediamatters.org/video/2016/07/18/tavis-smiley-blasts-political-sycophants-scapegoating-black-lives-matter/211670

Mehrabian, A. (1968). A relationship of attitude to seated posture orientation and distance. *Journal of Personality and Social Psychology, 10,* 26–30. doi:10.1037/h0026384

Mehrabian, A. (1971). *Silent messages.* Belmont, CA: Cengage Learning.

Mehrabian, A. (2007). *Nonverbal communication.* New Brunswick, NJ: Aldine Transaction.

Mehra, R., & Strohl, K. P. (2014). Pharmacology of sleep medicine. In K. Strohl (Ed.), *Competencies in sleep medicine* (pp. 27–44). New York, NY: Springer. doi:10.1007/978-1-4614-9065-4_3

Meier, M. H., Caspi, A., Cerdá, M., Hancox, R. J., Harrington, H., Houts, R., . . . Moffitt, T. E. (2016). Associations between cannabis use and physical health problems in early midlife: A longitudinal comparison of persistent cannabis vs tobacco. *JAMA Psychiatry, 73,* 731–740. doi:10.1001/jamapsychiatry.2016.0637

Meirick, P. C., & Schartel Dunn, S. (2015). Obama as exemplar: Debate exposure and implicit and explicit racial affect. *Howard Journal of Communications, 26,* 57–73. doi:10.1080/10646175.2014.986312

Meldrum, R. C., Barnes, J. C., & Hay, C. (2015). Sleep deprivation, low self-control, and delinquency: A test of the strength model of self-control. *Journal of Youth and Adolescence, 44,* 465–477. doi:10.1007/s10964-013-0024-4

Meletti, S. (2016). Emotion recognition. In M. Mula (Ed.), *Neuropsychiatric symptoms of epilepsy. Neuropsychiatric symptoms of neurological disease* (pp. 177–193). Cham, CH: Springer International Publishing. doi:10.1007/978-3-319-22159-5_11

Meltzoff, A. N., & Moore, M. K. (1977). Imitation of facial and manual gestures by human neonates. *Science, 198,* 75–78. doi:10.1126/science.198.4312.75

Meltzoff, A. N., & Moore, M. K. (1985). Cognitive foundations and social functions of imitation and intermodal representation in infancy. In J. Mehler & R. Fox (Eds.), *Neonate cognition: Beyond the blooming buzzing confusion* (pp. 139-156). Hillsdale, NJ: Erlbaum.

Meltzoff, A. N., & Moore, M. K. (1994). Imitation, memory, and the representation of persons. *Infant Behavior and Development, 17,* 83–99.

Melzack, R. (1999). Pain and stress: A new perspective. In R. J. Gatchel & D. C. Turk (Eds.), *Psychosocial factors in pain: Critical perspectives* (pp. 89–106). New York, NY: Guilford.

Melzack, R., & Wall, P. D. (1965). Pain mechanisms: A new theory. *Science, 150,* 971–979.

Memili, E., Chang, E. P. C., Kellermanns, F. W., & Welsh, D. H. B. (2015). Role conflicts of family members in family firms. *European Journal of Work and Organizational Psychology, 24,* 143–151. doi:10.1080/1359432X.2013.839549

Meredith, S. E., Jarvis, B. P., Raiff , B. R., Rojewski, A. M., Kurti, A., Cassidy, R. N., . . . Dallery, J. (2014). The ABCs of incentive-based treatment in health care: A behavior analytic framework to inform research and practice. *Psychology Research and Behavior Management, 7,* 103–114. doi:10.2147/PRBM.S59792

Mermelshtine, R., & Barnes, J. (2016). Maternal responsive–didactic caregiving in play interactions with 10-month-olds and cognitive development at 18 months. *Infant and Child Development, 25,* 296–316. http://dx.doi.org/10.1002/icd.1961

Metgud, D., & Honap, R. (2015). Comparison of kangaroo mother care and tactile kinesthetic stimulation in low birth weight babies—An experimental study. *International Journal on Disability and Human Development, 14,* 147-150. doi:10.1515/ijdhd-2014-0011

Mettler, E., Massey, C. M., & Kellman, P. J. (2016). A comparison of adaptive and fixed schedules of practice. *Journal of Experimental Psychology: General, 145,* 897-917. http://dx.doi.org/10.1037/xge0000170

Metzl, J., & MacLeish, K. T. (2015). Mental illness, mass shootings, and the politics of American firearms. *American Journal of Public Health, 105,* 240–249. doi:10.2105/AJPH.2014.302242

Meyer, U. (2016). Rodent models of multiple environmental exposures with relevance to schizophrenia. In M. V. Pletnikov & J. Waddington (Eds.), *Modeling the psychopathological dimensions of schizophrenia: From molecules to behavior* (pp. 361–371). San Diego, CA: Elsevier Academic Press.

Mezick, E. J., Matthews, K. A., Hall, M. H., Jennings, J. R., & Kamarck, T. W. (2014). Sleep duration and cardiovascular responses to stress in undergraduate men. *Psychophysiology, 51,* 88–96. doi:10.1111/psyp.12144

Michael, R. B., & Garry, M. (2016). Ordered questions bias eyewitnesses and jurors. *Psychonomic Bulletin & Review, 23,* 601–608. http://dx.doi.org/10.3758/s13423-015-0933-1

Mikels, J. A., & Shuster, M. M. (2016). The interpretative lenses of older adults are not rose-colored—just less dark: Aging and the interpretation of ambiguous scenarios. *Emotion, 16,* 94–100. http://dx.doi.org/10.1037/emo0000104

Miklikowska, M. (2015). Like parent, like child? Development of prejudice and tolerance towards immigrants. *British Journal of Psychology, 107,* 95–116. doi:10.1111/bjop.12124

Mikulincer, M., Shaver, P. R., Borgida, E., & Bargh, J. A. (Eds.). (2015a). *APA handbook of personality and social psychology, Vol. 1. Attitudes and social cognition.* Washington, DC: American Psychological Association. doi:10.1037/14341-000

Mikulincer, M., Shaver, P. R., Dovidio, J. F., & Simpson, J. A. (Eds.). (2015b). *APA handbook of personality and social psychology, Vol. 2. Group processes.* Washington, DC: American Psychological Association. doi:10.1037/14342-000

Milgram, S. (1963). Behavioral study of obedience. *Journal of Abnormal and Social Psychology, 67,* 371–378.

Milgram, S. (1974). *Obedience to authority: An experimental view.* New York, NY: Harper & Row.

Miller, A. A., & Spencer, S. J. (2014). Obesity and neuroinflammation: A pathway to cognitive impairment. *Brain, Behavior, and Immunity, 42,* 10–21. doi:10.1016/j.bbi.2014.04.001

Miller, B. R., & Hen, R. (2015). The current state of the neurogenic theory of depression and anxiety. *Current Opinion in Neurobiology, 30,* 51–58. doi:10.1007/978-94-017-9576-0

Miller, D. I., & Halpern, D. F. (2014). The new science of cognitive sex differences.*Trends in Cognitive Sciences, 18,* 37–45. doi:10.1016/j.tics.2013.10.011

Miller, D. P., & Brooks-Gunn, J. (2015). Obesity. In T. P. Gullotta, R. W. Plant, & M. A. Evans (Eds.), *Handbook of adolescent behavioral problems: Evidence-based approaches to prevention and treatment* (2nd ed., pp. 287–304). New York, NY: Springer. doi:10.1007/978-1-4899-7497-6_15

Miller, G. A. (1956). The magical number seven, plus or minus two: Some limits on our capacity for processing information. *Psychological Review, 63,* 81–97. doi:10.1037/h0043158

Miller, J. G., & Bersoff , D. M. (1998). The role of liking in perceptions of the moral responsibility to help: A cultural perspective. *Journal of Experimental Social Psychology, 34,* 443–469. doi:10.1006/jesp.1998.1359

Miller, J. L., Saklofske, D. H., Weiss, L. G., Drozdick, L., Llorente, A. M., Holdnack, J. A., & Prifitera, A. (2016). Issues related to the WISC-V assessment of cognitive functioning in clinical and special groups. In L. G. Weiss, D. H. Saklofske, J. A. Holdnack & A. Prifitera

(Eds.), *WISC-V assessment and interpretation: Scientist-practitioner perspectives* (pp. 287–343). San Diego, CA: Elsevier Academic Press. http://dx.doi.org/10.1016/B978-0-12-404697-9.00010-8

Miller, K. B., Lund, E., & Weatherly, J. (2012). Applying operant learning to the stay-leave decision in domestic violence. *Behavior and Social Issues, 21,* 135–151. doi:10.5210/bsi.v21i0.4015

Miller, S. D., Hubble, M. A., Chow, D. L., & Seidel, J. A. (2013). The outcome of psychotherapy: Yesterday, today, and tomorrow. *Psychotherapy, 50,* 88–97. http://dx.doi.org/10.1037/a0031097

Millings, A., Walsh, J., Hepper, E., & O'Brien, M. (2013). Good partner, good parent: Responsiveness mediates the link between romantic attachment and parenting style. *Personality and Social Psychology Bulletin, 39,* 170–180. doi:10.1177/0146167212468333

Mills, P. L., Redwine, L., Wilson, K., Pung, M. A., Chinh, K., Greenberg, B. H., . . . Chopra, D. (2013). The role of gratitude in spiritual well-being in asymptomatic heart failure patients. *Spirituality in Clinical Practice, 2,* 5–17. doi:http://dx.doi.org/10.1037/scp0000050

Milojev, P., Osborne, D., & Sibley, C. G. (2014). Personality resilience following a natural disaster. *Social Psychological and Personality Science, 5,* 760–768.

Miltenberger, R. G. (2011). *Behavior modification: Principles and procedures* (5th ed.). Belmont, CA: Cengage Learning.

Mindell, J. A., & Owens, J. A. (2015). *A clinical guide to pediatric sleep: Diagnosis and management of sleep problems* (3rd ed.). Alphen, Netherlands: Wolters Kluwer.

Mineka, S., & Oehlberg, K. (2008). The relevance of recent developments in classical conditioning to understanding the etiology and maintenance of anxiety disorders. *Acta Psychologica, 127,* 567–580.

Minzenberg, M. J., Lesh, T. A., Niendam, T. A., Yoon, J. H., Rhoades, R. N., & Carter, C. S. (2014). Frontal cortex control dysfunction related to long-term suicide risk in recent-onset schizophrenia. *Schizophrenia Research, 157,* 19–25. doi:10.1016/j.schres.2014.05.039

Mischel, W. (1966). Theory and research on the antecedents of self-imposed delay of reward. In B. A. Maher (Ed.), *Progress in experimental personality research* (pp. 85–131). New York, NY: Academic Press.

Mischel, W. (2014). *The marshmallow test: Mastering self-control.* New York, NY: Little, Brown, & Company.

Mischel, W., Ayduk, O., Berman, M. G., Casey, B. J., Gotlib, I. H., Jonides, J., . . . Shoda, Y. (2011). 'Willpower' over the life span: Decomposing self-regulation. *Social Cognitive and Affective Neuroscience, 6,* 252–256. doi:10.1093/scan/nsq08

Mischel, W., & Ebbesen, E. B. (1970). Attention in delay of gratification. *Journal of Personality and Social Psychology, 16,* 329–337. doi:10.1037/h0029815.

Mita, T. H., Dermer, M., & Knight, J. (1977). Reversed facial images and the mere-exposure hypothesis. *Journal of Personality and Social Psychology, 35,* 597–601.

Mitchell, J. M., O'Neil, J. P., Janabi, M., Marks, S. M., Jagust, W. J., & Fields, H. L. (2012). Alcohol consumption induces endogenous opioid release in the human orbitofrontal cortex and nucleus accumbens. *Science Translational Medicine, 4*: 116ra6. doi:10.1126/scitranslmed.3002902

Mitchell, M., & Heads, G. (2015). Staying well: A follow up of a 5-week mindfulness based stress reduction programme for a range of psychological issues. *Community Mental Health Journal, 51,* 897–902. http://dx.doi.org/10.1007/s10597-014-9825-5

Mithoefer, M. C., Grob, C. S., & Brewerton, T. D. (2016). Novel psychopharmacological therapies for psychiatric disorders: Psilocybin and MDMA. *The Lancet Psychiatry, 3,* 481–488.

Mohr, D. C., Ho, J., Duffecy, J., Reifler, D., Sokol, L., Burns, M. N., . . . Siddique, J. (2012). Effect of telephone-administered vs face-to-face cognitive behavioral therapy on adherence to therapy and depression outcomes among primary care patients: A randomized trial. *Journal of the American Medical Association, 307,* 2278–2285. doi:10.1001/jama.2012.5588

Mok, P. L. H., Webb, R. T., Appleby, L., & Pedersen, C. B. (2016). Full spectrum of mental disorders linked with childhood residential mobility. *Journal of Psychiatric Research, 78,* 57–64. http://dx.doi.org/10.1016/j.jpsychires.2016.03.011

Mokrova, I. L., O'Brien, M., Calkins, S. D., Leerkes, E. M., & Marcovitch, S. (2013). The role of persistence at preschool age in academic skills at kindergarten. *European Journal of Psychology of Education, 28,* 1495–1503. doi:10.1007/s10212-013-0177-2

Mokrysz, C., Landy, R., Gage, S. H., Munafò, M. R., Roiser, J. P., & Curran, H. V. (2016). Are IQ and educational outcomes in teenagers related to their cannabis use? A prospective cohort study. *Journal of Psychopharmacology, 30,* 159–168. doi:10.1177/0269881115622241

Møller, A. P., & Erritzøe, J. (2014). Predator-prey interactions, flight initiation distance and brain size. *Journal of Evolutionary Biology, 27,* 34–42. doi:10.1111/jeb.12272

Mondak, J. L., & Canache, D. (2014). Personality and political culture in the American states. *Political Research Quarterly, 67,* 26–41. doi:10.1177/1065912913495112

Monin, B. (2003). The warm glow heuristic: When liking leads to familiarity. *Journal of Personality and Social Psychology, 85,* 1035–1048.

Montag, J. L., Jones, M. N., & Smith, L. B. (2015). The words children hear: Picture books and the statistics for language learning. *Psychological Science, 26,* 1489–1496. doi:10.1177/0956797615594361

Moon, C., Lagercrantz, H., & Kuhl, P. K. (2013). Language experienced in utero affects vowel perception after birth: A two-country study. *ActaPaediatrica, 102,* 156–160. doi:10.1111/apa.12098

Moore, D. L. (2013). USA's Manteo Mitchell runs 4x400 relay on broken leg. *USA Today Sports.* Retrieved from http://usatoday30.usatoday.com/sports/olympics/london/track/story/2012-08-09/usa-man teo-mitchell-runs-4x400-relay-onbroken-leg/56915070/1

Moore, D. W. (2005). Three in four Americans believe in paranormal: Little change from similar results in 2001. *Americas.* Retrieved from http://www.gallup.com/poll/16915/three-four-americans-believe-paranormal.aspx

Moran, J. M., Jolly, E., & Mitchell, J. P. (2014). Spontaneous mentalizing predicts the fundamental attribution error. *Journal of Cognitive Neuroscience, 26,* 569–576. doi:10.1162/jocn_a_00513

Morelli, S. A., Lee, I. A., Arnn, M. E., & Zaki, J. (2015). Emotional and instrumental support provision interact to predict well-being. *Emotion, 15,* 484–493. http://dx.doi.org/10.1037/emo0000084

Morey, L. C. (2013). Measuring personality and psychopathology. In J. A. Schinka, W. F. Velicer, & I. B. Weiner (Eds.), *Handbook of psychology, Vol. 2. Research methods in psychology* (2nd ed., pp. 395–427). Hoboken, NJ: Wiley.

Morgan, C. A., & Southwick, S. (2014). Perspective: I believe what I remember, but it may not be true. *Neurobiology of Learning and Memory, 112,* 101–103. doi:10.1016/j.nlm.2013.12.011

Morgan, C. A., Southwick, S., Steffian, G., Hazlett, G. A., & Loftus, E. F. (2013). Misinformation can influence memory for recently experienced, highly stressful events. *International Journal of Law and Psychiatry, 36,* 11–17. doi:10.1016/j.ijlp.2012.11.002

Mori, K., Ito-Koyama, A., Arai, M., & Hanayama, A. (2014). Boys, be independent! Conformity development of Japanese children in the Asch experiment without using confederates. *Psychology, 5,* 617–623. doi:10.4236/psych.2014.57073.

Morin, C. M., & Edinger, J. D. (2015). Sleep-wake disorders. In P. H. Blaney, R. F. Krueger, & T. Millon (Eds.), *Oxford textbook of psychopathology* (3rd ed., pp. 566–588). New York, NY: Oxford University Press.

Morin, C. M., Savard, J., & Ouellet, M.-C. (2013). Nature and treatment of insomnia. In A. M. Nezu, C. M. Nezu, P. A. Geller, & I. B. Weiner (Eds.), *Handbook of psychology, Vol. 9. Health psychology* (2nd ed., pp. 318–339). Hoboken, NJ: Wiley.

Morin-Major, J. K., Marin, M.-F., Durand, N., Wan, N., Juster, R. P., & Lupien, S. J. (2016). Facebook behaviors associated with diurnal cortisol in adolescents: Is befriending stressful? *Psychoneuroendocrinology, 63,* 238–246. http://dx.doi.org/10.1016/j.psyneuen.2015.10.005

Morling, B. (2015). *Research methods in psychology: Evaluating a world of information* (2nd ed.). New York, NY: W.W. Norton & Company.

Morris, B. (2015). *Anthropology of the self: The individual in cultural perspective.* London, UK: Pluto.

Morrison, A. B., Goolsarran, M., Rogers, S. L., & Jha, A. P. (2013). Taming a wandering attention: Short-form mindfulness training in student cohorts. *Frontiers in Human Neuroscience, 7,* 897. http://doi.org/10.3389/fnhum.2013.00897

Morry, M. M., Kito, M., & Dunphy, L. (2014). How do I see you? Partner enhancement in dating couples. *Canadian Journal of Behavioural Science, 46,* 356–365. doi:10.1037/a0033167

Mosher, C., & Akins, S. (2014). *Drugs and drug policy* (2nd ed.). Thousand Oaks, CA: Sage.

Moskowitz, J. T., Epel, E. S., & Acree, M. (2008). Positive affect uniquely predicts lower risk of mortality in people with diabetes. *Health Psychology, 27,* S73–S82. doi:10.1037/0278-6133.27.1.S73

Moulding, N. (2016). *Gendered violence, mental health and recovery in everyday lives: Beyond trauma.* London, UK: Taylor & Francis.

Moutinho, A., Pereira, A., & Jorge, G. (2011). Biology of homosexuality. *European Psychiatry, 26,* 1741–1753.

Moutsiana, C., Johnstone, T., Murray, L., Fearon, P., Cooper, P. J., Pliatsikas, C., . . . Halligan, S. L. (2015). Insecure attachment during infancy predicts greater amygdala volumes in early adulthood. *Journal of Child Psychology and Psychiatry, 56,* 540–548. doi:10.1111/jcpp.12317

Mrazek, M. D., Franklin, M. S., Phillips, D. T., Baird, B., & Schooler, J. W. (2013). Mindfulness training improves working memory capacity and GRE performance while reducing mind wandering. *Psychological Science, 24,* 776–781. doi:10.1177/0956797612459659

Mueller, P. A., & Oppenheimer, D. M. (2014). The pen is mightier than the keyboard: Advantages of longhand over laptop note taking. *Psychological Science, 25,* 1159–1168. doi:10.1177/0956797614524581

Muise, A., Schimmack, U., & Impett, E. A. (2016). Sexual frequency predicts greater well-being, but more is not always better. *Social Psychological and Personality Science, 7,* 295–302. doi:10.1177/1948550615616462

Mujcic, R., & Frijters, P. (2013). Still not allowed on the bus: It matters if you're Black or White! *IZA Discussion Paper No. 7300.*

Mullen, N. W., Maxwell, H., & Bédard, M. (2015). Decreasing driver speeding with feedback and a token economy. *Transportation Research Part F: Traffic Psychology and Behaviour, 28,* 77–85. doi:10.1016/j.trf.2014.11.008

Muller, C. A., Schmitt, K., Barber, A. L. A., & Hubert, L. (2015). Dogs can discriminate emotional expressions of human faces. *Current Biology, 5,* 601–605. doi.org/10.1016/j.cub.2014.12.055

Müller, C. P., & Homberg, J. R. (2015). The role of serotonin in drug use and addiction. *Behavioural Brain Research, 277,* 146–192. doi:10.1016/j.bbr.2014.04.007

Müller, S., Mychajliw, C., Hautzinger, M., Fallgatter, A. J., Saur, R., & Leyhe, T. (2014). Memory for past public events depends on retrieval frequency but not memory age in Alzheimer's disease. *Journal of Alzheimer's Disease, 38,* 379–390. doi:10.3233/JAD-130923

Munoz, L., & Anastassiou-Hadjicharalambous, X. (2011). Disinhibited behaviors in young children: Relations with impulsivity and autonomic psychophysiology. *Biological Psychology, 86,* 349–359.

Munsey, C. (2006). Emerging adults: The in-between age. *Monitor on Psychology, 37,* 68. Retrieved from http://www.apa.org/monitor/jun06/emerging.aspx

Murayama, K., Perkrun, R., Lichtenfeld, S., & vomHofe, R. (2012). Predicting long-term growth in students' mathematics achievement: The unique contributions of motivation and cognitive strategies. *Child Development, 84,* 1475–1490. doi:10.1111/cdev.12036

Murdock, K. K. (2013). Texting while stressed: Implications for students' burnout, sleep, and well-being. *Psychology of Popular Media Culture, 2,* 207–221. doi:10.1037/ppm0000012

Murray, H. A. (1938). *Explorations in personality.* Oxford, UK: Oxford.

Nagasawa, M., Mitsui, S., En, S., Ohtani, N., Ohta, M., Sakuma, Y., . . . Kikusui, T. (2015). Oxytocin-gaze positive loop and the coevolution of human-dog bonds. *Science, 348,* 333–336. doi:10.1126/science.1261022.

Nairne, J. S., & Neath, I. (2013). Sensory and working memory. In A. F. Healy, R. W. Proctor, & I. B. Weiner (Eds.), *Handbook of psychology, Vol. 4. Experimental psychology* (2nd ed., pp. 419–445). Hoboken, NJ: Wiley.

Na, J., & Chan, M. Y. (2015). Culture, cognition, and intercultural relations. In J. E. Warnick & D. Landis (Eds.), *Neuroscience in intercultural contexts* (pp. 49–71). New York, NY: Springer Science + Business Media. http://dx.doi.org/10.1007/978-1-4939-2260-4_3

Nakai, Y., Nin, K., Noma, S. I., Hamagaki, S., Takagi, R., & Wonderlich, S. A. (2014). Outcome of eating disorders in a Japanese sample: A 4-to 9-year follow-up study. *European Eating Disorders Review, 22,* 206–211. doi:10.1002/erv.2290

Naneix, F., Darlot, F., Coutureau, E., & Cador, M. (2016). Long-lasting deficits in hedonic and nucleus accumbens reactivity to sweet rewards by sugar overconsumption during adolescence. *European Journal of Neuroscience, 43,* 671–680. doi:10.1111/ejn.13149

Naselaris, T., Olman, C. A., Stansbury, D. E., Ugurbil, K., & Gallant, J. L. (2015). A voxel-wise encoding model for early visual areas decodes mental images of remembered scenes. *NeuroImage, 105,* 215–228. doi:10.1016/j.neuroimage.2014.10.018

Nash, R. A., Nash, A., Morris, A., & Smith, S. L. (2016). Does rapport-building boost the eyewitness eye closure effect in closed questioning? *Legal and Criminological Psychology.* No Pagination Specified. doi:10.1111/lcrp.12073

National Alliance on Mental Health. (2015). People with mental illness enrich our lives. *National Alliance on Mental Illness.* Retrieved May 24, 2015 from http://www2.nami.org/Template.cfm?Section=Helpline1&template=/ContentManagement/ContentDisplay.cfm&ContentID=4858

National Institute of Mental Health (NIMH). (2016). Any anxiety disorder among adults. *NIMH.* Retrieved August 3, 2016 from http://www.nimh.nih.gov/health/statistics/index.shtml

National Institute of Mental Health (NIMH). (2014). Post-traumatic stress disorder. *NIH.gov.* Retrieved from http://www.nimh.nih.gov/health/publications/post-traumatic-stress-disorder-ptsd/index.shtml

National Sleep Foundation. (2012). *National sleep foundation sleepiness test.* Retrieved from https://sleepfoundation.org/quiz/national-sleep-foundation-sleepiness-test

Navarro, P., & Hurtado, I. (2015). Corporality and trauma. In M. Sáenz-Herrero (Ed.), *Psychopathology in women: Incorporating gender perspective into descriptive psychopathology* (pp. 161–183). Cham, CH: Springer International Publishing. doi:10.1007/978-3-319-05870-2

Neale, J. M., Oltmanns, T. F., & Winters, K. C. (1983). Recent developments in the assessment and conceptualization of schizophrenia. *Behavioral Assessment, 5,* 33–54.

Neher, A. (1991). Maslow's theory of motivation: A critique. *Journal of Humanistic Psychology, 31,* 89–112. doi:10.1177/0022167891313010

Neisser, U. (1967). *Cognitive psychology.* New York, NY: Appleton-Century-Crofts.

Nelson, C. A., Fox, N. A., & Zeanah, C. H. (2014). *Romania's abandoned children: Deprivation, brain development, and the struggle for recovery.* Cambridge, MA: Harvard University Press.

Ness, R. B. (2015). Promoting innovative thinking. *American Journal of Public Health, 105,* S114–S118. doi:10.2105/AJPH.2014.302365

Neubauer, A. C., Grabner, R. H., Freudenthaler, H. H., Beckmann, J. F., & Guthke, J. (2004). Intelligence and individual differences in becoming neurally efficient. *ActaPsychologica, 116,* 55–74. doi:10.1016/j.actpsy.2003.11.005

Neumann, A., & Walter, S. (2015). Depression as an adaptation: The infection–defense hypothesis and cytokine mechanisms. In T. Breyer (Ed.), *Epistemological dimensions of evolutionary psychology* (pp. 175–196). New York, NY: Springer. doi:10.1007/978-1-4939-1387-9_9

Newcombe, N. S. (2010). On tending to our scientific knitting: Thinking about gender in the context of evolution. In J. C. Chrisler & D. R. McCreary (Eds.), *Handbook of gender research in psychology, Vol. 1. Gender research in general and experimental psychology* (pp. 259–274). New York, NY: Springer.

New, J. J., & German, T. C. (2015). Spiders at the cocktail party: An ancestral threat that surmounts inattentional blindness. *Evolution and Human Behavior, 36,* 165–173. doi:10.1016/j.evolhumbehav.2014.08.004

Newman, B. W., & Newman, P. R. (2015). *Theories of human development* (2nd ed.). New York, NY: Psychology Press.

Ng, A. M., Chong, C. L. Y., Ching, J. Y. X., Beh, J. L., & Lim, P. P. F. (2015). A critical comparison of the psychoanalytic and humanistic theory. *Academia.edu.* Retrieved from http://www.academia.edu/7304762/A_Critical_Comparison_of_the_Psychoanalytic_and_Humanistic_Theory

Ng, H. B., Kao, K. L., Chan, Y. C., Chew, E., Chuang, K. H. & Chen, S. H. (2016). Modality specificity in the cerebro-cerebellar neurocircuitry during working memory. *Behavioural Brain Research, 305,* 164–173. doi:10.1016/j.bbr.2016.02.027

Ng, T. H., Chung, K.-F., Ho, F. Y.-Y., Yeung, W.-F., Yung, K.-P., & Lam, T.-H. (2015). Sleep-wake disturbance in interepisode bipolar disorder and high-risk individuals: A systematic review and meta-analysis. *Sleep Medicine Reviews, 20,* 46–58. doi:10.1016/j.smrv.2014.06.006

Nguyen, T., & Szymanski, B. (2012). Using location-based social networks to validate human mobility and relationships models. *Proceedings of the 2012 IEEE/ACM International Conference on Advances in Social Networks Analysis and Mining,* pp. 1247–1253.

Nichols, D. E. (2016). Psychedelics. *Pharmacological Reviews, 68,* 264–355. doi:10.1124/pr.115.011478

Nickerson, R. (1998). Confirmation bias: A ubiquitous phenomenon in many guises. *Review of General Psychology, 2,* 175–220. doi:10.1037/10892680.2.2.175

Nickerson, R. S., & Adams, M. J. (1979). Long-term memory for a common object. *Cognitive Psychology, 11,* 287–307. doi:10.1016/0010-0285(79)90013-6

Nicklaus, S. (2016). The role of food experiences during early childhood in food pleasure learning. *Appetite, 104,* 3–9. http://dx.doi.org/10.1016/j.appet.2015.08.022

Nicolaides, N. C., Kyratzi, E., Lamprokostopoulou, A., Chrousos, G. P., & Charmandari, E. (2015). Stress, the stress system and the role of glucocorticoids. *Neuroimmunomodulation, 22,* 6–19. doi:10.1159/000362736)

NIDA. (2016, May 14). Club drugs. *National Institute of Drug Abuse (NIDA).* Retrieved from https://www.drugabuse.gov/drugs-abuse/club-drugs

Nielsen, T., O'Reilly, C., Carr, M., Dumel, G., Godin, L., Solomonova, E., . . . Paquette, T. (2015). Overnight improvements in two REM sleep-sensitive tasks are associated with both REM and NREM sleep changes, sleep spindle features, and awakenings for dream recall. *Neurobiology of Learning and Memory, 122,* 88–97. doi:10.1016/j.nlm.2014.09.007

Nierenberg, B., Mayersohn, G., Serpa, S., Holovatyk, A., Smith, E., & Cooper, S. (2016). Application of well-being therapy to people with disability and chronic illness. *Rehabilitation Psychology, 61,* 32–43. http://dx.doi.org/10.1037/rep0000060

NIH. (2016). Infant and newborn development. *National Institute of Health.* Retrieved from https://www.nlm.nih.gov/medlineplus/infantandnewborndevelopment.html

Nishimoto, R. (1988). A cross-cultural analysis of psychiatric symptom expression using Langer's twenty-two item index. *Journal of Sociology and Social Welfare, 15,* 45–62.

Nishitani, S., Miyamura, T., Tagawa, M., Sumi, M., Takase, R., Doi, H., . . . Shinohara, K. (2009). The calming effect of a maternal breast milk odor on the human newborn infant. *Neuroscience Research, 63,* 66–71. doi:10.1016/j.neures.2008.10.007

Noble, K. G., Houston, S. M., Brito, N. H., Bartsch, H., Kan, E., Kuperman, J. M., . . . Sowell, E. R. (2015). Family income, parental education and brain structure in children and adolescents. *Nature Neuroscience, 18,* 773–778. doi:10.1038/nn.3983

Nolan, D., & Amico, C. (2016, February 23). How bad is the opiod epidemic? *Frontline.* Retrieved from http://www.pbs.org/wgbh/frontline/article/how-bad-is-the-opioid-epidemic/

Nolan, P. (2012). *Therapist and client: A relational approach to psychotherapy.* Malden, MA: Wiley-Blackwell.

Norbury, A., & Husain, M. (2015). Sensation-seeking: Dopaminergic modulation and risk for psychopathology. *Behavioural Brain Research, 288,* 79–93. http://dx.doi.org/10.1016/j.bbr.2015.04.015

Normandin, L., Ensink, K., & Kernberg, O. F. (2015). Transference-focused psychotherapy for borderline adolescents: A neurobiologically informed psychodynamic psychotherapy. *Journal of Infant, Child & Adolescent Psychotherapy, 14,* 98–110. doi:10.1080/15289168.2015.1006008

North, A. C., Sheridan, L. P., & Areni, C. S. (2016). Music congruity effects on product memory, perception, and choice. *Journal of Retailing, 92, 83–95.* doi:10.1016/j.jretai.2015.06.001

Northcote, J., & Livingston, M. (2011). Accuracy of self-reported drinking: Observational verification of "last occasion" drink estimates of young adults. *Alcohol and Alcoholism, 46,* 709–713. doi:10.1093/alcalc/agr138

Noval, L. J., & Stahl, G. K. (2015). Accounting for proscriptive and prescriptive morality in the workplace: The double-edged sword effect of mood on managerial ethical decision making. *Journal of Business Ethics.* No Pagination Specified. doi:10.1007/s10551-015-2767-1

Nowicki, S. (2016). *Choice or chance: Understanding your locus of control and why it matters.* New York, NY: Prometheus Books.

Oarga, C., Stavrova, O., & Fetchenhauer, D. (2015). When and why is helping others good for well-being? The role of belief in reciprocity and conformity to society's expectations. *European Journal of Social Psychology, 45,* 242–254. doi:10.1002/ejsp.2092

Obschonka, M., Schmitt-Rodermund, E., Silbereisen, R. K., Gosling, S. D., & Potter, J. (2013). The regional distribution and correlates of an entrepreneurship-prone personality profile in the United States, Germany, and the United Kingdom: A socioecological perspective. *Journal of Personality and Social Psychology, 105,* 104–122. doi:10.1037/a0032275

Ockerman, E. (2016, June 22). 'Infant trackers' help parents keep tables on their babies. *Time.* Retrieved from http://time.com/4376283/quantified-self-parents-apps/

O'Farrell, T. J., Schumm, J. A., Dunlap, L. J., Murphy, M. M., & Muchowski, P. (2016). A randomized clinical trial of group versus standard behavioral couples therapy plus individually based treatment for patients with alcohol dependence. *Journal of Consulting and Clinical Psychology, 84,* 497–510. http://dx.doi.org/10.1037/ccp0000089

Oglesby, M. E., Raines, A. M., Short, N. A., Capron, D. W., & Schmidt, N. B. (2016). Interpretation bias for uncertain threat: A replication and extension. *Journal of Behavior Therapy and Experimental Psychiatry, 51,* 35–42. http://dx.doi.org/10.1016/j.jbtep.2015.12.006

Ohayon, M. M., Mahowald, M. W., Dauvilliers, Y., Krystal, A. D., & Leger, D. (2012). Prevalence and comorbidity of nocturnal wandering in the US adult general population. *Neurology, 78,* 1583–1589.

Okouchi, H., Lattal, K., Sonoda, A., & Nakamae, T. (2014). Stimulus control and generalization of remote behavioral history. *Journal of the Experimental Analysis of Behavior, 101,* 275–287. doi:10.1002/jeab.75

Olds, J., & Milner, P. M. (1954). Positive reinforcement produced by electrical stimulation of septal area and other regions of rat brains. *Journal of Comparative and Physiological Psychology, 47,* 419–427.

Olenski, A. R., Abola, M. V., & Jena, A. B. (2015). Do heads of government age more quickly? Observational study comparing mortality between elected leaders and runners-up in national elections of 17 countries. *British Medical Journal, 351*:h6424. http://dx.doi.org/10.1136/bmj.h6424

Oller, J. W., Jr., Oller, S. D., & Oller, S. N. (2014). *Milestones: Normal speech and language development across the life span* (2nd ed.). San Diego, CA: Plural.

Ollmann, T., Péczely, L., László, K., Kovács, A., Gálosi, R., Berente, E., . . . Zoltán, L. L. (2015). Positive reinforcing effect of neurotensin microinjection into the ventralpallidum in conditioned place preference test. *Behavioural Brain Research, 278,* 470–475. doi:10.1016/j.bbr.2014.10.021

Olsen, L. R., Jensen, D. V., Noerholm, V., Martiny, K., & Bech, P. (2003). The internal and external validity of the Major Depression Inventory in measuring severity of depressive states. *Psychological Medicine, 33,* 351–356.

Olulade, O. A., Jamal, N. I., Koo, D. S., Perfetti, C. A., LaSasso, C., & Eden, G. F. (2016). Neuroanatomical evidence in support of the bilingual advantage theory. *Cerebral Cortex, 26,* 3196–3204. doi:10.1093/cercor/bhv152

O'Neil, J. M. (2015). *Men's gender role conflict: Psychological costs, consequences, and an agenda for change.* Washington, DC: American Psychological Association. http://dx.doi.org/10.1037/14501-000

O'Neill, J. W., & Davis, K. (2011). Work stress and well-being in the hotel industry. *International Journal of Hospitality Management, 30,* 385–390. doi:10.1016/j.ijhm.2010.07.007

Oppezzo, M., & Schwartz, D. L. (2014). Give your ideas some legs: The positive effect of walking on creative thinking. *Journal of Experimental Psychology: Learning, Memory, and Cognition, 40,* 1142–1152. doi:10.1037/a0036577

Oram, S., Trevillion, K., Feder, G., & Howard, L. M. (2013). Prevalence of experiences of domestic violence among psychiatric patients: Systematic review. *The British Journal of Psychiatry, 202,* 94–99.

Ormerod, T. C., & Dando, C. J. (2015). Finding a needle in a haystack: Toward a psychologically informed method for aviation security screening. *Journal of Experimental Psychology: General, 144,* 76–84. doi:10.1037/xge0000030

Orth-Gomér, K., Schneiderman, N., Vaccarino, V., & Deter, H.-C. (Eds.). (2015). *Psychosocial stress and cardiovascular disease in women: Concepts, findings, future perspectives.* Washington, DC: American Psychological Association. doi:10.1007/978-3-319-09241-6

Oswald, M. E., Bieneck, S., & Hupfeld-Heinemann, J. (Eds.). (2015). *Social psychology of punishment and crime.* Hoboken, NJ: Wiley-Blackwell.

Ottaviano, G., Marioni, G., Frasson, G., Zuccarello, D., Marchese-Ragona, R., Staffieri, C., . . . Staffieri, A. (2015). Olfactory threshold for bourgeonal and sexual desire in young adult males. *Medical Hypotheses, 84,* 437–441. doi:10.1016/j.mehy.2015.01.035

Ottavi, P., Passarella, T., Pasinetti, M., Salvatore, G., & Dimaggio, G. (2016). Adapting mindfulness for treating personality disorder. In W. J. Livesley, G. Dimaggio, & J. F. Clarkin (Eds.), *Integrated treatment for personality disorder: A modular approach* (pp. 282–302). New York, NY: Guilford.

Oudekerk, B. A., Allen, J. P., Hessel, E. T., & Molloy, L. E. (2015). The cascading development of autonomy and relatedness from adolescence to adulthood. *Child Development, 86,* 472–485. doi:10.1111/cdev.12313

Oudiette, D., Dealberto, M.-J., Uguccioni, G., Golmard, J.-L., Merino-Andreu, M., Tafti, M., . . . Arnulf, I. (2012). Dreaming without REM sleep. *Consciousness and Cognition: An International Journal, 21,* 1129–1140. doi:10.1016/j.concog.2012.04.010

Ozturk, O., Shayan, S., Liszkowski, U., & Majid, A. (2013). Language is not necessary for color categories. *Developmental Science, 16,* 111–115.

Pacek, L. R., Mauro, P. M., & Martins, S. S. (2015). Perceived risk of regular cannabis use in the United States from 2002 to 2012: Differences by sex, age, and race/ethnicity. *Drug and Alcohol Dependence, 149,* 232–244.

Pack, A. A. (2015). Experimental studies of dolphin cognitive abilities. In D. L. Herzing & C. M. Johnson (Eds.), *Dolphin communication and cognition: Past, present, and future* (pp. 175–200). Cambridge, MA: MIT Press.

Pagano, M. E., Wang, A. R., Rowles, B. M., Lee, M. T., & Johnson, B. R. (2015). Social anxiety and peer helping in adolescent addiction treatment. *Alcoholism: Clinical and Experimental Research, 39,* 887–895. doi:10.1111/acer.12691

Pagano, M. E., White, W. L., Kelly, J. F., Stout, R. L., & Tonigan, J. S. (2013). The 10-year course of AA participation and long-term outcomes: A follow-up study of outpatient subjects in Project MATCH. *Substance Abuse, Special Issue, 31,* 51–59.

Paiva, T., Gaspar, T., & Matos, M. G. (2015). Sleep deprivation in adolescents: Correlations with health complaints and health-related quality of life. *Sleep Medicine, 16,* 521–527. doi:10.1016/j.sleep.2014.10.010

Paivio, A. (1995). *Mental representations: A dual coding approach.* New York, NY: Oxford University Press.

Palermo, T. M., Law, E. F., Fales, J., Bromberg, M. H., Jessen-Fiddick, T., & Tai, G. (2016). Internet-delivered cognitive-behavioral treatment for adolescents with chronic pain and their parents: A randomized controlled multicenter trial. *Pain, 157,* 174–185. doi:10.1097/j.pain.0000000000000348.

Palgi, S., Klein, E., & Shamay-Tsoory, S. G. (2015). Intranasal administration of oxytocin increases compassion toward women. *Social Cognitive and Affective Neuroscience, 10,* 311–317. http://dx.doi.org/10.1093/scan/nsu040

Palombo, D. J., McKinnon, M. C., McIntosh, A. R., Anderson, A. K., Todd, R. M., & Levine, B. (2015). The neural correlates of memory for a life-threatening event: An fMRI study of passengers from flight AT236. *Clinical Psychological Science, 4,* 312–319. doi:10.1177/2167702615589308

Paluck, E. L., Shepherd, H., & Aronow, P. M. (2016). Changing climates of conflict: A social network experiment in 56 schools. *Proceedings of the National Academy of Sciences of the United States of America, 113,* 566–571. doi:10.1073/pnas.1514483113

Pandolfo, G., Gugliandolo, A., Gangemi, C., Arrigo, R., Currò, M., La Ciura, G., . . . Caccamo, D. (2015). Association of the COMT synonymous polymorphism Leu136Leu and missense variant Val158Met with mood disorders. *Journal of Affective Disorders, 177,* 108–113. doi:10.1016/j.jad.2015.02.016

Panja, D., & Bramham, C. R. (2014). BDNF mechanisms in late LTP formation: A synthesis and breakdown. *Neuropharmacology, 76,* 664–676. doi:10.1016/j.neuropharm.2013.06.024

Panova, T., & Lleras, A. (2016). Avoidance or boredom: Negative mental health outcomes associated with use of information and communication technologies depend on users' motivations. *Computers in Human Behavior, 58,* 249–258. doi:10.1016/j.chb.2015.12.062

Papageorgiou, C. (2013). Mental health promotion and prejudices. *Psychiatriki, 24,* 166–167.

Papathanasiou, I. V., Tsaras, K., Neroliatsiou, A., & Roupa, A. (2015). Stress: Concepts, theoretical models and nursing interventions. *American Journal of Nursing, 4,* 45–50. doi:10.11648/j.ajns.s.2015040201.19

Pape, A. D., Kurtz, K. J., & Sayama, H. (2015). Complexity measures and concept learning. *Journal of Mathematical Psychology, 64–65,* 66–75. doi:10.1016/j.jmp.2015.01.001

Paris, J. (2015). *A concise guide to personality disorders.* Washington, DC: American Psychological Association. doi:10.1037/14642-006

Park, A. (2016, April 11). 40% of former NFL players had brain injuries. *Time.* Retrieved from http://time.com/4289745/nfl-concussion-symptoms-treatment/

Park, G., Schwartz, H. A., Eichstaedt, J. C., Kern, M. L., Kosinski, M., Stillwell, D. J., . . . Seligman, M. E. P. (2015). Automatic personality assessment through social media language. *Journal of Personality and Social Psychology, 108,* 934–952. http://dx.doi.org/10.1037/pspp0000020

Partyka, M. L., Bond, R. F., Farrar, J., Falco, A., Cassens, B., Cruse, A., & Atwill, E. R. (2014). Quantifying the sensitivity of scent detection dogs to identify fecal contamination on raw produce. *Journal of Food Protection, 77,* 6–14. doi:10.4315/0362-028X.JFP-13-249

Paterson, H. M., Kemp, R. I., & Ng, J. R. (2011). Combating co-witness contamination:

Attempting to decrease the negative effects of discussion on eyewitness memory. *Applied Cognitive Psychology, 25,* 43–52. doi:10.1002/acp.1640

Pathman, T., & Bauer, P. J. (2013). Beyond initial encoding: Measures of the postencoding status of memory traces predict long-term recall during infancy. *Journal of Experimental Child Psychology, 114,* 321–338. doi:10.1016/j.jecp.2012.10.004

Patihis, L., Ho, L. Y., Tingen, I. W., Lilienfeld, S. O., & Loftus, E. F. (2014). Are the "memory wars" over? A scientist-practitioner gap in beliefs about repressed memory. *Psychological Science, 25,* 519–530. doi:10.1177/0956797613510718

Patra, B. N., & Balhara, Y. P. (2012). Creativity and mental disorder. *British Journal of Psychiatry, 200,* 346.

Patterson, F., & Linden, E. (1981). *The education of Koko.* New York, NY: Holt, Rinehart and Winston.

Patterson, P. (2002). Penny's journal: Koko wants to have a baby. *The Gorilla Foundation.* Retrieved from http://www.koko.org/world/journal.phtml?off set57

Pauen, S., & Hoehl, S. (2015). Preparedness to learn about the world: Evidence from infant research. In T. Breyer (Ed.), *Epistemological dimensions of evolutionary psychology* (pp. 159–173). New York, NY: Springer Science + Business Media. doi:10.1007/978-1-4939-1387-9_8

Pauletti, R. E., Menon, M., Cooper, P. J., Aults, C. D., & Perry, D. G. (2016). Psychological androgyny and children's mental health: A new look with new measures. *Sex Roles.* No Pagination Specified. http://dx.doi.org/10.1007/s11199-016-0627-9

Paul, M. A., Love, R. J., Hawton, A., Brett, K., McCreary, D. R., & Arendt, J. (2015). Sleep deficits in the high Arctic summer in relation to light exposure and behaviour: Use of melatonin as a countermeasure. *Sleep Medicine, 16,* 406–413. doi:10.1016/j.sleep.2014.12.012

Paul, M., Lech, R. K., Scheil, J., Dierolf, A. M., Suchan, B., & Wolf, O. T. (2016). Acute stress influences the discrimination of complex scenes and complex faces in young healthy men. *Psychoneuroendocrinology, 66,* 125–129. http://dx.doi.org/10.1016/j.psyneuen.2016.01.007

Pearce, N., Gallo, V., & McElvenny, D. (2015). Head trauma in sport and neurodegenerative disease: An issue whose time has come? *Neurobiology of Aging, 36,* 1383–1389. doi:10.1016/j.neurobiolaging.2014.12.024

Pear, J. J. (2016). *The science of learning* (2nd ed.). New York, NY: Psychology Press.

Pearson, C. M., Wonderlich, S. A., & Smith, G. T. (2015). A risk and maintenance model for bulimia nervosa: From impulsive action to compulsive behavior. *Psychological Review, 122,* 516–535. doi:10.1037/a0039268

Peleg, G., Katzir, G., Peleg, O., Kamara, M., Brodsky, L., Hel-Or, H., . . . Nevo, E. (2006). Hereditary family signature of facial expression. *Proceedings of the National Academy of Sciences of the United States of America, 103,* 15921–15926. doi:10.1073/pnas.0607551103

Pellegrino, R., Kavakli, I. H., Goel, N., Cardinale, C. J., Dinges, D. F., Kuna, S. T., . . . Pack, A. I. (2014). A novel BHLHE41 variant is associated with short sleep and resistance to sleep deprivation in humans. *Sleep, 37,* 1327–1336. doi:10.5665/sleep.3924

Pennebaker, J. W., Gosling, S. D., & Ferrell, J. D. (2013). Daily online testing in large classes: Boosting college performance while reducing achievement gaps. *PLoS ONE, 8:* e79774. doi:10.1371/journal.pone.0079774

Peper, J. S., de Reus, M. A., van den Heuvel, M. P., & Schutter, D. J. L. G. (2015). Short fused? Associations between white matter connections, sex steroids, and aggression across adolescence. *Human Brain Mapping, 36,* 1043–1052. doi:10.1002/hbm.22684

Pérez, P., & Gaviña, J. (2015). Affective disorders. In M. Sáenz-Herrero (Ed.), *Psychopathology in women: Incorporating gender perspective into descriptive psychopathology* (pp. 527–559). Cham, CH: Springer International Publishing. doi:10.1007/978-3-319-05870-2

Perkmen, S., & Sahin, S. (2013). Who should study instructional technology? Vocational personality approach. *British Journal of Educational Technology, 44,* 54–65. doi:10.1111/j.1467-8535.2012.01293.x

Pérusse, L., Rice, T. K., & Bouchard, C. (2014). Genetic component to obesity. In G. Bray & C. Bouchard (Eds.), *Handbook of obesity: Epidemiology, etiology, and physiopathology* (pp. 91–101). Boca Raton, FL: Taylor & Francis Group.

Peter, C. J., Fischer, L. K., Kundakovic, M., Garg, P., Jakovcevski, M., Dincer, A., . . . Akbarian, S. (2016). DNA methylation signatures of early childhood malnutrition associated with impairments in attention and cognition. *Biological Psychiatry.* No Pagination Specified. http://dx.doi.org/10.1016/j.biopsych.2016.03.2100

Peteros, R. G., & Maleyeff, J. (2015). Using Lean Six Sigma to improve investment behavior. *International Journal of Lean Six Sigma, 6,* 59–72. doi:10.1108/IJLSS-03-2014-0007

Petrocchi, N., & Couyoumdjian, A. (2016). The impact of gratitude on depression and anxiety: The mediating role of criticizing, attacking, and reassuring the self. *Self and Identity, 15,* 191–205. doi:http://dx.doi.org/10.1080/15298868.2015.1095794

Petrosini, L., Cutuli, D., & De Bartolo, P. (2013). Environmental influences on development of the nervous system. In R. J. Nelson, S. J. Y. Mizumori, & I. B. Weiner (Eds.), *Handbook of psychology,* Vol. 3. *Behavioral neuroscience* (2nd ed., pp. 461–479). Hoboken, NJ: Wiley.

Pew Research Center. (2016, May 12). Changing attitudes on gay marriage. Retrieved from http://www.pewforum.org/2016/05/12/changing-attitudes-on-gay-marriage/

Pfattheicher, S., & Keller, J. (2014). Towards a biopsychological understanding of costly punishment: The role of basal cortisol. *PLoS ONE, 9:* e85691.

Phan, H. P., & Ngu, B. H. (2016). Sources of self-efficacy in academic contexts: A longitudinal perspective. *School Psychology Quarterly.* No Pagination Specified. http://dx.doi.org/10.1037/spq0000151

Phillip, A. (2015, February 25). For Chris Kyle's killer, Eddie Ray Routh, life in prison may make jail an asylum. *The Washington Post.* Retrieved from http://www.washingtonpost.com/news/morning-mix/wp/2015/02/25/for-chris-kyles-killerlife-in-prison-may-make-prison-an-asylum/

Phillips, R. O., Fyhri, A., & Sagberg, F. (2011). Risk compensation and bicycle helmets. *Risk Analysis, 31,* 1187–1195. doi:10.1111/j.1539-6924.2011.01589.x

Phillips, S. T., & Ziller, R. C. (1997). Toward a theory and measure of the nature of non-prejudice. *Journal of Personality and Social Psychology, 72,* 420–434.

Piaget, J. (1952). *The origins of intelligence in children.* New York, NY: Oxford University Press.

Pines, A. (2014). Surgical menopause and cognitive decline. *Climacteric, 17,* 580–582. doi:10.3109/13697137.2014.883244

Piomelli, D. (2015). Neurobiology of marijuana. In M. Galanter, H. D. Kleber, & K. T. Brady (Eds.), *The American Psychiatric Publishing textbook of substance abuse treatment* (5th ed., pp. 335–350). Arlington, VA: American Psychiatric Publishing.

Planas-Sitjà, I., Deneubourg, J.-L., Gibon, C., & Sempo, G. (2015). Group personality during collective decision-making: A multilevel approach. *Proceedings of the Royal Society B, 282.* doi:10.1098/rspb.2014.2515.

Plassmann, H., O'Doherty, J., Shiv, B., & Rangel, A. (2008). Marketing actions can modulate neural representations of experienced pleasantness. *Proceedings of the National Academy of Sciences of the United States of America, 105,* 1050–1054.

Platt, J. M., Prins, S. J., Bates, L. M., & Keyes, K. M. (2016). Unequal depression for equal work? How the wage gap explains gendered disparities in mood disorders. *Social Science & Medicine, 149,* 1–8. http://dx.doi.org/10.1016/j.socscimed.2015.11.056

Plattner, F., Hernández, A., Kistler, T. M., Pozo, K., Zhong, P., Yuen, E. Y., . . . Bibb, J. A. (2014). Memory enhancement by targeting Cdk5 regulation of NR2B. *Neuron, 81,* 1070–1083. doi:10.1016/j.neuron.2014.01.022

Plomin, R., & Deary, I. J. (2015). Genetics and intelligence differences: Five special findings.

Molecular Psychiatry, 20, 98–108. doi:10.1038/mp.2014.105

Plomin, R., DeFries, J. C., Knopik, V. S., & Neiderhiser, J. M. (2016). Top 10 replicated findings from behavioral genetics. *Perspectives on Psychological Science, 11,* 3–23. http://dx.doi.org/10.1177/1745691615617439

Plucker, J. A., & Esping, A. (2014). *The psych 101 series: Intelligence 101.* New York, NY: Springer.

Pohl, R. F., Erdfelder, E., Hilbig, B. E., Liebke, L., & Stahlberg, D. (2013). Effort reduction after self-control depletion: The role of cognitive resources in use of simple heuristics. *Journal of Cognitive Psychology, 25,* 267–276. doi:10.1080/20445911.2012.758101

Pokhrel, P., Herzog, T. A., Black, D. S., Zaman, A., Riggs, N. R., & Sussman, S. (2013). Adolescent neurocognitive development, self-regulation, and school-based drug use prevention. *Prevention Science, 14,* 218–228. doi:10.1007/s11121-012-0345-7

Polanco-Roman, L., Gomez, J., Miranda, R., & Jeglic, E. (2016). Stress-related symptoms and suicidal ideation: The roles of rumination and depressive symptoms vary by gender. *Cognitive Therapy and Research.* No Pagination Specified. http://dx.doi.org/10.1007/s10608-016-9782-0

Polito, V., Barnier, A. J., Woody, E. Z., & Connors, M. H. (2014). Measuring agency change across the domain of hypnosis. *Psychology of Consciousness: Theory, Research, and Practice, 1,* 3–19. doi:10.1037/cns0000010

Pollock, N. C., Noser, A. E., Holden, C. J., & Zeigler-Hill, V. (2016). Do orientations to happiness mediate the associations between personality traits and subjective well-being? *Journal of Happiness Studies, 17,* 713–729. http://dx.doi.org/10.1007/s10902-015-9617-9

Pomerantz, E. M., & Kempner, S. G. (2013). Mothers' daily person and process praise: Implications for children's theory of intelligence and motivation. *Developmental Psychology, 49,* 2040–2046. doi:10.1037/a0031840

Pomponio, A. T. (2002). *Psychological consequences of terror.* Hoboken, NJ: Wiley.

Pope, K. S., & Vasquez, M. J. T. (2011). *Ethics in psychotherapy and counseling: A practical guide* (4th ed.). Hoboken, NJ: Wiley.

Pope, L., & Harvey, J. (2015). The impact of incentives on intrinsic and extrinsic motives for fitness-center attendance in college first-year students. *American Journal of Health Promotion, 29,* 192–199. doi:10.4278/ajhp.140408-QUAN-135

Porritt, F., Shapiro, M., Waggoner, P., Mitchell, E., Thomson, T., Nicklin, S., & Kacelnik, A. (2015). Performance decline by search dogs in repetitive tasks, and mitigation strategies. *Applied Animal Behaviour Science, 166,* 112–122. doi:10.1016/j.applanim.2015.02.013

Portrat, S., Guida, A., Phénix, T., & Lemaire, B. (2016). Promoting the experimental dialogue between working memory and chunking: Behavioral data and simulation. *Memory & Cognition, 44,* 420–434. http://dx.doi.org/10.3758/s13421-015-0572-9

Possemato, K., Bergen-Cico, D., Treatman, S., Allen, C., Wade, M., & Pigeon, W. (2016). A randomized clinical trial of primary care brief mindfulness training for veterans with PTSD. *Journal of Clinical Psychology, 72,* 179–193. http://dx.doi.org/10.1002/jclp.22241

Posthuma, D., de Geus, E. J. C., & Boomsma, D. I. (2001). Perceptual speed and IQ are associated through common genetic factors. *Behavior Genetics, 31,* 593–602. doi:10.1023/A:1013349512683

Poulin, M. J., Holman, E. A., & Buffone, A. (2012). The neurogenetics of nice: Receptor genes for oxytocin and vasopressin interact with threat to predict prosocial behavior. *Psychological Science, 23,* 446–452. doi:10.1177/0956797611428471

Prather, A. A., Janicki-Deverts, D., Hall, M. H., & Cohen, S. (2015). Behaviorally assessed sleep and susceptibility to the common cold. *Sleep, 38,* 1353–1959. doi:10.5665/sleep.4968.

Prati, F., Vasiljevic, M., Crisp, R. J., & Rubini, M. (2015). Some extended psychological benefits of challenging social stereotypes: Decreased dehumanization and a reduced reliance on heuristic thinking. *Group Processes & Intergroup Relations, 18,* 801–816. doi:10.1177/1368430214567762

Preckel, K., Scheele, D., Kendrick, K. M., Maier, W., & Hurlemann, R. (2014). Oxytocin facilitates social approach behavior in women. *Frontiers in Behavioral Neuroscience, 8,* Article ID 191. doi:10.3389/fnbeh.2014.00191

Prenderville, J. A., Kennedy, P. J., Dinan, T. G., & Cryan, J. F. (2015). Adding fuel to the fire: The impact of stress on the ageing brain. *Trends in Neurosciences, 38,* 13–25. doi:10.1016/j.tins.2014.11.001

Presti, D. E. (2016). *Foundational concepts in neuroscience: A brain-mind odyssey. The Norton series on interpersonal neurobiology.* New York, NY: W. W. Norton.

Price, J., Lefgren, L., & Tappen, H. (2013). Interracial workplace cooperation: Evidence from the NBA. *Economic Inquiry, 51,* 1026–1034. doi:10.1111/j.1465-7295.2011.00438.x

Price, T. J., & Prescott, S. A. (2015). Inhibitory regulation of the pain gate and how its failure causes pathological pain. *Pain, 156,* 789–792. doi:10.1097/j.pain.0000000000000139

Prichard, I., Polivy, J., Provencher, V., Herman, C. P., Tiggemann, M., & Cloutier, K. (2014). Brides and young couples: Partners' weight, weight change, and perceptions of attractiveness. *Journal of Social and Personal Relationships, 32,* 263–278. doi:10.11177/0265407514529068

Primeau, M., & O'Hara, R. (2015). Sleep-wake disorders. In L. W. Roberts & A. K. Louie (Eds.), *Study guide to DSM-5®* (pp. 267–290). Arlington, VA: American Psychiatric Publishing.

Prkachin, K. M., & Silverman, B. E. (2002). Hostility and facial expression in young men and women: Is social regulation more important than negative affect? *Health Psychology, 21,* 33–39. doi:10.1037/0278-6133.21.1.33

Prot, S., Gentile, D. A., Anderson, C. A., Suzuki, K., Swing, E., Lim, K. M., . . . Lam, B. C. (2014). Long-term relations among prosocial-media use, empathy, and prosocial behavior. *Psychological Science, 25,* 358–368. doi:10.1177/0956797613503854.

Protzko, J., Aronson, J., & Blair, C. (2013). How to make a young child smarter: Evidence from the database of raising intelligence. *Perspectives on Psychological Science, 8,* 25–40. doi:10.1177/1745691612462585

Proyer, R. T., Ruch, W., & Buschor, C. (2013). Testing strengths-based interventions: A preliminary study on the effectiveness of a program targeting curiosity, gratitude, hope, humor, and zest for enhancing life satisfaction. *Journal of Happiness Studies, 14,* 275–292. doi:10.1007/s10902-012-9331-9

Przybylski, A. K., & Weinstein, N. (2013). Can you connect with me now? How the presence of mobile communication technology influences face-to-face conversation quality. *Journal of Social and Personal Relationships, 30,* 237–246.

Psychology Matters. (2006, June 30). Pushing buttons. Retrieved from http://www.psychologymatters.org/pushbutton.

Pullum, G. K. (1991). *The great Eskimo vocabulary hoax and other irreverent essays on the study of language.* Chicago, IL: University of Chicago Press.

Putwain, D., & Remedios, R. (2014). The scare tactic: Do fear appeals predict motivation and exam scores? *School Psychology Quarterly, 29,* 503–516. doi:10.1037/spq0000048

Qian, Z., Zhang, D., & Wang, L. (2013). Is aggressive trait responsible for violence? Priming effects of aggressive words and violent movies. *Psychology, 4,* 96–100.

Qin, S., Young, C. B., Duan, X., Chen, T., Supekar, K., & Menon, V. (2014). Amygdala subregional structure and intrinsic functional connectivity predicts individual differences in anxiety during early childhood. *Biological Psychiatry, 75,* 892–901. doi:10.1016/j.biopsych.2013.10.006.

Quas, J. A., Rush, E. B., Yim, I. S., Edelstein, R. S., Otgaar, H., & Smeets, T. (2016). Stress and emotional valence effects on children's versus adolescents' true and false memory. *Memory, 24,* 696–707. http://dx.doi.org/10.1080/09658211.2015.1045909

Quiano, K. (2016, March 21). Living in chains: In Indonesia, mentally ill kept shackled in filthy cells. *CNN World.* Retrieved from http://www.cnn.com/2016/03/20/asia/indonesia-mental-health/

Quick, J. C., Wright, T. A., Adkins, J. A., Nelson, D. L., & Quick, J. D. (2013). Primary prevention for individuals: Managing and coping with stressors. In J. C. Quick, T. A. Wright, J. A. Adkins, D. L. Nelson, & J. D. Quick (Eds.), *Preventive stress management in organizations* (2nd ed., pp. 147–163). Washington, DC: American Psychological Association.

Raaska, H., Elovainio, M., Sinkkonen, J., Stolt, S., Jalonen, I., Matomaki, J., . . . Lapinleimu, H. (2013). Adopted children's language difficulties and their relation to symptoms of reactive attachment disorder: FinAdo study. *Journal of Applied Developmental Psychology, 34,* 152–160. doi:10.1016/j.appdev.2012.12.003

Rabellino, D., Densmore, M., Frewen, P. A., Théberge, J., & Lanius, R. A. (2016). The innate alarm circuit in post-traumatic stress disorder: Conscious and subconscious processing of fear- and trauma-related cues. *Psychiatry Research: Neuroimaging, 248,* 142–150. http://dx.doi.org/10.1016/j.pscychresns.2015.12.005

Radhika, P., Murthy, P., Sarin, A., & Jain, S. (2015). Psychological symptoms and medical responses in nineteenth-century India. *History of Psychiatry, 26,* 88–97. doi:10.1177/0957154X14530815

Radvansky, G. A., & Ashcraft, M. H. (2016). *Cognition* (6th ed.). Upper Saddle River, NJ: Pearson.

Raffin, E., Richard, N., Giraux, P., & Reilly, K. T. (2016). Primary motor cortex changes after amputation correlate with phantom limb pain and the ability to move the phantom limb. *NeuroImage, 130,* 134–144. http://dx.doi.org/10.1016/j.neuroimage.2016.01.063

Rahafar, A., Maghsudloo, M., Farhangnia, S., Vollmer, C., & Randler, C. (2016). The role of chronotype, gender, test anxiety, and conscientiousness in academic achievement of high school students. *Chronobiology International, 33,* 1–9. http://dx.doi.org/10.3109/07420528.2015.1107084

Ramchand, R., Ayer, L., Geyer, L., & Kofner, A. (2016). Factors that influence chaplains' suicide intervention behavior in the army. *Suicide and Life-Threatening Behavior, 46,* 35–45. doi:10.1111/sltb.12170

Ramler, T. R., Tennison, L. R., Lynch, J., & Murphy, P. (2016). Mindfulness and the college transition: The efficacy of an adapted mindfulness-based stress reduction intervention in fostering adjustment among first-year students. *Mindfulness, 7,* 179–188. http://dx.doi.org/10.1007/s12671-015-0398-3

Ramsay, C. E., Stewart, T., & Compton, M. T. (2012). Unemployment among patients with newly diagnosed first-episode psychosis: Prevalence and clinical correlates in a US sample. *Social Psychiatry and Psychiatric Epidemiology, 47,* 797–803. doi:10.1007/s00127-011-0386-4

Ramsay, I. S., & MacDonald, A. W. III (2015). Brain correlates of cognitive remediation in schizophrenia: Activation likelihood analysis shows preliminary evidence of neural target engagement. *Schizophrenia Bulletin, 41,* 1276–1284. doi:10.1093/schbul/sbv025

Ramscar, M., Hendrix, P., Shaoul, C., Milin, P., & Baayen, H. (2014). The myth of cognitive decline: Non-linear dynamics of lifelong learning. *Topics in Cognitive Science, 6,* 5–42. doi:10.1111/tops.12078

Randi, J. (2014, January 7). It's not a contest. *James Randi Educational Foundation.* Retrieved from http://www.randi.org/site/index.php/swift-blog/2304-its-not-a-contest.html

Rasmussen, P. R., & Aleksandrof, D. (2015). Depression and bipolar disorders. In L. Sperry, J. Carlson, J. D. Sauerheber, & J. Sperry (Eds.), *Psychopathology and psychotherapy: DSM-5 diagnosis, case conceptualization, and treatment* (3rd ed., pp. 95–122). New York, NY: Routledge/Taylor & Francis Group.

Rass, O., Ahn, W.-Y., & O'Donnell, B. F. (2016). Resting-state EEG, impulsiveness, and personality in daily and nondaily smokers. *Clinical Neurophysiology, 127,* 409–418. http://dx.doi.org/10.1016/j.clinph.2015.05.007

Ratner, K. G., & Amodio, D. M. (2013). Seeing "us vs. them": Minimal group effects on the neural encoding of faces. *Journal of Experimental Social Psychology, 49,* 298–301.

Rattan, A., Savani, K., Chugh, D., & Dweck, C. S. (2015). Leveraging mindsets to promote academic achievement: Policy recommendations. *Perspectives on Psychological Science, 10,* 721–726. doi:http://dx.doi.org/10.1177/1745691615599383

Ray, A. L., Ullmann, R., & Francis, M. C. (2015). Pain as a perceptual experience. In T. R. Deer, M. S. Leong, & A. L. Ray (Eds.), *Treatment of chronic pain by integrative approaches: The American Academy of Pain Medicine textbook on patient management* (pp. 1–13). New York, NY: Springer-Verlag. doi:10.1007/978-1-4939-1821-8_1

Ray, D. C., & Jayne, K. M. (2016). Humanistic psychotherapy with children. In D. J. Cain, K. Keenan, & S. Rubin (Eds.), *Humanistic psychotherapies: Handbook of research and practice* (2nd ed., pp. 387–417). Washington, DC: American Psychological Association. http://dx.doi.org/10.1037/14775-013

Ray, W. J. (2015). *Abnormal psychology: Neuroscience perspectives on human behavior and experience.* Thousand Oaks, CA: Sage.

Raynald, Li, Y., Yu, H., Huang, H., Guo, M., Hua, R., . . . An, Y. (2016). The heterotransplantation of human bone marrow stromal cells carried by hydrogel unexpectedly demonstrates a significant role in the functional recovery in the injured spinal cord of rats. *Brain Research, 1634,* 21–33. doi:10.1016/j.brainres.2015.10.038

Reardon, S. (2015). Rave drug tested against depression: Companies and clinicians turn to ketamine to treat mental-health disorder as pipeline of new drugs dries up. *Nature, 517,* 130–131. doi:10.1038/517130a

Rebok, F., Teti, G. L., Fantini, A. P., Cárdenas-Delgado, C., Rojas, S. M., Derito, M. N. C., & Daray, F. M. (2015). Types of borderline personality disorder (BPD) in patients admitted for suicide-related behavior. *Psychiatric Quarterly, 86,* 49–60. doi:10.1007/s11126-014-9317-3

Redondo, M. T., Beltrán-Brotóns, J. L., Reales, J. M., & Ballesteros, S. (2015). Word-stem priming and recognition in type 2 diabetes mellitus, Alzheimer's disease patients and healthy older adults. *Experimental Brain Research, 233,* 3163–3174. http://dx.doi.org/10.1007/s00221-015-4385-7

Reed, A. E., Chan, L., & Mikels, J. A. (2014). Meta-analysis of the age-related positivity effect: Age differences in preferences for positive over negative information. *Psychology and Aging, 29,* 1–15. doi:10.1037/a0035194

Reed, M. (2015). Obesity. In R. M. McCarron, G. L. Xiong, C. R. Keenan, & H. A. Nasrallah (Eds.), *Preventive medical care in psychiatry: A practical guide for clinicians* (pp. 143–160). Arlington, VA: American Psychiatric Publishing.

Rees, C. S., Breen, L. J., Cusack, L., & Hegney, D. (2015). Understanding individual resilience in the workplace: The international collaboration of workforce resilience model. *Frontiers in Psychology, 6,* 73. doi:10.3389/fpsyg.2015.00073

Regan, P. (1998). What if you can't get what you want? Willingness to compromise ideal mate selection standards as a function of sex, mate value, and relationship context. *Personality and Social Psychology Bulletin, 24,* 1294–1303.

Regan, P. (2011). *Close relationships.* New York, NY: Routledge/Taylor & Francis Group.

Reicher, S. (2014). In praise of activism: Rethinking the psychology of obedience and conformity. In C. Antaki & S. Condor (Eds.), *Rhetoric, ideology and social psychology: Essays in honour of Michael Billig* (pp. 94–109). New York, NY: Routledge.

Rentfrow, P. J. (2014). Geographical differences in personality. In P. J. Rentfrow (Ed.), *Geographical psychology: Exploring the interaction of environment and behavior* (pp. 115–137). Washington, DC: American Psychological Association. doi:10.1037/14272-007

Rentfrow, P. J., Gosling, S. D., & Potter, J. (2008). A theory of the emergence, persistence, and expression of geographic variation in psychological characteristics. *Perspectives on Psychological Science, 3,* 339–369. doi:10.1111/j.1745-6924.2008.00084.x

Resnick, B. (2016, April 8). These scientists can prove it's possible to reduce prejudice. *Vox: Science & Health.* Retrieved from http://www.vox.com/2016/4/7/11380974/reduce-prejudice-science-transgender

Rest, J., Narvaez, D., Bebeau, M., & Thoma, S. (1999). A neo-Kohlbergian approach: The DIT and schema theory. *Educational Psychology Review, 11,* 291–324.

Reuben, E., Sapienza, P., & Zingales, L. (2014). How stereotypes impair women's careers in science. *Proceedings of the National Academy of Sciences of the United States of America, 111,* 4403–4408.

Rhee, S. H., & Waldman, I. D. (2011). Genetic and environmental influences on aggression. In P. R. Shaver & M. Mikulincer (Eds.), *Human aggression and violence: Causes, manifestations, and consequences* (pp. 143–163). Washington, DC: American Psychological Association.

Rhudy, J. L. (2016). Emotional modulation of pain. In M. al'Absi & M. A. Flaten (Eds.), *The neuroscience of pain, stress, and emotion: Psychological and clinical implications* (pp. 51–75). San Diego, CA: Elsevier Academic Press. http://dx.doi.org/10.1016/B978-0-12-800538-5.00003-0

Rice, S. M., Fallon, B. J., Aucote, H. M., Möller-Leimkühler, A., Treeby, M. S., & Amminger, G. P. (2014). Longitudinal sex differences of externalising and internalising depression symptom trajectories: Implications for assessment of depression in men from an online study. *International Journal of Social Psychiatry, 61,* 236–240. doi:10.1177/0020764014540149

Richardson, R. C. (2015). Evolutionary psychology, altruism, and kin selection. In T. Breyer (Ed.), *Epistemological dimensions of evolutionary psychology* (pp. 103–115). New York, NY: Springer. doi:10.1007/978-1-4939-1387-9

Riediger, M., & Luong, G. (2016). Happy to be unhappy? Pro- and contrahedonic motivations from adolescence to old age. In A. D. Ong & C. E. Löckenhoff (Eds.), *Emotion, aging, and health. Bronfenbrenner series on the ecology of human development* (pp. 97–118). Washington, DC: American Psychological Association. http://dx.doi.org/10.1037/14857-006

Rimmele, U., Davachi, L., & Phelps, E. A. (2012). Memory for time and place contributes to enhanced confidence in memories for emotional events. *Emotion, 12,* 834–846. doi:10.1037/a0028003

Risman, B. J., & Davis, G. (2013). From sex roles to gender structure. *Current Sociology, 61,* 733–755. doi:10.1177/0011392113479315

Rivers, S. E., Brackett, M. A., Reyes, M. R., Elbertson, N. A., & Salovey, P. (2013). Improving the social and emotional climate of classrooms: A clustered randomized controlled trial testing the RULER Approach. *Prevention Science, 14,* 77–87. doi:10.1007/s11121-012-0305-2.

Rizvi, S. L., & Salters-Pedneault, K. (2013). Borderline personality disorder. In W. O'Donohue & S. O. Lilienfeld (Eds.), *Case studies in clinical psychological science: Bridging the gap from science to practice* (pp. 301–322). New York, NY: Oxford University Press.

Rizzolatti, G. (2014). Confounding the origin and function of mirror neurons. *Behavioral and Brain Sciences, 37,* 218–219. doi:10.1017/S0140525X13002471

Rizzolatti, G., Fadiga L., Fogassi L., & Gallese V. (1996). Premotor cortex and the recognition of motor actions. *Cognitive Brain Research, 3,* 131–141. doi:10.1016/0926-6410(95)00038-0

Rizzolatti, G., Sinigaglia, C., & Anderson, F. (2008). *Mirrors in the brain: How our minds share actions and emotions.* New York, NY: Oxford University Press.

Robbins, L. (2013). Neuralstem's stem cells give spinal injury patients hope. Retrieved from http://www.gazette.net/article/20130114/NEWS/130119667/neuralstemx2019-s-stemcells-give-spinal-injury-patients-hope&template=gazette

Robbins, S. P. (1996). *Organizational behavior: Concepts, controversies, and applications.* Englewood Cliffs, NJ: Prentice Hall.

Robin, F., Dominguez, J, & Tilford, M. (2008). *Your money or your life: 9 steps to transforming your relationship with money and achieving financial independence.* New York, NY: Penguin Books.

Robinson, F. P. (1970). *Effective study* (4th ed.). New York, NY: Harper & Row.

Robinson, K. J., Hoplock, L, B., & Cameron, J. J. (2015). When in doubt, reach out: Touch is a covert but effective mode of soliciting and providing social support. *Social Psychological and Personality Science, 6,* 831–839. http://dx.doi.org/10.1177/1948550615584197

Robinson, P. H., & Nicholls, D. (Eds.). (2015). *Critical care for anorexia nervosa: The MARSIPAN guidelines in practice.* Cham, CH: Springer. doi:10.1007/978-3-319-08174-8

Robins, S. K. (2016). Misremembering. *Philosophical Psychology, 29,* 432–447. http://dx.doi.org/10.1080/09515089.2015.1113245

Robnett, R. D., & Leaper, C. (2013). "Girls don't propose! Ew.": A mixed-methods examination of marriage tradition preferences and benevolent sexism in emerging adults. *Journal of Adolescent Research, 28,* 96–121. doi:10.1177/0743558412447871

Rode, L., Nordestgaard, B. G., & Bojesen, S. E. (2015). Peripheral blood leukocyte telomere length and mortality among 64,637 individuals from the general population. *Journal of the National Cancer Institute, 107,* djv074. doi:10.1093/jnci/djv074

Rodkey, E. N., & Riddell, R. P. (2013). The infancy of infant pain research: The experimental origins of infant pain denial. *The Journal of Pain, 14,* 338–350. doi:10.1016/j.jpain.2012.12.017

Rodriguez, C. M., Tucker, M. C., & Palmer, K. (2015). Emotion regulation in relation to emerging adults' mental health and delinquency: A multi-informant approach. *Journal of Child and Family Studies, 25,* 1916–1925. http://dx.doi.org/10.1007/s10826-015-0349-6

Roepke, A. M., & Seligman, M. E. P. (2016). Depression and prospection. *British Journal of Clinical Psychology, 55,* 23–48. http://dx.doi.org/10.1111/bjc.12087

Rogers, C. R. (1961). *On becoming a person.* Boston, MA: Houghton Mifflin.

Rogers, C. R. (1980). *A way of being.* Boston, MA: Houghton Mifflin.

Rogge, R. D., Cobb, R. J., Lawrence, E., Johnson, M. D., & Bradbury, T. N. (2013). Is skills training necessary for the primary prevention of marital distress and dissolution? A 3-year experimental study of three interventions. *Journal of Consulting and Clinical Psychology, 81,* 949–961. http://dx.doi.org/10.1037/a0034209

Rohlfs Domínguez, P. (2014). Promoting our understanding of neural plasticity by exploring developmental plasticity in early and adult life. *Brain Research Bulletin, 107,* 31–36. doi:10.1016/j.brainresbull.2014.05.006

Rokke, P. D., & Lystad, C. M. (2014). Mood-specific effects in the allocation of attention across time. *Cognition & Emotion, 29,* 27–50. doi:10.1080/02699931.2014.893865

Romero, C., Master, A., Paunesku, D., Dweck, C. S., & Gross, J. J. (2014). Academic and emotional functioning in middle school: The role of implicit theories. *Emotion, 14,* 227–234. doi:10.1037/a0035490

Ronan, K. R., Kelly, B., LeBlanc, J., & Burke, S. (2015). Community health and disaster recovery. In E. Mpofu (Ed.), *Community-oriented health services: Practices across disciplines* (pp. 243–269). New York, NY: Springer.

Rood, L., Roelofs, J., Bögels, S. M., & Meesters, C. (2012). Stress-reactive rumination, negative cognitive style, and stressors in relationship to depressive symptoms in non-clinical youth. *Journal of Youth and Adolescence, 41,* 414–425. doi:10.1007/s10964-011-9657-3

Roozen, S., Peters, G. J., Kok, G., Townend, D., Nijhuis, J., & Curfs, L. (2016). Worldwide prevalence of fetal alcohol spectrum disorders: A systematic literature review including meta-analysis. *Alcoholism, Clinical and Experimental Research, 40,* 18–32. doi:10.1111/acer.12939

Rosch, E. (1978). Principles of categorization. In E. Rosch & B. B. Lloyd (Eds.), *Cognition and categorization* (pp. 27–48). Hillsdale, NJ: Erlbaum.

Rosch, E. H. (1973). Natural categories. *Cognitive Psychology, 4,* 328–350. doi:10.1016/0010-0285(73)90017-0

Rosenhan, D. L. (1973). On being sane in insane places. *Science, 179,* 250–258. doi:10.1126/science.179.4070.250

Rosenthal, R. (1965). *Clever Hans: A case study of scientific method, introduction to Clever Hans.* New York, NY: Holt, Rinehart & Winston.

Rosenzweig, M. R., Bennett, E. L., & Diamond, M. C. (1972). Brain changes in response to experience. *Scientific American, 226,* 22–29. doi:10.1038/scientificamerican0272-22

Roskey, J. W. (2013). The (f)utility of post-conviction polygraph testing. *Sexual Abuse:*

Journal of Research and Treatment, 25,* 259–281. doi:10.1177/1079063212455668

Rosner, T. M., D'Angelo, M. C., MacLellan, E., & Milliken, B. (2015). Selective attention and recognition: Effects of congruency on episodic learning. *Psychological Research, 79,* 411–424. doi:10.1007/s00426-014-0572-6

Ross, L. (1977). The intuitive psychologist and his shortcomings: Distortions in the attribution process. In L. Berkowitz (Ed.), *Advances in experimental social psychology* (Vol. 10, pp. 173–220). New York, NY: Academic Press.

Rothbaum, F., Kakinuma, M., Nagaoka, R., & Azuma, H. (2007). Attachment and amae: Parent-child closeness in the United States and Japan. *Journal of Cross-Cultural Psychology, 38,* 465–486. doi:10.1177/0022022107302315

Rothgerber, H., & Wolsiefer, K. (2014). A naturalistic study of stereotype threat in young female chess players. *Group Processes & Intergroup Relations, 17,* 79–90. doi:10.1177/1368430213490212

Rotter, J. B. (1954). *Social learning and clinical psychology.* Englewood Cliffs, NJ: Prentice Hall.

Rotter, J. B. (1966). Generalized expectancies for internal versus external control of reinforcement. *Psychological Monographs: General & Applied, 80,* 1–28.

Rotter, J. B. (1990). Internal versus external control of reinforcement: A case history of a variable. *American Psychologist, 45,* 489–493.

Rouder, J. N., Morey, R. D., & Province, J. M. (2013). A Bayes factor meta-analysis of recent extrasensory perception experiments: Comment on Storm, Tressoldi, and Di Risio (2010). *Psychological Bulletin, 139,* 241–247.

Rubin, L. H., Wu, M., Sundermann, E. E., Meyer, V. J., Smith, R., Weber, K. M., . . . Maki, P. M. (2016). Elevated stress is associated with prefrontal cortex dysfunction during a verbal memory task in women with HIV. *Journal of Neurovirology.* No Pagination Specified. http://dx.doi.org/10.1007/s13365-016-0446-3

Ruffman, T., O'Brien, K. S., Taumoepeau, M., Latner, J. D., & Hunter, J. A. (2016). Toddlers' bias to look at average versus obese figures relates to maternal anti-fat prejudice. *Journal of Experimental Child Psychology, 142,* 195–202. doi:10.1016/j.jecp.2015.10.008

Ruini, C., & Fava, G. A. (2014). Increasing happiness by well-being therapy. In K. M. Sheldon & R. E. Lucas (Eds.), *Stability of happiness: Theories and evidence on whether happiness can change* (pp. 147–166). San Diego, CA: Elsevier Academic Press.

Ruiz-Aranda, D., Extremera, N., & Pineda-Galán, C. (2014). Emotional intelligence, life satisfaction and subjective happiness in female student health professionals: The mediating effect of perceived stress. *Journal of Psychiatric and Mental Health Nursing, 21,* 106–113. doi:10.1111/jpm.12052

Rumbaugh, D. M., von Glasersfeld, E. C., Warner, H., Pisani, P., & Gill, T. V. (1974). Lana (chimpanzee) learning language: A progress report. *Brain and Language,* 1, 205–212. doi:10.1016/0093-934X(74)90035-2

Rumschlag, G., Palumbo, T., Martin, A., Head, D., George, R., & Commissaris, R. L. (2015). The effects of texting on driving performance in a driving simulator: The influence of driver age. *Accident Analysis & Prevention, 74,* 145–149. doi:10.1016/j.aap.2014.10.009

Ruocco, A. C., Amirthavasagam, S., Choi-Kain, L. W., & McMain, S. F. (2013). Neural correlates of negative emotionality in borderline personality disorder: An activation-likelihood-estimation meta-analysis. *Biological Psychiatry, 73,* 153–160.

Rushton, J. P., & Jensen, A. R. (2010). Race and IQ: A theory-based review of the research in Richard Nisbett's Intelligence and how to get it. *The Open Psychology Journal, 3,* Article 9-35. http://dx.doi.org/10.2174/1874350101003010009

Russ, S. (2014). Play, culture, and the modern world. In S. W. Russ (Ed.), *Pretend play in childhood: Foundation of adult creativity* (pp. 153–171). Washington, DC: American Psychological Association.

Russ, S., & Wallace, C. E. (2013). Pretend play and creative processes. *American Journal of Play, 6,* 136–148.

Russell, V. A., Zigmond, M. J., Dimatelis, J. J., Daniels, W. M. U., & Mabandla, M. V. (2014). The interaction between stress and exercise, and its impact on brain function. *Metabolic Brain Disease, 29,* 255–260. doi:10.1007/s11011-013-9479-y

Rutland, A., & Killen, M. (2015). A developmental science approach to reducing prejudice and social exclusion: Intergroup processes, social-cognitive development, and moral reasoning. *Social Issues and Policy Review, 9,* 121–154. doi:10.1111/sipr.12012

Ruzzoli, M., & Soto-Faraco, S. (2014). Alpha stimulation of the human parietal cortex attunes tactile perception to external space. *Current Biology, 24,* 329–332. doi:10.1016/j.cub.2013.12.029

Ryan, R. M., & Deci, E. L. (2013). Toward a social psychology of assimilation: Self-determination theory in cognitive development and education. In B. W. Sokol, F. M. E. Grouzet, & U. Muller (Eds.), *Self-regulation and autonomy: Social and developmental dimensions of human conduct* (pp. 191–207). Cambridge, UK: Cambridge University Press. doi:10.1017/cbo9781139152198.014

Rychlowska, M., Miyamoto, Y., Matsumoto, D., Hess, U., Gilboa-Schechtman, E., Kamble, S., . . . Niedenthal, P. M. (2015). Heterogeneity of long-history migration explains cultural differences in reports of emotional expressivity and the functions of smiles. *Proceedings of the National Academy of Sciences of the United States of America, 112,* E2429–E2436. doi:10.1073/pnas.1413661112

Rydé, K., & Hjelm, K. (2016). How to support patients who are crying in palliative home care: An interview study from the nurses' perspective. *Primary Health Care Research and Development.* No Pagination Specified. http://dx.doi.org/10.1017/S1463423616000037

Rymer, R. (1993). *Genie: An abused child's first flight from silence.* New York, NY: Harper-Collins.

Sachsenweger, M. A., Fletcher, R. B., & Clarke, D. (2015). Pessimism and homework in CBT for depression. *Journal of Clinical Psychology, 71,* 1153–1172. http://dx.doi.org/10.1002/jclp.22227

Sacks, O. (2015). *On the move: A life.* New York, NY: Knopf.

Sáenz Herrero, M. (2015). *Psychopathology in women: Incorporating gender perspective into descriptive psychopathology.* New York, NY: Springer.

Safer, M. A., Murphy, R. P., Wise, R. A., Bussey, L., Millett, C., & Holfeld, B. (2016). Educating jurors about eyewitness testimony in criminal cases with circumstantial and forensic evidence. *International Journal of Law and Psychiatry, 47,* 86–92. http://dx.doi.org/10.1016/j.ijlp.2016.02.041

Sagong, B., Bae, J. W., Rhyu, M. R., Kim, U. K., & Ye, M. K. (2014). Multiplex minisequencing screening for PTC genotype associated with bitter taste perception. *Molecular Biology Reports, 41,* 1563–1567. doi:10.1007/s11033-013-3002-8

Saito, S., Kobayashi, T., & Kato, S. (2014). Management and treatment of eating disorders with severe medical complications on a psychiatric ward: A study of 9 inpatients in Japan. *General Hospital Psychiatry, 36,* 291–295. doi:10.1016/j.genhosppsych.2014.02.001

Saletan, W. (2016, January 15). Gun nuts. *Slate.* Retrieved from http://www.slate.com/articles/news_and_politics/politics/2016/01/gop_presidential_candidates_have_a_paranoid_fear_of_gun_laws_and_gun_confiscation.html

Salovey, P., & Mayer, J. D. (1990). Emotional intelligence. *Imagination, Cognition, and Personality, 9,* 185–211.

Salvi, C., Bricolo, E., Kounios, J., Bowden, E., & Beeman, M. (2016). Insight solutions are correct more often than analytic solutions. *Thinking and Reasoning, 22,* 1814–1819. doi:10.1080/13546783.2016.1141798

Salzman, J. P., Kunzendorf, R. G., Saunders, E., & Hulihan, D. (2014). The Primary Attachment Style Questionnaire: A brief measure for assessing six primary attachment styles before and after age twelve. *Imagination, Cognition and Personality, 33,* 113–149.

Sampaio, C. V. S., Lima, M. G., & Ladeia, A. M. (2016). Meditation, health and scientific investigations: Review of the literature.

Journal of Religion and Health. No Pagination Specified. http://dx.doi.org/10.1007/s10943-016-0211-1

Samuels, B. A., Mendez-David, I., Faye, C., David, S. A., Pierz, K. A., Gardier, A. M., . . . David, D. J. (2016). Serotonin 1A and serotonin 4 receptors: Essential mediators of the neurogenic and behavioral actions of antidepressants. *The Neuroscientist, 22*, 26–45. http://dx.doi.org/10.1177/1073858414561303

Sanbonmatsu, D. M., Uchino, B. N., & Birmingham, W. (2011). On the importance of knowing your partner's views: Attitude familiarity is associated with better interpersonal functioning and lower ambulatory blood pressure in daily life. *Annals of Behavioral Medicine, 41*, 131–137.

Sánchez-Villegas, A., Toledo, E., de Irala, J., Ruiz-Canela, M., Pla-Vidal, J., & Martínez-González, M. A. (2011). Fast-food and commercial baked goods consumption and the risk of depression. *Public Health Nutrition, 15*, 424–432.

Sanders, A. R., Martin, E. R., Beecham, G. W., Guo, S., Dawood, K., Rieger, G., . . . Bailey, J. M. (2015). Genome-wide scan demonstrates significant linkage for male sexual orientation. *Psychological Medicine, 45*, 1379–1388. doi:10.1017/S0033291714002451

Sanderson, C. A. (2013). *Health psychology* (2nd ed.). Hoboken, NJ: Wiley.

Sandner, B., Prang, P., Blesch, A., & Weidner, N. (2015). Stem cell-based therapies for spinal cord regeneration. In H. Kuhn & A. Eisch (Eds.), *Neural stem cells in development, adulthood and disease* (pp. 155–174). New York, NY: Springer.

Sándor, P., Szakadát, S., & Bódizs, R. (2014). Ontogeny of dreaming: A review of empirical studies. *Sleep Medicine Reviews, 18*, 435–449. doi:10.1016/j.smrv.2014.02.001

Sand, R. S. (2014). *Dialog-on-Freud series. The unconscious without Freud.* Lanham, MD: Rowman & Littlefield.

Sanjuán, P., & Magallares, A. (2014). Coping strategies as mediating variables between self-serving attributional bias and subjective well-being. *Journal of Happiness Studies, 15*, 443–453. doi:10.1007/s10902-013-9430-2

Sankar, A., Scott, J., Paszkiewicz, A., Giampietro, V. P., Steiner, H., & Fu, C. H. Y. (2015). Neural effects of cognitive–behavioural therapy on dysfunctional attitudes in depression. *Psychological Medicine, 45*, 1425–1433. doi:10.1017/S0033291714002529

Santos, T. O. (2016). Cognitive changes in aging: Implications for discourse processing. In L. S. Carozza (Ed.), *Communication and aging: Creative approaches to improving the quality of life* (pp. 25–65). San Diego, CA: Plural Publishing.

Sargent, J. D., Tanski, S., & Stoolmiller, M. (2012). Influence of motion picture rating on adolescent response to movie smoking. *Pediatrics, 130*, 228–236. doi:10.1542/peds.2011-1787

Satterly, M. V., & Anitescu, M. (2015). Opioids and substance abuse. In A. D. Kaye, N. Vadivelu, & R. D. Urman (Eds.), *Substance abuse: Inpatient and outpatient management for every clinician* (pp. 179–192). New York, NY: Springer.

Saucier, G., Kenner, J., Iurino, K., Malham, P. B., Chen, Z., Thalmayer, A. G., . . . Altschul, C. (2015). Cross-cultural differences in a global "Survey of World Views." *Journal of Cross-Cultural Psychology, 46*, 53–70. doi:10.1177/0022022114551791

Savage-Rumbaugh, E. S. (1990). Language acquisition in a nonhuman species: Implications for the innateness debate. *Developmental Psychobiology, 23*, 599–620. doi:10.1002/dev.420230706

Saxon, S. V., Etten, M. J., & Perkins, E. A. (2014). *Physical change and aging: A guide for the helping professions* (6th ed.). New York, NY: Springer.

Sayal, K., Heron, J., Maughan, B., Rowe, R., & Ramchandani, P. (2014). Infant temperament and childhood psychiatric disorder: Longitudinal study. *Child: Care, Health and Development, 40*, 292–297. doi:10.1111/cch.12054

Schachter, S., & Singer, J. E. (1962). Cognitive, social, and physiological determinants of emotional state. *Psychological Review, 69*, 379–399.

Schaeffer, E. L., Cerulli, F. G., Souza, H. O. X., Catanozi, S., & Gattaz, W. F. (2014). Synergistic and additive effects of enriched environment and lithium on the generation of new cells in adult mouse hippocampus. *Journal of Neural Transmission, 121*, 695–706. doi:10.1007/s00702-014-1175-5

Schare, M. L., Wyatt, K. P., Skolnick, R. B., Terjesen, M., Haak Bohnenkamp, J., Lai, B. S., . . . Ehrlich, C. J. (2015). Cognitive and behavioral interventions. In R. Flanagan, K. Allen, & E. Levine (Eds.), *Cognitive and behavioral interventions in the schools: Integrating theory and research into practice* (pp. 249–283). New York, NY: Springer. doi:10.1007/978-1-4939-1972-7

Scharrer, E., & Ramasubramanian, S. (2015). Intervening in the media's influence on stereotypes of race and ethnicity: The role of media literacy education. *Journal of Social Issues, 71*, 171–185. doi:10.1111/josi.12103

Scheele, D., Striepens, N., Güntürkün, O., Deutschländer, S., Maier, W., Kendrick, K. M., & Hurlemann, R. (2012). Oxytocin modulates social distance between males and females. *The Journal of Neuroscience, 32*, 16074–16079.

Scheele, D., Wille, A., Kendrick, K. M., Stoffel-Wagner, B., Becker, B., Güntürkün, O., . . . Hurlemann, R. (2013). Oxytocin enhances brain reward system responses in men viewing the face of their female partner. *Proceedings of the National Academy of Science of the United States of America, 110*, 20308–20313. doi:10.1073/pnas.1314190110

Scherman, D. (2014). *Advanced textbook on gene transfer, gene therapy and genetic pharmacology: Principles, delivery and pharmacological and biomedical applications of nucleotide-based therapies.* London, UK: Imperial College Press.

Schick, T., Jr., & Vaughn, L. (2014). *How to think about weird things: Critical thinking for a new age* (7th ed.). New York, NY: McGraw-Hill.

Schiffer, B., Pawliczek, C., Müller, B., Forsting, M., Gizewski, E., Leygraf, N., & Hodgins, S. (2014). Neural mechanisms underlying cognitive control of men with lifelong antisocial behavior. *Psychiatry Research: Neuroimaging, 222*, 43–51. doi:10.1016/j.pscychresns.2014.01.008

Schilling, C., Kühn, S., Sander, T., & Gallinat, J. (2014). Association between dopamine D4 receptor genotype and trait impulsiveness. *Psychiatric Genetics, 24*, 82. doi:10.1097/YPG.0000000000000005

Schimmel, P. (2014). *Sigmund Freud's discovery of psychoanalysis: Conquistador and thinker.* New York, NY: Routledge/Taylor & Francis Group.

Schlichting, M. L., & Preston, A. R. (2014). Memory reactivation during rest supports upcoming learning of related content. *Proceedings of the National Academy of Sciences of the United States of America, 111*, 15845–15850. doi:10.1073/pnas.1404396111

Schmidt, S. R. (2012). *Essays in cognitive psychology. Extraordinary memories for exceptional events.* New York, NY: Psychology Press.

Schmitgen, M. M., Walter, H., Drost, S., Rückl, S., & Schnell, K. (2016). Stimulus-dependent amygdala involvement in affective theory of mind generation. *NeuroImage, 129*, 450–459. http://dx.doi.org/10.1016/j.neuroimage.2016.01.029

Schmitt, D. P. (2015). *The evolution of sexuality.* Cham, CH: Springer International Publishing.

Schnack, H. G., Nieuwenhuis, M., Haren, N. E., Abramovic, L., Scheewe, T. W., Brouwer, R. M., . . . Kahn, R. S. (2014). Can structural MRI aid in clinical classification? A machine learning study in two independent samples of patients with schizophrenia, bipolar disorder and healthy subjects. *NeuroImage, 84*, 299–306. doi:10.1016/j.neuroimage.2013.08.05

Schneider, K., Fraser Pierson, J., & Bugenta, J. (2015). *The handbook of humanistic psychology* (2nd ed.). Thousand Oaks, CA: Sage.

Schneider, M. F. (2015). Eating disorders. In L. Sperry, J. Carlson, J. D. Sauerheber, & J. Sperry (Eds.), *Psychopathology and psychotherapy: DSM-5 diagnosis, case conceptualization, and treatment* (3rd ed., pp. 151–175). New York, NY: Routledge/Taylor & Francis Group.

Schneidman, E. S. (1969). Suicide, lethality and the psychological autopsy. *International Psychiatry Clinics, 6*, 225–250.

Schoenmaker, C., Juffer, F., van IJzendoorn, M. H., & Bakermans-Kranenburg, M. J. (2014). Does family matter? The well-being of children growing up in institutions, foster care and adoption. In A. Ben-Arieh, F., Casas, I., Frønes, & J. Korbin (Eds.), *Handbook of child well-being* (pp. 2197–2228). Houston, TX: Springer Netherlands. doi:1007/978-90-4819063-8_179

Schoenmaker, C., Juffer, F., van IJzendoorn, M. H., van den Dries, L., Linting, M., Vander voort, A., & Bakermans-Kranenburg, M. J. (2015). Cognitive and health-related outcomes after exposure to early malnutrition: The Leiden longitudinal study of international adoptees. *Children and Youth Services Review, 48,* 80–86. doi:10.1016/j.childyouth.2014.12.010

Schofield, T. P., Creswell, J. D., & Denson, T. F. (2015). Brief mindfulness induction reduces inattentional blindness. *Conscious Cognition, 37,* 63–70. doi:10.1016/j.concog.2015.08.007

Schonert-Reichl, K. A., Oberle, E., Lawlor, M. S., Abbott, D., Thomson, K., Oberlander, T. F., & Diamond, A. (2015). Enhancing cognitive and social–emotional development through a simple-to-administer mindfulness-based school program for elementary school children: A randomized controlled trial. *Developmental Psychology, 51,* 52–66. http://doi.org/10.1037/a0038454

Schoon, A., Fjellanger, R., Kjeldsen, M., & Goss, K. U. (2014). Using dogs to detect hidden corrosion. *Applied Animal Behaviour Science, 15,* 43–52. doi:10.1016/j.applanim.2014.01.001.

Schroeder, D. A., & Graziano, W. G. (Eds.). (2015). *The Oxford handbook of prosocial behavior.* Oxford, UK: Oxford University Press.

Schroers, W. (2014). Memory improvement—spaced repetition. *Field-theory.org.* Retrieved from http://www.field-theory.org/articles/memory/spaced_repetition.html

Schroll, H., Horn, A., Gröschel, C., Brücke, C., Lütjens, G., Schneider, G.-H., . . . Hamker, F. H. (2015). Differential contributions of the globus pallidus and ventral thalamus to stimulus–response learning in humans. *NeuroImage, 122,* 233–245. doi:10.1016/j.neuroimage.2015.07.061

Schulze, L., Schmahl, C., & Niedtfeld, I. (2016). Neural correlates of disturbed emotion processing in borderline personality disorder: A multimodal meta-analysis. *Biological Psychiatry, 79,* 97–106. doi:10.1016/j.biopsych.2015.03.027

Schulz, H. M. (2015). Reference group influence in consumer role rehearsal narratives. *Qualitative Market Research: An International Journal, 18,* 210–229. doi:10.1108/QMR-02-2012-0009

Schunk, D. H., & Zimmerman, B. J. (2013). Self-regulation and learning. In W. M. Reynolds, G. E. Miller, & I. B. Weiner (Eds.), *Handbook of psychology, Vol. 7. Educational psychology* (2nd ed., pp. 45–68). Hoboken, NJ: Wiley.

Schüz, B., Bower, J., & Ferguson, S. G. (2015). Stimulus control and affect in dietary behaviours. An intensive longitudinal study. *Appetite, 87,* 310–317. doi:10.1016/j.appet.2015.01.002

Schwartz, B., & Krantz, J. (2016). *Sensation and perception.* Thousand Oaks, CA: Sage.

Scott, C. (2015). *Learn to teach: Teach to learn.* New York, NY: Cambridge University Press.

Scott-Phillips, T. C. (2015). Nonhuman primate communication, pragmatics, and the origins of language. *Current Anthropology, 56,* 56–80.

Scribner, S. (1977). Modes of thinking and ways of speaking: Culture and logic reconsidered. In P. N. Johnson-Laird & P. C. Wason (Eds.), *Thinking: Readings in cognitive science* (pp. 324–339). New York, NY: Cambridge University Press.

Sdrulla, A. D., Chen, G., & Mauer, K. (2015). Definition and demographics of addiction. In A. Kaye, N. Vadivelu, & R. Urman (Eds.), *Substance abuse* (pp. 1–15). New York, NY: Springer.

Seay, T. A., & Sun, C. T. L. (2016). Psychotherapies: What can be done when the mind is unwell? In C. Tien-Lun Sun (Ed.), *Psychology in Asia: An introduction* (pp. 395–422). Boston, MA: Cengage Learning.

Sebelius, K. (2014). *The health consequences of smoking—50 years of progress: A report of the Surgeon General.* Atlanta, GA: US Department of Health and Human Services, Centers for Disease Control and Prevention, National Center for Chronic Disease Prevention and Health Promotion, Office on Smoking and Health. Retrieved from http://www.surgeongeneral.gov/library/reports/50-years-of-progress/execsummary.Pdf

Sedikides, C., & Alicke, M. D. (2012). Self-enhancement and self-protection motives. In R. M. Ryan (Ed.), *The Oxford handbook of human motivation* (pp. 303–322). New York, NY: Oxford University Press.

Seebauer, L., Froß, S., Dubaschny, L., Schönberger, M., & Jacob, G. A. (2014). Is it dangerous to fantasize revenge in imagery exercises? An experimental study. *Journal of Behavior Therapy and Experimental Psychiatry, 45,* 20–25.

Seedat, S., Scott, K. M., Angermeyer, M. C., Berglund, P., Bromet, E. J., Brugha, T. S., . . . Kessler, R. C. (2009). Cross-national associations between gender and mental disorders in the World Health Organization World Mental Health Surveys. *Archives of General Psychiatry, 66,* 785–795.

Seedman, A. A., & Hellman, P. (2014). *Fifty years after Kitty Genovese: Inside the case that rocked our faith in each other.* New York, NY: The Experiment.

Seeley, R. J., & Berridge, K. C. (2015). The hunger games. *Cell, 16,* 805–806. doi:10.1016/j.cell.2015.02.028

Sehgal, P. (2015, December 1). The profound emptiness of "resilience." *The New York Times Magazine.* Retrieved from http://www.nytimes.com/2015/12/06/magazine/the-profoundemptiness-of-resilience.html?_r=1

Seifer, R., Dickstein, S., Parade, S., Hayden, L. C., Magee, K. D., & Schiller, M. (2014). Mothers' appraisal of goodness of fit and children's social development. *International Journal of Behavioral Development, 38,* 86–97. doi:10.1177/0165025413507172

Sekiguchi, A., Kotozaki, Y., Sugiura, M., Nouchi, R., Takeuchi, H., Hanawa, S., . . . Kawashima, R. (2014). Long-term effects of postearthquake distress on brain microstructural changes. *BioMed Research International, Volume 2014,* Article ID 180468. http://doi.org/10.1155/2014/180468

Seligman, M. (2011). *Learned optimism: How to change your mind and your life.* New York, NY: Random House.

Seligman, M. E. P. (1975). *Helplessness: On depression, development, and death.* San Francisco, CA: Freeman.

Seligman, M. E. P. (2003). The past and future of positive psychology. In C. L. M. Keyes & J. Daidt (Eds.), *Flourishing: Positive psychology and the life well-lived* (pp. xi–xx). Washington, DC: American Psychological Association.

Seligman, M. E. P. (2007). Coaching and positive psychology. *Australian Psychologist, 42,* 266–267.

Seligman, M. E. P. (2012). *Flourish: A visionary new understanding of happiness and well being.* Riverside, NJ: Atria.

Seligman, M. E. P. (2015). Chris Peterson's unfinished masterwork: The real mental illnesses. *The Journal of Positive Psychology, 10,* 3–6. doi:10.1080/17439760.2014.888582

Seligman, M. E. P., & Maier, S. F. (1967). Failure to escape traumatic shock. *Journal of Experimental Psychology, 74,* 1–9. doi:10.1037/h0024514

Selvi, F. F., Karakaş, S. A., Boysan, M., & Selvi, Y. (2015). Effects of shift work on attention deficit, hyperactivity, and impulsivity, and their relationship with chronotype. *Biological Rhythm Research, 46,* 53–61. doi:10.1080/09291016.2014.948299

Selye, H. (1936). A syndrome produced by diverse nocuous agents. *Nature, 138,* 32.

Selye, H. (1974). *Stress without distress.* Philadelphia, PA: Saunders.

Selye, H. (1983). The stress concept: Past, present, and future. In C. L. Cooper (Ed.), *Stress research* (pp. 1–20). New York, NY: Wiley.

Semlyen, J., King, M., Varney, J., & Hagger-Johnson, G. (2016). Sexual orientation and symptoms of common mental disorder or low wellbeing: Combined meta-analysis of 12 UK population health surveys. *BMC Psychiatry, 16,* Article 67.

Sénécal, V., Deblois, G., Beauseigle, D., Schneider, R., Brandenburg, J., Newcombe, J., . . . Arbour, N. G. (2016). Production of IL-27 in multiple sclerosis lesions by astrocytes and myeloid cells: Modulation of local immune responses. *Glia, 64*, 553–569. doi:10.1002/glia.22948

Shakoor, S., Zavos, H. M. S., McGuire, P., Cardno, A. G., Freeman, D., & Ronald, A. (2015). Psychotic experiences are linked to cannabis use in adolescents in the community because of common underlying environmental risk factors. *Psychiatry Research, 227,* 144–151. doi:10.1016/j.psychres.2015.03.041

Shakya, A., Soni, U. K., Rai, G., Chatterjee, S. S., & Kumar, V. (2015).Gastro-protective and anti-stress efficacies of monomethyl fumarate and a fumaria indica extract in chronically stressed rats. *Cellular and Molecular Neurobiology, 36*, 621–635. http://dx.doi.org/10.1007/s10571-015-0243-1

Shand, G. (2013). Culture and the self: A comparison of attitudes to study among English and Japanese students in state secondary education. *Compare: A Journal of Comparative and International Education, 43,* 857–858. doi:10.1080/03057925.2012.752623

Shannon, P. J., Wieling, E., McCleary, J. S., & Becher, E. (2015). Exploring the mental health effects of political trauma with newly arrived refugees. *Qualitative Health Research, 25,* 443–457. doi:10.1177/1049732314549475

Sharma, V. K., Rango, J., Connaughton, A. J., Lombardo, D. J., & Sabesan, V. J. (2015). The current state of head and neck injuries in extreme sports. *Orthopaedic Journal of Sports Medicine*, *3*:2325967114564358. doi:10.1177/2325967114564358

Sharma, V., & Shakeel, M. (2015). Illusion versus reality: An empirical study of overconfidence and self-attribution bias in business management students. *Journal of Education for Business, 90,* 199–207. doi:10.1080/08832323.2015.1014458

Shaw, A. M., Timpano, K. R., Tran, T. B., & Joormann, J. (2015). Correlates of Facebook usage patterns: The relationship between passive Facebook use, social anxiety symptoms, and brooding. *Computers in Human Behavior, 48,* 575–580. http://dx.doi.org/10.1016/j.chb.2015.02.003

Shaw, J., & Porter, S. (2015). Constructing rich false memories of committing crime. *Psychological Science, 26,* 291–301. doi:10.1177/0956797614562862

Shaw, N. D., Butler, J. P., McKinney, S. M., Nelson, S. A., Ellenbogen, J. M., & Hall, J. E. (2012). Insights into puberty: The relationship between sleep stages and pulsatile LH secretion. *Journal of Clinical Endocrinology & Metabolism, 97,* E2055–E2062. doi:10.1210/jc.2012-2692

Shenkman, R. (2016). *Political animals: How our Stone-Age brain gets in the way of smart politics*. New York, NY: Basic Books.

Sherif, M. (1966). *In common predicament: Social psychology of intergroup conflict and cooperation.* Boston, MA: Houghton Mifflin.

Sherif, M. (1998). Experiments in group conflict. In J. M. Jenkins, K. Oatley, & N. L. Stein (Eds.), *Human emotions: A reader* (pp. 245–252). Malden, MA: Blackwell.

Sherman, G. D., Lee, J. J., Cuddy, A. J. C., Renshon, J., Oveis, C., Gross, J. J., & Lerner, J. S. (2012). Leadership is associated with lower levels of stress. *Proceedings of the National Academy of Sciences of the United States of America, 109,* 17903–17907. doi:10.1073/ pnas.1207042109

Sherman, R. A., Rauthmann, J. F., Brown, N. A., Serfass, D. G., & Jones, A. B. (2015). The independent effects of personality and situations on real-time expressions of behavior and emotion. *Journal of Personality and Social Psychology, 109,* 872–888.

Shiban, Y., Peperkorn, H., Alpers, G. W., Pauli, P., & Mühlberger, A. (2016). Influence of perceptual cues and conceptual information on the activation and reduction of claustrophobic fear. *Journal of Behavior Therapy and Experimental Psychiatry, 51*, 19–26. http://dx.doi.org/10.1016/j.jbtep.2015.11.002

Shiraev, E. (2015). *A history of psychology: A global perspective* (2nd ed.). Thousand Oaks, CA: Sage.

Short, F., & Thomas, P. (2015). *Core approaches in counselling and psychotherapy.* New York, NY: Routledge/Taylor & Francis Group.

Shweder, R. A. (2011). Commentary: Ontogenetic cultural psychology. In L. A. Jensen (Ed.), *Bridging cultural and developmental approaches to psychology: New syntheses in theory, research, and policy* (pp. 303–310). New York, NY: Oxford University Press.

Siegel, A. B. (2010). Dream interpretation in clinical practice: A century after Freud. *Sleep Medicine Clinics, 5,* 299–313.

Siegel, J. M. (2000, January). Narcolepsy. *Scientific American,* 76–81. doi:10.1038/scientificamerican0100-76.

Sierksma, J., Thijs, J., & Verkuyten, M. (2015). In-group bias in children's intention to help can be overpowered by inducing empathy. *British Journal of Developmental Psychology, 33,* 45–56. doi:10.1111/bjdp.12065

Sievert, L., Morrison, L. A., Reza, A. M., Brown, D. E., Kalua, E., & Tefft, H. T. (2007). Age-related differences in health complaints: The Hilo women's health study. *Women & Health, 45,* 31–51. doi:10.1300/J013v45n03-03

Sigalow, E., & Fox, N. S. (2014). Perpetuating stereotypes: A study of gender, family, and religious life in Jewish children's books. *Journal for the Scientific Study of Religion, 53,* 416–431. doi:10.1111/jssr.12112

Silber, K. (2014). *Schizophrenia.* Basingstoke, UK: Palgrave Macmillan.

Silverstein, M. L. (2013). *Personality assessment in depth: A casebook.* New York, NY: Routledge.

Simm, A., & Klotz, L.-O. (2015). Stress and biological aging: A double-edged sword. *Zeitschrift für Gerontologie und Geriatrie, 48,* 505–510. http://dx.doi.org/10.1007/s00391-015-0928-6

Simmons, S. M., Hicks, A., & Caird, J. K. (2016). Safety-critical event risk associated with cell phone tasks as measured in naturalistic driving studies: A systematic review and meta-analysis. *Accident Analysis and Prevention, 87,* 161–169. http://dx.doi.org/10.1016/j.aap.2015.11.015

Simons, D. J., & Chabris, C. F. (1999). Gorillas in our midst: Sustained inattentional blindness for dynamic events. *Perception, 28,* 1059–1074. doi:10.1068/p2952

Simons, L. G., Wickrama, K. A. S., Lee, T. K., Landers-Potts, M., Cutrona, C., & Conger, R. D. (2016). Testing family stress and family investment explanations for conduct problems among African American adolescents. *Journal of Marriage and Family, 78,* 498–515. http://dx.doi.org/10.1111/jomf.12278

Siniscalchi, A., Bonci, A., Biagio Mercuri, N., De Siena, A., De Sarro, G., Malferrari, G., . . . Gallelli, L. (2015). Cocaine dependence and stroke: Pathogenesis and management. *Current Neurovascular Research, 12,* 163–172. doi:10.2174/ 1567202612666150305110144

Situala, S., Amador, A., & Burris, T. P. (2016). The circadian clock as a drug target. In M. L. Gumz (Ed.), *Circadian clocks: Role in health and disease* (pp. 335–366). New York, NY: Springer Science + Business Media. http://dx.doi.org/10.1007/978-1-4939-3450-8_12

Skinner, B. F. (1956). A case history in the scientific method. *American Psychologist,* 11, 221–233. doi:10.1037/h0047662

Skinner, B. F. (1961). Diagramming schedules of reinforcement. *Journal of the Experimental Analysis of Behavior, 1,* 67–68.

Slane, J. D., Klump, K. L., McGue, M., & Iacono, G. (2014). Genetic and environmental factors underlying comorbid bulimic behaviours and alcohol use disorders: A moderating role for the dysregulated personality cluster? *European Eating Disorders Review, 22,* 159–169. doi:10.1002/erv.2284

Smalheiser, N. R., Zhang, H., & Dwivedi, Y. (2014). Enoxacin elevates microRNA levels in rat frontal cortex and prevents learned helplessness. *Frontiers in Psychiatry, 5,* 6. doi:10.3389/fpsyt.2014.00006

Smart, R., & Tsong, Y. (2014). Weight, body dissatisfaction, and disordered eating: Asian American women's perspectives. *Asian American Journal of Psychology, 5,* 344–352. doi:10.1037/a0035599

Smith, D., Mackie, D., & Claypool, H. (2015). *Social psychology* (4th ed.). New York, NY: Routledge.

Smith, K. Z., Smith, P. H., Cercone, S. A., McKee, S. A., & Homish, G. G. (2016). Past year non-medical opioid use and abuse and PTSD diagnosis: Interactions with sex and associations with symptom clusters. *Addictive*

Behaviors, 58, 167–174. http://dx.doi.org/10.1016/j.addbeh.2016.02.019

Smith, L. E., Bernal, D. R., Schwartz, B. S., Whitt, C. L., Christman, S. T., Donnelly, S., . . . Kobetz, E. (2014). Coping with vicarious trauma in the aftermath of a natural disaster. *Journal of Multicultural Counseling and Development, 42,* 2–12. doi:10.1002/j.2161-1912.2014.00040.x

Smith, L. S. (2016). Family-based therapy for parent-child reunification. *Journal of Clinical Psychology, 72,* 498–512. http://dx.doi.org/10.1002/jclp.22259

Smith, M. L., & Glass, G. V. (1977). Meta-analysis of psychotherapy outcome studies. *American Psychologist, 32,* 752–760. http://dx.doi.org/10.1037/0003-066X.32.9.752

Smith, M. L., Glass, G. V., & Miller, T. I. (1980). *The benefits of psychotherapy.* Baltimore, MD: Johns Hopkins University Press.

Smith, M., Robinson, L., & Segal, R. (2012). How much sleep do you need? Sleep cycles and stages, lack of sleep, and getting the hours you need. Retrieved from http://helpguide.org/life/ sleeping.htm

Smith, R. L. (Ed.). (2015). *Treatment strategies for substance and process addictions.* Alexandria, VA: American Counseling Association.

Snarey, J. R. (1995). In communitarian voice: The sociological expansion of Kohlbergian theory, research, and practice. In W. M. Kurtines & J. L. Gerwirtz (Eds.), *Moral development: An introduction* (pp. 109–134). Boston, MA: Allyn & Bacon.

Snider, S. E., Quisenberry, A. J., & Bickel, W. K. (2016). Order in the absence of an effect: Identifying rate-dependent relationships. *Behavioural Processes, 127,* 18-24. doi:10.1016/j.beproc.2016.03.012

Sobral, M., Pestana, M. H., & Constanca, P. (2015). The impact of cognitive reserve on neuropsychological and functional abilities in Alzheimer's disease patients. *Psychology & Neuroscience, 8,* 39–55. doi:10.1037/h0101022

Sofer, C., Dotsch, R., Wigboldus, D. H. J., & Todorov, A. (2015). What is typical is good: The influence of face typicality on perceived trustworthiness. *Psychological Science, 26,* 39–47. doi:10.1177/0956797614554955

Solms, M. (1997). *The neuropsychology of dreams.* Hillsdale, NJ: Erlbaum.

Solnit, R. (2009). *A paradise built in hell: The extraordinary communities that arise in disaster.* New York, NY: Penguin.

Solomon, G. S., & Zuckerman, S. L. (2015). Chronic traumatic encephalopathy in professional sports: Retrospective and prospective views. *Brain Injury, 29,* 164–170. doi:10.3109/02699052.2014.965205

Song, M. J., & Bharti, K. (2016). Looking into the future: Using induced pluripotent stem cells to build two and three dimensional ocular tissue for cell therapy and disease modeling. *Brain Research, 1638(Pt A),* 2–14. doi:10.1016/j.brainres.2015.12.011

Song, T. M., An, J-Y., Hayman, L. L., Woo, J.-M., & Yom, Y.-H. (2016). Stress, depression, and lifestyle behaviors in Korean adults: A latent means and multi-group analysis on the Korea health panel data. *Behavioral Medicine, 42,*72–81. http://dx.doi.org/10.1080/08964289.2014.943688

Son, H., Banasr, M., Choi, M., Chae, S. Y., Licznerski, P., Lee, B., . . . Duman, R. S. (2012). Neuritin produces antidepressant actions and blocks the neuronal and behavioral deficits caused by chronic stress. *Proceedings of the National Academy of Sciences of the United States of America, 109,* 11378–11383. doi:10.1073/pnas.1201191109

Sotiropoulos, I., Silva, J., Kimura, T., Rodrigues, A. J., Costa, P., Almeida, O. F. X., . . . Takashima, A. (2015). Female hippocampus vulnerability to environmental stress, a precipitating factor in tau aggregation pathology. *Journal of Alzheimer's Disease, 43,* 763–774.

Southwick, S., & Watson, P. (2015). The emerging scientific and clinical literature on resilience and psychological first aid. In N. C. Bernardy & M. J. Friedman (Eds.), *A practical guide to PTSD treatment: Pharmacological and psychotherapeutic approaches* (pp. 21–33). Washington, DC: American Psychological Association. doi:10.1037/14522-003

Souza, A. L., Conroy-Beam, D., & Buss, D. M. (2016). Mate preferences in Brazil: Evolved desires and cultural evolution over three decades. *Personality and Individual Differences, 95,* 45–49. http://dx.doi.org/10.1016/j.paid.2016.01.053

Spano, R., Koenig, T. L., Hudson, J. W., & Leiste, M. R. (2010). East meets west: A nonlinear model for understanding human growth and development. *Smith College Studies in Social Work, 80,* 198–214.

Spearman, C. (1923). *The nature of "intelligence" and the principles of cognition.* London, UK: Macmillan.

Sperling, G. (1960). The information available in brief visual presentations. *Psychological Monographs, 74,* 1–29. doi:10.1037/h0093759

Spiegel, D. (2015). Hypnosis and pain control. In T. R. Deer, M. S. Leong, & A. L. Ray (Eds.), *Treatment of chronic pain by integrative approaches: The American Academy of Pain Medicine textbook on patient management* (pp. 115–122). New York, NY: Springer. doi:10.1007/978-1-4939-1821-8

Spiegel, D., Lewis-Fernández, R., Lanius, R., Vermetten, E., Simeon, D., & Friedman, M. (2013). Dissociative disorders in DSM-5. *Annual Review of Clinical Psychology, 9,* 299–326. doi:10.1146/annurev-clinpsy-050212-185531

Spiegel, D., & Simeon, D. (2015). Dissociative disorders. In L. W. Roberts & A. K. Louie (Eds.), *Study guide to DSM-5®* (pp. 195–210). Arlington, VA: American Psychiatric Publishing.

Spiegler, M. (2016). *Contemporary behavior therapy* (6th ed.). Boston, MA: Cengage Learning.

Spinazzola, J., Hodghon, H., Liang, L. J., Ford, J. D., Layne, C. M., Pynoos, R. S., . . . Kisiel, C. (2014). Unseen wounds: The contribution of psychological maltreatment to child and adolescent mental health and risk outcomes. *Psychological Trauma: Theory, Research, Practice, and Policy, 6,* S18–S28. doi:10.1037/a0037766

Sprecher, S., & Fehr, B. (2011). Dispositional attachment and relationship-specific attachment as predictors of compassionate love for a partner. *Journal of Social and Personal Relationships, 28,* 558–574. doi:10.1177/0265407510386190

Sprecher, S., Felmlee, D., Metts, S., & Cupach, W. (2015). Relationship initiation and development. In M. Mikulincer, P. R. Shaver, J. A. Simpson, & J. F. Dovidio (Eds.), *APA handbook of personality and social psychology, Vol. 3. Interpersonal relations* (pp. 211–245). Washington, DC: American Psychological Association. doi:10.1037/14344-008

Srinivasan, V., Singh, J., Brzezinski, A., Zakaria, R., Shillcutt, S. D., & Brown, G. M. (2014). Jet lag: Use of melatonin and melatonergic drugs. In V. Srinivasan, A. Brzezinski, S. Oter, & S. Shillcutt (Eds.), *Melatonin and melatonergic drugs in clinical practice* (pp. 367–378). Tamilnadu, IN: Springer. doi:10.1007/978-81-322-0825-9_26

Stadler, M., Aust, M., Becker, N., Niepel, C., & Greiff, S. (2016). Choosing between what you want now and what you want most: Self-control explains academic achievement beyond cognitive ability. *Personality and Individual Differences, 94,* 168–172. http://dx.doi.org/10.1016/j.paid.2016.01.029

Stamatakis, A. M., Van Swieten, M., Basiri, M. L., Blair, G. A., Kantak, P., & Stuber, G. D. (2016). Lateral hypothalamic area glutamatergic neurons and their projections to the lateral habenula regulate feeding and reward. *The Journal of Neuroscience, 36,* 302–311. doi:10.1523/JNEUROSCI.1202-15.2016

Stange, M., Graydon, C., & Dixon, M. J. (2016). "I was that close": Investigating players' reactions to losses, wins, and near-misses on scratch cards. *Journal of Gambling Studies, 32,* 187–203. doi:10.1007/s10899-015-9538-x

Stanley, I. H., Hom, M. A., & Joiner, T. E. (2016). A systematic review of suicidal thoughts and behaviors among police officers, firefighters, EMTs, and paramedics. *Clinical Psychology Review, 44,* 25–44. http://dx.doi.org/10.1016/j.cpr.2015.12.002

Stanovich, K. E. (2015). Rational and irrational thought: The thinking that IQ tests miss. *Scientific American, 23,* 12–17. doi:10.1038/scientificamericangenius0115-12

Starr, C. R., & Zurbriggen, E. L. (2016). Sandra Bem's gender schema theory after 34 years: A review of its reach and impact. *Sex Roles.* No Pagination Specified. http://dx.doi.org/10.1007/s11199-016-0591-4

Stavropoulos, V., Kuss, D., Griffiths, M., & Motti-Stefanidi, F. (2016). A longitudinal study of adolescent Internet addiction: The role of conscientiousness and classroom hostility. *Journal of Adolescent Research, 31,* 442–473. http://dx.doi.org/10.1177/0743558415580163

Steele, C. M., & Aronson, J. (1995). Stereotype threat and the intellectual test performance of African Americans. *Journal of Personality and Social Psychology, 69,* 797–811.

Steers, M-L. N., Wickham, R. E., & Acitelli, L. K. (2014). Seeing everyone else's highlight reels: How Facebook usage is linked to depressive symptoms. *Journal of Social and Clinical Psychology, 33,* 701–731. doi:10.1521/jscp.2014.33.8.701

Stefanek, E., Strohmeier, D., Fandrem, H., & Spiel, C. (2012). Depressive symptoms in native and immigrant adolescents: The role of critical life events and daily hassles. *Anxiety, Stress and Coping, 25,* 201–217. doi:10.1080/10615806.2011.605879

Steiner, K. L., Pillemer, D. B., Thomsen, D. K., & Minigan, A. P. (2014). The reminiscence bump in older adults' life story transitions. *Memory, 22,* 1002–1009. doi:10.1080/09658211.2013.86335

Stein, S. J., & Deonarine, J. M. (2015). Current concepts in the assessment of emotional intelligence. In S. Goldstein, D. Princiotta, & J. A. Naglieri (Eds.), *Handbook of intelligence: Evolutionary theory, historical perspective, and current concepts* (pp. 381–402). New York, NY: Springer. doi:10.1007/978-1-4939-1562-0_24

Sternberg, K. (2014). *Psychology of love 101.* New York, NY: Springer.

Sternberg, R. J. (1985). *Beyond IQ: A triarchic theory of human intelligence.* New York, NY: Cambridge University Press.

Sternberg, R. J. (1986). A triangular theory of love. *Psychological Review, 93,* 119–135.

Sternberg, R. J. (1988). *The triangle of love.* New York, NY: Basic Books.

Sternberg, R. J. (2006). A duplex theory of love. In R. J. Sternberg & K. Weis (Eds.), *The new psychology of love* (pp. 184–199). New Haven, CT: Yale University Press.

Sternberg, R. J. (2014). Teaching about the nature of intelligence. *Intelligence, 42,* 176–179. doi:10.1016/j.intell.2013.08.010

Sternberg, R. J. (2015). Multiple intelligences in the new age of thinking. In S. Goldstein, D. Princiotta, & J. A. Naglieri (Eds.), *Handbook of intelligence: Evolutionary theory, historical perspective, and current concepts* (pp. 229–241). New York, NY: Springer. doi:10.1007/978-1-4939-1562-0_16

Stets, J. E., & Carter, M. J. (2012). A theory of the self for the sociology of morality. *American Sociological Review, 77,* 120–140. doi:10.1177/0003122411433762

Stiles, N. R. B., Zheng, Y., & Shimojo, S. (2015). Length and orientation constancy learning in 2-dimensions with auditory sensory substitution: The importance of self-initiated movement. *Frontiers in Psychology, 6,* Article 842.

Stoll, J. L., & Brooks, J. (2015). Behavior therapy. In F. Chan, N. L. Berven, & K. R. Thomas (Eds.), *Counseling theories and techniques for rehabilitation and mental health professionals* (2nd ed., pp. 133–155). New York, NY: Springer.

Stone, M. H. (2014). The spectrum of borderline personality disorder: A neurophysiological view. *Current Topics in Behavioral Neurosciences, 21,* 23–46. doi:10.1007/7854_2014_308

Stoner, J. A. (1961). A comparison of individual and group decisions involving risk. Unpublished master's thesis, School of Industrial Management, MIT, Cambridge, MA.

Stopper, C. M., & Floresco, S. B. (2015). Dopaminergic circuitry and risk/reward decision making: Implications for schizophrenia. *Schizophrenia Bulletin, 41,* 9–14. doi:10.1093/schbul/sbu165

Strack, F., Martin, L. L., & Stepper, S. (1988). Inhibiting and facilitating conditions of the human smile: A nonobstrusive test of the facial feedback hypothesis. *Journal of Personality and Social Psychology, 54,* 768–777.

Strasburger, V. C., Donnerstein, E., & Bushman, B. J. (2014). Why is it so hard to believe that media influence children and adolescents? *Pediatrics, 133,* 571–573. doi:10.1542/peds.2013-2334

Stratton, G. M. (1896). Some preliminary experiments on vision without inversion of the retinal image. *Psychological Review, 3,* 611–617. doi:10.1037/h0072918

Straub, R. O. (2014). *Health psychology* (4th ed.). New York, NY: Worth.

Strauss, B. M., Shapiro, D. A., Barkham, M., Parry, G., & Machado, P. P. P. (2015). "The times they are a-changin": 25 years of psychotherapy research—A European and Latin American perspective. *Psychotherapy Research, 25,* 294–308. doi:10.1080/10503307.2014.1002439

Stricker, L. J., & Rock, D. A. (2015). An "Obama effect" on the GRE General Test? *Social Influence, 10,* 11–18. doi:10.1080/15534510.2013.878665

Sue, D., Sue, D., Sue, S., & Sue, D. (2016). *Understanding abnormal behavior* (11th ed.). Stamford, CT: Cengage Learning.

Suerken, C. K., Reboussin, B. A., Egan, K. L., Sutfin, E. L., Wagoner, K. G., Spangler, J., & Wolfson, M. (2016). Marijuana use trajectories and academic outcomes among college students. *Drug & Alcohol Dependence, 162,* 137–145. http://dx.doi.org/10.1016/j.drugalcdep.2016.02.041

Sugar, J. A., Riekse, R. J., Holstege, H., & Faber, M. A. (2014). *Introduction to aging: A positive, interdisciplinary approach.* New York, NY: Springer.

Sugarman, H., Impey, C., Buxner, S., & Antonellis, J. (2011). Astrology beliefs among undergraduate students. *Astronomy Education Review, 10.* doi:10.3847/AER2010040

Suhay, E. (2015). Explaining group influence: The role of identity and emotion in political conformity and polarization. *Political Behavior, 37,* 221–251. doi:10.1007/s11109-014-9269-1

Suher, J., Raj R., & Hoyer, W. (2016). Eating healthy or feeling empty? How the "Healthy = Less Filling" intuition influences satiety. *The Journal of the Association for Consumer Research, 1.* No Pagination Specified.

Suicide Basic Facts. (2015). Suicide: 2015 facts and figures. American Foundation for Suicide Prevention. Retrieved from http://www.afsp.org/news-events/in-the-news/suicide-2015-facts-and-figures-infographic

Suissa, A. J. (2015). Cyber addictions: Toward a psychosocial perspective. *Addictive Behaviors, 43,* 28–32. doi:10.1016/j.addbeh.2014.09.020

Sung, J., Beijers, R., Garstein, M. A., de Weerth, C., & Putnam, S. P. (2015). Exploring temperamental differences in infants from the USA and the Netherlands. *European Journal of Developmental Psychology, 12,* 15–28.

Sun, H., Liu, Z., & Ma, X. (2016). Interactions between astrocytes and neurons in the brainstem involved in restraint water immersion stress-induced gastric mucosal damage. *NeuroReport: For Rapid Communication of Neuroscience Research, 27,* 151–159.

Super, C., & Harkness, S. (2015). Charting infant development: Milestones along the way. In L. A. Jensen (Ed.), *The Oxford handbook of human development and culture: An interdisciplinary perspective* (pp. 79–93). New York, NY: Oxford University Press.

Suso-Ribera, C., & Gallardo-Pujol, D. (2016). Personality and health in chronic pain: Have we failed to appreciate a relationship? *Personality and Individual Differences, 96,* 7–11. http://dx.doi.org/10.1016/j.paid.2016.02.063

Sussman, T. J., Szekely, A., Hajcak, G., & Mohanty, A. (2016). It's all in the anticipation: How perception of threat is enhanced in anxiety. *Emotion, 16,* 320–327. http://dx.doi.org/10.1037/emo0000098

Sutin, A. R., Stephan, Y., Carretta, H., & Terracciano, A. (2015). Perceived discrimination and physical, cognitive, and emotional health in older adulthood. *The American Journal of Geriatric Psychiatry, 23,* 171–179. doi:10.1016/j.jagp.2014.03.007

Sutin, R., Terracciano, A., Milaneschi, Y., An, Y., Ferrucci, L., & Zonderman, A. B. (2013). The effect of birth cohort on well-being: The legacy of economic hard times. *Psychological Science, 24,* 379–385. doi:10.1177/0956797612459658

Suzuki, H., & Lucas, L. R. (2015). Neurochemical correlates of accumbal dopamine d2 and amygdaloid 5-ht1b receptor densities on observational learning of aggression. *Cognitive, Affective & Behavioral Neuroscience, 15,* 460–474. doi:10.3758/s13415-015-0337-8

Suzuki, L. A., Naqvi, S., & Hill, J. S. (2014). Assessing intelligence in a cultural context. In F. T. L. Leong, L. Comas-Díaz, G. C. Nagayama Hall, V. C. McLoyd, & J. E. Trimble (Eds.), *APA handbook of multicultural psychology, Vol. 1: Theory and research* (pp. 247–266). Washington, DC: American Psychological Association. doi:10.1037/14189-013

Suzuk, Y., Tamesue, D., Asahi, K., & Ishikawa, Y. (2015). Grit and work engagement: A cross-sectional study. *PLoS ONE, 10:* e0137501.

Svetina, M. (2014). Resilience in the context of Erikson's theory of human development. *Current Psychology: A Journal for Diverse Perspectives on Diverse Psychological Issues, 33,* 393–404. doi:10.1007/s12144-014-9218-5

Swaab, D. F. (2014). *We are our brains: A neurobiography of the brain, from the womb to Alzheimer's.* (J. Hedley-Prôle, Trans.). New York, NY: Spiegel & Grau/Random House.

Swami, V. (2011). *Evolutionary psychology: A critical introduction.* Chichester, West Sussex, UK: Wiley-Blackwell.

Swami, V. (2012). Mental health literacy of depression: Gender differences and attitudinal antecedents in a representative British sample. *PLoS ONE, 7*: e49779.

Sweeney, S., Air, T., Zannettino, L., & Galletly, C. (2015). Gender differences in the physical and psychological manifestation of childhood trauma and/or adversity in people with psychosis. *Frontiers in Psychology, 6*, Article 1768.

Sylvestre, A., & Mérette, C. (2010). Language delay in severely neglected children: A cumulative or specific effect of risk factors? *Child Abuse & Neglect, 34,* 414–428. doi:10.1016/j.chiabu.2009.10.003

Szabo, T. G., Long, D. M., Villatte, M., & Hayes, S. C. (2015). Mindfulness in contextual cognitive-behavioral models. In K. W. Brown, J. D. Creswell, & R. M. Ryan (Eds.), *Handbook of mindfulness: Theory, research, and practice* (pp. 130–147). New York, NY: Guilford.

Szkodny, L. E., & Newman, M. G. (2014). Generalized anxiety disorder. In S. G. Hofmann, D. J. A. Dozois, W. Rief, & J. A. J. Smits (Eds.), *The Wiley handbook of cognitive behavioral therapy* (Vols. 1–3, pp. 1001–1022). Malden, MA: Wiley-Blackwell.

Takarangi, M. K. T., & Loftus, E. F. (2016). Suggestion, placebos, and false memories. In A. Raz & C. S. Harris (Eds.), *Placebo talks: Modern perspectives on placebos in society* (pp. 204–226). New York, NY: Oxford University Press.

Tamagawa, R., Speca, M., Stephen, J., Pickering, B., Lawlor-Savage, L., & Carlson, L. E. (2015). Predictors and effects of class attendance and home practice of yoga and meditation among breast cancer survivors in a Mindfulness-Based Cancer Recovery (MBCR) Program. *Mindfulness,* 1–10. doi:10.1007/s12671-014-0381-4

Tamir, M., Bigman, Y. E., Rhodes, E., Salerno, J., & Schreier, J. (2015). An expectancy-value model of emotion regulation: Implications for motivation, emotional experience, and decision making. *Emotion, 15,* 90–103. doi:10.1037/emo0000021

Tan, G., Rintala, D. H., Jensen, M. P., Fukui, T., Smith, D., & Williams, W. (2015). A randomized controlled trial of hypnosis compared with biofeedback for adults with chronic low back pain. *European Journal of Pain, 19,* 271–280. doi:10.1002/ejp.545

Tang, W. Y., & Fox, J. (2016). Men's harassment behavior in online video games: Personality traits and game factors. *Aggressive Behavior.* No Pagination Specified. http://dx.doi.org/10.1002/ab.21646

Tang, Y., Newman, L. S., & Huang, L. (2014). How people react to social-psychological accounts of wrongdoing: The moderating effects of culture. *Journal of Cross-Cultural Psychology, 45,* 752–763. doi:10.1177/0022022114527343

Tang, Y. Y., Posner, M. I., & Rothbart, M. K. (2014). Meditation improves self-regulation over the life span. *Annals of the New York Academy of Sciences, 1307,* 104–111. doi:10.1111/nyas.12227

Tan, H. S. G., Fischer, A. R., Tinchan, P., Stieger, M., Steenbekkers, L. P. A., & van Trijp, H. C. (2015). Insects as food: Exploring cultural exposure and individual experience as determinants of acceptance. *Food Quality and Preference, 42,* 78–89. doi:10.1016/j.foodqual.2015.01.013

Tan, X., Alén, M., Cheng, S. M., Mikkola, T. M., Tenhunen, J., Lyytikäinen, A., . . . Cheng, S. (2015). Associations of disordered sleep with body fat distribution, physical activity and diet among overweight middle-aged men. *Journal of Sleep Research, 24,* 414–424. doi:10.1111/jsr.12283

Tanzer, M., Freud, E., Ganel, T., & Avidan, G. (2014). General holistic impairment in congenital prosopagnosia: Evidence from Garner's speeded-classification task. *Cognitive Neuropsychology, 30,* 429–445. doi:10.1080/02643294.2013.873715

Tarafdar, M., Tu, Q., & Ragu-Nathan, T. S. (2010). Impact of technostress on end-user satisfaction and performance. *Journal of Management Information Systems, 27,* 303–334. doi:10.2753/MIS0742-1222270311

Tarr, B., Launay, J., & Dunbar, R. I. M. (2016). Silent disco: Dancing in synchrony leads to elevated pain thresholds and social closeness. *Evolution and Human Behavior, 37,* 343–349. doi:10.1016/j.evolhumbehav.2016.02.004

Taub, E. (2004). Harnessing brain plasticity through behavioral techniques to produce new treatments in neurorehabilitation. *American Psychologist, 59,* 692–704. doi:10.1037/0003-066X.59.8.692

Taub, E., Uswatte, G., & Mark, V. W. (2014). The functional significance of cortical reorganization and the parallel development of CI therapy. *Frontiers in Human Neuroscience, 8,* Article 396.

Tavassolie, T., Dudding, S., Madigan, A. L., Thorvardarson, E., & Winsler, A. (2016). Differences in perceived parenting style between mothers and fathers: Implications for child outcomes and marital conflict. *Journal of Child and Family Studies, 25,* 2055–2068. http://dx.doi.org/10.1007/s10826-016-0376-y

Tavernier, R., Choo, S. B., Grant, K., & Adam, E. K. (2016). Daily affective experiences predict objective sleep outcomes among adolescents. *Journal of Sleep Research, 25,* 62–69. http://dx.doi.org/10.1111/jsr.12338

Tayama, J., Li, J., & Munakata, M. (2016). Working long hours is associated with higher prevalence of diabetes in urban male Chinese workers: The Rosai Karoshi study. *Stress and Health, 32,* 84–87. http://dx.doi.org/10.1002/smi.2580

Tay, L., & Diener, E. (2011). Needs and subjective well-being around the world. *Journal of Personality and Social Psychology, 101,* 354–365. doi:10.1037/a0023779

Taylor-Clift, A., Holmgreen, L., Hobfoll, S. E., Gerhart, J. I., Richardson, D., Calvin, J. E., & Powell, L. H. (2016). Traumatic stress and cardiopulmonary disease burden among low-income, urban heart failure patients. *Journal of Affective Disorders, 190,* 227–234. http://dx.doi.org/10.1016/j.jad.2015.09.023

Taylor, D. J., Zimmerman, M. R., Gardner, C. E., Williams, J. M., Grieser, E. A., Tatum, J. I., . . . Ruggero, C. (2014). A pilot randomized controlled trial of the effects of cognitive-behavioral therapy for insomnia on sleep and daytime functioning in college sudents. *Behavior Therapy, 45,* 376–389. doi:10.1016/j.beth.2013.12.010

Taylor, K. N., & Abba, N. (2015). Mindfulness meditation in cognitive-behavioral therapy for psychosis. In B. A. Gaudiano (Ed.), *Incorporating acceptance and mindfulness into the treatment of psychosis: Current trends and future directions* (pp. 170–200). New York, NY: Oxford University Press.

Taylor, L., Chrismas, B. C. R., Dascombe, B., Chamari, K., & Fowler, P. M. (2016). Sleep medication and athletic performance—The evidence for practitioners and future research directions. *Frontiers in Physiology, 7,* 83. http://doi.org/10.3389/fphys.2016.00083

Taylor, S. E. (2006). Tend and befriend: Biobehavioral bases of affiliation under stress. *Current Directions in Psychological Science, 15,* 273–277. doi:10.1111/j.1467-8721.2006.00451.x

Taylor, S. E. (2012). Tend and befriend theory. In P. A. M. Van Lange, A. W. Kruglanski, & E. T. Higgins (Eds.), *Handbook of theories of social psychology* (Vol. 1, pp. 32–49). Thousand Oaks, CA: Sage.

Tebbe, E. A., & Moradi, B. (2016). Suicide r isk in trans populations: An application of minority stress theory. *Journal of Counseling Psychology*. No Pagination Specified. http://dx.doi.org/10.1037/cou0000152

Tedeschi, R. G., & Blevins, C. L. (2015). From mindfulness to meaning: Implications for the theory of posttraumatic growth. *Psychological Inquiry, 26*, 373–376. http://dx.doi.org/10.1080/1047840X.2015.1075354

Tei, S., Becker, C., Sugihara, G., Kawada, R., Fujino, J., Sozu, T., . . . Takahashi, H. (2015). Sense of meaning in work and risk of burnout among medical professionals. *Psychiatry and Clinical Neurosciences, 69*, 123–124. http://dx.doi.org/10.1111/pcn.12217

Tellegen, A. (1985). Structures of mood and personality and their relevance to assessing anxiety with an emphasis on self-report. In A. H. Tuma & J. D. Maser (Eds.), *Anxiety and the anxiety disorders* (pp. 681–706). Hillsdale, NJ: Erlbaum.

Templeton, J. A., Dixon, M. J., Harrigan, K. A., & Fugelsang, J. A. (2015). Upping the reinforcement rate by playing the maximum lines in multi-line slot machine play. *Journal of Gambling Studies, 31*, 949–964. doi:10.1007/s10899-014-9446-5

Tennen, H., Suls, J., & Weiner, I. B. (Eds.). (2013). *Handbook of psychology, Vol. 5. Personality and social psychology* (2nd ed.). Hoboken, NJ: Wiley.

Teo, A. R., Choi, H., & Valenstein, M. (2013). Social relationships and depression: Ten-year follow-up from a nationally representative study. *PLoS ONE, 8*: e62396. http://doi.org/10.1371/journal.pone.0062396

Terman, L. M. (1916). *The measurement of intelligence.* Boston, MA: Houghton Mifflin.

Terman, L. M. (1925). *Genetic studies of genius: Vol. 1. Mental and physical traits of a thousand gifted children.* Palo Alto, CA: Stanford University Press.

Terman, L. M. (1954). Scientists and nonscientists in a group of 800 gifted men. *Psychological Monographs, 68*, 1–44.

Terrace, H. S. (1979, November). How Nim-Chimpsky changed my mind. *Psychology Today*, 65–76.

Tesarz, J., Schuster, A. K., Hartmann, M., Gerhardt, A., & Eich, W. (2012). Pain perception in athletes compared to normally active controls: A systematic review with meta-analysis. *Pain, 153*, 1253–1262.

Tetrick, L. E., & Peiró, J. M. (2016). Health and safety: Prevention and promotion. In M. J. Grawitch & D. W. Ballard (Eds.), *The psychologically healthy workplace: Building a win-win environment for organizations and employees* (pp. 199–229). Washington, DC: American Psychological Association. http://dx.doi.org/10.1037/14731-010

Teunissen, H. A., Spijkerman, R., Prinstein, M. G., Cohen, G. L., Engles, R. C., & Scholte, R. H. (2012). Adolescents' conformity to their peers' pro-alcohol and anti-alcohol norms: The power of popularity. *Alcoholism: Clinical and Experimental Research, 36*, 1257–1267.

Thames, A. D., Arbid, N., & Sayegh, P. (2014). Cannabis use and neurocognitive functioning in a non-clinical sample of users. *Addictive Behaviors, 39*, 994–999. doi:10.1016/j.addbeh.2014.01.019

The Amazing Meeting. (2011). The amazing one: James Randi. Retrieved from http://www.amazingmeeting.com/speakers#randi

Thomas, A., & Chess, S. (1977). *Temperament and development.* New York, NY: Brunner/Mazel.

Thomas, A., & Chess, S. (1987). Round-table: What is temperament: Four approaches. *Child Development, 58*, 505–529.

Thomas, J., Raynor, M., & Bahussain, E. (2016). Stress reactivity, depressive symptoms, and mindfulness: A Gulf Arab perspective. *International Perspectives in Psychology: Research, Practice, Consultation, 5*, 156–166. http://dx.doi.org/10.1037/ipp0000055

Thomason, T. (2014). Issues in the diagnosis of Native American culture-bound syndromes. *Arizona Counseling Journal.* Retrieved from http://works.bepress.com/cgi/viewcontent.cgi?article=1181&context=timothy_thomason

Thompson, E. (2015). *Waking, dreaming, being: Self and consciousness in neuroscience, meditation, and philosophy.* New York, NY: Columbia University Press.

Thorndike, E. L. (1898). Animal intelligence. *Psychological Review Monograph, 2*(8).

Thorndike, E. L. (1911). *Animal intelligence.* New York, NY: Macmillan.

Thorn, R. (2013). *12 tips for surviving personal crisis.* Retrieved from http://www.huffingtonpost.com/rayanne-thorn/mindfulness-practice_b_4026593.html

Thrailkill, E. A., & Bouton, M. E. (2015). Contextual control of instrumental actions and habits. *Journal of Experimental Psychology: Animal Learning and Cognition, 41*, 69–80. doi:10.1037/xan0000045

Thurstone, L. L. (1938). *Primary mental abilities.* Chicago, IL: University of Chicago Press.

Tips for Coping with Crisis. (2015). Northeastern University. University Health and Counseling Services. Retrieved June 10, 2015 from http://www.northeastern.edu/uhcs/health-and-wellness/tips-coping-crisis-traumatic-events/

Todd, P. M., & Gigerenzer, G. (2000). Precis of simple heuristics that make us smart. *Behavioral and Brain Sciences, 23*, 727. doi:10.1017/S0140525X00003447

Toepfer, S. M., & Walker, K. (2009). Letters of gratitude: Improving well-being through expressive writing. *Journal of Writing Research, 1*, 181–198.

Toll, B. A., Rojewski, A. M., Duncan, L. R., Latimer-Cheung, A. E., Fucito, L. M., Boyer, J. L., . . . Herbst, R. S. (2014). "Quitting smoking will benefit your health": The evolution of clinician messaging to encourage tobacco cessation. *Clinical Cancer Research, 20*, 301–309. doi:10.1158/10780432.CCR-13-2261

Tolman, E. C., & Honzik, C. H. (1930). Introduction and removal of reward and maze performance in rats. *University of California Publications in Psychology, 4*, 257–275.

Tomash, J. J., & Reed, P. (2013). The generalization of a conditioned response to deception across the public/private barrier. *Learning and Motivation, 44*, 196–203. doi:10.1016/j.lmot.2012.12.001

Topham, G. L., Hubbs-Tait, L., Rutledge, J. M., Page, M. C., Kennedy, T. S., Shriver, L. H., & Harrist, A. W. (2011). Parenting styles, parental response to child emotion, and family emotional responsiveness are related to child emotional eating. *Appetite, 56*, 261–264.

Torrens, M., & Rossi, P. (2015). Mood disorders and addiction. In G. Dom & F. Moggi (Eds.), *Co-occurring addictive and psychiatric disorders: A practice-based handbook from a European perspective* (pp. 103–117). New York, NY: Springer-Verlag. doi:10.1007/978-3-642-45375-5_8

Tousseyn, T., Bajsarowicz, K., Sánchez, H., Gheyara, A., Oehler, A., Geschwind, M., . . . DeArmond, S. J. (2015). Prion disease induces Alzheimer disease—Like neuropathologic changes. *Journal of Neuropathology and Experimental Neurology, 74*, 873–888. http://dx.doi.org/10.1097/NEN.0000000000000228

Tran, D. M., & Westbrook, R. F. (2015). Rats fed a diet rich in fats and sugars are impaired in the use of spatial geometry. *Psychological Science, 26*, 1947–1957. doi:10.1177/0956797615608240

Trautmann-Lengsfeld, S. A., & Herrmann, C. S. (2014). Virtually simulated social pressure influences early visual processing more in low compared to high autonomous participants. *Psychophysiology, 51*, 124–135. http://dx.doi.org/10.1111/psyp.12161

Travers, K. M., Creed, P. A., & Morrissey, S. (2015). The development and initial validation of a new scale to measure explanatory style. *Personality and Individual Differences, 81*, 1–6. doi:10.1016/j.paid.2015.01.045

Treffert, D. A. (2014). Savant syndrome: Realities, myths and misconceptions. *Journal of Autism and Developmental Disorders, 44*, 564–571. doi:10.1007/s10803-013-1906-8

Tropp, L. R., & Page-Gould, E. (2015). Contact between groups. In M. Mikulincer, P. R. Shaver, J. F. Dovidio, & J. A. Simpson (Eds.), *APA handbook of personality and social psychology, Vol. 2. Group processes* (pp. 535–560). Washington, DC: American Psychological Association. doi:10.1037/14342-020

Trull, T. J., Carpenter, R. W., & Widiger, T. A. (2013). Personality disorders. In G. Stricker, T. A. Widiger, & I. B. Weiner (Eds.), *Handbook of*

psychology, Vol. 8. Clinical psychology (2nd ed., pp. 94–120). Hoboken, NJ: Wiley.

Trumbo, M. C., Leiting, K. A., McDaniel, M. A., & Hodge, G. K. (2016). Effects of reinforcement on test-enhanced learning in a large, diverse introductory college psychology course. *Journal of Experimental Psychology: Applied, 9,* 54–57. doi:10.1037/xap0000082

Tsai, K. C. (2015). All work and no play makes an adult a dull learner. *Journal of Education and Training, 2,* 184–191. doi:10.5296/jet.v2i1.6979

Tsai, Y., Lu, B., Ljubimov, A. V., Girman, S., Ross-Cisneros, F. N., Sadun, A. A., . . . Wang, S. (2014). Ocular changes in TgF344-AD rat model of Alzheimer's disease. *Investigative Ophthalmology & Visual Science, 55,* 521–534. doi:10.1167/iovs.13-12888

Tsien, J. Z. (2000, April). Building a brainier mouse. *Scientific American, 282,* 62–68. doi:10.10789248

Tsimakouridze, E. V., Alibhai, F. J., & Martino, T. A. (2015). Therapeutic applications of circadian rhythms for the cardiovascular system. *Frontiers in Pharmacology, 6,* 77. doi:10.3389/fphar.2015.00077

Tsoukalas, I. (2012). The origin of REM sleep: A hypothesis. *Dreaming, 22,* 253–283.

Tucker, S., Pek, S., Morrish, J., & Ruf, M. (2016). Prevalence of texting while driving and other risky driving behaviors among young people in Ontario, Canada: Evidence from 2012 and 2014. *Accident Analysis and Prevention, 84,* 144–152. http://dx.doi.org/10.1016/j.aap.2015.07.011

Tulving, E., & Thompson, D. M. (1973). Encoding specificity and retrieval processes in episodic memory. *Psychological Review, 80,* 352–373. doi:10.1037/h0020071

Turkheimer, E., Pettersson, E., & Horn, E. E. (2014). A phenotypic null hypothesis for the genetics of personality. *Annual Review of Psychology, 65,* 515–540. doi:10.1146/annurev-psych-113011-143752

Tversky, A., & Kahneman, D. (1974). Judgment under uncertainty: Heuristics and biases. *Science, 185,* 1124–1131. doi:10.1126/science.185.4157.1124

Tversky, A., & Kahneman, D. (1993). Probabilistic reasoning. In A. I. Goldman (Ed.), *Readings in philosophy and cognitive science* (pp. 43–68). Cambridge, MA: MIT Press.

Tyner, S., Brewer, A., Helman, M., Leon, Y., Pritchard, J., & Schlund, M. (2016). Nice doggie! Contact desensitization plus reinforcement decreases dog phobias for children with autism. *Behavior Analysis in Practice, 9,* 54–57. doi:10.1007/s40617-016-0113-4

Tyson, P. J., Jones, D., & Elcock, J. (2011). *Psychology in social context: Issues and debates.* Malden, MA: Wiley-Blackwell.

Ulrich, R. E., Stachnik, T. J., & Stainton, N. R. (1963). Student acceptance of generalized personality interpretations. *Psychological Reports, 13,* 831–834. doi:10.2466/pr0.1963.13.3.831

Underwood, E. (2013). Sleep: The brain's housekeeper? *Science, 342,* 301. doi:10.1126/science.342.6156.301

Unsworth, N., Spillers, G. J., & Brewer, G. A. (2012). Dynamics of context-dependent recall: An examination of internal and external context change. *Journal of Memory and Language, 66,* 1–16. doi:10.1016/j.jml.2011.05.001

Urbanová, L., Vyhnánková, V., Krisová, Š., Pacík, D., & Nečas, A. (2015). Intensive training technique utilizing the dog's olfactory abilities to diagnose prostate cancer in men. *Acta Veterinaria Brno, 84,* 77–82. doi:10.2754/avb201585010077

Urriza, J., Arranz-Arranz, B., Ulkatan, S., Téllez, M.J., & Deletis, V. (2016). Integrative action of axonal membrane explored by trains of subthreshold stimuli applied to the peripheral nerve. *Clinical Neurophysiology, 127,* 1707–1709. http://dx.doi.org/10.1016/j.clinph.2015.07.024

Uvnäs-Moberg, K., Handlin, L., & Petersson, M. (2015). Self-soothing behaviors with particular reference to oxytocin release induced by non-noxious sensory stimulation. *Frontiers in Psychology, 5,* Article 1529.

Vacharkulksemsuk, T., Reit, E., Khambatta, P., Eastwick, P. W., Finkel, E. J., & Carney, D. R. (2016). Dominant, open nonverbal displays are attractive at zero-acquaintance. *Proceedings of the National Academy of Sciences of the United States of America, 113,* 4009–4014. doi:10.1073/pnas.1508932113

Vaillant, G. E. (2012). *Triumphs of experience: The men of the Harvard Grant Study.* Cambridge, MA: Harvard University Press.

Valchev, V. H., van de Vijver, F. J. R., Meiring, D., Nel, J. A., Hill, C., Laher, S., & Adams, B. G. (2014). Beyond agreeableness: Social-relational personality concepts from an indigenous and cross-cultural perspective. *Journal of Research in Personality, 48,* 17–32. doi:10.1016/j.jrp.2013.10.003

Valentine, K. A., Li, N. P., Penke, L., & Perrett, D. I. (2014). Judging a man by the width of his face: The role of facial ratios and dominance in mate choice at speed-dating events. *Psychological Science, 25,* 806–811. doi:10.1177/0956797613511823

Vallejo-Torres, L., Castilla, I., González, N., Hunter, R., Serrano-Pérez, P., & Perestelo-Pérez, L. (2015). Cost-effectiveness of electroconvulsive therapy compared to repetitive transcranial magnetic stimulation for treatment-resistant severe depression: A decision model. *Psychological Medicine, 45,* 1459–1470. doi:10.1017/S0033291714002554

van Avesaat, M., Troost, F. J., Ripken, D., Hendriks, H. F., & Masclee, A. A. M. (2015). Ileal brake activation: Macronutrient-specific effects on eating behavior? *International Journal of Obesity, 39,* 235–243. doi:10.1038/ijo.2014.112

Van Belle, G., Lefèvre, P., & Rossion, B. (2015). Face inversion and acquired prosopagnosi a reduce the size of the perceptual field of view. *Cognition, 136,* 403–408. doi:10.1016/j.cognition.2014.11.037

Van de Carr, F. R., & Lehrer, M. (1997). *While you are expecting: Your own prenatal classroom.* New York, NY: Humanics.

van de Kamp, M.-T., Admiraal, W., van Drie, J., & Rijlaarsdam, G. (2015). Enhancing divergent thinking in visual arts education: Effects of explicit instruction of metacognition. *British Journal of Educational Psychology, 85,* 47–58. doi:10.1111/bjep.12061

Vandeleur, C. L., Rothen, S., Lustenberger, Y., Glaus, J., Castelao, E., & Preisig, M. (2015). Inter-informant agreement and prevalence estimates for mood syndromes: Direct interview vs. family history method. *Journal of Affective Disorders, 171,* 120–127. doi:10.1016/j.jad.2014.08.048

van den Akker, K., Havermans, R. C., & Jansen, A. (2015). Effects of occasional reinforced trials during extinction on the reacquisition of conditioned responses to food cues. *Journal of Behavior Therapy and Experimental Psychiatry, 48,* 50–58. doi:10.1016/j.jbtep.2015.02.001

van den Berg, S. M., de Moor, M. H. M., Verweij, K. J. H., Krueger, R. F., Luciano, M., Arias Vasquez, A., . . . Boomsma, D. I. (2016). Meta-analysis of genome-wide association studies for extraversion: Findings from the genetics of personality consortium. *Behavior Genetics, 46,* 170–182. http://dx.doi.org/10.1007/s10519-015-9735-5

Vandenbosch, L., & Eggermont, S. (2011). Temptation Island, The Bachelor, Joe Millionaire: A prospective cohort study on the role of romantically themed reality television in adolescents' sexual development. *Journal of Broadcasting & Electronic Media, 56,* 563–580.

van der Lely, S., Frey, S., Garbazza, C., Wirz-Justice, A., Jenni, O. G., Steiner, R., . . . Schmidt, C. (2015). Blue blocker glasses as a countermeasure for alerting effects of evening light-emitting diode screen exposure in male teenagers. *Journal of Adolescent Health, 56,* 113–119. doi:10.1016/j.jadohealth.2014.08.002

van der Pligt, J., & Vliek, M. (2016). *The psychology of influence.* New York, NY: Psychology Press.

van der Weiden, A., Prikken, M., & van Haren, N. E. M. (2015). Self-other integration and distinction in schizophrenia: A theoretical analysis and a review of the evidence. *Neuroscience and Biobehavioral Reviews, 57,* 220–237. doi:10.1016/j.neubiorev.2015.09.004

van Dijk, S. J., Molloy, P. L., Varinli, H., Morrison, J. L., Muhlhausler, B. S., Buckley, M., . . . Tellam, R. L. (2015). Epigenetics and human obesity. *International Journal of Obesity, 39,* 85–97. doi:10.1038/ijo.2014.34

van Dongen, J., Willemsen, G., Heijmans, B. T., Neuteboom, J., Kluft, C., Jansen, R., . . . Boomsma, D. I. (2015). Longitudinal weight differences, gene expression and blood biomarkers in BMI-discordant identical twins. *International Journal of Obesity, 39,* 899–909. doi:10.1038/ijo.2015.24

van IJzendoorn, M. H., & Bakermans-Kranenburg, M. J. (2010). Invariance of adult attachment across gender, age, culture, and socioeconomic status? *Journal of Social and Personal Relationships, 27,* 200–208. doi: 10.1177/0265407509360908

van Lenthe, F. J., Jansen, T., & Kamphuis, C. (2015). Understanding socio-economic inequalities in food choice behaviour: Can Maslow's pyramid help? *British Journal of Nutrition, 113,* 1139–1147. doi:10.1017/S0007114515000288

van Meurs, B., Wiggert, N., Wicker, I., & Lissek, S. (2014). Maladaptive behavioral consequences of conditioned fear-generalization: A pronounced, yet sparsely studied, feature of anxiety pathology. *Behaviour Research and Therapy, 57,* 29–37. doi:10.1016/j.brat.2014.03.009

van Name, M., Giannini, C., Santoro, N., Jastreboff , A. M., Kubat, J., Li, F., . . . Caprio, S. (2015). Blunted suppression of acyl-ghrelin in response to fructose ingestion in obese adolescents: The role of insulin resistance. *Obesity, 23,* 653–661. doi:10.1002/oby.21019

van Ommen, M. M., van Beilen, M., Cornelissen, F. W., Smid, H. G. O. M., Knegtering, H., Aleman, A., . . . GROUP Investigators. (2016). The prevalence of visual hallucinations in non-affective psychosis, and the role of perception and attention. *Psychological Medicine, 46,* 1735–1747. http://dx.doi.org/10.1017/S0033291716000246

Van Tilburg, W. A. P., & Igou, E. R. (2014). From Van Gogh to Lady Gaga: Artist eccentricity increases perceived artistic skill and art appreciation. *European Journal of Social Psychology, 44,* 93–103. doi:10.1002/ejsp.1999

Vassoler, F. M., Byrnes, E. M., & Pierce, R. C. (2014). The impact of exposure to addictive drugs on future generations: Physiological and behavioral effects. *Neuropharmacology, 76,* 269–275. doi:10.1016/j.neuropharm.2013.06.016

Vecchione, M., Dentale, F., Alessandri, G., Imbesi, M. T., Barbaranelli, C., & Schnabel, K. (2016). On the applicability of the big five implicit association test in organizational settings. *Current Psychology,* 1–10. http://dx.doi.org/10.1007/s12144-016-9455-x

Venables, P. H., & Raine, A. (2016). The impact of malnutrition on intelligence at 3 and 11 years of age: The mediating role of temperament. *Developmental Psychology, 52,* 205–220. http://dx.doi.org/10.1037/dev0000046

Ventriglio, A., Ayonrinde, O., & Bhugra, D. (2016). Relevance of culture-bound syndromes in the 21st century. *Psychiatry and Clinical Neurosciences, 70,* 3–6. http://dx.doi.org/10.1111/pcn.12359

Vermetten, E., & Spiegel, D. (2014). Trauma and dissociation: Implications for borderline personality disorder. *Current Psychiatry Reports, 16,* 1–10. doi:10.1007/s11920-013-0434-8

Vezzali, L., Stathi, S., Giovannini, D., Capozza, D., & Trifiletti, E. (2015). The greatest magic of Harry Potter: Reducing prejudice. *Journal of Applied Social Psychology, 45,* 105–121. doi:10.1111/jasp.12279

Vidal, F., Meckler, C., & Hasbroucq, T. (2015). Basics for sensorimotor information processing: Some implications for learning. *Frontiers in Psychology, 6,* 33. doi:10.3389/fpsyg.2015.00033

Vinall, J., & Grunau, R. E. (2014). Impact of repeated procedural pain-related stress in infants born very preterm. *Pediatric Research, 75,* 584–587. doi:10.1038/pr.2014.16

Vishwanath, A. (2015). Habitual Facebook use and its impact on getting deceived on social media. *Journal of Computer-Mediated Communication, 20,* 83–98. doi:10.1111/jcc4.12100

Viviani, R., Nagl, M., & Buchheim, A. (2015). Psychotherapy outcome research and neuroimaging. In O. C. G. Gelo, A. Pritz, & B. Rieken (Eds.), *Psychotherapy research: Foundations, process, and outcome* (pp. 611–634). New York, NY: Springer. doi:10.1007/978-3-7091-1382-0_30

Vliegenthart, J., Noppe, G., van Rossum, E. F. C., Koper, J. W., Raat, H., & van den Akker, E. L. T. (2016). Socioeconomic status in children is associated with hair cortisol levels as a biological measure of chronic stress. *Psychoneuroendocrinology, 65,* 9–14. http://dx.doi.org/10.1016/j.psyneuen.2015.11.022

Vokey, J. R., & Read, J. D. (1985). Subliminal messages: Between the devil and the media. *American Psychologist, 40,* 1231–1239.

Volz, B. D. (2016). Race and quarterback survival in the National Football League. *Journal of Sports Economics.* No Pagination Specified.

von Dawans, B., Fischbacher, U., Kirschbaum, C., Fehr, E., & Heinrichs, M. (2012). The social dimension of stress reactivity: Acute stress increases prosocial behavior in humans. *Psychological Science, 23,* 651–660. doi:10.1177/0956797611431576

von Hofsten, C. (2013). Action in infancy: A foundation for cognitive development. In W. Prinz, M. Beisert, & A. Herwig (Eds.), *Action science foundation of an emerging discipline* (pp. 255–280). New York, NY: Oxford University Press.

Vonmoos, M., Hulka, L. M., Preller, K. H., Minder, F., Baumgartner, M. R., & Quednow, B. B. (2014). Cognitive impairment in cocaine users is drug-induced but partially reversible: Evidence from a longitudinal study. *Neuropsychopharmacology, 39,* 2200–2210. doi:10.1038/npp.2014.71

Von Stumm, S., & Plomin, R. (2015). Socioeconomic status and the growth of intelligence from infancy through adolescence. *Intelligence, 48,* 30–36. doi:10.1016/j.intell.2014.10.002

Vorster, A. P., & Born, J. (2015). Sleep and memory in mammals, birds and invertebrates. *Neuroscience and Biobehavioral Reviews, 50,* 103–119. doi:10.1016/j.neubiorev.2014.09.020

Vozzola, E. C. (2014). *Moral development: Theory and applications.* New York, NY: Routledge/Taylor & Francis Group.

Vrij, A., Granhag, P. A., & Porter, S. (2010). Pitfalls and opportunities in nonverbal and verbal lie detection. *Psychological Science in the Public Interest, 11,* 89–121. doi:10.1177/1529100610390861

Vrticka, P., Simioni, S., Fornari, E., Schluep, M., Vuilleumier, P., & Sander, D. (2013). Neural substrates of social emotion regulation: A fMRI study on imitation and expressive suppression to dynamic facial signals. *Frontiers in Psychology, 4,* Article ID 95. doi:10.3389/fpsyg.2013.00095

Vygotsky, L. S. (1962). *Thought and language.* Cambridge, MA: MIT Press.

Vyplelová, P., Vokálek, V., Pinc, L., Pacáková, Z., Bartoš, L., Santariová, M., & Čapková, Z. (2014). Individual human odor fallout as detected by trained canines. *Forensic Science International, 234,* 13–15. doi:10.1016/j.forsciint.2013.10.018

Wagner, F. L., Rammsayer, T. H., Schweizer, K., & Troche, S. J. (2014). Relations between the attentional blink and aspects of psychometric intelligence: A fixed-links modeling approach. *Personality and Individual Differences, 58,* 122–127. doi:10.1016/j.paid.2013.10.023

Walker, A. K., Rivera, P. D., Wang, Q., Chuang, J. C., Tran, S., Osborne-Lawrence, S., . . . Zigman, J. M. (2015). The P7C3 class of neuroprotective compounds exerts antidepressant efficacy in mice by increasing hippocampal neurogenesis. *Molecular Psychiatry, 20,* 500–508. doi:10.1038/mp.2014.34

Walker, H. M., & Gresham, F. M. (2016). *Handbook of evidence-based practices for emotional and behavioral disorders* (Reprint edition). New York, NY: Guilford Press.

Walker, J. V., III, & Lampropoulos, G. K. (2014). A comparison of self-help (homework) activities for mood enhancement: Results from a brief randomized controlled trial. *Journal of Psychotherapy Integration, 24,* 46–64. http://dx.doi.org/10.1037/a0036145

Wallack, L., & Thornburg, K. (2016). Developmental origins, epigenetics, and equity: Moving upstream. *Maternal and Child Health Journal, 20,* 935–940. http://dx.doi.org/10.1007/s10995-016-1970-8

Walsh, K., & Cross, W. (2013). Depression: Classification, culture and the westernisation of mental illness. In N. Kocabasoglu (Ed.), *Mood disorders.* Retrieved from http://cdn.intechopen.com/pdfs/42233/InTech-Depression_classification_culture_and_the_westernisation_of_mental_illness.pdf

Walsh, R., Teo, T., & Baydala, A. (2014). *A critical history of psychology and philosophy.* Cambridge, UK: Cambridge University Press.

Walton, G. M., & Cohen, G. L. (2011). A brief social-belonging intervention improves academic and health outcomes of minority students. *Science, 331,* 1447–1451. doi:10.1126/science.1198364

Walton, G. M., Logel, C., Peach, J. M., Spencer, S. J., & Zanna, M. P. (2015). Two brief interventions to mitigate a "chilly climate" transform women's experience, relationships, and achievements in engineering. *Journal of Educational Psychology, 10,* 468–485. doi:10.1037/a0037461

Wamsley, E. J., & Stickgold, R. (2010). Dreaming and offline memory processing. *Current Biology, 20,* 1010–1013. doi:10.1016/j.cub.2010.10.045

Wang, M.-T., & Kenny, S. (2014). Longitudinal links between fathers' and mothers' harsh verbal discipline and adolescents' conduct problems and depressive symptoms. *Child Development, 85,* 908–923. doi:10.1111/cdev.12143

Wang, Q. (2011). Autobiographical memory and culture. Online readings in psychology and culture, 5. http://dx.doi.org/10.9707/2307-0919.1047

Wassing, R., Benjamins, J. S., Dekker, K., Moens, S., Spiegelhalder, K., Feige, B., . . . Van Someren, E. J. W. (2016). Slow dissolving of emotional distress contributes to hyperarousal. *Proceedings of the National Academy of Sciences of the United States of America, 113,* 2538–2543. doi:10.1073/pnas.1522520113

Watkins, C. E., Jr. (2016). Listening, learning, and development in psychoanalytic supervision: A self psychology perspective. *Psychoanalytic Psychology, 33,* 437–471. http://dx.doi.org/10.1037/a0038168

Watkins, P. C., Uhder, J., & Pichinevskiy, S. (2015). Grateful recounting enhances subjective well-being: The importance of grateful processing. *The Journal of Positive Psychology, 10,* 91–98. doi:10.1080/17439760.2014.927909

Watson, D., Beer, A., & McDade-Montez, E. (2014). The role of active assortment in spousal similarity. *Journal of Personality, 82,* 116–129. doi:10.1111/jopy.12039

Watson, J. B. (1913). Psychology as the behaviorist views it. *Psychological Review, 20,* 158–177. doi:10.1037/h0074428

Watson, J. B., & Rayner, R. (1920). Conditioned emotional reactions. *Journal of Experimental Psychology, 3,* 1–14. doi:10.1037/h0069608

Watts, B. V., Zayed, M. H., Llewellyn-Thomas, H., & Schnurr, P. P. (2016). Understanding and meeting information needs for patients with posttraumatic stress disorder. *BMC Psychiatry, 16,* Article 21. http://dx.doi.org/10.1186/s12888-016-0724-x

Weaver, M. F., Hopper, J. A., & Gunderson, E. W. (2015). Designer drugs 2015: Assessment and management. *Addiction Science and Clinical Practice, 10,* 1–9. doi:10.1186/s13722-015-0024-7

Webb, B., Hine, A, C., & Bailey, P. E. (2016). Difficulty in differentiating trustworthiness from untrustworthiness in older age. *Developmental Psychology, 52,* 985–995. http://dx.doi.org/10.1037/dev0000126

Webber, D., Schimel, J., Faucher, E. H., Hayes, J., Zhang, R., & Martens, A. (2015). Emotion as a necessary component of threat-induced death thought accessibility and defensive compensation. *Motivation and Emotion, 39,* 142–155. doi:10.1007/s11031-014-9426-1

Webb, S. (2016). Schizophrenia. In A. Breland-Noble, C. S. Al-Mateen, & N. N. Singh (Eds.), *Handbook of mental health in African American youth* (pp. 249–259). Cham, CH: Springer International Publishing. http://dx.doi.org/10.1007/978-3-319-25501-9_15

Wechsler, D. (1944). *The measurement of adult intelligence* (3rd ed.). Baltimore, MD: Williams & Wilkins.

Wechsler, D. (1977). *Manual for the Wechsler Intelligence Scale for Children* (Rev.). New York, NY: Psychological Corporation.

Weeks, B. E., & Garrett, R. K. (2014). Electoral consequences of political rumors: Motivated reasoning, candidate rumors, and vote choice during the 2008 US presidential election. *International Journal of Public Opinion Research, 26,* 401–422. doi:10.1093/ijpor/edu005

Weems, C. F., Scott, B. G., Banks, D. M., & Graham, R. A. (2012). Is TV traumatic for all youths? The role of preexisting posttraumatic stress symptoms in the link between disaster coverage and stress. *Psychological Science, 23,* 1293–1297. doi:10.1177/0956797612446952

Weiler, L. M., Lyness, K. P., Haddock, S. A., & Zimmerman, T. S. (2015). Contextual issues in couple and family therapy: Gender, sexual orientation, culture, and spirituality. In J. L. Wetchler & L. L. Hecker (Eds.), *An introduction to marriage and family therapy* (2nd ed., pp. 65–116). New York, NY: Routledge/Taylor & Francis Group.

Weiner, B. (1972). *Theories of motivation.* Chicago, IL: Rand-McNally.

Weiner, B. (2015). On the cross-cultural trail, searching for (non)-replication. *International Journal of Psychology, 50,* 303–307. http://dx.doi.org/10.1002/ijop.12156

Weingart, P., Mitchell, S. D., Richerson, P. J., & Maasen, S. (Eds.). (2013). *Human by nature: Between biology and the social sciences.* New York, NY: Psychology Press.

Weinstein, D., Launay, J., Pearce, E., Dunbar, R.I.M., & Stewart, L. (2016). Singing and social bonding: Changes in connectivity and pain threshold as a function of group size. *Evolution and Human Behavior, 37,* 152–158. doi:10.1016/j.evolhumbehav.2015.10.002

Weinstein, N., Ryan, W. S., DeHaan, C. R., Przybylski, A. K., Legate, N., & Ryan, R. M. (2012). Parental autonomy support and discrepancies between implicit and explicit sexual identities: Dynamics of self-acceptance and defense. *Journal of Personality and Social Psychology, 102,* 815–832. doi:10.1037/a0026854

Weinstein, Y., Nunes, L. D., & Karpicke, J. D. (2016). On the placement of practice questions during study. *Journal of Experimental Psychology: Applied, 22,* 72–84. doi:10.1037/xap0000071

Weintraub, K. (2016). Young and sleep deprived. *Monitor on Psychology, 47,* 46. Retrieved from http://www.apa.org/monitor/2016/02/sleep-deprived.aspx

Weir, K. (2014, October). Mind games. *Monitor on Psychology, 45.* No Pagination Specified. doi:10.1037/e577942014-009

Weisman, O., Zagoory-Sharon, O., & Feldman, R. (2012). Oxytocin administration to parent enhances infant physiological and behavioral readiness for social engagement. *Biological Psychiatry, 72,* 982–989.

Weiss, A., Gartner, M. C., Gold, K. C., & Stoinski, T. S. (2013). Extraversion predicts longer survival in gorillas: An 18-year longitudinal study. *Proceedings of the Royal Society B-Biological Sciences, 280,* 1–5. doi:10.1098/rspb.2012.2231

Weiss, A., Staes, N., Pereboom, J. J., Inoue-Murayama, M., Stevens, J. M., & Eens, M. (2015). Personality in bonobos. *Psychological Science, 26,* 1430–1439. doi:10.1177/0956797615589933.

Weitkamp, K., Daniels, J. K., Hofmann, H., Timmermann, H., Romer, G., & Wiegand-Grefe, S. (2014). Psychoanalytic psychotherapy for children and adolescents with severe depressive psychopathology: Preliminary results of an effectiveness trial. *Psychotherapy, 51,* 138–147. doi:10.1037/a0034178

Weitlauf, J. C., Cervone, D., Smith, R. E., & Wright, P. M. (2001). Assessing generalization in perceived self-efficacy: Multidomain and global assessments of the effects of self-defense training for women. *Personality and Social Psychology Bulletin, 27,* 1683–1691. doi:10.1177/01461672012712011

Wergård, E.-M., Westlund, K., Spångberg, M., Fredlund, H., & Forkman, B. (2016). Training success in group-housed long-tailed macaques (Macaca fascicularis) is better explained by personality than by social rank. *Applied Animal Behaviour Science, 177,* 52–58. http://dx.doi.org/10.1016/j.applanim.2016.01.017

Werner, K. B., Few, L. R., & Bucholz, K. K. (2015). Epidemiology, comorbidity, and behavioral genetics of antisocial personality disorder and psychopathy. *Psychiatric Annals, 45,* 195–199. doi:10.3928/00485713-20150401-08

Werner, K. H., Roberts, N. A., Rosen, H. J., Dean, D. L., Kramer, J. H., Weiner, M. W., . . . Levenson, R. W. (2007). Emotional reactivity and emotion recognition in frontotemporal lobar degeneration. *Neurology, 69,* 148–155.

Werner, S., & Roth, D. (2014). Stigma in the field of intellectual disabilities: Impact and initiatives for change. In P. W. Corrigan (Ed.), *The stigma of disease and disability: Understanding causes and overcoming injustices* (pp. 73–91). Washington, DC: American Psychological Association. doi:10.1037/14297-005

Wertli, M. M., Burgstaller, J. M., Weiser, S., Steurer, J., Kofmehl, R., & Held, U. (2014). Influence of catastrophizing on treatment outcome in patients with nonspecific low back pain: A systematic review. *Spine, 39,* 263–273. doi:10.1097/BRS.0000000000000110

Westfall, J., Van Boven, L., Chambers, J. R., & Judd, C. M. (2015). Perceiving political polarization in the United States: Party identity strength and attitude extremity exacerbate the perceived partisan divide. *Perspectives on Psychological Science, 10,* 145–158. doi:10.1177/1745691615569849

West, J. P. (2015). Combating age discrimination: Legal and regulatory issues, challenges, and opportunities. In R. R. Sims & W. I. Sauser (Eds.), *Legal and regulatory issues in human resources management. Contemporary human resources management: Issues, challenges, and opportunities* (pp. 169–205). Charlotte, NC: Information Age.

West, T. V., Magee, J. C., Gordon, S. H., & Gullett, L. (2014). A little similarity goes a long way: The effects of peripheral but self-revealing similarities on improving and sustaining interracial relationships. *Journal of Personality and Social Psychology, 107,* 81–100. doi:10.1037/a0036556

Wetterling, T., Dibbelt, L., Wetterling, G., G.der, R., Wurst, F., Margraf, M., & Junghanns, K. (2014). Ethyl glucuronide (EtG): Better than breathalyser or self-reports to detect covert short-term relapses into drinking. *Alcohol and Alcoholism, 49,* 51–54. doi:10.1093/alcalc/agt155

Whillans, A. V., Weidman, A. C., & Dunn, E. W. (2016). Valuing time over money is associated with greater happiness. *Social Psychological and Personality Science, 7,* 213–222. doi:10.1177/1948550615623842

Whitbourne, S. K., & Whitbourne, S. B. (2014). *Adult development and aging: Biological perspectives* (5th ed.). Hoboken, NJ: Wiley.

White, T., Andreasen, N. C., & Nopoulos, P. (2002). Brain volumes and surface morphology in monozygotic twins. *Cerebral Cortex, 12,* 486–493. doi:10.1093/cercor/12.5.486

Whorf, B. L. (1956). *Language, thought, and reality.* New York, NY: Wiley.

Wiggin, K. L., & Yalch, R. F. (2015). Whose fault is it? Effects of relational self-views and outcome counterfactuals on self-serving attribution biases following brand policy changes. *Journal of Consumer Psychology, 25,* 459–472. doi:10.1016/j.jcps.2015.02.004

Wild, J., & Clark, D. M. (2015). Experiential exercises and imagery rescripting in social anxiety disorder: New perspectives on changing beliefs. In N. C. Thoma & D. McKay (Eds.), *Working with emotion in cognitive-behavioral therapy: Techniques for clinical practice* (pp. 216–236). New York, NY: Guilford.

Wilkie, G., Sakr, B., & Rizack, T. (2016). Medical marijuana use in oncology: A review. *JAMA Oncology, 2,* 670–675. doi:10.1001/jamaoncol.2016.0155.

Wilkins, C. L., Wellman, J. D., Babbitt, L. G., Toosi, N. R., & Schad, K. D. (2015). You can win but I can't lose: Bias against high-status groups increases their zero-sum beliefs about discrimination. *Journal of Experimental Social Psychology, 57,* 1–14. doi:10.1016/j.jesp.2014.10.008

Williams, C. L., & Lally, S. J. (2016). MMPI-2, MMPI-2-RF, and MMPI-A administrations (2007–2014): Any evidence of a "new standard?" *Professional Psychology: Research and Practice.* No Pagination Specified. http://dx.doi.org/10.1037/pro0000088

Williams, D. L. (2014). Neural integration of satiation and food reward: Role of GLP-1 and orexin pathways. *Physiology & Behavior, 136,* 194–199. doi:10.1016/j.physbeh.2014.03.013

Williamson, A. A., Guerra, N. G., & Tynan, W. D. (2014). The role of health and mental health care providers in gun violence prevention. *Clinical Practice in Pediatric Psychology, 2,* 88–98. doi:10.1037/cpp0000055

Williamson, J. M., Lounsbury, J. W., & Han, L. D. (2013). Key personality traits of engineers for innovation and technology development. *Journal of Engineering Technology Management, 30,* 157–168.

Williamson, J. N., & Williamson, D. G. (2015). Sleep-wake disorders. In L. Sperry, J. Carlson, J. D. Sauerheber, & J. Sperry (Eds.), *Psychopathology and psychotherapy: DSM-5 diagnosis, case conceptualization, and treatment* (3rd ed., pp. 243–264). New York, NY: Routledge/Taylor & Francis Group.

Williams, S. C. P. (2013, July 15). Obesity gene linked to hunger hormone. *Science NOW.* Retrieved from http://news.sciencemag.org/sciencenow/2013/07/obesitygene-linked-to-hunger-ho.html? ref=em#.UeTHLsf3tP0.email

Williams, S. S. (2001). Sexual lying among college students in close and casual relationships. *Journal of Applied Social Psychology, 31,* 2322–2338.

Willyard, C. (2011). Men: A growing minority. *grad-PSYCH, 9,* 40–44. doi:10.1037/e669902010-010

Wilson, D. S. (2015). *Does altruism exist? Culture, genes, and the welfare of others.* New Haven, CT: Yale University Press.

Wilson, E. O. (1975). *Sociobiology: The new synthesis.* Cambridge, MA: Harvard University Press.

Wilson, E. O. (1978). *On human nature.* Cambridge, MA: Harvard University Press.

Wilson, E. O. (2013). *The social conquest of earth.* New York, NY: Liveright.

Wilson, L. M., Tang, E. A., Chander, G., Hutton, H. E., Odelola, O. A., Elf, J. L., . . . Apelberg, B. J. (2012). Impact of tobacco control interventions on smoking initiation, cessation, and prevalence: A systematic review. *Journal of Environmental and Public Health, Volume 2012,* Article ID 961724. http://dx.doi.org/10.1155/2012/961724

Wilson, M. (2015b, June 5). A Manhattan fortune teller cost him fortune after fortune. *New York Times.* http://www.nytimes.com/2015/06/06/nyregion/he-went-to-thefortune-teller-now-his-fortune-is-gone.html?

Witelson, S. F., Kigar, D. L., & Harvey, T. (1999). The exceptional brain of Albert Einstein. *The Lancet, 353,* 2149–2153. doi:10.1016/S0140-6736(05)70590-0

Wixted, J. T., Mickes, L., Clark, S. E., Gronlund, S. D., & Roediger, H. L. III. (2015). Initial eyewitness confidence reliably predicts eyewitness identification accuracy. *American Psychologist, 70,* 515–526. http://dx.doi.org/10.1037/a0039510

Wolfgang, B. (2016, March 6). Bernie Sanders suggests GOP presidential candidates are mentally ill. *The Washington Times.* Retrieved from http://www.washingtontimes.com/news/2016/mar/6/berniesanders-suggests-republican-presidential-ca/

Wollan, M. (2015, August 16). How to brush a gorilla's teeth. *The New York Times Magazine,* p. 25.

Wollan, M. (2015). How to beat a polygraph test. *The New York Times Magazine.* Retrieved from http://www.nytimes.com/2015/04/12/magazine/how-to-beat-apolygraph-test.html?_r=0

Wolpe, J., & Plaud, J. J. (1997). Pavlov's contributions to behavior therapy. *American Psychologist, 52,* 966–972.

Woodin, E. M., Sukhawathanakul, P., Caldeira, V., Homel, J., & Leadbeater, B. (2016). Pathways to romantic relational aggression through adolescent peer aggression and heavy episodic drinking. *Aggressive Behavior.* No Pagination Specified. doi:10.1002/ab.21651

Woodley of Menie, M. A., & Madison, G. (2015). The association between g and K in a sample of 4246 Swedish twins: A behavior genetic analysis. *Personality and Individual Differences, 74,* 270–274. doi:10.1016/j.paid.2014.10.027

Woodley of Menie, M. A., Peñaherrera, M. A., Fernandes, H. B. F., Becker, D., & Flynn, J. R. (2016). It's getting bigger all the time: Estimating the Flynn effect from secular brain mass increases in Britain and Germany. *Learning and Individual Differences, 45,* 95–100. http://dx.doi.org/10.1016/j.lindif.2015.11.004

Wood, M. (2016, February 17). Electronic devices, kids and sleep: How screen time keeps them awake. *ScienceLife.* Retrieved from https://sciencelife.uchospitals.edu/2016/02/17/electronic-devices-kids-and-sleep-how-screen-time-keeps-them-awake/

Woods, R. J., & Wilcox, T. (2013). Posture support improves object individuation in infants.

Developmental Psychology, 49, 1413–1424. http://doi.org/10.1037/a0030344

Woodward, N. D., & Heckers, S. (2015). Brain structure in neuropsychologically defined subgroups of schizophrenia and psychotic bipolar disorder. *Schizophrenia Bulletin, 41,* 1349–1359. doi:10.1093/schbul/sbv048

World Health Organization. (2011). *Depression.* Retrieved from http://www.who.int/topics/depression/en/

Wright, K. P., Drake, A. L., Frey, D. J., Fleshner, M., Desouza, C. A., Gronfier, C., & Czeisler, C. A. (2015). Influence of sleep deprivation and circadian misalignment on cortisol, inflammatory markers, and cytokine balance. *Brain, Behavior, and Immunity, 47,* 24–34. doi:10.1016/j.bbi.2015.01.004

Wright, T. J., Boot, W. R., & Brockmole, J. R. (2015). Functional fixedness: The functional significance of delayed disengagement based on attention set. *Journal of Experimental Psychology: Human Perception and Performance, 41,* 17–21. doi:10.1037/xhp0000016

Wrzesniewski, A., Schwartz, B., Cong, X., Kane, M., Omar, A., & Kolditz, T. (2014). Multiple types of motives don't multiply the motivation of West Point cadets. *Proceedings of the National Academy of Sciences of the United States of America, 111,* 10990–10995. doi:10.1073/pnas.1405298111

Wu, J., Perry, D. C., Bupp, J. E., Jiang, F., Polgar, W. E., Toll, L., & Zaveri, N. T. (2014). [125I] AT-1012, a new high affinity radioligand for the α3β4 nicotinic acetylcholine receptors. *Neuropharmacology, 77,* 193–199. doi:10.1016/j.neuropharm.2013.09.023

Wu, X. N., Zhang, T., Qian, N. S., Guo, X. D., Yang, H. J., Huang, K. B., . . . Pan, S. Y. (2015). Antinociceptive effects of endomorphin-2: Suppression of substance P release in the inflammatory pain model rat. *Neurochemistry international, 82,* 1–9. doi:10.1016/j.neuint.2015.01.004

Wyman, A. J., & Vyse, S. (2008). Science versus the stars: A double-blind test of the validity of the NEO Five Factor Inventory and computer-generated astrological natal charts. *Journal of General Psychology, 135,* 287–300.

Xi, J., Lee, M., LeSuer, W., Barr, P., Newton, K., & Poloma, M. (2016). Altruism and existential well-being. *Applied Research in Quality of Life.* No Pagination Specified. http://dx.doi.org/10.1007/s11482-016-9453-z

Xiao, K., & Yamauchi, T. (2016). Subliminal semantic priming in near absence of attention: A cursor motion study. *Consciousness and Cognition, 38,* 88–98. http://dx.doi.org/10.1016/j.concog.2015.09.013

Xie, L., Kang, H., Xu, Q., Chen, M. J., Liao, Y., Thiyagarajan, M., . . . Nedergaard, M. (2013). Sleep drives metabolite clearance from the human brain. *Science, 342,* 373–377. doi:10.1126/science.1241224

Xu, L., & Barnes, L. (2011). Measurement invariance of scores from the inventory of school motivation across Chinese and U.S. college students. *International Journal of Testing, 11,* 178–210. doi: 10.1080/15305058.2010.542357

Xue, S. W., Tang, Y. Y., Tang, R., & Posner, M. I. (2014). Short-term meditation induces changes in brain resting EEG theta networks. *Brain and Cognition, 87,* 1–6. doi:10.1016/j.bandc.2014.02.008

Yadollahpour, A., Hosseini, S. A., & Shakeri, A. (2016). Rtms for the treatment of depression: A comprehensive review of effective protocols on right dlpfc. *International Journal of Mental Health and Addiction, 14,* 539–549. http://dx.doi.org/10.1007/s11469-016-9669-z

Yamada, H. (1997). *Different games, different rules: Why Americans and Japanese misunderstand each other.* London, UK: Oxford University Press.

Yamaguchi, K., Inoue, Y., Ohki, N., Satoya, N., Inoue, F., Maeda, Y., . . . Nagai, A. (2014). Gender-specific impacts of apnea, age, and BMI on parasympathetic nerve dysfunction during sleep in patients with obstructive sleep apnea. *PLoS ONE, 9,* 1–11. doi:10.1371/journal.pone.0092808

Yamazaki, T., Nagao, S., Lennon, W., & Tanaka, S. (2015). Modeling memory consolidation during posttraining periods in cerebellovestibular learning. *Proceedings of the National Academy of Sciences of the United States of America, 112,* 3541–3546. doi:10.1073/pnas.1413798112

Yang, J., Hou, X., Wei, D., Wang, K., Li, Y., & Qiu, J. (2016). Only-child and non-only-child exhibit differences in creativity and agreeableness: Evidence from behavioral and anatomical structural studies. *Brain Imaging and Behavior.* No Pagination Specified. http://dx.doi.org/10.1007/s11682-016-9530-9

Yang, J., Peek-Asa, C., Covassin, T., & Torner, J. C. (2015). Post-concussion symptoms of depression and anxiety in Division I collegiate athletes. *Developmental Neuropsychology, 40,* 18–23. doi:10.1080/87565641.2014.973499

Yang, J., Watanabe, J., Kanazawa, S., Nishida, S.'y., & Yamaguchi, M. K. (2015). Infants' visual system nonretinotopically integrates color signals along a motion trajectory. *Journal of Vision, 15,* Article ID 25. doi:10.1167/15.1.25

Yang, T. (2016). Image schemas in verb-particle constructions: Evidence from a behavioral experiment. *Journal of Psycholinguistic Research, 45,* 379–393. http://dx.doi.org/10.1007/s10936-015-9354-6

Yapko, M. D. (2015). *Essentials of hypnosis* (2nd ed.). New York, NY: Routledge/Taylor & Francis Group.

Yasnitsky, A. (2015). *Vygotsky: An intellectual biography.* Boca Raton, FL: Taylor & Francis Group.

Yetish, G., Kaplan, H., Gurven, M., Wood, B., Pontzer, H., Manger, P. R., . . . Siegel, J. M. (2015). Natural sleep and its seasonal variations in three pre-industrial societies. *Current Biology, 25,* 2862–2868. http://dx.doi.org/10.1016/j.cub.2015.09.046

Yin, H., Pantazatos, S. P., Galfalvy, H., Huang, Y.-Y., Rosoklija, G. B., Dwork, A. J., . . . Mann, J. J. (2016). A pilot integrative genomics study of GABA and glutamate neurotransmitter systems in suicide, suicidal behavior, and major depressive disorder. *American Journal of Medical Genetics Part B: Neuropsychiatric Genetics, 171,* 414–426. http://dx.doi.org/10.1002/ajmg.b.32423

Yoon, K. L., LeMoult, J., & Joormann, J. (2014). Updating emotional content in working memory: A depression-specific deficit? *Journal of Behavior Therapy & Experimental Psychiatry, 45,* 368–374. doi:10.1016/j.jbtep.2014.03.004

Yoshimoto, S., Imai, H., Kashino, M., & Takeuchi, T. (2014). Pupil response and the subliminal mere exposure effect. *PLoS ONE,* 9: e90670. doi:10.1371/journal. pone.0090670

Young, S. G., Brown, C. M., & Ambady, N. (2012). Priming a natural or human-made environment directs attention to context-congruent threatening stimuli. *Cognition & Emotion,* 26, 927–933. doi:10.1080/02699931.2011.625399

Young, T. (1802). On the theory of light and colours. *Philosophical Transactions of the Royal Society, 92,* 12–48.

Youyou, W., Kosinski, M., & Stillwell, D. (2015). Computer-based personality judgments are more accurate than those made by humans. *Proceedings of the National Academy of Sciences of the United States of America, 112,* 1036–1040. doi:10.1073/pnas.1418680112

Yu, C. K.-C. (2012). Dream motif scale. *Dreaming, 22,* 18–52. doi:10.1037/a0026171

Zaremohzzabieh, Z., Samah, B. A., Omar, S. Z., Bolong, J., & Kamarudin, N. A. (2014). Addictive Facebook use among university students. *Asian Social Science, 10,* 107–116.

Zarrindast, M. R., Ownegh, V., Rezayof, A., & Ownegh, F. (2014). The involvement of dorsal hippocampus in dextromethorphan-induced state-dependent learning in mice. *Pharmacology Biochemistry and Behavior, 116,* 90–95. doi:10.1016/j.pbb.2013.11.015

Zeanah, C. H., & Gleason, M. M. (2015). Annual research review: Attachment disorders in early childhood—clinical presentation, causes, correlates, and treatment. *Journal of Child Psychology and Psychiatry, 56,* 207–222. doi: 10.1111/jcpp.12347

Zentner, M., & Mitura, K. (2012). Stepping out of the caveman's shadow: Nations' gender gap predicts degree of sex differentiation in mate preferences. *Psychological Science, 23,* 1176–1185. doi:10.1177/0956797612441004

Zerbe Enns, C., Rice, J. K., & Nutt, R. L. (Eds.). (2015). *Psychological practice with*

women: Guidelines, diversity, empowerment. Washington, DC: American Psychological Association. doi:10.1037/14460-008

Zerwas, S., Larsen, J. T., Petersen, L., Thornton, L. M., Mortensen, P. B., & Bulik, C. M. (2015). The incidence of eating disorders in a Danish Nationwide Register Study: Associations with suicide risk and mortality. *Journal of Psychiatric Research, 65,* 16–22. doi:10.1016/j.jpsychires.2015.03.003

Zhang, B., Tian, D., Yu, C., Zhang, J., Tian, X., von Deneen, K. M., . . . Liu, Y. (2015). Altered baseline brain activities before food intake in obese men: A resting state fMRI study. *Neuroscience Letters, 584,* 156–161.

Zhang, H. (2015). Moderate tolerance promotes tag-mediated cooperation in spatial Prisoner's dilemma game. *Physica A: Statistical Mechanics and its Applications, 424,* 52–61. doi:10.1016/j.physa.2015.01.005

Zhang, M. W., Harris, K. M., & Ho, R. C. (2016). Is off-label repeat prescription of ketamine as a rapid antidepressant safe? Controversies, ethical concerns, and legal implications. *BMC Medical Ethics, 17,* Article 4. http://dx.doi.org/10.1186/s12910-016-0087-3

Zhang, Q.-F., Yuan, Y.-T., Ren, Q.-T., & Lu, Y.-Z. (2014). A randomized single-blind controlled trial of combination of Naikan and Morita therapy (NMT) in patients with generalized anxiety. *Chinese Mental Health Journal, 28,* 651–656.

Zhang, W., Liu, H., Jiang, X., Wu, D., & Tian, Y. (2014). A longitudinal study of posttraumatic stress disorder symptoms and its relationship with coping skill and locus of control in adolescents after an earthquake in China. *PLoS ONE, 9:* e88263. doi:10.1371/journal.pone.0088263

Zhang, Y. Q., Zhu, D., Zhou, X. Y., Liu, Y. Y., Qin, B., Ren, G. P., & Xie, P. (2015). Bilateral repetitive transcranial magnetic stimulation for treatment-resistant depression: A systematic review and meta-analysis of randomized controlled trials. *Brazilian Journal of Medical and Biological Research, 48,* 198–206. doi:10.1590/1414-431X20144270

Zhao, J., & Wood, J. N. (2015). Glycine at the gate—from model to mechanism. *Neuron, 85,* 152–1154. doi:10.1016/j.neuron.2015.03.012

Zhong, W., Li, Y., Li, P., Xu, G., & Mo, L. (2015). Short-term trained lexical categories produce preattentive categorical perception of color: Evidence from ERPs. *Psychophysiology, 52,* 98–106. doi:10.1111/psyp.12294

Zhou, B., Gao, W., Lv, J., Yu, C., Wang, S., Liao, C., . . . Li, L. (2015). Genetic and environmental influences on obesity-related phenotypes in Chinese twins reared apart and together. *Behavior Genetics, 45,* 427–437. doi:10.1007/s10519-015-9711-0

Zhou, X., Hu, X., Zhang, C., Wang, H., Zhu, X., Xu, L., . . . Yu, Y. (2016). Aberrant functional connectivity and structural atrophy in subcortical vascular cognitive impairment: Relationship with cognitive impairments. *Frontiers in Aging Neuroscience, 8,* Article 14. doi:10.3389/fnagi.2016.00014

Zhou, X., & Wu, X. (2016). The relationship between rumination, posttraumatic stress disorder, and posttraumatic growth among Chinese adolescents after earthquake: A longitudinal study. *Journal of Affective Disorders, 193,* 242–248. http://dx.doi.org/10.1016/j.jad.2015.12.076

Zhu, B., Chen, C., Loftus, E. F., He, Q., Chen, C., Lei, D., . . . Dong, Q. (2012). Brief exposure to misinformation can lead to long-term false memories. *Applied Cognitive Psychology, 26,* 301–307. doi:10.1002/acp.1825

Zilhão, N. R., Smit, D. J. A., den Braber, A., Dolan, C. V., Willemsen, G., Boomsma, D. I., & Cath, D. C. (2015). Genetic and environmental contributions to stability in adult obsessive compulsive behavior. *Twin Research and Human Genetics, 18,* 52–60. http://dx.doi.org/10.1017/thg.2014.77

Zimbardo, P. G. (1993). Stanford prison experiment: A 20-year retrospective. Invited presentation at the meeting of the Western Psychological Association, Phoenix, AZ.

Zimbardo, P. G. (2007). *The Lucifer effect: Understanding how good people turn evil.* New York, NY: Random House.

Zimbardo, P. G., Ebbeson, E. B., & Maslach, C. (1977). *Influencing attitudes and changing behavior.* Reading, MA: Addison-Wesley.

Zinbarg, R. E., Anand, D., Lee, J. K., Kendall, A. D., & Nuñez, M. (2015). Generalized anxiety disorder, panic disorder, social anxiety disorder, and specific phobias. In P. H. Blaney, R. F. Krueger, & T. Millon (Eds.), *Oxford textbook of psychopathology* (3rd ed., pp. 133–162). New York, NY: Oxford University Press.

Zinzow, H. M., & Thompson, M. (2015). Factors associated with use of verbally coercive, incapacitated, and forcible sexual assault tactics in a longitudinal study of college men. *Aggressive Behavior, 41,* 34–43. doi:10.1002/ab.21567

Zorrilla, I., López-Zurbano, S., Cano, A. I., & González-Pinto, A. (2015). Schizophrenia and gender. In M. Sáenz-Herrero (Ed.), *Psychopathology in women: Incorporating gender perspective into descriptive psychopathology* (pp. 621–639). Cham, CH: Springer International Publishing. doi:10.1007/978-3-319-05870-2

Zourbanos, N., Papaioannou, A., Argyropoulou, E., & Hatzigeorgiadis, A. (2014). Achievement goals and self-talk in physical education: The moderating role of perceived competence. *Motivation and Emotion, 38,* 235–251. doi:10.1007/s11031-013-9378-x

Zuberbühler, K. (2015). Linguistic capacity of non-human animals. *WIREs Cognitive Science,* 6, 313–321. doi:10.1002/wcs.1338

Zuckerman, M. (1978, February). The search for high sensation. *Psychology Today,* 38–46.

Zuckerman, M. (1979). *Sensation seeking: Beyond the optimal level of arousal.* Hillsdale, NJ: Erlbaum.

Zuckerman, M. (1994). *Behavioral expressions and biosocial bases of sensation seeking.* New York, NY: Cambridge University Press.

Zuckerman, M. (2004). The shaping of personality: Genes, environments, and chance encounters. *Journal of Personality Assessment, 82,* 11–22.

Zuckerman, M. (2014). Sensation seeking, impulsivity and the balance between behavioral approach and inhibition. *Personality and Individual Differences, 60,* S4. doi:10.1016/j.paid.2013.07.150

Zuckerman, M., & Aluja, A. (2015). Measures of sensation seeking. In G. J. Boyle, D. H. Saklofske, & G. Matthews (Eds.), *Measures of personality and social psychological constructs* (pp. 352–380). San Diego, CA: Elsevier Academic Press. doi:10.1016/B978-0-12-386915-9.00013-9

Zuurbier, L. A., Luik, A. I., Hofman, A., Franco, O. H., Van Someren, E. J., & Tiemeier, H. (2015). Fragmentation and stability of circadian activity rhythms predict mortality: The Rotterdam Study. *American Journal of Epidemiology, 181,* 54–63. doi:10.1093/aje/kwu245

Zysberg, L., Orenshtein, C., Gimmon, E., & Robinson, R. (2016). Emotional intelligence, personality, stress, and burnout among educators. *International Journal of Stress Management.* No Pagination Specified. http://dx.doi.org/10.1037/str0000028

Glossary

Abnormal behavior The patterns of behaviors, thoughts, or emotions considered pathological (diseased or disordered) for one or more of these four reasons: deviance, dysfunction, distress, and/or danger.

Absolute threshold The minimum amount of stimulation necessary to consciously detect a stimulus 50% of the time.

Accommodation According to Piaget, the process of adjusting (accommodating) existing schemas to incorporate new definition (Chapter 9).

Accommodation The process by which the eye's ciliary muscles change the shape (thickness) of the lens so that light is focused on the retina; adjustment of the eye's lens permitting focusing on near and distant objects (Chapter 4).

Achievement motivation The desire to excel, especially in competition with others.

Acquisition (in classical conditioning) Learning that occurs (is acquired) when an organism involuntarily links a neutral stimulus (NS) with an unconditioned stimulus (US), which in turn elicits the conditioned response (CR).

Acquisition (in operant conditioning) Learning that occurs (is acquired) when an organism voluntarily links a response with a consequence, such as a reward.

Action potential A neural impulse, or brief electrical charge, that carries information along the axon of a neuron; movement is generated when positively charged ions move in and out through channels in the axon's membrane.

Activation–synthesis theory of dreams The theory that dreams are a by-product of random, spontaneous stimulation of brain cells during sleep, which the brain combines (synthesizes) into coherent patterns, known as dreams.

Active listening A communication technique that requires listening with total attention to what another is saying; techniques include reflecting, paraphrasing, and clarifying what the person says and means.

Actor–observer effect The tendency to attribute other people's behavior to personality factors, while seeing our own behavior as caused by the situation.

Acute stress A short-term state of arousal, in response to a perceived threat or challenge that has a definite endpoint.

Adaptation-level phenomenon A tendency to judge a new situation or stimuli relative to a neutral, "normal" level based on our previous experiences; we then adapt to this new level and it becomes the new "normal."

Adaptation/protection theory of sleep The theory that sleep evolved to conserve energy and provide protection from predators.

Addiction A broad term that describes describing a condition in which the body requires a drug (or specific activity) in order to function without physical and psychological reactions to its absence; it is often the outcome of tolerance and dependence.

Ageism A form of prejudice or discrimination based on physical age; similar to racism and sexism in its negative stereotypes.

Age-related positivity effect The relative preference in older adults for positive over negative information in attention and memory.

Aggression Any behavior intended to cause psychological or physical harm to another individual.

Agonist drug A substance that binds to a receptor and triggers a response that mimics or enhances a neurotransmitter's effect.

Algorithm A logical, step-by-step procedure that, if followed correctly, will always eventually solve the problem.

All-or-nothing principle The principle that a neuron's response to a stimulus is either to fire with a full-strength response or not at all; also known as the all-or-none law.

Alternate state of consciousness (ASC) A temporary mental state, other than ordinary waking consciousness, that occurs during sleep, dreaming, psychoactive drug use, and hypnosis.

Altruism Prosocial behaviors designed to help or benefit others.

Amygdala A part of the limbic system linked to the production and regulation of emotions—especially aggression and fear.

Androgyny [an-DRAH-juh-nee] Exhibiting both traditional masculine and feminine traits; from the Greek *andro* for "male" and *gyn* for "female."

Anorexia nervosa An eating disorder characterized by an obsessive fear of obesity, a need for control, self-imposed starvation, and a severe loss of weight.

Antagonist drug A substance that binds to a receptor and triggers a response that blocks a neurotransmitter's effect.

Anterograde amnesia The inability to form new memories; forward-acting amnesia.

Antisocial personality disorder (ASPD) A personality disorder characterized by egocentrism and a lack of conscience, remorse, or empathy for others.

Anxiety disorder One of a group of psychological disorders characterized by disabling (uncontrollable and disruptive) fear or anxiety, accompanied by physiological arousal and related behavioral disturbances.

Applied research A type of research primarily conducted to solve practical, real world problems; generally conducted outside the laboratory.

Approach–approach conflict A forced choice between two options, both of which have equally desirable characteristics.

Approach–avoidance conflict A forced choice involving one option with equally desirable and undesirable characteristics.

Archetypes Jung's term for the collective, universal images and patterns, residing in the unconscious, that have symbolic meaning for all people.

Archival research A descriptive research technique that studies existing data to find answers to research questions.

Assimilation In Piaget's theory, the incorporation (assimilation) of new information into existing schemas.

Association areas The "quiet" areas in the cerebral cortex involved in interpreting, integrating, and acting on information processed by other parts of the brain.

Associative learning Learning that two events occur or happen together.

Attachment A strong emotional bond with special others that endures over time.

Attitude The learned predisposition to respond positively or negatively to a particular object, person, or event.

Attribution The explanations we make about the causes of behaviors or events.

Audition The sense or act of hearing.

Automatic processes The mental activities that require minimal attention and generally have little impact on other activities.

Autonomic nervous system (ANS) The subdivision of the peripheral nervous system (PNS) that controls the body's involuntary motor responses; it connects the sensory receptors to the central nervous system (CNS) and the CNS to the smooth muscle, cardiac muscle, and glands.

Availability heuristic A cognitive strategy (or shortcut) that estimates the frequency or likelihood of an event based on information that is readily available in our memory.

Aversion therapy A type of behavior therapy that pairs an aversive (unpleasant) stimulus with a maladaptive behavior in order to elicit a negative reaction to the target stimulus.

Avoidance–avoidance conflict A forced choice between two options, both of which have equally undesirable characteristics.

Axon A long, tube-like structure that conveys impulses away from a neuron's cell body toward other neurons or to muscles or glands.

Basic anxiety According to Horney, feelings of helplessness and insecurity that adults experience because as children they felt alone and isolated in a hostile environment.

Basic research A type of research primarily conducted to advance core scientific knowledge; most often conducted in universities and research laboratories.

Behavioral genetics The study of the relative effects of heredity and the environment on behavior and mental processes.

Behavioral perspective A modern approach to psychology that emphasizes objective, observable, environmental influences on overt behavior.

Behavior therapies A group of therapies that uses learning principles to reduce or eliminate maladaptive behaviors; techniques are based on classical and operant conditioning, along with observational learning.

Binge-eating disorder An eating disorder characterized by recurrent episodes of consuming large amounts of food (bingeing), but not followed by purge behaviors.

Binocular cues Visual input from two eyes, which allows perception of depth or distance.

Biological perspective A modern approach to psychology that focuses on genetics and biological processes.

Biological preparedness The built-in (innate) readiness to form associations between certain stimuli and responses.

Biomedical therapies A group of therapies designed to alter brain functioning with biological or physical techniques, such as drugs, electroconvulsive therapy, and psychosurgery.

Biopsychosocial model An integrative, unifying theme of modern psychology that sees biological, psychological, and social processes as interrelated and interacting influences.

Bipolar disorder A psychological disorder characterized by repeated episodes of mania (unreasonable elation, often with hyperactivity) alternating with depression.

Blind spot The point at which the optic nerve leaves the eye, which contains no receptor cells for vision—thus creating a "blind spot."

Borderline personality disorder (BPD) A psychological disorder characterized by severe instability in emotions, relationships, and self-image, along with impulsive and self-destructive behaviors.

Bottom-up processing Information processing that starts at the "bottom" with an analysis of smaller features, and then builds on them to create complete perceptions; data-driven processing that moves from the parts to the whole.

Brainstem A diffuse, stem-shaped area of the brain, including much of the midbrain, pons, and medulla; responsible for automatic survival functions, such as respiration and heartbeat.

Bulimia nervosa An eating disorder characterized by recurrent episodes of consuming large quantities of food (bingeing), followed by self-induced vomiting or laxative use (purging).

Burnout A state of psychological and physical exhaustion resulting from chronic exposure to high levels of stress, with little personal control.

Bystander effect A phenomenon in which the greater the number of bystanders, the less likely it is that any one individual will feel responsible for seeking help or giving aid to someone who is in need of help.

Cannon-Bard theory A theory proposing that emotions and physiological changes occur simultaneously ("I'm crying and feeling sad at the same time"); in this view, all emotions are physiologically similar.

Case study A descriptive research technique involving an in-depth study of a single research participant or a small group of individuals.

Cataclysmic event A stressful occurrence that occurs suddenly and generally affects many people simultaneously.

Cell body The part of a neuron that contains the cell nucleus and other structures that help the neuron carry out its functions; also known as the soma.

Central nervous system (CNS) The part of the nervous system consisting of the brain and spinal cord.

Cerebellum The hindbrain structure responsible for coordinating fine muscle movement, balance, and some perception and cognition.

Cerebral cortex The thin surface layer on the cerebral hemispheres that regulates most complex behavior, including sensations, motor control, and higher mental processes.

Chromosome A threadlike molecule of DNA (deoxyribonucleic acid) that carries genetic information.

Chronic stress A continuous state of arousal in which demands are perceived as greater than the inner and outer resources available for dealing with them.

Chunking A memory technique involving grouping separate pieces of information into larger, more manageable units (or chunks).

Circadian rhythm The internal, biological clock governing bodily activities, such as the sleep/wake cycle, temperature, that occur on a 24- to 25-hour cycle. (*Circa* means "about," and *dies* means "day.")

Classical conditioning Learning that develops through involuntarily paired associations; a previously neutral stimulus (NS) is paired (associated) with an unconditioned stimulus (US) to elicit a conditioned response (CR).

Client-centered therapy A form of talk therapy, developed by Carl Rogers, that provides a warm, supportive atmosphere that encourages self-actualization and improves the client's self-concept; techniques include empathy, unconditional positive regard, genuineness, and active listening.

Cochlea [KOK-lee-uh] The fluid-filled, coiled tube in the inner ear that contains the receptors for hearing.

Coding The process in which neural impulses travel by different routes to different parts of the brain; it allows us to detect various physical stimuli as distinct sensations.

Cognition The mental activities involved in acquiring, storing, retrieving, and using knowledge.

Cognitive-behavior therapy (CBT) A type of therapy, developed by Aaron Beck, that combines cognitive therapy (changing faulty thinking) with behavior therapy (changing maladaptive behaviors).

Cognitive dissonance The unpleasant psychological tension we experience after noticing contradictions between our thoughts, feelings, and/or actions.

Cognitive map A mental image of a three-dimensional space that an organism has navigated.

Cognitive perspective A modern approach to psychology that focuses on the mental processes used in thinking, knowing, remembering, and communicating.

Cognitive restructuring A therapeutic process of learning to identify and dispute irrational or maladaptive thought patterns.

Cognitive-social learning theory A theory that emphasizes the roles of thinking and social learning.

Cognitive therapies A group of talk therapies that focuses on changing faulty thought processes (cognitions); based on the assumption that thoughts intervene between events and reactions.

Cognitive view of dreams The perspective that dreaming is a type of information processing that helps us organize and interpret our everyday experiences.

Collective unconscious Jung's name for the deepest layer of the unconscious, which contains universal memories and archetypes shared by all people due to our common ancestral past.

Comorbidity The co-occurrence of two or more disorders in the same person at the same time, as when a person suffers from both depression and alcoholism.

Companionate love A type of strong and enduring love characterized by deep trust, caring, tolerance, and friendship.

Concrete operational stage Piaget's third stage of cognitive development (roughly ages 7 to 11), in which the child can think logically about concrete, tangible objects and events.

Conditioned emotional response (CER) An emotion, such as fear, that becomes a learned, conditioned response to a previously neutral stimulus (NS), such as a loud noise.

Conditioned response (CR) A learned reaction to a conditioned stimulus (CS) that occurs after previous repeated pairings with an unconditioned stimulus (US).

Conditioned stimulus (CS) A previously neutral stimulus (NS) that, after repeated pairings with an unconditioned stimulus (US), comes to elicit a conditioned response (CR).

Conditioning The process of learning associations between stimuli and behavioral responses.

Conduction hearing loss A type of hearing loss that results from damage to the mechanical system that conducts sound waves to the cochlea; also called conduction deafness.

Cones Retinal receptor cells with high sensitivity to color and detail, but low sensitivity in dim light.

Confirmation bias The tendency to prefer information that confirms our preexisting positions or beliefs and to ignore or discount contradictory evidence; also known as remembering the 'hits' and ignoring the 'misses.'

Conflict A forced choice between two or more incompatible goals or impulses.

Conformity A change in thoughts, feelings, or actions because of real or imagined group pressure.

Conscious In Freudian terms, thoughts or motives that a person is currently aware of or is remembering.

Consciousness Our awareness of ourselves and our environment.

Conservation According to Piaget, the understanding that certain physical characteristics (such as volume) remain unchanged, even though appearances may change; a hallmark of Piaget's concrete operational stage.

Consolidation The process by which LTM memories become stable in the brain; neural changes that take place when a memory is formed.

Constructive process The process of organizing and shaping information during encoding, storage, and retrieval of memories.

Consummate love Sternberg's strongest and most enduring type of love, based on a balanced combination of intimacy, passion, and commitment.

Continuous reinforcement Every correct response is reinforced.

Control group The group that is not manipulated (i.e., receives no treatment) during an experiment; participants who are NOT exposed to the independent variable (IV).

Controlled processes The mental activities that require focused attention and generally interfere with other ongoing activities.

Convergence A binocular depth cue in which the eyes turn inward (or converge) to fixate on an object.

Convergent thinking A type of thinking that seeks the single best solution to a problem.

Corpus callosum A bundle of neural fibers that connects the brain's two hemispheres.

Correlation coefficient A number from −1.00 to +1.00 that indicates the direction and strength of the relationship between two variables.

Correlational research A type of research that examines possible relations between variables; designed to meet the goal of *prediction*.

Creativity The ability to produce original, appropriate, and valued outcomes in a novel way; consists of three characteristics—originality, fluency, and flexibility.

Critical period A specific time during which an organism must experience certain stimuli in order to develop properly in the future.

Critical thinking The process of objectively evaluating, comparing, analyzing, and synthesizing information.

Cross-sectional design In developmental psychology, a research technique that measures individuals of various ages at one point in time and provides information about age differences.

Crystallized intelligence (*gc*) The store of knowledge and skills gained through experience and education; gc tends to increase over the life span.

Debriefing A discussion procedure conducted at the end of an experiment or study; participants are informed of the study's design and purpose, possible misconceptions are clarified, questions are answered, and explanations are provided for any possible deception.

Defense mechanisms Freud's term for the strategies the ego uses to reduce anxiety by unconsciously distorting reality.

Deindividuation The reduced self-consciousness, inhibition, and personal responsibility that sometimes occurs in a group, particularly when the members feel anonymous.

Delusion A false or irrational belief maintained despite clear evidence to the contrary.

Dendrites The branching fibers of neurons that receive neural impulses from other neurons and convey impulses toward the cell body.

Dependent variable (DV) The variable that is observed and measured for change; the factor that is affected by (or dependent on) the independent variable.

Depressant A drug that decreases bodily processes and overall responsiveness.

Depressive disorders A group of psychological disorders characterized by sad, empty, or irritable moods that interfere with the ability to function.

Depth perception The ability to perceive three-dimensional space and to accurately judge distance.

Descriptive research A type of research that systematically observes and records behavior and mental processes without manipulating variables; designed to meet the goal of *description*.

Developmental psychology The study of age-related behavior and mental processes from conception to death.

Diagnostic and Statistical Manual of Mental Disorders (DSM) A manual developed by the American Psychiatric Association that is used primarily to classify psychological disorders.

Diathesis-stress model A hypothesis about the cause of certain disorders, such as schizophrenia, which suggests that people inherit a predisposition (or "diathesis") that increases their risk for psychological disorders when exposed to certain extremely stressful life experiences.

Difference threshold The smallest physical difference between two stimuli that is consciously detectable 50% of the time; also called the *just noticeable difference* (*JND*).

Diffusion of responsibility The dilution (diffusion) of personal responsibility for acting when others are present.

Discrimination An unjustifiable, negative action directed toward members of a group; also the behavioral component of prejudice (Chapter 14).

Discrimination (in classical conditioning) A learned ability to distinguish (discriminate) between similar stimuli so as NOT to involuntarily respond to a new stimulus as if it were the previously conditioned stimulus (CS); the opposite of generalization.

Discrimination (in operant conditioning) A learned ability to distinguish (discriminate) between similar stimuli based on whether the response to the stimuli is reinforced or punished, and then to voluntarily respond accordingly; the opposite of generalization.

Dissociative disorder One of a group of psychological disorders characterized by a sudden break (*dissociation*) in conscious awareness, self-identity, and/or memory.

Dissociative identity disorder (DID) A psychological disorder characterized by the presence of two or more distinct personality systems (or identities) in the same individual; previously known as multiple personality disorder (MPD).

Distress The unpleasant, undesirable stress caused by aversive conditions.

Distributed practice A learning strategy in which studying or practice is broken up into a number of short sessions over a period of time; also known as spaced repetition.

Divergent thinking A type of thinking that produces many solutions to the same problem.

DNA The main constituent of chromosomes found in all living organisms, which transmits hereditary characteristics from parents to children; short for *deoxyribonucleic acid*.

Double-blind study An experimental technique in which both the researcher and the participants are unaware of (blind to) who is in the experimental or control groups.

Dream analysis In psychoanalysis, interpretation of the underlying true meaning of dreams to reveal unconscious processes.

Drive-reduction theory The theory that motivation begins with a physiological need (a lack or deficiency) that elicits a drive toward behavior that will satisfy the original need; once the need is met, a state of balance (homeostasis) is restored, and motivation decreases.

Drug abuse A type of drug taking that causes emotional or physical harm to the drug user or others.

Eclectic approach A perspective that combines elements of various therapies to find the most appropriate treatment; also known as integrative therapy.

Ego In Freud's theory, the second personality structure that is largely conscious, and the "executive," which deals with the demands of reality; it operates on the reality principle.

Egocentrism In cognitive development, the inability to take the perspective of another person; a hallmark of Piaget's preoperational stage.

Egoistic model of helping A proposed explanation for helping that suggests we help because of anticipated gain—later reciprocation, increased self-esteem, or avoidance of distress and guilt.

Elaborative rehearsal A process of forming numerous connections of new information to material already stored in long-term memory (LTM); process of storing information that results in more durable, lasting memories.

Electroconvulsive therapy (ECT) A biomedical therapy based on passing electrical current through the brain; it is used almost exclusively to treat serious depression when drugs and psychotherapy have failed.

Embryonic period The second stage of prenatal development, which begins after uterine implantation and lasts through the eighth week.

Emerging adulthood The age period from approximately 18–25 in which individuals in modern cultures have left the dependency of childhood, but not yet assumed adult responsibilities.

Emotion A complex pattern of feelings that includes arousal (heart pounding), cognitions (thoughts, values, and expectations), and expressive behaviors (smiles, frowns, and gestures).

Emotional Intelligence (EI) The ability to perceive, understand, manage, and utilize emotions accurately and appropriately.

Emotion-focused coping The strategies we use to relieve or regulate our emotional reactions to a stressful situation.

Empathy In Rogerian terms, a sensitive understanding and sharing of another's inner experience.

Empathy–altruism hypothesis A proposed explanation for helping that suggests we help because of empathy for someone in need.

Encoding The first step of the ESR memory model; process of moving sensory information into memory storage.

Encoding-specificity principle The principle that retrieval of information is improved if cues received at the time of recall are consistent with those present at the time of encoding.

Encoding, storage, and retrieval (ESR) model A memory model that involves three processes: *encoding* (getting information in), *storage* (retaining information for future use), and *retrieval* (recovering information).

Endocrine system A network of glands located throughout the body that manufacture and secrete hormones into the bloodstream.

Endorphin A chemical substance in the nervous system similar in structure and action to opiates; involved in pain control, pleasure, and memory.

Epigenetics The study of how non-genetic factors, such as age, environment, lifestyle, or disease, affect how (and if) genes are expressed; "epi" means "above" or "outside of."

Episodic memory A subsystem of long-term memory (LTM) that stores autobiographical events and the contexts in which they occurred; a mental diary of a person's life.

Ethnocentrism The belief that one's culture is typical of all cultures; also, viewing one's own ethnic group (or culture) as central and "correct" and judging others according to this standard.

Eustress The pleasant, desirable stress that arouses us to persevere and accomplish challenging goals.

Evolutionary perspective A modern approach to psychology that stresses natural selection, adaptation, and reproduction.

Evolutionary theory of helping A theory suggesting that altruism is an instinctual behavior, which has evolved because it favors survival of the helper's genes.

Experimental group The group that is manipulated (i.e., receives treatment) in an experiment; participants who are exposed to the independent variable (IV).

Experimental research A type of research that involves the manipulation and control of variables to determine cause and effect; designed to meet the goal of *explanation*.

Experimenter bias A bias that occurs when a researcher influences research results in the expected direction.

Explicit/declarative memory A subsystem within long-term memory (LTM) that involves conscious, easily described (declared) memories; consists of semantic memories (facts) and episodic memories (personal experiences).

External locus of control The belief that chance or outside forces beyond our control determine our fate.

Extinction (in classical conditioning) The gradual diminishing of a conditioned response (CR) when the unconditioned stimulus (US) is withheld or removed.

Extinction (in operant conditioning) The gradual diminishing of a conditioned response when it is no longer reinforced.

Extrasensory perception (ESP) The perceptual, so-called "psychic," abilities that supposedly go beyond the known senses (for example, telepathy, clairvoyance, and precognition).

Extrinsic motivation A type of motivation for a task or activity based on external incentives, such as rewards and punishments.

Facial-feedback hypothesis The hypothesis that movements of the facial muscles produce and/or intensify our subjective experience of emotion.

Feature detectors Neurons in the brain's visual system that respond to specific characteristics of stimuli, such as shape, angle, or movement.

Fetal period The third, and final, stage of prenatal development (eight weeks to birth).

Five-factor model (FFM) A model of personality traits that includes five basic dimensions: openness, conscientiousness, extraversion, agreeableness, and neuroticism; informally called the Big Five.

Fixed interval (FI) schedule A reinforcer is delivered for the first response made after a fixed period of time.

Fixed ratio (FR) schedule A reinforcer is delivered for the first response made after a fixed number of responses.

Flashbulb memory (FBM) A vivid, detailed, and near-permanent memory of an emotionally significant moment or event; memory resulting from a form of automatic encoding, storage, and later retrieval.

Fluid intelligence (*gf*) The ability to think speedily and abstractly, and to solve novel problems; gf tends to decrease over the life span.

Foot-in-the-door technique A process in which an initial, small request is used as a setup for a later, larger request.

Forebrain The collection of upper-level brain structures including the cerebral cortex, limbic system, thalamus, and hypothalamus.

Formal operational stage Piaget's fourth stage of cognitive development (around age 11 and beyond), characterized by abstract and hypothetical thinking.

Fovea A tiny pit in the center of the retina that is densely filled with cones; it is responsible for sharp vision.

Free association In psychoanalysis, reporting whatever comes to mind without monitoring its contents.

Frequency theory for hearing The theory that pitch perception depends on how often the auditory nerve fires.

Frontal lobes The two lobes at the front of the brain that govern motor control, speech production, and higher functions, such as thinking, personality, emotion, and memory.

Frustration The unpleasant tension, anxiety, and heightened sympathetic activity resulting from a blocked goal.

Functional fixedness A barrier to problem solving that comes from thinking about objects as functioning only in their usual or customary way.

Fundamental attribution error (FAE) The tendency of observers to overestimate the influence of internal, dispositional factors on a person's behavior, while underestimating the impact of external, situational factors.

Gate-control theory of pain The theory that pain sensations are processed and altered by certain cells in the spinal cord, which act as gates to interrupt and block some pain signals while sending others on to the brain.

Gender A psychological and sociocultural phenomenon referring to learned, sex-related thoughts, feelings, and actions of men and women.

Gender roles A set of learned, societal expectations for thoughts, feelings, and actions considered "appropriate" for men and women, and expressed publicly by the individual.

Gene A segment of DNA (deoxyribonucleic acid) that occupies a specific place on a particular chromosome, and carries the code for hereditary transmission.

General adaptation syndrome (GAS) Selye's three-stage (alarm, resistance, exhaustion) reaction to chronic stress; a pattern of nonspecific, adaptational responses to a continuing stressor.

General intelligence (*g*) Spearman's term for a common skill set that underlies all intellectual behavior.

Generalization (in classical conditioning) A conditioned response (CR) spreads (generalizes) and comes to be involuntarily elicited not only by the conditioned stimulus (CS), but also by stimuli similar to the CS; the opposite of discrimination.

Generalization (in operant conditioning) Voluntarily responding to a new stimulus as if it were the original, previously conditioned stimulus (CS); the opposite of discrimination.

Generalized anxiety disorder (GAD) An anxiety disorder characterized by persistent, uncontrollable, and free-floating, nonspecified anxiety.

Genuineness In Rogerian terms, being personally authentic and sincere; the awareness of one's true inner thoughts and feelings and the ability to share them honestly with others.

Germinal period The first stage of prenatal development, beginning with ovulation and followed by conception and implantation in the uterus; the first two weeks of pregnancy.

Glial cells The cells that provide structural, nutritional, and other functions for neurons; also called glia or neuroglia.

Grammar The set of rules (syntax and semantics) governing the use and structure of language.

Grit A psychological term referring perseverance and passion in the pursuit of long-term goals.

Group polarization The tendency for the decisions and opinions of group members to become more extreme (either riskier or more conservative), depending on the members' initial dominant tendency.

Group therapies A form of therapy in which a number of people with similar concerns meet together to work toward therapeutic goals.

Groupthink The faulty decision making that occurs when maintaining group harmony becomes more important than making a good decision.

Growth/development theory of sleep The theory that deep sleep (Stage 3) is correlated with physical development, including changes in the structure and organization of the brain; infants spend far more time in Stage 3 sleep than adults.

Growth mindset A psychological term referring to a self-perception or set of beliefs about abilities and the potential to change.

Gustation The sense or act of tasting; receptors are located in the tongue's taste buds.

Habituation The brain's learned tendency to ignore or stop responding to unchanging information; an example of top-down processing.

Hallucination A false, imaginary sensory perception that occurs without an external, objective source, such as hearing voices that do not actually exist.

Hallucinogen A drug that produces sensory or perceptual distortions.

Hassles The small problems of daily living that may accumulate and become a major source of stress.

Health psychology A subfield of psychology that studies how people stay healthy, why they become ill, and how they respond when they become ill.

Heuristic An educated guess, or "rule of thumb," often used as a shortcut for problem solving; does not guarantee a solution to a problem but does narrow the alternatives.

Hierarchy of needs Maslow's view that basic human motives form a hierarchy; the lower motives (such as physiological and safety needs) must be met before advancing to higher needs (such as belonging and self-actualization).

Higher-order conditioning A new conditioned stimulus (CS) is created by pairing it with a previously conditioned stimulus (CS); also known as second-order conditioning.

Hindbrain The lower or hind region of the brain; collection of structures including the medulla, pons, and cerebellum.

Hippocampus The seahorse shaped part of the limbic system involved in forming and retrieving memories.

Homeostasis Our body's tendency to maintain equilibrium, or a steady state of internal balan.

Hormone Chemical messengers manufactured and secreted by the endocrine glands, which circulate in the bloodstream to produce bodily changes or maintain normal bodily functions.

HPA axis Our body's delayed stress response, involving the hypothalamus, pituitary, and adrenal cortex; also called the hypothalamic–pituitary–adrenocortical (HPA) axis.

Humanistic perspective A modern approach to psychology that perceives human nature as naturally positive and growth seeking; it emphasizes free will and self-actualization.

Humanistic therapies A group of talk therapies that emphasizes maximizing a client's inherent capacity for self-actualization by providing a nonjudgmental, accepting atmosphere.

Hypnosis An alternate state of consciousness (ASC) characterized by deep relaxation and a trance-like state of heightened suggestibility and intense focus.

Hypothalamus The small brain structure beneath the thalamus that helps govern drives (hunger, thirst, sex, and aggression) and hormones.

Hypothesis A tentative and testable explanation (or "educated guess") about the relationship between two or more variables; a testable prediction or question.

Id According to Freud, the first personality structure that is present at birth, completely unconscious, and striving to meet basic drives, such as hunger, thirst, sex, and aggression; it operates on the pleasure principle.

Illusion A false or misleading perception shared by others in the same perceptual environment.

Illusory correlation A mistaken perception that a relationship exists between variables when no such relationship actually exists.

Implicit bias A hidden, automatic attitude that may guide behaviors independent of a person's awareness or control.

Implicit/nondeclarative memory A subsystem within long-term memory (LTM) that contains memories independent of conscious recall; consists of procedural motor skills, priming, and simple classically conditioned responses.

Imprinting The process by which attachments are formed during critical periods in early life.

Inattentional blindness The failure to notice a fully visible, but unexpected stimulus, when our attention is directed elsewhere; also known as perceptual blindness.

Incentive theory The theory that motivation results from external stimuli that "pull" an organism in certain directions.

Independent variable (IV) The variable that is manipulated and controlled by the experimenter to determine its causal effect on the dependent variable; also called the treatment variable.

Inferiority complex Adler's idea that feelings of inferiority develop from early childhood experiences of helplessness and incompetence.

Informational social influence A type of conforming based on the need for information and direction.

Informed consent A participant's agreement to take part in a study after being told what to expect.

Ingroup favoritism The tendency to judge members of the ingroup more positively than members of an outgroup.

Inner ear The semicircular canals, vestibular sacs, and cochlea, which generate neural signals that are sent to the brain.

Insanity The legal (not clinical) designation for a situation in which an individual cannot be held responsible for his or her actions or is incompetent to manage his or her own affairs because of mental illness.

Insight A sudden understanding or realization of how a problem can be solved.

Insomnia A sleep disorder characterized by persistent problems in falling asleep, staying asleep, or awakening too early.

Instinct The fixed, unlearned response patterns found in almost all members of a species.

Instinctive drift The tendency for conditioned responses to revert (drift back) to innate response patterns.

Intelligence The global capacity to think rationally, act purposefully, profit from experience, and deal effectively with the environment.

Intelligence quotient (IQ) An index of intelligence initially derived from standardized tests, which is computed by dividing mental age (MA) by chronological age (CA) and then multiplying by 100; now derived by comparing individual scores with the scores of others of the same age.

Internal locus of control The belief that we control our own fate.

Interpretation A psychoanalyst's explanation of a client's free associations, dreams, resistance, and transference; more generally, any statement by a therapist that presents a problem in a new way.

Intrinsic motivation A type of motivation for a task or activity based on internal incentives, such as enjoyment and personal satisfaction.

James-Lange theory A theory of emotion suggesting that the subjective experience of emotion results from physiological arousal, rather than being its cause ("I feel sad because I'm crying"); in this view, each emotion is physiologically distinct.

Kinesthesis The sense that provides information about the location, orientation, and movement of individual body parts relative to each other; receptors are located in muscles, joints, and tendons.

Language A form of communication using sounds or symbols combined according to specified rules.

Language acquisition device (LAD) According to Chomsky, an innate mechanism within the brain, which enables a child to analyze language and extract the basic rules of grammar.

Latent content of dreams According to Freud, a dream's unconscious, hidden meaning is transformed into symbols within the dream's manifest content (story line).

Latent learning Hidden learning that exists without behavioral signs.

Law of effect Thorndike's rule that any behavior followed by pleasant consequences is likely to be repeated, whereas any behavior followed by unpleasant consequences is likely to be stopped.

Learned helplessness Seligman's term for a state of helplessness, or resignation, in which human or nonhuman animals fail to act to escape from a situation due to a history of repeated failures in the past.

Learning A relatively permanent change in behavior or mental processes caused by experience.

Learning/memory theory of sleep The theory that sleep is important for learning and for the consolidation, storage, and maintenance of memories.

Levels of processing A continuum of memory processing ranging from shallow to intermediate to deep, with deeper processing leading to improved encoding, storage, and retrieval.

Limbic system The interconnected group of forebrain structures involved with emotions, drives, and memory; its two most important structures are the hippocampus and amygdala.

Lobotomy An outmoded neurosurgical procedure for mental disorders, which involved cutting nerve pathways between the frontal lobes and the thalamus and hypothalamus.

Long-term memory (LTM) The third stage of memory, which stores information for long periods of time; the capacity is virtually limitless, and the duration is relatively permanent.

Long-term potentiation (LTP) A long-lasting increase in neural sensitivity; a biological mechanism for learning and memory.

Longitudinal design In developmental psychology, a research design that measures individuals over an extended period and gives information about age changes.

Maintenance rehearsal The act of repeating information over and over to maintain it in short-term memory (STM).

Manifest content of dreams In Freudian dream analysis, the "surface," or remembered, story line, which contains symbols that mask the dream's latent content (the true meaning).

Massed practice A study technique in which time spent learning is grouped (or massed) into long, unbroken intervals; also called cramming.

Meditation A group of techniques generally designed to focus attention, block out distractions, and produce an alternate state of consciousness (ASC); it's believed to enhance self-knowledge and well-being through reduced self-awareness.

Medulla The hindbrain structure responsible for vital, automatic functions, such as respiration and heartbeat.

Memory The persistence of learning over time; process by which information is encoded, stored, and retrieved.

Mental age (MA) An individual's level of mental development relative to that of others; mental age was initially used in comparison to chronological age (CA) to calculate IQ.

Mental set A fixed-thinking approach to problem solving that only sees solutions that have worked in the past.

Meta-analysis A statistical technique for combining and analyzing data from many studies in order to determine overall trends.

Midbrain The collection of structures in the middle of the brain responsible for coordinating movement patterns, sleep, and arousal.

Middle ear The hammer, anvil, and stirrup structures of the ear, which concentrate eardrum vibrations onto the cochlea's oval window.

Mindfulness-based stress reduction (MBSR) A stress reduction strategy based on developing a state of consciousness that attends to ongoing events in a receptive and non-judgmental way.

Minnesota Multiphasic Personality Inventory (MMPI) The most widely researched and clinically used self-report method of personality assessment; originally designed to reveal abnormal personality traits and behaviors, but also used for various screening purposes.

Mirror neurons Neurons that fire (or are activated) when an action is performed, as well as when observing the actions or emotions of another; believed to be responsible for empathy, imitation, language, and the deficits of some mental disorders.

Misinformation effect A memory error resulting from misleading information being presented after an event, which alters memories of the event itself.

Mnemonic A strategy or device that uses familiar information during the encoding of new information to enhance later recall.

Modeling therapy A type of therapy characterized by watching and imitating models that demonstrate desirable behaviors.

Monocular cues Visual input from a single eye alone that contributes to perception of depth or distance.

Morpheme The smallest meaningful unit of language; formed from a combination of phonemes.

Motivation A set of factors that activate, direct, and maintain behavior, usually toward some goal.

Myelin sheath The layer of fatty insulation wrapped around the axon of some neurons that increases the rate at which neural impulses travel along the axon.

Narcolepsy A sleep order characterized by uncontrollable sleep attacks. (*Narco* means "numbness," and *lepsy* means "seizure.")

Natural selection Darwin's principle of an evolutionary process in which heritable traits that increase an organism's chances of survival or reproduction are more likely to be passed on to succeeding generations.

Naturalistic observation A descriptive research technique that observes and records behavior and mental processes in a natural, real-world setting.

Nature–nurture controversy An ongoing dispute about the relative contributions of nature (heredity) and nurture (environment) in determining the development of behavior and mental processes.

Negative punishment A process by which taking away (or removing) a stimulus following a response decreases the likelihood that the response will be repeated.

Negative reinforcement A process by which taking away (or removing) a stimulus following a response increases the likelihood that the response will be repeated.

Neurogenesis The formation (generation) of new neurons.

Neuron The basic building block (nerve cell) of the nervous system; responsible for receiving, processing, and transmitting electrochemical information.

Neuroplasticity The brain's lifelong ability to reorganize and change its structure and function by forming new neural connections.

Neurosis An outmoded term and category dropped from the DSM, in which a person does not have signs of brain abnormalities and does not display grossly irrational thinking or violate basic norms but does experience subjective distress.

Neurotransmitter A chemical messenger released by neurons that travels across the synapse and allows neurons to communicate with one another.

Neutral stimulus (NS) A stimulus that, before conditioning, does not naturally bring about the response of interest.

Nightmares The anxiety-arousing dreams that generally occur near the end of the sleep cycle, during REM sleep.

Non-rapid-eye-movement (NREM) sleep The sleep stages (1 through 3) during which a sleeper does not show rapid eye movements.

Normal distribution A statistical term used to describe how traits are distributed within a population; IQ scores usually form a symmetrical, bell-shaped curve, with most scores falling near the average, and fewer scores near the extremes.

Normative social influence A type of conforming based on the need to be liked, accepted, and approved of by others.

Obedience The act of following direct commands, usually from an authority figure.

Obesity An eating problem involving a body mass index of 30 or above, based on height and weight.

Object permanence According to Piaget, an understanding that objects continue to exist even when they cannot be seen, heard, or touched directly; a hallmark of Piaget's preoperational stage.

Observational learning The learning of new behaviors or information by watching and imitating others (also known as social learning or modeling).

Obsessive-compulsive disorder (OCD) A psychological disorder characterized by persistent, unwanted, fearful thoughts (obsessions) and/or irresistible urges to perform repetitive and/or ritualized behaviors (compulsions).

Occipital lobes The two lobes at the back of the brain that are primarily responsible for vision and visual perception.

Oedipus complex According to Freud, during the phallic stage (ages 3 to 6 years), a young boy develops a sexual attraction to his mother and rivalry with his father.

Olfaction The sense or act of smelling; receptors are located in the nose's nasal cavity.

Operant conditioning Learning through voluntary behavior and its subsequent consequences; consequences that are reinforcing increase behavioral tendencies, whereas consequences that are punishing decrease them.

Operational definition A precise description of how the variables in a study will be observed, manipulated, and measured.

Opiate/opiod A drug derived from opium that numbs the senses and relieves pain.

Opponent-process theory of color The theory that all color perception is based on three systems, each of which contains two color opposites (red versus green, blue versus yellow, and black versus white).

Optimal-arousal theory The theory that organisms are motivated to achieve and maintain an optimal level of arousal, which maximizes their performance.

Optimism A tendency to expect the best and to see the best in all things.

Outer ear The pinna, auditory canal, and eardrum structures, which funnel sound waves to the middle ear.

Outgroup homogeneity effect The tendency to judge members of an outgroup as more alike and less diverse than members of the ingroup.

Panic disorder An anxiety disorder in which sufferers experience repeated, sudden onsets of intense terror and inexplicable panic attacks; symptoms include severe heart palpitations, dizziness, trembling, difficulty breathing, and feelings of impending doom.

Parasympathetic nervous system The subdivision of the autonomic nervous system (ANS) that is responsible for calming the body and conserving energy.

Parietal lobes The two lobes located at the top of the brain in which bodily sensations are received and interpreted.

Partial (intermittent) reinforcement Some but not all, correct responses are reinforced.

Participant bias A bias that occurs when a research participant contaminates research results.

Perception The process of selecting, organizing, and interpreting sensory information into meaningful objects and events.

Perceptual constancy The tendency to perceive the environment as stable, despite changes in the sensory input.

Perceptual set The readiness to perceive in a particular manner, based on expectations.

Peripheral nervous system (PNS) The part of the nervous system composed of the nerves and neurons connecting the central nervous system (CNS) to the rest of the body.

Personality Our unique and relatively stable pattern of thoughts, feelings, and actions.

Personality disorder A psychological disorder characterized by chronic, inflexible, maladaptive personality traits, which cause significant impairment of social and occupational functioning.

Pheromones [FARE-oh-mones] Chemical signals released by organisms that trigger certain responses, such as aggression or mating, in other members of the same species.

Phobia A persistent and intense, irrational fear and avoidance of a specific object, activity, or situation.

Phoneme The smallest basic unit of speech or sound in any given language.

Physical dependence The changes in bodily processes that make a drug necessary for minimal functioning.

Place theory for hearing The theory that pitch perception is linked to the particular spot on the cochlea's basilar membrane that is most stimulated.

Placebo An inactive substance or fake treatment used as a control technique in experiments; often used in drug research.

Placebo effect A change that occurs when a participant's expectations or beliefs, rather than the actual drug or treatment, cause a particular experimental outcome.

Polygraph An instrument that measures sympathetic arousal (heart rate, respiration rate, blood pressure, and skin conductivity) to detect emotional arousal, which in turn supposedly reflects lying versus truthfulness.

Pons The hindbrain structure involved in respiration, movement, waking, sleep, and dreaming.

Positive affect The experience or expression of positive feelings (affect), including happiness, joy, enthusiasm, and contentment.

Positive psychology The study of optimal human functioning; it emphasizes positive emotions, traits, and institutions.

Positive punishment A process by which adding (or presenting) a stimulus following a response decreases the likelihood that the response will be repeated.

Positive reinforcement A process by which adding (or presenting) a stimulus following a response increases the likelihood that the response will be repeated.

Posttraumatic stress disorder (PTSD) A long-lasting, trauma- and stressor-related disorder that overwhelms an individual's ability to cope.

Preconscious Freud's term for thoughts, motives, or memories that exist just beneath the surface of awareness and can be called to consciousness when necessary.

Prejudice A learned, unjustified negative attitude toward members of a particular group; it includes thoughts (stereotypes), feelings, and behavioral tendencies (discrimination).

Preoperational stage Piaget's second stage of cognitive development (roughly ages 2 to 7) it is characterized by significant language, but the child lacks operations (reversible mental processes), and thinking is egocentric and animistic.

Primary punisher Any unlearned, innate stimulus, such as hunger or thirst, that punishes a response and thus decreases the probability that it will recur.

Primary reinforcer Any unlearned, innate stimulus (like food, water, or sex) that reinforces a response and thus increases the probability that it will recur.

Priming An exposure (often unconscious) to previously stored information that predisposes (or primes) our response to related stimuli.

Proactive interference A memory problem that occurs when old information disrupts (*interferes* with) the recall of new information; forward-acting interference.

Problem-focused coping The strategies we use to deal directly with a stressor to eventually decrease or eliminate it.

Projective test A method of personality assessment that uses a standardized set of ambiguous stimuli, such as inkblots or abstract drawings, which allow test takers to "project" their underlying motives, conflicts, and personality traits onto the test materials.

Prototype A mental image or best example that embodies the most typical features of a concept or category.

Psychiatry The branch of medicine that deals with the diagnosis, treatment, and prevention of mental disorders.

Psychoactive drug A chemical that changes mental processes, such as conscious awareness, mood, and perception.

Psychoanalysis A type of talk therapy, originated by Sigmund Freud, that emphasizes analysis and bringing unconscious thoughts and conflicts into conscious awareness.

Psychoanalytic perspective An earlier approach to psychology developed by Sigmund Freud, which focuses on unconscious processes, unresolved conflicts, and past experiences.

Psychodynamic perspective A modern approach to psychology that emphasizes unconscious dynamics, motives, conflicts, and past experiences; based on the psychoanalytic approach, but focuses more on social and cultural factors, and less on sexual drives.

Psychodynamic therapies A newer group of talk therapies that focuses on conscious processes and current problems; briefer, more directive, and more modern forms of psychoanalysis.

Psychological dependence The psychological desire or craving to achieve a drug's effect.

Psychology The scientific study of behavior and mental processes.

Psychoneuroimmunology The interdisciplinary field that studies the effects of psychological and other factors on the immune system.

Psychopharmacology The use of drugs to relieve or control the major symptoms of psychological disorders.

Psychophysics The study of the link between the physical characteristics of stimuli and the psychological experience of them.

Psychosexual stages In Freudian theory, five developmental periods (oral, anal, phallic, latency, and genital) during which particular kinds of pleasures must be gratified if personality development is to proceed normally.

Psychosis A serious psychological disorder characterized by extreme mental disruption and defective or lost contact with reality.

Psychosocial stages Erikson's theory that identifies eight developmental stages, each involving a crisis that must be successfully resolved for proper future development.

Psychosurgery A form of biomedical therapy that involves alteration of the brain to bring about desirable behavioral, cognitive, or emotional changes, which is generally used when clients have not responded to other forms of treatment.

Psychotherapy Any of a group of therapies used to treat psychological disorders and to improve psychological functioning and adjustment to life.

Puberty The biological changes during adolescence that lead to sexual maturation and the ability to reproduce.

Punishment Adding or removing a stimulus following a response decreases the likelihood that the response will be repeated.

Random assignment A research technique for assigning participants to experimental or control conditions so that each participant has an equal chance of being in either group; minimizes the possibility of biases or preexisting differences within or between the groups.

Rapid-eye-movement (REM) sleep The fourth stage of sleep, marked by rapid eye movements, irregular breathing, high-frequency brain waves, paralysis of large muscles, and often dreaming.

Rational-emotive behavior therapy (REBT) A form of talk therapy, developed by Albert Ellis, that focuses on eliminating negative emotional reactions through logic, confrontation, and examination of irrational beliefs.

Reciprocal determinism Bandura's belief that internal personal factors, the environment, and the individual's behavior all work as interacting (reciprocal) determinants of each other.

Reference groups Any group that individuals use as a standard for evaluating themselves.

Reflex An innate, automatic response to a stimulus that has a biological relevance for an organism (for example, knee-jerk reflex).

Reinforcement Adding or removing a stimulus following a response increases the likelihood that the response will be repeated.

Reliability The degree to which a test produces similar scores each time it is used; stability or consistency of the scores produced by an instrument.

Repair/restoration theory of sleep The theory that sleep allows organisms to repair their bodies or recuperate from depleting daily waking activities.

Repetitive transcranial magnetic stimulation (rTMS) A biomedical treatment that uses repeated magnetic field pulses targeted at specific areas of the brain.

Representativeness heuristic A cognitive strategy (or shortcut) that involves making judgments based on how well something matches (represents) an existing prototype or stereotype.

Resilience The ability to recover from or adapt effectively in the face of adversity.

Resistance In psychoanalysis, the client's inability or unwillingness of a client to discuss or reveal certain memories, thoughts, motives, or experiences.

Reticular formation The diffuse set of neurons that helps screen incoming information and helps control arousal.

Retina The light-sensitive inner surface of the back of the eye, which contains the receptor cells for vision (rods and cones).

Retinal disparity The binocular cue of distance in which the separation of the eyes causes different images to fall on each retina.

Retrieval The third step of the ESR memory model; recovery of information from memory storage.

Retrieval cues A prompt or stimulus that aids recall or retrieval of a stored piece of information from long-term memory (LTM).

Retroactive interference A memory problem that occurs when new information disrupts (*interferes* with) the recall of old, "retro" information; backward-acting interference.

Retrograde amnesia The inability to retrieve information from the past; backward-acting amnesia.

Rods Retinal receptor cells with high sensitivity in dim light, but low sensitivity to details and color.

Romantic love An intense feeling of attraction to another in an erotic context.

Rorschach Inkblot Test The most widely used projective personality test, which is based on interpretations of test takers' projections of their underlying motives, conflicts, and personality traits onto 10 inkblots.

Saliency bias A type of attributional bias in which people tend to focus on the most noticeable (salient) factors when explaining the causes of behavior.

SAM system Our body's initial, rapid-acting stress response, involving the sympathetic nervous system and the adrenal medulla; called the sympatho–adreno–medullary (SAM) system.

Sample bias A bias that may occur when research participants are unrepresentative of the larger population.

Schedules of reinforcement Specific patterns of reinforcement (either fixed or variable) that determine when a behavior will be reinforced.

Schema A Piagetian term for a cognitive framework, or "blueprint," formed through interaction with an object or event.

Schizophrenia A group of severe psychological disorders involving major disturbances in perception, language, thought, emotion, and/or behavior.

Scientific method The cyclical and cumulative research process used for gathering and interpreting objective information in a way that minimizes error and yields dependable results.

Secondary punisher Any learned stimulus, such as poor grades or a parking ticket, that punishes a response and thus decreases the probability that it will recur.

Secondary reinforcer Any learned stimulus (like money, praise, or attention) that reinforces a response and thus increases the probability that it will recur.

Selective attention The process of focusing conscious awareness onto a specific stimulus, while filtering out a range of other stimuli occurring simultaneously.

Self-actualization The humanistic term for the inborn drive to develop all one's talents and capabilities.

Self-concept The image of oneself that develops from interactions with significant others and life experiences.

Self-efficacy Bandura's term for a person's learned expectation of success in a given situation; another term for self-confidence.

Self-help group A leaderless or non-professionally guided group in which members assist each other with a specific problem, as in Alcoholics Anonymous.

Self-serving bias The tendency to credit success to internal, personality factors, while blaming failure on external, situational factors.

Semantic memory A subsystem of long-term memory (LTM) that stores general knowledge; a mental encyclopedia or dictionary.

Sensation The process of detecting, converting, and transmitting raw sensory information from the external and internal environments to the brain.

Sensorimotor stage Piaget's first stage of cognitive development (birth to approximately age 2), in which schemas are developed through sensory and motor activities.

Sensorineural hearing loss A type of hearing loss resulting from damage to cochlea's receptor (hair) hearing cells or to the auditory nerve; also called nerve deafness.

Sensory adaptation The sensory receptors' innate tendency to fatigue and stop responding to unchanging stimuli; an example of bottom-up processing.

Sensory memory The initial memory stage, which holds sensory information; it has relatively large capacity, but the duration is only a few seconds.

Serial-position effect A characteristic of memory retrieval in which information at the beginning and end of a series is remembered better than material in the middle.

Sexual orientation A primary erotic attraction toward members of the same sex (homosexual, gay, lesbian), both sexes (bisexual), or the other sex (heterosexual).

Sexual prejudice A negative attitude toward an individual because of her or his sexual orientation.

Sexual response cycle A four-stage bodily response to sexual arousal, which consists of excitement, plateau, orgasm, and resolution.

Shaping Reinforcement is delivered for successive approximations of the desired response.

Short-term memory (STM) The second memory stage, which temporarily stores sensory information and sends and receives information to and from long-term memory (LTM); its capacity is limited to five to nine items, and it has a duration of about 30 seconds.

Single-blind study An experimental technique in which only the participants are unaware of (blind to) who is in the experimental or control groups.

Sleep apnea A sleep disorder of the upper respiratory system that causes a repeated interruption of breathing during sleep; it also leads to loud snoring, poor-quality sleep, and excessive daytime sleepiness.

Sleep terrors The abrupt awakenings from NREM (non-rapid-eye-movement) sleep accompanied by intense physiological arousal and feelings of panic.

Social psychology The branch of psychology that studies how others influence our thoughts, feelings, and actions.

Sociocultural perspective A modern approach to psychology that emphasizes social interaction and the cultural determinants of behavior and mental processes.

Somatic nervous system (SNS) A subdivision of the peripheral nervous system (PNS) that connects the central nervous system (CNS) to sensory receptors and controls skeletal muscles.

Source amnesia A memory error caused by forgetting the origin of a previously stored memory; also called source confusion or source misattribution.

Split-brain surgery The cutting of the corpus callosum to separate the brain's two hemispheres; used medically to treat severe epilepsy; also provides information on the functions of the two hemispheres.

Spontaneous recovery The reappearance of a previously extinguished conditioned response (CR).

SQ4R method A study technique based on six steps: Survey, Question, Read, Recite, Review, and wRite.

Standardization A set of uniform procedures for administering and scoring a test; also, establishing norms by comparison with scores of a pretested group.

Statistical significance A statistical statement of how likely it is that a study's result occurred merely by chance.

Stem cells Immature (uncommitted) cells that have the potential to develop into almost any type of cell, depending on the chemical signals they receive.

Stereotype threat The awareness of a negative stereotype directed toward a group, which leads members of that group to respond in a self-fulfilling way that impairs their performance.

Stereotypes The overgeneralized beliefs about members of a group; also the cognitive component of prejudice.

Stimulant A drug that increases overall activity and general responsiveness.

Storage The second step of the ESR memory model; retention of encoded information over time.

Stress The interpretation of specific events, called *stressors*, as threatening or challenging the physical and psychological reactions to stress, known as the *stress response*.

Stressor A trigger or stimulus that induces stress.

Subliminal perception The detection of stimuli below the absolute threshold for conscious awareness.

Superego In Freud's theory, is the third personality structure that serves as the center of morality, providing internalized ideals and standards for judgment; often referred to as the "conscience."

Survey/interview A descriptive research technique that questions a large sample of people to assess their behaviors and mental processes.

Sympathetic nervous system The subdivision of the autonomic nervous system (ANS) that is responsible for arousing the body and mobilizing its energy during times of stress; also called the "fight-flight-freeze" system.

Synapse The gap between the axon tip of the sending neuron and the dendrite and/or cell body of the receiving neuron; during an action potential, neurotransmitters are released and flow across the synapse.

Systematic desensitization A behavior therapy technique in which a client is first asked to create a hierarchy of ordered fears and then taught to relax while gradually confronting the feared stimulus.

Taste aversion A classically conditioned dislike for, and avoidance of, a specific food whose ingestion is followed by illness.

Technostress A feeling of anxiety or mental pressure from overexposure or involvement with technology; stress caused by an Inability to cope with modern technology.

Temperament An individual's characteristic manner and intensity of emotional response.

Temporal lobes The two lobes on each side of the brain above the ears that are involved in audition (hearing), language comprehension, memory, and some emotional control.

Teratogen Any factor that causes damage or fetal death during prenatal development; comes from the Greek word *teras*, meaning "malformation."

Thalamus The forebrain structure at the top of the brainstem that relays sensory messages to and from the cerebral cortex.

Thematic Apperception Test (TAT) A projective personality test, which is based on interpretations of test takers' projections of their underlying motives, conflicts, and personality traits revealed through the stories they make up about ambiguous scenes.

Theory A well-substantiated explanation for a phenomenon or a group of facts that have been repeatedly confirmed by previous research.

Third-variable problem A situation in which a variable that has not been measured accounts for a relationship between two or more other variables; also known as a problem of confounding.

Three-stage memory model A memory model based on the passage of information through three stages (sensory, short-term, and long-term memory).

Tip-of-the-tongue (TOT) phenomenon A strong, confident feeling of knowing something, while not being able to retrieve it at the moment.

Tolerance The bodily adjustment to continued use of a drug in which the drug user requires greater dosages to achieve the same effect.

Top-down processing Information processing that starts at the "top" with higher-level analysis (prior knowledge and expectations), and then works "down" to recognize individual features as a unified whole; conceptually driven processing that moves from the whole to the parts.

Trait A relatively stable personality characteristic that describes a pattern of thinking, feeling, and acting.

Transduction The process of converting sensory stimuli into neural impulses that are sent along to the brain (for example, transforming light waves into neural impulses).

Transference In psychoanalysis, the process by which a client attaches (transfers) to the therapist emotional reactions related to someone else in the client's life.

Triangular theory of love Sternberg's theory that different stages and types of love result from three basic components—*intimacy*, *passion*, and *commitment*; Sternberg's consummate love is a combination of all three components.

Triarchic theory of intelligence Sternberg's theory that intelligence involves three forms: analytical, creative, and practical.

Trichromatic theory of color The theory that color perception results from three types of cones in the retina, each most sensitive to either red, green, or blue; other colors result from a mixture of these three.

Two-factor theory Schachter and Singer's theory that emotion depends upon two factors—physiological arousal and cognitive labeling of that arousal.

Unconditional positive regard Rogers's term for love and acceptance with no "strings" (contingencies) attached.

Unconditioned response (UR) An unlearned reaction to an unconditioned stimulus (US) that occurs without previous conditioning.

Unconditioned stimulus (US) A stimulus that elicits an unconditioned response (UR) without previous conditioning.

Unconscious Freud's term for the reservoir of largely unacceptable thoughts, feelings, memories, and other information that lies beneath conscious awareness (Chapter 11); in modern terms, subliminal processing that lies beneath the absolute threshold (Chapter 4).

Validity The degree to which a test measures what it is intended to measure.

Variable interval (VI) schedule A reinforcer is delivered for the first response made after a variable period of time whose average is predetermined.

Variable ratio (VR) schedule A reinforcer is delivered for the first response made after a variable number of responses whose average is predetermined.

Vestibular sense The sense that provides information about balance and movement; receptors are located in the inner ear.

Volley principle for hearing An explanation for pitch perception suggesting that clusters of neurons take turns firing in a sequence of rhythmic volleys, and that pitch depends on the frequency of these volleys.

Well-being therapy (WBT) A newer form of psychotherapy aimed at enhancing psychological well-being by focusing on the personal growth and noticing and savoring the positive aspects of life.

Wish-fulfillment view of dreams The Freudian belief that dreams provide an outlet for unacceptable desires.

Withdrawal The discomfort and distress, including physical pain and intense cravings, experienced after stopping the use of an addictive drug.

Working memory A newer understanding of short-term memory (STM) that emphasizes the active processing of information.

Yerkes-Dodson law The law stating that maximum performance is related to levels of arousal; complex tasks require a relatively low level of arousal, whereas simple tasks require a relatively high arousal level.

Zone of proximal development (ZPD) Vygotsky's concept of the difference between what children can accomplish on their own and what they can accomplish with the help of others who are more competent.

Name Index

C

D

M

Q

R

S

T

Subject Index

Note: Page numbers followed by a "t" indicate the entry may be found within a table. Page numbers followed by an "f" may be found within a figure.

N

O

R

T